America Reads

ROBERT C. POOLEY, *General Editor*

Projection in Literature

Counterpoint in Literature

Outlooks Through Literature

Exploring Life Through Literature

The United States in Literature

England in Literature

Composition Guide by **DON OTTO**, *Saint Cloud State College, Saint Cloud, Minnesota.*
Novel Discussion Guides by **KENNETH SICKAL**, *Cary Grove High School, Cary, Illinois.*
Picture Editor, **L. G. G. RAMSEY**, *Editor of* The Connoisseur, *London.* *Fellow*
of the Society of Antiquaries of London. *Editor of* The Connoisseur Encyclopaedia
of Antiques. *Coeditor of* The Connoisseur Period Guides (*Tudor to Victorian*).
Consultant for this revision, **JAMES E. MILLER**, **JR.**, *University of Chicago.*

SCOTT, FORESMAN AND COMPANY

England *in* Literature

ROBERT C. POOLEY
Professor of English, University of Wisconsin.
Director, Wisconsin English-Language Arts Curriculum Project.
First Chairman of the Board of Trustees of the Research Foundation
of the National Council of Teachers of English. First Recipient
of the W. Wilbur Hatfield Award for extraordinary
contributions to the teaching of English.

GEORGE K. ANDERSON
Professor of English, Brown University. Visiting Professor,
Bread Loaf School of English, Middlebury College. Author of
The Literature of the Anglo-Saxons *and* Old and Middle English Literature.

PAUL FARMER
Georgia Institute of Technology, Consultant in the teaching of English.
Formerly Coordinator of Language Arts, Atlanta Public Schools, Atlanta, Georgia.
Trustee of the Research Foundation of the National Council of Teachers
of English. Contributor to The English Journal.

HELEN THORNTON
Formerly Head of the English Department, Arsenal Technical High School,
Indianapolis, Indiana. Contributor to The English Journal.
Director of Literary Journeys to the British Isles.

Cover: The Vicar and Churchwardens of Fairfield Church, Gloucestershire.
Acknowledgments for pictures appearing on the title page:
Suit of armor—Her Majesty's Tower of London Armouries
Detail from the painting, "The Marriage Fete"—Courtesy the Marquess of Salisbury
Trinity Church, Stratford—Photo by Lon McKee
Winston Churchill—Photo Courtesy British Information Services

Contents

A Graphic Chronology of English Literature and Life, page 2

chapter six

The Triumph of Romantic Revolt

342

The Victorian Age

Anglo-Saxon England 449-1066

The history of English literature is a long and fascinating pageant. It begins roughly sixteen hundred years ago when the Roman legions abandoned the province of Britain and left the native Celts a prey to conquest by Anglo-Saxon tribes from the north of Europe. A primitive, warlike people who fought among themselves, against invading tribes of Danes, and against the harsh British climate, the Anglo-Saxons became known for their hearty feasts, skill in handicrafts, and long, heroic tales, as well as for their brooding, introspective blending of pagan beliefs with Christian teachings. Before they were absorbed by the conquering Normans from France, the Anglo-Saxons had produced the grim epic poem *Beowulf* and lyrics which sound for the first time in English literature the fascination of the English with the sea.

Stole, 10th century

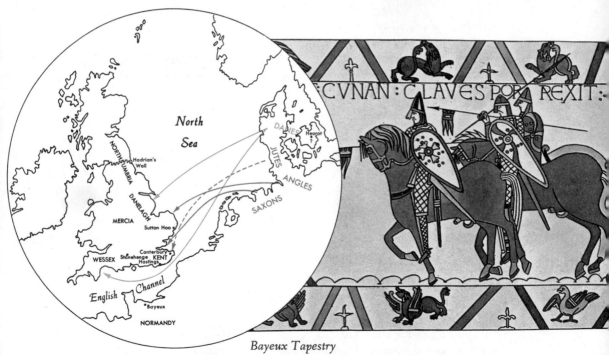

Bayeux Tapestry

Medieval England 1066-1485

Celtic fancy, Anglo-Saxon solidity, and Norman vivacity—these were the original ingredients of English life and letters. The third of these was brought into England from northern France by William the Conqueror and his Norman knights and churchmen. Castles and feudalism, jousts and duels, cathedrals and monasteries, chivalry and adventure were the contributions of these aristocratic newcomers whose knightly code is preserved for all time in the romances of King Arthur and the Round Table. Medieval life was harsh for aristocrat and common man alike. Feudal lords waged constant war on one another. The Black Death swept the land. Medieval folk ballads convey the heavy air of poverty and tragedy that hung over the lowly life of serf and vassal. But to the people of the Age of Faith, God had ordained all —the angels in heaven, the sun in the universe, the King in the castle, the lord in the manor, the yeoman in the wood, the serf in his hut, the beast in his lair, the plant in the earth, the pebble on the shore, and Satan in hell—and if man's life was hard it was because he was journeying through a vale of tears to a better life after death. Geoffrey Chaucer captured the spirit of this age just as it was ending.

The Elizabethan Age 1485-1625

Thomas Cranmer, Archbishop of Canterbury, acknowledged Henry VIII as head of the Church of England

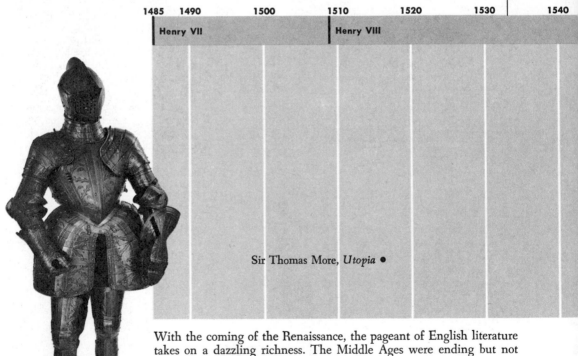

1485	1490	1500	1510	1520	1530	1540
Henry VII			**Henry VIII**			

Sir Thomas More, *Utopia* ●

With the coming of the Renaissance, the pageant of English literature takes on a dazzling richness. The Middle Ages were ending but not over, and the modern world had not yet arrived. England was both feudal and national, agricultural and commercial, devout and worldly. Her people were superstitious and skeptical, reverent and critical, courteous and bumptious, humble and immensely proud. Out of the exciting turmoil of English life there emerged a long and crowded parade of song writers, sonneteers, and dramatists who were led but not eclipsed by the prodigious figure of William Shakespeare. This was the age of monarchy, and the most regal monarch of all was "the mightie

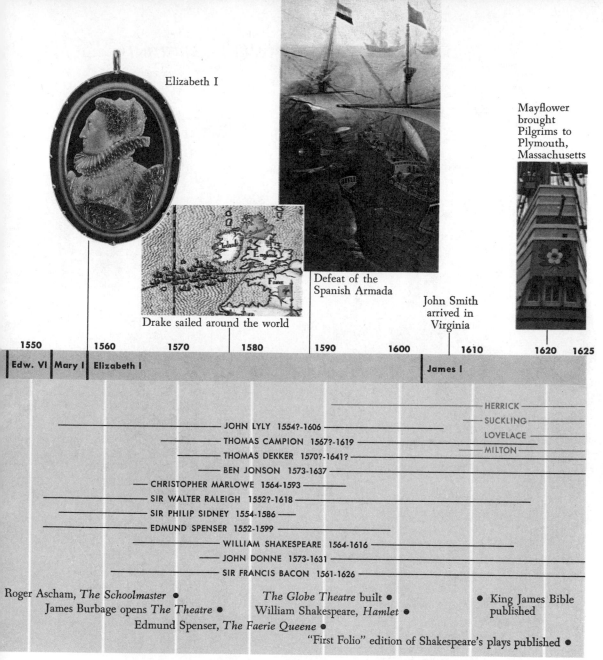

Elizabeth I

Defeat of the
Spanish Armada

Drake sailed around the world

John Smith
arrived in
Virginia

Mayflower
brought
Pilgrims to
Plymouth,
Massachusetts

| 1550 | 1560 | 1570 | 1580 | 1590 | 1600 | 1610 | 1620 | 1625 |

| Edw. VI | Mary I | Elizabeth I | | | | James I | | |

HERRICK
SUCKLING
LOVELACE
MILTON

JOHN LYLY 1554?-1606
THOMAS CAMPION 1567?-1619
THOMAS DEKKER 1570?-1641?
BEN JONSON 1573-1637
CHRISTOPHER MARLOWE 1564-1593
SIR WALTER RALEIGH 1552?-1618
SIR PHILIP SIDNEY 1554-1586
EDMUND SPENSER 1552-1599
WILLIAM SHAKESPEARE 1564-1616
JOHN DONNE 1573-1631
SIR FRANCIS BACON 1561-1626

Roger Ascham, *The Schoolmaster* •
James Burbage opens *The Theatre* •
Edmund Spenser, *The Faerie Queene* •

The Globe Theatre built •
William Shakespeare, *Hamlet* •

• King James Bible
published

"First Folio" edition of Shakespeare's plays published •

and magnificent Empresse Elizabeth," who inspired her people to live in peace after centuries of feuding, who chopped off their heads if they did not live in peace, and who cared not if a man were of high birth or low so long as he had talent. It was also the high age of aristocracy, when the old feudal families converted moats and castles into gardens and palaces. These people opened their minds to the expanding worlds of art, scholarship, and science. They led expeditions of swashbuckling sailors to the New World and against the Spanish Armada. And they lived in peace with the ever growing number of middle-class merchants, bankers, and lawyers who would soon displace both monarch and aristocrat. Death by disease or violence still lay close at hand, but by comparison with past times the Elizabethans lived in merry ease and comfort.

5

The Seventeenth Century 1625-1700

St. Clement Danes (Wren)

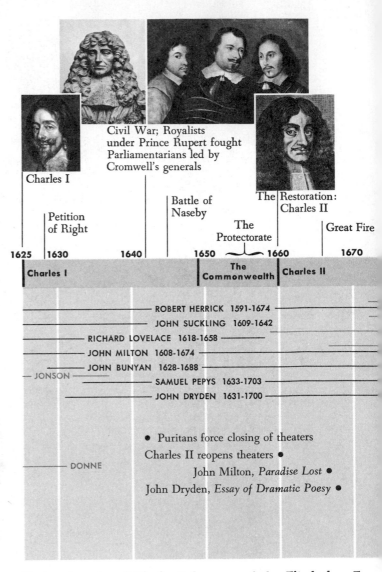

Civil War; Royalists under Prince Rupert fought Parliamentarians led by Cromwell's generals

Charles I

The Restoration: Charles II

Petition of Right

Battle of Naseby

The Protectorate

Great Fire

1625	1630	1640	1650	1660	1670
Charles I			The Commonwealth	Charles II	

ROBERT HERRICK 1591-1674

JOHN SUCKLING 1609-1642

RICHARD LOVELACE 1618-1658

JOHN MILTON 1608-1674

JOHN BUNYAN 1628-1688

JONSON

SAMUEL PEPYS 1633-1703

JOHN DRYDEN 1631-1700

DONNE

- Puritans force closing of theaters
- Charles II reopens theaters •
- John Milton, *Paradise Lost* •
- John Dryden, *Essay of Dramatic Poesy* •

During the reign of Charles I the peace of the Elizabethan Era was shattered by a devastating civil war. On one side were the elegant Cavaliers who went to battle for the King, the Established Church of England, and the old luxurious life of the aristocracy. On the other were the Puritans who fought for Parliament, a reformed church, and a simpler, less "sinful" way of life. Scarlets and plumes and Cavalier curls stood out in marked contrast to the dark, plain dress of Puritan protest. Wine, women, theater, and song vied with Bible readings, Sabbath walks, and the hard work required to run an ever growing world of commerce. Writers felt

An ACCOUNT of the
FORMALITIES
Of the CITIZENS of the Honourable CITY of
LONDON,
In their RECEPTION of
His Most Sacred Majesty,
King WILLIAM,
At His RETURN from FLANDERS.

Notice of
London reception
for King William

Sedan chair of the period

The
Glorious
Revolution

Newton
published
work on law
of universal
gravitation

War of Palatinate
brought to conclusion
with the Peace
of Ryswick

Bill of
Rights

1680   1690   1700

| Jas. II | William and Mary |

ADDISON
STEELE
DEFOE
SWIFT

POPE

● John Bunyan,
   Pilgrim's Progress

   ● Sir Isaac Newton,
      Principia

*Fountain Court,
designed by
Sir Christopher Wren
for the official
residence of
William and Mary
at Hampton
Court*

obliged to take sides in the century's great schism; and
courtly poets like Richard Lovelace and John Suckling
were challenged by the sterner voices of John Milton and
John Bunyan. Later in the century the Plague of 1665
and the Great Fire of London the following year added to
the woes of an England already chastened and exhausted
by civil war. When William and Mary came to power in
1688, they found a nation in which the power of the
aristocracy had been broken forever by the growth of commerce and the emergence of a strong middle class.

Badly shaken by the passions and convulsions of the seventeenth century, the men of the eighteenth century were determined to lead quiet, orderly, reasonable lives. Propriety, decorum, correctness, gentility, and common sense were the key words of the day. Enthusiasm of any kind was mercilessly lampooned. Gardens were carefully planned and pruned. City life was preferable to the country. People danced the minuet, purchased silhouettes, and sipped tea and coffee. Buildings were balanced, formal, and precise. So were chairs and tables, paintings, speech, prose and poetry. In politics, Parliament, Cabinet, and Prime Minister took over leadership from the King. Whigs and Tories fought it out. Old aristocratic families merged with wealthy middle-class ones to form a new high society. Anyone who was not a part of this society did not advance. A writer who did not address himself to this society on genteel subjects and in a genteel fashion did not get read. Powdered wigs, public literature, and pompous Doctor Samuel Johnson were the ideals of the century that looked upon itself as the first civilized period in English history. Englishmen had refined themselves at last. England itself was supposed to be running as smoothly as Newton's universe of planets and gravitational forces, and English letters were thought to be just as good as the much admired literature of classical Greece and Rome. To the Age of Reason and Neoclassicism, it was the best of all possible worlds, and anyone who dared say otherwise was either a lunatic or a boor. But toward the end of the eighteenth century, men began to question the perfections of a civilization which reserved its privileges for the few and disregarded the wants of the many. A new age was at hand.

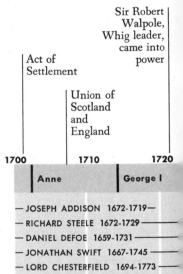

Act of Settlement

Sir Robert Walpole, Whig leader, came into power

Union of Scotland and England

1700	1710	1720
Anne		George I

— JOSEPH ADDISON 1672-1719—
— RICHARD STEELE 1672-1729 ———
— DANIEL DEFOE 1659-1731 ———
— JONATHAN SWIFT 1667-1745 ———
— LORD CHESTERFIELD 1694-1773 ———
— ALEXANDER POPE 1688-1744 ———
——— PEPYS ———

• Defoe founds *The Review* first English newspaper

• First issue of Addison and Steele's *Spectator*

• Alexander Pope *Essay on Criticism*

Daniel Defoe, • *Robinson Crusoe*

Century 1700-1798

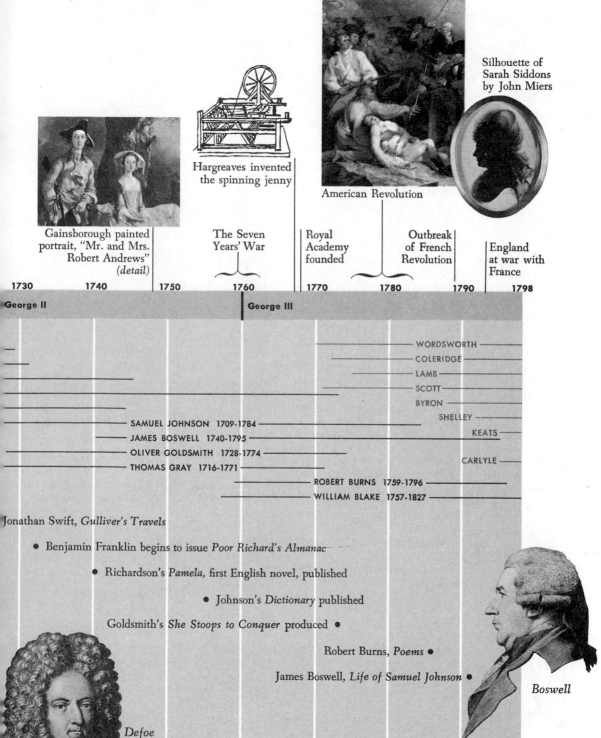

Silhouette of Sarah Siddons by John Miers

Hargreaves invented the spinning jenny

American Revolution

Gainsborough painted portrait, "Mr. and Mrs. Robert Andrews" *(detail)*

The Seven Years' War

Royal Academy founded

Outbreak of French Revolution

England at war with France

| 1730 | 1740 | 1750 | 1760 | 1770 | 1780 | 1790 | 1798 |

George II

George III

WORDSWORTH
COLERIDGE
LAMB
SCOTT
BYRON
SHELLEY
KEATS

SAMUEL JOHNSON 1709-1784
JAMES BOSWELL 1740-1795
OLIVER GOLDSMITH 1728-1774
THOMAS GRAY 1716-1771

CARLYLE

ROBERT BURNS 1759-1796
WILLIAM BLAKE 1757-1827

Jonathan Swift, *Gulliver's Travels*

• Benjamin Franklin begins to issue *Poor Richard's Almanac*

• Richardson's *Pamela*, first English novel, published

• Johnson's *Dictionary* published

Goldsmith's *She Stoops to Conquer* produced •

Robert Burns, *Poems* •

James Boswell, *Life of Samuel Johnson* •

Boswell

Defoe

9

The Romantic Movement 1798-1837

Shropshire countryside

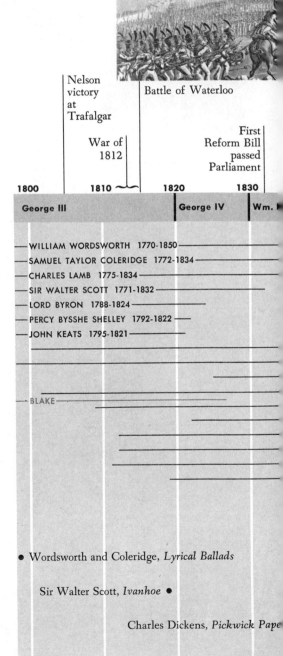

To the revolutionaries of the early nineteenth century, the eighteenth century had been unbearably stuffy and undemocratic; it was high time that men gave up their narrow-mindedness and extended the democratic ideal of brotherhood to all peoples. The Americans had revolted against the mother country as far back as 1776. The French Revolution had broken out thirteen years later. And at last the English were clamoring for an extension of the suffrage to people other than the privileged and wealthy few. The nineteenth century also disagreed with the eighteenth-century belief that life could be explained as neatly and simply as Newton had explained the physical universe. Romantic poets pointed to the wild, unfathomable beauties of nature, the elusive, supernatural visions of mystics, and the mysterious atmosphere of religion that had cast such celestial light about the Middle Ages. To the Romantics, man was aflame with too many passions to be explained by a few cold scientific formulas. By the time that Queen Victoria came to the throne, this romantic fever had somewhat burned itself out. Men had turned their attention to the far reaching implications of the Industrial Revolution, which was at last transforming the entire surface and structure of England. This was the time of enormously wealthy industrialists, the first factory towns, the first steamships and railways, and the British Empire on which the sun never set. It was also the time of overstuffed sitting rooms, bric-a-brac ornaments, high bodices, bustle skirts, and fireside readings from the novels of Dickens and Thackeray. Although much of Victorian England disappeared with the two World Wars, many of its aspects are still with us today.

Nelson

Nelson victory at Trafalgar

Battle of Waterloo

War of 1812

First Reform Bill passed Parliament

| 1800 | 1810 | 1820 | 1830 |

| George III | | George IV | Wm. |

— WILLIAM WORDSWORTH 1770-1850 —
— SAMUEL TAYLOR COLERIDGE 1772-1834 —
— CHARLES LAMB 1775-1834 —
— SIR WALTER SCOTT 1771-1832 —
— LORD BYRON 1788-1824 —
— PERCY BYSSHE SHELLEY 1792-1822 —
— JOHN KEATS 1795-1821 —

— BLAKE —

• Wordsworth and Coleridge, *Lyrical Ballads*

Sir Walter Scott, *Ivanhoe* •

Charles Dickens, *Pickwick Pape*

The Victorian Age 1837-1900

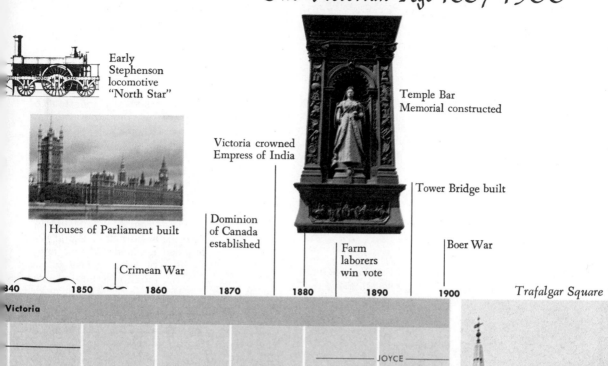

Early Stephenson locomotive "North Star"

Temple Bar Memorial constructed

Victoria crowned Empress of India

Houses of Parliament built

Tower Bridge built

Dominion of Canada established

Crimean War

Farm laborers win vote

Boer War

840   1850   1860   1870   1880   1890   1900

Trafalgar Square

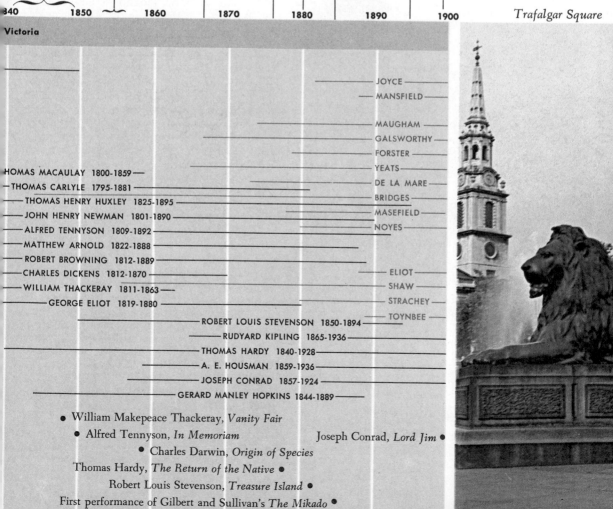

Victoria

JOYCE
MANSFIELD

MAUGHAM
GALSWORTHY
FORSTER
YEATS
DE LA MARE
BRIDGES
MASEFIELD
NOYES

HOMAS MACAULAY 1800-1859
THOMAS CARLYLE 1795-1881
THOMAS HENRY HUXLEY 1825-1895
JOHN HENRY NEWMAN 1801-1890
ALFRED TENNYSON 1809-1892
MATTHEW ARNOLD 1822-1888
ROBERT BROWNING 1812-1889
CHARLES DICKENS 1812-1870
WILLIAM THACKERAY 1811-1863
GEORGE ELIOT 1819-1880

ELIOT
SHAW
STRACHEY
TOYNBEE

ROBERT LOUIS STEVENSON 1850-1894
RUDYARD KIPLING 1865-1936
THOMAS HARDY 1840-1928
A. E. HOUSMAN 1859-1936
JOSEPH CONRAD 1857-1924
GERARD MANLEY HOPKINS 1844-1889

- William Makepeace Thackeray, *Vanity Fair*
- Alfred Tennyson, *In Memoriam*
- Charles Darwin, *Origin of Species*
- Thomas Hardy, *The Return of the Native*
- Robert Louis Stevenson, *Treasure Island*
- First performance of Gilbert and Sullivan's *The Mikado*

Joseph Conrad, *Lord Jim* •

During the last quarter of the nineteenth century England was the richest, most powerful, and most fully industrialized nation in the world. But even as the nation settled back under Victoria's son, Edward VII, to enjoy its position, the tide of nationalism was rising fast in places like India and Germany. It was the tide of nationalism that gradually washed away the Empire, leaving a Commonwealth of newly independent nations, and that swept England from her "splendid isolation" into the maelstrom of World War I. Scarcely had England had time to enjoy the fruits of peace when it was plunged into a series of severe economic crises, culminating in the world-wide depression of 1929. These economic crises aggravated social unrest in England, and, in Europe, aided the rise of communism and fascism, which set the stage for World War II. When the smoke cleared, Europe counted the cost: dead — over twenty million in both wars; price—ranging in the trillions of dollars. The power and wealth that had for centuries made Europe the center of Western civilization had all but vanished in forty-five years. Of all the major nations, England had suffered most, for, because of her small size and few resources, she could least afford the loss of men, wealth, and trade. Small wonder that many who lived through this age of violence thought they saw the very fabric of civilization unraveling before their eyes. The traditional teachings of politics, economics, philosophy, even religion, seemed to many to be singularly inapplicable to this new world. Even the old certainties of Newtonian physics and Euclidean geometry were shaken by the theories of relativity and curving space. Moreover, science had developed the atomic bomb, making the total destruction of all civilization a real possibility. Writers expressed the full range of men's reactions to this "brave new world": rage, retreat, despair, or escape for some; for others, a wide-ranging search for new sets of values.

The new Coventry Cathedral, replacing the structure (above) which was destroyed during a 1940 bombing raid

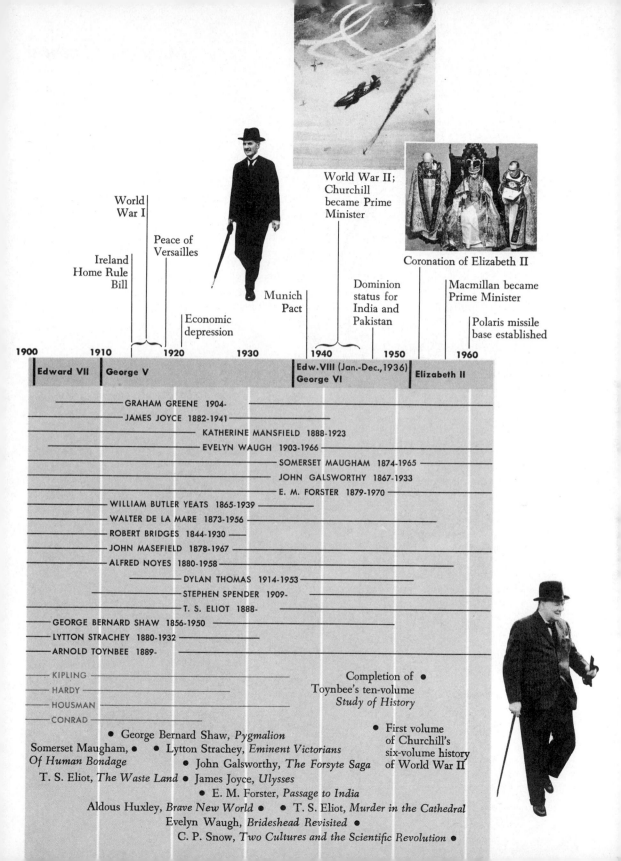

World War II;
Churchill became Prime Minister

World War I

Peace of Versailles

Ireland Home Rule Bill

Economic depression

Munich Pact

Dominion status for India and Pakistan

Coronation of Elizabeth II

Macmillan became Prime Minister

Polaris missile base established

| 1900 | 1910 | 1920 | 1930 | 1940 | 1950 | 1960 |

| Edward VII | George V | | Edw. VIII (Jan.-Dec., 1936) / George VI | Elizabeth II |

GRAHAM GREENE 1904-
JAMES JOYCE 1882-1941
KATHERINE MANSFIELD 1888-1923
EVELYN WAUGH 1903-1966
SOMERSET MAUGHAM 1874-1965
JOHN GALSWORTHY 1867-1933
E. M. FORSTER 1879-1970
WILLIAM BUTLER YEATS 1865-1939
WALTER DE LA MARE 1873-1956
ROBERT BRIDGES 1844-1930
JOHN MASEFIELD 1878-1967
ALFRED NOYES 1880-1958
DYLAN THOMAS 1914-1953
STEPHEN SPENDER 1909-
T. S. ELIOT 1888-
GEORGE BERNARD SHAW 1856-1950
LYTTON STRACHEY 1880-1932
ARNOLD TOYNBEE 1889-

KIPLING
HARDY
HOUSMAN
CONRAD

Completion of Toynbee's ten-volume *Study of History*

First volume of Churchill's six-volume history of World War II

• George Bernard Shaw, *Pygmalion*
Somerset Maugham, • • Lytton Strachey, *Eminent Victorians*
Of Human Bondage
• John Galsworthy, *The Forsyte Saga*
T. S. Eliot, *The Waste Land* • James Joyce, *Ulysses*
• E. M. Forster, *Passage to India*
Aldous Huxley, *Brave New World* • • T. S. Eliot, *Murder in the Cathedral*
Evelyn Waugh, *Brideshead Revisited* •
C. P. Snow, *Two Cultures and the Scientific Revolution* •

Acknowledgments for Graphic Chronology pictures:

page 2 Rocky Seacoast, detail—Photo by James Ballard
Stole—Courtesy The Durham Cathedral Library
Bayeaux Tapestry, detail—Courtesy The British Museum

page 3 Pectoral Cross—The John Hunt Collection, Dublin
Statue—Photo by Lon McKee
Stained Glass, detail—The Vicar and Churchwardens of Fairford Church, Gloucestershire
Helmet—The Victoria and Albert Museum

page 4 Suit of Armor—Her Majesty's Tower of London Armouries
Thomas Cranmer—National Portrait Gallery, London

page 5 Queen Elizabeth I—Reproduced by Gracious Permission of Her Majesty Queen Elizabeth II
Drake Map, detail—The Trustees of the National Maritime Museum, Greenwich
Painting "Battle of the Armada," detail—From the Collection of the Late Captain Eric Palmer
Mayflower II, detail—Photo by James Ballard

page 6 St. Clement Danes—Photo by Lon McKee
Charles I—Private Collection, London
Prince Rupert—Courtesy The British Museum
Generals Fairfax, Ireton, and Essex—Private Collection, London
Charles II—Private Collection, London

page 7 17th century Broadsheet—The Society of Antiquaries of London
Sedan Chair—The London Museum
Fountain Court—Photo by Lon McKee

page 8 Hampton Court Formal Garden—Photo by Lon McKee

page 9 Gainsborough Painting, detail—Messrs. Sotheby's, London
Painting "Battle of Bunker Hill" by John Trumbull, detail—Yale University Art Gallery
Defoe—National Portrait Gallery, London
Boswell—National Portrait Gallery, London

page 10 Shropshire Country Scene—A. F. Kersting
Lord Nelson—Lloyd's, London
Painting "Battle of Waterloo," detail—The Parker Gallery, London

page 11 Locomotive—Radio Times Hulton Picture Library
Houses of Parliament—A. F. Kersting
Statue of Queen Victoria—Photo by Lon McKee
Trafalgar Square—Photo by Lon McKee

page 12 Coventry Cathedral, ruins and new structure—Courtesy British Travel Association

page 13 Neville Chamberlain—The Times, London
Painting "The Battle of Britain" by Roy Nockolds—Imperial War Museum, London
Coronation of Queen Elizabeth II—Central Press Photos Ltd., London
Winston Churchill—Courtesy British Information Services

part one THE
DEVELOPMENT
of ENGLISH
LITERATURE

chapter one

ANGLO-SAXON ENGLAND

c. 450-1066

Stonehenge, standing shrouded in mystery on barren Salisbury Plain, suggests the ancient, unknown history of England. Who built it and when it was built are still riddles, as are the names of the races who inhabited Britain before the beginnings of recorded history. The first mention of Britain occurs in the writings of the ancient Greeks, to whom it was a remote and legendary land; but only in the time of Julius Caesar did the classical world begin its real acquaintance with the island. When Caesar, in the course of one of his Gallic Wars, crossed the English Channel to Britain in 55 B.C., the land was occupied by the Celts, a people related to the Gauls of Western Europe. Caesar made no attempt to colonize the island, and the development of a Roman province there did not begin until nearly a century later. Then the Roman emperor Claudius, in 43 A.D., led a campaign which overcame the Celtic Britons and established Roman rule.

A. F. KERSTING

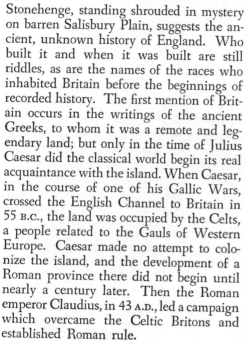

PHOTO BY LON MC KEE

Left: Monumental Stonehenge stands as a reminder of England's prehistory.
Above: England's history begins with the coming of the Romans, who, under the Emperor Hadrian, built this wall across the narrow part of the island.
Opposite: The Anglo-Saxons started the long tradition of English literature. This iron helmet is from the most important archaeological remains of the Anglo-Saxons, the Sutton Hoo treasure (see page 34).

17

For nearly four hundred years, Britain remained a part of the mighty Roman Empire. Romans and Britons intermarried, towns grew and prospered, magnificent roads fanned out over the province, and peace was maintained under Roman law. When, under repeated attacks by barbarians, the Roman Empire began to fall apart early in the fifth century, the Romans abandoned the province. The Romanized Britons, left without the defense of the Roman legions, were soon involved in conflicts with other Celtic tribes—Irishmen from the west, Scots and Picts from the north. Eventually, however, the remnants of the Roman province of Britain were conquered by Germanic invaders from across the North Sea.

These invaders, to be referred to throughout this chapter as the Anglo-Saxons, were actually of three major tribes—the Angles, the Saxons, and the Jutes. Their homelands had been areas along the northwest coast of Germany and the Danish peninsula. When the Huns came pouring into Europe from the East in the fourth and fifth centuries, they pushed the Germanic tribes of Central Europe farther west. These in turn exerted pressures on the Anglo-Saxons, who became for a time Vikings, or sea-rovers. For many years they made sporadic raids on the coast of Britain. Then, according to tradition, in 449 the Jutes under Hengest and Horsa landed on the coast of Kent to begin the actual conquest of Britain. Within a century and a half, all of England had fallen to the conquerors.

The history of England from about 600 to 850 is the story of the rise and fall of petty Anglo-Saxon kingdoms and the efforts of successive states to unify England. First Kent became the strongest of the kingdoms under the rule of King Ethelbert. From about 650 to 750 Northumbria, the

Below left: This tombstone of a Roman centurion was found at Colchester, site of the first Roman colony in Britain. Below middle: Also from Colchester is this excellent piece of Roman pottery, showing a gladiatorial combat. Below right: Map shows routes of the Germanic tribes that invaded England when the Romans left.

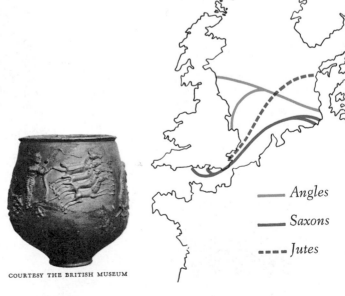

—— *Angles*

—— *Saxons*

---- *Jutes*

kingdom of the Angles, achieved political eminence and a considerable tradition of literary culture. Power then moved to the Angles of Mercia, until Wessex, settled by the Saxons, attained supremacy early in the ninth century.

ANGLO-SAXON SOCIETY When the Anglo-Saxons invaded England they were an agricultural, semi-nomadic people. They recognized two classes of society: the *earls* of the ruling class, who could claim kinship to the founder of the tribe; and the *churls*, who were bondmen tracing their ancestry only to some unfortunate former captive of the tribe. For centuries the Anglo-Saxons had lived amid hostile neighbors, and therefore they admired greatly the individual warrior leader and the ideals of courage required of him. At the same time, even at the time of their invasion, they understood the concept of a social organization greater than the individual since they had strict laws and a certain degree of social consciousness.

The warrior occupied a preëminent position in Anglo-Saxon society. The prestige of the successful warrior was immense. Even the king was essentially a warrior. Although he ruled absolutely, he was attentive to the advice of his assembly of elders, the *Witan* ("wise men"). This group of prominent earls was later known as the *Witenagemot* ("meeting of wise men").

The churls were responsible for the hard labor that sustained the predominantly agricultural community. They spent their days tilling the soil, hunting and fishing and fowling, working metal and weaving. They were bound to the service of the earls unless they could earn possessions and special royal favor which could transform them into the relatively small group of *freemen*, or independent landholders.

The place of women in the social scale was unimportant. A queen, the wife of a powerful earl, or, later, a churchwoman occupied a position of honor and power. But most women were regarded as valuable only for domestic duties.

Although life among the Anglo-Saxons was primitive, an appreciation of craftsmanship developed early. The warrior always prized a masterly specimen of metalwork or jewelry, a heroic sword "doughty of edge," and he could appreciate a tapestry woven cunningly by "maiden's craft."

Great feasts were also a part of Anglo-Saxon life. To celebrate the deeds of a hero there had been from ancient times the professional bard, called the *scop*, who combined in his person the rôles of chief entertainer, antiquarian, poet laureate, and press agent for the king and tribe. At the feast the *scop* would come forward to regale the company with legends relating to the deeds of great Germanic heroes of the past. He delivered his story in a rhythmic kind of chant, accompanied by occasional chords on his harp. The form of his story was fixed by tradition in elastic, alliterative verses. There were occasional descriptive touches, and sometimes a lyrical note crept in most effectively, but on the whole his epic lay was straightforward narrative verse on the subject of a great warrior and his deeds. The audience of earls would listen attentively to these tales; the queen and her retinue would hospitably pass the ceremonial mead-cup and then discreetly retire; the warriors would listen to more stories and enjoy more mead.

The Anglo-Saxon, while he lived on the continent of Europe, had surrounded himself with greater and lesser deities—forces of nature or personifications of the supernatural which he could comprehend only as animal or human agencies of superior strength. In Britain, he came into contact with Christianity. Some Christians had actually been in Britain during the latter years of the Roman occupation, and Christian missionaries from Ireland had set up little centers in the northern part of the island as early as the first part of the sixth century. But the full flow of Christianity into England came straight from Rome when, in 597, Pope Gregory the Great sent his emissary Augustine to convert King Ethelbert of Kent. According to a memorable story, when Gregory was a young deacon he saw a group of fair-skinned, golden-haired youths being sold as slaves in the market place in Rome. Upon inquiring where they had come from, he was told they were Angles. "Not Angles but Angels," he replied. Years later, when he became Pope, he sent Augustine to convert this faraway people to Christianity. To the Anglo-Saxon who heard the message of Christian teachers, the new religion that promised something more certain than his pagan deities offered seemed worthy to be followed. Augustine became the first Archbishop of Canterbury, and within a generation or two Christianity had spread the length and breadth of England.

The conversion of the Anglo-Saxon to Christianity widened his spiritual and intellectual outlook. In the schools that grew up as the monasteries spread, the young Anglo-Saxon learned not only the Scriptures but also the classical writings of Vergil and of the ancient Greeks. He traveled to Rome on pilgrimages or to increase his knowledge of learning and literature. As his human experience increased, his mental and his spiritual powers broadened and deepened.

In spite of the widespread effects of Christianity on the Anglo-Saxons, the un-

Detail of the embroidery on an early tenth-century stole showing the figure of Jonah. The stole was part of the vestments of Frithestan, Bishop of Winchester.

derlying paganism of the people shows here and there in telltale fashion in the written records. It is particularly evident in the surviving folk-lore, some of which endures even today in such heathen relics as the Yule log and the Christmas tree, the mistletoe, the names of the days of the week, in the charms to cure illness or to help agriculture, or in the books of remedies or "leechdoms." If traces of paganism show in the written records, which have come down to us for the greatest part from priestly traditions, how much more these ancient beliefs must have affected the day-by-day living of men, women, and children of the Anglo-Saxon period.

KING ALFRED AND THE DANISH INVASIONS Around 850 in the kingdom of Wessex there emerged the figure of King Alfred the Great, most remarkable of the Anglo-Saxon kings. Strong and skillful ruler though he was, his reign was nevertheless one of critical strife in the island. His enemies were Viking Danes, who were following the pattern set by the Anglo-Saxons four hundred years earlier. Beginning with swift raids at the end of the eighth century, the Vikings had advanced farther and farther into the northern and central portions of England, pillaging and burning. Raids had been followed by settlements, until during the reign of Alfred the Danes were threatening the entire island. Alfred checked the Danish menace. To establish peace, however, he had to cede to the Danes the northern and central portions of England then known as the Danelagh (Danelaw).

The Danelagh was gradually won back by the Anglo-Saxons during the tenth century, so that one can at last begin to think of a unified English nation. However, the power of the West Saxon kings declined late in the century, new waves of Danish invaders assaulted the island, and in 1014 the Danes conquered England. More unrest followed, the Anglo-Saxons returned to rule in 1042, and in 1066 the Norman Conquest put an end to the Anglo-Saxon history of England. But that introduces the next chapter in the story.

Left: The Abingdon Sword. Right: The tower of the church of Earls Barton, which dates from the tenth century, has been called "the most noteworthy architectural monument of the Saxon period."

The Changing English Language

The most widely distributed of all the languages of the western world, English is spoken by more than 260 million people and is understood by many more. As the official language of nations like Great Britain, Canada, Australia, and the United States, in addition to many smaller nations, English is a principal language in diplomatic affairs; it is also the medium of communication for peoples from many lands at international conferences. Considering the importance of English today, and its probable future as one of the chief languages of the world, it is amazing to recall that this great tongue had its beginnings among scattered tribes of invading Germanic peoples who crossed the English Channel and made their homes in England only fifteen

First page of Beowulf manuscript, most famous survival of Old English literature.

hundred years ago. In this and subsequent sections we shall trace the story of our language from its humble origins to its major position in the world today.

In the development of this story we shall be concerned with four periods of time. The first will treat of the ancestry of English and will include from about 2000 B.C. to 450 A.D., the approximate date of the invasion of England by Germanic tribes. The next period is called Old English, and comprises roughly the years 450 A.D. to 1100 A.D. Because of important changes and developments in English, the period from 1100 to 1500, which stands between Old English and Modern English, is called Middle English. Modern English is dated from 1500 to the present.

THE ANCESTRY OF ENGLISH

A large group of culturally related human beings living before 2000 B.C. in central and southeastern Europe have been given the name Indo-Europeans by language scholars. Seeking food and possibly grazing lands, these people spread all over Europe and penetrated into India. During the course of many centuries they became isolated from each other. Their language, once understood by all the group, developed distinct characteristics in distinct areas, giving rise to what are today called "branches" of the Indo-European language. Two branches which have strongly influenced modern English are the *Italic*, from which developed Latin, Italian, Spanish, and French; and *Hellenic*, from which developed the Greek language. However, the branch from which English comes is called *Germanic*, and was the speech of early peoples of Europe. Groups of this Germanic-speaking people also scattered, bringing about changes in the form of their speech which we identify as "divisions" of the Germanic branch: (1) an eastern division which has disappeared, leaving only some written documents in a language called Gothic; (2) a northern division from which have developed Icelandic, Norwegian, Swedish, and Danish; and (3) a western division from which came German, Dutch, Flemish, and English. Hence scholars call English a language derived from the western division of the Germanic branch of the Indo-European family of languages. But the vocabulary of English has been greatly enriched by words from other branches.

ENGLAND BEFORE THE ENGLISH

Not long before the beginning of the Christian era England was invaded and settled by a people from Western Europe called Celts, related to the Gauls about whom Julius Caesar wrote. They spread out over the British Isles. These people spoke languages derived from another branch of the Indo-European family of languages, called the *Celtic* branch. From this branch developed Cornish (now no longer spoken); Welsh, the language of Wales; Erse, the language of Ireland; and Scots, the surviving ancient tongue of the Scottish Highlanders.

These Celtic people in time contributed richly to the literature of Great Britain. For centuries their literature was oral, but from it have sprung not only the great romantic legends of Arthur and Tristram but also a delicate quality of the imagination that is found in some of the most gifted of the English poets. It is this fairylike loveliness of the Celtic literature that produced such a description as:

And they saw a tall tree by the side of the river, one half of which was in flames from the root to the top, and the other half was green and in full leaf.

By legend, by romantic stories of love and adventure, and by special qualities of delicate imagination our literature is linked to the prehistoric Celtic occupants of England, Scotland, and Wales.

During the nearly four hundred years that Britain was part of the Roman Empire the camps of the legions dotted the countryside, particularly along the borders of Roman rule. Their presence or influence survives in names of towns ending in *-chester*, *-cester*, and *-caster*, from *castra*, the Latin word for *camp*. A map of England today quickly reveals the names

Colchester and *Chester*, the latter an important camp on the Welsh border; *Lancaster*, *Doncaster*, and *Manchester* in northern England; *Worcester*, *Gloucester*, and *Leicester* in central England; and *Dorchester* on the south coast. These are only a few of the many English cities whose names reflect the Roman occupation.

Although most of the Latin words in Modern English came into our language long after the Roman occupation of England, a few words have perhaps survived from these times by being passed on from the Romanized Celts to the Anglo-Saxons. It is supposed that *port*, *mile*, *wine*, and *street* were known to the Celts and also to the invading Germanic peoples from their contacts with the Romans. However, it was in the later Old English period that the first notable additions of Latin words to English were made.

OLD ENGLISH

When the Germanic invaders spread over England from 449 onward, they formed three dialectal groups whose pronunciation and usage of their common language differed in specific ways. The largest group, the Angles, inhabited the lands from the Thames River to the north of England. It is from this group that the names *England* (*Angleland*) and *English* (*Anglisc*) are derived. However, since in the Danish invasions of the eighth and ninth centuries the libraries and books of the Angles were destroyed, few documents in this dialect survive. The Saxons, who lived south of the Thames, spoke the variety of Old English in which most of the surviving documents are written. In Kent were the Jutes, whose dialect gave us such words as *vat*, a Kentish form of *fat*, and *vixen*, the female *fox*. In the rural districts of England there are still traces of these dialect differences today, though such distinctions are rapidly disappearing.

Old English was enriched in two ways after Augustine and his missionaries arrived from Rome in 597. Words related to church and Christian life were borrowed from Latin and became a part of English; for example, *alms, altar, candle, disciple, mass, organ,* and *temple.* In addition to the strictly religious influence, contact with the Roman form of Christianity brought a general advancement of culture, which may be seen in the adoption of such words as *school, master, grammar, notary*; and *cap, chest, plant, circle*, and *place*. The advance in culture also developed Anglo-Saxon words to express the new ideas, such as *dyppan* (literally "to dip") for *baptism*, and *fēond* ("fiend") as a synonym for *devil*. Thus Christianity and Roman culture started that extensive borrowing of words from Latin sources which has persisted to our own day; for only yesterday we borrowed our new word *radio* from Latin *radius*.

Old English in the north of England was greatly altered by the Danish invasions. Since Old English and the language of the invaders were much alike, as Anglo-Saxon and Dane intermingled they tended to mix their forms of speech. Some Scandinavian words, such as *law, egg*, and *window*, were borrowed outright, replacing the English equivalents. English took over the Scandinavian pronouns *they, their*, and *them*. Some Old English words that had fallen into disuse were revived because of Scandinavian parallels.

One clear evidence of Scandinavian settlement survives in place names in the north of England. There we find *Grimsby, Whitby*, and *Derby*, formed from the root word *-by*, meaning "a farm or town." There are over five hundred English towns with names ending in *-by*. (This Scandinavian root word survives also in *bylaw*.) There are several hundred names like *Gremelthorpe, Linthorp*, and *Cleethorpe*, from the Scandinavian *-thorp*, "a village"; and almost as many like *Thistlethwaite* and *Braithwaite* from *-thwaite*, "land off by itself." The greatest number of these names will be found in modern Yorkshire and Lincolnshire, which are counties in the north of England.

With borrowings from the Latin and the Scandinavian, Old English was modified and to some extent simplified. However, it was still a language characterized by many inflections, or changes in words to show tense, case, number, gender, and person. There were several declensions of nouns, with distinctive endings to show gender, number, and case.

The adjective, which had two declensions, agreed with its noun in gender, number, and case. Verbs, too, were highly inflected, and in most of them the vowel changed in the principal parts, as in modern *sing, sang, sung*. There was also a group of "weak" verbs which indicated change of time by adding *d* or *t*; these set the pattern for the majority of our verbs today, like *look, looked, looked*, which we call "regular" verbs.

Fewer than a fourth of the words we use today are derived from Old English; but among these are our most commonly used nouns and verbs, pronouns, connectives, and articles. Their frequent use gives them an importance out of proportion to their number.

The following passage is an example of Old English prose. It was probably written by King Alfred before 900 A.D., and was inserted by him into a translation he was making of the *Compendious History of the World*, by Orosius, a Latin author. This text is therefore Old English of late West Saxon dialect.

Ōhtere sǣde his hlāforde, Ælfrēde cyninge, þæt hē ealra Norðmonna norðmest būde. Hē cwæð þæt hē būde on þǣm lande norðweardum wið þā Westsǣ. Hē sǣde þēah þæt þæt land sīe swīðe lang norð þonan; ac hit is eall wēste, būton on fēawum stōwum styccemǣlum wīciað Finnas, on huntoðe on wintra, ond on sumera on fiscaðe be þǣre sǣ. Hē sǣde þæt hē æt sumum cirre wolde fandian hū longe þæt land norðryhte lǣge, oððe hwæðer ǣnig monn be norðan þǣm wēstenne būde.

TRANSLATION:

Ohtere said to his lord, Alfred the king, that he of all Northmen northmost dwelt. He said that he dwelt on that land northward along the West Sea. He said, though, that that land is very long north thence [from there], but it is all waste except that in a few places stickmeal [here and there] live Finns [in] hunting in winter and in the summer [in] fishing by that sea. He said that he at a certain time wanted to find how far that land northward lay, or whether any man to the north of the waste dwelt.

BEOWULF—AN ANGLO-SAXON EPIC

Belief in a hero has always been an important article in the social and political faith of the Germanic peoples, whether they were Christian or not. The fact that such a hero could be related to the figure of Christ no doubt attracted the sympathy of many a cleric toward heroic legends. Almost certainly the one who first cast the epic Beowulf legend into coherent and artistic form and wrote it down in the language we now call Old English was a Christian cleric who was evidently Norse in his sympathies and interests, if not in his nationality. This unknown author, who flourished probably in the first half of the eighth century, is known as the Beowulf Poet.

It is generally supposed that *Beowulf* was a heroic Scandinavian epic legend, a story of the type the *scop* chanted to the warriors assembled in the great hall. The only surviving full-length heroic epic in Old English, *Beowulf* tells of Scandinavian kings and heroes. Its presence in Anglo-Saxon England can be explained simply by saying that the Viking Danes brought the legend to England, or that it may derive from classical sources. However, legendry of this type is common to all Germanic nations. The probabilities are strong that there were extant on the Continent a large number of epics comparable in length and scope to *Beowulf* which have unfortunately been lost, either because they were not lucky enough to survive the destructiveness of time or because no one ever wrote them down.

In *Beowulf* a truly non-Christian story of monsters and mighty sea beasts and firedragons is blended, although rather incongruously, with serious thoughts about the dispensations of a wise God, the necessity for praying to a Christian deity, the fate that will befall the evil, and the reward that is promised to the righteous. Through the story stalks the impressive and noble figure of Beowulf, in whom pagan fatalism mingles strangely with Christian qualities.

The Beowulf Poet possessed a sense of drama, an ear for music, and the power to create effective word-pictures. There is no end rhyme, but by regularly dividing each line into two parts and by extensive use of alliteration, the poet achieved a rhythmic, musical effect. Most striking is his use of *kennings*, poetic synonyms that are often metaphorical compounds. They were probably drawn from a large stock of formula-phrases characteristic of Anglo-Saxon verse. Thus the king is the "ring-giver," the rough sea is the "whale-road," the smooth sea is the "swan-road," the boat is the "wave-rider," the dragon is the "shadow-walker," and the ocean is "the mingling of the waves."

This great drinking horn, reconstructed from the Sutton Hoo findings, reflects the splendor of Anglo-Saxon feasts, which included recitation of the long epics.

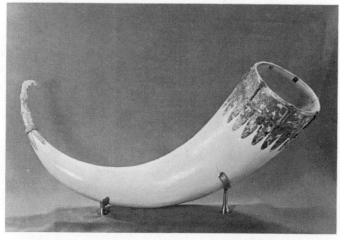

COURTESY THE BRITISH MUSEUM

from BEOWULF

Translated by Charles W. Kennedy

The story of Beowulf *begins in the land of the Danes during the reign of King Hrothgar (hrōth'gär). The King had built a great hall called Heorot (hā'ə rot), where the earls feasted and listened to hero tales chanted by the* scop. *Then one night Grendel, a monster of human shape but superhuman size, appeared and slew thirty men. For twelve years he haunted the land, killing and devouring, while Heorot stood deserted and men lived in terror.*

In southern Sweden the warrior Beowulf, who was the nephew of Hygelac (hig'ə läk), ruler of the Geats (gā'atz), heard of Grendel's ravages. With fourteen companions he sailed to Denmark to fight the monster. After a great feast in Heorot, Beowulf and his men lay down in the hall to await Grendel's approach. Beowulf boasted he would overcome Grendel without weapons. Then, while all slept, Grendel appeared.

BEOWULF'S FIGHT WITH GRENDEL

From the stretching moors, from the misty hollows,
Grendel came creeping, accursed of God,
A murderous ravager minded to snare
Spoil of heroes in high-built hall. . . .
Storming the building he burst the portal,   5
Though fastened of iron, with fiendish strength;
Forced open the entrance in savage fury
And rushed in rage o'er the shining floor.
A baleful glare from his eyes was gleaming
Most like to a flame. He found in the hall   10
Many a warrior sealed in slumber,
A host of kinsmen. His heart rejoiced;
The savage monster was minded to sever
Lives from bodies ere break of day,
To feast his fill of the flesh of men.   15
But he was not fated to glut his greed
With more of mankind when the night was ended!
The hardy kinsman of Hygelac waited
To see how the monster would make his attack.
The demon delayed not, but quickly clutched   20
A sleeping thane in his swift assault,
Tore him in pieces, bit through the bones,
Gulped the blood, and gobbled the flesh,
Greedily gorged on the lifeless corpse,
The hands and the feet. Then the fiend stepped nearer,   25
Sprang on the Sea-Geat[1] lying outstretched,
Clasping him close with his monstrous claw.
But Beowulf grappled and gripped him hard,
Struggled up on his elbow; the shepherd of sins
Soon found that never before had he felt   30
In any man other in all the earth
A mightier hand-grip; his mood was humbled,
His courage fled; but he found no escape!
He was fain to be gone; he would flee to the darkness,
The fellowship of devils. Far different his fate   35
From that which befell him in former days!
The hardy hero, Hygelac's kinsman,
Remembered the boast he had made at the banquet,
He sprang to his feet, clutched Grendel fast,
Though fingers were cracking, the fiend pulling free.   40
The earl pressed after; the monster was minded
To win his freedom and flee to the fens.
He knew that his fingers were fast in the grip
Of a savage foe. Sorry the venture,
The raid that the ravager made on the hall. . . .   45
    The walls resounded, the fight was fierce,
Savage the strife as the warriors struggled.
The wonder was that the lofty wine-hall
Withstood the struggle, nor crashed to earth,
The house so fair; it was firmly fastened   50
Within and without with iron bands
Cunningly smithied; though men have said
That many a mead-bench gleaming with gold
Sprang from its sill as the warriors strove.

From *Beowulf, The Oldest English Epic*, translated by Charles W. Kennedy. Copyright 1940 by Oxford University Press, Inc. Used by permission.
1. *Sea-Geat*, Beowulf.

The Scylding[2] wise men had never weened [55]
That any ravage could wreck the building,
Firmly fashioned and finished with bone,
Or any cunning compass its fall,
Till the time when the swelter and surge of
    fire
Should swallow it up in a swirl of flame. [60]
  Continuous tumult filled the hall;
A terror fell on the Danish folk
As they heard through the wall the horrible
    wailing,
The groans of Grendel, the foe of God
Howling his hideous hymn of pain, [65]
The hell-thane shrieking in sore defeat.
He was fast in the grip of the man who was
    greatest
Of mortal men in the strength of his might,
Who would never rest while the wretch was
    living,
Counting his life-days a menace to man. [70]
  Many an earl of Beowulf brandished
His ancient iron to guard his lord,
To shelter safely the peerless prince.
They had no knowledge, those daring thanes,
When they drew their weapons to hack and
    hew, [75]
To thrust to the heart, that the sharpest sword,
The choicest iron in all the world,
Could work no harm to the hideous foe.
On every sword he had laid a spell,
On every blade; but a bitter death [80]
Was to be his fate; far was the journey
The monster made to the home of fiends.
  Then he who had wrought such wrong to
    men,
With grim delight as he warred with God,
Soon found that his strength was feeble and
    failing [85]
In the crushing hold of Hygelac's thane.
Each loathed the other while life should last!
There Grendel suffered a grievous hurt,
A wound in the shoulder, gaping and wide;
Sinews snapped and bone-joints broke,[3] [90]
And Beowulf gained the glory of battle.
Grendel, fated, fled to the fens,
To his joyless dwelling, sick unto death.
He knew in his heart that his hours were
    numbered,
His days at an end. For all the Danes [95]
Their wish was fulfilled in the fall of Grendel.

The stranger from far, the stalwart and strong,
Had purged of evil the hall of Hrothgar.

*The next morning Hrothgar and his men came
to rejoice at Beowulf's victory. There was
feasting in Heorot and the mead-cup passed
from hand to hand. But at night terror returned. Grendel's mother came from her
cavern under the sea to avenge her dead son.
She burst into the hall, seized a sleeping
thane, and made off across the moor bearing
the thane and Grendel's arm. Vowing revenge
for the death of the thane, Beowulf with his
men followed the sea-troll's bloody tracks to a
loathsome pool. Into it Beowulf plunged.*

BEOWULF'S FIGHT WITH GRENDEL'S MOTHER

  Nigh unto a day he endured the depths
Ere he first had view of the vast sea-bottom. [100]
Soon she found, who had haunted the flood,
A ravening hag, for a hundred half-years,
Greedy and grim, that a man was groping
In daring search through the sea-troll's home.
Swift she grappled and grasped the warrior [105]
With horrid grip, but could work no harm,
No hurt to his body; the ring-locked byrny[4]
Cloaked his life from her clutching claw;
Nor could she tear through the tempered mail
With her savage fingers. The she-wolf bore [110]
The ring-prince down through the watery
    depths
To her den at the bottom; nor could Beowulf
    draw
His blade for battle, though brave his mood.
Many a sea-beast, strange sea-monsters,
Tasked him hard with their menacing tusks, [115]
Broke his byrny and smote him sore.
  Then he found himself in a fearsome hall
Where water came not to work him hurt,
But the flood was stayed by the sheltering
    roof.
There in the glow of firelight gleaming [120]
The hero had view of the huge sea-troll.
He swung his war-sword with all his strength,
Withheld not the blow, and the savage blade
Sang on her head its hymn of hate. [124]

2. *Scylding* (shil′ding), Danish. Scyld was the mythical
founder of the Danish royal line. 3. *Sinews . . . broke.*
Beowulf wrenched Grendel's arm from his body. 4. *ring-
locked byrny* (bĕr′ni), coat of mail made of metal rings
locked together.

But the bold one found that the battle-flasher
Would bite no longer, nor harm her life. . . .
But fixed of purpose and firm of mood
Hygelac's earl was mindful of honor;
In wrath, undaunted, he dashed to earth
The jeweled sword with its scrolled design, 130
The blade of steel; staked all on strength,
On the might of his hand, as a man must do
Who thinks to win in the welter of battle
Enduring glory; he fears not death.
The Geat-prince joyed in the straining
    struggle, 135
Stalwart-hearted and stirred to wrath,
Gripped the shoulder of Grendel's dam
And headlong hurled the hag to the ground.
But she quickly clutched him and drew him
    close,
Countered the onset with savage claw. 140
The warrior staggered, for all his strength,
Dismayed and shaken and borne to earth.
She knelt upon him and drew her dagger,
With broad bright blade, to avenge her son,
Her only issue. But the corselet's steel 145
Shielded his breast and sheltered his life,
Withstanding entrance of point and edge. . . .
    Swift the hero sprang to his feet;
Saw mid the war-gear a stately sword,
An ancient war-brand of biting edge, 150
Choicest of weapons worthy and strong,
The work of giants, a warrior's joy,
So heavy no hand but his own could hold it,
Bear to battle or wield in war. 154
Then the Scylding warrior, savage and grim,
Seized the ring-hilt and swung the sword,
Struck with fury, despairing of life,
Thrust at the throat, broke through the
    bone-rings;
The stout blade stabbed through her fated
    flesh.
She sank in death; the sword was bloody; 160
The hero joyed in the work of his hand.
The gleaming radiance shimmered and shone
As the candle of heaven shines clear from the
    sky. . . .
The blade had failed not the battle-prince;
A full requital he firmly planned 165
For all the injury Grendel had done
In numberless raids on the Danish race,
When he slew the hearth-companions of
    Hrothgar,

Devoured fifteen of the Danish folk
Clasped in slumber, and carried away 170
As many more spearmen, a hideous spoil.
All this the stout-heart had stern requited;
And there before him bereft of life
He saw the broken body of Grendel
Stilled in battle, and stretched in death, 175
As the struggle in Heorot smote him down.
The corpse sprang wide as he struck the blow,
The hard sword-stroke that severed the head.
    Then the tried retainers, who there with
        Hrothgar
Watched the face of the foaming pool, 180
Saw that the churning reaches were reddened,
The eddying surges stained with blood.
And the gray, old spearmen spoke of the hero,
Having no hope he would ever return
Crowned with triumph and cheered with
    spoil. 185
Many were sure that the savage sea-wolf
Had slain their leader. At last came noon.
The stalwart Scyldings forsook the headland;
Their proud gold-giver[5] departed home.
But the Geats sat grieving and sick in spirit, 190
Stared at the water with longing eyes,
Having no hope they would ever behold
Their gracious leader and lord again.
    Then the great sword, eaten with blood of
        battle,
Began to soften and waste away 195
In iron icicles, wonder of wonders,
Melting away most like to ice
When the Father looses the fetters of frost,
Slackens the bondage that binds the wave,
Strong in power of times and seasons; 200
He is true God! Of the goodly treasures
From the sea-cave Beowulf took but two,
The monster's head and the precious hilt
Blazing with gems; but the blade had melted,
The sword dissolved, in the deadly heat, 205
The venomous blood of the fallen fiend.
    Then he who had compassed the fall of his
        foes
Came swimming up through the swirling
    surge.
Cleansed were the currents, the boundless
    abyss,
Where the evil monster had died the death 210
And looked her last on this fleeting world.

5. gold-giver, Hrothgar, the Danish king.

With sturdy strokes the lord of the seamen
To land came swimming, rejoiced in his spoil,
Had joy of the burden he brought from the
    depths.
And his mighty thanes came forward to meet
    him,   215
Gave thanks to God they were granted to see
Their well-loved leader both sound and safe.

*To celebrate Beowulf's final victory over the
monsters, a great feast was held in Heorot
and the hero was given rich gifts. The next
morning he set sail for his own country, where,
after the death of his uncle, he became king.
For fifty years he ruled wisely and well. Then
a dragon, aroused by the theft of a golden cup
from the treasure hoard he was guarding, began to lay waste the land. In age as in youth,
Beowulf was ready to risk his life for the
people. With a small band, including his
kinsman and loyal companion, Wiglaf, he
sought out the dragon, who was guarding his
treasure in his barrow beneath a cliff.*

BEOWULF'S DEATH AND BURIAL

                    . . . The stalwart king,
Gold-friend of the Geats, took seat on the
    headland,
Hailed his comrades and wished them well. 220
Sad was his spirit, restless and ready,
And the march of Fate immeasurably
    near; . . .
  For the last time Beowulf uttered his
    boast:
"I came in safety through many a conflict
In the days of my youth; and now even yet, 225
Old as I am, I will fight this feud,
Do manful deeds, if the dire destroyer
Will come from his cavern to meet my sword."
The king for the last time greeted his
    comrades, . . .   229
"I would bear no sword nor weapon to battle
With the evil worm, if I knew how else
I could close with the fiend, as I grappled
    with Grendel.
From the worm I look for a welling of fire,
A belching of venom, and therefore I bear
Shield and byrny. Not one foot's space   235
Will I flee from the monster, the ward of the
    mound.

It shall fare with us both in the fight at the
    wall
As Fate shall allot, the lord of mankind." . . .
    Then the stalwart rose with his shield upon
    him,
Bold under helmet, bearing his sark   240
Under the stone-cliff; he trusted the strength
Of his single might. Not so does a coward!
He who survived through many a struggle,
Many a combat and crashing of troops,
Saw where a stone-arch stood by the wall   245
And a gushing stream broke out from the
    barrow.
Hot with fire was the flow of its surge,
Nor could any abide near the hoard unburned,
Nor endure its depths, for the flame of the
    dragon.
Then the lord of the Geats in the grip of his
    fury   250
Gave shout of defiance; the strong-heart
    stormed.
His voice rang out with the rage of battle,
Resounding under the hoary stone.
Hate was aroused; the hoard-warden knew
'Twas the voice of a man. No more was there
    time   255
To sue for peace; the breath of the serpent,
A blast of venom, burst from the rock.
The ground resounded; the lord of the Geats
Under the barrow swung up his shield
To face the dragon; the coiling foe   260
Was gathered to strike in the deadly strife.
The stalwart hero had drawn his sword,
His ancient heirloom of tempered edge;
In the heart of each was fear of the other!
The shelter of kinsmen stood stout of heart 265
Under towering shield as the great worm
    coiled;
Clad in his war-gear he waited the rush.
In twisting folds the flame-breathing dragon
Sped to its fate. The shield of the prince
For a lesser while guarded his life and his
    body   270
Than heart had hoped. For the first time then
It was not his portion to prosper in war;
Fate did not grant him glory in battle!
Then lifted his arm the lord of the Geats   274
And smote the worm with his ancient sword
But the brown edge failed as it fell on bone,
And cut less deep than the king had need

In his sore distress. Savage in mood
The ward of the barrow countered the blow
With a blast of fire; wide sprang the flame. 280
The ruler of Geats had no reason to boast;
His unsheathed iron, his excellent sword,
Had weakened as it should not, had failed in
the fight. . . .
  Then Wiglaf dashed through the deadly
reek
In his battle-helmet to help his lord.   285
Brief were his words: "Beloved Beowulf,
Summon your strength, remember the vow
You made of old in the years of youth
Not to allow your glory to lessen
As long as you lived. With resolute heart, 290
And dauntless daring, defend your life
With all your force. I fight at your side!"
  Once again the worm, when the words were
spoken,
The hideous foe in a horror of flame,
Rushed in rage at the hated men.   295
Wiglaf's buckler was burned to the boss
In the billows of fire; his byrny of mail
Gave the young hero no help or defense.
But he stoutly pressed on under shield of his
kinsman
When his own was consumed in the scorching
flame.   300
Then the king once more was mindful of
glory,
Swung his great sword-blade with all his
might
And drove it home on the dragon's head. . . .
The kinsmen together had killed the dragon.

*Knowing his fated time had come, Beowulf
bade Wiglaf bring to him the treasure that
he might see what he had won for his people.*

  Beowulf spoke, as he gazed on the gold; 305
"For this goodly treasure whereon I gaze
I give my thanks to the Lord of all,
To the Prince of glory, Eternal God,
Who granted me grace to gain for my people
Such dower of riches before my death.   310
I gave my life for this golden hoard.
Heed well the wants, the need of my people;
My hour is come, and my end is near.
Bid warriors build, when they burn my body,
A stately barrow on the headland's height. 315

It shall be for remembrance among my people
As it towers high on the Cape of the Whale,
And sailors shall know it as Beowulf's
Barrow. . . ."
  The Geat folk fashioned a peerless pyre 319
Hung round with helmets and battle-boards,[6]
With gleaming byrnies as Beowulf bade.
In sorrow of soul they laid on the pyre
Their mighty leader, their well-loved lord.
The warriors kindled the bale on the barrow,
Wakened the greatest of funeral fires.   325
Dark o'er the blaze the wood-smoke mounted;
The winds were still, and the sound of
weeping
Rose with the roar of the surging flame
Till the heat of the fire had broken the body.
With hearts that were heavy they chanted
their sorrow,   330
Singing a dirge for the death of their
lord; . . .
They sang their dirge and spoke of the hero
Vaunting his valor and venturous deeds. . . .
Said he was kindest of worldly kings,
Mildest, most gentle, most eager for fame. 335

---

6. *battle-boards*, shields.

❋ To increase understanding

1. Cite in as much detail as possible ways in
which the life pictured in the poem *Beowulf* con-
forms to the description of Anglo-Saxon society given
in the introduction to this chapter (page 19).

2. (*a*) What are Beowulf's outstanding characteristics? (*b*) Explain the relationship between these
characteristics and the Anglo-Saxon ideal of a hero.

3. In the introduction to the selections from
Beowulf you read that pagan and Christian elements
are blended in this epic. Point out passages that
show (*a*) the pagan foundation, (*b*) the Christian
influence.

4. When an Old English epic is translated into
Modern English, many changes in the poetry necessarily occur. However, in translating *Beowulf*,
Charles W. Kennedy did retain two important sty-
listic devices of Old English—alliteration and kennings. (*a*) Point out several good examples of
alliteration. (*b*) Point out and explain the meaning
of several kennings. (Remember that a kenning is a
poetic synonym in which the name of a person or
thing is replaced by a compound word or phrase
describing it; for example, *whale-road*, for "rough
sea.")

ANGLO-SAXON LYRICS

The Anglo-Saxon lyric, like the epic, owes much to the *scop*. But while the epics are filled with the deeds of dauntless warriors, the lyrics reflect the somberer aspects of life. The tone is usually *elegiac*—impersonal thoughts on the brevity of life, the terror of the northern winter, and the immensity and cruelty of the sea. In most of the lyrics the poetic style closely resembles that of the epic—the same alliterative verse form and the use of kennings.

While the warrior and the *scop* gave to literature these so-called elegiac poems, it is to the clergy we are indebted for their preservation. In the transmission of poems like *The Seafarer* (below) and *The Wanderer* through Christian hands, we may assume certain pagan elements were eliminated and Christian touches added. Thus the Old English poetry that has come down to us blends the traditions of the *scop* and the priest.

Purse lid found in the Anglo-Saxon burial ship at Sutton Hoo.

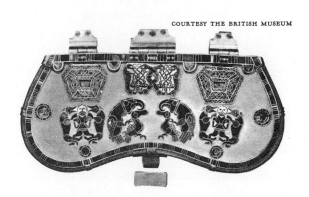

from THE SEAFARER

Translated by George K. Anderson

"The Seafarer" was probably composed early in the eighth century. It is found in the famous Exeter Book—one of the four important collections of the surviving poetry of the Anglo-Saxon period. It stresses a theme or motif that has recurred throughout the ages of English literature—the haunting beauty, the foreboding terror, and the unfathomed mystery of the sea. The poem is the monologue of an old sailor, who is torn between the fascination of the sea and resentment of the hardships and perils of life upon it. Some critics have interpreted it as a dialogue between a young man eager to follow the sea and an old sailor weary of its hardships.

I can make a true song of myself,
Tell of my travels, how I endured oft
Days of hardship and times of trouble;
Bitter breast-care I have experienced,
Made trial in a ship of many wretched
    quarters,   5
The dire dashing of waves, where the hard
    night-watch
Oft found me at the prow of the vessel,
As it tossed beside the cliffs. Pressed by
    the cold,
My feet were fettered by frost,
By cold claws; then I sighed my care   10
Hot about my heart; hunger rent within
The soul of the sea-weary. That the man
    knows not
Whom it befalls fairest in the world,
How I, careworn on the ice-cold sea,

Have spent the winter on paths of exile, ⁱ⁵
Bereft of joys, cut off from kinsmen,
Hung round with icicles—hail flew in
      showers.
There heard I naught save the booming sea,
The ice-cold pathway, sometimes the song of
      the swan.
I had my joy in the sporting of the gannet, ²⁰
In the cry of the curlew rather than the
      laughter of men,
In the scream of the seamew rather than
      the mead-drink.
There storms beat on the stone-cliff, there
      the tern replied
With icy feathers; oft the eagle cried out
Dewy of wings¹. . . No kinsman-protector ²⁵
Can sustain the destitute heart.
And so he little believes, who has the joy
      of life,
Abiding in the city, knowing few hardships,
Proud and wine-flushed, how I oft weary
Must linger, dwelling in the paths of ocean! ³⁰
The shadow of night grew dark; it snowed
      from the north;
Frost bound the earth; hail fell to the
      ground,
The coldest of grains.

So the thoughts of my heart
Stir within me, that I myself make trial ³⁵
Of the high streams, the sporting salt-waves;
The desire of my heart ever urges me on
To fare forth in my venture far hence,
To seek the home of alien people.
For there is no man on earth so proud, ⁴⁰
Nor so generous in giving nor in youth so
      bold,
Nor in deeds so daring, nor his lord to him
      so gracious,
That he has not always sorrow in seafaring,
As to what his Lord will bestow on him.
Not for him are thoughts of the harp, nor
      of ring-giving, ⁴⁵
Nor of the joy of woman, nor of delights
      in the world,
Nor of aught else but the dashing of waves;
Yet ever he has longing, who sets forth on
      the sea.
The groves put forth blossoms, the cities
      grow fair,

The meadows are beautiful, the world
      revives: ⁵⁰
All these urge a man's eager heart
To the journey, when he thus thinks
To depart forth on the flood-ways.
Likewise the cuckoo sad of voice
Urges in song, the harbinger of summer, ⁵⁵
Proclaims a sorrow bitter in her
      breast-hoard.
That the man knows not, the favored being,
What some endure, who must widely pace
The tracks of exile. Therefore my heart
      now
Stirs within my breast, my inner soul ⁶⁰
Moves with the sea-flood over the whale's
      home
Moves far over the world's expanse, comes
      again to me
Eager and greedy; the lone flier screams,
Urges the heart resistlessly over the
      whale-road,
Over the stretch of the sea. ⁶⁵

1. *wings.* At this point a line or two seems to be lost in
the original manuscript.

 To increase understanding

1. (*a*) What are some of the hardships and difficulties the seafarer has known in his years at sea?
Cite lines in which these hardships are vividly described. (*b*) Point out lines in which the seaman
mentions the joys of seafaring. (*c*) In your opinion
which lines best summarize the fascination of the sea?
2. What poetic devices used in *Beowulf* occur
also in "The Seafarer"? Cite examples to illustrate
your answer.
3. What elements of "The Seafarer," in addition
to its style, mark it as belonging to the Anglo-Saxon
period?

Extending interests

If you were to interpret "The Seafarer" as a dialogue
between an old sailor and a young man eager to
follow the sea, which lines would you give to each
character? With a classmate work out the poem as
a dialogue and prepare to read it to the class.
If you are interested in choral reading, you might
assemble two groups to read the poem. The heavier
voices would read the lines attributed to the old
sailor and the lighter voices the lines of the young
man.

RIDDLES

Translated by George K. Anderson

The English love of riddles goes far back into Anglo-Saxon times. The riddles printed here are from a collection of ninety-four which are found in the Exeter Book, *where they appear without titles. The solution of these riddles is often a matter of mere conjecture, but those printed here have caused no disagreement among the experts. How good would you have been at this Anglo-Saxon game?*

I am a lonely warrior, wounded by iron,
Stricken by a sword, weary of battle-works,
Tired of blades. Oft I see combat,
Fighting a brave foe, I cannot expect comfort,
Safety to come to me in saving struggle,   5
Before I perish entirely among men;
But the leavings of hammers[1] strike me,
The hard-edged, battle-sharp handiwork of
      smiths,
Bites me in the stronghold. I must await   9
A more hateful encounter. Never a physician
Could I find on the battlefield,
One who with herbs might heal my wounds;
But the blows of the swords grow greater
Through death-strokes, by day and by night.

My garment is silent when I tread the earth
Or inhabit the dwellings or stir up the
      waters.
Sometimes over the abodes of heroes
My trappings raise me, and this high air,
And the power of the clouds bears me then   5
Far above the folk. My adornments
Loudly resound and make melody,[2]
Singing clearly when I do not touch
Flood or earth as a traveling spirit.

A moth ate a word; that seemed to me
A curious fate, when I heard of that wonder,
That a worm should devour the song of a man,

(Thief in the night), the far-famed utterance
A thing established by a strong man.   5
The thievish guest was no whit the wiser
For having swallowed the words.

A creature came traveling, wondrous along
      the waves,
It called out in comeliness from ship to land,
Loud was its din; terrible its laughter,
Dreadful on earth; sharp were its edges.   4
It was fierce in malice, in battle too sluggish,
Bitter in battle-deeds; wooden walls[3] it
      shattered,
Cruel and ravaging. It spread about a
      baleful charm;
It spoke with cunning about its own nature:
"My mother is among maidens the dearest,
She is my daughter grown to greatness,   10
As is known to men among the people,
She shall stand with joy on the earth
      everywhere."[4]

---

1. *leavings of hammers,* a kenning for *swords.*
2. *adornments . . . melody.* It is a folk tradition that a swan in flight makes a musical sound because the wind whistles through its plumage.
3. *wooden walls,* presumably a kenning for the sides of a ship.
4. *My mother . . . everywhere.* This is a rather cryptic statement of the old folklore idea that ice derives from water and when it melts turns to water again. Hence the mother is also the daughter. Because of the importance of water as a life-giving element, she "shall stand with joy on the earth."

To increase understanding

1. (a) Which riddle or riddles can you solve? (b) Point out the clues which led to your solution.

2. "The Seafarer" and the riddles are eighth-century Anglo-Saxon compositions. What resemblances do you find in (a) feeling toward nature, (b) poetic devices?

Extending interests

The Old English riddles necessarily dealt with subjects familiar to the Anglo-Saxons. Are you able to write a riddle focused on some aspect of twentieth-century life? Try your skill at writing at least one riddle in the style of the Old English ones but with modern subject matter. See whether your classmates can solve it.

The Treasure of Sutton Hoo

Sutton Hoo is an estate in Suffolk on the eastern coast of England. Here in 1939 archaeologists began excavating a burial mound that lay on a cliff a hundred feet above the tidal estuary of the River Deben. As the painstaking work continued under the direction of the British Museum, archaeologists realized that they had uncovered the richest hoard of early Anglo-Saxon objects ever found. A sword, a shield, and a helmet, finely wrought golden jewelry, coins, silver bowls—these objects certainly must have been the treasure of a mighty king.

The treasure, scattered and corroded by time, lay within the hull of what once had been an eighty-six-foot wooden ship. Only the iron bolts and nails remained, but the outline of the ship was plainly visible in the sand. The ship had not been a grave but a cenotaph —a memorial to a king whose bones lay elsewhere. The treasure had been placed amidships in a wooden chamber or cabin, long since rotted away. From the evidence offered by the coins placed with the hoard, the burial has been dated as probably occurring during the last half of the seventh century.

Before the discoveries at Sutton Hoo, many graves had been excavated in Kent, Northumbria, and other sections of England, and from them *grave-goods* such as brooches, knives,

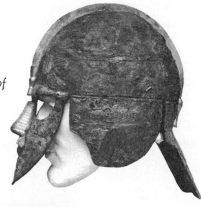

Below left: Imprint of the ship's hull after careful excavation. Below right: Silver "Saul and Paul" spoons from the far Byzantine Empire. Right: The king's helmet; the front view of this helmet appears on page 16.

COURTESY THE BRITISH MUSEUM

combs, and pottery had been recovered. But they gave only a fragmentary picture of Anglo-Saxon life. It took the discoveries at Sutton Hoo to establish the fact that the life described in *Beowulf* was a true picture of the way the warrior classes lived. Here were found fragments of the dress and equipment of a warrior—bits of a mail shirt, a sword with a gold pommel inlaid with garnets, a shield with dragon and bird figures, and an iron helmet ornamented with a silver crest. Here also were articles that spoke of great feasts in the mead-hall—nests of silver vessels, silver mounts that had once ornamented great drinking horns, and the fragments of a six-string harp.

The articles found at Sutton Hoo established the fact that Anglo-Saxon culture of the seventh century was far more advanced than students had previously imagined. The golden jewelry surpasses any Germanic work of the period found elsewhere. The brooches and buckles, finely designed and inlaid with garnets and mosaic glass, show the mastery of first-class craftsmen.

The Sutton Hoo hoard proves also that the Anglo-Saxons traded widely. The blade of the sword was probably forged in the Rhineland. Some of the silver bowls bear the stamp of Asia Minor and of Mediterranean lands. And there are two silver spoons bearing the names *Saul* and *Paul* in Greek.

Although much has been learned about the treasure of Sutton Hoo, some questions remain in dispute. What East Anglican king was honored by this magnificent cenotaph? Was he pagan or Christian? Until these and other questions are positively answered, this ancient detective story will continue to fascinate students of the past.

Jewelry of native Anglo-Saxon craftsmanship. Below left: belt mount (top); belt buckle (center); fasteners for sword knot (bottom). Below right: a hinged clasp.

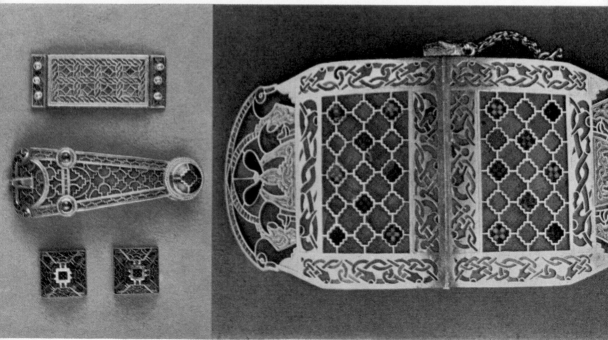

PROSE IN ANGLO-SAXON ENGLAND

Before the days of Alfred the Great (849-901), the most important prose writer in England was the Venerable Bede (673-735). Born and educated in Northumbria, this Benedictine monk more than any other scholar led Northumbria to its period of literary supremacy. (See page 18.) Among Bede's many works the *Ecclesiastical History of the English People* is still an invaluable source book for our knowledge of the earlier period of Anglo-Saxon rule. But Bede, as a churchman and scholar, wrote in Latin. Only because the *Ecclesiastical History* was translated into Old English by Alfred the Great is it considered a part of Anglo-Saxon prose.

Cross of gold inlaid with garnets worn by St. Cuthbert, a seventh-century bishop. Finding of the St. Cuthbert relics was described by Bede.

DURHAM CATHEDRAL LIBRARY

King Alfred is regarded as the greatest figure in Old English prose. After his heroic work in holding back the Danes, he turned his attention to the education of his people. The books he chose for translation and dissemination, including philosophy, general information, religion, and Bede's history, show the wide range of his interests. It is probable that Alfred translated these works himself, and he certainly added material of his own to some of them. He was also responsible for fostering the *Anglo-Saxon Chronicle*, a year-by-year account of English history, which had been kept spasmodically for some time. Under Alfred's sponsorship it became a tremendously valuable contemporary account of life in Anglo-Saxon England.

The last great figure in Old English literature is Abbot Aelfric of Eynsham (955?-1025?), like Bede a great Benedictine scholar and teacher. His works are many, but he is best known for his homilies, or sermons, his lives of the saints, and his amusing "Colloquy on the Occupations" (page 38). The colloquy differs from most Anglo-Saxon works in that it gives real insight into the humdrum life of the ordinary man—farmer, hunter, fisherman, and merchant. Aelfric is much more the conscious stylist than Alfred. His knowledge of the structure of Latin carries over into his writings in the vernacular. With Aelfric, Old English prose achieves balance and rhythm.

THE CONVERSION OF KING EDWIN

from Bede's ECCLESIASTICAL HISTORY OF THE ENGLISH PEOPLE
Translated by J. A. Giles

At this time the nation of the Northumbrians, that is, the nation of the Angles that live on the north side of the river Humber, with their king, Edwin, received the faith through the preaching of Paulinus.[1] . . .

For some time he [Edwin] delayed to receive the word of God at the preaching of Paulinus, and used to sit several hours alone, and seriously to ponder with himself what he was to do, and what religion he was to follow. Then the man of God came to him, laid his right hand on his head, and asked whether he knew

1. *Paulinus* (pô lin′əs), a missionary sent by Pope Gregory the Great to Northumbria in 601.

that sign.[2] The king in a trembling condition, was ready to fall down at his feet, but he raised him up, and in a familiar manner said to him, "Behold, by the help of God you have escaped the hands of the enemies whom you feared. Behold, you have of His gift obtained the kingdom which you desired. Take heed not to delay that which you promised to perform; embrace the faith, and keep the precepts of Him who, delivering you from the temporal adversity, has raised you to the honor of a temporal kingdom; and if, from this time forward, you shall be obedient to His will, which through me He signifies to you, He will not only deliver you from the everlasting torments of the wicked, but also make you partaker with Him of His eternal kingdom in Heaven."

The king, hearing these words, answered that he was both willing and bound to receive the faith which he taught; but that he would confer about it with his principal friends and counselors, to the end that if they also were of his opinion, they might all together be cleansed in Christ the Fountain of Life. Paulinus consenting, the king did as he said; for, holding a council with the wise men, he asked of every one in particular what he thought of the new doctrine, and the new worship that was preached. To which the chief of his own priests, Coifi, immediately answered, "O king, consider what this is which is now preached to us; for I verily declare to you that the religion which we have hitherto professed has, as far as I can learn, no virtue in it. For none of your people has applied himself more diligently to the worship of our gods than I, and all are more prosperous in all their undertakings. Now if the gods were good for any thing, they would rather forward me, who have been more careful to serve them. It remains, therefore, that if upon examination you find those new doctrines which are now preached to us better and more efficacious, we immediately receive them without delay."

Another of the king's chief men, approving of his words and exhortations, presently added: "The present life of man, O king, seems to me, in comparison to that time which is unknown to us, like to the swift flight of a sparrow through the room wherein you sit at supper in the winter, with your commanders and ministers, and a good fire in the midst, whilst the storms of rain and snow prevail abroad; the sparrow, flying in at one door and immediately out at another, while he is within, is safe from the wintry storm; but after a short space of fair weather, he immediately vanishes out of your sight, into the dark winter from which he had emerged. So this life of man appears for a short space, but of what went before, or what is to follow, we are utterly ignorant. If, therefore, this new doctrine contains something more certain, it seems justly to deserve to be followed." The other elders and king's counselors, by Divine inspiration, spoke to the same effect.

But Coifi added that he wished more attentively to hear Paulinus discourse concerning the God whom he preached; which he having by the king's command performed, Coifi, hearing his words, cried out: "I have long since been sensible that there was nothing in that which we worshiped; because the more diligently I sought after truth in the worship, the less I found it. But now I freely confess, that such truth evidently appears in this preaching as can confer on us the gifts of life, of salvation, and of eternal happiness. For which reason I advise, O king, that we instantly abjure and set fire to those temples and altars which we have consecrated without reaping any benefit from them." In short, the king publicly gave his license to Paulinus to preach the Gospel, and renouncing idolatry, declared that he received the faith of Christ, and when he inquired of the high priest who should first profane the altars and temples of their idols, with the enclosures that were about them, he answered: "I. For who can more properly than myself destroy those things which I worshiped through ignorance, for an example to all others, through the wisdom which has been given me by the true God?" Then immediately, in contempt of his

---

2. *asked . . . sign.* The ceremony of the laying on, or imposition, of hands, which Paulinus had just performed, signified the transmitting of spiritual powers and graces to Edwin.

former superstitions, he desired the king to furnish him with arms and a stallion; and mounting the same, he set out to destroy the idols; for it was not lawful before for the high priest either to carry arms or to ride on any but a mare. Having therefore girt a sword about him, with a spear in his hand, he mounted the king's stallion and proceeded to the idols. The multitude, beholding it, concluded he was mad; but he lost no time, for as soon as he drew near the temple he profaned the same, casting into it the spear which he held; and rejoicing in the knowledge of the worship of the true God, he commanded his companions to destroy the temple, with all its enclosures, by fire. The place where the idols were is still shown, not far from York, to the eastward, beyond the river Derwent, and is now called Godmunding-ham,[3] where the high priest, by the inspiration of the true God, profaned and destroyed the altars which he had himself consecrated.

King Edwin, therefore, with all the nobility of the nation, and a large number of the common sort, received the faith, and the washing of regeneration in the eleventh year of his reign, which is the year of the incarnation of our Lord 627, and about one hundred and eighty after the coming of the English into Britain. . .

✤ To increase understanding

1. (a) Earlier you read the Anglo-Saxon term for "the council of the wise men." What was it? (b) What fact about Anglo-Saxon civilization is brought out by Edwin's deferring to the opinions of these men?
2. What arguments did the wise men advance as reasons for adopting the new religion?
3. What details about the pagan religion of the Anglo-Saxons can you learn from this selection?
4. The passage beginning "The present life of man . . ." (page 37) is one of the most famous in Old English literature. Why do you think this is so?

A COLLOQUY ON THE OCCUPATIONS   Abbot Aelfric

Translated by George K. Anderson

Aelfric, as you have learned, usually wrote in Old English. However, because he was interested in teaching Latin, he wrote the "Colloquy" in Latin as a dialogue for the student to read to his teacher. Between the lines of the Latin text, some unknown writer of the eleventh century placed the Anglo-Saxon translation.

1

Pupil: We children pray thee, O teacher, that thou teach us to speak aright, for we are untutored and speak corruptly.

Master: What would ye talk about?

Pupil: What care we what we talk about, provided it be right and fitting, not idle or wicked?

Master: Would ye be chastised in your learning?

Pupil: We had liefer be chastised for the sake of learning than not to know; but we know thee to be kind, loath to inflict a flogging unless thou art forced by our stupidity.

Master: I ask thee, what sort of stuff art thou saying? What occupation hast thou?

Pupil: I am a confessed monk, and I sing each day seven times[1] with my brothers, and I am busied with reading and singing; but even so I should like to learn to speak Latin.

Master: What do these thy companions know?

Pupil: Some are farmers, some shepherds, some cowherds; some indeed are hunters, some fishers, some fowlers, some merchants, some cobblers, salt-workers,[2] bakers.

2

Master: What sayest thou, farmer, how goest thou about thy work?

Farmer: Alas, dear master, I am sorely in need; I go out at dawn, forcing my oxen to

---

CONVERSION OF KING EDWIN. 3. *Godmundingham*, present-day Godmanham, near Market Weighton in Yorkshire.

COLLOQUY. 1. *seven times.* A duty of the Benedictine monks was singing the Divine Office, which was divided into seven parts, each part to be sung at a specified time. 2. *salt-workers*, men who obtained salt from brine.

the field, and I yoke them to the plow; there is no winter so severe that I dare lounge about my home for fear of my lord; but with yoked oxen and affixed plowshare and coulter with the plow, every day I must cultivate a full acre or more.

Master: Hast thou any companions?

Farmer: I have a boy who urges on the oxen with his goad, who is now hoarse from cold and bawling.

Master: What more dost thou in a day?

Farmer: Well, I certainly do more. I must fill the bin of the oxen with hay, and water them, and carry out their dung.

Master: Hey! Hey! That is a lot of labor.

Farmer: Yea, master; it is a great labor, for I am not free.

3

Master: Well, cowherd, what kind of work dost thou do?

Cowherd: Alas, my lord, I labor very hard: when the farmer unhitches the oxen, I lead them to pasture, and all night I stand watching over them against thieves, and then in the early morning I give them back to the farmer well filled and watered.

Master: Knowest thou anything?

Hunter: I know a trade.

Master: Which one?

Hunter: I am a hunter.

Master: Whose?

Hunter: The king's.

Master: How dost thou go about thy business?

Hunter: I take my nets, and set them in all sorts of places, and I urge on my hounds, that they harry the wild beasts until they come in unforeseen fashion into the nets, so that they are trapped; then I kill them off in the nets.

Master: Canst thou not hunt except with nets?

Hunter: Yea, I can hunt without nets.

Master: How?

Hunter: With swift hounds I ensnare the wild beasts.

Master: What kind of wild animals dost thou most often catch?

Hunter: I catch harts and bears and stags and roes, and sometimes hares.

Master: Wert thou hunting today?

From an illustrated Anglo-Saxon calendar. First two columns of letters to the left of text show the dates according to the Roman method of counting backward. For example, vii ID, *is the seventh day before the idus, or middle of the month.* NON *stands for nonae, or ninth day before the idus. Days after the ides are numbered back from the Calendae, or first day, of the next month.*

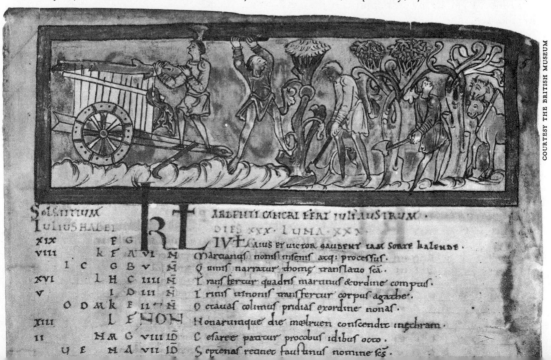

Hunter: I was not, for today is Sunday, but yesterday I was hunting.

Master: What didst thou catch?

Hunter: Two harts and a bear.

Master: How didst thou catch them?

Hunter: The harts I caught in the nets, and the bear I killed myself.

Master: How wert thou so bold as to stab the bear?

Hunter: The hounds drove him towards me, and I there, standing up to him, suddenly stabbed him to death.

Master: Truly thou wert very brave.

Hunter: No hunter can be fearful, because various wild beasts live in the woods.

Master: What dost thou do about thy kill?

Hunter: I give to the king whatsoever I catch, because I am his hunter.

Master: What does he give to thee?

Hunter: He clothes me well and feeds me, and sometimes he gives me a horse or ring, that I may the more joyfully go about my trade.

5

Master: Which trade dost thou know?

Fisher: I am a fisher.

Master: What dost thou derive from thy trade?

Fisher: Sustenance and clothing and cattle.

Master: How dost thou catch fish?

Fisher: I get in my ship, and cast my nets in the sea, and I throw my fishhook and basket, and whatsoever they bring up, I take it.

Master: Where dost thou sell thy fish?

Fisher: In the town.

Master: What kind of fish dost thou catch?

Fisher: Eels and pikes, minnows and eel-pouts, trout and lampreys, and whatsoever swims in the water.

Master: Why dost thou never fish in the ocean?

Fisher: Sometimes I do, but seldom, because it is hard rowing for me to go to the ocean.

Master: What dost thou catch in the ocean?

Fisher: Herring and salmon, porpoises and sturgeons, oysters and crabs, mussels, peri-winkles, cockles, plaices and flounders, and lobsters, and many other such.

Master: Couldst thou catch a whale?

Fisher: Not I.

Master: Why not?

Fisher: Because it is a dangerous thing to catch a whale. Safer it is for me to go to the ocean with my ships, than to go with many ships hunting after whales.

Master: Why so?

Fisher: Because I had liefer catch a fish which I could slay, than one that with one blow could sink and drown not only myself but my companions also.

Master: And yet many catch whales, and escape the dangers, and get a great deal of money for it.

Fisher: Thou sayest the truth, but I dare not, out of the ignorance of my mind.

6

Master: What sayest thou, fowler? How dost thou trap birds?

Fowler: In many ways I ensnare birds: sometimes with nets, sometimes with nooses, sometimes with birdlime, sometimes by whistling, sometimes with hawks, sometimes with traps.

Master: Hast thou a hawk?

Fowler: I have.

Master: Dost thou know how to tame it?

Fowler: Yea, I know how. What good would they do me, if I did not know how to tame them?

Master: How dost thou feed thy hawk?

Fowler: They feed both themselves and me in the winter, and in the spring I let them fly away to the woods, and catch my birds in the autumn and tame them.

Master: And why dost thou let the tamed ones fly away from thee?

Fowler: Because I am not willing to feed them in summer, because they eat excessively.

Master: And yet many feed the tame hawks through the summer, so that they may have them all ready in the autumn.

Fowler: Yea, so they do, but I am not willing to worry over one of them, because I can catch others, not that one, and many more if I need.

7

Master: Well, merchant, what sayest thou?

Merchant: I say that I am necessary to the

king, and to the nobles and the wealthy, and to all people.

Master: And why?

Merchant: I get in my ship with my cargoes, and I row over the watery wastes, and I sell my goods and buy valuable goods in return, which are unknown in this land, and I bring them hither to you with great risk over the sea, and sometimes I suffer shipwreck with the loss of all my goods, myself barely escaping alive.

Master: What sort of things dost thou bring us?

Merchant: Robes of pall[3] and silk, precious jewels, and gold; strange booty, and spices, wine, and oil, ivory and brass, bronze and tin, sulphur and glass, and many other such things.

Master: Wilt thou sell thy goods here, for the same price as thou didst buy them there?

Merchant: I will not. What profit would there be for me from my labors? But I will sell them here at a greater price than that for which I bought them there, that I may get some advantage from it, whence I can feed myself and my wife and my son.

8

Master: What sayest thou, wise man? Which trade, as it seems to thee, is more important among all these people? Which, as it seems to thee, holds sovereignty among all the trades of the world?

Councilor: Tilling of the earth, because the farmer feeds us all.

Smith: Whence does the farmer get his plowshare or his coulter, who does not even have a goad except from my trade? Whence does the fisher get his fishhook, or the cobbler his awl, or the tailor his needle? Is it not from my works?

Councilor: Truly thou speakest rightly: but we had all liefer live with the farmer than with thee; because the farmer gives us bread and drink; thou—what dost thou give us in thy smithy, except iron sparks and the sounding of beating sledges and blowing bellows?

Carpenter: Which one of you has no need of my trade? I make thy house and many a vessel, and ships for all of you.

Smith: O carpenter, why dost thou speak so, when not even one hole couldst thou make in thy business without the fruit of my labor?

9

Councilor: O companions and good laboring men: let us leave immediately this controversy, and let there be peace and harmony among us, and let each do for the other according to his trade, and agree with the farmer, whence we have food for ourselves and fodder for our horses. And this thought I give to all workers, that each one of you go about his business with pleasure, because he who abandons his profession is abandoned by that profession. Whosoever thou mayest be, mass-priest, monk, churl, warrior, observe this rule for thyself: be what thou art, for it is a great shame and abasement for a man not to be what he is and what he ought to be.

10

Master: Thou, boy, what didst thou today?

Pupil: I did many things. In the night, when I heard the bell, I arose from my bed and went to church and sang matins[4] with the brothers; after that we sang about all the saints and the daily lauds; after that we sang prime-service and seven psalms with the litany and early morning mass; after that we sang midday mass and ate and drank and slept, and again we arose and sang nones; and now we are here before thee ready to hear what thou hast to tell us.

Master: When will you sing evensong or compline?

Pupil: When it is time.

Master: Wert thou scourged today?

Pupil: I was not, for I behaved circumspectly.

Master: What eatest thou by day?

Pupil: I still enjoy meat, because I am a child leading my life under the rod.[5]

Master: What more dost thou eat?

Pupil: Roots and eggs, fish and cheese, butter and beans, and all clean things I eat with much gratitude.

Master: Thou must be very eager to grow,

---

3. *pall,* a rich purple cloth. 4. *matins,* the first part of the Divine Office. (See footnote 1.) *Lauds, prime-service, nones,* and *compline,* mentioned later, are also parts of the Office. 5. *enjoy meat . . . under the rod.* Although the Benedictine monks abstained from meat, the pupil is still a boy and not expected to follow this part of the rule.

when thou eatest all things that are put before thee.

Pupil: I enjoy sometimes this dish and sometimes that dish in moderation, as befits a monk, not with greed, because I am not a glutton.

Master: And what dost thou drink?

Pupil: Ale, if I have any; or water, if I have no ale.

Master: Dost thou not drink wine?

Pupil: I am not so well-to-do that I can buy wine for myself; and wine is not a drink for children or foolish people, but for the old and wise.

Master: Where dost thou sleep?

Pupil: In the dormitory with the brothers.

Master: Who wakens thee for matins?

Pupil: Sometimes I hear the sound of the bell and arise; sometimes my master wakens me sternly with the rod.

Master: O all ye good children and delightful pupils, your master admonishes you that you obey the laws of God, and keep yourselves excellent wherever you may be. Go with devotion when you hear the church-bell, and go into the church and bow yourselves humbly before the holy altar, and stand with devotion and sing wholeheartedly and pray for all your sins, and depart without foolishness to the cloister or to study.

❈ To increase understanding

1. Is the farmer in the "Colloquy" a churl or a freeman?

2. What is the difference between a hunter and a fowler?

3. (*a*) In what ways do the experiences of the merchant differ from those of the farmer and the fisher? (*b*) How should this difference affect the merchant's outlook on life?

4. Describe the life of a boy studying to become a monk.

5. (*a*) What purpose do you think the master has in asking which is the most important occupation? (*b*) How does the councilor show himself truly a "wise man"?

6. List in order the probable position in Anglo-Saxon society of each of the following: (*a*) the farmer; (*b*) the cowherd; (*c*) the hunter; (*d*) the merchant; (*e*) the councilor. Be ready to defend your answers.

The Larger View

The selections below represent some of the types of Anglo-Saxon literature you have studied in this chapter. After you have read them carefully, write a paragraph about each, explaining (1) whether you believe the selection was pagan or Christian in origin, and (2) whether it is from an epic, an elegiac poem, or a prose historical work. Pay particular attention to citing the clues on which you base your decision.

I. Often I must alone, each early dawn
Bewail my woes; now is no man alive
To whom I dare the thoughts of my mind
Plainly relate. I know of a truth
That with an earl is a noble custom,
To hold firmly his feelings within him,
To keep his treasure-chest, let him think as he will.
Nor may the weary heart withstand this Wyrd
Nor a savage spirit bring any solace;
Though eager for justice, a mournful heart
He must therefore restrain within his breast-hoard.
And so the thoughts of my heart I must
(Though often wretched, bereft of my native land)
Seal up in fetters, far from my free kinsmen,
Since long ago my gold-giver
The covering of earth enwrapped, and I thence abject,
Winter-troubled, traversed the mingling of the waves,
Sadly sought the hall of the dispenser of treasure,
Where I, far or near, might be able to find
Him who in mead-hall would show me favor
Or would console me friendless and treat me kindly.

II. By his verses the minds of many were often excited to despise the world, and to aspire to heaven. Others after him attempted, in the English nation, to compose religious poems, but none could ever compare with him, for he did not learn the art of poetry from men, but from God; for which reason he never could compose any trivial or vain poem, but only those which relate to religion suited his religious tongue; for having lived in a secular habit till he was well advanced in years, he had never learned anything of versifying; for which reason being sometimes at entertainments, when it was agreed for the sake of mirth that all present should sing in their turns,

when he saw the instrument come towards him,
he rose up from table and returned home.

III. He of mankind was strongest in power
in that day of this life, noble and vigorous.
He bade for himself a good wave-rider
to be prepared; said he would go
over the swan-road to seek the war-king,
the prince renowned, since men he had need of.
Dear tho' he was, his prudent liegemen
little blamed him for that voyage,
whetted him rather, and noted the omen.
Then the good chief chose him champions
of the Geat-folk, whomso bravest
he could find, and, fourteen with him,
sought the vessel. Then the hero,
the sea-crafty man, led the way to the shore.
Time passed; the floater was on the waves,
the boat 'neath the hill; the ready warriors
stepped on the prow; the streams surged
the sea 'gainst the sand; the warriors bare
into the bark's bosom bright arms,
a rich war-array. The men shoved out
on the welcome voyage the wooden bark.
Most like to a bird the foamy-necked floater,
impelled by the wind, then flew o'er the waves
till about the same time on the second day
the twisted prow had sailed so far
that the voyagers land descried,
shining ocean-shores, mountains steep,
spacious sea-nesses. Then was the floater
at the end of its voyage. Up thence quickly
the Weders' people stept on the plain;
the sea-wood tied; their mail-shirts shook,
their martial weeds; thanked God that to them
the paths of the waves had been made easy.

Bibliography

BEOWULF, retold by Rosemary Sutcliff. (Dutton) This is a masterly recreation of *Beowulf*. Rosemary Sutcliff so uses a rich vocabulary and cadenced prose that the reader senses the spirit that animates this oldest of English epics.

COOLIDGE, OLIVIA, *Legends of the North*. (Houghton) "Song of Beowulf" and "Beowulf and the Fire Dragon" are included in this well-written collection of old tales from the northern countries of Europe. There are bold illustrations in keeping with the courage of the times.

DUGGAN, ALFRED, *The Right Line of Cerdic*. (Pantheon) Alfred the Great comes alive both as a man and as a ruler in this vivid and lively account of a most decisive period in English history.

LEIGHTON, MARGARET, *Journey for a Princess*. (Farrar, Straus) Princess Elstrid, youngest child of Alfred the Great, is loved by two men —one a Viking, the other a Frank—but she cares for neither suitor. Her story is exciting and romantic, and presents a good picture of old England.

PARKER, RICHARD, *The Sword of Ganelon*. (McKay) A tale of ninth-century England, this book will captivate the attention of readers with its powerful blending of action and character study.

PRICE, CHRISTINE, *The Dragon and the Book*. (McKay) Wilfred, a young monk of the ninth century, helps to translate the Book of Psalms for King Alfred—and just as the work is completed, the Danes invade England. Wilfred escapes with the Psalter and sets out to search for Alfred.

QUENNELL, MARJORIE, *Everyday Life in Roman and Anglo-Saxon Times*. (Putnam) The contributions of the Romans, Anglo-Saxons, Danes, Norwegians, and Normans to early British civilization are examined and explained by the author. Her use of many new findings in archeology makes the book especially interesting.

SHORE, MAXINE, *The Captive Princess*. (McKay) No student should miss this lovely story of England's first Christian princess, who was held in captivity by the Romans.

SUTCLIFF, ROSEMARY, *Dawn Wind*, *The Eagle of the Ninth*, and *The Lantern Bearers*. (Walck) Rosemary Sutcliff is one of the few contemporary authors to write extensively about early Britain. *Dawn Wind*, set in sixth-century Britain, is a convincing story of a young orphan boy who gives himself as a thrall to the Saxons in order to save the life of a friend. *The Eagle of the Ninth* is an authentic picture of life in the first century A.D., when Britain was under Roman occupation. The fast-paced *The Lantern Bearers* tells of a fifth-century England invaded and tormented by legions of foreign tribes, and shows how, despite ruthless and bitter power struggles, people from enemy tribes gradually merged.

TREECE, HENRY, *The Road to Mikelgard*. (Criterion) Constantinople—called Mikelgard by the Vikings—is the colorful setting of much of the action in this suspenseful story of Harold, British king and adventurer.

chapter two

MEDIEVAL ENGLAND

1066-1485

To many readers the words "medieval England" and "feudalism" suggest all the romance of the past. Into mind flash images of King Arthur and his peerless knights, of minstrels singing in castle halls, of Sir Walter Scott's Norman villains and Saxon heroes battling before a besieged castle, and of Chaucer's pilgrims wending their slow way toward Canterbury Cathedral. These literary images of the Middle Ages are true but woefully incomplete. They omit the serfs, living with their livestock in dirt-floored huts. They overlook the fact that terrible plagues kept the cathedral bells tolling night and day as funeral followed funeral. They fail to recognize the dominant part the Church played in the life of king and serf, knight and freeman. If we are to understand the literature of medieval England, we must be able to re-create in imagination the world that produced folk ballads and Chaucer's tales, the verse romances of the wandering minstrels and Malory's *Morte Darthur*.

THE FEUDAL SYSTEM In 1066 the purely Anglo-Saxon history of England came to an end. In that year William the Conqueror and his Norman warriors invaded England and overcame the Anglo-Saxons at the Battle of Hastings. Originally the Normans, like the Danes who had overrun eastern England in the ninth century, had been Vikings. A hundred years earlier they had invaded that part of France which has since been called Normandy and gradually adopted the culture, customs, and language of the French. At the time they conquered England, their civilization was more highly organized and more elaborate than Anglo-Saxon culture. Its foundation was the feudal system, a system based upon the holding of land. Immediately upon conquering England, William laid claim to all the land in the realm. Dispossessing its Anglo-Saxon owners, he granted large areas to his lords, who, in return, promised William their services and those of their retainers. The lords, in turn, might grant portions of their lands to knights pledged to assist them in battle. At the bottom of the social scale were the serfs, who belonged to the land. They eked out a scanty and

Detail from one of the famous stained-glass windows of the Fairford Church, Gloucestershire. These windows, of English design and workmanship, were executed in the late fifteenth century.

THE VICAR AND CHURCHWARDENS OF FAIRFORD CHURCH, GLOUCESTERSHIRE

often desolate existence, paying goods and services to the lord in return for the land they farmed.

This system of organizing men into specific classes was accepted even by the feudal serf because medieval man believed that full equality could not exist on earth. In this mortal life each man assumed the place in society for which God had destined him. The earthly hierarchy was a reflection of the divine order in which God held the highest position, followed by angels, men, animate and inanimate objects, and finally, in the lowest position, Satan.

Feudal society was essentially a society geared to war. Disputes arose not only between one country and another but between rival barons in the same land. A king possessed only a little more power than the strongest lords. National unity as we know it today did not exist. A man thought of himself as first the subject of the lord from whom he held his lands and then as a subject of the king.

CHIVALRY The feudal system revolved about the knight—the mounted warrior who became the symbol of chivalry. In fact, it was from *chevalier*, the French word for "mounted soldier," that the word *chivalry* evolved.

The training of a knight began in early childhood. At about the age of seven the well-born boy left his own home for service first as page, then as squire at some lord's castle. The lady of the castle taught him the elaborate code of courtesy and manners that a knight must follow. With other pages he was trained in horsemanship and the use of the shield, sword, and lance. When he became a squire, he waited upon his lord and, if need arose, followed him into battle. Finally he was dubbed knight and swore to uphold the code of chivalry—loyalty toward Church and King, reverence toward women.

The institution of chivalry softened the harshness of medieval life. It bound the often lawless warrior by a code, violating which meant loss of honor. In combination with a wave of devotion to the Virgin Mary which

Left: Woodcut from the press of Wynkyn de Worde, successor to England's first printer, William Caxton (see page 83).
Below: Seal of William the Conqueror. The obverse (left) shows William as Chief of the Normans; the reverse (right), as King of the English.

swept across Europe late in the eleventh century, it raised the status of woman and gained her a larger rôle both in life and in literature.

THE MEDIEVAL CHURCH The pageantry of chivalry with its flashing tournaments, its banquets at which minstrels sang of valorous deeds, its elaborate ritual of courtly love, brightened the lives of only a relatively small number of upper-class Englishmen. The mass of people—the serfs, and the artisans in the growing towns—lived a life different in every respect. Only in the Church were Englishmen of all classes united.

The magnificent cathedrals which throughout the Middle Ages raised their towers above the towns of England testified to the fact that these ages were centuries of faith. In a world of war, plague, and violent death, medieval man clung to the Church's teaching that the world in which he lived was relatively unimportant while the world to come was of vast importance. Membership in the Church also secured him his place in society. If, for a serious transgression, he was excommunicated, prohibited from participating in any of the rites of the Church, he lost his status. Excommunication was equivalent to being condemned to a life of total isolation.

In Norman England as in Saxon England, education was the province of the Church. In the long centuries before the printing press was invented, manuscripts were painstakingly copied by hand in the monasteries. Monks and priests passed the culture of Greek and Roman scholars as well as the teachings of the Church on to young students who flocked to the monasteries to learn. From such beginnings in the twelfth and thirteenth centuries came the formal organization of Oxford and Cambridge as universities.

The Church was also intimately bound up with political affairs. In medieval thought Church and King were necessary instruments of the divine scheme for maintaining order in society: They were, in medieval terms, the "two swords of God." The question of which sword was indeed the greater on this earth was a major source of dispute. The most famous quarrel between Church and King in Medieval England was that of Thomas à Becket, Archbishop of Canterbury, and Henry II. It was Henry's belief that certain rights exercised by the Church belonged to the King. Confident that he could bring about the changes he desired if a man sympathetic to his views were Archbishop of Canterbury, Henry had Becket, his chancellor and close friend, appointed to this position. But once he had become Archbishop, Becket stanchly upheld the rights of the Church. By 1170 matters had reached a climax. According to an often told story, one day Henry in exasperation exclaimed to a group of his followers, "Will not one of you avenge me of this turbulent priest?" Four knights straightway dashed off to Canterbury, found the Archbishop at his prayers in the cathedral, and struck him down with their daggers. The Christian world was shocked; Henry II himself deplored the killing and did penance; and the tomb of Thomas à Becket at Canterbury became the favorite place of pilgrimage for Englishmen of all classes.

JOHN HUNT COLLECTION, DUBLIN

Small cross of exquisite workmanship, containing a relic of Thomas à Becket. This is a pectoral cross, designed to be worn by a bishop or an abbot.

Right: Illustration from an early fifteenth-century manuscript showing Richard I captured by a margrave of the Emperor Henry VI. Richard was attempting to pass through Austria in disguise on his return to England from the Holy Land. He was later released on payment of a king's ransom—120,000 pounds of silver. Below: Inside and outside of two medieval castles. Photo on left shows the great hall of Bunratty Castle, an important stronghold of the west coast of Ireland from 1440 through the eighteenth century. Photo on right shows the keep of Dover Castle, known since medieval times as the "Key of England" from its important position at the narrowest part of the Straits. The Romans built a fortress here about 50 A.D., and during World War II the casemates of the castle sheltered the people of Dover from the continuous shellfire. The keep of the castle was built by Henry II between 1181 and 1187.

THE CRUSADES The widespread religious zeal of the Middle Ages inspired the great religious movement known as the Crusades, whose object was to retake the Holy Land from the Mohammedans. Kings, knights, and commoners flocked to take up their swords in this Holy War. Leader of one of the Crusades was Richard the Lion-Hearted, King of England, son of Henry II, and one of the most dazzling figures produced by the Age of Chivalry.

The First Crusade was launched in 1095; and for almost the next two hundred years wave after wave of men from every Christian country battered against the Moslems. While the Crusades were ultimately unsuccessful in their efforts to liberate the Holy Land from the Turks, they had a profound effect on all of Europe. For the first time since the fall of the Roman Empire, great numbers of men traveled widely. Knights from the bleak fortress castles of England saw the palaces of Venice, the opulent cities of Asia Minor. Scholars rediscovered the literature of ancient Greece and Rome. The horizons of men were widened and civilization took a great step toward the modern world.

THE BEGINNINGS OF NATIONAL GOVERNMENT During the more than four centuries commonly covered by the term "Medieval England," England was ruled by two royal families: the Normans, including William the Conqueror and his direct successors (1066-1154), and the Plantagenets, beginning with Henry II (1154-1485). Three important events in the slow progress toward a national government occurred during this period: judicial reform, the granting of the Magna Charta, and the beginnings of Parliament.

When Henry II ascended the throne in 1154, nearly a hundred years after the Norman Conquest, he found a confused and corrupt system of justice. Some of the courts were administered by the King's justices; others were under the jurisdiction of feudal barons; still others followed the old Anglo-Saxon judicial code. Resolved that the King's justice must be the

same for all people in every section of England, Henry divided the country into districts, appointed judges to administer justice in each circuit, and expanded the functions of the jury.

King John, son of Henry II, totally disregarded the provisions for justice his father had guaranteed by charter. He jailed men on trumped-up charges and refused them trials; he impoverished the country by ruinous taxes. Exasperated beyond endurance, barons and knights banded together, and in 1215 at Runnymede on the banks of the Thames River forced John to sign the Magna Charta, or Great Charter. This document, which established by law certain liberties of Englishmen, was revolutionary in its implication that the King, like his people, was subject to the rule of law.

During the reign of Edward I, grandson of John, the rights of Englishmen were again extended. For some time *parliaments* (from the French word *parler*, "to speak") had been held. Edward called the first Parliament—the Great Parliament of 1295—in which all classes of the kingdom from barons to the lower clergy were included. This Parliament became in time the most significant governmental body developed by the English, the ancestor of the Congress of the United States and of representative assemblies the world over.

WARFARE For centuries it had been the dream of English kings to bring the entire island of Britain under one dominion. Edward I spent most of his reign (1272-1307) trying to achieve this goal. He successfully subdued the Welsh; but the struggle against the Scots, a freedom-loving Celtic people toughened by centuries of border warfare with Romans, Saxons, and English, dragged on and on. Edward I died with Scotland still unconquered.

During the fifty-year reign of Edward III (1327-1377), the grandson of Edward I, commerce developed and England prospered. Particularly important was the wool trade. Wool from English sheep was shipped to Flanders to be woven into cloth for English markets. So important was this trade that the export duty on raw wool was the chief financial mainstay of the English government. This prosperous trade irked the King of France to such a degree that he began to seize English wool ships. In retaliation, Edward III revived an old claim to the crown of France. The war thus begun in 1337 was waged intermittently for a hundred years and is known as the Hundred Years' War.

Eight years after war was declared, the Battle of Crécy (1346) marked the beginning of the end of the Age of Chivalry and the emergence of the common man. For at Crécy the English longbowmen dramatically routed the French cavalry and proved that the unarmored foot soldier was the equal of the horseman in armor. Ultimately England lost the war and relinquished her claims to French territory. But the war had one beneficial effect. No longer was there friction between Normans and Anglo-Saxons; henceforth all were Englishmen.

Instead of the needed period of peace to recover from the war with France, the second half of the fifteenth century was marked by warfare between the descendants of the Duke of York and the Duke of Lancaster, who were both sons of Edward III. Because the House of Lancaster had a red rose as its emblem and the House of York a white rose, this civil war is called the War of the Roses. After a period of bitter warfare during which the crown changed hands several times, the Earl of Richmond of the House of Lancaster married Elizabeth, heiress of the House of York, and ascended the throne in 1485 as Henry VII, the first of the Tudors.

THE RISE OF THE COMMON MAN During the declining years of the Middle Ages the pageantry of chivalry with its armored knights jousting in tournaments still dazzled the people but no longer blinded them. The great lords of the castles and the powerful religious leaders could no longer hold the poor villagers in complete subservience. The common man began his slow rise. In mid-fourteenth century the terrible Black Death killed an estimated forty percent of the population, and serfs, left without masters, escaped to a freer life in the growing towns. Other serfs were driven from the manors when the lords turned to sheep raising, which required fewer workers. In towns and villages families deprived of home and work became vagabonds and robbers. Out of the desperation of the laborers emerged the Peasants' Revolt of 1381, which was savagely crushed by the nobles.

During this same century a middle class of merchants and craftsmen began its rise to power and stability. Craftsmen were prospering and were establishing guilds—the forerunners of unions or trade organizations—to protect their rights. Many of these guilds—such as the weavers, the carpenters, the haberdashers—had fine halls, and their members dressed in gay, distinctive liveries.

Along with the social upheaval came a change in the attitude toward the Church. The way was being paved for a new phase in English history. The country was moving toward nationalism, a more modern economy, a more questioning attitude toward the powers of the Church, and above all toward the idea that a man's place in society was not necessarily a fixed thing nor was his earthly life so unimportant. The first whisper of the Renaissance was in the air.

Opposite: Edward I. Below: A vigorous picture of the work of the common man stands in contrast to the otherworldly text in this fourteenth-century Psalter.

iudicia tua domine
Quoniam tu dominus altissimus
super omnem terram: nimis exalta
tus es super omnes deos

Medieval England 51

POPULAR BALLADS

Because ballads were sung for centuries before they were written down, exactly when or how they originated and developed is unknown. But from references in old documents and from the character of the ballads themselves, we know that they were sung by the simple, unlettered people of the Middle Ages. The fact that the word *ballad* comes from an old French word which means "dance song" suggests that at one time people danced to ballads. In their directness, in their swift-moving narratives, and in the way they present the elemental themes—love, courage, enmity, death—the ballads reflect the lives of people who snatched eagerly at intervals of happiness and faced tragedy with cold-blooded calm.

There are three basic types of ballad: the *folk ballad*, the *minstrel ballad*, and the *coronach*. Folk ballads, the oldest of these types, were probably composed by a local singer to commemorate some event of importance to the community. As generations of singers passed on the song, a word was changed here and there, stanzas were omitted, and differing versions of the same ballad often appeared. Certain basic characteristics also developed. Because the listeners were most interested in rapid and dramatic action, story is more important than characters or setting. The introductory material is sketched in briefly and the action moves swiftly to its climax. The general tone is usually tragic. The ballads often end in death by accident, murder, or suicide, or with the return of the dead. In them death is viewed impersonally. Tragedy was part of the pattern of medieval life.

In the folk ballad *repetition* of various types adds to the melody, provides emphasis, and heightens the emotional effect. *Incremental repetition*, or the repetition of lines containing some small addition or increment, is used to build to a climax. Many of the oldest ballads also make use of a *refrain*. Both types of repetition may be observed in the opening stanzas of "Lord Randal."

> "O where ha you been, Lord Randal, my son?
> And where ha you been, my handsome young man?"
> "I ha been at the greenwood; Mother, mak my bed soon,
> For I'm wearied wi huntin, and fain wad lie down."
>
> "And wha met ye there, Lord Randal, my son?
> And wha met ye there, my handsome young man?"
> "O I met wi my true-love; Mother, mak my bed soon,
> For I'm wearied wi huntin, and fain wad lie down."

The minstrel ballad takes its name from the fact that its originators were often minstrels who both composed and sang their ballads. Some minstrels may have had experience in the halls of noblemen; others traveled with the bands of Scottish and English in the years of Border warfare. Although they used the same themes as the community bards had sung in the folk ballads, they were more conscious artists in the handling of these themes. Often they added a description of the countryside or an account of a character's thoughts and feelings. Minstrel ballads, consequently, are often longer and less direct than the older folk ballads and have a more literary flavor.

The coronach, or lament, is the most personal type of ballad. To the narrative tradition of the folk ballad and the descriptive touches of the minstrel ballad it adds a lyric note—a personal reaction to tragedy. This lyric strain is strong in "Bonnie George Campbell" (page 58), the fragment of a coronach that describes one of the Campbell clan lost in a Border battle.

All English ballads are divided into stanzas. The *ballad stanza*, so called because it is the most frequently used ballad form, consists of four iambic lines with four accents in the first and third lines, three in the rhyming second and fourth lines. When read, the meter of ballads often seems crude and irregular. This is because ballads were meant to be sung, and the rhythms of song differ from speech rhythms. To understand the popularity of ballads in medieval England, one must imagine the skilled folk singer singing the ballad exactly as his grandfather had sung it before him, using traditional variations in the refrains and so building up in the listeners a familiar emotional response.

In 1327 this room in Berkeley Castle witnessed the brutal murder of Edward II through a conspiracy between his wife and Roger Mortimer.

EDWARD

"Why dois your brand[1] sae[2] drap wi bluid,
        Edward, Edward,
Why dois your brand sae drap wi bluid,
  And why sae sad gang[3] yee O?"
"O I hae killed my hauke sae guid,   5
        Mither, mither,
O I hae killed my hauke sae guid,
  And I had nae mair bot hee O.[4]"

"Your haukis bluid was nevir sae reid,[5]
        Edward, Edward,   10
Your haukis bluid was nevir sae reid,
  My deir son I tell thee O."
"O I hae killed my reid-roan steid,[6]
        Mither, mither,
O I hae killed my reid-roan steid,   15
  That erst was sae fair and frie O."

"Your steid was auld, and ye hae gat mair,
        Edward, Edward,
Your steid was auld, and ye hae gat mair,
  Sum other dule ye drie[7] O."   20

---

1. *brand*, sword. 2. *sae*, so. 3. *gang*, walk, or go.
4. *nae . . . hee O*, none other but him. 5. *reid*, red.
6. *reid-roan steid*, roan-red horse. 7. *dule ye drie*, sorrow you suffer.

"O I hae killed my fadir deir,
    Mither, mither,
O I hae killed my fadir deir,
    Alas, and wae[8] is mee O!"   24

"And whatten penance[9] wul ye drie for that,
    Edward, Edward?
And whatten penance wul ye drie for that?
    My deir son, now tell me O."
"Ile[10] set my feit in yonder boat,
    Mither, mither,   30
Ile set my feit in yonder boat,
    And Ile fare ovir the sea O."

"And what wul ye doe wi your towirs and
    your ha,[11]
        Edward, Edward,
And what wul ye doe wi your towirs and
    your ha,   35
    That were sae fair to see O?"
"Ile let thame stand tul they doun fa,[12]
    Mither, mither,
Ile let thame stand tul they doun fa,
    For here nevir mair maun[13] I bee O."   40

"And what wul ye leive to your bairns[14] and
    your wife,
        Edward, Edward?
And what wul ye leive to your bairns and
    your wife,
    Whan ye gang ovir the sea O?"   44
"The warldis room,[15] late them beg thrae life,
    Mither, mither,
The warldis room, late them beg thrae life,
    For thame nevir mair wul I see O."

"And what wul ye leive to your ain mither
    deir?
        Edward, Edward?   50
And what wul ye leive to your ain mither
    deir?
    My deir son, now tell me O."
"The curse of hell frae me sall ye beir,[16]
    Mither, mither,
The curse of hell frae me sall ye beir,   55
    Sic[17] counseils ye gave to me O."

SIR PATRICK SPENS

*Although no mention of Sir Patrick Spens can
be found in old Scottish or English records,
most authorities agree that this ballad records
an actual historical event. While there is disagreement as to what event the ballad commemorates, evidence points toward the ill-fated
return voyage of the ship that in 1281 had
carried Margaret, daughter of King Alexander
III of Scotland, to Norway to marry Eric,
King of Norway.*

The king sits in Dunfermline[1] toune
    Drinking the blude-red wine:
"O whar will I get guid sailor,
    To sail this schip of mine?"

Up and spak an eldern knicht,   5
    Sat at the kings richt kne:
"Sir Patrick Spens is the best sailor
    That sails upon the se."

The king has written a braid letter,[2]
    And signed it wi his hand,   10
And sent it to Sir Patrick Spens,
    Was walking on the sand.

The first line that Sir Patrick red,
    A loud lauch lauched[3] he;
The next line that Sir Patrick red,   15
    The teir blinded his ee.[4]

"O wha is this has don this deid,
    This ill deid don to me,
To send me out this time o' the yeir,
    To sail upon the se!   20

"Mak haste, mak haste, my mirry men all,
    Our guid schip sails the morne":
"O say na sae,[5] my master deir,
    For I feir a deadlie storme.

EDWARD. 8. *wae,* woe. 9. *whatten penance,* what kind
of penance. 10. *Ile,* I will. 11. *towirs . . . ha,* towers and
your castle. 12. *fa,* fall. 13. *maun,* must. 14. *bairns,*
children. 15. *The warldis room,* the world's room.
16. *sall ye beir,* shall you bear. 17. *Sic,* such.
SIR PATRICK SPENS. 1. *Dunfermline* (dun ferm'lin), a
town in Scotland near Edinburgh. 2. *a braid letter,* a
lengthy letter or a letter written on a broad sheet of paper.
3. *lauch lauched,* laugh laughed. 4. *ee,* eye. 5. *na sae,*
not so.

"Late late yestreen[6] I saw the new moone,   25
  Wi the auld moone in hir arme,
And I feir, I feir, my deir master,
  That we will cum to harme."

O our Scots nobles wer richt laith[7]
  To weet their cork-heild schoone[8];   30
Bot lang owre[9] a' the play wer playd,
  Thair hats they swam aboone.[10]

O lang, lang may their ladies sit,
  Wi thair fans into their hand,
Or eir they se Sir Patrick Spens   35
  Cum sailing to the land.

O lang, lang may the ladies stand,
  Wi thair gold kems[11] in their hair,
Waiting for thair ain deir lords,
  For they'll se thame na mair.   40

Haf owre, haf owre to Aberdour,[12]
  It's fiftie fadom deip,
And thair lies guid Sir Patrick Spens,
  Wi the Scots lords at his feit.

THE WIFE OF USHER'S WELL

There lived a wife at Usher's well,
  And a wealthy wife was she;
She had three stout and stalwart sons,
  And sent them o'er the sea.

They hadna been a week from her,   5
  A week but barely ane,[1]
When word came to the carline wife[2]
  That her three sons were gane.

They hadna been a week from her,
  A week but barely three,   10
When word came to the carline wife
  That her sons she'd never see.

"I wish the wind may never cease,
  Nor fashes[3] in the flood,
Till my three sons come hame to me   15
  In earthly flesh and blood!"

It fell about the Martinmas,[4]
  When nights are lang and mirk,

The carline wife's three sons came hame,
  And their hats were o' the birk.[5]   20

It neither grew in syke[6] nor ditch,
  Nor yet in ony sheugh[7];
But at the gates o' Paradise
  That birk grew fair eneugh.

"Blow up the fire, my maidens!   25
  Bring water from the well!
For a' my house shall feast this night,
  Since my three sons are well."

And she has made to them a bed,
  She's made it large and wide[8];   30
And she's ta'en her mantle her about,
  Sat down at the bedside.

Up then crew the red, red cock,[9]
  And up and crew the gray;
The eldest to the youngest said,   35
  " 'Tis time we were away."

The cock he hadna crawed but once,
  And clapped his wings at a',
When the youngest to the eldest said,
  "Brother, we must awa'."   40

"The cock doth craw, the day doth daw,[10]
  The channerin'[11] worm doth chide;
Gin[12] we be missed out o' our place,
  A sair[13] pain we maun bide."

"Lie still, lie still but a little wee while,   45
  Lie still but if we may;

SIR PATRICK SPENS. 6. *yestreen*, yesterday. 7. *richt laith*, right loath, or extremely unwilling. 8. *weet . . . schoone*, to wet their cork-heeled shoes. 9. *owre*, before. 10. *Thair . . . aboone*, their hats were floating above their bodies. 11. *kems*, combs. 12. *haf . . . Aberdour*, halfway on the return journey to Aberdour, or halfway home.

THE WIFE OF USHER'S WELL. 1. *ane*, one. 2. *carline wife*, old woman. 3. *fashes*, storms. 4. *Martinmas*, November 11, the feast of St. Martin. 5. *birk*, birch. An old tradition says that a man returning from the dead wears on his head some plant from Paradise to forestall the power of earthly winds. 6. *syke*, trench. 7. *sheugh*, furrow. 8. *bed . . . large and wide*. According to ballad conventions, any reference to making a bed "large and wide" or "deep and narrow" or "soon" means that someone is about to die. 9. *crew . . . cock*. The dead arose from their graves at midnight and remained above ground until the cock crowed at dawn. 10. *daw*, dawn. 11. *channerin'*, devouring. 12. *Gin*, if. 13. *sair*, sore.

Gin my mother should miss us when she
    wakes,
  She'll go mad ere it be day."

"Fare ye weel, my mother dear!
  Fareweel to barn and byre!   50
And fare ye weel, the bonny lass
  That kindles my mother's fire."

THE BATTLE OF OTTERBOURNE

*This famous Border ballad tells of a battle be-
tween the Scottish Douglas and the English
Percy on August 19, 1338. It makes use of a
common ballad technique called* leaping *and*
lingering, *which means simply "leaping" over
unimportant events and "lingering" on scenes
that are colorful and dramatic. Although use
of this technique makes it difficult to follow
the transitions from scene to scene, a striking
dramatic effect is gained.*

It fell about the Lammas tide,[1]
  When the muir-men win their hay.[2]
The doughty Douglas bound him to ride
  Into England, to drive a prey.

He chose the Gordons and the Graemes,   5
  With them the Lindesays, light and gay;
But the Jardines wald not with him ride,
  And they rue it to this day.

And he has burn'd the dales of Tyne,[3]
  And part of Bambroughshire;   10
And three good towers on Reidswire fells,[4]
  He left them all on fire,

And he march'd up to Newcastle,
  And rode it round about;
"O wha's the lord of this castle,   15
  Or wha's the lady o't?"

But up spake proud Lord Percy then,
  And O but he spake hie!
"I am the lord of this castle,
  My wife's the lady gay."   20

"If thou'rt the lord of this castle,
  Sae weel it pleases me!

For, ere I cross the Border fells,
  The tane[5] of us shall die."

He took a lang spear in his hand,   25
  Shod with the metal free,
And for to meet the Douglas there,
  He rode right furiouslie.

But O how pale his lady look'd,
  Frae aff the castle wa',   30
When down before the Scottish spear
  She saw proud Percy fa'.

"Had we twa been upon the green,
  And never an eye to see,
I wad hae had you, flesh and fell[6];   35
  But your sword sall gae wi' me."

"But gae ye up to Otterbourne,
  And wait there dayis three;
And if I come not ere three dayis end,
  A fause knight ca' ye me."   40

"The Otterbourne's a bonnie burn[7];
  'Tis pleasant there to be;
But there is nought at Otterbourne,
  To feed my men and me.

"The deer rins wild on hill and dale,   45
  The birds fly wild from tree to tree;
But there is neither bread nor kale,[8]
  To fend[9] my men and me.

"Yet I will stay at Otterbourne,
  Where you shall welcome be;   50
And if ye come not at three dayis end,
  A fause lord I'll ca' thee."

"Thither will I come," proud Percy said,
  "By the might of Our Ladye!"
"There will I bide thee," said the Douglas; 55
  "My troth I plight[10] to thee."

---

1. *Lammas tide*, August 1. A harvest festival was formerly held on this day. **2.** *muir-men . . . hay*, men from
the highlands gather their hay. **3.** *dales of Tyne*, valleys
along the River Tyne in north England. **4.** *Bambroughshire . . . Reidswire fells*, places in Northumberland, a county in northeastern England. A *fell* is a hill. **5.** *tane*, one.
6. *fell*, skin or hide. **7.** *burn*, brook. **8.** *kale*, green
leafy vegetables from which soup is made. **9.** *fend*, provide for. **10.** *troth I plight*, pledge I give.

They lighted high on Otterbourne,
　Upon the bent[11] sae brown;
They lighted high on Otterbourne,
　And threw their pallions[12] down.　　　　60

And he that had a bonnie boy,
　Sent out his horse to grass;
And he that had not a bonnie boy,
　His ain servant he was.

But up then spake a little page,　　　　65
　Before the peep of dawn,
"O waken ye, waken ye, my good lord,
　For Percy's hard at hand."

"Ye lie, ye lie, ye liar loud!
　Sae loud I hear ye lie;　　　　　　70
For Percy had not men yestreen
　To dight[13] my men and me.

"But I have dream'd a dreary dream,
　Beyond the Isle of Sky;
I saw a dead man win a fight,　　　　75
　And I think that man was I."

He belted on his guid braid sword,
　And to the field he ran;
But he forgot the helmet good,
　That should have kept his brain.　　　80

When Percy wi' the Douglas met,
　I wat he was fu' fain[14];
They swakked[15] their swords till sair they
　　swat,[16]
　And the blood ran down like rain.

But Percy with his good broadsword,　　85
　That could so sharply wound,
Has wounded Douglas on the brow,
　Till he fell to the ground.

Then he call'd on his little foot-page,
　And said, "Run speedilie,　　　　90
And fetch my ain dear sister's son,
　Sir Hugh Montgomery.

"My nephew good," the Douglas said,
　"What recks the death of ane!
Last night I dream'd a dreary dream,　　95
　And I ken the day's thy ain.

"My wound is deep; I fain would sleep;
　Take thou the vanguard of the three,
And hide me by the braken bush,
　That grows on yonder lilye lee.[17]　　100

"O bury me by the braken bush,
　Beneath the blooming brier,
Let never living mortal ken
　That ere a kindly Scot lies here."

He lifted up that noble lord,　　　　105
　Wi' the saut tear in his ee;
He hid him in the braken bush,
　That his merrie-men might not see.

The moon was clear, the day drew near,
　The spears in flinders[18] flew,　　　110
But mony a gallant Englishman
　Ere day the Scotsmen slew.

The Gordons good, in English blood
　They steep'd their hose and shoon;
The Lindsays flew like fire about　　　115
　Till all the fray was done.

The Percy and Montgomery met,
　That either of other were fain[19];
They swapped swords, and they twa swat,
　And aye the blood ran down between.　120

"Now yield thee, yield thee, Percy," he said,
　"Or else I vow I'll lay thee low!"
"To whom must I yield," quoth Earl Percy.
　Now that I see it must be so?"

"Thou shalt not yield to lord nor loun,[20]　125
　Nor yet shalt thou yield to me;
But yield thee to the braken bush,
　That grows upon yon lilye lee."

"I will not yield to a braken bush,
　Nor yet will I yield to a brier;　　　130

---

11. *bent*, field. 12. *pallions*, tents. 13. *dight*, deal
with. 14. *wat . . . fu' fain*, know he was very glad. 15.
swakked, struck. 16. *sair they swat*, sorely (very much)
they sweated. 17. *lilye lee*. A lee is a meadow or grassy
field; *lilye* in this context probably means "lovely," although
it may also mean "lily." 18. *flinders*, pieces. 19. *That
either . . . fain*. The approximate meaning of this is that
both Percy and Montgomery were glad the battle had begun. 20. *loun*, a man of lowly station.

But I would yield to Earl Douglas,
  Or Sir Hugh the Montgomery, if he were
    here."

As soon as he knew it was Montgomery,
  He struck his sword's point in the gronde;
The Montgomery was a courteous knight, 135
  And quickly took him by the honde.

This deed was done at the Otterbourne,
  About the breaking of the day;
Earl Douglas was buried at the braken bush,
  And the Percy led captive away.   140

BONNIE GEORGE CAMPBELL

High upon Highlands,[1]
  And low upon Tay,[2]
Bonnie George Campbell
  Rode out on a day.

He saddled, he bridled,   5
  And gallant rode he,
And hame cam his guid horse,
  But never cam he.

Out cam his mother dear,
  Greeting fu sair,[3]   10
And out came his bonnie bride,
  Riving her hair.

"The meadow lies green,
  The corn is unshorn,
But Bonnie George Campbell   15
  Will never return."

Saddled and bridled
  And booted rode he,
A plume in his helmet,
  A sword at his knee.   20

But toom[4] cam his saddle,
  All bloody to see,
Oh, hame cam his guid horse,
  But never cam he!

---

1. *Highlands*, the mountainous region of northern and western Scotland. 2. *Tay*, a river in central Scotland. 3. *Greeting fu sair*, weeping full sore (very bitterly). 4. *toom*, empty.

✹ To increase understanding

1. Briefly tell the story of "Edward."
2. Would you classify "Edward" as a folk ballad, a minstrel ballad, or a coronach? Give reasons to support your answer.
3. The *legacy*, or inheritance, is a convention in many ballads. (*a*) Name each legacy and the person to whom it is willed in "Edward." (*b*) Which legacy constitutes the climax of the tale? (*c*) Explain the way in which incremental repetition is used to build to this climax.
4. Versions of "Edward" have been found not only in England, Scotland, and the United States, but also in Finland and Germany. How do you suppose this ballad became so widely diffused?
5. In your opinion what qualities have made "Sir Patrick Spens" one of the most popular of all ballads?
6. (*a*) What similarities do you find between "Sir Patrick Spens" and "Edward"? (*b*) What differences do you find? (*c*) Which ballad do you think is older? Explain your answer.
7. (*a*) What is the occurrence in "The Wife of Usher's Well" to which everything else is subordinated? (*b*) Why does the ballad not dwell upon the mother's emotions?
8. (*a*) In "The Wife of Usher's Well" we learn through a ballad convention that the three sons did not return "in earthly flesh and blood." What is this convention? (*b*) Point out two other conventions used in this ballad and explain the meaning of each. (Use the footnotes for hints in answering this question.)
9. (*a*) Briefly tell the story of the Battle of Otterbourne. (*b*) Is the story told from the Scottish or the English point of view? Give evidence to prove your point.
10. (*a*) Cite the lines in "The Battle of Otterbourne" that give the substance of Douglas' dream. (*b*) How is the dream fulfilled? (*c*) What is the function of the dream in the ballad?
11. In folk and minstrel ballads exterior appearances are often given rather than feelings or abstract ideas; for example, when Lady Percy sees her lord fall, the reader is told not how she feels but how she looks. Find other examples of this device in this and other ballads, for example, the way the reader learns that the Battle of Otterbourne is fought at night.
12. "Bonnie George Campbell" is a fragment of a coronach; "The Battle of Otterbourne" is a minstrel ballad. Both describe tragedies that result from Border warfare. Note as many differences as possible between these two ballads.
13. Each of the ballads you have read is tragic in theme. (*a*) Explain the prominence of tragedies

among ballads. (*b*) Why does "Bonnie George Campbell" have a greater emotional impact than any of the other ballads?

14. (*a*) Of the ballads you have studied, which are written in typical ballad stanzas? (*b*) Chart on the blackboard the scansion of a stanza from one or more of the ballads. (*c*) How do you account for roughness of meter in many stanzas?

15. *Alliteration* is a characteristic ballad device. (*a*) Point out examples of alliteration in the ballads you have read. (*b*) Why do you think alliteration was so frequently used by the ballad writers?

16. Folk beliefs and superstitions have an important place in many ballads. Give examples of such beliefs in the ballads you have studied.

17. Which ballad do you like best? Explain the reasons for your choice with reference to (*a*) the story itself, (*b*) ballad conventions and devices, and (*c*) the poetry of the ballad.

 Extending interests

1. "Edward" and "The Battle of Otterbourne" offer particularly good opportunities for choral reading. "Edward" may be presented as a dialogue. The refrains "Edward, Edward" and "Mither, mither,"

if read in a tone appropriate to the context of the stanza in which they appear, will heighten the dramatic effect. The oral presentation should also make clear which person was ultimately responsible for the murder.

To present "The Battle of Otterbourne," readers are needed for the following parts: the narrator, Douglas, Percy, Sir Hugh Montgomery, and the Page. For variety, three to five students might join with the narrator in reading the lines describing the events which were probably witnessed by soldiers.

2. When some of America's first settlers came to the New World, they brought with them many of the traditional English and Scottish ballads. As the ballads were changing in the British Isles, they were also changing, along different lines, in the American colonies. Consequently numerous versions of the same ballad came into existence. Trace the history of one or two of the more popular early ballads, such as "Edward" or "Barbara Allen." Good sources to consult are *The Ballad Book*, edited by MacEdward Leach, and *Folk Songs of North America*, by Alan Lomax. Report your findings to the class.

3. To appreciate the full value of a popular ballad, one must hear it sung by an authentic ballad singer. Bring authentic folk-song records to class. Try to find recordings of the same basic ballad in different versions or sung to different melodies.

The Changing English Language

William the Conqueror and his Normans, as you have read (see page 44), were of Viking stock. But having lived in northern France for a hundred years, they had acquired a northern variety of the French language. The invasion force of seven thousand Normans in seven hundred ships that William the Conqueror led across the English Channel to Pevensey represented a civilization that was more highly cultured and more organized than that of the Anglo-Saxons. It is not surprising that after the great Norman victory at Hastings this disciplined and organized people became the ruling class in England and that their French supplanted Old English as the official language. The proud Norman barons and their followers spoke only French, their children learned French at home and in school, and all governmental, legal, and mili-

tary matters were conducted in French. As a national language, English seemed doomed to extinction.

But amazingly English was victorious. It took about three centuries for this victory over French to be accomplished and many different kinds of influences to bring it about. In the first place, ordinary Englishmen clung stubbornly to their language. They did not willingly speak French, though as time went on it became necessary for the leading English people to be able to use French. In the second place, the English were the majority, greatly outnumbering the Normans. But perhaps the leading factor in the ultimate victory of the English language was a gradually developing nationalism in which as time went on all the people living in England shared. Both the Norman and the Plantagenet kings claimed lands in France. To retain these lands they had to fight the kings of France. In these recurrent wars the Norman warriors from England increasingly began to think of France as an alien land and of themselves as Englishmen. Some of the Norman kings invited lords from France to come to England and bestowed lands and wealth upon them. Such gifts to "foreigners" were bitterly resented by the descendants of the original Norman invaders, who regarded themselves as Englishmen in contrast to these newcomers. This national spirit and the resentment of foreigners at court advanced a growing tolerance of things English, including the language.

Another factor in the victory of English was the advance in status of the native English people. At first little better than serfs, in generation after generation a greater number of Englishmen rose to positions of influence and respect. Because they were part of the majority of the people, their use of English for the affairs of government and business seemed natural and right. Increasingly English was so used, until in 1362, almost exactly three hundred years after the Normans landed in England, the English language was declared by royal decree the official language of the courts of law. In the schools English was in use by 1350 and by 1385 was the language of all the people.

Early in the fourteenth century the growing status of English is indicated by the fact that writers were turning by preference to English as their vehicle for writing. The following extract from a poem written about 1325 illustrates this viewpoint and affords a sample of the English of the time.

Riʒt is, þat Inglische Inglische vnderstond,
Þat was born in Inglond;
Freynsche vse þis gentilman,
Ac euerich Inglische can.
Mani noble ich haue yseiʒe
Þat no Freynsche couþe seye.[1]

About the same time that English became official in the courts, the victory of the native tongue was clinched by the decision of one of the greatest of all English-born authors to write his poems in English. His name was Geoffrey Chaucer. (See pages 65-66.)

THE DEVELOPMENT OF MIDDLE ENGLISH

When the Scandinavians and English mingled in the eighth and ninth centuries, they spoke languages derived from a common, close ancestor tongue. Since the grammar of these languages was fairly parallel, no conflict in grammar developed. But when Norman-French and English mixed, the speakers used languages much more remotely related with entirely different types of grammar. As a result, French and English could not blend or fuse; one or the other grammatical type would have to be adopted, and it was the English grammatical plan which emerged. The influence of French grammar on English is negligible, but the influence of French words upon our vocabulary was and is one of the great formative forces in Middle and Modern English.

In the first century following the Norman invasion of 1066 the adoption of French words into English was slight. It was not until about 1250, when the English had lost Normandy to the French king and the new English nationalism had made itself felt, that the inflow of French words into English became considerable. From this time on, borrowing from French accelerated to the extent that by 1400 the English vocabulary was enlarged and enriched by a very great number of French words. It was only natural that as English was increasingly used as the prevailing pattern of speech, the vocabulary of the alternate language would increasingly become a part of the victorious language.

Words borrowed from French before 1250 show the relationships between a ruling class and a subordinate class; the English people began to use words like *noble, dame, servant, feast, messenger,* and large numbers of words connected with religion, such as *sermon, com-*

---

1. From *A History of the English Language,* 2nd ed., Albert C. Baugh (New York, Appleton-Century-Crofts, 1957, page 173). The translation of this passage is as follows: It is right that the English people understand English, (the people) that was born in England; this (particular) gentleman uses French, but everybody knows English. Many a noble have I seen that could speak no French.

munion, *confession, clergy, abbey,* and *convent*. Most of these words were of Latin origin but were absorbed into English from the French forms. An interesting example of the relation between the French and English peoples emerges from the names of food animals which the English tended, and the French ate as meats on the dinner table. Thus *deer* or *stag* is eaten as *venison; pig* or *hog* is *pork* on the table; *cow* or *bull* becomes *beef; calf* becomes *veal,* and *sheep* is eaten as *mutton*.

French words adopted into English after 1250 show the merging of interests and activities of the two peoples. Many words connected with government, law, and business, such as *crown, state, realm, courtier, justice, equity, warrant, felony, manor, bill, petition, estate,* and *executor,* were taken over from the French by the English. As the cultural interests and opportunities of the English increased, more words from literature, art, medicine, fashion, and social life were absorbed from the French. Thus by the close of Middle English we find an English language still English in grammar, but vastly enriched in words and ideas from the cultural resources of French. Nor has this borrowing from French ever ceased, as is illustrated by such recent words as *chauffeur, garage,* and *barrage*.

The English language between the years 1000 and 1400 was greatly simplified in structure. In essence, it changed from being a fairly highly inflected language to a language of relatively few inflections. This change is called the *leveling* of inflections. It means that forms of words, principally endings, which once were sharply distinct from each other in order to express grammatical relationships, lost these distinctions until they merged into a few, or sometimes one, single, surviving form. For example, the adjective *good,* which in King Alfred's day had at least ten different forms, had been leveled by Chaucer's time to two forms, and not long after to one. Hence today we use the adjective *good* to modify *boy, girl, tree, boy's, girls', trees,* with no change of form for number, gender, or case. Another example of leveling is seen in the verb *help,* which in Old English had four principal parts (*healpan, healp, hulpon, holpen*) with five

or more additional endings, and today has only two principal parts (*help, helped*) with one additional ending. As endings were gradually confused and lost, the grammatical relationships which they expressed were taken over by patterns and arrangements of words, so that Modern English has become a phrasal language more than an inflected language. When we say "My friend's house," we are using a possessive case form, all that remains of an older genitive. But when we say "The house of my friend," we use a pattern of words to express the same idea. In Modern English, therefore, the order and arrangement of words becomes very important because by word order we express relationships formerly indicated by endings.

THE SOURCE OF MODERN ENGLISH

As you learned in studying the growth of Old English (page 23), in different parts of England distinct Anglo-Saxon dialects emerged. During the Middle Ages these dialects gradually developed into four Middle English dialect groups, of which the most important is called East Midland. This dialect was spoken by the people between the Thames and the Humber rivers, an area which included the city of London, the rapidly growing center of government and commerce. Because of the importance of London and the gathering there of people from all parts of England, the East Midland speech gradually came to be looked upon as "the King's English," the official dialect of England. About 1370, when Chaucer chose to write in English, he used this dialect, thus giving it literary status. A century later, when Caxton introduced printing to England, he was troubled by the diversity of dialects, but chose to use the speech of London as the standard for printing, thus further establishing this dialect. In this way the speech of a particular region by chance became "standard English," and Modern English, including American English, is descended from this East Midland dialect.

In subsequent chapters of this book will be found references to the growth of Modern English and its various changes, from the times of the Tudor kings to the present.

The Cathedrals of Medieval England

Because the Middle Ages were centuries of faith, the cathedral became the most typical artistic expression of the time. While the Norman castles were rising as feudal strongholds, the Norman cathedrals were also taking shape. Square-towered, with rounded arches and relatively small windows and enormously thick stone walls, they were fortresslike in their strength and massiveness. Indeed, in times of peril Norman cathedrals like Durham were used for defense.

By the time the Plantagenet kings had succeeded the Normans, Gothic cathedrals were taking the place of the earlier Norman structures. (Most of the earlier English churches are a fusion of both.) No longer were churches needed for defense, and the increasing knowledge of architecture made it possible for the master craftsmen to plan buildings with less massive walls, with pointed arches and ribbed vaulting, with much larger window expanses, and with tall airy towers spiring upward. The Gothic cathedrals of the thirteenth century echoed in stone and glass, iron and wood, the temper of people who had emerged from the terrors of invasion and civil strife and had thankfully turned their enormously increased skills to the task of glorifying God.

More than any artistic works of succeeding centuries, the cathedrals stand as monuments to thousands of anonymous craftsmen—men like the guildsmen whom Chaucer was to celebrate in his *Canterbury Tales*. The work was usually under the direction of a master craftsman, or architect, whose name may often be found in old records. Occasionally the names of artisans, such as Robert Lyen and John Thornton, the master glaziers who executed some of the great windows at York Minster, are listed in the records of business transactions. But for the most part no one knows who patterned the brilliant windows with their pictured Bible stories and placed them as messages for all who came to worship; or wove the tapestries that covered the interior walls; or carved the stone and wood into commemorative figures, shrines, screens, choir stalls, and canopies. The alabasters, enamels, ivories, jeweled coffers, and wrought metal devices remain as mute testimonies to the men, fathers and sons, who often labored for several generations to complete the building of a cathedral. For what was time to craftsmen engaged in the task of glorifying God on earth and preparing for their salvation in heaven!

Below: The medieval cathedral provided a rich field for the sculptor. Carved effigies are fitted to the design of the tomb of Sir John Beauchamp, steward to household of Richard II, and his wife in Worcester Cathedral. Right: Canterbury Cathedral, begun in 1070 and completed in 1503.

A. F. KERSTING

Below: One of the medieval windows in Canterbury Cathedral (top). The ambulatory—area between the chancel and outside wall—of Norwich Cathedral (bottom). Right: The towers of Lincoln Cathedral (above) and Durham Cathedral (below).

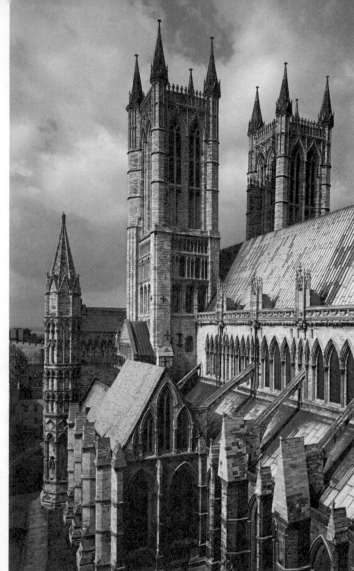

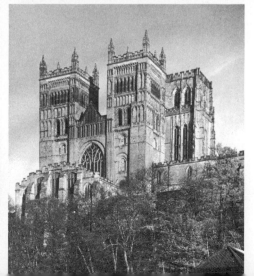

Geoffrey Chaucer 1340?-1400

Chaucer's life and career seem to epitomize the history of the later Middle Ages. His name, being French for *shoemaker* (the French *chausseur* means "cobbler"), suggests that his family had followed that trade, but for as far back as his ancestors can be traced on English soil, they had been vintners. As the son of a well-to-do wine merchant living in London, and later as a customs official, Chaucer was a member of the rising middle class.

Most of his life Chaucer was associated in one way or another with the royal household. Through his father's court connections he probably was given his first position as page in the service of Elizabeth, Countess of Ulster, daughter-in-law of Edward III. While still in her service he went as a soldier to France in the division of Prince Lionel, Elizabeth's husband and third son of the King. Here he had the misfortune to be captured by the French, but he was soon ransomed by King Edward. Later Chaucer became one of the King's esquires, which in those days meant that he worked in the administrative department of the King's government. One of his duties was to act as a government envoy on foreign diplomatic missions, carrying on such work as that performed by embassies of our day. His diplomatic missions took him first to France and later to Italy. While in France Chaucer came in contact with French literature, and from his very earliest writings through 1370 a French influence is noticeable. To the French period can be assigned many of his lyrics, which follow models laid down by earlier and contemporary French poets.

In 1372 Chaucer was sent to Genoa to arrange a commercial treaty. As he became acquainted with Italian life and culture, he discovered that a new interest in the learning of the past, in the literature of Greece and Rome, was sweeping over the Italian towns—the Renaissance had begun. Chaucer became acquainted with the classical Latin writing of Virgil and Ovid, with the newer Italian works of Dante and Petrarch, perhaps with the tales of Boccaccio. In Chaucer's own writing the French models of his early years gave way to this Italian influence.

On his return to London in 1374 Chaucer became Comptroller of Customs and Subsidy of Wool, Skins, and Leather in the port of London. As one of the benefits of this position the government provided him with free lodgings above Aldgate, one of the gates in the wall around London, on condition that he "kepe in goode repayre" his home. There he liked to retire "as an hermyte," he says, after his working day was done, to write or read (for he loved the world of books as much as the world of men), or to look down upon the colorful throng that passed through the gateway beneath him. There, no doubt, he saw merchants with their pack trains, jovial peddlers with their wares, minstrels in their motley costumes, acrobats and jugglers, bearwards leading their trained animals, beggars— all taking the highway across the open fields beyond the wall toward the fairs, the chief centers of domestic trade. Always there were churchmen in the procession; often there were students. In contrast to the drably dressed students were the guild members garbed in bright new liveries.

Chaucer gave up his comptrollership and left his home above Aldgate in 1386—the year in which it is believed he began composing *The Canter-*

Opposite: Canterbury has been the center of the Church in England since the time of Augustine (see page 20). The cathedral became the most revered shrine in England after the murder of Thomas à Becket here in 1170.

bury Tales. Subsequently he represented Kent in Parliament, and beginning in 1389 again served the King, first as Clerk of the King's Works, or supervisor of repairs of royal property, and then as Deputy Forester of the great royal forest in Somersetshire. When he died in 1400, he was buried in Westminster Abbey in a section which later became established as the Poets' Corner.

THE CANTERBURY TALES   The varied experiences of Chaucer's crowded life—royal commissions, travel abroad, contacts with Londoners and country folk—went into his *Canterbury Tales,* on which he worked intermittently for at least ten years. In fact, the "Prologue," in which he introduces a group of pilgrims bound for the shrine of Thomas à Becket at Canterbury, is considered a source book of information on fourteenth-century England. It is composed of character sketches of the pilgrims, as seen through the eyes of Chaucer himself. The tales these pilgrims tell show Chaucer's wide knowledge of literature from classical and medieval European sources and from the Orient. Unfortunately he lived to complete only about one fifth of the one hundred twenty tales he planned to present.

The framework of *The Canterbury Tales* is the pilgrimage, in Chaucer's day a popular religious devotion. While most pilgrimages were undertaken in penance for sins or for other serious purposes, some pilgrims undoubtedly visited the shrines in the spirit of Chaucer's famous Wife of Bath, as much for the fun of the journey as for the saving of their souls.

Opposite: A facsimile of the Ellesmere manuscript. The full value of this, the most reliable of the existing manuscripts of the Canterbury Tales, *was not discovered until mid-nineteenth century. Prior to that time, people generally accepted Dryden's estimate of Chaucer's language as "rude sweetness," not appreciating its polished form. This page shows Chaucer beginning his own "Tale of Melibee."*

Chaucer's pilgrims meet at the Tabard Inn in Southwark, a suburb of London on the south bank of the Thames River. The inn, which stood near the southern end of London Bridge, was a customary point at which to rest and eat before setting out on the fifty-nine-mile journey to Canterbury. Harry Bailey, host of the Tabard, is so taken with the lively company that he offers to join their pilgrimage and to act as guide and master of ceremonies. For entertainment along the way he suggests a program of storytelling—two stories apiece for each pilgrim each way, the prize for the best to be a dinner, at the expense of the group, back at his inn. The pilgrims draw straws to determine who shall tell the first tale. The Knight, the top-ranking member of the party, wins the draw, as all people in a fourteenth-century audience expected.

Through his pilgrims Chaucer gives far more than an unforgettable group of character sketches and a collection of stories. He uses the pilgrims to comment subtly but powerfully on the social problems of his time. His view is that of a man who, to an unusual degree, sees life clearly and sees it whole. Writing *The Canterbury Tales* in the last period of his life, he had the wisdom of years to guide his judgment. Furthermore, his native tolerance and sense of humor helped him to understand men and the forces that motivate them. He realized that the disorders and confusions of the age in which he lived marked the decline of the Age of Chivalry, and the beginnings of a new era—an era in which the lot of the common man was improving, the merchant class was prospering, and a Parliament was functioning. Chaucer looked upon this new order and found it good. This optimism colors the mood of Chaucer's pilgrims as they set forth for Canterbury on an April morning.

Ther fore lordynges alle I yow biseche
If þt yow thynke I varie as in my speche
As this though that I telle somwhat moore
Of þuibes than ye han herd bifoore
Comprehended in this litel tretys heere
To enforce with theffect of my mateere
And though I nat the same wordes seye
As ye han herd yet to yow alle I preye
Blameth me nat for as in my sentence
Shul ye nowher fynden difference
Fro the sentence of this tretys lyte
After the which this murie tale I write
And therfore herkneth what þt I shal seye
And lat me tellen al my tale I preye

Explicit

Heere bigynneth Chaucers tale of Melibee

A Yong man called Melibeus myghty and riche bigat
vp on his wyf that called was prudence a doghter
which that called was Sophie vpon a day bifel þt
he for his desport is went in to the feldes hym to pleie
his wyf and eek his doghter hath he left inwith his hous of which
the dores weren faste yshette thre of hise olde foos han it espyed
and setten laddres to the walles of his hous and by wyndowes
been entred and betten his wyf and wounded his doghter with
fyue mortal woundes in fyue sondry places this is to seyn in
hir feet in hir handes in hir eris in hir nose and in hir mouth
And lesten hir for deed and wenten awey Whan Melibeus re
tourned was in to his hous and saugh al this meschief he lyk a
mad man rentynge his clothes gan to wepe and crie And Pru
dence his wyf as ferforth as she dorste bisoghte hym of his wepyng
for to stynte but nat for thy he gan to crie and wepen euere lenger
the moore This noble wyf Prudence remembred hir vpon this
sentence of Ouide in his book that cleped is the remedie of loue
Wher as he seith he is a fool that destourbeth the mooder to wepen in
the deeth of hir child til she haue wept hir fille as for a certein
tyme And thanne shal man doon his diligence with amyable
wordes hir to reconforte and preyen hir of hir wepyng for to
stynte After which resoun this noble wyf Prudence suffred hir
housbonde for to wepe and crie as for a certein space and whan
she saugh hir tyme she seyde hym in this wise Allas my
lord quod she why make ye youre self for to be lyk a fool for sooth
the it apperteineth nat to a wys man to maken with a sorwe youre

from THE PROLOGUE TO THE CANTERBURY TALES

Geoffrey Chaucer

COURTESY THE BRITISH MUSEUM

Whan that Aprillë with his shourës sootë
The droghte of Marche hath percëd to the
    rootë,
And bathëd every veyne in swich licour,
Of which vertu engendrëd is the flour;
Whan Zephirus eek with his swetë breeth
Inspirëd hath in every holt and heeth
The tendrë croppës, and the yongë sonnë
Hath in the Ram his halfë cours yronnë,
And smalë fowlës maken melodyë,
That slepen al the night with open yë—
So priketh hem nature in hir coragës:
Than longen folk to goon on pilgrimages,
And palmers for to seken straungë strondës,
To fernë halwës, couthe in sondry londës;
And specially, from every shirës endë
Of Engelond, to Caunterbury they wendë,
The holy, blisful martir for to sekë,
That hem hath holpen whan that they
    were sekë.

*The first eighteen lines of the "Prologue" in
Middle English. The drawing, from a medieval
manuscript, is of the pilgrims returning from
Canterbury. Since Chaucer never completed all
the Tales, it was customary in medieval times
to include in the same book tales by other
authors. This illustration accompanies* The
Siege of Thebes, *written by John Lydgate
as the first tale of the knight on the return.*

As soon as April pierces to the root
    The drought of March, and
    bathes each bud and shoot
Through every vein of sap with gentle
    showers
From whose engendering liquor spring the
    flowers;   4
When zephyrs have breathed softly all about
Inspiring every wood and field to sprout,
And in the zodiac the youthful sun
His journey halfway through the Ram has
    run[1];
When little birds are busy with their song
Who sleep with open eyes the whole night
    long   10
Life stirs their hearts and tingles in them so,
On pilgrimages people long to go
And palmers[2] to set out for distant strands
And foreign shrines renowned in many lands,
And specially in England people ride   15
To Canterbury from every countryside
To visit there the blessed martyred saint[3]
Who gave them strength when they were
    sick and faint.
    In Southwark at the Tabard one spring
    day
It happened, as I stopped there on my way, [20]
Myself a pilgrim with a heart devout
Ready for Canterbury to set out,
At night came all of twenty-nine assorted
Travelers, and to that same inn resorted,
Who by a turn of fortune chanced to fall   25
In fellowship together, and they were all
Pilgrims who had it in their minds to ride
Toward Canterbury. The stable doors were
    wide,
The rooms were large, and we enjoyed the
    best,   29

From *The Portable Chaucer*, selected, translated, and
edited by Theodore Morrison. Copyright, 1949, by
Theodore Morrison. Reprinted by permission of The
Viking Press, Inc., New York.

1. *in the zodiac . . . run.* Since the Ram, the first sign of
the zodiac begins its run about March 21, Chaucer dates
the pilgrimage as early in April. 2. *palmers.* Pilgrims
who had been to the Holy Land were called palmers because of the crossed palm leaves they wore as a sign of their
pilgrimage. 3. *blessed martyred saint.* See page 47.

And shortly, when the sun had gone to rest,
I had so talked with each that presently
I was a member of their company
And promised to rise early the next day
To start, as I shall show, upon our way.
    But none the less, while I have time and
       space,   35
Before this tale has gone a further pace,
I should in reason tell you the condition
Of each of them, his rank and his position,
And also what array they all were in;
And so then, with a knight I will begin. 40

THE KNIGHT
A Knight was with us, and an excellent
    man,
Who from the earliest moment he began
To follow his career loved chivalry,
Truth, open-handedness, and courtesy. 44
He was a stout man in the king's campaigns
And in that cause had gripped his horse's
    reins
In Christian lands and pagan through the
    earth,
None farther, and always honored for his
    worth.
He was on hand at Alexandria's fall.[4]
He had often sat in precedence to all . 50
The nations at the banquet board in Prussia.
He had fought in Lithuania and in Russia,
No Christian knight more often; he had
    been
In Moorish Africa at Benmarin,
At the siege of Algeciras in Granada, 55
And sailed in many a glorious armada
In the Mediterranean, and fought as well
At Ayas and Attalia when they fell
In Armenia and on Asia Minor's coast.
Of fifteen deadly battles he could boast, 60
And in Algeria, at Tremessen,
Fought for the faith and killed three
    separate men
In single combat. He had done good work
Joining against another pagan Turk 64
With the king of Palathia. And he was wise,
Despite his prowess, honored in men's eyes,
Meek as a girl and gentle in his ways.
He had never spoken ignobly all his days
To any man by even a rude inflection.
He was a knight in all things to perfection. 70

He rode a good horse, but his gear was
    plain,
For he had lately served on a campaign.
His tunic was still spattered by the rust
Left by his coat of mail, for he had just
Returned and set out on his pilgrimage. 75

THE SQUIRE
His son was with him, a young Squire,
    in age
Some twenty years as near as I could guess.
His hair curled as if taken from a press.
He was a lover and would become a knight.
In stature he was of a moderate height 80
But powerful and wonderfully quick.
He had been in Flanders, riding in the thick
Of forays in Artois and Picardy,
And bore up well for one so young as he,
Still hoping by his exploits in such places 85
To stand the better in his lady's graces.
He wore embroidered flowers, red and
    white,
And blazed like a spring meadow to the
    sight.
He sang or played his flute the livelong day.
He was as lusty as the month of May. 90
His coat was short, its sleeves were long and
    wide.
He sat his horse well, and knew how to ride,
And how to make a song and use his lance,
And he could write and draw well, too, and
    dance. 94
So hot his love that when the moon rose pale
He got no more sleep than a nightingale.
He was modest, and helped whomever he
    was able,
And carved as his father's squire at the table.

THE YEOMAN
But one more servant had the Knight
    beside,
Choosing thus simply for the time to ride: 100
A Yeoman,[5] in a coat and hood of green.
His peacock-feathered arrows, bright and
    keen,

---

4. *Alexandria's fall.* Here, and in the following lines
Chaucer mentions the Knight's campaigns, which were
scattered over most of the then known world, from Asia
Minor to Moorish Africa. Judging by the places mentioned,
the knight must have been for the most part in the service of
King Edward III. 5. *Yeoman,* attendant of a king or lord.

He carried under his belt in tidy fashion.
For well-kept gear he had a yeoman's
     passion.   104
No draggled feather might his arrows show,
And in his hand he held a mighty bow.
He kept his hair close-cropped, his face was
     brown.
He knew the lore of woodcraft up and
     down.
His arm was guarded from the bowstring's
     whip   109
By a bracer,[6] gaily trimmed. He had at hip
A sword and buckler, and at his other side
A dagger whose fine mounting was his pride,
Sharp-pointed as a spear. His horn he bore
In a sling of green, and on his chest he wore
A silver image of St. Christopher[7]   115
His patron, since he was a forester.

THE PRIORESS

There was also a Nun, a Prioress,
Whose smile was gentle and full of
     guilelessness.
"By St. Loy!"[8] was the worst oath she would
     say.
She sang mass well, in a becoming way,   120
Intoning through her nose the words divine,
And she was known as Madame Eglantine.
She spoke good French, as taught at
     Stratford-Bow,[9]
For the Parisian French she did not know.
She was schooled to eat so primly and so well
That from her lips no morsel ever fell.   126
She wet her fingers lightly in the dish
Of sauce, for courtesy was her first wish.
With every bite she did her skillful best
To see that no drop fell upon her breast.   130
She always wiped her upper lip so clean
That in her cup was never to be seen
A hint of grease when she had drunk her
     share.
She reached out for her meat with comely
     air.
She was a great delight, and always tried   135
To imitate court ways, and had her pride,
Both amiable and gracious in her dealings.
As for her charity and tender feelings,
She melted at whatever was piteous.
She would weep if she but came upon a
     mouse   140

Caught in a trap, if it were dead or bleeding.
Some little dogs that she took pleasure
     feeding
On roasted meat or milk or good wheat
     bread
She had, but how she wept to find one dead
Or yelping from a blow that made it smart,
And all was sympathy and loving heart.   146
Neat was her wimple in its every plait,
Her nose well formed, her eyes as gray as
     slate.
Her mouth was very small and soft and red.
She had so wide a brow I think her head   150
Was nearly a span broad, for certainly
She was not undergrown, as all could see.
She wore her cloak with dignity and charm,
And had her rosary about her arm,   154
The small beads coral and the larger green,
And from them hung a brooch of golden
     sheen,
On it a large A and a crown above;
Beneath, "All things are subject unto love."
     A Priest accompanied her toward
          Canterbury,
And an attendant Nun, her secretary.   160

THE MONK

There was a Monk, and nowhere was his
     peer,
A hunter, and a roving overseer.
He was a manly man, and fully able
To be an abbot. He kept a hunting stable,
And when he rode the neighborhood could
     hear   165
His bridle jingling in the wind as clear
And loud as if it were a chapel bell.
Wherever he was master of a cell
The principles of good St. Benedict,[10]
For being a little old and somewhat strict, 170
Were honored in the breach, as past their
     prime.

---

6. *bracer,* a guard for the left wrist and arm. 7. *St. Christopher,* the patron saint of travel and the protector against storms and accidents. 8. *By St. Loy.* Loy, or Eligius, refused to swear upon sacred relics. Therefore, to swear by St. Loy was to swear very mildly or not at all. 9. *good French . . . Stratford-Bow.* Stratford-Bow was a nunnery in Bromley, Middlesex. The implication is clear; the prioress spoke the inferior kind of French heard in a nunnery in England, not the French of Paris. 10. *St. Benedict,* founder of the Benedictine religious order, which was governed by strict rules.

He lived by the fashion of a newer time.
He would have swapped that text for a
	plucked hen[11]
Which says that hunters are not holy men,
Or a monk outside his discipline and rule
Is too much like a fish outside his pool; 176
That is to say, a monk outside his cloister.
But such a text he deemed not worth an
	oyster.
I told him his opinion made me glad.
Why should he study always and go mad, 180
Mewed in his cell with only a book for
	neighbor?
Or why, as Augustine[12] commanded, labor
And sweat his hands? How shall the world
	be served?
To Augustine be all such toil reserved!
And so he hunted, as was only right. 185
He had greyhounds as swift as birds in flight
His taste was all for tracking down the hare,
And what his sport might cost he did not
	care.
His sleeves I noticed, where they met his
	hand,
Trimmed with gray fur, the finest in the
	land 190
His hood was fastened with a curious pin
Made of wrought gold and clasped beneath
	his chin,
A love knot at the tip. His head might pass,
Bald as it was, for a lump of shining glass,
And his face was glistening as if anointed. 195
Fat as a lord he was, and well appointed.
His eyes were large, and rolled inside his
	head
As if they gleamed from a furnace of hot
	lead.
His boots were supple, his horse superbly
	kept.
He was a prelate to dream of while you
	slept. 200
He was not pale nor peaked like a ghost.
He relished a plump swan as his favorite
	roast.
He rode a palfrey brown as a ripe berry.

THE FRIAR

A Friar was with us, a gay dog and a
	merry,
Who begged his district with a jolly air. 205

No friar in all four orders[13] could compare
With him for gallantry; his tongue was
	wooing.
Many a girl was married by his doing,
And at his own cost it was often done.
He was a pillar, and a noble one, 210
To his whole order. In his neighborhood
Rich franklins[14] knew him well, who served
	good food,
And worthy women welcomed him to town;
For the license that his order handed down,
He said himself, conferred on him
	possession 215
Of more than a curate's power of confession.
Sweetly the list of frailties he heard,
Assigning penance with a pleasant word.
He was an easy man for absolution 219
Where he looked forward to a contribution,
For if to a poor order a man has given
It signifies that he has been well shriven,
And if a sinner let his purse be dented
The Friar would stake his oath he had
	repented.
For many men become so hard of heart 225
They cannot weep, though conscience makes
	them smart.
Instead of tears and prayers, then, let the
	sinner
Supply the poor friars with the price of
	dinner.
For pretty women he had more than shrift.
His cape was stuffed with many a little gift,
As knives and pins and suchlike. He could
	sing 231
A merry note, and pluck a tender string,
And had no rival at all in balladry.
His neck was whiter than a fleur-de-lis,
And yet he could have knocked a strong man
	down. 235
He knew the taverns well in every town.
The barmaids and innkeepers pleased his
	mind

---

11. *plucked hen.* In this context, *plucked hen* is used symbolically to represent worthlessness. 12. *Augustine,* St. Augustine (d. 430 A.D.), who advised monks to practice manual labor. Do not confuse him with the St. Augustine, (d. 604 A.D.), who was the first Archbishop of Canterbury. 13. *Friar . . . four orders.* The four orders of friars were the Franciscans, the Dominicans, the Carmelites, and the Augustinians. A friar could obtain a license to beg in a limited district. 14. *franklins,* landowners of the middle class, who were just below the gentry in rank.

Better than beggars and lepers and their
    kind.
In his position it was unbecoming   **239**
Among the wretched lepers to go slumming.
It mocks all decency, it sews no stitch[15]
To deal with such riffraff; but with the rich,
With sellers of victuals, that's another thing.
Wherever he saw some hope of profiting,
None so polite, so humble. He was good,   **245**
The champion beggar of his brotherhood.
Should a woman have no shoes against the
    snow,
So pleasant was his *"In principio"*[16]
He would have her widow's mite before he
    went.
He took in far more than he paid in rent   **250**
For his right of begging within certain
    bounds.
None of his brethren trespassed on his
    grounds!
He loved as freely as a half-grown whelp.
On arbitration-days[17] he gave great help, **254**
For his cloak was never shiny nor threadbare
Like a poor cloistered scholar's. He had an
    air
As if he were a doctor or a pope.
It took stout wool to make his semicope[18]
That plumped out like a bell for portliness.
He lisped a little in his rakishness   **260**
To make his English sweeter on his tongue,
And twanging his harp to end some song
    he'd sung
His eyes would twinkle in his head as bright
As the stars twinkle on a frosty night.
Hubert this gallant Friar was by name.   **265**

THE MERCHANT

Among the rest a Merchant also came.
He wore a forked beard and a beaver hat
From Flanders. High up in the saddle he sat,
In figured cloth, his boots clasped
    handsomely,
Delivering his opinions pompously,   **270**
Always on how his gains might be increased.
At all costs he desired the sea policed
From Middleburg in Holland to Orwell.[19]
He knew the exchange rates, and the time
    to sell
French currency, and there was never yet **275**
A man who could have told he was in debt

So grave he seemed and hid so well his
    feelings
With all his shrewd engagements and close
    dealings.
You'd find no better man at any turn;   **279**
But what his name was I could never learn.

THE STUDENT

There was an Oxford Student too, it
    chanced,
Already in his logic well advanced.
He rode a mount as skinny as a rake,
And he was hardly fat. For learning's sake
He let himself look hollow and sober
    enough.   **285**
He wore an outer cloak of threadbare stuff,
For he had no benefice[20] for his enjoyment
And was too unworldly for some lay
    employment.
He much preferred to have beside his bed
His twenty volumes bound in black or red **290**
All packed with Aristotle from end to middle
Than a sumptuous wardrobe or a merry
    fiddle.
For though he knew what learning had to
    offer
There was little coin to jingle in his coffer.
Whatever he got by touching up[21] a
    friend   **295**
On books and learning he would promptly
    spend
And busily pray for the soul of anybody
Who furnished him the wherewithal for
    study.
His scholarship was what he truly heeded.
He never spoke a word more than was
    needed,   **300**
And that was said with dignity and force,

---

15. *it sews no stitch*, it accomplishes nothing. 16. *In principio* (prin sip'i ō), "In the beginning (was the Word, and the Word was with God, and the Word was God)—" (John 1:1) The Friar spoke these opening words of the Gospel of John in greeting to those he met. These words were considered to have special soul saving value, and almost magical power. 17. *arbitration-days*, days on which disputes could be settled by umpires out of court. Friars often acted as umpires and accepted "gifts" for their services. 18. *semicope*, a short cape. 19. *Orwell*, then a town on the English coast directly opposite Middleburg. This was a direct route for the wool trade with the Low Countries. 20. *benefice* (ben'i fis), an appointment in the church, which paid a salary. 21. *touching up*, borrowing from.

And quick and brief. He was of grave
  discourse,
Giving new weight to virtue by his speech,
And gladly would he learn and gladly teach.

THE LAWYER

There was a Lawyer, cunning and
  discreet,
Who had often been to St. Paul's porch²²
  to meet   306
His clients. He was a Sergeant of the Law,²³
A man deserving to be held in awe,
Or so he seemed, his manner was so wise.
He had often served as Justice of Assize   310
By the king's appointment, with a broad
  commission,
For his knowledge and his eminent position.
He had many a handsome gift by way of fee.
There was no buyer of land as shrewd as he.
All ownership to him became fee simple.²⁴
His titles were never faulty by a pimple.   316
None was so busy as he with case and cause,
And yet he seemed much busier than he
  was.
In all cases and decisions he was schooled
That were of record since King William²⁵
  ruled.   320
No one could pick a loophole or a flaw
In any lease or contract he might draw.
Each statute on the books he knew by rote.
He traveled in a plain, silk-belted coat.

THE FRANKLIN

A Franklin traveled in his company.
Whiter could never daisy petal be   326
Than was his beard. His ruddy face gave
  sign
He liked his morning sop of toast in wine.
He lived in comfort, as he would assure us,
For he was a true son of Epicurus²⁶   330
Who held the opinion that the only measure
Of perfect happiness was simply pleasure.
Such hospitality did he provide,
He was St. Julian²⁷ to his countryside.   334
His bread and ale were always up to scratch.
He had a cellar none on earth could match.
There was no lack of pasties in his house,
Both fish and flesh, and that so plenteous
That where he lived it snowed of meat and
  drink.   339

With every dish of which a man can think,
After the various seasons of the year,
He changed his diet for his better cheer.
He had coops of partridges as fat as cream,
He had a fish pond stocked with pike and
  bream.
Woe to his cook for an unready pot   345
Or a sauce that wasn't seasoned and spiced
  hot!
A table in his hall stood on display
Prepared and covered through the livelong
  day.²⁸
He presided at court sessions for his bounty
And sat in Parliament often for his county.
A well-wrought dagger and a purse of silk 351
Hung at his belt, as white as morning milk.
He had been a sheriff and county auditor.
On earth was no such rich proprietor!

THE GUILDSMEN

There were five Guildsmen, in the livery
Of one august and great fraternity,   356
A Weaver, a Dyer, and a Carpenter,
A Tapestry-maker and a Haberdasher.
Their gear was furbished new and clean as
  glass.
The mountings of their knives were not of
  brass   360
But silver. Their pouches were well made
  and neat,
And each of them, it seemed, deserved a seat
On the platform at the Guildhall,²⁹ for each
  one
Was likely timber to make an alderman.
They had goods enough, and money to be
  spent,   365

---

22. *St. Paul's porch.* It was customary for lawyers to
meet their clients in the porch of St. Paul's Cathedral.
23. *Sergeant of the Law,* a legal servant of the King who
had been a lawyer for at least sixteen years. 24. *fee
simple.* The lawyer knew how to get all property in un-
restricted possession so that heirs of any social class
might inherit an estate. 25. *King William,* William the
Conqueror. 26. *Epicurus* (ep′ə kūr′əs), a noted Greek
philosopher (342?-270 B.C.), who believed in the pursuit
of pleasure. 27. *St. Julian,* the patron saint of hospitality. 28. *Prepared . . . livelong day.* The Franklin's
table, unlike most tables of his time, was a permanent
affair, always provided with food and drink in abundance. 29. *And . . . Guildhall.* A guildhall was the
building in which the members of a particular trade guild
regularly met. In these meetings, the head of the guild,
called the mayor, and his council, the aldermen, sat on
the platform.

Also their wives would willingly consent
And would have been at fault if they had
  not.
For to be "Madamed" is a pleasant lot,
And to march in first at feasts for being well
  married,
And royally to have their mantles carried. 370

THE COOK

For the pilgrimage these Guildsmen brought
  their own
Cook to boil their chicken and marrow bone
With seasoning powder and capers and sharp
  spice.
In judging London ale his taste was nice.
He well knew how to roast and broil and fry,
To mix a stew, and bake a good meat pie, 376
Or capon creamed with almond, rice, and
  egg.
Pity he had an ulcer on his leg!

THE SKIPPER

A Skipper was with us, his home far in the
  west.
He came from the port of Dartmouth, as I
  guessed.   380
He sat his cart horse pretty much at sea
In a coarse smock that joggled on his knee.
From his neck a dagger on a string hung
  down
Under his arm. His face was burnished
  brown
By the summer sun. He was a true good
  fellow.   385
Many a time he had tapped a wine cask
  mellow
Sailing from Bordeaux while the owner
  slept.
Too nice a point of honor he never kept.
In a sea fight, if he got the upper hand,
Drowned prisoners floated home to every
  land.   390
But in navigation, whether reckoning tides,
Currents, or what might threaten him
  besides,
Harborage, pilotage, or the moon's demeanor,
None was his like from Hull to Cartagena.[30]
He knew each harbor and the anchorage
  there   395
From Gotland to the Cape of Finisterre

And every creek in Brittany and Spain,
And he had called his ship the *Madeleine*.

THE PHYSICIAN

With us came also an astute Physician.
There was none like him for a disquisition 400
On the art of medicine or surgery,
For he was grounded in astrology.[31]
He kept his patient long in observation,
Choosing the proper hour for application
Of charms and images by intuition   405
Of magic, and the planets' best position.
For he was one who understood the laws
That rule the humors,[32] and could tell the
  cause
That brought on every human malady,
Whether of hot or cold, or moist or dry.   410
He was a perfect medico, for sure.
The cause once known, he would prescribe
  the cure,
For he had his druggists ready at a motion
To provide the sick man with some pill or
  potion—
A game of mutual aid, with each one
  winning.   415
Their partnership was hardly just
  beginning! . . .
He urged a moderate fare on principle,
But rich in nourishment, digestible;
Of nothing in excess would he admit.
He gave but little heed to Holy Writ.   420
His clothes were lined with taffeta; their hue
Was all of blood red and of Persian blue,
Yet he was far from careless of expense.
He saved his fees from times of pestilence,
For gold is a cordial,[33] as physicians hold, 425
And so he had a special love for gold.

THE WIFE OF BATH

A worthy woman there was from near the
  city

---

30. *from Hull to Cartegena* (kär′tə jĕ′nə), from a seaport
in northern England to a seaport in southern Spain. These
references and others indicate how widely traveled the
Skipper was. 31. *astrology.* Since it was believed that
the position of the planets determined the best time for
treatment of a patient, physicians were students of astrology. 32. *the humors,* the four bodily fluids—blood,
choler, phlegm, and melancholy—which, according to
medieval belief, determined a person's health and disposition. 33. *gold is a cordial.* Gold in solution was used as
a remedy in desperate diseases.

Of Bath, but somewhat deaf, and more's the
    pity.
For weaving she possessed so great a bent
She outdid the people of Ypres and of
    Ghent.[34]   430
No other woman dreamed of such a thing
As to precede her at the offering,
Or if any did, she fell in such a wrath
She dried up all the charity in Bath.   434
She wore fine kerchiefs of old-fashioned air,
And on a Sunday morning, I could swear,
She had ten pounds of linen on her head.
Her stockings were of finest scarlet-red,
Laced tightly, and her shoes were soft
    and new.   439
Bold was her face, and fair, and red in hue.
She had been an excellent woman all her
    life.
Five men in turn had taken her to wife,
Omitting other youthful company—
But let that pass for now! Over the sea
She had traveled freely; many a distant
    stream   445
She crossed, and visited Jerusalem
Three times. She had been at Rome and at
    Boulogne,
At the shrine of Compostella, and at
    Cologne.[35]
She had wandered by the way through many
    a scene.   449
Her teeth were set with little gaps between.
Easily on her ambling horse she sat.
She was well wimpled, and she wore a hat
As wide in circuit as a shield or targe.
A skirt swathed up her hips, and they were
    large.   454
Upon her feet she wore sharp-roweled spurs.
She was a good fellow; a ready tongue was
    hers.
All remedies of love she knew by name,
For she had all the tricks of that old game.

THE PARSON

There was a good man of the priest's
    vocation,
A poor town Parson of true consecration,   460
But he was rich in holy thought and work.
Learned he was, in the truest sense a clerk[36]
Who meant Christ's gospel faithfully to
    preach

And truly his parishioners to teach.
He was a kind man, full of industry,   465
Many times tested by adversity
And always patient. If tithes were in arrears,
He was loth to threaten any man with fears
Of excommunication; past a doubt
He would rather spread his offering about   470
To his poor flock, or spend his property.
To him a little meant sufficiency.
Wide was his parish, with houses far
    asunder,
But he would not be kept by rain or thunder,
If any had suffered a sickness or a blow,   475
From visiting the farthest, high or low,
Plodding his way on foot, his staff in hand.
He was a model his flock could understand,
For first he did and afterward he taught.
That precept from the Gospel he had
    caught,   480
And he added as a metaphor thereto,
"If the gold rusts, what will the iron do?"
For if a priest is foul, in whom we trust,
No wonder a layman shows a little rust.
A priest should take to heart the shameful
    scene   485
Of shepherds filthy while the sheep are
    clean.
By his own purity a priest should give
The example to his sheep, how they should
    live.
He did not rent his benefice for hire,
Leaving his flock to flounder in the mire,   490
And run to London, happiest of goals,
To sing paid masses in St. Paul's for souls,
Or as chaplain from some rich guild take his
    keep,
But dwelt at home and guarded well his
    sheep
So that no wolf should make his flock
    miscarry.   495
He was a shepherd, and not a mercenary.
And though himself a man of strict vocation
He was not harsh to weak souls in
    temptation,
Not overbearing nor haughty in his speech,

---

34. *Ypres* (ē′prə) . . . *Ghent* (gent), Flemish cities famous
for the ability of their weavers and as markets of the
wool trade. **35.** *Rome . . . Cologne* (kə lōn′). The Wife
of Bath had visited the most famous shrines in Italy,
France, Spain, and Germany. **36.** *clerk,* a scholar, a learned
man. In the Middle Ages, most scholars were clergymen.

But wise and kind in all he tried to teach. 500
By good example and just words to turn
Sinners to heaven was his whole concern.
But should a man in truth prove obstinate,
Whoever he was, of rich or mean estate,
The Parson would give him a snub to meet
    the case. 505
I doubt there was a priest in any place
His better. He did not stand on dignity
Nor affect in conscience too much nicety,
But Christ's and his disciples' word he sought
To teach, and first he followed what he
    taught. 510

THE PLOWMAN

There was a Plowman with him on the
    road,
His brother, who had forked up many a load
Of good manure. A hearty worker he,
Living in peace and perfect charity.
Whether his fortune made him smart or
    smile, 515
He loved God with his whole heart all the
    while
And his neighbor as himself. He would
    undertake,
For every luckless poor man, for the sake
Of Christ to thresh and ditch and dig by
    the hour
And with no wage, if it was in his power. 520
His tithes on goods and earnings he paid
    fair.
He wore a coarse, rough coat and rode a
    mare.
    There also were a Manciple, a Miller,
A Reeve, a Summoner, and a Pardoner,
And I—this makes our company complete. 525

THE MILLER

As tough a yokel as you care to meet
The Miller was. His big-beefed arms and
    thighs
Took many a ram put up as wrestling prize.
He was a thick, squat-shouldered lump of
    sins.
No door but he could heave it off its pins 530
Or break it running at it with his head.
His beard was broader than a shovel, and red
As a fat sow or fox. A wart stood clear
Atop his nose, and red as a pig's ear

A tuft of bristles on it. Black and wide 535
His nostrils were. He carried at his side
A sword and buckler. His mouth would open
    out
Like a great furnace, and he would sing and
    shout
His ballads and jokes of harlotries and
    crimes.
He could steal corn and charge for it three
    times, 540
And yet was honest enough, as millers come,
For a miller, as they say, has a golden
    thumb.[37]
In white coat and blue hood this lusty
    clown,
Blowing his bagpipes, brought us out of
    town.

THE MANCIPLE

The Manciple[38] was of a lawyer's college,
And other buyers might have used his
    knowledge 546
How to be shrewd provisioners, for whether
He bought on cash or credit, altogether
He managed that the end should be the
    same:
He came out more than even with the game.
Now isn't it an instance of God's grace 551
How a man of little knowledge can keep
    pace
In wit with a whole school of learned men?
He had masters to the number of three times
    ten
Who knew each twist of equity and tort; 555
A dozen in that very Inn of Court[39]
Were worthy to be steward of the estate
To any of England's lords, however great,
And keep him to his income well confined 559
And free from debt, unless he lost his mind,
Or let him scrimp, if he were mean in
    bounty;
They could have given help to a whole
    county

---

37. *a golden thumb.* A miller's thumb was considered
worth its weight in gold because he used it to weight the
scales containing grain or flour, thus giving the customers
short measure. **38.** *Manciple,* a purchasing agent for a
medieval institution. **39.** *Inn of Court.* The Inns of
Court, located in London, are four sets of buildings which
house the four societies of lawyers. These societies alone
admit practitioners of the law of England to practice at
the bar.

In any sort of case that might befall;
And yet this Manciple could cheat them all!

THE REEVE

The Reeve[40] was a slender, fiery-tempered
    man.   565
He shaved as closely as a razor can.
His hair was cropped about his ears, and
    shorn
Above his forehead as a priest's is worn.
His legs were very long and very lean.   569
No calf on his lank spindles could be seen.
But he knew how to keep a barn or bin,
He could play the game with auditors and
    win.
He knew well how to judge by drought and
    rain
The harvest of his seed and of his grain.   574
His master's cattle, swine, and poultry flock,
Horses and sheep and dairy, all his stock,
Were altogether in this Reeve's control.
And by agreement, he had given the sole
Accounting since his lord reached twenty
    years.
No man could ever catch him in arrears.   580
There wasn't a bailiff, shepherd, or farmer
    working
But the Reeve knew all his tricks of cheating
    and shirking.
He would not let him draw an easy breath.
They feared him as they feared the very
    death.   584
He lived in a good house on an open space,
Well shaded by green trees, a pleasant place.
He was shrewder in acquisition than his lord.
With private riches he was amply stored.
He had learned a good trade young by work
    and will.
He was a carpenter of first-rate skill.   590
On a fine mount, a stallion, dappled gray,
Whose name was Scot, he rode along the
    way.
He wore a long blue coat hitched up and tied
As if it were a friar's, and at his side   594
A sword with rusty blade was hanging down.
He came from Norfolk, from nearby the
    town
That men call Bawdswell. As we rode the
    while,
The Reeve kept always hindmost in our file.

THE SUMMONER

A Summoner[41] in our company had his
    place.
Red as the fiery cherubim his face. . . .   600
His brows were scabby and black, and thin
    his beard.
His was a face that little children feared. . . .
No salve nor ointment that will cleanse or
    bite
Could cure him of his blotches, livid white,
Or the nobs and nubbins sitting on his
    cheeks.   605
He loved his garlic, his onions, and his leeks.
He loved to drink the strong wine down
    blood-red.
Then would he bellow as if he had lost his
    head,
And when he had drunk enough to parch
    his drouth,
Nothing but Latin issued from his
    mouth. . . .   610
He had the young men and girls in his
    control
Throughout the diocese; he knew the soul
Of youth, and heard their every last
    design.
A garland big enough to be the sign
Above an alehouse balanced on his head,   615
And he made a shield of a great round loaf
    of bread.

THE PARDONER

There was a Pardoner[42] of Rouncivalle
With him, of the Blessed Mary's hospital,[43]
But now come straight from Rome (or so
    said he).   619
Loudly he sang, "Come hither, love, to me,"
While the Summoner's counterbass trolled
    out profound—
No trumpet blew with half so vast a sound.
This Pardoner had hair as yellow as wax,
But it hung as smoothly as a hank of flax.
His locks trailed down in bunches from his
    head,   625

---

40. *Reeve*, manager of an estate. 41. *Summoner*. His
job was to call delinquents to appear before the ecclesiastical
court. 42. *Pardoner*, a clergyman licensed to grant in-
dulgences (pardon for punishment due to sin) as a return
for money offered to the church. 43. *hospital*, located at
Rouncivalle (roun'si vəl) in London.

And he let the ends about his shoulders
  spread,
But in thin clusters, lying one by one.
Of hood, for rakishness, he would have none,
For in his wallet he kept it safely stowed.
He traveled, as he thought, in the latest
  mode,   630
Disheveled. Save for his cap, his head was
  bare,
And in his eyes he glittered like a hare.
A Veronica[44] was stitched upon his cap,
His wallet lay before him in his lap
Brimful of pardons from the very seat   635
In Rome. He had a voice like a goat's
  bleat. . . .
No pardoner could beat him in the race,
For in his wallet he had a pillowcase
Which he represented as Our Lady's veil;
He said he had a piece of the very sail   640
St. Peter, when he fished in Galilee
Before Christ caught him, used upon the sea.
He had a latten cross embossed with stones
And in a glass he carried some pig's bones,
And with these holy relics, when he found
Some village parson grubbing his poor
  ground,   646
He would get more money in a single day
Than in two months would come the
  parson's way.
Thus with his flattery and his trumped-up
  stock
He made dupes of the parson and his
  flock.   650
But though his conscience was a little plastic
He was in church a noble ecclesiastic.
Well could he read the Scripture or saint's
  story,
But best of all he sang the offertory,
For he understood that when this song was
  sung,   655
Then he must preach, and sharpen up his
  tongue
To rake in cash, as well he knew the art,
And so he sang out gaily, with full heart.
  Now I have set down briefly, as it was,
Our rank, our dress, our number, and the
  cause   660
That made our sundry fellowship begin
In Southwark, at this hospitable inn
Known as the Tabard, not far from the Bell.

from THE PARDONER'S TALE

While the pilgrims rest on the road to Canterbury, the Pardoner tells his tale. Warmed and refreshed by ale, he delivers a long sermon in which he reveals with astonishing frankness how he fools the public with his "pigges' bones" and other counterfeit relics.

To illustrate the text of his sermon—"Avarice is the root of all evil"—the Pardoner introduces a short but powerful "moral tale." In this tale, which follows, Chaucer has given us one of the best short stories ever written.

These three young roisterers of
    whom I tell
    Long before prime had rung from
    any bell
Were seated in a tavern at their drinking,
And as they sat, they heard a bell go
  clinking
Before a corpse being carried to his grave.   5
One of these roisterers, when he heard it,
  gave
An order to his boy: "Go out and try
To learn whose corpse is being carried by.
Get me his name, and get it right. Take
  heed."
  "Sir," said the boy, "there isn't any need. 10
I learned before you came here, by two
  hours.
He was, it happens, an old friend of yours,
And all at once, there on his bench upright
As he was sitting drunk, he was killed last
  night.
A sly thief, Death men call him, who
  deprives   15
All the people in this country of their lives,
Came with his spear and smiting his heart in
  two
Went on his business with no more ado.
A thousand have been slaughtered by his
  hand

PROLOGUE. **44.** *Veronica,* a representation of the face of Christ. It was so called from the imprint of Christ's face left on the handkerchief Veronica offered Him on the way to Calvary.

PARDONER'S TALE. From *The Portable Chaucer,* selected, translated, and edited by Theodore Morrison. Copyright, 1949, by Theodore Morrison. Reprinted by permission of The Viking Press, Inc., New York.

During this plague.[1] And, sir, before you
    stand   20
Within his presence, it should be necessary,
It seems to me, to know your adversary.
Be evermore prepared to meet this foe.
My mother taught me thus; that's all I
    know."
   "Now by St. Mary," said the innkeeper, 25
"This child speaks truth. Man, woman,
    laborer,
Servant, and child the thief has slain this
    year
In a big village a mile or more from here.
I think it is his place of habitation.
It would be wise to make some preparation 30
Before he brought a man into disgrace."
   "God's arms!" this roisterer said. "So that's
    the case!
Is it so dangerous with this thief to meet?
I'll look for him by every path and street,
I vow it, by God's holy bones! Hear me, 35
Fellows of mine, we are all one, we three.
Let each of us hold up his hand to the other
And each of us become his fellow's brother.
We'll slay this Death, who slaughters and
    betrays,   39
He shall be slain whose hand so many slays,

*Dance of Death. These moralistic
drawings of death were very common.*

By the dignity of God, before tonight!"
   The three together set about to plight
Their oaths to live and die each for the other
Just as though each had been to each born
    brother,
And in their drunken frenzy up they get 45
And toward the village off at once they set
Which the innkeeper had spoken of before,
And many were the grisly oaths they swore.
They rent Christ's precious body limb from
    limb—
Death shall be dead, if they lay hands on
    him!   50
   When they had hardly gone the first half
    mile,
Just as they were about to cross a stile,
An old man, poor and humble, met them
    there.
The old man greeted them with a meek air
And said, "God bless you, lords, and be
    your guide."   55
   "What's this?" the proudest of the three
    replied.
"Old beggar, I hope you meet the evil grace!
Why are you all wrapped up except your
    face?
What are you doing alive so many a year?"
   The old man at these words began to peer
Into this gambler's face. "Because I can, 61
Though I should walk to India, find no
    man,"
He said, "in any village or any town,
Who for my age is willing to lay down
His youth. So I must keep my old age still 65
For as long a time as it may be God's will.
Nor will Death take my life from me, alas!
Thus like a restless prisoner I pass
And on the ground, which is my mother's
    gate,[2]   69
I walk and with my staff both early and late
I knock and say, 'Dear mother, let me in!
See how I vanish, flesh, and blood, and skin!
Alas, when shall my bones be laid to rest?
I would exchange with you my clothing
    chest,
Mother, that in my chamber long has been 75
For an old haircloth rag to wrap me in.'

---

1. *This plague.* Chaucer doubtless has in mind the Black
Death of 1348-1349. **2.** *mother's gate,* the grave, the entrance to "mother earth."

And yet she still refuses me that grace.
All white, therefore, and withered is my
        face.
   "But, sirs, you do yourselves no courtesy
To speak to an old man so churlishly   80
Unless he had wronged you either in word
        or deed.
As you yourselves in Holy Writ may read,
'Before an aged man whose head is hoar
Men ought to rise.' I counsel you, therefore,
No harm nor wrong here to an old man
        do,   85
No more than you would have men do to
        you
In your old age, if you so long abide.
And God be with you, whether you walk
        or ride!
I must go yonder where I have to go."   89
   "No, you old beggar, by St. John, not so,"
Said another of these gamblers. "As for me,
By God, you won't get off so easily!
You spoke just now of that false traitor,
        Death,
Who in this land robs all our friends of
        breath.   94
Tell where he is, since you must be his spy,
Or you will suffer for it, so say I
By God and by the holy sacrament.
You are in league with him, false thief, and
        bent
On killing us young folk, that's clear to my
        mind."
   "If you are so impatient, sirs, to find   100
Death," he replied, "turn up this crooked
        way,
For in that grove I left him, truth to say,
Beneath a tree, and there he will abide.
No boast of yours will make him run and
        hide.
Do you see that oak tree? Just there you
        will find   105
This Death, and God, who bought again
        mankind,
Save and amend you!" So said this old man;
And promptly each of these three gamblers
        ran
Until he reached the tree, and there they
        found
Florins of fine gold, minted bright and
        round,   110

Nearly eight bushels of them, as they
        thought.
And after Death no longer then they sought.
Each of them was so ravished at the sight,
So fair the florins glittered and so bright,
That down they sat beside the precious
        hoard.   115
The worst of them, he uttered the first word.
   "Brothers," he told them, "listen to what
        I say.
My head is sharp, for all I joke and play.
Fortune has given us this pile of treasure
To set us up in lives of ease and pleasure.   120
Lightly it comes, lightly we'll make it go.
God's precious dignity! Who was to know
We'd ever tumble on such luck today?
If we could only carry this gold away,   124
Home to my house, or even one of yours—
For well you know that all this gold is ours—
We'd touch the summit of felicity.
But still, by daylight that can hardly be.
People would call us thieves, too bold for
        stealth,
And they would have us hanged for our
        own wealth.   130
It must be done by night, that's our best plan,
As prudently and slyly as we can.
Hence my proposal is that we should all
Draw lots, and let's see where the lot will
        fall,
And the one of us who draws the shortest
        stick   135
Shall run back to the town, and make it
        quick,
And bring us bread and wine here on the
        sly,
And two of us will keep a watchful eye
Over this gold; and if he doesn't stay   139
Too long in town, we'll carry this gold away
By night, wherever we all agree it's best."
   One of them held the cut out in his fist
And had them draw to see where it would
        fall,
And the cut fell on the youngest of them all.
At once he set off on his way to town,   145
And the very moment after he was gone
The one who urged this plan said to the
        other:
"You know that by sworn oath you are my
        brother.

I'll tell you something you can profit by.   149
Our friend has gone, that's clear to any eye,
And here is gold, abundant as can be,
That we propose to share alike, we three.
But if I worked it out, as I could do,
So that it could be shared between us two,
Wouldn't that be a favor, a friendly one?"   155
   The other answered, "How that can be
      done,
I don't quite see. He knows we have the
      gold.
What shall we do, or what shall he be told?"
   "Will you keep the secret tucked inside
      your head?   159
And in a few words," the first scoundrel said,
"I'll tell you how to bring this end about."
   "Granted," the other told him. "Never
      doubt,
I won't betray you, that you can believe."
   "Now," said the first, "we are two, as you
      perceive,
And two of us must have more strength
      than one.   165
When he sits down, get up as if in fun
And wrestle with him. While you play this
      game
I'll run him through the ribs. You do the
      same
With your dagger there, and then this gold
      shall be   169
Divided, dear friend, between you and me.
Then all that we desire we can fulfill,
And both of us can roll the dice at will."
Thus in agreement these two scoundrels fell
To slay the third, as you have heard me tell.
   The youngest, who had started off to town,
Within his heart kept rolling up and down   176
The beauty of these florins, new and bright.
"O Lord," he thought, "were there some way
      I might
Have all this treasure to myself alone,
There isn't a man who dwells beneath
      God's throne   180
Could live a life as merry as mine should be!"
And so at last the fiend, our enemy,
Put in his head that he could gain his ends
If he bought poison to kill off his friends.
Finding his life in such a sinful state,   185
The devil was allowed to seal his fate.
For it was altogether his intent

To kill his friends, and never to repent.
So off he set, no longer would he tarry,
Into the town, to an apothecary,   190
And begged for poison; he wanted it because
He meant to kill his rats; besides, there was
A polecat living in his hedge, he said,
Who killed his capons; and when he went
      to bed   194
He wanted to take vengeance, if he might,
On vermin that devoured him by night.
   The apothecary answered, "You should
      have
A drug that as I hope the Lord will save
My soul, no living thing in all creation,
Eating or drinking of this preparation   200
A dose no bigger than a grain of wheat,
But promptly with his death-stroke he shall
      meet.
Die, that he will, and in a briefer while
Than you can walk the distance of a mile,
This poison is so strong and virulent."   205
   Taking the poison, off the scoundrel went,
Holding it in a box, and next he ran
To the neighboring street, and borrowed
      from a man
Three generous flagons. He emptied out his
      drug
In two of them, and kept the other jug   210
For his own drink; he let no poison lurk
In that! And so all night he meant to work
Carrying off the gold. Such was his plan,
And when he had filled them, this accursed
      man   214
Retraced his path, still following his design,
Back to his friends with his three jugs of
      wine.
   But why dilate upon it any more?
For just as they had planned his death
      before,
Just so they killed him, and with no delay.
When it was finished, one spoke up to
      say: 220
"Now let's sit down and drink, and we can
      bury
His body later on. First we'll be merry,"
And as he said the words, he took the jug
That, as it happened, held the poisonous
      drug,
And drank, and gave his friend a drink
      as well,   225

And promptly they both died. But truth to
    tell,
In all that Avicenna[3] ever wrote
He never described in chapter, rule, or note
More marvelous signs of poisoning, I
    suppose,
Than appeared in these two wretches at
    the close.   230
Thus they both perished for their homicide,
And thus the traitorous poisoner also died.

3. *Avicenna* (av′i sen′ə), an Arabic philosopher of the
eleventh century, famous for his medical studies.

 To increase understanding

1. The "Prologue" to *The Canterbury Tales* has
long been considered a striking picture of the varied
types of people that made up fourteenth-century
society. (*a*) With your text as guide, discuss the
place of each pilgrim in medieval society. (*b*) Explain why Chaucer was able to cover the society
of his day with such completeness.

2. Why may the "Prologue" be considered "a
source book of information on fourteenth-century
England"?

3. In your opinion are the pilgrims types or individuals? Explain your answer by analyzing Chaucer's description of one pilgrim.

4. (*a*) What is the plot of "The Pardoner's
Tale"? (*b*) What is the theme?

5. Is the old man whom the three roisterers meet
a real person or a symbol? Explain your answer.

6. Critics consider "The Pardoner's Tale" one of
the best short stories ever written. Explain why you
agree or disagree with this judgment, taking into
consideration (*a*) the development of plot, (*b*) the
characterization, and (*c*) the pace of the narrative.

7. Like most of Chaucer's tales, "The Pardoner's
Tale" is a retelling of an old story, in this case one
that originated in the Orient. Why was its setting
in a plague-infested land particularly chilling to men
of Chaucer's day?

 Better reading

The tone of Chaucer's Prologue

When the thoughtful reader has finished Chaucer's
"Prologue," he has gained not only vivid mental images of twenty-nine pilgrims but also a clear idea of
Chaucer's attitude toward these widely varying individuals. This attitude of an author as evidenced in
his work is called *tone.* The tone of an author may

be sentimental, tragic, comic, idealistic, ironic, or a
combination of these or of still other tones. Chaucer's tone in the "Prologue" is largely *ironic; that is,*
he says one thing while he is actually implying another. He pretends to be a mere innocent observer,
supplying details about each pilgrim in haphazard
manner; yet these seemingly random details, when
carefully weighed, have a telling ironic force. Consider the Prioress. Here is a gentle, guileless nun
moving serenely toward Canterbury with her attendants. Now scrutinize the details. In what is
the Prioress really interested? The portrait that
emerges is that of a nun whose chief concern is to
impress the other pilgrims with her gentility. Thus
Chaucer, through the use of irony, makes his comment on the worldliness that in the later Middle
Ages was becoming increasingly prevalent in the
Church.

Of all the pilgrims, only three—the Knight, the
poor Parson, and the Plowman—are treated without
any irony at all. The Knight represents the ideals of
the Age of Chivalry, in Chaucer's time long past its
greatest days. The poor Parson is the ideal churchman. The Plowman is the finest type of English
workingman. These three are contrasted with people
of all classes of society and of several degrees of
virtue. Chaucer calls none of them rascals, but his
ironic tone tells the reader that he knows many of
them are. But whether he is writing of saints or
sinners, his tone clearly tells us also that he enjoys
his fellowmen and sympathizes with their difficulties.
His irony is blended with humor and compassion.

Compare Chaucer's portrait of the Knight with
those of the Franklin, the Skipper, and the Reeve.
Explain why the sketch of the Knight may be considered idealized. What touches of irony do you find
in the descriptions of the others?

What details in the character sketch of the poor
Parson show that Chaucer regards him as the ideal
priest? What is the poet's opinion of the Monk,
the Friar, the Summoner, and the Pardoner? Why
do the sketches of these four amuse us while that
of the Parson does not?

Select a pilgrim you find interesting and discuss
the tone or tones Chaucer uses in describing this
individual.

 Words!

Words are not static! Many words Chaucer used in
the Middle Ages have gradually changed their meanings to suit the changing needs of the people. The
history of many a word—its origin, or beginnings,
and gradual changes of meaning over a long period

of time—makes a fascinating story. The word *clerk*, for example, which appears in the description of the parson on page 75, originally meant "a man in a religious order, a cleric or clergyman." Since the scholarship of the Middle Ages was practically limited to the clergy, and these men performed all the writing, notarial, and secretarial work of the time, the name *clerk* came to be equivalent to *scholar*. Later, as education spread and the ability to read and write tended to be less significant, the word *clerk* became more general in its application, indicating anyone who performed minor tasks such as keeping records or perhaps looking after a shop. In addition to becoming generalized in its application, the word descended in connotation; from a term of praise the word dropped to one of merely factual description.

While some words descended in connotation, others ascended. For example, the word *marshal*, which originally meant a groom or stable servant, today may be used to denote an officer in a royal household, a law officer, or a high-ranking military figure. Words may also specialize or become narrowed in their range of application; for example, *deer* at one time meant any animal.

Below are given a few words that have interesting stories to tell and which also show at least one of the meaning changes just described: *generalization, specialization, ascended* or *descended connotation*. Look the words up in an etymological dictionary, an unabridged dictionary, or one of the following books: *Picturesque Word Origins* (published by G. and C. Merriam Company); *Dictionary of Word Origins*, by Joseph T. Shipley. Tell the story of each word as vividly and dramatically as you can, including the type of meaning change that occurred.

bedlam	curfew	melancholy	pecuniary
calculate	enthralling	neighbor	tawdry
canter	lady	pagan	villain
chivalry	lord	palace	

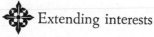 Extending interests

The tales told by Chaucer's pilgrims differ as widely as the pilgrims themselves. Among the most interesting tales are the Nun's Priest's, the Oxford Student's (or Clerk's), the Nun's, the Wife of Bath's, the Knight's, and the Man of Law's. Read one of these tales and report on it to the class. Let your classmates decide whether or not this is the type of story they would expect this pilgrim to tell. You will find good modern translations of *The Canterbury Tales* listed in the chapter bibliography on page 89.

William Caxton and the Printing Press

Chaucer says in one of his poems that he possessed sixty books, and if this is an autobiographical statement, Chaucer had a library to be proud of. Many a college library at Oxford or Cambridge had fewer and still considered itself well equipped. Since manuscript volumes were rare and expensive, usually costing the equivalent of forty to sixty dollars today, they were generally inaccessible to most men. In fact, they were so valuable that libraries sometimes chained them to the walls in order to baffle thieves. Within one hundred years of Chaucer's death the introduction of movable type to England had reduced the price of books to one fifth of their former cost. The man who brought about this historic change was William Caxton.

Although William Caxton (1422?-1491?) was at an early age apprenticed to one of England's richest cloth merchants and ultimately became a wealthy merchant himself, it is with printing that his name is forever associated. Vacationing in the German city of Cologne in the summer of 1471, he for the first time saw a printing press at work. Gutenberg's invention of printing from movable type, though not over fifty years old at the time, had already spread to nearly every country in Europe. It so excited the interest of Caxton that he learned the whole printing trade, from typesetting to the production of the finished book. On his return to England he established the first English press at Westminster in 1476. One third of the books he issued were his own translations, and to them he contributed prefaces. Among Caxton's hundred printed books are Chaucer's *Canterbury Tales* and Malory's *Morte Darthur,* to the latter of which he contributed an excellent preface. He also printed translations of classical works in Greek and Latin. Caxton and the printers who followed him made directly available to Englishmen the treasures of the past that Chaucer had earlier encountered in Italy.

The early printers made the printed page

look as much like manuscript as possible, painting in illuminated initials by hand in the case of the most prized volumes, particularly in sacred works. But although the manuscript-like type kept the number of words on a page small, the substitution of paper for the sheep- or lambskin which the scribes had used cut down the weight, size, and cost. Since books became both less cumbersome and less expensive, and since many different titles were printed, for the first time it became worthwhile for the average man to learn to read. Thus to a great extent the invention of printing brought England to the close of the Middle Ages and ushered in the Renaissance.

Below: A typical fifteenth-century printing house.
Right: A sample of printing from Caxton's press. Since paper was very expensive at this time, printers often combined cover, frontispiece, and title page with the first page of text.

Here foloweth The lyf of Saynt Jherome And first of his name

Jherome is sayd of Jera that is hooly / And of nemus / that is to saye a wood / And soo Jherome is as moche to saye as an hooly wood

Sir Thomas Malory *and the prose romance*

Throughout the Middle Ages, the dominant form of literature among the feudal aristocracy was the *romance*. Originated by the troubadours who wandered across France, the romance spread to Germany, Spain, and Italy, and finally across the channel to England. There the troubadours were called *minstrels;* as they chanted their long verse tales of courtly love and knightly adventure in the great halls of the Norman castles, they were as welcome as the *scops* had been in Anglo-Saxon England. As time passed, the romances, like the ballads, changed. An English minstrel might add new elements to a French troubadour's tale, and many of the verse romances were filled out in prose versions.

Shortly before Chaucer's death, when both feudalism and chivalry were faltering institutions, a man was born who sought to capture in his writings the medieval ideal of knighthood. This man was Sir Thomas Malory (1394?-1471). Little is known about his life beyond the fact that he was a knight who fought in the last years of the Hundred Years' War, was elected to Parliament in 1445, became involved in the Wars of the Roses, and spent the last twenty years of his life in prison for crimes of which he may not have been guilty. Fortunately for succeeding generations, he was imprisoned at Newgate Gaol, a London prison which happened to be across the road from the Gray Friars monastery. The monastery had a collection of manuscripts, about twenty of them being legends of Arthur, mostly French. Malory was allowed to draw upon this treasure in writing his version of the Arthurian legends, the *Morte Darthur* (*The Death of Arthur*).

Malory's *Morte Darthur* is the most complete single version of the tales of King Arthur and his court that has been written in English. It represents the drawing together, arranging, and clarifying of tales from various English and French versions, many of them contradictory. The historical sources of the Arthurian legend remain obscure. Arthur was probably a Celtic chieftain who lived in Britain during the fifth century and fought the invading Anglo-Saxons, Picts, and Scots. Twelfth-century accounts of Arthur which are extant mention the Round Table and a following of a few knights. Sometime during the height of the Middle Ages the Celtic folk hero Arthur became associated with the code of chivalry and with medieval French romances about Lancelot and the Holy Grail. Through these diverse sources Arthur ultimately emerged in song and story as the embodiment of the ideal knight. It is this Arthur that Malory tried to record, so that men who lived in the days when chivalry was a lost ideal might recall fondly the glamorous yesterdays of knighthood.

A medieval knight is represented in this fourteenth-century chess piece.

from *Malory's* MORTE DARTHUR

The following selection occurs near the end of the Morte Darthur, *when the unity of the Round Table has been disrupted by the ambitions of Arthur's nephew, Mordred. Rallying a band of knights around him, the traitor attempts to seize Arthur's crown. Ultimately the two factions meet in a battle which brings about the death of all the knights of the kingdom except the loyal Sir Bedivere. Mordred is killed by Arthur, who is himself mortally wounded. It is left to Bedivere to carry out his King's last wishes.*

BOOK 21, CHAPTER 5

How King Arthur Commanded to Cast His Sword Excalibur into the Water, and How He was Delivered to Ladies in a Barge

". . . But my time hieth fast," said the king. "Therefore," said Arthur unto Sir Bedivere, "take thou Excalibur, my good sword, and go with it to yonder water side, and when thou comest there I charge thee throw my sword in that water, and come again and tell me what

King Arthur, as represented in a fourteenth-century tapestry.

thou there seest." "My lord," said Bedivere, "your commandment shall be done, and lightly bring you word again." So Sir Bedivere departed, and by the way he beheld that noble sword, that the pommel and the haft was all of precious stones; and then he said to himself: "If I throw this rich sword in the water, thereof shall never come good, but harm and loss." And then Sir Bedivere hid Excalibur under a tree. And so, as soon as he might, he came again unto the king, and said he had been at the water, and had thrown the sword in the water. "What saw thou there?" said the king. "Sir," he said, " I saw nothing but waves and winds." "That is untruly said of thee," said the king, "therefore go thou lightly[1] again and do my commandment; as thou art to me lief and dear, spare not, but throw it in." Then Sir Bedivere returned again, and took the sword in his hand; and then him thought sin and shame to throw away that noble sword, and so efte he hid the sword and returned again, and told to the king that he had been at the water and done his commandment. "What saw thou there?" said the king. "Sir," he said, "I saw nothing but the waters wappe and the waves wanne."[2] "Ah, traitor untrue," said King Arthur, "now hast thou betrayed me twice. Who would have weened that thou that hast been to me so lief and dear, and thou art named a noble knight, and would betray me for the richness of the sword. But now go again lightly, for thy long tarrying putteth me in great jeopardy of my life, for I have taken cold. And but if[3] thou do now as I bid thee, if ever I may see thee, I shall slay thee with mine own hands; for thou wouldst for my rich sword see me dead." Then Sir Bedivere departed, and went to the sword, and lightly took it up, and went to the water side; and there he bound the girdle about the hilts, and then he threw the sword as far into the water as he might; and there came an arm and an hand above the water and met it, and caught it, and so shook it thrice and brandished, and then vanished away the hand with the sword in the water. So Sir Bedivere came again to the king, and told him what he saw. "Alas!" said the king, "help me hence, for I dread me I have tarried over long." Then Sir Bedivere

took the king upon his back, and so went with him to that water side. And when they were at the water side, even fast by the bank hoved a little barge with many fair ladies in it, and among them all was a queen, and all they had black hoods, and all they wept and shrieked when they saw King Arthur. "Now put me into the barge," said the king. And so he did softly; and there received him three queens with great mourning; and so they set them down, and in one of their laps King Arthur laid his head. And then that queen said: "Ah, dear brother, why have ye tarried so long from me? alas, this wound on your head hath caught over-much cold." And so then they rowed from the land, and Sir Bedivere beheld all those ladies go from him. Then Sir Bedivere cried: "Ah my lord Arthur, what shall become of me, now ye go from me and leave me here alone among mine enemies?" "Comfort thyself," said the king, "and do as well as thou mayest, for in me is no trust for to trust in; for I will into the vale of Avilion to heal me of my grievous wound; and if thou hear never more of me, pray for my soul." But ever the queens and ladies wept and shrieked, that it was pity to hear. And as soon as Sir Bedivere had lost the sight of the barge, he wept and wailed, and so took the forest; and so he went all that night, and in the morning he was ware betwixt two holts hoar,[4] of a chapel and an hermitage.

CHAPTER 6

How Sir Bedivere Found Him on the Morrow Dead in an Hermitage, and How He Abode There with the Hermit

Then was Sir Bedivere glad, and thither he went; and when he came into the chapel, he saw where lay an hermit grovelling on all four, there fast by a tomb was new graven. When the hermit saw Sir Bedivere, he knew him well, for he was but little tofore Bishop of Canterbury, that Sir Mordred flemed.[5] "Sir," said Bedivere, "what man is there interred that

1. *go thou lightly*, go quickly. 2. *wappe . . . wanne*, lap and ebb. 3. *but if*, unless. 4. *holts hoar*, old gray woods. 5. *flemed*, put to flight.

ye pray so fast for?" "Fair son," said the hermit, "I wot not verily, but by deeming.[6] But this night, at midnight, here came a number of ladies, and brought hither a dead corpse, and prayed me to bury him; and here they offered an hundred tapers, and they gave me an hundred besants."[7] "Alas!" said Sir Bedivere, "that was my lord King Arthur, that here lieth buried in this chapel." Then Sir Bedivere swooned; and when he awoke he prayed the hermit he might abide with him still there, to live with fasting and prayers. "For from hence will I never go," said Sir Bedivere, "by my will, but all the days of my life here to pray for my lord Arthur." . . . So there bode Sir Bedivere with the hermit that was tofore Bishop of Canterbury, and there Sir Bedivere put upon him poor clothes and served the hermit full lowly in fasting and in prayers. . . . More of the death of King Arthur could I never find, but that ladies brought him to his burials; and such one was buried there, that the hermit bare witness that sometime was Bishop of Canterbury, but yet the hermit knew not in certain that he was verily the body of King Arthur; for this tale Sir Bedivere, knight of the Table Round, made it to be written.

CHAPTER 7

Of the Opinion of Some Men of the Death of King Arthur

Yet some men say in many parts of England that King Arthur is not dead, but had by the will of our Lord Jesu into another place; and men say that he shall come again, and he shall win the holy cross. I will not say it shall be so, but rather I will say, here in this world he changed his life. But many men say that there is written upon his tomb this verse: *Hic jacet Arthurus Rex, quondam Rexque Futurus.*[8] Thus leave I here Sir Bedivere with the hermit, that dwelled that time in a chapel beside Glastonbury, and there was his hermitage . . .

---

6. *I wot . . . deeming,* I do not actually know; I can only speculate. 7. *besants,* gold coins. 8. *Hic . . . Futurus,* a Latin inscription meaning, "Here lies King Arthur, king that was and is to be."

To increase understanding

1. (*a*) What is a *romance?* (*b*) Drawing for examples on the selection from the *Morte Darthur,* explain why the romance was popular with the knightly classes.

2. In this selection we learn about Arthur principally from the reactions of others toward him. (*a*) What can you deduce from the behavior of the three queens? (*b*) What do you learn about Arthur from the actions of Sir Bedivere?

3. (*a*) Compare Sir Bedivere with Chaucer's Knight. (*b*) Which comes closer to the medieval concept of the ideal knight? In what respects?

4. The English have long had a legend that in time of great peril Arthur will return to save England. Explain how this belief probably originated.

5. What is the tone of this selection from the *Morte Darthur?*

6. (*a*) What is the probable historical foundation of the Arthurian romance? (*b*) Why do you think this romance is still popular today?

7. (*a*) What was Malory's purpose in writing the *Morte Darthur?* (*b*) By writing it what service did he perform for English literature? (*c*) How did he aid historians?

Extending interests

1. In the centuries since Malory wrote his *Morte Darthur* many versions in prose and in poetry have been published. *The Boy's King Arthur; Sir Thomas Malory's History of King Arthur and His Knights of the Round Table,* edited for boys by Sidney Lanier, follows the *Morte Darthur* more closely than any other edition does. *The Story of King Arthur and His Knights,* by Howard Pyle, is a vigorous prose retelling that follows Malory in tone. *The Once and Future King,* by T. H. White, treats the story with twentieth-century humor and realism. The most famous retelling in poetry is Tennyson's *Idylls of the King.* One student might read each of these books, or several students might divide a book among them. A panel discussion on the varying treatments of the Arthurian legend might subsequently be held.

2. The hero of French romance is Roland, whose story, like Arthur's, is based on history. You may find the origins and an outline of the legend in an encyclopedia. Two easily understood versions of the romance are *The Story of Roland,* by James Baldwin, and *The Song of Roland,* translated from the *Chanson de Roland* by Merriam Sherwood.

The Larger View

One of the great values of reading the literature of the past is the light it throws upon the people, the history, and the culture of other ages.

A. Draw upon the knowledge you have gained from studying the text selections (ballads, the "Prologue" to The Canterbury Tales and "The Pardoner's Tale," and the selection from the Morte Darthur), as well as upon additional literature of the Middle Ages you have read, to talk over the following subjects:
    (a) Classes of society in feudal times
    (b) Warfare
    (c) The ideals of chivalry
    (d) The dominant position of the Church
    (e) Customs and superstitions

B. Studying the selections in the first and second chapters should have made you aware of some of the great differences between Anglo-Saxon and Medieval England. Prepare to discuss the following areas of difference:
    (a) Occupations and classes of society, as shown in Chaucer's "Prologue" and Aelfric's "Colloquy on the Occupations"
    (b) The ideal of the hero, as represented by Chaucer's Knight, King Arthur, and Beowulf
    (c) Social customs, as represented in Chaucer's Canterbury Tales, Malory's Morte Darthur, and Beowulf
    (d) Types of literature produced in each age

Bibliography

BOLTON, IVY MAY, Son of the Land. (Messner) This fast-moving and dramatic account of the stirring days of the Peasant's Revolt in fourteenth-century England centers on a young serf and his struggle for freedom.

CHAUCER, GEOFFREY, The Canterbury Tales, edited by Daniel Cook. (•Anchor) Professor Cook presents the first great English classic in its original Middle English, and on facing pages explains the meanings of words and phrases which are now obsolete.

CHAUCER, GEOFFREY, The Portable Chaucer, selected, translated, and edited by Theodore Morrison. (••Viking) In this collection by Theodore Morrison, author of the selections from Chaucer in England in Literature, you will find the "Prologue" to The Canterbury Tales; twelve of the best tales; summaries of the other tales; all the linking material; and in addition a brilliant translation of Troilus and Cressida.

CHUTE, MARCHETTE, Geoffrey Chaucer of England. (•Everyman's) The author presents a fascinating account of Chaucer as a many-sided, likable personality, and an excellent background for understanding his works.

COSTAIN, THOMAS, The Conquerors. (Doubleday) Mr. Costain's greatest talent is the ability to make history read like an exciting novel. This study of English history from the days of the Norman conquest through the rule of King John is absorbing reading.

MAC LEOD, MARY, King Arthur and His Noble Knights. (Lippincott) The King Arthur tales of Sir Thomas Malory are retold in a simple and enjoyable style.

MUNTZ, HOPE, The Golden Warrior. (Scribner) This stirring novel based on the life of Harold II, the last of the Saxon kings, ends with the memorable battle of Hastings in 1066.

QUENNELL, MARJORIE, and CHARLES H. B., The History of Everyday Things in England. (Putnam) The social life and customs of England are examined in this authoritative four-volume series. Refer to volume I (1066-1499) for information on the Medieval Period.

RICKERT, EDITH (compiler), Chaucer's World. (••Columbia) Combining the use of old records and diaries with pictures from contemporary sources, Edith Rickert presents a fascinating and realistic picture of life in the London of the fourteenth century. The book is both entertaining and enlightening.

SANDOZ, EDOUARD, Twice Besieged. (Walck) Using factual material from French and English sources, Sandoz tells a forceful and intriguing story of eleventh-century crusaders.

SETON, ANYA, Katherine. (Houghton •Pocket Books) The Katherine in this engrossing story was Chaucer's sister-in-law and (with John of Gaunt) the founder of the royal line which included Henry VII, Henry VIII, and Elizabeth I.

TEY, JOSEPHINE, The Daughter of Time. (•Berkley) Did Richard III really murder his nephews? That's the question that intrigues Allan Grant, a twentieth-century detective. This psychological mystery has been called one of the best ever written.

•paperback only   ••paperback and hardcover

chapter three THE

ELIZABETHAN

Action between the British Royal Ark (right) and the flagship of the Spanish Armada off the Isle of Wight as shown in a painting by Vroom. Because the British here abandoned the custom of grappling and boarding for the practice of standing off and firing, they revolutionized naval warfare, and became the masters of the sea.

Behold the threaden sails,
Borne with the invisible and creeping wind,
Draw the huge bottoms through the furrow'd sea,
Breasting the lofty surge.
(Shakespeare, *Henry V*, III, *Prologue*)

AGE
1485-1625

The Elizabethan Age might very well be called the Age of the Sea. Not only did the swashbuckling English sea-dogs come to rule the waves of both the Old World and the recently discovered New World, but England as a whole was embarked upon a great voyage in Time. Behind lay the Middle Ages. Ahead lay the modern world we know today. And the time in between, the sixteenth century, was a surging tumult of old and new. The medieval baron, the knight, the serf, and the Catholic prelate were no longer the dominant types in English society. Steadily becoming more important were the agent of the national government, the wealthy urban merchant, the Protestant reformer, and the worldly scholar. This mingling of the old with the new also characterized the Elizabethan outlook on life. Englishmen in the sixteenth century were as devoutly religious as their medieval ancestors, but they also threw themselves passionately into

Below: Portrait of Henry VIII by court painter Hans Holbein, a great master of realism.
Right: The emphasis of painter Marc Gheeraerts is, in contrast, decorative and symbolic.
This is his celebrated "Armada" portrait of Queen Elizabeth.

the worldliest of projects and pastimes. They were still superstitious enough to believe in witches but rejected as total nonsense such questions as how many angels could fit on the head of a pin. They were great respecters of authority yet violently critical of their medieval ancestors for accepting it. And while they were conscious of being born into certain stations in life, they proclaimed the right of men of natural talent to rise to the top of the social ladder.

This upheaval that was taking place in every phase of English life lasted for a period of about a century and a half, starting with the reign of the first Tudor king, Henry VII (1485-1509), continuing through the reigns of Henry VIII (1509-1547) and his three children, Edward VI (1547-1553), Mary (1553-1558), and Elizabeth I (1558-1603), and terminating with the reign of the first Stuart king, James I (1603-1625).

The entire period bears the name of Queen Elizabeth for several reasons. Not only did she rule longer than any of the other Tudors, but the tremendous political, religious, economic, and intellectual changes that had been in the making under her father and grandfather finally came to a climax during her reign and burst forth in what has been called the finest flowering of the arts in all English history. Elizabeth was also the greatest of the Tudor monarchs. When she came to the throne, England was perilously close to capsizing under the pressure of dangers from within and from without, but Elizabeth met these dangers with the kind of high statesmanship that alone brings countries safely through stormy times.

Above all, the entire age takes its name from Elizabeth because she was the living embodiment of its spirit. Both the Queen and the age were madly in love with life in all its aspects. The breathtaking activity of the court with its swarms of royal agents, foreign ambassadors, churchmen, scholars, poets, actors, musicians, cooks, porters, and chambermaids was faithfully reproduced in the city of London as a whole. Here carts and coaches, laughing and quarreling throngs of men, women, and children jostled up and down the streets to such an extent that posts had to be set up to keep houses from falling down. Elizabeth's tastes as well as those of her subjects ran the gamut from public hangings, witch burnings, bearbaitings, and bawdy jokes on up into the rarer atmosphere of exquisite jewels, silks, and brocades, stately dances, and elevated discussions of Christian theology, Greek philosophy, and Italian poetry. Just as

Elizabeth could slap and spit at her associates one moment and discuss the elegancies of Italian poetry the next, so her subjects could stop in at the Paris Garden, where mastiffs tore at Harry Hunks, the bear, and then pass on to the Globe Theater next door, where Romeo's moon-magic words dropped gently into Juliet's ears.

If the Elizabethans loved one thing more than anything else it was England. ". . . I know I have the body of a weak feeble woman, but I have the heart and stomach of a King—and a King of England, too, and think foul scorn that Parma[1] or Spain or any Prince of Europe should dare to invade the borders of my realm." These were Elizabeth's words to her troops on the eve of meeting the Spanish Armada. They reveal the same intense patriotism as John of Gaunt's famous speech in Shakespeare's *Richard II*:

> This happy breed of men, this little world,
> This precious stone set in the silver sea,
> Which serves it in the office of a wall
> Or as a moat defensive to a house,
> Against the envy of less happier lands,
> This blessed plot, this earth, this realm, this England.

THE NEW NATIONAL MONARCHY It is often hard for the twentieth century to understand just why the Elizabethans were so exuberant. In politics, for example, we take for granted the existence of a national government with sufficient power to impose law and order. But for the Elizabethans this was something *new*. The Middle Ages had been a time of wars between feudal barons. Although feudal families decreased in numbers and in power during the later Middle Ages, it was not until the reigns of the Tudor monarchs that Englishmen knew what it was like to live for long periods of time in peace and harmony. Under the intelligent, strong-arm rule of the Tudors, England was kept from civil strife for over a hundred years.

The greatest threat to the new national monarchy came from Philip II of Spain, who did not look too kindly on the plundering of Spanish treasure galleons by English ships and who as the head of a Catholic country greatly resented the rise of English Protestantism. When "the Master Thief of the unknown world," Sir Francis Drake, singed Philip's very beard by sailing into and sacking the harbor of Cádiz, Philip decided it was time to teach the English a lesson, and in July of 1588 he sent his Invincible

An engraving of courtiers dancing by Theodore de Brie, sixteenth-century book illustrator.

---

1. Parma. The Duke of Parma was one of the ablest generals in the employ of Philip II of Spain. Philip had ordered him to collect a huge flotilla of transports and to keep his army ready for Spain's contemplated invasion of England.

í aulica fuada,   *Et lepor, & vita generofa modeftia glifcit*   *Quid mirúm, divas vltrò fi diâ fequant*

Armada sailing up into the English Channel. Much to his consternation the renowned Spanish fleet was savagely raked by the new long-range guns of Drake and Hawkins and then completely routed by the autumn gales off the coasts of Scotland and Ireland. The threat of the great armada had ended, and Englishmen were beside themselves with joy. Not only did Britannia bask in the bright air and sunshine of domestic peace; she also rode in safest majesty on the waters of the world.

A source of strength, however, can also be a source of weakness. In their overwhelming desire for political unification and international supremacy, the Tudors sent a steady stream of "dissenters" to the gallows, the stake, and the chopping block. Among them was Mary Queen of Scots, who as a Catholic and as heir to the throne after Elizabeth was an invitation to rebellion from within and aggression from without on the part of persons interested in toppling England's Protestant monarchy. Persuaded by her advisers that her cousin's death was a political necessity, Elizabeth set in motion a chain of events whose tragic conclusion took place at Fotheringhay castle:

Mary had arrayed herself superbly for the final scene. As she disrobed for the headsman's act, her garments of black satin, removed by the weeping handmaids, revealed a bodice and petticoat of crimson velvet. One of her ladies handed her a pair of crimson sleeves, which she put on. Thus the unhappy Queen halted, for one last moment, standing blood-red from head to foot against the black scaffold. There was a deathly hush throughout the hall. She knelt, and at the second stroke the final blow was delivered. The awed assembly had fulfilled its task. In death the majestic illusion was shattered. The head of an aging woman with false hair was held up by the executioner. A lap dog crept out from beneath the clothes of the bleeding trunk.[2]

2. Churchill, Winston S., *A History of the English-Speaking Peoples*, Vol. II, p. 119. Copyright 1956 by Dodd, Mead & Company, Inc., New York.

RADIO TIMES HULTON PICTURE LIBRARY

Above top: The Lennox jewel, made for the Countess of Lennox, whose husband was Regent of Scotland and whose son married Mary Stuart. Above bottom: Elizabeth attending a wedding in June 1600, engraved after a painting by Gheeraerts.
Right: "The Feathers," an inn at Ludlow dating from 1521.

THE NEW THEOLOGIES Religion was obviously one of the issues that threatened to put an end to domestic peace. In the Middle Ages all Europeans, including Englishmen, had looked to the Catholic Church in Rome as the supreme authority in matters of religion. There had been individuals prior to the Elizabethan Age who had preached that the Scriptures and not the Church were supreme, but it was not until 1517 when Martin Luther nailed his ninety-five theses on the church door at Wittenberg in Germany that this idea burst into flame and spread across Europe. The Protestant Reformation entered England within a decade of Luther's historic act—via the lusty personality of Henry VIII. When the Pope refused to give Henry permission to divorce his first wife, Catherine, of the ruling house of Spain, in order to marry Anne Boleyn, Henry put through Parliament a number of bills that severed relations with the Catholic Church and set him up as the head of the Anglican Church of England. Years of disturbance in religion followed as reign succeeded reign. Henry's son by a third marriage, Edward VI, was a sickly boy of nine when he came to the throne, and his advisers were able to tip the balance that his father had maintained between Catholic and Anglican theology and worship in favor of the Anglican Church. Mary, as the daughter of Catherine of Aragon, tipped things back again to Catholicism. Queen Elizabeth, daughter of Anne Boleyn, reëstablished the Anglican Church once and for all on a base broad enough to attract both "high" Anglicans, who were close in spirit to Catholicism, and "low" Anglicans, who were closer to the more radical Protestant sects loosely grouped under the heading of "Puritan." The childless Elizabeth was ironically succeeded by James I, son of Mary Queen of Scots. Although James I's high-church Anglicanism was one of the factors that led to the great civil war of the next century, it was under his direction that the greatest of the English Bible translations was conducted and completed.

Left: Queen Elizabeth is thought to have inherited this, the Boleyn Cup, from her mother. Below: A very rare map showing the route of Drake's raid on the Spanish possessions in America, 1585.

THE NEW PROSPERITY   During the Tudor period Bartolomeu Dias made the first voyage around Africa, Vasco da Gama anchored in the harbor of Calicut, Christopher Columbus reached the Bahamas, and Sir Francis Drake sailed around the world. During James I's reign the first permanent English settlement in the New World was established at Jamestown, Virginia. As a result of the great explorations of the sixteenth century, England emerged from the position of a small, rather bleak, and primarily agricultural island to one of a resplendent, commercial nation leading all others in the race for empire. The waters about London were afloat with strange vessels laden with the riches of distant countries. The English middle class, which had begun to rise in the time of Chaucer and which was composed primarily of urban merchants, now became so wealthy that its members began to replace the feudal aristocracy in positions of political power.

THE RENAISSANCE   National strength and pride, a variety of religious beliefs, and an abundance of wealth—all of this was new and tremendously stimulating to the Elizabethans. So too was the proposition that man is the measure, if not of all things, at least of most. This idea came into England as a part of the movement historians call the Renaissance, or the "rebirth" of ancient Greek and Roman culture.

A middle-class marriage celebration is shown in this painting by Hoefnagle. Across the Thames in the distance is the Tower of London.

When the Roman Empire disintegrated and Europe was overrun by barbaric tribes, many Greek and Latin manuscripts were either lost or forgotten. Unearthed from their hiding places in the fourteenth and fifteenth centuries and reproduced by the newly invented printing press,

these manuscripts set off a wave of admiration for classical ideas which swept through Italy first, then France, and finally England.

The basic message that the ancient Greeks and Romans imparted to the Elizabethans was that life was not, as the Middle Ages had thought, a "journey through a vale of tears" to a better world after death, but rather a beautiful and exciting end-in-itself. The Renaissance Englishman, like his contemporaries on the Continent, was overwhelmed by the sheer wonder of himself: "What a piece of work is a man! how noble in reason! how infinite in faculty! in form and moving how express and admirable! in action how like an angel! in apprehension how like a god!"[3] He was also overcome by the beauty of the things around him—a feeling which he often found expressed in such Italian Renaissance writings as Castiglione's *The Courtier:* "It (the world) is praised in saying the beautiful heaven, beautiful earth, beautiful sea, beautiful rivers, beautiful woods, trees, gardens, beautiful cities, beautiful churches, houses, armies." The message of the Renaissance confirmed what the Tudor accomplishments had suggested, that the world was not only the place where man was disciplined for eternity; it was also the stage on which he could display his amazing creative faculties.

Appropriately enough, the men who adopted this man-centered point of view were called *humanists.* Strictly speaking, the humanists were the university experts in Greek and Latin such as Sir Thomas More and Roger Ascham. But humanism in its broadest sense meant what the twentieth century means by the humanities, or liberal arts: a concern for *all* subjects of human interest. The humanist could read not only Greek and Latin, but Italian, French, and Spanish as well. He felt just as at home accompanying his own songs on the lute as he did participating in a wide variety of physical sports. He was not only up to date on the developments in speculative philosophy or theology; he was also aware of what was going on in natural philosophy or science.

The Elizabethan zest for living could not last forever. During the final years of Elizabeth's reign and throughout the reign of James I men began to question whether the world was really as wonderful as they had thought. Civil war was threatening again. The new theories of astronomy of Copernicus and Galileo were convincing more and more people that the sun, not the earth, was at the center of the universe. Having tasted deeply of the pleasures of the world, some men turned with disgust and revulsion against them. As you will see from some of the selections in the chapter, especially *Hamlet,* the later Elizabethans became disenchanted with life to the same extent that the early Elizabethans had been enchanted by it.

Below left: James I. Below right: Hampton Court, favorite royal residence from the time of Henry VIII. View is of Anne Boleyn's gateway from the Green Court.

3. William Shakespeare, *Hamlet,* II, ii.

ELIZABETHAN SONGS

Stimulated by the excitement of the Renaissance, the Elizabethan world came alive with the sound of music. For the Elizabethan gentleman skill in music was as indispensable as skill in sports and in reading Latin. Ordinary men and women were ashamed if they could not take part in the singing of a madrigal. As one writer of the time put it, even a journeyman shoemaker had to be able "to sound the trumpet, or play upon the flute, and bear his part in a three-man's song, and readily reckon his tools in rhyme."

There is no better way to understand the violent contrasts of the Renaissance than to turn from the coarse and often brutal masculinity of Elizabethan life to the delicate and often exquisite femininity of Elizabethan songs. The city that quartered its criminals alive could also print untold numbers of song books with such titles as *The Paradise of Dainty Devices* and *A Gorgeous Gallery of Gallant Inventions*. The dramatist Ben Jonson could slay an actor in a duel and also whisper to some lady, "Drink to me only with thine eyes." As you will see from the following selections, some Elizabethan songs are beautifully, almost limpidly clear, especially those interspersed throughout the plays of the time. More often than not, however, the Elizabethans turned out songs that were as fantastic and elaborate as the frills and furbelows of courtly dress.

CHERRY-RIPE *Thomas Campion*

There is a garden in her face
  Where roses and white lilies grow;
A heavenly paradise is that place,
  Wherein all pleasant fruits do flow.
There cherries grow that none may buy,   5
Till "Cherry-ripe" themselves do cry.

Those cherries fairly do enclose
  Of orient pearl a double row,
Which when her lovely laughter shows,
  They look like rosebuds filled with snow. 10
Yet them no peer nor prince may buy,
Till "Cherry-ripe" themselves do cry.

Her eyes like angels watch them still;
  Her brows like bended bows do stand,
Threat'ning with piercing frowns to kill   15
  All that attempt with eye or hand
Those sacred cherries to come nigh,
Till "Cherry-ripe" themselves do cry!

APELLES' SONG *John Lyly*

Cupid and my Campaspe[1] played
  At cards for kisses; Cupid paid.
  He stakes his quiver, bows and
    arrows,
His mother's doves and team of sparrows[2];
Loses them too; then down he throws   5
The coral of his lip, the rose
Growing on's cheek (but none knows how);
With these, the crystal of his brow,
And then the dimple of his chin;
All these did my Campaspe win.   10
At last he set her both his eyes;
She won, and Cupid blind did rise.
O Love, has she done this to thee?
What shall, alas! become of me?

APELLES' SONG **1.** *Campaspe* (kam pas′pē), a beautiful woman of ancient Greece who was loved by the Greek painter Apelles (ə pel′ez). **2.** *His mother's . . . sparrows.* In classical mythology Cupid's mother was Aphrodite (af rə di′ti), or Venus, goddess of love and beauty. Doves and sparrows were considered sacred to her.

THE TRIUMPH OF CHARIS *Ben Jonson*

See the chariot at hand here of Love,
    Wherein my lady rideth!
Each that draws is a swan or a dove,
    And well the car Love guideth.
As she goes, all hearts do duty   5
        Unto her beauty;
And enamor'd, do wish, so they might
        But enjoy such a sight,
That they still were to run by her side,
Through swords, through seas, whither she
        would ride.   10

Do but look on her eyes, they do light
    All that Love's world compriseth!
Do but look on her hair, it is bright
    As Love's star when it riseth!
Do but mark, her forehead smoother   15
        Than words that soothe her;
And from her arched brows, such a grace
        Sheds itself through the face
As alone there triumphs to the life
All the gain, all the good, of the elements'
        strife.   20

Have you seen but a bright lily grow,
    Before rude hands have touched it?
Have you marked but the fall of the snow
    Before the soil hath smutched it?
Have you felt the wool of the beaver?   25
        Or swan's down ever?
Or have smelt o' the bud of the briar?[1]
        Or the nard[2] in the fire?
Or have tested the bag of the bee?
O so white! O so soft! O so sweet is she!   30

SONG TO CELIA *Ben Jonson*

Drink to me only with thine eyes,
    And I will pledge with mine;
Or leave a kiss but in the cup,
    And I'll not look for wine.
The thirst that from the soul doth rise   5
    Doth ask a drink divine;
But might I of Jove's nectar sup,
    I would not change for thine.

I sent thee late a rosy wreath,
    Not so much honoring thee   10
As giving it a hope, that there
    It could not withered be.
But thou thereon didst only breathe,
    And sent'st it back to me;
Since when it grows, and smells, I swear, 15
    Not of itself, but thee.

SONGS *by William Shakespeare*

UNDER THE GREENWOOD TREE
from AS YOU LIKE IT

Under the greenwood tree
    Who loves to lie with me,
And turn his merry note
Unto the sweet bird's throat,
Come hither, come hither, come hither!   5
    Here shall he see
    No enemy
But winter and rough weather.

Who doth ambition shun,
    And loves to live i' the sun,   10
Seeking the foods he eats,
    And pleased with what he gets,
Come hither, come hither, come hither!
    Here shall he see
    No enemy   15
But winter and rough weather.

WHO IS SILVIA?
from THE TWO GENTLEMEN OF VERONA

Who is Silvia? What is she
    That all our swains commend her?
Holy, fair, and wise is she;
    The heaven such grace did lend her
That she might admirèd be.   5

Is she kind as she is fair?
    For beauty lives with kindness.
Love doth to her eyes repair,
    To help him of his blindness.
And, being helped, inhabits there.   10

THE TRIUMPH OF CHARIS **1.** *bud of the briar*, the wild
rose. **2.** *nard*, an aromatic substance.

Then to Silvia let us sing
  That Silvia is excelling;
She excels each mortal thing
  Upon the dull earth dwelling.
To her let us garlands bring.   15

SIGH NO MORE
from MUCH ADO ABOUT NOTHING

Sigh no more, ladies, sigh no more,
  Men were deceivers ever;
One foot in sea, and one on shore,
  To one thing constant never.
    Then sigh not so,   5
    But let them go,
  And be you blithe and bonny,
Converting all your sounds of woe
  Into Hey nonny, nonny.

Sing no more ditties, sing no moe   10
  Of dumps so dull and heavy;
The fraud of men was ever so,
  Since summer first was leavy.
    Then sigh not so,
    But let them go,   15
  And be you blithe and bonny,
Converting all your sounds of woe
  Into Hey nonny, nonny.

THERE IS A LADY SWEET AND KIND
Anonymous

There is a lady sweet and kind,
Was never face so pleased my mind;
I did but see her passing by,
And yet I love her till I die.

Her gesture, motion, and her smiles,   5
Her wit, her voice, my heart beguiles,
Beguiles my heart, I know not why,
And yet I love her till I die. . . .

Cupid is wingèd and doth range,
Her country so my love doth change: 10
But change she earth, or change she sky,
Yet will I love her till I die.

LULLABY   *Thomas Dekker*

Golden slumbers kiss your eyes,
Smiles awake you when you rise;
Sleep, pretty wantons, do not cry,
And I will sing a lullaby:
Rock them, rock them, lullaby.   5

Care is heavy, therefore sleep you;
You are care, and care must keep you;
Sleep, pretty wantons, do not cry,
And I will sing a lullaby:
Rock them, rock them, lullaby.   10

Christopher Marlowe 1564-1593 and
Sir Walter Raleigh 1552?-1618

Christopher Marlowe and Walter Raleigh were perhaps the most adventurous and hot-tempered of all the Elizabethans. Marlowe's secret-service work brought about his early death in a tavern brawl. Raleigh died under the executioner's ax after a lifetime of fighting on the Continent, the high seas, and in the dangerous world of court intrigue. But like true men of the Renaissance, Marlowe and Raleigh managed to combine daring adventures with scholarly and literary pursuits. Marlowe achieved fame as a dramatist and as the author of "The Passionate Shepherd to His Love," one of the most melodic love songs of all time. Raleigh wrote an incomplete yet impressive history of the world as well as lyric poems characterized by refreshing notes of realism. His "Nymph's Reply to the Shepherd" is the best of the many sequels to Marlowe's popular poem.

THE PASSIONATE SHEPHERD TO HIS LOVE

Christopher Marlowe

Come live with me and be my Love,
And we will all the pleasures prove
That hills and valleys, dales and
    fields,
Or woods or steepy mountain yields.

And we will sit upon the rocks,   5
And see the shepherds feed their flocks
By shallow rivers, to whose falls
Melodious birds sing madrigals.

And I will make thee beds of roses
And a thousand fragrant posies;   10
A cap of flowers, and a kirtle
Embroidered all with leaves of myrtle;

A gown made of the finest wool
Which from our pretty lambs we pull;
Fair-linèd slippers for the cold,   15
With buckles of the purest gold;

A belt of straw and ivy buds
With coral clasps and amber studs—
And if these pleasures may thee move,
Come live with me and be my Love.   20

The shepherd swains shall dance and sing
For thy delight each May morning—
If these delights thy mind may move,
Then live with me and be my Love.

THE NYMPH'S REPLY TO THE SHEPHERD

Sir Walter Raleigh

If all the world and love were young,
And truth in every shepherd's tongue,
These pretty pleasures might me move,
To live with thee and be thy love.

Time drives the flocks from field to fold,   5
When rivers rage, and rocks grow cold;
And Philomel[1] becometh dumb;
The rest complain of cares to come.

The flowers do fade, and wanton fields
To wayward winter reckoning yields;   10
A honey tongue, a heart of gall,
Is fancy's spring, but sorrow's fall.

Thy gowns, thy shoes, thy bed of roses,
Thy cap, thy kirtle, and thy posies,
Soon break, soon wither, soon forgotten; 15
In folly ripe, in reason rotten.

Thy belt of straw and ivy buds,
Thy coral clasps and amber studs,
All these in me no means can move,
To come to thee and be thy love.   20

But could youth last, and love still breed,
Had joys no date, nor age no need,
Then these delights my mind might move
To live with thee and be thy love.

THE NYMPH'S REPLY TO THE SHEPHERD **1.** *Philomel* (fil'ə mel), the nightingale. In Greek mythology Philomela (fil'ə mē′lə) was the daughter of a king of Athens. When pursued by her sister's husband, she was transformed into a nightingale.

To increase understanding

(a) Which of the songs that you have read are clear and simple? (b) Which are highly decorative and elaborate? (c) What evidence of the Renaissance do you find in them?

2. Elizabethan writers made frequent use of what is called a *conceit*—a fanciful and often far-fetched image such as the card game in Lyly's "Apelles' Song." (a) What is the conceit in Campion's "Cherry-Ripe"? (b) How is Campion's description of his lady similar to Lyly's? (c) Do these ladies seem real to you? (d) What is the difference in tone between these two songs and Ben Jonson's "Song to Celia"?

3. (a) What is the main point of Jonson's "The Triumph of Charis"? (b) In which of the three stanzas of the poem are the images most concrete? (c) What do these images have in common besides their concreteness?

4. (a) What kind of life is described by Marlowe's shepherd? (b) Why specifically does Raleigh's nymph consider this kind of life unrealistic? (c) Where in her reply does she denounce the shepherd's outlook with particular vehemence? (d) What attitude does she express in the last stanza of the poem?

Pastoral poetry speaks of the light loves and labors of shepherds in idyllic country settings. It was first developed by the Greek poet Theocritus (c. 270 B.C.) and later by the Roman poet Vergil (70-19 B.C.). Why do you think pastoral poems like Marlowe's "The Passionate Shepherd to His Love" were so much in vogue during the Renaissance? Which of the songs of Shakespeare that you read is a pastoral poem? Judging from these poems, what are some of the conventional images of pastoral poetry?

Elizabethan lyrics have been set to music many times over. The nineteenth-century Austrian composer Franz Schubert was particularly interested in writing new music for the songs from Shakespeare's plays. Especially popular during Elizabethan times was the madrigal which, like the sonnet, had originated in Italy. The harmonies of the madrigal were generally complex and were sung without instrumental accompaniment. In order to hear Elizabethan lyrics as they were heard by the Elizabethans, try to obtain recordings of musical settings by the London Madrigal Group, the Robert Shaw Chorale, or the Pro Musica Antiqua of New York.

The Elizabethan Manor House

The sixteenth century was the great age of patronage when writers and artists of all kinds looked to members of the nobility for financial support and friendly encouragement. Freed from the burdens of civil war, in many cases accomplished scholars and artists in their own right, the noblemen of the sixteenth century were as eager to surround themselves with writers as the writers were to secure patrons. Their country homes or manor houses soon became well-known centers of cultural activity. Plays, readings, and pageants were put on in the great halls to entertain the Queen when she progressed with full retinue throughout her kingdom. It is said that Shakespeare acted in *As You Like It* at Wilton House,

home of Sir Philip Sidney's sister, the Countess of Pembroke. Writers like Edmund Spenser and Ben Jonson had easy access to several of England's stately manors.

Elizabethan manor houses differed as much from the castles of the Middle Ages as the Elizabethan noblemen-scholars did from the medieval barons. Ponds and brilliant gardens replaced the moats that had been necessary to defend the medieval castle. The slits in the castle walls gave way to windows that brought light and air to the rooms within. Windows steadily increased in size until the remark was made of a late sixteenth-century manor, "Hardwick Hall, more glass than wall."

Inside his home the Elizabethan nobleman

Hardwick Hall, one of the noblest Elizabethan mansions, was built between 1590 and 1597.

enjoyed a comfort and an elegance that would have amazed his medieval ancestors. Rooms were paneled with highly polished wood and hung with rich tapestries and portraits in oils. Ceilings, beams, staircases, balconies, and furnishings of all sorts displayed the work of expert plasterers and woodcarvers. The fireplace in the great hall, which in medieval times had stood in the middle of the room, sending its smoke up to "cure" the timbers of the ceiling (see page 48), now took its place in the wall and was surrounded by elaborate carvings in wood and stone that often reached from the floor to the ceiling. Like the literature of the age, the Elizabethan manor house reflected the Englishman's increasing delight in himself and in the good things of the world about him.

Above: Oxborough Castle, built in the fifteenth century. Below right: Sulgrave Manor, home of the Washington family from 1539 to 1626. Note Gilbert Stuart portrait of George Washington. Right, the Marble Hall, and, below left, the Armory of Hatfield House, erected 1610-1611.

Sir Philip Sidney 1554-1586

The sixteenth century was the age of the song writer and the sonneteer. The sonnet, which had originated in Italy in the twelfth century and which became famous in the hands of the Italian Renaissance poet Petrarch (1304-1374), was introduced into England in the early sixteenth century by Sir Thomas Wyatt and Henry Howard, Earl of Surrey. It was not until the publication of Sir Philip Sidney's *Astrophel and Stella* in 1591, however, that the great flood of Elizabethan sonnet sequences began.

Sidney came as close as anyone could to the Renaissance ideal of the complete man. As scholar, critic, and poet, courtier, diplomat, and soldier, he was a man of thought and a man of action, as expert in the gentler pursuits of life as he was in the more hardy ones. As could have been expected, Sidney ended his life with a flourish of bravery and courtesy: he was fatally wounded during a battle in Holland but instead of taking the water offered him, he passed it to another wounded man with the words, "Thy necessity is greater than mine."

Sidney's *Astrophel and Stella* is a sequence of 108 sonnets which took its inspiration from Petrarch and which inspired other Elizabethan poets, including Shakespeare, to write similar sequences. Within the general framework of *Astrophel and Stella*, which records the poet's hopeless love for a beautiful lady, Sidney gave expression to his various states of feeling, as in the following well-known sonnets.

Portrait of Sidney by an unknown artist.

SONNET 31

With how sad steps, O Moon, thou climb'st the skies!
How silently, and with how wan a face!
What, may it be that even in heavenly place
That busy archer his sharp arrows tries?
Sure, if that long-with-love-acquainted eyes   5
Can judge of love, thou feel'st a lover's case.
I read it in thy looks; thy languished grace,
To me that feel the like, thy state descries.
Then, even of fellowship, O Moon, tell me,
Is constant love deemed there but want of wit?   10
Are beauties there as proud as here they be?
Do they above love to be loved, and yet
Those lovers scorn whom that love doth possess?
Do they call virtue there ungratefulness?

SONNET 41 Having this day my horse, my hand, my lance
Guided so well that I obtained the prize,
Both by the judgment of the English eyes
And of some sent from that sweet enemy France,
Horsemen my skill in horsemanship advance,   5
Town folks my strength; a daintier judge applies
His praise to sleight which from good use doth rise;
Some lucky wits impute it but to chance;
Others, because of both sides I do take
My blood from them who did excel in this,   10
Think Nature me a man-at-arms did make.
How far they shot awry! the true cause is,
Stella looked on, and from her heavenly face
Sent forth the beams which made so fair my race.

Oldest known portrait of Spenser.

Edmund Spenser 1552-1599

Unlike Sidney, Spenser was not "born to the purple" but came from a middle-class family of clothmakers whose good fortune enabled their son to graduate from Cambridge into the household of the Earl of Leicester, Elizabeth's favorite courtier and Philip Sidney's uncle. After four years in the rarefied atmosphere of courtly circles, Spenser took a government post in Ireland, where he remained until shortly before his death.

It was in Ireland that Spenser wrote his masterpiece *The Faerie Queene*, dedicated and duly presented to "the mightie and magnificent Empresse Elizabeth." One of the few works in the history of English literature that manage to bring together all the major trends of a particular time, *The Faerie Queene* gave poetic form to the classical, medieval, and Renaissance ideas that made up the Elizabethan Age.

Because it is the longest poem in the English language and because its beauty is remote and dreamlike in quality, *The Faerie Queene* has not attracted as many readers as Spenser's sonnet sequence *Amoretti*. The sonnets, which were addressed to the woman Spenser eventually married, convey a greater sense of immediate, personal feeling than *The Faerie Queene* without losing the smoothness and loftiness of tone that is regarded as the distinguishing mark of Spenser's work.

SONNET 34

Like as a ship, that through the ocean wide
By conduct of some star doth make her way
Whenas a storm hath dimmed her trusty
   guide,
Out of her course doth wander far astray;
So I, whose star, that wont with her bright
   ray   **5**
Me to direct, with clouds is overcast,
Do wander now in darkness and dismay,
Through hidden perils round about me
   placed.
Yet hope I well, that when this storm is past,
My Helicé, the lodestar of my life,   **10**
Will shine again, and look on me at last,
With lovely light to clear my cloudy grief;
   Till then I wander careful, comfortless,
   In secret sorrow and sad pensiveness.

SONNET 75

One day I wrote her name upon the strand,
But came the waves and washéd it away:
Again I wrote it with a second hand,
But came the tide and made my pains his
   prey.
Vain man, said she, that dost in vain assay **5**
A mortal thing so to immortalize,
For I myself shall like to this decay,
And eke my name be wipèd out likewise.
Not so, (quoth I) let baser things devise
To die in dust, but you shall live by fame; **10**
My verse your virtues rare shall eternize,
And in the heavens write your glorious name.
Where, whenas death shall all the world
   subdue,
Our love shall live, and later life renew.

To increase understanding

1. (*a*) What is Sidney's mood in the first two lines of Sonnet 31? (*b*) What is his mood throughout the rest of the sonnet? (*c*) How does the mood of this sonnet differ from the mood expressed in Sonnet 41?

2. (*a*) Upon what figure of speech does Spenser build his Sonnet 34? (*b*) Explain the figure in detail.

3. (*a*) Explain the comparison in lines 7-8 of Spenser's Sonnet 75. (*b*) How does this comparison lead the poet to his main point?

4. Which of the two poets—Sidney or Spenser—uses more concrete and conversational diction? Which poet is more abstract and detached? Give as many reasons as you can for your answer.

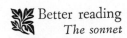

Better reading
The sonnet

Because its pattern has been fixed by tradition, the sonnet is one of the most challenging of poetic forms. You have just read sonnets by Sidney and Spenser and you are about to turn to the finest sonneteer of them all, William Shakespeare. Each of these men used a slightly different sonnet pattern. Sidney's came closest to the original pattern developed by the Italian Renaissance poet Petrarch. Spenser, who was a gifted narrative poet, worked out his own more fluid pattern. And Shakespeare used the pattern developed and adopted by the majority of Elizabethan poets.

All sonnets have two things in common. They are made up of fourteen lines, and each line is written in *iambic pentameter*—ten syllables with the stress on every second syllable.

The Italian or Petrarchan sonnet is divided into two parts, the *octave* or first eight lines, and the *sestet* or last six lines. The rhyme scheme of the Italian sonnet is usually *abbaabba/cdecde*. With this pattern the theme of the sonnet is naturally presented in two parts whose ideas either oppose or complement each other.

The Shakespearean or English sonnet is divided into three four-line parts or quatrains and a concluding couplet. The rhyme scheme of the English sonnet is *abab/cdcd/efef/gg*. Each quatrain develops a different aspect of the theme and the final couplet provides the clinching or summing up statement.

Trace the rhyme scheme of Sidney's Sonnet 31 and explain what part of the theme is developed in the octave. What part of the theme is developed in the sestet?

What is the theme of Sidney's Sonnet 41? Does this sonnet observe the division between the octave and the sestet? What effect does this produce?

How does Sidney's rhyme scheme vary slightly from the traditional rhyme scheme of the Italian sonnet?

Trace the rhyme scheme adopted by Spenser. Why is this rhyme scheme particularly suitable for narrative?

William Shakespeare 1564-1616

The best Elizabethan songs, sonnets and plays came from the teeming imagination and lightning pen of William Shakespeare. It is ironic that the man who best understood his age and who captured it so dazzlingly in words should have left behind him so few traces of his own part in it, but such is the case: our knowledge of Shakespeare's life is full of gaps; he is a much more elusive figure than either Sidney or Spenser.

We do know that Shakespeare's ancestors were Warwickshire farmers, and that when William's father moved to the town of Stratford-on-Avon, he took up the genteel and profitable profession of glove-making, married into a distinguished family, and eventually donned the robes of high bailiff or mayor. It is likely that young Will attended Stratford's free grammar-school with its long hours and rigorous program of classical studies. It is also likely that at thirteen he was apprenticed to some local trade as a result of his father's declining fortunes. We know that he married Anne Hathaway when he was eighteen and she twenty-six, and that their first child, Susanna, was born in 1583, followed by twins, Hamnet and Judith, in 1585. But then for some reason Shakespeare left Stratford, and until he emerges as a rising London playwright in 1592 we hear nothing of him.

The 1590's were without a doubt the most exciting years in the history of the English theater—thanks largely to a group of young playwrights known as the "University Wits." John Lyly, Robert Greene, George Peele, Thomas Lodge, Thomas Nashe, Thomas Kyd, and Christopher Marlowe had all graduated from Oxford or Cambridge. Sensing the Elizabethan thirst for drama, these brilliant and often recklessly Bohemian young men began turning out sophisticated plays for courtiers and sensational plays for the general public. Londoners were particularly thrilled by Kyd's *Spanish Tragedy*, with its blood and thunder treatment of murder and revenge, and by Marlowe's *Tamburlaine, Dr. Faustus,* and *The Jew of Malta,* whose titanic heroes went crashing to their destruction as a result of their insatiable thirst for power. Though not a university man, Shakespeare stepped into this tradition and carried it forward with such success that Greene, piqued at being outdone by an outsider, called him an "upstart crow, beautified with our feathers."

Within two decades the "upstart crow" had regaled London with an incredible variety of plays—thirty-seven in all. The comedies appeared throughout his career, starting with the early, lighthearted romances and farces, such as *A Midsummer-Night's Dream* and *The Taming of the Shrew,* and ending with the late comedies that threaten in some scenes to turn into tragedies, such as *Measure for Measure* and *All's Well That Ends Well.* The histories, such as *Henry V* and *Richard II,* appeared during the last decade of the sixteenth century when the defeat of the Spanish Armada had set off a wave of patriotic pride and interest in the past. And with the exception of *Titus Andronicus* and *Romeo and Juliet,* the tragedies, such as the incomparable *Hamlet, Othello, King Lear,* and *Macbeth,* appeared during the first decade of the seventeenth century.

Playwriting, however, was a poorly paying business in the age of Elizabeth. In order to get in on the excellent profits of the box office, a man had to be one of the *house-sharers* (persons who hired or built and then maintained the theater structure) or one of the *actor-sharers* (persons who commissioned or selected and then performed the plays). Shakespeare was both, which quickly dispels any idea of his being an ivory-tower kind of genius. With a theater to run, parts to memorize, rehearsals to go to, actors to train, court performances to squeeze in, he had no time for long, leisurely hours with pen and paper. There are no records to tell us

Left: The "Chandos" portrait, attributed to Richard Burbage, one of the chief actors of the Globe Theater in Shakespeare's time. As with many Shakespeare portraits, the identity is in doubt, but this portrait has been held in high esteem since the early seventeenth century. Below: The Avon. In background, Trinity Church where Shakespeare is buried.

where and when the plays were written, but a safe guess would be that it was in the very midst of the London theatrical fray and during odd hours snatched from money-making activities. And Shakespeare did make money. When he retired to Stratford a few years before his death, it was to the second largest house in town and with a newly purchased coat-of-arms which elevated his family to the rank of gentlemen.

Succeeding generations have had their own particular opinions about Shakespeare. In the three and a half centuries since his death he has been revered and disparaged many times over. But no one has ever disputed his power—the kind of power that comes when a writer is at one and the same time a master poet and a master dramatist. Shakespeare's sonnets, especially the later ones, are as dramatic as his plays. They catch the reader up in the quick twists and turns that occur at the deepest level of a person's experience. And his best plays, such as *Hamlet*, achieve the same powerful impact as poetry through a richly suggestive interplay between what is seen and what is heard on the stage.

SONNET 18

Shall I compare thee to a summer's day?
Thou art more lovely and more temperate:
Rough winds do shake the darling buds of May,
And summer's lease hath all too short a date:
Sometime too hot the eye of heaven shines,   5
And often is his gold complexion dimmed;
And every fair from fair sometimes declines,
By chance or nature's changing course untrimmed;
But thy eternal summer shall not fade,
Nor lose possession of that fair thou owest[1];   10
Nor shall Death brag thou wander'st in his shade,
When in eternal lines to time thou growest:
   So long as men can breathe, or eyes can see,
   So long lives this, and this gives life to thee.

SONNET 29

When, in disgrace with fortune and men's eyes,
I all alone beweep my outcast state,
And trouble deaf heaven with my bootless cries
And look upon myself, and curse my fate,
Wishing me like to one more rich in hope,   5
Featured like him, like him with friends possessed,
Desiring this man's art and that man's scope,
With what I most enjoy contented least;
Yet in these thoughts myself almost despising,
Haply I think on thee—and then my state,   10
Like to the lark at break of day arising
From sullen earth, sings hymns at heaven's gate;
   For thy sweet love remembered such wealth brings
   That then I scorn to change my state with kings.

SONNET 18 **1.** *of that fair thou owest*, of your beauty.

SONNET 116

Let me not to the marriage of true minds
Admit impediments. Love is not love
Which alters when it alteration finds,
Or bends with the remover to remove.[1]
Oh, no! it is an ever-fixèd mark   5
That looks on tempests and is never shaken;
It is the star to every wandering bark,
Whose worth's unknown, although his height be taken.[2]
Love's not Time's fool, though rosy lips and cheeks
Within his bending sickle's compass come;   10
Love alters not with his brief hours and weeks,
But bears it out even to the edge of doom.
    If this be error and upon me proved,
    I never writ, nor no man ever loved.

SONNET 146

Poor soul, the center of my sinful earth—
Thrall to these rebel powers that thee array[1]—
Why dost thou pine within and suffer dearth,
Painting thy outward walls so costly gay?
Why so large cost, having so short a lease,   5
Dost thou upon thy fading mansions spend?
Shall worms, inheritors of this excess,
Eat up thy charge?[2] Is this thy body's end?
Then, soul, live thou upon thy servant's loss,
And let that pine to aggravate[3] thy store;   10
Buy terms divine[4] in selling hours of dross;
Within be fed, without be rich no more:
    So shalt thou feed on Death, that feeds on men,
    And Death once dead, there's no more dying then.

SONNET 116   1. *Or bends . . . remove*, or wavers when anyone tries to change it.   2. *Whose worth's . . . taken.* Just as we cannot know what a star really is although we can measure its elevation, so we cannot know what love really is although its extent can be determined.
SONNET 146   1. *Thrall . . . array*, slave to the body, which houses the soul.   2. *charge*, possessions.   3. *aggravate*, increase.   4. *terms divine*, eternity.

To increase understanding

One of the favorite themes of the Elizabethans—and of poets of all times—is that, by writing poems, a person confers immortality on himself and the people he writes about. (*a*) Which of Shakespeare's sonnets that you have read develops this theme? (*b*) In what other Elizabethan sonnet that you have read is this theme developed? (*c*) In your opinion which of these two sonnets is more concrete and vivid? Give as many reasons as you can for your answer.

2. (*a*) In Sonnet 29 why does the poet feel like an outcast? (*b*) How, in the second quatrain, does he increase his misery? (*c*) What brings him out of his depression? (*d*) Explain the simile in lines 10–12.

3. Analyze the organization of Sonnet 116. (*a*) What ideas announced in the first quatrain are developed in the second and third quatrains respectively? (*b*) What is the function of the concluding couplet?

4. (*a*) Explain in detail the basic metaphor of Sonnet 146. (*b*) State the theme of the sonnet in one or two sentences. (*c*) How does it differ from the themes of the preceding sonnets?

The Growth of the Theater in England

Let us imagine that we are in the center of London on a summer afternoon in 1601. Across the Thames on the south bank flags are flying from the tops of the theaters in which performances are being given. We go over by boat and then are swept by a crushing crowd to the very door of the Globe Theater, where Shakespeare is principal playwright, part owner, and actor. (It is rumored that he will take the part of the ghost in today's performance of *Hamlet*.) Paying a penny, we manage to push our way into the eight-sided auditorium, which is open to the air except for a thatched roof over the jutting stage and over the tiers of galleries that line the walls. Another penny gets us seats in one of the galleries away from the terrible smell of the greasy, food-munching "groundlings," or standing spectators, who have just set up a tremendous howl at the sight of a satin-clad courtier striding across to a corner of the stage and disposing himself on a stool to watch the play. Trumpets sound. The "stinkards" grow quiet. A boy appears on the stage with a sign saying that the play's first scene takes place on the ramparts of the royal castle in Denmark. Two soldiers appear, and the play begins:

> *Bernardo.* Who's there?
> *Francisco.* Nay, answer me: stand,
> and unfold yourself.

This image of the Elizabethan theater crowd tumbling all over itself in order to hear the most exciting plays in all English history has become so fixed in our minds that we tend to forget that the English theater did not always present such an aspect—nor did it do so for long.

English drama had its beginnings with the church plays and pantomimes of the Middle Ages. Introduced by the clergy in order to help the unlettered congregation understand the Latin church service, these plays eventually became so elaborate and so filled with secular or humorous incidents that they were moved to the church porch. When this too became inadequate, they were moved to the church lawn or graveyard. Out in the open the plays lost even more of their religious solemnity. Audiences became unruly. Church property was destroyed. An irate clergy eventually threw up its hands in disgust and banned the production of plays from church property altogether.

After losing the patronage of the church, the plays were taken up by the flourishing trade guilds, who came to regard good productions as a matter of civic pride. Guildsmen provided funds for costumes, stage properties, and the payment of actors on condition that the acting was creditable and that the actors would attend rehearsals or be subject to fines. The plays, which had originally been called *miracle* plays, in time acquired the name *mystery* plays, probably because of a certain ritualism associated with the guilds. They were put on in *cycles*, a cycle being a group

of short plays forming one long narrative (usually the entire Christian story from the Creation to the Last Judgment). Under guild management each individual play was placed on a wagon. Spectators gathered at prearranged spots and the wagons, moving in succession, brought the entire cycle to the waiting crowds.

While the miracle or mystery play was still in its heyday, another medieval dramatic form emerged. This was the *morality* play, which differs from the miracle play in that its characters are personified abstractions of vices and virtues competing for the possession of man's soul. The most famous of these plays is the fifteenth-century *Everyman*, in which a character representing all men encounters Good Deeds, Strength, Discretion, Five Wits, and various others as he goes on the long journey to which Death has summoned him.

Both in its technical and literary aspects the morality play forms a direct link between medieval and Elizabethan drama. Designed for more educated audiences than the miracle plays, morality plays were performed at schools and colleges and especially in the courtyards of inns. These innyards were unroofed inner courts surrounded by rooms on the lowest floor, above which were two or more tiers of galleries opening from the upper rooms. A stage was easily constructed by placing planks across trestles or sawhorses and by dropping a curtain at the back to conceal the actors until they made their entrances. This platform was usually placed opposite the innyard entrance.

In 1576, when the Elizabethan actor James Burbage built England's first public playhouse (called simply "The Theatre"), he used the innyard as a model, transforming the makeshift platform into a permanent, three-sided stage that jutted almost half way out into the auditorium. This kind of stage explains in part the bubbling excitement of the Elizabethan theater-goer, for with the actors and action virtually thrust into his lap, he became not just a spectator but in a sense a participant caught up in the passions of actors who were almost close enough to touch.

It was also a natural step from the simplified characters of the medieval morality play, who possessed only one trait (Strength, Honesty, Greed, etc.), to the complex characters of the Elizabethan drama, who combined many personality traits. This transition away

The Wagon

from personified abstractions to characters drawn from real-life men and women was given impetus by the Renaissance idea that individual human beings were fascinating objects of study. It helped produce a veritable torrent of playwrights who were eager to try their hand at creating real-life stage characters. It also brought the Elizabethans flocking to the new playhouses in droves, for what could be more stimulating than to see in some actor the reflection of one's own personality! The crowning glory of this new kind of theater was William Shakespeare. Voraciously curious about human beings, keenly aware of their infinite depth and variety, and supremely capable of finding words that would accurately portray them, he created a roster of characters who often seem more real than our own friends and acquaintances.

This kind of theater did not last long, however. In the middle of the seventeenth century (see Chapter IV) the Puritans succeeded in closing all the public playhouses. When they reopened again at the end of the seventeenth century during a period in history known as the Restoration, their entire aspect was changed. They were rectangular instead

of round and no longer open to the sky. Artificial lighting was necessary for the first time. Women's parts, which in Elizabethan times had been played by boys, were now played by women. The bare Elizabethan stage, whose setting had been left to the descriptive skill of the playwright and the imaginative skill of the audience, was now filled with movable scenery. Above all, the jutting, three-sided Elizabethan stage began to recede into a stage that looked like a box left open on one side, or a framed canvas with actors painted on it. Only a deep apron in front of the stage served to remind audiences of the older Elizabethan structure. During the eighteenth century the stage apron was foreshortened considerably. It was done away with entirely in the nineteenth century, and a curtain was put up to conceal the stage from the audience until show time. This new stage produced a new kind of theater experience. Audience and actor were no longer caught up together in a single emotional experience as they had been in the Age of Elizabeth. Instead, the actor withdrew into his world inside the picture-frame stage and the audience withdrew into its world within the rectangular auditorium.

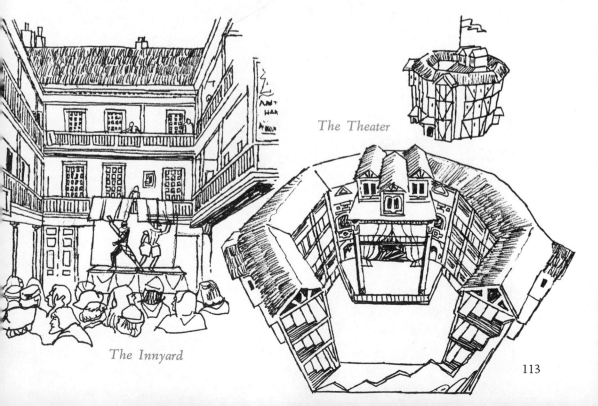

The Theater

The Innyard

GERTRUDE, Queen of Denmark,
and mother to Hamlet.

CLAUDIUS,
King of Denmark.

HAMLET, son to the late,
and nephew to the present king.

POLONIUS,
lord chambe

HORATIO, friend to Hamlet.

HAMLET *Prince of Denmark*

by William Shakespeare

Ghost of Hamlet's father.

VOLTIMAND,
CORNELIUS,
ROSENCRANTZ,
GUILDENSTERN, } courtiers.
OSRIC,
A GENTLEMAN,
A PRIEST.
MARCELLUS, } officers.
BERNARDO,
FRANCISCO, a soldier.
REYNALDO, servant to Polonius.
PLAYERS.
TWO CLOWNS, grave diggers.
FORTINBRAS, Prince of Norway.
A CAPTAIN.
ENGLISH AMBASSADORS.

LORDS, LADIES, OFFICERS,
SOLDIERS, SAILORS, MESSENGERS,
and other ATTENDANTS.

SCENE: *Denmark.*

LAERTES, son to Polonius.
OPHELIA, daughter to Polonius.

ACT ONE

FRANCISCO *at his post. Enter to him*
BERNARDO.

Ber. Who's there?
Fran. Nay, answer me: stand, and unfold
    yourself.
Ber. Long live the king!
Fran. Bernardo?
Ber. He.
Fran. You come most carefully upon your
    hour.
Ber. 'Tis now struck twelve; get thee to bed,
    Francisco.
Fran. For this relief much thanks; 'tis bitter
    cold,
And I am sick at heart.
    Ber. Have you had quiet guard?
    Fran.   Not a mouse stirring.   10
    Ber. Well, good night.
If you do meet Horatio and Marcellus,
The rivals² of my watch, bid them make haste.
    Fran. I think I hear them. Stand, ho! Who's
    there?

Enter HORATIO *and* MARCELLUS.

    Hor. Friends to this ground.
    Mar.   And liegemen to the Dane.
    Fran. Give you good night.
    Mar.   O, farewell, honest soldier:
Who hath relieved you?
    Fran.   Bernardo has my place.
Give you good night.   [*Exit.*
    Mar.   Holla! Bernardo!
    Ber.   Say,
What, is Horatio there?
    Hor.   A piece of him.
    Ber. Welcome, Horatio: welcome, good
    Marcellus.   20
    Mar. What, has this thing appear'd again
    to-night?
    Ber. I have seen nothing.
    Mar. Horatio says 'tis but our fantasy,
And will not let belief take hold of him
Touching this dreaded sight, twice seen of us:

Therefore I have entreated him along
With us to watch the minutes of this night;
That if again this apparition come,
He may approve³ our eyes and speak to it.
    Hor. Tush, tush, 'twill not appear.
    Ber.   Sit down awhile;   30
And let us once again assail your ears,
That are so fortified against our story
What we have two nights seen.
    Hor.   Well, sit we down,
And let us hear Bernardo speak of this.
    Ber. Last night of all,
When yond same star that's westward from
    the pole
Had made his course to illume that part of
    heaven
Where now it burns, Marcellus and myself,
The bell then beating one,—

Enter GHOST.

    Mar. Peace, break thee off; look, where it
    comes again!   40
    Ber. In the same figure, like the king that's
    dead.
    Mar. Thou art a scholar⁴; speak to it,
    Horatio.
    Ber. Looks it not like the king? mark it,
    Horatio.
    Hor. Most like: it harrows me with fear and
    wonder.
    Ber. It would be spoke to.
    Mar.   Question it, Horatio.
    Hor. What art thou that usurp'st this time
    of night,
Together with that fair and warlike form
In which the majesty of buried Denmark
Did sometimes march? by heaven I charge
    thee, speak!
    Mar. It is offended.
    Ber.   See, it stalks⁵ away!   50
    Hor. Stay! speak, speak! I charge thee,
    speak!   [*Exit* GHOST.
    Mar. 'Tis gone, and will not answer.
    Ber. How now, Horatio! you tremble and
    look pale:

---

1. *platform,* a level space on the battlements of the royal castle at Elsinore, a Danish seaport; now Helsignör. 2. *rivals,* partners. 3. *approve,* confirm. 4. *scholar,* a man who can speak Latin, which was the language used to exorcise, or drive out, evil spirits. 5. *stalks,* slips.

Is not this something more than fantasy?
What think you on 't?

   Hor. Before my God, I might not this
    believe
Without the sensible and true avouch
Of mine own eyes.

   Mar.   Is it not like the king?

   Hor. As thou art to thyself:
Such was the very armor he had on   60
When he the ambitious Norway[6] combated;
So frown'd he once, when, in an angry parle,
He smote the sledded Polacks[7] on the ice.
'Tis strange.

   Mar. Thus twice before, and jump[8] at this
    dead hour,
With martial stalk hath he gone by our watch.

   Hor. In what particular thought to work I
    know not;
But in the gross and scope[9] of my opinion,
This bodes some strange eruption to our state.

   Mar. Good now, sit down, and tell me, he
    that knows,   70
Why this same strict and most observant
    watch
So nightly toils the subject of the land,[10]
And why such daily cast[11] of brazen cannon
And foreign mart[12] for implements of war;
Why such impress[13] of shipwrights, whose
    sore task
Does not divide the Sunday from the week;
What might be toward, that this sweaty haste
Doth make the night joint-laborer with the
    day:
Who is 't that can inform me?

   Hor.   That can I;
At least, the whisper goes so. Our last king,   80
Whose image even but now appear'd to us,
Was, as you know, by Fortinbras of Norway,
Thereto prick'd on[14] by a most emulate[15] pride,
Dared to the combat; in which our valiant
    Hamlet—
For so this side of our known world esteem'd
    him—
Did slay this Fortinbras; who, by a seal'd
    compact,
Well ratified by law and heraldry,[16]
Did forfeit, with his life, all those his lands
Which he stood seized[17] of, to the conqueror:
Against the which, a moiety competent[18]   90
Was gaged[19] by our king; which had return'd

To the inheritance of Fortinbras,
Had he been vanquisher; as, by the same
    covenant,
And carriage[20] of the article design'd,
His fell to Hamlet. Now, sir, young Fortinbras,
Of unimproved mettle[21] hot and full,
Hath in the skirts of Norway here and there
Shark'd up a list of lawless resolutes,[22]
For food and diet, to some enterprise
That hath a stomach in 't; which is no other—
As it doth well appear unto our state—   101
But to recover of us, by strong hand
And terms compulsatory, those foresaid lands
So by his father lost: and this, I take it,
Is the main motive of our preparations,
The source of this our watch and the chief
    head
Of this post-haste and romage[23] in the land.

   Ber. I think it be no other but e'en so:
Well may it sort[24] that this portentous figure
Comes armed through our watch; so like the
    king   110
That was and is the question of these wars.

   Hor. A mote it is to trouble the mind's eye.
In the most high and palmy state of Rome,
A little ere the mightiest Julius fell,
The graves stood tenantless and the sheeted
    dead
Did squeak and gibber in the Roman streets:
As stars with trains of fire[25] and dews of blood,
Disasters in the sun; and the moist star
Upon whose influence Neptune's empire
    stands[26]
Was sick almost to doomsday with eclipse: 120
And even the like precurse of fear'd events,

---

6. *Norway*, the king of Norway. It was customary to refer to the king of a country by the name of the country (Norway, Denmark, etc.). 7. *when . . . sledded Polacks*, when in an encounter he struck down the Polish soldiers in sleds. 8. *jump*, precisely. 9. *gross and scope*, general drift. 10. *toils . . . land*, wearies the Danish people. 11. *cast*, casting, founding. 12. *foreign mart*, trade abroad. 13. *impress*, conscription. 14. *prick'd on*, incited, or stirred up. 15. *emulate*, ambitious. 16. *law and heraldry*, civil law and also the courts of chivalry. 17. *seized*, possessed. 18. *moiety competent*, adequate portion. 19. *gaged*, pledged. 20. *carriage*, import, bearing. 21. *unimproved mettle*, courage not hitherto turned to account. 22. *Shark'd up . . . resolutes*, got together in haphazard fashion a group of lawless men. 23. *romage*, bustle, commotion. 24. *Well may it sort*, it may well be appropriate. 25. *stars with trains of fire*, meteors. 26. *moist star . . . stands.* The "moist star" is the moon, so called because it affects the tides. Thus it governs the empire of Neptune, Roman god of the sea.

As harbingers preceding still the fates
And prologue to the omen coming on,
Have heaven and earth together demonstrated
Unto our climatures and countrymen.—
But soft, behold! lo, where it comes again!

Re-enter GHOST.

I'll cross²⁷ it, though it blast me. Stay, illusion!
If thou hast any sound, or use of voice,
Speak to me:
If there be any good thing to be done,   130
That may to thee do ease and grace to me,
Speak to me: [*Cock crows.*
If thou art privy to thy country's fate,
Which, happily, foreknowing may avoid,
O, speak!
Or if thou hast uphoarded in thy life
Extorted treasure in the womb of earth,
For which, they say, you spirits oft walk in
    death,
Speak of it: stay, and speak! Stop it, Marcellus.
    Mar. Shall I strike at it with my partisan?²⁸
    Hor. Do, if it will not stand.
    Ber.   'Tis here!
    Hor.   'Tis here!   141
    Mar. 'Tis gone!   [*Exit* GHOST.
We do it wrong, being so majestical,
To offer it the show of violence;
For it is, as the air, invulnerable,
And our vain blows malicious mockery.
    Ber. It was about to speak, when the cock
    crew.
    Hor. And then it started like a guilty thing
Upon a fearful summons. I have heard,
The cock, that is the trumpet to the morn, ¹⁵⁰
Doth with his lofty and shrill-sounding throat
Awake the god of day; and, at his warning,
Whether in sea or fire, in earth or air,
The extravagant and erring²⁹ spirit hies
To his confine: and of the truth herein
This present object made probation.³⁰
    Mar. It faded on the crowing of the cock.
Some say that ever 'gainst³¹ that season comes
Wherein our Saviour's birth is celebrated, ¹⁵⁹
The bird of dawning singeth all night long:
And then, they say, no spirit dare stir abroad;
The nights are wholesome; then no planets
    strike,³²
No fairy takes, nor witch hath power to charm,
So hallow'd and so gracious is the time.

Hor. So have I heard and do in part believe
    it.
But, look, the morn, in russet mantle clad,
Walks o'er the dew of yon high eastward hill:
Break we our watch up; and by my advice,
Let us impart what we have seen to-night
Unto young Hamlet; for, upon my life,   170
This spirit, dumb to us, will speak to him.
Do you consent we shall acquaint him with it,
As needful in our loves, fitting our duty?³³
    Mar. Let's do 't, I pray; and I this morning
    know
Where we shall find him most conveniently.
                        [*Exeunt.*

SCENE II. *A room of state in the castle.*

Enter the KING, QUEEN, HAMLET, POLONIUS,
LAERTES, VOLTIMAND, CORNELIUS, LORDS, *and*
ATTENDANTS.

King. Though yet of Hamlet¹ our dear
    brother's death
The memory be green, and that it us befitted
To bear our hearts in grief and our whole
    kingdom
To be contracted in one brow of woe,
Yet so far hath discretion fought with nature
That we with wisest sorrow think on him,
Together with remembrance of ourselves.
Therefore our sometime² sister, now our
    queen,
The imperial jointress³ to this warlike state,
Have we, as 'twere with a defeated joy,—   10
With an auspicious and a dropping eye,⁴
With mirth in funeral and with dirge in
    marriage,
In equal scale weighing delight and dole,—
Taken to wife: nor have we herein barr'd
Your better wisdoms, which have freely gone

SCENE I **27.** *cross*, meet, face. **28.** *partisan*, long-
handled weapon, like a pike or spear. **29.** *extravagant and
erring*, wandering. Both mean the same thing. **30.** *made
probation*, proved. **31.** *'gainst*, just before. **32.** *planets strike*. It was believed that planets could exert an
evil influence on men. **33.** *As needful . . . duty*, as be-
fitting the behavior of friends.
SCENE II **1.** *Hamlet*, the elder Hamlet, brother of the
present king, and father of young Hamlet, Prince of Denmark. **2.** *sometime*, former. **3.** *jointress*, dowager, wife
who holds an estate settled on her to be enjoyed after her
husband's death. **4.** *With . . . dropping eye*, joyfully yet
tearfully.

With this affair along. For all, our thanks.
Now follows, that you know, young
    Fortinbras,
Holding a weak supposal[5] of our worth,
Or thinking by our late dear brother's death
Our state to be disjoint and out of frame,   20
Colleagued with the dream of his advantage,[6]
He hath not fail'd to pester us with message,
Importing[7] the surrender of those lands
Lost by his father, with all bonds of law,
To our most valiant brother. So much for him.
Now for ourself and for this time of meeting:
Thus much the business is: we have here writ
To Norway, uncle of young Fortinbras,—
Who, impotent and bed-rid, scarcely hears
Of this his nephew's purpose,—to suppress   30
His further gait[8] herein; in that the levies,
The lists and full proportions, are all made
Out of his subject[9]: and we here dispatch
You, good Cornelius, and you, Voltimand,
For bearers of this greeting to old Norway;
Giving to you no further personal power
To business with the king, more than the
    scope
Of these delated[10] articles allow.
Farewell, and let your haste commend your
    duty.
  Cor.) In that and all things will we show
  Vol.⟩   our duty.   40
King. We doubt it nothing: heartily
    farewell.
            [Exeunt VOLTIMAND and CORNELIUS.
And now, Laertes, what 's the news with you?
You told us of some suit; what is 't, Laertes?
You cannot speak of reason to the Dane,
And lose your voice[11]: what wouldst thou beg,
    Laertes,
That shall not be my offer, not thy asking?
The head is not more native to the heart,
The hand more instrumental to the mouth,
Than is the throne of Denmark to thy father.
What wouldst thou have, Laertes?
  Laer.   My dread lord,   50
Your leave and favor to return to France;
From whence though willingly I came to
    Denmark,
To show my duty in your coronation,
Yet now, I must confess, that duty done,
My thoughts and wishes bend again toward
    France

And bow them to your gracious leave and
    pardon.
  King. Have you your father's leave? What
    says Polonius?
  Pol. He hath, my lord, wrung from me my
    slow leave
By laborsome petition, and at last
Upon his will I seal'd my hard consent: 60
I do beseech you, give him leave to go.
  King. Take thy fair hour,[12] Laertes; time
    be thine,
And thy best graces spend it at thy will!
But now, my cousin Hamlet, and my son,—
  Ham. [Aside] A little more than kin, and
    less than kind.[13]
  King. How is it that the clouds still hang
    on you?
  Ham. Not so, my lord; I am too much i' the
    sun.[14]
  Queen. Good Hamlet, cast thy nighted color
    off,
And let thine eye look like a friend on
    Denmark.
Do not for ever with thy vailed lids   70
Seek for thy noble father in the dust:
Thou know'st 'tis common; all that lives must
    die,
Passing through nature to eternity.
  Ham. Ay, madam, it is common.
  Queen.   If it be,
Why seems it so particular with thee?
  Ham. Seems, madam! nay, it is; I know not
    "seems."
'Tis not alone my inky cloak, good mother,
Nor customary suits of solemn black,
Nor windy suspiration of forced breath,
No, nor the fruitful river in the eye,   80
Nor the dejected 'havior of the visage,

5. *weak supposal*, low estimate. 6. *Colleagued . . . advantage*, allied with his visionary hope of success. 7. *Importing*, pertaining to. 8. *gait*, proceeding. 9. *subject*, subjects, people of Norway. 10. *delated*, expressly stated. 11. *speak of . . . voice*, speak reasonably to the King of Denmark and not be heeded. 12. *Take thy fair hour*, make the most of your youth. 13. *A little more . . . kind.* Hamlet mutters that he and his uncle are closer than kinsmen usually are (because related as uncle and nephew, stepfather and stepson) and yet there is little kindred feeling between them. 14. *I am . . . sun.* This line has several possible interpretations: I am too much out of doors; I am too much in the sun of your grace (ironical); you have put me out of my inheritance; and especially (punning), I am too much of a *son* to you.

Together with all forms, moods, shapes of grief,
That can denote me truly: these indeed seem,
For they are actions that a man might play:
But I have that within which passeth show;
These but the trappings and the suits of woe.
    King. 'Tis sweet and commendable in your nature, Hamlet,
To give these mourning duties to your father:
But, you must know, your father lost a father;
That father lost, lost his, and the survivor bound   90
In filial obligation for some term
To do obsequious[15] sorrow: but to persever
In obstinate condolement[16] is a course
Of impious stubbornness; 'tis unmanly grief;
It shows a will most incorrect to heaven,
A heart unfortified, a mind impatient,
An understanding simple and unschool'd:
For what we know must be and is as common
As any the most vulgar thing to sense,[17]
Why should we in our peevish opposition   100
Take it to heart? Fie! 'tis a fault to heaven,
A fault against the dead, a fault to nature,
To reason most absurd; whose common theme
Is death of fathers, and who still hath cried,
From the first corse till he that died to-day,
"This must be so." We pray you, throw to earth
This unprevailing[18] woe, and think of us
As of a father: for let the world take note,
You are the most immediate to our throne;
And with no less nobility of love   110
Than that which dearest father bears his son,
Do I impart toward you. For your intent
In going back to school in Wittenberg,[19]
It is most retrograde[20] to our desire:
And we beseech you, bend you to remain
Here, in the cheer and comfort of our eye,
Our chiefest courtier, cousin, and our son.
    Queen. Let not thy mother lose her prayers, Hamlet:
I pray thee, stay with us; go not to Wittenberg.
    Ham. I shall in all my best obey you, madam.   120
    King. Why, 'tis a loving and a fair reply:
Be as ourself[21] in Denmark. Madam, come;
This gentle and unforced accord of Hamlet
Sits smiling to my heart: in grace whereof,[22]
No jocund health that Denmark drinks to-day,
But the great cannon to the clouds shall tell,

And the king's rouse[23] the heaven shall bruit[24] again,
Re-speaking earthly thunder. Come away.
                [*Exeunt all but* HAMLET.
    Ham. O, that this too too solid flesh would melt,
Thaw and resolve itself into a dew!   130
Or that the Everlasting had not fix'd
His canon 'gainst self-slaughter! O God! God!
How weary, stale, flat and unprofitable,
Seem to me all the uses of this world!
Fie on 't! ah fie! 'tis an unweeded garden,
That grows to seed; things rank and gross in nature
Possess it merely. That it should come to this!
But two months dead: nay, not so much, not two:
So excellent a king; that was, to this,
Hyperion[25] to a satyr[26]; so loving to my mother
That he might not beteem[27] the winds of heaven   141
Visit her face too roughly. Heaven and earth!
Must I remember? why, she would hang on him,
As if increase of appetite had grown
By what it fed on: and yet, within a month—
Let me not think on 't—Frailty, thy name is woman!—
A little month, or ere those shoes were old
With which she follow'd my poor father's body,
Like Niobe,[28] all tears:—why she, even she—
O God! a beast, that wants discourse of reason,
Would have mourn'd longer—married with my uncle,   151
My father's brother, but no more like my father
Than I to Hercules[29]: within a month:

---

15. *obsequious,* dutiful. 16. *obstinate condolement,* persistent sorrowing. 17. *the most . . . sense,* the most familiar thing in our experience. 18. *unprevailing,* unavailing. 19. *Wittenberg,* famous German university founded in 1502. 20. *retrograde,* contrary. 21. *Be as ourself,* behave with the freedom of the king himself. 22. *in grace whereof,* in honor of which. 23. *rouse,* draft of liquor, carousal. 24. *bruit,* echo, report. 25. *Hyperion* (hī-pēr'i ʌn), the sun god. 26. *satyr,* a creature half man, half goat, ugly and lecherous. 27. *might not beteem,* could not permit. 28. *Niobe* (nī'ō bē), in Greek mythology, a mother whose fourteen beautiful children were slain because she boasted about them. She was changed by Zeus into a stone that appeared to weep continually. 29. *Hercules,* in Greek and Roman mythology, a hero famous for his great strength.

Ere yet the salt of most unrighteous tears
Had left the flushing in her galled eyes,
She married. O, most wicked speed, to post
With such dexterity to incestuous[30] sheets!
It is not nor it cannot come to good:
But break, my heart; for I must hold my
    tongue.

Enter HORATIO, MARCELLUS, *and* BERNARDO.

Hor. Hail to your lordship!
Ham.   I am glad to see you well: 160
Horatio,—or I do forget myself.
Hor. The same, my lord, and your poor
    servant ever.
Ham. Sir, my good friend; I'll change that
    name with you[31]:
And what make you from Wittenberg,[32]
    Horatio? Marcellus?
Mar. My good lord—
Ham. I am very glad to see you. Good
    even, sir.
But what, in faith, make you from
    Wittenberg?
Hor. A truant disposition, good my lord.
Ham. I would not hear your enemy say so,
Nor shall you do mine ear that violence,   171
To make it truster of your own report
Against yourself: I know you are no truant.
But what is your affair in Elsinore?
We'll teach you to drink deep ere you depart.
Hor. My lord, I came to see your father's
    funeral.
Ham. I pray thee, do not mock me,
    fellow-student;
I think it was to see my mother's wedding.
Hor. Indeed, my lord, it follow'd hard
    upon.
Ham. Thrift, thrift, Horatio! the funeral
    baked meats   180
Did coldly furnish forth the marriage tables.
Would I had met my dearest foe in heaven
Or ever I had seen that day, Horatio!
My father!—methinks I see my father.
Hor. Where, my lord?
Ham.   In my mind's eye, Horatio.
Hor. I saw him once; he was a goodly king.
Ham. He was a man, take him for all in all,
I shall not look upon his like again.
Hor. My lord, I think I saw him
    yesternight.

Ham. Saw? who?   190
Hor. My lord, the king your father.
Ham.   The king my father!
Hor. Season your admiration[33] for a while
With an attent ear, till I may deliver,
Upon the witness of these gentlemen,
This marvel to you.
Ham.   For God's love, let me hear.
Hor. Two nights together had these
    gentlemen,
Marcellus and Bernardo, on their watch,
In the dead vast and middle of the night,
Been thus encounter'd. A figure like your
    father,
Armed at point exactly cap-a-pe,[34]   200
Appears before them, and with solemn march
Goes slow and stately by them: thrice he
    walk'd
By their oppress'd and fear-surprised eyes,
Within his truncheon's length; whilst they,
    distill'd
Almost to jelly with the act of fear,
Stand dumb and speak not to him. This to
    me
In dreadful secrecy impart they did;
And I with them the third night kept the
    watch:
Where, as they had deliver'd, both in time,
Form of the thing, each word made true and
    good,   210
The apparition comes: I knew your father;
These hands are not more like.
Ham.   But where was this?
Mar. My lord, upon the platform where we
    watch'd.
Ham. Did you not speak to it?
Hor.   My lord, I did;
But answer made it none: yet once methought
It lifted up it head and did address
Itself to motion, like as it would speak;
But even then the morning cock crew loud,
And at the sound it shrunk in haste away,   219
And vanish'd from our sight.
Ham.   'Tis very strange.
Hor. As I do live, my honor'd lord, 'tis true;

---

30. *incestuous.* Marriage with a deceased husband's brother was forbidden by the medieval Church. **31.** *I'll change . . . you,* I'll exchange the name of friend with you. **32.** *what . . . Wittenberg,* what are you doing away from Wittenberg. **33.** *Season your admiration,* restrain your astonishment. **34.** *cap-a-pe* (kap′ə pē′), head to foot.

And we did think it writ down in our duty
To let you know of it.

Ham. Indeed, indeed, sirs, but this troubles me.
Hold you the watch to-night?

Mar.
Ber. } We do, my lord.

Ham. Arm'd, say you?

Mar.
Ber. } Arm'd, my lord.

Ham. From top to toe?

Mar.
Ber. } My lord, from head to foot.

Ham. Then saw you not his face?

Hor. O yes, my lord; he wore his beaver[35] up.   230

Ham. What, look'd he frowningly?

Hor. A countenance more in sorrow than in anger.

Ham. Pale or red?

Hor. Nay, very pale.

Ham.   And fix'd his eyes upon you?

Hor. Most constantly.

Ham.   I would I had been there.

Hor. It would have much amazed you.

Ham. Very like, very like. Stay'd it long?

Hor. While one with moderate haste might tell a hundred.

Mar.
Ber. } Longer, longer.

Hor. Not when I saw 't.

Ham.   His beard was grizzled,—no?

Hor. It was, as I have seen it in his life, [241]
A sable silver'd.

Ham.   I will watch to-night;
Perchance 'twill walk again.

Hor.   I warrant it will.

Ham. If it assume my noble father's person,
I'll speak to it, though hell itself should gape
And bid me hold my peace. I pray you all,
If you have hitherto conceal'd this sight,
Let it be tenable[36] in your silence still;
And whatsoever else shall hap to-night,
Give it an understanding, but no tongue: 250
I will requite your loves. So, fare you well:
Upon the platform, 'twixt eleven and twelve,
I'll visit you.

All.   Our duty to your honor.

Ham. Your loves, as mine to you: farewell.
                              [*Exeunt all but* HAMLET.

My father's spirit in arms! all is not well;
I doubt some foul play: would the night were come!
Till then sit still, my soul: foul deeds will rise,
Though all the earth o'erwhelm them, to men's eyes.   [*Exit.*

SCENE III. *A room in Polonius' house.*

Enter LAERTES *and* OPHELIA.

Laer. My necessaries are embark'd: farewell:
And, sister, as the winds give benefit
And convoy is assistant,[1] do not sleep,
But let me hear from you.

Oph.   Do you doubt that?

Laer. For Hamlet and the trifling of his favor,
Hold it a fashion[2] and a toy in blood,[3]
A violet in the youth of primy nature,
Forward,[4] not permanent, sweet, not lasting,
The perfume and suppliance of a minute[5];
No more.

Oph. No more but so?

Laer.   Think it no more: 10
For nature, crescent,[6] does not grow alone
In thews and bulk, but, as this temple[7] waxes,
The inward service of the mind and soul
Grows wide withal. Perhaps he loves you now,
And now no soil nor cautel[8] doth besmirch
The virtue of his will: but you must fear,
His greatness weigh'd,[9] his will is not his own;
For he himself is subject to his birth:
He may not, as unvalued persons do,
Carve for himself[10]; for on his choice depends   20
The sanity and health of this whole state;
And therefore must his choice be circumscribed
Unto the voice and yielding of that body

SCENE II   **35.** *beaver,* visor on the helmet. **36.** *tenable,* held, contained.

SCENE III   **1.** *as the winds . . . assistant,* when the winds are favorable and convoy is available. **2.** *fashion,* custom, fad. **3.** *toy in blood,* a passing fancy rather than true love. **4.** *Forward,* early, precocious. **5.** *suppliance of a minute,* pastime. **6.** *crescent,* growing, waxing. **7.** *temple,* body. **8.** *no soil nor cautel,* no blemish or crafty device. **9.** *His greatness weigh'd,* considering his noble birth. **10.** *Carve for himself,* follow his own inclination.

Whereof he is the head. Then if he says he
    loves you,
It fits your wisdom so far to believe it
As he in his particular act and place
May give his saying deed; which is no further
Than the main voice of Denmark goes withal.
Then weigh what loss your honor may
    sustain,
If with too credent ear you list his songs,   30
Fear it, Ophelia, fear it, my dear sister,
And keep you in the rear of your affection,[11]
Out of the shot and danger of desire.
The chariest maid is prodigal enough,
If she unmask her beauty to the moon:
Be wary then; best safety lies in fear:
Youth to itself rebels, though none else
    near.[12]
    Oph. I shall the effect of this good lesson
    keep,
As watchman to my heart. But, good my
    brother,
Do not, as some ungracious pastors do,   40
Show me the steep and thorny way to heaven;
Whiles, like a puff'd and reckless libertine,
Himself the primrose path of dalliance treads,
And recks not his own rede.[13]
    Laer.   O, fear me not.
I stay too long: but here my father comes.

Enter POLONIUS.

A double blessing is a double grace;
Occasion smiles upon a second leave.
    Pol. Yet here, Laertes! aboard, aboard, for
    shame!
The wind sits in the shoulder of your sail,
And you are stay'd for. There; my blessing
    with thee!   50
And these few precepts in thy memory
Look thou character.[14] Give thy thoughts no
    tongue,
Nor any unproportion'd thought his act.[15]
Be thou familiar, but by no means vulgar.
Those friends thou hast, and their adoption
    tried,
Grapple them to thy soul with hoops of steel;
But do not dull thy palm with entertainment
Of each new-hatch'd, unfledged comrade.
    Beware
Of entrance to a quarrel, but being in,

Bear 't that the opposed may beware of thee. 60
Give every man thy ear, but few thy voice;
Take each man's censure,[16] but reserve thy
    judgment.
Costly thy habit as thy purse can buy,
But not express'd in fancy; rich, not gaudy;
For the apparel oft proclaims the man,
And they in France of the best rank and
    station
Are of a most select and generous chief in that.
Neither a borrower nor a lender be;
For loan oft loses both itself and friend,
And borrowing dulls the edge of husbandry. 70
This above all: to thine own self be true,
And it must follow, as the night the day,
Thou canst not then be false to any man.
Farewell: my blessing season this in thee!
    Laer. Most humbly do I take my leave, my
    lord.
    Pol. The time invites you; go; your servants
    tend.
    Laer. Farewell, Ophelia; and remember well
What I have said to you.
    Oph.   'Tis in my memory lock'd,
And you yourself shall keep the key of it.
    Laer. Farewell.   [*Exit.*
    Pol. What is 't, Ophelia, he hath said to
    you?
    Oph. So please you, something touching the
    Lord Hamlet.   82
    Pol. Marry, well bethought:
'Tis told me, he hath very oft of late
Given private time to you; and you yourself
Have of your audience been most free and
    bounteous:
If it be so, as so 't is put on me,
And that in way of caution, I must tell you,
You do not understand yourself so clearly
As it behooves my daughter and your honor. 90
What is between you? give me up the truth.
    Oph. He hath, my lord, of late made many
    tenders[17]
Of his affection to me.

---

11. *keep you in the rear of your affection,* don't let your
emotions lead you astray. 12. *Youth to itself . . . near,*
youth tends to do what it shouldn't at the slightest temptation. 13. *recks . . . rede,* heeds not his own counsel.
14. *precepts . . . character,* be certain you inscribe these
precepts in your memory. 15. *Nor . . . act,* nor act upon
any unrestrained thought. 16. *censure,* opinion. 17.
tenders, offers. Note how Shakespeare plays on the word
tenders in the following lines.

Pol. Affection! pooh! you speak like a green girl,
Unsifted[18] in such perilous circumstance.
Do you believe his tenders, as you call them?
  Oph. I do not know, my lord, what I should think.
  Pol. Marry, I'll teach you: think yourself a baby;
That you have ta'en these tenders[19] for true pay,
Which are not sterling. Tender yourself more
    dearly;   100
Or—not to crack the wind of the poor phrase,
Running it thus—you'll tender me a fool.[20]
  Oph. My lord, he hath importuned me with love
In honorable fashion.
  Pol. Ay, fashion you may call it; go to, go to.
  Oph. And hath given countenance to his speech, my lord,
With almost all the holy vows of heaven.
  Pol. Ay, springes to catch woodcocks.[21] I do know,
When the blood burns, how prodigal the soul
Lends the tongue vows: these blazes, daughter,
Giving more light than heat, extinct in both,
Even in their promise, as it is a-making,   112
You must not take for fire. From this time
Be somewhat scanter of your maiden presence;
Set your entreatments[22] at a higher rate
Than a command to parley.[23] For Lord
    Hamlet,
Believe so much in him, that he is young,
And with a larger tether may he walk
Than may be given you: in few, Ophelia,
Do not believe his vows; for they are
    brokers,[24]   120
Not of that dye[25] which their investments[26]
    show,
But mere implorators[27] of unholy suits,
Breathing like sanctified and pious bawds,
The better to beguile. This is for all[28]:
I would not, in plain terms, from this time
    forth,
Have you so slander any moment leisure,
As to give words or talk with the Lord
    Hamlet.
Look to 't, I charge you: come your ways.
  Oph. I shall obey, my lord.   [*Exeunt.*

SCENE IV. *The platform.*

Enter HAMLET, HORATIO, *and* MARCELLUS.

  Ham. The air bites shrewdly; it is very cold.
  Hor. It is a nipping and an eager air.
  Ham. What hour now?
  Hor.   I think it lacks of twelve.
  Mar. No, it is struck.
  Hor. Indeed? I heard it not: then it draws
    near the season
Wherein the spirit held his wont to walk.
            [*A flourish of trumpets, and
              ordnance shot off, within.*
What does this mean, my lord?
  Ham. The king doth wake[1] to-night and
    takes his rouse,
Keeps wassail, and the swaggering up-spring[2]
    reels;
And, as he drains his draughts of Rhenish
    down,   10
The kettle-drum and trumpet thus bray out
The triumph of his pledge.[3]
  Hor.   Is it a custom?
  Ham. Ay, marry, is 't:
But to my mind, though I am native here
And to the manner born, it is a custom
More honor'd in the breach than the
    observance.
This heavy-headed revel east and west
Makes us traduced and tax'd[4] of other nations:
They clepe[5] us drunkards, and with swinish
    phrase[6]
Soil our addition[7]; and indeed it takes   20
From our achievements, though perform'd at
    height,
The pith and marrow of our attribute.[8]

SCENE III **18.** *Unsifted,* untried. **19.** *tenders,* promises to pay. **20.** *tender me a fool,* offer me a fool for a daughter. **21.** *springes . . . woodcocks.* Since woodcocks are supposedly stupid birds who are easily trapped, by this expression Polonius is suggesting Ophelia is stupid in believing Hamlet's vows. **22.** *entreatments,* negotiations to surrender. **23.** *command to parley,* mere invitation to talk. **24.** *brokers,* go-betweens, procurers. **25.** *dye,* color or sort. **26.** *investments,* clothing. **27.** *implorators,* solicitors. **28.** *This is for all,* these are your orders.
SCENE IV **1.** *doth wake,* stays awake. **2.** *up-spring,* a German dance, particularly associated with drunken parties. **3.** *pledge,* a pledge of health and then a draining of the drinking cup in one swallow. **4.** *traduced and tax'd,* slandered and censured. **5.** *clepe,* call. **6.** *with swinish phrase,* by speaking of us as swine. **7.** *addition,* title. **8.** *attribute,* reputation.

So, oft it chances in particular men,
That for some vicious mole of nature[9] in
  them,
As, in their birth—wherein they are not guilty,
Since nature cannot choose his origin—
By the o'ergrowth of some complexion,[10]
Oft breaking down the pales and forts of
  reason,
Or by some habit that too much o'er-leavens
The form of plausive[11] manners, that these
  men,   30
Carrying, I say, the stamp of one defect,
Being nature's livery,[12] or fortune's star,[13]—
Their virtues else—be they as pure as grace,
As infinite as man may undergo—
Shall in the general censure take corruption
From that particular fault: the dram of eale[14]
Doth all the noble substance of a doubt[15]
To his own scandal.
  Hor.   Look, my lord, it comes!

Enter GHOST.

  Ham. Angels and ministers of grace defend
    us!
Be thou a spirit of health or goblin damn'd, 40
Bring with thee airs from heaven or blasts
    from hell,
Be thy intents wicked or charitable,
Thou comest in such a questionable shape
That I will speak to thee: I'll call thee
    Hamlet,
King, father, royal Dane: O, answer me!
Let me not burst in ignorance; but tell
Why thy canonized bones, hearsed in death,
Have burst their cerements; why the
    sepulchre,
Wherein we saw thee quietly interr'd,
Hath oped his ponderous and marble jaws, 50
To cast thee up again. What may this mean,
That thou, dead corse, again in complete steel
Revisit'st thus the glimpses of the moon,[16]
Making night hideous; and we fools of
    nature
So horridly to shake our disposition
With thoughts beyond the reaches of our
    souls?
Say, why is this? wherefore? what should we
    do?
                    [GHOST *beckons* HAMLET.

  Hor. It beckons you to go away with it,
As if it some impartment[17] did desire
To you alone.
  Mar.   Look, with what courteous action
It waves you to a more removed ground: 61
But do not go with it.
  Hor.   No, by no means.
  Ham. It will not speak; then I will follow it.
  Hor. Do not, my lord.
  Ham.   Why, what should be the fear?
I do not set my life at a pin's fee;
And for my soul, what can it do to that,
Being a thing immortal as itself?
It waves me forth again: I'll follow it.
  Hor. What if it tempt you toward the flood,
    my lord,
Or to the dreadful summit of the cliff   70
That beetles o'er his base into the sea,
And there assume some other horrible form,
Which might deprive your sovereignty of
    reason[18]
And draw you into madness? think of it:
The very place puts toys of desperation,[19]
Without more motive, into every brain
That looks so many fathoms to the sea
And hears it roar beneath.
  Ham.   It waves me still.
Go on; I'll follow thee.
  Mar. You shall not go, my lord.
  Ham.   Hold off your hands.   80
  Hor. Be ruled; you shall not go.
  Ham.   My fate cries out,
And makes each petty artery in this body
As hardy as the Nemean lion's[20] nerve.
Still am I call'd. Unhand me, gentlemen.
By heaven, I'll make a ghost of him that lets
    me!
I say, away! Go on; I'll follow thee.
                    [*Exeunt* GHOST *and* HAMLET.

---

9. *mole of nature*, natural blemish in one's constitution.
10. *complexion*, temperament, trait. 11. *plausive*, pleasing. 12. *nature's livery*, nature's endowment. 13. *fortune's star*, the position in which one is placed by fortune.
14. *dram of eale*, small measure of evil. 15. *of a doubt*.
There have been several spellings of this phrase. The meaning is probably in the sense of "erase" or "counteract."
16. *the glimpses of the moon*, the earth by night. 17. *impartment*, communication. 18. *deprive your sovereignty
of reason*, take away the supremacy of your reason. 19.
toys of desperation, notions of suicide. 20. *Nemean*
(ni mē′ ən) *lion's*. According to Greek and Roman mythology, Hercules, a hero famous for his strength, had to slay
the Nemean lion as one of his twelve tasks.

Hor. He waxes desperate with imagination.

Mar. Let's follow; 'tis not fit thus to obey him.

Hor. Have after. To what issue will this come?

Mar. Something is rotten in the state of Denmark.   90

Hor. Heaven will direct it.

Mar.   Nay, let's follow him.

[*Exeunt.*

SCENE V. *Another part of the platform.*

Enter GHOST *and* HAMLET.

Ham. Whither wilt thou lead me? speak;
I'll go no further.

Ghost. Mark me.

Ham.   I will.

Ghost.   My hour is almost come,
When I to sulphurous and tormenting flames
Must render up myself.

Ham.   Alas, poor ghost!

Ghost. Pity me not, but lend thy serious hearing
To what I shall unfold.

Ham.   Speak; I am bound to hear.

Ghost. So art thou to revenge, when thou shalt hear.

Ham. What?

Ghost. I am thy father's spirit,
Doom'd for a certain term to walk the night, 10
And for the day confined to fast in fires,
Till the foul crimes done in my days of nature
Are burnt and purged away. But that I am forbid
To tell the secrets of my prison-house,
I could a tale unfold whose lightest word
Would harrow up thy soul, freeze thy young blood,
Make thy two eyes, like stars, start from their spheres,
Thy knotted and combined locks to part
And each particular hair to stand an end,
Like quills upon the fretful porpentine[1]:   20
But this eternal blazon[2] must not be
To ears of flesh and blood. List, list, O, list!
If thou didst ever thy dear father love—

Ham. O God!

Ghost. Revenge his foul and most unnatural murder.[3]

Ham. Murder!

Ghost. Murder most foul, as in the best it is;
But this most foul, strange and unnatural.

Ham. Haste me to know 't, that I, with wings as swift
As meditation or the thought of love,   30
May sweep to my revenge.

Ghost.   I find thee apt;
And duller shouldst thou be than the fat weed
That roots itself in ease on Lethe wharf,[4]
Wouldst thou not stir in this. Now, Hamlet, hear:
'Tis given out that, sleeping in my orchard,
A serpent stung me; so the whole ear of Denmark
Is by a forged process of my death
Rankly abused: but know, thou noble youth,
The serpent that did sting thy father's life
Now wears his crown.

Ham.   O my prophetic soul! 40
My uncle!

Ghost. Ay, that incestuous, that adulterate[5] beast,
With witchcraft of his wit, with traitorous gifts,—
O wicked wit and gifts, that have the power
So to seduce!—won to his shameful lust
The will of my most seeming-virtuous queen:
O Hamlet, what a falling-off was there!
From me, whose love was of that dignity
That it went hand in hand even with the vow
I made to her in marriage, and to decline   50
Upon a wretch whose natural gifts were poor
To those of mine!
But, soft! methinks I scent the morning air;
Brief let me be. Sleeping within my orchard,
My custom always of the afternoon,
Upon my secure hour thy uncle stole,
With juice of cursed hebenon[6] in a vial,
And in the porches of my ears did pour
The leperous distillment; whose effect

---

1. *porpentine*, porcupine. 2. *eternal blazon*, revelation of the hereafter. 3. *unnatural murder*, murder of a brother, fratricide. 4. *fat weed . . . Lethe* (lē'thi) *wharf*, a plant, never clearly identified, growing along the wharves of Lethe, the river of forgetfulness in Hades. 5. *adulterate*, adulterous. 6. *hebenon*, probably *henbane*, a poisonous plant, coarse and bad-smelling.

Holds such an enmity with blood of man   60
That swift as quicksilver it courses through
The natural gates and alleys of the body,
And with a sudden vigor it doth posset[7]
And curd, like eager droppings into milk,
The thin and wholesome blood: so did it
   mine;
And a most instant tetter bark'd about,
Most lazar-like,[8] with vile and loathsome
   crust,
All my smooth body.
Thus was I, sleeping, by a brother's hand
Of life, of crown, of queen, at once
   dispatch'd[9]:   70
Cut off even in the blossoms of my sin,
Unhousel'd, disappointed, unaneled,[10]
No reckoning made, but sent to my
   account
With all my imperfections on my head:
O, horrible! O, horrible! most horrible!
If thou hast nature in thee, bear it not;
Let not the royal bed of Denmark be
A couch for luxury and damned incest.
But, howsoever thou pursuest this act,
Taint not thy mind, nor let thy soul
   contrive   80
Against thy mother aught: leave her to
   heaven
And to those thorns that in her bosom lodge,
To prick and sting her. Fare thee well at
   once!
The glow-worm shows the matin to be near,
And 'gins to pale his uneffectual fire:
Adieu, adieu! Hamlet, remember me.   [*Exit.*
   Ham. O all you host of heaven! O earth!
   what else?
And shall I couple hell? O, fie! Hold, hold,
   my heart;
And you, my sinews, grow not instant old,
But bear me stiffly up. Remember thee!   90
Ay, thou poor ghost, while memory holds a
   seat
In this distracted globe.[11] Remember thee!
Yea, from the table of my memory
I'll wipe away all trivial fond[12] records,
All saws of books, all forms, all pressures[13]
   past,
That youth and observation copied there;
And thy commandment all alone shall live
Within the book and volume of my brain,

Unmix'd with baser matter: yes, by heaven!
O most pernicious woman!   100
O villain, villain, smiling, damned villain!
My tables,[14]—meet it is I set it down,
That one may smile; and smile, and be a
   villain;
At least I'm sure it may be so in Denmark:
   [*Writing.*
So, uncle, there you are. Now to my word;
It is "Adieu, adieu! remember me."
I have sworn 't.
   Mar.⎱ [*Within*] My lord, my lord,—
   Hor.⎰
   Mar.   [*Within*] Lord Hamlet,—
   Hor.   [*Within*] Heaven secure him!
   Ham. So be it!
   Mar. [*Within*] Hillo, ho, ho,[15] my lord!   110
   Ham. Hillo, ho, ho, boy! come, bird, come.

Enter HORATIO *and* MARCELLUS.

   Mar. How is 't, my noble lord?
   Hor.   What news, my lord?
   Ham. O, wonderful!
   Hor.   Good my lord, tell it.
   Ham. No; you'll reveal it.
   Hor. Not I, my lord, by heaven.
   Mar.   Nor I, my lord.
   Ham. How say you, then; would heart of
   man once think it?
But you'll be secret?
   Hor.⎱
   Mar.⎰   Ay, by heaven, my lord.
   Ham. There's ne'er a villain dwelling in all
   Denmark
But he's an arrant knave.
   Hor. There needs no ghost, my lord, come
   from the grave   120
To tell us this.
   Ham.   Why, right; you are i' the right;
And so, without more circumstance at all,
I hold it fit that we shake hands and part:

---

7. *posset*, coagulate, curdle. 8. *tetter bark'd about . . . lazar-like*, the skin became covered with a barklike substance similar to leprosy. 9. *dispatch'd*, deprived of. 10. *Unhousel'd . . . unaneled*, without having received Communion, unprepared for death, without having received extreme unction. 11. *distracted globe*, confused head. 12. *fond*, foolish. 13. *saws . . . pressures*, maxims, images, impressions. 14. *tables*, writing tablet. 15. *Hillo, ho, ho*, a falconer's call to a hawk in air.

You, as your business and desire shall point
    you;
For every man has business and desire,
Such as it is; and for mine own poor part,
Look you, I'll go pray.
   Hor. These are but wild and whirling words,
    my lord.
   Ham. I'm sorry they offend you, heartily;
Yes, 'faith, heartily.
   Hor.   There's no offence, my lord.
   Ham. Yes, by Saint Patrick,[16] but there is,
    Horatio,   131
And much offence too. Touching this vision
    here,
It is an honest ghost, that let me tell you:
For your desire to know what is between us,
O'ermaster 't as you may. And now, good
    friends,
As you are friends, scholars and soldiers,
Give me one poor request.
   Hor. What is 't, my lord? we will.
   Ham. Never make known what you have
    seen to-night.
   Hor. ⎱
   Mar. ⎰ My lord, we will not.
   Ham.   Nay, but swear 't.
   Hor.   In faith,   140
My lord, not I.
   Mar.   Nor I, my lord, in faith.
   Ham. Upon my sword.
   Mar.   We have sworn, my lord, already.
   Ham. Indeed, upon my sword, indeed.
   Ghost. [*Beneath*] Swear.
   Ham. Ah, ha, boy! say'st thou so? art thou
    there, truepenny?[17]
Come on—you hear this fellow in the
    cellarage—
Consent to swear.
   Hor.   Propose the oath, my lord.
   Ham. Never to speak of this that you have
    seen,
Swear by my sword.
   Ghost. [*Beneath*] Swear.   150
   Ham. Hic et ubique?[18] then we'll shift our
    ground.
Come hither, gentlemen,
And lay your hands again upon my sword:
Swear by my sword,
Never to speak of this that you have
    heard.

   Ghost. [*Beneath*] Swear by his sword.
   Ham. Well said, old mole! canst work i' the
    earth so fast?
A worthy pioner![19] Once more remove, good
    friends.
   Hor. O day and night, but this is wondrous
    strange!
   Ham. And therefore as a stranger give it
    welcome.   160
There are more things in heaven and earth,
    Horatio,
Than are dreamt of in your philosophy.
But come;
Here, as before, never, so help you mercy,
How strange or odd soe'er I bear myself,
As I perchance hereafter shall think meet
To put an antic[20] disposition on,
That you, at such times seeing me, never
    shall,
With arms encumber'd[21] thus, or this
    head-shake,
Or by pronouncing of some doubtful
    phrase,
As "Well, well, we know," or "We could, an
    if we would,"   171
Or "If we list to speak," or "There be, an if
    they might,"
Or such ambiguous giving out, to note
That you know aught of me: this not to do,
So grace and mercy at your most need help
    you,
Swear.
   Ghost. [*Beneath*] Swear.
   Ham. Rest, rest, perturbed spirit! [*They
    swear.*] So, gentlemen,
With all my love I do commend me to you:
And what so poor a man as Hamlet is   180
May do, to express his love and friending to
    you,
God willing, shall not lack. Let us go in
    together;
And still your fingers on your lips, I pray.
The time is out of joint: O cursed spite,
That ever I was born to set it right!
Nay, come, let 's go together.   [*Exeunt.*

---

16. *Saint Patrick.* St. Patrick was keeper of Purgatory and
patron saint of all blunders and confusion. 17. *truepenny,*
good old boy, or the like. 18. *Hic et ubique,* here and
everywhere. 19. *pioner,* digger, miner. 20. *antic,* fantastic. 21. *encumber'd,* folded or entwined.

❊ To increase understanding
Act I, Scene 1

1. Unlike the short-story writer or novelist, who can devote paragraphs to *exposition*, the dramatist must use dialogue alone to convey necessary information about past events and about the initial situation. (*a*) What is the scene as the play opens? (*b*) Why are the soldiers uneasy? (*c*) How does their dialogue reveal their uneasiness? (*d*) What conflict exists between the state of Denmark and the state of Norway? (*e*) What effect is this conflict having on Denmark? (*f*) What sort of man had King Hamlet been?

2. What indication of future action do you find in this scene?

Scene 2

1. (*a*) What do you learn in this scene about the present King of Denmark? (*b*) Contrast him with Hamlet's father.

2. What is Hamlet's reaction to the Queen's marriage to the present King?

3. (*a*) Cite lines that reveal Hamlet's general state of mind. (*b*) Explain why he feels as he does.

4. How does this scene advance the action concerning the enmity between Denmark and Norway?

Scene 3

1. (*a*) How do Laertes and Polonius regard Hamlet's courtship of Ophelia? (*b*) What advice do they give Ophelia?

2. (*a*) Summarize the advice Polonius gives to his son. (*b*) Explain the implications of the statement "Give thy thoughts no tongue, /Nor any unproportion'd thought his act" (lines 52–53). (*c*) Do you think Polonius' advice is sound? Why, or why not?

Scene 4

1. What seems to be the purpose of this short scene?

2. Explain Hamlet's comparison of the state and the individual in lines 23–38.

Scene 5

1. What revelation does the Ghost make to Hamlet?

2. Reread the conversation between Hamlet, Horatio, and Marcellus (lines 112–186). (*a*) How would you describe Hamlet's speeches in this conversation? (*b*) Upon what subject does Hamlet pledge his friends to secrecy? (*c*) Do you see any connection between his desire for secrecy and his behavior? (*d*) Do you see any connection between Hamlet's behavior and the things that have happened to him and his family?

Act I in Review

1. (*a*) What major conflict is set in motion in Act I? (*b*) Do you foresee any additional conflicts?

2. What function does the Ghost serve in the development of the plot?

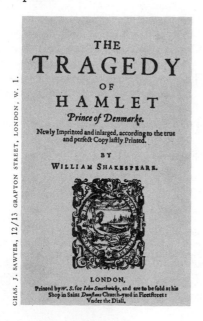

A facsimile of the fourth quarto edition title page, printed about 1630.

ACT TWO

SCENE I. *A room in Polonius' house.*

Enter POLONIUS *and* REYNALDO.

Pol. Give him this money and these notes,
Reynaldo.
Rey. I will, my lord.
Pol. You shall do marvelous wisely, good
Reynaldo,
Before you visit him, to make inquire
Of his behavior.
Rey.   My lord, I did intend it.
Pol. Marry, well said; very well said. Look
you, sir,
Inquire me first what Danskers[1] are in Paris;
And how, and who, what means, and where
they keep,
What company, at what expense; and finding
By this encompassment and drift of question[2] [10]
That they do know my son, come you more
nearer
Than your particular demands[3] will touch it:
Take you, as 'twere, some distant knowledge
of him;
As thus, "I know his father and his friends,
And in part him:" do you mark this,
Reynaldo?
Rey. Ay, very well, my lord.
Pol. "And in part him; but" you may say
"not well:
But, if 't be he I mean, he's very wild;
Addicted so and so:" and there put on him
What forgeries[4] you please; marry, none so
rank   20
As may dishonor him; take heed of that;
But, sir, such wanton, wild and usual slips
As are companions noted and most known
To youth and liberty.
Rey.   As gaming, my lord.
Pol. Ay, or drinking, fencing, swearing,
quarreling,
Drabbing[5]: you may go so far.
Rey. My lord, that would dishonor him.
Pol. 'Faith, no; as you may season it in the
charge.[6]
You must not put another scandal on him,
That he is open to incontinency;   30

That's not my meaning: but breathe his
faults so quaintly
That they may seem the taints of liberty,
The flash and outbreak of a fiery mind,
A savageness in unreclaimed blood,
Of general assault.[7]
Rey.   But, my good lord,—
Pol. Wherefore should you do this?
Rey.   Ay my lord,
I would know that.
Pol.   Marry, sir, here's my drift;
And, I believe, it is a fetch of wit[8]:
You laying these slight sullies on my son,
As 'twere a thing a little soil'd i' the
working,   40
Mark you,
Your party in converse, him you would
sound,
Having ever seen in the prenominate[9] crimes
The youth you breathe of guilty, be assured
He closes with you in this consequence[10];
"Good sir," or so, or "friend," or "gentleman,"
According to the phrase or the addition
Of man and country.
Rey.   Very good, my lord.
Pol. And then, sir, does he this—he does—
what was I about to say? By the mass, I was
about to say something: where did I leave?   51
Rey. At "closes in the consequence," at
"friend or so," and "gentleman."
Pol. At "closes in the consequence," ay,
marry;
He closes thus: "I know the gentleman;
I saw him yesterday, or t' other day,
Or then, or then; with such, or such; and, as
you say,
There was a' gaming; there o'ertook in 's
rouse[11];
There falling out at tennis." See you now;
Your bait of falsehood takes this carp of
truth: 60
And thus do we of wisdom and of reach,[12]

---

1. *Danskers,* Danes.   2. *encompassment and drift of question,* roundabout, gradual inquiry.   3. *particular demands,* direct questions.   4. *forgeries,* fabrications.   5. *Drabbing,* associating with immoral women.   6. *season it in the charge,* soften the charge by the way in which you state it.   7. *savageness . . . of general assault,* a tendency common to untamed youth.   8. *fetch of wit,* clever trick.   9. *prenominate,* previously named.   10. *closes . . . consequence,* agrees with you as follows.   11. *o'ertook in's rouse,* overcome by liquor.   12. *reach,* comprehension.

With windlasses[13] and with assays of bias,[14]
By indirections find directions out:
So by my former lecture and advice,
Shall you my son. You have me, have you
    not?
  Rey. My lord, I have.
  Pol.   God be wi' you; fare you well.
  Rey. Good my lord!
  Pol. Observe his inclination in yourself.[15]
  Rey. I shall, my lord.   69
  Pol. And let him ply his music.
  Rey.   Well, my lord.
  Pol. Farewell!   [*Exit* REYNALDO.

Enter OPHELIA.

      How now, Ophelia! what's the matter?
  Oph. O, my lord, my lord, I have been so
  affrighted!
  Pol. With what, i' the name of God?
  Oph. My lord, as I was sewing in my
  closet,[16]
Lord Hamlet, with his doublet all unbraced;
No hat upon his head; his stockings foul'd,
Ungarter'd, and down-gyved[17] to his ankle;
Pale as his shirt; his knees knocking each
    other;
And with a look so piteous in purport
As if he had been loosed out of hell   80
To speak of horrors,—he comes before me.
  Pol. Mad for thy love?
  Oph.   My lord, I do not know;
But truly, I do fear it.
  Pol.   What said he?
  Oph. He took me by the wrist and held
  me hard;
Then goes he to the length of all his arm;
And, with his other hand thus o'er his brow,
He falls to such perusal of my face
As he would draw it. Long stay'd he so;
At last, a little shaking of mine arm
And thrice his head thus waving up and
    down,   90
He raised a sigh so piteous and profound
As it did seem to shatter all his bulk
And end his being: that done, he lets me go:
And, with his head over his shoulder turn'd,
He seem'd to find his way without his eyes;
For out o' doors he went without their helps,
And, to the last, bended their light on me.

  Pol. Come, go with me: I will go seek the
  king.
This is the very ecstasy of love,
Whose violent property fordoes itself[18]   100
And leads the will to desperate undertakings
As oft as any passion under heaven
That does afflict our natures. I am sorry.
What, have you given him any hard words
  of late?
  Oph. No, my good lord, but, as you did
  command,
I did repel his letters and denied
His access to me.
  Pol.   That hath made him mad.
I am sorry that with better heed and
  judgment
I had not quoted [19] him: I fear'd he did but
  trifle,
And meant to wreck thee; but, beshrew my
  jealousy![20]   110
By heaven, it is as proper to our age
To cast beyond ourselves in our opinions
As it is common for the younger sort
To lack discretion. Come, go we to the king:
This must be known; which, being kept
  close, might move
More grief to hide than hate to utter love.[21]
                    [*Exeunt.*

SCENE II. *A room in the castle.*

Enter KING, QUEEN, ROSENCRANTZ,
GUILDENSTERN, *and* ATTENDANTS.

  King. Welcome, dear Rosencrantz and
  Guildenstern!
Moreover that we much did long to see you,
The need we have to use you did provoke
Our hasty sending. Something have you
  heard
Of Hamlet's transformation; so call it,

---

13. *windlasses,* here used to mean "circuitous paths."
14. *assays of bias,* oblique approaches (a term from bowling). 15. *in yourself,* with your own eyes. 16. *closet,*
private chamber. 17. *down-gyved,* fallen. 18. *Whose*
violent property fordoes itself, whose violent nature destroys
itself. 19. *quoted,* observed. 20. *beshrew my jealousy,*
curse my suspicion. 21. *might . . . love,* might cause more
grief to others than hatred of me and my family. Polonius
is worried that the king and queen will disapprove of
Hamlet's loving someone of a lower rank.

Sith nor the exterior nor the inward man
Resembles that it was. What it should be,
More than his father's death, that thus hath
    put him
So much from the understanding of himself,
I cannot dream of: I entreat you both,   10
That, being of so young days brought up
    with him,
And sith so neighbor'd to his youth and
    havior,
That you vouchsafe your rest[1] here in our
    court
Some little time: so by your companies
To draw him on to pleasures, and to gather,
So much as from occasion you may glean,
Whether aught, to us unknown, afflicts him
    thus,
That, open'd, lies within our remedy.
    Queen. Good gentlemen, he hath much
        talk'd of you;
And sure I am two men there are not living [20]
To whom he more adheres. If it will please
    you
To show us so much gentry and good will
As to expend your time with us awhile,
For the supply and profit of our hope,
Your visitation shall receive such thanks
As fits a king's remembrance.
    Ros.   Both your majesties
Might, by the sovereign power you have of
    us,
Put your dread pleasures more into command
Than to entreaty.
    Guil.   But we both obey,
And here give up ourselves, in the full bent [30]
To lay our service freely at your feet,
To be commanded.
    King. Thanks, Rosencrantz and gentle
        Guildenstern.
    Queen. Thanks, Guildenstern and gentle
        Rosencrantz:
And I beseech you instantly to visit
My too much changed son. Go, some of you,
And bring these gentlemen where Hamlet is.
    Guil. Heavens make our presence and our
        practices
Pleasant and helpful to him!
    Queen.   Ay, amen!
        [*Exeunt* ROSENCRANTZ, GUILDENSTERN,
                and some ATTENDANTS.

Enter POLONIUS.

    Pol. The ambassadors from Norway, my
        good lord,   40
Are joyfully return'd.
    King. Thou still has been the father of
        good news.
    Pol. Have I, my lord? I assure my good
        liege,
I hold my duty, as I hold my soul,
Both to my God and to my gracious king:
And I do think, or else this brain of mine
Hunts not the trail of policy so sure
As it hath used to do, that I have found
The very cause of Hamlet's lunacy.
    King. O, speak of that; that do I long to
        hear.   50
    Pol. Give first admittance to the
        ambassadors;
My news shall be the fruit[2] to that great
    feast.
    King. Thyself do grace to them, and
        bring them in.   [*Exit* POLONIUS.
He tells me, my dear Gertrude, he hath found
The head and source of all your son's
    distemper.
    Queen. I doubt it is no other but the main;
His father's death, and our o'erhasty
    marriage.
    King. Well, we shall sift him.

Re-enter POLONIUS, *with* VOLTIMAND *and*
CORNELIUS.

                    Welcome, my good friends!
Say, Voltimand, what from our brother
    Norway?
    Volt. Most fair return of greetings and
        desires.   60
Upon our first,[3] he sent out to suppress
His nephew's levies; which to him appear'd
To be a preparation 'gainst the Polack;
But, better look'd into, he truly found
It was against your highness: whereat grieved,
That so his sickness, age and impotence
Was falsely borne in hand,[4] sends out arrests
On Fortinbras; which he, in brief, obeys;

---

1. *vouchsafe your rest*, deign to stay.   2. *fruit*, dessert.
3. *Upon our first*, at our first audience.   4. *falsely borne
in hand*, deceived.

Receives rebuke from Norway, and in fine
Makes vow before his uncle never more   70
To give the assay of arms against your
   majesty.
Whereon old Norway, overcome with joy,
Gives him three score thousand crowns in
   annual fee,
And his commission to employ those soldiers,
So levied as before, against the Polack:
With an entreaty, herein further shown,
               [*Giving a paper.*
That it might please you to give quiet pass
Through your dominions for this enterprise,
On such regards of safety and allowance
As therein are set down.
   King.   It likes[5] us well;   80
And at our more consider'd time we'll read,
Answer, and think upon this business.
Meantime we thank you for your well-took
   labor:
Go to your rest; at night we'll feast together:
Most welcome home!
       [*Exeunt* VOLTIMAND *and* CORNELIUS.
   Pol.   This business is well ended.
My liege, and madam, to expostulate
What majesty should be, what duty is,
Why day is day, night night, and time is time,
Were nothing but to waste night, day and
   time.
Therefore, since brevity is the soul of wit,[6] 90
And tediousness the limbs and outward
   flourishes,
I will be brief: your noble son is mad:
Mad call I it; for, to define true madness,
What is 't but to be nothing else but mad?
But let that go.
   Queen.   More matter, with less art.
   Pol. Madam, I swear I use no art at all.
That he is mad, 'tis true: 'tis true 'tis pity;
And pity 'tis 'tis true: a foolish figure[7];
But farewell it, for I will use no art.
Mad let us grant him, then: and now
   remains   100
That we find out the cause of this effect,
Or rather say, the cause of this defect,
For this effect defective comes by cause:
Thus it remains, and the remainder thus.
Perpend.[8]
I have a daughter—have while she is mine—
Who, in her duty and obedience, mark,

Hath given me this: now gather, and
   surmise.   [*Reads.*
To the celestial and my soul's idol, the most
beautified Ophelia—   110
That's an ill phrase, a vile phrase; *beautified*
is a vile phrase: but you shall hear. Thus:
                          [*Reads.*
In her excellent white bosom, these, &c.
   Queen. Came this from Hamlet to her?
   Pol. Good madam, stay awhile; I will be
   faithful.   [*Reads.*
   Doubt thou the stars are fire;
     Doubt that the sun doth move;
   Doubt truth to be a liar;
     But never doubt I love.   119
O dear Ophelia, I am ill at these numbers[9];
I have not art to reckon my groans[10]: *but that*
I love thee best, O most best, believe it. Adieu.
     Thine evermore, most dear lady, whilst
         this machine[11] *is to him,* HAMLET.
This, in obedience, hath my daughter shown
   me,
And more above, hath his solicitings,
As they fell out by time, by means and place,
All given to mine ear.
   King.   But how hath she
Received his love?
   Pol.   What do you think of me?
   King. As of a man faithful and honorable.
   Pol. I would fain prove so. But what might
   you think,   131
When I had seen this hot love on the wing—
As I perceived it, I must tell you that,
Before my daughter told me—what might
   you,
Or my dear majesty your queen here, think,
If I had play'd the desk or table-book,[12]
Or given my heart a winking,[13] mute and
   dumb,
Or look'd upon this love with idle sight;
What might you think? No, I went round to
   work,
And my young mistress thus I did
   bespeak: 140

---

5. *likes*, pleases. **6.** *wit*, wisdom, understanding. **7.** *figure*, figure of speech. **8.** *Perpend*, consider. **9.** *ill at these numbers*, unskilled in writing verses. **10.** *reckon my groans*, sum up my love. **11.** *machine*, body. **12.** *play'd the desk or table-book*, remained shut up, concealed the information. **13.** *given my heart a winking*, given my heart a signal to keep quiet.

"Lord Hamlet is a prince, out of thy star[14];
This must not be:" and then I prescripts
    gave her,
That she should lock herself from his resort,
Admit no messengers, receive no tokens.
Which done, she took the fruits of my
    advice;
And he, repelled—a short tale to make—
Fell into a sadness, then into a fast,
Thence to a watch, thence into a weakness,
Thence to a lightness, and, by this
    declension,[15]
Into the madness wherein now he raves,   150
And all we mourn for.
    King.   Do you think 'tis this?
    Queen. It may be, very like.
    Pol. Hath there been such a time—I 'd
        fain know that—
That I have positively said " 'Tis so,"
When it proved otherwise?
    King.   Not that I know.
    Pol. [*Pointing to his head and shoulder*]
Take this from this, if this be otherwise:
If circumstances lead me, I will find
Where truth is hid, though it were hid
    indeed
Within the center.
    King.   How may we try it further?
    Pol. You know, sometimes he walks four
        hours together   160
Here in the lobby.
    Queen.   So he does indeed.
    Pol. At such a time I'll loose my daughter
        to him:
Be you and I behind an arras then;
Mark the encounter: if he love her not
And be not from his reason fall'n thereon,
Let me be no assistant for a state,
But keep a farm and carters.
    King.   We will try it.
    Queen. But, look, where sadly the poor
        wretch comes reading.
    Pol. Away, I do beseech you, both away:
I'll board him presently.

    [*Exeunt* KING, QUEEN, *and* ATTENDANTS.

   Enter HAMLET, *reading.*

          O, give me leave: 170
How does my good Lord Hamlet?

    Ham. Well, God-a-mercy.
    Pol. Do you know me, my lord?
    Ham. Excellent well; you are a fishmonger.
    Pol. Not I, my lord.
    Ham. Then I would you were so honest a
man.
    Pol. Honest, my lord!
    Ham. Ay, sir; to be honest, as this world
goes, is to be one man picked out of ten
thousand.   181
    Pol. That 's very true, my lord.
    Ham. For if the sun breed maggots in a
dead dog, being a god kissing carrion,[16]—Have
you a daughter?
    Pol. I have, my lord.
    Ham. Let her not walk i' the sun: con-
ception is a blessing: but not as your daughter
may conceive. Friend, look to 't.   189
    Pol. [*Aside*] How say you by that? Still
harping on my daughter: yet he knew me not
at first; he said I was a fishmonger: he is far
gone: and truly in my youth I suffered much
extremity for love; very near this. I'll speak to
him again. What do you read, my lord?
    Ham. Words, words, words.
    Pol. What is the matter, my lord?
    Ham. Between who?
    Pol. I mean, the matter that you read, my
lord.   200
    Ham. Slanders, sir: for the satirical rogue
says here that old men have grey beards, that
their faces are wrinkled, their eyes purging
thick amber and plum-tree gum and that they
have a plentiful lack of wit, together with most
weak hams: all which, sir, though I most powerfully and potently believe, yet I hold it not
honesty to have it thus set down, for yourself,
sir, should be old as I am, if like a crab you
could go backward.   210
    Pol. [*Aside*] Though this be madness, yet
there is method in 't. Will you walk out of the
air, my lord?
    Ham. Into my grave.
    Pol. Indeed, that is out o' the air. [*Aside*]
How pregnant sometimes his replies are! a
happiness that often madness hits on, which

---

14. *out of thy star,* above you in rank. 15. *declension,*
decline. 16. *god kissing carrion,* the sun god shining on
a dead body. Elizabethans believed that maggots and other
organisms were generated directly by the sun.

reason and sanity could not so prosperously be delivered of. I will leave him, and suddenly contrive the means of meeting between him and my daughter.—My honorable lord, I will most humbly take my leave of you.   222

Ham. You cannot, sir, take from me any thing that I will more willingly part withal: except my life, except my life, except my life.

Pol. Fare you well, my lord.

Ham. These tedious old fools!

Enter ROSENCRANTZ *and* GUILDENSTERN.

Pol. You go to seek the Lord Hamlet; there he is.   230

Ros. [*To Polonius*] God save you, sir!
                                    [*Exit* POLONIUS.

Guil. My honored lord!

Ros. My most dear lord!

Ham. My excellent good friends! How dost thou, Guildenstern? Ah, Rosencrantz! Good lads, how do ye both?

Ros. As the indifferent children of the earth.

Guil. Happy, in that we are not over-happy; On fortune's cap we are not the very button. 240

Ham. Nor the soles of her shoe?

Ros. Neither, my lord.

Ham. What's the news?

Ros. None, my lord, but that the world's grown honest.

Ham. Then is doomsday near: but your news is not true. Let me question more in particular: what have you, my good friends, deserved at the hands of fortune, that she sends you to prison hither?   250

Guil. Prison, my lord!

Ham. Denmark's a prison.

Ros. Then is the world one.

Ham. A goodly one; in which there are many confines, wards and dungeons, Denmark being one o' the worst.

Ros. We think not so, my lord.

Ham. Why, then, 'tis none to you; for there is nothing either good or bad, but thinking makes it so: to me it is a prison.   260

Ros. Why then, your ambition makes it one; 'tis too narrow for your mind.

Ham. O God, I could be bounded in a nutshell and count myself a king of infinite space, were it not that I have bad dreams.

Guil. Which dreams indeed are ambition, for the very substance of the ambitious is merely the shadow of a dream.

Ham. A dream itself is but a shadow.   269

Ros. Truly, and I hold ambition of so airy and light a quality that it is but a shadow's shadow.

Ham. Then are our beggars bodies, and our monarchs and outstretched heroes the beggars' shadows.[17] Shall we to the court? for, by my fay, I cannot reason.

Ros. ⎫
Guil. ⎬ We'll wait upon you.   278

Ham. No such matter: I will not sort you with the rest of my servants, for, to speak to you like an honest man, I am most dreadfully attended. But, in the beaten way of friendship,[18] what make you at Elsinore?

Ros. To visit you, my lord; no other occasion.

Ham. Beggar that I am, I am even poor in thanks; but I thank you: and sure, dear friends, my thanks are too dear a halfpenny. Were you not sent for? Is it your own inclining? Is it a free visitation? Come, deal justly with me: come, come; nay, speak.   291

Guil. What should we say, my lord?

Ham. Why, any thing, but to the purpose. You were sent for; and there is a kind of confession in your looks which your modesties have not craft enough to color: I know the good king and queen have sent for you.

Ros. To what end, my lord?   298

Ham. That you must teach me. But let me conjure you, by the rights of our fellowship, by the consonancy of our youth, by the obligation of our ever-preserved love, and by what more dear a better proposer could charge you withal, be even and direct with me, whether you were sent for, or no?

Ros. [*Aside to Guil.*] What say you?

Ham. [*Aside*] Nay, then, I have an eye of you.—If you love me, hold not off.

Guil. My lord, we were sent for.   309

Ham. I will tell you why; so shall my anticipation prevent your discovery, and your se-

---

17. *beggars bodies . . . beggars' shadows,* if ambition is but the shadow of a shadow, then beggars, who have no ambition, are solid substance and kings and heroes, who are ruled by ambition, are shadows. **18.** *in the . . . friendship,* as old friends.

crecy to the king and queen moult no feather. I have of late—but wherefore I know not—lost all my mirth, forgone all custom of exercises; and indeed it goes so heavily with my disposition that this goodly frame, the earth, seems to me a sterile promontory, this most excellent canopy, the air, look you, this brave o'erhanging firmament, this majestical roof fretted with golden fire, why, it appears no other thing to me than a foul and pestilent congregation of vapors. What a piece of work is a man! how noble in reason! how infinite in faculty! in form and moving how express and admirable! in action how like an angel! in apprehension how like a god! the beauty of the world! the paragon of animals! And yet, to me, what is this quintessence of dust? man delights not me: no, nor woman neither, though by your smiling you seem to say so.   330

Ros. My lord, there was no such stuff in my thoughts.

Ham. Why did you laugh then, when I said "man delights not me"?

Ros. To think, my lord, if you delight not in man, what lenten entertainment the players shall receive from you: we coted[19] them on the way; and hither are they coming, to offer you service.   339

Ham. He that plays the king shall be welcome; his majesty shall have tribute of me; the adventurous knight shall use his foil and target[20]; the lover shall not sigh gratis; the humorous man[21] shall end his part in peace; the clown shall make those laugh whose lungs are tickle o' the sere[22]; and the lady shall say her mind freely, or the blank verse shall halt for 't. What players are they?

Ros. Even those you were wont to take delight in, the tragedians of the city.   350

Ham. How chances it they travel? their residence, both in reputation and profit, was better both ways.

Ros. I think their inhibition[23] comes by the means of the late innovation.[24]

Ham. Do they hold the same estimation they did when I was in the city? are they so followed?

Ros. No, indeed, are they not.   359

Ham. How comes it? do they grow rusty?

Ros. Nay, their endeavor keeps in the wonted pace: but there is, sir, an aery of children, little eyases, that cry out on the top of question,[25] and are most tyrannically[26] clapped for 't: these are now the fashion, and so berattle the common stages—so they call them—that many wearing rapiers are afraid of goosequills and dare scarce come thither.[27]   368

Ham. What, are they children? who maintains 'em? how are they escoted?[28] Will they pursue the quality no longer than they can sing?[29] will they not say afterwards, if they should grow themselves to common players—as it is most like, if their means are no better—their writers do them wrong, to make them exclaim against their own succession?   376

Ros. 'Faith, there has been much to do on both sides; and the nation holds it no sin to tarre[30] them to controversy: there was, for a while, no money bid for argument,[31] unless the poet and the player went to cuffs in the question.

Ham. Is 't possible?

Guil. O, there has been much throwing about of brains.

Ham. Do the boys carry it away?

Ros. Ay, that they do, my lord; Hercules and his load too.[32]   383

Ham. It is not very strange; for mine uncle is king of Denmark, and those that would make mows[33] at him while my father lived, give twenty, forty, fifty, an hundred ducats a-piece for his picture in little.[34] 'Sblood, there is something in this more than natural, if philosophy could find it out.

---

19. *coted,* passed. **20.** *foil and target,* sword and shield. **21.** *humorous man,* the man who plays a particular "humor" (disposition) as, for example, "melancholy." **22.** *tickle o' the sere,* easy on the trigger. **23.** *inhibition,* formal prohibition (from acting in the city). **24.** *innovation,* the increased popularity of the acting company at Blackfriars Theatre, which was composed entirely of children. **25.** *cry out on the top of question,* declaim in shrill voices. **26.** *tyrannically,* outrageously. **27.** *many wearing . . . thither,* many men of fashion do not attend the public playhouses for fear of being satirized by the poets writing for the boy actors at Blackfriars. **28.** *escoted,* supported. **29.** *pursue . . . can sing,* follow the profession only until their voices change. **30.** *tarre,* incite. **31.** *no money bid for argument,* no play accepted (for production). **32.** *Hercules and his load too.* Shakespeare's own company (the Globe Theater, whose sign was that of Hercules bearing the world on his shoulders) seems to have suffered from the competition of the boy actors. **33.** *mows,* grimaces. **34.** *picture in little,* miniature. This refers to the many miniatures in Elizabethan times.

[Flourish of trumpets within.

Guil. There are the players.   397

Ham. Gentlemen, you are welcome to Elsinore. Your hands, come then: the appurtenance of welcome is fashion and ceremony: let me comply with you in this garb,[35] lest my extent[36] to the players, which, I tell you, must show fairly outward, should more appear like entertainment than yours. You are welcome: but my uncle-father and aunt-mother are deceived.

Guil. In what, my dear lord?

Ham. I am but mad north-north-west: when the wind is southerly I know a hawk from a handsaw.[37]   410

Re-enter POLONIUS.

Pol. Well be with you, gentlemen!

Ham. Hark you, Guildenstern; and you too: at each ear a hearer: that great baby you see there is not yet out of his swaddling-clouts.

Ros. Happily[38] he 's the second time come to them; for they say an old man is twice a child.

Ham. I will prophesy he comes to tell me of the players; mark it.—You say right, sir: o' Monday morning; 'twas so indeed.   421

Pol. My lord, I have news to tell you.

Ham. My lord, I have news to tell you. When Roscius[39] was an actor in Rome,—

Pol. The actors are come hither, my lord.

Ham. Buz, buz!

Pol. Upon mine honor,—   427

Ham. Then came each actor on his ass,—

Pol. The best actors in the world, either for tragedy, comedy, history, pastoral, pastoral-comical, historical-pastoral, tragical-historical, tragical-comical-historical-pastoral, scene individable,[40] or poem unlimited[41]: Seneca[42] cannot be too heavy, nor Plautus[43] too light. For the law of writ and the liberty,[44] these are the only men.

Ham. O Jephthah,[45] judge of Israel, what a treasure hadst thou!

Pol. What a treasure had he, my lord?

Ham. Why,   440

One fair daughter, and no more,
    The which he loved passing well.

Pol. [*Aside*] Still on my daughter.

Ham. Am I not i' the right, old Jephthah?

Pol. If you call me Jephthah, my lord, I have a daughter that I love passing well.

Ham. Nay, that follows not.

Pol. What follows, then, my lord?

Ham. Why,   449

As by lot, God wot,

and then, you know,

It came to pass, as most like it was,—

the first row[46] of the pious chanson will show you more; for look, where my abridgement[47] comes.   455

Enter four or five PLAYERS.

You are welcome, masters; welcome, all. I am glad to see thee well. Welcome, good friends. O, my old friend! thy face is valanced[48] since I saw thee last: comest thou to beard me in Denmark? What, my young lady and mistress![49] By 'r lady, your ladyship is nearer to heaven than when I saw you last, by the altitude of a chopine.[50] Pray God, your voice, like a piece of uncurrent gold, be not cracked within the ring.[51] Masters, you are all welcome. We'll e'en to 't like French falconers, fly at any thing we see: we'll have a speech straight: come, give us a taste of your quality; come, a passionate speech.   470

First Play. What speech, my lord?

Ham. I heard thee speak me a speech once, but it was never acted; or, if it was, not above once; for the play, I remember, pleased not

35. *comply . . . garb*, observe the formalities of courtesy. 36. *extent*, extension of courtesy. 37. *I am but . . . handsaw*, I am only partly mad; at times I am as clear-headed as anyone. 38. *Happily*, perhaps. 39. *Roscius*, a famous Roman actor. This is Hamlet's way of saying that Polonius' news is old. 40. *scene individable*, a play that observes the unities which were laid down by the writers of classical antiquity. 41. *poem unlimited*, a play that disregards the classical unities. 42. *Seneca* (sen'ə kə), Roman dramatist whose "blood-and-thunder" tragedies were imitated by Elizabethan playwrights. 43. *Plautus* (plô'təs), Roman writer of farcical comedies. 44. *law of writ and the liberty*, following the rules faithfully or improvising. 45. *Jephthah*. Hamlet proceeds to quote a ballad about Jephthah's sacrifice of his daughter. (Judges 11:34-39.) 46. *row*, stanza. 47. *abridgement*, opportunity for cutting the conversation short. 48. *valanced*, fringed (with a beard). 49. *mistress*. Women's parts were played by boys in Elizabethan times. 50. *chopine*, a shoe with a thick sole. 51. *uncurrent . . . ring*. Gold pieces that were cracked through the ring surrounding the image of the ruling sovereign could not be lawfully passed.

the million; 'twas caviare to the general: but it was—as I received it, and others, whose judgments in such matters cried in the top of mine[52]—an excellent play, well digested in the scenes, set down with as much modesty as cunning. I remember, one said there were no sallets[53] in the lines to make the matter savory, nor no matter in the phrase that might indict the author of affectation; but called it an honest method, as wholesome as sweet, and by very much more handsome than fine. One speech in it I chiefly loved: 'twas Æneas'[54] tale to Dido[55]; and thereabout of it especially, where he speaks of Priam's[56] slaughter: if it live in your memory, begin at this line: let me see, let me see—   490

The rugged Pyrrhus,[57] like the Hyrcanian beast,[58]—

It is not so:—it begins with Pyrrhus:—

The rugged Pyrrhus, he whose sable arms,[59]

Black as his purpose, did the night resemble

When he lay couched in the ominous horse,[60]

With his eyes like carbuncles,[61] the hellish Pyrrhus

Old grandsire Priam seeks.

So, proceed you.

Pol. 'Fore God, my lord, well spoken, with good accent and good discretion.   500

First Play.   Anon he finds him

Striking too short at Greeks; his antique sword,

Rebellious to his arm, lies where it falls,

Repugnant to command: unequal match'd,

Pyrrhus at Priam drives; in rage strikes wide;

But with the whiff and wind of his fell sword

The unnerved father falls. Then senseless Ilium,[62]

Seeming to feel this blow, with flaming top

Stoops to his base, and with a hideous crash

Takes prisoner Pyrrhus' ear; for, lo! his sword,   510

Which was declining on the milky head

Of reverend Priam, seem'd i' the air to stick:

So, as a painted tyrant, Pyrrhus stood,

And like a neutral to his will and matter,

Did nothing.

But, as we often see, against some storm,

A silence in the heavens, the rack stand still,

The bold winds speechless and the orb below

As hush as death, anon the dreadful thunder

Doth rend the region, so, after Pyrrhus' pause,   520

Aroused vengeance sets him new a-work;

And never did the Cyclops' hammers fall

On Mars's armor forged for proof eterne[63]

With less remorse than Pyrrhus' bleeding sword

Now falls on Priam.

Out, out, thou strumpet, Fortune! All you gods,

In general synod, take away her power;

Break all the spokes and fellies[64] from her wheel,

And bowl the round nave down the hill of heaven,

As low as to the fiends!   530

Pol. This is too long.

Ham. It shall be to the barber's, with your beard. Prithee, say on: he 's for a jig or a tale of bawdry, or he sleeps: say on: come to Hecuba.[65]

First Play. But who, O, who had seen the mobled[66] queen—

Ham. "The mobled queen?"

Pol. That 's good; "mobled queen" is good.

First Play. Run barefoot up and down, threatening the flames

With bisson rheum,[67] a clout upon that head   540

---

52. *cried in the top of mine*, exceeded mine.   53. *sallets*, spicy bits.   54. *Aeneas* (i nē'əs), the Trojan hero of Vergil's *Aeneid*.   55. *Dido* (dī'dō), queen of Carthage.   56. *Priam* (prī'əm), king of Troy.   57. *Pyrrhus* (pir'əs), a Greek hero of the Trojan War.   58. *Hyrcanian* (hẻr kā'ni ən) *beast*, the tiger.   59. *sable arms*, the black heraldic device on his shield.   60. *ominous horse*, the wooden horse used by the Greeks to trick the Trojans.   61. *like carbuncles*, glowing red.   62. *senseless Ilium*, insensible Troy, the city now in flames.   63. *Cyclops' . . . proof eterne*. In Greek mythology, the Cyclops, or one-eyed giants, assisted Vulcan, the blacksmith for the other gods. Mars was the Roman god of war whose armor could resist assault eternally.   64. *fellies*, sections forming the rim of a wheel.   65. *Hecuba* (hek'ū bə), wife of Priam.   66. *mobled*, muffled.   67. *bisson rheum*, blinding tears.

Where late the diadem stood, and for a
*   robe,*
A blanket, in the alarm of fear caught up;
Who this had seen, with tongue in venom
*   steep'd,*
'Gainst Fortune's state would treason have
*   pronounced:*
But if the gods themselves did see her
*   then*
When she saw Pyrrhus make malicious
*   sport*
In mincing with his sword her husband's
*   limbs,*
The instant burst of clamor that she made,
Unless things mortal move them not at all,
Would have made milch[68] the burning
*   eyes of heaven,*   550
And passion in the gods.

Pol. Look, whether he has not turned his
color and has tears in 's eyes. Pray you, no
more.

Ham. 'Tis well; I'll have thee speak out the
rest soon. Good my lord, will you see the
players well bestowed? Do you hear, let them
be well used; for they are the abstract and
brief chronicles of the time: after your death
you were better have a bad epitaph than their
ill report while you live.   561

Pol. My lord, I will use them according to
their desert.

Ham. God's bodykins, man, much better:
use every man after his desert, and who should
'scape whipping? Use them after your own
honor and dignity: the less they deserve, the
more merit is in your bounty. Take them in.

Pol. Come, sirs.   569

Ham. Follow him, friends: we'll hear a play
to-morrow. [*Exit* POLONIUS *with all the* PLAY-
ERS *but the* FIRST.] Dost thou hear me, old
friend; can you play the Murder of Gonzago?

First Play. Ay, my lord.

Ham. We'll ha 't to-morrow night. You
could, for a need, study a speech of some
dozen or sixteen lines, which I would set down
and insert in 't, could you not?

First Play. Ay, my lord.   579

Ham. Very well. Follow that lord; and look
you mock him not. [*Exit* FIRST PLAYER.] My
good friends, I'll leave you till night: you are
welcome to Elsinore.

Ros. Good my lord!

Ham. Ay, so, God be wi' ye; [*Exeunt* ROSEN-
CRANTZ *and* GUILDENSTERN.] Now I am
alone.
O, What a rogue and peasant slave am I!
Is it not monstrous that this player here,   589
But in a fiction, in a dream of passion,
Could force his soul so to his own conceit[69]
That from her working all his visage wann'd,
Tears in his eyes, distraction in 's aspect,
A broken voice, and his whole function
    suiting
With forms to his conceit? and all for
    nothing!
For Hecuba!
What 's Hecuba to him, or he to Hecuba,
That he should weep for her? What would
    he do,
Had he the motive and the cue for passion
That I have? He would drown the stage
    with tears   600
And cleave the general ear with horrid
    speech,
Make mad the guilty and appal the free,
Confound the ignorant, and amaze indeed
The very faculties of eyes and ears.
Yet I,
A dull and muddy-mettled rascal, peak,[70]
Like John-a-dreams,[71] unpregnant of[72] my
    cause,   607
And can say nothing; no, not for a king,
Upon whose property and most dear life
A damn'd defeat was made. Am I a coward?
Who calls me villain? breaks my pate across?
Plucks off my beard, and blows it in my
    face?
Tweaks me by the nose? gives me the lie i'
    the throat,
As deep as to the lungs? who does me this?
Ha!
'Swounds, I should take it: for it cannot be
But I am pigeon-liver'd and lack gall
To make oppression bitter,[73] or ere this
I should have fatted all the region kites   619
With this slave's offal: bloody, bawdy villain!

---

68. *milch*, moist with tears. 69. *Could force his soul . . .
conceit*, could make his whole being respond to his thought.
70. *peak*, mope. 71. *John-a-dreams*, Elizabethan expression for a dreamer. 72. *unpregnant of*, not quickened by.
73. *I am . . . bitter*, I am unable to feel the bitterness of
oppression.

Remorseless, treacherous, lecherous, kindless[74]
   villain!
O, vengeance!
Why, what an ass am I! This is most brave,
That I, the son of a dear father murder'd,
Prompted to my revenge by heaven and hell,
Must, like a whore, unpack my heart with
   words,
And fall a-cursing, like a very drab,
A scullion!
Fie upon 't! foh! About, my brain! I have
   heard
That guilty creatures sitting at a play   630
Have by the very cunning of the scene
Been struck so to the soul that presently
They have proclaim'd their malefactions;
For murder, though it have no tongue, will
   speak
With most miraculous organ. I'll have these
   players
Play something like the murder of my father
Before mine uncle: I'll observe his looks; 637
I'll tent[75] him to the quick: if he but blench,
I know my course. The spirit that I have seen
May be the devil: and the devil hath power
To assume a pleasing shape; yea, and perhaps
Out of my weakness and my melancholy,
As he is very potent with such spirits,[76]
Abuses[77] me to damn me: I'll have grounds
More relative[78] than this: the play's the
   thing
Wherein I'll catch the conscience of the king.
                        [*Exit.*

---

74. *kindless*, unnatural. **75.** *tent*, probe. **76.** *spirits*, moods. **77.** *Abuses*, deceives. **78.** *relative*, definite.

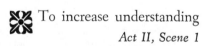 To increase understanding

Act II, Scene 1

1. (*a*) What is the idea underlying Polonius' conversation with Reynaldo? (*b*) Does this dialogue make Polonius a more or less admirable character than you had judged from his behavior in Act I, Scene 2? Explain.

2. (*a*) Describe Hamlet's change in behavior toward Ophelia. (*b*) How does Polonius interpret this change? (*c*) Is Polonius' interpretation correct?

Scene 2

1. (*a*) What request does the King make of Rosencrantz and Guildenstern in the opening lines of this scene? (*b*) How does the Ghost's revelation to Hamlet shed light on the reason behind the King's request? (*c*) Are Rosencrantz and Guildenstern successful in their mission? Explain. (*d*) What is Polonius' plan for testing his theory about Hamlet's mad behavior?

2. (*a*) What message do Voltimand and Cornelius bring from Norway? (*b*) Why does the King find the message reassuring? (*c*) Does the plan involve any elements of danger? (*d*) What is it that young Fortinbras and young Hamlet now have in common?

3. Hamlet's soliloquy at the end of this long scene (pages 139–140) indicates his state of uncertainty and his plans for determining his "true course." (*a*) Are there any indications of madness? (*b*) What train of thought is he following when he cries out "What's Hecuba to him, or he to Hecuba/ That he should weep for her?" (*c*) Why does he refer to himself as "pigeon-liver'd"? (*d*) What reason does he offer for his delay in avenging his father's murder? (*e*) What course of action has the presence of the players suggested to him?

Act II in Review

1. Speaking of Hamlet's madness, Polonius says "Though this be madness, yet there is method in 't." Just as the fools or clowns in Shakespeare's other plays often prove wiser than the normal characters, so Hamlet in his "madness" comes closer to the truth than do the "sane" characters. (*a*) Find indications of Hamlet's wisdom in his conversation with Polonius (Act II, Scene 2, lines 170–227). (*b*) Comment on Hamlet's remarks in his conversation with Rosencrantz and Guildenstern (Act II, Scene 2, lines 232–410). Do they suggest madness? (*c*) How would you reconcile his speech in these lines with his behavior as reported to Polonius by Ophelia (Act II, Scene 1, lines 72-97)?

2. At this point in the play is your opinion of Polonius higher or lower than it was at his first appearance? Cite lines to support your answer.

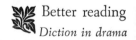 Better reading

Diction in drama

A good playwright constantly seeks ways to sustain the interest of his audience and to make their time in the theater as stimulating as possible. One of the ways of doing this is to include in his play a wide variety of dictions, or styles of speaking. By having each character speak in a way that is peculiar to him, the playwright not only creates character but also varies the pace of his play by the passage from one level of diction to another.

Reread the speech of Marcellus and that of Horatio at the end of Act I, Scene 1 (lines 157–173). How do they differ from the preceding speeches in the play? What is it about Horatio's speech that reveals his scholarly and poetic turn of mind?

Contrast the speeches of Marcellus and Horatio with the King's speech at the opening of Act I, Scene 2 (lines 1–39). Consider in your answer length of sentences, complexity and formality of sentence structure, and use of abstract and concrete words. How is the King's speech in keeping with his character?

Reread Polonius' speeches at the end of Act I, Scene 3 (lines 94–128). How is Polonius' diction in keeping with his moralizing nature? How is it in keeping with his tendency to treat life as a business affair?

The speech of the First Player (Act II, Scene 2, lines 501–530, 539–551) greatly amused Elizabethan audiences because it was intended as a parody of another Elizabethan play, *Dido, Queen of Carthage*, by Christopher Marlowe and Thomas Nashe. Point out examples of overblown language and exaggeration in these lines. What effect does Shakespeare achieve by surrounding these lines with prose speeches?

Contrast Hamlet's diction (Act I, Scene 2, lines 129–159, Act II, Scene 2, lines 310–330, 588–646) with the diction of such characters as the King and Polonius. What gives these speeches their tormented, baffled quality? What makes them the speeches of a highly imaginative, intelligent young man whose powers of observation and reasoning are sharper than those of other characters?

 Words!

The words *wit* and *humor* are often stumbling blocks in our understanding of the literature of the Elizabethan Age. When Hamlet speaks of the group of traveling players and says, "the *humorous* man shall end his part in peace," he is not referring to a comical or funny character, as we would suspect, but rather to a character who exhibits one of the several basic human temperaments. When Hamlet says of himself, "My *wit's* diseased," he does not mean that there is something wrong with his ability to make sharp, amusing remarks but rather that something has gone wrong with his intelligence or understanding. With the aid of an unabridged or etymological dictionary, determine the origins of *wit* and *humor*. How did the Elizabethan definitions of *wit* and *humor* develop from these original words? How did the twentieth-century definitions of *wit* and *humor* develop from the Elizabethan definitions? Do any of the types of meaning change described on pages 82–83 apply to the words *wit* and *humor*?

Falconry. This engraving made in 1578 shows a group of noblemen engaged in this popular aristocratic sport.

ACT THREE

SCENE I. *A room in the castle.*

Enter KING, QUEEN, POLONIUS, OPHELIA,
ROSENCRANTZ, *and* GUILDENSTERN.

King. And can you, by no drift of
    conference,[1]
Get from him why he puts on this confusion,
Grating so harshly all his days of quiet
With turbulent and dangerous lunacy?
    Ros. He does confess he feels himself
    distracted;
But from what cause he will by no means
    speak.
    Guil. Nor do we find him forward[2] to be
    sounded,
But, with a crafty madness, keeps aloof,
When we would bring him on to some
    confession
Of his true state.
    Queen.   Did he receive you well? 10
    Ros. Most like a gentleman.
    Guil. But with much forcing of his
    disposition.
    Ros. Niggard of question[3]; but, of our
    demands,
Most free in his reply.
    Queen.   Did you assay[4] him
To any pastime?
    Ros. Madam, it so fell out, that certain
    players
We o'er-raught[5] on the way: of these we told
    him;
And there did seem in him a kind of joy
To hear of it: they are about the court,
And, as I think, they have already order 20
This night to play before him.
    Pol.   'Tis most true:
And he beseech'd me to entreat your
    majesties
To hear and see the matter.
    King. With all my heart; and it doth much
    content me
To hear him so inclined.
Good gentlemen, give him a further edge,[6]
And drive his purpose on to these delights.
    Ros. We shall, my lord.

[*Exeunt* ROSENCRANTZ *and* GUILDENSTERN.
    King.   Sweet Gertrude, leave us too;
For we have closely[7] sent for Hamlet hither,
That he, as 'twere by accident, may here 30
Affront Ophelia:
Her father and myself, lawful espials,[8]
Will so bestow ourselves that, seeing, unseen,
We may of their encounter frankly judge,
And gather by him, as he is behaved,
If 't be the affliction of his love or no
That thus he suffers for.
    Queen.   I shall obey you.
And for your part, Ophelia, I do wish
That your good beauties be the happy cause
Of Hamlet's wildness: so shall I hope your
    virtues 40
Will bring him to his wonted way again,
To both your honors.
    Oph.   Madam, I wish it may.
                 [*Exit* QUEEN.
    Pol. Ophelia, walk you here. Gracious,[9] so
    please you,
We will bestow ourselves. [*To Ophelia*]
    Read on this book;
That show of such an exercise may color
Your loneliness.[10] We are oft to blame in
    this,—
'Tis too much proved—that with devotion's
    visage
And pious action we do sugar o'er
The devil himself.
    King.   [*Aside*] O, 'tis too true!
How smart a lash that speech doth give my
    conscience! 50
The harlot's cheek, beautied with plastering
    art,
Is not more ugly to the thing[11] that helps it
Than is my deed to my most painted word:
O heavy burthen!
    Pol. I hear him coming; let's withdraw, my
    lord.   [*Exeunt* KING *and* POLONIUS.

Enter HAMLET.

---

1. *drift of conference*, device of conversation. 2. *forward*, willing. 3. *Niggard of question*, sparing of conversation. 4. *assay*, tempt, challenge. 5. *o'er-raught*, overtook. 6. *edge*, incitement, urging on. 7. *closely*, secretly. 8. *espials*, spies. 9. *Gracious*, your grace. Polonius is addressing the king. 10. *That show ... loneliness*, that your solitude may appear more natural. 11. *to the thing*, compared to the cosmetic.

Ham. To be, or not to be: that is the
    question:
Whether 'tis nobler in the mind to suffer
The slings and arrows of outrageous fortune,
Or to take arms against a sea of troubles,   59
And by opposing end them? To die: to sleep;
No more; and by a sleep to say we end
The heart-ache and the thousand natural
    shocks
That flesh is heir to, 'tis a consummation
Devoutly to be wish'd. To die, to sleep;
To sleep: perchance to dream: ay, there 's
    the rub;
For in that sleep of death what dreams may
    come
When we have shuffled off this mortal coil,[12]
Must give us pause: there 's the respect
That makes calamity of so long life[13];
For who would bear the whips and scorns of
    time,   70
The oppressor's wrong, the proud man's
    contumely,
The pangs of despised love, the law's delay,
The insolence of office and the spurns
That patient merit of the unworthy takes,
When he himself might his quietus[14] make
With a bare bodkin?[15] who would fardels[16]
    bear,
To grunt and sweat under a weary life,
But that the dread of something after death,
The undiscover'd country from whose bourn
No traveler returns, puzzles the will   80
And makes us rather bear those ills we have
Than fly to others that we know not of?
Thus conscience does make cowards of us all;
And thus the native hue of resolution
Is sicklied o'er with the pale cast of thought,
And enterprises of great pith and moment
With this regard their currents turn awry,
And lose the name of action.—Soft you now!
The fair Ophelia! Nymph, in thy orisons
Be all my sins remember'd.
    Oph.   Good my lord.   90
How does your honor for this many a day?
    Ham. I humbly thank you; well, well,
    well.
    Oph. My lord, I have remembrances of
    yours,
That I have longed long to re-deliver;
I pray you, now receive them.

    Ham.   No, not I:
I never gave you aught.
    Oph. My honor'd lord, you know right
    well you did;
And, with them, words of so sweet breath
    composed
As made the things more rich: their perfume
    lost,
Take these again; for to the noble mind   100
Rich gifts wax poor when givers prove
    unkind.
There, my lord.
    Ham. Ha, ha! are you honest?
    Oph. My lord?
    Ham. Are you fair?
    Oph. What means your lordship?
    Ham. That if you be honest and fair, your
honesty should admit no discourse to your
beauty.[17]   110
    Oph. Could beauty, my lord, have better
commerce than with honesty?
    Ham. Ay, truly; for the power of beauty
will sooner transform honesty from what it is
to a bawd than the force of honesty can translate beauty into his likeness: this was sometime a paradox, but now the time gives it
proof. I did love you once.
    Oph. Indeed, my lord, you made me believe
so.   120
    Ham. You should not have believed me; for
virtue cannot so inoculate our old stock but
we shall relish of it[18]: I loved you not.
    Oph. I was the more deceived.
    Ham. Get thee to a nunnery: why wouldst
thou be a breeder of sinners? I am myself indifferent honest[19]; but yet I could accuse me
of such things that it were better my mother
had not borne me: I am very proud, revenge-
ful, ambitious, with more offences at my beck[20]

---

12. *shuffled off this mortal coil,* sloughed off this turmoil
that is life. *Coil* might mean "body" in the sense that it is
wound around the soul like a rope. **13.** *That makes . . .
life,* that makes us live out a long life of calamity. **14.**
quietus (kwī ē′təs), acquittance; here, death. **15.** *bare
bodkin,* mere (or unsheathed) dagger. **16.** *fardels,* burdens.
17. *That if you . . . beauty.* In Elizabethan times *honest*
meant both "truthful" and "pure." *Fair* meant both "honorable" and "beautiful." Hence Hamlet is saying to
Ophelia that if she is pure and beautiful, she had better
not let beauty destroy her purity. **18.** *virtue . . . of it,*
virtue cannot be grafted upon old stock to thereby change
its wickedness. **19.** *indifferent honest,* reasonably virtuous. **20.** *beck,* command.

than I have thoughts to put them in, imagination to give them shape, or time to act them in. What should such fellows as I do crawling between earth and heaven? We are arrant knaves, all; believe none of us. Go thy ways to a nunnery. Where 's your father?   136

Oph. At home, my lord.

Ham. Let the doors be shut upon him, that he may play the fool no where but in 's own house. Farewell.

Oph. O, help him, you sweet heavens!

Ham. If thou dost marry, I'll give thee this plague for thy dowry: be thou as chaste as ice, as pure as snow, thou shalt not escape calumny. Get thee to a nunnery, go: farewell. Or, if thou wilt needs marry, marry a fool; for wise men know well enough what monsters[21] you make of them. To a nunnery, go, and quickly too. Farewell.

Oph. O heavenly powers, restore him!   150

Ham. I have heard of your paintings too, well enough; God has given you one face, and you make yourselves another: you jig, you amble, and you lisp, and nick-name God's creatures, and make your wantonness your ignorance.[22] Go to, I'll no more on 't; it hath made me mad. I say, we will have no more marriages: those that are married already, all but one, shall live; the rest shall keep as they are. To a nunnery, go.   [*Exit.* 160

Oph. O, what a noble mind is here o'er-thrown!
The courtier's, soldier's, scholar's, eye, tongue, sword;
The expectancy and rose of the fair state,
The glass of fashion and the mould of form,
The observed of all observers, quite, quite down!
And I, of ladies most deject and wretched,
That suck'd the honey of his music vows,
Now see that noble and most sovereign reason,
Like sweet bells jangled, out of tune and harsh;
That unmatch'd form and feature of blown[23] youth   170
Blasted with ecstasy[24]: O, woe is me,
To have seen what I have seen, see what I see!

Re-enter KING *and* POLONIUS.

King. Love! his affections do not that way tend;
Nor what he spake, though it lack'd form a little,
Was not like madness. There 's something in his soul,
O'er which his melancholy sits on brood;
And I do doubt the hatch and the disclose
Will be some danger: which for to prevent,
I have in quick determination   180
Thus set it down: he shall with speed to England,
For the demand of our neglected tribute:
Haply the seas and countries different
With variable objects shall expel
This something-settled matter in his heart,
Whereon his brains still beating puts him thus
From fashion of himself. What think you on 't?

Pol. It shall do well: but yet do I believe
The origin and commencement of his grief
Sprung from neglected love. How now, Ophelia!   190
You need not tell us what Lord Hamlet said;
We heard it all. My lord, do as you please;
But, if you hold it fit, after the play
Let his queen mother all alone entreat him
To show his grief: let her be round[25] with him;
And I'll be placed, so please you, in the ear
Of all their conference. If she find him not,
To England send him, or confine him where
Your wisdom best shall think.

King.   It shall be so:
Madness in great ones must not unwatch'd go.   [*Exeunt.* 200

SCENE II. *A hall in the castle.*

Enter HAMLET *and* PLAYERS.

Ham. Speak the speech, I pray you, as I pronounced it to you, trippingly on the tongue:

---

21. *monsters*, an allusion to the horns of the cuckold. 22. *make your wantonness your ignorance*, excuse your wantonness on the grounds of ignorance. 23. *blown*, blooming. 24. *ecstasy*, madness. 25. *round*, plain-spoken.

but if you mouth it, as many of your players do, I had as lief the town-crier spoke my lines. Nor do not saw the air too much with your hand, thus, but use all gently; for in the very torrent, tempest, and, as I may say, the whirlwind of your passion, you must acquire and beget a temperance that may give it smoothness. O, it offends me to the soul to hear a robustious periwig-pated[1] fellow tear a passion to tatters, to very rags, to split the ears of the groundlings, who for the most part are capable of[2] nothing but inexplicable dumb-shows and noise: I would have such a fellow whipped for o'er-doing Termagant[3]; it out-herods Herod[4]: pray you, avoid it.   17

First Play. I warrant[5] your honor.

Ham. Be not too tame neither, but let your own discretion be your tutor: suit the action to the word, the word to the action; with this special observance, that you o'er-step not the modesty of nature: for any thing so overdone is from the purpose of playing, whose end, both at the first and now, was and is, to hold, as 't were, the mirror up to nature; to show virtue her own feature, scorn her own image, and the very age and body of the time his form and pressure. Now this overdone, or come tardy off, though it make the unskillful laugh, cannot but make the judicious grieve; the censure of the which one must in your allowance o'er-weigh a whole theater of others. O, there be players that I have seen play, and heard others praise, and that highly, not to speak it profanely, that, neither having the accent of Christians nor the gait of Christian, pagan, nor man, have so strutted and bellowed that I have thought some of nature's journeymen[6] had made men and not made them well, they imitated humanity so abominably.   41

First Play. I hope we have reformed that indifferently[7] with us, sir.

Ham. O, reform it altogether. And let those that play your clowns speak no more than is set down for them; for there be of them that will themselves laugh, to set on some quantity of barren[8] spectators to laugh too; though, in the mean time, some necessary question of the play be then to be considered: that 's villainous, and shows a most pitiful ambition in the fool that uses it. Go, make you ready.

[*Exeunt* PLAYERS.

Enter POLONIUS, ROSENCRANTZ, *and* GUILDENSTERN.

How now, my lord! will the king hear this piece of work?

Pol. And the queen too, and that presently.

Ham. Bid the players make haste.
[*Exit* POLONIUS.

Will you two help to hasten them?

Ros. ⎫
Guil. ⎬ We will, my lord.

[*Exeunt* ROSENCRANTZ *and* GUILDENSTERN.

Ham. What ho! Horatio!

Enter HORATIO.

Hor. Here, sweet lord, at your service.

Ham. Horatio, thou art e'en as just a man
As e'er my conversation coped withal.   68

Hor. O, my dear lord,—

Ham.   Nay, do not think I flatter;
For what advancement may I hope from
    thee
That no revenue hast but thy good spirits,
To feed and clothe thee? Why should the
    poor be flatter'd?
No, let the candied[9] tongue lick absurd pomp,
And crook the pregnant hinges of the knee
Where thrift may follow fawning. Dost thou
    hear?
Since my dear soul was mistress of her
    choice
And could of men distinguish her election,
S' hath seal'd thee for herself; for thou hast
    been
As one, in suffering all, that suffers nothing,
A man that fortune's buffets and rewards   80
Hast ta'en with equal thanks: and blest are
    those
Whose blood and judgment are so well
    commeddled,[10]
That they are not a pipe for fortune's finger

---

1. *periwig-pated,* wig-wearing. 2. *capable of,* susceptible to. 3. *Termagant* (tèr′mə gənt), a Saracen god who appears as a fiend in early morality plays. 4. *Herod,* a rôle played with great noise and fury in early drama. 5. *warrant,* promise. 6. *journeymen,* laborers not yet masters in their trade. 7. *indifferently,* fairly, tolerably. 8. *barren,* i.e., of wit. 9. *candied,* sugared, honeyed. 10. *commeddled,* commingled, blended.

To sound what stop she please. Give me that man
That is not passion's slave, and I will wear him
In my heart's core, ay, in my heart of heart,
As I do thee.—Something too much of this.—
There is a play to-night before the king;
One scene of it comes near the circumstance
Which I have told thee of my father's death:
I prithee, when thou seest that act afoot,   91
Even with the very comment of thy soul
Observe mine uncle: if his occulted[11] guilt
Do not itself unkennel in one speech,
It is a damned[12] ghost that we have seen,
And my imaginations are as foul
As Vulcan's stithy.[13] Give him heedful note;
For I mine eyes will rivet to his face,
And after we will both our judgments join
In censure of his seeming.[14]

Hor.   Well, my lord: 100
If he steal aught the whilst this play is playing,
And 'scape detecting, I will pay the theft.

Ham. They are coming to the play; I must be idle:
Get you a place.

Danish march. A flourish. Enter KING,
QUEEN, POLONIUS, OPHELIA, ROSENCRANTZ,
GUILDENSTERN, *and others.*

King. How fares our cousin Hamlet?

Ham. Excellent, i' faith; of the chameleon's dish[15]: I eat the air, promise-crammed: you cannot feed capons so.

King. I have nothing with this answer, Hamlet; these words are not mine.[16]   110

Ham. No, nor mine now. [*To Polonius*] My lord, you played once i' the university, you say?

Pol. That did I, my lord; and was accounted a good actor.

Ham. What did you enact?

Pol. I did enact Julius Cæsar: I was killed i' the Capitol; Brutus killed me.

Ham. It was a brute part of him to kill so capital a calf there. Be the players ready?   120

Ros. Ay, my lord; they stay upon your patience.

Queen. Come hither, my dear Hamlet, sit by me.

Ham. No, good mother, here's metal more attractive.

Pol. [*To the King*] O, ho! do you mark that?

Ham. Lady, shall I lie in your lap?   129
[*Lying down at Ophelia's feet.*

Oph. You are merry, my lord.

Ham. Who, I?

Oph. Ay, my lord.

Ham. O God, your only jig-maker.[17] What should a man do but be merry? for, look you, how cheerfully my mother looks, and my father died within these two hours.   137

Oph. Nay, 'tis twice two months, my lord.

Ham. So long? Nay then, let the devil wear black, for I'll have a suit of sables. O heavens! die two months ago, and not forgotten yet? Then there's hope a great man's memory may outlive his life half a year: but, by 'r lady, he must build churches, then; or else shall he suffer not thinking on, with the hobby-horse, whose epitaph is "For, O, for, O, the hobby-horse is forgot."[18]   [*Exeunt.*

Enter PROLOGUE.

Pro. For us, and for our tragedy,
Here stooping to your clemency   149
We beg your hearing patiently. [*Exit.*

Ham. Is this a prologue, or the posy[19] of a ring?

Oph. 'Tis brief, my lord.

Ham. As woman's love.

Enter two PLAYERS, KING *and* QUEEN.

P. King. Full thirty times hath Phoebus' cart[20] gone round

---

11. *occulted*, hidden.   12. *damned*, in league with Satan. 13. *Vulcan's stithy*, the forge of Vulcan, Roman god of war.   14. *In censure of his seeming*, in judgment of his appearance or behavior.   15. *chameleon's dish*. The chameleon, a type of lizard, was supposed to feed on air. 16. *are not mine*, do not fit my question.   17. *your only jig-maker*, only your composer of jigs.   18. *For . . . forgot*, line from a song occurring in *Love's Labours Lost*. 19. *posy*, motto.   20. *Phoebus'* (fē'bəs) *cart*, the chariot of the sun god.

Neptune's salt wash[21] and Tellus' orbed
      ground,[22]
And thirty dozen moons with borrow'd sheen
About the world have times twelve thirties
      been,
Since love our hearts and Hymen[23] did our
      hands   159
Unite commutual[24] in most sacred bonds.
      P. Queen. So many journeys may the sun
      and moon
Make us again count o'er ere love be done!
But, woe is me, you are so sick of late,
So far from cheer and from your former state,
That I distrust you.[25] Yet, though I distrust,
Discomfort you, my lord, it nothing must:
For women's fear and love holds quantity;
In neither aught, or in extremity.
Now, what my love is, proof hath made you
      know;
And as my love is sized, my fear is so: 170
Where love is great, the littlest doubts are
      fear;
Where little fears grow great, great love
      grows there.
      P. King. 'Faith, I must leave thee, love, and
      shortly too;
My operant[26] powers their functions leave[27]
      to do:
And thou shalt live in this fair world
      behind,
Honor'd, beloved; and haply one as kind
For husband shalt thou—
      P. Queen.   O, confound the rest!
Such love must needs be treason in my
      breast:
In second husband let me be accurst!   179
None wed the second but who kill'd the first.
      Ham. [Aside] Wormwood, wormwood.
      P. Queen. The instances that second
      marriage move
Are base respects of thrift, but none of love.
      P. King. I do believe you think what now
      you speak;
But what we do determine oft we break.
What to ourselves in passion we propose,
The passion ending, doth the purpose lose.
The violence of either grief or joy
Their own enactures with themselves destroy:
Where joy most revels, grief doth most
      lament;   190

Grief joys, joy grieves, on slender accident.
This world is not for aye, nor 'tis not strange
That even our loves should with our fortunes
      change;
For 'tis a question left us yet to prove,
Whether love lead fortune, or else fortune
      love.
The great man down, you mark his favorite
      flies;
The poor advanced makes friends of enemies.
And hitherto doth love on fortune tend;
For who not needs shall never lack a friend,
And who in want a hollow friend doth try,
Directly seasons him his enemy.   201
But, orderly to end where I begun,
Our wills and fates do so contrary run
That our devices still are overthrown;
Our thoughts are ours, their ends none of
      our own:
So think thou wilt no second husband wed;
But die thy thoughts when thy first lord is
      dead.
      P. Queen. Nor earth to me give food, nor
      heaven light!
Sport and repose lock from me day and night!
To desperation turn my trust and hope!   210
An anchor's[28] cheer in prison be my scope!
Each opposite[29] that blanks the face of joy
Meet what I would have well and it destroy!
Both here and hence pursue me lasting strife,
If, once a widow, ever I be wife!
      Ham. If she should break it now!
      P. King. 'Tis deeply sworn. Sweet, leave me
      here awhile;
My spirits grow dull, and fain I would
      beguile
The tedious day with sleep.   [Sleeps.
      P. Queen.   Sleep rock thy brain;
And never come mischance between us
      twain!   [Exit. 220
      Ham. Madam, how like you this play?
      Queen. The lady doth protest too much,
methinks.
      Ham. O, but she'll keep her word.

---

21. Neptune's salt wash, the sea. 22. Tellus' orbed
ground, the earth (Tellus was the Roman goddess of the
earth). 23. Hymen (hi'mən), god of matrimony. 24.
commutual, intensely mutual. 25. distrust you, am anxious about you. 26. operant, active. 27. leave, cease.
28. anchor, anchorite, or hermit. 29. opposite, adversary.

King. Have you heard the argument? Is there no offence in 't?

Ham. No, no, they do but jest, poison in jest; no offence i' the world.

King. What do you call the play? 229

Ham. The Mouse-trap. Marry, how? Tropically.[30] This play is the image of a murder done in Vienna: Gonzago is the duke's name; his wife, Baptista: you shall see anon; 't is a knavish piece of work: but what o' that? your majesty and we that have free souls, it touches us not: let the galled jade wince, our withers are unwrung.[31]

Enter LUCIANUS.

This is one Lucianus, nephew to the king. 238

Oph. You are as good as a chorus, my lord.

Ham. Begin, murderer; pox, leave thy damnable faces, and begin. Come: "the croaking raven doth bellow for revenge."

Luc. *Thoughts black, hands apt, drugs fit, and time agreeing;*
Confederate season, else no creature seeing;
Thou mixture rank, of midnight weeds collected,
With Hecate's ban[32] thrice blasted, thrice infected,
Thy natural magic and dire property,
On wholesome life usurp immediately. 250

[*Pours the poison into the sleeper's ears.*

Ham. He poisons him i' the garden for 's estate. His name 's Gonzago: the story is extant, and writ in choice Italian: you shall see anon how the murderer gets the love of Gonzago's wife.

Oph. The king rises.

Ham. What, frighted with false fire![33]

Queen. How fares my lord?

Pol. Give o'er the play.

King. Give me some light: away! 260

All. Lights, lights, lights!

[*Exeunt all but* HAMLET *and* HORATIO.

Ham. Why, let the stricken deer go weep,*
The hart ungalled play;
For some must watch, while some must sleep:
So runs the world away.

Would not this, sir, and a forest of feathers[34]—
if the rest of my fortunes turn Turk with[35] me

—with two Provincial roses on my razed shoes,[36] get me a fellowship in a cry[37] of players, sir?

Hor. Half a share.[38] 272

Ham. A whole one, I.
For thou dost know, O Damon[39] dear,
This realm dismantled was
Of Jove himself; and now reigns here
A very, very—pajock.[40]

Hor. You might have rhymed. 280

Ham. O good Horatio, I'll take the ghost's word for a thousand pound. Didst perceive?

Hor. Very well, my lord.

Ham. Upon the talk of the poisoning?

Hor. I did very well note him.

Ham. Ah, ah! Come, some music! come, the recorders!
For if the king like not the comedy,*
Why then, belike, he likes it not, perdy.
Come, some music! 290

Re-enter ROSENCRANTZ *and* GUILDENSTERN.

Guil. Good my lord, vouchsafe me a word with you.

Ham. Sir, a whole history.

Guil. The king, sir,—

Ham. Ay, sir, what of him?

Guil. Is in his retirement marvelous distempered.

Ham. With drink, sir?

Guil. No, my lord, rather with choler. 300

Ham. Your wisdom should show itself more richer to signify this to his doctor; for, for me to put him to his purgation would perhaps plunge him into far more choler.

Guil. Good my lord, put your discourse into some frame[41] and start not so wildly from my affair.

Ham. I am tame, sir: pronounce.

Guil. The queen, your mother, in most great

---

30. *Tropically,* figuratively. 31. *let the . . . unwrung,* let the guilty worry; our consciences are clear. 32. *Hecate's* (hek'ə tiz) *ban,* the curse of Hecate, goddess of witchcraft. 33. *false fire,* fireworks, or a blank discharge. 34. *forest of feathers,* an allusion to the plumes the Elizabethan actors were fond of wearing. 35. *turn Turk with,* go back on. 36. *Provincial . . . shoes,* rosettes of ribbons on my slashed shoes (by way of ornament). 37. *cry,* pack (as of hounds). 38. *Half a share,* i.e., in the acting company. 39. *Damon* (dā'mən). In Roman legend, Damon and Pythias (pith'i əs) were noted for their close friendship. 40. *pajock,* peacock, a repulsive creature according to Elizabethan natural history. 41. *frame,* order.

affliction of spirit, hath sent me to you.   310

Ham. You are welcome.

Guil. Nay, good my lord, this courtesy is not of the right breed. If it shall please you to make me a wholesome⁴² answer, I will do your mother's commandment: if not, your pardon and my return shall be the end of my business.

Ham. Sir, I cannot.

Guil. What, my lord?   318

Ham. Make you a wholesome answer; my wit 's diseased: but, sir, such answer as I can make, you shall command; or, rather, as you say, my mother: therefore no more, but to the matter: my mother, you say,—

Ros. Then thus she says; your behavior hath struck her into amazement and admiration.

Ham. O wonderful son, that can so astonish a mother! But is there no sequel at the heels of this mother's admiration? Impart.

Ros. She desires to speak with you in her closet, ere you go to bed.   330

Ham. We shall obey, were she ten times our mother. Have you any further trade with us?

Ros. My lord, you once did love me.

Ham. So I do still, by these pickers and stealers.⁴³

Ros. Good my lord, what is your cause of distemper? You do, surely, bar the door upon your own liberty, if you deny your griefs to your friend.

Ham. Sir, I lack advancement.   340

Ros. How can that be, when you have the voice of the king himself for your succession in Denmark?

Ham. Ay, sir, but "While the grass grows,"⁴⁴ —the proverb is something musty.

Re-enter PLAYERS *with recorders.*

O, the recorders! let me see one. To withdraw⁴⁵ with you:—why do you go about to recover the wind of me, as if you would drive me into a toil?⁴⁶   350

Guil. O, my lord, if my duty be too bold, my love is too unmannerly.⁴⁷

Ham. I do not well understand that. Will you play upon this pipe?

Guil. My lord, I cannot.

Ham. I pray you.

Guil. Believe me, I cannot.

Ham. I do beseech you.

Guil. I know no touch of it, my lord.   359

Ham. 'Tis as easy as lying: govern these ventages with your fingers and thumb, give it breath with your mouth, and it will discourse most eloquent music. Look you, these are the stops.

Guil. But these cannot I command to any utterance of harmony; I have not the skill.

Ham. Why, look you now, how unworthy a thing you make of me! You would play upon me; you would seem to know my stops; you would pluck out the heart of my mystery; you would sound me from my lowest note to the top of my compass: and there is much music, excellent voice, in this little organ; yet cannot you make it speak. 'Sblood, do you think I am easier to be played on than a pipe? Call me what instrument you will, though you can fret⁴⁸ me, yet you cannot play upon me.   377

Enter POLONIUS.

God bless you, sir!

Pol. My lord, the queen would speak with you, and presently.

Ham. Do you see yonder cloud that's almost in shape of a camel?

Pol. By the mass, and 'tis like a camel, indeed.

Ham. Methinks it is like a weasel.

Pol. It is backed like a weasel.

Ham. Or like a whale?

Pol. Very like a whale.   389

Ham. Then I will come to my mother by and by. They fool me to the top of my bent.⁴⁹ I will come by and by.

Pol. I will say so.

Ham. By and by is easily said.

                            [*Exit* POLONIUS.

Leave me, friends.   [*Exeunt all but* HAMLET.

---

42. *wholesome*, sensible. 43. *these pickers and stealers*, hands, so called from the catechism, "to keep my hands from picking and stealing." 44. *While the grass grows.* The proverb continues "the horse starves." 45. *withdraw*, speak in private. 46. *why . . . into a toil*, why do you try to maneuver about me as if to drive me into a trap. 47. *if . . . unmannerly*, if I am using an unmannerly boldness, it is my love that causes it. 48. *fret*, quibble on meaning "irritate" and the raised parts of stringed instruments that regulate fingering. 49. *top of my bent*, limit of my endurance.

'Tis now the very witching time of night,
When churchyards yawn and hell itself
    breathes out
Contagion to this world: now could I drink
    hot blood,   400
And do such bitter business as the day
Would quake to look on. Soft! now to my
    mother.
O heart, lose not thy nature; let not ever
The soul of Nero⁵⁰ enter this firm bosom:
Let me be cruel, not unnatural:
I will speak daggers to her, but use none;
My tongue and soul in this be hypocrites;
How in my words soever she be shent,⁵¹
To give them seals⁵² never, my soul, consent!
                                            [Exit.

SCENE III. *A room in the castle.*

Enter KING, ROSENCRANTZ, *and*
GUILDENSTERN.

King. I like him not, nor stands it safe
    with us
To let his madness range. Therefore prepare
    you;
I your commission will forthwith dispatch,
And he to England shall along with you:
The terms of our estate¹ may not endure
Hazard so near us as doth hourly grow
Out of his lunacies.
    Guil.   We will ourselves provide:
Most holy and religious fear it is
To keep those many many bodies safe
That live and feed upon your majesty.   10
    Ros. The single and peculiar² life is bound,
With all the strength and armor of the mind,
To keep itself from noyance³; but much more
That spirit upon whose weal depend and rest
The lives of many. The cease of majesty
Dies not alone; but, like a gulf, doth draw
What 's near it with it: is a massy wheel,
Fix'd on the summit of the highest mount,
To whose huge spokes ten thousand lesser
    things
Are mortised and adjoin'd; which, when it
    falls,   20
Each small annexment, petty consequence,
Attends the boisterous ruin. Never alone

Did the king sigh, but with a general groan.
    King. Arm⁴ you, I pray you, to this speedy
    voyage;
For we will fetters put about this fear,
Which now goes too free-footed.
    Ros. ⎫
    Guil. ⎰   We will haste us.
        [*Exeunt* ROSENCRANTZ *and* GUILDENSTERN.

Enter POLONIUS.

    Pol. My lord, he 's going to his mother's
    closet:
Behind the arras I'll convey myself,
To hear the process; I'll warrant she'll tax him
    home⁵:
And as you said, and wisely was it said,   30
'Tis meet that some more audience than a
    mother,
Since nature makes them partial, should
    o'erhear
The speech, of vantage. Fare you well, my
    liege:
I'll call upon you ere you go to bed,
And tell you what I know.
    King.   Thanks, dear my lord.
                                [*Exit* POLONIUS.
O, my offence is rank, it smells to heaven;
It hath the primal eldest curse⁶ upon 't,
A brother's murder. Pray can I not,
Though inclination be as sharp as will:
My stronger guilt defeats my strong intent; ⁴⁰
And, like a man to double business bound,
I stand in pause where I shall first begin,
And both neglect. What if this cursed hand
Were thicker than itself with brother's blood,
Is there not rain enough in the sweet heavens
To wash it white as snow? Whereto serves
    mercy
But to confront the visage of offence?
And what 's in prayer but this two-fold force,
To be forestalled ere we come to fall,
Or pardon'd being down? Then I'll look up; ⁵⁰

SCENE II   **50.** *Nero,* Roman emperor who murdered his
mother.   **51.** *shent,* rebuked.   **52.** *give them seals,* confirm them with deeds.
    SCENE III   **1.** *terms . . . estate,* the circumstances of our
state (as king).   **2.** *peculiar,* personal, private.   **3.** *noy-
ance,* harm.   **4.** *Arm,* prepare.   **5.** *tax him home,* rebuke
him severely.   **6.** *primal eldest curse,* the curse put upon
Cain for slaying his brother Abel.

My fault is past. But, O, what form of prayer
Can serve my turn? "Forgive me my foul
    murder"?
That cannot be: since I am still possess'd
Of those effects for which I did the murder,
My crown, mine own ambition and my
    queen.
May one be pardon'd and retain the offence?
In the corrupted currents of this world
Offence's gilded hand[7] may shove by justice,
And oft 'tis seen the wicked prize itself
Buys out the law: but 'tis not so above;   60
There is no shuffling,[8] there the action lies
In his true nature; and we ourselves
    compell'd,
Even to the teeth and forehead of our faults,
To give in evidence. What then? what rests?
Try what repentance can: what can it not?
Yet what can it when one can not repent?
O wretched state! O bosom black as death!
O limed[9] soul, that, struggling to be free,
Art more engaged! Help, angels! Make assay,
Bow, stubborn knees; and, heart with strings
    of steel,   70
Be soft as sinews of the new-born babe!
All may be well.   [*Retires and kneels.*

Enter HAMLET.

Ham. Now might I do it pat, now he is
    praying;
And now I'll do 't. And so he goes to heaven;
And so am I revenged. That would be
    scann'd[10]:
A villain kills my father; and for that,
I, his sole son, do this same villain send
To heaven.
O, this is hire and salary, not revenge.
He took my father grossly, full of bread[11];   80
With all his crimes broad blown, as flush as
    May;
And how his audit stands who knows save
    heaven?
But in our circumstance and course of
    thought,
'Tis heavy with him: and am I then
    revenged,
To take him in the purging of his soul,
When he is fit and season'd for his passage?
No!

Up, sword; and know thou a more horrid
    hent:
When he is drunk asleep, or in his rage,
At gaming, swearing, or about some act   90
That has no relish of salvation in 't;
Then trip him, that his heels may kick at
    heaven,
And that his soul may be as damn'd and
    black
As hell, whereto it goes. My mother stays[12]:
This physic[13] but prolongs thy sickly days.
                                    [*Exit.*

    King. [*Rising*] My words fly up, my
        thoughts remain below:
Words without thoughts never to heaven go.
                                    [*Exit.*

SCENE IV. *The* QUEEN's *closet.*

Enter QUEEN *and* POLONIUS.

    Pol. He will come straight. Look you lay
        home to him:
Tell him his pranks have been too broad to
    bear with,
And that your grace hath screen'd and stood
    between
Much heat and him. I'll sconce[1] me even
    here.
Pray you, be round with him.
    Ham. [*Within*] Mother, mother, mother!
    Queen.   I'll warrant you,
Fear me not: withdraw, I hear him coming.
            [POLONIUS *hides behind the arras.*

Enter HAMLET.

    Ham. Now, mother, what 's the matter?
    Queen. Hamlet, thou hast thy father much
        offended.
    Ham. Mother, you have my father much
        offended.   10

SCENE III **7.** *Offence's gilded hand,* hand offering a bribe.
8. *shuffling,* escape by trickery. **9.** *limed,* caught, as a
bird is caught with birdlime. **10.** *would be scann'd,* needs
to be looked into. **11.** *grossly, full of bread,* still attached
to this earthly life; without confession and absolution.
12. *stays,* awaits. **13.** *physic,* purging; in the case of
the king, by prayer.
SCENE IV **1.** *sconce,* hide.

Queen. Come, come, you answer with an idle tongue.

Ham. Go, go, you question with a wicked tongue.

Queen. Why, how now, Hamlet!

Ham.　　　　　What's the matter now?

Queen. Have you forgot me?

Ham.　　　　　No, by the rood,[2] not so:
You are the queen, your husband's brother's wife;
And—would it were not so!—you are my mother.

Queen. Nay, then, I'll set those to you that can speak.

Ham. Come, come, and sit you down; you shall not budge;
You go not till I set you up a glass[3]
Where you may see the inmost part of you. 20

Queen. What wilt thou do? thou will not murder me?
Help, help, ho!

Pol. [*Behind*] What, ho! help, help, help!

Ham. [*Drawing*] How now! a rat? Dead, for a ducat, dead!

　　　　　[*Makes a pass through the arras.*

Pol. [*Behind*] O, I am slain!

　　　　　　　　　　[*Falls and dies.*

Queen. O me, what hast thou done?

Ham.　　　　　Nay, I know not:
Is it the king?

Queen. O, what a rash and bloody deed is this!

Ham. A bloody deed! almost as bad, good mother,
As kill a king, and marry with his brother.

Queen. As kill a king!

Ham.　　　　　Ay, lady, 'twas my word. 30

[*Lifts up the arras and discovers* POLONIUS.

Thou wretched, rash, intruding fool, farewell!
I took thee for thy better: take thy fortune;
Thou find'st to be too busy is some danger.
Leave wringing of your hands: peace! sit you down,
And let me wring your heart; for so I shall,
If it be made of penetrable stuff,
If damned custom have not brass'd it so
That it be proof and bulwark against sense.

Queen. What have I done, that thou darest wag thy tongue
In noise so rude against me?

Ham.　　　　　　Such an act　　40
That blurs the grace and blush of modesty,
Calls virtue hypocrite, takes off the rose
From the fair forehead of an innocent love
And sets a blister there, makes marriage-vows
As false as dicers' oaths: O, such a deed
As from the body of contraction[4] plucks
The very soul, and sweet religion makes
A rhapsody of words: heaven's face doth glow;
Yea, this solidity and compound mass,[5]
With heated visage, as against the doom,　　50
Is thought-sick at the act.

Queen.　　　　　Ay me, what act,
That roars so loud, and thunders in the index?[6]

Ham. Look here, upon this picture, and on this.
The counterfeit presentment[7] of two brothers.
See, what a grace was seated on this brow;
Hyperion's[8] curls; the front of Jove himself;
An eye like Mars, to threaten and command;
A station[9] like the herald Mercury
New-lighted on a heaven-kissing hill;
A combination and a form indeed,　　60
Where every god did seem to set his seal,
To give the world assurance of a man:
This was your husband. Look you now, what follows:
Here is your husband; like a mildew'd ear,[10]
Blasting his wholesome brother. Have you eyes?
Could you on this fair mountain leave to feed,
And batten on this moor?[11] Ha! have you eyes?
You cannot call it love; for at your age
The hey-day in the blood is tame, it 's humble,
And waits upon the judgment: and what judgment　　70
Would step from this to this? Sense,[12] sure, you have,

---

2. *rood*, cross.　3. *glass*, mirror.　4. *contraction*, betrothal.　5. *solidity and compound mass*, the earth.　6. *index*, prelude or preface.　7. *counterfeit presentment*, portrait. On stage the portraits are sometimes presented as miniatures, sometimes as pictures on the wall.　8. *Hyperion*, the sun god.　9. *station*, manner of standing, bearing.　10. *mildew'd ear*. See Genesis 41:5-7.　11. *batten on this moor*, grow fat on barren uplands.　12. *Sense*, sensory perception.

Else could you not have motion; but sure, that sense
Is apoplex'd[13]; for madness would not err,
Nor sense to ecstasy was ne'er so thrall'd
But it reserved some quantity of choice,
To serve in such a difference. What devil was 't
That thus hath cozen'd you at hoodman-blind?[14]
Eyes without feeling, feeling without sight,
Ears without hands or eyes, smelling sans[15] all,
Or but a sickly part of one true sense   80
Could not so mope.
O shame! where is thy blush! Rebellious hell,
If thou canst mutine[16] in a matron's bones,
To flaming youth let virtue be as wax,
And melt in her own fire.
    Queen.   O Hamlet, speak no more:
Thou turn'st mine eyes into my very soul;
And there I see such black and grained spots
As will not leave their tinct.   89
These words, like daggers, enter in mine ears;
No more, sweet Hamlet!
    Ham.   A murderer and a villain;
A slave that is not twentieth part the tithe
Of your precedent lord; a vice of kings[17];
A cutpurse of the empire and the rule,
That from a shelf the precious diadem stole,
And put it in his pocket!
    Queen.   No more!
Ham. A king of shreds and patches,[18]—

Enter GHOST.

Save me, and hover o'er me with your wings,
You heavenly guards! What would your gracious figure?
    Queen. Alas, he 's mad!   100
Ham. Do you not come your tardy son to chide,
That, lapsed in time and passion, lets go by
The important acting of your dread command?
O, say!
    Ghost. Do not forget: this visitation
Is but to whet thy almost blunted purpose.
But, look, amazement[19] on thy mother sits:

O, step between her and her fighting soul:
Conceit[20] in weakest bodies strongest works:
Speak to her, Hamlet.
    Ham.   How is it with you, lady?   110
    Queen. Alas, how is 't with you,
That you do bend your eye on vacancy
And with the incorporal air do hold discourse?
Forth at your eyes your spirits wildly peep;
And, as the sleeping soldiers in the alarm,
Your bedded[21] hair, like life in excrements,[22]
Start up, and stand an end. O gentle son,
Upon the heat and flame of thy distemper
Sprinkle cool patience. Whereon do you look?
    Ham. On him, on him! Look you, how pale he glares!   120
His form and cause conjoin'd, preaching to stones,
Would make them capable.[23] Do not look upon me;
Lest with this piteous action you convert
My stern effects[24]: then what I have to do
Will want true color; tears perchance for blood.
    Queen. To whom do you speak this?
    Ham.   Do you see nothing there?
    Queen. Nothing at all; yet all that is I see.
    Ham. Nor did you nothing hear?
    Queen.   No, nothing but ourselves.
    Ham. Why, look you there! look, how it steals away!
My father, in his habit[25] as he lived!   130
Look, where he goes, even now, out at the portal!   [*Exit* GHOST.
    Queen. This is the very coinage of your brain:
This bodiless creation ecstasy[26]
Is very cunning in.
    Ham.   Ecstasy!

---

13. *apoplex'd,* paralyzed. 14. *hoodman-blind,* blindman's buff. 15. *sans,* without. 16. *mutine,* mutiny, rebel. 17. *vice of kings,* buffoon of kings, a reference to the Vice, or clown, of the morality plays. 18. *shreds and patches,* i.e., motley, the traditional costume of the Vice. 19. *amazement,* frenzy, distraction. 20. *Conceit,* imagination. 21. *bedded,* laid smoothly. 22. *excrements.* The hair was considered an excrement or voided part of the body. 23. *capable,* susceptible to emotional appeal. 24. *convert my stern effects,* divert me from my stern duty. 25. *habit,* dress. 26. *ecstasy,* frenzy, madness.

My pulse, as yours, doth temperately keep time,
And makes as healthful music: it is not madness
That I have utter'd: bring me to the test,
And I the matter will re-word, which madness
Would gambol from. Mother, for love of grace,
Lay not that flattering unction to your soul, 140
That not your trespass, but my madness speaks:
It will but skin and film the ulcerous place,
Whiles rank corruption, mining all within,
Infects unseen. Confess yourself to heaven;
Repent what 's past; avoid what is to come;
And do not spread the compost on the weeds,
To make them ranker. Forgive me this my virtue;
For in the fatness of these pursy²⁷ times
Virtue itself of vice must pardon beg,
Yea, curb²⁸ and woo for leave to do him good. 150
    Queen. O Hamlet, thou hast cleft my heart in twain.
    Ham. O, throw away the worser part of it,
And live the purer with the other half.
Good night: but go not to mine uncle's bed;
Assume a virtue, if you have it not.
And when you are desirous to be bless'd,
I'll blessing beg of you. For this same lord,
            [Pointing to POLONIUS.
I do repent: but heaven hath pleased it so,
To punish me with this and this with me,
That I must be their scourge and minister. 160
I will bestow him, and will answer well
The death I gave him. So, again, good night.
I must be cruel, only to be kind:
Thus bad begins and worse remains behind.
One word more, good lady.
    Queen.   What shall I do?
    Ham. Not this, by no means, that I bid you do:
Let the bloat king tempt you again to bed;
Make you to ravel all this matter out,
That I essentially am not in madness,
But mad in craft. 'Twere good you let him know; 170
For who, that 's but a queen, fair, sober, wise,

Would from a paddock,²⁹ from a bat, a gib,³⁰
Such dear concernings hide? who would do so?
    Queen. Be thou assured, if words be made of breath,
And breath of life, I have no life to breathe
What thou hast said to me.
    Ham. I must to England; you know that?
    Queen.   Alack,
I had forgot: 'tis so concluded on.
    Ham. There 's letters seal'd: and my two schoolfellows,
Whom I will trust as I will adders fang'd, 180
They bear the mandate; they must sweep my way,
And marshal me to knavery. Let it work;
For 'tis the sport to have the enginer
Hoist with his own petar³¹: and 't shall go hard
But I will delve one yard below their mines,
And blow them at the moon: O, 'tis most sweet,
When in one line two crafts directly meet.
This man shall set me packing:
I'll lug the guts into the neighbor room.
Mother, good night. Indeed this counselor 190
Is now most still, most secret and most grave,
Who was in life a foolish prating knave.
Come, sir, to draw toward an end with you.
Good night, mother.
            [Exeunt severally; Hamlet
            dragging in Polonius.

27. *pursy*, physically and morally slack. 28. *curb*, bow.
29. *paddock*, toad. 30. *gib*, tomcat. 31. *enginer . . .
petar*, artilleryman blown up with his own explosives.

To increase understanding
Act III, Scene 1

1. Just as Hamlet has resolved to use the play to discover whether the King did in fact murder his father, so the King is trying to determine whether or not Hamlet is a threat to him. (a) What indications of the King's uneasiness do you get at the opening of this scene? (b) Cite the lines in which the King definitely admits his guilt to the audience. (c) Hidden behind the arras, the King and Polonius overhear Hamlet say to Ophelia ". . . those that are married already, all but one shall live; the rest shall keep as they are." Do you think the King interprets this as the ravings of a madman or as something

else? Explain. (*d*) What do you infer from the King's determination to send Hamlet to England?

2. (*a*) Describe Hamlet's behavior toward Ophelia. (*b*) What is the significance of Ophelia's remarks in lines 161–172?

3. How do you know that Polonius still clings to his original theory about the cause of Hamlet's madness?

Scene 2

1. (*a*) What aspect of Horatio's character does Hamlet particularly admire (lines 67–87)? (*b*) Is Hamlet's estimate of Horatio consistent with what you have already learned of him in Act I, Scene 1? (*c*) How does Hamlet show that he trusts Horatio completely?

2. (*a*) Outline the plot of the play within the play. (*b*) What is the King's reaction? (*c*) What is the Queen's reaction?

3. When Rosencrantz and Guildenstern inquire once more into the reasons for his strange behavior, Hamlet asks the players for a flutelike instrument called a *recorder* and uses it as the basis for his answer (lines 347–377). Explain this answer.

Scene 3

1. What is the subject of the King's conversation with Rosencrantz and Guildenstern?

2. The King's soliloquy (lines 36–72) explains his state of mind to the audience. (*a*) How does he feel about the murder he has committed? (*b*) What stands in the way of his being forgiven? (*c*) What comparison does he make between earthly and heavenly justice?

3. Why does Hamlet not take advantage of this opportunity for killing the King?

Scene 4

1. (*a*) How does Polonius meet his death? (*b*) Do you think this is an appropriate end for him? Why, or why not?

2. (*a*) What does Hamlet try to accomplish in his conversation with his mother? (*b*) Does he believe she had been involved in the murder? (*c*) Do you think she had? Cite lines to prove your point. (*d*) Why is Hamlet's encounter with his mother particularly dramatic?

3. What is Hamlet's plan of action as Act III ends?

Act III in Review

1. The episodes involving the traveling players—their arrival at court, Hamlet's advice to them, and their performance of *The Murder of Gonzago*—

are interesting in themselves and also vital to the unfolding of the play. (*a*) What aspects of the acting profession does Hamlet take up in his advice to the players (Act III, Scene 2)? (*b*) What does Hamlet mean when he says that the function of drama is "to hold, as t'were, the mirror up to nature; to show virtue her own feature, scorn her own image, and the very age and body of the time his form and pressure" (Act III, Scene 2, lines 25–29)? (*c*) What historical facts of Shakespeare's own time are recalled by the reason the players give for leaving the city (Act II, Scene 2)? (*d*) The device of the play within a play (Act III, Scene 3) is often used by a dramatist to invest the larger play with a greater sense of reality and to make audiences forget that they are watching the unfolding of fictitious events. Explain why the play within a play tends to produce this effect. (*e*) What position does the play within a play occupy in the unfolding of the plot of *Hamlet?*

2. As you have seen, much of *Hamlet* is concerned with getting behind appearances to the truth of things. Hamlet tries to penetrate behind the King's courtly behavior to find out whether he is a murderer. The King, in turn, tries to unmask the cause of Hamlet's strange behavior. Do you see any connection between this problem and the fact that Shakespeare devotes considerable stage time to the traveling players or actors, and to the techniques of acting?

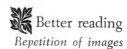 Better reading

Repetition of images

The power of *Hamlet*—and, for that matter, of most of Shakespeare's plays—derives largely from the repetition of certain images. By constantly repeating certain *images* (words or phrases that arouse or stimulate any of the listener's or reader's five senses), Shakespeare was able to buttress or reinforce the basic themes of his play.

One of the themes of *Hamlet*, for example, is that of appearance and reality: "Is the Ghost my father or is it a devil?" Hamlet asks. "Is the King really a murderer?" "Are Rosencrantz and Guildenstern really my friends?" "Is Ophelia as innocent as she appears or, like my mother, weak and corrupt?" And on the King's part, "Is Hamlet really mad?" This theme—the extreme difficulty of getting behind appearances to the truth about people and situations —is kept constantly before the reader by the repetition of images based on *clothes* and *paint*, which are suggestive of "covering up" or "concealing."

Consider, for example, Hamlet's words to his mother,

> Seems, madam! nay, it is; I know not 'seems.'
> 'Tis not alone my *inky cloak*, good mother,
> Nor customary *suits of solemn black*,
> . . .
> That can denote me truly. . . .
> (Act I, Scene 2, lines 76–83)

And in his first soliloquy, Hamlet says,

> . . . Frailty, thy name is woman!—
> A little month, or ere those *shoes* were old
> With which she follow'd my poor father's body,
> Like Niobe, all tears. . . .
> (Act I, Scene 2, lines 146–149)

Again, Polonius tells Ophelia that Hamlet's vows are false or deceptive apparel,

> Not of that *dye* which their *investments* show,
> But mere implorators of unholy *suits*. . . .
> (Act I, Scene 3, lines 121–122)

The King, stung by guilt, says,

> The harlot's *cheek*, beautied with *plastering* art,
> Is not more ugly to the thing that helps it
> Than is my deed to my most *painted word*. . . .
> (Act III, Scene 1, lines 51–53)

And Hamlet says of women,

> I have heard of your *paintings* too, well enough;
> God has given you one *face*, and you make yourselves another. . . .
> (Act III, Scene 1, lines 151–153

Other themes in *Hamlet* are handled in the same way. Turn to the following passages in the play and explain the imagery that connects them: Act I, Scene 4, lines 23–38; Act I, Scene 4, lines 90–91; Act III, Scene 4, lines 141–144. How are these and other similar images related to the events of *Hamlet*? What theme do these images buttress or reinforce?

The images of ulcers or abscesses which burst and spread infection and disease occur through the play, but they become more frequent—and more repulsive—in the second half. Watch for them as you read Acts IV and V. Watch also for dramatic symbols related to these images, that is, for actual props and bits of action which stand for or symbolize the idea of corruption and decay.

The George Inn, the only surviving gallery inn in London. Dating from before 1500, it was destroyed by fire in 1676. The present building dates from 1677. Tudor actors performed their plays in the courtyards.

ACT FOUR

SCENE I. *A room in the castle.*

Enter KING, QUEEN, ROSENCRANTZ, *and*
GUILDENSTERN.

King. There 's matter in these sighs, these
  profound heaves:
You must translate: 'tis fit we understand
  them.
Where is your son?
  Queen. Bestow this place on us a little
  while.
  [*Exeunt* ROSENCRANTZ *and* GUILDENSTERN.
Ah, mine own lord, what have I seen
  to-night!
  King. What, Gertrude? How does Hamlet?
  Queen. Mad as the sea and wind, when
  both contend
Which is the mightier: in his lawless fit,
Behind the arras hearing something stir,
Whips out his rapier, cries, "A rat, a rat!"   10
And, in this brainish apprehension,[1] kills
The unseen good old man.
  King.   O heavy deed!
It had been so with us, had we been there:
His liberty is full of threats to all;
To you yourself, to us, to every one.
Alas, how shall this bloody deed be
  answer'd?
It will be laid to us, whose providence
Should have kept short,[2] restrain'd and out of
  haunt,[3]
This mad young man: but so much was our
  love,
We would not understand what was most fit;
But, like the owner of a foul disease,   21
To keep it from divulging,[4] let it feed
Even on the pith of life. Where is he gone?
  Queen. To draw apart the body he hath
  kill'd:
O'er whom his very madness, like some ore
Among a mineral of metals base,
Shows itself pure; he weeps for what is done.
  King. O Gertrude, come away!
The sun no sooner shall the mountains touch,
But we will ship him hence: and this vile
  deed   30

We must, with all our majesty and skill,
Both countenance and excuse. Ho,
  Guildenstern!

Re-enter ROSENCRANTZ *and* GUILDENSTERN.

Friends both, go join you with some further
  aid:
Hamlet in madness hath Polonius slain,
And from his mother's closet hath he dragg'd
  him:
Go seek him out; speak fair, and bring the
  body
Into the chapel. I pray you, haste in this.
  [*Exeunt* ROSENCRANTZ *and* GUILDENSTERN.
Come, Gertrude, we'll call up our wisest
  friends;
And let them know, both what we mean to
  do,
And what 's untimely done   40
Whose whisper o'er the world's diameter,
As level as the cannon to his blank,[5]
Transports his poison'd shot, may miss our
  name,
And hit the woundless[6] air. O, come away!
My soul is full of discord and dismay.
                                      [*Exeunt.*

SCENE II. *Another room in the castle.*

Enter HAMLET.

  Ham. Safely stowed.
  Ros. }
  Guil. } [*Within*] Hamlet! Lord Hamlet!
  Ham. But soft, what noise? who calls on
Hamlet? O, here they come.

Enter ROSENCRANTZ *and* GUILDENSTERN.

  Ros. What have you done, my lord, with
the dead body?
  Ham. Compounded it with dust, whereto
'tis kin.

SCENE I **1.** *brainish apprehension*, brainsick imagination.
2. *kept short*, i.e., kept on a short tether. **3.** *out of haunt*,
secluded. **4.** *divulging*, becoming evident. **5.** *As level
...blank*, as well aimed as the cannon to its target.
6. *woundless*, invulnerable.

Ros. Tell us where 'tis, that we may take it thence 10
And bear it to the chapel.

Ham. Do not believe it.

Ros. Believe what?

Ham. That I can keep your counsel[1] and not mine own. Besides, to be demanded of[2] a sponge! what replication[3] should be made by the son of a king? 17

Ros. Take you me for a sponge, my lord?

Ham. Ay, sir, that soaks up the king's countenance, his rewards, his authorities. But such officers do the king best service in the end: he keeps them, like an ape an apple, in the corner of his jaw; first mouthed, to be last swallowed: when he needs what you have gleaned, it is but squeezing you, and sponge, you shall be dry again. 26

Ros. I understand you not, my lord.

Ham. I am glad of it: a knavish speech sleeps in a foolish ear.

Ros. My lord, you must tell us where the body is, and go with us to the king.

Ham. The body is with the king, but the king is not with the body. The king is a thing—

Guil. A thing, my lord!

Ham. Of nothing: bring me to him. Hide fox, and all after.[4] [*Exeunt.* 36

SCENE III. *Another room in the castle.*

Enter KING, *attended.*

King. I have sent to seek him, and to find the body.
How dangerous is it that this man goes loose!
Yet must not we put the strong law on him:
He's loved of the distracted multitude,
Who like not in their judgment, but their eyes;
And where 'tis so, the offender's scourge is weigh'd,
But never the offence. To bear all smooth and even,
This sudden sending him away must seem
Deliberate pause[1]: diseases desperate grown
By desperate appliance are relieved, 10
Or not at all.

Enter ROSENCRANTZ.

How now! what hath befall'n?

Ros. Where the dead body is bestow'd, my lord,
We cannot get from him.

King.   But where is he?

Ros. Without, my lord; guarded, to know your pleasure.

King. Bring him before us.

Ros. Ho, Guildenstern! bring in my lord.

Enter HAMLET *and* GUILDENSTERN.

King. Now, Hamlet, where 's Polonius?

Ham. At supper.

King. At supper! where? 19

Ham. Not where he eats, but where he is eaten: a certain convocation of politic worms are e'en at him. Your worm is your only emperor for diet: we fat all creatures else to fat us, and we fat ourselves for maggots: your fat king and your lean beggar is but variable service, two dishes, but to one table: that's the end.

King. Alas, alas!

Ham. A man may fish with the worm that hath eat of a king, and eat of the fish that hath fed of that worm. 31

King. What dost thou mean by this?

Ham. Nothing but to show you how a king may go a progress[2] through the guts of a beggar.

King. Where is Polonius?

Ham. In heaven; send thither to see: if your messenger find him not there, seek him i' the other place yourself. But indeed, if you find him not within this month, you shall nose him as you go up the stairs into the lobby. 41

King. Go seek him there.
                    [*To some* ATTENDANTS.

Ham. He will stay till you come.
                    [*Exeunt* ATTENDANTS.

SCENE II **1.** *keep your counsel.* Hamlet is aware of their treachery but says nothing of it. **2.** *to be demanded of,* being questioned by. **3.** *replication,* reply. **4.** *Hide fox, and all after,* an old signal cry in the game of hide-and-seek.
SCENE III **1.** *deliberate pause,* considered action. **2.** *progress,* royal journey of state.

King. Hamlet, this deed, for thine especial safety,—
Which we do tender,[3] as we dearly grieve
For that which thou hast done,—must send thee hence
With fiery quickness: therefore prepare thyself;
The bark is ready, and the wind at help,
The associates tend, and everything is bent
For England.

Ham.   For England!

King.   Ay, Hamlet.

Ham.   Good.   50

King. So is it, if thou knew'st our purposes.

Ham. I see a cherub that sees them.[4] But, come; for England! Farewell, dear mother.

King. Thy loving father, Hamlet.

Ham. My mother: father and mother is man and wife; man and wife is one flesh; and so, my mother. Come, for England!   [*Exit.*

King. Follow him at foot; tempt him with speed aboard;
Delay it not; I'll have him hence to-night;
Away! for every thing is seal'd and done   60
That else leans on the affair: pray you, make haste.

    [*Exeunt* ROSENCRANTZ *and* GUILDENSTERN.

And, England, if my love thou hold'st at aught—
As my great power thereof may give thee sense,
Since yet thy cicatrice looks raw and red
After the Danish sword, and thy free awe
Pays homage to us—thou mayst not coldly set
Our sovereign process; which imports at full,
By letters congruing[5] to that effect,
The present death of Hamlet. Do it, England;   70
For like the hectic[6] in my blood he rages,
And thou must cure me: till I know 'tis done,
Howe'er my haps,[7] my joys were ne'er begun.

    [*Exit.*

SCENE IV. *A plain in Denmark.*

Enter FORTINBRAS, *a* CAPTAIN, *and* SOLDIERS, *marching.*

For. Go, captain, from me greet the Danish king;
Tell him that, by his license, Fortinbras
Craves the conveyance of a promised march
Over his kingdom. You know the rendezvous.
If that his majesty would aught with us,
We shall express our duty in his eye[1];
And let him know so.

Cap.   I will do 't, my lord.

For. Go softly[2] on.

    [*Exeunt* FORTINBRAS *and* SOLDIERS.

Enter HAMLET, ROSENCRANTZ, GUILDENSTERN, *and others.*

Ham. Good sir, whose powers are these?

Cap. They are of Norway, sir.   10

Ham. How purposed, sir, I pray you?

Cap. Against some part of Poland.

Ham. Who commands them, sir?

Cap. The nephew to old Norway, Fortinbras.

Ham. Goes it against the main of Poland, sir,
Or for some frontier?

Cap. Truly to speak, and with no addition,
We go to gain a little patch of ground
That hath in it no profit but the name.   19
To pay five ducats, five, I would not farm it[3];
Nor will it yield to Norway or the Pole
A ranker rate, should it be sold in fee.[4]

Ham. Why, then the Polack never will defend it.

Cap. Yes, it is already garrison'd.

Ham. Two thousand souls and twenty thousand ducats
Will not debate the question of this straw[5]:
This is the imposthume[6] of much wealth and peace,
That inward breaks, and shows no cause without
Why the man dies. I humbly thank you, sir.

Cap. God be wi' you, sir.   [*Exit.*

Ros.   Will 't please you go, my lord? 30

SCENE III **3.** *tender,* regard, hold dear. **4.** *I see . . . them,* I suspect your real intentions. **5.** *congruing,* according. **6.** *hectic,* fever. **7.** *haps,* fortunes.

SCENE IV **1.** *in his eye,* in his presence. **2.** *softly,* slowly. **3.** *farm it,* take a lease of it. **4.** *in fee,* outright. **5.** *debate the . . . straw,* settle this trifling matter. **6.** *imposthume,* festering abscess.

Ham. I'll be with you straight. Go a little
  before.   [*Exeunt all except* HAMLET.
How all occasions do inform against me,[7]
And spur my dull revenge! What is a man,
If his chief good and market of his time
Be but to sleep and feed? a beast, no more.
Sure, he that made us with such large
  discourse,[8]
Looking before and after, gave us not
That capability and god-like reason
To fust[9] in us unused. Now, whether it be
Bestial oblivion, or some craven scruple   40
Of thinking too precisely on the event,
A thought which, quarter'd, hath but one
  part wisdom
And ever three parts coward, I do not know
Why yet I live to say "This thing 's to do;"
Sith[10] I have cause and will and strength and
  means
To do 't. Examples gross as earth exhort me:
Witness this army of such mass and charge
Led by a delicate and tender prince,
Whose spirit with divine ambition puff'd
Makes mouths at the invisible event,   50
Exposing what is mortal and unsure
To all that fortune, death and danger dare,
Even for an egg-shell. Rightly to be great
Is not to stir without great argument,
But greatly to find quarrel in a straw
When honor's at the stake. How stand I
  then,
That have a father kill'd, a mother stain'd,
Excitements of my reason and my blood,
And let all asleep? while, to my shame, I see
The imminent death of twenty thousand
  men,   60
That, for a fantasy and trick of fame,
Go to their graves like beds, fight for a plot
Whereon the numbers cannot try the cause,
Which is not tomb enough and continent
To hide the slain? O, from this time forth,
My thoughts be bloody, or be nothing worth!
      [*Exit.*

SCENE V. *Elsinore. A room in the castle.*

Enter QUEEN, HORATIO, *and a* GENTLEMAN.

Queen. I will not speak with her.

Gent. She is importunate, indeed distract:
Her mood will needs be pitied.
  Queen.   What would she have?
  Gent. She speaks much of her father; says
  she hears
There 's tricks i' the world; and hems, and
  beats her heart;
Spurns enviously at straws[1]; speaks things in
  doubt,
That carry but half sense: her speech is
  nothing,
Yet the unshaped[2] use of it doth move
The hearers to collection[3]; they yawn[4] at it,
And botch the words up fit to their own
  thoughts;   10
Which, as her winks, and nods, and gestures
  yield them,
Indeed would make one think there might be
  thought,
Though nothing sure, yet much unhappily.[5]
  Hor. 'Twere good she were spoken with:
  for she may strew
Dangerous conjectures in ill-breeding minds.
  Queen. Let her come in.   [*Exit* HORATIO.
To my sick soul, as sin's true nature is,
Each toy seems prologue to some great amiss:
So full of artless jealousy is guilt,
It spills itself in fearing to be spilt.[6]   20

Re-enter HORATIO, *with* OPHELIA.

  Oph. Where is the beauteous majesty of
  Denmark?
  Queen. How now, Ophelia!
  Oph. [*Sings*]
      *How should I your true love know
          From another one?*
      By his cockle hat and staff,[7]
          And his sandal shoon.
  Queen. Alas, sweet lady, what imports this
  song?
  Oph. Say you? nay, pray you, mark.

SCENE IV   **7.** *How all . . . me,* how all events conspire
against me. **8.** *discourse,* power of thought. **9.** *fust,*
grow moldy. **10.** *Sith,* since.
SCENE V   **1.** *Spurns enviously at straws,* shies suspiciously
at trifles. **2.** *unshaped,* artless, unformed. **3.** *collection,*
inference. **4.** *yawn,* wonder. **5.** *much unhappily,* expression of much unhappiness. **6.** *So full . . . spilt,* guilt
betrays itself in fearing to be betrayed. **7.** *cockle hat and
staff,* the garb of a pilgrim to the shrine of St. James of
Compostella in Spain; also a conventional disguise for lovers.

[*Sings*] *He is dead and gone, lady,*
    He is dead and gone;   30
At his head a grass-green turf,
    At his heels a stone.
Queen. Nay, but, Ophelia,—
Oph. Pray you, mark.
[*Sings*] *White his shroud as the mountain*
    snow,—

Enter KING.

Queen. Alas, look here, my lord.
Oph. [*Sings*] *Larded*⁸ *all with flowers;*
    Which bewept to the grave did not go
    with true-love showers.
King. How do you, pretty lady?   40
Oph. Well, God 'ild⁹ you! They say the owl
was a baker's daughter. Lord, we know what
we are, but know not what we may be. God
be at your table!
King. How long hath she been thus?
Oph. I hope all will be well. We must be
patient: but I cannot choose but weep, to
think they should lay him i' the cold ground.
My brother shall know of it: and so I thank
you for your good counsel. Come, my coach!
Good night, ladies; good night, sweet ladies;
good night, good night.   [*Exit.* 52
King. Follow her close; give her good watch,
    I pray you.   [*Exit* HORATIO.
O, this is the poison of deep grief; it springs
All from her father's death. O Gertrude,
    Gertrude,
When sorrows come, they come not single
    spies,
But in battalions. First, her father slain:
Next, your son gone; and he most violent
    author
Of his own just remove: the people muddied,
Thick and unwholesome in their thoughts
    and whispers,   60
For good Polonius' death; and we have done
    but greenly,¹⁰
In hugger-mugger¹¹ to inter him: poor
    Ophelia
Divided from herself and her fair judgment,
Without the which we are pictures, or mere
    beasts:
Last, and as much containing as all these,
Her brother is in secret come from France;

Feeds on his wonder, keeps himself in clouds,
And wants not buzzers¹² to infect his ear
With pestilent speeches of his father's
    death;
Wherein necessity, of matter beggar'd,   70
Will nothing stick¹³ our person to arraign
In ear and ear. O my dear Gertrude, this,
Like to a murdering-piece,¹⁴ in many places
Gives me superfluous death. [*A noise within.*
    Queen.   Alack, what noise is this?
    King. Where are my Switzers?¹⁵ Let them
    guard the door.

Enter another GENTLEMAN.

What is the matter?
    Gent.   Save yourself, my lord:
The ocean, overpeering of his list,¹⁶
Eats not the flats with more impetuous haste
Than young Laertes, in a riotous head,¹⁷
O'erbears your officers. The rabble call him
    lord;   80
And, as the world were now but to begin,
Antiquity forgot, custom not known,
The ratifiers and props of every word,¹⁸
They cry "Choose we: Laertes shall be king":
Caps, hands, and tongues, applaud it to the
    clouds:
"Laertes shall be king, Laertes king!"
    Queen. How cheerfully on the false trail
    they cry!
O, this is counter, you false Danish dogs!
    King. The doors are broke.   [*Noise within.*

Enter LAERTES, *armed;* DANES *following.*

Laer. Where is this king? Sirs, stand you
    all without.   90
Danes. No, let's come in.
Laer.   I pray you, give me leave.
Danes. We will, we will.
    [*They retire without the door.*

---

8. *Larded,* decorated. 9. *God'ild,* God yield or reward.
10. *greenly,* foolishly. 11. *hugger-mugger,* secrecy.
12. *wants not buzzers,* is not lacking for gossips. 13. *noth-*
ing stick, not hesitate. 14. *murdering-piece,* a cannon using scattered shot. 15. *Switzers,* Swiss guards. 16. *over-*
peering of his list, overflowing its boundary. 17. *in a*
riotous head, heading a riotous force. 18. *ratifiers and . . .*
word, i.e., antiquity and custom are the foundation of civil
life, or government.

Laer. I thank you: keep the door. O thou vile king,
Give me my father!
  Queen.   Calmly, good Laertes.
  King.   What is the cause, Laertes,
That thy rebellion looks so giant-like?
Let him go, Gertrude; do not fear our person:
There 's such divinity doth hedge a king,
That treason can but peep[19] to what it would,
Acts little of his will. Tell me, Laertes,   100
Why thou art thus incensed. Let him go, Gertrude.
Speak, man.
  Laer. Where is my father?
  King.   Dead.
  Queen.   But not by him.
  King. Let him demand his fill.
  Laer. How came he dead? I'll not be juggled with:
To hell, allegiance! vows, to the blackest devil!
Conscience and grace, to the profoundest pit!
I dare damnation. To this point I stand,
That both the worlds I give to negligence,[20]
Let come what comes; only I'll be revenged   110
Most throughly[21] for my father.
  King.   Who shall stay you?
  Laer. My will, not all the world:
And for my means, I'll husband them so well,
They shall go far with little.
  King.   Good Laertes,
If you desire to know the certainty
Of your dear father's death, is 't writ in your revenge,
That, swoopstake,[22] you will draw both friend and foe,
Winner and loser?
  Laer. None but his enemies.
  King.   Will you know them then?
  Laer. To his good friends thus wide I'll ope my arms;   120
And like the kind life-rendering pelican,[23]
Repast them with my blood.
  King.   Why, now you speak
Like a good child and a true gentleman.
That I am guiltless of your father's death,
And am most sensibly in grief for it,

It shall as level to your judgment 'pear
As day does to your eye.
  Danes.   [*Within*] Let her come in.
  Laer. How now! what noise is that?

Re-enter OPHELIA.

O heat, dry up my brains! tears seven times salt,
Burn out the sense and virtue of mine eye! 130
By heaven, thy madness shall be paid with weight,
Till our scale turn the beam. O rose of May!
Dear maid, kind sister, sweet Ophelia!
O heavens! is 't possible, a young maid's wits
Should be as mortal as an old man's life?
Nature is fine in love,[24] and where 'tis fine,
It sends some precious instance of itself
After the thing it loves.
  Oph. [*Sings*]
    They bore him barefaced on the bier;
    Hey non nonny, nonny, hey nonny; 140
    And in his grave rain'd many a tear:—
Fare you well, my dove!
  Laer. Hadst thou thy wits, and didst persuade revenge,
It could not move thus.
  Oph. [*Sings*]
    You must sing a-down a-down,
    An you call him a-down-a.
O, how the wheel[25] becomes it! It is the false steward, that stole his master's daughter.
  Laer. This nothing 's more than matter. 149
  Oph. There 's rosemary, that 's for remembrance; pray, love, remember: and there is pansies, that 's for thoughts.
  Laer. A document in madness, thoughts and remembrance fitted.
  Oph. There 's fennel for you, and columbines: there 's rue for you; and here 's some for me: we may call it herb of grace o' Sundays: O, you must wear your rue with a dif-

---

19. *peep*, look from a distance. **20.** *both the worlds . . . negligence*, I despise both this world and the one to come. **21.** *throughly*, thoroughly. **22.** *swoopstake*, indiscriminately. **23.** *pelican*, a reference to the belief that the pelican feeds its young with its own blood. **24.** *Nature is fine in love*, human nature is noble in love. **25.** *wheel*. Ophelia recalls songs she heard sung by women working at their spinning wheels.

ference. There 's a daisy: I would give you some violets,[26] but they withered all when my father died: they say he made a good end,—
[Sings] *For bonny sweet Robin is all my joy.*

Laer. Thought and affliction, passion, hell itself,
She turns to favor and to prettiness.

Oph. [Sings]
And will he not come again?
And will he not come again?
No, No, he is dead:
Go to thy death-bed:
He never will come again.

His beard was as white as snow,   170
All flaxen was his poll:
He is gone, he is gone,
And we cast away moan:
God ha' mercy on his soul!

And of all Christian souls, I pray God. God be wi' ye.   [*Exit.*

Laer. Do you see this, O God?

King. Laertes, I must commune with your grief,
Or you deny me right. Go but apart,
Make choice of whom your wisest friends you will,   180
And they shall hear and judge 'twixt you and me:
If by direct or by collateral hand
They find us touch'd,[27] we will our kingdom give,
Our crown, our life, and all that we call ours,
To you in satisfaction; but if not,
Be you content to lend your patience to us,
And we shall jointly labor with your soul
To give it due content.

Laer.   Let this be so;
His means of death, his obscure funeral—
No trophy, sword, nor hatchment o'er his bones,   190
No noble rite nor formal ostentation—
Cry to be heard, as 'twere from heaven to earth,
That I must call 't in question.

King.   So you shall;
And where the offence is let the great axe fall.

I pray you, go with me.   [*Exeunt.*

SCENE VI. *Another room in the castle.*

Enter HORATIO *and a* SERVANT.

Hor. What are they that would speak with me?

Serv. Sailors, sir: they say they have letters for you.

Hor. Let them come in.   [*Exit* SERVANT.
I do not know from what part of the world
I should be greeted, if not from lord Hamlet.

Enter SAILORS.

First Sail. God bless you, sir.

Hor. Let him bless thee too.

First Sail. He shall, sir, an 't please him. There 's a letter for you, sir; it comes from the ambassador that was bound for England; if your name be Horatio, as I am let to know it is.   12

Hor. [*Reads*] *Horatio, when thou shalt have overlooked this, give these fellows some means[1] to the king: they have letters for him. Ere we were two days old at sea, a pirate of very warlike appointment gave us chase. Finding ourselves too slow of sail, we put on a compelled valor, and in the grapple I boarded them: on the instant they got clear of our ship; so I alone became their prisoner. They have dealt with me like thieves of mercy[2]: but they knew what they did; I am to do a good turn for them. Let the king have the letters I have sent; and repair thou to me with as much speed as thou wouldst fly death. I have words to speak in thine ear will make thee dumb; yet are they much too light for the bore[3] of the matter. These good fellows will bring thee where I am. Rosencrantz and Guildenstern hold their course for England: of them I have much to tell thee. Farewell.*   32

He that thou knowest thine, HAMLET.

SCENE V   **26.** *fennel ... violets.* Plants were regarded as emblems: *fennel* stood for flattery; *columbines* for disloyalty and ingratitude; *rue* for repentance (when mingled with holy water, rue was known as *herb of grace*); *daisies* for infidelity; and *violets* for faithfulness. **27.** *touch'd,* implicated.
SCENE VI **1.** *means,* means of access. **2.** *thieves of mercy,* merciful thieves. **3.** *bore,* caliber, importance.

Come, I will make you way for these your
  letters;
And do 't the speedier, that you may direct
  me
To him from whom you brought them.
                                    [*Exeunt.*

SCENE VII. *Another room in the castle.*

  Enter KING *and* LAERTES.

  King. Now must your conscience my
    acquittance seal,
And you must put me in your heart for
    friend,
Sith you have heard, and with a knowing
    ear,
That he which hath your noble father slain
Pursued my life.
  Laer.   It well appears: but tell me
Why you proceeded not against these feats,
So criminal and so capital in nature,
As by your safety, wisdom, all things else,
You mainly[1] were stirr'd up.
  King.   O, for two special reasons;
Which may to you, perhaps, seem much
    unsinew'd,   10
But yet to me they are strong. The queen his
    mother
Lives almost by his looks; and for myself—
My virtue or my plague, be it either which—
She 's so conjunctive[2] to my life and soul,
That, as the star moves not but in his
    sphere,[3]
I could not but by her. The other motive,
Why to a public count I might not go,
Is the great love the general gender[4] bear
    him;
Who, dipping all his faults in their affection,
Would, like the spring that turneth wood to
    stone,[5]   20
Convert his gyves[6] to graces; so that my
    arrows,
Too slightly timber'd[7] for so loud a wind,
Would have reverted to my bow again,
And not where I had aim'd them.
  Laer. And so have I a noble father lost;
A sister driven into desperate terms,
Whose worth, if praises may go back again,

Stood challenger on mount of all the age
For her perfections: but my revenge will
    come.
  King. Break not your sleeps for that: you
    must not think   30
That we are made of stuff so flat and dull
That we can let our beard be shook with
    danger
And think it pastime. You shortly shall hear
    more:
I loved your father, and we love ourself;
And that, I hope, will teach you to imagine—

  Enter a MESSENGER.

How now! what news?
  Mess.   Letters, my lord, from Hamlet:
This to your majesty; this to the queen.
  King. From Hamlet! who brought them?
  Mess. Sailors, my lord, they say; I saw
    them not:
They were given me by Claudio; he received
    them   40
Of him that brought them.
  King.   Laertes, you shall hear them.
Leave us.   [*Exit* MESSENGER.
  [*Reads*] *High and mighty, You shall know
I am set naked*[8] *on your kingdom. To-morrow
shall I beg leave to see your kingly eyes: when
I shall, first asking your pardon thereunto, re-
count the occasion of my sudden and more
strange return.*   HAMLET.
What should this mean? Are all the rest come
    back?   50
Or is it some abuse, and no such thing?
  Laer. Know you the hand?
  King.   'Tis Hamlet's character. "Naked!"
And in a postscript here, he says "alone."
Can you advise me?
  Laer. I 'm lost in it, my lord. But let him
    come;
It warms the very sickness in my heart,

---

1. *mainly*, greatly. 2. *conjunctive*, joined with. 3.
sphere. According to the Ptolemaic (tol'ə mā'ik) system
of astronomy (which held that the earth was the fixed center of the universe), the planets moved within a hollow
sphere. 4. *general gender*, common people. 5. *the spring
. . . stone*, i.e., one heavily charged with lime. 6. *gyves*
(jivz), fetters. 7. *slightly timber'd*, light. 8. *naked*, unprovided (with retinue).

That I shall live and tell him to his teeth,
"Thus didst thou."
    King.   If it be so, Laertes—
As how should it be so? how otherwise?—
Will you be ruled by me?
    Laer.   Ay, my lord;   60
So you will not o'errule me to a peace.
    King. To thine own peace. If he be now
    return'd,
As checking at[9] his voyage, and that he
    means
No more to undertake it, I will work him
To an exploit, now ripe in my device,
Under the which he shall not choose but
    fall:
And for his death no wind of blame shall
    breathe,
But even his mother shall uncharge the
    practice[10]
And call it accident.
    Laer.   My lord, I will be ruled;
The rather, if you could devise it so   70
That I might be the organ.[11]
    King.   It falls right.
You have been talk'd of since your travel
    much,
And that in Hamlet's hearing, for a quality
Wherein, they say, you shine: your sum of
    parts
Did not together pluck such envy from him
As did that one, and that, in my regard,
Of the unworthiest siege.[12]
    Laer.   What part is that, my lord?
    King. A very riband in the cap of youth,
Yet needful too; for youth no less becomes
The light and careless livery that it wears   80
Than settled age his sables and his weeds,
Importing health and graveness. Two months
    since,
Here was a gentleman of Normandy:—
I've seen myself, and served against, the
    French,
And they can well on horseback: but this
    gallant
Had witchcraft in 't; he grew unto his seat;
And to such wondrous doing brought his
    horse,
As had he been incorpsed and demi-natured[13]
With the brave beast: so far he topp'd my
    thought,

That I, in forgery of shapes and tricks,[14]   90
Come short of what he did.
    Laer.   A Norman was 't?
    King. A Norman.
    Laer. Upon my life, Lamond.
    King.   The very same.
    Laer. I know him well: he is the brooch
    indeed
And gem of all the nation.
    King. He made confession of you,[15]
And gave you such a masterly report
For art and exercise in your defense
And for your rapier most especial,   99
That he cried out, 'twould be a sight indeed,
If one could match you: the scrimers[16] of
    their nation,
He swore, had neither motion, guard, nor
    eye,
If you opposed them. Sir, this report of his
Did Hamlet so envenom with his envy
That he could nothing do but wish and beg
Your sudden coming o'er, to play with him.
Now, out of this,—
    Laer.   What out of this, my lord?
    King. Laertes, was your father dear to you?
Or are you like the painting of a sorrow,
A face without a heart?
    Laer.   Why ask you this? 110
    King. Not that I think you did not love
    your father;
But that I know love is begun by time;
And that I see, in passages of proof,[17]
Time qualifies the spark and fire of it.
There lives within the very flame of love
A kind of wick or snuff that will abate it;
And nothing is at a like goodness still;
For goodness, growing to a plurisy,[18]
Dies in his own too much: that we would do,
We should do when we would; for this
    "would" changes   120
And hath abatements and delays as many
As there are tongues, are hands, are accidents;
And then this "should" is like a spendthrift
    sigh,

---

9. *checking at,* shying from. 10. *uncharge the practice,* acquit the method. 11. *organ,* agent. 12. *siege,* rank. 13. *incorpsed and demi-natured,* of one body and nearly of one nature. 14. *in forgery ... tricks,* in imagining feats of horsemanship. 15. *made confession of you,* said he knew you. 16. *scrimers* (skrim'ẽrz), fencers. 17. *passages of proof,* proved instances. 18. *plurisy,* excess.

That hurts by easing. But, to the quick o'
    the ulcer[19]:—
Hamlet comes back: what would you
    undertake,
To show yourself your father's son in deed
More than in words?
    Laer.   To cut his throat i' the church.
    King. No place, indeed, should murder
    sanctuarize[20];
Revenge should have no bounds. But, good
    Laertes,
Will you do this, keep close within your
    chamber.   130
Hamlet return'd shall know you are come
    home:
We'll put on those shall praise your
    excellence
And set a double varnish on the fame
The Frenchman gave you, bring you in fine
    together
And wager on your heads: he, being remiss,
Most generous and free from all contriving,
Will not peruse the foils; so that, with ease,
Or with a little shuffling, you may choose
A sword unbated,[21] and in a pass of practice[22]
Requite him for your father.
    Laer.   I will do 't: 140
And, for that purpose, I'll anoint my sword.
I bought an unction of a mountebank,
So mortal that, but dip a knife in it,
Where it draws blood no cataplasm[23] so rare,
Collected from all simples[24] that have virtue
Under the moon, can save the thing from
    death
That is but scratched withal: I'll touch my
    point
With this contagion, that, if I gall[25] him
    slightly,
It may be death.
    King   Let 's further think of this;
Weigh what convenience both of time and
    means   150
May fit us to our shape[26]: if this should fail,
And that our drift[27] look through our bad
    performance,
'Twere better not assay'd: therefore this
    project
Should have a back or second, that might
    hold,
If this should blast in proof. Soft! let me see:

We'll make a solemn wager on your
    cunnings:
I ha 't:
When in your motion you are hot and dry—
As make your bouts more violent to that
    end—
And that he calls for drink, I'll have prepared
    him   160
A chalice for the nonce,[28] whereon but
    sipping,
If he by chance escape your venom'd stuck,
Our purpose may hold there.

    Enter QUEEN.

                    How now, sweet queen!
    Queen. One woe doth tread upon another's
    heel,
So fast they follow: your sister 's drown'd,
    Laertes.
    Laer. Drown'd! O, where?
    Queen. There is a willow grows aslant a
    brook,
That shows his hoar leaves in the glassy
    stream;
There with fantastic garlands did she make
Of crow-flowers, nettles, daisies, and long
    purples: 170
There, on the pendent boughs her coronet
    weeds
Clambering to hang, an envious sliver[29]
    broke;
When down her weedy trophies and herself
Fell in the weeping brook. Her clothes spread
    wide;
And, mermaid-like, awhile they bore her up:
Which time she chanted snatches of old
    tunes;
As one incapable[30] of her own distress,
Or like a creature native and indued
Unto that element: but long it could not be
Till that her garments, heavy with their
    drink,   180

---

19. *quick o' the ulcer*, heart of the difficulty. **20.** *sanctuarize*, protect from punishment, an allusion to the fact that certain religious places were invested with the right of sanctuary. **21.** *unbated*, not blunted. **22.** *pass of practice*, treacherous thrust. **23.** *cataplasm*, plaster or poultice. **24.** *simples*, herbs. **25.** *gall*, graze, wound. **26.** *shape*, part we propose to act. **27.** *drift*, intention. **28.** *for the nonce*, for such an occasion. **29.** *sliver*, branch. **30.** *incapable*, unaware.

Pull'd the poor wretch from her melodious
    lay
To muddy death.
    Laer.   Alas then, she is drown'd?
    Queen. Drown'd, drown'd.
    Laer. Too much of water hast thou, poor
    Ophelia,
And therefore I forbid my tears: but yet
It is our trick[31]; nature her custom holds,
Let shame say what it will: when these are
    gone,
The woman will be out. Adieu, my lord:
I have a speech of fire, that fain would blaze,
But that this folly douts[32] it.   [*Exit.*
    King.   Let's follow, Gertrude: 190
How much I had to do to calm his rage!
Now fear I this will give it start again;
Therefore let 's follow.   [*Exeunt.*

---

31. *trick*, way. 32. *douts*, extinguishes.

To increase understanding
Act IV, Scenes 1-4

1. (*a*) With what problem does the death of
Polonius confront the King? (*b*) What action does
he take?

2. (*a*) Describe Hamlet's encounter with the
army of Fortinbras. (*b*) What effect does this encounter have on Hamlet?

3. Reread lines 27–29 in Scene 4. (*a*) What
do they mean in context? (*b*) What do they mean
in terms of the play as a whole?

Scene 5

1. What has happened to Ophelia?

2. (*a*) How have the Danish people reacted to
Polonius' death? (*b*) How has Laertes reacted? (*c*)
In what way is the King responsible for the increased
state of turmoil?

Scenes 6-7

1. (*a*) What news does Horatio have from Hamlet? (*b*) What does he do on receipt of this news?

2. Scene 7 opens in the middle of a conversation. (*a*) How do you think the King has explained
Polonius' death to Laertes? (*b*) How does he justify
not moving faster against Hamlet? (*c*) Describe in
detail the plan agreed upon by the King and Laertes
when news of Hamlet's return reaches them.

3. What is the irony of lines 127–129, Scene 7?

4. With what tragic event does the act end?

Act IV in Review

1. By the end of Act IV what has happened to,
or what is the situation of: (*a*) the conflict between
the King and Hamlet; (*b*) the affairs of Polonius
and his family; (*c*) the relations between Denmark
and Norway?

2. When the King says that sorrows come "not
single spies, /But in battalions," he is referring to
the deaths and disorder that have already befallen
the state of Denmark. What other "sorrows" are
likely to lie ahead?

Better reading
Puns

Shakespeare's plays, like many Elizabethan writings,
are full of *puns*—plays on words that sound alike
but have different meanings. The eighteenth-century prose writer Joseph Addison, whom you will read
in Chapter V, looked upon the Elizabethan habit of
punning as merely a means of producing a low-grade
kind of humor. And, indeed, when Shakespeare has
one comical character say to another (Act V, Scene
1) that Adam must have been a gentleman because
he bore arms (knightly arms—limbs), audiences today tend to groan.

What Addison did not realize, however, was that
the Elizabethans not only punned for fun but also,
in many cases, in all seriousness. Perhaps more so
than any Englishmen before them, and any Englishmen since, the Elizabethans were aware that people
think and feel in several ways at the same time
(anger, fear, joy, etc.) and that events do not just
have single causes and single effects. Punning
proved an admirable way of pointing up this complexity of any given life situation. Thus Shakespeare's contemporary John Donne, whom you will
read in this chapter, in an effort to express his
complex feelings about the thought of his own death,
asks God to swear

                  that at my death Thy *Son*
Shall shine as he shines now, and heretofore;
    And, having done that, Thou hast *done*;
      I fear no more.

By *Son*, Donne means both "sunshine" and "Christ";
done means "finished" and also "John Donne."

Turn back to the following serious puns in *Hamlet* and explain what multiple effects Shakespeare is
trying to achieve with each:

A little more than kin, and less than *kind*.
                (Act I, Scene 2, line 65)

I am too much i' the *sun*.
                (Act I, Scene 2, line 67)

Ay, madam, it is *common*.

(Act I, Scene 2, line 74)

Not of that dye which their *investments* show,
But mere implorators of unholy *suits*.

(Act I, Scene 3, lines 121–122)

This man shall set me *packing*.

(Act III, Scene 4, line 188)

 Words!

The following words have changed meaning since Elizabethan times either through generalization, specialization, or ascended or descended connotation, or by some combination of these processes. (See the discussion of these modes of change, pages 82–83.) By referring to a standard work on etymology, explain how these words came to mean what they do today.

erring, honest, rash, fond, counterfeit,
picture, affection, virtue, vice

This illuminated letter "T" contains a miniature portrait of Mr. Tarlton, a famous clown in the days of Queen Elizabeth I. Mr. Tarlton is said to have been the original of Yorick, the jester of whom Hamlet speaks in the following scene (lines 215-239).

ACT FIVE

SCENE I. *A churchyard.*

Enter two CLOWNS,[1] *with spades, &c.*

First Clo. Is she to be buried in Christian burial that willfully seeks her own salvation?

Sec. Clo. I tell thee she is; and therefore make her grave straight[2]: the crowner[3] hath sat on her, and finds it Christian burial.

First Clo. How can that be, unless she drowned herself in her own defense?

Sec. Clo. Why, 'tis found so. 10

First Clo. It must be *se offendendo*[4]; it cannot be else. For here lies the point: if I drown myself wittingly, it argues an act: and an act hath three branches; it is, to act, to do, and to perform: argal,[5] she drowned herself wittingly.

Sec. Clo. Nay, but hear you, goodman delver,—

First Clo. Give me leave. Here lies the water; good: here stands the man; good: if the man go to this water, and drown himself, it is, will he, nill he, he goes,—mark you that; but if the water come to him and drown him, he drowns not himself: argal, he that is not guilty of his own death shortens not his own life. 25

Sec. Clo. But is this law?

First Clo. Ay, marry, is 't; crowner's quest[6] law.

Sec. Clo. Will you ha' the truth on 't? If this had not been a gentlewoman, she should have been buried out o' Christian burial. 31

First Clo. Why, there thou say'st: and the more pity that great folk should have countenance[7] in this world to drown or hang themselves, more than their even[8] Christian. Come, my spade. There is no ancient gentlemen but gardeners, ditchers, and grave-makers: they hold up Adam's profession.

Sec. Clo. Was he a gentleman? 39

---

1. *Clowns.* The word *clown* was used to denote peasants as well as humorous characters; here applied to the rustic type of clown. **2.** *straight,* straightway. **3.** *crowner,* coroner. **4.** *se offendendo,* for *se defendendo,* a common legal phrase meaning "in self-defense." **5.** *argal,* corruption of *ergo,* Latin for "therefore." **6.** *crowner's quest,* coroner's inquest. **7.** *countenance,* privilege. **8.** *even,* fellow.

First Clo. A' was the first that ever bore arms.

Sec. Clo. Why, he had none.

First Clo. What, art a heathen? How dost thou understand the Scripture? The Scripture says "Adam digged": could he dig without arms? I'll put another question to thee: if thou answerest me not to the purpose, confess thyself[9]—

Sec. Clo. Go to.　　　　　　　　　　49

First Clo. What is he that builds stronger than either the mason, the shipwright, or the carpenter?

Sec. Clo. The gallows-maker: for that frame outlives a thousand tenants.

First Clo. I like thy wit well, in good faith: the gallows does well; but how does it well? it does well to those that do ill: now thou dost ill to say the gallows is built stronger than the church: argal, the gallows may do well to thee. To 't again, come.　　　　60

Sec. Clo. 'Who builds stronger than a mason, a shipwright, or a carpenter?'

First Clo. Ay, tell me that, and unyoke.[10]

Sec. Clo. Marry, now I can tell.

First Clo. To 't.

Sec. Clo. Mass,[11] I cannot tell.

Enter HAMLET *and* HORATIO, *at a distance.*

First Clo. Cudgel thy brains no more about it, for your dull ass will not mend his pace with beating; and, when you are asked this question next, say "a grave-maker": the houses that he makes last till doomsday. Go, get thee in, and fetch me a stoup of liquor. [*Exit* SEC. CLOWN.
　　　　　　　　　　[*He digs, and sings.*
　In youth,[12] *when I did love, did love,*
　　Methought it was very sweet,
　To contract, O, the time, for, ah, my
　　　behove,　　　　80
　O, methought, there was nothing
　　meet.

Ham. Has this fellow no feeling of his business, that he sings at grave-making?

Hor. Custom hath made it in him a property of easiness.[13]

Ham. 'Tis e'en so: the hand of little employment hath the daintier sense.

First Clo. [*Sings*]

　But age, with his stealing steps,
　　Hath claw'd me in his clutch,　　90
　And hath shipped me into the land,
　　As if I had never been such.
　　　　　　　[*Throws up a skull.*

Ham. That skull had a tongue in it, and could sing once: how the knave jowls[14] it to the ground, as if it were Cain's jaw-bone,[15] that did the first murder! It might be the pate of a politician, which this ass now o'er-reaches; one that would circumvent God, might it not?

Hor. It might, my lord.　　　　100

Ham. Or of a courtier; which could say "Good morrow, sweet lord! How dost thou, good lord?" This might be my lord such-a-one, that praised my lord such-a-one's horse, when he meant to beg it; might it not?

Hor. Ay, my lord.

Ham. Why, e'en so: and now my Lady Worm's; chapless,[16] and knocked about the mazzard[17] with a sexton's spade: here 's fine revolution, an we had the trick to see 't. Did these bones cost no more the breeding, but to play at loggats[18] with 'em? mine ache to think on 't.　　　　113

First Clo. [*Sings*]
　A pick-axe, and a spade, a spade,
　　For and a shrouding sheet:
　O, a pit of clay for to be made
　　For such a guest is meet.　　　118
　　　　　　　[*Throws up another skull.*

Ham. There 's another: why may not that be the skull of a lawyer? Where be his quiddities now, his quillets,[19] his cases, his tenures, and his tricks? why does he suffer this rude knave now to knock him about the sconce[20] with a dirty shovel, and will not tell him of his action of battery? Hum! This fellow might be in 's time a great buyer of land, with his statutes, his recognizances, his fines, his double

---

9. *confess thyself,* ". . . and be hanged" completes the proverb. 10. *unyoke,* unharness, your work's done. 11. *Mass,* by the Mass. 12. *In youth.* This and the two following stanzas, with nonsensical variations, are from *Tottel's Miscellany,* the first of the many collections of Elizabethan lyrics. 13. *Custom . . . easiness,* it is a matter of habit with him now. 14. *jowls,* dashes. 15. *jaw-bone,* allusion to the old tradition that Cain slew Abel with the jaw-bone of an ass. 16. *chapless,* having no lower jaw. 17. *mazzard,* head. 18. *loggats,* a game in which sticks are thrown as near a fixed stake as possible. 19. *quiddities . . . quillets,* logical subtleties and quibbles. 20. *sconce,* head.

vouchers, his recoveries: is this the fine[21] of his fines, and the recovery of his recoveries, to have his fine pate full of fine dirt? will his vouchers vouch him no more of his purchases, and double ones too, than the length and breadth of a pair of indentures? The very conveyances of his lands will hardly lie in this box; and must the inheritor himself have no more, ha? 137

Hor. Not a jot more, my lord.

Ham. Is not parchment made of sheep-skins?

Hor. Ay, my lord, and of calf-skins too.

Ham. They are sheep and calves which seek out assurance in that. I will speak to this fellow. Whose grave 's this, sirrah?

First Clo. Mine, sir.

[*Sings*] O, *a pit of clay for to be made*
    For such a guest is meet.

Ham. I think it be thine, indeed; for thou liest in 't. 149

First Clo. You lie out on 't, sir, and therefore it is not yours: for my part, I do not lie in 't, and yet it is mine.

Ham. Thou dost lie in 't, to be in 't and say it is thine: 'tis for the dead, not for the quick; therefore thou liest.

First Clo. 'Tis a quick lie, sir; 'twill away again, from me to you.

Ham. What man dost thou dig it for?

First Clo. For no man, sir.

Ham. What woman, then? 160

First Clo. For none, neither.

Ham. Who is to be buried in 't?

First Clo. One that was a woman, sir: but, rest her soul, she 's dead.

Ham. How absolute[22] the knave is! we must speak by the card,[23] or equivocation will undo us. By the Lord, Horatio, these three years I have taken note of it; the age is grown so picked[24] that the toe of the peasant comes so near the heel of the courtier, he galls his kibe.[25] How long hast thou been a grave-maker? 172

First Clo. Of all the days i' the year, I came to 't that day that our last king Hamlet overcame Fortinbras.

Ham. How long is that since?

First Clo. Cannot you tell that? every fool can tell that: it was the very day that young Hamlet was born; he that is mad, and sent into England. 180

Ham. Ay, marry, why was he sent into England?

First Clo. Why, because he was mad: he shall recover his wits there; or, if he do not, it 's no great matter there.

Ham. Why?

First Clo. 'Twill not be seen in him there; there the men are as mad as he.

Ham. How came he mad?

First Clo. Very strangely, they say. 190

Ham. How strangely?

First Clo. Faith, e'en with losing his wits.

Ham. Upon what ground?

First Clo. Why, here in Denmark: I have been sexton here, man and boy, thirty years.

Ham. How long will a man lie i' the earth ere he rot?

First Clo. I' faith, if he be not rotten before he die—as we have many pocky[26] corses now-a-days, that will scarce hold the laying in—he will last you some eight year or nine year: a tanner will last you nine year. 202

Ham. Why he more than another?

First Clo. Why, sir, his hide is so tanned with his trade, that he will keep out water a great while; and your water is a sore decayer of your dead body. Here's a skull now hath lain you i' th' earth three and twenty years.

Ham. Whose was it? 209

First Clo. A mad fellow's it was: whose do you think it was?

Ham. Nay, I know not.

First Clo. A pestilence on him for a mad rogue! a' poured a flagon of Rhenish on my head once. This same skull, sir, was Yorick's skull, the king's jester.

Ham. This?

First Clo. E'en that. 218

Ham. Let me see. [*Takes the skull.*] Alas, poor Yorick! I knew him, Horatio: a fellow of infinite jest, of most excellent fancy: he hath borne me on his back a thousand times; and now, how abhorred in my imagination it

---

21. *fine*, end. Notice that Hamlet plays with four different meanings of *fine* in this sentence. **22.** *absolute*, positive, precise. **23.** *by the card*, to the point. **24.** *picked*, refined, fastidious. **25.** *galls his kibe*, grazes his chilblain. **26.** *pocky*, diseased.

is! my gorge rises at it. Here hung those lips that I have kissed I know not how oft. Where be your gibes now? your gambols? your songs? your flashes of merriment, that were wont to set the table on a roar? Not one now, to mock your own grinning? quite chap-fallen? Now get you to my lady's chamber, and tell her, let her paint an inch thick, to this favor she must come; make her laugh at that. Prithee, Horatio, tell me one thing.   233

Hor. What 's that, my lord?

Ham. Dost thou think Alexander[27] looked o' this fashion i' the earth?

Hor. E'en so.

Ham. And smelt so? pah!

                            [*Puts down the skull.*

Hor. E'en so, my lord.   240

Ham. To what base uses we may return, Horatio! Why may not imagination trace the noble dust of Alexander, till he find it stopping a bung-hole?

Hor. 'Twere to consider too curiously,[28] to consider so.

Ham. No, faith, not a jot; but to follow him thither with modesty enough, and likelihood to lead it: as thus: Alexander died, Alexander was buried, Alexander returneth into dust; the dust is earth; of earth we make loam[29]; and why of that loam, whereto he was converted, might they not stop a beerbarrel?

Imperious Cæsar, dead and turn'd to clay,
Might stop a hole to keep the wind away:
O, that that earth, which kept the world
    in awe,
Should patch a wall to expel the winter's
    flaw![30]

But soft! but soft! aside: here comes the king,

Enter PRIESTS, &c. *in procession; the*
Corpse of OPHELIA, LAERTES *and*
MOURNERS, *following;* KING, QUEEN,
their trains, &c.

The queen, the courtiers: who is this they
    follow?
And with such maimed rites? This doth
    betoken
The corse they follow did with desperate
    hand

Fordo it[31] own life: 'twas of some estate.
Couch[32] we awhile, and mark.   270

                 [*Retiring with* HORATIO.

Laer. What ceremony else?

Ham.   That is Laertes,
A very noble youth: mark.

Laer. What ceremony else?

First Priest. Her obsequies have been as far
    enlarged[33]
As we have warranty: her death was
    doubtful;
And, but that great command o'ersways the
    order,[34]
She should in ground unsanctified have
    lodged
Till the last trumpet; for charitable prayers,
Shards, flints and pebbles should be thrown
    on her:
Yet here she is allow'd her virgin crants,[35]
Her maiden strewments and the bringing
    home
Of bell and burial.   282

Laer. Must there no more be done?

First Priest.   No more be done:
We should profane the service of the dead
To sing a requiem and such rest to her
As to peace-parted souls.

Laer.   Lay her i' the earth:
And from her fair and unpolluted flesh
May violets spring! I tell thee, churlish priest,
A ministering angel shall my sister be,
When thou liest howling.[36]

Ham.   What, the fair Ophelia! 290

Queen. Sweets to the sweet: farewell!

                 [*Scattering flowers.*

I hoped thou shouldst have been my Hamlet's
    wife;
I thought thy bride-bed to have deck'd, sweet
    maid,
And not have strew'd thy grave.

---

27. *Alexander,* Alexander the Great, king of Macedonia from 336 to 323 B.C. He conquered the Greek city-states and the whole Persian empire, from the coasts of Asia Minor and Egypt to India. 28. *curiously,* ingeniously. 29. *loam,* clay paste for brickmaking. 30. *flaw,* gust of wind. 31. *Fordo it,* destroy it. 32. *Couch,* hide. 33. *enlarged,* extended, referring to the fact that suicides are not given full burial rites. 34. *death was doubtful . . . order.* The priest reluctantly accepts the king's claim that Ophelia died by accident and not by suicide. 35. *crants,* garlands customarily hung upon the bier of an unmarried woman. 36. *howling,* i.e., in hell.

Laer.   O, treble woe
Fall ten times treble on that cursed head,
Whose wicked deed thy most ingenious
        sense[37]
Deprived thee of! Hold off the earth awhile,
Till I have caught her once more in mine
        arms: [*Leaps into the grave.*
Now pile your dust upon the quick and dead,
Till of this flat a mountain you have made,
To o'ertop old Pelion,[38] or the skyish head 301
Of blue Olympus.
    Ham. [*Advancing*] What is he whose grief
Bears such an emphasis? whose phrase of
        sorrow
Conjures the wandering stars, and makes
        them stand
Like wonder-wounded hearers? This is I,
Hamlet the Dane.   [*Leaps into the grave.*
    Laer.   The devil take thy soul!
                    [*Grappling with him.*
    Ham. Thou pray'st not well.
I prithee, take thy fingers from my throat;
For, though I am not splenitive[39] and rash,
Yet have I in something dangerous,   310
Which let thy wiseness fear: hold off thy
        hand.
    King. Pluck them asunder.
    Queen.   Hamlet, Hamlet!
    All. Gentlemen,—
    Hor.   Good my lord, be quiet.
            [*The Attendants part them, and
                they come out of the grave.*
    Ham. Why, I will fight with him upon
        this theme
Until my eyelids will no longer wag.
    Queen. O my son, what theme?
    Ham. I loved Ophelia: forty thousand
        brothers
Could not, with all their quantity of love,
Make up my sum. What wilt thou do for
        her?
    King. O, he is mad, Laertes.   320
    Queen. For love of God, forbear him.[40]
    Ham. 'Swounds, show me what thou 'lt do:
Woo 't weep? woo 't fight? woo 't fast? woo 't
        tear thyself?
Woo 't drink up eisel?[41] eat a crocodile?
I'll do 't. Dost thou come here to whine?
To outface me with leaping in her grave?
Be buried quick with her, and so will I:

And, if thou prate of mountains, let them
        throw
Millions of acres on us, till our ground,   329
Singeing his pate against the burning zone,
Make Ossa like a wart! Nay, an thou 'lt
        mouth,
I'll rant as well as thou.
    Queen.   This is mere madness:
And thus awhile the fit will work on him;
Anon, as patient as the female dove,
When that her golden couplets[42] are
        disclosed,
His silence will sit drooping.
    Ham.   Hear you, sir;
What is the reason that you use me thus?
I loved you ever: but it is no matter;
Let Hercules himself do what he may,   339
The cat will mew and dog will have his day.
                                [*Exit.*
    King. I pray you, good Horatio, wait upon
        him.   [*Exit* HORATIO.
[*To Laertes*] Strengthen your patience in our
        last night's speech;
We'll put the matter to the present push.
Good Gertrude, set some watch over your
        son.
This grave shall have a living monument:
An hour of quiet shortly shall we see;
Till then, in patience our proceeding be.
                                [*Exeunt.*

SCENE II. *A hall in the castle.*

Enter HAMLET *and* HORATIO.

    Ham. So much for this, sir: now shall you
        see the other;
You do remember all the circumstance?
    Hor. Remember it, my lord!
    Ham. Sir, in my heart there was a kind of
        fighting,
That would not let me sleep: methought I lay

---

37. *thy most ingenious sense*, thy reason. **38.** *Pelion.* The giants of Greek mythology piled Mount Pelion on Mount Ossa in an effort to reach Olympus. This exaggerated statement is Laertes' way of expressing his utter grief at Ophelia's death. **39.** *splenitive*, quick-tempered. **40.** *forbear him*, let him alone. **41.** *eisel*, vinegar. **42.** *golden couplets.* The dove's two fledglings are covered with golden down.

Worse than the mutines in the bilboes.[1]
  Rashly,
And praised be rashness for it, let us know,
Our indiscretion sometimes serves us well,
When our deep plots do pall[2]: and that
    should teach us
There 's a divinity that shapes our ends,   10
Rough-hew them how we will,—
    Hor.   That is most certain.
    Ham. Up from my cabin.
My sea-gown scarf'd about me, in the dark
Groped I to find out them; had my desire,
Finger'd[3] their packet, and in fine withdrew
To mine own room again; making so bold,
My fears forgetting manners, to unseal
Their grand commission; where I found,
    Horatio,—
O royal knavery!—an exact command,
Larded with many several sorts of reasons   20
Importing Denmark's health and England's
    too,
With, ho! such bugs and goblins in my life,[4]
That, on the supervise, no leisure bated,[5]
No, not to stay the grinding of the axe,
My head should be struck off.
    Hor.   Is 't possible?
    Ham. Here 's the commission: read it at
    more leisure.
But wilt thou hear me how I did proceed?
    Hor. I beseech you.
    Ham. Being thus be-netted round with
    villainies,—
Ere I could make a prologue to my brains,   30
They had begun the play[6]—I sat me down,
Devised a new commission, wrote it fair[7]:
I once did hold it, as our statists[8] do,
A baseness to write fair and labor'd much
How to forget that learning, but, sir, now
It did me yeoman's[9] service: wilt thou know
The effect of what I wrote?
    Hor.   Ay, good my lord.
    Ham. An earnest conjuration from the
    king,
As England was his faithful tributary,
As love between them like the palm might
    flourish,   40
As peace should still her wheaten garland
    wear
And stand a comma[10] 'tween their amities,
And many such-like "As"es[11] of great charge,

That, on the view and knowing of these
    contents,
Without debatement further, more or less,
He should the bearers put to sudden death,
Not shriving-time[12] allow'd.
    Hor.   How was this seal'd?
    Ham. Why, even in that was heaven
    ordinant.[13]
I had my father's signet in my purse,
Which was the model of that Danish seal;   50
Folded the writ up in form of the other,
Subscribed it, gave 't the impression, placed
    it safely,
The changeling[14] never known. Now, the
    next day
Was our sea-fight; and what to this was
    sequent
Thou know'st already.
    Hor. So Guildenstern and Rosencrantz go
    to 't.
    Ham. Why, man, they did make love to
    this employment;
They are not near my conscience; their
    defeat
Does by their own insinuation[15] grow:
'Tis dangerous when the baser nature comes   60
Between the pass and fell incensed[16] points
Of mighty opposites.
    Hor.   Why, what a king is this!
    Ham. Does it not, thinks 't thee, stand me
    now upon[17]—
He that hath kill'd my king and whored my
    mother,
Popp'd in between the election[18] and my
    hopes,
Thrown out his angle[19] for my proper life,
And with such cozenage[20]—is 't not perfect
    conscience,

---

1. *mutines in the bilboes,* mutineers in shackles. 2. *pall,*
fail. 3. *Finger'd,* pilfered. 4. *such . . . life,* such exaggerated dangers in my continued existence. 5. *on the
supervise . . . bated,* on perusing it no delay was allowable.
6. *Ere . . . play,* before I could begin to think, my mind had
made its decision. 7. *fair,* in the hand of a professional
clerk. 8. *statists,* statesmen. 9. *yeoman's,* faithful.
10. *comma,* i.e., connector. 11. *As'es,* probably the
"whereases" of a formal document. 12. *shriving-time,*
time for absolution. 13. *ordinant,* directing. 14. *changeling,* exchange. 15. *insinuation,* interference. 16. *pass
and fell incensed,* thrust and fiercely angered. 17. *Does
it . . . upon,* is it not now my obligation. 18. *election,*
a reference to the fact that the Danish throne was filled by
election. 19. *angle,* fishhook. 20. *cozenage,* trickery.

To quit him with this arm? and is 't not to be
    damn'd,
To let this canker of our nature come
In further evil?   70
   Hor. It must be shortly known to him from
    England
What is the issue of the business there.
   Ham. It will be short: the interim is mine;
And a man's life 's no more than to say "One."
But I am very sorry, good Horatio,
That to Laertes I forgot myself;
For, by the image of my cause, I see
The portraiture of his: I'll court his favors:
But, sure, the bravery[21] of his grief did put
    me
Into a towering passion.
   Hor.   Peace! who comes here? 80

Enter OSRIC.

   Osr. Your lordship is right welcome back to
Denmark.
   Ham. I humbly thank you, sir. Dost know
this water-fly?[22]
   Hor. No, my good lord.
   Ham. Thy state is the more gracious; for 'tis
a vice to know him. He hath much land, and
fertile: let a beast be lord of beasts, and his
crib shall stand at the king's mess[23]: 'tis a
chough[24]; but, as I say, spacious in the possession of dirt.   91
   Osr. Sweet lord, if your lordship were at
leisure, I should impart a thing to you from
his majesty.
   Ham. I will receive it, sir, with all diligence
of spirit. Put your bonnet to his right use; 'tis
for the head.
   Osr. I thank your lordship, it is very hot.
   Ham. No, believe me, 'tis very cold; the
wind is northerly.   100
   Osr. It is indifferent[25] cold, my lord, indeed.
   Ham. But yet methinks it is very sultry and
hot for my complexion.
   Osr. Exceedingly, my lord; it is very sultry,
—as 'twere,—I cannot tell how. But, my lord,
his majesty bade me signify to you that he has
laid a great wager on your head: sir, this is
the matter,—
   Ham. I beseech you, remember—   109
    [HAMLET *moves him to put on his hat.*

   Osr. Nay, good my lord; for mine ease, in
good faith. Sir, here is newly come to court
Laertes; believe me, an absolute gentleman,
full of most excellent differences,[26] of very
soft society and great showing: indeed, to
speak feelingly of him, he is the card or calendar of gentry,[27] for you shall find in him the
continent of what part a gentleman would
see.[28]   119
   Ham. Sir, his definement[29] suffers no perdition in you; though, I know, to divide him
inventorially would dizzy the arithmetic of
memory, and yet but yaw neither, in respect
of his quick sail.[30] But, in the verity of extol-
ment, I take him to be a soul of great article[31];
and his infusion[32] of such dearth and rare-
ness, as, to make true diction[33] of him, his
semblable[34] is his mirror; and who else would
trace[35] him, his umbrage,[36] nothing more.
   Osr. Your lordship speaks most infallibly
of him.   131
   Ham. The concernancy,[37] sir? why do we
wrap the gentleman in our more rawer
breath?[38]
   Osr. Sir?
   Hor. Is 't not possible to understand in another tongue? You will do 't,[39] sir, really.
   Ham. What imports the nomination of this
gentleman?
   Osr. Of Laertes?   140
   Hor. His purse is empty already; all 's
golden words are spent.
   Ham. Of him, sir.
   Osr. I know you are not ignorant—
   Ham. I would you did, sir; yet, in faith, if
you did, it would not much approve me. Well,
sir?

---

21. *bravery*, showiness. 22. *water-fly*, showy idler.
23. *let a beast . . . mess*, any fool with enough money
can get admitted to court. 24. *chough*, chattering jack-
daw. 25. *indifferent*, somewhat. 26. *differences*, distinguishing qualities. 27. *card or calendar of gentry*, a
veritable handbook of good breeding. 28. *the continent
. . . see*, to possess those qualities one gentleman expects of
another. 29. *definement*, definition. 30. *to divide . . .
sail*, one would get dizzy before coming to the end of a list-
ing of all his qualities. 31. *great article*, many excellencies.
32. *infusion*, character. 33. *diction*, description. 34. *semblable*, only true image. 35. *trace*, emulate. 36. *umbrage*, shadow. 37. *concernancy*, import, meaning.
38. *why . . . breath*, why do we speak of him in words,
which cannot match his fineness. 39. *do't*, outdo Osric
by using language even more extravagant than he uses.

Osr. You are not ignorant of what excellence Laertes is—   149

Ham. I dare not confess that, lest I should compare with him in excellence; but, to know a man well, were to know himself.

Osr. I mean, sir, for his weapon; but in the imputation laid on him by them, in his meed[40] he 's unfellowed.[41]

Ham. What 's his weapon?

Osr. Rapier and dagger.   157

Ham. That 's two of his weapons: but, well.

Osr. The king, sir, hath wagered with him six Barbary horses; against the which he has imponed,[42] as I take it, six French rapiers and poniards, with their assigns,[43] as girdle, hangers, and so: three of the carriages, in faith, are very dear to fancy,[44] very responsive [45] to the hilts, most delicate carriages, and of very liberal conceit.[46]

Ham. What call you the carriages?

Hor. I knew you must be edified by the margent[47] ere you had done.

Osr. The carriages, sir, are the hangers. 170

Ham. The phrase would be more german[48] to the matter, if we could carry cannon by our sides: I would it might be hangers till then. But, on: six Barbary horses against six French swords, their assigns, and three liberal-conceited carriages; that 's the French bet against the Danish. Why is this "imponed," as you call it?   178

Osr. The king, sir, hath laid, that in a dozen passes between yourself and him, he shall not exceed you three hits: he hath laid on twelve for nine; and it would come to immediate trial, if your lordship would vouchsafe the answer.

Ham. How if I answer "no"?

Osr. I mean, my lord, the opposition of your person in trial.

Ham. Sir, I will walk here in the hall: if it please his majesty, 't is the breathing time of day with me; let the foils be brought, the gentleman willing, and the king hold his purpose, I will win for him an I can; if not, I will gain nothing but my shame and the odd hits. 192

Osr. Shall I re-deliver you e'en so?

Ham. To this effect, sir; after what flourish your nature will.

Osr. I commend my duty to your lordship.

Ham. Yours, yours. [*Exit* OSRIC.] He does well to commend it himself; there are no tongues else for 's turn.   200

Enter a LORD.

Lord. My lord, his majesty commended him to you by young Osric, who brings back to him, that you attend him in the hall: he sends to know if your pleasure hold to play with Laertes, or that you will take longer time.

Ham. I am constant to my purposes; they follow the king's pleasure: if his fitness speaks, mine is ready; now or whensoever, provided I be so able as now.   209

Lord. The king and queen and all are coming down.

Ham. In happy time.

Lord. The queen desires you to use some gentle entertainment[49] to Laertes before you fall to play.

Ham. She well instructs me.   [*Exit* LORD.

Hor. You will lose this wager, my lord.

Ham. I do not think so; since he went into France, I have been in continual practice; I shall win at the odds. But thou wouldst not think how ill all 's here about my heart: but it is no matter.   222

Hor. Nay, good my lord,—

Ham. It is but foolery; but it is such a kind of gain-giving,[50] as would perhaps trouble a woman.

Hor. If your mind dislike any thing, obey it: I will forestall their repair hither, and say you are not fit.   229

Ham. Not a whit, we defy augury: there 's a special providence in the fall of a sparrow. If it be now, 'tis not to come; if it be not to come, it will be now; if it be not now, yet it will come: the readiness is all: since no man has aught of what he leaves, what is 't to leave betimes? Let be.

---

40. *meed,* merit. 41. *unfellowed,* unmatched. 42. *imponed,* wagered. 43. *assigns,* accessories. *Girdle* (sword belt) and *hangers* (straps) were regarded as accessories of the rapier. 44. *dear to fancy,* fancifully made. 45. *responsive,* close in design. 46. *liberal conceit,* elaborate design. 47. *margent,* marginal comment. 48. *german,* germane, appropriate. 49. *use some gentle entertainment,* greet with courtesy. 50. *gain-giving,* misgiving.

Enter KING, QUEEN, LAERTES, LORDS, OSRIC, *and* ATTENDANTS *with foils, &c.*

King. Come, Hamlet, come, and take this
hand from me.
[*The King puts Laertes' hand into Hamlet's.*
Ham. Give me your pardon, sir: I've done
you wrong;
But pardon 't, as you are a gentleman.
This presence[51] knows,
And you must needs have heard, how I am
punish'd
With sore distraction. What I have done,
That might your nature, honor and
exception[52]   250
Roughly awake, I here proclaim was madness.
Was 't Hamlet wrong'd Laertes? Never
Hamlet:
If Hamlet from himself be ta'en away,
And when he 's not himself does wrong
Laertes,
Then Hamlet does it not, Hamlet denies it.
Who does it, then? His madness: if 't be so,
Hamlet is of the faction that is wrong'd;
His madness is poor Hamlet's enemy.
Sir, in this audience,
Let my disclaiming from a purposed evil   260
Free me so far in your most generous
thoughts,
That I have shot mine arrow o'er the house,
And hurt my brother.
Laer.   I am satisfied in nature,[53]
Whose motive, in this case, should stir me
most
To my revenge: but in my terms of honor
I stand aloof; and will no reconcilement,
Till by some elder masters, of known honor,
I have a voice and precedent of peace,
To keep my name ungored.[54] But till that
time,
I do receive your offer'd love like love,   270
And will not wrong it.
Ham.   I embrace it freely;
And will this brother's wager frankly play.
Give us the foils. Come on.
Laer.   Come, one for me.
Ham. I'll be your foil,[55] Laertes: in mine
ignorance
Your skill shall, like a star i' the darkest
night,

Stick fiery off indeed.
Laer.   You mock me, sir.
Ham. No, by this hand.
King. Give them the foils, young Osric.
Cousin Hamlet,
You know the wager?
Ham.   Very well, my lord;
Your grace hath laid the odds o' the weaker
side.   280
King. I do not fear it; I have seen you
both:
But since he is better'd, we have therefore
odds.
Laer. This is too heavy, let me see another.
Ham. This likes me well. These foils have
all a length?[56]   [*They prepare to play.*
Osr. Ay, my good lord.
King. Set me the stoups of wine upon that
table.
If Hamlet give the first or second hit,
Or quit[57] in answer of the third exchange,
Let all the battlements their ordnance fire;
The king shall drink to Hamlet's better
breath;   290
And in the cup an union[58] shall he throw,
Richer than that which four successive kings
In Denmark's crown have worn. Give me the
cups;
And let the kettle[59] to the trumpet speak,
The trumpet to the cannoneer without,
The cannons to the heavens, the heavens to
earth,
"Now the king drinks to Hamlet." Come,
begin:
And you, the judges, bear a wary eye.
Ham. Come on, sir.
Laer.   Come, my lord.   [*They play.*
Ham.   One.
Laer.   No.
Ham.   Judgment.
Osr. A hit, a very palpable hit.
Laer.   Well; again.   300
King. Stay; give me drink. Hamlet, this
pearl[60] is thine;

---

51. *presence,* royal assembly.   **52.** *exception,* disapproval.
53. *in nature,* as far as my personal feelings are concerned.
54. *ungored,* unmarred.   **55.** *foil,* rapier; also a background which sets something off.   **56.** *have all a length,*
are all the same length.   **57.** *quit,* repay.   **58.** *union,*
pearl.   **59.** *kettle,* kettledrum.   **60.** *pearl.* The pearl
carried the poison.

Here 's to thy health.
[*Trumpets sound, and cannon shot off within.*
                    Give him the cup.
  Ham. I'll play this bout first; set it by
    awhile.
Come. [*They play.*] Another hit; what say
    you?
  Laer. A touch, a touch, I do confess 't.
  King. Our son shall win.
  Queen.   He 's fat,[61] and scant of breath.
Here, Hamlet, take my napkin, rub thy
    brows:
The queen carouses to thy fortune, Hamlet.
  Ham. Good madam!
  King.   Gertrude, do not drink.
  Queen. I will, my lord; I pray you, pardon
    me.   310
  King. [*Aside*] It is the poison'd cup: it is
    too late.
  Ham. I dare not drink yet, madam; by and
    by.
  Queen. Come, let me wipe thy face.
  Laer. My lord, I'll hit him now.
  King.   I do not think 't.
  Laer. [*Aside*] And yet 'tis almost 'gainst my
    conscience.
  Ham. Come, for the third, Laertes: you but
    dally;
I pray you, pass with your best violence;
I am afeard you make a wanton of me.[62]
  Laer. Say you so? come on.   [*They play.*
  Osr. Nothing, neither way.   320
  Laer. Have at you now!
            [*Laertes wounds Hamlet; then, in
              scuffling, they change rapiers,
              and Hamlet wounds Laertes.*
  King.   Part them; they are incensed.
  Ham. Nay, come, again. [*The Queen falls.*
  Osr.   Look to the queen there, ho!
  Hor. They bleed on both sides. How is it,
    my lord?
  Osr. How is 't, Laertes?
  Laer. Why, as a woodcock to mine own
    springe, Osric;
I am justly kill'd with mine own treachery.
  Ham. How does the queen?
  King.   She swounds to see them bleed.
  Queen. No, no, the drink, the drink,—O
    my dear Hamlet,—
The drink, the drink! I am poison'd. [*Dies.*

  Ham. O villainy! Ho! let the door be
    lock'd:
Treachery! Seek it out.   331
  Laer. It is here, Hamlet: Hamlet, thou art
    slain;
No medicine in the world can do thee good;
In thee there is not half an hour of life;
The treacherous instrument is in thy hand,
Unbated and envenom'd: the foul practice
Hath turn'd itself on me; lo, here I lie,
Never to rise again: thy mother 's poison'd:
I can no more: the king, the king 's to blame.
  Ham. The point envenom'd too!   340
Then, venom, to thy work. [*Stabs the King.*
  All. Treason! treason!
  King. O, yet defend me, friends; I am but
    hurt.
  Ham. Here, thou incestuous, murderous,
    damned Dane,
Drink off this potion. Is thy union here?
Follow my mother.   [*King dies.*
  Laer.   He is justly served;
It is a poison temper'd by himself.
Exchange forgiveness with me, noble Hamlet:
Mine and my father's death come not upon
    thee,
Nor thine on me!   [*Dies.* 350
  Ham. Heaven make thee free of it! I
    follow thee.
I am dead, Horatio. Wretched queen, adieu!
You that look pale and tremble at this
    chance,
That are but mutes or audience to this act,
Had I but time—as this fell sergeant, death,
Is strict in his arrest—O, I could tell you—
But let it be. Horatio, I am dead;
Thou livest; report me and my cause aright
To the unsatisfied.
  Hor.   Never believe it:
I am more an antique Roman[63] than a
    Dane: 360
Here 's yet some liquor left.
  Ham.   As thou 'rt a man,
Give me the cup: let go; by heaven, I'll
    have 't.

---

61. *fat.* The Queen probably means that Hamlet is out of
training. 62. *make a wanton of me,* toy with me. Hamlet
believes that Laertes can win the match whenever he really
tries. 63. *antique Roman.* Horatio is referring to the
practice common in ancient Rome of servants or slaves following their masters in death.

O God! Horatio, what a wounded name,
Things standing thus unknown, shall live
    behind me!
If thou didst ever hold me in thy heart,
Absent thee from felicity awhile,
And in this harsh world draw thy breath in
    pain,
To tell my story.
                    [*March afar off, and shot within.*
                    What warlike noise is this?
    Osr. Young Fortinbras, with conquest come
        from Poland,
To the ambassadors of England gives   370
This warlike volley.
    Ham.   O, I die, Horatio;
The potent poison quite o'er-crows[64] my spirit:
I cannot live to hear the news from England;
But I do prophesy the election lights
On Fortinbras: he has my dying voice;
So tell him, with the occurrents,[65] more and
    less,
Which have solicited.[66] The rest is silence.
                                        [*Dies.*
    Hor. Now cracks a noble heart. Good
        night, sweet prince;
And flights of angels sing thee to thy rest!
Why does the drum come hither?
                                [*March within.*

Enter FORTINBRAS, *the* ENGLISH
AMBASSADORS, *and others.*

    Fort. Where is this sight?
    Hor.   What is it ye would see?   381
If aught of woe or wonder, cease your search.
    Fort. This quarry cries on havoc.[67] O proud
        death,
What feast is toward in thine eternal cell,
That thou so many princes at a shot
So bloodily hast struck?
    First Amb.   The sight is dismal;
And our affairs from England come too late:
The ears are senseless that should give us
    hearing,
To tell him his commandment is fulfill'd,   389
That Rosencrantz and Guildenstern are dead:
Where should we have our thanks?
    Hor.   Not from his mouth,
Had it the ability of life to thank you:
He never gave commandment for their death.

But since, so jump[68] upon this bloody
    question,
You from the Polack wars, and you from
    England,
Are here arrived, give order that these bodies
High on a stage be placed to the view;
And let me speak to the yet unknowing
    world
How these things came about: so shall you
    hear
Of carnal, bloody, and unnatural acts,   400
Of accidental judgments, casual slaughters,
Of deaths put on by cunning and forced
    cause,
And, in this upshot, purposes mistook
Fall'n on the inventors' heads: all this can I
Truly deliver.
    Fort.   Let us haste to hear it,
And call the noblest to the audience.
For me, with sorrow I embrace my fortune:
I have some rights of memory in this
    kingdom,
Which now to claim my vantage doth invite
    me.
    Hor. Of that I shall have also cause to
        speak,   410
And from his mouth whose voice will draw
    on more[69]:
But let this same be presently perform'd,
Even while men's minds are wild; lest more
    mischance,
On plots and errors, happen.
    Fort.   Let four captains
Bear Hamlet, like a soldier, to the stage;
For he was likely, had he been put on,[70]
To have proved most royal: and, for his
    passage,
The soldiers' music and the rites of war
Speak loudly for him.
Take up the bodies: such a sight as this   420
Becomes the field, but here shows much
    amiss.
Go, bid the soldiers shoot.
            [*A dead march. Exeunt, bearing off
                the dead bodies; after which a
                peal of ordnance is shot off.*

---

64. *o'er-crows*, triumphs over. **65.** *occurrents*, events, incidents. **66.** *solicited*, moved, urged. **67.** *This ... havoc*, this heap of bodies bespeaks merciless slaughter. **68.** *jump*, exactly. **69.** *whose ... more*, whose authority will cause others to follow. **70.** *put on*, tried.

1. The writers of the eighteenth century felt that the grave-digger scene was inappropriate in a play as serious as *Hamlet*. (*a*) By referring to specific speeches, explain the serious issues behind the comic repartee in this scene. (*b*) Are tragedy and comedy necessarily incompatible? (*c*) What does Shakespeare gain by placing this scene in its particular position? (*d*) Might the grave diggers symbolize or stand for one of the themes of the play? Which theme? (*e*) Do you agree or disagree with the eighteenth-century criticism?

2. Reread lines 177–188. What effect would these lines have had on an Elizabethan audience?

3. Explain why Hamlet is angered by Laertes' behavior at Ophelia's funeral.

Scene 2

1. Reread lines 10–11, 230–236. (*a*) What do these lines mean in context? (*b*) What do they mean in terms of the play as a whole?

2. What has been the fate of Rosencrantz and Guildenstern?

3. What type of Elizabethan does Shakespeare satirize in the character of Osric?

4. Describe the final action of the play, beginning with Hamlet's apology to Laertes (line 245).

The Play in Review

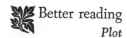 Better reading
Plot

Like the short-story writer and the novelist, the dramatist usually tells a tale or story that has a beginning, middle, and end, i.e., he is concerned with *plot*. The plot of a work of fiction usually falls into three divisions: the *exposition*, or explanation, in which characters and situations are introduced; the *rising action* in which one force gains ascendancy over another; and the *falling action* in which the opposite force takes over and precipitates a *denouement*, or untying of the plot. The highest point in the rising action—the point where one force wins but then relinquishes control to the opposing force—is called the *technical climax* of the work. This is not to be confused with the *dramatic climax*, or point of greatest excitement for the reader or audience, although in some works of fiction these two climaxes coincide.

The collision of forces or *conflict* within a work of fiction may take various forms. It may be the conflict between two or more individuals; between individuals and fate or destiny, or perhaps nature. Or it may be the conflict that is carried on within the individual himself. In more complex works which deal with the human situation in all its depth and breadth each of these basic types of conflict may be present.

1. The most obvious conflict in *Hamlet* is between two individuals, Hamlet and the King. (*a*) State the nature of their struggle in one or two sentences. (*b*) Where in the play does Shakespeare bring the exposition of characters and situations to an end, i.e., what event begins the rising action of the play? (*c*) Who is in ascendancy during the rising action? (*d*) Where and what is the technical climax? (*e*) What two events begin the falling action of the play? (*f*) What is the denouement? (*g*) Is the technical climax of the play also the dramatic climax? Explain.

2. Conflict produces two basic types of suspense: the pure suspense of the mystery story in which the reader does not know who the guilty party is; and the suspense of knowing that certain characters are headed for destruction but not knowing when and how. (*a*) Which kind of suspense is produced by the conflict between Hamlet and the King? Explain. (*b*) Is there any suspense created by the actions of the Queen? If so, what kind?

3. The simple unfolding of the conflict between the King and Hamlet is complicated by the conflict going on inside Hamlet himself. (*a*) What is Hamlet's inner conflict? (*b*) Does Hamlet resolve this conflict himself or is it resolved for him by outside events and circumstances? Explain your answer.

4. The conflict between the King and Hamlet and the conflict within Hamlet himself are part of a larger conflict between man and fate. The presence of doom or fate hangs heavy over the play from the outset, giving audiences and readers the impression that no matter how hard they try, the people at the court of Denmark cannot ward off their destruction. (*a*) What are some of the indications of doom or fate in the opening scenes of the play? (*b*) Where does Hamlet reveal that he is aware of the presence of fate? (*c*) Is Denmark destroyed by its own internal corruption? from without by the forces of Fortinbras? by fate? Explain your answer.

Characterization

In portraying character, the writer of short stories or novels has at his disposal many resources. He may tell us directly how characters usually behave, what sort of individuals they are, or what they and their surroundings look like. He may also characterize by quoting typical speeches, or by showing us characters in action. Or he may even assume the rôle of an all-knowing person who can step inside his characters' minds and reveal their thoughts. The dramatist, on the other hand, portrays character through dialogue and action alone. What a character does or does not do, what a character says about himself, about others, and what others say about him—these things are of primary importance in creating and understanding the characters in a play.

This difference in technique was less great in Shakespeare's time than in our own, for Shakespeare and his fellow dramatists made frequent use of what is called a *soliloquy*—a dramatic convention whereby the audience "overhears" a character talking to himself. By using soliloquies, Shakespeare, like short-story writers and novelists of today, was able to reveal his characters' inmost thoughts.

The following questions will help you arrive at a general understanding of the major characters in *Hamlet*. Refer to specific actions, specific passages of dialogue, or to the soliloquies to support your answers.

The King

1. One of Shakespeare's greatest and most consistent achievements was his creation of characters who are neither all bad nor all good but human, i.e., both good and bad. (*a*) How does the King's soliloquy (Act III, Scene 3, lines 36–72) soften our impression of him as a debauched and hypocritical villain? (*b*) How competent is the King in conducting the affairs between Denmark and Norway?

2. Would you characterize the King as a *materialist*—a person who cares too much for the things of the world and neglects his spiritual needs—or as an *idealist*—a person who neglects practical matters to follow his spiritual promptings? Explain your answer.

The Queen

1. Is the Queen as "bad" as the King? Explain.

2. (*a*) What are the Queen's good points and what are her failings? (*b*) Does she realize what she has done and the effect it has had on her son Hamlet?

Polonius, Laertes, and Ophelia

1. (*a*) How would you characterize Polonius? (*b*) Do you consider him a fitting lord chamberlain for the King? (*c*) What is it that softens our impression of Polonius?

2. Does the phrase "like father like son" apply to Laertes? Explain your answer.

3. (*a*) What sort of person is Ophelia when Shakespeare first introduces her? (*b*) What effect does the advice of Polonius and Laertes have upon her? (*c*) Who or what is responsible for her madness and death? (*d*) Do you think Shakespeare intended Ophelia as a sympathetic character? Explain your answer.

Horatio, Rosencrantz, and Guildenstern

1. These three young men are all schoolfellows of Hamlet. (*a*) Compare Horatio with the other

two. (*b*) Would you consider all three of them as genuine friends of Hamlet? Explain.

2. Horatio does not appear as often as many other characters but, because Hamlet regards him as the ideal man, understanding Horatio is vital to an understanding of Hamlet's own character. Reread Hamlet's description of Horatio (Act III, Scene 2, lines 67–87). What ideal does Horatio represent?

Hamlet

Like men and women in real life, Hamlet is an extremely complex character whose thoughts and feelings cannot be pigeon-holed or explained by any one theory. Generations of critics and actors have tried their hands at explaining or interpreting Hamlet—sometimes with great, but never with complete, success.

1. (*a*) What was Hamlet like before the death of his father and his mother's hasty marriage to his uncle? (*b*) What does Hamlet's first soliloquy (Act I, Scene 2, lines 129–159) reveal about his way of looking at the world?

2. Is Hamlet really mad? Consider in your answer Hamlet's own thoughts and his interaction with Polonius, Rosencrantz and Guildenstern, Horatio, Ophelia, and the Queen.

3. Why does Hamlet treat Ophelia as he does?

4. Does Hamlet's second soliloquy (Act II, Scene 2, lines 588–646) reveal a man who can only "unpack his heart with words" or one who can also act upon the promptings of his heart? Explain.

5. Reread Hamlet's third soliloquy (Act III, Scene 1, lines 56–88). (*a*) What does it reveal about the way Hamlet looks at the world? (*b*) Why would a man who thinks as Hamlet does in this soliloquy admire a man like Horatio?

6. What is the significance of Hamlet's fourth soliloquy (Act IV, Scene 4, lines 32–66)?

7. Does Hamlet ever achieve the ideal represented by Horatio? Explain your answer.

8. Compare Hamlet with Polonius and the King.

9. (*a*) In what sense is Hamlet justified in plotting against and killing the King? (*b*) In what sense is he not justified? (*c*) Is Shakespeare trying to tell us something about the nature of violence by having Hamlet refrain from killing the King until practically forced to in the very last scene of the play? If so, what is he trying to tell us?

Tragedy

Although different ages have had different theories about what constitutes a tragedy, all ages have agreed on certain basic qualities of tragedy. Most tragedies end unhappily, indeed disastrously, usually with the death of at least the hero or the heroine. This final catastrophe is not something that is merely tacked on at the end of a work; rather, it represents the logical, inevitable outcome of preceding struggles or conflicts. The conflict that precipitates the final catastrophe—whether it be between individuals or between individuals and some greater power—must be regarded by the author and his audience as vital and highly serious.

In spite of the fact that tragedy deals with human pain and suffering, it is looked upon as the highest literary type, the one that leaves audiences with the greatest sense of satisfaction. This powerful after-effect of tragedy has been variously described as a catharsis or purgation of emotion, a sense of calm, a sense of exultation, and a sense of emotional understanding. Just exactly how this effect is produced

The art of the miniature was introduced into England by Nicholas Hilliard. Portraits at right of George Clifford III (left) and Sir Francis Drake (right) are by Hilliard, as is the unidentified man against a background of flames on the opposite page. The left portrait (opposite) is by Hans Holbein, one of the great painters of the age, who was also one of the early miniaturists.

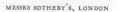

MESSRS SOTHEBY'S, LONDON   KUNSTHISTORISCHES-MUSEUM, VIENNA

has never been wholly explained, but most critics agree that it is related to the universal significance of tragedy. The problems probed in a great tragedy are the problems of all people. In pitying the suffering hero and sharing in his fear of the inevitable disaster, the members of the audience become drained of pity and fear and are ready to take up their own lives with clearer and wiser heads.

1. To what extent are the three basic qualities of tragedy present in *Hamlet*?

2. (*a*) In what sense are the problems of *Hamlet* your problems? (*b*) Why do you pity Hamlet? (*c*) Why do you fear for him?

3. Many critics have tried to describe the necessary attributes of a tragic hero. The Greek philosopher Aristotle, who dealt with tragedy in his *Poetics*, described the tragic hero as a man of high estate; that is, a well-known, well-intentioned man, whose misfortune results from some error in judgment or some flaw of character (called a tragic flaw). Others have described the tragic hero as a man who, from whatever station in life, climbs slowly upward toward some ideal, and who realizes this ideal at or near the moment of his death. Does Hamlet fit either of these descriptions? Why, or why not?

The Changing English Language

When Caxton introduced the printing press to England in 1476, the English language began to settle down to a relatively stable, standardized form of expression. Chaucer would not have been able to read the Old English of *Beowulf*. Shakespeare would have found the Middle English of Chaucer strange. But we, fortunately enough, can read the Modern English of Shakespeare. To be sure, pronunciation in Shakespeare's day differed in many ways from our own; new words have entered the language in the intervening centuries; other words such as *yare* ("ready") and *compt* ("neat") are now obsolete; still others have changed meaning (see page 168). But these differences are more than offset by the fact that Shakespeare's grammar and spelling are essentially our own.

Paradoxically enough, the printing press worked not only for uniformity of language; it also worked for unrestrained variety. Confronted with the printed page and tremendously stimulated by the new experiences and ideas of the Renaissance, the Elizabethans became intoxicated with words and the fantastic things that could be done with them. They loved extravagant expressions, complicated figures of speech, and such rollicking verbal free-for-alls as Hamlet's encounter with the grave diggers and with the delightfully foolish Osric. They made up words by the dozens, such as *to fool, disgraceful, barefaced, countless, critic, bump, gloomy, laughable*, which

Shakespeare is credited with, and *dimension, conscious, jovial, scientific, rascality, audacious, obscure*, which came from other writers of the time.

The Elizabethans also borrowed words as freely as some housewives borrow ingredients. These borrowings were not the result of invasions by people of alien tongues, as had been the case in Anglo-Saxon and medieval times, but were rather a product of the tremendous geographical and intellectual expansion of the Renaissance. Most of the borrowings were a result of the Elizabethan's passionate interest in the pagan literature and culture of ancient Greece and Rome: for example, *antipathy, appendix, comprehensible, denunciation, dogma, emanate, emphasis, epitome, implacable, lexicon, monopoly, obstruction, pathetic, pretext, reliance*, and *submerge*. From Italian came *cameo, grotto*, and *violin*. From French came *detail, ticket*, and *explore*. Arabic and American Indian words came in via Spanish: *apricot, cocoa, embargo, potato, tobacco. Calico* came from India; *mammoth* and *sable* from Russia; *gingham* and *indigo* from Siam and the Malay coasts; *caravan* from Persia; *tea* from China; *tulip* from Turkey; and *alpaca* from South America.

The growth of the English language in the Elizabethan Age reveals what we now regard as the typical pattern of language growth during peaceful, prosperous times: minor changes in grammar; major changes in vocabulary.

John Donne 1573-1631

One of the first persons to realize the difficulties inherent in the Renaissance idea of living primarily for this world was the lyric poet John Donne. A brilliant and dashing young student, European traveler, soldier, and man about town, Donne tasted deeply of the things the world had to offer—and then turned with bitter disillusionment against them. This change of attitude is reflected in his considerable body of poetry, many of the early lyrics being devoted to the concerns of "Jack" Donne, the man about town, many of the later ones revealing John Donne's concern for the state of his soul.

Though Donne eventually took orders in the Anglican Church and, as Dean of St. Paul's, became a well-known preacher and writer of religious prose, the conflict he experienced between the world of the spirit and the world of the flesh never seems to have entirely resolved itself. As a result, much of Donne's religious prose and poetry is characterized by tension, the kind of tension that comes when a man strives to attain a certain spiritual understanding and serenity but does not quite succeed in doing so.

In "Song" Donne made fun of the earlier Elizabethan poets —including Sidney and Spenser—who bemoaned the fact that their ladies were not constant. "Death Be Not Proud" is one of his nineteen *Holy Sonnets*. "Meditation 17" is one of several devotions written during a long and serious illness.

NATIONAL PORTRAIT GALLERY, LONDON

Above: Copy of a portrait by Isaac Oliver (1556?-1617). Right: Woodcut from a book published in 1563 showing a family at prayer.

RADIO TIMES HULTON PICTURE LIBRARY

SONG

Go and catch a falling star,
  Get with child a mandrake root,[1]
Tell me where all past years are,
  Or who cleft the devil's foot;
Teach me to hear mermaids singing,   5
Or to keep off envy's stinging,
    And find
    What wind
Serves to advance an honest mind.

If thou be'st born to strange sights,   10
  Things invisible to see,
Ride ten thousand days and nights
  Till Age snow white hairs on thee;
Thou, when thou return'st, wilt tell me
All strange wonders that befell thee,   15
    And swear
    No where
Lives a woman true and fair.

If thou find'st one, let me know;
  Such a pilgrimage were sweet.   20
Yet do not; I would not go,
  Though at next door we might meet.
Though she were true when you met her,
And last, till you write your letter,
    Yet she   25
    Will be
False, ere I come, to two or three.

DEATH, BE NOT PROUD

Death, be not proud, though some have
    called thee
Mighty and dreadful, for thou art not so;
For those whom thou think'st thou dost
    overthrow
Die not, poor Death; nor yet canst thou kill
    me.
From rest and sleep, which but thy picture
    be,   5
Much pleasure; then from thee much more
    must flow;
And soonest our best men with thee do go—
Rest of their bones and souls' delivery!
Thou'rt slave to fate, chance, kings, and
    desperate men,

And dost with poison, war, and sickness
    dwell;   10
And poppy[1] or charms can make us sleep as
    well
And better than thy stroke. Why swell'st
    thou then?
One short sleep past, we wake eternally,
And Death shall be no more: Death, thou
    shalt die.

from MEDITATION 17

Nunc lento sonitu dicunt, Morieris.
Now, this Bell tolling softly for
another, says to me, Thou must die.

Perchance he for whom this *Bell*
tolls, may be so ill, as that he knows
not it tolls for him; And perchance
I may think myself so much better
than I am, as that they who are
about me, and see my state, may have caused
it to toll for me, and I know not that. The
Church is *Catholic, universal*, so are all her
Actions; *All* that she does, belongs to *all.*
When she *baptizes a child*, that action concerns me; for that child is thereby connected
to that *Head* which is my *Head* too, and en-
graffed into that *body*, whereof I am a *member*. And when she *buries a Man*, that action
concerns me: All *mankind* is of one *Author*,
and is one *volume*; when one Man dies, one
Chapter is not *torn* out of the *book*, but *translated* into a better *language*; and every *Chapter* must be so *translated*; *God* employs several
translators; some pieces are translated by *age*,
some by *sickness*, some by *war*, some by *justice*; but *God's* hand is in every *translation*;
and his hand shall bind up all our scattered
leaves again, for that *Library* where every
book shall lie open to one another: As therefore the *Bell* that rings to a *Sermon*, calls not
upon the *Preacher* only, but upon the *Congregation* to come; so this *Bell* calls us all: but

---

SONG **1.** *Get...mandrake root.* The mandrake, or
mandragora, is a European herb with a forked root, fancied
to resemble the figure of a man. It was believed that if
women ate this herb, they would be able to conceive children. Donne suggests that an even greater impossibility
would be for the mandrake to conceive a child.
DEATH BE NOT PROUD **1.** *poppy.* Opium is made from
one kind of poppy plant.

how much more me, who am brought so near the *door* by this *sickness*.

There was a *contention* as far as a *suit* (in which both *piety* and *dignity*, *religion*, and *estimation*, were mingled) which of the religious *Orders* should ring to *prayers* first in the *Morning*; and it was *determined*, that *they should ring first that rose earliest*. If we understand aright the *dignity* of this *Bell* that tolls for our *evening prayer*, we would be glad to make it ours, by rising early, in that *application*, that it might be ours, as well as his, whose indeed it is. The *Bell* doth toll for him that *thinks* it doth; and though it *intermit* again, yet from that *minute*, that that occasion wrought upon him, he is united to *God*. Who casts not up his *Eye* to the *Sun* when it rises? but who takes off his *Eye* from a *Comet* when that breaks out? Who bends not his *ear* to any *bell*, which upon any occasion rings? but who can remove it from that *bell*, which is passing a *piece of himself* out of this *world*? No man is an *Island*, entire of itself; every man is a piece of the *Continent*, a part of the *main*; if a *Clod* be washed away by the *Sea, Europe* is the less, as well as if a *Promontory* were, as well as if a *Manor* of thy *friends* or of *thine own* were; any man's *death* diminishes *me*, because I am involved in *Mankind*; And therefore never send to know for whom the *bell* tolls; It tolls for *thee*.

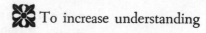 To increase understanding

1. (*a*) In "Song" what is the common quality of the tasks the poet asks us to perform? (*b*) What attitude toward women does this quality help convey? (*c*) Is this poem written in the spirit of "Jack" Donne or John Donne?

2. How is the attitude toward women expressed in this poem different from the attitude expressed in the sonnets of Sidney and Spenser?

3. (*a*) Why are *snow* (line 13) and *pilgrimage* (line 20) particularly effective words? (*b*) How does the rhythm of the last stanza of "Song" contribute to the flippant tone of the poem?

4. (*a*) In "Death Be Not Proud" what reasons does Donne give for believing that death is not powerful? (*b*) Which of these reasons is most important? (*c*) How does this sonnet differ from "Song" in subject matter and tone?

5. Which of Shakespeare's sonnets does Donne's sonnet remind you of, and why?

6. People often betray their uncertainty about something by insisting too strongly that they do believe it and by offering too many reasons why. Does this remark apply to Donne's sonnet? Explain.

7. (*a*) What is the main idea of *Meditation 17*? (*b*) What striking images does Donne use to convey this idea?

8. Would you describe the language of *Meditation 17* as smooth and serene? Consider in your answer (*a*) length and structure of sentences, (*b*) transitions from one thought to another, and (*c*) choice of words.

9. To whom is *Meditation 17* addressed?

Sir Francis Bacon 1561-1626

Like so many of the Elizabethan courtiers, Francis Bacon was a man of tremendous political ambition. Under Elizabeth he managed to rise from a minor post at the English embassy in France to a seat in Parliament and a position on the Queen's Learned Council. Under James I he moved rapidly through a succession of offices until he finally reached the much coveted position of Lord Chancellor, whose power was second only to the King's. But Bacon seems to have regarded all his offices as only the means which would enable him to carry out his literary-scientific projects. The greatest of these was his incomplete yet monumental *Instauratio Magna*, or Great Renewal of Science, which discussed for the first time the importance of inductive reasoning, or drawing a principle from direct observation, in the scientific process. It was Bacon's contention that if men wished to gain control over nature they would have to stop looking at her through the eyes of past authorities and start observing her themselves. This was a revolutionary idea in the sixteenth and early seventeenth centuries, and Bacon's eloquent statement of it won him the title of Father (or Prophet) of Modern Science.

The most literary of Bacon's works is his famous collection of fifty-eight *Essays*, which were published in three installments over a period of a quarter of a century (from 1597-1625). These essays met with immediate success for several reasons. They represented the first use of the essay as a literary form in England. They were written in a sharp, concentrated prose that gave rise to many "quotable quotes." And they covered a wide variety of subjects, ranging from abstractions, such as "truth" and "beauty," to concrete, personal matters, such as "marriage and single life" and "parents and children." Just as Bacon's scientific-philosophical writings attempted to show men how they could become the masters of nature, so the *Essays* were intended to show them how they could make best use of their social environment.

Portrait of Bacon by an unknown artist.

OF STUDIES

Studies serve for delight, for ornament, and for ability. Their chief use for delight is in privateness and retiring; for ornament, is in discourse; and for ability, is in the judgment and disposition of business; for expert[1] men can execute, and perhaps judge of particulars, one by one; but the general counsels, and the plots and marshaling of affairs come best from those that are learned. To spend too much time in studies is sloth; to use them too much for ornament is affectation; to make judgment wholly by their rules is the humor[2] of a scholar. They perfect nature, and are perfected by experience; for natural abilities are like natural plants, that need pruning by study; and studies themselves do give forth directions too much at large, except they be bounded in by experience. Crafty[3] men contemn studies, simple men admire them, and wise men use them; for they teach not their own use; but that is a wisdom without them

1. *expert*, practical (as opposed to theoretical). 2. *humor*, whim, disposition. 3. *Crafty*, skilled in crafts, practical.

and above them, won by observation. Read not to contradict and confute, nor to believe and take for granted, nor to find talk and discourse, but to weigh and consider. Some books are to be tasted, others to be swallowed, and some few to be chewed and digested; that is, some books are to be read only in parts; others to be read but not curiously,[4] and some few to be read wholly, and with diligence and attention. Some books also may be read by deputy, and extracts made of them by others; but that would be only in the less important arguments and the meaner sort of books; else distilled books are, like common distilled waters, flashy[5] things. Reading maketh a full man; conference a ready man; and writing an exact man. And, therefore, if a man write little, he had need have a great memory; if he confer little, he had need have a present wit[6]; and if he read little, he had need have much cunning, to seem to know that he doth not. Histories make men wise; poets, witty; the mathematics, subtile; natural philosophy, deep; moral, grave; logic and rhetoric, able to contend: *Abeunt studia in mores!*[7] Nay, there is no stand or impediment in the wit but may be wrought out by fit studies; like as diseases of the body may have appropriate exercises. Bowling is good for the stone[8] and reins, shooting for the lungs and breast, gentle walking for the stomach, riding for the head, and the like. So if a man's wit be wandering, let him study the mathematics; for in demonstrations, if his wit be called away never so little, he must begin again. If his wit be not apt to distinguish or find differences, let him study the schoolmen, for they are *cymini sectores!*[9] If he be not apt to beat over matters, and to call up one thing to prove and illustrate another, let him study the lawyers' cases. So every defect of the mind may have a special receipt.

4. *curiously,* thoroughly. 5. *flashy,* tasteless, flat. 6. *wit,* used throughout the essay in the sense of intelligence. 7. *Abeunt . . . mores,* studies develop into habits. 8. *stone,* a disease of the kidneys (reins). 9. *schoolmen . . . cymini sectores.* Medieval scholars, or schoolmen, were famous for long involved discussions of what the Renaissance considered trivial subjects. Hence, Bacon calls them *cymini sectores,* which means splitters of cuminseeds (seeds from a small plant), or hairsplitters.

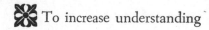 To increase understanding

1. (*a*) What, according to Bacon, are the chief uses of studies? (*b*) What does he feel are their chief dangers? (*c*) As a firm believer in the importance of inductive reasoning, which of these dangers does Bacon consider the greatest?

2. Name several books that you feel should be (*a*) tasted (*b*) swallowed (*c*) digested.

3. (*a*) What, according to Bacon, is the relationship between studies and the human personality? (*b*) Have you had any experiences that confirm this idea?

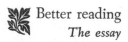 Better reading
The essay

Bacon wrote prose in an age of poetry, when all around him men were composing songs, sonnets, and dramas in verse. England, however, was soon to move out of the Elizabethan Age of great poetry into a new age of great prose (see Chapter V) and Bacon's *Essays* are regarded as one of the first important steps in this new direction.

The essay was and still is the most flexible of the prose composition forms, its length, subject matter, and structure depending entirely upon the needs and intentions of the essayist. Usually the term is applied to a work of moderate length in which a writer tries to develop his own thoughts on some subject.

Although essays had been written since the time of the ancient Greeks and Romans, it was not until 1580 when the Frenchman Montaigne called his prose pieces *essais* or "attempts" that the form received its name. Because of their personal, rambling quality, Montaigne's essays belong to the *informal* tradition in essay writing. Bacon's essays, which are more impersonal and more highly organized, are examples of the *formal* essay.

Although many of Bacon's essays consist of only one paragraph, they usually divide naturally into three or more groups of ideas. How would you divide "Of Studies" into paragraphs? Explain your reasons for dividing the essay in this way.

Bacon's essays are composed mainly of *aphorisms* —terse sentences expressing general thoughts or maxims. What are some of the more effective aphorisms in "Of Studies"? How does this kind of sentence make it difficult to get at the formal pattern of the essay?

What is the tone of "Of Studies"?

THE KING JAMES BIBLE

During the early years of the seventeenth century the differences between the various groups of English Protestants became more and more acute. In an effort to resolve these differences, James I called a conference of religious leaders at Hampton Court in 1604. The conference did not succeed in uniting the Protestants, but it did authorize the undertaking of a new translation of the Bible. Fifty-four of England's greatest scholars and churchmen set to work at Oxford, Cambridge, and Westminster. Reading from previous English translations by Wycliffe, Tyndale, and Coverdale and also from the original Bibles in Hebrew, Greek, and Latin, they finally produced in 1611 the Authorized King James Version, which was written in an English "understanded of the people." So great was the popularity of the new translation that it ran through fourteen printings in three years—and today it continues to outsell all other books in English.

The King James Bible is regarded as one of the outstanding literary achievements of the English Renaissance, not only because of its tremendous scope but also because of its brilliant use of language. Like the original Hebrew Bible, the Authorized English Version makes extensive use of concrete terms and images. Straightforward phrases, sentences, and passages create an overall tone of dignified simplicity. And frequent use of questions and answers and repeated ideas gives rise to the rhythmical cadence of poetry. This language has so profoundly affected succeeding generations of writers and has so thoroughly stamped itself in the minds of ordinary people that today it forms a basic part of our everyday speech.

Title page of the first edition.

THE GOOD SAMARITAN
Luke 10:25–37

And, behold, a certain lawyer stood up, and tempted him, saying, Master, what shall I do to inherit eternal life?

26 He said unto him, What is written in the law? how readest thou?

27 And he answering said, Thou shalt love the Lord thy God with all thy heart, and with all thy soul, and with all thy strength, and with all thy mind; and thy neighbor as thyself.

28 And he said unto him, Thou hast answered right: this do, and thou shalt live.

29 But he, willing[1] to justify himself, said unto Jesus, And who is my neighbor?

30 And Jesus answering said, A certain man went down from Jerusalem to Jericho, and fell among thieves, which stripped him of his raiment, and wounded him, and departed, leaving him half dead.

31 And by chance there came down a certain priest that way: and when he saw him, he passed by on the other side.

32 And likewise a Levite,[2] when he was at the place, came and looked on him, and passed by on the other side.

33 But a certain Samaritan,[3] as he journeyed, came where he was: and when he saw him, he had compassion on him,

34 And went to him, and bound up his wounds, pouring in oil and wine, and set him on his own beast, and brought him to an inn, and took care of him.

35 And on the morrow when he departed, he took out two pence, and gave them to the host, and said unto him, Take care of him; and whatsoever thou spendest more, when I come again, I will repay thee.

36 Which now of these three, thinkest thou, was neighbor unto him that fell among the thieves?

37 And he said, He that shewed mercy on him. Then said Jesus unto him, Go, and do thou likewise.

CHARITY
I Corinthians 13

Though I speak with the tongues of men and of angels, and have not charity, I am become as sounding brass, or a tinkling cymbal.

2 And though I have the gift of prophecy, and understand all mysteries, and all knowledge; and though I have all faith, so that I could remove mountains, and have not charity, I am nothing.

3 And though I bestow all my goods to feed the poor, and though I give my body to be burned, and have not charity, it profiteth me nothing.

4 Charity suffereth long, and is kind; charity envieth not; charity vaunteth not itself, is not puffed up,

5 Doth not behave itself unseemly, seeketh not her own, is not easily provoked, thinketh no evil;

6 Rejoiceth not in iniquity, but rejoiceth in the truth;

7 Beareth all things, believeth all things, hopeth all things, endureth all things.

8 Charity never faileth: but whether there be prophecies, they shall fail; whether there be tongues, they shall cease; whether there be knowledge, it shall vanish away.

9 For we know in part, and we prophesy in part.

10 But when that which is perfect is come, then that which is in part shall be done away.

11 When I was a child, I spake as a child, I understood as a child, I thought as a child: but when I became a man, I put away childish things.

12 For now we see through a glass, darkly; but then face to face: now I know in part; but then shall I know even as also I am known.

13 And now abideth faith, hope, charity, these three; but the greatest of these is charity.

THE GOOD SAMARITAN **1.** *willing*, wishing. **2.** *Levite*, member of the tribe of Levi from which assistants to the Jewish priests were chosen. **3.** *Samaritan*, a man from Samaria.

PSALM 1

Blessed is the man that walketh not in the counsel of the ungodly, nor standeth in the way of sinners, nor sitteth in the seat of the scornful.

2 But his delight is in the law of the Lord; and in his law doth he meditate day and night.

3 And he shall be like a tree planted by the rivers of water, that bringeth forth his fruit in his season; his leaf also shall not wither; and whatsoever he doeth shall prosper.

4 The ungodly are not so: but are like the chaff which the wind driveth away.

5 Therefore the ungodly shall not stand in the judgment, nor sinners in the congregation of the righteous.

6 For the Lord knoweth the way of the righteous: but the way of the ungodly shall perish.

PSALM 24

The earth is the Lord's, and the fulness thereof; the world, and they that dwell therein.

2 For he hath founded it upon the seas, and established it upon the floods.

3 Who shall ascend into the hill of the Lord? or who shall stand in his holy place?

4 He that hath clean hands, and a pure heart; who hath not lifted up his soul unto vanity, nor sworn deceitfully.

5 He shall receive the blessing from the Lord, and righteousness from the God of his salvation.

6 This is the generation of them that seek him, that seek thy face, O Jacob.

7 Lift up your heads, O ye gates; and be ye lift up, ye everlasting doors; and the King of glory shall come in.

8 Who is this King of glory? The Lord strong and mighty, the Lord mighty in battle.

9 Lift up your heads, O ye gates; even lift them up, ye everlasting doors; and the King of glory shall come in.

10 Who is this King of glory? The Lord of hosts, he is the King of glory.

PSALM 91

He that dwelleth in the secret place of the most High shall abide under the shadow of the Almighty.

2 I will say of the Lord, He is my refuge and my fortress: my God; in him will I trust.

3 Surely he shall deliver thee from the snare of the fowler, and from the noisome pestilence.

4 He shall cover thee with his feathers, and under his wings shalt thou trust: his truth shall be thy shield and buckler.

5 Thou shalt not be afraid for the terror by night; nor for the arrow that flieth by day;

6 Nor for the pestilence that walketh in darkness; nor for the destruction that wasteth at noonday.

7 A thousand shall fall at thy side, and ten thousand at thy right hand; but it shall not come nigh thee.

8 Only with thine eyes shalt thou behold and see the reward of the wicked.

9 Because thou hast made the Lord, which is my refuge, even the most High, thy habitation;

10 There shall no evil befall thee, neither shall any plague come nigh thy dwelling.

11 For he shall give his angels charge over thee, to keep thee in all thy ways.

12 They shall bear thee up in their hands, lest thou dash thy foot against a stone.

13 Thou shalt tread upon the lion and adder: the young lion and the dragon shalt thou trample under feet.

14 Because he hath set his love upon me, therefore will I deliver him: I will set him on high, because he hath known my name.

15 He shall call upon me, and I will answer him: I will be with him in trouble; I will deliver him, and honor him.

16 With long life will I satisfy him, and shew him my salvation.

Make a joyful noise unto the Lord, all ye lands.

2 Serve the Lord with gladness: come before his presence with singing.

3 Know ye that the Lord he is God: it is he that hath made us, and not we ourselves; we are his people, and the sheep of his pasture.

4 Enter into his gates with thanksgiving, and into his courts with praise: be thankful unto him, and bless his name.

5 For the Lord is good; his mercy is everlasting; and his truth endureth to all generations.

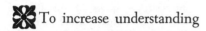 To increase understanding

1. "The Good Samaritan" is an example of a *parable*—a short fictitious narrative from which a spiritual or moral lesson can be drawn. (*a*) Explain the parable of "The Good Samaritan." (*b*) Why are parables particularly effective in teaching?

2. "Charity" is an *epistle*, or letter, by St. Paul to members of the church at Corinth. (*a*) What does St. Paul's epistle have in common with the parable of "The Good Samaritan"? (*b*) How does it differ from the parable?

3. (*a*) Explain the simile in the first sentence of St. Paul's epistle. (*b*) Reread verse 12 of the epistle. What is meant by the phrase "For now we see through a glass, darkly"?

4. The Bible's one hundred and fifty Psalms or songs were written for a variety of religious purposes. For example, some are petitions, some meditations, and so on. What would you say was the intended purpose of each of the Psalms you have read?

5. These Psalms exhibit a number of literary qualities. Cite examples of effective use of (*a*) contrast, (*b*) comparison, (*c*) repetition, (*d*) question and answer, (*e*) imagery.

The Larger View

A. In order to arrive at a better understanding of the Elizabethan Age as a whole and of its place in the long chronology of English literature, review the literary works of this period you have studied and the lives of the men who wrote them. Prepare to discuss the following questions.

1. How did the Renaissance outlook on life differ from the medieval outlook? What architectural structures might stand as symbols of these two different points of view?

2. How do the selections you have read reflect the spirit of the Renaissance?

3. Did the spirit of the Renaissance persist throughout the Elizabethan Age? Explain.

B. The exuberance of the Elizabethan Age shines out clearly in the Elizabethan songs, the sonnets of Sidney and Spenser, and many of Shakespeare's sonnets. A different, more somber and questioning tone is apparent in *Hamlet*, Sonnet 146 by Shakespeare, and the poems and prose of John Donne.

Study the following poems or parts of poems carefully. Notice the diction, the nature of the figurative language, the ideas expressed, and the tone. Then decide which poems exhibit the spirit of the earlier part of the Elizabethan Age and which represent the spirit of the later part. Be prepared to give evidence to support your answers.

I. Sister, awake, close not your eyes,
   The day her light discloses;
And the bright morning doth arise
   Out of her bed of roses.
See the clear sun, the world's bright eye,
   In at our window peeping;
Lo, how he blushes to espy
   Us idle wenches sleeping.
Therefore awake, make haste I say,
   And let us without staying
All in our gowns of green so gay
   Into the park a-maying.

II. Tomorrow, and tomorrow, and tomorrow,
Creeps in this petty pace from day to day,
To the last syllable of recorded time;
And all our yesterdays have lighted fools
The way to dusty death. Out, out, brief
      candle!
Life's but a walking shadow, a poor player
That struts and frets his hour upon the stage
And then is heard no more: it is a tale
Told by an idiot, full of sound and fury,
Signifying nothing.

III. Love guards the roses of thy lips
And flies about them like a bee;
If I approach he forward skips,
And if I kiss he stingeth me.
Love in thine eyes doth build his bower,
And sleeps within their pretty shine;
And if I look the boy will lour,
And from their orbs shoot shafts divine.
Love works thy heart within his fire,
And in my tears doth firm the same;
And if I tempt it will retire,
And of my plaints doth make a game.
Love, let me cull her choicest flowers,
And pity me, and calm her eye,
Make soft her heart, dissolve her lours,
Then will I praise thy deity.
But if thou do not, Love, I'll truly serve her
In spite of thee, and by firm faith deserve her.

IV. This is my play's last scene, here heavens
        appoint
My pilgrimage's last mile; and my race
Idly, yet quickly, run, hath this last pace,
My span's last inch, my minute's latest point,
And gluttonous Death will instantly unjoint
My body, and soul, and I shall sleep a space,
But my ever-waking part shall see that face,
Whose fear already shakes my every joint:
Then, as my soul, to Heaven, her first seat, takes
        flight,
And earth-born body, in the earth shall dwell,
·So, fall my sins, that all may have their right,
To where they are bred, and would press me, to
        Hell.
Impute me righteous, thus purged of evil,
For thus I leave the world, the flesh, the devil.

Bibliography

ANDERSON, MAXWELL, *Eleven Verse Plays*. (Harcourt) Included in this collection you will find *Elizabeth the Queen*, which shows Elizabeth as a strong character who chose to sacrifice personal consideration in order to safeguard her power as a ruler. *Mary of Scotland*, also included, deals with one of the most mysterious and tragic figures in English history.

AULT, NORMAN (editor), *Elizabethan Lyrics from the Original Texts*. (••Putnam) Here is a fine collection of Elizabethan lyrics for you to enjoy.

BACON, FRANCIS, *Essays*. (•Dolphin) Bacon's brief essays are both witty and wise; they have been read and enjoyed for well over three centuries.

BARNES, MARGARET CAMPBELL, *King's Fool*. (Macrae, Smith) Henry VIII is viewed through the eyes of Will Somers, king's fool and confidante, in this colorful and historically accurate novel about the Tudor period.

BUCKMASTER, HENRIETTA, *All the Living*. (Random) The elusive life of Shakespeare is enough to stir the imagination of any novelist, and this book, concerned primarily with Shakespeare in his thirty-seventh year, will completely capture the attention of its readers.

CHUTE, MARCHETTE, *Ben Jonson of Westminster*. (Dutton •Everyman's) One of the most interesting studies of the life and times of Ben Jonson, this spirited book is an excellent example of Marchette Chute's ability to combine research and imagination.

CHUTE, MARCHETTE, *Shakespeare of London*. (Dutton •Everyman's) Using documentary material, all of which was written before 1635, the author presents Shakespeare as a man rather than as an immortal in this very readable biography.

CLEMENS, SAMUEL LANGHORNE, *The Prince and the Pauper*. (Harper •Grosset) You will find the plot interesting: the boy king, Edward VI, switches places with a poor boy who impersonates him as king. There are plenty of exciting adventures as well as a lively description of English court life.

DAVIS, WILLIAM STEARNS, *Life in Elizabethan Days*. (Harper) The author gives a simple and vital portrayal of a typical English community at the end of the sixteenth century.

HAYCRAFT, MOLLY, *The Reluctant Queen*. (Lippincott) Mary Tudor, sister of Henry VIII, is the subject of this romantic historical novel. The sad story of Mary's love for her brother's best friend is offset by the pomp and pageantry of tournaments and coronations.

JONSON, BEN, *Bartholomew Fair*, edited by E. A. Horsman. (Harvard) Laid against the background of the famous Bartholomew Fair formerly held in Smithfield, England, this excellent example of Elizabethan comedy tells the story of John Littlewit, a proctor who issues marriage licenses. Littlewit wants to see the fair but meets considerable opposition from his mother-in-law.

JONSON, BEN, *Volpone*, edited by V. F. Hopper and Cedric Gale. (• • Barron's) Jonson's subject in this "humor comedy" is greed. Volpone leads three greedy friends to believe he is dying in order to test their loyalty. This is one of Jonson's best works and should be read by any student interested in Shakespeare's contemporaries in the theater.

KINGSLEY, CHARLES, *Westward Ho!* (Dodd • Everyman's) This famous story of adventure tells of sea fights with the Spaniards in the time of Queen Elizabeth. The defeat of the powerful Spanish Armada is dealt with, as well as Hawkins, Drake, and other British naval heroes of the time.

MARLOWE, CHRISTOPHER, *Dr. Faustus*, edited by R. H. Robbins. (• Barron's) Based on an old German legend about a man who enters into a bargain with the devil and sells his soul to him, *Dr. Faustus* is a brilliant example of the eloquence and imagination of the Elizabethan theater.

NORMAN, CHARLES, *The Playmaker of Avon*. (McKay) This biography uses passages from Shakespeare's plays to reconstruct unknown parts of his life. It makes Shakespeare a real and convincing person, describes the theater of his day, and shows the influence on him of such important figures as Queen Elizabeth and Christopher Marlowe.

OGBURN, DOROTHY, and CHARLTON, JR., *Shakespeare; The Man Behind the Name*. (Morrow) Possessing all the elements of a good mystery story, this intriguing book is bound to stir up arguments in many quarters. "Who *really* wrote Shakespeare's plays"? ask the Ogburns. They claim it was Edward De Vere, the seventeenth-century Earl of Oxford, and they present some interesting evidence to back up their statement.

QUENNELL, MARJORIE, and CHARLES H. B., *The History of Everyday Things in England*. (Putnam) Refer to the second volume of this four-volume series for information on the Elizabethan Age. This book is one of the most authoritative of its kind.

SHAKESPEARE, WILLIAM, *Complete Works*, edited by Hardin Craig. (Scott, Foresman) Comedy, tragedy, intrigue, satire, mystery, ghost stories—what's your taste in plays? Whatever it is, you will find something to satisfy your appetite in this well-presented collection of Shakespeare's works.

SITWELL, EDITH, *Fanfare for Elizabeth*. (• Macmillan) The greatest woman ruler in history could have no better biographer than Dame Edith Sitwell, well-known poet and author. Anyone who reads this book will enjoy it. If you prefer a more fictionalized account of the life of Elizabeth, read *The Queens and the Hive* (Little) by the same author. The Queens here are Elizabeth, Mary Tudor, and Mary Queen of Scots, and the hive is England.

SPENSER, EDMUND, *Selected Poetry*, edited by Leo Kirschbaum. (• Holt, Rinehart & Winston) Spenser, long ranked as "the poet's poet," will prove absorbing reading for any student interested in great poetry.

SUTCLIFF, ROSEMARY, *Lady in Waiting*. (Coward) A book with a definite appeal for girls, this well-written novel tells the sometimes stormy, sometimes tragic story of Sir Walter Raleigh and his wife Bess.

TREASE, GEOFFREY, *Sir Walter Raleigh, Captain and Adventurer*. (Vanguard) Boys especially will enjoy this biography of Raleigh, for it reads like a dramatic adventure story. The arrogant, able Sir Walter is pictured as a master of himself in every situation, including his own execution.

VANCE, MARGUERITE, *Lady Jane Grey, Reluctant Queen*. (Dutton) This dramatic biography tells the romantic and tragic story of Lady Jane Grey, who was queen of England for only nine days.

WHITE, ANNE TERRY, *Will Shakespeare and the Globe Theater*. (Random) Opening with the twenty-two-year-old Shakespeare setting out to seek his fortune on the stage, this colorful biography tells about the part he played in the building of the Globe Theater and about his associates in Elizabethan London.

WILSON, JOHN DOVER, *Through Elizabethan Eyes*. (Cambridge U.P.) This abridgment of the author's *Life in Shakespeare's England* presents an authentic and thoroughly enjoyable picture of England as the Elizabethans knew it.

WINWAR, FRANCES, *Queen Elizabeth and the Spanish Armada*. (Random) The author tells how, in one of the most daring naval maneuvers in history, Elizabeth's tiny navy defeated the 114 ships of the Spanish Armada.

• paperback only   • • paperback and hardcover

chapter four THE SEVENTEENTH CENTURY

1625·1700

London on the last night of the Great Fire. The painting, by an anonymous eyewitness, shows the Tower (right) and St. Paul's in flames (center).

The Age of Elizabeth had been an exciting and dangerous one. Too much political ambition had sent many a swashbuckling courtier to the executioner's block and the "wrong" religious views had sent many a citizen to the stake. But the age had been a merry one as well. Firmly united by the first warm stirrings of patriotic pride, the Elizabethans had managed to laugh, dance, and love their way through the turmoil of their time with more childlike gusto than any Englishmen before them or any Englishmen since. In the seventeenth century this feeling of unity and merriment came to an end. For the first time since the War of the Roses over a hundred and fifty years earlier, Englishmen took up arms against Englishmen in one of the bloodiest civil wars in history. Faced with catastrophe, the kings and courtiers of the seventeenth century withdrew into their private world of refined elegance. The rest of the country came down from the exuberant heights attained during Elizabethan times to lead cautious and sober lives.

The great issues that split England asunder in the seventeenth century could have been, and probably were, foreseen by the more forward-looking of the Elizabethans. Elizabeth's subjects probably realized that the peace between the Anglican Protestants and the Puritans—those persons who wished to "purify" the Anglican Church—was an uneasy one and depended largely on the Queen's own lenient and magnetic personality and on the diverting activities of her reign. When Elizabeth died, the whole question was thrown open: Was England to become an Anglican or a Puritan nation? Elizabethans probably also realized that the peace between an authoritarian monarch and a Parliament whose seats were being increasingly filled by the new and prosperous middle class depended largely on the tact exercised by both sides. If either monarch or Parliament bluntly stated that it was the only authority in the land, then war was inevitable.

The first of the Stuart kings to rule England, James I, about whom you read in the preceding chapter, was succeeded in 1625 by his son Charles I. It was during Charles' reign that the long-threatened civil war broke out, ending in 1649 with the tragic beheading of the King. Then for an interlude of eleven years England was ruled by Oliver Cromwell, a Puritan and a leader in Parliament. In 1660 the Stuart family was restored to the throne. Charles II (1660-1685) was succeeded by his brother James II (1685-1688). When James was deposed in 1688, the crown passed to his daughter Mary and her husband William of Orange, who reigned from 1689 to 1702.

PURITANS
AND
CAVALIERS
In England Puritanism was the last step in the great church-reform movement, called the Reformation, which swept over Europe in the sixteenth and seventeenth centuries. The first step had been Henry VIII's creation of the Church of England, also called the Anglican Church, which refused to recognize the authority of the Roman Catholic Pope but which sought only slight changes in the ritual of the Church itself. The Puritans wanted radical changes, such as the elimination of vestments, processionals, chanting, kneeling, organ music, and the burning of incense—all of which, they felt, contributed to the spiritual emptiness of the Anglican service. Even John Milton, the greatest writer of the period, whose views were much less radical than those of most Puritans, described

the Anglican clergy as "blind mouths" to whom congregations, like "hungry sheep, look up and are not fed."[1]

The Puritans were serious and industrious people, possessed of that straining for perfection which brings about great improvements in the world but which presents problems for the less saintly persons who make up the greater portion of mankind. In his *Essay on Milton* the nineteenth-century writer Macaulay speaks of the defects of the Puritans—their contempt of human learning and amusements, their gloomy minds and habits, and their fanatical intolerance of other religions. But for their active stand against the greatest sources of tyranny in their day, most certainly the King and the Church of England, Macaulay pronounces the Puritans "a brave, a wise, an honest, and a useful body."

On the Anglican side of the struggle were the Stuarts and their followers, who, because they resembled the courtiers of the King's cavalry, were called "Cavaliers." They were elegant gallants clad in satins and velvets, lace collars, and hats with great flowing plumes. Their bright finery and long curly locks stood out in marked contrast to the somber, practical garb of the Puritans, whose habit of wearing their hair short earned them the nickname "Roundheads." Trying to see both sides of the question, Macaulay tells us that there were many Cavaliers who were immoral "horseboys, gamblers, and bravoes" but that there were also "honest old Cavaliers" who fought for "the old banner which had waved in so many battles over the heads of their fathers, and for the altars at which they had received the hands of their brides. . . . With many of the vices of the Round Table they had also many of its virtues—courtesy, generosity, veracity, tenderness, and respect for women. They had far more both of profound and polite learning than the Puritans. Their manners were more engaging, their tempers more amiable, their tastes more elegant, and their households more cheerful."

CIVIL WAR Both James I and his son Charles I were dogmatic Anglicans who sought to correct the "errors" and the "treason" of the Puritans by force. One man, for instance, who had written a book attacking plays and actors, was deprived of his degree from Oxford, barred from his profession of law, made to stand in the pillory, subjected to having both ears cut off, fined five thousand pounds, and imprisoned for life. "I will make them conform," said James I as he left the conference that authorized the translation of the King James Bible, "or I will harry them out of the land." And harry them out he did. In 1620 a band of Puritans took flight to New England aboard the *Mayflower*. Within twenty years of that historic trip, which must have had the same awesome fascination in the seventeenth century as

Portrait of Charles I by Daniel Mytens, 1631.

---

1. John Milton, "Lycidas," lines 119-125.

Above: Oliver Cromwell.
Below: Engraving showing the
turning point in the Battle of
Naseby. The Earl of
Carneworth is shown turning
Charles I from his panic-stricken
troops.

space travel in the twentieth, more than twenty thousand Puritans had set sail for the American wilderness.

James I and Charles I were just as blunt in matters of politics. They claimed that the king was God's representative on earth and therefore the highest authority in the land. Parliament showed its hostility toward this theory (known as the Divine Right of Kings) by refusing to grant Charles' desperate requests for money. By August of 1642 all hope of coöperation had vanished, and Puritans and Parliamentarians ranged themselves against Anglicans and Royalists on the field of battle.

At first the Cavaliers, with their superior training in horsemanship and the use of arms, were the victors. But then there rose from the Puritan ranks a military genius by the name of Oliver Cromwell, who fanned his troops into such an intense flame of religious fervor that the Cavaliers were doomed. "God made them stubble to our swords," were his words at the bloody battle of Marston Moor (1644). At Naseby (1645) Charles I watched in anguish as Cromwell's terrifying Ironside Army drove all before it. A tragic fate awaited Charles. When the war was over, the victorious Ironsides clamored for his death—and they got it. On the afternoon of January 30, 1649, after having been refused permission to speak at his trial, Charles mounted the scaffold and helped the executioner to arrange his hair under a cap. Upon his own signal the ax fell.

Finding himself swept to power by the military machine he had created, Oliver Cromwell tried hard to assemble Parliaments that would coöperate with him in the task of governing the new Commonwealth of England. His efforts failed, however, and he found that he was ruling England just as absolutely as any of the Stuart monarchs. The welfare of the country was always uppermost in Cromwell's mind—naval and merchant shipping flourished, colonization was encouraged, and the Dutch and the Spanish were defeated at sea—but during the eleven years of his rule Englishmen were subjected to the intense prying and spying of Puritan officials. Not only were theaters and alehouses shut down and betting games suppressed, but "swearing was an offense punishable by a graduated scale of fines: a duke paid 30s., a baron 20s., and a squire 10s. Common people could relieve their feelings at 3s. 4d.[2] Not much was allowed for their money; one man was fined for saying 'God is my witness,' another for saying 'Upon my life.' "[3] Christmas festivities were considered irreligious, and on Christmas Day soldiers were ordered to seize the meat cooking in the kitchens of private homes. Walking on the Sabbath (except to and from church), Maypole celebrations, sports, and ornamental attire were forbidden. During this time many Cavaliers set sail for the New World out of the same sense of oppression that had prompted the Puritans to emigrate some twenty years earlier. Englishmen soon grew tired of Puri-

---

2. *30s. . . . 4d.* In English currency *s.* stands for shilling, *d.* (from the Latin *denarii*) for pence. **3.** Churchill, Winston S., *A History of the English-Speaking Peoples*, Vol. II, p. 312. Copyright 1956 by Dodd, Mead & Company, Inc., New York.

Above: The reverse side of the second Great Seal of the Commonwealth, showing the House of Commons. Right: Cavalier and Roundhead, extreme examples of each. On the right, the man known as "Oliver Cromwell's porter," a Puritan religious fanatic. On the left, one of the officers in attendance on Charles I, reproduced from Battles of the English Civil War, *by Austin Woolrych, published by Messrs. B. T. Batsford, London.*

tan perfection, however. When Cromwell died and his son Richard had been in office only five months, the Stuart King Charles II, son of the executed Charles I, was invited back to the throne from his exile in France.

THE RESTORATION Great was the rejoicing as Charles II entered London on the afternoon of May 29, 1660. Flowers were flung in the streets, bells were rung, tapestries were hung from balconies crowded with ladies, and wine ran from the fountains. The people eventually settled back to sober, everyday living, but the Court did not. Anybody would have appeared immoral in contrast with the stern figures of the Puritan interlude, but the Cavaliers who came back from France to enjoy an Indian summer under Charles II appeared particularly so. Gaiety, frivolity, and licentiousness were the order of the day, and the poor Puritans became the objects of much of the satirical writing that was one of the chief characteristics of the Restoration.

Charles immediately reopened the theaters, which had been closed for nearly twenty years. The new plays were either witty, sophisticated comedies, usually dealing with the battle of the sexes, or extravagant, declamatory heroic tragedies, whose theme was the conflict between love and duty. Both types were written exclusively for and by courtiers and had little, if any, appeal for ordinary Englishmen. The "groundlings," or "stinkards," who had lent such boisterous color to the Elizabethan theaters, were no longer present to boo and hiss at elegant courtiers. Even the courtiers conducted themselves in a more refined manner than their Elizabethan counterparts. Instead of strutting and posturing before the audience as a whole in the manner of Sir Walter Raleigh and his friends, Restoration gallants carried on elaborate flirtations with ladies in boxes or indulged in witty but quiet conversations with their neighbors. This birth of the "polite" theater was accompanied by the birth of the "divided" theater, the jutting Elizabethan stage giving way to a picture-frame stage that tended to separate the audience and the actors into two different worlds.

Packwood House, Warwickshire. The house was finished in its present form and the remarkable garden laid out during the Restoration period.

One of the outstanding events of the Restoration was the founding in 1660 of England's first scientific society, the Royal Society of London. Francis Bacon would have been immensely pleased could he have attended the meetings of this society, composed both of men of letters and scientists, for they had as their primary purpose the carrying out of experiments and the exchange of scientific findings with men of all countries. The seventeenth century was in fact so full of powerful intellects, most of whom dealt either directly or indirectly with science, that it has been called the Century of Genius. The astronomer Galileo was working in Italy when the first Stuarts were on the throne in England. About the same time, the English physician William Harvey was discovering how the blood circulates in the body. Around mid-century, Robert Boyle worked on the properties of gases. And the great Newton, who was the Royal Society's president for over twenty years, published his work on the theory of gravity of 1687.

The Restoration years were also a time of mass death. In 1665 there came a ferocious outbreak of the bubonic plague—the worst since the days of the Black Death in the fourteenth century—which killed a quarter of the citizens of London. The eighteenth-century writer-journalist Daniel Defoe, who is best known as the author of *Robinson Crusoe*, was not an eyewitness of the plague (being only five years old at the time), but with the journalist's gift for collecting detailed information he composed in 1722 a *Journal of the Plague Year* that gives us a good idea of what a ghostly city London

Above: Silver tankard made in London for Charles II, 1684. Below: London in the seventeenth century.
Opposite: Marble bust of Charles II by Honoré Pellé, 1682.

S. PAULES CHURCH

THAMESIS

must have been. "Whole streets seemed to be desolated, and not to be shut up only, but to be emptied of their inhabitants; doors were left open, and windows stood shattering with the wind in empty houses for want of people to shut them." And as if this were not enough, the Great Fire, which you will read about in the diary of Samuel Pepys (page 230), swept through the city in the following year, destroying close to thirteen thousand dwellings, whole sections of the city, and many historic monuments, including the thirteenth-century Cathedral of St. Paul.

It was indeed an exhausted and chastened citizenry that William and Mary came from Holland to govern in 1688. They came because Charles II had left no legitimate heir and because his brother James II, who ruled from 1685 to 1688, was an avowed Catholic, which Protestant England did not want. The island, however, had learned its lesson, for the Glorious Revolution that chased James II from the country and that set his daughter and son-in-law on the throne was a bloodless one, celebrated by the passage of a Bill of Rights similar to the first ten amendments to the Constitution of the United States. The remaining twelve years of the century are largely a story of William's wars against the Sun King of France, Louis XIV. In England the Puritan and Cavalier epoch came to a close. Henceforth, these two powerful contestants would fight it out not on the battlefield but in Parliament—one going by the name of Whig, the other by the name of Tory.

LUVIUS

The Cavalier Poets

The poets who most perfectly expressed the graceful elegance of the
Stuart courts were a group of young men known, appropriately enough,
as the Cavalier Poets. Devoted Royalists, these gallant young men wrote
verses that were as gay and smooth and polished as their courtly surroundings. Their model and idol was the Elizabethan poet and playwright
Ben Jonson (1573?-1637), who had been a gay blade himself, and who
in the midst of the rough-and-tumble crudeness of much Elizabethan life
and literature had spoken out in favor of the classical ideals of refined
living and refined writing.

> Ah, Ben!
> Say how or when
> Shall we, thy guests,
> Meet at those lyric feasts
> Made at the Sun,
> The Dog, the Triple Tun?
> Where we such clusters had
> As made us nobly wild, not mad;
> And yet each verse of thine
> Outdid the meat, outdid the frolic wine.

This is a famous stanza by Robert Herrick (1591-1674), the most accomplished of all the "Sons of Ben." After a career as a jeweler and a Cambridge scholar, Herrick joined Jonson and his "tribe" at the Sun, the
Triple Tun, and other taverns. In 1629, having taken orders in the
Anglican Church, he accepted Charles I's offer of a position as parish
priest in the west-country county of Devon. He was removed from this
post by Cromwell's government but restored to it when Charles II took
the throne. To London-born Herrick, Devonshire seemed a dull place—
one story has it that he once threw his sermon at his half-sleeping, half-
gossiping congregation. But Herrick soon discovered that the country had
its own special kind of "lyric feasts." The innocent, half-pagan charm of
country players, dancers, and milkmaids, of harvest carts, winter revels,
and spring Maypoles soon worked its magic on him. In a book entitled
Hesperides, from the Greek word meaning "people of the West," Herrick
expressed his delight in the country and his belief in living for the present
in over eleven hundred poems that are as delicately carved and as jewel-
encrusted as the rings and brooches he had made as a young man.

The most elegant of all the Cavalier Poets were Richard Lovelace
(1618-1658) and John Suckling (1609-1642). Lovelace was much more
the "honest old Cavalier" than Suckling (see page 205), but both led the
devil-may-care kind of life for which their generation is famous. Suckling
was the greatest gamester of his day (cribbage was one of his inventions)
and he managed to squander the large fortune left to him by his father
in extravagant adventures on the Continent and in England. The troop
of a hundred horsemen that was his contribution to one of the campaigns
of Charles I was outfitted in a blaze of scarlet and white finery. Lovelace
was just as rich as Suckling but less fortunate. After playing the rôle of
the beautiful knight who goes to battle for his king dressed in cloth of

silver, Lovelace was thrown into prison by the Puritans, where he wrote his best-known poems, "To Althea" and "To Lucasta." Released from prison, he spent the last ten years of his life in extreme poverty, searching in alleys for food and dying of consumption in a cellar.

Opposite: Richard Lovelace. Below: Syon House, seat of the Duke of Northumberland, a son of Charles II. The house is seen across the Thames a few miles west of London.

The Cavalier Poets were not the only kind of poets in the seventeenth century. Men like George Herbert, Richard Crashaw, and Henry Vaughan wrote intensely personal religious lyrics that are close in spirit to the sacred poems of John Donne (page 184). Henry King, John Cleveland, and Abraham Cowley wrote poems that are reminiscent of Donne in his more worldly moods. Andrew Marvell combined the best of Ben Jonson and John Donne in poems of striking originality. And John Milton wove the classical, Christian, and Renaissance ideas of his time into the greatest poetic masterpieces of the age.

THE DUKE OF NORTHUMBERLAND, K. G.

THE ARGUMENT OF HIS BOOK
from HESPERIDES
Robert Herrick

I sing of brooks, of blossoms, birds and
    bowers,
Of April, May, of June and July
    flowers;
I sing of Maypoles, hock-carts, wassails,
    wakes,
Of bridegrooms, brides, and of their bridal
    cakes;
I write of youth, of love, and have access   5
By these to sing of cleanly wantonness;
I sing of dews, of rains, and piece by piece
Of balm, of oil, of spice and ambergris;
I sing of times trans-shifting, and I write
How roses first came red and lilies white;   10
I write of groves, of twilight, and I sing
The Court of Mab,[1] and of the Fairy King;
I write of hell; I sing (and ever shall)
Of heaven, and I hope to have it after all.

TO THE VIRGINS TO MAKE MUCH OF TIME   *Robert Herrick*

Gather ye rosebuds while ye may,
    Old Time is still a-flying;
And this same flower that smiles today,
    Tomorrow will be dying.

The glorious lamp of heaven, the sun,   5
    The higher he's a-getting,
The sooner will his race be run,
    And nearer he's to setting.

That age is best which is the first,
    When youth and blood are warmer;   10
But being spent, the worse and worst
    Times still succeed the former.

Then be not coy, but use your time,
    And while ye may, go marry;
For, having lost but once your prime,   15
    You may forever tarry.

TO LUCASTA, ON GOING TO THE WARS   *Richard Lovelace*

Tell me not, sweet, I am unkind,
    That from the nunnery
Of thy chaste breast and quiet mind
    To war and arms I fly.

True, a new mistress now I chase,   5
    The first foe in the field;
And with a stronger faith embrace
    A sword, a horse, a shield.

Yet this inconstancy is such
    As thou too shalt adore;
I could not love thee, dear, so much   10
    Loved I not honor more.

THE ARGUMENT OF HIS BOOK   **1.** Mab, the Fairy Queen.

Engraved frontispiece to Hesperides *showing Robert Herrick. This, Herrick's only book, containing all his poems, was not published until 1648, eight years after its completion.*

*Sir John Suckling.
This painting by
Theodore Russel is a
copy of a portrait by
Van Dyke. One of the
great portrait painters,
he was court painter
to Charles I.*

TO ALTHEA, FROM PRISON
Richard Lovelace

When Love with unconfinèd wings
  Hovers within my gates,
And my divine Althea brings
  To whisper at the grates;
When I lie tangled in her hair   5
  And fettered to her eye,
The birds that wanton in the air
  Know no such liberty.

When flowing cups run swiftly round
  With no allaying Thames,[1]   10
Our careless heads with roses bound,
  Our hearts with loyal flames;
When thirsty grief in wine we steep,
  When healths and drafts go free,   15
Fishes that tipple in the deep
  Know no such liberty.

When, like committed linnets, I
  With shriller throat will sing
The sweetness, mercy, majesty,
  And glories of my King;   20
When I shall voice aloud how good
  He is, how great should be,
Enlargèd winds, that curl the flood,
  Know no such liberty.

Stone walls do not a prison make,   25
  Nor iron bars a cage;
Minds innocent and quiet take
  That for an hermitage;
If I have freedom in my love
  And in my soul am free,   30
Angels alone, that soar above,
  Enjoy such liberty.

THE CONSTANT LOVER
Sir John Suckling

Out upon it, I have loved
  Three whole days together!
And am like to love three more,
  If it prove fair weather.

Time shall molt away his wings   5
  Ere he shall discover
In the whole wide world again
  Such a constant lover.

But the spite on't is, no praise
  Is due at all to me: 10
Love with me had made no stays,
  Had it any been but she.

Had it any been but she,
  And that very face,
There had been at least ere this   15
  A dozen dozen in her place.

WHY SO PALE AND WAN?
Sir John Suckling

Why so pale and wan, fond lover?
  Prithee, why so pale?
Will, when looking well can't move her,
  Looking ill prevail?
  Prithee, why so pale?   5

Why so dull and mute, young sinner?
  Prithee, why so mute?
Will, when speaking well can't win her,
  Saying nothing do't?
  Prithee, why so mute?   10

Quit, quit for shame! This will not move,
  This cannot take her.
If of herself she will not love,
  Nothing can make her:
  The devil take her!   15

TO ALTHEA, FROM PRISON. **1.** *no allaying Thames,* no
diluting water from the Thames River.

✻ To increase understanding

1. (*a*) What are Herrick's poetic intentions as announced in "The Argument of His Book"? (*b*) How do you think a Puritan would have reacted to such aims?

2. (*a*) What is the literal meaning of the first two stanzas of "To the Virgins to Make Much of Time"? (*b*) What is the meaning of the last two stanzas? (*c*) How do the last two stanzas force a symbolic interpretation of stanzas 1 and 2; e.g., in the light of the last two stanzas, what do rosebuds stand for or symbolize? What does the course of the day symbolize? (*d*) Does stanza 4 tell the reader everything that the rosebud symbolizes or just one thing? Explain.

3. The *carpe diem* (kär′pi dī′em), or "enjoy the present," theme of "To the Virgins to Make Much of Time" was extremely popular in seventeenth-century England. To what do you attribute its popularity?

4. The poems by Lovelace make use of a literary device known as *paradox*, a contradiction which when examined appears entirely plausible. (*a*) What is the paradox in "To Lucasta"? (*b*) How is it resolved? (*c*) What is the paradox in "To Althea"? (*d*) How is it developed in each of the first three stanzas? (*e*) How is it resolved? (*f*) What effects does Lovelace achieve through the use of paradox?

5. (*a*) What ironical effect does Suckling achieve by titling his poem "The Constant Lover"? (*b*) Is Suckling's intent to discredit love or is he paying a compliment to his lady?

6. What does Suckling's poem "Why So Pale and Wan?" have in common with John Donne's "Song" (page 184)?

7. What is the difference in tone between the poems of Lovelace and the poems of Suckling?

Portrait of Inigo Jones.

The Masque

The spirit of lavish elegance which pervaded the Stuart courts and which angered the somber Puritans found expression in the masque, or court spectacle. Originally associated with primitive religious rites and folk ceremonies, the masque eventually became the exclusive concern of the upper classes—a kind of after-dinner show of music, dancing, rich costumes, painted scenery, and some poetry, in which royal or noble persons often took part. It originated in this form in Renaissance Italy, moved on to France, and then to England and the court of Henry VIII. Later it developed into grand opera.

Queen Elizabeth had been entertained with masques during her many progresses, but it was not until the reigns of her seventeenth-century successors James I and Charles I that court spectacles were taken as seriously as the drama proper. In 1634 John Milton combined

Two costume drawings by Inigo Jones.
Below: Lady Wynter as Candace in The Masque
of Queens, *by Ben Jonson. Left: King*
Charles I in the masque Salmacida Spolia,
by Sir William Davenant.

his poetic skill with the musical talents of Henry Lawes to produce *Comus*—a masque whose variety of sights, sounds, and verse delighted its aristocratic participants and spectators at Ludlow Castle. During the latter part of his career the poet-playwright Ben Jonson devoted himself almost exclusively to writing masques for the royal household.

Jonson's partner was the architect and artist Inigo Jones, whose visual tastes eventually overruled Jonson's literary ones. Feeling that it was more important to appeal to the eye than to the imagination, Jones made the masque almost purely a matter of sumptuous spectacle. His costumes and sets, often designed after Italian models, helped to establish him as one of the foremost artists of the time. Their lavishness, however, only emphasized the ever widening gulf between the Cavaliers at court and the large Puritan populace.

John Milton 1608-1674

Most of the poets of the seventeenth century were on the side of the King and the Church of England. The greatest poet of the century, however, was a Puritan—but a Puritan of a very special sort. Born in London, John Milton was given the best education that his cultured and prosperous father could provide. A product of Renaissance England himself, the elder Milton passed on to his son an intense love of learning and the arts. The Milton home provided good books, good music, and stimulating companionship among members of the family and friends. Henry Lawes, one of the century's most talented composers, was a frequent visitor to the house. The elder Milton was himself an accomplished musician. He played upon the organ which he had in the home and trained his son John to play also. John's formal education began at the age of eight with a private tutor; then followed several years of schooling at St. Paul's in preparation for Cambridge University, which he entered at sixteen and left at twenty-three, receiving the degree of Master of Arts.

Milton spent the next six years of his life quietly on his father's country estate at Horton near London, in leisurely reading of the Greek and Latin writers whom he admired so much, and in further preparation for the high calling of poet, to which he had felt dedicated since his early youth. During these years he wrote two of his best-known short poems, "L'Allegro" and "Il Penseroso" (pages 210 and 213) and his masque *Comus* (see page 206). Like most of Milton's works, *Comus* reveals a mingling of Renaissance and Puritan elements; it presents mythological characters in an idealized setting for the development of a Puritan theme: the power of temperance and chastity over intemperance and sensuality.

Another important poem belonging to Milton's Horton period is the elegy "Lycidas." It was written as a contribution to a collection of poems composed by Cambridge students in memory of a classmate who had drowned crossing the Irish Sea soon after his graduation from the university. He and Milton had intended to enter the ministry. The reasons for Milton's decision not to take Holy Orders are expressed in "Lycidas" in lines of scathing criticism of the Anglican clergy (see page 196).

Though Milton was nearly thirty years old by the close of the years at Horton, his father gave him the year abroad with which every young man who had the means finished his education. By this time (1638), Milton had established his reputation as a young man of letters, and with it he gained entrance into the circles of the most learned men in Europe, especially in France and Italy. One of his interviews was with the famous astronomer Galileo in a villa just outside of Florence. When he learned in Naples that civil war was imminent in England, Milton decided to return home. "I thought it base," he explained, "that I should be traveling for intellectual diversion while friends at home were fighting for liberty."

Milton began life on his own by taking London lodgings large enough

Opposite above: Milton at age twenty-one. Opposite below: Milton's cottage in Chalfont-St. Giles, where he completed Paradise Lost. *Right:* Milton Dictating to His Daughters. *This painting by George Romney, made about one hundred years after the event, illustrates the popular view of Milton's tyranny over his daughters.*

MAJOR SIMON WHITBREAD

to accommodate himself and his sister's two sons, who came to him for tutelage. He lived there throughout the war years, taking on a few additional students, and giving up his own scholarly and literary pursuits (except for a few sonnets) in order to write hard-hitting and sometimes violent prose pamphlets in the Puritan cause. *Areopagitica*, a plea for freedom of the press, is one of the best of these. In 1643, Milton made the mistake of marrying the daughter of a Cavalier, a girl half his age, who in no way understood him, and who soon left him for a period of about three years. Milton was bitterly hurt by the separation, but he soon lost himself in his new duties as Latin secretary (correspondent for foreign affairs) under the Commonwealth—a post given to him by Cromwell in recognition of his powers of the pen. For some years Milton had been losing his sight. Now, in 1651, in spite of doctors' warnings, he chose to sacrifice his sight in service to the state. The strain of preparing a pamphlet entitled *A Defense of the English People*, which was the reply to European attacks on England for having executed Charles I, caused Milton to lose his sight completely. Though blind, he continued his secretarial duties by dictation until Cromwell's death and the close of the Puritan interlude.

With the restoration of the monarchy, Milton's life was in danger. He was imprisoned for a short time, and some of his pamphlets were burned. But, except for these indignities, he escaped without serious reprisals. Until his death in 1674 he and his three daughters lived in comparative obscurity in London except for a brief sojourn in a nearby village, Chalfont-St. Giles, during the plague. Wherever he was, his many friends and admirers sought him out, and eager pupils came to the man now recognized as one of England's greatest men of letters. The only cloud that darkened Milton's remaining years was his relationship with his daughters, who had never had much sympathy for their stern Puritan parent. Nevertheless, he taught them to pronounce, but not understand, several different languages, so that he might have readers.

It was in this last period that Milton produced the poetic masterpieces for which he is most famous. The epic poem *Paradise Lost* was published in 1667. Its sequel, *Paradise Regained*, appeared in 1671, followed by *Samson Agonistes* in the same year. All of Milton's poems, but particularly these last ones, reveal a loftiness and musicality of language that countless numbers of poets have sought to imitate. They also reveal one of those rare minds that are capable of ranging freely and easily among the several great sources of Western civilization. The Hebraic, the classical, the Christian, and the Renaissance worlds of thought were all within Milton's grasp and were woven by him into poetic tapestries that are among the richest in the English language.

For years readers have been charmed by the crisp, fresh images of the English countryside and the wealth of classical allusions in Milton's companion poems "L'Allegro" and "Il Penseroso." The titles of these poems are typical of John Milton, the linguist and the musician, for they are Italian terms used in music to mean, respectively, "quick and light-hearted," "slow and thoughtful." Each poem describes a man in one of these two basic moods.

L'ALLEGRO

Hence, loathèd Melancholy,
Of Cerberus[1] and blackest Midnight born
In Stygian[2] cave forlorn
  'Mongst horrid shapes, and shrieks, and
    sights unholy!
Find out some uncouth[3] cell,   5
  Where brooding Darkness spreads his
    jealous wings,
And the night-raven sings;
  There, under ebon shades and low-browed
    rocks,
As ragged as thy locks,
  In dark Cimmerian[4] desert ever dwell.   10
But come, thou Goddess fair and free,
In heaven ycleped Euphrosyne,
And by men heart-easing Mirth,
Whom lovely Venus at a birth
With two sister Graces more   15
To ivy-crownèd Bacchus bore[5];
Or whether (as some sager sing)
The frolic Wind that breathes the spring,
Zephyr[6] with Aurora[7] playing,
As he met her once a-Maying,   20
There on beds of violets blue,
And fresh-blown roses washed in dew,
Filled her with thee, a daughter fair,
So buxom, blithe, and debonair.
Haste thee, nymph, and bring with thee   25
Jest, and youthful Jollity,
Quips, and cranks, and wanton wiles,
Nods, and becks, and wreathèd smiles,
Such as hang on Hebe's[8] cheek,
And love to live in dimple sleek;   30
Sport that wrinkled Care derides,
And Laughter holding both his sides,
Come, and trip it as you go,
On the light fantastic toe;
And in thy right hand lead with thee   35
The mountain nymph, sweet Liberty;
And, if I give thee honor due,
Mirth, admit me of thy crew,

To live with her, and live with thee,
In unreprovèd pleasures free;   40
To hear the lark begin his flight,
And, singing, startle the dull night,
From his watch-tower in the skies,
Till the dappled dawn doth rise;
Then to come, in spite of sorrow,   45
And at my window bid good-morrow,
Through the sweet-briar or the vine,
Or the twisted eglantine;
While the cock with lively din,
Scatters the rear of darkness thin;   50
And to the stack, or the barn-door,
Stoutly struts his dames before;
Oft listening how the hounds and horn
Cheerly rouse the slumbering morn,
From the side of some hoar hill,   55
Through the high wood echoing shrill;
Sometime walking, not unseen,
By hedgerow elms[9], on hillocks green,
Right against the eastern gate,
Where the great Sun begins his state,   60
Robed in flames and amber light,
The clouds in thousand liveries dight;
While the plowman, near at hand,
Whistles o'er the furrowed land,
And the milkmaid singeth blithe,   65
And the mower whets his scythe,
And every shepherd tells his tale[10]
Under the hawthorn in the dale.
Straight mine eye hath caught new pleasures,
Whilst the landscape round it measures: 70
Russet lawns, and fallows gray,
Where the nibbling flocks do stray;
Mountains on whose barren breast
The laboring clouds do often rest;
Meadows trim with daisies pied;   75
Shallow brooks, and rivers wide.
Towers and battlements it sees

---

1. *Cerberus* (sẽr'bər əs), the three-headed dog of classical mythology who guarded the entrance to Hades, or hell. 2. *Stygian* (stij'i ən), pertaining to the Styx, one of the four rivers of Hades. 3. *uncouth*, unknown (an obsolete definition). 4. *Cimmerian* (sə mēr'i ən). In Cimmeria, a land described in Homer's *Odyssey*, "never does the shining sun look down." 5. *Euphrosyne* (ū frŏs'ə nē) . . . *Bacchus* (bak'əs) *bore*. Euphrosyne and her sister Graces, Aglaia and Thalia, were goddesses of joy. They were the daughters of Venus, the goddess of love and beauty, and Bacchus, the god of wine. 6. *Zephyr*, the west wind. 7. *Aurora*, the goddess of the dawn. 8. *Hebe* (hē'bi), the goddess of youth. 9. *hedgerow elms*, trees planted close together to form a hedge. 10. *tells his tale*, counts his sheep.

Bosomed high in tufted trees,
Where perhaps some beauty lies,
The cynosure of neighboring eyes. 80
Hard by, a cottage chimney smokes
From betwixt two agèd oaks,
Where Corydon and Thyrsis[11] met,
Are at their savory dinner set
Of herbs and other country messes, 85
Which the neat-handed Phyllis dresses;
And then in haste her bower she leaves,
With Thestylis to bind the sheaves;
Or, if the earlier season lead,
To the tanned haycock in the mead. 90
Sometimes, with secure delight,
The upland hamlets will invite,
When the merry bells ring round,
And the jocund rebecks sound
To many a youth and many a maid 95
Dancing in the checkered shade;
And young and old come forth to play
On a sunshine holiday,
Till the livelong daylight fail;
Then to the spicy nut-brown ale, 100
With stories told of many a feat,
How Faery Mab the junkets eat;
She was pinched and pulled, she said;
And he, by Friar's lantern led,
Tells how the drudging goblin sweat 105
To earn his cream-bowl duly set,
When, in one night, ere glimpse of morn,
His shadowy flail hath threshed the corn
That ten day-laborers could not end;
Then lies him down the lubber fiend, 110
And, stretched out all the chimney's length,
Basks at the fire his hairy strength,
And crop-full out of doors he flings,
Ere the first cock his matin rings.[12]
Thus done the tales, to bed they creep, 115
By whispering winds soon lulled asleep.
Towered cities please us then,
And the busy hum of men,
Where throngs of knights and barons bold,
In weeds[13] of peace, high triumphs hold, 120
With store of ladies, whose bright eyes
Rain influence,[14] and judge the prize
Of wit or arms, while both contend
To win her grace whom all commend.
There let Hymen[15] oft appear 125
In saffron robe, with taper clear,
And pomp, and feast, and revelry,

With mask[16] and antique pageantry;
Such sights as youthful poets dream
On summer eves by haunted stream. 130
Then to the well-trod stage anon,
If Jonson's learnèd sock[17] be on,
Or sweetest Shakespeare, Fancy's child,
Warble his native wood-notes wild.
And ever, against eating cares, 135
Lap me in soft Lydian[18] airs,
Married to immortal verse,
Such as the meeting soul may pierce
In notes with many a winding bout
Of linkèd sweetness long drawn out, 140
With wanton heed and giddy cunning,
The melting voice through mazes running,
Untwisting all the chains that tie
The hidden soul of harmony;
That Orpheus' self may heave his head 145
From golden slumber on a bed
Of heaped Elysian flowers, and hear
Such strains as would have won the ear
Of Pluto to have quite set free
His half-regained Eurydice.[19] 150
These delights if thou canst give,
Mirth, with thee I mean to live.

---

11. *Corydon* (kôr′i don) *and* Thyrsis (thėr′sis), traditional names for shepherds in pastoral poetry. *Phyllis* (line 86) and *Thestylis* (thes′ti lis) (line 88) are names of shepherd-esses. **12.** *With stories . . . rings.* The company listens to tales about Faery Mab, a common figure from Welsh folklore, mentioned by Shakespeare in *Romeo and Juliet*, who was supposed to make off with the junkets, or milk products, of the dairy. One storyteller (*she* line 103) claims to have been pinched and pulled by fairy creatures. Another (*he* line 104), who was led astray by Friar's lantern, a flickering light in the marshes, tells the familiar tale of Robin Goodfellow (*the drudging goblin* and *lubber-fiend*, or clumsy sprite), who earns a bowl of cream by grinding the corn in one night. **13.** *weeds*, garments. **14.** *eyes . . . influence.* The eyes are thought of as stars (which were supposed to exert an occult power over human affairs). **15.** *Hymen* (hī′mən), the god of marriage. **16.** *mask*, the masque, or court spectacle (see page 206). **17.** *Jonson's learned sock.* Ben Jonson's considerable scholarship came through in his plays. The sock, or low-heeled slipper worn by actors in Greek and Roman comedies, is used as the symbol of comedy in general. **18.** *Lydian* (lid′i ən), the softest of the modes (varieties) in ancient Greek music. **19.** *Orpheus* (ôr′fi əs) . . . *Eurydice* (ū rid′ə sē). In Greek mythology, Orpheus was such a wonderful musician that animals and even inanimate objects followed him when he played upon his lyre. The greatest proof of his power was his visit to the lower regions. From Pluto, the king of the dead, he won permission to take to the upper world his young wife Eurydice on condition that he should not look back at her until they had both reached the upper air. Near the end of the journey, Orpheus did look back and Eurydice was lost forever. When Orpheus died, he went to the Elysian fields, the abode of the blessed after death.

IL PENSEROSO

Hence, vain, deluding Joys,
  The brood of Folly without father bred!
How little you bested,[1]
  Or fill the fixèd mind with all your toys!
Dwell in some idle brain,   5
  And fancies fond with gaudy shapes
        possess,
As thick and numberless
  As the gay motes that people the sunbeams,
Or likest hovering dreams,   9
  The fickle pensioners of Morpheus'[2] train.
But, hail! thou Goddess sage and holy!
Hail, divinest Melancholy!
Whose saintly visage is too bright
To hit the sense of human sight,
And therefore to our weaker view,   15
O'erlaid with black, staid Wisdom's hue;
Black, but such as in esteem
Prince Memnon's[3] sister might beseem,
Or that starred Ethiop queen that strove
To set her beauty's praise above   20
The Sea-Nymph's, and their powers
        offended.[4]
Yet thou art higher far descended;
Thee bright-haired Vesta long of yore
To solitary Saturn bore;
His daughter she; in Saturn's reign,[5]   25
Such mixture was not held a stain.
Oft in glimmering bowers and glades
He met her, and in secret shades
Of woody Ida's inmost grove,
Whilst yet there was no fear of Jove.[6]   30
Come, pensive Nun, devout and pure,
Sober, steadfast, and demure,
All in a robe of darkest grain,[7]
Flowing with majestic train,
And sable stole of cypress lawn   35
Over thy decent shoulders drawn.
Come; but keep thy wonted state,
With even step, and musing gait,
And looks commercing with[8] the skies,
Thy rapt soul sitting in thine eyes;   40
There, held in holy passion still,
Forget thyself to marble, till
With a sad leaden downward cast
Thou fix them on the earth as fast.

And join with thee calm Peace and Quiet,   45
Spare Fast, that oft with gods doth diet,
And hears the Muses[9] in a ring
Aye round about Jove's altar sing;
And add to these retirèd Leisure,
That in trim gardens takes his pleasure;   50
But, first and chiefest, with thee bring
Him that yon soars on golden wing,
Guiding the fiery-wheelèd throne,
The Cherub Contemplation[10];
And the mute Silence hist along,   55
'Less Philomel[11] will deign a song,
In her sweetest saddest plight,
Smoothing the rugged brow of Night,
While Cynthia checks her dragon yoke[12]
Gently o'er th' accustomed oak.   60
Sweet bird, that shunn'st the noise of folly,
Most musical, most melancholy!
Thee, chauntress, oft the woods among
I woo, to hear thy even-song;
And, missing thee, I walk unseen   65
On the dry smooth-shaven green,
To behold the wandering moon
Riding near her highest noon,
Like one that had been led astray
Through the heaven's wide pathless way,   70
And oft, as if her head she bowed,
Stooping through a fleecy cloud.
Oft, on a plat of rising ground,
I hear the far-off curfew sound,
Over some wide-watered shore,   75
Swinging slow with sullen roar;
Or, if the air will not permit,

---

1. bested, avail. **2.** Morpheus (môr′fĭ əs), the Greek god of dreams. **3.** Prince Memnon (mem′non), the beautiful black Ethiopian king of classical mythology. **4.** Ethiop queen . . . offended. In classical mythology, the beautiful wife of Cepheus, king of the Ethiopians, boasted that she was more beautiful than the Sea-Nymphs. The nymphs sent a sea-monster to ravage the country. When the Queen died, the gods transformed her into a star. **5.** Vesta . . . Saturn's reign. Vesta was the goddess of the hearth and daughter of Saturn, the ancient god of agriculture, whom Milton identifies with Cronus (krō′nəs), the king of the gods before Jove. **6.** Ida's . . . no fear of Jove. Saturn, or Cronus, was overthrown by his son Jove after the infant god had been concealed from his father and brought up in the caves of Mount Ida in Crete. **7.** grain, dye. **8.** commercing with, communing with, directed at. **9.** Muses, the nine Greek goddesses of the fine arts and sciences. **10.** fiery-wheeled . . . Cherub Contemplation. The Cherubim attended the fiery, wheeled throne of God. To them was attributed knowledge, to the Seraphim, love. **11.** Philomel (fĭl′ə mel), the nightingale. **12.** Cynthia checks her dragon yoke, Diana, goddess of the moon, reins in her dragon-drawn car to listen to the nightingale.

Some still removèd place will fit,
Where glowing embers through the room
Teach light to counterfeit a gloom,　　　　80
Far from all resort of mirth,
Save the cricket on the hearth,
Or the bellman's drowsy charm[13]
To bless the doors from nightly harm.
Or let my lamp, at midnight hour,　　　　85
Be seen in some high lonely tower,
Where I may oft outwatch the Bear,[14]
With thrice great Hermes,[15] or unsphere
The spirit of Plato,[16] to unfold
What worlds or what vast regions hold　　　90
The immortal mind that hath forsook
Her mansion in this fleshly nook;
And of those demons that are found
In fire, air, flood, or underground
Whose power hath a true consent　　　　95
With planet or with element.
Sometime let gorgeous Tragedy
In sceptered pall come sweeping by,
Presenting Thebes,[17] or Pelops'[18] line,
Or the tale of Troy divine.　　　　　　100
Or what (though rare) of later age
Ennobled hath the buskined stage.[19]
But, O sad Virgin! that thy power
Might raise Musaeus[20] from his bower;
Or bid the soul of Orpheus[21] sing　　　105
Such notes as, warbled to the string,
Drew iron tears down Pluto's cheek,
And made Hell grant what love did seek;
Or call up him[22] that left half told
The story of Cambuscan bold,　　　　　110
Of Camball, and of Algarsife,
And who had Canace to wife,
That owned the virtuous ring and glass,
And of the wondrous horse of brass
On which the Tartar king did ride;　　　115
And if aught else great bards beside
In sage and solemn tunes have sung,
Of tourneys, and of trophies hung,
Of forests, and enchantments drear,
Where more is meant than meets the ear.　120
Thus, Night, oft see me in thy pale career,
Till civil-suited Morn appear,
Not tricked and frounced, as she was wont
With the Attic boy[23] to hunt,
But kerchieft in a comely cloud,　　　　125
While rocking winds are piping loud,
Or ushered with a shower still,

When the gust hath blown his fill,
Ending on the rustling leaves,
With minute-drops from off the eaves.　　　130
And, when the sun begins to fling
His flaring beams, me, Goddess, bring
To archèd walks of twilight groves,
And shadows brown, that Sylvan loves,
Of pine, or monumental oak,　　　　　135
Where the rude ax with heavèd stroke
Was never heard the nymphs to daunt,
Or fright them from their hallowed haunt.
There in close covert, by some brook,
Where no profaner eye may look,　　　　140
Hide me from day's garish eye,
While the bee with honeyed thigh,
That at her flowery work doth sing,
And the waters murmuring,
With such consort as they keep,　　　　145
Entice the dewy-feathered Sleep.
And let some strange mysterious dream
Wave at his wings, in airy stream
Of lively portraiture displayed,
Softly on my eyelids laid;　　　　　　150
And, as I wake, sweet music breathe
Above, about, or underneath,
Sent by some Spirit to mortals good,
Or the unseen Genius of the wood.[24]
But let my due feet never fail　　　　155
To walk the studious cloister's pale,
And love the high embowèd roof,
With antique pillars massy-proof,

---

13. *bellman's drowsy charm*, the night watchman's hourly
call of "All's well." **14.** *outwatch the Bear*. The Great
Bear, or Big Dipper, never sets in England. **15.** *thrice
great Hermes*. Hermes Trismegistus (triz mə jis′təs), mythical Egyptian king, reputed author of a number of learned
books, is here mentioned to indicate an interest in forgotten
lore. **16.** *unsphere . . . Plato*, call the spirit of the Greek
philosopher Plato from its sphere in the heavens; literally,
to find out by close study what he means. **17.** *Thebes*
(thēbz), a Greek city, setting of several of the great Greek
tragedies. **18.** *Pelops* (pē′lops), the ancestor of several
great characters in Greek tragedy. **19.** *buskined stage*.
The buskin was a thick-soled boot worn by Greek and Roman tragic actors to give them stature; it has become the
symbol of tragedy. **20.** *Musaeus* (mū zē′əs), a mythical
singer. **21.** *Orpheus*, see page 212, note 19. **22.** *him*,
Chaucer, who left "The Squire's Tale" unfinished. *Cambuscan* (line 110) was a king of Tartary; *Camball* (line 111)
and *Algarsife* (line 111) were his sons, and *Canace* (line 112)
his daughter. The ring, mirror, and brass horse (lines 113-
115) were gifts from the king of Arabia and possessed magic
properties. **23.** *Attic boy*, Cephalus (sef′ə ləs), an Athenian (Attic) huntsman beloved of Aurora (Dawn), here described as "civil-suited Morn" (line 122). **24.** *Genius of
the wood*, the presiding deity of the locality.

And storied windows richly dight,
Casting a dim religious light. 160
There let the pealing organ blow,
To the full-voiced quire below,
In service high and anthems clear,
As may with sweetness, through mine ear,
Dissolve me into ecstasies, 165
And bring all Heaven before mine eyes.
And may at last my weary age
Find out the peaceful hermitage,
The hairy gown and mossy cell,
Where I may sit and rightly spell 170
Of every star that heaven doth shew,
And every herb that sips the dew,
Till old experience do attain
To something like prophetic strain.
These pleasures, Melancholy, give, 175
And I with thee will choose to live.

COURTESY THE BRITISH MUSEUM

MILTON'S SONNETS

*Although Milton wrote only twenty-three son-
nets during a period of approximately thirty
years, he was an expert in the use of this
literary form. "On His Having Arrived at
the Age of Twenty-Three" is a sonnet that
was found among Milton's Cambridge manuscripts. He had inserted it in a letter to a
friend who had remonstrated with him, apparently, upon his aimless student life. In
reply, Milton wrote: "That you may see
that I am something suspicious of myself,
or do take notice of a certain belatedness in
me, I am the bolder to send you some of
my nightward thoughts some little while ago,*

*made up in a Petrarchan stanza which I told
you of."*

*The second sonnet you will read is the nine-
teenth of the collection and was written sometime after Milton, at only forty-five years of
age, had become completely blind.*

ON HIS HAVING ARRIVED AT THE
AGE OF TWENTY-THREE

How soon hath Time, the subtle thief
of youth,
Stolen on his wing my three and
twentieth year!
My hasting days fly on with full career,
But my late spring no bud or blossom
shew'th.[1]
Perhaps my semblance might deceive the
truth 5
That I to manhood am arrived so near;
And inward ripeness doth much less appear,
That some more timely-happy spirits
endu'th.[2]
Yet be it less or more, or soon or slow,
It shall be still in strictest measure even 10
To that same lot, however mean or high,
Toward which Time leads me, and the will
of Heaven;
All is, if I have grace to use it so,
As ever in my great Task-Master's eye.

ON HIS BLINDNESS

When I consider how my light is spent
Ere half my days in this dark world and
wide,
And that one talent[1] which is death to hide
Lodged with me useless, though my soul
more bent
To serve therewith my Maker, and present 5
My true account, lest He returning chide;
"Doth God exact day-labor, light denied?"
I fondly ask. But Patience, to prevent

ON HIS HAVING ARRIVED AT THE AGE OF TWENTY-THREE
1. *shew'th*, shows. 2. *endu'th*, endows.

ON HIS BLINDNESS 1. *one talent*, the gift of writing. This
refers to Jesus' parable of the talents, or coins, which tells
of the "unprofitable servant" who was condemned for hiding his one talent in the earth. (Matthew 25:15-30)

That murmur, soon replies, "God doth not
     need   9
Either man's work or His own gifts. Who
     best
Bear His mild yoke, they serve Him best.
     His state
Is kingly: thousands at His bidding speed,
And post o'er land and ocean without rest;
They also serve who only stand and wait."

To increase understanding
L'Allegro and Il Penseroso

1. In lines 1-24 of "L'Allegro" Milton describes the birth of Melancholy and of Mirth. (*a*) Contrast the details used in telling of the birth of Melancholy with those describing that of Mirth. (*b*) Why does Milton prefer the second parentage of Mirth?

2. Lines 25-36 enumerate members of Mirth's crew. (*a*) Who are they? (*b*) Why do you think Liberty is included?

3. Lines 41-116 deal with country pleasures. (*a*) In what order are these pleasures arranged? (*b*) What are some of these pleasures? (*c*) What quality or feeling is conveyed by the images in this section of the poem?

4. The last section of "L'Allegro" speaks of the city pleasures that appeal to the light-hearted, active man. (*a*) What kind of drama does he prefer? (*b*) What distinction does Milton make between Jonson and Shakespeare? (*c*) What sort of music is emphasized?

5. (*a*) Compare the first ten lines of "L'Allegro" and "Il Penseroso" as to subject matter, rhythm, and rhyme scheme. (*b*) How does the body of each poem differ from the opening section in rhyme and rhythm? (*c*) What effect does the change produce?

6. (*a*) How does the Melancholy pictured in lines 11-44 of "Il Penseroso" differ from the Melancholy described in the opening lines of "L'Allegro"? (*b*) Who are Melancholy's companions as described in "Il Penseroso" (lines 45-55)? (*c*) Is this the usual conception of melancholy? Explain.

7. Compare lines 56-76 of "Il Penseroso" with lines 41-68 of "L'Allegro." (*a*) What is the subject of each passage? (*b*) How is the subject of the passage related to the poem as a whole?

8. Lines 77-120 of "Il Penseroso" deal with the evening activities of the contemplative man. (*a*) How do they differ from the evening activities of the light-hearted, active man? (*b*) What sort of literature does the contemplative man prefer? Cite specific authors.

9. (*a*) Compare the description of early morning in "Il Penseroso" with that in the companion poem. (*b*) What aspects of nature does the contemplative man prefer?

10. What kind of music is emphasized in "Il Penseroso"?

11. (*a*) What is the contemplative man's hope for his later years? (*b*) Why does he look to the future whereas the light-hearted man does not?

12. Milton is often spoken of as the last Renaissance man. What evidence of the Renaissance do you find in "L'Allegro" and "Il Penseroso"? Explain.

Milton's Sonnets

1. As Milton said in the letter concerning his poem "On Having Arrived at the Age of Twenty-Three," he favored the Petrarchan form of the sonnet. Review the Petrarchan form (page 106); then analyze the relationship of form and thought in the two sonnets by Milton.

2. (*a*) What is the poet's mood in each of the two sonnets? (*b*) What evidence do you find that the man of forty-five retained the attitudes expressed by the youth of twenty-three?

 Words!

Since the Renaissance English writers have borrowed freely from the myths of ancient Greece and Rome. Milton's poems, as you have seen, are often veritable storehouses of allusions to classical gods, goddesses, demigods, and heroes. Partly as a result of these borrowings and partly because a direct study of classical lore has long been a basic part of Western education, the names of mythological figures have become the roots of words in our everyday—or almost everyday—vocabulary.

Below are seven words derived from some of the mythological figures that appear in "L'Allegro" and "Il Penseroso," followed by references to the lines or passages in which these figures appear. Try to determine the meanings of the seven words from your own knowledge of classical mythology or from Milton's allusions in "L'Allegro" and "Il Penseroso." Check your definitions against those in the dictionary.

bacchanalian ("L'Allegro," line 16)
zephyrean ("L'Allegro," lines 17-24)
auroral ("L'Allegro," lines 17-24)
hymeneal ("L'Allegro," lines 125-128)
plutonian ("L'Allegro," lines 145-150)
morphetic ("Il Penseroso," lines 9-10)
sylvan ("Il Penseroso," lines 132-139)

Milton's PARADISE LOST

Like all epic poems, Milton's *Paradise Lost* is a long narrative of events on a grand scale. In the case of *Paradise Lost*, the scale is one of the grandest possible, for the poem has as its setting the entire universe. The main characters are God, His Son, Adam and Eve, and Satan. And the theme is the fall of man as embodied in the Biblical story of the temptation of Adam and Eve and their expulsion from Paradise.

Milton's story begins in a pre-Creation period when there was only a high Heaven filled with angels and ruled over by a benign God in the manner of an earthly king. As if inspired by the earthly event of civil war in his own time and place, Milton envisions a civil war in Heaven, arising over God's appointment of His Son to the seat of honor and power at His right hand. Satan, one of the archangels, desires the exalted position for himself, and with a third of the other angels he wages war against God and His followers. God's forces prove superior; Satan and his rebel host are sent plunging down through space into Hell, the place that God had prepared for them, as far removed from Heaven as possible.

From this point on Satan vows eternal vengeance. He has heard of God's plan to fashion a new creature called man and to place him in a new region called the world. Why not strike back at God through the corruption of this latest creature of His handiwork? After persuading Sin and Death to open the gates of Hell, Satan "swims, or sinks, or wades, or creeps, or flies" his way through Chaos, until at last

> The sacred influence
> Of light appears, and from the walls of heaven
> Shoots far into the bosom of dim night
> A glimmering dawn . . .
> And, fast by, hanging in a golden chain,
> This pendent world, in bigness as a star
> Of smallest magnitude close by the moon.
> (Book III, lines 1034-1053)

The story of Satan's meeting with Adam and Eve in the Garden of Eden follows, in the main, the Bible story. Satan tempts Eve, who in turn persuades Adam to eat the forbidden fruit of the Tree of Knowledge. For their disobedience Adam and Eve are driven from Paradise out into the world. The twelfth and last book of the poem closes with the pair standing hand in hand upon the threshold of the world. Paradise, "so late their happy home," lies behind them. Sadly and penitently they face the future, their punishment softened only by the promise of the ultimate redemption of man by Christ.

Milton did not develop his story chronologically. Instead he adopted the traditional epic technique of beginning *in medias res*, or in the middle of the action, waiting until later in the poem to provide a narrative of the earlier events of his story. Thus in Book I the reader is confronted with the terrifying scenes of Satan and his "horrid crew" "rolling in the fiery gulf" of Hell and of Satan hurling thundering speeches of defiance at the Almighty.

from PARADISE LOST

from BOOK I

Of man's first disobedience, and the
 fruit
Of that forbidden tree, whose
 mortal taste
Brought death into the world, and all our
 woe,
With loss of Eden, till one greater man
Restore us, and regain the blissful seat,   5
Sing heavenly muse, that on the secret top
Of Oreb, or of Sinai, didst inspire
That shepherd, who first taught the
 chosen seed,[1]
In the beginning how the heavens and earth
Rose out of chaos: Or if Sion hill[2]   10
Delight thee more, and Siloa's brook[3]
 that flowed
Fast by the oracle of God; I thence
Invoke thy aid to my adventurous song,
That with no middle flight intends to soar   14
Above the Aonian mount,[4] while it pursues
Things unattempted yet in prose or rhyme.
And chiefly thou, O spirit[5] that dost prefer
Before all temples the upright heart and
 pure,
Instruct me, for thou knowest; thou from
 the first
Wast present, and, with mighty wings
 outspread   20

---

1. *heavenly muse . . . seed.* Of the nine Greek muses who
presided over the various arts and sciences, Milton chose to
invoke Urania (ū rā′ni ə), the muse of astronomy, to help
him in his great task of writing a poem about the entire universe. As a man of the Renaissance, Milton had no difficulty in thinking both in pagan and Biblical terms; hence,
Urania is thought of as having inspired *that shepherd*
(Moses) who received the word of God on the twin peaks
of *Horeb* (hô′reb) and *Sinai* (si′nī) and who interpreted it to
the *chosen seed* (the Israelites). 2. *Sion hill*, the height
upon which Jerusalem was built. 3. *Siloa's brook*, the
stream which flowed near the hill on which the temple was
erected in Jerusalem. 4. *Aonian* (ā ō′ni ən) *mount*, Mount
Helicon, representing Greek poetry, which Milton, by
writing a Christian poem, endeavored to surpass.
5. *spirit*, the Holy Spirit, which descended "in a bodily
shape like a dove. . . ." (Luke 3:22)

Milton's Cosmography

The word *cosmography* comes from the Greek
kosmographia (*kosmos* world + *graphein*
write) meaning "description or view of the
world or universe." Milton's cosmography,
which is essentially the same as that of the
Renaissance and the Middle Ages, is based on
a combination of various ancient philosophies
which were built around the theory that the
earth was the fixed center of the universe. It
must be remembered that the systems of Copernicus (1473-1543) and Galileo (1564-
1642), which were based on the idea that the
sun, not the earth, was at the center of the
universe, had not received general acceptance
in Milton's time, and that Milton therefore
had some warrant in clinging to the older
theories.

According to the older view, the universe
was composed first, of Heaven, or the Empy-
rean. Below Heaven lay Chaos, or infinite
space, filled with atoms and warring elements
in ceaseless flux. Below or far down in Chaos
lay Hell, a vast continent which was cut off
from Chaos by walls of enormous thickness.
Hanging by a chain from the floor of the Em-
pyrean was the World, or created universe,
which was composed of nine concentric
spheres through which the planets and fixed
stars moved in their courses around the central
earth.

This view of the universe was elaborated
and filled out with many details. The earth was
thought of as surrounded by spherical layers
of water, air, and fire. Everything above the
moon was eternal and perfect, everything below the moon imperfect and subject to change.
Milton envisioned an opening at the top of
the created universe which enabled angels
and also Satan to travel to and from the earth.

Though it is strange to us today, this view
of the universe was accepted for many hundreds of years—not so firmly in Milton's time

Dove-like satest brooding on the vast abyss
And madest it pregnant: What in me is
    dark
Illumine, what is low raise and support;
That to the height of this great argument
I may assert eternal providence,   25
And justify the ways of God to men.
    Say first, for heaven hides nothing from
        thy view,
Nor the deep tract of hell, says first what
    cause
Moved our grand parents in that happy state,
Favored of heaven so highly, to fall off   30
From their Creator, and transgress His will
For one restraint, lords of the world besides?
Who first seduced them to that foul revolt?
The infernal serpent; he it was, whose guile
Stirred up with envy and revenge,
    deceived   35
The mother of mankind, what time his pride
Had cast him out from heaven, with all his
    host
Of rebel angels, by whose aid aspiring
To set himself in glory above his peers,

He trusted to have equaled the most High, 40
If He opposed; and with ambitious aim
Against the throne and monarchy of God
Raised impious war in heaven and battle
    proud
With vain attempt. Him the almighty power
Hurled headlong flaming from the ethereal
    sky   45
With hideous ruin and combustion down
To bottomless perdition, there to dwell
In adamantine chains and penal fire,
Who durst defy the omnipotent to arms.
Nine times the space that measures day and
    night   50
To mortal men, he with his horrid crew
Lay vanquished, rolling in the fiery gulf
Confounded though immortal: But his doom
Reserved him to more wrath; for now the
    thought
Both of lost happiness and lasting pain   55
Torments him; round he throws his baleful
    eyes
That witnessed[6] huge affliction and dismay
Mixed with obdurate pride and steadfast
    hate:
At once as far as angels' ken he views
The dismal situation waste and wild,   60
A dungeon horrible, on all sides round
As one great furnace flamed, yet from those
    flames
No light, but rather darkness visible
Served only to discover sights of woe,
Regions of sorrow, doleful shades, where
    peace   65
And rest can never dwell, hope never comes
That comes to all; but torture without end
Still urges, and a fiery deluge, fed
With ever-burning sulphur unconsumed:
Such place eternal justice had prepared   70
For those rebellious, here their prison
    ordained
In utter darkness, and their portion set
As far removed from God and light of
    heaven
As from the center thrice to the utmost pole.[7]
O how unlike the place from whence they
    fell!   75

6. *witnessed*, gave evidence of. 7. *center . . . pole*, three
times the distance from the earth (center) to the farthest
vault of the universe.

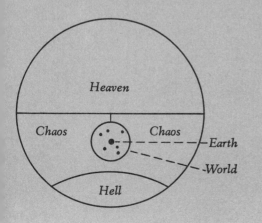

as during the Renaissance or Middle Ages,
but a popular conception during the seventeenth century none the less. It was not a
scientific view, but it did serve the important
function of providing a framework for the
imaginations of writers and artists of all kinds.

There the companions of his fall, o'erwhelmed
With floods and whirlwinds of tempestuous fire,
He soon discerns, and weltering by his side
One next himself in power, and next in crime,
Long after known in Palestine, and named [80]
Beelzebub.[8] To whom the arch-enemy,
And thence in heaven called Satan, with bold words
Breaking the horrid silence thus began.

Addressing Beelzebub, Satan boldly declares that though he has been thrown into Hell, he will continue to fight God with all his might. Beelzebub is afraid that God is too strong to be overcome. Satan, chiding him for his fears, begins to make plans.

"Seest thou yon dreary plain, forlorn and wild,
The seat of desolation, void of light, [85]
Save what the glimmering of these livid flames
Casts pale and dreadful? Thither let us tend
From off the tossing of these fiery waves,
There rest, if any rest can harbor there,
And reassembling our afflicted powers, [90]
Consult how we may henceforth most offend
Our enemy, our own loss how repair,
How overcome this dire calamity,
What reinforcement we may gain from hope,
If not what resolution from despair." [95]
    Thus Satan talking to his nearest mate
With head uplift above the wave, and eyes
That sparkling blazed, his other parts besides
Prone on the flood, extended long and large
Lay floating many a rood,[9] in bulk as huge
As whom the fables name of monstrous size,
Titanian,[10] or earth-born, that warred on [102]
    Jove,
Briareos or Typhon,[11] whom the den
By ancient Tarsus held, or that sea-beast
Leviathan,[12] which God of all his works [105]
Created hugest that swim the ocean stream:
Him haply slumbering on the Norway foam
The pilot of some small night-foundered skiff,
Deeming some island, oft, as seamen tell,
With fixed anchor in his scaly rind [110]

Moors by his side under the lee, while night
Invests the sea, and wished morn delays:
So stretched out huge in length the archfiend lay
Chained on the burning lake, nor ever thence
Had risen or heaved his head, but that the will [115]
And high permission of all-ruling heaven
Left him at large to his own dark designs,
That with reiterated crimes he might
Heap on himself damnation, while he sought
Evil to others, and enraged might see [120]
How all his malice served but to bring forth
Infinite goodness, grace and mercy shown
On man by him seduced, but on himself
Treble confusion, wrath and vengeance poured.
Forthwith upright he rears from off the pool [125]
His mighty stature; on each hand the flames
Driven backward slope their pointing spires, and rolled
In billows, leave in the midst a horrid vale.
Then with expanded wings he steers his flight
Aloft, incumbent on the dusky air [130]
That felt unusual weight, till on dry land
He lights, if it were land that ever burned
With solid, as the lake with liquid fire;
And such appeared in hue, as when the force
Of subterranean wind transports a hill [135]
Torn from Pelorus,[13] or the shattered side
Of thundering Etna, whose combustible
And fueled entrails thence conceiving fire,
Sublimed with mineral fury, aid the winds,
And leave a singed bottom all involved [140]

8. *Beelzebub* (bi el′zə bub), from Hebrew meaning "Lord of Flies." In the time of Jesus, Beelzebub was "prince of the demons." (Matthew 12:24; Luke 11:15) In certain medieval literature he was a chief associate of Satan. 9. *rood*, usually seven or eight yards. 10. *Titanian* (tī ta′ni ən), like the Titans, giants descended from Heaven, or Uranus (ūr′ə nəs), and Earth, or Gaea (jē′ə). 11. *Briareos* (brī ār′i əs) *or Typhon* (tī′fən), in Greek mythology, two monsters, the first with a hundred hands, the second with a hundred fire-breathing heads, who attempted to overthrow the dynasty of Jove. Typhon lived in Cilicia (sə lish′ə), of which *Tarsus* (tär′səs) (line 104) was the capital. 12. *Leviathan*, a huge sea-monster mentioned in the Bible. 13. *Pelorus* (pə lôr′əs), the northeastern promontory of Sicily near the volcano of Mount *Etna* (line 137).

With stench and smoke: Such resting found the sole
Of unblest feet. Him followed his next mate,
Both glorying to have scaped the Stygian[14] flood
As gods, and by their own recovered strength,
Not by the sufferance of supernal power.   145
  "Is this the region, this the soil, the clime,"
Said then the lost archangel, "this the seat
That we must change for heaven, this mournful gloom
For that celestial light? Be it so, since He
Who now is sovereign can dispose and bid   150
.What shall be right: farthest from Him is best
Whom reason hath equaled, force hath made supreme
Above His equals. Farewell happy fields
Where joy forever dwells: Hail horrors, hail
Infernal world, and thou profoundest hell 155
Receive thy new possessor: One who brings
A mind not to be changed by place or time.
The mind is its own place, and in itself
Can make a heaven of hell, a hell of heaven.
What matter where, if I be still the same, 160
And what I should be, all but less than He
Whom thunder hath made greater? Here at least
We shall be free; the Almighty hath not built
Here for his envy, will not drive us hence:
Here we may reign secure, and in my choice   165
To reign is worth ambition though in hell:
Better to reign in hell, than serve in heaven.
But wherefore let we then our faithful friends,
The associates and copartners of our loss
Lie thus astonished on the oblivious pool, 170
And call them not to share with us their part
In this unhappy mansion, or once more
With rallied arms to try what may be yet
Regained in heaven, or what more lost in hell?"
  So Satan spake, and him Beelzebub   175
Thus answered. "Leader of those armies bright,

Which but the omnipotent none could have foiled
If once they hear that voice, their liveliest pledge
Of hope in fears and dangers, heard so oft
In worst extremes, and on the perilous edge
Of battle when it raged, in all assaults   180
Their surest signal, they will soon resume
New courage and revive, though now they lie
Groveling and prostrate on yon lake of fire,
As we erewhile, astounded and amazed,   185
No wonder, fallen such a pernicious height."
  He scarce had ceased when the superior Fiend
Was moving toward the shore; his ponderous shield
Ethereal temper, massy, large and round,
Behind him cast; the broad circumference 190
Hung on his shoulders like the moon, whose orb
Through optic glass the Tuscan artist views
At evening from the top of Fesole,
Or in Valdarno,[15] to descry new lands,
Rivers or mountains in her spotty globe.   195
His spear, to equal which the tallest pine
Hewn on Norwegian hills, to be the mast
Of some great ammiral,[16] were but a wand,
He walked with to support uneasy steps
Over the burning marl, not like those steps
On heaven's azure, and the torrid clime   200
Smote on him sore besides, vaulted with fire;
Nathless he so endured, till on the beach
Of that inflamed sea, he stood and called
His legions, angel forms, who lay entranced
Thick as autumnal leaves that strew the   205
brooks
In Vallombrosa,[17] where the Etrurian shades
High over arched embower; or scattered sedge

---

14. *Stygian* (stij'i ən), of the river Styx, one of the four rivers in Hades. 15. *optic ... Valdarno.* The optic glass is the telescope of Galileo, whom Milton refers to as a Tuscan because he lived in Tuscany, a region in central Italy which includes Florence. *Fesole* (Fiesole, fē e'zō lä) is a city on a hill near Florence. *Valdarno* (val där'nō) is the valley of the River Arno in which Florence is situated. 16. *ammiral*, admiral, the flagship bearing the commander of the fleet. 17. *Vallombrosa* (val lom brō'sə), a valley twenty miles east of Florence. Florence and the surrounding country are in ancient *Etruria* (i trür'i ə) (line 206).

Afloat, when with fierce winds Orion[18] armed
Hath vexed the Red Sea coast, whose waves
o'erthrew   210
Busiris and his Memphian chivalry,
While with perfidious hatred they pursued
The sojourners of Goshen,[19] who beheld
From the safe shore their floating carcasses
And broken chariot wheels, so thick
bestrewn   215
Abject and lost lay these, covering the flood,
Under amazement of their hideous change.
He called so loud, that all the hollow deep
Of hell resounded. "Princes, potentates
Warriors, the flower of heaven, once yours,
now lost,   220
If such astonishment as this can seize
Eternal spirits; or have ye chosen this place
After the toil of battle to repose
Your wearied virtue, for the ease you find
To slumber here, as in the vales of
heaven?   225
Or in this abject posture have ye sworn
To adore the conqueror? who now beholds
Cherub and seraph rolling in the flood
With scattered arms and ensigns, till anon
His swift pursuers from heaven gates
discern   230
The advantage, and descending tread us
down
Thus drooping, or with linked thunderbolts
Transfix us to the bottom of this gulf.
Awake, arise, or be forever fallen."

*First to rise from the burning lake are the
leaders of the fallen angels. Followed by the
multitude, they wing their way to the plain
and assemble in military formation before
their "dread commander," Satan.*

He above the rest   235
In shape and gesture proudly eminent
Stood like a tower; his form had yet not lost
All her original brightness, nor appeared
Less than archangel ruined, and the excess
Of glory obscured: As when the sun
new risen   240
Looks through the horizontal misty air
Shorn of his beams, or from behind the
moon
In dim eclipse disastrous twilight sheds
On half the nations, and with fear of change

Perplexes monarchs. Darkened so, yet
shone   245
Above them all the archangel: but his face
Deep scars of thunder had intrenched, and
care
Sat on his faded cheek, but under brows
Of dauntless courage, and considerate pride
Waiting revenge: cruel his eye, but cast   250
Signs of remorse and passion to behold
The fellows of his crime, the followers rather
(Far other once beheld in bliss) condemned
Forever now to have their lot in pain.

*In his speech to the army, Satan announces
his intention of seeking revenge by fraud or
guile, not force. Book I ends with the building of the palace of Pandemonium and with
preparations for a council of war.*

---

18. *Orion*, in Greek mythology, a hunter who became a
constellation upon his death. When the constellation rises
late (in November) it is supposed to cause storms. **19.**
Busiris (bü sī′rəs) . . . *Goshen* (gō′shən). Busiris was a
mythical king of Egypt (Goshen). Milton considers him the
Pharaoh who with his cavalry pursued the children of Israel
into the Red Sea. (Exodus 14)

To increase understanding

1. (*a*) Cite the lines in which Milton announces
the theme of *Paradise Lost*. (*b*) Whom does he call
upon for aid in writing his poem? (*c*) Cite the lines
in which he sets forth the purpose of his poem. (*d*)
What is the connection between Milton's purpose in
writing *Paradise Lost* and his early desire to take
orders in the church?

2. (*a*) In what lines does Milton survey the action
of the entire poem? (*b*) What is the action of Book
I? (*c*) Relate the action of Book I to the diagram of
the universe on page 219. (*d*) How does this conception of the universe differ from the one generally held today?

3. What references in this selection from *Paradise
Lost* suggest Milton's travels?

4. It has often been said that through his magnificent treatment of Satan, Milton inadvertently
made him the hero of *Paradise Lost*. Cite lines that
might have given rise to this opinion.

5. (*a*) What aspect of Satan's character is stressed
as the source of his downfall? (*b*) Do any changes
take place in Satan's appearance in Book I? (*c*) What
foreshadowing of his future course of action is given?

(*d*) Is there any difference in mind and character between Satan and Beelzebub?

6. Turn to the following lines in the selection from *Paradise Lost*:

The mind is its own place, and in itself
Can make a heaven of hell, a hell of heaven.
(lines 158-159)
Better to reign in hell, than serve in heaven.
(line 167)

What is it that distinguishes these lines from the rest of the passage and puts them in the category of "quotable quotes"?

7. (*a*) Tennyson called Milton the "God-gifted organ voice of England." To what extent is this an appropriate label for him? (*b*) *Sublime* is an adjective often applied to Milton's verse. Give evidence of its appropriateness.

8. On the basis of all the selections by Milton you have studied discuss (*a*) Milton's Puritanism, and (*b*) the ways in which he differed from the typical Puritan.

 Extending interests

Read and report on other selections from *Paradise Lost,* such as: War Council in Hell, Book II, lines 1-487; Gates of Hell, Book II, lines 629-810; Hymn to Light, Book III, lines 1-55; Satan's First View of Eden and Adam and Eve, Book IV, lines 131-171, 288-357; Adam's Account of His Creation, Book VIII, lines 250-559.

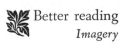 Better reading
Imagery

Sensory imagery plays an important part in the unfolding of *Paradise Lost*—not only as a means of achieving the striking effects one expects of poetry, but also as a way of bringing within the experience of the reader the unfamiliar place, characters, and events of a cosmic drama. Hell, for example, as a place, is not within our experience. But when Milton stimulates our sense of touch by telling us how painful it was for Satan to stand for the first time on the ever-burning ground of his new kingdom (Book I, lines 129-142), the infernal regions suddenly come alive for us.

Reread the selection from *Paradise Lost* with an eye for the sensory details that help bring the poem within our experience. Which lines or passages appeal to your sense of sight? What other senses are appealed to, and where?

Many of Milton's most effective images are contained in his *heroic similes*—comparisons that are usually sustained for several lines and that are suggestive of heroic stature or proportions. How, for example, does Milton give us an idea of Satan's size? To what does he compare Satan's shield; his spear; his ruined but still bright appearance? What similes give the reader an idea of the vast numbers and the helplessness of the fallen angels on the burning lake?

John Bunyan 1628-1688

By Thomas Sadler, 1684.

The life and work of John Bunyan stand out in marked contrast to those of his fellow Puritan John Milton. Bunyan was of humble birth and little schooling; he traveled only as required by his trade of itinerant tinker in and about his native Bedfordshire. Unlike Milton, who dipped many times into most—if not all—of the great books of Western civilization, Bunyan read chiefly in one book, the new and immensely popular Authorized King James Bible. As a result, Milton addressed himself to the broadly educated, while Bunyan spoke to and for the masses. While both men believed in the Parliamentary cause and Puritanism, they reacted to them differently. Milton fought with his pen, and Bunyan fought as a foot soldier in Cromwell's Ironsides Army, later using his pen to serve the Puritan cause.

From boyhood Bunyan seems to have been troubled by an overactive conscience. In his spiritual autobiography, *Grace*

Abounding to the Chief of Sinners, he tells of his early love of games, dancing, bell-ringing, swearing, and drinking, and of his sudden awareness that all of this was sinful. While playing one day on the village green, says Bunyan, "A voice did suddenly dart from Heaven into my soul, which said, 'Wilt thou leave thy sins and go to Heaven, or have thy sins and go to Hell?'" Some people have difficulty answering this question, but Bunyan did not. He changed his ways, received baptism in 1653, and took time out from his mending of pots and kettles to preach to whoever would listen to him—usually small groups of common folk who gathered in woods, private homes, and barns.

With the Restoration of Charles II, an old statute against those who refused to conform to the Anglican Church was invoked against Bunyan, with the result that he spent twelve years and six months in Bedford jail. With writing materials provided by his fairly lenient jailers, Bunyan wrote first *Grace Abounding to the Chief of Sinners* and then his most famous work, *The Pilgrim's Progress,* which is a fictional version of the earlier autobiography.

In *The Pilgrim's Progress* Bunyan witnesses "in the similitude of a dream" the progress of the pilgrim Christian as he journeys from the City of Destruction to the Celestial City. The story is an allegory with characters such as Faithful, Obstinate, and Goodwill. The landscape is that of seventeenth-century England with its castles, dungeons, fairs, markets, highways, and byways. Sloughs of Despond, like those through which Christian struggles, were plentiful in the marshlands around Elstow, Bunyan's birthplace. Castle Dangerous and Palace Beautiful he had grown up with: the one, the sinister and romantic ruins of a Norman stronghold that had once dominated the town of Bedford; the other, either the stone mansion of the local squire or an even grander house of the neighborhood. The Pilgrim's Way, which led to Canterbury along the crest of the North Downs where Bunyan may have plied his trade, could have suggested the title for his book, while the South Downs, viewed from the Way across a wide, pleasant valley, may have become the story's Delectable Mountains.

Pilgrim's Progress met with immediate success, much to its author's surprise. Its touches of humor, as in the name-choosings and the use of imaginative creatures such as dragons and giants, made Bunyan feel almost guilty for the fun the writing had given him. Puritans were not supposed to have fun! That Bunyan did not feel too guilty to write his book is fortunate, for *Pilgrim's Progress,* with its translating of theological ideas into vivid, realistic, contemporary terms, reflecting the daily life of ordinary people, marks an important step toward the first flowering of the English novel which occurred in the middle of the eighteenth century. Bunyan's book also contributed substantially—along with *Paradise Lost* and the Bible—to the high moral tone of the New Englanders across the Atlantic who were soon to take part in the founding of a new nation.

The following selection from *Pilgrim's Progress* relates the experiences of Christian and Faithful in the town of Vanity.

from THE PILGRIM'S PROGRESS

Then I saw in my dream that when they were got out of the wilderness they presently saw a town before them, and the name of that town is Vanity. And at the town there is a fair kept, called Vanity Fair; it is kept all the year long; it beareth the name of Vanity Fair, because the town where 'tis kept is lighter than vanity; and also because all that is there sold, or that cometh thither, is vanity. As is the saying of the wise, "All that cometh is vanity."

This fair is no new-erected business, but a thing of ancient standing; I will show you the original of it.

Almost five thousand years agone, there were pilgrims walking to the celestial city, as these two honest persons are; and Beelzebub, Apollyon, and Legion,[1] with their companions, perceiving by the path that the pilgrims made, that their way to the city lay through this town of Vanity, they contrived here to set up a fair; a fair wherein should be sold all sorts of vanity, and that it should last all the year long. Therefore at this fair are all such merchandise sold, as houses, lands, trades, places, honors, preferments, titles, countries, kingdoms, lusts, pleasures, and delights of all sorts, as lives, blood, bodies, souls, silver, gold, pearls, precious stones, and what not.

And moreover, at this fair there is at all times to be seen juggling, cheats, games, plays, fools, apes, knaves, and rogues, and that of all sorts. . . .

Now these pilgrims [Christian and Faithful] must needs go through this fair. Well, so they did; but behold, even as they entered into the fair, all the people in the fair were moved and the town itself as it were in a hubbub about them; and that for several reasons; for,

First: The pilgrims were clothed with such kind of raiment as was diverse from the raiment of any that traded in that fair. The people therefore of the fair made a great gazing upon them; some said they were fools, some they were bedlams,[2] and some they were outlandish-men.[3]

Secondly: And as they wondered at their apparel, so they did likewise at their speech; for few could understand what they said. They naturally spoke the language of Canaan,[4] but they that kept the fair were the men of this world; so that from one end of the fair to the other they seemed barbarians each to the other.

Thirdly: But that which did not a little amuse the merchandisers was that these pilgrims set very light by all their wares; they cared not so much as to look upon them; and if they called upon them to buy, they would put their fingers in their ears, and cry, "Turn away mine eyes from beholding vanity," and look upward, signifying that their trade and traffic was in heaven.

One chanced, mockingly, beholding the carriages of the men, to say unto them, "What will ye buy?" But they, looking gravely upon him, answered, "We buy the Truth." At that there was an occasion taken to despise the men the more; some mocking, some taunting, some speaking reproachfully, and some calling upon others to smite them. At last things came to a hubbub and a great stir in the fair, insomuch that all order was confounded. Now was word presently brought to the great one of the fair, who quickly came down and deputed some of his most trusty friends to take those men into examination, about whom the fair was almost overturned.

So the men were brought to examination; and they that sat upon them asked them whence they came, whither they went, and what they did there in such an unusual garb. The men told them that they were pilgrims and strangers in the world, and that they were going to their own country, which was the heavenly Jerusalem; and that they had given no occasion to the men of the town, nor yet to the merchandisers, thus to abuse them, and to let them in their journey, except it was for that, when one asked them what they would buy, they said they would buy the Truth.

---

1. *Beelzebub, Apollyon, and Legion*, other names for the devil, here indicating a number of devils. 2. *bedlams*, lunatics. 3. *outlandish-men*, foreigners. 4. *the language of Canaan*, the heavenly tongue.

But they that were appointed to examine them did not believe them to be any other than bedlams and mad, or else such as came to put all things into a confusion in the fair. Therefore they took them and beat them, and besmeared them with dirt, and then put them into a cage that they might be made a spectacle to all the men of the fair. There therefore they lay for some time and were made the objects of any man's sport, or malice, or revenge, the great ones of the fair laughing still at all that befell them. But the men being patient, and not rendering railing for railing, but contrariwise blessing, and giving good words for bad, and kindness for injuries done, some men in the fair, that were more observing and less prejudiced than the rest, began to check and blame the baser sort for their continual abuses done by them to the men; they therefore in angry manner let fly at them again, counting them as bad as the men in the cage, and telling them that they seemed confederates, and should be made partakers of their misfortunes. The others replied that for aught they could see, the men were quiet, and sober, and intended nobody any harm; and that there were many that traded in their fair that were more worthy to be put into the cage, yea, and pillory, too, than were the men that they had abused. Thus, after divers words had passed on both sides—the men behaving themselves all the while very wisely and soberly before them— they fell to some blows among themselves and did harm one to another.

Then were these two poor men brought before their examiners again and there charged as being guilty of the late hubbub that had been in the fair. So they beat them pitifully and hanged irons upon them, and led them in chains up and down the fair, for an example and a terror to others, lest any should speak in their behalf, or join themselves unto them. But Christian and Faithful behaved themselves yet more wisely and received the ignominy and shame that were cast upon them with so much meekness and patience that it won to their side (though but a few in comparison of the rest) several of the men in the fair.

This put the other party yet into a greater rage, insomuch that they concluded the death of these two men. Wherefore they threatened that neither cage nor irons should serve their turn, but they should die, for the abuse they had done, and for deluding the men of the fair.

Then were they remanded to the cage again, until further order should be taken with them. So they put them in and made their feet fast in the stocks.

Then, a convenient time being appointed, they brought them forth to their trial, in order to their condemnation. When the time was come, they were brought before their enemies and arraigned. The judge's name was Lord Hategood. Their indictment was one and the same in substance, though somewhat varying in form, the content whereof was this:

That they were enemies to and disturbers of their trade; that they had made commotions and divisions in the town and had won a party to their own most dangerous opinions, in contempt of the law of their prince.

Then Faithful began to answer that he had only set himself against that which had set itself against Him that is higher than the highest. And said he, "As for disturbance, I make none, being myself a man of peace; the parties that were won to us were won by beholding our truth and innocence, and they are only turned from the worse to the better. And as to the king you talk of, since he is Beelzebub, the enemy of our Lord, I defy him and all his angels."

Then proclamation was made that they that had aught to say for their Lord the King against the prisoner at the bar should forthwith appear and give in their evidence. So there came in three witnesses, to wit, Envy, Superstition, and Pickthank. They were then asked if they knew the prisoner at the bar and what they had to say for their Lord the King against him.

Then stood forth Envy and said to this effect: "My Lord, I have known this man a long time and will attest upon my oath before this honorable Bench that he is——"

"Hold!" said the Judge. "Give him his oath." So they sware him. Then he said, "My

Lord, this man, notwithstanding his plausible name, is one of the vilest men in our country. He neither regardeth prince nor people, law nor custom; but doth all that he can to possess all men with certain of his disloyal notions, which he in the general calls principles of faith and holiness. And in particular, I heard him once myself affirm that Christianity and the customs of our town of Vanity were diametrically opposite and could not be reconciled. By which saying, my Lord, he doth at once not only condemn all our laudable doings, but us in the doing of them."

Then did the Judge say to him, "Hast thou any more to say?"

"My Lord," replied Envy, "I could say much more, only I would not be tedious to the Court. Yet if need be, when the other gentlemen have given in their evidence, rather than anything shall be wanting that will dispatch him, I will enlarge my testimony against him." So he was bid stand by.

Then they called Superstition and bid him look upon the prisoner. They also asked what he could say for their Lord the King against him. Then they sware him; so he began:

"My Lord, I have no great acquaintance with this man, nor do I desire to have further knowledge of him; however, this I know, that he is a very pestilent fellow, from some discourse that the other day I had with him in this town; for then talking with him, I heard him say that our religion was naught, and such by which a man could by no means please God. Which sayings of his, my Lord, your Lordship very well knows what necessarily thence will follow, to wit, that we still do worship in vain, are yet in our sins, and finally shall be damned; and this is that which I have to say."

Then was Pickthank sworn and bid say what he knew in behalf of their Lord the King against the prisoner at the bar.

"My Lord and you gentlemen all," said Pickthank, "this fellow I have known of a long time and have heard him speak things that ought not to be spoke; for he hath railed on our noble Prince Beelzebub and hath spoken contemptibly of his honorable friends, whose names are the Lord Old Man, the Lord Carnal Delight, the Lord Luxurious, the Lord Desire of Vainglory, my old Lord Lechery, Sir Having Greedy, with all the rest of our nobility; and he hath said, moreover, that if all men were of his mind, if possible, there is not one of these noblemen should have any longer a being in this town; besides, he hath not been afraid to rail on you, my Lord, who are now appointed to be his judge, calling you an ungodly villain, with many other such-like vilifying terms, with which he hath bespattered most of the gentry of our town."

When this Pickthank had told his tale, the Judge directed his speech to the prisoner at the bar, saying, "Thou runagate, heretic, and traitor, hast thou heard what these honest gentlemen have witnessed against thee?"

"May I speak a few words in my own defense?" asked Faithful.

"Sirrah, sirrah," answered the Judge, "thou deservest to live no longer, but to be slain immediately upon the place; yet that all men may see our gentleness toward thee, let us see what thou hast to say."

Faithful spoke: "1. I say then, in answer to what Mr. Envy hath spoken, I never said aught but this, that what rule, or laws, or custom, or people were flat against the Word of God are diametrically opposite to Christianity. If I have said amiss in this, convince me of my error, and I am ready here before you to make my recantation.

"2. As to the second, to wit, Mr. Superstition, and his charge against me, I said only this, that in the worship of God there is required a divine faith, but there can be no divine faith without a divine revelation of the will of God; therefore, whatever is thrust into the worship of God that is not agreeable to divine revelation cannot be done but by a human faith, which faith will not profit to eternal life.

"3. As to what Mr. Pickthank hath said, I say (avoiding terms, as that I am said to rail, and the like) that the prince of this town, with all the rabblement his attendants, by this gentleman named, are more fit for a being in hell than in this town and country; and so, the Lord have mercy upon me."

Then the Judge called to the jury (who all

this while stood by, to hear and observe), "Gentlemen of the Jury, you see this man about whom so great an uproar hath been made in this town; you have also heard what these worthy gentlemen have witnessed against him; also you have heard his reply and confession. It lieth now in your breasts to hang him or save his life; but yet I think meet to instruct you into our law.

"There was an act made in the days of Pharaoh the Great, servant to our Prince, that lest those of a contrary religion should multiply and grow too strong for him, their males should be thrown into the river.[5] There was also an act made in the days of Nebuchadnezzar the Great, another of his servants, that whoever would not fall down and worship his golden image should be thrown into a fiery furnace.[6] There was also an act made in the days of Darius that whoso, for some time, called upon any God but him should be cast into the lions' den.[7] Now the substance of these laws this rebel has broken, not only in thought (which is not to be borne) but also in word and deed, which must therefore needs be intolerable.

"For that of Pharaoh, his law was made upon a supposition, to prevent mischief, no crime being yet apparent; but here is a crime apparent. For the second and third, you see he disputeth against our religion; and for the treason he hath confessed, he deserveth to die the death."

Then went the jury out, whose names were Mr. Blind-man, Mr. No-good, Mr. Malice, Mr. Love-lust, Mr. Live-loose, Mr. Heady, Mr. High-mind, Mr. Enmity, Mr. Liar, Mr. Cruelty, Mr. Hate-light, and Mr. Implacable, who every one gave in his private verdict against him among themselves and afterwards unanimously concluded to bring him in guilty before the Judge.

And first Mr. Blind-man, the foreman, said, "I see clearly that this man is a heretic." Then said Mr. No-good, "Away with such a fellow from the earth." "Aye," said Mr. Malice, "for I hate the very looks of him." Then said Mr. Love-lust, "I could never endure him." "Nor I," said Mr. Live-loose, "for he would always be condemning my way." "Hang him, hang him," said Mr. Heady. "A sorry scrub," said Mr. High-mind. "My heart riseth against him," said Mr. Enmity. "He is a rogue," said Mr. Liar. "Hanging is too good for him," said Mr. Cruelty. "Let us dispatch him out of the way," said Mr. Hate-light. Then said Mr. Implacable, "Might I have all the world given me, I could not be reconciled to him; therefore, let us forthwith bring him in guilty of death."

And so they did; therefore, he was presently condemned, to be had from the place where he was to the place from whence he came, and there to be put to the most cruel death that could be invented.

They therefore brought him out, to do with him according to their law; and first they scourged him, then they buffeted him, then they lanced his flesh with knives; after that they stoned him with stones, then pricked him with their swords; and last of all they burned him to ashes at the stake. Thus came Faithful to his end.

Now I saw that there stood behind the multitude a chariot and a couple of horses, waiting for Faithful, who (so soon as his adversaries had dispatched him) was taken up into it, and straightway was carried up through the clouds, with sound of trumpet, the nearest way to the Celestial Gate.

But as for Christian, he had some respite and was remanded back to prison; so he there remained for a space. But He that overrules all things, having the power of their rage in his own hand, so wrought it about that Christian for that time escaped them and went his way. And as he went he sang, saying,

Well Faithful, thou hast faithfully professed
Unto thy Lord; with Him thou shalt be
    blessed
When faithless ones, with all their vain delights,
Are crying out under their hellish plights;
Sing, Faithful, sing, and let thy name
    survive;
For though they killed thee, thou art yet alive.

---

5. *Pharaoh the Great . . . river.* This story is told in chapter 1 of Exodus. 6. *Nebuchadnezzar . . . furnace.* The decree of Nebuchadnezzar is the subject of Daniel 3. 7. *Darius . . . den.* The story of Daniel in the lion's den occurs in Daniel 6.

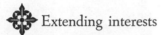 To increase understanding

1. (a) What is the initial situation in the selection from *Pilgrim's Progress*? (b) How does paragraph 3 expand the meaning of the term *Vanity Fair*?

2. (a) Why do Christian and Faithful cause so much consternation as they enter the fair? (b) What is it that incites the people at the fair to mistreat the two travelers even further? (c) Are Christian and Faithful sympathetic characters? Explain. (d) Do they have any counterparts in contemporary life? If so, who are their counterparts?

3. As a thoroughgoing Puritan, Bunyan was well acquainted with the Bible. How do the references and language of *Pilgrim's Progress* reflect Bunyan's interest in the Bible?

4. Compare and contrast the selections by Milton with the selection by Bunyan. Consider in your answer themes, influences, and diction.

Extending interests

Read and report on other adventures of Christian in *Pilgrim's Progress*. The most interesting include: The Slough of Despond, The Meeting with Mr. Worldly Wiseman, The Interpreter's House, Christian Loses His Burden, The Hill of Difficulty, The Palace Beautiful, Apollyon and the Valley of Humiliation, Doubting Castle, and Giant Despair.

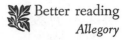 Better reading

Allegory

An *allegory* is a narrative whose characters or figures represent types, moral qualities, or abstract ideas, and whose main purpose is to teach a lesson or prove a point. An allegory may be a play, such as the fifteenth-century *Everyman;* a poem, such as Spenser's *Faerie Queene;* or a prose narrative, such as Bunyan's *Pilgrim's Progress.*

In Bunyan's allegory what does Christian represent? What do the people in the town represent? What moral lesson is contained in the account of Christian's experiences at Vanity Fair?

Good allegory is difficult to achieve, for a writer must work on two levels—the concrete, narrative level, and the abstract, moral one. If he errs on the side of the concrete, his moral philosophy may not come through; and if he errs on the side of the abstract, he may find that he has written a dull sermon without sufficient narrative detail to move and convince his readers.

How successful is Bunyan in maintaining a balance between the concrete and the abstract? Consider in your answer (a) setting, (b) plot, and (c) characterization.

Samuel Pepys 1633-1703

With the Restoration of Charles II in 1660 and the return of a court even more licentious than Bunyan's Vanity Fair, the strict atmosphere of the Puritan interlude gave way to an indulgent acceptance of worldly ways. This attitude comes across clearly in the work of two great diarists of the Restoration, John Evelyn (ēv′lin) and Samuel Pepys (pēps, peps, pep′is). Though far from the depraved characters so often thought of in connection with the Restoration, Evelyn and Pepys present themselves in their diaries as men of the world with no overwhelming desire to improve people's morals.

The diaries of both Evelyn and Pepys abound in the concrete, realistic details that have made diaries the object of both literary and historical interest. Both men, for example, give eyewitness accounts of the plague of 1665 and the Great Fire of London. It is to Pepys' diary, however, that most readers are inclined to return, for unlike Evelyn, Pepys never intended his diary to be published. Pepys wrote his diary in a secret code from 1660 to 1669, and it was not until 1825 that it was found and its code deciphered. As a result Pepys' diary is filled with the artless, unconscious revelations of character that give the reader the uncanny sensation of dealing with a contemporary individual instead of someone of a time long since past.

The son of a tailor, Pepys was helped through Cambridge by his kinsman and patron, Sir Edward Montagu, first Earl of Sandwich. Through Montagu's aid, he received his first minor post in the Navy. Eventually he achieved the high post of Secretary of the Admiralty, where with incredibly good judgment and efficiency he became "perhaps the greatest administrator in the history of the British Navy." As for Pepys' personality, there are no better comments than his own.

Right: Portrait by John Halys. Opposite: Photo of Pepys' Diary showing his unique shorthand.

from the DIARY

Oct. 13, 1660. To my Lord's[1] in the morning, where I met with Captain Cuttance, but my Lord not being up I went out to Charing Cross, to see Major-General Harrison[2] hanged, drawn, and quartered; which was done there, he looking as cheerful as any man could do in that condition. He was presently cut down, and his head and heart shown to the people, at which there was great shouts of joy. It is said that he said that he was sure to come shortly at the right hand of Christ to judge them that now had judged him; and that his wife do expect his coming again. Thus it was my chance to see the King beheaded at Whitehall Palace, and to see the first blood shed in revenge for the blood of the King at Charing Cross. After that I went by water home, where I was angry with my wife for her things lying about, and in my passion kicked the little fine basket, which I bought her in Holland, and broke it, which troubled me after I had done it.

Apr. 23, 1661. (Coronation Day.) About 4 I rose and got to the Abbey,[3] where I followed Sir J. Denham, the Surveyor, with some company that he was leading in. And with much ado, by the favor of Mr. Cooper, his man, did get up into a great scaffold across the north end of the Abbey, where with a great deal of patience I sat from past 4 till 11 before the King came in. And a great pleasure it was to see the Abbey raised in the middle, all covered with red, and a throne (that is a chair) and footstool on the top of it; and all the officers of all kinds, so much as the very fiddlers, in red vests.

At last comes in the Dean and prebends of Westminster, with the Bishops (many of them in cloth-of-gold copes), and after them the nobility, all in their Parliament robes, which was a most magnificent sight. Then the Duke, and the King with a scepter (carried by my Lord Sandwich) and sword and mond[4] before him, and the crown too. The King in his robes, bareheaded, which was very fine. And after all had placed themselves, there was a sermon and the service; and then in the choir at the high altar, the King passed through all the ceremonies of the Coronation, which to my great grief I and most in the Abbey could not see. The crown being put upon his head, a great shout begun, and he came forth to the throne, and there passed more ceremonies, as taking the oath, and having things read to

1. *my Lord,* Pepys' cousin, Sir Edward Montagu. 2. *Major-General Harrison.* Harrison was condemned to die for his part in the deposition of Charles I. 3. *the Abbey,* Westminster Abbey. 4. *mond,* an orb or ball of gold, intended to represent the globe of the earth, forming part of the insignia of royalty.

him by the Bishop, and his lords (who put on their caps as soon as the King put on his crown) and bishops come and kneeled before him. And three times the King at Arms went to the three open places on the scaffold, and proclaimed that if any one could show any reason why Charles Stuart should not be King of England, that now he should come and speak. And a general pardon also was read by the Lord Chancellor, and medals flung up and down by my Lord Cornwallis, of silver, but I could not come by any. But so great a noise that I could make but little of the music; and, indeed, it was lost to everybody.

Jan. 13, 1663. My poor wife rose by five o'clock in the morning, before day, and went to market and bought fowls and many other things for dinner, with which I was highly pleased. . . .

Things being put in order, and the cook come, I went to the office, where we sat till noon and then broke up, and I home; whither by and by comes Dr. Clerke and his lady, his sister and a she-cousin, and Mr. Pierce and his wife; which was all my guests. I had for them, after oysters, at first course a hash of rabbits, a lamb, and a rare chine of beef. Next a great dish of roasted fowl, cost me about 30 shillings, and a tart; and then fruit and cheese. My dinner was noble and enough. I had my house mighty clean and neat; my room below with a good fire in it; my dining room above, and my chamber being made a withdrawing chamber; and my wife's a good fire also. I find my new table very proper, and will hold nine or ten people well, but eight with great room.

After dinner the women to cards in my wife's chamber, and the Dr. and Mr. Pierce in mine, because the dining room smokes unless I keep a good charcoal fire, which I was not then provided with. At night to supper, had a good sack posset and cold meat, and sent my guests away about ten o'clock at night, both them and myself highly pleased with our management of this day; and indeed their company was very fine, and Mrs. Clerke a very witty, fine lady, though a little conceited and proud. So weary, so to bed. I believe this day's feast will cost me near £5.

Oct. 16, 1665.[5] Took boat and down to the Tower, where I hear the Duke of Albemarle is. To Lumbarde Street, but can get no money. So upon the Exchange. The news for certain that the Dutch are come with their fleet[6] before Margett, and some men were

---

5. *1665*, the year of the plague.   6. *Dutch . . . fleet.* During the year 1665-66 England was engaged in a naval war with Holland as a result of the growing colonial aspirations of both powers.

A Looking-glasse for City and Country:
Wherein is to be feene many fearfull examples in the time of this grievous Visitation, with an admonition to our Londoners flying from the City; and a perswasion Country to be more pitifull to such as come for succor amongst them.

endeavoring to come on shore when the post come away, perhaps to steal some sheep. Thence I walked to the Tower. But, Lord! how empty the streets are and melancholy, so many poor sick people in the streets full of sores; and so many sad stories overheard as I walk, everybody talking of this dead, and that man sick, and so many in this place, and so many in that. And they tell me that in Westminster there is never a physician and but one apothecary left, all being dead; but that there are great hopes of a great decrease this week: God send it!

Aug. 14, 1666. (Thanksgiving day.[7]) After dinner with my wife and Mercer to the Bear Garden, where I have not been, I think, of many years, and saw some good sport of the bull's tossing of the dogs, one into the very boxes. But it is a very rude and nasty pleasure.

Sept. 2, 1666. (Lord's Day.) Some of our maids sitting up late last night to get things ready against our feast today, Jane called us up about three in the morning to tell us of a great fire they saw in the City. So I rose and slipped on my nightgown and went to her window, and thought it to be on the back side of Markelane at the farthest; but, being unused to such fires as followed, I thought it far enough off; and so went to bed again and to sleep. About seven rose again to dress myself, and there looked out at the window and saw the fire not so much as it was, and further off. So to my closet to set things to rights after yesterday's cleaning.

By and by Jane comes and tells me that she hears that above 300 houses have been burned down tonight by the fire we saw, and that it is now burning down all Fish Street, by London Bridge. So I made myself ready presently and walked to the Tower, and there got up upon one of the high places, Sir J. Robinson's little son going up with me; and there I did see the houses at that end of the bridge all on fire, and an infinite great fire on this and the other side the end of the bridge. So with my heart full of trouble, I down to the waterside, and there got a boat and through bridge, and there saw a lamentable fire. Poor Michell's house, as far as the Old Swan, already burned that way, and the fire running further. Everybody endeavoring to remove their goods, and flinging into the river or bringing them into lighters that lay off; poor people staying in their houses as long as till the very fire touched them, and then running into boats, or clambering from one pair of stairs by the waterside to another. And among other things the poor pigeons, I perceive, were loth to leave their houses, but hovered about the windows and balconies till they were, some of them, burned, their wings, and fell down.

Having stayed, and in an hour's time seen the fire rage every way, and nobody, to my sight, endeavoring to quench it, but to remove their goods and leave all to the fire; and having seen it get as far as the Steeleyard, and the wind mighty high and driving it into the City, and everything after so long a drought proving combustible, even the very stones of churches, I to Whitehall and there up to the King's closet in the Chapel, where people come about me and I did give them an account dismayed them all, and word was carried in to the King.

So I was called for and did tell the King and Duke of York what I saw, and that unless his Majesty did command houses to be pulled down nothing could stop the fire. They seemed much troubled, and the King commanded me to go to my Lord Mayor from him and command him to spare no houses, but to pull down before the fire every way. The Duke of York bid me tell him that if he would have any more soldiers he shall.

Here meeting with Captain Cocke, I in his coach which he lent me, and Creed with me to Paul's, and there walked along Watling Street as well as I could, every creature coming away loaden with goods to save, and here and there sick people carried away in beds. Extraordinary good goods carried in carts and on backs. At last met my Lord Mayor in Canning Street like a man spent, with a handkercher about his neck. To the King's message he cried, like a fainting woman, "Lord! what

---

7. *Thanksgiving day,* a day set aside for celebrating the recent victory at sea over the Dutch.

can I do? I am spent; people will not obey me. I have been pulling down houses, but the fire overtakes us faster than we can do it." That he needed no more soldiers; and that, for himself, he must go and refresh himself, having been up all night.

So he left me, and I him, and walked home, seeing people all almost distracted; and no manner of means used to quench the fire. . . .

Met with the King and Duke of York in their barge, and with them to Queenhithe, and there called Sir Richard Browne to them. Their order was only to pull down houses apace; and so below bridge at the waterside, but little was or could be done, the fire coming upon them so fast. River full of lighters and boats taking in goods, and good goods swimming in the water. . . .

Having seen as much as I could now, I away to Whitehall by appointment, and there walked to St. James' Park, and there met my wife and Creed, and walked to my boat; and there upon the water again, and to the fire up and down, it still increasing, and the wind great. So near the fire as we could for smoke; and all over the Thames, with one's face in the wind, you were almost burned with a shower of firedrops. This is very true; so as houses were burned by these drops and flakes of fire, three or four, nay, five or six houses, one from another.

When we could endure no more upon the water, we to a little alehouse on the Bankside, over against the Three Cranes, and there stayed till it was dark almost, and saw the fire grow; and, as it grew darker, appeared more and more, and in corners and upon steeples, and between churches and houses as far as we could see up the hill of the City, in a most horrid malicious bloody flame, not like the fine flame of an ordinary fire. We stayed till, it being darkish, we saw the fire as only one entire arch of fire from this to the other side the bridge, and in a bow up the hill for an arch of above a mile long. It made me weep to see it. The churches, houses and all on fire and flaming at once; and a horrid noise the flames made, and the cracking of houses at their ruins.

So home with a sad heart, and there find poor Tom Hater come with some few of his goods saved out of his house, which is burned. I invited him to lie at my house and did receive his goods, but was deceived in his lying there, the news coming every moment of the growth of the fire; so as we were forced to begin to pack up our own goods and prepare for their removal; and did by moonshine (it being brave dry and moonshine and warm weather) carry much of my goods into the garden, and Mr. Hater and I did remove my money and iron chests into my cellar, as thinking that the safest place. And got my bags of gold into my office ready to carry away, and my chief papers of accounts also there, and my tallies into a box by themselves. So great was our fear, as Sir W. Batten hath carts come out of the country to fetch away his goods this night. We did put Mr. Hater, poor man, to bed a little; but he got but very little rest, so much noise being in my house taking down of goods.

To increase understanding

1. From the diary entries you have read, characterize Pepys' reactions to the events of his time.

2. More than any other kind of writing, the diary reveals the character of the man who writes it. Point out passages in Pepys' diary that reveal (a) his impulsive nature, (b) his Restoration sympathies, (c) his Epicureanism (d) his pride in his accomplishments, (e) his thrift, (f) his practicality and his passion for order, (g) his administrative bent, and (h) his preoccupation with material possessions.

Extending interests

For more about the Great Fire of London, read Pepys' diary entries for September 3-7, 1666.

Compare Pepys' account of the plague (July 17-22, August 10-16, August 28-31, 1665) with John Evelyn's diary account (July 16-December 31, 1665) and with *A Journal of the Plague Year* by Daniel Defoe (see page 260). Make your comparison from the point of view of realistic detail, both personal and objective.

For an account of how another prose writer of the seventeenth century occupied his time, read portions of *The Compleat Angler* by Izaak Walton. Compare Walton's occupations and outlook on life with those of Pepys and Evelyn.

The Art of Grinling Gibbons

One evening in December 1671 as the diarist John Evelyn was on his way home, he was attracted by a light shining through the windows of a thatched cottage. Inside a young man was carving in wood an exquisite copy of a famous painting of the Crucifixion. Evelyn succeeded in introducing the young man to Charles II and also invited him to dinner to meet Samuel Pepys and the leading architect of the day, Sir Christopher Wren. In this way the public became aware of one of the greatest wood carvers of all times, Grinling Gibbons.

Wren invited Gibbons to help with the interior decorations of the new St. Paul's Cathedral, after the old had been destroyed in the Great Fire. The two men also worked together on other London churches, Hampton Court Palace, and various buildings at Cambridge and Oxford, and Gibbons went on to decorate with his carvings many of the great English country houses. His work was unique, stemming mainly from his great love and detailed knowledge of plant and animal life. In Gibbons' hands a piece of wood turned into a delicate array of petals, leaves, tendrils, bouquets, birds, shells, and fishes that often seemed more real than their natural models.

Below: Gibbons' carving in the chapel of Belton House, Lincolnshire. Right: Snipe, lace cravat, foliage, and medallion portrait that may be a copy of Kneller's work (see caption, next page).

John Dryden 1631-1700

Portrait by Godfrey Kneller, most renowned portrait painter of his time. Charles II sat for him, as did nine other reigning monarchs.

The work of John Dryden signals the approach of a new and great age. This new age did not come into its own until the eighteenth century, which is the subject of the next chapter, but it had its beginnings in the society of the Restoration. Its chief characteristic, as heralded by Dryden, was a preference for rules and regulations, in life as well as in art, as opposed to the youthful zest and enthusiasm of the Elizabethans.

Brought up in a Puritan and antimonarchial family, Dryden made his literary debut in the last year of the Puritan interlude with a poem in praise of Oliver Cromwell. During the first year of the Restoration, however, he came out in favor of the Anglican Church and the monarchy by publishing a poem in praise of Charles II. After the succession of Charles' Catholic brother James II, Dryden became a convert to Catholicism.

Although Englishmen were no longer fighting for their religious and political beliefs on the battlefield, they continued to fight vigorously with their pens. Dryden served the royal family by writing several verse satires, the most famous of which is a defense of the Catholic Church entitled *The Hind and the Panther*. With the exception of his odes and lyrics, Dryden's poems are written in heroic couplets (pairs of rhyming iambic pentameter lines)—a verse form that is associated with certain fixed rules and regulations.

One of the most prolific dramatists of the Restoration, Dryden turned out comedies, tragedies, and heroic plays for the newly opened theaters. As always, he sought to conform to the special literary rules that Restoration writers and critics were holding up as formulas for good literature. There were three rules for drama, called the three unities: the action of a play had to take place in twenty-four hours; it had to involve only one place or location; and it had to be a single action without subplots. *All for Love*, which is Dryden's best play, is a pruning of Shakespeare's *Antony and Cleopatra* according to the three dramatic unities.

When the "Glorious Revolutions" of 1688 brought Protestant William and Mary to the throne, Dryden, after years of changing with the political and religious tides, refused to give up his Catholic convictions and was deprived of the offices and pensions that had been bestowed upon him under Charles II. Thrown back on his pen for support, he continued to write plays, odes, prose prefaces, and numerous translations of ancient Greek and Roman authors. His evenings were spent at Will's, one of the new coffee houses, where he was recognized as the literary dictator of his day. Like Ben Jonson before him and Samuel Johnson after him (see page 274), Dryden was surrounded by a number of disciples who went on to establish literary reputations of their own. Among his admirers were the Restoration dramatists Congreve and Wycherley, the eighteenth-century prose writers Addison and Swift, and the then twelve-year-old aspirant to poetic fame, Alexander Pope.

Dryden is thought of today not only as the chief poet and playwright of the Restoration but also as the father of modern English prose. In his various prefaces and essays he turned away from the ornate rhetoric of the Elizabethans to write the first English prose that has a familiar ring to modern ears. In so doing, he helped to lay the foundations upon which the great eighteenth-century prose experiments were based.

A SONG FOR ST. CECILIA'S DAY

A Christian martyr of the third century, St. Cecilia is the patron saint of music and by tradition the inventor of the pipe organ. At an annual London music festival held on St. Cecilia's Day (November 22), it was customary to present an original ode set to music. Dryden wrote the following poem for this purpose. In this poem he attempts to translate the effects of various instruments into poetry.

From harmony, from heavenly harmony,
   This universal frame began:
  When Nature underneath a heap
    Of jarring atoms lay,
And could not heave her her head,   5
The tuneful voice was heard from high:
    "Arise, ye more than dead."

Then cold and hot and moist and dry[1]
  In order to their stations leap,
   And Music's power obey.   10
From harmony, from heavenly harmony,
   This universal frame began:
    From harmony to harmony
Through all the compass of the notes it ran,
The diapason closing full in Man.   15

What passion cannot Music raise and quell!
   When Jubal struck the chorded shell,[2]
  His listening brethren stood around,
   And wondering, on their faces fell
To worship that celestial sound.   20
Less than a god they thought there could
    not dwell
  Within the hollow of that shell
  That spoke so sweetly and so well.
What passion cannot Music raise and quell!

   The trumpet's loud clangor   25
    Excites us to arms
  With shrill notes of anger
    And mortal alarms.
  The double, double, double beat
    Of the thundering drum   30
    Cries: "Hark! the foes come;
Charge, charge, 'tis too late to retreat!'

  The soft complaining flute
   In dying notes discovers
    The woes of hopeless lovers,   35

---

1. *cold . . . dry*, air, fire, water, and earth, which were the four elements of the universe according to classical and medieval natural philosophy. 2. *Jubal . . . chorded shell.* Jubal is referred to in the Bible as "the father of all such as handle the harp and pipe." (Genesis 4:21)

Whose dirge is whispered by the warbling
    lute.
    Sharp violins proclaim
Their jealous pangs and desperation,
Fury, frantic indignation,
Depth of pain, and height of passion,   40
    For the fair, disdainful dame.

But oh! what art can teach,
What human voice can reach
    The sacred organ's praise?
    Notes inspiring holy love,   45
Notes that wing their heavenly ways
    To mend the choirs above.
Orpheus[3] could lead the savage race;
And trees unrooted left their place,
    Sequacious[4] of the lyre;   50
But bright Cecilia raised the wonder
    higher:
When to her organ vocal breath was given,
An angel heard, and straight appeared,
    Mistaking earth for heaven.

GRAND CHORUS
As from the power of sacred lays   55
    The spheres began to move,[5]
And sung the great Creator's praise
    To all the blessed above;
So when the last and dreadful hour
This crumbling pageant shall devour,   60
The trumpet shall be heard on high,
The dead shall live, the living die,
And Music shall untune the sky.

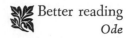

To increase understanding

1. (a) What does Dryden mean by "universal
frame" (line 2)? (b) What idea does he develop in
the first two stanzas of the poem? (c) Explain lines
14-15.
2. (a) What idea is developed in the third stanza?
(b) How are stanzas 4-6 related to this idea? (c)
What comparison of pagan and Christian music does
Dryden make in stanza 6? (d) What is the concluding idea of the poem?
3. Dryden was an expert at *onomatopoeia*, or the
use of words in which sound echoes sense (as in
murmur and *boom*). What words sound like (a) the
plucking of a harp in stanza 3, (b) a trumpet and
drum in stanza 4, (c) an organ in stanza 6?

Better reading
Ode

"A Song for St. Cecilia's Day" is called an *ode*, a
name applied to an exalted, often rapturous lyric
poem, on a lofty subject, with complex or irregular
stanzas. Although English odes are not meant to be
sung by a chorus performing a formal dance as were
the original odes of ancient Greece, they should
nevertheless be read aloud, since their special effect
is due to varying lines and varying arrangements
of rhymes.
    How does stanza 4 of Dryden's ode differ from the
other stanzas in line length, meter, and rhyme?
What does Dryden achieve by these variations? In
what other stanzas does rhyme recur fairly rapidly?
    Which two stanzas of the ode are the most exalted
and rapturous? How is this effect achieved?

from AN ESSAY
OF DRAMATIC POESY

*In his prefaces and essays Dryden tried to
make English prose into a clear, precise instrument of expression. His success is evident in
the following portion of* An Essay of Dramatic
Poesy—*a work regarded by many as the first
important achievement in the field of English
literary criticism.*

To begin then with Shakespeare.
He was the man who of all modern, and perhaps ancient, poets,
had the largest and most comprehensive soul. All the images of
nature were still[1] present to him, and he drew
them not laboriously, but luckily; when he
describes anything, you more than see it, you
feel it too. Those who accuse him to have
wanted learning give him the greater commendation. He was naturally learned; he

---

A SONG FOR ST. CECILIA'S DAY. **3.** *Orpheus.* See footnote
number 19, page 212. **4.** *Sequacious*, following after. **5.**
spheres . . . move. It was believed that the stars made music
as they revolved in their spheres.
AN ESSAY OF DRAMATIC POESY. **1.** *still*, always.

needed not the spectacles of books to read nature; he looked inward, and found her there. I cannot say he is everywhere alike; were he so, I should do him injury to compare him with the greatest of mankind. He is many times flat, insipid; his comic wit[2] degenerating into clenches,[3] his serious swelling into bombast. But he is always great when some great occasion is presented to him; no man can say he ever had a fit subject for his wit, and did not then raise himself as high above the rest of poets,

Quantum lenta solent inter viburna cupressi.[4]

The consideration of this made Mr. Hales of Eaton say that there was no subject of which any poet ever writ but he would produce it much better done in Shakespeare; and however others are now generally preferred before him, yet the age wherein he lived, which had contemporaries with him, Fletcher[5] and Jonson, never equaled them to him in their esteem. And in the last king's court, when Ben's reputation was at highest, Sir John Suckling, and with him the greater part of the courtiers, set our Shakespeare far above him.

Beaumont and Fletcher, of whom I am next to speak, had, with the advantage of Shakespeare's wit, which was their precedent, great natural gifts, improved by study; Beaumont especially being so accurate a judge of plays that Ben Jonson, while he lived, submitted all his writings to his censure, and 'tis thought, used his judgment in correcting, if not contriving, all his plots. What value he had for him appears by the verses he writ to him; and therefore I need speak no farther of it. The first play that brought Fletcher and him[6] in esteem was their *Philaster;* for before that they had written two or three very unsuccessfully; as the like is reported of Ben Jonson, before he writ *Every Man in His Humor.* Their plots were generally more regular[7] than Shakespeare's especially those which were made before Beaumont's death; and they understood and imitated the conversation of gentlemen much better; whose wild debaucheries, and quickness of wit in repartees, no poet before them could paint as they have done. Humor,

which Ben Jonson derived from particular persons, they made it not their business to describe. They represented all the passions very lively, but above all, love. I am apt to believe the English language in them arrived to its highest perfection; what words have since been taken in are rather superfluous than ornamental. Their plays are now the most pleasant and frequent entertainments of the stage; two of theirs being acted through the year for one of Shakespeare's or Jonson's. The reason is, because there is a certain gayety in their comedies, and pathos in their more serious plays, which suits generally with all men's humors. Shakespeare's language is likewise a little obsolete, and Ben Jonson's wit comes short of theirs.

As for Jonson, to whose character I am now arrived, if we look upon him while he was himself (for his last plays were but his dotages), I think him the most learned and judicious writer which any theater ever had. He was a most severe judge of himself, as well as others. One cannot say he wanted wit, but rather that he was frugal of it. In his works you find little to retrench or alter. Wit and language, and humor also in some measure, we had before him; but something of art was wanting to the drama, till he came. He managed his strength to more advantage than any who preceded him. You seldom find him making love in any of his scenes, or endeavoring to move the passions; his genius was too sullen and saturnine to do it gracefully, especially when he knew he came after those who had performed both to such an height. Humor was his proper sphere; and in that he delighted most to represent mechanic people.[8] He was deeply conversant in the ancients, both Greek and Latin, and he borrowed boldly from them. There is scarce a poet or historian among the Roman authors of those times

---

2. *wit.* This word is used throughout the essay to mean imaginative intelligence. 3. *clenches,* puns. 4. *Quantum . . . cupressi,* as do the tall cypresses above the low-growing shrubs. (Vergil, *Eclogues* I, 26) 5. *Fletcher,* John Fletcher, one of the best dramatists in the reign of James I. He collaborated on several occasions with another dramatist, Francis *Beaumont.* 6. *him,* Beaumont. 7. *regular,* observing the dramatic unities. (See page 235.) 8. *mechanic people,* mechanics, workingmen.

whom he has not translated in *Sejanus* and *Catiline*.[9] But he has done his robberies so openly that one may see he fears not to be taxed by any law. He invades authors like a monarch; and what would be theft in other poets is only victory in him. With the spoils of these writers he so represents old Rome to us, in its rites, ceremonies, and customs, that if one of their poets had written either of his tragedies, we had seen less of it than in him. If there was any fault in his language, it was that he weaved it too closely and laboriously, in his comedies especially. Perhaps, too, he did a little too much Romanize our tongue, leaving the words which he translated almost as much Latin as he found them; wherein, though he learnedly followed their language, he did not enough comply with the idiom of ours. If I would compare him with Shakespeare, I must acknowledge him the more correct poet, but Shakespeare the greater wit. Shakespeare was the Homer, or father, of our dramatic poets; Jonson was the Vergil, the pattern of elaborate writing; I admire him, but I love Shakespeare. To conclude of him: as he has given us the most correct plays, so in the precepts which he has laid down in his *Discoveries*,[10] we have as many and profitable rules for perfecting the stage as any wherewith the French can furnish us.

---

9. *Sejanus* (sə ja′nəs) . . . *Catiline*, two of Jonson's plays.
10. *Discoveries*, Jonson's collection of notes, extracts, and reflections made from his wide reading.

❈ To increase understanding

1. (a) What opinions does Dryden express concerning Shakespeare? (b) To what extent do you agree with Dryden's evaluation of Shakespeare? Cite passages from *Hamlet* to support your position.
2. What comparisons does Dryden make between Beaumont and Fletcher, and Shakespeare?
3. (a) What particular merits does Dryden ascribe to Jonson? (b) What fault does he find in Jonson's language? (c) What rules is Dryden referring to in the last sentence of the essay? (d) In what sense is Shakespeare not a "correct" poet?
4. Compare Dryden's essay with that of Francis Bacon from the point of view of (a) clearness of arrangement, and (b) clarity and ease of diction.

The Changing English Language

Englishmen of the seventeenth century, especially those who lived during the latter half of the period, became increasingly dissatisfied with the exuberant language of the Elizabethan Age. The Royal Society (see page 200) objected to the Elizabethan love of verbal gymnastics on the grounds that it was unscientific, and demanded of its members instead "a close, naked, natural way of speaking; positive expressions, clear senses, a native easiness, bringing as near the mathematical plainness as they can." The scientists were supported in this matter by the Puritans, who objected to display of any kind, whether in matters of religion, dress, or language; and also by John Dryden and his followers, who wanted to make English into an instrument as clear and precise as the classical languages they so admired.

English continued to be enriched by words from other languages. Increased commercial rivalry with the Dutch brought in such terms as *bowsprit*, *brandy*, *cruise*, *freight*, *keel*, *smack*, and *sloop*. From the American colonies came such words as *canoe*, *maize*, *papoose*, and *squaw*. The popularity of Italian music in the latter half of the century gave rise to terms such as *aria*, *allegro*, *contralto*, *cantata*, *opera*, *oratorio*, *piano*, *soprano*, and *trombone*. The main change, however, as Dryden's *Essay of Dramatic Poesy* reveals, was increased ease and lucidity of expression.

The Larger View

Match the following authors with the following poems, parts of poems, or prose passages. In each instance explain the reasons why you associate a particular author with a particular quotation.

a. Robert Herrick
b. John Milton
c. John Bunyan
d. Samuel Pepys
e. John Dryden

I. They heard, and were abashed, and up they
    sprung
Upon the wing . . .
Nor did they not perceive the evil plight
In which they were, or the fierce pains not feel;
Yet to their General's voice they soon obeyed
Innumerable. As when the potent rod
Of Amram's son, in Egypt's evil day,
Waved round the coast, up-called a pitchy cloud
Of locusts, warping on the eastern wind,
That o'er the realm of impious Pharaoh hung
Like Night, and darkened all the land of Nile;
So numberless were those bad Angels seen
Hovering on wing under the cope of Hell
'Twixt upper, nether, and surrounding fires;
Till, as a signal given, the uplifted spear
Of their great Sultan waving to direct
Their course, in even balance down they light
On the firm brimstone, and fill all the plain.

II. Fair daffodils, we weep to see
  You haste away so soon;
As yet the early-rising sun
  Has not attained his noon.
    Stay, stay
Until the hasting day
  Has run
But to the evensong;
And, having prayed together, we
  Will go with you along.
We have short time to stay, as you,
  We have as short a spring;
As quick a growth to meet decay,
  As you, or anything.
    We die
As your hours do, and dry
    Away
Like to the summer's rain;
Or as the pearls of morning's dew,
  Ne'er to be found again.

III. I could produce, even in Shakespeare's and Fletcher's works, some plays which are almost exactly formed; as *The Merry Wives of Windsor*, and *The Scornful Lady*: but because (generally speaking), Shakespeare, who writ first, did not perfectly observe the laws of comedy, and Fletcher, who came nearer to perfection, yet through carelessness made many faults, I will take the pattern of a perfect play from Ben Jonson, who was a careful and learned observer of the dramatic laws.

IV. Soon as dined, I and Moone away, and walked through the city, the streets full of nothing but people and horses and carts loaden with goods, ready to run over one another, and removing goods from one burned house to another. They now removing out of Canning Street, which received goods in the morning, into Lumbard Street, and further; and among others, I now saw my little goldsmith Stokes receiving some friends goods, whose house itself was burned the day after.

V. Now, when they were gone over the stile, they began to contrive with themselves what they should do at that stile, to prevent those that should come after, from falling into the hands of Giant Despair. So they consented to erect there a pillar, and to engrave upon the side thereof this sentence—"Over this stile is the way to Doubting Castle, which is kept by Giant Despair, who despiseth the King of the Celestial Country, and seeks to destroy his holy pilgrims." Many, therefore, that followed after, read what was written, and escaped the danger.

Bibliography

BARNES, MARGARET CAMPBELL, *Mary of Carisbrooke*. (Macrae, Smith) Charles I's imprisonment on the Isle of Wight is the subject of this historical romance. Its pleasant blending of romance and adventure will appeal to girls.

BLACKMORE, RICHARD DODDRIDGE, *Lorna Doone*. (Dutton •Everyman's) The mysterious, wild moorlands of Exmoor in western England provide the setting for this romantic love story, long a favorite with young people.

BUNYAN, JOHN, *The Pilgrim's Progress*. (Lippincott •Everyman's) Whether you read it as a symbolic narrative or an interesting story, Bunyan's famous tale of Christian and his troubled journey is one that you will not soon forget.

DARINGER, HELEN, *Pilgrim Kate*. (Harcourt) Through the eyes of a teen-age girl the author relates the story of a family's last year in a small English town before sailing to America to find religious freedom. It is a well-written and historically accurate novel that will appeal to anyone who enjoys historical fiction.

DOYLE, ARTHUR CONAN, *Micah Clarke*. (Transatlantic) Careful research and the ability to tell a good story (as anyone who has ever read *Sherlock Holmes* well knows) make Doyle a favorite writer of many. He is at his best in this stirring adventure story of how the Duke of Monmouth attempted to seize the British throne in 1685.

DRYDEN, JOHN, *Poetry of John Dryden*, edited by Richard Wilbur. (•Dell) This well-edited edition of Dryden's works will satisfy the demands of any student who wishes to read more of this famous seventeenth-century poet.

DU MAURIER, DAPHNE, *The King's General*. (Doubleday •Pocket Books) Honor Harris, eighteen and in love with Sir Richard Grenville, Charles I's general in the West, is caught up in the stress and strife of Britain's Civil War. This fascinating story is told from the Cavalier point of view.

GRAVES, ROBERT, *Wife to Mr. Milton*. (•Noonday) In the form of a detailed diary, the author tells the story of Mary Powell, John Milton's first wife. Only sixteen when she married the thirty-three-year-old Milton, the lighthearted girl and the stern Puritan have an unhappy marriage, which is described up to her death at twenty-six. Graves' conception of Milton is particularly interesting.

HAWES, C. B., *The Dark Frigate*. (Little) In an authentic seventeenth-century setting, a well-born English lad runs away to sea, is captured by pirates, and barely escapes hanging.

HERRICK, ROBERT, *Robert Herrick*, edited by John Hayward. (•Penguin) Selections from *Hesperides* and *Noble Numbers* are included in this collection of Herrick's poetry. Mr. Hayward's skillful editing helps to make the book a very interesting and enjoyable collection.

KNIGHT, FRANK, *The Last of Lallows*. (St. Martin's) Mr. Knight has written an absorbing and exciting tale of a family divided by political beliefs. The love story Knight portrays against this political and military background will appeal to feminine readers.

MACAULAY, THOMAS BABINGTON, *Macaulay's Essays on Milton and Addison*, Lake English Classics. (Scott, Foresman) The essay on Milton contains vivid descriptions of both Puritans and Cavaliers as well as a fine account of Milton. Macaulay is a master at recreating the spirit of a vanished age.

MARRYAT, FREDERICK, *Children of the New Forest*. (Dutton) Here is another absorbing story of England during the civil wars, written from the Royalist point of view.

MILTON, JOHN, *Paradise Lost, Samson Agonistes, Lycidas*. (•Mentor) The serious student who would like to read more poetry by the greatest poet of the seventeenth century will enjoy this collection. The title poems are included in their complete form. There is also a good biographical introduction by Edward Le Comte.

SAVERY, CONSTANCE, *Emeralds for the King*. (Longmans) This is a tale of Roundheads and Royalists during the time of the Puritan Revolution. The story covers the period from 1630 to 1658.

TREASE, GEOFFREY, *Seven Kings of England*. (Vanguard) Simple, informal character sketches of Charles I and Charles II are included in this study of reigns that are of special interest in the history of Great Britain.

VARBLE, RACHEL, *Three Against London*. (Doubleday) Here is an especially good picture of seventeenth-century London at the time of the plague and the Great Fire. The simply written story of two waterfront boys and a kitchen maid in the Samuel Pepys household is one of suspense and adventure.

WELCH, RONALD, *For the King*. (Criterion) Studious Neil Carey felt that the cause of neither the Roundheads nor the Royalists was right, but he decides to remain loyal to the King. With color and credibility Mr. Welch tells of the young man's experiences through three years of war.

WILSON, CHARLES G., *Guns in the Wilderness*. (Washburn) In 1665 Noell Goffe is in hiding because of his family's connection with the Cromwell revolt. He escapes to America and fights through King Philip's War. The vigorous and fast-moving story is based on an accurate historical background.

WINSLOW, OLA ELIZABETH, *John Bunyan*. (Macmillan) Miss Winslow, a Pulitzer Prize winner, is at her best in this three-dimensional biography of John Bunyan.

•paperback only

chapter five

THE
EIGHTEENTH
CENTURY

1700-1798

Opposite: The salon at Houghton Hall, Norfolk, originally conceived and built by Sir Robert Walpole between 1722 and 1731.
Right: Tapestry portrait in silk and wool of George II made in Dublin in 1738.

Like change in the seasons, the change from one ideal of life to another is always gradual. We do not say, "Yesterday it was summer; today it is winter." After a time of almost imperceptible or unnoticed alteration in nature we at length look upon a world that has been transformed. So it was in England around 1700. Men awoke one day to find themselves in a new age. They found that they were responding less eagerly, even negatively, to the burning idealism and passionate enthusiasm that had characterized both the unified society of the Elizabethans and the war-torn society of the seventeenth century. The dramas of Shakespeare, for example, seemed indeed the work of genius, but it was a wild and romantic genius, in need of pruning and restraint. The powerful passions of the tragedies were thought of as monstrous and unreal, the mixing of tragic and comic elements was regarded as a sin against good taste, and the unmerited death of a noble character like Hamlet did not seem a tragedy but merely a violation of the rules of poetic justice. *Hamlet* was criticized because the Prince of Denmark fought a duel with Laertes, who was beneath him in rank, and because such vulgar creatures as grave diggers were permitted to appear on the same platform with a prince of the blood. In short, the eighteenth century—at least the first half of it—was the Age of Reason, for it had rigid rules for everything from the "taming" of Shakespeare to the pruning of gardens and the way in which people should conduct themselves on social occasions. These rules were upheld in the name of correctness, propriety, decorum, and common sense—all of which reigned so inflexibly that even their first champion, John Dryden, was taken to task for his occasional lapses into enthusiasm.

It is not hard to see why the eighteenth century became the Age of Reason. The seventeenth century with its Puritan fanaticism, Cavalier debaucheries, and all-out civil war had been a painful lesson in what happens when people let their passions get the best of them. Calling themselves the Augustans, after the Roman Emperor Augustus, who stabilized and expanded the Roman Empire, the men of the eighteenth century looked upon their Puritan and Cavalier forefathers as barbarians and upon themselves as the first civilized Englishmen. "We are refined," wrote Lord Chesterfield to his son, "and plain manners, plain dress, and plain diction, would as little do in life, as acorns, herbage, and the water of the neighboring well, would do at table."

The elegant but often smothering formality of the Augustans did not last throughout the whole of the eighteenth century. Somewhere in the second half Englishmen began throwing off the Augustan rules. But this was the prelude to another new age.

SCIENCE The tendency of the Augustans to cherish law and reason received a powerful impetus from the advancement of science, for it was during the eighteenth century that the achievements of Newton began to capture the imagination of great numbers of people.

> Nature and Nature's laws lay hid in night;
> God said, Let Newton be! and all was light.

This couplet by the most famous eighteenth-century poet, Alexander Pope, was only one of many such hymns of praise that rose up throughout the length and breadth of the Western world, extending even as far as the newly organized colonies in America. The men of the eighteenth century were fairly unanimous in their conviction that after centuries of darkness the ideas of Newton had ushered in a new and glorious Enlightenment. They figured that if reason had enabled Newton to discover the natural laws of the universe and thereby predict its operation, then reason could also discover the natural laws of society and thereby predict its progress.

These three words—*reason, natural laws,* and *progress*— caused as much excitement in the eighteenth century as *astronaut, spaceship,* and *rocket* have in the twentieth. Many men felt that the age of Enlightenment had already come, that society was at last functioning as reasonably and naturally as it possibly could. Many others felt that the age of Enlightenment was yet to come and that the organization of society was unreasonable and unnatural. The first social scientists began making their appearance—men like the economist Adam Smith, advocate of the system of private enterprise, and the historian Edward Gibbon, author of *The Decline and Fall of the Roman Empire.* In literature satire· became the dominant form, for when men think of society as a reasonable operation but find that it is just as irrational and crude as ever, they quite naturally turn to satirical writing. Eighteenth-century satire, as you will learn as you study this chapter, varied with the temperaments of the men producing it—from the mild and smiling admonitions of Joseph Addison and Richard Steele to the bitterly disillusioned, searing condemnations of Jonathan Swift.

THE MIDDLE CLASS The passing of the reins of government from the monarchy and the aristocracy to the *bourgeoisie*, or middle class, was another reason that eighteenth-century society became exceedingly rule-conscious. England's middle class, which was made up of merchants, bankers, lawyers, and other town businessmen, had been in the making ever since the time of Chaucer. By mid-seventeenth century it had been powerful enough to bring success to the armies of the Commonwealth, and in the Glorious Revolution of 1688 it had forced a king to flee and had replaced his rule with that of Parliament. When it came to matters of polite social intercourse, however, England's new leaders felt awkward and ignorant. They had not yet worked out a code of behavior to replace the old aristocratic ideal of chivalry or courtliness. This problem was thrashed out for the most part in the London coffee houses, which sprang up with the same rapidity in the eighteenth century as had theaters and taverns in the time of Elizabeth. As Macaulay tells us in his *History of England*, it was in the "eternal fog and stench" of the tobacco-filled coffee houses that the boorish middle class could rub shoulders with England's men of letters

Below: The eighteenth-century ideal of elegance in manners, dress, and surroundings is illustrated in this picture of a minuet at a fashionable ball. Opposite: The prevailing taste for elegant ornament extended even to details. The upper photograph shows a pair of enameled goblets, bearing the arms of the Earls of Pembroke and Montgomery; the lower is of a Chinese painted looking glass set in an English gilded frame.

and with the members of the hereditary aristocracy. The result was a new ideal of behavior which came to be known as *gentility*.

At the same time that its rough edges were being polished, the middle class was dazzling itself and the world with its meteoric accumulation of wealth. Improved inventions increased manufacture of cloth in the North. Potteries developed in the West. Farming became more scientific. Colonial trade and the first free trade among nations produced a boom in shipping and seaports. The empire builders were at work unfurling the British flag around the globe—in Canada, India, Gibraltar, the West Indies, and in Africa. England was indeed plagued with wars, mostly with the French, who, like the Spaniards in the time of Elizabeth, had become England's greatest rivals; but they were all fought (and mostly won) on foreign soil and so did not impede the growing prosperity. Even the loss of the American colonies did not make much of a dent in eighteenth-century British expansion and smugness.

The music room of Mellerstain, the Scottish home of the Earl of Haddington. The ceiling of this room, along with the house itself, was designed by Robert Adam, who was the architect to George III. Adam interiors and furniture design helped set the neoclassical style of the entire age.

The working class meanwhile—the ever increasing number of men working in mines and factories and at heavy labor, whose voices began to be heard in the eighteenth century as those of the middle class had begun to be heard some four centuries earlier—benefited little if any from England's new riches. The same was true even for great numbers of people who considered themselves middle class. In London, for example, which received the bulk of the great population shift from country to town, the inequality in the distribution of wealth was appalling. In the streets the silks, powdered headdresses, gold coaches, and brocaded sedan chairs of the rich moved against a background of rags, filth, stench, and general despair worse than that of a present-day slum. Beaux and belles attended plays at Drury Lane Theater, heard Italian operas, sipped wine in the arbors of Vauxhall or Ranelagh Gardens, or watched fireworks, while hundreds of people wondered where their next meal was coming from. Sir Joshua Reynolds and Thomas Gainsborough turned out elegant portraits of prosperous ladies and gentlemen, while William Hogarth satirized the wealthy, and in his grotesque paintings and engravings of the London slums protested against the lot of the poor. For most Englishmen the poverty and uncertainty of life was such that, as the eighteenth century's great literary dictator Dr. Johnson said, "He that sees before him to his third dinner, has a long prospect."

GOVERNMENT
BY CABINET

Below left: a cabinetmaker's trade card. From the ranks of such unpretentious craftsmen rose the great English furniture makers: Chippendale, Adam, Hepplewhite, Sheraton. Below right: Mereworth Castle shows the classical architecture of Colin Campbell.

The progress of the middle class, or town gentry, to a position of political dominance, was gradual. During the opening years of the eighteenth century England was still controlled by the aristocracy, or landed gentry. By the end of the century, however, the members of this aristocracy were forced to admit that there was no longer anything to distinguish them from the middle class. Intermarriage between aristocracy and wealthy middle class, a common reverence for property, and common political aims had fused members of the two groups into one larger group. The spokesman for this enlarged middle class was the Whig Party. It was the Whigs who dominated the Parliaments of the eighteenth century and who, overcoming the Tory, or aristocratic party, established once and for all the supremacy of the majority cabinet in Parliament over the King.

After the deaths of William and Mary (see page 201), the crown passed to Mary's sister Anne, who reigned from 1702 to 1714. When Anne died leaving no heirs, the Whigs threw the Tories out of office and brought the Stuart monarchy to an end by arranging for the succession of Anne's cousins from the small German kingdom of Hanover. The first kings of

A. F. KERSTING

the House of Hanover, George I (1714-1727) and George II (1727-1760), did not particularly want the crown that had been thrust upon them. Homesick for Hanover and ill at ease in England (they never did learn to speak the English language), the first two Georges gladly passed the reins of government to the Whig cabinet ministers in Parliament. One of these ministers, Sir Robert Walpole, governed England so long (from 1721 to 1742) and so successfully that he is thought of today as having made the Prime Minister of the ruling party into the highest official in the land. When George III (1760-1820) took the throne, he tried with the aid of the Tories to undo the precedent set by Walpole and to reassert the supremacy of the King, but because he was unable to keep the French out of the West Indies and the Americans in the British Empire, he was ultimately unsuccessful. During the closing years of the century George III was "wandering the corridors of Windsor in the darkness of insanity" and England was governed by the Cabinet.

ENGLISH INFLUENCE ON AMERICAN CULTURE

There is much in eighteenth-century England that seems familiar to us in America today. When we recall that the eighteenth century coincides with the Colonial Period in our history and that our original thirteen colonies were peopled largely by English settlers, the reason for this familiarity is clear. Many of the settlers were sons of English aristocrats who decided to carve out estates for themselves in the New World, especially in the South. Still other Englishmen became merchants and shipbuilders in the budding seaport towns along the coastline from Maine to the Carolinas. When they built their homes and when they began constructing the public buildings of the new American nation, these English settlers quite naturally used as a model the type of architecture then popular in England.

Like the painting and the literature of the period, eighteenth-century English architecture, known as Georgian architecture after the Georges of the House of Hanover, was neoclassical in style. To the eighteenth-century Englishman, whether in England or America, the arts of classical antiquity, with their emphasis on formality, balance, and precision, were not only a tribute to man's rationality; they also expressed the power and grandeur of human civilization. Neoclassical precision and balance can be seen today in such widely scattered buildings as St. Paul's Cathedral in London, which was redesigned by Sir Christopher Wren after its destruction in the Great Fire of 1666; the pillared and porticoed mansion of the plantation owner in the American South; the tall, three-storied home of the early New England merchant; and the massive, high-domed Capitol building in Washington. The neoclassical style also dominates in the work of the great eighteenth-century English craftsmen Adam, Chippendale, Hepplewhite, Sheraton, and Wedgwood, whose interior decorations and furnishings of all sorts continue to lend orderly elegance to many English and American homes.

America inherited not only the appearance of eighteenth-century England; it also inherited its thoughts. When people speak, for example, of the merits of the private-enterprise system, they are harking back to the eighteenth-century English economists. When they speak of the right of each individual to "life, liberty, and the pursuit of happiness," they are associating themselves with an outstanding group of English social philosophers, especially John Locke (1632-1704), who is regarded by many as the "Newton of society." Three popular forms of literature in America today—the newspaper, the magazine, and the novel—likewise had their origins in eighteenth-century England. And the formal style of the first great English prose writers (which corresponds to the formality in every other aspect of eighteenth-century English life) still claims a host of American admirers and imitators.

THE PARKER GALLERY, LONDON

Opposite: A Sheraton cabinet originally owned by the engineer, inventor, and industrialist, Sir Richard Arkwright. Above: Engraving of Sir Robert Walpole. Right: Prospect of Dryham Park, Gloucestershire, which was redesigned early in the century.

THE NATIONAL TRUST, ENGLAND

The Coffee House

From the Restoration of 1660 through the reigns of the first Georges of the House of Hanover, the London coffee house was the center of English social life. At a time when journalism was in its infancy and the London business world was only beginning to realize its economic and political strength, the coffee house served as the repository of news and the meeting place of businessman and client. Coffee was being imported from the Far East for the first time in large quantities, and it afforded a genteel refreshment for a wide variety of club activities, ranging from gossip and games of checkers to the buying and selling of goods and the formulation of political policy.

No one was excluded from the coffee houses —a condition which hastened the union of the middle class and the aristocracy—and yet every profession and every shade of political and religious opinion had its own particular meeting place. Whigs went to St. James' Coffee House, Tories to the Cocoa Tree Chocolate House. The Grecian served the world of scholarship, Truby's the clergy, Lloyd's the merchants, and White's the fashionable dandies of high society. In the reign of Queen Anne at the opening of the eighteenth century a partial list of coffee houses runs to nearly five hundred names.

One of the most celebrated houses was Will's, frequented by poets, critics, and men-of-letters. Will's boasted the patronage of such people as John Dryden, Joseph Addison, and Alexander Pope. It was there that the much admired literature and literary criticism of classical antiquity were discussed; and there the considerable body of neoclassical rules and regulations were formulated and enforced.

Below: So popular were the coffee houses that a floating one was built to operate on the Thames.
Left: More conventional coffee houses were identified by signs such as this lion's head which was erected outside Button's Coffee House by editor Richard Steele, who used Button's as the office for the Guardian. Aspiring authors submitted copy by dropping it through the opening in the lion's mouth. The inscription at the bottom of the sign reads: These claws are curved for proud necks; this beast feeds only on the chosen.

Top: An etching, thought to be of Lloyd's Coffee House, the birthplace of the now world-famous insurance exchange. Above: Moll King, keeper of King's Coffee House.
Left: Illustration from a satire called Coffee House Mob.

Two popular authors painted by the most renowned portrait artists of the time. The Addison portrait (left) is a copy of a work by Kneller (see caption, page 235). The Steele portrait is by Kneller's successor in public favor, Jonathan Richardson.

Joseph Addison 1672-1719 and *Richard Steele* 1672-1729

One day in 1709 there appeared in the London coffee houses a single news sheet called *The Tatler,* which bore the motto: "Whatever men do is the subject of this book." Its author was an impulsive Irishman by the name of Richard Steele, who had decided to make the education of the newly arrived middle class his main life task. "I own myself of the Society for Reformation of Manners," said Steele in the third *Tatler* (the paper appeared three times a week). "Therefore, as I design to have notices from all public assemblies, I shall take upon me only indecorums, improprieties, and negligences, in such as shall give us better examples. After this declaration, if a fine lady thinks fit to giggle in church, or a great beau to come in drunk to a play, either shall be sure to hear of it in my ensuing paper; for merely as a well-bred man I cannot bear such enormities." An even more serious statement of his purpose in Number 39—"to stem, as far as I can, the prevailing torrent of vice and ignorance" —served only to whet the appetites of the new reading public. The *Tatler's* news items and essays were soon being read by practically everybody—women as well as men—for the members of the fair sex, who were conversing and reasoning around the tea tables at home as were their husbands around the coffee tables, seemed to Steele to be in particular need of criticism and instruction.

One issue of *The Tatler* found its way to Ireland, where the Englishman Joseph Addison, a former schoolmate of Steele and a fellow Whig, was employed in government service. Addison thought he recognized the *Tatler's* anonymous author and forthwith sent him a contribution for its columns. This was the beginning of a famous literary partnership, for Addison and Steele had a common aim (the education of the middle class) and complementary talents. As the more warm-hearted of the two men, Steele jollied his readers along in a style that was very much like their own way of speaking, and as the sociable man-about-town, he contributed most of the *Tatler's* newsy items. Addison was more reserved and scholarly. He contributed many serious literary essays and he wrote in a highly polished, formal style. Both men had a gift for deft and delicate satire.

When *The Tatler* was discontinued in 1711 because of political difficulties, Addison and Steele founded a daily paper called *The Spectator*. Still writing anonymously, the authors offered their comments on manners, morals, and literature through the kindly character of "the Spectator." Around him they organized a club of representative eighteenth-century types, such as the famous Sir Roger de Coverley. This lovable old country gentleman, who was created by Addison and Steele in a deliberate attempt to make the landed aristocracy sympathetic to the town businessmen, was one of the main reasons for the *Spectator's* enormous success.

Addison and Steele take their place among the pioneers in English literature for several reasons. Their Roger de Coverley essays, when put together, constitute one of the steps in the development of the English novel. The chatty essays on topical subjects in both *The Tatler* and *The Spectator* mark the beginning of the familiar, journalistic essay that appears frequently in many English and American newspapers today. And the various collections made of these essays gave birth to the idea of the magazine.

THE SPECTATOR CLUB

The Spectator, No. 2, March 2, 1711
Richard Steele

———Ast alii sex,
Et plures uno conclamant ore.[1]

The first of our society is a gentleman of Worcestershire, of ancient descent, a baronet, his name Sir Roger de Coverley. His great-grandfather was inventor of that famous country-dance which is called after him. All who know that shire are very well acquainted with the parts and merits of Sir Roger. He is a gentleman that is very singular in his behavior, but his singularities proceed from his good sense and are contradictions to the manners of the world only as he thinks the world is in the wrong. However, this humor creates him no enemies, for he does nothing with sourness or obstinacy; and his being unconfined to modes and forms makes him but the readier and more capable to please and oblige all who know him.

When he is in town, he lives in Soho Square. It is said he keeps himself a bachelor by reason he was crossed in love by a perverse, beautiful widow of the next county to him. Before this disappointment Sir Roger was what you call a fine gentleman, had often supped

---

1. *Ast . . . ore*, "But six others and more cry out together with one voice." This is a quotation from the Roman satirist Juvenal (60?-140? A.D.).

with my Lord Rochester and Sir George Etherege,[2] fought a duel upon his first coming to town, and kicked Bully Dawson[3] in a public coffee house for calling him "youngster." But being ill-used by the above-mentioned widow, he was very serious for a year and a half; and though, his temper being naturally jovial, he at last got over it, he grew careless of himself, and never dressed afterwards. He continues to wear a coat and doublet of the same cut that were in fashion at the time of his repulse, which, in his merry humors, he tells us, has been in and out twelve times since he first wore it.

He is now in his fifty-sixth year, cheerful, gay, and hearty; keeps a good house both in town and country; a great lover of mankind; but there is such a mirthful cast in his behavior that he is rather beloved than esteemed. His tenants grow rich, his servants look satisfied, all the young women profess love to him, and the young men are glad of his company. When he comes into a house, he calls the servants by their names, and talks all the way upstairs to a visit. I must not omit that Sir Roger is a justice of the quorum,[4] that he fills the chair at a quarter-session[5] with great abilities; and three months ago gained universal applause by explaining a passage in the Game Act.

The gentleman next in esteem and authority among us is another bachelor, who is a member of the Inner Temple,[6] a man of great probity, wit, and understanding; but he has chosen his place of residence rather to obey the direction of an old humorsome father than in pursuit of his own inclinations. He was placed there to study the laws of the land, and is the most learned of any of the house in those of the stage. Aristotle and Longinus are much better understood by him than Littleton and Coke.[7] He knows the argument of each of the orations of Demosthenes and Tully,[8] but not one case in the reports of our own courts. No one ever took him for a fool, but none, except his intimate friends, know he has a great deal of wit. This turn makes him at once both disinterested and agreeable. As few of his thoughts are drawn from business, they are most of them fit for conversation. His taste of books is a little too just[9] for the age he lives

in; he has read all, but approves of very few. His familiarity with the customs, manners, actions, and writings of the ancients makes him a very delicate observer of what occurs to him in the present world. He is an excellent critic, and the time of the play is his hour of business. Exactly at five he passes through New Inn, crosses through Russell Court, and takes a turn at Will's[10] till the play begins. He has his shoes rubbed and his periwig powdered at the barber's as you go into the Rose.[11] It is for the good of the audience when he is at a play, for the actors have an ambition to please him.

The person of next consideration is Sir Andrew Freeport, a merchant of great eminence in the city of London, a person of indefatigable industry, strong reason, and great experience. His notions of trade are noble and generous, and, as every rich man has usually some sly way of jesting which would make no great figure were he not a rich man, he calls the sea the British Common.

He is acquainted with commerce in all its parts and will tell you that it is a stupid and barbarous way to extend dominion by arms; for true power is to be got by arts and industry. He will often argue that if this part of our trade were well cultivated, we should gain from one nation; and if another, from another. I have heard him prove that diligence makes more lasting acquisitions than valor and that sloth has ruined more nations than the sword. He abounds in several frugal maxims, among which the greatest favorite is, "A penny saved is a penny got."

A general trader of good sense is pleasanter

2. *Lord Rochester and Sir George Etherege,* a poet and a dramatist, respectively, during the Restoration. 3. *Bully Dawson,* a notorious London swindler of the seventeenth century. 4. *justice of the quorum,* justice of the peace. 5. *quarter-session,* a meeting of the court every three months. 6. *Inner Temple,* one of the four Inns of Court in London which control the admitting of persons to practice at the bar. 7. *Aristotle . . . Coke.* Aristotle and Longinus were famous Greek critics whose opinions were held in high esteem during the eighteenth century. Littleton (1402-1481) was perhaps the greatest English jurist of the Middle Ages; Coke (1552-1634) held the position of Lord Chief Justice. 8. *Demosthenes* (di mos'tha nēz) *and Tully* (tul'i). The former was the most famous orator of ancient Greece. The latter was Marcus Tullius Cicero, a famous Roman orator. 9. *just,* correct, proper. 10. *takes . . . Will's,* plays a game or so of cards at Will's Coffee House. 11. *the Rose,* a tavern adjoining Drury Lane Theater.

company than a general scholar; and Sir Andrew having a natural, unaffected eloquence, the perspicuity of his discourse gives the same pleasure that wit would in another man. He has made his fortunes himself and says that England may be richer than other kingdoms by as plain methods as he himself is richer than other men; though at the same time I can say this of him, that there is not a point in the compass but blows home a ship in which he is an owner.

Next to Sir Andrew in the club room sits Captain Sentry, a gentleman of great courage, good understanding, but invincible modesty. He is one of those that deserve very well, but are very awkward at putting their talents within the observation of such as should take notice of them. He was some years a captain and behaved himself with great gallantry in several engagements and at several sieges; but having a small estate of his own, and being next heir to Sir Roger, he has quitted a way of life in which no man can rise suitably to his merit who is not something of a courtier as well as a soldier.

I have heard him often lament that in a profession where merit is placed in so conspicuous a view, impudence should get the better of modesty. When he has talked to this purpose I never heard him make a sour expression, but frankly confess that he left the world because he was not fit for it. A strict honesty and an even, regular behavior are in themselves obstacles to him that must press through crowds who endeavor at the same end with himself—the favor of a commander. He will, however, in this way of talk, excuse generals for not disposing according to men's desert, or inquiring into it. "For," says he, "that great man who has a mind to help me has as many to break through to come at me as I have to come at him." Therefore he will conclude that the man who would make a figure, especially in a military way, must get over all false modesty and assist his patron against the importunity of other pretenders by a proper assurance in his own vindication. He says it is a civil cowardice to be backward in asserting what you ought to expect, as it is a military fear to be slow in attacking when it is your duty.

With this candor does the gentleman speak of himself and others. The same frankness runs through all his conversation. The military part of his life has furnished him with many adventures, in the relation of which he is very agreeable to the company; for he is never overbearing, though accustomed to command men in the utmost degree below him; nor ever too obsequious from an habit of obeying men highly above him.

But that our society may not appear a set of humorists,[12] unacquainted with the gallantries and pleasures of the age, we have among us the gallant Will Honeycomb, a gentleman who according to his years should be in the decline of his life, but having ever been very careful of his person and always had a very easy fortune, time has made but very little impression either by wrinkles on his forehead or traces in his brain. His person is well turned, of a good height. He is very ready at that sort of discourse with which men usually entertain women.

He has all his life dressed very well, and remembers habits[13] as others do men. He can smile when one speaks to him, and laughs easily. He knows the history of every mode and can inform you from which of the French king's wenches our wives and daughters had this manner of curling their hair, that way of placing their hoods; whose frailty was covered by such a sort of petticoat, and whose vanity to show her foot made that part of the dress so short in such a year. In a word, all his conversation and knowledge has been in the female world.

This way of talking of his very much enlivens the conversation among us of a more sedate turn; and I find there is not one of the company but myself, who rarely speak at all, but speaks of him as of that sort of man who is usually called a well-bred, fine gentleman. To conclude his character, where women are not concerned, he is an honest, worthy man.

I cannot tell whether I am to account him whom I am next to speak of as one of our company, for he visits us but seldom; but when he does, it adds to every man else a new enjoy-

---

12. *humorists*, eccentric characters. 13. *habits*, styles.

ment of himself. He is a clergyman, a very philosophic man, of general learning, great sanctity of life, and the most exact good breeding. He has the misfortune to be of a very weak constitution and consequently cannot accept of such cares and business as preferments in his functions would oblige him to. He is therefore among divines what a chamber-counselor[14] is among lawyers. The probity of his mind and the integrity of his life create him followers, as being eloquent or loud advances others. He seldom introduces the subject he speaks upon; but we are so far gone in years that he observes, when he is among us, an earnestness to have him fall on some divine topic, which he always treats with much authority, as one who has no interest in this world, as one who is hastening to the object of all his wishes and conceives hope from his decays and infirmities.

These are my ordinary companions.

WILL WIMBLE

The Spectator, No. 108, July 4, 1711
Joseph Addison

Gratis anhelans, multa agendo nihil agens.[1]

As I was yesterday morning walking with Sir Roger before his house, a country fellow brought him a huge fish, which, he told him, Mr. William Wimble had caught that very morning; and that he presented it, with his service, to him, and intended to come and dine with him. At the same time he delivered a letter, which my friend read to me as soon as the messenger left him.

SIR ROGER:

I desire you to accept of a jack[2] which is the best I have caught this season. I intend to come and stay with you a week and see how the perch bite in the Black River. I observed, with some concern, the last time I saw you upon the bowling green, that your whip wanted a lash to it. I will bring half a dozen with me that I twisted last week, which I hope will serve you all the time you are in the country. I have not been out of the saddle for six days last past, having been at Eton with Sir John's eldest son. He takes to his learning hugely.

I am, Sir, your humble servant,
WILL WIMBLE

This extraordinary letter and message that accompanied it made me very curious to know the character and quality of the gentleman who sent them, which I found to be as follows:

Will Wimble is younger brother to a baronet and descended of the ancient family of the Wimbles. He is now between forty and fifty; but being bred to no business and born to no estate, he generally lives with his elder brother as superintendent of his game. He hunts a pack of dogs better than any man in the country and is very famous for finding out a hare. He is extremely well versed in all the little handicrafts of an idle man. He makes a May fly to a miracle and furnishes the whole country with angle rods. As he is a good-natured, officious[3] fellow and very much esteemed upon account of his family, he is a welcome guest at every house and keeps up a good correspondence among all the gentlemen about him. He carries a tulip root in his pocket from one to another or exchanges a puppy between a couple of friends that live perhaps in the opposite sides of the county.

Will is a particular favorite of all the young heirs, whom he frequently obliges with a net that he has weaved or a setting dog that he has made himself.[4] He now and then presents a pair of garters of his own knitting to their mothers or sisters and raises a great deal of mirth among them by inquiring, as often as he meets them, *how they wear*. These gentlemenlike manufactures and obliging little humors make Will the darling of the country.

Sir Roger was proceeding in the character of him when we saw him make up to us with two or three hazel twigs in his hand that he had cut in Sir Roger's woods as he came

---

THE SPECTATOR CLUB. **14.** *chamber-counselor,* a lawyer who gives opinions in private, but does not appear in court.
WILL WIMBLE. **1.** *Gratis ... agens.* "Out of breath to no purpose, and very busy about nothing," a quotation from a Roman writer of fables. **2.** *jack,* a pike. **3.** *officious,* eager to serve or please. **4.** *made himself,* that he himself has carved.

through them, in his way to the house. I was very much pleased to observe on one side the hearty and sincere welcome with which Sir Roger received him and on the other the secret joy which his guest discovered at sight of the good old knight.

After the first salutes were over, Will desired Sir Roger to lend him one of his servants to carry a set of shuttlecocks he had with him in a little box to a lady that lived about a mile off, to whom it seems he had promised such a present for above this half year. Sir Roger's back was no sooner turned but honest Will began to tell me of a large cock pheasant that he had sprung in one of the neighboring woods, with two or three other adventures of the same nature. Odd and uncommon characters are the game that I look for and most delight in; for which reason I was as much pleased with the novelty of the person that talked to me as he could be for his life with the springing of a pheasant, and therefore listened to him with more than ordinary attention.

In the midst of his discourse the bell rung to dinner, where the gentleman I have been speaking of had the pleasure of seeing the huge jack he had caught served up for the first dish in a most sumptuous manner. Upon our sitting down to it he gave us a long account how he had hooked it, played with it, foiled it, and at length drew it out upon the bank, with several other particulars that lasted all the first course. A dish of wild fowl that came afterwards furnished conversation for the rest of the dinner, which concluded with a late invention of Will's for improving the quail pipe.

Upon withdrawing into my room after dinner I was secretly touched with compassion toward the honest gentleman that had dined with us and could not but consider with a great deal of concern how so good a heart and such busy hands were wholly employed in trifles, that so much humanity should be so little beneficial to others, and so much industry so little advantageous to himself. The same temper of mind and application to affairs might have recommended him to the public esteem and have raised his fortune to another station of life. What good to his country or himself might not a trader or merchant have done with such useful though ordinary qualifications?

Will Wimble's is the case of many a younger brother of a great family, who had rather see their children starve like gentlemen than thrive in a trade or profession that is beneath their quality. This humor fills several parts of Europe with pride and beggary. It is the happiness of a trading nation like ours that the younger sons, though uncapable of any liberal art or profession, may be placed in such a way of life as may perhaps enable them to vie with the best of their family. Accordingly, we find several citizens that were launched into the world with narrow fortunes rising by an honest industry to greater estates than those of their elder brothers. It is not improbable but Will was formerly tried at divinity, law, or physic; and that, finding his genius did not lie that way, his parents gave him up at length to his own inventions. But certainly, however improper he might have been for studies of a higher nature, he was perfectly well turned for the occupations of trade and commerce.

PARTY PATCHES

The Spectator, No. 81, June 2, 1711
Joseph Addison

Qualis ubi audito venantum murmure tigris
Horruit in maculas——[1]

About the middle of last winter I went to see an opera at the theater in the Haymarket, where I could not but take notice of two parties of very fine women that had placed themselves in the opposite side boxes and seemed drawn up in a kind of battle array one against another.

After a short survey of them, I found they were *patched* differently, the faces on one hand being spotted on the right side of the

---

PARTY PATCHES. 1. *Qualis ... maculas.* "Like the tigress when, at the sound of the hunters, spots appear upon her skin," from the Roman poet Statius.

forehead and those upon the other on the left. I quickly perceived that they cast hostile glances upon one another and that their patches were placed in those different situations as party signals to distinguish friends from foes. In the middle boxes between these two opposite bodies were several ladies who patched indifferently on both sides of their faces and seemed to sit there with no other intention but to see the opera.

Upon inquiry I found that the body of Amazons[2] on my right hand were Whigs, and those on my left, Tories; and that those who had placed themselves in the middle boxes were a neutral party, whose faces had not yet declared themselves. These last, however, as I afterwards found, diminished daily, and took their party with one side or the other; insomuch that I observed in several of them the patches which were before dispersed equally are now all gone over to the Whig or Tory side of the face.

The censorious say that the men whose hearts are aimed at are very often the occasions that one part of the face is thus dishonored and lies under a kind of disgrace, while the other is so much set off and adorned by the owner; and that the patches turn to the right or to the left according to the principles of the man who is most in favor. But whatever may be the motives of a few fantastical coquettes, who do not patch for the public good so much as for their own private advantage, it is certain that there are several women of honor who patch out of principle and with an eye to the interest of their country. Nay, I am informed that some of them adhere so steadfastly to their party and are so far from sacrificing their zeal for the public to their passion for any particular person that in a late draft of marriage articles a lady has stipulated with her husband that, whatever his opinions are, she shall be at liberty to patch on which side she pleases.

I must here take notice that Rosalinda, a famous Whig partisan, has most unfortunately a very beautiful mole on the Tory part of her forehead; which, being very conspicuous, has occasioned many mistakes and given a handle to her enemies to misrepresent her face, as though it had revolted from the Whig interest. But, whatever this natural patch may seem to intimate, it is well known that her notions of government are still the same. This unlucky mole, however, has misled several coxcombs and, like the hanging out of false colors, made some of them converse with Rosalinda in what they thought the spirit of her party, when on a sudden she has given them an unexpected fire that has sunk them all at once.

If Rosalinda is unfortunate in her mole, Nigranilla is as unhappy in a pimple, which forces her, against her inclinations, to patch on the Whig side.

I am told that many virtuous matrons, who formerly have been taught to believe that this artificial spotting of the face was unlawful, are now reconciled by a zeal for their cause to what they could not be prompted by a concern for their beauty. This way of declaring war upon one another puts me in mind of what is reported of the tigress, that several spots rise in her skin when she is angry; or, as Mr. Cowley has imitated the verses that stand as the motto of this paper,

> ——She swells with angry pride,
> And calls forth all her spots on ev'ry side.[3]

When I was in the theater the time abovementioned, I had the curiosity to count the patches on both sides, and found the Tory patches to be about twenty stronger than the Whig; but to make amends for this small inequality, I the next morning found the whole puppet show filled with faces spotted after the Whiggish manner. Whether or no the ladies had retreated hither in order to rally their forces I cannot tell; but the next night they came in so great a body to the opera that they outnumbered the enemy.

This account of party patches will, I am afraid, appear improbable to those who live at a distance from the fashionable world; but as it is a distinction of a very singular nature, and what perhaps may never meet with a

2. *Amazons*, an ancient race of female warriors famous in literature for their contests with the Greeks. 3. *She swells . . . side*, from the *Davideis*, an epic poem by the seventeenth-century poet Abraham Cowley.

parallel, I think I should not have discharged the office of a faithful Spectator had I not recorded it.

I have, in former papers, endeavored to expose this party-rage in women, as it only serves to aggravate the hatreds and animosities that reign among men, and in a great measure deprives the fair sex of those peculiar charms with which nature has endowed them.

When the Romans and Sabines[4] were at war and just upon the point of giving battle, the women who were allied to both of them interposed with so many tears and entreaties that they prevented the mutual slaughter which threatened both parties and united them together in a firm and lasting peace.

I would recommend this noble example to our British ladies at a time when their country is torn with so many unnatural divisions that if they continue it will be a misfortune to be born in it. The Greeks thought it so improper for women to interest themselves in competitions and contentions that for this reason, among others, they forbade them, under pain of death, to be present at the Olympic games, notwithstanding these were the public diversions of all Greece.

As our English women excel those of all nations in beauty, they should endeavor to outshine them in all other accomplishments proper to the sex and to distinguish themselves as tender mothers and faithful wives rather than as furious partisans. Female virtues are of a domestic turn. The family is the proper province for private women to shine in. If they must be showing their zeal for the public, let it not be against those who are perhaps of the same family, or at least of the same religion or nation, but against those who are the open, professed, undoubted enemies of their faith, liberty, and country.

When the Romans were pressed with a foreign enemy, the ladies voluntarily contributed all their rings and jewels to assist the government under a public exigence, which appeared so laudable an action in the eyes of their countrymen that from thenceforth it was permitted by a law to pronounce public orations at the funeral of a woman in praise of the deceased person, which till that time was peculiar to men. Would our English ladies, instead of sticking on a patch against those of their own country, show themselves so truly public-spirited as to sacrifice every one her necklace against the common enemy, what decrees ought not to be made in favor of them?

Since I am recollecting upon this subject such passages as occur to my memory out of ancient authors, I cannot omit a sentence in the celebrated funeral oration of Pericles,[5] which he made in honor of those brave Athenians that were slain in a fight with the Lacedaemonians.[6] After having addressed himself to the several ranks and orders of his countrymen, and shown them how they should behave themselves in the public cause, he turns to the female part of his audience: "And as for you (says he) I shall advise you in very few words: Aspire only to those virtues that are peculiar to your sex; follow your natural modesty, and think it your greatest commendation not to be talked of one way or other."

---

4. *Romans and Sabines.* The Sabines were an ancient people living in central Italy who were conquered by the Romans. 5. *Pericles* (per′ə klēz), 490?-429 B.C., Athenian statesman, orator, and military commander. 6. *Lacedaemonians* (las′ə di mo′ni ənz), Spartans. Sparta was the great rival of Athens among the ancient Greek cities.

❈ To increase understanding

1. (a) What was the purpose of Addison and Steele in writing the *Tatler* and *Spectator* papers? (b) How is this purpose carried out in the three *Spectator* papers you have read?

2. (a) Describe Sir Roger de Coverley. (b) Characterize the other members of the Spectator Club. (c) How does the attitude of Addison and Steele toward Sir Roger differ from their attitude toward the other members of the Club? (d) How does this difference reflect the changing positions of the English aristocracy and the English middle class?

3. In what way is Will Wimble a typical product of eighteenth-century English society?

4. Compare the paper by Steele with the papers by Addison. Which man do you find more kindly and humorous, which more severe and serious? Cite passages to support your answer.

5. (a) Compare the members of the Spectator Club with Chaucer's pilgrims of corresponding occupations. (b) Which group of characters seem individuals to you and which seem types? (c) How would you account for this difference?

Daniel Defoe 1659-1731

Defoe was first and foremost a journalist. His *Review*, which came out three times a week between 1704 and 1713, is regarded as the first English newspaper (Steele's *Tatler* did not appear until 1709). During the last twenty years of his life Defoe turned from writing news to writing stories, but even these reveal the hand of an expert press reporter. *Robinson Crusoe*, which has become the most famous fictional account of the ship-wrecked man on a desert island, is written with such careful attention to concrete detail and in such a straightforward manner that it sounds like factual truth. The same qualities make *A Journal of the Plague Year* sound like an eyewitness account of the Great Plague of London, although it occurred in 1665 when Defoe was but a child.

Defoe's passion for the issues of the day and his liberal outlook often made him a center of controversy. He defended William of Orange against those who thought that only a pure-blooded Englishman should be King, and he spoke up against the Church of England's intolerance of dissenters. (While in the pillory for this last offense, Defoe was pelted with flowers by friends who sang the poem he had written for the occasion entitled "Hymn to the Pillory.") In his *Essay on Projects* Defoe showed that he was far ahead of his time by proposing a host of practical schemes for social progress, among them an academy for the higher education of women.

THE EDUCATION OF WOMEN

I have often thought of it as one of the most barbarous customs in the world, considering us as a civilized and a Christian country, that we deny the advantages of learning to women. We reproach the sex every day with folly and impertinence, while I am confident, had they the advantages of education equal to us, they would be guilty of less than ourselves.

One would wonder, indeed, how it should happen that women are conversable at all, since they are only beholding to natural parts for all their knowledge. Their youth is spent to teach them to stitch and sew or make baubles. They are taught to read, indeed, and perhaps to write their names or so, and that is the height of a woman's education. And I would but ask any who slight the sex for their understanding, what is a man (a gentleman, I mean) good for that is taught no more?

I need not give instances or examine the character of a gentleman with a good estate and of a good family and with tolerable parts, and examine what figure he makes for want of education.

The soul is placed in the body like a rough diamond and must be polished, or the luster of it will never appear; and 'tis manifest that as the rational soul distinguishes us from brutes, so education carries on the distinction and makes some less brutish than others. This is too evident to need any demonstration. But why then should women be denied the benefit of instruction? If knowledge and understanding had been useless additions to the sex, God

Almighty would never have given them capacities, for He made nothing needless. Besides, I would ask such what they can see in ignorance that they should think it a necessary ornament to a woman? or how much worse is a wise woman than a fool? or what has the woman done to forfeit the privilege of being taught? Does she plague us with her pride and impertinence? Why did we not let her learn, that she might have had more wit? Shall we upbraid women with folly, when 'tis only the error of this inhuman custom that hindered them being made wiser?

The capacities of women are supposed to be greater and their senses quicker than those of the men; and what they might be capable of being bred to is plain from some instances of female wit, which this age is not without; which upbraids us with injustice, and looks as if we denied women the advantages of education for fear they should vie with the men in their improvements.

To remove this objection, and that women might have at least a needful opportunity of education in all sorts of useful learning, I propose the draft of an academy for that purpose. . . .

The academy I propose would differ but little from public schools,[1] wherein such ladies as were willing to study should have all the advantages of learning suitable to their genius. But since some severities of discipline more than ordinary would be absolutely necessary to preserve the reputation of the house, that persons of quality and fortune might not be afraid to venture their children thither, I shall venture to make a small scheme by way of essay.

The house I would have built in a form by itself, as well as in a place by itself. The building should be of three plain fronts, without any jettings or bearing-work,[2] that the eye might at a glance see from one coign to the other; the gardens walled in the same triangular figure, with a large moat, and but one entrance. When thus every part of the situation was contrived as well as might be for discovery, and to render intriguing dangerous, I would have no guards, no eyes, no spies set over the ladies, but shall expect them to be tried by the principles of honor and strict virtue. . . .

In this house, the persons who enter should be taught all sorts of breeding suitable both to their genius and quality, and in particular, music and dancing, which it would be cruelty to bar the sex of, because they are their darlings; but besides this, they should be taught languages, as particularly French and Italian; and I would venture the injury of giving a woman more tongues than one. They should, as a particular study, be taught all the graces of speech and all the necessary air of conversation, which our common education is so defective in that I need not expose it. They should be brought to read books, and especially history; and so to read as to make them understand the world and be able to know and judge of things when they hear of them.

To such whose genius would lead them to it, I would deny no sort of learning; but the chief thing, in general, is to cultivate the understandings of the sex, that they may be capable of all sorts of conversation; that, their parts and judgments being improved, they may be as profitable in their conversation as they are pleasant.

Women, in my observation, have little or no difference in them, but as they are or are not distinguished by education. Tempers, indeed, may in some degree influence them, but the main distinguishing part is their breeding.

The whole sex are generally quick and sharp. I believe I may be allowed to say generally so, for you rarely see them lumpish and heavy when they are children, as boys will often be. If a woman be well-bred, and taught the proper management of her natural wit, she proves generally very sensible and retentive; and without partiality, a woman of sense and manners is the finest and most delicate part of God's creation, the glory of her Maker, and the great instance of His singular regard to man, His darling creature, to whom

---

1. *public schools.* British public schools, such as Rugby and Eton, are what Americans would call private schools. 2. *jettings or bearing-work.* Jettings were parts jutting out from the perpendicular walls; bearing-works were the supports for these parts.

He gave the best gift either God could bestow or man receive. And 'tis the sordidest piece of folly and ingratitude in the world to withhold from the sex the due luster which the advantage of education gives to the natural beauty of their minds.

A woman well-bred and well taught, furnished with the additional accomplishments of knowledge and behavior, is a creature without comparison; her society is the emblem of sublimer enjoyments; her person is angelic and her conversation heavenly; she is all softness and sweetness, peace, love, wit, and delight. She is every way suitable to the sublimest wish, and the man that has such a one to his portion has nothing to do but rejoice in her and be thankful.

On the other hand, suppose her to be the very same woman, and rob her of the benefit of education, and it follows thus:

If her temper be good, want of education makes her soft and easy. Her wit, for want of teaching, makes her impertinent and talkative. Her knowledge, for want of judgment and experience, makes her fanciful and whimsical. If her temper be bad, want of breeding makes her worse, and she grows haughty, insolent, and loud. If she be passionate, want of manners makes her termagant and a scold, which is much at one with lunatic. If she be proud, want of discretion (which still is breeding) makes her conceited, fantastic, and ridiculous. And from these she degenerates to be turbulent, clangorous, noisy, nasty, and the devil.

Methinks mankind for their own sakes— since, say what we will of the women, we all think fit at one time or other to be concerned with them—should take some care to breed them up to be suitable and serviceable, if they expected no such thing as delight from them. Bless us! what care do we take to breed up a good horse and to break him well! and what a value do we put upon him when it is done, and all because he should be fit for our use! and why not a woman? Since all her ornaments and beauty without suitable behavior is a cheat in nature, like the false tradesman who puts the best of his goods uppermost, that the buyer may think the rest are of the same goodness. . . .

The great distinguishing difference which is seen in the world between men and women is in their education, and this is manifested by comparing it with the difference between one man or woman and another.

And herein it is that I take upon me to make such a bold assertion that all the world are mistaken in their practice about women; for I cannot think that God Almighty ever made them so delicate, so glorious creatures, and furnished them with such charms, so agreeable and so delightful to mankind, with souls capable of the same accomplishments with men, and all to be only stewards of our houses, cooks, and slaves.

Not that I am for exalting the female government in the least; but, in short, I would have men take women for companions, and educate them to be fit for it. A woman of sense and breeding will scorn as much to encroach upon the prerogative of the man as a man of sense will scorn to oppress the weakness of the woman. But if the women's souls were refined and improved by teaching, that word would be lost; to say the *weakness of the sex* as to judgment would be nonsense, for ignorance and folly would be no more found among women than men. I remember a passage which I heard from a very fine woman. She had wit and capacity enough, an extraordinary shape and face, and a great fortune, but had been cloistered up all her time, and, for fear of being stolen, had not had the liberty of being taught the common necessary knowledge of women's affairs. And when she came to converse in the world, her natural wit made her so sensible of the want of education that she gave this short reflection on herself: "I am ashamed to talk with my very maids," says she, "for I don't know when they do right or wrong. I had more need go to school than be married."

I need not enlarge on the loss the defect of education is to the sex, nor argue the benefit of the contrary practice; 'tis a thing will be more easily granted than remedied. This chapter is but an essay at the thing, and I refer the practice to those happy days, if ever they shall be, when men shall be wise enough to mend it.

To increase understanding

1. (a) Describe the physical aspects of Defoe's proposed academy for women. (b) Of what would the course of study consist? (c) Cite passages that show Defoe's interest in concrete detail.

2. (a) How do Defoe's ideas about women differ from those of Addison as expressed in "Party Patches"? (b) How are they similar?

3. (a) What, according to Defoe, is the chief aim of education? (b) How does Defoe's aim differ from that of Sir Francis Bacon in "Of Studies" (page 186)? (c) How are Bacon's ideas typical of the Elizabethan or humanistic outlook on life? (d) How do Defoe's ideas fit in with the Augustan outlook on life?

Words!

Eighteenth-century writers were fond of using "big," formal-sounding words in place of smaller, less dignified ones. However, they also had a tendency to place these words in such a way in long, formal sentences that the context helped to make their meaning clear. Listed are five sentences from the selections by Addison, Steele, and Defoe. Try to gain at least a partial meaning of the italicized words in each from their use in context. Then check your definitions against those in the Glossary for a more precise meaning.

1. A general trader of good sense is pleasanter company than a general scholar; and Sir Andrew having a natural, unaffected eloquence, the *perspicuity* of his discourse gives the same pleasure that wit would in another man.

2. Therefore he will conclude that the man who would make a figure, especially in a military way, must get over all false modesty and assist his patron against the *importunity* of other pretenders by a proper assurance in his own *vindication*.

3. The *censorious* say that the men whose hearts are aimed at are very often the occasions that one part of the face is thus dishonored and lies under a kind of disgrace, while the other is so much set off and adorned by the owner.

4. When the Romans were pressed with a foreign enemy, the ladies voluntarily contributed all their rings and jewels to assist the government under a public *exigence*. . . .

5. A woman of sense and breeding will scorn as much to encroach upon the *prerogative* of the man as a man of sense will scorn to oppress the weakness of the woman.

Jonathan Swift 1667-1745

Charles Jervas, a student of Kneller and a tutor of Alexander Pope, executed this portrait of Swift.

One of the most tragic figures in English literature is the eighteenth-century satirist Jonathan Swift. As a product of the Enlightenment, Swift believed strongly in the idea of men living together in a society that functioned as harmoniously and as reasonably as Newton's universe. As a sensitive observer, however, Swift saw that eighteenth-century English society was filled with corruption, brutality, and ignorance. This disparity between what ought to be and what *was*, plus an overwhelming sense of frustrated ambition, led Swift to lash out at the world with a bitterness unequaled by any other English satirist.

Born in Ireland of a distinguished but penniless English family, Swift lived first on the charity of his uncle and then, after a period of study at Trinity College, Dublin, he served as secretary (with servant status) in the household of Sir William Temple in London. Hoping for political preferment from the Tories, who were in power during the reign of Queen Anne, Swift worked his way to a position of high eminence in the newly powerful London press by means of many excellent pamphlets and essays. When the Tories fell from power after the death of Queen Anne, Swift's chances for political office fell with them and he returned to Ireland a bitterly disillusioned man. There he devoted himself to writing and to his work as Dean of St. Patrick's Cathedral, Dublin (Church of England), a post that had been bestowed upon him under Queen Anne.

The only light in Swift's dark, self-tortured life was his deep love for a young woman named Esther Johnson, who was the recipient of the often embarrassingly tender letters contained in the *Journal to Stella*. (*Esther* is the Hebrew for *star*, *Stella* the Latin.) Soon after Esther died, the once brilliant Swift fell prey to a madness from which he never recovered. "To think of him," said the nineteenth-century novelist Thackeray, "is like thinking of the ruin of a great empire."

Ironically enough, the work that contains Swift's most savage satire has become a favorite book with children. *Gulliver's Travels*, published in 1726, is filled with such marvelous inventions—little people six inches high, giants, flying islands, talking horses—and its narrative is so vivid and direct that generations of younger readers have looked upon it as a wonderful adventure story. Actually, Swift used his marvelous inventions to level a devastating attack on the pettiness, grossness, and folly of humanity in general and eighteenth-century Englishmen in particular. In Book One, the shipwrecked Captain Gulliver finds himself in the country of Lilliput, whose citizenry appear ridiculous to him because of their tiny size. In Book Two, the situation is reversed; it is Gulliver who appears ridiculous in the land of the giant Brobdingnags. The third voyage takes the sea captain to Laputa and other countries which are inhabited by hopelessly scatterbrained scholars, scientists, philosophers, inventors, and professors, one of whom has devoted eight years to the project of extracting sunbeams from cucumbers. Gulliver then proceeds to the country of the Houyhnhnms, where reasonable horses govern and where the filthy, debased humans or Yahoos serve.

The following episode occurs early in the voyage to Lilliput. Gulliver has been shipwrecked, captured by the little people just six inches high, brought before their king, and housed in an ancient temple, which is the only building big enough for him.

This painting is by Samuel Scott, who at one time collaborated with Hogarth (see page 284). It shows London as it was in Swift's time. In the foreground can be seen the rebuilding of Westminster Bridge.

from GULLIVER'S TRAVELS

My gentleness and good behavior had gained so far on the Emperor and his court, and indeed upon the army and people in general, that I began to conceive hopes of getting my liberty in a short time. I took all possible methods to cultivate this favorable disposition. The natives came, by degrees, to be less apprehensive of any danger from me. I would sometimes lie down and let five or six of them dance on my hand; and, at the last, the boys and girls would venture to come and play at hide and seek in my hair. I had now made a good progress in understanding and speaking their language.

The Emperor had a mind, one day, to entertain me with several of the country shows, wherein they exceed all nations I have known, both for dexterity and magnificence. I was diverted with none so much as that of the rope-dancers performed upon a slender white thread, extended about two feet, and twelve inches from the ground. Upon which I shall desire liberty to enlarge a little.

This diversion is only practiced by those persons who are candidates for great employments and high favor at court. They are trained in this art from their youth, and are not always of noble birth, or liberal education. When a great office is vacant, either by death or disgrace (which often happens), five or six of those candidates petition the Emperor to entertain his Majesty and the court with a dance on the rope, and whoever jumps the highest, without falling, succeeds in the office.

Very often the chief ministers themselves are commanded to show their skill, and to convince the Emperor that they have not lost their faculty. Flimnap,[1] the treasurer, is allowed to cut a caper on the straight rope at least an inch higher than any other lord in the whole empire. I have seen him do the somersault several times together, upon a trencher fixed on the rope, which is no thicker than a common packthread in England. My friend Reldresal, principal secretary for private affairs, is, in my opinion, if I am not partial, the second after the treasurer; the rest of the great officers are much upon a par.

These diversions are often attended with fatal accidents, whereof great numbers are on record. I myself have seen two or three candidates break a limb. But the danger is much greater when the ministers themselves are commanded to show their dexterity; for, by contending to excel themselves and their fellows, they strain so far that there is hardly one of them who hath not received a fall, and some of them two or three. I was assured that, a year or two before my arrival, Flimnap would have infallibly broken his neck if one of the king's cushions, that accidentally lay on the ground, had not weakened the force of his fall.

There is likewise another diversion, which is only shown before the Emperor and Empress, and first minister, upon particular occasions. The Emperor lays on the table three fine silken threads of six inches long; one is blue, the other red, and the third green.[2] These threads are proposed as prizes for those persons whom the Emperor hath a mind to distinguish by a peculiar mark of his favor. The ceremony is performed in his Majesty's great chamber of state, where the candidates are to undergo a trial of dexterity very different from the former, and such as I have not observed the least resemblance of in any other country of the Old or New World. The Emperor holds a stick in his hands, both ends parallel to the horizon, while the candidates advancing, one by one, sometimes leap over the stick, sometimes creep under it backwards and forwards several times, according as the stick is advanced or depressed. Sometimes the Emperor holds one end of the stick, and his first minister the other; sometimes the minister has it entirely to himself. Whoever performs his part with most agility, and holds out the longest in leaping and creeping, is rewarded with the blue-colored silk, the red is given to the next, and the green to the third, which they all wear girt twice around about the middle.

1. *Flimnap*, a reference to Sir Robert Walpole, who was at one time First Lord of the Treasury. (See page 248.)
2. *The Emperor . . . green.* The three threads refer to the badges for the Order of the Garter, the Order of the Bath, and the Order of the Thistle.

The horses of the army, and those of the royal stables, having been daily led before me, were no longer shy, but would come up to my very feet without starting. The riders would leap them over my hand as I held it on the ground, and one of the Emperor's huntsmen, upon a large courser, took my foot, shoe and all: which was, indeed, a prodigious leap.

I had the good fortune to divert the Emperor, one day, after a very extraordinary manner. I desired he would order several sticks of two feet high, and the thickness of an ordinary cane, to be brought me; whereupon his Majesty commanded the master of his woods to give directions accordingly, and the next morning six woodsmen arrived with as many carriages, drawn by eight horses to each. I took nine of these sticks, and fixing them firmly in the ground, in a quadrangular figure, two feet and a half square, I took four other sticks, and tied them parallel at each corner, about two feet from the ground; then I fastened my handkerchief to the nine sticks that stood erect, and extended it on all sides till it was as tight as the top of a drum; and the four parallel sticks, rising about five inches higher than the handkerchief, served as ledges on each side.

When I had finished my work, I desired the Emperor to let a troop of his best horses, twenty-four in number, come and exercise upon this plain. His Majesty approved of the proposal, and I took them up one by one in my hands, ready mounted and armed, with the proper officers to exercise them. As soon as they got in order, they divided into two parties, performed mock skirmishes, discharged blunt arrows, drew their swords, fled and pursued, attacked and retired, and in short discovered the best military discipline I ever beheld. The parallel sticks secured them and their horses from falling over the stage; and the Emperor was so much delighted that he ordered this entertainment to be repeated several days, and once was pleased to be lifted up, and give the word of command; and, with great difficulty, persuaded even the Empress herself to let me hold her in her close chair within two yards of the stage, from whence she was able to view the whole performance.

It was by good fortune that no ill accident happened in these entertainments; only once a fiery horse, that belonged to one of the captains, pawing with his hoof, struck a hole in my handkerchief, and his foot slipping, he overthrew his rider and himself; but I immediately relieved them both, and covering the hole with one hand, I set down the troop with the other, in the same manner as I took them up. The horse that fell was strained in the left shoulder, but the rider got no hurt, and I repaired my handkerchief as well as I could; however, I would not trust to the strength of it any more in such dangerous enterprises.

About two or three days before I was set at liberty,[3] there arrived an express to inform his Majesty that some of his subjects, riding near where I was first taken up, had seen a great black substance lying on the ground, very oddly shaped, extending its edges round as wide as his Majesty's bedchamber, and rising up in the middle as high as a man; that, by mounting upon each other's shoulders, they had got to the top, which was flat and even, and, stamping upon it, they found it was hollow; that they humbly conceived it might be something belonging to the Man-Mountain, and, if his Majesty pleased, they would undertake to bring it with only five horses.

I presently knew what they meant, and was glad at heart to receive this intelligence. It seems upon my first reaching the shore, after our shipwreck, I was in such confusion that, before I came to the place where I went to sleep, my hat, which I had fastened with a string to my head while I was rowing, and had stuck on all the time I was swimming, fell off after I came to land; the string, as I conjecture, breaking by some accident which I never observed, but thought my hat had been lost at sea. I entreated his Imperial Majesty to give orders it might be brought to me as soon as possible, describing to him the use and nature of it; and the next day the wagoners arrived with it, but not in a very good condition; they had bored two holes in the brim, within an inch and a half of the edge, and fastened two hooks in the holes; these hooks were tied by a long cord to the harness,

3. *before I was set at liberty.* The Lilliputians had chained Gulliver's left leg.

and thus my hat was dragged along for above half an English mile; but, the ground in that country being extremely smooth and level, it received less damage than I expected.

I had sent so many memorials and petitions for my liberty that his Majesty at length mentioned the matter first in the cabinet, and then in a full council, where it was opposed by none, except Skyresh Bolgolam, who was pleased, without any provocation, to be my mortal enemy. But it was carried against him by the whole board, and confirmed by the Emperor. That minister was *galbet*, or admiral of the realm, very much in his master's confidence, and a person well versed in affairs, but of a morose and sour complexion.[4] However, he was at length persuaded to comply; but prevailed that the articles and conditions upon which I should be set free, and to which I must swear, should be drawn up by himself. These articles were brought to me by Skyresh Bolgolam in person, attended by two under-secretaries, and several persons of distinction.

After they were read, I was demanded to swear to the performance of them; first in the manner of my own country, and afterwards in the method described by their laws, which was to hold my right foot in my left hand and to place the middle finger of my right hand on the crown of my head, and my thumb on the tip of my right ear. But, because the reader may be curious to have some idea of the style and manner of expression peculiar to that people, as well as to know the articles upon which I recovered my liberty, I have made a translation of the whole instrument, word for word, as near as I was able, which I here offer.

"GOLBASTO MOMAREN EVLAME GURDILO SHEFIN MULLY ULLY GUE, most mighty Emperor of Lilliput, delight and terror of the universe, whose dominions extend five thousand *blustrugs* (about twelve miles in circumference), to the extremities of the globe; monarch of all monarchs, taller than the sons of men; whose feet press down to the center, and whose head strikes against the sun; at whose nod the princes of the earth shake their knees; pleasant as the spring, comfortable as the summer, fruitful as autumn, dreadful as winter. His most sublime Majesty proposeth to the Man-Mountain, lately arrived to our celestial dominions, the following articles, which, by a solemn oath, he shall be obliged to perform:

"1st. The Man-Mountain shall not depart from our dominions without our license under our great seal.

"2d. He shall not presume to come into our metropolis without our express order; at which time the inhabitants shall have two hours of warning to keep within their doors.

"3d. The said Man-Mountain shall confine his walks to our principal high roads, and not offer to walk or lie down in a meadow or field of corn.

"4th. As he walks the said roads, he shall take the utmost care not to trample upon the bodies of any of our loving subjects, their horses, or carriages, nor take any of our subjects into his hands without their own consent.

"5th. If an express requires extraordinary dispatch, the Man-Mountain shall be obliged to carry in his pocket the messenger and horse a six days' journey once in every moon, and return the said messenger back (if so required) safe to our imperial presence.

"6th. He shall be our ally against our enemies in the Island of Blefuscu,[5] and do his utmost to destroy their fleet, which is now preparing to invade us.

"7th. That the said Man-Mountain shall, at his times of leisure, be aiding and assisting our workmen, in helping to raise certain great stones, toward covering the wall of the principal park, and other of our royal buildings.

"8th. That the said Man-Mountain shall, in two moons' time, deliver an exact survey of the circumference of our dominions, by a computation of his own paces around the coast.

"Lastly, That, upon his solemn oath to observe all the above articles, the said Man-Mountain shall have a daily allowance of meat and drink sufficient for the support of 1728 of our subjects, with free access to our royal person, and other marks of our favor. Given at our palace at Belfaborac, the twelfth day of the ninety-first moon of our reign."

I swore and subscribed to these articles with great cheerfulness and content, although some

4. *complexion*, disposition. 5. *Blefuscu*, a reference to France.

of them were not so honorable as I could have wished, which proceeded wholly from the malice of Skyresh Bolgolam, the high admiral; whereupon my chains were immediately unlocked, and I was at full liberty. The Emperor himself in person did me the honor to be by at the whole ceremony. I made my acknowledgments by prostrating myself at his Majesty's feet, but he commanded me to rise; and after many gracious expressions, which, to avoid the censure of vanity, I shall not repeat, he added that he hoped I should prove a useful servant, and well deserve all the favors he had already conferred upon me, or might do for the future.

The reader may please to observe that, in the last article for the recovery of my liberty, the Emperor stipulates to allow me a quantity of meat and drink sufficient for the support of 1728 Lilliputians. Some time after, asking a friend at court how they came to fix on that determinate number, he told me that his Majesty's mathematicians, having taken the height of my body by the help of a quadrant, and finding it to exceed theirs in the proportion of twelve to one, they concluded, from the similarity of their bodies, that mine must contain, at least 1728 of theirs, and, consequently, would require as much food as was necessary to support that number of Lilliputians. By which, the reader may conceive an idea of the ingenuity of that people, as well as the prudent and exact economy of so great a prince.

To increase understanding

1. Review the following episodes in the selection from *Gulliver's Travels*: the dancers on the "slender white thread"; the contest for the blue, red, and green threads; the horsemen on Gulliver's handkerchief; Gulliver's hat; and the proclamation concerning Gulliver's release. (a) Why would these episodes appeal to young readers? (b) How would they have been read by adults in the eighteenth century?

2. What is the irony of the remarks "I repaired my handkerchief as well as I could; however, I would not trust to the strength of it any more in such dangerous enterprises" (page 266, column 2, lines 10-13); and "most mighty Emperor of Lilliput, delight and terror of the universe" (page 267, column 1, paragraph 3)?

Better reading

Satire

Just as the Elizabethan Age was the great age of lyric and dramatic poetry, so the eighteenth century was the great age of satire. There were several reasons why this was so. The eighteenth century was the time when the rational model of the universe elaborated by Newton and his fellow scientists began to capture the imaginations of ordinary men and to persuade them that perhaps society could be made over according to similarly reasonable, well-functioning models. Satire was one way of pointing up how irrational society actually was. The eighteenth century was also a time when men were sharply divided on political, religious, and personal issues, and writers of satire proved useful in attacking and defending various people and ideas. Finally, most of the writers of the eighteenth century saw themselves as the guardians of civilization and in certain instances as the victims of the cruelty and barbarism of the age. They were eager to ridicule anyone—especially the awkward and ignorant members of the newly arrived middle class—who did not measure up to the refined standard of morality of the London coffee houses.

Unlike writers of pure fiction whose primary aim is to create a world of the imagination in which readers may lose themselves, satirists are mainly concerned with having some direct effect on this world of here and now. Their aim may be to discredit their personal enemies, or to eliminate certain social institutions or conventions, or they may level their attack against the callousness, egotism, and cruelty of human society in general. The tone of their attack depends largely on the extent of their outrage. Some satirists are content to criticize merely by poking fun in the spirit of light comedy. Others feel compelled to wound with malicious barbs of wit and sarcasm or to lash out at the world with intense and bitter irony. Despite the frequently topical, newslike character of its subject matter, satire has proved to be an enduring form of literature, for it satisfies the human desire not only to disapprove but to disapprove with stinging wit and force.

To what extent is Swift's satire in the selection from *Gulliver's Travels* an attack on specific individuals and specific social conventions? To what extent is it an attack on mankind in general?

Why is the presence of a Man-Mountain among tiny people a particularly effective satirical device?

What is the tone of Swift's satire?

Compare Addison, Steele, and Swift as satirists. How do they differ in intention? How do they differ in tone? Which satirist probably had the greatest effect on his audience and why?

Lord Chesterfield 1694-1773

Portrait by William Hoare (see caption on next page).

Another critic of eighteenth-century society was Philip Stanhope, Lord Chesterfield. Unlike Addison and Steele, Defoe, and Swift, Chesterfield belonged to the old courtly aristocracy, whose power was steadily diminishing but whose pride remained solidly intact. After a short time at Cambridge and the traditional Continental tour, Chesterfield took his father's place in the House of Lords, where he became an influential leader, even against the powerful prime minister Walpole. He joined the ranks of authors in his *Letters* addressed to his son. Like so many of his contemporaries, Chesterfield regarded the rituals and conventions of society as the sole concern of man. "The epithet I should covet the most," he remarked, "would be that of well-bred." It is this emphasis on manners and fashions that gives unity to Chesterfield's letters and that makes them one of the most perfect expressions of Augustan formality and sophistication.

THE EDUCATION OF A GENTLEMAN

November 9, 1745

Now that the Christmas breaking-up draws near, I have ordered Mr. Desnoyers to go to you, during that time, to teach you to dance. I desire that you will particularly attend to the graceful motion of your arms; which with the manner of putting on your hat, and giving your hand, is all that a gentleman need attend to.

Dancing is in itself a very trifling, silly thing; but it is one of those established follies to which people of sense are sometimes obliged to conform; and then they should be able to do it well. And though I would not have you a dancer, yet when you do dance, I would have you dance well; as I would have you do everything you do, well. There is no one thing so trifling, but which (if it is to be done at all) ought to be done well; and I have often told you that I wish you even played at pitch and cricket better than any boy at Westminster.

For instance, dress is a very foolish thing; and yet it is a very foolish thing for a man not to be well dressed, according to his rank and way of life; and it is so far from being disparagement to any man's understanding, that it is rather a proof of it, to be as well dressed as those whom he lives with. The difference in this case between a man of sense and a fop is that the fop values himself upon his dress; and the man of sense laughs at it, at the same time that he knows he must not neglect it.

There are a thousand foolish customs of this kind, which not being criminal, must be complied with, and even cheerfully, by men of sense. Diogenes the cynic[1] was a wise man for despising them; but a fool for showing it. Be wiser than other people if you can; but do not tell them so.

---

1. *Diogenes* (dī oj'ə nēz) *the cynic.* The Cynics were a group of ancient Greek philosophers who taught that self-control is the essential part of virtue. They despised pleasure, money, and personal comfort.

To increase understanding

1. (*a*) What were some of the accomplishments expected of an eighteenth-century gentleman? (*b*) In what, according to Lord Chesterfield, did the importance of these accomplishments lie?
2. How does Lord Chesterfield's idea of a gentleman differ from the gentlemanly ideal of Elizabethan times?

Alexander Pope 1688-1744

Crayon portrait of Pope, attributed to William Hoare, who is reputed to be the first English artist to study in Rome. He was one of the original members of the Royal Academy of Art.

Pope was a hunchback in an age which took great delight in laughing at all kinds of deformity. He was a Roman Catholic at a time when Catholics could neither attend universities nor hold public office. And he was a commoner in a society that did not pay too much attention to a man without a title. With such provocation, it is no wonder that Pope came to be known as "the wicked wasp of Twickenham." By the time he was seventeen, he had equipped himself with such immense learning that the aging literary dictators of John Dryden's generation were forced to admit him to their company. While still a young man in his twenties, he demonstrated a gift for satire which, unlike the kindly criticism of Steele and the white-hot anger of Swift, had a malicious, rapierlike quality. Pope's satirical writings and his scholarly works were so much in demand (particularly his translation of Homer's *Iliad*) that by the age of thirty he had acquired enough money to retire with his parents to Twickenham on the Thames River. Here he spent the rest of his life engaged in landscape gardening, writing, and receiving visits from Swift and other prominent Tories.

As a poet, Pope has been called the high priest and magistrate of the Age of Reason. His poems were such perfect embodiments of the eighteenth-century's poetic rules and regulations that they became the fixed models for anyone aspiring to literary fame. His first important poem, *An Essay on Criticism* (1711), is a neat exposition of the eighteenth century's three basic rules for poetry: (1) Follow "nature"; write about things that are common to all people at all times; do not write about things that are uncommon, or odd, or strange in any way. (2) Imitate the poems of the ancient Greeks and Romans, especially those of Homer, Vergil, and Horace. (3) State the general truths of life with greater control and polish than any previous writer has done. In *An Essay on Criticism*, Pope achieved the control and polish he so admired by using heroic couplets (pairs of rhyming iambic pentameter lines) as the basic units of expression and by working and reworking each couplet until it glittered with precision.

All of Pope's poems can be understood in terms of the rules contained in *An Essay on Criticism*. For example, *The Rape of the Lock* (1712, 1714), which was his second important work, deals with the general conflict between men and women: a young man cuts a lock of hair from the head of a young lady who greatly resents the liberty. To point up the silliness of the quarrel, which was based on an actual incident in Augustan society, Pope developed it in exactly the same way that Homer and Vergil had developed truly great conflicts in their epic poems (thus creating what is known as a *mock epic*). More than any other of Pope's poems, *The Rape of the Lock* dazzled readers with a display of brilliantly manipulated heroic couplets.

Next to Shakespeare, Pope is the most frequently quoted of

English poets. "To err is human; to forgive divine." "A little learning is a dangerous thing." "Hope springs eternal in the human breast." "The proper study of mankind is man." "Fools rush in where angels fear to tread." These and many other lines from Pope have taken their place in the body of English proverbs. In part this is due to Pope's ability to express a complete thought or feeling in a tightly wrapped line or couplet. In part it is due to his preoccupation with the moral sentiments of Augustan society, which are neatly summed up in his last important poem, *An Essay on Man* (1733). It is also due to his unrivaled gift for the kind of satire that is so sharp and sure that even its victims are forced into admiration.

from AN ESSAY ON CRITICISM

[*from Part I*]

T is hard to say, if greater want of skill
Appear in writing or in judging ill;
But, of the two, less dangerous is th' offense
To tire our patience than mislead our sense.
Some few in that, but numbers err in this,   5
Ten censure wrong for one who writes amiss.
A fool might once himself alone expose;
Now one in verse makes many more in prose.
'Tis with our judgments as our watches; none
Go just alike, yet each believes his own.   10
In poets as true genius is but rare,
True taste as seldom is the critic's share;
Both must alike from heaven derive their light,
These born to judge, as well as those to write.
Let such teach others who themselves excel,   15
And censure freely who have written well.
Authors are partial to their wit, 'tis true,
But are not critics to their judgment, too?

. . . .

First follow nature, and your judgment frame
By her just standard, which is still the same; 20
Unerring nature, still divinely bright,
One clear, unchanged, and universal light,
Life, force, and beauty, must to all impart,
At once the source, and end, and test of Art.
Art from that fund each just supply provides,
Works without show, and without pomp
     presides.   26

In some fair body thus th' informing[1] soul
With spirits feeds, with vigor fills the whole,
Each motion guides, and every nerve sustains;
Itself unseen, but in th' effects, remains.   30
Some, to whom Heaven in wit[2] has been profuse,
Want as much more,[3] to turn it to its use;
For wit and judgment often are at strife,
Though meant each other's aid, like man and wife.
'Tis more to guide than spur the Muse's steed; 35
Restrain his fury, than provoke his speed;
The wingéd courser, like a generous[4] horse,
Shows most true mettle when you check his course.
Those rules of old discovered, not devised,
Are nature still, but nature methodized;   40
Nature, like liberty, is but restrained
By the same laws which first herself ordained.

. . . .

You, then, whose judgment the right course would steer,
Know well each Ancient's[5] proper character;
His fable, subject, scope in every page;   45
Religion, country, genius of his age.
Without all these at once before your eyes,

---

1. *informing*, inspiring or animating. 2. *wit*, imagination.
3. *Want . . . more*, need as much judgment in addition.
4. *generous*, thoroughbred. 5. *each Ancient*, the ancient
Greek and Roman writers.

Cavil you may, but never criticize.
Be Homer's works your study and delight,
Read them by day, and meditate by night;   50
Thence form your judgment, thence your
      maxims bring,
And trace the Muses upward to their spring.
Still with itself compared, his text peruse;
And let your comment be the Mantuan Muse.[6]
   When first young Maro[7] in his boundless
      mind   55
A work[8] t' outlast immortal Rome designed,
Perhaps he seemed above the critic's law,
And but from nature's fountains scorned to
      draw;
But when t' examine every part he came,   59
Nature and Homer were, he found, the same.
Convinced, amazed, he checks the bold
      design,
And rules as strict his labored work confine,
As if the Stagirite[9] o'erlooked each line.
Learn hence for ancient rules a just esteem:
To copy nature is to copy them.   65
   Some beauties yet no precepts can declare,
For there's a happiness as well as care.
Music resembles poetry; in each
Are nameless graces which no methods teach,
And which a master-hand alone can reach.   70
If, where the rules not far enough extend
(Since rules were made but to promote
      their end),
Some lucky license answer to the full
Th' intent proposed, that license is a rule.
Thus Pegasus,[10] a nearer way to take   75
May boldly deviate from the common track;
From vulgar bounds with brave disorder
      part,
And snatch a grace beyond the reach of art,
Which, without passing through the
      judgment, gains
The heart, and all its end at once attains. 80
In prospects thus, some objects please our
      eyes,
Which out of nature's common order rise,
The shapeless rock, or hanging precipice.
Great wits sometimes may gloriously offend,
And rise to faults true critics dare not mend.
But though the Ancients thus their rules
      invade   86
(As kings dispense with laws themselves
      have made),

Moderns, beware! Or if you must offend
Against the precept, ne'er transgress its end:
Let it be seldom and compelled by need,   90
And have, at least, their precedent to plead.
The critic else proceeds without remorse,
Seizes your fame, and puts his laws in force.
   I know there are, to whose presumptuous
      thoughts
Those freer beauties, e'en in them, seem
      faults.   95
Some figures monstrous and misshaped
      appear,
Considered singly, or beheld too near,
Which, but proportioned to their light or
      place,
Due distance reconciles to form and grace.
A prudent chief not always must display   100
His powers in equal ranks and fair array,
But with th' occasion and the place comply,
Conceal his force, nay, seem sometimes to fly.
Those oft are stratagems which errors seem,
Nor is it Homer nods, but we that dream.   105

PORTRAIT OF ADDISON

*Pope and Addison were originally great friends,
but they quarreled because Addison criticized
Pope's plan to revise and enlarge* The Rape of
the Lock. *Pope's "portrait" of Addison is one
of several brief stinging character descriptions
contained in the long poem* Epistle to Dr.
Arbuthnot.

Peace to all such! but were there one
      whose fires
      True genius kindles, and fair fame
      inspires;
Blessed with each talent and each art to
      please,
And born to write, converse, and live
      with ease—
Should such a man, too fond to rule alone,   5

AN ESSAY ON CRITICISM   **6.** *Mantuan Muse*, Vergil, born
near Mantua.   **7.** *Maro*, Vergil (Publius Vergilius Maro).
8. *A work*, the *Aeneid*.   **9.** *Stagirite*, Aristotle (384-322
B.C.), born at Stagira in Macedonia. His *Poetics* was the
beginning and still is a foundation of literary criticism.
10. *Pegasus*, the winged horse of the Muses.

Bear, like the Turk, no brother near the
    throne,
View him with scornful, yet with jealous,
    eyes,
And hate for arts that caused himself to rise;
Damn with faint praise, assent with civil
    leer,
And without sneering, teach the rest to
    sneer;   10
Willing to wound, and yet afraid to strike,
Just hint a fault, and hesitate dislike;
Alike reserved to blame, or to commend,
A timorous foe, and a suspicious friend;
Dreading e'en fools, by flatterers besieged, 15
And so obliging that he ne'er obliged;
Like Cato,[1] give his little senate laws,
And sit attentive to his own applause;
While wits and templars[2] every sentence
    raise,
And wonder with a foolish face of praise— 20
Who but must laugh, if such a man
    there be?
Who would not weep, if Atticus[3] were he!

---

1. *Cato*, Roman statesman, general, and writer (234-119
B.C.), the hero of Addison's classical tragedy *Cato*, for which
Pope had written the prologue. 2. *templars*, law stu-
dents. 3. *Atticus*, Pope's name for Addison.

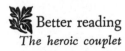

To increase understanding

Essay on Criticism

·1. Lines 1-18 reveal Pope's attitude toward literary criticism. (*a*) Which does he regard as more
important, the presence of good writers in a society
or the presence of good critics? (*b*) What, according
to Pope, is the function of the literary critic? Do
you agree with this definition? Why, or why not?
(*c*) What is Pope's test for a critic?

2. (*a*) What does Pope mean by "nature" (lines
19-24)? (*b*) What does he mean by "art" (lines
25-30)? (*c*) Explain Pope's idea about the relation
between art and nature. (*d*) What is his idea about
the relation between wit or imagination and judgment or reason (lines 31-38)?

3. Line 39 begins the famous passage on the importance of using the ancient Greeks and Romans as
literary models. The "rules" referred to are those
that Aristotle had laid down in his treatise on poetry.
Pope is right in saying that they were "discovered";
that is, Aristotle examined the best Greek dramas of
his time and drew certain conclusions from them as

to what constitutes good drama. But the Latin poet
Horace and the neoclassical critics of the sixteenth
and seventeenth centuries had greatly extended the
rules so that they covered different kinds of poetry
in great detail. In what he says about "methodized"
nature (line 40), Pope has in mind the difference,
for example, between the wild growth of a forest and
the trim formal nature of a cultivated garden. Milton,
you remember, spoke in "L'Allegro" about the "native
wood-notes" of Shakespeare, and in Pope's day
Shakespeare was spoken of as a natural genius, wanting art. With these points in mind, explain (*a*)
Pope's remarks about Homer and Vergil (lines 49-
63); (*b*) his remarks about ancient vs. modern
authors (lines 66-93); and (*c*) his attitude toward
those who find faults in the great classical writers
(lines 94-105).

Portrait of Addison

1. (*a*) What impression of Addison does Pope
convey? (*b*) On which of Addison's faults does Pope
concentrate his attack?

2. Pope was an expert at assuming various satirical poses, such as that of the fearless champion of
truth, or the graceful, light-hearted mocker of follies,
or the hard-headed man of reason. How would you
describe the pose he assumes in his description of
Addison?

Better reading

The heroic couplet

Heroic couplets, or pairs of rhyming iambic-pentam-
eter lines, were first introduced into English poetry
by Chaucer and have been used by countless numbers of English poets ever since. They are particularly associated with the age of Dryden and Pope,
however, because it was then that the heroic couplet
became the exclusive form of poetic expression.

That the eighteenth century should have been
interested in only one verse form is not surprising,
for it was an age that encouraged uniformity and
discouraged variety. That the heroic couplet should
have been the one accepted form is also understandable, for, with the addition of certain rules, the
heroic couplet was made into an appropriate vehicle
for the moralistic and satiric sentiments of the age.

The rules imposed on the heroic couplet by the
neoclassicists were chiefly two: (1) the line or couplet had to be end-stopped—that is, the line or couplet
had to contain a complete thought; (2) each line
had to be balanced or divided into two parts. Bal-

ance was achieved by various means. Sometimes the same word forms were used in the same sequence in both parts of the line, as in the line:

To *tire our patience* than *mislead our sense.*

This repeats the sequence *verb, pronoun, noun.* Other lines were made to contain a comparison or contrast of idea, as when Pope compares the presence of many bad critics with the presence of a few bad writers in:

Ten censure wrong for one who writes amiss.

Still other lines were balanced by causing the caesura (//), or pause felt by the reader, to occur in the middle of the line, as in the following couplet:

Let such teach others // who themselves excel,
And censure freely // who have written well.

Analyze Pope's "Portrait of Addison" and lines 1-18 of *An Essay on Criticism.* Is each line or couplet end-stopped? Which lines strike you as being the most perfectly balanced? How is this effect achieved in each?

How does Pope keep his couplets from sounding monotonous?

Why is the tightly wrapped, divided couplet an effective way of expressing moralistic and satiric sentiments?

Samuel Johnson 1709-1784

NATIONAL PORTRAIT
GALLERY, LONDON

The lives of John Dryden, Alexander Pope, and Samuel Johnson mark, respectively, the beginning, middle, and end of the Age of Reason in English literature. Dryden was the first writer to follow the literary rules and regulations derived from the ancient Greeks and Romans; Pope carried the neoclassical rules to their final perfection; and Johnson, despite the increasing number of people who were becoming dissatisfied with neo-classicism, kept it alive by the sheer weight of his personality.

The son of a learned but penniless bookseller, Johnson spent the first thirty years of his adult life in extreme poverty. After leaving Oxford for lack of funds, he became a hack writer, first in his native town of Lichfield and then in London's Grub Street, where, according to Macaulay, Johnson's already bearish nature became almost savage: "Being frequently under the necessity of wearing shabby coats and dirty shirts, he became a confirmed sloven. Being often very hungry when he sat down to his meals, he contracted a habit of eating with ravenous greediness. Even to the end of his life, and even at the tables of the great, the sight of food affected him as it affects wild beasts and birds of prey."

Johnson's reputation as a scholar and writer was established in 1755 with the publication of his voluminous *Dictionary*, which, as is evident from the following excerpts, was as much a revelation of its author's personality as it was an attempt to stabilize the English language.

Grub Street: The name of a Street in London, much inhabited by writers of small histories, dictionaries, and temporary poems: whence any mean production is called *Grub Street.*

Lexicographer: A writer of dictionaries, a harmless drudge.

Oats: A grain which in England is generally given to horses but in Scotland supports the people.

Network: Anything reticulated or decussated at equal distances with interstices between the intersections.

Tory [Johnson's party]: One who adheres to the ancient constitution of the State and the apostolical hierarchy of the Church of England; opposed to Whig.

Whig: The name of a faction.
Pension: An allowance made to anyone without an equivalent.
In England it is generally understood to mean pay given to
a state hireling for treason to his country.
Pensioner: A slave of state hired by a stipend to obey his master.

When Johnson later accepted a pension from the government, people were quick to throw up to him his own definition of the word *pensioner*. Johnson replied in characteristic fashion: "I wish my pension were twice as large that they might make twice as much noise."

In all his works Johnson carried the neoclassical rules for prose writing to an extreme. His smooth-flowing, well-balanced sentences are so long and are filled with so many words derived from Latin that they read like the ponderous, grandiose pronouncements of an orator. As Oliver Goldsmith put it, "His little fishes talked like whales." Or, in the words of James Boswell, "He writes like a teacher. He dictates to his readers from an academical chair."

Few of Johnson's writings are read today, partly because of their academic quality and partly because Johnson's greatest works were those that he "wrote out loud." By the time he was fifty, Johnson was well known in the taverns and coffee houses for his vigorous utterances in defense of the neoclassical approach to literature and life. When the much-talked-about pension put an end to his poverty in 1762, Johnson and the well-known painter Sir Joshua Reynolds founded their famous Literary Club, which has come to be regarded as one of the most brilliant assemblies of all times. Meeting originally at the Turk's Head Tavern on Monday evenings, Johnson's Club boasted such "good fellows" as Oliver Goldsmith, poet, playwright, and novelist; Edmund Burke, statesman, political philosopher, and advocate of American independence; David Garrick, the Shakespearean actor; Edward Gibbon, the historian; Adam Smith, the economist; Richard Sheridan, the playwright; and James Boswell, the biographer, who immortalized the Club in his *Life of Samuel Johnson.* All these men were good talkers, but Johnson held the primacy in an assembly of kings. Alone, or with his pen in hand, Johnson was often morose, lethargic, unable to force himself to work; but at these intellectual tennis matches he rolled and puffed with excitement, dropped the ponderous style that plagued his writings, and said things so full of character, common sense, humor, and learning that they constitute his unique claim to distinction.

JOHNSON'S
LETTER TO LORD
CHESTERFIELD
Samuel Johnson played a central rôle in the changing status of the English writer in the eighteenth century. When the undertaking of the *Dictionary* was proposed, Johnson tried to work within the long-established system of patronage by applying to Lord Chesterfield for financial help. Since Chesterfield left no account of his meetings with Johnson, his side of the story is unknown. Boswell wrote of the meetings in his *Life of Samuel Johnson,* and this version is the basis for the following famous account, written by Macaulay in the nineteenth century.

[Chesterfield] received Johnson's homage with the most winning affability and requited it with a few guineas, bestowed doubtless in a very graceful manner, but was by no means desirous to see all his carpets blackened with the London mud, and his soups and wines thrown to right and left over the gowns of fine ladies and the waistcoats of fine gentlemen, by an absent, awkward scholar, who gave strange starts and uttered strange growls, who dressed like a scarecrow and ate like a cormorant. During this time Johnson continued to call on his patron, but, after being repeatedly told by the porter that his lordship was not at home, took the hint, and ceased to present himself at the inhospitable door.

Eight years later, when the *Dictionary* had been completed, Lord Chesterfield expressed the desire to be regarded as its patron. By refusing, Johnson announced the end of patronage by the aristocracy.

SAMUEL JOHNSON'S LETTER TO CHESTERFIELD

To the Right Honorable
the Earl of Chesterfield

February 7, 1755.

My Lord: I have lately been informed by the proprietor of *The World*,[1] that two papers, in which my *Dictionary* is recommended to the public, were written by your lordship. To be so distinguished is an honor which, being very little accustomed to favors from the great, I know not well how to receive, or in what terms to acknowledge.

When, upon some slight encouragement, I first visited your lordship, I was overpowered, like the rest of mankind, by the enchantment of your address; and I could not forbear to wish that I might boast myself "*Le vainqueur du vainqueur de la terre*"[2]; that I might obtain that regard for which I saw the world contending; but I found my attendance so little encouraged, that neither pride nor modesty would suffer me to continue it. When I had once addressed your lordship in public, I had exhausted all the art of pleasing which a retired and uncourtly scholar can possess. I had done all that I could; and no man is well pleased to have his all neglected, be it ever so little.

Seven years, my lord, have now passed, since I waited in your outward rooms, or was repulsed from your door; during which time I have been pushing on my work through difficulties, of which it is useless to complain, and have brought it at last to the verge of publication, without one act of assistance, one word of encouragement, or one smile of favor.

Such treatment I did not expect, for I never had a patron before.

The shepherd in Vergil grew at last acquainted with Love, and found him a native of the rocks.[3]

Is not a patron, my lord, one who looks with unconcern on a man struggling for life in the water, and, when he has reached ground, encumbers him with help? The notice which you have been pleased to take of my labors, had it been early, had been kind; but it has been delayed till I am indifferent and cannot enjoy it; till I am solitary, and cannot impart it; till I am known, and do not want it. I hope it is no very cynical asperity not to confess obligations where no benefit has been received, or to be unwilling that the public should consider me as owing that to a patron, which Providence has enabled me to do for myself.

Having carried on my work thus far with so little obligation to any favorer of learning, I shall not be disappointed though I should conclude it, if less be possible, with less; for I have been long wakened from that dream of hope, in which I once boasted myself with so much exaltation,

My Lord,
Your Lordship's most humble,
Most Obedient servant,

SAM. JOHNSON

1. *The World*, a newspaper run by a friend of Johnson. 2. *Le vainqueur . . . de la terre.* "The conqueror of the conqueror of the world." 3. *The shepherd . . . rocks.* Johnson is referring to a pastoral poem by Vergil which speaks of the cruelty and inhumanity of love.

James Boswell 1740-1795

Greater than any book that Johnson ever wrote is the book that was written about him by his disciple James Boswell. Boswell was born in Scotland of an old aristocratic family. He graduated from the universities of Edinburgh and Glasgow, toyed for a while with thoughts of studying law and of joining the army, and finally made the Grand Tour of the Continent that was customary for a man of his position and wealth. Upon his return he entered into a close friendship with his long-time hero and idol Samuel Johnson, whose open dislike for Scotland seems only to have brought the two men closer together. The result of this unusual friendship was Boswell's extensive *Life of Samuel Johnson*, which is unanimously accepted as the greatest of all English biographies. By constantly following his mentor around (Boswell was jokingly called Johnson's "little Scotch burr") and by tirelessly recording the great man's conversations, either on the spot or at some later time, Boswell was able to put together a portrait so vivid that Johnson would have lived for posterity if he had never written a word.

The portrait of Johnson and Boswell contained in the famous biography was confirmed and deepened by the discovery, in the twentieth century, of Boswell's *London Journal, 1762-1763*.

from THE LIFE OF SAMUEL JOHNSON

BOSWELL'S INTRODUCTION TO JOHNSON (1763)

Mr. Thomas Davies the actor, who then kept a bookseller's shop in Russell Street, Covent Garden, told me that Johnson came frequently to his house, where he more than once invited me to meet him; but by some unlucky accident or other he was prevented from coming to us.

Mr. Thomas Davies was a man of good understanding and talents, with the advantage of a liberal education. Though somewhat pompous, he was an entertaining companion and his literary performances have no inconsiderable share of merit. He was a friendly and very hospitable man. Both he and his wife, who has been celebrated for her beauty, though upon the stage for many years, maintained an uniform decency of character; and Johnson esteemed them, and lived in as easy an intimacy with them as with any family which he used to visit. Mr. Davies recollected several of Johnson's remarkable sayings, and was one of the best of the many imitators of his voice and manner, while relating them. He increased my impatience more and more to see the extraordinary man whose works I highly valued, and whose conversation was reported to be so excellent.

At last, on Monday the 16th of May, when I was sitting in Mr. Davies' back parlor, after having drunk tea with him and Mrs. Davies, Johnson unexpectedly came into the shop; and Mr. Davies having perceived him through the glass door in the room in which we were sitting, advancing toward us—he announced his awful approach to me, somewhat in the manner of an actor in the part of Horatio when he addresses Hamlet on the appearance of his father's ghost, "Look, my Lord, it comes." I found that I had a very perfect idea of Johnson's figure, from the portrait of him painted by Sir Joshua Reynolds soon after he had published his *Dictionary*, in the attitude of sitting in his easy chair in deep meditation. Mr. Davies mentioned my name, and respectfully introduced me to him. I was much agitated and recollecting his prejudice against the Scotch, of which I had heard much, I said to Davies, "Don't tell where I come from." —"From Scotland," cried Davies, roguishly. "Mr. Johnson," said I, "I do indeed come from Scotland, but I cannot help it." I am willing to flatter myself that I meant this as light pleasantry to soothe and conciliate him, and not as an humiliating abasement at the expense of my country. But however that might be, this speech was somewhat unlucky for he seized the expression "come from Scotland," and retorted, "That, sir, I find, is what a very great many of your countrymen cannot help." This stroke stunned me a good deal and when we had sat down, I felt myself not a little embarrassed, and apprehensive of what might come next. He then addressed himself to Davies: "What do you think of Garrick? He has refused me an order for the play for Miss Williams, because he knows the house will be full, and that an order would be worth three shillings." Eager to take any opening to get into conversation with him, I ventured to say, "Oh, sir, I cannot think Mr. Garrick would grudge such a trifle to you." "Sir," said he, with a stern look, "I have known David Garrick longer than you have done, and I know no right you have to talk to me on the subject." Perhaps I deserved this check, for it was rather presumptuous in me, an entire stranger, to express any doubt of the justice of his animadversion upon his old acquaintance and pupil.[1] I now felt myself much mortified, and began to think that the hope which I had long indulged of obtaining his acquaintance was blasted. And, in truth, had not my ardor been uncommonly strong, and my resolution uncommonly persevering, so rough a reception might have deterred me forever from making any further attempts.

Fortunately, however, I remained upon the field not wholly discomfited, and was soon rewarded by hearing some of his conversation, of which I preserved the following short minute without marking the questions and observations by which it was produced.

"People," he remarked, "may be taken in once, who imagine that an author is greater in private life than other men. Uncommon parts require uncommon opportunities for their exertion.

"In barbarous society, superiority of parts is of real consequence. Great strength or great wisdom is of much value to an individual. But in more polished times there are people to do everything for money, and then there are a number of other superiorities, such as those of birth and fortune and rank, that dissipate men's attention and leave no extraordinary share of respect for personal and intellectual superiority. This is wisely ordered by Providence, to preserve some equality among mankind."

BOSWELL'S FIRST CALL UPON JOHNSON (1763)

A few days afterwards I called on Davies, and asked him if he thought I might take the liberty of waiting on Mr. Johnson at his chambers in the Temple.[2] He said I certainly might, and that Mr. Johnson would take it as a compliment. So upon Tuesday the 24th of May, I boldly repaired to Johnson. His chambers were on the first floor of No. 1, Inner Temple Lane, and I entered them with an impression given me by the Reverend Dr. Blair, of Edinburgh, who had been introduced to him not long before, and described his having "found the Giant in his den." . . .

He received me very courteously, but it must be confessed that his apartment and furniture and morning dress were sufficiently uncouth. His brown suit of clothes looked very rusty; he had on a little, old, shriveled, unpowdered wig, which was too small for his head; his shirt-neck and knees of his breeches were loose; his black, worsted stockings ill drawn up, and he had a pair of unbuckled

---

1. *pupil.* David Garrick had been one of Johnson's pupils when Johnson was teaching school in Lichfield. 2. *the Temple*, the area where the law courts are located.

shoes by way of slippers. But all these slovenly particularities were forgotten the moment that he began to talk. Some gentlemen, whom I do not recollect, were sitting with him, and when they went away, I also rose, but he said to me, "Nay, don't go."—"Sir," said I, "I am afraid that I intrude upon you. It is benevolent to allow me to sit and hear you." He seemed pleased with this compliment, which I sincerely paid him, and answered, "Sir, I am obliged to any man who visits me."

JOHNSON AND GOLDSMITH (1763)

As Dr. Oliver Goldsmith will frequently appear in this narrative, I shall endeavor to make my readers in some degree acquainted with his singular character. He was a native of Ireland and a contemporary with Mr. Burke[3] at Trinity College, Dublin, but did not then give much promise of future celebrity. He, however, observed to Mr. Malone, that "though he made no great figure in mathematics, which was a study in much repute there, he could turn an ode of Horace[4] into English better than any of them." He afterwards studied physic at Edinburgh and upon the Continent, and, I have been informed, was enabled to pursue his travels on foot, partly by demanding at Universities to enter the lists as a disputant,[5] by which, according to the custom of many of them, he was entitled to the premium of a crown when luckily for him his challenge was not accepted, so that, as I once observed to Dr. Johnson, he *disputed* his passage through Europe. He then came to England and was employed successively in the capacities of an usher to an academy, a corrector of the press, a reviewer, and a writer for a newspaper. He had sagacity enough to cultivate assiduously the acquaintance of Johnson. To me and many others it appeared that he studiously copied the manner of Johnson, though, indeed, upon a smaller scale. . . .

No man had the art of displaying with more advantage as a writer, whatever literary acquisitions he made. *"Nihil quod tetigit non ornavit."*[6] His mind resembled a fertile, but thin, soil. There was a quick, but not a strong vegetation, of whatever chanced to be thrown upon it. No deep root could be struck. The oak of the forest did not grow there, but the elegant shrubbery and the fragrant parterre appeared in gay succession. It has been generally circulated and believed that he was a mere fool in conversation; but, in truth, this has been greatly exaggerated. He had, no doubt, a more than common share of that hurry of ideas which we often find in his countrymen, and which sometimes produces a laughable confusion in expressing them. He was very much what the French call *un étourdi,*[7] and from vanity and an eager desire of being conspicuous wherever he was, he frequently talked carelessly without knowledge of the subject, or even without thought. . . .

He, I am afraid, had no settled system of any sort, so that his conduct must not be strictly scrutinized, but his affections were social and generous, and when he had money he gave it away very liberally. His desire of imaginary consequence predominated over his attention to truth. He boasted to me of the power of his pen in commanding money, which I believe was true in a certain degree, though in the instance he gave he was by no means correct. He told me that he had sold a novel for four hundred pounds. This was his *Vicar of Wakefield.* But Johnson informed me that he had made the bargain for Goldsmith, and the price was sixty pounds. . . .

Mrs. Piozzi and Sir John Hawkins[8] have strangely misstated the history of Goldsmith's situation and Johnson's friendly interference when this novel was sold. I shall give it authentically from Johnson's own exact narration:

"I received one morning a message from poor Goldsmith that he was in great distress, and as it was not in his power to come to me, begging that I would come to him as soon as

---

3. *Mr. Burke,* Edmund Burke, statesman and political philosopher and one of the members of Johnson's Club. 4. *Horace,* Roman poet and satirist. 5. *disputant,* debater. 6. *Nihil . . . ornavit.* "He touched nothing that he did not adorn." 7. *un étourdi* (ən ā tür dē'), a rattle-brained blunderer. [French] 8. *Mrs. Piozzi and Sir John Hawkins.* Mrs. Piozzi, an intimate friend of Johnson, relates the Goldsmith incident in her *Anecdotes of Johnson.* Sir John Hawkins, a London attorney, gives an account of the incident in his biography of Johnson.

possible. I sent him a guinea, and promised to come to him directly. I accordingly went as soon as I was dressed, and found that his landlady had arrested him for his rent, at which he was in a violent passion. I perceived that he had already changed my guinea, and had got a bottle of Madeira and a glass before him. I put the cork into the bottle, desired he would be calm, and began to talk to him of the means by which he might be extricated. He then told me that he had a novel ready for the press, which he produced to me. I looked into it, and saw its merit; told the landlady I should soon return, and having gone to a bookseller, sold it for sixty pounds. I brought Goldsmith the money, and he discharged his rent, not without rating his landlady in a high tone for having used him so ill. . . ."

(1773)

Goldsmith's incessant desire of being conspicuous in company was the occasion of his sometimes appearing to such disadvantage as one should hardly have supposed possible in a man of his genius. One evening, in a circle of wits, he found fault with me for talking of Johnson as entitled to the honor of unquestionable superiority. "Sir," said he, "you are for making a monarchy of what should be a republic." He was still more mortified when, talking in a company with fluent vivacity, a German who sat next to him and perceived Johnson rolling himself as if about to speak, suddenly stopped him, saying, "Stay, stay—Toctor Shonson is going to say something." This was, no doubt, very provoking, especially to one so irritable as Goldsmith, who frequently mentioned it with strong expressions of indignation.

It may also be observed that Goldsmith was sometimes content to be treated with an easy familiarity, but, upon occasions, would be consequential and important. An instance of this occurred in a small particular. Johnson had a way of contracting the names of his friends; as Beauclerk, *Beau*; Boswell, *Bozzy*; Langton, *Lanky*; Murphy, *Mur*; Sheridan, *Sherry*. I remember one day, when Tom Davies was telling that Dr. Johnson said, "We are all in labor for a name to Goldy's play,"

Goldsmith seemed displeased that such a liberty should be taken with his name, and said, "I have often desired him not to call me *Goldy*." Tom was remarkably attentive to the most minute circumstance about Johnson. I recollect his telling me once, on my arrival in London, "Sir, our great friend has made an improvement on his appellation of old Mr. Sheridan. He calls him now *Sherry derry*."

LONDON JOURNAL, 1762-1763

Wednesday 6 July. . . . I had engaged Mr. Johnson and some more company to sup at my lodgings, and as my having the parlor of an evening was a favor from my landlord, I would by no means think of it.[1] I went to Mr. Johnson and told him my distress. He laughed and bid me consider how little a distress it would appear a twelvemonth hence. He said that if my landlord insisted that the bargain should stand and the lodgings be mine for a year, that I could certainly use them as I pleased. "So, Sir," said he, "you may quarter two Life Guard men[2] upon him; or you may get the greatest scoundrel you can find and send into his house; or you may say that you want to make some experiments in natural philosophy[3] and may burn a large quantity of asafoetida in his house." Such ludicrous fertility can this great man throw out!

I made myself easy as to my company by letting them know that they were to consider the Mitre Tavern as my lodgings for the night. Accordingly, I ordered supper there, and I had as my guests Mr. Samuel Johnson, Dr. Goldsmith, Mr. Ogilvie, Mr. Davies, bookseller, and Mr. Eccles, an Irish gentleman of fortune, a good ingenious sort of man. I was well dressed and in excellent spirits, neither muddy nor flashy. I sat with much secret pride, thinking of my having such a company with me. I

Selections from *Boswell's London Journal, 1762-1763,* edited by Frederick A. Pottle. Copyright, 1950, by Yale University. Reprinted by permission of McGraw-Hill Book Company, Inc. and William Heinemann Ltd.
1. Boswell was having trouble with his landlord and had just determined to find lodgings elsewhere. 2. *Life Guard men,* soldiers belonging to the royal household. 3. *natural philosophy,* physical science.

behaved with ease and propriety, and did not attempt at all to show away; but gently assisted conversation by those little arts which serve to make people throw out their sentiments with ease and freedom.

Ogilvie was rapt in admiration of the Stupendous Johnson. Goldsmith was in his usual style, too eager to be bright. . . .

We talked of Scotland. Ogilvie, who is a rank Scot, defended his native land with all the powers that he could muster up. I was diverted to see how great a man a London wit is in comparison of one of your country swans who sing ever so *bonnily*. Ogilvie said there was very rich country round Edinburgh. "No, no," said Goldsmith, with a sneering laugh; "it is not rich country."[4] Ogilvie then said that Scotland had a great many noble wild prospects. "Sir," said Johnson, "I believe you have a great many noble wild prospects. Norway too has some noble wild prospects; and Lapland is remarkable for prodigious noble wild prospects. But, Sir, I believe the noblest prospect that a Scotsman ever sees is the road which leads him to England!"

We gave a roar of applause to this most excellent sally of strong humor. At the same time, I could not help thinking that Mr. Johnson showed a want of taste in laughing at the wild grandeur of nature, which to a mind undebauched by art conveys the most pleasing, awful, sublime ideas. . . .

Mr. Johnson was exceeding good company all this evening. We parted at one. I was very happy.

Thursday 14 July. Mr. Johnson and I met at the Mitre by ourselves. He was in most excellent humor, though the night was very rainy. I said it was good for the vegetable part of the creation. "Aye, Sir," said he, "and for the animals who eat those vegetables, and for the animals who eat those animals." We had a good supper, which made us very comfortable.

I said, "You and I, Sir, are very good companions, but my father and I are not so. Now what can occasion this? For you are as old a man as my father, and you are certainly as learned and as knowing." "Sir," said he, "I am a man of the world. I live in the world, and I take in some measure the color of the world as it moves along. But your father is a judge in a remote part of the country, and all his notions are taken from the old world. Besides, there must always be a struggle between a father and son, while the one aims at power and the other at independency." I told him that I was afraid of my father's forcing me to be a lawyer. "Why, Sir," said he, "you need not be afraid of his forcing you to be a laborious practicing lawyer. That is not in his power. For, as the proverb says, 'One man may lead a horse to the water, but twenty cannot make him drink.' He may be displeased, but it will not go far. If he only insists on your having as much law as is necessary for a man of property, and endeavors to get you into Parliament, he is quite in the right." . . .

He said he would not advise a plan of study, for he had never pursued one two days. "And a man ought just to read as inclination leads him, for what he reads as a task will do him little good. Idleness is a disease which must be combated. A young man should read five hours every day, and so may acquire a great deal of knowledge."

Saturday 16 July. At my last meeting with Mr. Johnson, he . . . advised me to keep a journal of my life, fair and undisguised. He said it would be a very good exercise, and would yield me infinite satisfaction when the ideas were faded from my remembrance. I told him that I had done so ever since I left Scotland. He said he was very happy that I pursued so good a plan. And now, O my journal! art thou not highly dignified? Shalt thou not flourish tenfold? No former solicitations or censures could tempt me to lay thee aside; and now is there any argument which can outweigh the sanction of Mr. Samuel Johnson? He said indeed that I should keep it private, and that I might surely have a friend who would burn it in case of my death. For my own part, I have at present such an affection for this my journal that it shocks me to think of burning it. I rather encourage the idea of having it carefully laid up among the

---

4. Goldsmith had studied medicine at the University of Edinburgh.

archives of Auchinleck.[5] However, I cannot judge fairly of it now. Some years hence I may. I told Mr. Johnson that I put down all sorts of little incidents in it. "Sir," said he, "there is nothing too little for so little a creature as man. It is by studying little things that we attain the great knowledge of having as little misery and as much happiness as possible."

Friday 22 July. . . . At night Mr. Johnson and I had a room at the Turk's Head Coffeehouse, which he encouraged because the mistress of the house is a good civil woman and wants business. And indeed we found better entertainment here than at the Mitre, and as reasonable. . . .

Mr. Johnson said he loved the acquaintance of young people. "Because," said he, "in the first place, I don't like to think myself turning old. In the next place, young acquaintances must last longest, if they do last; and in the next place, young men have more virtue than old men. They have more generous sentiments in every respect. I love the young dogs of this age: they have more wit and humor and knowledge of life than we had. But then the dogs are not so good scholars. Sir, in my early years I read very hard. It is a hard enough reflection, but a true one, that I knew almost as much at eighteen as I do now. My judgment, to be sure, was not so good, but I had all the facts. I remember very well when I was about five and twenty an old gentleman at Oxford said to me, 'Young man, ply your book diligently now and acquire a stock of knowledge; for when years come upon you, you will find that poring upon books will be but an irksome task.'"

I complained to Mr. Johnson that I was much afflicted with melancholy, which was hereditary in our family. He said that he himself had been greatly distressed with it, and for that reason had been obliged to fly from study and meditation to the dissipating variety of life. He advised me to have constant occupation of mind, to take a great deal of exercise, and to live moderately; especially to shun drinking at night.

"Melancholy people," said he, "are apt to fly to intemperance, which gives a momentary relief but sinks the soul much lower in misery." He observed that laboring men who work much and live sparingly are seldom or never troubled with low spirits. It gave me great relief to talk of my disorder with Mr. Johnson; and when I discovered that he himself was subject to it, I felt that strange satisfaction which human nature feels at the idea of participating distress with others; and the greater person our fellow sufferer is, so much the more good does it do us.

---

5. *Auchinleck,* Boswell's home in Scotland.

To increase understanding
Johnson's Letter to Lord Chesterfield

1. Why is Johnson's letter to Lord Chesterfield an important document in the history of English literature?

2. What does the letter reveal about (*a*) Johnson's character, (*b*) his style of writing?

Boswell's Life of Samuel Johnson

1. What do you learn about Johnson's personality from Boswell's account of (*a*) his introduction to Johnson, (*b*) his first visit to Johnson, (*c*) Johnson's relationship with Goldsmith?

2. (*a*) What does Boswell tell us about Johnson's Club? (*b*) What position did Oliver Goldsmith occupy in the famous group?

Boswell's London Journal

1. (*a*) How would you characterize Boswell? (*b*) What accounts for his close friendship with Johnson?

2. What evidences of Johnsonian humor do you find in the selections from the *London Journal?*

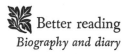 Better reading
Biography and diary

Biographies, autobiographies, memoirs, letters, and diaries are all concerned with the recording of actual events and the revelation of actual personalities. In the case of biographies, the author takes as his subject the life of some other person. In the case of autobiographies, memoirs, letters, and diaries, the author writes about his own life. Of these various forms the diary or journal is regarded as the most subjective, for the diarist writes not only *about* himself—he usually writes exclusively *for* himself, with little if any thought of publication. Whereas the biographer, for example, may write for any number of purposes, ranging from the strictly factual recording of someone's life to the commemoration of a hero, the diarist is moved by a need to record his daily routine and confess his innermost thoughts. Although a purely private record taken up and left off more or less arbitrarily, the diary makes up in immediacy and frankness what it lacks in artistic shape and coherence.

What do you think was Boswell's purpose in writing his biography of Johnson? How well does Boswell succeed in the selections you have read?

Explain the connection between Boswell's purpose in writing his biography and the thoughts he confesses in his diary or journal. Which gives us the more immediate impression of Boswell's relationship with Johnson? Explain.

Do you think Boswell had any idea that his diary would be published? Which strikes you as the more frank and intimate diary, Pepys' or Boswell's?

The Changing English Language

During the eighteenth century the movement away from the exuberant language of Elizabethan times to a more deliberate and precise manner of expression was carried to completion. Of the various influences at work in this new movement (see page 243), neoclassicism was perhaps the most decisive. Men like Joseph Addison, Jonathan Swift, and Samuel Johnson deliberately tried to make the English language conform to the patterns of Latin—a language that lends itself to long, smoothly flowing sentences, the sense or meaning of which is suspended until the last word or clause. Johnson in particular carried this Latinizing tendency to an extreme in such sentences as,

The reverence due to writings that have long subsisted arises therefore not from any credulous confidence in the superior wisdom of past ages, or gloomy persuasion of the degeneracy of mankind, but is the consequence of acknowledged and indubitable positions, that what has been longest known has been most considered, and what is most considered is best understood.

The Latinate quality of the above sentence is due not only to its structure; it is due also to the preponderance of words derived from Latin: *reverence, subsisted, credulous, confidence, superior, persuasion, degeneracy, consequence, indubitable, positions, considered.* The fact that the eighteenth century welcomed the use of words derived from Latin greatly increased a writer's chances to say precisely what he had in mind, especially if what he had in mind was fairly abstract, since English tends to form words that denote abstract ideas by combining words of Latin origin. In Johnson's writings, however, and in the writings of other neoclassical figures, the number of words derived from Latin are so many that the effect is often not precision but long-windedness.

In the long run neoclassicism proved to be more interested in dignity and formality than in precision. Latin words were preferred because they were longer and more formal-sounding. Shorter, sharper, Anglo-Saxon words were usually discredited on the grounds that they were too low and slangy. Johnson even tried to get rid of such pungent words as *to coax, stingy,* and *fun,* and Swift looked down on *banter, sham, bubble, mob, bully,* and *bamboozle.* The neoclassical desire to set and preserve standards of purity did lead to the first important English dictionaries (Johnson's *Dictionary* of 1755 was based on Nathaniel Bailey's thorough and comprehensive *English Dictionary* of 1721). Neoclassicism also did much to tone down the bizarre and freakish speech habits that often make the Elizabethans obscure and incomprehensible to modern readers. But by making Latin into the queen of all languages, neoclassicism also put a temporary end to the spirit of variety and experimentation that has done so much to make the English language into a rich and vital instrument.

Eighteenth-Century English Painters

One of Samuel Johnson's many distinguished friends was the portrait painter and first president of England's Royal Academy of Art, Sir Joshua Reynolds (1723-1792). A solid, conservative painter who upheld the rules and regulations of the old masters, Reynolds turned out portraits of well-known and well-bred people that are as elegant and polished—and often as stuffy—as the neoclassical prose of Johnson. His reputation as England's leading painter was threatened only by Thomas Gainsborough (1727-1788), whose own portraits of fashionable people exhibit as much ease, charm, and natural talent as Reynolds' do hard work and industry. Thanks to Gainsborough, Reynolds, and a large group of lesser figures like Thomas Lawrence and Henry Raeburn, the eighteenth century became the golden age of English portraiture.

Two eighteenth-century painters stood against the mainstream. One of them, William Hogarth (1697-1764), penetrated through the elegant world of Reynolds and Gainsborough to the same layer of immorality, corruption, and cruelty that outraged writers like Jonathan Swift. In a number of narrative series of paintings which he later made into etchings, Hogarth exposed the artificiality and vice that lay under the surface of much eighteenth-century society.

The other dissenter was William Blake (1757-1827), who was so infuriated by the elegant, highly rational art of the time that he unceremoniously spoke of Sir Joshua Reynolds as "Sir Sloshua." Blake's paintings and poetry (pages 337-340) are shaped and animated by an intensely personal vision that recognizes no boundary between fact and fancy.

Above left: Lady Waldegrove by Reynolds. Above right: the famous actor David Garrick by Thomas Gainsborough. Left: General MacGregor by Sir Henry Raeburn, a noted follower of Reynolds and Gainsborough. Opposite: A part of the famous sequence of paintings by Hogarth, The Rake's Progress. *The first scene shows the young rake as he inherits his father's fortune and rejects his truelove; the next two show him wasting his fortune on a life of debauchery; the last shows him beginning to reap the consequences of his brief life in debtor's prison, where his constant sweetheart has followed him.*

Oliver Goldsmith 1728-1774

Here lies Nolly Goldsmith, for shortness called Noll,
Who wrote like an angel, but talked like poor Poll.

David Garrick's assessment of Oliver Goldsmith is a just one: he was
too whimsical and scatterbrained to hold his own in the verbal combats of
Johnson's Club (see Boswell's comments on Goldsmith, pages 279-280),
but he was without a doubt the best of the later neoclassical writers. Possessed of a rare versatility, Goldsmith produced a novel (*The Vicar of
Wakefield*), a long poem (*The Deserted Village*), and a play (*She Stoops
to Conquer*) that have the honor of being among the most frequently read
works in the English language.

Like Dryden, Pope, and Johnson, Goldsmith wrote within the confines
of the neoclassical rules and regulations: the heroic couplet is the basic
unit in his poetry; smooth-flowing, high-sounding sentences dominate his
prose. But there is also in Goldsmith's work a new note of feeling, particularly in *The Deserted Village*, which wistfully longs for things of the
past and which speaks with warm compassion of humble country folk. Pope
would have ridiculed this feeling as a vulgar outburst of emotion incompatible with a hard-headed, reasonable approach to life. It is also likely
that Pope would not have approved of Goldsmith's play *She Stoops to
Conquer* on the grounds that its moments of exuberant high spirits were
but coarse extravagance. By writing such a play, Goldsmith, and after
him Richard Sheridan (1751-1816), attempted to revitalize the English
theater, which had been offering nothing but heavy melodrama ever since
the opening of the eighteenth century.

*Portrait of Goldsmith by
the studio of Reynolds.*

DRAMATIS PERSONAE

DRAMATIS PERSONAE

MR. RICHARD HARDCASTLE, *a country squire*

MRS. DOROTHY HARDCASTLE, *his wife*

MISS KATE HARDCASTLE, *Mr. Hardcastle's daughter by his first wife*

TONY LUMPKIN, *Mrs. Hardcastle's son by her first husband*

MISS CONSTANCE NEVILLE, *Mrs. Hardcastle's niece*

DIGGORY, *a servant in the Hardcastle home*

SIR CHARLES MARLOW, *a friend of Mr. Hardcastle*

YOUNG CHARLES MARLOW, *his son*

GEORGE HASTINGS, *a close friend of young Charles Marlow*

The LANDLORD at an inn, a MAID, SERVANTS, etc.

BY COMMAND OF
Their MAJESTIES.
At the Theatre-Royal, Covent-Garden,
This present WEDNESDAY, October 11, 1775,
She STOOPS to CONQUER.
Hardcastle by Mr. WILSON,
Being his FIRST APPEARANCE in that Character.
Tony Lumpkin by Mr. QUICK,
Marlow by Mr. LEE LEWES,
HASTINGS, with a Song,
By Mr. DU-BELLAMY,
Sir Charles Marlow, Mr. FEARON,
Mrs. Hardcastle by Mrs. GREEN,
Miss Neville, Mrs. LESSINGHAM,
Miss Hardcastle by Mrs. BULKLEY.
End of Act II. a New Grand Ballet, called the Italian Gardeners,
And End of the Comedy, a New Dance, called the Gamesters,
By Signor and Signora ZUCHELLI,
Being their FIRST APPEARANCE in ENGLAND.
To which (BY COMMAND) will be added a FARCE, call'd
St. PATRICK'S DAY.
Lieutenant O'Connor by Mr. CLINCH,
Justice Credulous by Mr. LEE LEWES,
Doctor Rosy by Mr. QUICK,
Serjeant Trounce by Mr. DUNSTALL,
Bridget by Mrs. PITT,
And Lauretta by Miss BROWN.
In which Character will be introduced a Song.
The Doors to be opened at FIVE o'Clock, and to begin exactly at SIX.
To-morrow ZARA, Osman (First Time) by Mr. AICKIN,
Lusignan and Zara by Mr. and Mrs. BARRY, being their First Appearance this Season.

ENTHOVEN THEATER COLLECTION, VICTORIA AND ALBERT MUSEUM

SHE STOOPS TO CONQUER

ACT ONE

SCENE I. *A chamber in an old-fashioned house*

Enter MRS. HARDCASTLE *and* MR. HARDCASTLE

Mrs. Hardcastle. I vow, Mr. Hardcastle, you're very particular. Is there a creature in the whole country but ourselves that does not take a trip to town now and then, to rub off the rust a little? There's the two Miss Hoggs and our neighbor Mrs. Grigsby go to take a month's polishing every winter.

Hardcastle. Aye, and bring back vanity and affectation to last them the whole year. I wonder why London cannot keep its own fools at home. In my time the follies of the town crept slowly among us, but now they travel faster than a stagecoach. Its fopperies come down not only as inside passengers, but in the very basket.[1]

Mrs. Hardcastle. Aye, your times were fine times indeed; you have been telling us of them for many a long year. Here we live in an old rumbling mansion, that looks for all the world like an inn, but that we never see company. Our best visitors are old Mrs. Odd-fish, the curate's wife, and little Cripplegate, the lame dancing master; and all our entertainment your old stories of Prince Eugene and the Duke of Marlborough.[2] I hate such old-fashioned trumpery.

Hardcastle. And I love it. I love everything that's old—old friends, old times, old manners, old books, old wine; and, I believe, Dorothy (*taking her hand*), you'll own I've been pretty fond of an old wife.

Mrs. Hardcastle. Lord, Mr. Hardcastle, you're forever at your Dorothys and your old wives. You may be a Darby, but I'll be no

---

1. *basket,* the overhanging back compartment on the outside of a stagecoach. 2. *Prince Eugene and the Duke of Marlborough.* These two famous generals, the former in charge of the Austrian army and the latter in charge of the English army, were allies in the Battle of Blenheim (1704) where they won a signal victory over the French.

Joan,[3] I promise you. I'm not so old as you'd make me, by more than one good year. Add twenty to twenty, and make money of that.

Hardcastle. Let me see; twenty added to twenty—makes just fifty and seven.

Mrs. Hardcastle. It's false, Mr. Hardcastle; I was but twenty when I was brought to bed of Tony, that I had by Mr. Lumpkin, my first husband; and he's not come to years of discretion yet.

Hardcastle. Nor ever will, I dare answer for him. Aye, you have taught him finely.

Mrs. Hardcastle. No matter. Tony Lumpkin has a good fortune. My son is not to live by his learning. I don't think a boy wants much learning to spend fifteen hundred a year.

Hardcastle. Learning, quotha![4] a mere composition of tricks and mischief. .

Mrs. Hardcastle. Humor, my dear; nothing but humor. Come, Mr. Hardcastle, you must allow the boy a little humor.

Hardcastle. I'd sooner allow him a horsepond. If burning the footmen's shoes, frightening the maids, and worrying the kittens be humor, he has it. It was but yesterday he fastened my wig to the back of my chair, and when I went to make a bow, I popped my bald head in Mrs. Frizzle's face.

Mrs. Hardcastle. And am I to blame? The poor boy was always too sickly to do any good. A school would be his death. When he comes to be a little stronger, who knows what a year or two's Latin may do for him?

Hardcastle. Latin for him! A cat and fiddle. No, no; the alehouse and the stable are the only schools he'll ever go to.

Mrs. Hardcastle. Well, we must not snub the poor boy now, for I believe we shan't have him long among us. Anybody that looks in his face may see he's consumptive.

Hardcastle. Aye, if growing too fat be one of the symptoms.

Mrs. Hardcastle. He coughs sometimes.

Hardcastle. Yes, when his liquor goes the wrong way.

Mrs. Hardcastle. I'm actually afraid of his lungs.

Hardcastle. And truly, so am I; for he sometimes whoops like a speaking trumpet— (TONY *hallooing behind the scenes*)—Oh, there he goes—a very consumptive figure, truly!

Enter TONY, *crossing the stage*

Mrs. Hardcastle. Tony, where are you going, my charmer? Won't you give Papa and I a little of your company, lovee?

Tony. I'm in haste, Mother; I cannot stay.

Mrs. Hardcastle. You shan't venture out this raw evening, my dear; you look most shockingly.

Tony. I can't stay, I tell you. *The Three Pigeons* expects me down every moment. There's some fun going forward.

Hardcastle. Aye; the alehouse, the old place; I thought so.

Mrs. Hardcastle. A low, paltry set of fellows.

Tony. Not so low, neither. There's Dick Muggins, the exciseman; Jack Slang, the horse doctor; little Aminadab, that grinds the music box; and Tom Twist, that spins the pewter platter.[5]

Mrs. Hardcastle. Pray, my dear, disappoint them for one night, at least.

Tony. As for disappointing them, I should not so much mind; but I can't abide to disappoint myself.

Mrs. Hardcastle. You shan't go.

Tony. I will, I tell you.

Mrs. Hardcastle. I say you shan't.

Tony. We'll see which is strongest, you or I.
(*Exit, hauling her out.*)

Hardcastle (*alone*). Aye, there goes a pair that only spoil each other. But is not the whole age in a combination to drive sense and discretion out of doors? There's my pretty darling, Kate! The fashions of the times have almost infected her, too. By living a year or two in town, she is as fond of gauze and French frippery as the best of them.

Enter KATE HARDCASTLE

Hardcastle. Blessings on my pretty inno-

---

3. *Darby . . . Joan,* humorous names commonly used for an elderly, deeply devoted husband and wife. 4. *quotha,* indeed! 5. *Tom Twist . . . platter.* Tom Twist's work was to spin or turn a lathe used in shaping pewter articles.

cence! Dressed out as usual, my Kate. Goodness! What a quantity of superfluous silk hast thou got about thee, girl! I could never teach the fools of this age that the indigent world could be clothed out of the trimmings of the vain.

Kate. You know our agreement, sir. You allow me the morning to receive and pay visits, and to dress in my own manner; and in the evening I put on my housewife's dress, to please you.

Hardcastle. Well, remember, I insist on the terms of our agreement; and, by the by, I believe I shall have occasion to try your obedience this very evening.

Kate. I protest, sir, I don't comprehend your meaning.

Hardcastle. Then, to be plain with you, Kate, I expect the young gentleman I have chosen to be your husband, from town this very day. I have his father's letter, in which he informs me his son is set out and that he intends to follow, himself, shortly after.

Kate. Indeed! I wish I had known something of this before. Bless me, how shall I behave? It's a thousand to one I shan't like him; our meeting will be so formal and so like a thing of business that I shall find no room for friendship or esteem.

Hardcastle. Depend upon it, child, I'll never control your choice; but Mr. Marlow, whom I have pitched upon, is the son of my old friend, Sir Charles Marlow, of whom you have heard me talk so often. The young gentleman has been bred a scholar, and is designed for an employment in the service of his country. I am told he's a very generous man.

Kate. I believe I shall like him.

Hardcastle. Young and brave.

Kate. I'm sure I shall like him.

Hardcastle. And very handsome.

Kate. My dear Papa, say no more (*kissing his hand*); he's mine—I'll have him.

Hardcastle. And to crown all, Kate, he's one of the most bashful and reserved young fellows in all the world.

Kate. Eh! you have frozen me to death again. That word *reserved* has undone all the rest of his accomplishments. A reserved lover, it is said, always makes a suspicious husband.

Hardcastle. On the contrary, modesty seldom resides in a breast that is not enriched with nobler virtues. It was the very feature in his character that first struck me.

Kate. He must have more striking features to catch me, I promise you. However, if he be so young, so handsome, and so everything as you mention, I believe he'll do still.

Hardcastle. Aye, Kate, but there is still an obstacle. It's more than an even wager he may not have you.

Kate. My dear Papa, why will you mortify one so?—Well, if he refuses, instead of breaking my heart at his indifference, I'll only break my glass for its flattery, set my cap to some newer fashion, and look out for some less difficult admirer.

Hardcastle. Bravely resolved! In the meantime, I'll go prepare the servants for his reception. As we seldom see company, they want as much training as a company of recruits the first day's muster. (*Exit.*)

Kate (*alone*). Lud,[6] this news of Papa's puts me all in a flutter. Young, handsome— these he put last, but I put them foremost. Sensible, good-natured—I like all that. But then, reserved and sheepish—that's much against him. Yet, can't he be cured of his timidity by being taught to be proud of his wife? Yes, and can't I—but I vow I'm disposing of the husband before I have secured the lover.

Enter CONSTANCE NEVILLE

Kate. I'm so glad you're come, Neville, my dear. Tell me, Constance, how do I look this evening? Is there anything whimsical about me? Is it one of my well-looking days, child? Am I in face today?

Constance. Perfectly, my dear. Yet now I look again—bless me!—surely no accident has happened among the canary birds or the goldfishes? Has your brother or the cat been meddling? Or has the last novel been too moving?

Kate. No; nothing of all this. I have been threatened—I can scarce get it out—I have been threatened with a lover.

---

6. **Lud,** a corrupt form of *Lord,* used as an exclamation.

Constance. And his name—

Kate. Is Marlow.

Constance. Indeed!

Kate. The son of Sir Charles Marlow.

Constance. As I live, the most intimate friend of Mr. Hastings, my admirer. They are never asunder. I believe you must have seen him when we lived in town.

Kate. Never.

Constance. He's a very singular character, I assure you. Among women of reputation and virtue, he is the modestest man alive; but his acquaintance gives him a very different character among creatures of another stamp; you understand me.

Kate. An odd character, indeed. I shall never be able to manage him. What shall I do? Pshaw, think no more of him, but trust to occurrences for success. But how goes on your own affair, my dear? Has my mother been courting you for my brother Tony, as usual?

Constance. I have just come from one of our agreeable tête-à-têtes. She has been saying a hundred tender things, and setting off her pretty monster as the very pink of perfection.

Kate. And her partiality is such that she actually thinks him so. A fortune like yours is no small temptation. Besides, as she has the sole management of it, I'm not surprised to see her unwilling to let it go out of the family.

Constance. A fortune like mine, which chiefly consists in jewels, is no such mighty temptation. But, at any rate, if my dear Hastings be but constant, I make no doubt to be too hard for her at last. However, I let her suppose that I am in love with her son; and she never once dreams that my affections are fixed upon another.

Kate. My good brother holds out stoutly. I could almost love him for hating you so.

Constance. It is a good-natured creature at bottom, and I'm sure would wish to see me married to anybody but himself. But my aunt's bell rings for our afternoon's walk round the improvements. *Allons!*[7] Courage is necessary, as our affairs are critical.

Kate. Would it were bedtime, and all were well. (*Exeunt.*)

SCENE II. *An alehouse room*

Several shabby fellows with punch and tobacco. TONY *at the head of the table, a little higher than the rest, a mallet in his hand*

All. Hurrah! Hurrah! Hurrah! Bravo!

First Fellow. Now, gentlemen, silence for a song. The squire is going to knock himself down for a song.

All. Aye, a song, a song!

Tony. Then I'll sing you, gentlemen, a song I made upon this alehouse, "The Three Pigeons."

SONG

Let schoolmasters puzzle their brain
  With grammar, and nonsense, and learning;
Good liquor, I stoutly maintain,
  Gives *genus*[1] a better discerning.
Let them brag of their heathenish gods,
  Their Lethes, their Styxes, and Stygians,[2]
Their *quis*, and their *quaes*, and their *quods*,[3]
  They're all but a parcel of Pigeons.[4]
          Toroddle, toroddle, toroll.

When Methodist preachers come down,
  A-preaching that drinking is sinful,
I'll wager the rascals a crown,
  They always preach best with a skinful.
But when you come down with your pence,
  For a slice of their scurvy religion,
I'll leave it to all men of sense,
  But you, my good friend, are the Pigeon.
          Toroddle, toroddle, toroll.

Then come, put the jorum about,
  And let us be merry and clever;
Our hearts and our liquors are stout,
  Here's the Three Jolly Pigeons forever.
Let some cry up woodcock or hare,
  Your bustards, your ducks, and your widgeons;
But of all the birds in the air,
  Here's a health to the Three Jolly Pigeons.
          Toroddle, toroddle, toroll.

SCENE I. **7.** Allons (ä lŏn′), let's go. [*French*]
SCENE II. **1.** *genus*, kind, race, here the human race. **2.** *Lethe, Styx, Stygian.* Lethe and Styx are rivers of Hades. Stygian is formed from *Styx.* **3.** *quis ... quaes ... quods*, plural forms of the Latin pronoun meaning "who" or "which." **4.** *Pigeons*, dupes.

All. Bravo, bravo!

First Fellow. The squire has got spunk in him.

Second Fellow. I loves to hear him sing, bekeays he never gives us nothing that's low.[5]

Third Fellow. Oh, damn anything that's low; I cannot bear it.

Fourth Fellow. The genteel thing is the genteel thing any time; if so be that a gentleman bees in a concatenation[6] accordingly.

Third Fellow. I like the maxum of it, Master Muggins. What, though I am obligated to dance a bear,[7] a man may be a gentleman for all that. May this be my poison, if my bear ever dances but to the very genteelest of tunes—"Water Parted" or "The Minuet in Ariadne."[8]

Second Fellow. What a pity it is the squire is not come to his own. It would be well for all the publicans within ten miles round of him.

Tony. Ecod,[9] and so it would, Master Slang. I'd then show what it was to keep choice of company.

Second Fellow. Oh, he takes after his own father for that. To be sure, old Squire Lumpkin was the finest gentleman I ever set eyes on. For winding the straight horns,[10] or beating a thicket for a hare, he never had his fellow. It was a saying in the place that he kept the best horses and dogs in the county.

Tony. Ecod, and when I'm of age I'll be no bastard, I promise you. I have been thinking of Bet Bouncer and the miller's gray mare to begin with. But come, my boys, drink about and be merry, for you pay no reckoning. Well, Stingo, what's the matter?

Enter LANDLORD

Landlord. There be two gentlemen in a post chaise at the door. They have lost their way upo' the forest; and they are talking something about Mr. Hardcastle.

Tony. As sure as can be, one of them must be the gentleman that's coming down to court my sister. Do they seem to be Londoners?

Landlord. I believe they may. They look woundily[11] like Frenchmen.

Tony. Then desire them to step this way, and I'll set them right in a twinkling. (*Exit* LANDLORD.) Gentlemen, as they mayn't be good enough company for you, step down for a moment, and I'll be with you in the squeezing of a lemon. (*Exeunt mob.*)

Tony (*alone*). Father-in-law[12] has been calling me whelp and hound this half year. Now, if I pleased, I could be so revenged upon the old grumbletonian. But then I'm afraid—afraid of what? I shall soon be worth fifteen hundred a year, and let him frighten me out of *that* if he can.

Enter LANDLORD, *conducting* MARLOW *and* HASTINGS

Marlow. What a tedious, uncomfortable day have we had of it! We were told it was but forty miles across the country, and we have come above threescore!

Hastings. And all, Marlow, from that unaccountable reserve of yours, that would not let us inquire more frequently on the way.

Marlow. I own, Hastings, I am unwilling to lay myself under an obligation to everyone I meet, and often stand the chance of an unmannerly answer.

Hastings. At present, however, we are not likely to receive any answer.

Tony. No offense, gentlemen. But I'm told you have been inquiring for one Mr. Hardcastle, in these parts. Do you know what part of the country you are in?

Hastings. Not in the least, sir, but should thank you for information.

Tony. Nor the way you come?

Hastings. No, sir; if you can inform us——

Tony. Why, gentlemen, if you know neither the road you are going, nor where you are, nor the road you came, the first thing I have to inform you is that—you have lost your way.

---

5. *nothing that's low,* a satirical reference to Augustan snobbery which insisted that only highborn people were fit subjects for a play. 6. *concatenation,* a connected series. The speaker does not know the meaning but thinks it sounds genteel. 7. *to dance a bear,* to make a bear dance for money. 8. *"Water . . . Ariadne,"* songs from operas. 9. *Ecod,* a mild oath. 10. *winding . . . horns,* blowing the hunting horn. 11. *woundily,* exceedingly. 12. *Father-in-law,* stepfather.

Marlow. We wanted no ghost to tell us that.

Tony. Pray, gentlemen, may I be so bold as to ask the place from whence you came?

Marlow. That's not necessary toward directing us where we are to go.

Tony. No offense; but question for question is all fair, you know. Pray, gentlemen, is not this same Hardcastle a cross-grained, old-fashioned, whimsical fellow with an ugly face, a daughter, and a pretty son?

Hastings. We have not seen the gentleman; but he has the family you mention.

Tony. The daughter, a tall, traipsing, trolloping, talkative maypole; the son, a pretty, well-bred, agreeable youth, that everybody is fond of!

Marlow. Our information differs in this. The daughter is said to be well-bred and beautiful; the son, an awkward booby, reared up and spoiled at his mother's apron-string.

Tony. He-he-hem!—Then, gentlemen, all I have to tell you is that you won't reach Mr. Hardcastle's house this night, I believe.

Hastings. Unfortunate!

Tony. It's a damned long, dark, boggy, dirty, dangerous way. Stingo, tell the gentlemen the way to Mr. Hardcastle's (*winking upon the* LANDLORD)—Mr. Hardcastle's of Quagmire Marsh, you understand me?

Landlord. Master Hardcastle's! Lack-a-daisy, my masters, you're come a deadly deal wrong. When you came to the bottom of the hill, you should have crossed down Squash Lane.

Marlow. Cross down Squash Lane!

Landlord. Then you were to keep straight forward, till you came to four roads.

Marlow. To where four roads meet?

Tony. Aye; but you must be sure to take only one of them.

Marlow. Oh, sir, you're facetious.

Tony. Then, keeping to the right, you are to go sideways till you come upon Crackskull Common; there you must look sharp for the track of the wheel, and go forward till you come to Farmer Murrain's barn. Coming to the farmer's barn, you are to turn to the right, and then to the left, and then to the right again, till you find out the old mill——

Marlow. Zounds, man! we could as soon find out the longitude.[13]

Hastings. What's to be done?

Marlow. This house promises but a poor reception; though, perhaps, the landlord can accommodate us.

Landlord. Alack, master, we have but one spare bed in the whole house.

Tony. And to my knowledge, that's taken up by three lodgers already. (*After a pause in which the rest seem disconcerted.*) I have it. Don't you think, Stingo, our landlady could accommodate the gentlemen by the fireside, with—three chairs and a bolster?

Hastings. I hate sleeping by the fireside.

Marlow. And I detest your three chairs and a bolster.

Tony. You do, do you?—then, let me see —what if you go on a mile farther, to the Buck's Head; the old Buck's Head on the hill, one of the best inns in the whole country?

---

13. *longitude.* This was a timely reference, because the government had recently paid a large reward to a man who had figured out how to determine longitude.

The cramped sedan chair, carried by two men, was a common mode of transportation through the dangerous city streets.

MESSRS MALLETT & SON, LONDON

Hastings. O ho! so we have escaped an adventure for this night, however!

Landlord (apart to TONY). Sure, you ben't sending them to your father's as an inn, be you?

Tony. Mum, you fool, you. Let *them* find that out. (*To them.*) You have only to keep on straight forward till you come to a large old house by the roadside. You'll see a pair of large horns over the door. That's the sign. Drive up the yard and call stoutly about you.

Hastings. Sir, we are obliged to you. The servants can't miss the way?

Tony. No, no; but I tell you, though, the landlord is rich and going to leave off business; so he wants to be thought a gentleman, saving your presence, he! he! he! He'll be for giving you his company; and, ecod, if you mind him, he'll persuade you that his mother was an alderman and his aunt a justice of peace.

Landlord. A troublesome old blade, to be sure; but he keeps as good wines as any in the whole country.

Marlow. Well, if he supplies us with these, we shall want no further connection. We are to turn to the right, did you say?

Tony. No, no, straight forward. I'll just step myself and show you a piece of the way. (*To the* LANDLORD.) Mum!

Landlord. Ah, bless your heart, for a pleasant, mischievous son. (*Exeunt.*)

❀ To increase understanding

1. Mr. Hardcastle, a country squire, and his wife have differing opinions about country life versus city life. What do you learn about their characters from this disagreement?

2. (*a*) What is the practical joke Tony plays on Marlow and Hastings? (*b*) What do you anticipate will be the results?

3. The authors of both *The Spectator*, written early in the eighteenth century, and *She Stoops to Conquer*, published in 1773, poke gentle fun at the foibles of men and women of various social classes. Point out similarities and differences between (*a*) Sir Roger de Coverley and Mr. Hardcastle; (*b*) Will Wimble and Tony Lumpkin; (*c*) the women described in "Party Patches" and Mrs. Hardcastle.

ACT TWO

SCENE: *An old-fashioned house*

Enter HARDCASTLE, *followed by three or four awkward Servants*

Hardcastle. Well, I hope you are perfect in the table exercise I have been teaching you these three days. You all know your posts and your places, and can show that you have been used to good company, without ever stirring from home.

All. Aye, aye.

Hardcastle. When company comes, you are not to pop out and stare, and then run in again, like frighted rabbits in a warren.

All. No, no.

Hardcastle. You, Diggory, whom I have taken from the barn, are to make a show at the side table; and you, Roger, whom I have advanced from the plow, are to place yourself behind my chair. But you're not to stand so, with your hands in your pockets. Take your hands from your pockets, Roger; and from your head, you blockhead, you. See how Diggory carries his hands. They're a little too stiff indeed, but that's no great matter.

Diggory. Aye, mind how I hold them. I learned to hold my hands this way when I was upon drill for the militia. And so being upon drill——

Hardcastle. You must not be so talkative, Diggory. You must be all attention to the guests. You must hear us talk, and not think of talking; you must see us drink, and not think of drinking; you must see us eat, and not think of eating.

Diggory. By the laws, your worship, that's perfectly unpossible. Whenever Diggory sees yeating going forward, ecod, he's always wishing for a mouthful himself.

Hardcastle. Blockhead! Is not a bellyful in the kitchen as good as a bellyful in the parlor? Stay your stomach with that reflection.

Diggory. Ecod, I thank your worship, I'll make a shift to stay my stomach with a slice of cold beef in the pantry.

Hardcastle. Diggory, you are too talkative. Then, if I happen to say a good thing or tell a good story at table, you must not all burst out a-laughing, as if you made part of the company.

Diggory. Then, ecod, your worship must not tell the story of Ould Grouse in the gunroom. I can't help laughing at that—he! he! he!—for the soul of me! We have laughed at that these twenty years—ha! ha! ha!

Hardcastle. Ha! ha! ha! The story *is* a good one. Well, honest Diggory, you may laugh at that—but still remember to be attentive. Suppose one of the company should call for a glass of wine, how will you behave? A glass of wine, sir, if you please.—(*To* DIGGORY.) Eh, why don't you move?

Diggory. Ecod, your worship, I never have courage till I see the eatables and drinkables brought upo' the table, and then I'm as bauld as a lion.

Hardcastle. What, will nobody move?

First Servant. I'm not to leave this place.

Second Servant. I'm sure it's no pleace of mine.

Third Servant. Nor mine, for sartin.

Diggory. Wauns,[1] and I'm sure it canna be mine.

Hardcastle. You numskulls! and so, while, like your betters, you are quarreling for places, the guests must be starved. O you dunces! I find I must begin all over again—But don't I hear a coach drive into the yard? To your posts, you blockheads! I'll go in the meantime and give my old friend's son a hearty reception at the gate.   (*Exit* HARDCASTLE.)

Diggory. By the elevens, my pleace is gone quite out of my head.

Roger. I know that my pleace is to be everywhere.

First Servant. Where the devil is mine?

Second Servant. My pleace is to be nowhere at all; and so I'ze go about my business. (*Exeunt Servants, running about as if frightened, several ways.*)

Enter SERVANT, *with candles, showing in* MARLOW *and* HASTINGS

Servant. Welcome, gentlemen, very welcome! This way.

Hastings. After the disappointments of the day, welcome once more, Charles, to the comforts of a clean room and a good fire. Upon my word, a very well-looking house; antique but creditable.

Marlow. The usual fate of a large mansion. Having first ruined the master by good housekeeping, it at last comes to levy contributions as an inn.

Hastings. As you say, we passengers are to be taxed to pay all these fineries. I have often seen a good sideboard or a marble chimney piece, though not actually put in the bill, inflame a reckoning[2] confoundedly.

Marlow. Travelers, George, must pay in all places. The only difference is that in good inns you pay dearly for luxuries; in bad inns you are fleeced and starved.

Hastings. You have lived pretty much among them. In truth, I have been often surprised that you who have seen so much of the world, with your natural good sense, and your many opportunities, could never yet acquire a requisite share of assurance.

Marlow. The Englishman's malady. But tell me, George, where could I have learned that assurance you talk of? My life has been chiefly spent in a college or an inn, in seclusion from that lovely part of the creation that chiefly teach men confidence. I don't know that I was ever familiarly acquainted with a single modest woman—except my mother—but among females of another class, you know——

Hastings. Aye, among them you are impudent enough, of all conscience!

Marlow. They are of *us*, you know.

Hastings. But in the company of women of reputation I never saw such an idiot, such a trembler; you look for all the world as if you wanted an opportunity of stealing out of the room.

Marlow. Why, man, that's because I *do* want to steal out of the room. Faith, I have often formed a resolution to break the ice and rattle away at any rate. But I don't know how; a single glance from a pair of fine eyes has totally overset my resolution. An impudent fellow may counterfeit modesty, but I'll

---

1. *Wauns,* wounds (a mild oath).   2. *inflame a reckoning,* increase the bill.

be hanged if a modest man can ever counterfeit impudence.

Hastings. If you could but say half the fine things to them that I have heard you lavish upon the barmaid of an inn——

Marlow. Why, George, I can't say fine things to them; they freeze, they petrify me. They may talk of a comet, or a burning mountain, or some such bagatelle; but to me a modest woman, dressed out in all her finery, is the most tremendous object of the whole creation.

Hastings. Ha! ha! ha! At this rate, man, how can you ever expect to marry?

Marlow. Never; unless, as among kings and princes, my bride were to be courted by proxy. If indeed, like an Eastern bridegroom, one were to be introduced to a wife he never saw before, it might be endured. But to go through all the terrors of a formal courtship, together with the episode of aunts, grandmothers, and cousins, and at last to blurt out the broad staring question of, "Madam, will you marry me?" No, no, that's a strain much above me, I assure you.

Hastings. I pity you. But how do you intend behaving to the lady you are come down to visit at the request of your father?

Marlow. As I behave to all other ladies. Bow very low, answer "Yes" or "No" to all her demands—but for the rest, I don't think I shall venture to look in her face till I see my father's again.

Hastings. I'm surprised that one who is so warm a friend can be so cool a lover.

Marlow. To be explicit, my dear Hastings, my chief inducement down was to be instrumental in forwarding your happiness, not my own. Miss Neville loves you, the family don't know you; as my friend you are sure of a reception, and let honor do the rest.

Hastings. My dear Marlow! But I'll suppress the emotion. Were I a wretch, meanly seeking to carry off a fortune, you should be the last man in the world I would apply to for assistance. But Miss Neville's person is all I ask, and that is mine, both from her deceased father's consent and her own inclination.

Marlow. Happy man! You have talents and art to captivate any woman. I'm doomed to adore the sex, and yet to converse with the

only part of it I despise. This stammer in my address, and this awkward, unprepossessing visage of mine can never permit me to soar above the reach of a milliner's 'prentice or one of the duchesses of Drury Lane.[3] Pshaw! this fellow here to interrupt us.

Enter HARDCASTLE

Hardcastle. Gentlemen, once more you are heartily welcome. Which is Mr. Marlow? Sir, you are heartily welcome. It's not my way, you see, to receive my friends with my back to the fire. I like to give them a hearty reception in the old style at my gate. I like to see their horses and trunks taken care of.

Marlow (aside). He has got our names from the servants already. (*To him.*) We approve your caution and hospitality, sir. (*To* HASTINGS.) I have been thinking, George, of changing our traveling dresses in the morning. I am grown confoundedly ashamed of mine.

Hardcastle. I beg, Mr. Marlow, you'll use no ceremony in this house.

Hastings. I fancy, Charles, you're right; the first blow is half the battle. I intend opening the campaign with the white and gold.

Hardcastle. Mr. Marlow—Mr. Hastings—gentlemen—pray be under no restraint in this house. This is Liberty Hall, gentlemen. You may do just as you please here.

Marlow. Yet, George, if we open the campaign too fiercely at first, we may want ammunition before it is over. I think to reserve the embroidery to secure a retreat.

Hardcastle. Your talking of a retreat, Mr. Marlow, puts me in mind of the Duke of Marlborough, when we went to besiege Denain.[4] He first summoned the garrison——

Marlow. Don't you think the *ventre d'or*[5] waistcoat will do with the plain brown?

Hardcastle. He first summoned the garrison, which might consist of about five thousand men——

---

3. *duchesses of Drury Lane,* flashily dressed women who try to pass themselves off for persons of rank. 4. *Denain,* a town in northern France, where the French won a victory over Prince Eugene's troops in 1712. Marlborough was not at this battle. 5. *ventre d'or* (vän′ trə dôr′), gold front. [*French*]

Hastings. I think not; brown and yellow mix but very poorly.

Hardcastle. I say, gentlemen, as I was telling you, he summoned the garrison, which might consist of about five thousand men—

Marlow. The girls like finery.

Hardcastle. Which might consist of about five thousand men well appointed with stores, ammunition, and other implements of war. "Now," says the Duke of Marlborough to George Brooks, that stood next to him—you must have heard of George Brooks—"I'll pawn my dukedom," says he, "but I take that garrison without spilling a drop of blood." So—

Marlow. What, my good friend, if you gave us a glass of punch in the meantime, it would help us to carry on the siege with vigor.

Hardcastle. Punch, sir! (*Aside.*) This is the most unaccountable kind of modesty I ever met with.

Marlow. Yes, sir, punch! A glass of warm punch, after our journey, will be comfortable. This is Liberty Hall, you know.

Hardcastle. Here's a cup,[6] sir.

Marlow (*aside*). So this fellow, in his Liberty Hall, will only let us have just what he pleases.

Hardcastle (*taking the cup*). I hope you'll find it to your mind. I have prepared it with my own hands, and I believe you'll own the ingredients are tolerable. Will you be so good as to pledge me, sir? Here, Mr. Marlow, here is to our better acquaintance! (*Drinks.*)

Marlow (*aside*). A very impudent fellow, this. But he's a character, and I'll humor him a little. Sir, my service to you. (*Drinks.*)

Hastings (*aside*). I see this fellow wants to give us his company, and forgets that he's an innkeeper, before he has learned to be a gentleman.

Marlow. From the excellence of your cup, my old friend, I suppose you have a good deal of business in this part of the country. Warm work, now and then, at elections, I suppose?

Hardcastle. No, sir, I have long given that work over. Since our betters have hit upon the expedient of electing each other, there is no business "for us that sell ale."

Hastings. So, then, you have no turn for politics, I find.

Hardcastle. Not in the least. There was a time, indeed, I fretted myself about the mistakes of government, like other people; but finding myself every day grow more angry and the government growing no better, I left it to mend itself. Since that, I no more trouble my head about Hyder Ally, or Ally Cawn,[7] than about Ally Croaker.[8] Sir, my service to you.

Hastings. So that, with eating above stairs and drinking below, with receiving your friends within and amusing them without, you lead a good, pleasant, bustling life of it.

Hardcastle. I do stir about a great deal, that's certain. Half the differences of the parish are adjusted in this very parlor.

Marlow (*after drinking*). And you have an argument in your cup, old gentleman, better than any in Westminster Hall.[9]

Hardcastle. Aye, young gentleman, that, and a little philosophy.

Marlow (*aside*). Well, this is the first time I ever heard of an innkeeper's philosophy.

Hastings. So then, like an experienced general, you attack them on every quarter. If you find their reason manageable, you attack it with your philosophy; if you find they have no reason, you attack them with this. Here's your health, my philosopher. (*Drinks.*)

Hardcastle. Good, very good, thank you; ha! ha! Your generalship puts me in mind of Prince Eugene, when he fought the Turks at the battle of Belgrade. You shall hear.

Marlow. Instead of the battle of Belgrade, I believe it's almost time to talk about supper. What has your philosophy got in the house for supper?

Hardcastle. For supper, sir! (*Aside.*) Was ever such a request to a man in his own house!

Marlow. Yes, sir, supper, sir; I begin to feel an appetite. I shall make devilish work tonight in the larder, I promise you.

Hardcastle (*aside*). Such a brazen dog, sure, never my eyes beheld. (*To him.*) Why, really, sir, as for supper I can't well tell. My Dorothy and the cookmaid settle these things

6. *cup*, wine sweetened and flavored and usually iced.   7. *Hyder Ally, or Ally Cawn*, Hyder Ali Khan, Maharajah of Mysore in India, who defeated the English in 1767.   8. *Ally Croaker*, a popular Irish song.   9. *Westminster Hall*, hall where the arguments of the law courts were held.

between them. I leave these kind of things entirely to them.

Marlow. You do, do you?

Hardcastle. Entirely. By the by, I believe they are in actual consultation upon what's for supper this moment in the kitchen.

Marlow. Then I beg they'll admit me as one of their privy council. It's a way I have got. When I travel I always choose to regulate my own supper. Let the cook be called. No offense, I hope, sir?

Hardcastle. Oh, no, sir, none in the least; yet I don't know how; our Bridget, the cook-maid, is not very communicative upon these occasions. Should we send for her, she might scold us all out of the house.

Hastings. Let's see your list of the larder, then. I ask it as a favor. I always match my appetite to my bill of fare.

Marlow (*to* HARDCASTLE, *who looks at them with surprise*). Sir, he's very right, and it's my way, too.

Hardcastle. Sir, you have a right to command here. Here, Roger, bring us the bill of fare for tonight's supper; I believe it's drawn out. (*Exit* ROGER.) Your manner, Mr. Hastings, puts me in mind of my uncle, Colonel Wallop. It was a saying of his that no man was sure of his supper till he had eaten it.

Hastings (*aside*). All upon the high ropes! His uncle a colonel! We shall soon hear of his mother being a justice of the peace. (*To* MARLOW.) But let's hear the bill of fare.

Marlow (*perusing*). What's here? For the first course; for the second course; for the dessert. The devil, sir, do you think we have brought down the whole Joiners' Company, or the Corporation of Bedford, to eat up such a supper? Two or three little things, clean and comfortable, will do.

Hastings. But let's hear it.

Marlow (*reading*). For the first course, at the top, a pig and prune sauce.

Hastings. Damn your pig, I say!

Marlow. And damn your prune sauce, say I!

Hardcastle. And yet, gentlemen, to men that are hungry, pig with prune sauce is very good eating.

Marlow. At the bottom, a calf's tongue and brains.

Hastings. Let your brains be knocked out, my good sir; I don't like them.

Marlow. Or you may clap them on a plate by themselves. I do.

Hardcastle (*aside*). Their impudence confounds me. (*To them.*) Gentlemen, you are my guests; make what alterations you please. Is there anything else you wish to retrench or alter, gentlemen?

Marlow. Item: A pork pie, a boiled rabbit and sausages, a florentine,[10] a shaking pudding,[11] and a dish of tiff—taff—taffety cream![12]

Hastings. Confound your made dishes![13] I shall be as much at a loss in this house as at a green and yellow dinner at the French ambassador's table. I'm for plain eating.

Hardcastle. I'm sorry, gentlemen, that I have nothing you like, but if there be anything you have a particular fancy to——

Marlow. Why, really, sir, your bill of fare is so exquisite that any one part of it is full as good as another. Send us what you please. So much for supper. And now to see that our beds are aired and properly taken care of.

Hardcastle. I entreat you'll leave all that to me. You shall not stir a step.

Marlow. Leave that to you! I protest, sir, you must excuse me; I always look to these things myself.

Hardcastle. I must insist, sir, you'll make yourself easy on that head.

Marlow. You see, I am resolved on it—— (*Aside.*) A very troublesome fellow this, as ever I met with.

Hardcastle. Well, sir, I'm resolved at least to attend you. (*Aside.*) This may be modern modesty, but I never saw anything look so like old-fashioned impudence.

(*Exeunt* MARLOW *and* HARDCASTLE.)

Hastings (*alone*). So I find this fellow's civilities begin to grow troublesome. But who can be angry at those assiduities which are meant to please him? Ha! what do I see? Miss Neville, by all that's happy!

Enter CONSTANCE NEVILLE

---

10. *florentine,* a baked pudding. **11.** *shaking pudding,* a jelly. **12.** *taffety cream,* a cream pudding with a velvety texture. **13.** *made dishes,* dishes composed of several ingredients.

Constance. My dear Hastings! To what unexpected good fortune, to what accident, am I to ascribe this happy meeting?

Hastings. Rather let me ask the same question, as I could never have hoped to meet my dearest Constance at an inn.

Constance. An inn! sure you mistake; my aunt, my guardian, lives here. What could induce you to think this house an inn?

Hastings. My friend, Mr. Marlow, with whom I came down, and I have been sent here as to an inn, I assure you. A young fellow whom we accidentally met at a house hard by directed us hither.

Constance. Certainly it must be one of my hopeful cousin's tricks, of whom you have heard me talk so often; ha! ha! ha!

Hastings. He whom your aunt intends for you? He of whom I have such just apprehensions?

Constance. You have nothing to fear from him, I assure you. You'd adore him if you knew how heartily he despises me. My aunt knows it, too, and has undertaken to court me for him, and actually begins to think she has made a conquest.

Hastings. Thou dear dissembler! You must know, my Constance, I have just seized this happy opportunity of my friend's visit here to get admittance into the family. The horses that carried us down are now fatigued with their journey, but they'll soon be refreshed; and, then, if my dearest girl will trust her faithful Hastings, we shall soon be landed in France, where even among slaves the laws of marriage are respected.

Constance. I have often told you that though ready to obey you, I yet should leave my little fortune behind with reluctance. The greatest part of it was left me by my uncle, the India director, and chiefly consists in jewels. I have been for some time persuading my aunt to let me wear them. I fancy I'm very near succeeding. The instant they are put into my possession, you shall find me ready to make them and myself yours.

Hastings. Perish the baubles! Your person is all I desire. In the meantime, my friend Marlow must not be let into his mistake. I know the strange reserve of his temper is such

that if abruptly informed of it, he would instantly quit the house before our plan was ripe for execution.

Constance. But how shall we keep him in the deception? Miss Hardcastle is just returned from walking; what if we still continue to deceive him?—This, this way——(*They confer.*)

Enter MARLOW

Marlow. The assiduities of these good people tease me beyond bearing. My host seems to think it ill manners to leave me alone, and so he claps not only himself but his old-fashioned wife on my back. They talk of coming to sup with us, too; and then, I suppose, we are to run the gauntlet through all the rest of the family.—What have we got here?

Hastings. My dear Charles! Let me congratulate you!—The most fortunate accident! —Who do you think is just alighted?

Marlow. Cannot guess.

Hastings. Our mistresses, boy, Miss Hardcastle and Miss Neville. Give me leave to introduce Miss Constance Neville to your acquaintance. Happening to dine in the neighborhood, they called on their return to take fresh horses here. Miss Hardcastle has just stepped into the next room, and will be back in an instant. Wasn't it lucky? Eh!

Marlow (*aside*). I have just been mortified enough of all conscience, and here comes something to complete my embarrassment.

Hastings. Well, but wasn't it the most fortunate thing in the world?

Marlow. Oh, yes! Very fortunate—a most joyful encounter——But our dresses, George, you know, are in disorder——What if we should postpone the happiness till tomorrow? —Tomorrow at her own house——It will be every bit as convenient—and rather more respectful——Tomorrow let it be. (*Offering to go.*)

Constance. By no means, sir. Your ceremony will displease her. The disorder of your dress will show the ardor of your impatience. Besides, she knows you are in the house, and will permit you to see her.

Marlow. Oh, the devil! How shall I support it? Hem! Hem! Hastings, you must not go. You are to assist me, you know. I shall be confoundedly ridiculous. Yet, hang it! I'll take courage.

Hastings. Pshaw, man! it's but the first plunge, and all's over. She's but a woman, you know.

Marlow. And, of all women, she that I dread most to encounter.

Enter KATE HARDCASTLE, *as returned from walking, a bonnet, etc.*

Hastings (introducing them). Miss Hardcastle, Mr. Marlow; I'm proud of bringing two persons of such merit together, that only want to know, to esteem each other.

Kate (aside). Now for meeting my modest gentleman with a demure face, and quite in his own manner. *(After a pause in which he appears very uneasy and disconcerted.)* I'm glad of your safe arrival, sir. I'm told you had some accidents by the way.

Marlow. Only a few, madam. Yes, we had some. Yes, madam, a good many accidents, but should be sorry—madam—or rather glad of any accidents—that are so agreeably concluded. Hem!

Hastings (to him). You never spoke better in your whole life. Keep it up, and I'll insure you the victory.

Kate. I'm afraid you flatter, sir. You that have seen so much of the finest company can find little entertainment in an obscure corner of the country.

Marlow (gathering courage). I have lived, indeed, in the world, madam, but I have kept very little company. I have been but an observer upon life, madam, while others were enjoying it.

Constance. But that, I am told, is the way to enjoy it at last.

Hastings (to him). Cicero never spoke better. Once more, and you are confirmed in assurance forever.

Marlow (to him). Hem! Stand by me then, and when I'm down, throw in a word or two to set me up again.

Kate. An observer, like you, upon life, were, I fear, disagreeably employed, since you must have had much more to censure than to approve.

Marlow. Pardon me, madam. I was always willing to be amused. The folly of most people is rather an object of mirth than uneasiness.

Hastings (to him). Bravo, bravo! Never spoke so well in your whole life. Well, Miss Hardcastle, I see that you and Mr. Marlow are going to be very good company. I believe our being here will but embarrass the interview.

Marlow. Not in the least, Mr. Hastings. We like your company of all things. *(To him.)* Zounds! George, sure you won't go? How can you leave us?

Hastings. Our presence will but spoil conversation; so we'll retire to the next room. *(To him.)* You don't consider, man, that we are to manage a little tête-à-tête of our own.

(Exeunt CONSTANCE *and* HASTINGS.*)*

Kate (after a pause). But you have not been wholly an observer, I presume, sir; the ladies, I should hope, have employed some part of your addresses.

Marlow (relapsing into timidity). Pardon me, madam, I—I—I—as yet have studied—only —to—deserve them.

Kate. And that, some say, is the very worst way to obtain them.

Marlow. Perhaps so, madam. But I love to converse only with the more grave and sensible part of the sex.—But I'm afraid I grow tiresome.

Kate. Not at all, sir; there is nothing I like so much as grave conversation myself; I could hear it forever. Indeed, I have often been surprised how a man of sentiment[14] could ever admire those light, airy pleasures, where nothing reaches the heart.

Marlow. It's—a disease—of the mind, madam. In the variety of tastes there must be some who, wanting a relish—for—um—a—um——

Kate. I understand you, sir. There must be some who, wanting a relish for refined pleasures, pretend to despise what they are incapable of tasting.

Marlow. My meaning, madam, but infinite-

---

14. *man of sentiment,* a man of feeling or sensitivity who is aware of the deeper moral issues in life. (See page 303 for a discussion of the cult of sentiment.)

ly better expressed. And I can't help observing —a——

Kate (aside). Who could ever suppose this fellow impudent upon some occasions! (*To him.*) You were going to observe, sir——

Marlow. I was observing, madam—I protest, madam, I forget what I was going to observe.

Kate (aside). I vow and so do I! (*To him.*) You were observing, sir, that in this age of hypocrisy——

Marlow. Yes, madam. In this age of hypocrisy there are few who upon strict inquiry do not—a—a—a——

Kate. I understand you perfectly, sir.

Marlow (aside). Egad! and that's more than I do myself.

Kate. You mean that in this hypocritical age there are few who do not condemn in public what they practice in private, and think they pay every debt to virtue when they praise it.

Marlow. True, madam; those who have most virtue in their mouths have least of it in their bosoms. But I'm sure I tire you, madam.

Kate. Not in the least, sir; there's something so agreeable and spirited in your manner, such life and force—pray, sir, go on.

Marlow. Yes, madam, I was saying—that there are some occasions—when a total want of courage, madam, destroys all the—and puts us —upon—a—a—a——

Kate. I agree with you entirely; a want of courage upon some occasions assumes the appearance of ignorance, and betrays us when we most want to excel. I beg you'll proceed.

Marlow. Yes, madam. Morally speaking, madam—but I see Miss Neville expecting us in the next room. I would not intrude for the world.

Kate. I protest, sir, I never was more agreeably entertained in all my life. Pray, go on.

Marlow. Yes, madam, I was—but she beckons us to join her. Madam, shall I do myself the honor to attend you?

Kate. Well, then, I'll follow.

Marlow (aside). This pretty, smooth dialogue has done for me. (*Exit.*)

Kate (alone). Ha! ha! ha! Was there ever such a sober, sentimental interview? I'm certain he scarce looked in my face the whole time. Yet the fellow, but for his unaccountable bashfulness, is pretty well, too. He has good sense, but then so buried in his fears that it fatigues one more than ignorance. If I could teach him a little confidence, it would be doing somebody that I know of a piece of service. But who is that somebody?—That, faith, is a question I can scarce answer. (*Exit.*)

Enter TONY *and* CONSTANCE, *followed by* MRS. HARDCASTLE *and* HASTINGS

Tony. What do you follow me for, cousin Con? I wonder you're not ashamed to be so very engaging.

Constance. I hope, cousin, one may speak to one's own relations and not be to blame.

Tony. Aye, but I know what sort of a relation you want to make me, though; but it won't do. I tell you, cousin Con, it won't do; so I beg you'll keep your distance. I want no nearer relationship. (*She follows, coquetting him, to the back scene.*)

Mrs. Hardcastle. Well! I vow, Mr. Hastings, you are very entertaining. There's nothing in the world I love to talk of so much as London, and the fashions, though I was never there myself.

Hastings. Never there! You amaze me! From your air and manner, I concluded you had been bred all your life either at Ranelagh, St. James', or Tower Wharf.[15]

Mrs. Hardcastle. Oh, sir! you're only pleased to say so. We country persons can have no manner at all. I'm in love with the town, and that serves to raise me above some of our neighboring rustics; but who can have a manner that has never seen the Pantheon, the Grotto Gardens, the Borough,[16] and such places where the nobility chiefly resort? All I can do is to enjoy London at second hand. I take care to know every tête-à-tête from the *Scandalous Magazine,* and have all the fash-

---

15. *Ranelagh, St. James', or Tower Wharf.* The first was a garden, the second a park—both fashionable resorts of high society; but Tower Wharf was a slum district near the Tower of London. 16. *the Pantheon, the Grotto Gardens, the Borough.* The Pantheon was a rival resort of Ranelagh, but Grotto Gardens and the Borough of Southwark, south of the Thames, were not places frequented by high society.

ions, as they come out, in a letter from the two Miss Rickets of Crooked Lane. Pray, how do you like this head,[17] Mr. Hastings?

Hastings. Extremely elegant and *dégagée*,[18] upon my word, madam. Your *friseur*[19] is a Frenchman, I suppose?

Mrs. Hardcastle. I protest, I dressed it myself from a print in the *Ladies' Memorandumbook* for the last year.

Hastings. Indeed! Such a head in a side box, at the playhouse, would draw as many gazers as my Lady Mayoress at a City Ball.

Mrs. Hardcastle. I vow, since inoculation began, there is no such thing to be seen as a plain woman; so one must dress a little particular, or one may escape in the crowd.

Hastings. But that can never be your case, madam, in any dress. (*Bowing.*)

Mrs. Hardcastle. Yet, what signifies my dressing, when I have such a piece of antiquity by my side as Mr. Hardcastle; all I can say will never argue down a single button from his clothes. I have often wanted him to throw off his great flaxen wig, and where he was bald, to plaster it over, like my Lord Pately, with powder.

Hastings. You are right, madam; for, as among the ladies there are none ugly, so among the men there are none old.

Mrs. Hardcastle. But what do you think his answer was? Why, with his usual Gothic[20] vivacity, he said I only wanted him to throw off his wig to convert it into a *tête*[21] for my own wearing!

Hastings. Intolerable! At your age you may wear what you please, and it must become you.

Mrs. Hardcastle. Pray, Mr. Hastings, what do you take to be the most fashionable age about town?

Hastings. Some time ago, forty was all the mode; but I'm told the ladies intend to bring up fifty for the ensuing winter.

Mrs. Hardcastle. Seriously? Then I shall be too young for the fashion!

Hastings. No lady begins now to put on jewels till she's past forty. For instance, miss there, in a polite circle, would be considered as a child, a mere maker of samplers.

Mrs. Hardcastle. And yet Mistress Niece thinks herself as much a woman, and is as fond of jewels, as the oldest of us all.

Hastings. Your niece, is she? And that young gentleman—a brother of yours, I should presume?

Mrs. Hardcastle. My son, sir. They are contracted to each other. Observe their little sports. They fall in and out ten times a day, as if they were man and wife already. (*To them.*) Well, Tony, child, what soft things are you saying to your cousin Constance this evening?

Tony. I have been saying no soft things; but that it's very hard to be followed about so. Ecod! I've not a place in the house now that's left to myself but the stable.

Mrs. Hardcastle. Never mind him, Con, my dear. He's in another story behind your back.

Constance. There's something generous in my cousin's manner. He falls out before faces to be forgiven in private.

Tony. That's a damned confounded—crack.

Mrs. Hardcastle. Ah! he's a sly one. Don't you think they're like each other about the mouth, Mr. Hastings? The Blenkinsop mouth to a T. They're of a size, too. Back to back, my pretties, that Mr. Hastings may see you. Come, Tony.

Tony. You had as good not make me, I tell you. (*Measuring.*)

Constance. O lud! he has almost cracked my head.

Mrs. Hardcastle. Oh, the monster! For shame, Tony. You a man, and behave so!

Tony. If I'm a man, let me have my fortin. Ecod! I'll not be made a fool of no longer.

Mrs. Hardcastle. Is this, ungrateful boy, all that I'm to get for the pains I have taken in your education? I that have rocked you in your cradle and fed that pretty mouth with a spoon! Did not I work that waistcoat to make you genteel? Did not I prescribe for you every day and weep while the receipt was operating?

Tony. Ecod! you had reason to weep, for

---

17. *head*, headdress. 18. *dégagée* (dā gä zhā'), graceful. [French] 19. *friseur* (frē zœr'), hairdresser. [French] 20. *Gothic*, barbaric. 21. *tête* (tet), a pun (*head-wig*). [French]

you have been dosing me ever since I was born. I have gone through every receipt in the *Complete Huswife* ten times over; and you have thoughts of coursing me through Quincy[22] next spring. But, ecod! I tell you, I'll not be made a fool of no longer.

Mrs. Hardcastle. Wasn't it all for your good, viper? Wasn't it all for your good?

Tony. I wish you'd let me and my good alone, then. Snubbing this way when I'm in spirits! If I'm to have any good, let it come of itself; not to keep dinging it, dinging it into one so.

Mrs. Hardcastle. That's false; I never see you when you're in spirits. No, Tony, you then go to the alehouse or kennel. I'm never to be delighted with your agreeable wild notes, unfeeling monster!

Tony. Ecod! Mamma, your own notes are the wildest of the two.

Mrs. Hardcastle. Was ever the like? But I see he wants to break my heart, I see he does.

Hastings. Dear madam, pray permit me to lecture the young gentleman a little. I'm certain I can persuade him to his duty.

Mrs. Hardcastle. Well! I must retire. Come, Constance, my love. You see, Mr. Hastings, the wretchedness of my situation. Was ever poor woman so plagued with a dear, sweet, pretty, provoking, undutiful boy? (*Exeunt* MRS. HARDCASTLE *and* CONSTANCE.)

Tony (*singing*). "There was a young man riding by, and fain would have his will. Rang do didlo dee." Don't mind her. Let her cry. It's the comfort of her heart. I have seen her and sister cry over a book for an hour together, and they said they liked the book better the more it made them cry.

Hastings. Then you're no friend to the ladies, I find, my pretty young gentleman?

Tony. That's as I find 'um.

Hastings. Not to her of your mother's choosing, I dare answer? And she appears to me a pretty, well-tempered girl.

Tony. That's because you don't know her as well as I. Ecod! I know every inch about her; and there's not a more bitter cantankerous toad in all Christendom!

Hastings (*aside*). Pretty encouragement this for a lover!

Tony. I have seen her since the height of that. She has as many tricks as a hare in a thicket, or a colt the first day's breaking.

Hastings. To me she appears sensible and silent.

Tony. Aye, before company. But when she's with her playmates, she's as loud as a hog in a gate.

Hastings. But there is a meek modesty about her that charms me.

Tony. Yes, but curb her never so little, she kicks up and you're flung in a ditch.

Hastings. Well, but you must allow her a little beauty.—Yes, you must allow her some beauty.

Tony. Bandbox! She's all a made-up thing, mun. Ah! could you but see Bet Bouncer of these parts, you might then talk of beauty. Ecod! she has two eyes as black as sloes, and cheeks as broad and red as a pulpit cushion. She'd make two of she.

Hastings. Well, what say you to a friend that would take this bitter bargain off your hands?

Tony. Anon![23]

Hastings. Would you thank him that would take Miss Neville, and leave you to happiness and your dear Betsy?

Tony. Aye; but where is there such a friend, for who would take her?

Hastings. I am he. If you but assist me, I'll engage to whip her off to France, and you shall never hear more of her.

Tony. Assist you! Ecod, I will, to the last drop of my blood. I'll clap a pair of horses to your chaise that shall trundle you off in a twinkling and maybe get you a part of her fortin besides, in jewels, that you little dream of.

Hastings. My dear squire, this looks like a lad of spirit.

Tony. Come along, then, and you shall see more of my spirit before you have done with me. (*Singing.*)

We are the boys
That fears no noise,
Where the thundering cannons roar.

(*Exeunt.*)

---

22. *Complete Huswife . . . Quincy,* compilations of popular remedies.   23. *Anon!,* an expression of surprise.

1. What is the first result of Tony's practical joke?

2. (a) How does Goldsmith contrive to keep Marlow ignorant of the fact that he is not at an inn, while Hastings becomes aware of the actual situation? (b) Why does not Hastings enlighten Marlow at once?

3. What is the status of each of the two love stories now developing side by side?

❧ Better reading
The cult of sentiment

In the eighteenth century the word *sentiment* referred to those exaggerated feelings of pity and tenderness that we today would call *sentimentality*. This is the meaning Kate has in mind when, tongue in cheek, she tells Marlow that she is amazed that "a man of *sentiment* could ever admire those light, airy pleasures, where nothing reaches the heart" (Act II, page 299, column 2, lines 36-38).

Goldsmith was much concerned about the rise of sentiment and the decline of comedy in the English theater. The lively but immoral plays of the Restoration had given way in the opening decades of the eighteenth century to middle-class, Puritan plays in which moral reform became more important than comic effect. The hero of such a play was usually a rakish gallant who was made to see the folly of his "light, airy pleasures" and the wisdom of following virtue largely through the efforts of a tearful, tender-hearted woman. Another stock character was the completely virtuous son, who had no bad habits, who never dreamed of disobeying his family—in short, who stood as the high example to which all those who had fallen might aspire. This cult of sentiment dominated not only the English theater, but it affected the English novel as well. It was paralleled in philosophy by a new school of thought which held that man was basically good and in possession of an innate moral sense that led him toward virtue. Although Goldsmith was too much a man of his time not to be influenced by the cult of sentiment, he deplored its negative effect on the traditionally light-hearted, spicy quality of English comedy.

Where in Acts I and II does Goldsmith directly ridicule the cult of sentiment? How is Kate's conversation with Marlow in Act II a reversal of the stock situation between men and women in sentimental comedies? To what extent is Tony Lumpkin the virtuous son in reverse?

Reread the alehouse scene in Act I and the scenes between Hardcastle and his servants and Hardcastle and his guests in Act II. How are these scenes opposite in spirit to sentimental comedy?

Engraving showing the airy pleasures of Vauxhall, favorite resort of sophisticated Londoners.

ACT THREE

SCENE: *The house*

Enter HARDCASTLE, *alone*

Hardcastle. What could my old friend Sir Charles mean by recommending his son as the modestest young man in town? To me he appears the most impudent piece of brass that ever spoke with a tongue. He has taken possession of the easy chair by the fireside already. He took his boots off in the parlor and desired me to see them taken care of. I'm desirous to know how his impudence affects my daughter. She will certainly be shocked at it.

Enter KATE, *plainly dressed*

Hardcastle. Well, my Kate, I see you have changed your dress, as I bade you; and yet, I believe, there was no great occasion.

Kate. I find such a pleasure, sir, in obeying your commands that I take care to observe them without ever debating their propriety.

Hardcastle. And yet, Kate, I sometimes give you some cause, particularly when I recommended my modest gentleman to you as a lover today.

Kate. You taught me to expect something extraordinary, and I find the original exceeds the description.

Hardcastle. I was never so surprised in my life! He has quite confounded all my faculties!

Kate. I never saw anything like it; and a man of the world, too!

Hardcastle. Aye, he learned it all abroad—what a fool was I to think a young man could learn modesty by traveling. He might as soon learn wit at a masquerade.

Kate. It seems all natural to him.

Hardcastle. A good deal assisted by bad company and a French dancing master.

Kate. Sure, you mistake, Papa! A French dancing master could never have taught him that timid look—that awkward address—that bashful manner.

Hardcastle. Whose look? Whose manner, child?

Kate. Mr. Marlow's; his *mauvaise honte*,[1] his timidity, struck me at the first sight.

Hardcastle. Then your first sight deceived you; for I think him one of the most brazen first sights that ever astonished my senses.

Kate. Sure, sir, you rally! I never saw anyone so modest.

Hardcastle. And can you be serious? I never saw such a bouncing, swaggering puppy since I was born. Bully Dawson[2] was but a fool to him.

Kate. Surprising! He met me with a respectful bow, a stammering voice, and a look fixed on the ground.

Hardcastle. He met me with a loud voice, a lordly air, and a familiarity that made my blood freeze again.

Kate. He treated me with diffidence and respect; censured the manners of the age; admired the prudence of girls that never laughed; tired me with apologies for being tiresome; then left the room with a bow and "Madam, I would not for the world detain you."

Hardcastle. He spoke to me as if he knew me all his life before; asked twenty questions, and never waited for an answer; interrupted my best remarks with some silly pun; and when I was in my best story of the Duke of Marlborough and Prince Eugene, he asked if I had not a good hand at making punch. Yes, Kate, he asked your father if he was a maker of punch!

Kate. One of us must certainly be mistaken.

Hardcastle. If he be what he has shown himself, I'm determined he shall never have my consent.

Kate. And if he be the sullen thing I take him, he shall never have mine.

Hardcastle. In one thing, then, we are agreed—to reject him.

Kate. Yes—but upon conditions. For if you should find him less impudent and I more presuming; if you find him more respectful and I more importunate—I don't know—the fellow is well enough for a man—certainly we don't meet many such at a horse race in the country.

---

1. *mauvaise honte* (mô′vez ONT′), bashfulness. [*French*]
2. *Bully Dawson*, the notorious swashbuckler of the seventeenth century mentioned by Steele on page 254.

Hardcastle. If we should find him so—but that's impossible. The first appearance has done my business. I'm seldom deceived in that.

Kate. And yet there may be many good qualities under the first appearance.

Hardcastle. Aye, when a girl finds a fellow's outside to her taste, she then sets about guessing the rest of his furniture. With her a smooth face stands for good sense, and a genteel figure for every virtue.

Kate. I hope, sir, a conversation begun with a compliment to my good sense won't end with a sneer at my understanding?

Hardcastle. Pardon me, Kate. But if young Mr. Brazen can find the art of reconciling contradictions, he may please us both, perhaps.

Kate. And as one of us must be mistaken, what if we go to make further discoveries?

Hardcastle. Agreed. But depend on't, I'm in the right.

Kate. And depend on't, I'm not much in the wrong. (*Exeunt.*)

Enter TONY, *running in with a jewelry casket*

Tony. Ecod! I have got them. Here they are. My cousin Con's necklaces, bobs and all. My mother shan't cheat the poor souls out of their fortin neither. Oh, my genus! is that you?

Enter HASTINGS

Hastings. My dear friend, how have you managed with your mother? I hope you have amused her with pretending love for your cousin, and that you are willing to be reconciled at least? Our horses will be refreshed in a short time, and we shall soon be ready to set off.

Tony. And here's something to bear your charges by the way (*giving the casket*)—your sweetheart's jewels. Keep them; and hang those, I say, that would rob you of one of them!

Hastings. But how have you procured them from your mother?

Tony. Ask me no questions, and I'll tell you no fibs. I procured them by the rule of thumb. If I had not a key to every drawer in Mother's bureau, how could I go to the alehouse so often as I do? An honest man may rob himself of his own at any time.

Hastings. Thousands do it every day. But to be plain with you: Miss Neville is endeavoring to procure them from her aunt this very instant. If she succeeds, it will be the most delicate way at least of obtaining them.

Tony. Well, keep them until you know how it will be. But I know how it will be well enough; she'd as soon part with the only sound tooth in her head.

Hastings. But I dread the effects of her resentment when she finds she has lost them.

Tony. Never you mind her resentment; leave *me* to manage that. I don't value her resentment the bounce of a cracker. Zounds! here they are! Morrice![3] Prance!

(*Exit* HASTINGS.)

Enter MRS. HARDCASTLE *and* CONSTANCE

Mrs. Hardcastle. Indeed, Constance, you amaze me. Such a girl as you want jewels? It will be time enough for jewels, my dear, twenty years hence, when your beauty begins to want repairs.

Constance. But what will repair beauty at forty will certainly improve it at twenty, madam.

Mrs. Hardcastle. Yours, my dear, can admit of none. That natural blush is beyond a thousand ornaments. Besides, child, jewels are quite out at present. Don't you see half the ladies of our acquaintance, my Lady Killdaylight, and Mrs. Crump, and the rest of them, carry their jewels to town, and bring nothing but paste and marcasites back?

Constance. But who knows, madam, but somebody that shall be nameless would like me best with all my little finery about me?

Mrs. Hardcastle. Consult your glass, my dear, and then see if, with such a pair of eyes, you want any better sparklers. What do you think, Tony, my dear? Does your Cousin Con want any jewels, in your eyes, to set off her beauty?

---

3. *Morrice!* Be off!

Tony. That's as thereafter may be.

Constance. My dear aunt, if you know how it would oblige me.

Mrs. Hardcastle. A parcel of old-fashioned rose and table-cut things. They would make you look like the court of King Solomon at a puppet show. Besides, I believe I can't readily come at them. They may be missing, for aught I know to the contrary.

Tony (*apart to* MRS. HARDCASTLE). Then why don't you tell her so at once, as she's so longing for them? Tell her they're lost. It's the only way to quiet her. Say they're lost, and call me to bear witness.

Mrs. Hardcastle (*apart to* TONY). You know, my dear, I'm only keeping them for you. So if I say they're gone, you'll bear me witness, will you? He! he! he!

Tony (*apart to* MRS. HARDCASTLE). Never fear me. Ecod! I'll say I saw them taken out with my own eyes.

Constance. I desire them but for a day, madam. Just to be permitted to show them as relics, and then they may be locked up again.

Mrs. Hardcastle. To be plain with you, my dear Constance, if I could find them, you should have them. They're missing, I assure you. Lost, for aught I know; but we must have patience wherever they are.

John Quick as Tony Lumpkin in the original London production.

ENTHOVEN THEATER COLLECTION, VICTORIA AND ALBERT MUSEUM

Constance. I'll not believe it; this is but a shallow pretense to deny me. I know they were too valuable to be so slightly kept, and as you are to answer for the loss——

Mrs. Hardcastle. Don't be alarmed, Constance. If they be lost, I must restore an equivalent. But my son knows they are missing and not to be found.

Tony. That I can bear witness to. They are missing and not to be found; I'll take my oath on't.

Mrs. Hardcastle. You must learn resignation, my dear; for though we lose our fortune, yet we should not lose our patience. See me, how calm I am.

Constance. Aye, people are generally calm at the misfortunes of others.

Mrs. Hardcastle. Now, I wonder a girl of your good sense should waste a thought upon such trumpery. We shall soon find them; and, in the meantime, you shall make use of my garnets till your jewels be found.

Constance. I detest garnets!

Mrs. Hardcastle. The most becoming things in the world to set off a clear complexion. You have often seen how well they look upon me. You *shall* have them.   (*Exit.*)

Constance. I dislike them of all things. You shan't stir. Was ever anything so provoking, to mislay my own jewels, and force me to wear her trumpery?

Tony. Don't be a fool. If she gives you the garnets, take what you can get. The jewels are your own already. I have stolen them out of her bureau, and she does not know it. Fly to your spark; he'll tell you more of the matter. Leave me to manage her.

Constance. My dear cousin!

Tony. Vanish. She's here and has missed them already. (*Exit* CONSTANCE.) Zounds! how she fidgets and spits about like a Catherine wheel.[4]

Enter MRS. HARDCASTLE

Mrs. Hardcastle. Confusion! Thieves! Robbers! We are cheated, plundered, broke open, undone.

---

4. *Catherine wheel*, a pinwheel type of fireworks.

Tony. What's the matter, what's the matter, Mamma? I hope nothing has happened to any of the good family!

Mrs. Hardcastle. We are robbed. My bureau has been broken open, the jewels taken out, and I'm undone.

Tony. Oh! is that all? Ha! ha! ha! By the laws, I never saw it better acted in my life. Ecod, I thought you was ruined in earnest, ha! ha! ha!

Mrs. Hardcastle. Why, boy, I *am* ruined in earnest. My bureau has been broken open and all taken away.

Tony. Stick to that; ha! ha! ha! stick to that. I'll bear witness, you know; call me to bear witness.

Mrs. Hardcastle. I tell you, Tony, by all that's precious, the jewels are gone, and I shall be ruined forever.

Tony. Sure, I know they're gone, and I am to say so.

Mrs. Hardcastle. My dearest Tony, but hear me. They're gone, I say.

Tony. By the laws, Mamma, you make me for to laugh, ha! ha! I know who took them well enough, ha! ha! ha!

Mrs. Hardcastle. Was there ever such a blockhead, that can't tell the difference between jest and earnest! I can tell you I'm not in jest, booby!

Tony. That's right, that's right; you must be in a bitter passion, and then nobody will suspect either of us. I'll bear witness that they are gone.

Mrs. Hardcastle. Was there ever such a cross-grained brute, that won't hear me! Can you bear witness that you're no better than a fool? Was ever poor woman so beset with fools on one hand and thieves on the other!

Tony. I can bear witness to that.

Mrs. Hardcastle. Bear witness again, you blockhead, you, and I'll turn you out of the room directly. My poor niece, what will become of her? Do you laugh, you unfeeling brute, as if you enjoyed my distress?

Tony. I can bear witness to that.

Mrs. Hardcastle. Do you insult me, monster? I'll teach you to vex your mother, I will!

Tony. I can bear witness to that. (*He runs off; she follows him.*)

Enter KATE *and* MAID

Kate. What an unaccountable creature is that brother of mine, to send them to the house as an inn, ha! ha! I don't wonder at his impudence.

Maid. But what is more, madam, the young gentleman, as you passed by in your present dress, asked me if you were the barmaid. He mistook you for the barmaid, madam!

Kate. Did he? Then, as I live, I'm resolved to keep up the delusion. Tell me, Pimple, how do you like my present dress? Don't you think I look something like Cherry in *The Beaux' Stratagem?*[5]

Maid. It's the dress, madam, that every lady wears in the country but when she visits or receives company.

Kate. And are you sure he does not remember my face or person?

Maid. Certain of it!

Kate. I vow I thought so; for though we spoke for some time together, yet his fears were such that he never once looked up during the interview. Indeed, if he had, my bonnet would have kept him from seeing me.

Maid. But what do you hope from keeping him in his mistake?

Kate. In the first place, I shall be seen, and that is no small advantage to a girl who brings her face to market. Then I shall perhaps make an acquaintance, and that's no small victory gained over one who never addresses any but the wildest of her sex. But my chief aim is to take my gentleman off his guard and, like an invisible champion of romance, examine the giant's force before I offer to combat.

Maid. But are you sure you can act your part and disguise your voice so that he may mistake that, as he has already mistaken your person?

Kate. Never fear me. I think I have got the true bar cant.—Did your honor call?—Attend the Lion there.—Pipes and tobacco for the

---

5. *The Beaux' Stratagem,* a play by the Restoration dramatist George Farquhar. Cherry is the daughter of a tavern keeper.

Angel.—The Lamb[6] has been outrageous this half hour.

Maid. It will do, madam. But he's here.

(*Exit* MAID.)

Enter MARLOW

Marlow. What a bawling in every part of the house! I have scarce a moment's repose. If I go to the best room, there I find my host and his story; if I fly to the gallery, there we have my hostess with her curtsy down to the ground. I have at last got a moment to myself, and now for recollection. (*Walks and muses.*)

Kate. Did you call, sir? Did your honor call?

Marlow (*musing*). As for Miss Hardcastle, she's too grave and sentimental for me.

Kate. Did your honor call? (*She still places herself before him, he turning away.*)

Marlow. No, child! (*Musing.*) Besides, from the glimpse I had of her, I think she squints.

Kate. I'm sure, sir, I heard the bell ring.

Marlow. No, no! (*Musing.*) I have pleased my father, however, by coming down, and I'll tomorrow please myself by returning. (*Taking out his tablets and perusing.*)

Kate. Perhaps the other gentleman called, sir?

Marlow. I tell you no.

Kate. I should be glad to know, sir. We have such a parcel of servants!

Marlow. No, no, I tell you. (*Looks full in her face.*) Yes, child, I think I did call. I wanted—I wanted——I vow, child, you are vastly handsome!

Kate. O la, sir, you'll make one ashamed.

Marlow. Never saw a more sprightly, malicious eye. Yes, yes, my dear, I did call. Have you got any of your—a—what d'ye call it, in the house?

Kate. No, sir, we have been out of that these ten days.

Marlow. One may call in this house, I find, to very little purpose. Suppose I should call for a taste, just by way of trial, of the nectar of your lips; perhaps I might be disappointed in that, too?

Kate. Nectar? Nectar? That's a liquor there's no call for in these parts. French, I suppose. We sell no French wines here, sir.

Marlow. Of true English growth, I assure you.

Kate. Then it's odd I should not know it. We brew all sorts of wines in this house, and I have lived here these eighteen years.

Marlow. Eighteen years! Why, one would think, child, you kept the bar before you were born. How old are you?

Kate. Oh! sir, I must not tell my age. They say women and music should never be dated.

Marlow. To guess at this distance, you can't be much above forty. (*Approaching.*) Yet nearer, I don't think so much. (*Approaching.*) By coming close to some women, they look younger still; but when we come very close indeed——(*Attempting to kiss her.*)

Kate. Pray, sir, keep your distance. One would think you wanted to know one's age as they do horses, by mark of mouth.

Marlow. I protest, child, you use me extremely ill. If you keep me at this distance, how is it possible you and I can be ever acquainted?

Kate. And who wants to be acquainted with you? I want no such acquaintance, not I. I'm sure you did not treat Miss Hardcastle, that was here a while ago, in this obstropalous[7] manner. I'll warrant me, before her you looked dashed and kept bowing to the ground, and talked for all the world as if you was before a justice of peace.

Marlow (*aside*). Egad, she has hit it, sure enough! (*To her.*) In awe of her, child? Ha! ha! ha! A mere awkward, squinting thing! No, no! I find you don't know me. I laughed and rallied her a little; but I was unwilling to be too severe. No, I could not be too severe, curse me!

Kate. Oh, then, sir, you are a favorite, I find among the ladies?

Marlow. Yes, my dear, a great favorite. And yet, hang me, I don't see what they find in me to follow. At the Ladies' Club in town I'm called their agreeable Rattle. Rattle, child, is not my real name, but one I'm known by. My name is Solomons; Mr. Solomons, my

6. *Lion . . . Angel . . . Lamb*, names of private rooms in an inn. 7. *obstropalous*, obstreperous.

dear, at your service. (*Offering to salute her.*)

Kate. Hold, sir; you are introducing me to your club, not to yourself. And you're so great a favorite there, you say?

Marlow. Yes, my dear. There's Mrs. Mantrap, Lady Betty Blackleg, the Countess of Sligo, Mrs. Langhorns, old Miss Biddy Buckskin, and your humble servant, keep up the spirit of the place.

Kate. Then it's a very merry place, I suppose?

Marlow. Yes, as merry as cards, suppers, wine, and old women can make us.

Kate. And their agreeable Rattle, ha! ha!

Marlow (*aside*). Egad! I don't quite like this chit. She looks knowing, methinks. You laugh, child?

Kate. I can't but laugh to think what time they all have for minding their work or their family.

Marlow (*aside*). All's well; she don't laugh at me. (*To her.*) Do you ever work, child?

Kate. Aye, sure. There's not a screen or a quilt in the whole house but what can bear witness to that.

Marlow. Odso! Then you must show me your embroidery. I embroider[8] and draw patterns myself a little. If you want a judge of your work, you must apply to me. (*Seizing her hand.*)

Enter HARDCASTLE, *who stands in surprise*

Kate. Aye, but the colors don't look well by candlelight. You shall see all in the morning. (*Struggling.*)

Marlow. Why not now, my *angel*? Such beauty fires beyond the power of resistance. ——Pshaw! the father here! My old luck; I never nicked seven that I did not throw ambsace three times following.[9] (*Exit* MARLOW.)

Hardcastle. So, madam! So I find *this* is your *modest* lover. This is your humble admirer, that kept his eyes fixed on the ground and only adored at humble distance. Kate, Kate, art thou not ashamed to deceive your father so?

Kate. Never trust me, dear Papa, but he's still the modest man I first took him for; you'll be convinced of it as well as I.

Hardcastle. By the hand of my body, I believe his impudence is infectious! Didn't I see him haul you about like a milkmaid? And now you talk of his respect and his modesty, forsooth!

Kate. But if I shortly convince you of his modesty, that he has only the faults that will pass off with time and the virtues that will improve with age, I hope you'll forgive him.

Hardcastle. The girl would actually make one run mad! I tell you I'll not be convinced. I am convinced. He has scarce been three hours in the house, and he has already encroached on all my prerogatives. You may like his impudence and call it modesty; but my son-in-law, madam, must have very different qualifications.

Kate. Sir, I ask but this night to convince you.

Hardcastle. You shall not have half the time, for I have thoughts of turning him out this very hour.

Kate. Give me that hour, then, and I hope to satisfy you.

Hardcastle. Well, an hour let it be then. But I'll have no trifling with your father. All fair and open, do you mind me?

Kate. I hope, sir, you have ever found that I considered your commands as my pride; for your kindness is such that my duty as yet has been inclination. (*Exeunt.*)

---

8. *I embroider.* In those days it was the custom for men of fashion to embroider. **9.** *I never . . . following,* I never made a lucky throw at dice without following three times with the lowest throw.

To increase understanding

1. (*a*) How does Marlow's second interview with Kate differ from his first one? (*b*) What has made the difference in his attitude and manner? (*c*) How does this scene between Marlow and Kate explain the title of the play?

2. The term *dramatic irony* is sometimes applied to a situation in a play or story in which facts known to some of the characters and to the spectators or readers are unknown to other characters. (*a*) Explain how the scene in which Mrs. Hardcastle, Constance, and Tony discuss Constance's jewels makes use of dramatic irony. (*b*) What is humorous about Tony's often-repeated line, "I can bear witness to that"?

ACT FOUR

SCENE: *The house*

Enter HASTINGS *and* CONSTANCE

Hastings. You surprise me; Sir Charles Marlow expected here this night! Where have you had your information?

Constance. You may depend upon it. I just saw his letter to Mr. Hardcastle, in which he tells him he intends setting out a few hours after his son.

Hastings. Then, my Constance, all must be completed before he arrives. He knows me, and should he find me here, would discover my name and perhaps my designs to the rest of the family.

Constance. The jewels, I hope, are safe?

Hastings. Yes, yes. I have sent them to Marlow, who keeps the keys of our baggage. In the meantime, I'll go to prepare matters for our elopement. I have had the squire's promise of a fresh pair of horses, and, if I should not see him again, will write him further directions. (*Exit.*)

Constance. Well, success attend you! In the meantime, I'll go amuse my aunt with the old pretense of a violent passion for my cousin. (*Exit.*)

Enter MARLOW, *followed by a* SERVANT

Marlow. I wonder what Hastings could mean by sending me so valuable a thing as a casket to keep for him, when he knows the only place I have is the seat of a post coach at an inn door. Have you deposited the casket with the landlady, as I ordered you? Have you put it into her own hands?

Servant. Yes, your honor.

Marlow. She said she'd keep it safe, did she?

Servant. Yes; she said she'd keep it safe enough; she asked me how I came by it; and she said she had a great mind to make me give an account of myself. (*Exit* SERVANT.)

Marlow. Ha! ha! ha! They're safe, however. What an unaccountable set of beings have we got amongst! This little barmaid, though, runs in my head most strangely and drives out the absurdities of all the rest of the family. She's mine, she must be mine, or I'm greatly mistaken.

Enter HASTINGS

Hastings. Bless me! I quite forgot to tell her that I intended to prepare at the bottom of the garden. Marlow here, and in spirits, too!

Marlow. Give me joy, George! Crown me, shadow me with laurels! Well, George, after all, we modest fellows don't want for success among the women.

Hastings. Some women, you mean. But what success has your honor's modesty been crowned with now, that it grows so insolent upon us?

Marlow. Didn't you see the tempting, brisk, lovely little thing that runs about the house with a bunch of keys to its girdle?

Hastings. Well, and what then?

Marlow. She's mine, you rogue, you. Such fire, such motion, such eyes, such lips—but, egad! she would not let me kiss them, though.

Hastings. But you are so very sure of her?

Marlow. Why, man, she talked of showing me her work above stairs, and I am to approve the pattern.

Hastings. But how can you, Charles, go about to rob a woman of her honor?

Marlow. Pshaw! Pshaw! We all know the honor of the barmaid of an inn. I don't intend to rob her, take my word for it.

Hastings. I believe the girl has virtue.

Marlow. And if she has, I should be the last man in the world that would attempt to corrupt it.

Hastings. You have taken care, I hope, of the casket I sent you to lock up? It's in safety?

Marlow. Yes, yes. It's safe enough. I have taken care of it. But how could you think the seat of a post coach at an inn door a place of safety? Ah! numskull! I have taken better precautions for you than you did for yourself —I have——

Hastings. What?

Marlow. I have sent it to the landlady to keep for you.

Hastings. To the landlady!

Marlow. The landlady.

Hastings. You did!

Marlow. I did. She's to be answerable for its forthcoming, you know.

Hastings. Yes, she'll bring it forth with a witness.

Marlow. Wasn't I right? I believe you'll allow that I acted prudently upon this occasion.

Hastings (aside). He must not see my uneasiness.

Marlow. You seem a little disconcerted though, methinks. Sure, nothing has happened?

Hastings. No, nothing. Never was in better spirits in all my life. And so you left it with the landlady, who, no doubt, very readily undertook the charge?

Marlow. Rather too readily. For she not only kept the casket, but, through her great precaution, was going to keep the messenger, too. Ha! ha! ha!

Hastings. He! he! he! They're safe, however.

Marlow. As a guinea in a miser's purse.

Hastings (aside). So now all hopes of fortune are at an end, and we must set off without it. (*To him.*) Well, Charles, I'll leave you to your meditations on the pretty barmaid, and, he! he! he!, may you be as successful for yourself as you have been for me. (*Exit.*)

Marlow. Thank ye, George; I ask no more.

Enter HARDCASTLE

Hardcastle. I no longer know my own house. It's turned all topsy-turvy. His servants have got drunk already. I'll bear it no longer; and yet, from my respect for his father, I'll be calm. (*To him.*) Mr. Marlow, your servant. I'm your very humble servant. (*Bowing low.*)

Marlow. Sir, your humble servant. (*Aside.*) What is to be the wonder now?

Hardcastle. I believe, sir, you must be sensible, sir, that no man alive ought to be more welcome than your father's son, sir. I hope you think so?

Marlow. I do from my soul, sir. I don't want much entreaty. I generally make my father's son welcome wherever he goes.

Hardcastle. I believe you do, from my soul, sir. But though I say nothing to your own conduct, that of your servants is insufferable. Their manner of drinking is setting a very bad example in this house, I assure you.

Marlow. I protest, my very good sir, that is no fault of mine. If they don't drink as they ought, they are to blame. I ordered them not to spare the cellar. I did, I assure you. (*To the side scene.*) Here, let one of my servants come up. (*To him.*) My positive directions were that, as I did not drink myself, they should make up for my deficiencies below.

Hardcastle. Then they had your orders for what they do? I'm satisfied!

Marlow. They had, I assure you. You shall hear it from one of themselves.

Enter SERVANT, *drunk*

Marlow. You, Jeremy! Come forward, sirrah! What were my orders? Were you not told to drink freely and call for what you thought fit, for the good of the house?

Hardcastle (aside). I begin to lose my patience.

Jeremy. Please your honor, liberty and Fleet Street forever! Though I'm but a servant, I'm as good as another man. I'll drink for no man before supper, sir, damme! Good liquor will sit upon a good supper, but a good supper will not sit upon—hiccup—upon my conscience, sir.
(*Exit.*)

Marlow. You see, my old friend, the fellow is as drunk as he can possibly be. I don't know what you'd have more, unless you'd have the poor devil soused in a beer barrel.

Hardcastle. Zounds! he'll drive me distracted, if I contain myself any longer. Mr. Marlow, sir, I have submitted to your insolence for more than four hours, and I see no likelihood of its coming to an end. I'm now resolved to be master here, sir, and I desire that you and your drunken pack may leave my house directly.

Marlow. Leave your house!—Sure, you jest, my good friend! What, when I am doing what I can to please you!

Hardcastle. I tell you, sir, you don't please me; so I desire you'll leave my house.

Marlow. Sure, you cannot be serious? At this time of night, and such a night? You only mean to banter me.

Hardcastle. I tell you, sir, I'm serious! And, now that my passions are roused, I say this house is mine, sir; this house is mine, and I command you to leave it directly.

Marlow. Ha! ha! ha! A puddle in a storm. I shan't stir a step, I assure you. (*In a serious tone.*) This your house, fellow! It's my house. This is my house. Mine, while I choose to stay. What right have you to bid me leave this house, sir? I never met with such impudence, curse me; never in my whole life before.

Hardcastle. Nor I, confound me if ever I did! To come to my house, to call for what he likes, to turn me out of my own chair, to insult the family, to order his servants to get drunk, and then to tell me, "This house is mine, sir." By all that's impudent, it makes me laugh. Ha! ha! ha! Pray, sir (*bantering*), as you take the house, what think you of taking the rest of the furniture? There's a pair of silver candlesticks, and there's a firescreen, and here's a pair of brazen-nosed bellows; perhaps you may take a fancy to them?

Marlow. Bring me your bill, sir; bring me your bill, and let's make no more words about it.

Hardcastle. There are a set of prints, too. What think you of the Rake's Progress[1] for your own apartment?

Marlow. Bring me your bill, I say; and I'll leave you and your infernal house directly.

Hardcastle. Then there's a mahogany table that you may see your face in.

Marlow. My bill, I say.

Hardcastle. I had forgot the great chair for your own particular slumbers, after a hearty meal.

Marlow. Zounds! bring me my bill, I say, and let's hear no more on't.

Hardcastle. Young man, young man, from your father's letter to me, I was taught to expect a well-bred, modest man as a visitor here, but now I find him no better than a coxcomb and a bully; but he will be down here presently, and shall hear more of it.   (*Exit.*)

Marlow. How's this! Sure, I have not mistaken the house? Everything looks like an inn. The servants cry, "Coming." The attendance is awkward; the barmaid, too, to attend us. But she's here, and will further inform me. Whither so fast, child? A word with you.

Enter KATE

Kate. Let it be short, then. I'm in a hurry. (*Aside.*) I believe he begins to find out his mistake. But it's too soon quite to undeceive him.

Marlow. Pray, child, answer me one question. What are you, and what may your business in this house be?

Kate. A relation of the family, sir.

Marlow. What, a poor relation?

Kate. Yes, sir. A poor relation, appointed to keep the keys, and to see that the guests want nothing in my power to give them.

Marlow. That is, you act as the barmaid of this inn.

Kate. Inn! O law!—What brought that into your head? One of the best families in the country keep an inn!—Ha! ha! ha! old Mr. Hardcastle's house an inn!

Marlow. Mr. Hardcastle's house! Is this Mr. Hardcastle's house, child?

Kate. Aye, sure. Whose else should it be?

Marlow. So, then, all's out, and I have been damnably imposed on. Oh, confound my stupid head, I shall be laughed at over the whole town. I shall be stuck up in caricature in all the printshops. The Dullissimo Macaroni.[2] To mistake this house of all others for an inn, and my father's old friend for an innkeeper! What a swaggering puppy must he take me for! What a silly puppy do I find myself! There again, may I be hanged, my dear, but I mistook you for the barmaid.

Kate. Dear me! dear me! I'm sure there's nothing in my *behavior* to put me upon a level with one of that stamp.

Marlow. Nothing, my dear, nothing. But

---

1. the Rake's Progress, a series of satirical paintings and engravings by William Hogarth. (See illustrations on page 284.) 2. *The Dullissimo Macaroni*, the most stupid of all dandies.

I was in for a list of blunders, and could not help making you a subscriber. My stupidity saw everything the wrong way. I mistook your assiduity for assurance and your simplicity for allurement. But it's over—this house I no more show *my* face in.

Kate. I hope, sir, I have done nothing to disoblige you. I'm sure I should be sorry to affront any gentleman who has been so polite, and said so many civil things to me. I'm sure I should be sorry (*pretending to cry*) if he left the family on my account. I'm sure I should be sorry people said anything amiss, since I have no fortune but my character.

Marlow (aside). By heaven! she weeps. This is the first mark of tenderness I ever had from a modest woman, and it touches me. (*To her.*) Excuse me, my lovely girl; you are the only part of the family I leave with reluctance. But to be plain with you, the difference of our birth, fortune, and education makes an honorable connection impossible; and I can never harbor a thought of seducing simplicity that trusted in my honor or bringing ruin upon one whose only fault was being too lovely.

Kate (aside). Generous man! I now begin to admire him. (*To him.*) But I am sure my family is as good as Miss Hardcastle's; and though I'm poor, that's no great misfortune to a contented mind; and until this moment I never thought that it was bad to want fortune.

Marlow. And why now, my pretty simplicity?

Kate. Because it puts me at a distance from one that if I had a thousand pounds I would give it all to.

Marlow (aside). This simplicity bewitches me so that if I stay I'm undone. I must make one bold effort, and leave her. (*To her.*) Your partiality in my favor, my dear, touches me most sensibly, and were I to live for myself alone, I could easily fix my choice. But I owe too much to the opinion of the world, too much to the authority of a father; so that—I can scarcely speak it—it affects me. Farewell!
(*Exit.*)

Kate. I never knew half his merit till now. He shall not go if I have power or art to detain him. I'll still preserve the character in which I *stooped to conquer*, but will undeceive my papa, who, perhaps, may laugh him out of his resolution.
(*Exit.*)

Enter TONY *and* CONSTANCE

Tony. Aye, you may steal for yourselves the next time. I have done my duty. She has got the jewels again, that's a sure thing; but she believes it was all a mistake of the servants.

Constance. But, my dear cousin, sure you won't forsake us in this distress? If she in the least suspects that I am going off, I shall certainly be locked up, or sent to my Aunt Pedigree's, which is ten times worse.

Tony. To be sure, aunts of all kinds are damned bad things. But what can I do? I have got you a pair of horses that will fly like Whistle-jacket,[3] and I'm sure you can't say but I have courted you nicely before her face. Here she comes; we must court a bit or two more, for fear she should suspect us. (*They retire and seem to fondle.*)

Enter MRS. HARDCASTLE

Mrs. Hardcastle. Well, I was greatly fluttered, to be sure. But my son tells me it was all a mistake of the servants. I shan't be easy, however, till they are fairly married, and then let her keep her own fortune. But what do I see? Fondling together, as I'm alive. I never saw Tony so sprightly before. Ah! have I caught you, my pretty doves? What, billing, exchanging stolen glances and broken murmurs? Ah!

Tony. As for murmurs, Mother, we grumble a little now and then, to be sure. But there's no love lost between us.

Mrs. Hardcastle. A mere sprinkling, Tony, upon the flame, only to make it burn brighter.

Constance. Cousin Tony promises to give us more of his company at home. Indeed, he shan't leave us any more. It won't leave us, cousin Tony, will it?

Tony. Oh, it's a pretty creature! No, I'd sooner leave my horse in a pound than leave you when you smile upon one so. Your laugh makes you so becoming.

Constance. Agreeable cousin! Who can

---

3. *Whistle-jacket,* a famous race horse.

help admiring that natural humor, that pleasant, broad, red, thoughtless (*patting his cheek*)—ah! it's a bold face!

Mrs. Hardcastle. Pretty innocence!

Tony. I'm sure I always loved cousin Con's hazel eyes and her pretty long fingers, that she twists this way and that over the haspicholls,[4] like a parcel of bobbins.

Mrs. Hardcastle. Ah! he would charm the bird from the tree. I was never so happy before. My boy takes after his father, poor Mr. Lumpkin, exactly. The jewels, my dear Con, shall be yours incontinently.[5] You shall have them. Isn't he a sweet boy, my dear? You shall be married tomorrow, and we'll put off the rest of his education, like Dr. Drowsy's sermons, to a fitter opportunity.

Enter DIGGORY

Diggory. Where's the squire? I have got a letter for your worship.

Tony. Give it to my mamma. She reads all my letters first.

Diggory. I had orders to deliver it into your own hands.

Tony. Who does it come from?

Diggory. Your worship mun ask that o' the letter itself. (*Exit* DIGGORY.)

Tony. I could wish to know, though. (*Turning the letter, and gazing on it.*)

Constance (*aside*). Undone! undone! A letter to him from Hastings. I know the hand. If my aunt sees it, we are ruined forever. I'll keep her employed a little, if I can. (*To* MRS. HARDCASTLE.) But I have not told you, madam, of my cousin's smart answer just now to Mr. Marlow. We so laughed—you must know, madam. This way a little, for he must not hear us. (*They confer.*)

Tony (*still gazing*). A damned cramp piece of penmanship as ever I saw in my life. I can read your print-hand very well. But here there are such handles, and shanks, and dashes that one can scarce tell the head from the tail. "To Anthony Lumpkin, Esquire." It's very odd, I can read the outside of my letters, where my own name is, well enough. But when I come to open it, it's all—buzz. That's hard—very hard; for the inside of the

letter is always the cream of the correspondence.

Mrs. Hardcastle. Ha! ha! ha! Very well, very well. And so my son was too hard for the philosopher.

Constance. Yes, madam; but you must hear the rest, madam. A little more this way, or he may hear us. You'll hear how he puzzled him again.

Mrs. Hardcastle. He seems strangely puzzled now himself, methinks.

Tony (*still gazing*). A damned up and down hand, as if it was disguised in liquor. (*Reading.*) "Dear Sir"—aye, that's that. Then there's an M, and a T, and an S, but whether the next be an izzard[6] or an R, confound me, I cannot tell.

Mrs. Hardcastle. What's that, my dear? Can I give you any assistance?

Constance. Pray, Aunt, let me read it. Nobody reads a cramp hand better than I. (*Twitching the letter from him.*) Do you know who it is from?

Tony. Can't tell, except from Dick Ginger, the feeder.[7]

Constance. Aye, so it is. (*Pretending to read.*) "Dear Squire, hoping that you're in health, as I am at this present. The gentlemen of the Shake-bag Club has cut the gentlemen of the Goose-green quite out of feather. The odds—um—odd battle—um—long fighting—um"—here, here, it's all about cocks and fighting; it's of no consequence; here put it up, put it up. (*Thrusting the crumpled letter upon him.*)

Tony. But I tell you, miss, it's of all the consequence in the world! I would not lose the rest of it for a guinea! Here, Mother, do you make it out. Of no consequence! (*Giving* MRS. HARDCASTLE *the letter.*)

Mrs. Hardcastle. How's this? (*Reads.*) "Dear Squire, I'm now waiting for Miss Neville, with a post chaise and a pair, at the bottom of the garden, but I find my horses yet unable to perform the journey. I expect you'll assist us with a pair of fresh horses, as you promised. Dispatch is necessary, as the *hag*—aye, the hag—your mother will otherwise

---

4. *haspicholls*, a corruption of *harpsichord.* 5. *incontinently,* at once. 6. *izzard,* the letter z. 7. *feeder,* trainer of cocks.

suspect us. Yours, Hastings." Grant me patience. I shall run distracted! My rage chokes me!

Constance. I hope, madam, you'll suspend your resentment for a few moments and not impute to me any impertinence or sinister design that belongs to another.

Mrs. Hardcastle (curtsying very low). Fine spoken, madam; you are most miraculously polite and engaging, and quite the very pink of courtesy and circumspection, madam. *(Changing her tone.)* And you, you great ill-fashioned oaf, with scarce sense enough to keep your mouth shut; were you, too, joined against me? But I'll defeat all your plots in a moment. As for you, madam, since you have got a pair of fresh horses ready, it would be cruel to disappoint them. So, if you please, instead of running away with your spark, prepare this very moment to run off with *me*. Your old Aunt Pedigree will keep you secure, I'll warrant me. You too, sir, may mount your horse and guard us upon the way. Here, Thomas, Roger, Diggory! I'll show you that I wish you better than you do yourselves.

(Exit.)

Constance. So, now I'm completely ruined.

Tony. Aye, that's a sure thing.

Constance. What better could be expected from being connected with such a stupid fool —and after all the nods and signs I made him!

Tony. By the laws, miss, it was your own cleverness, and not my stupidity, that did your business. You were so nice and so busy with your Shake-bags and Goose-greens that I thought you could never be making believe.

Enter HASTINGS

Hastings. So, sir, I find by my servant that you have shown my letter and betrayed us. Was this well done, young gentleman?

Tony. Here's another. Ask miss, there, who betrayed you. Ecod, it was her doing, not mine.

Enter MARLOW

Marlow. So I have been finely used here among you. Rendered contemptible, driven into ill manners, despised, insulted, laughed at.

Tony. Here's another. We shall have all Bedlam broke loose presently.

Constance. And there, sir, is the gentleman to whom we all owe every obligation.

Marlow. What can I say to him, a mere boy, an idiot, whose ignorance and age are a protection?

Hastings. A poor, contemptible booby that would but disgrace correction.

Constance. Yet with cunning and malice enough to make himself merry with all our embarrassments.

Hastings. An insensible cub.

Marlow. Replete with tricks and mischief.

Tony. Baw! damme, but I'll fight you both, one after the other—with baskets.[8]

Marlow. As for him, he's below resentment. But your conduct, Mr. Hastings, requires an explanation. You knew of my mistakes, yet would not undeceive me.

Hastings. Tortured as I am with my own disappointments, is this a time for explanations? It is not friendly, Mr. Marlow.

Marlow. But, sir—

Constance. Mr. Marlow, we never kept on your mistake till it was too late to undeceive you. Be pacified.

Enter SERVANT

Servant. My mistress desires you'll get ready immediately, madam. The horses are putting to. Your hat and things are in the next room. We are to go thirty miles before morning. *(Exit* SERVANT.*)*

Constance. Well, well; I'll come presently.

Marlow (to HASTINGS*).* Was it well done, sir, to assist in rendering me ridiculous? To hang me out for the scorn of all my acquaintance? Depend upon it, sir, I shall expect an explanation.

Hastings. Was it well done, sir, if you're upon that subject, to deliver what I entrusted to yourself, to the care of another, sir?

Constance. Mr. Hastings! Mr. Marlow! Why will you increase my distress by this

---

8. *basket*, a sword with a basket hilt for protecting the hand.

groundless dispute? I implore, I entreat you——

Enter SERVANT

Servant. Your cloak, madam. My mistress is impatient.

Constance. I come. (*Exit* SERVANT.) Pray be pacified. If I leave you thus, I shall die with apprehension!

Enter SERVANT

Servant. Your fan, muff, and gloves, madam. The horses are waiting.

Constance. Oh, Mr. Marlow! if you knew what a scene of constraint and ill nature lies before me, I'm sure it would convert your resentment into pity.

Marlow. I'm so distracted with a variety of passions that I don't know what I do. Forgive me, madam. George, forgive me. You know my hasty temper, and should not exasperate it.

Hastings. The torture of my situation is my only excuse.

Constance. Well, my dear Hastings, if you have that esteem for me that I think, that I am sure you have, your constancy for three years will but increase the happiness of our future connection. If——

Mrs. Hardcastle (within). Miss Neville. Constance, why, Constance, I say.

Constance. I'm coming. Well, constancy, remember, constancy is the word.

(*Exit, followed by* SERVANT.)

Hastings. My heart! how can I support this! To be so near happiness, and such happiness!

Marlow (to TONY). You see now, young gentleman, the effects of your folly. What might be amusement to you is here disappointment and even distress.

Tony (from a reverie). Ecod, I have hit it. It's here. Your hands. Yours, and yours, my poor Sulky. My boots there, ho! Meet me two hours hence at the bottom of the garden; and if you don't find Tony Lumpkin a more good-natured fellow than you thought for, I'll give you leave to take my best horse and Bet Bouncer into the bargain. Come along. My boots, ho! (*Exeunt.*)

❊ To increase understanding

1. (*a*) How does Marlow become aware of his error? (*b*) What at this point is the state of his relationship with Kate?

2. What causes Tony's plans to help Constance and Hastings to go awry?

Edward Shuter as Hardcastle, Mrs. Green as Mrs. Hardcastle, and John Quick as they appeared in the original production. This illustration shows Act V, scene ii (page 320).

ACT FIVE

Enter HASTINGS *and* SERVANT

Hastings. You saw the old lady and Miss Neville drive off, you say?

Servant. Yes, your honor. They went off in a post coach, and the young squire went on horseback. They're thirty miles off by this time.

Hastings. Then all my hopes are over.

Servant. Yes, sir. Old Sir Charles is arrived. He and the old gentleman of the house have been laughing at Mr. Marlow's mistake this half hour. They are coming this way.

Hastings. Then I must not be seen. So now to my fruitless appointment at the bottom of the garden. This is about the time. (*Exit.*)

Enter SIR CHARLES *and* HARDCASTLE

Hardcastle. Ha! ha! ha! The peremptory tone in which he sent for his sublime commands!

Sir Charles. And the reserve with which I suppose he treated all your advances.

Hardcastle. And yet he might have seen something in me above a common innkeeper, too.

Sir Charles. Yes, Dick, but he mistook you for an uncommon innkeeper; ha! ha! ha!

Hardcastle. Well, I'm in too good spirits to think of anything but joy. Yes, my dear friend, this union of our families will make our personal friendships hereditary; and though my daughter's fortune is but small——

Sir Charles. Why, Dick, will you talk of fortune to *me?* My son is possessed of more than a competence already, and can want nothing but a good and virtuous girl to share his happiness and increase it. If they like each other, as you say they do——

Hardcastle. *If*, man! I tell you they *do* like each other. My daughter as good as told me so.

Sir Charles. But girls are apt to flatter themselves, you know.

Hardcastle. I saw him grasp her hand in the warmest manner myself; and here he comes to put you out of your *ifs*, I warrant him.

Enter MARLOW

Marlow. I come, sir, once more, to ask pardon for my strange conduct. I can scarce reflect on my insolence without confusion.

Hardcastle. Tut, boy, a trifle! You take it too gravely. An hour or two's laughing with my daughter will set all to rights again. She'll never like you the worse for it.

Marlow. Sir, I shall be always proud of her approbation.

Hardcastle. Approbation is but a cold word, Mr. Marlow; if I am not deceived, you have something more than approbation thereabouts. You take me?

Marlow. Really, sir, I have not that happiness.

Hardcastle. Come, boy, I'm an old fellow and know what's what as well as you that are younger. I know what has passed between you; but mum.

Marlow. Sure, sir, nothing has passed between us but the most profound respect on my side and the most distant reserve on hers. You don't think, sir, that my impudence has been passed upon all the rest of the family?

Hardcastle. Impudence! No, I don't say that—not quite impudence—though girls like to be played with and rumpled a little, too, sometimes. But she has told no tales, I assure you.

Marlow. I never gave her the slightest cause.

Hardcastle. Well, well, I like modesty in its place well enough. But this is overacting, young gentleman. You *may* be open. Your father and I will like you the better for it.

Marlow. May I die, sir, if I ever——

Hardcastle. I tell you she don't dislike you; and as I'm sure you like her——

Marlow. Dear sir—I protest, sir——

Hardcastle. I see no reason why you should not be joined as fast as the parson can tie you.

Marlow. But hear me, sir——

Hardcastle. Your father approves the

match, I admire it; every moment's delay will be doing mischief, so——

Marlow. But why won't you hear me? By all that's just and true, I never gave Miss Hardcastle the slightest mark of my attachment or even the most distant hint to suspect me of affection. We had but one interview, and that was formal, modest, and uninteresting.

Hardcastle (aside). This fellow's modest impudence is beyond bearing.

Sir Charles. And you never grasped her hand or made any protestations?

Marlow. As heaven is my witness, I came down in obedience to your commands. I saw the lady without emotion, and parted without reluctance. I hope you'll exact no further proofs of my duty, nor prevent me from leaving a house in which I suffer so many mortifications. *(Exit.)*

Sir Charles. I'm astonished at the air of sincerity with which he parted.

Hardcastle. And I'm astonished at the deliberate intrepidity of his assurance.

Sir Charles. I dare pledge my life and honor upon his truth.

Hardcastle. Here comes my daughter, and I would stake my happiness upon her veracity.

Enter KATE

Hardcastle. Kate, come hither, child. Answer us sincerely and without reserve. Has Mr. Marlow made any professions of love and affection?

Kate. The question is very abrupt, sir! But since you require unreserved sincerity, I think he has.

Hardcastle (to SIR CHARLES*).* You see.

Sir Charles. And pray, madam, have you and my son had more than one interview?

Kate. Yes, sir, several.

Hardcastle (to SIR CHARLES*).* You see.

Sir Charles. But did he profess any attachment?

Kate. A lasting one.

Sir Charles. Did he talk of love?

Kate. Much, sir.

Sir Charles. Amazing! And all this formally?

Kate. Formally.

Hardcastle. Now, my friend, I hope you are satisfied.

Sir Charles. And how did he behave, madam?

Kate. As most professed admirers do: said some civil things of my face; talked much of his want of merit and the greatness of mine; mentioned his heart; gave a short, tragedy speech; and ended with pretended rapture.

Sir Charles. Now I'm perfectly convinced, indeed. I know his conversation among women to be modest and submissive. This forward, canting, ranting manner by no means describes him; and, I am confident, he never sat for the picture.

Kate. Then what, sir, if I should convince you to your face of my sincerity? If you and my papa, in about half an hour, will place yourselves behind that screen, you shall hear him declare his passion to me in person.

Sir Charles. Agreed. And if I find him what you describe, all my happiness in him must have an end. *(Exit.)*

Kate. And if you don't find him what I describe—I fear my happiness must never have a beginning. *(Exeunt.)*

SCENE II. *The back of the garden*

Enter HASTINGS

Hastings. What an idiot am I to wait here for a fellow who probably takes a delight in mortifying me. He never intended to be punctual, and I'll wait no longer. What do I see? It is he! And perhaps with news of my Constance.

Enter TONY, *booted and spattered*

Hastings. My honest squire! I now find you a man of your word. This looks like friendship.

Tony. Aye, I'm your friend, and the best friend you have in the world, if you knew but all. This riding by night, by the by, is cursedly tiresome. It has shook me worse than the basket of a stagecoach.

Hastings. But how? Where did you leave your fellow travelers? Are they in safety? Are they housed?

Tony. Five-and-twenty miles in two hours and a half is no such bad driving. The poor beasts have smoked for it. Rabbit me, but I'd rather ride forty miles after a fox than ten with such varment.[1]

Hastings. Well, but where have you left the ladies? I die with impatience.

Tony. Left them? Why, where should I leave them but where I found them?

Hastings. This is a riddle.

Tony. Riddle me this, then. What's that goes round the house and round the house, and never touches the house?

Hastings. I'm still astray.

Tony. Why, that's it, mon. I have led them astray. By jingo, there's not a pond or a slough within five miles of the place but they can tell the taste of.

Hastings. Ha! ha! ha! I understand; you took them in a round while they supposed themselves going forward, and so you have at last brought them home again.

Tony. You shall hear. I first took them down Feather-bed Lane, where we stuck fast in the mud. I then rattled them crack over the stones of Up-and-down Hill. I then introduced them to the gibbet on Heavy-tree Heath; and from that, with a circumbendibus,[2] I fairly lodged them in the horse pond at the bottom of the garden.

Hastings. But no accident, I hope?

Tony. No, no. Only Mother is confoundedly frightened. She thinks herself forty miles off. She's sick of the journey; and the cattle can scarce crawl. So, if your own horses be ready, you may whip off with cousin, and I'll be bound that no soul here can budge a foot to follow you.

Hastings. My dear friend, how can I be grateful?

Tony. Aye, now it's "dear friend," "noble squire." Just now, it was all "idiot," "cub," and run me through the guts. Damn *your* way of fighting, I say. After we take a knock in this part of the country, we kiss and be friends. But if you had run me through the guts, then I should be dead, and you might go kiss the hangman.

Hastings. The rebuke is just. But I must hasten to relieve Miss Neville; if you keep the old lady employed, I promise to take care of the young one.

Tony. Never fear me. Here she comes; vanish. (*Exit* HASTINGS.) She's got from the pond and draggled up to the waist.

Enter MRS. HARDCASTLE

Mrs. Hardcastle. Oh, Tony, I'm killed. Shook! Battered to death! I shall never survive it. That last jolt, that laid us against the quickset hedge, has done my business.

Tony. Alack, Mamma, it was all your own fault. You would be for running away by night without knowing one inch of the way.

Mrs. Hardcastle. I wish we were at home again. I never met so many accidents in so short a journey. Drenched in the mud, overturned in a ditch, stuck fast in a slough, jolted to a jelly, and at last to lose our way! Whereabouts do you think we are, Tony?

Tony. By my guess, we should be upon Crackskull Common, about forty miles from home.

Mrs. Hardcastle. O lud! O lud! The most notorious spot in all the country. We only want a robbery to make a complete night on't.

Tony. Don't be afraid, Mamma, don't be afraid. Two of the five that kept here are hanged, and the other three may not find us. Don't be afraid.——Is that a man that's galloping behind us? No; it's only a tree.——Don't be afraid.

Mrs. Hardcastle. The fright will certainly kill me.

Tony. Do you see anything like a black hat moving behind the thicket?

Mrs. Hardcastle. Oh, death!

Tony. No; it's only a cow. Don't be afraid, Mamma, don't be afraid.

Mrs. Hardcastle. As I'm alive, Tony, I see a man coming toward us. If he perceives us, we are undone.

---

1. *varment,* objectionable or troublesome persons. 2. *circumbendibus,* a roundabout course.

Tony (*aside*). Father-in-law, by all that's unlucky, come to take one of his night walks. (*To her.*) Ah, it's a highwayman, with pistols as long as my arm. A damned ill-looking fellow!

Mrs. Hardcastle. Good heaven defend us! He approaches.

Tony. Do you hide yourself in that thicket, and leave me to manage him. If there be any danger, I'll cough and cry hem. When I cough, be sure to keep close. (MRS. HARDCASTLE *hides behind a tree in the back scene.*)

Enter HARDCASTLE

Hardcastle. I'm mistaken, or I heard voices of people in want of help. Oh, Tony, is that you? I did not expect you so soon back. Are your mother and her charge in safety?

Tony. Very safe, sir, at my Aunt Pedigree's. Hem.

Mrs. Hardcastle (*from behind*). Ah, death! I find there's danger.

Hardcastle. Forty miles in three hours; sure, that's too much, my youngster.

Tony. Stout horses and willing minds make short journeys, as they say. Hem.

Mrs. Hardcastle (*from behind*). Sure, he'll do the dear boy no harm.

Hardcastle. But I heard a voice here; I should be glad to know from whence it came.

Tony. It was I, sir, talking to myself, sir. I was saying that forty miles in four hours was very good going. Hem. As to be sure it was. Hem. I have got a sort of cold by being out in the air. We'll go in, if you please. Hem.

Hardcastle. But if you talked to yourself, you did not answer yourself. I'm certain I heard two voices, and am resolved (*raising his voice*) to find the other out.

Mrs. Hardcastle (*from behind*). Oh! he's coming to find me out. Oh!

Tony. What need you go, sir, if I tell you? Hem. I'll lay down my life for the truth—hem—I'll tell you all, sir. (*Detaining him.*)

Hardcastle. I tell you I will not be detained. I insist on seeing. It's in vain to expect I'll believe you.

Mrs. Hardcastle (*running forward from behind*). O lud! he'll murder my poor boy, my

darling! Here, good gentleman, whet your rage upon me. Take my money, my life, but spare that young gentleman; spare my child, if you have any mercy.

Hardcastle. My wife, as I'm a Christian. From whence can she come? or what does she mean?

Mrs. Hardcastle (*kneeling*). Take compassion on us, good Mr. Highwayman. Take our money, our watches, all we have, but spare our lives. We will never bring you to justice; indeed we won't, good Mr. Highwayman.

Hardcastle. I believe the woman's out of her senses. What, Dorothy, don't you know me?

Mrs. Hardcastle. Mr. Hardcastle, as I'm alive! My fears blinded me. But who, my dear, could have expected to meet you here, in this frightful place, so far from home? What has brought you to follow us?

Hardcastle. Sure, Dorothy, you have not lost your wits? So far from home, when you are within forty yards of your own door! (*To him.*) This is one of your old tricks, you graceless rogue, you. (*To her.*) Don't you know the gate and the mulberry tree; and don't you remember the horse pond, my dear?

Mrs. Hardcastle. Yes, I shall remember the horse pond as long as I live; I have caught my death in it. (*To* TONY.) And is it to you, you graceless varlet, I owe all this? I'll teach you to abuse your mother, I will.

Tony. Ecod, Mother, all the parish says you have spoiled me, and so you may take the fruits on't.

Mrs. Hardcastle. I'll spoil you, I will. (*Follows him off the stage.*)

Hardcastle. There's morality, however, in his reply. (*Exit.*)

Enter HASTINGS *and* CONSTANCE

Hastings. My dear Constance, why will you deliberate thus? If we delay a moment, all is lost forever. Pluck up a little resolution, and we shall soon be out of the reach of her malignity.

Constance. I find it impossible. My spirits are so sunk with the agitations I have suffered that I am unable to face any new danger. Two or three years' patience will at last crown us with happiness.

Hastings. Such a tedious delay is worse than inconstancy. Let us fly, my charmer. Let us date our happiness from this very moment. Perish fortune! Love and content will increase what we possess beyond a monarch's revenue. Let me prevail!

Constance. No, Mr. Hastings, no. Prudence once more comes to my relief, and I will obey its dictates. In the moment of passion fortune may be despised, but it ever produces a lasting repentance. I'm resolved to apply to Mr. Hardcastle's compassion and justice for redress.

Hastings. But though he had the will, he has not the power to relieve you.

Constance. But he has influence, and upon that I am resolved to rely.

Hastings. I have no hopes. But since you persist, I must reluctantly obey you. (*Exeunt.*)

SCENE III. *A room at* MR. HARDCASTLE'S

Enter SIR CHARLES MARLOW *and* KATE

Sir Charles. What a situation am I in! If what you say appears, I shall then find a guilty son. If what he says be true, I shall then lose one that, of all others, I most wished for a daughter.

Kate. I am proud of your approbation; and to show I merit it, if you place yourselves as I directed, you shall hear his explicit declaration. But he comes.

Sir Charles. I'll to your father and keep him to the appointment.   (*Exit* SIR CHARLES.)

Enter MARLOW

Marlow. Though prepared for setting out, I come once more to take leave; nor did I, till this moment, know the pain I feel in the separation.

Kate (*in her own natural manner*). I believe these sufferings cannot be very great, sir, which you can so easily remove. A day or two longer, perhaps, might lessen your uneasiness by showing the little value of what you now think proper to regret.

Marlow (*aside*). This girl every moment improves upon me. (*To her.*) It must not be, madam; I have already trifled too long with my heart. My very pride begins to submit to my passion. The disparity of education and fortune, the anger of a parent, and the contempt of my equals begin to lose their weight; and nothing can restore me to myself but this painful effort of resolution.

Kate. Then go, sir; I'll urge nothing more to detain you. Though my family be as good as hers you came down to visit, and my education, I hope, not inferior, what are these advantages without equal affluence? I must remain contented with the slight approbation of imputed merit; I must have only the mockery of your addresses, while all your serious aims are fixed on fortune.

Enter HARDCASTLE *and* SIR CHARLES MARLOW *from behind*

Sir Charles. Here, behind this screen.

Hardcastle. Aye, aye; make no noise. I'll engage my Kate covers him with confusion at last.

Marlow. By heavens, madam, fortune was ever my smallest consideration. Your beauty at first caught my eye; for who could see that without emotion? But every moment that I converse with you steals in some new grace, heightens the picture, and gives it stronger expression. What at first seemed rustic plainness now appears refined simplicity. What seemed forward assurance now strikes me as the result of courageous innocence and conscious virtue.

Sir Charles. What can it mean? He amazes me!

Hardcastle. I told you how it would be. Hush!

Marlow. I am now determined to stay, madam, and I have too good an opinion of my father's discernment, when he sees you, to doubt his approbation.

Kate. No, Mr. Marlow, I will not, cannot detain you. Do you think I could suffer a connection in which there is the smallest room for repentance? Do you think I would take the mean advantage of a transient passion to load you with confusion? Do you think I could ever relish that happiness which was acquired by lessening yours?

Marlow. By all that's good, I can have no happiness but what's in your power to grant me! Nor shall I ever feel repentance but in not having seen your merits before. I will stay even contrary to your wishes; and though you should persist to shun me, I will make my respectful assiduities atone for the levity of my past conduct.

Kate. Sir, I must entreat you'll desist. As our acquaintance began, so let it end, in indifference. I might have given an hour or two to levity; but seriously, Mr. Marlow, do you think I could ever submit to a connection where I must appear mercenary and *you* imprudent? Do you think I could ever catch at the confident addresses of a secure admirer?

Marlow (kneeling). Does this look like security? Does this look like confidence? No, madam, every moment that shows me your merit only serves to increase my diffidence and confusion. Here let me continue——

SHE STOOPS TO CONQUER.

Mar. Madam every moment that shows me your merit only serves to encrease my diffidence.

Sir Charles. I can hold it no longer. Charles, Charles, how hast thou deceived me! Is this your indifference, your uninteresting conversation?

Hardcastle. Your cold contempt; your formal interview! What have you to say now?

Marlow. That I'm all amazement! What can it mean?

Hardcastle. It means that you can say and unsay things at pleasure; that you can address a lady in private and deny it in public; that you have one story for us and another for my daughter.

Marlow. Daughter!—this lady your daughter?

Hardcastle. Yes, sir, my only daughter; my Kate; whose else should she be?

Marlow. Oh, the devil!

Kate. Yes, sir, that very identical, tall, squinting lady you were pleased to take me for (*curtsying*); she that you addressed as the mild, modest, sentimental man of gravity, and the bold, forward, agreeable Rattle of the Ladies' Club. Ha! ha! ha!

Marlow. Zounds! There's no bearing this; it's worse than death!

Kate. In which of your characters, sir, will you give us leave to address you? As the faltering gentleman, with looks on the ground, that speaks just to be heard and hates hypocrisy; or the loud, confident creature, that keeps it up with Mrs. Mantrap and old Miss Biddy Buckskin till three in the morning? Ha! ha! ha!

Marlow. Oh, curse on my noisy head. I never attempted to be impudent yet that I was not taken down. I must be gone.

Hardcastle. By the hand of my body, but you shall not. I see it was all a mistake, and I am rejoiced to find it. You shall not, sir, I tell you. I know she'll forgive you. Won't you forgive him, Kate? We'll all forgive you. Take courage, man. (MARLOW *and* KATE *retire, she tormenting him, to the back scene.*)

Enter MRS. HARDCASTLE *and* TONY

Mrs. Hardcastle. So, so, they're gone off. Let them go; I care not.

Hardcastle. Who gone?

Mrs. Hardcastle. My dutiful niece and her gentleman, Mr. Hastings, from town. He who came down with our modest visitor here.

Sir Charles. Who, my honest George Hastings? As worthy a fellow as lives, and the girl could not have made a more prudent choice.

Hardcastle. Then, by the hand of my body, I'm proud of the connection.

Mrs. Hardcastle. Well, if he has taken away the lady, he has not taken her fortune; that remains in this family to console us for her loss.

Hardcastle. Sure, Dorothy, you would not be so mercenary?

Mrs. Hardcastle. Aye, that's my affair, not yours.

Hardcastle. But, you know, if your son, when of age, refuses to marry his cousin, her whole fortune is then at her own disposal.

Mrs. Hardcastle. Aye, but he's not of age, and she has not thought proper to wait for his refusal.

Enter HASTINGS *and* CONSTANCE

Mrs. Hardcastle (aside). What, returned so soon! I begin not to like it.

Hastings (to HARDCASTLE*).* For my late attempt to fly off with your niece, let my present confusion be my punishment. We are now come back to appeal from your justice to your humanity. By her father's consent, I first paid her my addresses, and our passions were first founded in duty.

Constance. Since his death, I have been obliged to stoop to dissimulation to avoid oppression. In an hour of levity, I was ready even to give up my fortune to secure my choice. But I am now recovered from the delusion, and hope from your tenderness what is denied me from a nearer connection.

Mrs. Hardcastle. Pshaw! Pshaw! this is all but the whining end of a modern novel.

Hardcastle. Be it what it will, I'm glad they're come back to reclaim their due. Come hither, Tony, boy. Do you refuse this lady's hand whom I now offer you?

Tony. What signifies my refusing? You know I can't refuse her till I'm of age, Father.

Hardcastle. While I thought concealing your age, boy, was likely to conduce to your improvement, I concurred with your mother's desire to keep it secret. But since I find she turns it to a wrong use, I must now declare you have been of age these three months.

Tony. Of age! Am I of age, Father?

Hardcastle. Above three months.

Tony. Then you'll see the first use I'll make of my liberty. *(Taking* CONSTANCE's *hand.)* Witness all men, by these presents, that I, Anthony Lumpkin Esquire, of BLANK place, refuse you, Constantia Neville, spinster, of no place at all, for my true and lawful wife. So Constance Neville may marry whom she pleases, and Tony Lumpkin is his own man again.

Sir Charles. O brave squire!

Hastings. My worthy friend!

Mrs. Hardcastle. My undutiful offspring!

Marlow. Joy, my dear George! And could I prevail upon my little tyrant here to be less arbitrary, I should be the happiest man alive, if you would return me the favor.

Hastings (to KATE*).* Come, madam, you are now driven to the very last scene of all your contrivances. I know you like him, I'm sure he loves you, and you must and shall have him.

Hardcastle (joining their hands). And I say so too. And, Mr. Marlow, if she makes as good a wife as she has a daughter, I don't believe you'll ever repent your bargain. So now to supper. Tomorrow we shall gather all the poor of the parish about us, and the mistakes of the night shall be crowned with a merry morning. So, boy, take her; and as you have been mistaken in the mistress, my wish is that you may never be mistaken in the wife.

(Exeunt ALL.*)*

❧ To increase understanding

1. Describe the outcome of the "trip to Aunt Pedigree's."

2. (*a*) How are both love stories brought to a satisfactory conclusion? (*b*) Which story did you find the more interesting, and why?

3. Do you think Marlow acted in character in the last scene? Explain your answer.

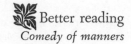 Better reading
Comedy of manners

She Stoops to Conquer is often called a *comedy of manners*. Although the term has been applied to any play dealing with the conventions of society, in its strictest sense it refers to plays that describe the fashions, manners, and conventions of a highly sophisticated, artificial society. In this sense the comedies of the Restoration dramatists of the seventeenth century are the first and the purest examples of the comedy of manners in English literature. A century later Oliver Goldsmith and Richard Brinsley Sheridan endeavored to revive Restoration comedy as a way of counteracting the cult of sentiment that was dominating the English stage (see page 303).

The plot of a true comedy of manners usually involves a series of clever, complicated intrigues. The characters are usually types instead of individuals and fall into categories as conforming or not conforming to the refined, elegant standards of the society of the time; those who do not conform become the play's main objects of satire. Both plot and characters are subordinate to the bright, intellectual atmosphere of the play, which is achieved largely through sharp, witty repartee or dialogue between pairs of lovers. The characters of a comedy of manners are usually so blasé and sophisticated that they treat obscenity and immorality lightly and cynically. Bawdy, common characters, however, are too low in the social scale to receive any recognition.

To what extent is the plot of *She Stoops to Conquer* a matter of complicated intrigue? Where in the plot does the intrigue turn into farce, or horseplay?

Describe some of the refined, sophisticated manners touched upon in the play.

Which of Goldsmith's characters come across more as individuals and which come across more as types in eighteenth-century English society? Which characters are the main objects of satire? Is Goldsmith's satire directed primarily at individuals who do not measure up to the standards of society, at the conventions of society, or at mankind in general? Explain your answer. What is the tone of Goldsmith's satire?

Where in the play is the dialogue at its sharpest and wittiest?

Is there any obscenity or immorality in Goldsmith's play? Are there any low, common characters?

To what extent is *She Stoops to Conquer* a true comedy of manners?

The Play in Review

She Stoops to Conquer is based upon an actual experience. On one of his travels Goldsmith wandered into a village, absent-mindedly asked to be directed to the best house, meaning inn, and was directed instead by a prankster to a fine country manor. There he ordered the squire about and otherwise acted the part of a citified guest at a country inn.

1. What plot elements does Goldsmith add in building his experience into a five-act play?

2. When Tony misdirects Marlow and Hastings on his first meeting with them he speaks of Crackskull Common and Farmer Murrain's barn. (*a*) How does Goldsmith again use this sort of humor in Tony's account of the trip to Aunt Pedigree's? (*b*) What evidence of humor can you find in the names of various characters?

3. (*a*) Which aspects of the play might be called universal? (*b*) Which belong especially to the eighteenth century?

The silhouette, which provided an easy method of obtaining an accurate likeness, was very popular before the invention of photography. In this era silhouettes were often very elaborate, reflecting the elegant manners of the time.

THE BEGINNINGS OF
THE ROMANTIC REVOLT

At the very time that Samuel Johnson and his Literary Club were insisting on the absolute perfection of the literature and social institutions of their generation, signs of revolt were at hand. The American colonists, whom Johnson described as a "race of convicts" who "ought to be thankful for anything we allow them short of hanging," were coming to the conclusion that they would rather hang or die in battle than put up with the rule of the mother country. The French people were about to plunge their country into a violent and bloody revolution in an effort to free themselves from the iron grip of a centuries-old monarchy and aristocracy. And in England there could be heard deep rumblings of discontent from the many citizens who had benefited in no way from the victory of the English Parliament over the English king. Throughout Western Europe and America the old philosophy of privilege for a fortunate few, which had given rise to the sophisticated, society literature of people like Alexander Pope, was about to be swept away by the new philosophy of the rights of all men. This new philosophy became one of the basic tenets of a new school of Romantic Poets, whose war on the literary dictatorship of Pope and Johnson was to prove as successful as that of the social revolutionaries on many an established government.

The Romantic Revolt in literature was not fully accomplished until the first three decades of the nineteenth century, which is the time span of the next chapter, but, like all important literary movements, it had its forerunners. Thomas Gray, Robert Burns, and William Blake lived during the second half of the eighteenth century when the neoclassical poetry of Alexander Pope was still very much in vogue. Like Oliver Goldsmith, these men produced poems that Pope would never have dreamed of writing and that later romantic poets looked back on in admiration.

Thomas Gray 1716-1771

Retiring and fastidious by nature, Gray turned his back on the elegant society that Pope had celebrated in his poems to lead instead the quiet life of a Cambridge professor. His best poem, the "Elegy Written in a Country Churchyard," though sufficiently neoclassical to draw praises from Samuel Johnson, reveals a similar departure from the prevailing tastes of the eighteenth century. Whereas Pope and his followers had spoken mostly of city life and, if they treated country life at all, did so only superficially, Gray infused the "Elegy" with his own delicate sensitivity to the beauties of the great outdoors. The people he wrote of were humble country folk who lived their quiet lives far from the glittering, active world of the metropolis. And in his reflections on the inevitability of death, Gray sounded a note of melancholy that is absent in the neoclassical poems on the same subject and that was to come through loud and clear in the poems of the nineteenth century.

The curfew tolls the knell of parting day,
　　The lowing herd wind slowly o'er the lea,
The plowman homeward plods his weary way,
　　And leaves the world to darkness and to me.

Now fades the glimmering landscape on the sight,　　5
　　And all the air a solemn stillness holds,
Save where the beetle wheels his droning flight,
　　And drowsy tinklings lull the distant folds;

Save that from yonder ivy-mantled tower
　　The moping owl does to the moon complain　　10
Of such as, wandering near her secret bower,
　　Molest her ancient solitary reign.

Beneath those rugged elms, that yew-tree's shade,
　　Where heaves the turf in many a moldering heap,
Each in his narrow cell forever laid,　　15
　　The rude forefathers of the hamlet sleep.

The breezy call of incense-breathing Morn,
　　The swallow twittering from the strawbuilt shed,
The cock's shrill clarion, or the echoing horn,[1]
　　No more shall rouse them from their lowly bed.　　20

For them no more the blazing hearth shall burn,
　　Or busy housewife ply her evening care;
No children run to lisp their sire's return,
　　Or climb his knees the envied kiss to share.

Oft did the harvest to their sickle yield,　　25
　　Their furrow oft the stubborn glebe has broke;
How jocund did they drive their team afield!
　　How bowed the woods beneath their sturdy stroke!

Let not Ambition mock their useful toil,
　　Their homely joys, and destiny obscure;　　30
Nor Grandeur hear, with a disdainful smile,
　　The short and simple annals of the poor.

The boast of heraldry, the pomp of power,
　　And all that beauty, all that wealth e'er gave,
Awaits alike the inevitable hour:　　35
　　The paths of glory lead but to the grave.

Nor you, ye proud, impute to these the fault,
　　If Memory o'er their tomb no trophies raise,

NATIONAL PORTRAIT GALLERY

---

1. *horn*, the huntsman's horn.

Where through the long-drawn aisle and fretted vault
    The pealing anthem swells the note of praise.   40

Can storied urn[2] or animated[3] bust
    Back to its mansion call the fleeting breath?
Can Honor's voice provoke the silent dust,
    Or Flattery soothe the dull cold ear of Death?

Perhaps in this neglected spot is laid   45
    Some heart once pregnant with celestial fire;
Hands that the rod of empire might have swayed,
    Or waked to ecstasy the living lyre.

But Knowledge to their eyes her ample page
    Rich with the spoils of time did ne'er unroll;   50
Chill Penury repressed their noble rage,
    And froze the genial current of the soul.

The church and churchyard of St. Giles at Stoke Poges. In this churchyard Gray is buried, and it is supposed that here the "Elegy" was conceived.

PHOTO BY DOROTHY BRACKEN

Full many a gem of purest ray serene
    The dark unfathomed caves of ocean bear;
Full many a flower is born to blush unseen,   55
    And waste its sweetness on the desert air.

Some village Hampden[4] that with dauntless breast
    The little tyrant of his fields withstood;
Some mute inglorious Milton here may rest,
    Some Cromwell guiltless of his country's blood.   60

The applause of listening senates to command,
    The threats of pain and ruin to despise,
To scatter plenty o'er a smiling land,
    And read their history in a nation's eyes,

Their lot forbade; nor circumscribed alone   65
    Their growing virtues, but their crimes confined;
Forbade to wade through slaughter to a throne,
    And shut the gates of mercy on mankind,

The struggling pangs of conscious truth to hide,
    To quench the blushes of ingenuous shame,   70
Or heap the shrine of Luxury and Pride
    With incense kindled at the Muse's flame.

Far from the madding crowd's ignoble strife,
    Their sober wishes never learned to stray;

---

2. *storied urn,* an urn inscribed with pictures that tell a story. (See Keats' "Ode on a Grecian Urn," page 398.) **3.** *animated,* lifelike. **4.** *Hampden,* John Hampden (1594-1643), member of the Puritan or Roundhead party who spoke out against royal taxes.

Along the cool sequestered vale of life   75
   They kept the noiseless tenor of their way.

Yet ev'n these bones from insult to protect
   Some frail memorial still erected nigh,
With uncouth⁵ rimes and shapeless sculpture decked,
   Implores the passing tribute of a sigh.   80

Their name, their years, spelt by the unlettered Muse,
   The place of fame and elegy supply;
And many a holy text around she strews,
   That teach the rustic moralist to die.

For who, to dumb Forgetfulness a prey,   85
   This pleasing anxious being e'er resigned,
Left the warm precincts of the cheerful day,
   Nor cast one longing, lingering look behind?

On some fond breast the parting soul relies,
   Some pious drops the closing eye requires;   90
Ev'n from the tomb the voice of Nature cries,
   Ev'n in our ashes live their wonted fires.

For thee,⁶ who mindful of the unhonored dead
   Dost in these lines their artless tale relate;
If chance, by lonely Contemplation led,   95
   Some kindred spirit shall inquire thy fate,

Haply some hoary-headed swain may say,
   "Oft have we seen him at the peep of dawn
Brushing with hasty steps the dews away
   To meet the sun upon the upland lawn,   100

"There at the foot of yonder nodding beech,
   That wreathes its old fantastic roots so high,
His listless length at noontide would he stretch,
   And pore upon the brook that babbles by.

"Hard by yon wood, now smiling as in scorn,   105
   Muttering his wayward fancies he would rove,
Now drooping, woeful wan, like one forlorn,
   Or crazed with care, or crossed in hopeless love.

"One morn I missed him on the customed hill,
   Along the heath, and near his favorite tree;   110
Another came; nor yet beside the rill,
   Nor up the lawn, nor at the wood was he;

---

5. *uncouth*, strange, odd. 6. *thee*, Gray himself.

"The next with dirges due in sad array
    Slow through the church-way path we saw him borne.
Approach and read (for thou canst read) the lay,   115
    Graved on the stone beneath yon aged thorn."

THE EPITAPH

Here rests his head upon the lap of Earth
    A youth to Fortune and to Fame unknown.
Fair Science frowned not on his humble birth,   120
    And Melancholy marked him for her own.

Large was his bounty, and his soul sincere,
    Heaven did a recompense as largely send;
He gave to Misery all he had, a tear,
    He gained from Heaven ('twas all he wished) a friend.

No farther seek his merits to disclose,   126
    Or draw his frailties from their dread abode.
(There they alike in trembling hope repose),
    The bosom of his Father and his God.

To increase understanding

1. (*a*) What is the function of stanzas 1-4 of Gray's "Elegy"? (*b*) What is the poet saying in lines 17-32? (*c*) How does he enlarge his theme in lines 33-44?

2. Lines 45-76 reveal Gray's humanitarian outlook. (*a*) Explain the metaphors contained in lines 53-56 and the references to Hampden, Milton, and Cromwell in lines 57-60. (*b*) What is it that keeps humble people from realizing their potentialities? (*c*) Does Gray regard all the activities of civilized man as praiseworthy? Explain.

3. What is Gray's attitude toward death in lines 77-92?

4. (*a*) In what sense do lines 93-129 represent a distinct break in the poem? (*b*) How would you describe the tone of these final lines?

5. Compare Gray's "Elegy" with the poems by Pope. How do they differ in verse form, subject matter, and tone?

Better reading
Elegy

In classical times an *elegy* was a poem written in a certain meter (couplets of hexameter and pentameter lines) expressing a writer's personal feelings on such subjects as love, war, and death. Today the term is applied to any poem that laments either the death of a specific person or the mortality of all men and the things they love.

As the nineteenth-century poet Coleridge remarked, "elegy is the form of poetry natural to the reflective mind," and, indeed, the elegiac poet presents himself for the most part in a mood of sad and melancholy contemplation. The tone of his poem is usually lofty and dignified, expressing generalized sentiments rather than passionate outbursts of feeling.

Would you describe Gray's "Elegy" as a personal lament or as a general lament for the death of all men?

Reread the first three stanzas. What time of day is the poet describing? What kinds of sound are suggested? What particular words impart a tone of mourning? How would you describe the movement of these stanzas? Why, in general, are these stanzas appropriate to the opening of an elegy?

What is meant by "incense-breathing Morn" (line 17), "pomp of power" (line 33), "inevitable hour" (line 35), "genial current" (line 52), "noiseless tenor" (line 76), "pious drops" (line 90)? How do such phrases contribute to the lofty tone of the poem?

Do the last eight stanzas add or detract from the dignity of the poem? Explain your answer.

Robert Burns 1759-1796

Unlike fashionable, "citified" poets like Alexander Pope, Scotland's "Bobbie" Burns led a vigorous, earthy kind of life. Until the age of sixteen he worked, as he himself said, "with the unceasing toil of a galley-slave" on the farms his father rented in the rocky Scottish Lowlands. By the time he was in his twenties, he had been in and out of several love affairs—and an even greater number of taverns. And though his last years were marked by poverty and illness, Burns undertook two rough journeys, one through northern England and the other through the Scottish Highlands, in an effort to uncover traditional songs and ballads.

Such a strenuous life was bound to be short, but before his death at thirty-seven, Burns was hailed as a new and exciting poet. His *Poems: Chiefly in the Scottish Dialect*, which he published in 1786 in hopes of getting enough money to start a new life in Jamaica, were so well received that he called off his Jamaica trip and accepted an invitation to join the fashionable, literary salons in Edinburgh. Edinburgh society, however, was still too enamored of the pedantry and polish of Alexander Pope to regard Burns as anything more than a rustic novelty, and Burns only made matters worse by acting the part of the arrogant, overly eager literary darling. He soon left the city to rejoin the "sons and daughters of labor and poverty" with whom he had grown up. In their eyes he was a great man—someone who not only spoke of the common people (as men like Thomas Gray were doing) but one who also spoke up for them in their own vigorous idiom of speech.

Next to being the poet of the people, Burns was the poet of love. The love he celebrates is not the witty, sophisticated kind of love that hovers almost unnoticed about the verses of the neoclassical poets, but rather the deeply personal lyrical kind of love that had welled up in many of the Elizabethan poets, and that Burns himself seems to have experienced with Jean Armour and Mary Campbell. In fact, all of Burns' poems, whether they are about love, or field mice, or the rights of man, possess a fine lyric quality. This is due in part to the fact that many of Burns' poems are based on Scottish folk songs. It is due above all to Burns' supreme ability to speak directly from the depths of his own experience.

The Old Kirk at Alloway. Alloway, Burns' birthplace, is the scene of "Tam o' Shanter."

Portrait of Burns by Alexander Nasmyth, a landscape painter who was an intimate friend of Burns.

MY JEAN

Of a' the airts[1] the wind can blaw,
    I dearly like the west,
For there the bonnie lassie lives,
    The lassie I lo'e best.
There wild woods grow, and rivers row,   5
    And monie a hill between;
But day and night my fancy's flight
    Is ever wi' my Jean.

I see her in the dewy flowers,
    I see her sweet and fair.   10
I hear her in the tunefu' birds,
    I hear her charm the air.
There's not a bonnie flower that springs
    By fountain, shaw,[2] or green;
There's not a bonnie bird that sings,   15
    But minds me o' my Jean.

A RED, RED ROSE

O my luve is like a red, red rose
    That's newly sprung in June.
O my luve is like the melodie
    That's sweetly played in tune.

As fair art thou, my bonie lass,   5
    So deep in luve am I,
And I will luve thee still, my dear,
    Till a' the seas gang dry.

Till a' the seas gang dry, my dear,
    And the rocks melt wi' the sun!   10
And I will luve thee still, my dear,
    While the sands o' life shall run.

And fare thee weel, my only luve,
    And fare thee weel a while!
And I will come again, my luve,   15
    Tho' it were ten thousand mile!

HIGHLAND MARY

Ye banks, and braes,[1] and streams around
    The castle o' Montgomery,
Green be your woods and fair your flowers,
    Your waters never drumlie![2]
There simmer first unfald her robes,   5
    And there the langest tarry;
For there I took the last fareweel,
    O' my sweet Highland Mary.

How sweetly bloom'd the gay green birk,[3]
    How rich the hawthorn's blossom   10
As underneath their fragrant shade
    I clasp'd her to my bosom!
The golden hours on angel wings
    Flew o'er me and my dearie;
For dear to me as light and life,   15
    Was my sweet Highland Mary.

Wi' monie a vow and lock'd embrace
    Our parting was fu' tender;
And, pledging aft[4] to meet again,
    We tore oursels asunder;   20
But O! fell Death's untimely frost,
    That nipt my flower sae early!
Now green's the sod, and cauld's the clay,
    That wraps my Highland Mary!

O pale, pale now, those rosy lips,   25
    I aft hae kiss'd sae fondly!
And clos'd for ay the sparkling glance,
    That dwalt on me sae kindly!
And moldering now in silent dust,
    That heart that lo'ed me dearly!   30
But still within my bosom's core
    Shall live my Highland Mary.

MY JEAN. 1. *airts*, quarters of the compass. 2. *shaw*, wood.
HIGHLAND MARY. 1. *braes*, hillsides. 2. *drumlie*, muddy. 3. *birk*, birch. 4. *aft*, often.

A MAN'S A MAN FOR A' THAT

Is there, for honest poverty,
    That hings his head, an' a' that?
The coward slave, we pass him by,
    We dare be poor for a' that!
For a' that, an' a' that,
    Our toils obscure, an' a' that;
The rank is but the guinea's stamp[1];
    The man's the gowd[2] for a' that.

What tho' on hamely fare we dine,
    Wear hodden-gray,[3] an' a' that;   10
Gie fools their silks, and knaves their wine,
    A man's a man for a' that.
        For a' that, an' a' that,
          Their tinsel show, an' a' that;
        The honest man, tho' e'er sae poor,   15
          Is king o' men for a' that.

Ye see yon birkie,[4] ca'd a lord,
    Wha struts, an' stares, an' a' that;
Tho' hundreds worship at his word,
    He's but a coof[5] for a' that.   20
        For a' that, an' a' that,
          His riband, star, an' a' that
        The man o' independent mind,
          He looks and laughs at a' that.

A prince can mak a belted knight,   25
    A marquis, duke, an' a' that;
But an honest man's aboon his might,[6]
    Guid faith he mauna fa'[7] that!
        For a' that, an' a' that,
          Their dignities, an' a' that,   30
        The pith o' sense, an' pride o' worth,
          Are higher rank than a' that.

Then let us pray that come it may,
    As come it will for a' that,
That sense and worth, o'er a' the earth,   35
    May bear the gree,[8] an' a' that.
        For a' that, an' a' that,
          It's coming yet, for a' that,
        That man to man, the warld o'er,
          Shall brothers be for a' that.   40

TO A MOUSE
*on turning her up in her nest
with the plow, November, 1785*

Wee, sleekit,[1] cowrin, tim'rous beastie,
Oh, what a panic's in thy breastie!
Thou need na start awa sae hasty
      Wi' bickering brattle![2]
I wad be laith[3] to rin an' chase thee,   5
      Wi' murdering pattle![4]

I'm truly sorry man's dominion
Has broken Nature's social union,
An' justifies that ill opinion
      Which makes thee startle   10
At me, thy poor, earth-born companion
      An' fellow mortal!

I doubt na, whyles,[5] but thou may thieve;
What then? poor beastie, thou maun live.
A daimen icker in a thrave[6]
      'S a sma' request;
I'll get a blessin wi' the lave,[7]
      An' never miss 't!

Thy wee-bit housie, too, in ruin!
Its silly wa's[8] the win's are strewin!   20
An' naething, now, to big[9] a new ane,
      O' foggage[10] green!
An' bleak December's win's ensuin,
      Baith snell[11] an' keen!

A MAN'S A MAN FOR A' THAT. 1. *guinea's stamp*, the imprint of the King's head on a coin as a statement of its value. 2. *gowd*, gold. 3. *hodden-gray*, coarse gray cloth. 4. *birkie*, fellow. 5. *coof*, fool. 6. *aboon his might*, above the prince's might. 7. *mauna fa'*, can't make. 8. *gree*, prize.
TO A MOUSE. 1. *sleekit*, sleek. 2. *Wi' . . . brattle*, with sudden scamper. 3. *wad be laith*, would be loath. 4. *pattle*, paddle for cleaning the plow. 5. *whyles*, at times. 6. *daimen . . . thrave*, an occasional ear or head of grain in a shock. 7. *lave*, rest. 8. *silly wa's*, simple walls. 9. *big*, build. 10. *foggage*, coarse grass. 11. *snell*, sharp, bitter.

Thou saw the fields laid bare an' waste,   25
An' weary winter comin' fast,
An' cozie here, beneath the blast,
     Thou thought to dwell,
Till, crash! the cruel coulter passed
     Out through thy cell.   30

That wee bit heap o' leaves an' stibble,
Has cost thee monie a weary nibble!
Now thou's turned out, for a' thy trouble,
     But house or hald,[12]
To thole[13] the winter's sleety dribble   35
     An' cranreuch[14] cauld!

But Mousie, thou art no thy lane,[15]
In proving foresight may be vain.
The best-laid schemes o' mice an' men
     Gang aft agley,[16]   40
An' lea'e us naught but grief an' pain,
     For promised joy!

Still thou art blest, compared wi' me!
The present only toucheth thee,
But och! I backward cast my e'e,   45
     On prospects drear!
An' forward, though I canna see,
     I guess an' fear!

TO A LOUSE
on seeing one on a lady's bonnet at church

Ha! whare ye gaun,[1] ye crowlin ferlie?[2]
Your impudence protects you sairly[3];
I canna say but ye strunt[4] rarely,
     Owre gauze and lace;
Though, faith! I fear ye dine but sparely   5
     On sic a place.

Ye ugly, creepin, blastit wonner,[5]
Detested, shunned by saunt an' sinner,
How daur ye set your fit[6] upon her—
     Sae fine a lady?   10
Gae somewhere else and seek your dinner
     On some poor body.

Swith! in some beggar's hauffet squattle[7];
There ye may creep, and sprawl, and sprattle,[8]

Wi' ither kindred, jumping cattle,   15
     In shoals and nations;
Whare horn nor bane[9] ne'er daur unsettle
     Your thick plantations.

Now haud[10] you there! ye're out o' sight,
Below the fatt'rils,[11] snug an' tight;   20
Na, faith ye yet! ye'll no be right
     'Till ye've got on it—
The vera tapmost, tow'ring height
     O' Miss's bonnet.

My sooth! right bauld ye set your nose out,   25
As plump an' gray as onie grozet[12];
O for some rank, mercurial rozet,[13]
     Or fell, red smeddum,[14]
I'd gie you sic a hearty dose o't,
     Wad dress your droddum.[15]   30

I wad na been surprised to spy
You on an auld wife's flainen toy[16];
Or aiblins[17] some bit duddie[18] boy,
     On's wyliecoat[19];
But Miss's fine Lunardi![20] fye!   35
     How daur ye do't?

O Jenny, dinna toss your head,
An' set your beauties a' abroad!
Ye little ken what cursèd speed
     The blastie's makin!   40
Thae winks an' finger-ends, I dread,
     Are notice takin!

O wad some Power the giftie gie us
To see oursels as ithers see us!
It wad frae monie a blunder free us,   45
     An' foolish notion.
What airs in dress an' gait wad lea'e us,
     An' ev'n devotion!

TO A MOUSE. 12. *But . . . hald*, without house or home. 13. *thole*, endure. 14. *cranreuch*, hoarfrost. 15. *no thy lane*, not alone. 16. *Gang aft agley*, often go awry.

TO A LOUSE 1. *gaun*, going. 2. *crowlin ferlie*, crawling wonder. 3. *sairly*, greatly. 4. *strunt*, strut. 5. *blastit wonner*, blasted wonder. 6. *fit*, foot. 7. *Swith! . . . squattle*. Quick! on some beggar's temple settle! 8. *sprattle*, scramble. 9. *horn nor bane*, comb nor poison. 10. *haud*, hold. 11. *fatt'rils*, ribbon-ends. 12. *grozet*, gooseberry. 13. *rozet*, rosin. 14. *smeddum*, powder. 15. *Wad dress your droddum*, would fix you proper. 16. *flainen toy*, flannel cap. 17. *aiblins*, perhaps. 18. *bit duddie*, small, ragged. 19. *wyliecoat*, undervest. 20. *Lunardi*, balloon bonnet, named after Lunardi, a famous balloonist.

TAM O' SHANTER

Toward the end of the eighteenth century people began to take a lively interest in things supernatural. At the request of a friend who had agreed to do a drawing of the place, Burns wrote the following witch-tale about the church at Alloway, where his father was buried. The tale comes from Scottish folklore, the hero from the real-life character of Douglas Graham, one of the more convivial souls in and about Alloway.

When chapman billies[1] leave the street,
And drouthy[2] neebors neebors meet,
As market-days are wearing late,
An' folk begin to take the gate[3];
While we sit bousing at the nappy,[4]   5
An' gettin' fou[5] and unco[6] happy,
We think na on the lang Scots miles,
The mosses, waters, slaps,[7] and stiles,
That lie between us and our hame,
Whare sits our sulky, sullen dame,   10
Gathering her brows like gathering storm,
Nursing her wrath to keep it warm.

This truth fand[8] honest Tam o' Shanter,
As he frae Ayr ae night did canter:
(Auld Ayr, wham ne'er a town surpasses,   15
For honest men and bonie lasses).

O Tam! had'st thou but been sae wise
As taen thy ain wife Kate's advice!
She tauld thee weel thou was a skellum,[9]
A bletherin, blusterin, drunken blellum[10];   20
That frae November till October,
Ae market-day thou was na sober;
That ilka melder[11] wi' the miller,
Thou sat as lang as thou had siller[12];
That ev'ry naig was ca'd[13] a shoe on,   25
The smith and thee gat roaring fou on;
That at the Lord's house, even on Sunday,
Thou drank wi' Kirkton[14] Jean till Monday.
She prophesied, that, late or soon,   29

Thou would be found deep drowned in Doon[15];
Or catched wi' warlocks[16] in the mirk,[17]
By Alloway's auld haunted kirk.

Ah, gentle dames! it gars me greet,[18]
To think how monie counsel sweet,
How monie lengthened sage advices,   35
The husband frae the wife despises!

But to our tale:—Ae market night,
Tam had got planted unco right,
Fast by an ingle, bleezing[19] finely,
Wi' reaming swats[20] that drank divinely;   40
And at his elbow, Souter[21] Johnie,
His ancient, trusty, drouthy cronie:
Tam loe'd him like a very brither;
They had been fou for weeks thegither.
The night drave on wi' sangs and clatter;   45
And ay the ale was growing better:
The landlady and Tam grew gracious
Wi' secret favors, sweet and precious:
The souter tauld his queerest stories;
The landlord's laugh was ready chorus: 50
The storm without might rair and rustle,
Tam did na mind the storm a whistle.

Care, mad to see a man sae happy,
E'en drowned himsel amang the nappy:
As bees flee hame wi' lades o' treasure,   55
The minutes winged their way wi' pleasure;
Kings may be blest, but Tam was glorious,
O'er a' the ills o' life victorious!

But pleasures are like poppies spread,
You seize the flow'r, its bloom is shed;   60
Or like the snow falls in the river,
A moment white—then melts forever;
Or like the borealis race,
That flit ere you can point their place;
Or like the rainbow's lovely form   65
Evanishing amid the storm.

---

1. *chapman billies*, peddler comrades. 2. *drouthy*, thirsty.
3. *take the gate*, go home. 4. *bousing at the nappy*, drinking ale. 5. *fou*, full, drunk. 6. *unco*, very. 7. *slaps*, fence gaps or gates. 8. *fand*, found. 9. *skellum*, good-for-nothing. 10. *blellum*, blabberer. 11. *ilka melder*, every grinding. 12. *siller*, silver. 13. *ca'd*, nailed. 14. *Kirkton*, any village near a church. 15. *Doon*, a small stream near Burns' birthplace. 16. *warlocks*, wizards or witches. 17. *mirk*, dark. 18. *gars me greet*, makes me weep. 19. *bleezing*, blazing. 20. *reaming swats*, foaming ale. 21. *Souter*, cobbler.

Nae man can tether time nor tide:
The hour approaches Tam maun ride—
That hour, o' night's black arch the
    keystane,²²
That dreary hour Tam mounts his beast in; 70
And sic a night he taks the road in,
As ne'er poor sinner was abroad in.

The wind blew as 'twad blawn its last;
The rattling showers rose on the blast;
The speedy gleams the darkness swallowed; 75
Loud, deep, and lang the thunder bellowed:
That night, a child might understand,
The Deil had business on his hand.

Weel mounted on his gray mare, Meg—
A better never lifted leg— 80
Tam skelpit²³ on thro' dub²⁴ and mire,
Despising wind and rain and fire;
Whiles holding fast his guid blue bonnet,
Whiles crooning o'er some auld Scots sonnet,
Whiles glow'ring round wi' prudent cares, 85
Lest bogles²⁵ catch him unawares.
Kirk-Alloway was drawing nigh,
Whare ghaists and houlets²⁶ nightly cry.

By this time he was cross the ford,
Whare in the snaw the chapman smoored²⁷; 90
And past the birks and meikle stane,²⁸
Whare drunken Charlie brak's neck-bane;
And thro' the whins,²⁹ and by the cairn,
Whare hunters fand the murdered bairn;
And near the thorn, aboon³⁰ the well, 95
Whare Mungo's mither hanged hersel.
Before him Doon pours all his floods;
The doubling storm roars thro' the woods;
The lightnings flash from pole to pole,
Near and more near the thunders roll; 100
When, glimmering thro' the groaning trees
Kirk-Alloway seemed in a bleeze:
Thro' ilka bore³¹ the beams were glancing,
And loud resounded mirth and dancing.

Inspiring bold John Barleycorn! 105
What dangers thou canst make us scorn!
Wi' tippenny³² we fear nae evil;
Wi' usquebae³³ we'll face the devil!
The swats sae reamed³⁴ in Tammie's noddle,
Fair play, he cared na deils a boddle.³⁵ 110
But Maggie stood right sair astonished,

Till, by the heel and hand admonished,
She ventured forward on the light;
And, wow! Tam saw an unco sight!

Warlocks and witches in a dance; 115
Nae cotillion brent-new frae France,
But hornpipes, jigs, strathspeys,³⁶ and reels
Put life and mettle in their heels:
A winnock bunker³⁷ in the east,
There sat Auld Nick in shape o' beast; 120
A towsie tyke,³⁸ black, grim, and large,
To gie them music was his charge;
He screwed the pipes and gart them skirl,³⁹
Till roof and rafters a' did dirl.⁴⁰
Coffins stood round like open presses, 125
That shawed the dead in their last dresses;
And by some devilish cantraip sleight⁴¹
Each in its cauld hand held a light,
By which heroic Tam was able
To note upon the haly table 130
A murderer's banes in gibbet airns⁴²;
Twa span-lang, wee, unchristened bairns;
A thief, new-cutted frae a rape⁴³—
Wi' his last gasp his gab⁴⁴ did gape;
Five tomahawks, wi' bluid red-rusted; 135
Five scymitars, wi' murder crusted;
A garter, which a babe had strangled;
A knife, a father's throat had mangled,
Whom his ain son o' life bereft—
The gray hairs yet stack to the heft; 140
Wi' mair o' horrible and awfu',
Which even to name wad be unlawfu'.

As Tammie glowered,⁴⁵ amazed and curious,
The mirth and fun grew fast and furious:
The piper loud and louder blew, 145
The dancers quick and quicker flew;
They reeled, they set, they crossed, they
    cleekit,⁴⁶

---

22. *hour . . . keystane*, midnight. 23. *skelpit*, clattered.
24. *dub*, puddle. 25. *bogles*, hobgoblins. 26. *houlets*,
owls. 27. *smoored*, smothered. 28. *meikle stane*, great
stone. 29. *whins*, furze, a prickly evergreen shrub. 30.
aboon, above. 31. *ilka bore*, every crevice. 32. *tip-
penny*, two-penny ale. 33. *usquebae*, whisky. 34. *swats
sae reamed*, ale so foamed. 35. *deils a boddle*, devil a farthing, not at all. 36. *strathspeys*, a Scottish dance. 37.
winnock bunker, window seat. 38. *towsie tyke*, shaggy cur.
39. *gart them skirl*, made them scream. 40. *dirl*, ring.
41. *cantraip sleight*, magic trick. 42. *banes in gibbet airns*,
bones in gibbet irons. 43. *rape*, rope. 44. *gab*, mouth.
45. *glowered*, stared. 46. *cleekit*, caught hold of each
other.

Till ilka carlin swat and reekit,[47]
And coost her duddies to the wark[48]
And linket at it in her sark![49]   150

    . . . .

    But Tam kend what was what fu' brawlie[50];
There was ae winsome wench and wawlie,[51]
That night enlisted in the core[52]
Lang after kend on Carrick shore
(For monie a beast to dead she shot,   155
An' perished monie a bonie boat,
And shook baith meikle corn and bear,[53]
And kept the countryside in fear).
Her cutty sark,[54] o' Paisley harn,[55]
That while a lassie she had worn,   160
In longitude tho' sorely scanty,
It was her best, and she was vauntie.[56]
Ah! little kend thy reverend grannie,
That sark she coft[57] for her wee Nannie,
Wi' twa pund Scots[58] ('twas a' her riches), 165
Wad ever graced a dance o' witches!

    But here my Muse her wing maun cour,[59]
Sic flights are far beyond her power;
To sing how Nannie lap and flang,[60]
(A souple jade she was and strang,)   170
And how Tam stood like ane bewitched,
And thought his very een enriched;
Even Satan glowered and fidged fu' fain,[61]
And hotched[62] and blew wi' might and main:
Till first ae caper, syne anither,   175
Tam tint[63] his reason a' thegither,
And roars out, "Weel done, Cutty-sark!"
And in an instant all was dark:
And scarcely had he Maggie rallied,
When out the hellish legion sallied.   180

    As bees bizz out wi' angry fyke,[64]
When plundering herds assail their byke[65];
As open pussie's[66] mortal foes,
When, pop! she starts before their nose;
As eager runs the market-crowd,   185
When "Catch the thief!" resounds aloud;
So Maggie runs, the witches follow,
Wi' monie an eldritch[67] skriech and hollo.

    Ah, Tam! ah, Tam! thou'll get thy fairin![68]
In hell they'll roast thee like a herrin!   190
In vain thy Kate awaits thy comin!
Kate soon will be a woefu' woman!
Now, do thy speedy utmost, Meg,

And win the keystane of the brig[69]:
There at them thou thy tail may toss,   195
A running stream they dare na cross.
But ere the keystane she could make,
The fient a tail she had to shake!
For Nannie, far before the rest,
Hard upon noble Maggie prest,   200
And flew at Tam wi' furious ettle[70];
But little wist she Maggie's mettle—
Ae spring brought aff her master hale,
But left behind her ain gray tail:
The carlin claught[71] her by the rump,   205
And left poor Maggie scarce a stump.

    Now, wha this tale o' truth shall read,
Ilk man and mother's son, take heed,
Whene'er to drink you are inclined,
Or cutty-sarks run in your mind,   210
Think, ye may buy the joys o'er dear,
Remember Tam o' Shanter's Mare.

---

47. *ilka . . . reekit*, each hag sweat and steamed. 48. *coost
. . . wark*, threw off her clothes for the work. 49. *linket
. . . sark*, danced in her shirt. 50. *fu' brawlie*, full well.
51. *wawlie*, buxom. 52. *core*, company. 53. *corn and
bear*, wheat and barley. 54. *cutty sark*, short shirt. 55.
Paisley harn, coarse linen made in the town of Paisley. 56.
vauntie, proud. 57. *coft*, bought. 58. *twa pund Scots*.
A pound Scots was worth about forty cents. 59. *maun
cour*, must lower. 60. *lap and flang*, jumped and kicked.
61. *fidged fu' fain*, fidgeted with pleasure. 62. *hotched*,
jerked. 63. *tint*, lost. 64. *fyke*, fuss. 65. *byke*, hive.
66. *pussie's*, the hare's. 67. *eldritch*, unearthly. 68.
fairin, reward, desserts. 69. *brig*, bridge. 70. *ettle*, aim,
intent. 71. *claught*, seized.

❀ To increase understanding

1. (*a*) What is the outstanding quality of Burns'
love songs? (*b*) How would you rank the three you
have read as to depth of emotion?

2. (*a*) What is the main idea of "A Man's a Man
for A' That"? (*b*) With what social movement
would Burns' poem have been associated upon its
publication in 1794?

3. "To a Mouse" and "To a Louse" are regarded
as companion poems. (*a*) What do they have in
common? (*b*) How do they differ from each other in
tone? (*c*) What is it that connects these two poems
with "A Man's a Man for A' That"?

4. (*a*) Relate the tale of "Tam o' Shanter."
(*b*) Cite as many reasons as you can which would
support the assertion that this poem is "one of the
most rollicking in the English language." (*c*) Why
would Pope never have considered writing a poem
of this kind?

William Blake 1757-1827

Blake was a more conscious rebel than Thomas Gray or Robert Burns. His occasional prose pieces contain ringing denunciations of the neoclassical theory that authors should write only for sophisticated people in a certain manner and on certain subjects, and his several books of poetry are vibrantly alive with the warm humanitarianism, the sensitivity to nature, the deeply felt emotion, and the high imaginativeness that are regarded as important signposts of romantic writing.

But Blake was not just a romantic rebel; he was a visionary and a mystic, a person who dwelt comfortably in the twilight world between fact and fancy, who could see God standing outside a window or sitting in a tree surrounded by angels. Mystical beliefs had always attracted Blake, particularly those of the Swedish philosopher and religious writer Emanuel Swedenborg, who claimed that the material things of the world were the symbols of an underlying spiritual reality. By the time he was a young married man

Left above: Portrait of Blake by Thomas Phillips, a professor at the Royal Academy. Left below: Part of Blake's Circle of the Life of Man. *Above: The frontispiece to* Europe, *one of Blake's early "Prophetic Books."*

in business for himself as an engraver and print-seller, Blake had become so steeped in mystical beliefs and had withdrawn so thoroughly into his visionary world that his wife is said to have remarked: "I have very little of Mr. Blake's company. He is always in Paradise."

Blake's series of mystical poems, called the "Prophetic Books," have proved too obscure for the general reader. His first book of poetry, however, entitled *Poetical Sketches,* and his second and his last works, entitled *The Songs of Innocence* and *The Songs of Experience,* contain some of the best-known poems in the English language. The *Poetical Sketches* are reminiscent of the delicate, spontaneous lyrics of the Elizabethans. *The Songs of Innocence* and *The Songs of Experience,* as the titles imply, deal with "the two contrary states of the human soul," the innocent, child-like state of exquisite joy, peace, and contentment, and the experienced, adult state which is full of corruption, distortion, and sadness but through which men must pass in order to arrive at a comprehensive vision of life.

With the exception of *Poetical Sketches,* Blake made all of his own books, etching the poems on copper plates, decorating them with his own drawings, and then printing and binding the volumes. These unique creations, plus his highly imaginative drawings for the Book of Job, Milton's *Paradise Lost,* and Dante's *Divine Comedy,* have secured Blake an important position in both the history of English art and the history of English literature.

The Raising of Lazarus, one of fifty illustrations which Blake was commissioned to do for an edition of the Bible.

HOW SWEET I ROAMED
from POETICAL SKETCHES

How sweet I roamed from field to
    field,
    And tasted all the summer's
    pride,
Till I the Prince of Love beheld,
  Who in the sunny beams did glide.

He showed me lilies for my hair,   5
  And blushing roses for my brow;
He led me through his gardens fair,
  Where all his golden pleasures grow.

With sweet May dews my wings were wet,
  And Phoebus[1] fired my vocal rage;   10
He caught me in his silken net,
  And shut me in his golden cage.

He loves to sit and hear me sing,
  Then, laughing, sports and plays with me;
Then stretches out my golden wing,   15
  And mocks my loss of liberty.

---

1. *Phoebus,* Apollo, the Greek god of the sun, who was also the god of music and poetry.

Little Lamb, I'll tell thee,
 Little Lamb, I'll tell thee:
He is callèd by thy name,
For He calls Himself a Lamb,
He is meek, and He is mild;   15
He became a little child.
I a child, and thou a lamb,
We are callèd by His name.
 Little Lamb, God bless thee!
 Little Lamb, God bless thee!   20

PIPING DOWN THE VALLEYS
from SONGS OF INNOCENCE

Piping down the valleys wild,
 Piping songs of pleasant glee,
 On a cloud I saw a child,
 And he laughing said to me:

"Pipe a song about a Lamb!"   5
So I piped with merry cheer.
"Piper, pipe that song again";
So I piped: he wept to hear.

"Drop thy pipe, thy happy pipe;
Sing thy songs of happy cheer":   10
So I sang the same again,
While he wept with joy to hear.

"Piper, sit thee down and write
In a book, that all may read."
So he vanished from my sight,   15
And I plucked a hollow reed,

And I made a rural[1] pen,
And I stained the water clear,[2]
And I wrote my happy songs
Every child may joy to hear.   20

THE LAMB
from SONGS OF INNOCENCE

Little Lamb, who made thee?
 Dost thou know who made thee?
Gave thee life, and bid thee feed,
By the streams and o'er the mead;
Gave thee clothing of delight,   5
Softest clothing, woolly, bright;
Gave thee such a tender voice,
Making all the vales rejoice?
 Little Lamb, who made thee?
 Dost thou know who made thee?   10

THE TIGER
from SONGS OF EXPERIENCE

Tiger! Tiger! burning bright
 In the forests of the night,
 What immortal hand or eye
 Could frame thy fearful symmetry?

In what distant deeps or skies   5
Burnt the fire of thine eyes?
On what wings dare he aspire?
What the hand dare seize the fire?

And what shoulder, and what art,
Could twist the sinews of thy heart?   10
And when thy heart began to beat,
What dread hand? and what dread feet?

What the hammer? what the chain?
In what furnace was thy brain?
What the anvil? what dread grasp   15
Dare its deadly terrors clasp?

When the stars threw down their spears,
And watered heaven with their tears,
Did He smile His work to see?
Did He who made the Lamb make thee?   20

Tiger! Tiger! burning bright
In the forests of the night,
What immortal hand or eye
Dare frame thy fearful symmetry?

PIPING DOWN THE VALLEYS. **1.** *rural,* crude. **2.** *stained
. . . clear,* made ink by dyeing the water with berries.

A NEW JERUSALEM
from MILTON

And did those feet in ancient time
  Walk upon England's mountain green?
And was the holy Lamb of God
  On England's pleasant pastures seen?

And did the Countenance Divine   5
  Shine forth upon our clouded hills?
And was Jerusalem builded here
  Among these dark Satanic mills?[1]

Bring me my bow of burning gold!
  Bring me my arrows of desire!   10
Bring me my spear! O clouds, unfold!
  Bring me my chariot of fire!

I will not cease from mental fight,
  Nor shall my sword sleep in my hand,
Till we have built Jerusalem   15
  In England's green and pleasant land.

---

1. *dark Satanic mills.* Blake is referring to the factories that were springing up in England during his time.

1. In what ways is Blake's poem "How Sweet I Roamed" reminiscent of the Elizabethan songs in Chapter III?

2. How does Blake convey the feeling of childhood peace and joy in "Piping Down the Valleys" and "The Lamb"?

3. "The Lamb" and "The Tiger" are companion poems, the one appearing in *Songs of Innocence,* the other in *Songs of Experience.* (*a*) What does each animal symbolize? (*b*) How does Blake convey his intense fascination with the tiger? (*c*) Why does the tiger fascinate him?

4. Gray, Burns, and Blake were among the first to give voice to the new philosophy of humanitarianism, but each expressed it in his own way. How does the humanitarianism of "A New Jerusalem" differ in tone or quality from the humanitarianism of "A Man's a Man for A' That" and "Elegy Written in a Country Churchyard"?

5. Would you describe Blake's poems as simple and direct or complicated and elaborate? Consider in your answer subject matter, imagery, meter, and rhyme scheme.

The Larger View

The subject of Augustan literature is predominantly man in his public aspects—general human nature—the permanent relations of human beings in society. Concerned with such matters, it would have occurred to no Augustan writer to give an account of the growth of a poet's mind . . . since it would never have occurred to him that a poet's mind was in any way peculiar or that an individual poet's mind was a fit object for public contemplation. . . . For the same reasons, Augustan literature is never intimate. When it turns to subjects like religion, or any of the great sources of human emotion, it tends to treat them in their public aspects: philosophical, social, moral.

> Maynard Mack, Ed., *The Augustans, 2nd Edition,* page 2. © 1961 by Prentice-Hall, Inc., and used with their permission.

The development of the English language in the period from Dryden to Johnson inevitably harmonized very closely with that of the literature and ideas of the age. When men desired stability in politics and society, they advocated stability in language. Since correctness and elegance became the ideals in literature, words and their usage had to be submitted to the same criteria. Order and harmony in life and thought must be reflected in the clear and graceful structure and cadence of sentences. The good breeding of a gentleman was impossible without well-bred speech free from affectation, pedantry, rusticity, and crudeness. As both the upper and professional classes and the growing mercantile middle class became increasingly conscious that material prosperity was a prime ideal to be pursued, language was required to be primarily useful, a clear, easy, precise means of communication.

> A. S. Collins, "Language 1660-1784," *From Dryden to Johnson,* edited by Boris Ford, page 125, Penguin Books, 1957. Used by permission of Mrs. A. S. Collins.

Choose one of the above quotations and prepare to discuss whether or not it is an appropriate description of the selections in this chapter. Support your ideas by referring to specific aspects of specific selections.

If your choice is the first quotation, include the following points in your discussion: (*a*) the aims of Addison and Steele and the kind of characters they created, (*b*) the objects of Swift's satire in *Gulliver's Travels,* (*c*) the nature of satire, (*d*) Pope's ideas about the function of the literary critic, (*e*) Goldsmith's handling of love in *She Stoops to Conquer.* Is the quotation an appropriate description of the poetry of Gray, Burns, and Blake? Why, or why not?

If your choice is the second quotation, consider the following points: (*a*) the relation between the heroic couplet and the ideas of the age, (*b*) the influence of Latin on the English language. Did the Augustans actually achieve a certain stability of language, i.e., is there a similarity between the early eighteenth-century prose of Addison and the late eighteenth-century prose of Johnson and Boswell? Was eighteenth-century English literature actually free from "affectation, pedantry, rusticity, and crudeness"? Cite passages to support your answers.

Bibliography

BURNEY, FANNY, *Evelina.* (•Dolphin) Written in the form of letters by one of the first women to attempt literary publication, this book pictures the pursuits of the gay social set of London in the latter part of the eighteenth century. Try Miss Burney's *Diary* (Dutton), too, especially the parts that sketch Samuel Johnson and David Garrick, the actor.

CLIFFORD, J. L., *Young Sam Johnson.* (Oxford) The forces that helped shape Johnson into the unusual man he became are given in this accurate account of his boyhood.

DEFOE, DANIEL, *Robinson Crusoe.* (Dodd •Signet) For generations the strange and fascinating tale of a shipwrecked sailor who lived on a desert island for twenty-eight years has been eagerly read by children and adults alike.

DE LA TORRE, LILLIAN, *The White Rose of Stuart.* (Nelson) The story tells how Flora Macdonald saved Bonnie Prince Charlie, Pretender to the English throne, after the Battle of Culloden in Scotland in 1746.

DOBSON, AUSTIN, *Eighteenth Century Vignettes.* (Oxford) These charming sketches of old London convey an authentic eighteenth-century atmosphere.

FALKNER, J. MEADE, *Moonfleet.* (Little •Grosset) Here is adventure for adventure's sake—a thrilling tale of smugglers in eighteenth-century England.

GOLDSMITH, OLIVER, *The Vicar of Wakefield.* (Dutton •Everyman's) If you feel inclined toward a rather gentle story steeped in eighteenth-century atmosphere, try this one about the unworldly Dr. Primrose and his delightful family.

NORDOFF, CHARLES BERNARD and JAMES NORMAN HALL, *The Bounty Trilogy: Mutiny on the Bounty; Men Against the Sea;* and *Pitcairn's Island.* (Little) This amazing story of the *Bounty's* voyage from England to the South Seas in 1787 is based on one of the strangest episodes in the history of the British Navy.

SHERIDAN, RICHARD, *The Rivals* and *The School for Scandal.* (••Barron's) These two famous comedies, written by a contemporary of Goldsmith, are satires on eighteenth-century society.

STEWART, ANNA BIRD, *Enter David Garrick.* (Lippincott) This vivid account traces David Garrick's rise from obscurity to the rôle of England's leading actor. It stresses his rich contributions to the theater of his day and following periods. In another book—*Young Miss Burney*—Miss Stewart provides a fresh and entertaining story of Fanny Burney's childhood and girlhood.

TARKINGTON, BOOTH, *Monsieur Beaucaire.* (Doubleday) In this gay story of the seaside resort of Bath in the eighteenth century, a French nobleman masquerades as a barber and falls in love with an English belle.

TREVELYAN, GEORGE, *The England of Queen Anne.* (Cambridge) Duels, market places, wages, elections, racing, the country gentleman—all are covered in this comprehensive and accurate book by an unquestioned authority on the period.

TURBERVILLE, A. S., *English Men and Manners in the Eighteenth Century.* (•Oxford) As the title indicates, this book provides a record of eighteenth-century social life in England.

•paperback only   ••paperback and hardcover

chapter six

THE TRIUMPH

OF

ROMANTIC REVOLT

1798-1837

The age-old feeling of romance which had pulsed so strongly during the Elizabethan Age and which had gone underground during the time of the Augustans welled up again with a new intensity in the opening decades of the nineteenth century. Having grown tired of Augustan dogmatism —of being told that the only place worth living in was London, the only life worth leading was that of high society, and the only authors worth reading were those who addressed themselves to London society in a certain manner and on certain subjects—Englishmen in the early nineteenth century threw off Augustan restraint in favor of a more daring and imaginative approach to both literature and life.

Oddly enough the Age of Reason contained the seeds of its own destruction. Having boasted that their social and literary achievements were the best because they were based on reason—the kind of reason that lay behind the scientific achievements of Newton—the Augustans could only sit back in bewilderment when men began using reason to expose the absurdities inherent in Augustan life itself. To the men of the early nineteenth century it was absurd to think, as had the Augustans, that a man of immense wealth and noble position was necessarily superior to a small businessman, a factory worker, or a farmer. It was equally absurd to regard the neoclassical writings of Pope and Johnson as superior to the less "civilized" works of Shakespeare or Robert Burns. In spite of all the claims of the Augustans to scientific reasonableness, it began to be apparent that they had merely used the prestige of scientific reasoning to buttress a basically snobbish way of life.

THE FRENCH REVOLUTION The collapse of fashionable eighteenth-century society was even more spectacular in France than it was in England. In France power was still in the hands of an absolute monarch and an overprivileged, dissolute aristocracy. For years the object of smoldering popular hatred, this Old French Regime came tumbling down in a series of fiery and bloody events that began with the storming of the Bastille prison in 1789, and that ended with the rise of Napoleon and his final defeat by a coalition of nations at the Battle of Waterloo in 1815.

English history in the late eighteenth and early nineteenth centuries is largely the story of England's involvement—either direct or indirect—with the French Revolution. For a time almost every important British man of letters responded warmly to the cry of the French people for "Liberty, Equality, Fraternity." William Wordsworth later declared:

The Lake Country made famous by Wordsworth and Coleridge.

> Bliss was it in that dawn to be alive,
> But to be young was very heaven!

When Napoleon set out on his conquest of Europe, early democratic ardors cooled, and from 1795 to 1815 England was allied with other nations in an all-out war against France. By the close of the year 1815 Napoleon was in final exile on the remote British island of St. Helena and the victorious allies had met in Vienna and had agreed on a massive reconstruction of the map of Europe.

343

Although the Napoleonic Wars had stifled the more ardent cries of "Liberty, Equality, Fraternity," one of the most significant aspects of nineteenth-century English life was the slow but steady application of the principles of democracy. Although England emerged from the eighteenth century a parliamentary state in which the Crown was largely a decorative post, the English Parliament was far from a truly representative body. The privileged peers in the House of Lords had almost equal power with the House of Commons, which in turn was elected by less than one sixth of the adult male population. No working-class people and only the wealthiest of the middle class had the right to vote. Particularly unfair was the fact that in the mushrooming factory towns of the North representation was practically nonexistent. After years of popular agitation Parliament finally passed the First Reform Bill of 1832. This bill extended the franchise to virtually all the middle class; it did not enfranchise the working class, which had to wait until the end of the century to benefit from the rising democratic tide.

THE SIDNEY SABIN GALLERIES, L

The Death of Nelson *by the portrait and historical painter William Drummond. Lord Nelson died while winning a great victory against the combined French and Spanish fleets off Cape Trafalgar in Spain. This brilliant naval victory removed the threat to England of an invasion by Napoleon throughout the remainder of the Napoleonic Wars.*

above: Girls carrying coal out of a mine. Below: Wood engraving by Thomas Bewick illustrates the new emphasis on emotion.

R. Johnson, del.   T. Bewick, sculp.

THE DEPARTURE.

Published January 1, 1804, by William Bulmer, at the
Shakspeare Printing Office, Cleveland Row.

THE NEED FOR SOCIAL CHANGE

The working class in England lived under deplorable conditions. As the Industrial Revolution gathered force, towns became cities; more and more villagers, forced by economic necessity to seek work in the growing factories, huddled together in filthy slums. Men, women, and children worked from sunrise to sunset for paltry wages. No child able to pull a cart in the suffocating coal mines or to sweep a floor in the textile factories was considered too young to work. For the children of the poor, religious training, medical care, and education were practically nonexistent.

Most Englishmen were apparently unconcerned by the plight of the workers, but among those who clearly saw the need for reform and who resolutely set out to bring it about were three young reformers—George Whitefield and John and Charles Wesley. As early as 1729 they had organized a little band of Oxford students for the practice of religion. Members of the group were dubbed *Methodists* because they resolved to conduct their lives and religious study by "rule and method." Although the three leaders never broke away from the Church of England, they created a great new religious movement whose message was the love and forgiveness of God. In the noisy, crowded factory towns of the North of England, in the filthy alleys of London, and even in the American colonies across the Atlantic, they sought out both the lonely and the wrongdoer to tell them of the wonders of "the new heaven and the new earth." Indirectly they awakened the church and the government to their responsibilities. Sunday schools were organized. Hospitals were built. Great movements were begun to reform the prisons, to free the slaves, and to regulate the conditions of child labor. Gradually English society began to awaken to its obligation to the miserable and the helpless.

ROMANTICISM

The effects of revolution abroad, the demand for a more democratic government, and a growing awareness of social injustice at home were all reflected in a new spirit that over a period of years affected practically every aspect of English life. The years characterized by this new attitude are known as the Age of Romanticism. Simplicity and naturalness rather than artificiality characterized this new era. To the Age of Reason nature had meant the well-laid-out formal garden with its neatly clipped hedges and patterned flower beds. Now there was a resurgence of interest in wild and lonely stretches of forest or mountain. The beautifully proportioned formal homes of the eighteenth century had been inspired by the columned buildings of classical Greece and the domes of ancient Rome; but the architects of the Romantic Age tried to recapture with bristling spires, arched windows, high vaulted ceilings, and general Gothic "gloomth" the mysterious atmosphere of the Middle Ages. In dress, the elaborate silks and satins of the Augustan Age were giving way to plain woolens and cotton cloth. Buckled knee breeches were being replaced by plain pantaloons. Powdered hair was seen less and less. Only judges, members of the clergy, and a few other professional persons continued to wear wigs. Over against the Augustan ideal of the elegant gentleman who never behaved unreasonably and who was never more content than when he could reduce life to a few clear rules and regulations stood the new romantic hero who valued freedom above all things and who longed for the unattainable.

The Romantic Revolt in England was part of a movement that affected all the countries of the Western World. France, Italy, and the German states were shaken by it, and even in the far-off United States its influence was felt. The forms of romanticism were so many and varied that it is difficult to speak of the movement as a whole. It did align itself with the humanitarian spirit of the democratic revolutionaries, but, as you will see from your study of nineteenth-century literature, romantics were not always democrats and democrats were not alway romantics. The only really safe thing to say is that romanticism represents a revolt against reason as the only and the supreme guide in all areas of living and rejects the idea that life can be reduced to a few scientific formulas.

THE ROMANTIC
REVOLT IN
LITERATURE
It is in literature that we can best see the emergence and growth of the romantic spirit in England. In the eighteenth century William Blake had listened not to reason but to intuition. Robert Burns had written of the joys and sorrows of humble village folk. Thomas Gray had rediscovered the beauties of nature. All of these strains—the belief in intuition, the emphasis on emotion rather than reason, the interest in humble life, and the rediscovery of the outdoor world—became progressively important as the Romantic Movement took form and became the dominant literary expression of the early nineteenth century.

Alexander Pope and the other poets of the Age of Reason showed little interest in the outdoor world. When they wrote of nature at all, they treated it artificially. In the nineteenth century William Wordsworth turned to contemplation of the unfathomable beauties of wild, untrammeled nature; and various aspects of man's relation to nature echo through the work of the other romantic poets. The people who appeared in the typical poetry of the eighteenth century belonged to the fashionable world, but Wordsworth, like Burns before him, wrote of humble life. Throughout the Augustan Age interest centered in the ancient classics of Greece and Rome, from which Pope and other leading writers drew up strict "rules" and standards as guides for their own writing. However, a few authors turned to other aspects of the past. Among them was Bishop Thomas Percy, who, in 1765, published *Reliques of Ancient English Poetry,* a collection of ballads dating back to medieval times. These forgotten evidences of England's past became extremely popular with the romantics. They relished the medieval atmosphere, the sense of mystery and the supernatural, the elemental themes of courage and valor, hatred and revenge, love and death. Sir Walter Scott, John Keats, and Samuel Taylor Coleridge all wrote ballads and all tried to recapture in other ways the mysterious atmosphere of the Middle Ages. But whether the romantics wrote odes to nature, sang lyrics of humble life, or gave themselves up to visions of far-off climes and distant times, they expressed emotions and wrote to create an emotional effect.

To some people romanticism with its emphasis on emotion seems a flight from reason and a cowardly attempt to escape from unpleasant reality. Others see it as an attempt to go beyond reality into the deeper, less obvious, and more elusive levels of human existence. Good and evil, beauty and deformity, tenderness and savagery, joy and death—these and other disturbing states are not entered in the notebook of the scientist or the ledger of the businessman, but they lie hidden behind his every word and gesture. It is this level of reality that the romantic seeks to explore and, if he is an artist, to uncover.

Opposite: These prints, contained in a didactic poem called The Landscape, *by R. P. Knight, illustrate the Augustan taste for nature brought under control (left) and the romantic taste for nature let run wild (right). Right: This illustration from a book called* The Principles of Gardening *gives a design for constructing a ruin "after the old Roman manner for the termination of walks, avenues &c."*

William Wordsworth 1770-1850 and Samuel Taylor Coleridge 1772-1834

WORDSWORTH The quiet dignity of Wordsworth's nature lyrics hardly suggests the hot-headed rebel the poet was in his childhood. He was a typical boy—a leader in rough games, a firm believer in the age-old theory that schooling serves no worthy purpose, and a constant source of concern to his family. He grew up among the mountains of the Lake District of northern England, and while the countryside did much to mold his character and teach him self-reliance, the young Wordsworth viewed his surroundings with a callousness typical of children. To him nature meant only two things: an ideal setting for countless games and a hiding place from the adult world. Years later he returned to that area, and inspired by its beauty, wrote some of his greatest poetry, thereby establishing himself as a leader among the Lake Poets. But this understanding and appreciation of nature did not begin to develop until he was seventeen and in his first year at Cambridge University.

The four years Wordsworth spent at Cambridge were lonely and restless. The classical curriculum did not suit his tastes; he found his independent reading much more absorbing. Since he preferred the simpler people he met in his wanderings about the countryside, he did not fit into the sophisticated social patterns of university life. But those were not wasted years, for it was through his readings and his wanderings that he began to formulate ideals and principles that became the basis of a whole new approach to poetry.

Upon graduating from Cambridge, Wordsworth journeyed to France, where he became very much aroused by the French fight for independence. Love of nature was temporarily subordinated to love of man and, spurred on by the claims of the Revolution, Wordsworth leapt into the fight for freedom. His anxious relatives imagined him headed for the guillotine, and in order to save his life they cut off his allowance, forcing his return to England.

Back in England Wordsworth found that his radical behavior and his failure to enter into a respectable profession had alienated everyone but his sister Dorothy. A fruitless search for employment, aimless wanderings about the country, a loss of close contact with nature, disillusionment in the Revolution as it ceased to be a struggle for human liberation and became a struggle for power, and the shock of war between England and France left him in an extreme state of depression.

Then, in January of 1795, a friend willed him a legacy of nine-hundred pounds. At the same time, another friend offered him, rent free, a house at Racedown, on the southern coast. Determined to put an end to his aimlessness and to devote his life to writing poetry, he moved to that lovely country with Dorothy. With her help he rediscovered an interest in nature, an interest that grew until Wordsworth became known primarily as a poet of nature. Fundamental in his nature poetry are his ideas of the relationship between man and nature and his belief that this relationship changes as man passes through the several stages of life. According to Wordsworth, the importance of nature is not realized in infancy or youth; understanding comes only with maturity. With full maturity comes a mystical state of harmony with nature in which man feels with extraordinary power the joy it offers. This idea is based on the poet's pantheistic belief that God and the universe are identical—a stone, a flower, "the round ocean" are all material manifestations of a Supreme Being.

COLERIDGE Besides nature, the most important influence upon the life and thought of Wordsworth was his association with Samuel Taylor Coleridge, whom he met in 1797.

The last-born of a family of fourteen, young Samuel Coleridge was the spoiled child of middle-aged parents. He was fretful and precocious, and so continually lost in fancies that before he was eight years old he was labeled as a "character" by other boys, and a "character" he remained. Until he was twenty-five, his life was a constant series of decisions and revisions. Everything influenced him—he read a medical dictionary, and

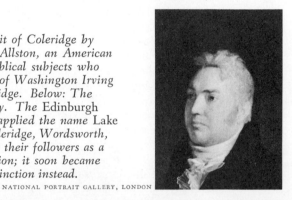

Right: Portrait of Coleridge by Washington Allston, an American painter of Biblical subjects who was a friend of Washington Irving and of Coleridge. Below: The Lake Country. The Edinburgh Review *first applied the name* Lake School *to Coleridge, Wordsworth, Southey, and their followers as a term of derision; it soon became a term of distinction instead.*

NATIONAL PORTRAIT GALLERY, LONDON

PHOTO BY EMILY BUTLER

decided to become a surgeon; he grew interested in the works of the French philosopher Voltaire, and planned a career in philosophy. Throughout his lifetime his mind was filled with countless uncompleted projects. He was a man possessed by an inexhaustible imagination that leapt far ahead of any human power of execution.

Although his family was poor, means were found to send Samuel to Cambridge. Here he read everything he thought worth his time, and fascinated the student body by his brilliant conversations and his eloquent monologues, full of mysticism and radical politics. He began to develop his poetic ability, one of his greatest inspirations being a Miss Mary Evans, with whom he was in love. He ran up many debts. Because the debts worried him and because he found university life somewhat boring, he recklessly left school in his second year and joined His Majesty's Fifteenth Light Dragoons, under the grotesque name of Silas Tomkyn Comberback. Unable to adjust to the harsh discipline of military life, he enlisted the aid of friends who paid his debts, got him out of the army, and had him reinstated in college. But he was not to remain long at the university.

For in June 1794, Coleridge met Robert Southey, a young poet greatly excited by the French Revolution. Coleridge immediately became converted to the idea of government for all by all. The two young men, spurred on by their beliefs, made elaborate plans to migrate to America and build a colony based on brotherly love and devoted to simple living and high thinking. The site of this colony was to be the Susquehanna River in Pennsylvania. Both felt they needed wives and companions, so Coleridge married Sara Fricker, and Southey married her sister. Because of the complications and expenses of caring for a family, they never reached America. Southey settled in Lisbon, and Coleridge, practically destitute and unable to adjust to this unfortunate turn of events, wandered about the English countryside.

His poetry at this time was a copy of that of his established contemporaries; and as these were second-rate poets, the result was sentimental and weak. But, in 1797 he met Wordsworth, and with his help Coleridge found himself as a poet.

LYRICAL BALLADS Wordsworth and Coleridge remained extremely good friends during the most productive years of their lives, and between them they wrought a revolution in poetry. Together they concocted a scheme that was to result in what the usually restrained *Encyclopaedia Britannica* calls the "most important event in the history of English poetry after Milton." The scheme was this: Wordsworth, with his sharp sense of reality, was to write poetry that transformed the everyday drama of ordinary men and women into art through the simple intensity of his imagination; Coleridge was to let his vagrant imagination rove over strange seas of thought and feeling, and give the appearance of truth to the wildest flights of his fancy. The outcome was a volume of poetry printed in September of 1798, modestly entitled *Lyrical Ballads*. The first and last poems, respectively, in this volume were "The Rime of the Ancient Mariner" and "Tintern Abbey," now considered among the greatest poems ever written in England. Ironically, the book was contemptuously received by critics and poets alike.

NATIONAL PORTRAIT
GALLERY, LONDON

Considering the bad reception that *Lyrical Ballads* received, it would not have been surprising if the poets, who by then were living in the Lake Country, had abandoned the whole idea. But they had become very dedicated to their purpose, and in 1800 they published a second, expanded volume, to which Wordsworth contributed a preface explaining his theories of poetry. In the Preface he writes:

The principal object, then, proposed in these poems was to choose incidents and situations from common life, and to relate or describe them throughout, as far as was possible, in a selection of language really used by men, and, at the same time, to throw over them a certain coloring of imagination, whereby ordinary things would be presented to the mind in an unusual aspect; and further, and above all, to make these incidents and situations interesting by tracing in them, truly though not ostentatiously, the primary laws of our nature: chiefly, as far as regards the manner in which we associate ideas in a state of excitement. Humble and rustic life was generally chosen, because, in that condition, the essential passions of the heart find a better soil in which they can attain their maturity, are under less restraint, and speak a plainer and more emphatic language. . . .

In describing this poetic process he states that "all good poetry is the spontaneous overflow of powerful feeling," but "poems to which any value can be attached were never produced on any variety of subjects but by a man who . . . had also thought long and deeply." He sees his poetry as distinguished from the popular poetry of the day by the fact that "the feeling therein developed gives importance to the action and situation, and not the action and situation to the feeling." He continues:

I have said that poetry is the spontaneous overflow of powerful feelings; it takes its origins from emotion recollected in tranquillity; the emotion is contemplated till, by a species of reaction, the tranquillity gradually disappears, and emotion, kindred to that which was before the subject of contemplation, is gradually produced, and does itself actually exist in the mind. In this mood successful composition generally begins. . . .

Opposite: Portrait of Wordsworth by B. R. Haydon. Haydon was a noted historical and portrait painter who fought against the stifling rules of the Royal Academy. Both Wordsworth and Keats addressed sonnets to him.

Compared to Wordsworth's contribution to *Lyrical Ballads,* Coleridge's was very small. In fact, in his entire life he composed only three poems that are often read today: "The Ancient Mariner," "Kubla Khan," and "Christabel." But in richness of sound, imagery, and command of rhythm and harmony these poems are unsurpassed in English poetry. Coleridge's contribution to the prose of the period is outstanding. He produced some of the loftiest, shrewdest, and most humane criticism of life and literature ever written, and his *Biographia Literaria* (see page 365) is the high point of romantic criticism. In both prose and poetry he was the equal of any writer of his time.

Although Wordsworth and Coleridge are commonly associated as literary figures, their greatness lies in different areas. Wordsworth created beauty from simple and commonplace things. His was a thrifty, retentive, and vigorously active mind, firmly anchored in the actual and the familiar. Coleridge, on the other hand, had the power to evoke an atmosphere of mystery, wonder, and pathos that seems at once strange, yet true. His was a soaring, effusive mind that delighted in the remote and the weird. Working together, these two men inspired and controlled each other, thereby greatly enlarging the scope of English poetry and determining its course for almost a hundred years.

Poems by Wordsworth

ONE SUMMER EVENING

The following selection is from Book I of the Prelude, a long autobiographical poem which has been called "the essential living document for the interpretation of Wordsworth's life and poetry." This passage deals with Wordsworth's boyhood in the Lake District of England.

One summer evening (led by her[1])
    I found
        A little boat tied to a willow tree
Within a rocky cave, its usual home.
Straight I unloosed her chain, and stepping in
Pushed from the shore. It was an act of
    stealth   5
And troubled pleasure, nor without the
    voice
Of mountain echoes did my boat move on,
Leaving behind her still, on either side,
Small circles glittering idly in the moon,
Until they melted all into one track   10
Of sparkling light. But now, like one who
    rows,
Proud of his skill, to reach a chosen point
With an unswerving line, I fixed my view
Upon the summit of a craggy ridge,
The horizon's utmost boundary; for above   15
Was nothing but the stars and the gray sky.
She was an elfin pinnace; lustily
I dipped my oars into the silent lake,
And, as I rose upon the stroke, my boat
Went heaving through the water like a
    swan;   20
When, from behind that craggy steep till
    then
The horizon's bound, a huge peak, black
    and huge,
As if with voluntary power instinct
Upreared its head. I struck and struck again,
And growing still in stature the grim shape 25
Towered up between me and the stars, and
    still,
For so it seemed, with purpose of its own

And measured motion like a living thing,
Strode after me. With trembling oars I
    turned,
And through the silent water stole my way 30
Back to the covert of the willow tree;
There in her mooring place I left my bark—
And through the meadows homeward went,
    in grave
And serious mood; but after I had seen
That spectacle, for many days my brain   35
Worked with a dim and undetermined sense
Of unknown modes of being; o'er my
    thoughts
There hung a darkness, call it solitude
Or blank desertion. No familiar shapes
Remained, no pleasant images of trees,   40
Of sea or sky, no colors of green fields;
But huge and mighty forms, that do not live
Like living men, moved slowly through the
    mind
By day, and were a trouble to my dreams.

TO A SKYLARK

Ethereal minstrel! pilgrim of the sky!
Dost thou despise the earth where cares
    abound?
Or, while the wings aspire, are heart and eye
Both with thy nest upon the dewy ground?
Thy nest which thou canst drop into at will, 5
Those quivering wings composed, that music
    still!

Leave to the nightingale her shady wood;
A privacy of glorious light is thine;
Whence thou dost pour upon the world a
    flood
Of harmony, with instinct more divine;   10
Type of the wise who soar, but never roam;
True to the kindred points of heaven and
    home!

---

1. *her*, nature.

LINES WRITTEN IN EARLY SPRING

I heard a thousand blended notes,
While in a grove I sate reclined,
In that sweet mood when pleasant thoughts
Bring sad thoughts to the mind.

To her fair works did Nature link   5
The human soul that through me ran;
And much it grieved my heart to think
What man has made of man.

Through primrose tufts, in that green bower,
The periwinkle trailed its wreaths;   10
And 'tis my faith that every flower
Enjoys the air it breathes.

The birds around me hopped and played,
Their thoughts I cannot measure—
But the least motion which they made,   15
It seemed a thrill of pleasure.

The budding twigs spread out their fan,
To catch the breezy air;
And I must think, do all I can,
That there was pleasure there.   20

If this belief from heaven be sent,
If such be Nature's holy plan,
Have I not reason to lament
What man has made of man?

Tintern Abbey.

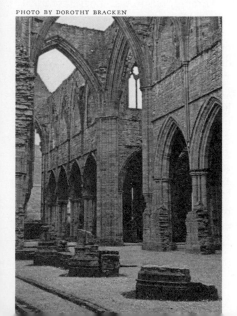

LINES COMPOSED A FEW MILES ABOVE TINTERN ABBEY

Wordsworth composed this poem while on a walking tour with his sister Dorothy along the River Wye, which winds back and forth across the border between England and Wales on its way to the Bristol Channel. The beautiful ruin of Tintern Abbey is located in a deep valley at the river's edge. Wordsworth had previously visited the Wye in 1793, five years before this poem was published in Lyrical Ballads.

Five years have past; five summers,
          with the length
     Of five long winters! and again I
          hear
These waters, rolling from their mountain
          springs
With a soft inland murmur. Once again
Do I behold these steep and lofty cliffs   5
That on a wild secluded scene impress
Thoughts of more deep seclusion and connect
The landscape with the quiet of the sky.
The day is come when I again repose
Here, under this dark sycamore, and view   10
These plots of cottage ground, these orchard
          tufts,
Which at this season, with their unripe fruits,
Are clad in one green hue, and lose themselves
Mid groves and copses. Once again I see
These hedgerows, hardly hedgerows, little
          lines   15
Of sportive wood run wild; these pastoral
          farms,
Green to the very door; and wreaths of
          smoke
Sent up, in silence, from among the trees,
With some uncertain notice, as might seem
Of vagrant dwellers in the houseless woods,   20
Or of some hermit's cave, where by his fire
The hermit sits alone.
                    These beauteous forms,
Through a long absence, have not been to
          me
As is a landscape to a blind man's eye;
But oft, in lonely rooms, and 'mid the din   25
Of towns and cities, I have owed to them,
In hours of weariness, sensations sweet,

William Wordsworth   353

Felt in the blood, and felt along the heart;
And passing even into my purer mind,
With tranquil restoration—feelings too   30
Of unremembered pleasure, such, perhaps,
As have no slight or trivial influence
On that best portion of a good man's life,
His little, nameless, unremembered acts
Of kindness and of love. Nor less, I trust,   35
To them I may have owed another gift,
Of aspect more sublime; that blessèd mood,
In which the burthen of the mystery,
In which the heavy and the weary weight
Of all this unintelligible world,   40
Is lightened—that serene and blessèd mood,
In which the affections gently lead us on—
Until, the breath of this corporeal frame
And even the motion of our human blood
Almost suspended, we are laid asleep   45
In body, and become a living soul;
While with an eye made quiet by the power
Of harmony, and the deep power of joy,
We see into the life of things.
                              If this
Be but a vain belief, yet, oh! how oft—   50
In darkness and amid the many shapes
Of joyless daylight; when the fretful stir
Unprofitable, and the fever of the world,
Have hung upon the beatings of my heart—
How oft, in spirit, have I turned to thee,   55
O sylvan Wye! thou wanderer through the
          woods,
How often has my spirit turned to thee!
And now, with gleams of half-extinguished
          thought,
With many recognitions dim and faint,
And somewhat of a sad perplexity,   60
The picture of the mind revives again;
While here I stand, not only with the sense
Of present pleasure, but with pleasing
          thoughts
That in this moment there is life and food
For future years. And so I dare to hope,   65
Though changed, no doubt, from what I was
          when first
I came among these hills, when like a roe
I bounded o'er the mountains, by the sides
Of the deep rivers, and the lonely streams,
Wherever nature led—more like a man   70
Flying from something that he dreads than
          one

Who sought the thing he loved. For nature
          then
(The coarser pleasures of my boyish days,
And their glad animal movements all gone
          by)
To me was all in all. —I cannot paint   75
What then I was. The sounding cataract
Haunted me like a passion; the tall rock,
The mountain, and the deep and gloomy
          wood,
Their colors and their forms, were then to me
An appetite, a feeling and a love,   80
That had no need of a remoter charm,
By thought supplied, nor any interest
Unborrowed from the eye. —That time is past,
And all its aching joys are now no more,
And all its dizzy raptures. Not for this   85
Faint I, nor mourn nor murmur; other gifts
Have followed; for such loss, I would believe,
Abundant recompense. For I have learned
To look on nature, not as in the hour
Of thoughtless youth, but hearing often times
The still, sad music of humanity,   91
Nor harsh nor grating, though of ample power
To chasten and subdue. And I have felt
A presence that disturbs me with the joy
Of elevated thoughts; a sense sublime   95
Of something far more deeply interfused,
Whose dwelling is the light of setting suns,
And the round ocean and the living air,
And the blue sky, and in the mind of man;
A motion and a spirit, that impels   100
All thinking things, all objects of all thought,
And rolls through all things. Therefore am I
          still
A lover of the meadows and the woods,
And mountains; and of all that we behold
From this green earth; of all the mighty
          world   105
Of eye, and ear—both what they half create,
And what perceive; well pleased to recognize
In nature and the language of the sense
The anchor of my purest thoughts, the nurse,
The guide, the guardian of my heart, and
          soul   110
Of all my moral being.
                              Nor perchance,
If I were not thus taught, should I the more
Suffer my genial spirits to decay;
For thou art with me here upon the banks

Of this fair river; thou my dearest friend, 115
My dear, dear friend; and in thy voice I catch
The language of my former heart, and read
My former pleasures in the shooting lights
Of thy wild eyes. Oh! yet a little while
May I behold in thee what I was once, 120
My dear, dear sister! and this prayer I make,
Knowing that nature never did betray
The heart that loved her; 'tis her privilege,
Through all the years of this our life, to lead
From joy to joy; for she can so inform 125
The mind that is within us, so impress
With quietness and beauty, and so feed
With lofty thoughts, that neither evil tongues,
Rash judgments, nor the sneers of selfish
        men, 129
Nor greetings where no kindness is, nor all
The dreary intercourse of daily life,
Shall e'er prevail against us, or disturb
Our cheerful faith, that all which we behold
Is full of blessings. Therefore let the moon
Shine on thee in thy solitary walk; 135
And let the misty mountain winds be free
To blow against thee; and, in after years,
When these wild ecstasies shall be matured
Into a sober pleasure, when thy mind
Shall be a mansion for all lovely forms, 140
Thy memory be as a dwelling place
For all sweet sounds and harmonies; oh!
        then,
If solitude, or fear, or pain, or grief,
Should be thy portion, with what healing
        thoughts
Of tender joy wilt thou remember me, 145
And these my exhortations! Nor, perchance—
If I should be where I no more can hear
Thy voice, nor catch from thy wild eyes these
        gleams
Of past existence—wilt thou then forget
That on the banks of this delightful stream 150
We stood together; and that I, so long
A worshiper of nature, hither came
Unwearied in that service—rather say
With warmer love—oh! with far deeper zeal
Of holier love. Nor wilt thou then forget 155
That after many wanderings, many years
Of absence, these steep woods and lofty cliffs,
And this green pastoral landscape, were to me
More dear, both for themselves and for thy
        sake!

THE SOLITARY REAPER

This poem is based in part on an actual experience Wordsworth had when visiting the Scottish Highlands with his sister Dorothy in 1803. According to Dorothy, Wordsworth also recalls in the poem an entry in Thomas Wilkinson's Tour in Scotland: *"Passed a female who was reaping alone; she sung in Erse, as she bended over her sickle; the sweetest human voice I ever heard: her strains were tenderly melancholy, and felt delicious, long after she was heard no more."*

Behold her, single in the field,
        Yon solitary Highland lass!
        Reaping and singing by herself;
        Stop here, or gently pass!
Alone she cuts and binds the grain, 5
And sings a melancholy strain;
O listen! for the vale profound
Is overflowing with the sound.

No nightingale did ever chaunt
More welcome notes to weary bands 10
Of travelers in some shady haunt,
Among Arabian sands:
A voice so thrilling ne'er was heard
In springtime from the cuckoo-bird,
Breaking the silence of the seas 15
Among the farthest Hebrides.

Will no one tell me what she sings?—
Perhaps the plaintive numbers flow
For old, unhappy, far-off things,
And battles long ago; 20
Or is it some more humble lay,
Familiar matter of today?
Some natural sorrow, loss, or pain,
That has been, and may be again?

Whate'er the theme, the maiden sang 25
As if her song could have no ending;
I saw her singing at her work,
And o'er the sickle bending;—
I listened, motionless and still;
And, as I mounted up the hill, 30
The music in my heart I bore,
Long after it was heard no more.

LONDON, 1802

Milton! thou shouldst be living at this hour.
England hath need of thee; she is a fen
Of stagnant waters: altar, sword, and pen,
Fireside, the heroic wealth of hall and bower,[1]
Have forfeited their ancient English dower 5
Of inward happiness. We are selfish men;
Oh! raise us up, return to us again,
And give us manners, virtue, freedom, power.
Thy soul was like a star, and dwelt apart:
Thou hadst a voice whose sound was like the
        sea; 10
Pure as the naked heavens, majestic, free,
So didst thou travel on life's common way,
In cheerful godliness; and yet thy heart
The lowliest duties on herself did lay.

THE WORLD IS TOO MUCH WITH US

The world is too much with us; late and
        soon,
Getting and spending, we lay waste our
        powers:
Little we see in Nature that is ours;
We have given our hearts away, a sordid
        boon!
The sea that bares her bosom to the moon; 5
The winds that will be howling at all hours,
And are up-gathered now like sleeping
        flowers;
For this, for everything, we are out of tune;
It moves us not. —Great God! I'd rather be
A Pagan suckled in a creed outworn; 10
So might I, standing on this pleasant lea,
Have glimpses that would make me less
        forlorn;
Have sight of Proteus rising from the sea;
Or hear old Triton[1] blow his wreathèd horn.

IT IS A BEAUTEOUS EVENING, CALM AND FREE

It is a beauteous evening, calm and free,
The holy time is quiet as a Nun
Breathless with adoration; the broad sun
Is sinking down in its tranquillity;
The gentleness of heaven broods o'er the
        Sea: 5
Listen! the mighty Being is awake,
And doth with his eternal motion make
A sound like thunder—everlastingly.
Dear Child![1] dear Girl; that walkest with me
        here, 9
If thou appear untouched by solemn thought,
Thy nature is not therefore less divine:
Thou liest in Abraham's bosom[2] all the year;
And worshipp'st at the temple's inner shrine,
God being with thee when we know it not.

MY HEART LEAPS UP

My heart leaps up when I behold
A rainbow in the sky:
So was it when my life began;
So is it now I am a man:
So be it when I shall grow old, 5
    Or let me die!
The Child is father of the Man;
And I could wish my days to be
Bound each to each by natural piety.[1]

LONDON, 1802. **1.** *hall and bower*, the resorts of knights
and ladies respectively.

THE WORLD IS TOO MUCH WITH US. **1.** *Proteus* (prō'ti əs)
... Triton (tri'tən), sea gods in Greek mythology.

IT IS A BEAUTEOUS EVENING. **1.** *Dear Child*, Wordsworth's daughter, Caroline. **2.** *in Abraham's bosom*, in
innocence; in the presence of God. See Luke 16:22.

MY HEART LEAPS UP. **1.** *piety*, reverence, affection.

*Scene in the
Lake Country.*

ODE ON INTIMATIONS OF IMMORTALITY
FROM RECOLLECTIONS OF EARLY CHILDHOOD

The full title of the ode suggests the poet's idea: that man's immortality is indicated by the fact that the child retains memories of a previous existence. As the child grows to manhood, these glimpses grow fainter until, as an adult, he can rely only on vague flashes of buried memory to reassure himself of his immortality. But maturity gives him the compensations of wisdom and a philosophic mind.

> *The Child is father of the man;*
> *And I could wish my days to be*
> *Bound each to each by natural piety.*

1

There was a time when meadow, grove, and stream,
　　The earth, and every common sight,
　　　　To me did seem
　　　Appareled in celestial light,
The glory and the freshness of a dream.　　　　　　　　5
It is not now as it hath been of yore;—
　　　Turn wheresoe'er I may,
　　　　By night or day,
The things which I have seen I now can see no more.

2

　　　The Rainbow comes and goes,　　　　　　　10
　　　And lovely is the Rose;
　　　The Moon doth with delight
Look round her when the heavens are bare;
　　　Waters on a starry night
　　　Are beautiful and fair;　　　　　　　　　15
　　The sunshine is a glorious birth;
　　But yet I know, where'er I go,
That there hath passed away a glory from the earth.

3

Now, while the birds thus sing a joyous song,
　　　And while the young lambs bound　　　　20
　　　　As to the tabor's sound,
To me alone there came a thought of grief:
A timely utterance gave that thought relief,
　　　And I again am strong:
The cataracts blow their trumpets from the steep;　　25
No more shall grief of mine the season wrong;
I hear the Echoes through the mountains throng,
The Winds come to me from the fields of sleep,
　　　And all the earth is gay;
　　　　Land and sea　　　　　　　　　30

Give themselves up to jollity,
      And with the heart of May
      Doth every Beast keep holiday;—
        Thou Child of Joy,
Shout round me, let me hear thy shouts, thou happy Shepherd-boy!   35

4

Ye blesséd Creatures, I have heard the call
      Ye to each other make; I see
The heavens laugh with you in your jubilee;
      My heart is at your festival,
      My head hath its coronal,   40
The fullness of your bliss, I feel—I feel it all.
      Oh, evil day! if I were sullen
      While Earth herself is adorning,
        This sweet May-morning,
      And the Children are culling   45
        On every side,
      In a thousand valleys far and wide,
Fresh flowers; while the sun shines warm,
And the Babe leaps up on his Mother's arm—
      I hear, I hear, with joy I hear!   50
      —But there's a Tree, of many, one,
A single Field which I have looked upon,
Both of them speak of something that is gone:
      The Pansy at my feet
      Doth the same tale repeat: 55
Whither is fled the visionary gleam?
Where is it now, the glory and the dream?

5

Our birth is but a sleep and a forgetting:
The Soul that rises with us, our life's Star,
      Hath had elsewhere its setting,   60
        And cometh from afar:
      Not in entire forgetfulness,
      And not in utter nakedness,
But trailing clouds of glory do we come
      From God, who is our home: 65
Heaven lies about us in our infancy!
Shades of the prison-house begin to close
      Upon the growing Boy,
But he beholds the light, and whence it flows
      He sees it in his joy;   70
The Youth, who daily farther from the east
      Must travel, still is Nature's priest,
      And by the vision splendid
      Is on his way attended;
At length the Man perceives it die away,   75
And fade into the light of common day.

6

Earth fills her lap with pleasures of her own;
Yearnings she hath in her own natural kind,
And even with something of a Mother's mind,
      And no unworthy aim,
      The homely Nurse doth all she can 80
To make her Foster-child, her Inmate Man,
      Forget the glories he hath known,
And that imperial palace whence he came.

7

Behold the Child among his new-born blisses, 85
A six years' Darling of a pigmy size!
See, where 'mid work of his own hand he lies,
Fretted by sallies of his mother's kisses,
With light upon him from his father's eyes!
See, at his feet, some little plan or chart, 90
Some fragment from his dream of human life,
Shaped by himself with newly-learnéd art;
      A wedding or a festival
      A mourning or a funeral,
          And this hath now his heart, 95
          And unto this he frames his song:
          Then will he fit his tongue
To dialogues of business, love, or strife;
      But it will not be long
      Ere this be thrown aside, 100
      And with new joy and pride
The little Actor cons another part[1];
Filling from time to time his "humorous[2] stage"
With all the Persons, down to palsied Age,
That Life brings with her in her equipage; 105
      As if his whole vocation
      Were endless imitation.

8

Thou, whose exterior semblance doth belie
      Thy Soul's immensity;
Thou best Philosopher, who yet dost keep 110
Thy heritage, thou Eye among the blind,
That, deaf and silent, read'st the eternal deep,[3]
Haunted forever by the eternal mind—
      Mighty Prophet! Seer blest!
      On whom those truths do rest, 115
Which we are toiling all our lives to find,

---

1. *Actor . . . part.* Lines 102-105 allude to Jaques' speech in Shakespeare's *As You Like It*, which begins, "All the world's a stage." 2. *humorous,* changeable, subject to varying moods, or humors. 3. *the eternal deep,* the mysteries of eternity.

In darkness lost, the darkness of the grave;
Thou, over whom thy Immortality
Broods like the Day, a Master o'er a Slave,
A Presence which is not to be put by;   120
Thou little Child, yet glorious in the might
Of heaven-born freedom on thy being's height,
Why with such earnest pains dost thou provoke
The years to bring the inevitable yoke,
Thus blindly with thy blessedness at strife;   125
Full soon thy Soul shall have her earthly freight,
And custom lie upon thee with a weight,
Heavy as frost, and deep almost as life!

                        9
            Oh, joy! that in our embers
            Is something that doth live,   130
            That nature yet remembers
            What was so fugitive!
The thought of our past years in me doth breed
Perpetual benediction: not indeed
For that which is most worthy to be blest;   135
Delight and liberty, the simple creed
Of Childhood, whether busy or at rest,
With new-fledged hope still fluttering in his breast—
            Not for these I raise
            The song of thanks and praise;   140
            But for those obstinate questionings
            Of sense and outward things,
            Fallings from us, vanishings;
            Blank misgivings of a Creature
Moving about in worlds not realized,[4]   145
High instincts before which our mortal nature
Did tremble like a guilty thing surprised:
            But for those first affections,
            Those shadowy recollections,
        Which, be they what they may,   150
Are yet the fountain light of all our day,
Are yet a master light of all our seeing;
    Uphold us, cherish, and have power to make
Our noisy years seem moments in the being
Of the eternal Silence: truths that wake,   155
            To perish never;
Which neither listlessness, nor mad endeavor,
            Nor Man nor Boy,
Nor all that is at enmity with joy,
Can utterly abolish or destroy!   160
            Hence in a season of calm weather
            Though inland far we be,

---

4. *not realized*, not yet truly understood.

Our Souls have sight of that immortal sea
      Which brought us hither,
      Can in a moment travel thither,   165
And see the Children sport upon the shore,
And hear the mighty waters rolling evermore.

      10
Then sing, ye Birds, sing, sing a joyous song!
      And let the young Lambs bound
      As to the tabor's sound!   170
We in thought will join your throng,
      Ye that pipe and ye that play,
      Ye that through your hearts today
      Feel the gladness of the May!
What though the radiance which was once so bright   175
Be now forever taken from my sight,
  Though nothing can bring back the hour
Of splendor in the grass, of glory in the flower;
      We will grieve not, rather find
      Strength in what remains behind;   180
      In the primal sympathy
      Which having been must ever be;
      In the soothing thoughts that spring
      Out of human suffering;
      In the faith that looks through death,   185
In years that bring the philosophic mind.

      11
And O, ye Fountains, Meadows, Hills, and Groves,
Forebode not any severing of our loves!
Yet in my heart of hearts I feel your might;
I only have relinquished one delight   190
To live beneath your more habitual sway.
I love the Brooks which down their channels fret,
Even more than when I tripped lightly as they;
The innocent brightness of a new-born Day
      Is lovely yet;   195
The Clouds that gather round the setting sun
Do take a sober coloring from an eye
That hath kept watch o'er man's mortality.
Another race hath been, and other palms are won.
Thanks to the human heart by which we live,   200
Thanks to its tenderness, its joys, and fears,
To me the meanest flower that blows can give
Thoughts that do often lie too deep for tears.

To increase understanding

One Summer Evening and *To a Skylark*

1. (*a*) Contrast the atmosphere of the summer evening and the boy's mood (lines 1-20). (*b*) In what way does the boy's mood foreshadow the appearance of the peak? (*c*) Is the peak real, or does the boy imagine it? Explain. (*d*) How do you account for the boy's feeling that the mountain is following him? (*e*) What effect does the experience have on the boy in the days that follow?

2. (*a*) What details or incidents in "One Summer Evening" suggest that Wordsworth was a typical boy? (*b*) What details or incidents suggest the emerging poet of nature?

3. (*a*) What question does the poet ask of the skylark in the first stanza of "To a Skylark"? (*b*) How is this question related to the idea stated in the last two lines of the poem? (*c*) What is the theme of the poem?

Lines Written in Early Spring,
Tintern Abbey, and *The Solitary Reaper*

1. In "Lines Written in Early Spring" Wordsworth declares, "And 'tis my faith that every flower/ Enjoys the air it breathes." (*a*) Cite other lines from the poem that expand this idea of nature. (*b*) What contrast between nature and man does the poet emphasize?

2. "Lines Written in Early Spring" was published in 1798. What experiences had Wordsworth recently undergone that would cause him "to lament/ What man has made of man"?

3. "Lines Composed a Few Miles Above Tintern Abbey" opens with a description of the countryside (lines 1-22). (*a*) What are the natural features of the scene? (*b*) What evidences of man does the poet find? (*c*) Cite phrases by which the poet indicates that nature is dominant here.

4. Wordsworth says that in his absence this countryside has *not* been to him "As is a landscape to a blind man's eye" (line 24). (*a*) What does this mean? (*b*) What effects have the memories of these "beauteous forms" had upon him?

5. In lines 65-111 the poet describes three phases of his developing attitude toward nature. (*a*) Cite the lines in which he tells how he regarded nature during his boyhood. (*b*) What was his attitude when he first visited the Wye? (*c*) How does his present attitude differ from his feeling then? (*d*) Locate the lines which best express Wordsworth's pantheistic beliefs and explain the reasons for your choice.

6. In the last section of the poem Wordsworth turns his attention to his sister Dorothy and her attitude toward nature. (*a*) At which phase of development in relation to nature does Dorothy now stand? (*b*) What are her brother's wishes for her?

7. (*a*) In "The Solitary Reaper" why is the poet unable to understand the girl's song? (*b*) What subjects suggest themselves to him as the subject of her song? Why? (*c*) What is the tone of the poem?

8. "The Solitary Reaper" is considered one of the most romantic poems Wordsworth ever wrote. Discuss the romantic elements it contains.

9. "Lines Written in Early Spring" and "Tintern Abbey" were first published in *Lyrical Ballads;* "The Solitary Reaper" was not. (*a*) Comment on how well each of these poems follows the theories Wordsworth set forth in the Preface to *Lyrical Ballads* as regards (1) language, (2) subject matter, and (3) imaginative quality. (*b*) What evidence is there that these poems originated in "emotion recollected in tranquillity"? (*c*) How does "The Solitary Reaper" compare with the other two poems in its adherence to the theories explained in the Preface?

Three sonnets

1. (*a*) What is the condition of England as Wordsworth describes it in "London, 1802"? (*b*) Why, from among all the great men of England's past, does the poet summon Milton?

2. Comment on the following statement: The primary purpose of "London, 1802" is not to mourn the stagnation of England but to praise Milton.

3. (*a*) What is the theme of "The World Is Too Much with Us"? (*b*) How does this sonnet resemble "London, 1802" in theme and tone?

4. (*a*) What is the setting of "It Is a Beauteous Evening"? (*b*) How does the setting affect the poet? (*c*) How does the child's attitude differ from his? (*d*) Why does the poet expect a different attitude in the child?

5. (*a*) In these sonnets does Wordsworth follow the English or the Italian form? (*b*) How do his rhyme schemes differ from the traditional?

6. Wordsworth is considered one of the greatest of the English sonneteers. Judging from the sonnets you have studied, explain why you think Wordsworth's sonnets are highly regarded.

My Heart Leaps Up and
Ode on Intimations of Immortality

1. (*a*) Why may line 7 of "My Heart Leaps Up" be considered a paradox? (*b*) What does this line mean? (*c*) How is it related to the preceding lines?

2. (*a*) To what time of life is Wordsworth referring in stanza 1 of the "Ode"? (*b*) How has his feeling changed since the days when "every com-

mon sight" seemed "Appareled in celestial light"? (c) What is meant by "the visionary gleam" (line 56)? (d) Cite lines which best capture the departed radiance of youth which the poet mourns.

3. In stanza 5 Wordsworth presents the central idea of the "Ode" as an extended metaphor in which the span of a human life from birth to maturity is compared to the first half of a day. The Soul, "our life's Star," is compared to the sun. (a) Explain the meaning of "The Soul that rises with us, our life's Star/Hath had elsewhere its setting." (b) What time of day do the "clouds of glory" (line 64) suggest? (c) What do they represent? (d) What is the light referred to in line 69? (e) What is the meaning of "the east" in line 71? (f) What does "the light of common day" (line 76) represent? (g) Explain the idea developed in this stanza.

4. (a) Why, in stanza 6, does Wordsworth speak of the earth as a "homely Nurse" (line 81) and of man as "her Foster-child"? (b) What is the "imperial palace" (line 84)? (c) What, according to this stanza, is man's true home?

5. What characteristic of childhood is emphasized in stanza 7?

6. In stanza 8 Wordsworth addresses the child as an "Eye among the blind" (line 111). (a) Why does he address him so? (b) Explain the significance of other terms used to describe the child in lines 110-122. (c) What is the meaning of the last three lines of the stanza?

7. In stanzas 1-8 Wordsworth traces man's progressive falling away from the recollections of immortality, and questions what consolation he may find on earth. In the last stanzas he answers the question. (a) Why does the thought of the past breed in him "Perpetual benediction" (line 134)? (b) What does he mean by "the fountain light of all our day" (line 151)? (c) How does possession of this light transform earthly life? (d) What causes for joy does he mention in stanza 10? (e) Cite lines that distinguish the feeling of maturity from "the gladness of the May."

8. (a) What changes in his attitude toward nature does the poet describe in stanza 11? (b) Compare this stanza with lines 72-111 of "Tintern Abbey."

9. (a) Why is the "Ode" prefaced by the last three lines of "My Heart Leaps Up"? (b) What relation is there between the short poem and the "Ode"?

10. Review the "Better Reading" article on the ode (page 237). (a) Does Wordsworth's "Ode on Intimations of Immortality" conform to the qualifications outlined there? Explain. (b) Cite passages in which the meter and line length are particularly appropriate to the tone.

Selections by Coleridge

KUBLA KHAN

"In Xamdu did Cubla Can build a stately Palace, encompassing sixteen miles of plaine ground with a wall, wherein are fertile Meddowes, pleasant springs, delightfull Streames, and all sorts of beasts of chace and game, and in the middest thereof a sumptuous house of pleasure, which may be removed from place to place." While reading these lines in the sixteenth-century edition of Samuel Purchas' Pilgrimage, a book about travels of Englishmen in foreign lands, Coleridge fell into a deep sleep. While sleeping, he had a vivid image of that scene. Upon awakening, he immediately began writing down his impression, but he was interrupted by a visitor. He was never able to recall the rest of the dream. Although "Kubla Khan" is only a fragment, it is considered one of the outstanding poems of the Romantic Movement.

In Xanadu[1] did Kubla Khan[2]
A stately pleasure-dome decree:
Where Alph, the sacred river, ran
Through caverns measureless to man
Down to a sunless sea.   5
So twice five miles of fertile ground
With walls and towers were girdled round;
And here were gardens bright with sinuous
        rills,
Where blossomed many an incense-bearing
        tree;
And here were forests ancient as the hills,   10
Enfolding sunny spots of greenery.

But oh! that deep romantic chasm which
        slanted

1. *Xanadu* (zan'ə dü), a region in Tartary, the ancient kingdom of the Tartars that included most of Russia and central and western Asia. 2. *Kubla Khan* (ordinarily pronounced kü'blə kän'; but, to rhyme correctly in this poem, the word *Khan* should be pronounced kan). The title refers to the Cham or Emperor Kublai (1214-1294), the Mongol conqueror of China.

Down the green hill athwart a cedarn cover!
A savage place! as holy and enchanted
As e'er beneath a waning moon was haunted 15
By woman wailing for her demon lover!
And from this chasm, with ceaseless turmoil
    seething,
As if this earth in fast, thick pants were
    breathing,
A mighty fountain momently was forced;
Amid whose swift half-intermitted burst   20
Huge fragments vaulted like rebounding hail,
Or chaffy grain beneath the thresher's flail;
And 'mid these dancing rocks at once and
    ever
It flung up momently the sacred river.
Five miles meandering with a mazy motion 25
Through wood and dale the sacred river ran,
Then reached the caverns measureless to man,
And sank in tumult to a lifeless ocean;
And 'mid this tumult Kubla heard from far
Ancestral voices prophesying war!   30

        The shadow of the dome of pleasure
        Floated midway on the waves;
        Where was heard the mingled measure
        From the fountain and the caves.
    It was a miracle of rare device,   35
    A sunny pleasure-dome with caves of ice!

        A damsel with a dulcimer
        In a vision once I saw:
        It was an Abyssinian maid,
        And on her dulcimer she played,   40
        Singing of Mount Abora.[3]
        Could I revive within me
        Her symphony and song,
        To such a deep delight 'twould win me
    That with music loud and long,   45
    I would build that dome in air,
    That sunny dome! those caves of ice!
    And all who heard should see them there,
    And all should cry, "Beware! Beware!
    His flashing eyes, his floating hair!   50
    Weave a circle round him thrice,
    And close your eyes with holy dread,
    For he on honey-dew hath fed,
    And drunk the milk of Paradise."

---

3. *Mount Abora* (ə bō rô′), either a mountain of Coleridge's
imagination or Mount Amara, the seat of a terrestrial paradise in Abyssinia. The words suggest romantic remoteness.

Better reading
Melody in "Kubla Khan"

Coleridge is celebrated for his power to stimulate the imagination through his imagery and his melody. He does not use strange words or sounds, or confusing rhymes or meters to achieve this effect; rather he transforms common language into mysterious and captivating melody by seemingly artless arrangements. Study, for instance, the following passage from "The Ancient Mariner:"

> Her lips were red, her looks were free,
> Her locks were yellow as gold,
> Her skin was white as leprosy,
> The nightmare Life-in-Death was she,
> Who thicks man's blood with cold.

These are ordinary words, the rhyme scheme is simple, yet this passage has an extraordinary effect on the imagination. The same is true of "Kubla Khan."

Three basic poetic devices add much to the musical quality of "Kubla Khan": *rhyme, alliteration*, and *assonance*. With easy grace Coleridge provides a pleasing flow of *rhyme,* and he heightens the musical effect of the rhyme by frequently changing its pattern. Compare the rhyme scheme of the first five lines with other sets of five lines. What effect do these frequent changes in pattern have on the sound and melody of the poem?

Coleridge is unsurpassed in the use of *alliteration*. Some lines hiss with *s*'s; others hum with *m*'s, such as

> Five *m*iles *m*eandering with a *m*azy *m*otion.

Cite other examples where Coleridge uses alliteration to add to the effectiveness of his writing.

Assonance, the third poetic device Coleridge frequently uses, literally means "resemblance of sound." Assonance in poetry is a substitute for rhyme in which the sounds of accented vowels are alike but the consonants differ (as in *sleep* and *feel*). To appreciate fully the musical effect of the repeated *i* sound in the line quoted below, one must remember that Coleridge was probably using the English pronunciation of *fertile*, which has the long *i*.

> So twice five miles of fertile ground.

Throughout "Kubla Khan" Coleridge uses these devices singly or in combination to heighten the melody. Which of the devices do you think adds most to the poem? Why? Which lines do you consider most beautiful from the standpoint of sound alone? Which do you feel is more important to the poem, its imagery or its melody? Are they at all dependent on each other? Explain.

from BIOGRAPHIA LITERARIA

Although on various occasions Coleridge had indicated his complete agreement with the critical ideas set forth by Wordsworth in the Preface to Lyrical Ballads, *when he wrote his* Biographia Literaria *in 1815-1816 he and Wordsworth were no longer working together. This circumstance gave him a more detached view of the Preface. Therefore, he devoted a considerable amount of* Biographia Literaria, *which may be roughly translated as "literary biography," to explaining points of agreement and difference. But first he felt it necessary to explain, as fundamental to his critical ideas, what a poem and a poet really are.*

During the first year that Mr. Wordsworth and I were neighbors, our conversations turned frequently on the two cardinal points of poetry, the power of exciting the sympathy of the reader by faithful adherence to the truth of nature, and the power of giving the interest of novelty by the modifying colors of imagination. The sudden charm, which accidents of light and shade, which moonlight or sunset diffused over a known and familiar landscape, appeared to represent the practicability of combining both. These are the poetry of nature. The thought suggested itself (to which of us I do not recollect) that a series of poems might be composed of two sorts. In the one, the incidents and agents were to be, in part at least, supernatural; and the excellence aimed at was to consist in the interesting of the affections by the dramatic truth of such emotions, as would naturally accompany such situations, supposing them real. And real in this sense they have been to every human being who, from whatever source of delusion, has at any time believed himself under supernatural agency. For the second class, subjects were to be chosen from ordinary life; the characters and incidents were to be such as will be found in every village and its vicinity, where there is a meditative and feeling mind to seek after them, or to notice them, when they present themselves.

In this idea originated the plan of the *Lyrical Ballads;* in which it was agreed, that my endeavor should be directed to persons and characters supernatural, or at least romantic; yet so as to transfer from our inward nature a human interest and a semblance of truth sufficient to procure for these shadows of imagination that willing suspension of disbelief for the moment, which constitutes poetic faith. Mr. Wordsworth, on the other hand, was to propose to himself as his object, to give the charm of novelty to things of every day, and to excite a feeling analogous to the supernatural, by awakening the mind's attention to the lethargy of custom, and directing it to the loveliness and the wonders of the world before us; an inexhaustible treasure, but for which, in consequence of the film of familiarity and selfish solicitude, we have eyes, yet see not, ears that hear not, and hearts that neither feel nor understand.

To the second edition he [Mr. Wordsworth] added a preface of considerable length, in which, notwithstanding some passages of apparently a contrary import, he was understood to contend for the extension of this style to poetry of all kinds, and to reject as vicious and indefensible all phrases and forms of speech that were not included in what he (unfortunately, I think, adopting an equivocal expression) called the language of real life.[1] From this preface, prefixed to poems in which it was impossible to deny the presence of original genius, however mistaken its direction might be deemed, arose the whole long-continued controversy. For from the conjunction of perceived power with supposed heresy, I explain the inveteracy and in some instances, I grieve to say, the acrimonious passions, with which the controversy has been conducted by the assailants.

Had Mr. Wordsworth's poems been the silly, the childish things, which they were

---

1. *language of real life.* Wordsworth's actual words were "the real language of men," and "the very language of men."

for a long time described as being; had they been really distinguished from the compositions of other poets merely by meanness of language and inanity of thought; had they indeed contained nothing more than what is found in the parodies and pretended imitations of them; they must have sunk at once, a dead weight, into the slough of oblivion, and have dragged the preface along with them. But year after year increased the number of Mr. Wordsworth's admirers. They were found, too, not in the lower classes of the reading public, but chiefly among young men of strong sensibility and meditative minds; and their admiration (inflamed perhaps in some degree by opposition) was distinguished by its intensity, I might almost say, by its religious fervor. These facts, and the intellectual energy of the author, which was more or less consciously felt, where it was outwardly and even boisterously denied, meeting with sentiments of aversion to his opinions, and of alarm at their consequences, produced an eddy of criticism, which would of itself have borne up the poems by the violence with which it whirled them round and round. With many parts of this preface in the sense attributed to them and which the words undoubtedly seem to authorize, I never concurred. . . . I think it expedient to declare once for all, in what points I coincide with the opinions supported in that preface, and in what points I altogether differ. But in order to render myself intelligible I must previously, in as few words as possible, explain my ideas, first, of a poem; and secondly, of poetry itself, in kind and in essence. . . .

A poem is that species of composition, which is opposed to works of science, by proposing for its immediate object pleasure, not truth; and from all other species (having this object in common with it) it is discriminated by proposing to itself such delight from the whole, as is compatible with a distinct gratification from each component part.

Controversy is not seldom excited in consequence of the disputants attaching each a different meaning to the same word; and in few instances has this been more striking, than in disputes concerning the present sub-

ject. If a man chooses to call every composition a poem, which is rhyme, or measure, or both, I must leave his opinion uncontroverted. The distinction is at least competent to characterize the writer's intention. If it were subjoined, that the whole is likewise entertaining or affecting, as a tale, or as a series of interesting reflections, I of course admit this as another fit ingredient of a poem, and an additional merit. But if the definition sought for be that of a legitimate poem, I answer, it must be one the parts of which mutually support and explain each other; all in their proportion harmonizing with, and supporting the purpose and known influences of metrical arrangement. The philosophic critics of all ages coincide with the ultimate judgment of all countries, in equally denying the praises of a just poem, on the one hand, to a series of striking lines or distiches, each of which, absorbing the whole attention of the reader to itself, disjoins it from its context, and makes it a separate whole, instead of a harmonizing part; and on the other hand, to an unsustained composition, from which the reader collects rapidly the general result unattracted by the component parts. The reader should be carried forward, not merely or chiefly by the mechanical impulse of curiosity, or by a restless desire to arrive at the final solution; but by the pleasurable activity of mind excited by the attractions of the journey itself. Like the motion of a serpent, which the Egyptians made the emblem of intellectual power; or like the path of sound through the air; at every step he pauses and half recedes, and from the retrogressive movement collects the force which again carries him onward. . . .

What is poetry? is so nearly the same question with, what is a poet? that the answer to the one is involved in the solution of the other. For it is a distinction resulting from the poetic genius itself, which sustains and modifies the images, thoughts, and emotions of the poet's own mind.

The poet, described in ideal perfection, brings the whole soul of man into activity, with the subordination of its faculties to each other according to their relative worth and dignity. He diffuses a tone and spirit of unity, that blends, and (as it were) fuses, each into each, by that synthetic and magical power, to which I would exclusively appropriate the name of imagination. This power, first put in action by the will and understanding, and retained under their irremissive, though gentle and unnoticed, control (*laxis effertur habenis*)[2] reveals itself in the balance or reconcilement of opposite or discordant qualities: of sameness, with difference; of the general, with the concrete; the idea, with the image; the individual, with the representative; the sense of novelty and freshness, with old and familiar objects; a more than usual state of emotion, with more than usual order; judgment ever awake and steady self-possession, with enthusiasm and feeling profound or vehement; and while it blends and harmonizes the natural and the artificial, still subordinates art to nature; the manner to the matter; and our admiration of the poet to our sympathy with the poetry.

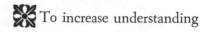 To increase understanding

1. What do Wordsworth and Coleridge believe are the main purposes of poetry?

2. (*a*) Outline the scheme of *Lyrical Ballads* as Coleridge presents it here. (*b*) Cite the expressions that best explain his idea of blending the natural and supernatural in poetry. (*c*) What is "poetic faith" as described by Coleridge? (*d*) What is its function?

3. (*a*) What controversy arose from the publication of the Preface? (*b*) What is Coleridge's defense of Wordsworth? (*c*) Is he in complete disagreement with the critics? Explain.

4. (*a*) Explain Coleridge's definition of poetry in your own words. (*b*) According to Coleridge, when is poetry not poetry? (*c*) What relation must the parts have to the whole in a good poem? (*d*) What reaction should a poem stimulate in a reader?

5. Explain what Coleridge means by imagination.

---

2. *laxis effertur habenis*, it is driven with reins relaxed. [Latin]

Charles Lamb 1775-1834

Although the romantic spirit found its greatest expression in lyric poetry, prose was also affected by the new influence. The essayist no longer felt he had to write in the scholarly style of the classicists. His writing became personal, whimsical, full of figure and fancy. The subjects bore no resemblance to those of eighteenth-century essays—they became only launching pads for the expression of personality. This new and exciting approach to prose writing is known as the *familiar essay*.

Charles Lamb was a master of this new art. Born in a medieval quarter of old London, he drew as much inspiration from the city as Wordsworth found in the countryside. London was the center of his world; here he lived, worked, and died. He was miserable only when well-meaning friends took him for visits to the country. Once there, he could not wait to return to London; to hear and see its swarms of people; to feel the hot pavement of its cobbled streets underfoot. He knew the city as well as Addison and Steele had ever known it; unlike them he saw nothing entertaining in ridiculing the customs or deploring the morals of something so dear to him.

Lamb, a friend to many figures of English romanticism, could talk for hours about the people he met in books or in real life, and liked nothing better than those Wednesday evenings when he played host to a group of literary men, among them Coleridge and Wordsworth. He was an easygoing, light-hearted man, yet his personal life was marred by frustration.

Because of a stammer, he was unable to take an examination at his preparatory school to qualify for a university. Lack of education forced him to take a job as a low-salaried clerk for the East India Tea Company, where he worked until 1825. There was a strain of insanity in Lamb's family; his sister Mary had several attacks of madness, during one of which she killed their mother. Rather than confine her to a miserable life in a sanitarium, Lamb abandoned dreams of marriage and devoted the rest of his life to her care and comfort.

Lamb did not really begin to find himself as a writer until he reached middle age. Up until that time he wrote very little, his only important work being *Tales from Shakespeare,* which was written in collaboration with Mary. The book was written for children and is a delightful retelling of Shakespeare's plays. It was not until he was forty-eight that he published his first book of essays. Entitled *Essays of Elia,* the book's humor, whimsy, and faint overtones of sadness made Lamb immediately popular with nineteenth-century readers. Ten years later, in 1833, he published a second volume, which was received even more enthusiastically than the first.

"Dream Children: A Reverie" is from the first volume of the *Essays.* More nostalgic in tone than most of his writing, the essay was prompted by the death of his brother John in 1821. Even though the two men had not been very friendly, John's death made Lamb aware of the loneliness of his life. Here Lamb dreams of what might have been if he had been able to marry Alice Winterton, his former sweetheart.

DREAM CHILDREN

Children love to listen to stories about their elders, when *they* were children; to stretch their imagination to the conception of a traditionary great-uncle, or grandame, whom they never saw. It was in this spirit that my little ones crept about me the other evening to hear about their great-grandmother Field, who lived in a great house in Norfolk[1] (a hundred times bigger than that in which they and papa lived) which had been the scene—so at least it was generally believed in that part of the country—of the tragic incidents which they had lately become familiar with from the ballad of "The Children in the Wood." Certain it is that the whole story of the children and their cruel uncle was to be seen fairly carved out in wood upon the chimney piece of the great hall, the whole story down to the Robin Redbreasts,[2] till a foolish rich person pulled it down to set up a marble one of modern invention in its

stead, with no story upon it. Here Alice put out one of her dear mother's looks, too tender to be called upbraiding.

Then I went on to say how religious and how good their great-grandmother Field was, how beloved and respected by everybody, though she was not indeed the mistress of this great house, but had only the charge of it (and yet in some respects she might be said to be mistress of it too) committed to her by the owner, who preferred living in a newer and more fashionable mansion which he had purchased somewhere in the adjoining county; but still she lived in it in a manner as if it had been her own and kept up the dignity of the great house in a sort while she lived, which afterward came to decay and was nearly

---

1. *their great-grandmother . . . Norfolk.* Lamb's grandmother, Mary Field, lived at Blakesware, Hertfordshire, not Norfolk. Her position in the "great house" was that of a trusted and much respected housekeeper. 2. *Robin Redbreasts.* At the end of the ballad the robins cover the bodies of the murdered children with leaves.

pulled down, and all its old ornaments were stripped and carried away to the owner's other house, where they were set up and looked as awkward as if someone were to carry away the old tombs they had seen lately at the Abbey[3] and stick them up in Lady C.'s tawdry gilt drawing room. Here John smiled, as much as to say, "That would be foolish, indeed."

And then I told how, when she came to die, her funeral was attended by a concourse of all the poor, and some of the gentry too, of the neighborhood for many miles round, to show their respect for her memory, because she had been such a good and religious woman—so good indeed, that she knew all the Psaltery[4] by heart, aye, and a great part of the Testament besides. Here little Alice spread her hands.

Then I told what a tall, upright, graceful person their great-grandmother Field once was, and how in her youth she was esteemed the best dancer—here Alice's little right foot played an involuntary movement, till upon my looking grave, it desisted—the best dancer, I was saying, in the county, till a cruel disease, called a cancer, came and bowed her down with pain; but it could never bend her good spirits, or make them stoop, because she was so good and religious.

Then I told how she was used to sleep by herself in a lone chamber of the great lone house, and how she believed that an apparition of two infants was to be seen at midnight gliding up and down the great staircase near where she slept, but she said "those innocents would do her no harm"; and how frightened I used to be, because I was never half so good or religious as she—and yet I never saw the infants. Here John tried to look courageous.

Then I told how good she was to all her grandchildren, having us to the great house in the holidays, where I in particular used to spend many hours by myself in gazing upon the old busts of the twelve Caesars that had been emperors of Rome, till the old marble heads would seem to live again or I to be turned into marble with them; how I never could be tired with roaming about that huge mansion with its vast, empty rooms, with their worn-out hangings, fluttering tapestry, and carved oaken panels, with the gilding almost rubbed out—sometimes in the spacious old-fashioned gardens, which I had almost to myself, unless when now and then a solitary gardening man would cross me—and how the nectarines and peaches hung upon the walls without my ever offering to pluck them, because they were forbidden fruits, unless now and then—and because I had more pleasure in strolling about among the old melancholy-looking yew trees, or the firs, and picking up the red berries and the fir apples,[5] which were good for nothing but to look at—or in lying about upon the fresh grass, with all the fine garden smells around me—or basking in the orangery, till I could almost fancy myself ripening too along with the oranges and the limes in that grateful warmth—or in watching the dace that darted to and fro in the fish-pond, at the bottom of the garden, with here and there a great sulky pike hanging midway down the water in silent state, as if it mocked at their impertinent friskings—I had more pleasure in these busy-idle diversions than in all the sweet flavors of peaches, nectarines, oranges, and suchlike common baits of children. Here John slyly deposited back upon the plate a bunch of grapes which, not unobserved by Alice, he had meditated dividing with her, and both seemed willing to relinquish them for the present as irrelevant.

Then in somewhat a more heightened tone, I told how, though their great-grandmother Field loved all her grandchildren, yet in an especial manner she might be said to love their uncle, John L———,[6] because he was so handsome and spirited a youth, and a king to the rest of us; and, instead of moping about in solitary corners, like some of us, he would mount the most mettlesome horse he could get, when but an imp no bigger than themselves, and make it carry him half over the county in a morning, and join the hunters when there were any out—and yet he loved the old great house and gardens too, but had

---

3. *Abbey*, Westminster Abbey in London, where many famous Englishmen are buried.   4. *Psaltery*, the version of the *Psalms* in the *Book of Common Prayer*.   5. *fir apples*, fir cones.   6. *John L....*, Lamb's brother John.

too much spirit to be always pent up within their boundaries—and how their uncle grew up to man's estate as brave as he was handsome, to the admiration of everybody, but of their great-grandmother Field most especially; and how he used to carry me upon his back when I was a lame-footed boy—for he was a good bit older than me—many a mile when I could not walk for pain; and how in after-life he became lame-footed too, and I did not always (I fear) make allowance enough for him when he was impatient, and in pain, nor remember sufficiently how considerate he had been to me when I was lame-footed; and how when he died, though he had not been dead an hour, it seemed as if he had died a great while ago, such a distance there is betwixt life and death; and how I bore his death as I thought pretty well at first, but afterward it haunted and haunted me; and though I did not cry or take it to heart as some do, and as I think he would have done if I had died, yet I missed him all day long, and knew not till then how much I had loved him. I missed his kindness, and I missed his crossness, and wished him to be alive again, to be quarreling with him (for we quarreled sometimes), rather than not have him again, and was as uneasy without him as he, their poor uncle, must have been when the doctor took off his limb. Here the children fell a-crying and asked if their little mourning, which they had on, was not for Uncle John; and they looked up and prayed me not to go on about their uncle, but to tell them some stories about their pretty dead mother.

Then I told how for seven long years, in hope sometimes, sometimes in despair, yet persisting ever, I courted the fair Alice W——n; and, as much as children could understand, I explained to them what coyness and denial meant in maidens—when suddenly, turning to Alice, the soul of the first Alice looked out at her eyes with such a reality of representment, that I became in doubt which of them stood there before me, or whose that bright hair was; and while I stood gazing, both the children gradually grew fainter to my view, receding, and still receding, till nothing at last but two mournful features were seen

in the uttermost distance, which, without speech, strangely impressed upon me the effects of speech: "We are not of Alice, nor of thee, nor are we children at all. We are nothing; less than nothing, and dreams. We are only what might have been, and must wait upon the tedious shores of Lethe[7] millions of ages before we have existence and a name"—and immediately awaking, I found myself quietly seated in my bachelor armchair, where I had fallen asleep, with the faithful Bridget unchanged by my side—but John L. (or James Elia[8]) was gone forever.

---

7. *Lethe* (lē'thi), the river of forgetfulness in Hades.
8. *Bridget . . . James Elia,* names given by Lamb to his sister Mary and his brother John.

To increase understanding

1. (*a*) Explain the title of the essay. (*b*) What details of the essay does Lamb draw from his own life? (*c*) What was Lamb's attitude toward John while he was alive? (*d*) How has that attitude changed?

2. In "Dream Children" Lamb makes the servant class interesting and important. (*a*) Point out the characteristics Lamb stresses in Grandmother Field. (*b*) How does this fit in with the ideals set forth in the Preface to *Lyrical Ballads*? (*c*) Lamb prefers the old house and the old furniture to the "tawdry gilt drawing room." What is romantic about this preference?

3. (*a*) What is Lamb's theme in this essay? (*b*) What is the tone? (*c*) What attitude does Lamb assume toward his readers? (*d*) Does Lamb ever become sentimental? Explain your answer.

Better reading
The familiar essay

The essayists of the romantic period—writers like Charles Lamb, William Hazlitt, Leigh Hunt, and Thomas De Quincey—felt the real business of the essay was to be personal. "Away with the dull and the dry!" cried these new, emancipated writers. They let their imaginations soar and spin and turn about. They caught at wisps of childhood memories. They picked over the literature of the preclassical period and collected whatever in diction, phrase, and imagery suited their fancy. They confessed, speculated, observed, and reflected on such things as dreams, death, friendship, roast pig, chimney sweeps, and old china. The pomposity, pretentiousness, and stiffness of the age of reason were abandoned. Wit crackled, whimsy was freed, pathos was gently touched upon, and personality reigned throughout.

Needless to say, the familiar essay is a highly individualistic thing, depending entirely on the personality and purpose of the writer. Success is his only when he is able to project that personality and purpose to the reader. When this is accomplished, as in the case of Lamb, the familiar essay becomes a literary gem. The writer can use any style he wants to impress the reader: he can write in short, rapid-fire sentences; he can ramble on—binding formlessness into satisfying unity by the invisible chain of mood or feeling; he can be happy or humorous, sad or sweet, harmonious or discordant. Nothing is outside the province of the familiar essay.

Are the ideas expressed in "Dream Children" interesting for their own sake or because of the personality of the writer? Explain. What kind of sentence structure does Lamb use in the essay? How is that structure related to the theme?

Review the article on the formal essay (page 187). Then compare the essays of Bacon and Lamb as to style, form, content, purpose, tone, vocabulary, imagery, and diction. Which of the two writers holds your attention more readily? Why?

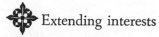 Extending interests

Lamb was not the only great essayist of the romantic period. Leigh Hunt, Thomas De Quincey, William Hazlitt, and Walter Savage Landor did much to develop the essay into a varied and personal form of literature. Each excelled in his own right. Hunt's love of literature shines through all he writes, and his critical essays cover everything from politics to poetry. De Quincey, somewhat influenced by the classicists, writes eloquent and at the same time intimate prose, his most famous work being *Confessions of an English Opium Eater.* Hazlitt was blessed with unusual critical abilities; his *Characters of Shakespeare* and *The Spirit of the Age* are animated and picturesque essays on Shakespeare and contemporary writers. Landor, in *Imaginary Conversations,* reproduces with extraordinary vividness dramatic conversations between such people as Lady Godiva and her merciless husband, and Henry VIII and Anne Boleyn on the eve of her execution.

Read several essays by one or more of the writers. Then choose one that appeals to you and prepare to discuss it in class. Consider the form and style of the essay, its theme and how it is developed, the author's attitude toward the idea, the author's personality, and the romantic aspects of the essay.

Sir Walter Scott 1771-1832

The founder of the modern historical novel was a lame, plump, sweet-faced man named Walter Scott. A descendant of a long line of swash-buckling freebooters with such names as Beardie and Auld Wat of Harden, he was the sheriff of Selkirkshire, the baronet of Abbotsford, and, unofficially, the prince of the romantics. He was the first major writer of the period to show a primary interest in medieval times. Born in Scotland, he grew up among the ballads and legends of the Highland clans, and spent his youth rambling about the country collecting its folklore and studying its landscape. At a time when the English reading public was clamoring for knowledge of Scotland, Scott was there to serve them. He undertook the gigantic task of unraveling the past of six centuries, and conquered the reading world with the results. His works are filled with optimism, action, and truth. His characters are feeling, breathing, flesh-and-blood people, and they assume every guise—from kings and queens to peasants and gypsies. His style is not flawless, his psychology does not penetrate, and his plots are not subtle or refined. Yet he exerted a great influence on such writers as James Fenimore Cooper, Washington Irving, Nathaniel Hawthorne, and Charles Dickens.

When Walter Scott was eighteen months old, an illness left him with a withered leg. A sickly child, he missed much school, and, left to his own resources, he turned to reading about Scotland's past. Parental pressure led him to study law, and although he was admitted to the bar, the practice of law was secondary to his love of literature. His first important work, the fine collection of Scotch ballads and legends known as *The Minstrelsy of the Scottish Border,* bore witness to the value of his early reading and his rambles about the country. His first popular success, *The Lay of the Last Minstrel* (1805), and the even more popular metrical romances that followed—*Marmion* (1806) and *The Lady of the Lake* (1810)—also drew on this Scottish background.

Scott's reputation rests most securely on his novels. *Waverley,* the first in a series of thirty-three novels including such works as *Ivanhoe, Kenilworth, The Heart of Midlothian,* and *Quentin Durward,* was published anonymously in 1814. For twelve years amidst increasing speculation as one novel after another appeared, Scott managed to conceal his identity. During these years he was living the life of a Scotch laird at Abbotsford, the mansion he had built on the banks of the Tweed River. Then, in 1826, a publishing firm in which he had a major interest failed. He could have declared bankruptcy and gone on living as a country gentleman. Instead he gave up Abbotsford, took lodgings in Edinburgh, and spent the rest of his life writing novels to pay his creditors.

Scott's life exemplified the two qualities that he glorified most in his writing—honor and heroism. His deeply felt patriotism is evident in "My Native Land," a selection from *The Lay of the Last Minstrel.*

PROUD MAISIE

In The Heart of Midlothian *(1818) the insane Madge Wildfire sings the following song upon her deathbed.*

P roud Maisie is in the wood,
    Walking so early;
Sweet Robin sits on the bush,
    Singing so rarely.

"Tell me, thou bonny bird,   5
    When shall I marry me?"
"When six braw gentlemen
    Kirkward shall carry ye."

"Who makes the bridal bed,
    Birdie, say truly?"   10
"The gray-headed sexton
    That delves the grave duly.

"The glowworm o'er grave and stone
    Shall light thee steady;
The owl from the steeple sing,   15
    'Welcome, proud lady.' "

Abbotsford.

PHOTO BY LUCIA RAUSCH

SOLDIER, REST! THY WARFARE O'ER

*The following selection is from the first canto
of* The Lady of the Lake. *Ellen Douglas, the
heroine, has just welcomed into her home on
Loch Katrine in Scotland an unfortunate
hunter who has strayed from his party and
lost his horse. The hunter introduces himself
and asks whose home he is in. Instead of answering him, Ellen sings the following song.*

Soldier, rest! thy warfare o'er,
   Sleep the sleep that knows not
      breaking;
   Dream of battled fields no more,
Days of danger, nights of waking.
In our isle's enchanted hall   5
   Hands unseen thy couch are strewing;
Fairy strains of music fall,
   Every sense in slumber dewing.
Soldier, rest! thy warfare o'er,
Dream of fighting fields no more;   10
Sleep the sleep that knows not breaking,
Morn of toil, nor night of waking.

No rude sound shall reach thine ear,
   Armor's clang, or war-steed champing;
Trump nor pibroch¹ summon here   15
   Mustering clan, or squadron tramping.
Yet the lark's shrill fife may come
   At the daybreak from the fallow,
And the bittern sound his drum,
   Booming from the sedgy shallow.   20
Ruder sounds shall none be near,
Guards nor warders challenge here,
Here's no war-steed's neigh and champing,
Shouting clans or squadrons stamping.

Huntsman, rest! thy chase is done;   25
   While our slumbrous spells assail ye,
Dream not, with the rising sun,
   Bugles here shall sound reveille.²
Sleep! the deer is in his den;
   Sleep! thy hounds are by thee lying: 30
Sleep! nor dream in yonder glen
   How thy gallant steed lay dying.
Huntsman, rest! thy chase is done;
Think not of the rising sun,
For at dawning to assail ye   35
Here no bugles sound reveille.

MY NATIVE LAND

Breathes there the man with soul so
      dead,
   Who never to himself hath said,
   "This is my own, my native land!"
Whose heart hath ne'er within him burned
As home his footsteps he hath turned   5
   From wandering on a foreign strand?
If such there breathe, go, mark him well;
For him no minstrel raptures swell;
High though his titles, proud his name,
Boundless his wealth as wish can claim;   10
Despite those titles, power, and pelf,
The wretch, concentered all in self,
Living, shall forfeit fair renown,
And, doubly dying, shall go down
To the vile dust from whence he sprung,   15
Unwept, unhonored, and unsung.

SOLDIER, REST! **1.** *Trump nor pibroch.* The trumpet
summoned lowland Scottish squadrons, while the pibroch
(pē′brok), a kind of musical piece performed on the bagpipe,
called the highland clans. **2.** *reveille,* generally pronounced
rev′ə li, but here pronounced rə vāl′yi to rhyme with assail
ye (ə sāl′yi).

❈ To increase understanding

1. In what ways does "Proud Maisie" resemble a
folk ballad?

2. In "Soldier Rest!" line 2 admits of two different interpretations. (*a*) What are these interpretations? (*b*) In the first two stanzas is there any
indication of which meaning is preferred? (*c*) How
does the third stanza differ from the other two?
Explain the reasons for this change.

3. "Soldier Rest!" is rich in the imagery of sound.
(*a*) Cite details that suggest the sounds of war.
(*b*) What sounds, according to the poem, are to
replace these sounds? (*c*) How would you describe
the tone of the poem?

4. "My Native Land" consists of a question and
its answer. (*a*) Cite the lines that comprise the
question and explain them. (*b*) What is the poet's
answer to the question?

5. (*a*) What is the meaning of "doubly dying"
(line 14)? (*b*) The last line of "My Native Land"
is frequently quoted. Why do you think it has
become famous?

6. What qualities of romanticism do you find in
these poems?

Romance in Art

Romantic painters as well as romantic writers revolted against the dictates of the eighteenth century. To the Augustan painters associated with the Royal Academy (see page 284), line and form were usually more important than color and light. A painting was judged good if it was well drawn and well balanced; it was especially good if it was a well-executed portrait of a fashionable lady or gentleman. To the painters of the romantic school, color and light were more interesting than line and form, and the beauties of nature were more exciting than the silks and satins of high society.

The leaders of this new school of painting were John Constable (1776-1837) and William Turner (1775-1851). Constable is often called the creator of the modern school of landscape painting. He was fascinated by the ever-changing moods of nature, and was the first landscape painter to consider it essential that a sketch be made directly from nature at one sitting, later to be enriched at the artist's leisure. His skies are an awe-inspiring drama filled with wind, sunlight, and clouds. He introduced green into landscape painting—the quiet greens of rolling hills, the lush greens of meadows, the bright, wild greens of foliage—and gave his works a spontaneity and force that remain unrivaled.

Turner was a man of turbulent visions. His Latin temperament belied his English origin. He catches hold of the imagination, not by what he paints, but by how he paints it. His subjects are only phantoms against a background of sensuous, unforgettable colors and brilliant effects of light. Turner does not paint nature; he paints his visions and his dreams, for which nature supplies the suggestions and the materials. His paintings, like Coleridge's poetry, stimulate belief in the unbelievable.

THE TATE GALLERY, LONDON

Opposite: Salisbury Cathedral, *by Constable.*
Below: Haystacks, *by Constable.*
Above: Shipping at Cowes, *by Turner.*
Right: Peasants and Horses near an Inn,
*by George Morland. George, the third
generation of Morland painters, first
exhibited at the Royal Academy when he
was ten. He became noted for his
treatment of low life and animals.*

COURTESY OF THE HAZLITT GALLERY, L.T.D., LONDON

PRIVATE COLLECTION THROUGH MESSRS THOS. AGNEW & SONS, LTD., LONDON

Lord Byron 1788-1824

George Gordon, Lord Byron was born lame, a fate to which he was never quite able to adjust. His father was a spendthrift and a playboy; his mother, a descendant of James I of Scotland, was slightly mad, abnormally vain, and extremely tempestuous. Born only remotely to nobility, he became an heir presumptive at the age of six, and the death of his great-uncle five years later brought him the title Lord Byron. When the young nobleman entered Cambridge at seventeen, he was well-read in Latin and Greek, excelled in swimming and boxing, and had already fallen in love at least twice. After graduation he traveled throughout Europe and Asia Minor until he was twenty-three. Returning to London, he took his seat in the House of Lords and published the first two cantos of *Childe Harold*, a disguised account of his travels as a confused pleasure seeker. This poem, plus a brilliant speech in the House defending workers who had wrecked machinery that threatened their jobs, made Byron famous overnight.

He was the "fair-haired boy" of London society, and he loved every minute of it. He dressed as he felt a poet should—complete with open collar and flowing tie—and worked hard to create an air of mystery about himself. In order to secure his place in society, he married the nobly born, very proper Annabella Milbanke. Annabella and Byron had completely different views on what constitutes a good husband, and she was shocked and horrified by his violent, egotistical behavior. Byron was merely bored.

Above: Portrait of Byron by Thomas Phillips, who also did the portrait of Blake on page 337. Right: Newstead Abbey, which Byron inherited from his great-uncle.

When at the end of the first year of marriage Annabella took their newly born daughter and returned to her parents, Byron was outraged. Londoners, appalled by the stories of his behavior told by Annabella, and by his apparent unconcern for anyone but himself, ostracized him from their company. Raving bitterly about the hypocrisies of society, he left England, never to return.

Byron wandered about the Continent, doing precisely as he pleased, faithful only to his own wayward impulses. His creative powers were more active than ever. He finished *Childe Harold* (1817), and began his masterpiece, *Don Juan*, besides writing many shorter poems. His verses sold well, but while his fortunes prospered, his health, always poor, failed.

More than any other romantic, Byron believed in the freedom of the individual. A foe of despotism anywhere, he was always ready to fight the oppressor. In 1821 he joined an Italian revolt that failed to materialize. In 1823 he joined the Greek war for independence from the Turks, devoting unlimited time and money to the effort. But before he could see battle, he caught fever and died in camp at Missolonghi embittered and old at thirty-six.

To this day he remains a legend. He was the hero of all his poems, but his real life was far more exciting than anything he wrote. He was a man possessed by self-pity, self-consciousness, and self-love. His life was a series of extremes and paradoxes. His impulses were constantly in opposition. He was a fiery rebel and a conventional aristocrat, an idealist and a cynic, a cad to his countrymen and a hero to the Greeks. But most important, he was a great poet, and his satire was the best produced in England since Pope. Not all of his poetry is good; some is cheap and showy and best remains forgotten. But that part which is good burns with the fire of genius.

STANZAS FOR MUSIC

There be none of Beauty's daughters
    With a magic like thee;
And like music on the waters
    Is thy sweet voice to me:
When, as if its sound were causing   5
The charmèd ocean's pausing,
The waves lie still and gleaming,
And the lulled winds seem dreaming.

And the midnight moon is weaving
  Her bright chain o'er the deep;   10
Whose breast is gently heaving,
  As an infant's asleep:
So the spirit bows before thee,
To listen and adore thee;
With a full but soft emotion,   15
Like the swell of Summer's ocean.

SHE WALKS IN BEAUTY

An old Hebrew melody and the sight of a lovely woman wearing a black dress with spangles—these were the inspirations for the following beautiful lyric.

She walks in beauty, like the night,
    Of cloudless climes and starry skies;
And all that's best of dark and bright
    Meet in her aspect and her eyes:
Thus mellowed to that tender light   5
  Which heaven to gaudy day denies.

One shade the more, one ray the less,
  Had half impaired the nameless grace
Which waves in every raven tress,
  Or softly lightens o'er her face;   10
Where thoughts serenely sweet express
  How pure, how dear their dwelling place.

And on that cheek, and o'er that brow,
  So soft, so calm, yet eloquent,
The smiles that win, the tints that glow,   15
  But tell of days in goodness spent,
A mind at peace with all below,
  A heart whose love is innocent!

SONNET ON CHILLON

*François de Bonnivard was a Swiss clergyman
and patriot of the sixteenth century. Because
of his efforts to free Geneva from the rule of
Charles III, Duke of Savoy, and make it a
republic, he was imprisoned in 1530 in the
dungeons of the Castle of Chillon, a gloomy
fortress on the shore of Lake Geneva. Six years
later he was released by members of his own
party.*

Eternal Spirit of the chainless Mind!
  Brightest in dungeons, Liberty! thou art;
  For there thy habitation is the heart—
The heart which love of thee alone can bind;
And when thy sons to fetters are consigned—
  To fetters, and the damp vault's dayless
    gloom,   6
Their country conquers with their martyrdom,
And Freedom's fame finds wings on every
    wind.
Chillon! thy prison is a holy place,
  And thy sad floor an altar— for 'twas
    trod,   10
Until his very steps have left a trace
  Worn, as if thy cold pavement were a sod,
By Bonnivard!—May none those marks efface!
  For they appeal from tyranny to God.

THE ISLES OF GREECE
from DON JUAN

The isles of Greece, the isles of
    Greece!
  Where burning Sappho[1] loved
    and sung,
Where grew the arts of war and peace,
  Where Delos rose, and Phoebus sprung![2]
Eternal summer gilds them yet,   5
But all, except their sun, is set.

The Scian and the Teian muse,[3]
  The hero's harp, the lover's lute,
Have found the fame your shores refuse:
  Their place of birth alone is mute   10
To sounds which echo further west
Than your sires' "Islands of the Blest."[4]

The mountains look on Marathon—[5]
  And Marathon looks on the sea;
And musing there an hour alone,   15
  I dreamed that Greece might still be free;
For standing on the Persians' grave,
I could not deem myself a slave.

A king sat on the rocky brow
  Which looks o'er sea-born Salamis[6];   20
And ships, by thousands, lay below,
  And men in nations;—all were his!
He counted them at break of day—
And when the sun set, where were they?

And where are they? and where art thou,   25
  My country?[7] On thy voiceless shore
The heroic lay is tuneless now—
  The heroic bosom beats no more!
And must thy lyre, so long divine,
Degenerate into hands like mine?   30

'Tis something, in the dearth of fame,
  Though linked among a fettered race,
To feel at least a patriot's shame,
  Even as I sing, suffuse my face;
For what is left the poet here?   35
For Greeks a blush—for Greece a tear.

Must *we* but weep o'er days more blest?
  Must *we* but blush?—Our fathers bled.

1. *Sappho* (saf'ō), the earliest celebrated poetess of Greece.
She lived about 600 B.C. 2. *Delos* (dē'los) . . . *sprung*, the
island of Delos, the reputed birthplace of Phoebus (fē'bəs),
god of the sun, and Artemis (är'tə mis) goddess of the hunt.
3. *Scian . . . muse.* The island of Scio (sī'ō) was the reputed
birthplace of Homer, the great epic poet of ancient Greece.
Teos (tē'ōs), on the coast of Asia Minor, was supposedly
the birthplace of Anacreon (ə nak'ri ən), a writer of love
poems and drinking songs. 4. "*Islands of the Blest,*" mythical islands in the Atlantic where heroes were said to dwell
after death. 5. *Marathon*, the plain where the Athenian
general Miltiades (mil ti'ə dēz) defeated the Persians in
490 B.C. 6. *A king . . . Salamis* (sal'ə mis), the scene of a
naval battle in 480 B.C. where the Greeks, led by Themis-
tocles (thə mis'tə klēz), cut to pieces the Persian fleet of
Xerxes (zėrk'sēz). 7. *my country.* As Byron wrote this,
the Greek war of independence was just beginning. He laments that England, the home of freedom, does not aid.

Earth! render back from out thy breast
　　A remnant of our Spartan dead![8]　　40
Of the three hundred grant but three,
To make a new Thermopylae!

What, silent still? and silent all?
　　Ah! no;—the voices of the dead
Sound like a distant torrent's fall,　　45
　　And answer, "Let one living head,
But one arise—we come, we come!"
'Tis but the living who are dumb.

In vain—in vain: strike other chords;
　　Fill high the cup with Samian[9] wine!　　50
Leave battles to the Turkish[10] hordes,
　　And shed the blood of Scio's vine!
Hark! rising to the ignoble call—
How answers each bold Bacchanal![11]

You have the Pyrrhic dance as yet;　　55
　　Where is the Pyrrhic phalanx[12] gone?
Of two such lessons, why forget
　　The nobler and the manlier one?
You have the letters Cadmus[13] gave—
Think ye he meant them for a slave?　　60

Fill high the bowl with Samian wine!
　　We will not think of themes like these!
It made Anacreon's song divine:
　　He served—but served Polycrates—[14]
A tyrant; but our masters then　　65
Were still, at least, our countrymen.

The tyrant of the Chersonese
　　Was freedom's best and bravest friend;
That tyrant was Miltiades![15]
　　Oh! that the present hour would lend　　70
Another despot of the kind!
Such chains as his were sure to bind.

Fill high the bowl with Samian wine!
　　On Suli's rock, and Parga's shore,[16]
Exists the remnant of a line　　75
　　Such as the Doric[17] mothers bore;
And there, perhaps, some seed is sown,
The Heracleidan[18] blood might own.

Trust not for freedom to the Franks—[19]
　　They have a king who buys and sells;　　80
In native swords, and native ranks,

The only hope of courage dwells:
But Turkish force, and Latin fraud,
Would break your shield, however broad.

Fill high the bowl with Samian wine!　　85
　　Our virgins dance beneath the shade—
I see their glorious black eyes shine;
　　But gazing on each glowing maid,
My own the burning tear-drop laves,
To think such breasts must suckle slaves.　　90

Place me on Sunium's marbled steep,[20]
　　Where nothing, save the waves and I,
May hear our mutual murmurs sweep;
　　There, swan-like, let me sing and die:
A land of slaves shall ne'er be mine—　　95
Dash down yon cup of Samian wine!

8. *Spartan dead*, a reference to the Spartan king Leonidas
(lē on'ə dəs) and his army, who were killed at Thermopylae
(thər mop'ə lē), while defending that mountain pass against
a great army of Persians. 9. *Samian* (sā'mi ən), from Samos, an island off the west coast of Asia Minor. 10. *Turkish*. When Byron wrote this, Greece was under Turkish
rule. 11. *Bacchanal* (bak'ə nal), worshipers of Bacchus,
god of wine. 12. *Pyrrhic* (pir'ik) *dance . . . Pyrrhic phalanx*. The Greeks kept the sensuous war dance but forgot
the world-conquering military formations that Phillip and
Alexander of Macedon (mas'ə don) had taught them. These
facts and the Samian and Scian wines help explain their present enslavement. 13. *Cadmus* (kad'məs), founder of the
Greek city of Thebes (thēbz). He supposedly introduced
the alphabet into Greece. 14. *Polycrates* (pō lik'rə tēz), a
Greek, not a foreign, tyrant who ruled Samos in the days of
Anacreon. He was a patron of literature and art. 15.
That tyrant . . . was Miltiades. Before his courageous efforts
to save Athens from the Persians, Miltiades had been the
tyrannical ruler in the Chersonese (kər'sō nēs'), an Athenian
colony. The colony is now called Gallipoli (gə lip'ə li) and
is located in the northwest part of Turkey. 16. *Suli's . . .
shore*. Suli and Parga are located in the extreme southern
part of Albania, and inhabited by a half-Greek population.
17. *Doric*. The Dorians lived in the mountainous country
of central Greece. They were a sturdy people. 18. *Heracleidan* (her'ə kli'dən), descended from Hercules. 19.
Franks, a Greek name for any foreign ruler. 20. *Sunium's
marbled steep*, the promontory at the southeastern extremity of Greece.

MAN AND NATURE
from CHILDE HAROLD

In Childe Harold Byron records impressions of the "countries of chivalry, history, and fable—Spain, Greece, Asia Minor, and Italy," emphasizing what is, to him, venerable and glorious. He explains that, in order to give "connection" to his work, he has invented a character who travels throughout these countries. Byron insisted that Childe Harold was fictitious; but his readers immediately identified him with the poet. In this passage he talks about his love of nature and drops the disguise.

There is a pleasure in the pathless
    woods,
    There is a rapture on the lonely
      shore,
There is society, where none intrudes,
By the deep sea, and music in its roar:
I love not Man the less, but Nature more,   **5**
From these our interviews, in which I steal
From all I may be or have been before,
To mingle with the universe, and feel
What I can ne'er express, yet cannot all
    conceal.   **9**

Roll on, thou deep and dark blue Ocean—
    roll!
Ten thousand fleets sweep over thee in vain;
Man marks the earth with ruin—his control
Stops with the shore; upon the watery plain

The wrecks are all thy deed, nor doth
    remain
A shadow of man's ravage, save his own,   **15**
When for a moment, like a drop of rain,
He sinks into thy depths with bubbling groan,
Without a grave, unknelled, uncoffined, and
    unknown.

His steps are not upon thy paths—thy fields
Are not a spoil for him—thou dost arise   **20**
And shake him from thee; the vile strength
    he wields
For earth's destruction thou dost all despise,
Spurning him from thy bosom to the skies,
And send'st him, shivering in thy playful
    spray
And howling, to his gods, where haply lies   **25**
His petty hope in some near port or bay,
And dashest him again to earth—there let
    him lay.

The armaments which thunderstrike the walls
Of rock-built cities, bidding nations quake
And monarchs tremble in their capitals,   **30**
The oak leviathans, whose huge ribs make
Their clay creator the vain title take
Of lord of thee and arbiter of war—
These are thy toys, and, as the snowy flake,   **34**
They melt into thy yeast of waves, which mar
Alike the Armada's pride or spoils of
    Trafalgar.[1]

1. *Armada's . . . Trafalgar* (trə fal'gər). In 1588 one-half of the Spanish Armada that sailed against England was destroyed by storms at sea. In 1805, during the Napoleonic Wars, the same fate overtook the French when they opposed the English under Lord Nelson.

PHOTO BY MARGARET RAUSCH

Thy shores are empires, changed in all save
  thee—
Assyria, Greece, Rome, Carthage,[2] what are
  they?
Thy waters washed them power while they
  were free,   39
And many a tyrant since; their shores obey
The stranger, slave, or savage; their decay
Has dried up realms to deserts—not so thou.
Unchangeable, save to thy wild waves' play,
Time writes no wrinkle on thine azure brow;
Such as creation's dawn beheld, thou rollest
  now.   45

Thou glorious mirror, where the Almighty's
  form
Glasses itself in tempests; in all time—
Calm or convulsed, in breeze, or gale, or
  storm,
Icing the pole, or in the torrid clime   49
Dark-heaving—boundless, endless, and
  sublime,
The image of eternity, the throne
Of the Invisible; even from out thy slime
The monsters of the deep are made; each zone
Obeys thee; thou goest forth, dread,
  fathomless, alone.

And I have loved thee, Ocean! and my joy   55
Of youthful sports was on thy breast to be
Borne, like thy bubbles, onward. From a boy
I wantoned with thy breakers—they to me
Were a delight; and if the freshening sea
Made them a terror—'twas a pleasing fear,   60
For I was as it were a child of thee,
And trusted to thy billows far and near,
And laid my hand upon thy mane—as I do
  here.

2. *Assyria, Greece, Rome, Carthage.* Each in its heyday
had been a powerful kingdom or empire, but the power of
each had long since vanished.

To increase understanding
Three lyrics

1. (a) What is the significance of the title of
"Stanzas for Music"? (b) How is the music created?
(c) Byron uses a sustained figure throughout this
lyric. What is that figure? (d) How and for what
purpose is it used? (e) What uses does Byron make

of imagery? (f) Are the rhythm and harmony of
sound appropriate to the theme?

2. (a) How does the first stanza of "She Walks
in Beauty" characterize as well as describe the
woman? (b) Why is her beauty appropriately compared to night? (c) How does the poet create the
aura of spirituality that surrounds the woman?

3. (a) What idea does Byron express in "Sonnet
on Chillon"? (b) How is this idea developed in the
octave? (c) Why is Liberty brightest in dungeons?
(d) How is the idea further developed in the sestet?

The Isles of Greece

1. (a) In the first five stanzas of "The Isles of
Greece" Byron contrasts the past glories of Greece
with what he regards as the shame of the present.
Explain the various references to the past made by
Byron and the respects in which the present differs
from the past. (b) What events of Byron's own
time probably occasioned the writing of the poem?

2. (a) Why does Byron feel "a patriot's shame"
(line 33)? (b) On what condition will "a remnant
of our Spartan dead" (line 40) return? (c) Is the
condition met? Explain.

3. In stanzas 9-11 (lines 49-66) Byron ridicules
the Greeks of his time. Cite examples he uses to
make the point.

4. (a) How did the word *tyrant* in ancient Greece
differ from the modern meaning? (b) Why does the
poet believe the Greeks need another Miltiades?

5. (a) In stanza 13 (lines 73-78) Byron expresses
a faint hope. What is it? (b) Judging from the following stanzas does he expect this hope to be realized? Explain.

6. (a) In what ways does this poem reflect
Byron's own life? (b) What aspects of romanticism
does it express?

Man and Nature

1. What aspects of nature does Byron emphasize
in "Man and Nature?"

2. Byron personifies the ocean. (a) According
to this personification, what is the ocean's attitude
toward man? Cite lines to prove your point. (b) Is
Byron's own attitude similar to or different from the
ocean's? Cite lines as evidence for your answer.

3. (a) Lines 37-45 contain one of the most important ideas in the poem. What is it? (b) What
contrast is drawn between man and the ocean?
(c) How does Byron indicate that the ocean is indifferent to man? (d) What striking figure of speech
does he use to show that the ocean remains unchanged by years?

4. (a) Byron calls the ocean a "glorious mirror," "The image of eternity," and a "throne of the invisible." Explain this imagery. (b) What is the tone of the last stanza? (c) Compare it to the tone of the rest of the poem.

 Words!

According to Wordsworth, one of the foundations of romantic poetry is its use of the everyday language of the people. In general, most poets do use that language, but occasionally every poet—even Wordsworth—uses language not ordinarily used in speech or prose writing. The dictionary labels such words *poetic* or *archaic*; they are words which were formerly a part of regular speech but which now have only a literary usage. The italicized words in the lines of poetry quoted below are examples of these types of words. Give the meaning of each as used here; then tell why you think the poet employed this word instead of a more commonly used word.

> I heard a thousand blended notes,
> While in a grove I *sate* reclined,
> > —*Lines Written in Early Spring*

> No nightingale did ever *chaunt*
> More welcome notes to weary bands
> Of travelers in some shady haunt,
> Among Arabian sands.
> > —*The Solitary Reaper*

> O listen! for the *vale* profound
> Is overflowing with the sound
> > —*The Solitary Reaper*

> Sleep the sleep that knows no breaking,
> *Morn* of toil, nor night of waking.
> > —*Soldier, Rest! Thy Warfare O'er*

> Whose heart hath ne'er within him burned
> As home his footsteps he hath turned
> From wandering on a foreign *strand*?
> > —*My Native Land*

> "Who makes the bridal bed,
> Birdie say truly?"
> "The gray-headed sexton
> That *delves* the grave duly."
> > —*Proud Maisie*

> She walks in beauty, like the night
> Of cloudless *climes* and starry skies;
> > —*She Walks in Beauty*

> I *wantoned* with thy breakers—
> > —*Man and Nature*

PHOTO BY LON MC KEE

A scene in Italy.

Percy Bysshe Shelley
1792-1822

Percy Shelley was the "black sheep" of a family bound by conventions. He stepped lightly over religious, political, social, and moral boundaries, seemingly unaware of their existence. To his wealthy parents his life seemed to be nothing but a long series of disgraces. He began this string of ig- nominies at Eton, a fashionable boys' school. A brilliant and hypersensitive student, he was completely resentful of all authority. School traditions meant nothing; he had no interest in sports or the games of the other boys, and did not hesitate in the ex- pression of his views on these matters. This nonconformist attitude put him at odds with everyone at the school—from head- master on down. He fared no better at Oxford University. There he developed a passion for metaphysics, a philosophical study of the nature of the universe, and published a pamphlet entitled *The Neces- sity of Atheism*. He was expelled.

Shelley's next imprudent move was to marry the very pretty but not very bright Harriet Westbrooke, daughter of an inn- keeper. By the time he was twenty-one he had become a father and published his first important poem, *Queen Mab*, a criticism of the structure of society. But by the third year of marriage he began to find Harriet dull. With characteristic aplomb he calmly announced to Harriet that since he no longer loved her he was leaving. Within two months he eloped with Mary God- win, daughter of the radical William God- win, with whom Shelley shared many revo- lutionary beliefs. They spent some time in Switzerland; their return to England was followed by Harriet's suicide. Although she had always threatened self-destruction, her death was a shock from which Shelley never fully recovered. Because of the inci- dent, the scorn of the English public fell upon him, and he and Mary left England for Italy. Like Byron, he never returned.

Portrait of Shelley by Amelia Curran.

NATIONAL PORTRAIT GALLERY, LONDON

Shelley wrote the bulk of his greatest poetry in the four short years he spent in Italy. He went there in 1818 and died there in 1822—an untimely and violent death before he reached the age of thirty. He and a friend were sailing in Shelley's boat when they were struck by a windstorm. Ten days later their bodies were found half buried in the sands of the beach. They were cremated on the spot, and, according to some accounts, Mary snatched her husband's heart from out of the ashes. The heart is buried in the Protestant cemetery in Rome under the inscription *"Cor Cordium!"* ("Heart of Hearts!").

Throughout his lifetime Shelley was filled with schemes for reforming the world, and was prepared to do it single-handed if necessary. Labeled everything from impractical to fanatic by society, Shelley remained a firm believer in the purity of his intentions and the soundness of his views, protected from alien attitudes by a strong armor of indifference. An uncompromising zealot, he preached a form of government that could only lead to anarchy. But this idea of lawless revolution that burns so strongly through much of Shelley's poetry is counterbalanced by strong idealism. A great lover of man and freedom, he believed in goodness, truth, and the power of love, and he glorified them in his writings.

Shelley's greatness lies not only in the great themes of which he wrote, but also in his powerful and fertile imagination, his instinctive, over-brimming lyric power, his superb sense of fancy, and his exquisite blending of mood and melody, thought and design. To him poetry was the best and happiest moments of the best and happiest minds—a device for making immortal all that is good and beautiful in the world.

SONG TO THE MEN OF ENGLAND

Men of England, wherefore plow
For the lords who lay ye low?
Wherefore weave with toil and
    care
The rich robes your tyrants wear?

Wherefore feed, and clothe, and save,   5
From the cradle to the grave,
Those ungrateful drones who would
Drain your sweat—nay, drink your blood?

Wherefore, bees of England, forge
Many a weapon, chain, and scourge,   10
That these stingless drones may spoil
The forced produce of your toil?

Have ye leisure, comfort, calm,
Shelter, food, love's gentle balm?
Or what is it ye buy so dear   15
With your pain and with your fear?

The seed ye sow, another reaps;
The wealth ye find, another keeps;
The robes ye weave, another wears;
The arms ye forge, another bears.   20

Sow seed—but let no tyrant reap;
Find wealth—let no impostor heap;
Weave robes—let not the idle wear;
Forge arms—in your defense to bear.

Shrink to your cellars, holes, and cells;   25
In halls ye deck another dwells.
Why shake the chains ye wrought? Ye see
The steel ye tempered glance on ye.

With plow and spade, and hoe and loom,
Trace your grave, and build your tomb,   30
And weave your winding sheet, till fair
England be your sepulcher.

OZYMANDIAS

According to an early Greek historian, Ozy-mandias (oz'i man'di əs) was an Egyptian ruler whose huge statue bore the following inscription: "I am Ozymandias, King of Kings; if anyone wishes to know what I am and where I lie, let him surpass me in some of my exploits."

I met a traveler from an antique land
    Who said: "Two vast and trunkless legs
      of stone
Stand in the desert. Near them, on the sand,
Half sunk, a shattered visage lies, whose
    frown,
And wrinkled lip, and sneer of cold
    command,   5
Tell that its sculptor well those passions read
Which yet survive, stamped on these lifeless
    things,
The hand that mocked them, and the heart
    that fed[1];
And on the pedestal these words appear:
'My name is Ozymandias, king of kings;   10
Look on my works, ye mighty, and despair.'
Nothing beside[2] remains. Round the decay
Of that colossal wreck, boundless and bare
The lone and level sands stretch far away."

TO——

One word is too often profaned
    For me to profane it,
One feeling too falsely disdained
    For thee to disdain it;
One hope is too like despair   5
    For prudence to smother,
And pity from thee more dear
    Than that from another.

I can give not what men call love,
    But wilt thou accept not   10
The worship the heart lifts above
    And the Heavens reject not—
The desire of the moth for the star,
    Of the night for the morrow,
The devotion to something afar   15
    From the sphere of our sorrow?

THE CLOUD

Mary Shelley wrote that the inspiration for this poem came to the poet "while he floated in his boat on the Thames," and "marked the cloud as it sped across the heavens."

I bring fresh showers for the thirsting
    flowers,
    From the seas and the streams;
I bear light shade for the leaves when laid
    In their noonday dreams.
From my wings are shaken the dews that
    waken   5
    The sweet buds every one,
When rocked to rest on their mother's breast,
    As she dances about the sun.
I wield the flail of the lashing hail,
    And whiten the green plains under,   10
And then again I dissolve it in rain,
    And laugh as I pass in thunder.

I sift the snow on the mountains below,
    And their great pines groan aghast;
And all the night 'tis my pillow white,   15
    While I sleep in the arms of the blast.
Sublime on the towers of my skyey bowers,
    Lightning, my pilot, sits;
In a cavern under is fettered the thunder,
    It struggles and howls at fits;   20
Over earth and ocean, with gentle motion,
    This pilot is guiding me,
Lured by the love of the genii that move
    In the depths of the purple sea;
Over the rills, and the crags, and the hills,   25
    Over the lakes and the plains,
Wherever he dream, under mountain or
    stream,
    The spirit he loves remains;
And I all the while bask in heaven's blue
    smile,
    Whilst he is dissolving in rains.   30

The sanguine Sunrise, with his meteor eyes,
    And his burning plumes outspread,

OZYMANDIAS. **1.** *The hand . . . fed.* The hand is that of the sculptor, who mockingly revealed the evil passions of Ozymandias. The heart that nourished ("fed") those passions belonged, of course, to Ozymandias himself. **2.** *be-side,* besides, else.

Leaps on the back of my sailing rack,[1]
    When the morning star shines dead;
As on the jag of a mountain crag,   35
    Which an earthquake rocks and swings,
An eagle alit one moment may sit
    In the light of its golden wings.
And when Sunset may breathe, from the lit
        sea beneath,
    Its ardors of rest and of love,   40
And the crimson pall of eve may fall
    From the depth of heaven above,
With wings folded I rest, on mine airy
        nest,
    As still as a brooding dove.

That orbèd[2] maiden with white fire laden,   45
    Whom mortals call the Moon,
Glides glimmering o'er my fleecelike floor,
    By the midnight breezes strewn;
And wherever the beat of her unseen feet,
    Which only the angels hear,   50
May have broken the woof of my tent's thin
        roof,
    The stars peep behind her and peer;
And I laugh to see them whirl and flee,
    Like a swarm of golden bees,
When I widen the rent in my wind-built tent,
    Till the calm rivers, lakes, and seas,   56
Like strips of the sky fallen through me on
        high,
    Are each paved with the moon and these.[3]

I bind the Sun's throne with a burning zone,[4]
    And the Moon's with a girdle of pearl;   60
The volcanoes are dim, and the stars reel and
        swim
    When the whirlwinds my banner unfurl.
From cape to cape, with a bridgelike shape,
    Over a torrent sea,
Sunbeam-proof, I hang like a roof—   65
    The mountains its columns be.
The triumphal arch through which I march
    With hurricane, fire, and snow,
When the Powers of the air chained to my
        chair,
    Is the million-colored bow;   70
The sphere fire above its soft colors wove,
    While the moist Earth was laughing below.

I am the daughter of Earth and Water,
    And the nursling of the Sky;
I pass through the ports of the ocean and
        shores;   75
    I change, but I cannot die.
For after the rain when with never a stain
    The pavilion of heaven is bare,
And the winds and sunbeams with their
        convex gleams
    Build up the blue dome of air,   80
I silently laugh at my own cenotaph,[5]
    And out of the caverns of rain,
Like a child from the womb, like a ghost from
        the tomb,
    I arise and unbuild it again.

TO A SKYLARK *According to Mrs. Shelley, "To a Skylark" was inspired as she and her
husband heard the skylark "on a beautiful summer evening while wandering among the lanes, whose myrtle hedges were bowers of fireflies."*

Hail to thee, blithe Spirit!
        Bird thou never wert,
    That from Heaven, or near it,
        Pourest thy full heart
In profuse strains of unpremeditated art.   5

    Higher still and higher
        From the earth thou springest
    Like a cloud of fire;

THE CLOUD. **1.** *rack,* broken portion of cloud. **2.** *orbèd,* from *orb,* a globe or sphere. **3.**
these, the stars. **4.** *zone,* girdle. **5.** *cenotaph,* an empty tomb erected in honor of someone who
is buried elsewhere; here, the blue dome of air.

The blue deep thou wingest,
And singing still dost soar, and soaring ever singest.   10

   In the golden lightning
     Of the sunken sun,
   O'er which clouds are bright'ning,
     Thou dost float and run;
Like an unbodied joy whose race is just begun.   15

   The pale purple even
     Melts around thy flight;
   Like a star of heaven,
     In the broad daylight
Thou art unseen, but yet I hear thy shrill delight,   20

   Keen as are the arrows
     Of that silver sphere,
   Whose intense lamp narrows
     In the white dawn clear
Until we hardly see—we feel that it is there.   25

   All the earth and air
     With thy voice is loud,
   As, when night is bare,
     From one lonely cloud
The moon rains out her beams, and heaven is overflowed.   30

   What thou art we know not;
     What is most like thee?
   From rainbow clouds there flow not
     Drops so bright to see
As from thy presence showers a rain of melody.   35

   Like a poet hidden
     In the light of thought,
   Singing hymns unbidden,
     Till the world is wrought
To sympathy with hopes and fears it heeded not;   40

   Like a highborn maiden
     In a palace tower,
   Soothing her love-laden
     Soul in secret hour
With music sweet as love, which overflows her bower;   45

   Like a glowworm golden
     In a dell of dew,
   Scattering unbeholden
     Its aëreal hue
Among the flowers and grass, which screen it from the view;   50

Like a rose embowered
    In its own green leaves,
By warm winds deflowered,
    Till the scent it gives
Makes faint with too much sweet those heavy-wingèd thieves;   55

Sound of vernal showers
    On the twinkling grass,
Rain-awakened flowers,
    All that ever was
Joyous, and clear, and fresh, thy music doth surpass.   60

Teach us, Sprite or Bird,
    What sweet thoughts are thine.
I have never heard
    Praise of love or wine
That panted forth a flood of rapture so divine.   65

Chorus hymeneal,
    Or triumphal chant,
Matched with thine would be all
    But an empty vaunt,
A thing wherein we feel there is some hidden want.   70

What objects are the fountains
    Of thy happy strain?
What fields, or waves, or mountains?
    What shapes of sky or plain?
What love of thine own kind? what ignorance of pain?   75

With thy clear, keen joyance
    Languor cannot be;
Shadow of annoyance
    Never came near thee;
Thou lovest—but ne'er knew love's sad satiety.   80

Waking or asleep,
    Thou of death must deem
Things more true and deep
    Than we mortals dream,
Or how could thy notes flow in such a crystal stream?   85

We look before and after,
    And pine for what is not;
Our sincerest laughter
    With some pain is fraught;
Our sweetest songs are those that tell of saddest thought.   90

Yet if we could scorn
    Hate, and pride, and fear;

If we were things born
  Not to shed a tear,
I know not how thy joy we ever should come near.   95

Better than all measures
  Of delightful sound,
Better than all treasures
  That in books are found,
Thy skill to poet were, thou scorner of the ground!   100

Teach me half the gladness
  That thy brain must know,
Such harmonious madness
  From my lips would flow
The world should listen then—as I am listening now.   105

ODE TO THE WEST WIND *Of the background for "Ode to the West Wind" Shelley himself wrote: "This poem was conceived and chiefly written in a wood that skirts the Arno, near Florence, and on a day when that tempestuous wind, whose temperature is at once mild and animating, was collecting the vapors which pour down the autumnal rains. They began, as I foresaw, at sunset with a violent tempest of hail and rain, attended by that magnificent thunder and lightning peculiar to the Cisalpine[1] regions."*

1

O wild West Wind, thou breath of Autumn's being,
  Thou, from whose unseen presence the leaves dead
  Are driven, like ghosts from an enchanter fleeing,

Yellow, and black, and pale, and hectic red,
Pestilence-stricken multitudes: O thou,   5
Who chariotest to their dark wintry bed

The wingèd seeds, where they lie cold and low,
Each like a corpse within its grave, until
Thine azure sister of the Spring[2] shall blow

Her clarion o'er the dreaming earth, and fill   10
(Driving sweet buds like flocks to feed in air)
With living hues and odors plain and hill:

Wild Spirit, which art moving everywhere;
Destroyer and preserver; hear, oh, hear!

ODE TO THE WEST WIND. **1.** *Cisalpine*, on the southern side of the Alps. **2.** *sister of the Spring*, the south wind.

2

Thou on whose stream, mid the steep sky's commotion,   15
Loose clouds like earth's decaying leaves are shed,
Shook from the tangled boughs of Heaven and Ocean,

Angels of rain and lightning: there are spread
On the blue surface of thine aëry surge,
Like the bright hair uplifted from the head   20

Of some fierce Maenad,[3] even from the dim verge
Of the horizon to the zenith's height,
The locks of the approaching storm. Thou dirge

Of the dying year, to which this closing night[4]
Will be the dome of a vast sepulcher,   25
Vaulted with all thy congregated might

Of vapors, from whose solid atmosphere
Black rain, and fire, and hail will burst: oh hear!

3

Thou who didst waken from his summer dreams
The blue Mediterranean, where he lay,   30
Lulled by the coil of his crystalline streams,

Beside a pumice isle in Baiae's bay,[5]
And saw in sleep old palaces and towers
Quivering within the wave's intenser day,

All overgrown with azure moss and flowers   35
So sweet, the sense faints picturing them! Thou
For whose path the Atlantic's level powers

Cleave themselves into chasms, while far below
The sea-blooms and the oozy woods which wear
The sapless foliage of the ocean, know   40

Thy voice, and suddenly grow gray with fear,
And tremble and despoil themselves:[6] oh, hear!

4

If I were a dead leaf thou mightest bear,
If I were a swift cloud to fly with thee;
A wave to pant beneath thy power, and share   45

---

3. *Maenad* (mē'nad), a priestess of Bacchus, god of wine. **4.** *closing night*, night sky closing down over the earth. **5.** *Baiae's* (bä'yäs) *bay*. The modern village of Baia (bä'yä) is a seaport about ten miles from Naples in Italy. Called *Baiae* by the Romans, the site is rich in ancient ruins. **6.** *sea-blooms . . . themselves*. In a note on these lines Shelley states that "the vegetation at the bottom of the sea, of rivers, and of lakes, sympathizes with that of the land in the change of seasons, and is consequently influenced by the winds which announce it."

The impulse of thy strength, only less free
Than thou, O uncontrollable! If even
I were as in my boyhood, and could be

The comrade of thy wanderings over Heaven,
As then, when to outstrip thy skyey speed   50
Scarce seemed a vision; I would ne'er have striven

As thus with thee in prayer in my sore need.
Oh, lift me as a wave, a leaf, a cloud!
I fall upon the thorns of life! I bleed!

A heavy weight of hours has chained and bowed   55
One too like thee: tameless, and swift, and proud.

5

Make me thy lyre, even as the forest is:
What if my leaves are falling like its own!
The tumult of thy mighty harmonies

Will take from both a deep, autumnal tone,   60
Sweet though in sadness. Be thou, Spirit fierce,
My spirit! Be thou me, impetuous one!

Drive my dead thoughts over the universe
Like withered leaves to quicken a new birth!
And, by the incantation of this verse,   65

Scatter, as from an unextinguished hearth
Ashes and sparks, my words among mankind!
Be through my lips to unawakened earth

The trumpet of a prophecy! O Wind,
If Winter comes, can Spring be far behind?   70

❀To increase understanding

1. Note that the first four stanzas of "Song to the Men of England" consist of questions. (*a*) What kind of questions are asked? (*b*) How and where are they answered? (*c*) How do you interpret the question in line 27? (*d*) What is the tone of the last six lines?

2. (*a*) What is the rhyme scheme of "Song to the Men of England"? (*b*) What is the meter? (*c*) Note the type of verbs and the frequency with which verbs are used. What effect does the use of verbs create?

3. Compare "Song to the Men of England" with Blake's "A New Jerusalem" (page 340). Consider (*a*) the basic situation, (*b*) emphasis, and (*c*) tone.

4. (*a*) Sum up the comment on tyranny made in "Ozymandias." (*b*) What is ironic about the situation described?

5. Compare the idea developed in "Ozymandias" with lines 37-45 of Byron's "Man and Nature" (page 381).

6. "To——" is often cited as one of Shelley's most melodious lyrics. (*a*) What devices create the melody? (*b*) The last four lines are often quoted. Why do you think this is so?

7. In "The Cloud" Shelley pictures clouds in

practically every imaginable situation. (*a*) Trace the changes in the situation of the cloud from first to last stanza. (*b*) What scientific truths are embodied in this imaginative treatment?

8. (*a*) Why might the entire poem be considered personification? (*b*) Cite lines that are notable for their imagery.

9. (*a*) In "To a Skylark" Shelley uses many similes in the first twelve stanzas. What do the similes describe? (*b*) What idea is developed in the first twelve stanzas? (*c*) How do the later stanzas of the poem differ from the first twelve?

10. (*a*) What conclusion is drawn in lines 96-105? (*b*) How are the last five lines especially typical of Shelley?

11. Compare Shelley's "To a Skylark" with Wordsworth's poem of the same name (page 352). (*a*) Wordsworth likens the skylark to people of high purpose and high ambition who never lose sight of ordinary things. What does Shelley's skylark symbolize? (*b*) In your opinion, which of the poems best uses the symbol of the skylark?

12. "Ode to the West Wind" is romantic in two ways: it is a nature poem, and it discusses a very romantic idea. (*a*) What is that idea? (*b*) What hope is expressed in the last two lines? (*c*) How does the first stanza of the ode prepare for this hint of hope? (*d*) What impression of Shelley do you get from the poem?

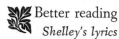 Better reading
Shelley's lyrics

There is perhaps no writer in whose works the lyric may be studied better than in the poetry of Shelley. Just what is a lyric? This is not a question that can be easily answered. The lyric may take many forms—ode, sonnet, ballad, elegy, song—and many themes—love, death, social sympathy, art, nature, patriotism. Three things are evident in all good lyrics: definite form, melody, and emotion.

Form: Shelley stands high among lyricists for his ability to fuse the form and content of a poem in perfect harmony. In "To a Skylark" Shelley reflects the spiral flight of the bird in the four short, alternately rhyming lines of each stanza. What part of the bird's flight does the long line at the end of each stanza represent? In your opinion, which stanza best represents soaring flight? Explain.

In "Ode to the West Wind" the poet uses *terza rima* (ter′tsä rē′mä), a series of three-line stanzas having the rhyme scheme *aba, bcb, cdc, ded,* etc. He divides the poem into sections, each section consisting of four stanzas followed by a couplet (for example,

lines 13-14 rhyming *ee*). How many sections are there in the poem? What is the topic of each section? Explain why the form is particularly appropriate for the thoughts expressed in the poem.

Melody: The two most important elements of melody are repetition and variation. In good melody these two are combined so as not to become too monotonous or too confusing. In "The Cloud" Shelley repeats particular sounds in various combinations and arrangements to emphasize certain words, to please the ear, and to give organization and structure to the poem. This sound pattern is achieved largely through the use of rhyme, assonance, and alliteration. Find examples of alliteration in the first six lines of the poem. What consonant sound predominates in these lines? Note the assonance created by the vowels in the first stanza. What sounds are dominant in lines 1-8? What change occurs in line 9? How does this change both affect the poem's melody and emphasize the change in atmosphere?

At times Shelley uses rhymes in which the vowel sounds do not exactly correspond, as in the words *love* and *move* in line 23 of "The Cloud." Rhymes of this type are known as *imperfect rhymes* or *slant rhymes.* Find other examples of this type of rhyme in "The Cloud." In each case explain why you think Shelley used this type of rhyme.

The fourth stanza of "The Cloud" is one of the most musical pieces of writing in the English language. Chart the rhyme scheme, including internal rhyme. What effect does this combination of internal rhyme with end rhyme achieve? What is the basic meter? Describe the melody created by this meter—is it soft, lilting, slow, fast-paced? Explain. If you were to choose an instrument to accompany the reading of the poem, what would it be? Why?

Emotion: Form and melody alone do not make a lyric great. Important as they are, they are only the mechanics of poetry. It is emotion that gives the lyric substance. "Ode to the West Wind" is not only a magnificent description of the effect of the wind in various seasons and different places; it is also the poet's anguished cry. Note that each of the first three sections ends with the words "oh, hear." What is the message that the poet wishes to speak?

The first section of the poem concentrates upon the action of the wind upon the leaves. Trace this idea through section 1. What various aspects of wind-driven clouds are pictured in section 2? Trace the action of the wind upon the sea in section 3. Show how in sections 4 and 5 Shelley relates leaves, clouds, and sea to his own life.

What is the overall emotional tone of the poem?

John Keats 1795-1821

John Keats was born in London, the first son of a cockney stable keeper. His father was killed in a riding accident when Keats was nine; six years later his mother died of tuberculosis—apparently a family affliction, for both Keats and a brother also died of it. At fifteen he was taken out of school and apprenticed to a physician; he began writing in the same year. He spent some time in London hospitals, but was prone to pay more attention to a ray of sunlight falling across a room than to the patients, and he finally abandoned medicine for literature.

With stanch support from such people as Leigh Hunt, Wordsworth, and Lamb, the twenty-one-year-old Keats began his literary career in earnest. He was hopeful and enthusiastic, full of the exuberance of youth. Suddenly came disappointment and tragedy. One brother left for America, the other died of tuberculosis. The publication of *Endymion*, his greatest effort to date, was met with vicious and unwarranted criticism. His cockney heritage and his physician's training were mocked and ridiculed. Critics advised, in not very polite terms, that he return to medicine and leave the writing of poetry to the cultured and capable. This bad publicity kept his poetry from selling and Keats was soon destitute. He began to feel the symptoms of the family disease; in 1818 his suspicions of tuberculosis were confirmed. At this point the ill and poverty-stricken Keats fell in love, but knowing he could never marry, he left England for the warmer climate of Italy. His sojourn there failed to arrest the disease and in less than six months Keats was dead. He was buried in Rome under the epitaph he himself had composed—"Here lies one whose name was writ in water."

Keats lived in a world fighting for freedom, but the French Revolution and various reform movements which played such a big part in the lives of the other romantics did not touch him. He did not in his writing advocate revolutionary ideas, as Shelley did, nor did he, like Wordsworth, develop an elaborate philosophy of nature. His concern was primarily with the relationship of truth and beauty.

One outstanding feature of Keats' poetry is his use of imagery, which in his hands becomes an all-purpose tool. With it he hammers out resonance and rhythm, blends explicit and figurative meanings, and fuses sight, sound, taste, smell, touch, and emotion. Keats' predecessors talked about spouting fountains, blooming plants, and blowing winds. Their use of adjectives was limited, the favorite being *sweet*—the sweet smell of a rose, the sweet taste of honey, the shy, sweet glances of a girl. But Keats seldom resorts to this standard "dictionary" of images. Freshness and vitality dominate his poetry. He possessed an uncluttered and expansive imagination that, like a kaleidoscope, produces a different picture every time.

England's storied past with its bold and romantic tales was a great inspiration to Keats. An ardent admirer of the Elizabethan poets, he adapted some of the sensuous pictorial qualities of Shakespeare and of Spenser to his own writings. His works, like the works of Spenser, are not to be read in great quantities at one time. They should be taken in small portions, savored, rolled around on the tongue, and sieved through the mind. Only then will their delicious, richly sweet, and mellow flavor be truly appreciated.

Not only medieval writings, but the works of the ancient Greeks influenced Keats and supplied him with background for his poetry. Charles Cowden Clarke, an old friend and former teacher, first introduced Keats to Greek literature when he presented him with George Chapman's spirited translation of Homer's *Iliad*. To Keats, who knew no Greek, it was a revelation and a delight; he spent the whole night reading it. About ten o'clock the next morning, Keats sent Clarke a communication. It was the following sonnet.

ON FIRST LOOKING INTO CHAPMAN'S HOMER

Much have I traveled in the realms of gold,[1]
And many goodly states and kingdoms seen;
Round many western islands have I been[2]
Which bards in fealty to Apollo[3] hold.
Oft of one wide expanse had I been told   5
That deep-browed Homer ruled as his
        demesne;
Yet did I never breathe its pure serene[4]
Till I heard Chapman speak out loud and
        bold.
Then felt I like some watcher of the skies
When a new planet swims into his ken;   10
Or like stout Cortez[5] when with eagle eyes
He stared at the Pacific—and all his men
Looked at each other with a wild surmise—
Silent, upon a peak in Darien.[6]

1. *traveled . . . gold*, read great books of poetry. 2. *Round . . . been*. Since Keats did not know Greek, he usually had to content himself with books by the bards (poets) of western countries, especially England. 3. *Apollo*, Greek god of poetry and music. 4. *serene*, serene air. 5. *Cortez*. Balboa, not Cortez, discovered the Pacific Ocean in 1513. 6. *Darien* (dar'i ən or dar i en'), a district forming the eastern part of the Isthmus of Panama.

Left above: Portrait of Keats by William Hilton is a copy of a miniature done by Joseph Severn. Severn, who was a gold medalist at the Royal Academy, accompanied Keats to Italy and attended him at his death. Left below: The house in Hampstead, London, where Keats lived with his brothers.

LA BELLE DAME SANS MERCI

*"La Belle Dame sans Merci" (lä bel däm' säN
mer'sē') translated from the French means
"the beautiful lady without pity." The poem
is probably based on the three-centuries-old
ballad "True Thomas," which tells how a man
was enchanted by the queen of Elfland and
lured to her home, where he had to serve her
for seven years. Keats takes up that story after
the seven years are over and the spell has
been broken. The situation in the poem is
considered symbolic of hopeless love and to
reflect the plight of Keats' own love affair.*

O what can ail thee, knight-at-arms!
    Alone and palely loitering!
The sedge has withered from the lake,
    And no birds sing.

"O what can ail thee, knight-at-arms!   5
    So haggard and so woebegone?
The squirrel's granary is full,
    And the harvest's done.

"I see a lily on thy brow
    With anguish moist and fever dew,   10
And on thy cheeks a fading rose
    Fast withereth too."

"I met a lady in the meads,
    Full beautiful—a faery's child,
Her hair was long, her foot was light,   15
    And her eyes were wild.

"I made a garland for her head,
    And bracelets too, and fragrant zone;
She looked at me as she did love,
    And made sweet moan.   20

"I set her on my pacing steed,
    And nothing else saw all day long.
For sidelong would she bend, and sing
    A faery's song.

"She found me roots of relish sweet,   25
    And honey wild and manna-dew;
And sure in language strange she said,
    'I love thee true.'

"She took me to her elfin grot,
    And there she wept and sighed full sore;   30
And there I shut her wild, wild eyes
    With kisses four.

"And there she lullèd me asleep,
    And there I dreamed—ah! woe betide!—
The latest dream I ever dreamed   35
    On the cold hillside.

"I saw pale kings, and princes too,
    Pale warriors, death-pale were they all;
They cried—'La Belle Dame sans Merci
    Hath thee in thrall!'   40

"I saw their starved lips in the gloam
    With horrid warning gapèd wide,
And I woke, and found me here
    On the cold hillside.

"And this is why I sojourn here   45
    Alone and palely loitering,
Though the sedge is withered from the lake,
    And no birds sing."

ODE TO A NIGHTINGALE

*After the death of his brother Tom, Keats
spent nearly a year with a friend, Charles
Armitage Brown, who described the circumstances surrounding the writing of the "Ode
to a Nightingale" as follows:*

*"In the spring a nightingale had built her
nest near my house. Keats felt a tranquil and
continual joy in her song; one morning he
took his chair from the breakfast table to the
grass plot under a plum tree, where he sat for
two or three hours. When he came into the
house, I perceived he had some scraps of paper
in his hand, and these he was quietly thrusting behind the books. On inquiry, I found
those scraps, four or five in number; the
writing was not well legible, and it was difficult to arrange the stanzas. With his assistance I succeeded, and this was his 'Ode to a
Nightingale.'"*

*The poem is a reverie inspired by the bird's
song. In the first stanza the poet is just sinking into the reverie; in the last stanza he comes*

out of it and back to consciousness of the real world. The first and last stanzas constitute a frame for the reverie proper.

My heart aches, and a drowsy numbness pains
    My sense, as though of hemlock[1] I had drunk,
    Or emptied some dull opiate to the drains
        One minute past, and Lethe-wards[2] had sunk.
'Tis not through envy of thy happy lot,   5
    But being too happy in thine happiness—
        That thou, light-wingèd Dryad[3] of the trees,
           In some melodious plot
Of beechen green, and shadows numberless,
        Singest of summer in full-throated ease.   10

O for a draft of vintage! that hath been
    Cooled a long age in the deep-delvèd earth,
Tasting of Flora[4] and the country green,
    Dance, and Provençal song,[5] and sunburnt mirth!
O for a beaker full of the warm South,   15
    Full of the true, the blushful Hippocrene,[6]
        With beaded bubbles winking at the brim,
           And purple-stainèd mouth;
That I might drink, and leave the world unseen,
        And with thee fade away into the forest dim—   20

Fade far away, dissolve, and quite forget
    What thou among the leaves hast never known,
The weariness, the fever, and the fret
    Here, where men sit and hear each other groan;
Where palsy shakes a few, sad, last gray hairs,   25
    Where youth grows pale, and specter-thin, and dies;
        Where but to think is to be full of sorrow
           And leaden-eyed despairs,
Where Beauty cannot keep her lustrous eyes,
        Or new love pine at them beyond tomorrow.   30

Away! away! for I will fly to thee,
    Not charioted by Bacchus[7] and his pards,
But on the viewless wings of poesy,[8]
    Though the dull brain perplexes and retards.
Already with thee! tender is the night,   35
    And haply the Queen-Moon is on her throne,
        Clustered around by all her starry fays;
           But here there is no light,

---

1. *hemlock*, a poison. 2. *Lethe-wards*, towards Lethe (lē'thi), the river of forgetfulness in Hades. 3. *Dryad*, a tree nymph. 4. *Flora*, goddess of the flowers and the spring. 5. *Provençal* (prō'vən säl') *song*. Provence in southern France was famous in the Middle Ages for the songs of its troubadours. 6. *Hippocrene* (hip'ə krēn), a fountain on Mt. Helicon, Greece, sacred to the Muses. 7. *Bacchus* (bak'əs), god of wine, who was often represented as riding in a carriage drawn by leopards (pards), tigers, or other wild beasts. 8. *viewless . . . poesy*, invisible wings of poetry.

Save what from heaven is with the breezes blown
   Through verdurous glooms and winding mossy ways.   40

I cannot see what flowers are at my feet,
   Nor what soft incense hangs upon the boughs,
But, in embalmèd[9] darkness, guess each sweet
   Wherewith the seasonable month endows
The grass, the thicket, and the fruit tree wild;   45
   White hawthorn, and the pastoral eglantine;
      Fast fading violets covered up in leaves;
         And mid-May's eldest child,
The coming muskrose, full of dewy wine,
   The murmurous haunt of flies on summer eves.   50

Darkling I listen; and, for many a time,
   I have been half in love with easeful Death,
Called him soft names in many a musèd rime,
   To take into the air my quiet breath;
Now more than ever seems it rich to die,   55
   To cease upon the midnight with no pain,
      While thou art pouring forth thy soul abroad
         In such an ecstasy!
Still wouldst thou sing, and I have ears in vain—
   To thy high requiem become a sod.   60

Thou wast not born for death, immortal Bird!
   No hungry generations tread thee down;
The voice I hear this passing night was heard
   In ancient days by emperor and clown[10];
Perhaps the selfsame song that found a path   65
   Through the sad heart of Ruth, when sick for home,
      She stood in tears amid the alien corn[11];
         The same that ofttimes hath
Charmed magic casements, opening on the foam
   Of perilous seas, in faery lands forlorn.   70

Forlorn! the very word is like a bell
   To toll me back from thee to my sole self.
Adieu! the fancy cannot cheat so well
   As she is famed to do, deceiving elf.
Adieu! adieu! thy plaintive anthem fades   75
   Past the near meadows, over the still stream,
      Up the hillside; and now 'tis buried deep
         In the next valley glades.
Was it a vision, or a waking dream?
      Fled is that music.—Do I wake or sleep?   80

---

9. *embalmèd*, sweet-smelling. 10. *clown*, peasant. 11. *Ruth . . . corn.* According to the Bible story, Ruth left her homeland to go with Naomi, her mother-in-law, to Judah, a foreign country to her, where she worked in the corn (wheat) fields. (Ruth 2: 1-23.)

About 1800 Thomas Bruce, Earl of Elgin, brought some of the classical sculptures which had for centuries adorned the Parthenon, a temple on the Acropolis at Athens, to England. They were purchased by the government in 1816 and exhibited in the British Museum, where they became known as the Elgin marbles. Here Keats saw them, and inspired by their enduring beauty, wrote the "Ode on a Grecian Urn," which expresses the very essence of his belief about the relationship of truth and beauty.

ODE ON A GRECIAN URN

Thou still unravished bride of quietness,
    Thou foster child of Silence and slow Time,
Sylvan historian, who canst thus express
    A flowery tale more sweetly than our rime—
What leaf-fringed legend haunts about thy shape   5
Of deities or mortals, or of both,
    In Tempe[1] or the dales of Arcady?[2]
What men or gods are these? What maidens loath?
What mad pursuit? What struggle to escape?
    What pipes and timbrels? What wild ecstasy?   10

Heard melodies are sweet, but those unheard
    Are sweeter; therefore, ye soft pipes, play on;
Not to the sensual ear, but, more endeared,
    Pipe to the spirit ditties of no tone.
Fair youth, beneath the trees, thou canst not leave   15
    Thy song, nor ever can those trees be bare;
      Bold lover, never, never canst thou kiss,
    Though winning near the goal—yet, do not grieve;
She cannot fade, though thou hast not thy bliss,
    Forever wilt thou love, and she be fair!   20

Ah, happy, happy boughs! that cannot shed
    Your leaves, nor ever bid the spring adieu;
And, happy melodist, unwearièd,
    Forever piping songs forever new.
More happy love! more happy, happy love!   25
    Forever warm and still to be enjoyed,
      Forever panting, and forever young;
All breathing human passion far above,
That leaves a heart high-sorrowful and cloyed,
    A burning forehead, and a parching tongue.   30

Who are these coming to the sacrifice?
    To what green altar, O mysterious priest,
Lead'st thou that heifer lowing at the skies,
    And all her silken flanks with garlands dressed?
What little town by river or seashore,   35
    Or mountain-built with peaceful citadel,

1. *Tempe* (tem'pi), a beautiful valley in Thessaly, Greece. 2. *Arcady* (är'kə di), Arcadia, a part of ancient Greece, celebrated in pastoral poetry as the home of an ideal shepherd life.

Is emptied of this folk, this pious morn?
And, little town, thy streets forevermore
Will silent be; and not a soul to tell
    Why thou art desolate, can e'er return.   40

O Attic shape!³ Fair attitude! with brede⁴
    Of marble men and maidens overwrought,
With forest branches and the trodden weed;
    Thou, silent form! dost tease us out of thought
As doth eternity: Cold pastoral!   45
    When old age shall this generation waste,
        Thou shalt remain, in midst of other woe
    Than ours, a friend to man, to whom thou say'st,
"Beauty is truth, truth beauty—that is all
    Ye know on earth, and all ye need to know."   50

THE EVE OF ST. AGNES

*"The Eve of St. Agnes" is a lavish and roman-
tic treatment of an old superstition. St. Agnes,
a saint of the Roman Catholic Church, was
martyred in Rome about the year 300. In
early days St. Agnes' Day (Jan. 21) was celebrated by the sacrifice of two lambs, their
wool to be woven later by chosen nuns. In
medieval times it was believed that a girl
could have a vision of her future husband on
St. Agnes' Eve (Jan. 20) if she performed a
certain ritual. The ritual was this: The girl
must fast all day, put on clean garments when
going to bed, and lie on her back as straight
as possible, with her hands under her head.
She must fall asleep as quickly as possible. If
she followed all these rules, her sweetheart
would appear before her in a dream, kiss her,
and feast with her.*

St. Agnes' Eve—Ah, bitter chill it was!
    The owl, for all his feathers, was
        a-cold;
The hare limped trembling through the
        frozen grass,
And silent was the flock in woolly fold:
Numb were the Beadsman's¹ fingers while he
        told   5
His rosary,² and while his frosted breath,
Like pious incense from a censer old,
Seemed taking flight for heaven, without a
        death,

Past the sweet Virgin's picture, while his
        prayer he saith.

His prayer he saith, this patient, holy man; 10
Then takes his lamp, and riseth from his
        knees,
And back returneth, meager, barefoot, wan,
Along the chapel aisle by slow degrees:
The sculptured dead, on each side, seem to
        freeze,
Imprisoned in black, purgatorial rails³: 15
Knights, ladies, praying in dumb orat'ries,
He passeth by, and his weak spirit fails
To think how they may ache in icy hoods
        and mails.

Northward he turneth through a little door,
And scarce three steps, ere Music's
        golden tongue   20
Flattered to tears this aged man and poor;
But no—already had his death-bell rung:
The joys of all his life were said and sung;
His was harsh penance on St. Agnes' Eve:
Another way he went, and soon among   25

ODE ON A GRECIAN URN. **3.** *Attic shape,* a shape representing the simple, elegant taste of Athens, in ancient
Greece. **4.** *brede,* embroidery.

THE EVE OF ST. AGNES. **1.** *Beadsman,* a dependent whose
whole duty was to pray for his benefactor. **2.** *told his rosary,* numbered the beads on his rosary during prayer. **3.**
black, purgatorial rails. Generally, it is assumed that *rails*
means *railings*—"black purgatorial" because the sculptured
dead are in Purgatory. But *rails* may mean *robes* (from Old
English *hraegl*). If so, the dead are sculptured in garments
appropriate for Purgatory.

Rough ashes sat he for his soul's reprieve,
And all night kept awake, for sinners' sake
    to grieve.

That ancient Beadsman heard the prelude
    soft;
And so it chanced, for many a door was wide,
From hurry to and fro. Soon, up aloft,   30
The silver, snarling trumpets 'gan to chide:
The level chambers, ready with their pride,
Were glowing to receive a thousand guests.
The carved angels, ever eager-eyed,
Stared, where upon their heads the cornice
    rests,   35
With hair blown back, and wings put
    crosswise on their breasts.

At length burst in the argent[4] revelry,
With plume, tiara, and all rich array,
Numerous as shadows haunting faerily
The brain new-stuffed, in youth, with
    triumphs gay   40
Of old romance. These let us wish away,
And turn, sole-thoughted, to one Lady there,
Whose heart had brooded, all that wintry day,
On love, and winged St. Agnes' saintly care,
As she had heard old dames full many times
    declare.   45

They told her how, upon St. Agnes' Eve,
Young virgins might have visions of delight,
And soft adorings from their loves receive
Upon the honeyed middle of the night,
If ceremonies due they did aright;   50
As, supperless to bed they must retire,
And couch supine their beauties, lily white;
Nor look behind, nor sideways, but require
Of Heaven with upward eyes for all that
    they desire.

Full of this whim was thoughtful Madeline: 55
The music, yearning like a god in pain,
She scarcely heard: her maiden eyes divine,
Fixed on the floor, saw many a sweeping train
Pass by—she heeded not at all: in vain
Came many a tiptoe, amorous cavalier,   60
And back retired; not cooled by high disdain,
But she saw not: her heart was otherwhere;
She sighed for Agnes' dreams, the sweetest
    of the year.

She danced along with vague, regardless eyes,
Anxious her lips, her breathing quick and
    short: 65
The hallowed hour was near at hand: she
    sighs
Amid the timbrels, and the thronged resort
Of whisperers in anger or in sport;
'Mid looks of love, defiance, hate, and scorn,
Hoodwinked with faery fancy; all amort,[5]   70
Save to St. Agnes and her lambs unshorn,[6]
And all the bliss to be before tomorrow morn.

So, purposing each moment to retire,
She lingered still. Meantime, across the moors,
Had come young Porphyro, with heart on fire
For Madeline. Beside the portal doors,   76
Buttressed from moonlight, stands he, and
    implores
All saints to give him sight of Madeline,
But for one moment in the tedious hours,
That he might gaze and worship all unseen; 80
Perchance speak, kneel, touch, kiss—in sooth
    such things have been.

He ventures in: let no buzzed whisper tell,
All eyes be muffled, or a hundred swords
Will storm his heart, Love's feverous citadel:
For him, those chambers held barbarian
    hordes,   85
Hyena foemen, and hot-blooded lords,
Whose very dogs would execrations howl
Against his lineage; not one breast affords
Him any mercy in that mansion foul,
Save one old beldame, weak in body and in
    soul.   90

Ah, happy chance! the aged creature came,
Shuffling along with ivory-headed wand,
To where he stood, hid from the torch's
    flame,
Behind a broad hall pillar, far beyond
The sound of merriment and chorus bland. 95
He startled her: but soon she knew his face,
And grasped his fingers in her palsied hand,
Saying, 'Mercy, Porphyro! hie thee from this
    place;
They are all here tonight, the whole blood-
    thirsty race!

---

4. *argent*, shining. 5. *amort*, deadened. 6. *lambs un-shorn*. See headnote.

"Get hence! get hence! there's dwarfish
    Hildebrand: 100
He had a fever late, and in the fit
He cursed thee and thine, both house and
    land:
Then there's that old Lord Maurice, not a
    whit
More tame for his gray hairs—Alas me! flit!
Flit like a ghost away."—"Ah, Gossip[7] dear, 105
We're safe enough; here in this arm-chair sit,
And tell me how—" "Good saints! not here,
    not here!
Follow me, child, or else these stones will be
    thy bier."

He followed through a lowly archèd way,
Brushing the cobwebs with his lofty
    plume;   110
And as she muttered "Well-a—well-a-day!"
He found him in a little moonlight room,
Pale, latticed, chill, and silent as a tomb.
"Now tell me where is Madeline," said he,
"O tell me, Angela, by the holy loom   115
Which none but secret sisterhood may see,
When they St. Agnes' wool are weaving
    piously."

"St. Agnes! Ah! it is St. Agnes' Eve—
Yet men will murder upon holy days.
Thou must hold water in a witch's sieve,[8] 120
And be liege-lord of all the Elves and Fays
To venture so: it fills me with amaze
To see thee, Porphyro!—St. Agnes' Eve!
God's help! my lady fair the conjurer plays
This very night: good angels her deceive! 125
But let me laugh awhile,—I've mickle time to
    grieve."

Feebly she laugheth in the languid moon,
While Porphyro upon her face doth look,
Like puzzled urchin on an aged crone
Who keepeth closed a wondrous riddle-
    book,   130
As spectacled she sits in chimney nook.
But soon his eyes grew brilliant, when she
    told
His lady's purpose; and he scarce could brook
Tears, at the thought of those enchantments
    cold,
And Madeline asleep in lap of legends old. 135

Sudden a thought came like a full-blown
    rose,
Flushing his brow, and in his pained heart
Made purple riot: then doth he propose
A stratagem, that makes the beldame start:
"A cruel man and impious thou art!   140
Sweet lady, let her pray, and sleep and dream
Alone with her good angels, far apart
From wicked men like thee. Go, go! I deem
Thou canst not surely be the same that thou
    didst seem."

"I will not harm her, by all saints I
    swear!"   145
Quoth Porphyro: "O may I ne'er find grace
When my weak voice shall whisper its last
    prayer,
If one of her soft ringlets I displace,
Or look with ruffian passion in her face.
Good Angela, believe me, by these tears; 150
Or I will, even in moment's space,
Awake, with horrid shout, my foemen's ears,
And beard them, though they be more fanged
    than wolves and bears."

"Ah! why wilt thou affright a feeble soul?
A poor, weak, palsy-stricken, churchyard
    thing,   155
Whose passing-bell may ere the midnight
    toll;
Whose prayers for thee, each morn and
    evening,
Were never missed." Thus plaining, doth she
    bring
A gentler speech from burning Porphyro;
So woeful, and of such deep sorrowing, 160
That Angela gives promise she will do
Whatever he shall wish, betide her weal or
    woe.

Which was, to lead him, in close secrecy,
Even to Madeline's chamber, and there hide
Him in a closet, of such privacy   165
That he might see her beauty unespied,
And win perhaps that night a peerless bride,
While legioned fairies paced the coverlet,
And pale enchantment held her sleepy-eyed.
Never on such a night have lovers met, 170

---

7. *Gossip,* friend. 8. *hold water . . . sieve.* This was
looked on as a sign of supernatural power.

Since Merlin paid his Demon all the
   monstrous debt.[9]

"It shall be as thou wishest," said the Dame:
"All cates and dainties shall be stored there
Quickly on this feast-night: by the tambour
   frame   174
Her own lute thou wilt see: no time to spare,
For I am slow and feeble, and scarce dare
On such a catering trust my dizzy head.
Wait here, my child, with patience: kneel in
   prayer
The while. Ah! thou must needs the lady wed,
Or may I never leave my grave among the
   dead."   180

So saying she hobbled off with busy fear.
The lover's endless minutes slowly passed;
The dame returned, and whispered in his ear
To follow her; with aged eyes aghast
From fright of dim espial. Safe at last   185
Through many a dusky gallery, they gain
The maiden's chamber, silken, hushed and
   chaste;
Where Porphyro took covert, pleased amain.
His poor guide hurried back with agues in
   her brain.

Her faltering hand upon the balustrade,   190
Old Angela was feeling for the stair,
When Madeline, St. Agnes' charmed maid,
Rose, like a missioned spirit, unaware:
With silver taper's light, and pious care,
She turned and down the aged gossip led   195
To a safe level matting. Now prepare,
Young Porphyro, for gazing on that bed;
She comes, she comes again, like ring-dove
   frayed[10] and fled.

Out went the taper as she hurried in;
Its little smoke, in pallid moonshine, died: 200
She closed the door, she panted, all akin
To spirits of the air, and visions wide:
No uttered syllable, or, woe betide!
But to her heart, her heart was voluble,
Paining with eloquence her balmy side;   205
As though a tongueless nightingale should
   swell
Her throat in vain, and die, heart-stifled, in
   her dell.

A casement high and triple-arched there was,
All garlanded with carven imageries,
Of fruits, and flowers, and bunches of knot-
   grass,   210
And diamonded with panes of quaint device,
Innumerable of stains and splendid dyes,
As are the tiger-moth's deep-damasked wings;
And in the midst, 'mong thousand heraldries,
And twilight saints, and dim emblazonings, 215
A shielded scutcheon blushed with blood of
   queens and kings.

Full on this casement shone the wintry moon,
And threw warm gules[11] on Madeline's fair
   breast,
As down she knelt for Heaven's grace and
   boon;   219
Rose-bloom fell on her hands, together prest,
And on her silver cross soft amethyst,
And on her hair a glory, like a saint:
She seemed a splendid angel, newly drest,
Save wings, for heaven:—Porphyro grew faint:
She knelt, so pure a thing, so free from
   mortal taint.   225

Anon his heart revives: her vespers done,
Of all its wreathed pearls her hair she frees;
Unclasps her warmed jewels one by one;
Loosens her fragrant bodice; by degrees
Her rich attire creeps rustling to her
   knees: 230
Half-hidden, like a mermaid in sea-weed,
Pensive awhile she dreams awake, and sees,
In fancy, fair St. Agnes in her bed,
But dares not look behind, or all the charm
   is fled.   234

Soon, trembling in her soft and chilly nest,
In sort of wakeful swoon, perplexed she lay,
Until the poppied warmth of sleep oppressed
Her soothed limbs, and soul fatigued away;
Flown, like a thought, until the morrow-day;
Blissfully havened both from joy and pain; 240
Clasped like a missal where swart Paynims
   pray[12];

---

9. *Since Merlin . . . debt.* Merlin, the famous wizard of King
Arthur's court, was supposedly descended from demons,
and paid for his existence by being killed by one of his own
spells. 10. *frayed,* frightened. 11. *gules,* red colors from
the stained glass. 12. *Clasped . . . pray,* shut like a prayer
book which pagans would have no occasion to unclasp.

Blinded alike from sunshine and from rain,
As though a rose should shut, and be a bud
  again.

Stolen to this paradise, and so entranced,
Porphyro gazed upon her empty dress,   245
And listened to her breathing, if it chanced
To wake into a slumberous tenderness;
Which when he heard, that minute did he
  bless,
And breathed himself: then from the closet
  crept,
Noiseless as fear in a wide wilderness,   250
And over the hushed carpet, silent, stept,
And 'tween the curtains peeped, where, lo!—
  how fast she slept.

Then by the bed-side, where the faded moon
Made a dim, silver twilight, soft he set
A table, and, half anguished, threw
  thereon   255
A cloth of woven crimson, gold and jet:—
O for some drowsy Morphean amulet![13]
The boisterous, midnight, festive clarion,
The kettle-drum, and far-heard clarinet,
Affray his ears, though but in dying
  tone:—   260
The hall-door shuts again, and all the noise
  is gone.

And still she slept an azure-lidded sleep,
In blanched linen, smooth, and lavendered,
While he from forth the closet brought a
  heap
Of candied apple, quince, and plum, and
  gourd;   265
With jellies soother[14] than the creamy curd,
And lucent syrops, tinct with cinnamon;
Manna and dates, in argosy transferred
From Fez[15]; and spiced dainties, every one,
From silken Samarcand[16] to cedared
  Lebanon.[17]   270

These delicates he heaped with glowing hand
On golden dishes and in baskets bright
Of wreathed silver: sumptuous they stand
In the retired quiet of the night,
Filling the chilly room with perfume
  light.—   275
"And now, my love, my seraph fair, awake!

Thou art my heaven, and I thine eremite[18]:
Open thine eyes, for meek St. Agnes' sake,
Or I shall drowse beside thee, so my soul
  doth ache."

Thus whispering, his warm, unnerved arm   280
Sank in her pillow. Shaded was her dream
By the dusk curtains:—'twas a midnight charm
Impossible to melt as iced stream:
The lustrous salvers in the moonlight gleam;
Broad golden fringe upon the carpet lies: 285
It seemed he never, never could redeem
From such a stedfast spell his lady's eyes;
So mused awhile, entoiled in woofed
  phantasies.[19]

Awakening up, he took her hollow lute,—
Tumultuous,—and, in chords that tenderest
  be,   290
He played an ancient ditty, long since mute,
In Provence called, "La belle dame sans
  mercy"[20]:
Close to her ear touching the melody;—
Wherewith disturbed, she uttered a soft
  moan;
He ceased—she panted quick—and suddenly   295
Her blue affrayed eyes wide open shone:
Upon his knees he sank, pale as smooth-
  sculptured stone.

Her eyes were open, but she still beheld,
Now wide awake, the vision of her sleep:
There was a painful change, that nigh
  expelled   300
The blisses of her dream so pure and deep
At which fair Madeline began to weep,
And moan forth witless words with many a
  sigh,
While still her gaze on Porphyro would keep;
Who knelt, with joined hands and piteous
  eye,   305
Fearing to move or speak, she looked so
  dreamingly.

---

13. *Morphean amulet*, a sleep producing charm. Morpheus
was the god of sleep. 14. *soother*, smoother. 15. *Fez*, a
province of Morocco. 16. *Samarcand*, a city in Turke-
stan, noted for its silks. 17. *Lebanon*, a mountain range in
Syria, famous for its cedars. 18. *eremite*, usually means
"hermit." Keats uses it to mean "devoted follower." 19.
woofed phantasies, confused daydreams. 20. *Provence . . .
mercy*. Alain Chartier, a medieval poet from Provence
wrote a poem with this title, as did Keats (see page 395).

"Ah, Porphyro!" said she, "but even now
Thy voice was at sweet tremble in mine ear,
Made tuneable with every sweetest vow;
And those sad eyes were spiritual and clear: 310
How changed thou art! how pallid, chill, and
    drear!
Give me that voice again, my Porphyro,
Those looks immortal, those complainings
    dear!
Oh, leave me not in this eternal woe,
For if thou diest, my Love, I know not where
    to go." 315

Beyond a mortal man impassioned far
At these voluptuous accents, he arose,
Ethereal, flushed, and like a throbbing star
Seen 'mid the sapphire heaven's deep repose;
Into her dream he melted, as the rose 320
Blendeth its odor with the violet,—
Solution sweet: meantime the frost-wind
    blows
Like Love's alarum, pattering the sharp sleet
Against the window-panes; St. Agnes' moon
    hath set.

'Tis dark: quick pattereth the flaw-blown
    sleet. 325
"This is no dream, my bride, my Madeline!"
'Tis dark: the iced gusts still rave and beat:
"No dream, alas! alas! and woe is mine!
Porphyro will leave me here to fade and
    pine.
Cruel! what traitor could thee hither bring? 330
I curse not, for my heart is lost in thine,
Though thou forsakest a deceived thing;—
A dove forlorn and lost with sick unpruned
    wing."

"My Madeline! sweet dreamer! lovely bride!
Say, may I be for aye thy vassal blest? 335
Thy beauty's shield, heart-shaped and
    vermeil-dyed?
Ah, silver shrine, here will I take my rest
After so many hours of toil and quest,
A famished pilgrim,—saved by miracle.
Though I have found, I will not rob thy
    nest,
Saving of thy sweet self; if thou think'st
    well 340
To trust, fair Madeline, to no rude infidel.

"Hark! 'tis an elfin-storm from faery land,
Of haggard sceming, but a boon indeed:
Arise—arise! the morning is at hand;— 345
The bloated wassailers will never heed;—
Let us away, my love, with happy speed;
There are no ears to hear, or eyes to see,—
Drowned all in Rhenish and the sleepy mead:
Awake! arise! my love, and fearless be, 350
For o'er the southern moors I have a home
    for thee."

She hurried at his words, beset with fears,
For there were sleeping dragons all around,
At glaring watch, perhaps, with ready
    spears—
Down the wide stairs a darkling way they
    found; 355
In all the house was heard no human sound.
A chain-drooped lamp was flickering by each
    door;
The arras, rich with horseman, hawk, and
    hound,
Fluttered in the besieging wind's uproar;
And the long carpets rose along the gusty
    floor. 360

They glide, like phantoms, into the wide
    hall;
Like phantoms, to the iron porch they glide,
Where lay the Porter, in uneasy sprawl,
With a huge empty flagon by his side:
The wakeful bloodhound rose, and shook his
    hide, 365
But his sagacious eye an inmate owns:
By one, and one the bolts full easy slide:—
The chains lie silent on the footworn stones;
The key turns, and the door upon its hinges
    groans.

And they are gone: aye, ages long ago 370
These lovers fled away into the storm.
That night the Baron dreamt of many a woe,
And all his warrior-guests with shade and
    form
Of witch, and demon, and large coffin-worm,
Were long be-nightmared. Angela the old 375
Died palsy-twitched, with meager face deform;
The Beadsman, after thousand aves told,
For aye unsought-for slept among his ashes
    cold.

To increase understanding
A sonnet and a ballad

1. (a) What metaphor does Keats use throughout the first octave of "On First Looking into Chapman's Homer"? (b) What idea does the sestet develop? (c) Is the comparison to "some watcher of the skies" (line 9) or "stout Cortez" (line 11) more effective in relation to the idea of the octave?

2. It was Balboa, not Cortez, who discovered the Pacific. Does this mistake alter the value of the poem? Explain.

3. "La Belle Dame sans Merci" is a *literary,* or *art ballad.* (a) In what ways does it resemble the medieval ballads? (b) How does it differ?

4. (a) What question is asked in this poem? (b) What answer is given?

5. (a) What season is the setting for the poem? (b) Cite details that emphasize this.

6. (a) What is the tone of the ballad? (b) Cite passages that are important in establishing this tone.

7. If the poem is symbolic of hopeless love and reflects Keats' own love affair, you may be able to find references to conditions in Keats' own life. (a) Are such references easily discovered? (b) What does this fact show about Keats' artistry?

Two odes

1. (a) In "Ode to a Nightingale" why does the poet's heart ache (line 1)? (b) How does he first prepare to achieve forgetfulness? (c) Cite the lines that explain why the poet wishes to escape life. (d) What means of escape is he considering in lines 33-34?

2. (a) What transition is indicated by the words "Already with thee!" (line 35)? (b) Cite images Keats uses in describing the forest. (c) To which senses do these images appeal?

3. In stanza 6 the poet realizes that he has been "half in love with easeful Death" (line 52). (a) What is the significance of the word *easeful?* (b) What other details in the stanza develop the idea it suggests?

4. Stanza 7 develops one of Keats' basic ideas—the permanence and changelessness of beauty. Explain how the poet uses the song of the nightingale to express this idea.

5. (a) What causes the end of Keats' reverie? (b) How does the last stanza differ from the preceding stanzas? (c) What effect is created by the closing words, "Do I wake or sleep"?

6. (a) Of five lines of poetry—lines 69-70 of "Ode to a Nightingale" and lines 14-16 of "Kubla Khan" (page 364)—Rudyard Kipling wrote: "These are the magic. These are the vision. The rest is only poetry." To what qualities of these lines do you think Kipling is referring? (b) Why are these lines said to be among the most romantic ever written?

7. (a) In the first three lines of "Ode on a Grecian Urn" what terms does the poet use to characterize the urn? (b) Explain each term.

8. Describe the two scenes pictured on the urn.

9. (a) How do the scenes of the urn differ from actual life? (b) How does the phrase "cold pastoral" (line 45) gather up and summarize the relationship between ideal and actual life?

10. What do the last lines of the ode mean?

11. Summarize the theme of the ode in one sentence.

12. Compare the ideas Keats draws from the urn with stanza 7 of "Ode to a Nightingale."

The Eve of St. Agnes

1. In "The Eve of St. Agnes" Keats devotes the first four stanzas to setting the scene. (a) Why is the first stanza often referred to as the coldest passage in English literature? (b) What does the beadsman represent? (c) What effect is gained by having the poem begin and end with the beadsman? (d) What is happening inside "The level chambers" (line 32)? (e) Why do you think the poet devotes so much attention to setting?

2. (a) How is the heroine introduced? (b) What is her attitude toward the revelry? (c) What is uppermost in her mind?

3. (a) Why does Porphyro come to the castle? (b) Why is it dangerous for him to enter Madeline's home? (c) Who is his one friend in the castle?

4. (a) What warning does the old nurse give to Porphyro? (b) What does she tell him Madeline is planning to do? (c) What decision does Porphyro make when he hears this? (d) What two methods does Porphyro use to make Angela agree to go along with his idea?

5. How does Madeline prepare for the vision she hopes to see?

6. Why do you think Keats describes the casement (lines 208-216) in detail?

7. (a) Describe the feast Porphyro sets. (b) How does the feast fit into the superstition about the Eve of St. Agnes?

8. (a) What is Madeline's reaction upon awakening and finding Porphyro in her room? (b) What plan do the lovers make?

9. Lines 352-369 describe the escape of the lovers. (a) What details in these lines show the danger that they face? (b) What details are added to create an atmosphere of danger?

10. The theme of this poem, the flowering of young love among feuding families, is romantic in itself. Keats heightens the romantic aspects of the poem by the addition of strangeness and beauty in both details and characters. (*a*) What romantic effects do the following lend to the poem: (*1*) the beadsman, (*2*) the old nurse, (*3*) the storm and the cold, and (*4*) the dreams of the drunken Baron and his friends? (*b*) What romantic appeal does the feast described in lines 264-275 have?

11. The plot of "The Eve of St. Agnes" is very similar to the plot of Shakespeare's *Romeo and Juliet.* Both stories are concerned with lovers of feuding families during medieval times. Both are based on an old Italian romance. (*a*) How does the manner in which the stories are told differ? (*b*) How do the endings differ?

Better reading
Keats and the Spenserian stanza

When Edmund Spenser wrote "The Faerie Queene" in the sixteenth century (page 105), he searched for a suitable stanza form among those then in existence. Unable to find one he felt fitted the poem, he invented his own. The Spenserian stanza, as it is called, contains nine iambic lines; each, except the last, contains ten syllables. The last line, which is called an *Alexandrine,* contains twelve syllables and has a pause after the sixth syllable. Only three rhymes are used in each stanza: *a b a b b c b c c.* The interlacing rhymes bind the two quatrains together and produce a feeling of unity; the Alexandrine is bound to the quatrains by rhyme, even while its length separates it from the quatrains, and adds dignity to the stanza. The long Alexandrine is often used to sum up the idea of a stanza. The variety and the differing effects of which the Spenserian stanza is capable make it very suitable for long poems.

When Byron undertook to write a poem about a knight in search of adventure, the Spenserian stanza, with its overtones of the Renaissance, was the natural choice. Byron brightened the romantic aspects of his tale by entitling it *Childe Harold* (*childe* being an archaic word for a youth of noble birth) and sprinkling the early cantos with old words found in "The Faerie Queene." ("Man and Nature," page 380, is taken from *Childe Harold.*)

Spenser was perhaps Keats' strongest literary influence. Keats associated Spenser with adventure and romance, and found the Spenserian stanza to be an ideal vehicle for telling the chivalrous and romantic story of "The Eve of St. Agnes." The poem is set in medieval times—an age when men were ruled by emotion, not reason; a time of bloody battles and family feuds. The Spenserian stanza allowed Keats the freedom necessary to express such feelings and emotions, and, at the same time, to retain the dignity due all old and noble tales.

"The Faerie Queene" is a deliberately slow-moving poem; Spenser probably felt this type of movement was necessary for full appreciation and understanding, and he used the stanza form to slow down the movement. But "The Eve of St. Agnes" is not a difficult or demanding piece of reading, and Keats dispensed with much of the slow movement. The narrative itself, the character interest, and the intensity of the approaching climax lend variety and liveliness to the poem and keep it moving at a fast pace.

Keats varies the pace of the Spenserian stanza by his selection of particular words used in combination and by frequent or infrequent pauses. For example, when in the second stanza he writes of the old beadsman, he creates a slowly moving rhythm through the actual syllable length of various words, through the meaning or the connotation of words, and through frequent pauses. What words in this stanza help create this slow rhythm? With the entrance of the hero the pace quickens. Read aloud lines 82-90. Explain why this stanza moves rapidly. How would you describe the movement of the stanza describing the casement (lines 208-216)? What is the movement of lines 352-369? Does this movement fit the thought expressed? How do these varying paces help to stimulate interest and understanding? Does the unvarying rhyme of the Spenserian stanza make the poem melodious or monotonous? Explain.

But even though Keats abandoned the continuous slow movement of the Spenserian stanza, he has captured much Spenserian flavor in the poem. Typically Spenserian is Keats' use of sensory imagery to add vividness and excitement to the narrative and to heighten the contrasts between the warmth of love and the cold cruelties which threaten it. What are some of the contrasts Keats makes in the poem? In each case, how is sensory imagery used to strengthen these contrasts? How are contrasts used to advance the story?

Keats, in keeping with the disciplined sensuality and richness of verse adapted from Spenser, uses old and archaic words for stylization, just as Spenser used words from Chaucer's time. Find examples of such words and explain their meanings. How do these words add flavor and color to the narrative? Would the present-day forms of the words have done as well?

Does Keats use the Alexandrine as Spenser intended it to be used? Explain by drawing examples from the poem.

The Changing English Language

The years prior to and including those of the Romantic Movement are notable for the beginnings of really serious attempts to improve and correct the spoken language—in other words, to set up a standard of pronunciation. In 1773 William Kendrick published the first dictionary that indicated vowel sounds, and he was quickly copied by both English and American lexicographers. Because many of these men felt that words should be pronounced as they are spelled, there was a tendency to reëstablish older pronunciations, especially in respect to unaccented syllables. This was especially true in America, which was establishing an English of its own. Americans rebelled against the pronunciations of Samuel Johnson, long the accepted English authority. Although Johnson's *Dictionary* (see page 274) had indicated no pronunciations, his poetry through its meter made clear which pronunciations he regarded as standard. Thus in his poem *The Vanity of Human Wishes* the following words obviously are to be pronounced with only two syllables: *venturous, treacherous, powerful, general, history, quivering, flattering,* and *slippery.* Yet, with the possible exception of *general,* they were three-syllable words in America.

It was not until the Romantic Age that Greek began to affect the English language directly. Many new philosophic and scientific names were being added to the language. Combining two or more words or roots from Latin or Greek became a common manner of forming scientific names. This process gave the language such words as *barometer* and *thermometer.* Another method of creating new words was adding Greek prefixes and suffixes such as *micro-* ("small"), *macro-* ("large"), *tele-* ("far"), *per-* ("maximum"), *-oid* ("like"), *-ic* ("smaller"), and *-ous* ("larger") to words already in use. In this manner words like *microscope, macrocosm, telepathy, peroxide, parotoid, sulphuric,* and *sulphurous* were produced.

Partly as a result of the interest of the romanticists in the Middle Ages, words belonging to the past were reintroduced into the language. The imitation of older ballads revived some archaic words found in such poems. Coleridge uses *eftsoons* for *at once, I wis* (from the Middle English *iwis*) for *certainly,* and *een* for *eye.* Keats uses *faeries,* the archaic spelling of *fairies, fay* in place of *faith,* and *sooth* to mean *smooth.* These words, not only old but odd, were scarcely likely to be adopted in conversation, but they served to acquaint readers with the language of England's past. In their search for color the romanticists also included slang and dialect terms, and although these forms are sparsely used in comparison with their use in literature today, they began to find acceptance in writing. Many of the romanticists liked to coin their own words; sometimes, as with *fuzzgig* and *critickasting,* these bordered on the ridiculous.

As you know, the romantic writers were very concerned with bringing naturalness and simplicity back into the language. Consequently some of them felt that borrowed or foreign words should be eliminated from the language because they corrupted the mother tongue. This discrimination against foreign words was not widespread, for English had become quite stabilized. The really outstanding contribution of the Romantic Period to the growth of the English language was its movement away from the rigidity in literature and conversation of the Augustan Age back to the colorful and flexible language of Elizabethan England.

The Larger View

The selections below are from the works of the various writers studied in this unit. Determine how each selection is typical of the writer and what aspects of romanticism it shows. In your analysis consider such points as subject matter, the writer's treatment of the subject, the implicit or explicit purpose of the passage, the construction, and other technical aspects of the selection.

And hark! how blithe the throstle sings!
He, too, is no mean preacher:
Come forth into the light of things,
Let nature be your teacher.

She has a world of ready wealth,
Our minds and hearts to bless—
Spontaneous wisdom breathed by health,
Truth breathed by cheerfulness.

One impulse from a vernal wood
May teach you more of man,
Of moral evil and of good,
Than all the sages can.

—William Wordsworth

It was a lovely sight to see
The lady Christabel, when she
Was praying at the old oak tree.
    Amid the jagged shadows
    Of mossy leafless boughs
    Kneeling in the moonlight,
    To make her gentle vows;
Her slender palms together prest,
Heaving sometimes on her breast;
Her face resigned to bliss or bale—
Her face, oh call it fair not pale,
And both her eyes more bright than clear,
Each about to have a tear.

—Samuel Taylor Coleridge

There is no flavor comparable, I will contend, to that of the crisp, tawny, well-watched, not over-roasted, *crackling*, as it is well called—the very teeth are invited to their share of the pleasure at this banquet in overcoming the coy, brittle resistance—with the adhesive oleaginous—O call it not fat!—but an indefinable sweetness growing up to it—the tender blossoming of fat—fat cropped in the bud—taken in the shoot—in the first inno- cence—the cream and quintessence of the child-pig's yet pure food—the lean, no lean, but a kind of animal manna—or, rather, fat and lean (if it must be so) blended and running into each other, that both together make but one ambrosian result or common substance.

—Charles Lamb

Waken, lords and ladies gay,
On the mountain dawns the day,
All the jolly chase is here,
With hawk and horse and hunting-spear!
Hounds are in their couples yelling,
Hawks are whistling, horns are knelling,
Merrily, merrily, mingle they,
"Waken lords and ladies gay."

—Sir Walter Scott

I have not loved the world, nor the world me;
I have not flattered its rank breath, nor bowed
To its idolatries a patient knee,
Nor coined my cheek to smiles, nor cried aloud
In worship of an echo; in the crowd
They could not deem me one of such; I stood
Amongst them, but not of them; in a shroud
Of thoughts which were not their thoughts,
    and still could,
Had I not filed my mind, which thus itself
    subdued.

—Lord Byron

Music, when soft voices die,
Vibrates in the memory;
Odors, when sweet violets sicken,
Live within the sense they quicken.

Rose leaves, when the rose is dead,
Are heaped for the beloved's bed;
And so thy thoughts, when thou art gone,
Love itself shall slumber on.

—Percy Bysshe Shelley

A thing of beauty is a joy for ever:
Its loveliness increases; it will never
Pass into nothingness; but will keep
A bower quiet for us, and a sleep
Full of sweet dreams, and health, and quiet
    breathing.

—John Keats

Bibliography

AUSLANDER, JOSEPH and FRANK E. HILL, *The Winged Horse.* (Doubleday) Quotations from the works of Byron, Keats, Shelley, and Wordsworth are included in these absorbing biographical sketches.

BENÉT, LAURA, *The Boy Shelley.* (Dodd) Shelley's rebellious boyhood and teen-age years are covered in this entertaining and informative biography.

COLERIDGE, SAMUEL TAYLOR, *The Portable Coleridge.* (••Viking) The poetry, literary criticisms, political essays, notebooks, and letters of Coleridge are well represented in this collection. The biographical sketch, written by I. A. Richards, is particularly interesting.

CRAIK, DINAH M., *John Halifax, Gentleman.* (Harper) John Halifax, a poor orphan, rises through hard work and nobility of character to wealth. His democratic ideals are shown in the assistance he gives factory workers in the early years of the Industrial Revolution.

CROSS, JOHN KEIR, *Blackadder: a Tale of the Days of Nelson and Trafalgar.* (Dutton) In this exciting story two boys identify a sinister smuggler spy. They are in a shipwreck, are captured and imprisoned, but escape and take part in the great sea battle at Trafalgar.

CUNCLIFFE, JOHN WILLIAM, *England in Picture, Song, and Story.* (Appleton) Portraits and brief sketches of famous English writers, together with illustrations of literary landmarks, make this an excellent background book.

KEATS, JOHN, *Poetical Works.* (••Oxford) Try reading Keats outside the classroom. You will find his quietly beautiful poetry extremely satisfying. Be sure to read "The Eve of St. Mark" and "Sleep and Poetry," two of his best and most famous works.

LAMB, CHARLES, *Essays of Elia, and Last Essays of Elia.* (Oxford •Dolphin) Lamb's wonderful essays on many, many subjects will delight and entertain you as only Lamb can.

LAMB, CHARLES and MARY, *Tales from Shakespeare.* (Dutton •Bantam) Twenty of Shakespeare's plays are retold in this great English classic. Charles Lamb worked on the tragedies, his sister on the comedies.

ORCZY, BARONESS EMMUSKA, *The Scarlet Pimpernel.* (Putnam •Dolphin) This famous tale of the French Revolution concerns a mysterious and elusive gentleman who helps many French royalists escape the guillotine.

PEARSON, HESKETH, *Sir Walter Scott: His Life and Personality.* (Harper) This biography reflects the heroic quality of Scott's life and his tremendous energy. You will find him to be a very human and likeable man.

QUENNELL, MARJORIE and CHARLES H. B., *The History of Everyday Things in England.* (Putnam) Volume 3 of this valuable series, entitled "The Rise of Industrialism, 1733-1851," deals with important inventions and improvements in agriculture, transportation, and trades.

SABATINI, RAFAEL, *Scaramouche.* (Houghton) Here is another colorful and romantic story of the French Revolution, by an author noted for his exciting plots.

SCOTT, SIR WALTER, *Ivanhoe.* (Nelson •Collier) Probably the most popular of Scott's novels, this is the story of a knight who lived in the period immediately following the Norman conquest of Britain. Fair ladies, attacks, counterattacks, and conspiracies can be found here in abundance. *Kenilworth* (Nelson •Collier), best known as a marvelous portrayal of Queen Elizabeth, also tells the intriguing story of the overly ambitious Earl of Leicester and the beautiful wife he ignores except to insult. *Quentin Durward* (Nelson •Collier) is not only a good history of France in the Middle Ages, but also tells the exciting story of a member of the Scottish guards and his love for a countess. *The Talisman* (Nelson) is laid against a background of the Crusades. Richard the Lion-Hearted and his enemy Saladin are the principal characters.

SELINKO, ANNEMARIE, *Désirée.* (Morrow •Pocket Books) Désirée, the woman who broke her engagement to Napoleon so that he might marry Josephine, is powerfully portrayed in this excellent novel. The author also describes in vivid detail the rise and fall of Napoleon, and his attempts to maneuver his family into positions of power in the government.

SHELLEY, PERCY BYSSHE, *Poetry.* (••Oxford) Shelley's fiery personality, his love of beauty, and his unmatched imagination are all evident in his poetry. If you like poetry with depth and feeling, you will like to read Shelley.

WORDSWORTH, WILLIAM, *Poetry.* (••Oxford.) To gain new understanding and appreciation of nature read Wordsworth's nature lyrics. These beautifully written poems were created by the poet to spread to others the joy he found in the outdoors.

•paperback only ••paperback and hardcover

THE
VICTORIAN
AGE 1837-1901

Annabelle and Caroline in their crinolines and ringlets sit beside a cozy fire with an edition of Thomas Bowdler's *Shakespeare* carefully expurgated for family reading. A bustled, high-bodiced matron glances up from some religious tract to survey her accumulation of overstuffed chairs, bric-a-brac, wax flowers, plaster busts, iron statuettes, glass ducks, and Landseer's painting of a dog. Enter father, the proud, prompt, methodical, sensible, enormously wealthy Captain of Industry, who glories in the thought that the sun never sets on the British Empire, who opposes any effort on the part of the government to regulate the business world, and who regards poverty solely as a consequence of improvidence, shiftlessness, immorality, and laziness. This exaggerated picture of the Victorian sitting room with its useless and prudish women and its smug men of business is, like all exaggerations, partly true and partly false. Many Victorians were so satisfied with their own comfortable positions that they could not see the poverty of others; and many were shocked and horrified by even minor infractions of the straight-laced code of respectability that they had set up; but, as you will see from your study of this chapter, other Victorians revolted against the typical trends of the time or quietly directed their attention elsewhere. Far from exhibiting a single style, the time spanned by the reign of Queen Victoria (1837-1901) was one of the most varied and diverse periods in the history of English life and letters.

THE NEW CODE OF CONDUCT In Victorian England those who wished to be thought respectable adhered to the regulations of a strict code. Sundays were observed not only by church attendance but also by almost puritanic prohibitions against amusements, even against reading anything but the Bible or tracts published by the Society for Promoting Christian Knowledge (known, in brief, as the SPCK) or similar groups.

The qualities of the model man and, especially, of the model female were described in other semireligious publications. Women were expected to be frail, fainting, proper creatures, the quintessence of uselessness and prudery (according to modern standards). Hannah More, a leader in the Sunday School movement and the most popular writer of books to teach propriety, offered advice upon the subject of earning a living, if the female was reduced to such circumstances. Under these unfortunate conditions she might teach, do social work, deliver Bibles and religious tracts, perhaps work in a milliner's shop or an undertaker's establishment, or fill other positions in which "she could protect her feminine sensibilities."

For the model male the code prescribed equally rigid rules and prohibitions. Gambling, swearing, drunkenness, sometimes even smoking, automatically removed a man from the ranks of the respectable. Many of the older forms of entertainment had fallen into disrepute. Ranelagh (see page 247) with its gambling pavilion had been closed in 1803. The old spectacles of public hangings and floggings had been abolished. Taverns were closed on Sundays and coffee houses were giving way to public reading rooms and clubs. Dr. Samuel Johnson would have called it a dull world.

Queen Victoria and the Prince Consort and their Eldest Children in 1846, by Frans Xavier Winterhalter.

QUEEN VICTORIA The Supreme symbol of respectability was the queen who gave her name to the age. Victoria had spent a sheltered childhood at Kensington Palace with her mother and her governess, both of whom had trained her in accordance with the prevailing code. She must read the Bible and works of Hannah More as well as sermons and religious tracts; she must attend Divine Service on Sunday; and she must diligently practice all the virtues prescribed for the model female. "I will be good," Victoria had said when, at the age of twelve, she was told that some day she would be Queen of England.

Victoria was eighteen when, in 1837, upon the death of her weak and incompetent old uncle William IV, she ascended the throne. Within three years she married Prince Albert of Saxe-Coburg. Her love for this quiet, scholarly, German-born prince and for her nine children endeared the Queen to her subjects, with whom she appeared to be in complete harmony. The climax of her reign came in 1897 with a Diamond Jubilee to celebrate the sixtieth anniversary of her coming to the throne. Four years later she died. So well attuned had she been throughout her long life to the ideas and ideals of the century in which she lived that the term *Victorian* has come to stand not only for a period of time but also for a particular outlook on life.

*Opposite: Queen Victoria
and the Duke of Wellington
reviewing the Life Guards,
by Sir Edwin Landseer. Most
famous for his paintings of
dogs, Landseer also did
numerous paintings of the
Royal Family. Below:
illustrations showing some of
the evils of the Industrial
Revolution.*

On May 1, 1851, Victoria opened the first world's fair—the "Great Exhibition of the Works of Industry of all Nations"—at the mammoth Crystal Palace in London, thereby announcing that the Industrial Revolution had come of age. Ushered in by the spinning jenny of Hargreaves in 1764, the improved spinning machines of Arkwright in 1779, and the power loom of Cartwright in 1784, the Industrial Revolution gathered force as the nineteenth century progressed, working profound changes on both the face and personality of the English nation. Sleepy villages, town criers, sailing vessels, and hand looms gave way within a hundred years to factory towns, cheap newspapers, railroads and steamships, and machines for mass production—all the mechanical paraphernalia that lie behind the enormous efficiency and prosperity of the modern Western world. The position in English society that had been held since the Middle Ages by the landed aristocracy gradually diminished in importance as the middle-class industrialists increased in numbers and in wealth; and the rural peasantry decreased while the wage-earning workers of the towns multiplied.

Foremost among the problems of the Victorian Age was that of coping with the seven deadly sins of the Industrial Revolution—filthy, dangerous factories; inhumanly long hours of work; child labor; exploitation of women workers; low wages; slums; and frequent unemployment. For many years these were the fiendish facts of life for workers in the growing industries. The dismal debut of this class onto the scene of history stands preserved in many Victorian writings, particularly the novels of Charles Dickens, who described the industrial center in *Hard Times* as

. . . a town of red brick, or of brick that would have been red if the smoke and ashes had allowed it; but as matters stood it was a town of unnatural red and black, like the painted face of a savage. It was a town of machinery and tall chimneys, out of which inter-

minable serpents of smoke trailed themselves for ever and ever, and never got
uncoiled. It had a black canal in it, and a river that ran purple with ill-smell-
ing dye, and vast piles of buildings full of windows where there was a rattling
and trembling all day long, and where the piston of the steam-engine worked
monotonously up and down, like the head of an elephant in a state of melancholy madness.

ENGLAND The responses to the problems of the Industrial Revolution were many
BECOMES A and varied. The Captains of Industry, who owned the mines and the
DEMOCRACY factories, supported a policy of *laissez faire*, or no regulation of trade and
industry by government. John Stuart Mill and other famous economists
believed that in general *laissez faire* was a good policy, but that it was
wrong to ignore completely the plight of the working classes. Mill advocated legislation that would improve factory conditions and give the
workers the right to vote. The Socialists went further than Mill, supporting not merely government regulation of factories but gradual government ownership of the industries themselves. Karl Marx and his followers
called for immediate and, if necessary, violent seizure of the entire industrial complex.

True to their age-old tradition of slow but steady change, the English
adopted the moderate position of people like John Stuart Mill. Through-
The House of out the Victorian era the Whig or Liberal party and the Tory or Con-
Commons in 1833. servative party vied with one another to see who would get credit for
Painting is by improving the social, economic, and political status not only of workers
Sir George but of people in general. Of the vast number of different reforms passed
Hayter, who was by the Victorian Parliaments, the two outstanding bills were those of 1867
made painter to and 1884-1885, the first extending the franchise to urban workers, the
the Queen in second enfranchising workers in agricultural districts. By 1911, the year
1837.

in which the House of Lords was deprived of all power except a delaying veto, England had become a modern democracy in which the people, through their representatives in the House of Commons, were politically sovereign.

SCIENCE In 1859 the biologist Charles Darwin published his *Origin of Species*, a book that was to produce a revolution in thought as radical and far-reaching as that brought about in the seventeenth century by the scientific discoveries of Galileo and Newton. In spite of the work of Charles Lyell (1797-1875) and other geologists demonstrating the great age of the earth, most people in mid-nineteenth century accepted literally the account of Creation given in the Bible, according to which all forms of life had appeared on earth about six thousand years ago in the space of a single week. Darwin went beyond his predecessors. After years of studying the work of earlier scientists and of collecting and analyzing his own biological data, he not only agreed with earlier conclusions about the age of the earth but also concluded that instead of all forms of life appearing at once complex forms had evolved from simpler ones during a great struggle for existence in which only the fittest survived. Although many people eventually came to see that there was no real conflict between the teachings of religion and the findings of the new biology, Darwin's work had the initial effect of throwing many individuals into doubts about their religious beliefs. Some people remained in a state of doubt. Others passed from doubt to despair. Still others reacted by renouncing science in favor of faith or giving up faith in favor of science.

Like the theories of Newton, Darwin's ideas were picked up by many nonscientists. The Captains of Industry, for example, were happy to hear that they were engaged in a struggle for existence with the members of the working class—a struggle in which the rich and hardworking were fit to survive and the poor and lazy were doomed to perish. The advocates of British imperialism felt that the struggle for existence was not so much between classes as it was between nations. To these people Britain was the nation fittest for survival, for the British flag had been carried into almost every part of the habitable world and was actually flying over a territory five times the size of all Europe.

"The Patent Impulsoria," an invention designed to replace the steam locomotive, and actually tried on the Southwestern Railway.

With such weighty problems as the Industrial Revolution and
Darwin's theory of evolution to disturb them, it is no wonder
that the Victorians abandoned the romantic vision attained by
people like Coleridge and Shelley to concentrate on the more
sober and practical aspects of life. They were supremely conscious of factories to build and run, machines to improve and
invent, legislation to pass, and the world of science to explore;
and to do all this well one had to have a pretty hard-headed
and realistic outlook. Nevertheless, romantic themes, particularly an interest in nature and in medievalism, did persist into
the Victorian era. Writers like Thomas Carlyle saw in the
Middle Ages a model on which contemporary life should pattern itself, while Alfred Lord Tennyson, William Morris, and
others retold for a Victorian audience the legends of King
Arthur and his Round Table.

The variety of attitudes and activities that make up the
Victorian Age is almost as bewildering as the array of what-nots
found in the Victorian sitting room, the sweep of gingerbread
decorations ornamenting the Victorian house, or the vistas of
stone statesmen and soldiers frowning down on Victorian
squares and parks. Realism and romanticism, poverty-stricken
workers and progressive legislation, hope and despair, faith
and doubt—these are but a few of the aspects of the highly
diverse age that immediately precedes our own even more
complex times.

In the midst of the irreducible variety of the later nineteenth century stood the figure of the Queen, who, like her predecessor Elizabeth, gave her name to an age. But while the aristocratic and Renaissance Queen Elizabeth had made merry with dancing, drinking, and singing and had ruled her country with an iron hand, Victoria practiced the pious and decorous arts of the housewife, leaving the affairs of the nation to such able ministers as Gladstone and Disraeli. In 1876 Disraeli bestowed upon Victoria the title of Empress of India, thus uniting in the person of the Queen both respectability and imperial might. Middle-class merchants and shopkeepers and tradesmen looking fondly on their beloved Queen might well ponder how far their class had come since the Middle Ages. From medieval guildsmen to Renaissance merchants, from Renaissance merchants to eighteenth- and nineteenth-century prime ministers and industrialists—the success of this long climb was testified to by the fact that Queen Victoria was a thoroughly middle-class monarch. In her home and in England at large there reigned a sense of pious respectability and of worldwide commercial leadership.

Below: The sitting room at Osborne, Queen Victoria's retreat on the Isle of Wight. Opposite above: A vase at Osborne House, gift of King Christian II of Denmark on the occasion of the 1887 Jubilee. Opposite, below: A view of the famous Crystal Palace during the Exhibition of 1851.

Thomas Babington Macaulay 1800-1859

Portrait of Macaulay by Sir Francis Grant, fashionable portrait painter and president of the Royal Academy.

By temperament and talents Thomas Babington Macaulay was admirably suited to become an eminent Victorian. Born a commoner, his work earned him a peerage as Baron Macaulay of Rothley (Rothley was his birthplace). His first contribution to the *Edinburgh Review*—the essay on Milton (see quotations from this essay, page 196)—brought him at the age of twenty-five immediate and widespread fame as a man of letters, a fame that endured throughout his life. He was equally successful in politics. Elected to Parliament in 1830, his brilliant first speech in favor of the Reform Bill of 1832 (see page 344) made him a valued member of the Whig party and led ultimately to various important political offices. Nor was money a problem. His *History of England* was immediately successful, was translated into many languages, and made him a wealthy man.

For the first part of his life Macaulay devoted most of his time and attention to public affairs. As a Whig and a believer in the *laissez-faire* theory of government, Macaulay was an enthusiastic spokesman for the Victorian middle class. His view was essentially optimistic. He saw industrial expansion, material accomplishments, and the growth of cities as synonymous with the progress of civilization. This viewpoint is strongly reflected in his great *History of England*.

From his childhood Macaulay had been drawn toward history. A precocious child, at the age of eight he had written *A Compendium of Universal History*. Significantly, another work of his childhood was a romance of three cantos in the style of Scott entitled *The Battle of Cheviot*. For Macaulay wrote history as Scott wrote novels—with zest, excitement, and a flair for telling a good story. Macaulay's skill as a storyteller is shown also in *The Lays of Ancient Rome* (1842), narrative poems that in their own time were as popular as his history.

The first two volumes of a *History of England from the Accession of James II*, which Macaulay regarded as his life work, appeared in 1848. Volumes III and IV were published in 1855. Macaulay was working on the fifth volume, which brought the history down to the death of William III, when he died in 1859. Macaulay saw history as a pageant of light and shadow, contrast and change, suspense and excitement. At times his desire for dramatic contrast led him to oversimplify. Factual material and human emotions that other historians had regarded as beneath the dignity of history made their way in rich, vast quantity from his astonishing memory into his account of the English past. His facts are accurate, but his interpretation of facts bears the impress of his attitudes and prejudices. The selection from the famous third chapter of the *History* is Macaulay at his vivid best.

ENGLAND IN 1685

from HISTORY OF ENGLAND, VOLUME I

The market place which the rustic can now reach with his cart in an hour was, a hundred and sixty years ago, a day's journey from him. The street which now affords to the artisan, during the whole night, a secure, a convenient, and a brilliantly lighted walk was, a hundred and sixty years ago, so dark after sunset that he would not have been able to see his hand, so ill-paved that he would have run constant risk of breaking his neck, and so ill-watched that he would have been in imminent danger of being knocked down and plundered of his small earnings. Every bricklayer who falls from a scaffold, every sweeper of a crossing who is run over by a carriage, may now have his wounds dressed and his limbs set with a skill such as, a hundred and sixty years ago, all the wealth of a great lord like Ormond, or of a merchant prince like Clayton, could not have purchased. Some frightful diseases have been extirpated by science; and some have been banished by police. The term of human life has been lengthened over the whole kingdom, and especially in the towns. The year 1685 was not accounted sickly; yet in the year 1685 more than one in twenty-three of the inhabitants of the capital died. At present only one inhabitant in forty dies annually. The difference in salubrity between the London of the nineteenth century and the London of the seventeenth century is very far greater than the difference between London in an ordinary season and London in the cholera.

Still more important is the benefit which all orders of society, and especially the lower orders, have derived from the mollifying influence of civilization on the national character. The groundwork of that character has indeed been the same through many generations, in the sense in which the groundwork of the character of an individual may be said to be the same when he is a rude and thoughtless schoolboy and when he is a refined and accomplished man. It is pleasing to reflect that the public mind of England has softened while it has ripened, and that we have, in the course of ages, become, not only a wiser, but also a kinder people. There is scarcely a page of the history or lighter literature of the seventeenth century which does not contain some proof that our ancestors were less humane than their posterity. The discipline of workshops, of schools, of private families, though not more efficient than at present, was infinitely harsher. Masters, well born and bred, were in the habit of beating their servants. Pedagogues knew no way of imparting knowledge but by beating their pupils. Husbands, of decent station, were not ashamed to beat their wives. The implacability of hostile factions was such as we can scarcely conceive. Whigs were disposed to murmur because Stafford[1] was suffered to die without seeing his bowels burned before his face. Tories reviled and insulted Russell as his coach passed from the Tower to the scaffold in Lincoln's Inn Fields.[2] As little mercy was shown by the populace to sufferers of a humbler rank. If an offender was put into the pillory, it was well if he escaped with life from the shower of brickbats and paving stones. If he was tied to the cart's tail, the crowd pressed round him, imploring the hangman to give it the fellow well, and make him howl. Gentlemen arranged parties of pleasure to Bridewell[3] on court days, for the purpose of seeing the wretched women who beat hemp[4] there whipped. A man pressed to death[5] for refusing to plead, a woman burned for coining,[6] excited less sympathy than is now felt for a galled horse or an over-

1. *Stafford.* William Howard, 1st Viscount Stafford (1614-1680), a member of the Tory party, was executed for high treason. 2. *Russell . . . Inn Fields.* William Russell (1639-1683), a member of the Whig party, was hanged at Lincoln's Inn Fields, London's largest public square, for high treason. 3. *Bridewell,* at the time this was written, a workhouse and house of correction. 4. *women who beat hemp.* Women sentenced to Bridewell were given the task of beating the rotted stems of hemp either with their fists or with wooden mallets to detach the fiber. 5. *pressed to death.* This was a form of punishment formerly inflicted on persons arraigned for serious crimes who refused to plead either guilty or not guilty. The body was pressed with heavy weights until the prisoner either pleaded or died. 6. *coining,* counterfeiting.

driven ox. Fights compared with which a boxing match is a refined and humane spectacle were among the favorite diversions of a large part of the town. Multitudes assembled to see gladiators hack each other to pieces with deadly weapons, and shouted with delight when one of the combatants lost a finger or an eye. The prisons were hells on earth, seminaries of every crime and of every disease. At the assizes the lean and yellow culprits brought with them from their cells to the dock an atmosphere of stench and pestilence which sometimes avenged them signally on bench, bar, and jury. But on all this misery society looked with profound indifference. Nowhere could be found that sensitive and restless compassion which has, in our time, extended a powerful protection to the factory child, to the Hindu widow, to the Negro slave, which pries into the stores and water-casks of every emigrant ship, which winces at every lash laid on the back of a drunken soldier, which will not suffer the thief in the hulks to be ill-fed or overworked, and which has repeatedly endeavored to save the life even of the murderer. It is true that compassion ought, like all other feelings, to be under the government of reason, and has, for want of such government, produced some ridiculous and some deplorable effects. But the more we study the annals of the past the more shall we rejoice that we live in a merciful age, in an age in which cruelty is abhorred, and in which pain, even when deserved, is inflicted reluctantly and from a sense of duty. Every class doubtless has gained largely by this great moral change: but the class which has gained most is the poorest, the most dependent, and the most defenseless.

The general effect of the evidence which

The Edinburgh Review

In October of 1802, three outspoken young men established a periodical which they called *The Edinburgh Review*. These men—Francis Jeffrey, Henry Brougham, and Sydney Smith —initiated a new era in literary criticism, for they adopted a highly independent and controversial tone that their predecessors had lacked. The *Review* commented on literature, art, science, politics, public events, and current books. These comments were very seldom filled with flattering opinions and nicely written platitudes; more often they were extremely critical—sometimes most unconstructively and unnecessarily so.

During its early years, contributors to the *Review* were conservatives, and one of their primary targets was the Lake Poets. They ridiculed, rebuked, and insulted the revolutionary poetry of Wordsworth and his followers at every opportunity. Their criticism was not limited to English writers, and about American literature Smith asked: "In the four quarters of the globe, who reads an American book? or goes to an American play? or looks at an American picture?"

At times the *Review* itself was assaulted. Following a harsh criticism of his first book of poetry, Byron attacked the *Review* with his brilliantly satirical *English Bards and Scotch Reviewers*. Of critics, he wrote "Fools are my theme, let satire be my song," and he continued:

And shall we own such judgment? no—as soon
Seek roses in December—ice in June;
Hope constancy in wind, or corn in chaff;
Believe a woman or an epitaph,
Or any other thing that's false, before
You trust in critics, who themselves are sore.

The *Edinburgh Review* is no longer published—the last issue appeared in 1929. During the Victorian Age it gradually became more liberal and less controversial. Ranked as one of the nations leading periodicals, it published some of the finest prose of the Victorian period. Among its contributors were Macaulay, Carlyle, and Arnold.

has been submitted to the reader seems hardly to admit of doubt. Yet, in spite of evidence, many will still imagine to themselves the England of the Stuarts as a more pleasant country than the England in which we live. It may at first sight seem strange that society, while constantly moving forward with eager speed, should be constantly looking backward with tender regret. But these two propensities, inconsistent as they may appear, can easily be resolved into the same principle. Both spring from our impatience of the state in which we actually are. That impatience, while it stimulates us to surpass preceding generations, disposes us to overrate their happiness. It is, in some sense, unreasonable and ungrateful in us to be constantly discontented with a condition which is constantly improving. But, in truth, there is constant improvement precisely because there is constant discontent. If we were perfectly satisfied with the present, we should cease to contrive, to labor, and to save with a view to the future. And it is natural that, being dissatisfied with the present, we should form a too favorable estimate of the past.

In truth we are under a deception similar to that which misleads the traveler in the Arabian desert. Beneath the caravan all is dry and bare: but far in advance, and far in the rear, is the semblance of refreshing waters. The pilgrims hasten forward and find nothing but sand where, an hour before, they had seen a lake. They turn their eyes and see a lake where, an hour before, they were toiling through sand. A similar illusion seems to haunt nations through every stage of the long progress from poverty and barbarism to the highest degrees of opulence and civilization. But, if we resolutely chase the mirage backward, we shall find it recede before us into the regions of fabulous antiquity. It is now the fashion to place the golden age of England in times when noblemen were destitute of comforts the want of which would be intolerable to a modern footman, when farmers and shopkeepers breakfasted on loaves the very sight of which would cause a riot in a modern workhouse, when men died faster in the purest country air than they now die in the most pestilential lanes of our towns, and when men

died faster in the lanes of our towns than they now die on the coast of Guiana.[7] We too shall, in our turn, be outstripped, and in our turn be envied. It may well be, in the twentieth century, that the peasant of Dorsetshire may think himself miserably paid with fifteen shillings a week; that the carpenter at Greenwich may receive ten shillings a day; that laboring men may be as little used to dine without meat as they now are to eat rye bread; that sanitary police and medical discoveries may have added several more years to the average length of human life; that numerous comforts and luxuries which are now unknown, or confined to a few, may be within the reach of every diligent and thrifty working man. And yet it may then be the mode to assert that the increase of wealth and the progress of science have benefited the few at the expense of the many, and to talk of the reign of Queen Victoria as the time when England was truly merry England, when all classes were bound together by brotherly sympathy, when the rich did not grind the faces of the poor, and when the poor did not envy the splendor of the rich.

---

7. *Guiana*, probably a reference to Dutch Guiana, which was plagued by yellow fever.

❋ To increase understanding

1. (*a*) Cite examples Macaulay uses to compare England in 1685 with Victorian England in the following areas: (1) transportation, (2) illumination, (3) health, (4) humaneness. (*b*) Which age does Macaulay see as having greater advantages? (*c*) How does this opinion reflect a typical Victorian viewpoint?

2. Concerning "the mollifying influence of civilization on the national character," Macaulay states that "the class which has gained most is the poorest, the most dependent, and the most defenseless" (page 420, column 2, line 17). Explain why you agree or disagree with this opinion.

3. Macaulay writes: ". . . in spite of evidence, many will still imagine to themselves the England of the Stuarts as a more pleasant country than the England in which we live" (page 421, column 1, line 2). (*a*) Why, according to Macaulay, is this a commonly held opinion? (*b*) In what way does he believe this manner of thinking advances society?

Thomas Carlyle 1795-1881

The dour Scotchman Thomas Carlyle differed in almost every respect from his affable and optimistic contemporary, Baron Macaulay. While Macaulay was comfortably at home in the prevailing moral and political thought of Victorian England, Carlyle rebelled against practically every aspect of contemporary life. A stormy individualist who was uncompromising in his beliefs, Carlyle raised his voice against materialism and the doctrine of *laissez faire*, against democracy and social reform. His constant emphasis was on the necessity of spiritual values.

Carlyle was born of humble parents in Ecclefechan, Dumfriesshire. The boy was strongly influenced by his father, later paying tribute to his "flash of just insight" and "sterling sincerity"; and undoubtedly the inspiration of his father's integrity was a strong element in the son's lifelong hatred of pretense and sham. Carlyle attended the University of Edinburgh, but left in 1814 without taking a degree. He was undetermined about his future. He abandoned the idea of becoming a minister, an idea his parents had long fostered; and after a year of teaching, he turned from this profession. He began to write; and his first works, among which are a life of Schiller and a translation from Goethe, reveal an interest in German thought which is apparent in many of his later works.

In 1826 Carlyle married the charming and brilliant Jane Welsh, and two years later they retired to her isolated farm at Craigenputtock for six years. While there Carlyle wrote *Sartor Resartus*, which contains the essence of his social philosophy, and his famous essay on Robert Burns. The years at Craigenputtock were among the most decisive in Carlyle's life. He went there an obscure writer; when he emerged, he was recognized as one of the foremost literary men in England.

Carlyle spent the rest of his long life in London. From his residence at 5 Cheyne Row, Chelsea, issued a long series of books, first of which was his *French Revolution* (1837), a brilliant history as exciting in style as in content. Carlyle, who was essentially undemocratic and did not believe that men were created equal, disapproved of the French Revolution and saw it as a failure of leadership. To use his own term, the Revolution lacked "heroes." He pursued this theme of the necessity of the hero and the importance of the individual in *On Heroes, Hero-Worship, and the Heroic in History* (1841). According to Carlyle, history is merely "the essence of innumerable biographies." Leaders create history; for good or evil they so plant their imprint upon it that a given age and its characteristics can be said to be a biography of its leader.

Past and Present (1843) is concerned with Carlyle's economic and industrial theories. Recognizing the grim reality of the problems facing Victorian society, he yet had no real faith in the efficacy of legislative and social action to right the wrongs. He believed reform must spring from spiritual sources. Taking inspiration from the social and religious structure of the Middle Ages, he cited the moral responsibility of the aristocracy and the Captains of Industry—the equivalents of the churchmen and nobles of the Middle Ages—to exert themselves to provide wise guidance and faithful compensation to the workers.

As Carlyle grew older, he became even more intolerant of the democratic process, coming in time to believe that a benevolent dictator was preferable to elected representatives. On this point he disagreed with his friend Ralph Waldo Emerson. While the two men agreed on the importance of the individual and the necessity of spiritual values, Emerson championed the American concept of the free choice of free men.

Charles Dickens and Alfred Tennyson, Matthew Arnold and Robert Browning were all to some extent influenced by Carlyle. He was the first great prophet of the Victorian Age. Often unreasonable, sometimes hysterical, but always worth reading, he struck out in his eccentric, vigorous style against complacency, materialism, and hypocrisy.

MIDAS

from PAST AND PRESENT

Opposite: Sketch by Daniel Maclise, a friend of Dickens and a noted illustrator of Dickens and Tennyson. Below: Carlyle's house in Chelsea, London.

The condition of England, on which many pamphlets are now in the course of publication, and many thoughts unpublished are going on in every reflective head, is justly regarded as one of the most ominous, and withal one of the strangest, ever seen in this world. England is full of wealth, of multifarious produce, supply for human want in every kind; yet England is dying of inanition. With unabated bounty the land of England blooms and grows; waving with yellow harvests; thick-studded with workshops, industrial implements, with fifteen millions of workers, understood to be the strongest, the cunningest and the willingest our earth ever had; these men are here; the work they have done, the fruit they have realized is here, abundant, exuberant on every hand of us: and behold, some baleful fiat as of Enchantment has gone forth, saying, "Touch it not, ye workers, ye master-workers,[1] ye master-idlers[2]; none of you can touch it, no man of you shall be the better for it; this is enchanted fruit!" On the poor workers such fiat falls first, in its rudest shape; but on the rich master-workers too it falls; neither can the rich master-idlers, nor any richest or highest man escape, but all are like to be brought low with it, and made "poor" enough, in the money sense or a far fataler one.

1. *master-workers*, industrial owners. 2. *master-idlers*, landowning aristocracy.

Of these successful skillful workers some two millions, it is now counted, sit in workhouses, poor-law prisons; or have "outdoor relief" flung over the wall to them[3]—the workhouse Bastille being filled to bursting, and the strong poor law broken asunder by a stronger. They sit there, these many months now; their hope of deliverance as yet small. In workhouses, pleasantly so-named, because work cannot be done in them. Twelve hundred thousand workers in England alone; their cunning right hand lamed, lying idle in their sorrowful bosom; their hopes, outlooks, share of this fair world, shut in by narrow walls. They sit there, pent up, as in a kind of horrid enchantment; glad to be imprisoned and enchanted, that they may not perish starved. The picturesque tourist, in a sunny autumn day, through this bounteous realm of Eng-

land, descries the union workhouse on his path. "Passing by the workhouse of St. Ives in Huntingdonshire, on a bright day last autumn," says the picturesque tourist, "I saw sitting on wooden benches, in front of their Bastille and within their ringwall and its railings, some half-hundred or more of these men. Tall robust figures, young mostly or of middle age; of honest countenance, many of them thoughtful and even intelligent-looking men. They sat there, nearby one another; but in a kind of torpor, especially in a silence, which was very striking. In silence: for, alas, what

---

3. *workhouses . . . them.* The able-bodied poor were sent to workhouses where they labored for very small salaries; those who refused to work in the workhouses except by force were sent to poor-law prisons; those who were unable to work were either kept in workhouses or were allowed to live in places of their own choosing and their needs were supplied by the parish or community.

The Legend of Midas

The colorful Greek myths have long been a source of inspiration to writers. The story of Midas is one that is well known to many people.

Old man Silenus (sī lē′ nəs), foster-father of Bacchus, had wandered away from a drinking party and gotten lost. He was found by King Midas, who entertained him royally for ten days and then returned him to Bacchus. Out of gratitude Bacchus offered Midas his choice of a reward, and Midas asked that whatever he touched might be turned into gold. His wish was granted.

Midas went about the country joyfully touching everything he came upon, and as soon as he returned to his home he ordered his servants to prepare a great feast of celebration. Much to his dismay bread turned to gold in his hands, and wine flowed down his throat like melted gold.

Whereupon Midas begged that Bacchus rid him of his questionable power. The merciful god told him to go to the River Pactolus (pak tō′ lús), plunge himself into it, and wash away the power. Midas did this; cured of his affliction he denounced wealth and splendor,

and went to live in the country where he became a worshipper of Pan, god of the fields.

Now Pan was very fond of playing on the syrinx, a type of shepherd's pipe, and fancied himself quite as talented as Apollo, god of music, who was renowned for his ability to play the lyre. Pan challenged Apollo to a contest to determine which was the better musician. Tmolus (mō′ ləs), god of mountains, was chosen as judge. Tmolus declared Apollo the winner, but Midas questioned the decision. Apollo did not feel that a pair of ears that heard so badly should be allowed to retain the human form. He caused them to increase in length, grow hairy, and movable in their roots; Midas' new ears very much resembled those of an ass.

In order to hide his shame Midas took to wearing turbans, and the only one who knew of his fate was his hairdresser, who was sworn to secrecy. But the secret was too much for the hairdresser to keep to himself. He went to a meadow, dug a hole, whispered the secret into it, and covered it up. Soon a big bed of reeds sprang up in the meadow, and now they tell Midas' secret to every passing breeze.

word was to be said? An earth all lying round, crying, Come and till me, come and reap me—yet we here sit enchanted! In the eyes and brows of these men hung the gloomiest expression, not of anger, but of grief and shame and manifold inarticulate distress and weariness; they returned my glance with a glance that seemed to say, 'Do not look at us. We sit enchanted here, we know not why. The sun shines and the earth calls; and, by the governing powers and impotences of this England, we are forbidden to obey. It is impossible, they tell us!' There was something that reminded me of Dante's Hell[4] in the look of all this; and I rode swiftly away."

So many hundred thousands sit in workhouses: and other hundred thousands have not yet got even workhouses; and in thrifty Scotland itself, in Glasgow or Edinburgh City, in their dark lanes, hidden from all but the eye of God, and of rare benevolence the minister of God, there are scenes of woe and destitution and desolation, such as, one may hope, the sun never saw before in the most barbarous regions where men dwelt. Competent witnesses, the brave and humane Dr. Alison,[5] who speaks what he knows, whose noble healing art in his charitable hands becomes once more a truly sacred one, report these things for us: these things are not of this year, or of last year, have no reference to our present state of commercial stagnation, but only to the common state. Not in sharp feverfits, but in chronic gangrene of this kind is Scotland suffering. A poor law, any and every poor law, it may be observed, is but a temporary measure; an anodyne, not a remedy: Rich and poor, when once the naked facts of their condition have come into collision, cannot long subsist together on a mere poor law. True enough. And yet, human beings cannot be left to die! Scotland too, till something better come, must have a poor law, if Scotland is not to be a byword among the nations. O, what a waste is there; of noble and thrice-noble national virtues; peasant stoicisms, heroisms; valiant manful habits, soul of a nation's worth, which all the metal of Potosi[6] cannot purchase back; to which the metal of Potosi, and all you can buy with *it*, is dross and dust!

Why dwell on this aspect of the matter? It is too indisputable, not doubtful now to any one. Descend where you will into the lower class, in town or country, by what avenue you will, by factory inquiries, agricultural inquiries, by revenue returns, by mining-laborer committees, by opening your own eyes and looking, the same sorrowful result discloses itself: you have to admit that the working body of this rich English nation has sunk or is fast sinking into a state, to which, all sides of it considered, there was literally never any parallel. At Stockport Assizes[7]—and this too has no reference to the present state of trade, being of date prior to that—a mother and a father are arraigned and found guilty of poisoning three of their children, to defraud a "burial-society" of some 3£. 8s.[8] due on the death of each child; they are arraigned, found guilty; and the official authorities, it is whispered, hint that perhaps the case is not solitary, that perhaps you had better not probe farther into that department of things. This is in the autumn of 1841; the crime itself is of the previous year or season. "Brutal savages, degraded Irish,"[9] mutters the idle reader of newspapers; hardly lingering on this incident. Yet it is an incident worth lingering on; the depravity, savagery and degraded Irishism being never so well admitted. In the British land, a human mother and father, of white skin and professing the Christian religion, had done this thing; they, with their Irishism and necessity and savagery, had been driven to do it. Such instances are like the highest mountain apex emerged into view; under which lies a whole mountain region and land, not yet emerged. A human mother and father had said to themselves, What shall we do to escape

4. *Dante's Hell*, a reference to the *Divine Comedy*, written by the Italian poet Dante about 1300. The epic poem tells of the writer's journey through Hell, Purgatory, and Heaven. 5. *Dr. Alison*, a Scottish physician who lived from 1790 to 1859. He sought to reform the archaic Scottish poor laws on the grounds that poverty was a major source of disease. 6. *Potosi*, a department, or city, in central Bolivia, once the world's richest source of silver. 7. *Stockport Assizes* (ə sīz'iz), country-court sessions held in Stockport, in the north of England. 8. *3£. 8s*, the abbreviated form for *three pounds, eight shillings*. 9. *degraded Irish*, the newspaper reader's term and attitude rather than Carlyle's.

starvation? We are deep sunk here, in our dark cellar; and help is far. Yes, in the Ugolino Hungertower stern things happen; best-loved little Gaddo fallen dead on his father's knees![10] The Stockport mother and father think and hint: Our poor little starveling Tom, who cries all days for victuals, who will see only evil and not good in this world: if he were out of misery at once; he well dead, and the rest of us perhaps kept alive? It is thought, and hinted; at last it is done. And now Tom being killed, and all spent and eaten, is it poor little starveling Jack that must go, or poor little starveling Will? What a committee of ways and means!

In starved sieged cities, in the uttermost doomed ruin of old Jerusalem fallen under the wrath of God, it was prophesied and said, "The hands of the pitiful women have sodden their own children."[11] The stern Hebrew imagination could conceive no blacker gulf of wretchedness; that was the ultimatum of degraded God-punished man. And we here, in modern England, exuberant with supply of all kinds, besieged by nothing if it be not by invisible Enchantments, are we reaching that? ——How come these things? Wherefore are they, wherefore should they be?

Nor are they of the St. Ives workhouses, of the Glasgow lanes, and Stockport cellars, the only unblessed among us. This successful industry of England, with its plethoric wealth, has as yet made nobody rich; it is an enchanted wealth, and belongs yet to nobody. We might ask, which of us has it enriched? We can spend thousands where we once spent hundreds; but can purchase nothing good with them. In poor and rich, instead of noble thrift and plenty, there is idle luxury alternating with mean scarcity and inability. We have sumptuous garnitures for our life, but have forgotten to *live* in the middle of them. It is an enchanted wealth; no man of us can yet touch it. The class of men who feel that they are truly better off by means of it, let them give us their name!

Many men eat finer cookery, drink dearer liquors—with what advantage they can report, and their doctors can—but in the heart of

them, if we go out of the dyspeptic stomach, what increase of blessedness is there? Are they better, beautifuler, stronger, braver? Are they even what they call "happier"?[12] Do they look with satisfaction on more things and human faces in this God's earth; do more things and human faces look with satisfaction on them? Not so. Human faces gloom discordantly, disloyally on one another. Things, if it be not mere cotton and iron things, are growing disobedient to man. The master-worker is enchanted, for the present, like his workhouse workman; clamors, in vain hitherto, for a very simple sort of "Liberty": the liberty "to buy where he finds it cheapest, to sell where he finds it dearest." With guineas jingling in every pocket, he was no whit richer; but now, the very guineas threatening to vanish, he feels that he is poor indeed. Poor master-worker! And the master-unworker,[13] is not he in a still fataler situation? Pausing amid his game preserves, with awful eye—as he well may! Coercing fifty-pound tenants[14]; coercing, bribing, cajoling; "doing what he likes with his own." His mouth full of loud futilities, and arguments to prove the excellence of his Corn Law,[15] and in his heart the blackest misgiving, a desperate half-consciousness that his excellent Corn Law is in-

10. *Ugolino . . . knees.* Ugolino della Gherardesca (ü'gō-lē'nō del'la gā rär des'kä), a thirteenth-century statesman of Pisa, Italy, was accused of betraying his city through negligence in battle. He was arrested and imprisoned in a tower with his sons and grandsons. Eventually they all died of starvation; Gaddo was one of the last to die. Dante, Chaucer, and Shelley all tell this story. 11. *doomed ruin . . . children.* In 586 b.c. Nebuchadnezzar (neb'ū kəd nez'ər), King of Babylon, and his troops captured Jerusalem. They surrounded the city so that no one could leave it and allowed no food to be brought in. The people of Jerusalem died of starvation in great numbers; some of them killed and ate other humans to keep from starving. The quotation is from the Old Testament, Lamentations 4:10, in which Jeremiah tells of the siege of the city. 12. *happier.* This term is often used in an ironical sense by Carlyle, who held that those whose principal purpose in life was happiness were aiming at a false standard. Satisfaction had to be *earned*, he maintained, through devoted work and responsibility. 13. *master-unworker*, a term like *master-idlers*, commonly used by Carlyle to denote the idle aristocracy. 14. *fifty-pound tenants*, tenants who earned only fifty pounds a year. 15. *Corn Law*, a law for regulating the importation and sometimes the exportation of wheat (corn). The system favored the landowners at the expense of the urban population for it caused the price of wheat to rise considerably. The law was repealed in 1846.

defensible, that his loud arguments for it are of a kind to strike men too literally *dumb*.

To whom, then, is this wealth of England wealth? Who is it that it blesses; makes happier, wiser, beautifuler, in any way better? Who has got hold of it, to make it fetch and carry for him, like a true servant, not like a false mock-servant; to do him any real service whatsoever? As yet no one. We have more riches than any nation ever had before; we have less good of them than any nation ever had before. Our successful industry is hitherto unsuccessful; a strange success, if we stop here! In the midst of plethoric plenty, the people perish; with gold walls, and full barns, no man feels himself safe or satisfied. Workers, master-workers, unworkers, all men, come to a pause; stand fixed, and cannot farther. Fatal paralysis spreading inwards, from the extremities, in St. Ives workhouses, in Stockport cellars, through all limbs, as if towards the heart itself. Have we actually got enchanted, then; accursed by some god?

Midas longed for gold, and insulted the Olympians. He got gold, so that whatsoever he touched became gold, and he, with his long ears, was little the better for it. Midas had misjudged the celestial music-tones; Midas had insulted Apollo and the gods: the gods gave him his wish, and a pair of long ears, which also were a good appendage to it. What a truth in these old fables!

❦ To increase understanding

1. Explain Carlyle's use of the Greek myth of Midas in this essay, paying particular attention to the following: (*a*) the author's frequent references to enchantment, (*b*) the last paragraph, (*c*) the title.

2. (*a*) State the basic idea developed in "Midas" in your own words. (*b*) What devices does Carlyle use to make this idea clear and forceful?

3. Carlyle writes: "This successful industry of England, with its plethoric wealth, has as yet made nobody rich; it is an enchanted wealth, and belongs yet to nobody" (page 426, column 1, paragraph 2). (*a*) Explain what Carlyle means by declaring this wealth has made nobody rich. (*b*) Why is it "an enchanted wealth"?

4. According to Carlyle, the master-worker clamors for the liberty "to buy where he finds it cheapest, to sell where he finds it dearest" (page 426, column 2, line 15). (*a*) To what doctrine is Carlyle here referring? (*b*) What is his attitude toward this theory? (*c*) Cite statements to prove your point and discuss the tone of these statements.

5. Compare and contrast the selection by Carlyle with that by Macaulay with regard to (*a*) basic idea, (*b*) ways of developing this idea, and (*c*) tone.

T. H. Huxley by his son-in-law, John Collier.

Thomas Henry Huxley 1825-1895

Huxley himself wrote of his childhood: "I had two years of a pandemonium of a school (between eight and ten) and after that neither help nor sympathy in any intellectual direction till I reached manhood." But in spite of young Huxley's lack of a formal education, his interest in science, particularly in biology, flourished. He began the study of medicine at Charing Cross College in London, and at about the same time he discovered the works of Carlyle. From Carlyle he gained a deep respect for honesty and integrity and a hatred of anything he considered false. After finishing his medical studies in 1845, he embarked as assistant surgeon on H.M.S. *Rattlesnake* for a scientific expedition to New Guinea and Australia. During the four-year voyage he sent many scientific articles to technical journals in London, and on his return discovered that publication of the articles had earned him a substantial reputation as a scientist.

In 1855 he was appointed Lecturer on Natural History to the London School of Science and Naturalist to the Geographical Survey. He settled down in London and devoted the remainder of his life to the teaching of science.

Following the publication of Darwin's *The Origin of Species* in 1859, Huxley, impressed by the theory of natural selection, offered his support to Darwin in publicizing the work. Subsequently he engaged in public debates, famous at the time, and wrote countless articles explaining and defending Darwin's work, thus earning the appellation "Darwin's bulldog."

Huxley's importance to the thought and development of the time, however, does not end with his Darwinian commentary. He also made important contributions to education, which, like most fields of endeavor, was caught up in the great ferment of the Victorian Age. He not only laid down the lines along which the teaching of biology developed but also established a pattern for elementary education which lasted well into the twentieth century.

Huxley was no gentle, cloistered scholar but a tireless, fearless champion of the ideas in which he believed. In both speaking and writing he combined the utmost lucidity of style with good humor and clearly understood examples. The following essay is typical of his technique and style in explaining scientific method to the public.

THE METHOD OF SCIENTIFIC INVESTIGATION

You have heard it repeated, I dare say, that men of science work by means of induction and deduction and that, by the help of these operations, they wring from nature certain other things (which are called natural laws and causes), and that out of these, by some cunning skill of their own, they build up hypotheses and theories. And it is imagined by many that the operations of the common mind can be by no means compared with these processes. To hear all these large words, you would think that the mind of a man of science must be constituted differently from that of his fellow men. But if you will not be frightened by terms, you will discover that you are quite wrong, and that all these terrible apparatus are being used by yourself every day of your life.

A very trivial circumstance will serve to exemplify this. Suppose you go into a fruiterer's shop, wanting an apple. You take up one, and on biting it, you find it is sour. You look at it and see that it is hard and green. You take up another one, and that too is hard, green, and sour. The shopman offers you a third; but, before biting it, you examine it and find that it is hard and green, and you immediately say that you will not have it, as it must be sour, like those you have already tried.

Nothing can be more simple than that, you think; but if you will take the trouble to analyze what has been done by your mind, you will be greatly surprised. In the first place, you have performed the operation of induction. You found that, in two experiences, hardness and greenness in apples went together with sourness. It was so in the first case, and it was confirmed by the second. True, it is a very small basis, but still it is enough to make an induction from; you generalize the facts, and you expect to find sourness in apples when you get hardness and greenness. You found upon that a general law—that all hard and green apples are sour; and this, so far as it goes, is a perfect induction.

Well, having got your natural law in this way, when you are offered another apple which you find is hard and green, you say, "All hard and green apples are sour; this apple is hard and green; therefore this apple is sour." That train of reasoning is what we call a syllogism, and has all its various parts and terms —its major premise, its minor premise, and its conclusion—and, by the help of further reasoning, you arrive at your final determination, "I will not have that apple." You see, you have, in the first place, established a law by induction, and upon that you have founded a deduction and reasoned out the special conclusion of the particular case.

Well, now, suppose, having got your law, that at some time afterward you are discussing the qualities of apples with a friend. You say to him, "It is a very curious thing, but I find that all hard and green apples are sour!" Your friend says to you, "But how do you know that?" You at once reply, "Oh, because I have tried them over and over again, and have always found them to be so." Well, if we were talking science instead of common sense, we should call that an experimental verification. And, if still opposed, you go further and say, "I have heard from the people in Somersetshire and Devonshire, where a large number of apples are grown, that they have observed the same thing. It is also found to be the case in Normandy and in North America. In short, I find it to be the universal experience of mankind wherever attention has been directed to the subject." Whereupon your friend, unless he is a very unreasonable man, agrees with you and is convinced that you are quite right in the conclusion you have drawn. He sees that the experiment has been tried under all sorts of conditions as to time, place, and people, with the same results; and he says with you, therefore, that the law you have laid down must be a good one and that he must believe it.

In science we do the same, though in a much more delicate manner. In scientific inquiry it becomes a matter of duty to expose a supposed law to every possible kind of verification and to take care, moreover, that this is done intentionally and not left to a mere accident, as in the case of the apples. And in science, as in common life, our confidence in a law is in exact proportion to the absence of variation in the result of our experimental verifications. For instance, if you let go your grasp of an article that you may have in your hand, it will immediately fall to the ground. This is a very common verification of one of the best established laws of nature—that of gravitation. The method by which men of science establish the existence of that law is exactly the same as that by which we have established the trivial proposition about the sourness of hard and green apples. But we believe it in such an extensive, thorough, and unhesitating manner because the universal experience of mankind verifies it, and we can verify it ourselves at any time; and that is the strongest possible foundation on which any natural law can rest.

So much, then, by the way of proof that the method of establishing laws in science is exactly the same as that pursued in common life. Let us now turn to another matter (though really it is but another phase of the same question), and that is, the method by which, from the relations of certain phenomena, we prove that some of these phenomena stand in the position of causes toward the other.

I want to put the case clearly before you, and will therefore show you what I mean by another familiar example. I will suppose that you, on coming down in the morning to the parlor of your house, find that a teapot and some spoons which had been left in the room on the previous evening are gone. The window is open and you observe the mark of a dirty hand on the window frame; and perhaps you notice the impress of a hobnailed shoe on the gravel outside. All these phenomena have struck your attention instantly, and before two seconds have passed you say, "Oh, somebody has broken open the window, entered the room, and run off with the spoons and the teapot!" That speech is out of your mouth in a moment. And you will probably add, "I know; I am quite sure of it!" You mean to say exactly what you know; but in reality you are giving expression to what is an hypothesis. You do not *know* it at all; it is nothing but an hypothesis rapidly founded on a long train of inductions and deductions.

What are those inductions and deductions, and how have you got at this hypothesis? You have observed, in the first place, that the window is open. But by a train of reasoning involving many inductions and deductions, you have probably arrived long before at the general law—and a very good one it is—that windows do not open of themselves; and you conclude that something has opened the window. A second general law that you have arrived at in the same way is this: that teapots and spoons do not go out of a window spontaneously; and you are satisfied that, since the teapot and the spoons are not now where you left them, they have been removed. In the third place, you look at the marks on the window sill and the shoe marks outside, and you say that in all previous experience the former kind of mark has never been produced by anything else but the hand of a human being; and the same experience shows that no other animal but man at present wears shoes with hobnails in them such as would produce the marks in the gravel.

You next reach the conclusion that, as these kinds of marks have not been left by any other animal than man, nor are liable to be formed in any other way than by a man's hand and shoe, the marks in question have been formed by a man in that way. You have, further, a general law, founded on observation and experience—that some men are thieves—and you assume at once from all these premises that the man who made the marks outside and on the window sill opened the window, got into the room, and stole your teapot and spoons. You have now arrived at a *vera causa*[1]; you have assumed a cause which, it is plain, is competent to produce all the phenomena you have observed. You can explain all these phenomena only by the hypothesis of a thief. But that is a hypothetical conclusion, of the justice of which you have no absolute proof at all; it is only rendered highly probable by a series of inductive and deductive reasonings.

I suppose your first action, assuming that you have established this hypothesis to your own satisfaction, will very likely be to go off for the police and set them on the track of the burglar, with the view to recovering your property. But just as you are starting with this object, some person comes in and, on learning what you are about, says, "My good friend, you are going on a great deal too fast. How do you know that the man who really made the marks took the spoons? It might have been a monkey that took them, and the man may have merely looked in afterward."

You would probably reply, "Well, that is all very well, but you see it is contrary to all experience of the way teapots and spoons are abstracted; so that, at any rate, your hypothesis is less probable than mine."

While you are talking the thing over in this way, another friend arrives, and he might say, "Oh, my dear sir, you are certainly going on a great deal too fast. You are most presumptuous. You admit that all these occurrences took place when you were fast asleep, at a time when you could not possibly have known anything about what was taking place. How do you know that the laws of nature are not suspended during the night? It may be that there has been some kind of supernatural interference in this case." In point of fact, he declares that your hypothesis is one of which you cannot at all demonstrate the truth.

Well, now, you cannot at the moment answer that kind of reasoning. You feel that your worthy friend has you somewhat at a disadvantage. You will feel perfectly convinced in your own mind, however, that you are quite right, and you say to him, "My good friend, I can be guided only by the natural probabilities of the case, and if you will be kind enough to step aside and permit me to pass, I will go and fetch the police." Well, we will suppose that your journey is successful and that by good luck you meet with a policeman, that eventually the burglar is found with your property on his person, and that the marks correspond to his hand and to his boots. Probably any jury would consider

1. *vera causa* (ver′ə kô′zə; *Latin,* wä′rä kou′sä), literally, a true cause.

those facts a very good experimental verification of your hypothesis and would act accordingly.

Now, in this supposed case, I have taken phenomena of a very common kind, in order that you might see what are the different steps in an ordinary process of reasoning. All the operations I have described, you will see, are involved in the mind of any man of sense in leading him to a conclusion as to the course he should take in order to make good a robbery and punish the offender. I say that you are led, in that case, to your conclusion by exactly the same train of reasoning as that which a man of science pursues when he is endeavoring to discover the origin and laws of the most occult phenomena. The process is, and always must be, the same. Precisely the same mode of reasoning was employed by Newton and Laplace[2] in their endeavors to discover and define the causes of the movements of the heavenly bodies as you, with your own common sense, would employ to detect a burglar. The only difference is this: that the nature of the inquiry being more abstruse, every step has to be most carefully watched, so that there may not be a single crack or flaw in your hypothesis. A flaw or crack in many of the hypotheses of daily life may be of little or no moment as affecting the general correctness of the conclusion at which we may arrive; but in a scientific inquiry, a fallacy, great or small, is always of importance and is sure to be, in the long run, productive of mischievous, if not fatal, results.

Do not allow yourself to be misled by the common notion that any hypothesis is untrustworthy simply because it is an hypothesis. It is often urged, in respect to some scientific conclusion, that, after all, it is only an hypothesis. But what more have we to guide us in nine-tenths of the most important affairs of daily life than hypotheses, and often very ill-based ones? Therefore, in science, where the evidence of an hypothesis is subjected to the most rigid examination, we may rightly pursue the same course. Every great step in our progress in discovering causes has been made in exactly the same way as that which I have detailed to you. When we observe the occurrence of certain facts and phenomena, we ask, naturally enough, "What process, what kind of operation known to occur in nature will, when applied to a particular case, unravel and explain the mystery?" Hence you have the scientific hypothesis; and its value will be proportionate to the care and completeness with which its basis has been tested and verified. It is as true in these matters as in the commonest affairs of practical life: the guess of the fool will be folly, while the guess of the wise man will contain wisdom. In all cases you see that the value of the result depends on the patience and faithfulness with which the investigator applies to his hypothesis every possible kind of verification.

---

2. *Newton and Laplace*, the English scientist, Sir Isaac Newton (1642-1727), who proved the law of gravitation; and the French scientist Pierre Simon Laplace (1749-1827), who made important discoveries in astronomy.

To increase understanding

1. What does Huxley set out to prove in his article? Quote sentences that summarize the idea.

2. (*a*) How does Huxley attempt to prove the point that he wishes to make? (*b*) Is his example appropriate and effective? Why?

3. Explain inductive and deductive reasoning, quoting examples from the essay to illustrate your explanation.

4. Huxley follows an inductive process first in his example, then deduces from his findings. What danger is there in using deductive reasoning exclusively or too early in an analytical problem?

5. What qualities as a teacher does Huxley reveal in this work?

 Words!

The word *syllogism* (page 429, column 1, paragraph 1) comes from the Greek prefix *syn-* meaning "together" and the Greek word *logos* meaning "a reckoning or a reasoning." Show how the idea of "a reasoning together" enters into the meaning of *syllogism* as Huxley uses the word.

Many English words have the prefix *syn-* (or *syl-*, as in *syllogism*) meaning "together." Show how this meaning appears in the following words (some of which you may wish to look up in the Glossary): *syllable, synchronize, syndicate, synthesis.*

John Henry Newman 1801-1890

Though born of wealthy parents, John Henry Newman never cared for the material things of the world. Even as a boy his mind was set on the unseen. Reading Scott's historical novels, he lived imaginatively in the Middle Ages; as he read the Bible, he peopled his world with angels. He attended Oxford, and after taking his degree he was ordained a clergyman in the Church of England. In 1828 he became vicar of St. Mary's at Oxford.

Long before Darwin published his *Origin of Species*, Victorian thinkers were disturbed by the difficulty of reconciling theology with science. At Oxford in the 1830's conflict arose between the liberal clergymen of the Anglican Church, who were influenced by new scientific theories, and those ministers who believed in a return to the authority of the church. This controversy came to a head in what is called the Oxford Movement. Beginning in 1833 a group of reformers, of whom Newman was the most prominent, issued ninety *Tracts for the Times*, advocating a strengthening of the authority of the Church of England and a return to many of the observances of the medieval church. Newman wrote twenty-nine of the tracts, including the famous Tract XC in 1842. This last tract was so critical of the Church of England that Newman felt obliged to resign his pulpit. Two years later he was received into the Roman Catholic Church. In 1879 he was made a cardinal.

Newman's leaving the Anglican Church inevitably aroused bitterness, and some scathing attacks upon him were made. To defend himself he wrote *Apologia pro Vita Sua* (1863), one of the finest spiritual autobiographies in the English language. This simple and moving account of one man's search for truth established his reputation as a master of English prose style.

Religious writings and a body of fine poems, most of them composed early in his career, form the bulk of Newman's work. However, educators know him particularly for an excellent series of lectures on university education, published in 1873 as *The Idea of a University*. The occasion of the lectures was the plan to establish a Roman Catholic university in Dublin, with Newman at its head. From an educational viewpoint Newman's lectures with their thoughtful analysis of the function of a university, learning and knowledge, and the necessity of a liberal education, have influenced educators from his time to the present day. From a literary viewpoint the lectures have continued to be regarded as models of clear, logical, and graceful prose, in which the style admirably serves the function.

Portrait of Cardinal Newman by Emmeline Deane, painted in 1889.

LEAD, KINDLY LIGHT

Lead, Kindly Light, amid the encircling gloom,
   Lead Thou me on!
The night is dark, and I am far from home—
   Lead Thou me on!
Keep Thou my feet; I do not ask to see
The distant scene—one step enough for me.

5

I was not ever thus, nor prayed that Thou
  Shouldst lead me on.
I loved to choose and see my path; but now
  Lead Thou me on!   10
I loved the garish day, and, in spite of fears,
Pride ruled my will; remember not past years.

So long Thy power hath blessed me, sure it still
  Will lead me on,
O'er moor and fen, o'er crag and torrent, till   15
  The night is gone;
And with the morn those angel faces smile
Which I have loved long since, and lost awhile.

from THE IDEA OF A UNIVERSITY

I suppose the *prima-facie*[1] view which the public at large would take of a university, considering it as a place of education, is nothing more or less than a place for acquiring a great deal of knowledge on a great many subjects. Memory is one of the first developed of the mental faculties; a boy's business when he goes to school is to learn, that is, to store up things in his memory. For some years his intellect is little more than an instrument for taking in facts, or a receptacle for storing them; he welcomes them as fast as they come to him; he lives on what is without; he has his eyes ever about him; he has a lively susceptibility of impressions; he imbibes information of every kind; and little does he make his own in a true sense of the word, living rather upon his neighbors all around him. He has opinions, religious, political, and literary, and, for a boy, is very positive in them and sure about them; but he gets them from his schoolfellows, or his masters, or his parents, as the case may be. Such as he is in his other relations, such also is he in his school exercises; his mind is observant, sharp, ready, retentive; he is almost passive in the acquisition of knowledge. I say this in no disparagement of the idea of a clever boy. Geography, chronology, history, language, natural history, he heaps up the matter of these studies as treasures for a future day. It is the seven years of plenty with him: he gathers in by handfuls, like the Egyptians,[2] without counting; and though, as time goes on, there is exercise for his argumentative powers in the elements of mathematics, and for his taste in the poets and orators, still, while at school, or at least, till quite the last years of his time, he acquires, and little more; and when he is leaving for the university, he is mainly the creature of foreign influences and circumstances, and made up of accidents, homogeneous or not, as the case may be. Moreover, the moral habits, which are a boy's praise, encourage and assist this result; that is, diligence, assiduity, regularity, dispatch, persevering application; for these are the direct conditions of acquisition, and naturally lead to it. Acquirements, again, are emphatically producible, and at a moment; they are a something to show, both for master and scholar; an audience, even though ignorant themselves of the subjects of an examination, can comprehend when questions are answered and when they are not. Here again is

THE IDEA OF A UNIVERSITY   **1.** *prima-facie* (prī′mə fā′-shi ē), at first view, before investigation.   **2.** *seven years . . . Egyptians.* This is a reference to the Old Testament, Genesis 41:1-36. The Pharaoh of Egypt had a dream interpreted for him by Joseph, a Hebrew slave. Joseph said the dream meant that Egypt would have seven years of plenty followed by seven years of famine, and advised the Pharaoh to set aside a fifth of the land of Egypt in the seven plenteous years and store the food grown on it for the seven years of famine. The Pharaoh took Joseph's advice; food was stored and the land of Egypt was saved from starvation.

a reason why mental culture is in the minds of men identified with the acquisition of knowledge.

The same notion possesses the public mind, when it passes on from the thought of a school to that of a university: and with the best of reasons so far as this, that there is no true culture without acquirements, and that philosophy presupposes knowledge. It requires a great deal of reading, or a wide range of information, to warrant us in putting forth our opinions on any serious subject; and without such learning the most original mind may be able indeed to dazzle, to amuse, to refute, to perplex, but not to come to any useful result or any trustworthy conclusion. There are indeed persons who profess a different view of the matter, and even act upon it. Every now and then you will find a person of vigorous or fertile mind, who relies upon his own resources, despises all former authors, and gives the world, with the utmost fearlessness, his views upon religion, or history, or any other popular subject. And his works may sell for a while; he may get a name in his day; but this will be all. His readers are sure to find on the long run that his doctrines are mere theories, and not the expression of facts, that they are chaff instead of bread, and then his popularity drops as suddenly as it rose.

Knowledge then is the indispensable condition of expansion of mind, and the instrument of attaining to it; this cannot be denied, it is ever to be insisted on; I begin with it as a first principle; however, the very truth of it carries men too far, and confirms to them the notion that it is the whole of the matter. A narrow mind is thought to be that which contains little knowledge; and an enlarged mind, that which holds a great deal; and what seems to put the matter beyond dispute is, the fact of the great number of studies which are pursued in a university, by its very profession. Lectures are given on every kind of subject; examinations are held; prizes awarded. There are moral, metaphysical, physical professors; professors of languages, of history, of mathematics, of experimental science. Lists of questions are published, wonderful for their range and depth, variety and difficulty; trea-

tises are written, which carry upon their very face the evidence of extensive reading or multifarious information; what then is wanting for mental culture to a person of large reading and scientific attainments? What is the grasp of mind but acquirement? Where shall philosophical repose be found, but in the consciousness and enjoyment of large intellectual possessions?

And yet this notion is, I conceive, a mistake, and my present business is to show that it is one, and that the end of a liberal education is not mere knowledge, or knowledge considered in its *matter;* and I shall best attain my object, by actually setting down some cases, which will be generally granted to be instances of the process of enlightenment or enlargement of mind, and others which are not, and thus, by the comparison, you will be able to judge for yourselves, whether knowledge, that is, acquirement, is after all the real principle of the enlargement, or whether that principle is not rather something beyond it.

For instance, let a person, whose experience has hitherto been confined to the more calm and unpretending scenery of these islands, whether here[3] or in England, go for the first time into parts where physical nature puts on her wilder and more awful forms, whether at home or abroad, as into mountainous districts; or let one, who has ever lived in a quiet village, go for the first time to a great metropolis —then I suppose he will have a sensation which perhaps he never had before. He has a feeling not in addition or increase of former feelings, but of something different in its nature. He will perhaps be borne forward, and find for a time that he has lost his bearings. He has made a certain progress, and he has a consciousness of mental enlargement; he does not stand where he did, he has a new center, and a range of thoughts to which he was before a stranger.

Again, the view of the heavens which the telescope opens upon us, if allowed to fill and possess the mind, may almost whirl it round

---

3. *here,* Ireland.

and make it dizzy. It brings in a flood of ideas, and is rightly called an intellectual enlargement, whatever is meant by the term.

And so again, the sight of beasts of prey and other foreign animals, their strangeness, the originality (if I may use the term) of their forms and gestures and habits and their variety and independence of each other, throw us out of ourselves into another creation, and as if under another Creator, if I may so express the temptation which may come on the mind. We seem to have new faculties, or a new exercise for our faculties, by this addition to our knowledge; like a prisoner, who, having been accustomed to wear manacles or fetters, suddenly finds his arms and legs free.

Hence physical science generally, in all its departments, as bringing before us the exuberant riches and resources, yet the orderly course, of the universe, elevates and excites the student, and at first, I may say, almost takes away his breath, while in time it exercises a tranquilizing influence upon him.

Again, the study of history is said to enlarge and enlighten the mind, and why? Because, as I conceive, it gives it a power of judging of passing events, and of all events, and a conscious superiority over them, which before it did not possess.

And in like manner, what is called seeing the world, entering into active life, going into society, traveling, gaining acquaintance with the various classes of the community, coming into contact with the principles and modes of thought of various parties, interests, and races, their views, aims, habits and manners, their religious creeds and forms of worship—gaining experience how various yet how alike men are, how low-minded, how bad, how opposed, yet how confident in their opinions; all this exerts a perceptible influence upon the mind, which it is impossible to mistake, be it good or be it bad, and is popularly called its enlargement. . . .

Now from these instances, to which many more might be added, it is plain, first, that the communication of knowledge certainly is either a condition or the means of that sense of enlargement or enlightenment, of which at this day we hear so much in certain quarters:

this cannot be denied; but next, it is equally plain, that such communication is not the whole of the process. The enlargement consists, not merely in the passive reception into the mind of a number of ideas hitherto unknown to it, but in the mind's energetic and simultaneous action upon and towards and among those new ideas, which are rushing in upon it. It is the action of a formative power, reducing to order and meaning the matter of our acquirements; it is a making the objects of our knowledge subjectively our own, or, to use a familiar word, it is a digestion of what we receive, into the substance of our previous state of thought; and without this no enlargement is said to follow. There is no enlargement, unless there be a comparison of ideas one with another, as they come before the mind, and a systematizing of them. We feel our minds to be growing and expanding *then*, when we not only learn, but refer what we learn to what we know already. It is not the mere addition to our knowledge that is the illumination; but the locomotion, the movement onwards, of that mental center, to which both what we know, and what we are learning, the accumulating mass of our acquirements, gravitates. And therefore a truly great intellect, and recognized to be such by the common opinion of mankind, such as the intellect of Aristotle, or of St. Thomas, or of Newton, or of Goethe,[4] (I purposely take instances within and without the Catholic pale, when I would speak of the intellect as such), is one which takes a connected view of old and new, past and present, far and near, and which has an insight into the influence of all these one on another; without which there is no whole, and no center. It possesses the knowledge, not only of things, but also of their mutual and true relations; knowledge, not merely considered as acquirement, but as philosophy.

Accordingly, when this analytical, distributive, harmonizing process is away, the mind experiences no enlargement, and is not reckoned as enlightened or comprehensive, what-

---

4. *Aristotle . . . Goethe* (goeʹtə). These were respectively an ancient Greek philosopher, a medieval theologian, a seventeenth-century English scientist, and a German writer of the late eighteenth and early nineteenth century.

ever it may add to its knowledge. For instance, a great memory, as I have already said, does not make a philosopher, any more than a dictionary can be called a grammar. There are men who embrace in their minds a vast multitude of ideas, but with little sensibility about their real relations towards each other. These may be antiquarians, analysts, naturalists; they may be learned in the law; they may be versed in statistics; they are most useful in their own place; I should shrink from speaking disrespectfully of them; still, there is nothing in such attainments to guarantee the absence of narrowness of mind. If they are nothing more than well-read men, or men of information, they have not what specially deserves the name of culture of mind, or fulfills the type of liberal education.

In like manner, we sometimes fall in with persons who have seen much of the world, and of the men who, in their day, have played a conspicuous part in it, but who generalize nothing, and have no observation, in the true sense of the word. They abound in information in detail, curious and entertaining, about men and things; and, having lived under the influence of no very clear or settled principles, religious or political, they speak of every one and every thing, only as so many phenomena, which are complete in themselves, and lead to nothing, not discussing them, or teaching any truth, or instructing the hearer, but simply talking. No one would say that these persons, well informed as they are, had attained to any great culture of intellect or to philosophy. . . .

Instances, such as these, confirm, by the contrast, the conclusion I have already drawn from those which preceded them. That only is true enlargement of mind which is the power of viewing many things at once as one whole, of referring them severally to their true place in the universal system, of understanding their respective values, and determining their mutual dependence. Thus is the form of universal knowledge, set up in the individual intellect, and constitutes its perfection. Possessed of this real illumination, the mind never views any part of the extended subject matter of knowledge without recollecting that it is but a part, or without the associations which spring from this recollection. It makes every thing in some sort lead to every thing else; it would communicate the image of the whole to every separate portion, till that whole becomes in imagination like a spirit, everywhere pervading and penetrating its component parts, and giving them one definite meaning. Just as our bodily organs, when mentioned, recall their function in the body, as the word *creation* suggests the Creator, and *subjects* a sovereign, so, in the mind of the philosopher, as we are abstractedly conceiving of him, the elements of the physical and moral world, sciences, arts, pursuits, ranks, offices, events, opinions, individualities, are all viewed as one, with correlative functions, and as gradually by successive combinations converging, one and all, to the true center.

To have even a portion of this illuminative reason and true philosophy is the highest state to which nature can aspire, in the way of intellect; it puts the mind above the influences of chance and necessity, above anxiety, suspense, unsettlement, and superstition, which is the lot of the many. Men, whose minds are possessed with some one object, take exaggerated views of its importance, are feverish in the pursuit of it, make it the measure of things which are utterly foreign to it, and are startled and despond if it happens to fail them. They are ever in alarm or in transport. Those on the other hand who have no object or principle whatever to hold by, lose their way, every step they take. They are thrown out, and do not know what to think or say, at every fresh juncture; they have no view of persons, or occurrences, or facts, which come suddenly upon them, and they hang upon the opinion of others, for want of internal resources. But the intellect, which has been disciplined to the perfection of its powers, which knows, and thinks while it knows, which has learned to leaven the dense mass of facts and events with the elastic force of reason, such an intellect cannot be partial, cannot be exclusive, cannot be impetuous, cannot be at a loss, cannot but be patient, collected, and majestically calm, because it discerns the end in every beginning, the origin in every end, the law in every interruption, the limit in each delay; because it ever knows where it stands, and how its path lies from one point to another. . . .

There are men who, when in difficulties, originate at the moment vast ideas or dazzling projects; who, under the influence of excitement, are able to cast a light, almost as if from inspiration, on a subject or course of action which comes before them; who have a sudden presence of mind equal to any emergency, rising with the occasion, and an undaunted magnanimous bearing, and an energy and keenness which is but made intense by opposition. This is genius, this is heroism; it is the exhibition of a natural gift, which no culture can teach, at which no institution can aim; here, on the contrary, we are concerned, not with mere nature, but with training and teaching. That perfection of the intellect, which is the result of education, and its *beau ideal*,[5] to be imparted to individuals in their respective measures, is the clear, calm, accurate vision and comprehension of all things, as far as the finite mind can embrace them, each in its place, and with its own characteristics upon it. It is almost prophetic from its knowledge of history; it is almost heart-searching from its knowledge of human nature; it has almost supernatural charity from its freedom from littleness and prejudice; it has almost the repose of faith, because nothing can startle it; it has almost the beauty and harmony of heavenly contemplation, so intimate is it with the eternal order of things and the music of the spheres.

---

5. *beau ideal*, beautiful idea.

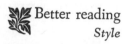 To increase understanding

1. The light Newman refers to in "Lead, Kindly Light" is the pillar of fire that guided the Israelites from Egypt. (Exodus 13) How does Newman adapt this idea of the guiding light to his own situation?

2. (*a*) Define *school* and *university* as Newman uses the terms. (*b*) How does the function of a school differ from that of a university?

3. (*a*) What does Newman mean by knowledge? (*b*) How is knowledge acquired? (*c*) Why does Newman insist that knowledge is not "the whole of the matter" (page 434, column 1, paragraph 2)?

4. According to Newman the purpose of a liberal education is not "knowledge considered in its *matter*" but "enlightenment or enlargement of mind" (page 434, column 2, paragraph 1). (*a*) Name some of the examples Newman uses as instances of "mental enlargement." (*b*) What part does knowledge play in this enlargement? (*c*) What is the vital principle of enlargement? (*d*) Cite the statement or statements which best summarize Newman's idea.

5. Newman writes: ". . . a great memory . . . does not make a philosopher, any more than a dictionary can be called a grammar" (page 436, column 1, line 2). (*a*) What does Newman mean by the word *philosopher*? (*b*) With this in mind, explain the meaning of the statement.

6. Reread the paragraph beginning: "To have even a portion of this illuminative reason and true philosophy. . ." (page 436, column 2) and answer the following questions. (*a*) What is characteristic of the mind "possessed with some one object"? (*b*) What happens to men "who have no object or principle whatever to hold by"? (*c*) What is the advantage of having a disciplined intellect?

7. What, according to Newman, is a liberal education?

8. Do you think the concept of education held by the American public today more closely resembles Newman's definition of knowledge or of enlightenment? Explain.

9. In your opinion are Newman's views on education valid today? Explain your answer.

Better reading
Style

According to Jonathan Swift, "Proper words in proper places make the true definition of a style," and Lord Chesterfield characteristically regarded style as "the dress of thoughts." The American essayist Ralph Waldo Emerson saw a man's style as "his mind's voice." An eighteenth-century Frenchman, Comte de Buffon, gave the most famous definition of all: "The style is the man himself." Taken together, these definitions attest to the fact that style not only distinguishes the writing of one man from another but often throws some light on the personality of the writer himself.

Carlyle's style is described on page 423 as eccentric and vigorous. On page 432 you read of Newman's "clear, logical, and graceful prose." What differences are there in the prose styles of these two great writers that lead to such contrasting appraisals? On what is a judgment of style based?

Your first glance at an essay or a piece of factual prose gives you some insight into an author's style. You may decide it looks hard or easy, interesting or uninteresting; and this judgment is probably based partially upon the length of the paragraphs. A preponderance of long paragraphs denotes long and often complex units of thought. The structure of the paragraph, which is the visual symbol of the author's arrangement of his material, is an aspect of style.

Study of the sentences which make up the paragraph affords a closer view of style. Sentences may be long or short, loose or periodic or balanced; they may contain a multiplicity of phrases and clauses or they may be structurally simple. The words of which a sentence is made up may be arranged in such a way that the effect is abrupt and jerky, or they may move with an easy rhythm. In some styles the sentences are stark and bare; in others they are rich with imagery, embroidered with figurative language, and studded with allusions.

The quality of individual words also has a major influence on the style. You may recall that according to Oliver Goldsmith, Samuel Johnson's "little fishes talked like whales" (page 275). It was Johnson's excessive use of long, Latinate words that provoked this comment. The style of other authors, particularly in the present day, may be notable for the use of many short, common words, for colloquial expressions, and for the skillful use of idioms.

Reread the first paragraphs of the selections by Macaulay, Carlyle, Huxley, and Newman and express your opinion on the following questions. After comparing the paragraphs as to length, decide which is easiest to understand. Do length and difficulty necessarily go together? Why, or why not? Which paragraph is most difficult? Is the difficulty primarily a matter of style or is it one of idea? In which paragraph is a logical progression of ideas most apparent?

How many sentences does each of these paragraphs contain? In general, are the sentences long or short? Which paragraph shows most variety in sentence length? In which paragraph are the individual sentences easiest to read? Is this primarily a matter of sentence structure or of vocabulary? In which paragraph is it most difficult to analyze the sentences according to grammatical principles? Which paragraph reads most smoothly?

Which paragraph gains most from the use of specific detail? What use do the paragraphs make of imagery, figurative language, and allusions? In which paragraph is the choice of words most pleasing?

Choose one of the four selections and study its style. Describe the style as accurately as possible, using examples from the selection to illustrate various points.

 Words!

A formal style such as that which Newman uses in *The Idea of a University* often makes extensive use of words derived from the Latin language. For example, when Newman talks about "the Catholic pale," he is referring to boundaries (*palus*). Show how the original meaning of each Latin word below has been retained in the sentence or phrase that follows it.

bibere, to drink
. . . he *imbibes* information of every kind . . .

pariare, to equalize
I say this in no *disparagement* of the idea of a clever boy.

assidere, to sit at
. . . encourage and assist this result; this is diligence, *assiduity* . . .

facere, to do
We seem to have new *faculties* . . .

uber, fertile
. . . as bringing before us the *exuberant* riches and resources . . .

lumen, light
It is not the mere addition of our knowledge that is the *illumination* . . .

loco, from a place
. . . but the *locomotion*, the movement onwards . . .

gravis, heavy
. . . and what we are learning, the accumulating mass of our requirements, *gravitates*.

relatus, brought back
. . . are all viewed as one, with *correlative* functions . . .

vadere, to go
. . . everywhere *pervading* and penetrating its component parts . . .

levare, to raise
. . . which has learned to *leaven* the dense mass of facts . . .

animus, spirit
. . . and an undaunted *magnanimous* bearing . . .

Alfred, Lord Tennyson 1809-1892

More than any other poet of the nineteenth century, Alfred Tennyson was the voice of the Victorian Age. English to the core of his being, he paid little attention to contemporary events outside his home island unless, like the Crimean War, they affected England itself. Like many of his fellow Victorians he was interested in science and troubled by the developing conflict between scientific thought and religion. In his poetry he displayed the seriousness and the high moral purpose the Victorians demanded. His appointment as poet laureate on the death of Wordsworth in 1850 was singularly appropriate, for he represented as few poets have the ideas and the aspirations of his age.

Alfred was the fourth of the twelve children of a rector in the little Lincolnshire village of Somersby. His father was a talented but moody man who brought his family up in an atmosphere of high thinking and lofty aspirations. The children took long walks in the pleasant countryside, played imaginative games drawn from tales of knight errantry, wrote continued stories in letter form, and acted old English plays. Before Alfred entered Trinity College, Cambridge, in 1828, he had already published a book of verse in conjunction with his brother.

At Cambridge Tennyson became associated with a group of brilliant students known as the "Apostles," who were distinguished by their acute intellectual curiosity, wit, and freedom of thought. One of the Apostles was Arthur Hallam, Tennyson's closest friend, who subsequently became engaged to Alfred's sister Emily.

A year before Tennyson left Cambridge, he published *Poems, Chiefly Lyrical*, and in 1832 he published still another volume, many of its poems being careful revisions of earlier work. The public liked these poems, which were romantic in spirit and showed the influence of Keats, and Tennyson was encouraged to go ahead in his chosen profession of poet.

Then in 1833 without warning came the most shattering blow ever to fall in Tennyson's life: Arthur Henry Hallam died in Vienna. The staggering impact of Hallam's death affected the young poet's health and spirits and left him with an overwhelming sense of bewilderment. For seventeen years he pondered over the death of his friend, struggling to make an adjustment between religious faith and scientific thought. Finally, in 1850, he published *In Memoriam;* here, in over a hundred lyrics, he showed the gradual evolution of his feelings from numb shock through despair to acceptance. Although *In Memoriam* was published almost a decade before Darwin's *Origin of Species*, it caught much of the thought about evolution that was troubling English thinkers. Throughout the poem there is evidence of Tennyson's effort to reconcile the orthodox religious faith his father had taught him with the radically different ideas which nineteenth-century science was bringing in its train.

While Tennyson was working on *In Memoriam*, he also turned his attention to other poems. He began work on *Idylls of the King*, a series of narrative poems in blank verse which retold the stories Malory had collected centuries before in the *Morte Darthur* (see page 86). In 1842 he published two volumes entitled *Poems*, which included "Ulysses" (page 443)

Farringford, Tennyson's home on the Isle of Wight.

and "Morte D'Arthur" (page 445). These volumes of poetry showed concretely the great effect Hallam's death had had on his friend's poetry.

During the year in which *In Memoriam* appeared, Tennyson married Emily Sellwood, his sweetheart of many years, and was appointed poet laureate. His affairs prospered; one volume of poetry after another was immediately successful. His dedication of an edition of *Idylls of the King* to the memory of Prince Albert, who died in 1861, delighted the Queen, and in 1884 Tennyson was raised to the peerage. As the years passed, he won the affection and recognition of Englishmen of all classes. Tall, gaunt, and distinguished, he filled the popular idea of how a poet should look. His life like his appearance was noble; in his character and his actions he seemed to embody the courtesy and dignity, the strength and courage, the high purpose and the devotion to duty that he wrote of in his tales of King Arthur and his noble knights. And the character that showed forth in his life is reflected in his poetry. When he died in 1892, he was buried in Westminster Abbey.

Sketch by Rossetti (see pages 464, 467) of Tennyson reading his highly successful poem "Maud."

FLOWER IN THE CRANNIED WALL

Flower in the crannied wall,
I pluck you out of the crannies,
I hold you here, root and all, in my hand,
Little flower—but *if* I could understand
What you are, root and all, and all in all,   5
I should know what God and man is.

BREAK, BREAK, BREAK

In this lyric the poet for the first time expressed his grief over the death of his friend Arthur Hallam. Tennyson tells us that he composed the poem "in a Lincolnshire lane at five o'clock in the morning between blossoming hawthorn hedges." However, the scene he pictures is the rocky coast of Somersetshire, viewed from the hill on which stands Clevedon Church, where Hallam is buried.

Break, break, break,
    On thy cold gray stones, O Sea!
And I would that my tongue could utter
    The thoughts that arise in me.

O well for the fisherman's boy,   5
    That he shouts with his sister at play!
O well for the sailor lad,
    That he sings in his boat on the bay!

And the stately ships go on
    To their haven under the hill;   10
But O for the touch of a vanished hand,
    And the sound of a voice that is still!

Break, break, break,
    At the foot of thy crags, O Sea!
But the tender grace of a day that is dead   15
    Will never come back to me.

from IN MEMORIAM A. H. H.

PROLOGUE

Strong son of God, immortal Love,
  Whom we, that have not seen Thy face,
  By faith, and faith alone, embrace,
Believing where we cannot prove;

Thine are these orbs¹ of light and shade;　　5
  Thou madest Life in man and brute;
  Thou madest Death; and lo, Thy foot
Is on the skull which Thou hast made.

Thou wilt not leave us in the dust:
  Thou madest man, he knows not why,　　10
  He thinks he was not made to die;
And Thou hast made him: Thou art just.

Thou seemest human and divine,
  The highest, holiest manhood, Thou.
  Our wills are ours, we know not how;　　15
Our wills are ours, to make them Thine.

Our little systems have their day;
  They have their day and cease to be;
  They are but broken lights of Thee,
And Thou, O Lord, art more than they.　　20

We have but faith: we cannot know,
  For knowledge is of things we see;
  And yet we trust it comes from Thee,
A beam in darkness: let it grow.

Let knowledge grow from more to more,　　25
  But more of reverence in us dwell;
  That mind and soul, according well,
May make one music as before,

But vaster. We are fools and slight;
  We mock Thee when we do not fear:　　30
  But help Thy foolish ones to bear;
Help Thy vain worlds to bear Thy light.

Forgive what seemed my sin in me,
  What seemed my worth since I began;
  For merit lives from man to man,　　35
And not from man, O Lord, to Thee.

Forgive my grief for one removed,
  Thy creature, whom I found so fair.
  I trust he lives in Thee, and there
I find him worthier to be loved.　　40

Forgive these wild and wandering cries,
  Confusions of a wasted youth;
  Forgive them where they fail in truth,
And in Thy wisdom make me wise.

54

O yet we trust that somehow good
  Will be the final goal of ill,
  To pangs of nature, sins of will,
Defects of doubt, and taints of blood;

That nothing walks with aimless feet;　　5
  That not one life shall be destroyed,
  Or cast as rubbish to the void,
When God hath made the pile complete;

That not a worm is cloven in vain;
  That not a moth with vain desire　　10
  Is shriveled in a fruitless fire,
Or but subserves another's gain.

Behold, we know not anything;
  I can but trust that good shall fall
  At last—far off—at last, to all,　　15
And every winter change to spring.

So runs my dream; but what am I?
  An infant crying in the night;
  An infant crying for the light,
And with no language but a cry.　　20

55

That wish, that of the living whole
  No life may fail beyond the grave,
  Derives it not from what we have
The likest God within the soul?

---

1. *orbs*, planets.

Are God and Nature then at strife,
  That Nature lends such evil dreams?
  So careful of the type she seems,
So careless of the single life,

That I, considering everywhere
  Her secret meaning in her deeds,
  And finding that of fifty seeds
She often brings but one to bear,

I falter where I firmly trod,
  And falling with my weight of cares
  Upon the great world's altar stairs
That slope through darkness up to God,

I stretch lame hands of faith, and grope,
  And gather dust and chaff, and call
  To what I feel is Lord of all,
And faintly trust the larger hope.

56

So careful of the type?" but no.
  From scarpèd cliff and quarried stone
  She cries, "A thousand types are gone;
I care for nothing, all shall go.

"Thou makest thine appeal to me,
  I bring to life, I bring to death;
  The spirit does but mean the breath.
I know no more." And he, shall he,

Man, her last work, who seemed so fair,
  Such splendid purpose in his eyes,
  Who rolled the psalm to wintry skies,
Who built him fanes of fruitless prayer,

Who trusted God was love indeed
  And love Creation's final law—
  Though Nature, red in tooth and claw
With ravine,[2] shrieked against his creed—

Who loved, who suffered countless ills,
  Who battled for the True, the Just,
  Be blown about the desert dust,
Or sealed within the iron hills?

No more? A monster then, a dream,
  A discord. Dragons of the prime,[3]

That tare[4] each other in their slime,
Were mellow music matched with him.

O life as futile, then as frail!
  O for thy voice[5] to soothe and bless!
  What hope of answer, or redress?
Behind the veil, behind the veil.

106

*In the third year following Hallam's death
Tennyson spent the Christmas holidays at his
new residence in Epping Forest. There were
no associations here to remind him of Hallam,
and he resolved to put aside his grief.*

Ring out, wild bells, to the wild sky,
  The flying cloud, the frosty light.
  The year is dying in the night;
Ring out, wild bells, and let him die.

Ring out the old, ring in the new,
  Ring, happy bells, across the snow.
  The year is going, let him go;
Ring out the false, ring in the true.

Ring out the grief that saps the mind,
  For those that here we see no more;
  Ring out the feud of rich and poor;
Ring in redress to all mankind.

Ring out a slowly dying cause,
  And ancient forms of party strife;
  Ring in the nobler modes of life,
With sweeter manners, purer laws.

Ring out the want, the care, the sin,
  The faithless coldness of the times;
  Ring out, ring out my mournful rhymes,
But ring the fuller minstrel in.

Ring out false pride in place and blood,
  The civic slander and the spite;
  Ring in the love of truth and right,
Ring in the common love of good.

---

2. *ravine* (rav'in), something seized and devoured as prey.
3. *Dragons of the prime*, prehistoric monsters. 4. *tare*,
tore. [*Scotch*] 5. *thy voice*, Hallam's voice.

Ring out old shapes of foul disease;   25
  Ring out the narrowing lust of gold;
  Ring out the thousand wars of old,
Ring in the thousand years of peace.

Ring in the valiant man and free,
  The larger heart, the kindlier hand;   30
  Ring out the darkness of the land,
Ring in the Christ that is to be.

ULYSSES

Homer's Odyssey is the story of the wanderings of the Greek hero Odysseus, or Ulysses, on his way home to his island kingdom of Ithaca after the siege of Troy. In this poem Tennyson imagines the reactions of the warrior, his life of high adventure behind him, now quietly at home with his wife Penelope, and his son Telemachus (tə lem'ə kəs).

It little profits that an idle king,
  By this still hearth, among these barren
    crags,
Matched with an aged wife, I mete and dole
Unequal laws unto a savage race,
That hoard, and sleep, and feed, and know
    not me.   5
I cannot rest from travel; I will drink
Life to the lees. All times I have enjoyed
Greatly, have suffered greatly, both with those
That loved me, and alone; on shore, and when
Through scudding drifts the rainy Hyades[1]   10
Vexed the dim sea. I am become a name;
For always roaming with a hungry heart
Much have I seen and known—cities of men
And manners, climates, councils, governments,
Myself not least, but honored of them all—   15
And drunk delight of battle with my peers,
Far on the ringing plains of windy Troy.
I am a part of all that I have met;
Yet all experience is an arch wherethrough
Gleams that untraveled world whose margin
    fades   20
Forever and forever when I move.
How dull it is to pause, to make an end,
To rust unburnished, not to shine in use!
As though to breathe were life! Life piled on
    life

Were all too little, and of one to me   25
Little remains; but every hour is saved
From that eternal silence, something more,
A bringer of new things; and vile it were
For some three suns to store and hoard myself,
And this gray spirit yearning in desire   30
To follow knowledge like a sinking star,
Beyond the utmost bound of human thought.
    This is my son, mine own Telemachus,
To whom I leave the scepter and the isle—
Well-loved of me, discerning to fulfill   35
This labor, by slow prudence to make mild
A rugged people, and through soft degrees
Subdue them to the useful and the good.
Most blameless is he, centered in the sphere
Of common duties, decent not to fail   40
In offices of tenderness, and pay
Meet adoration to my household gods,
When I am gone. He works his work, I mine.
    There lies the port; the vessel puffs her
      sail;
There gloom the dark, broad seas. My
    mariners,   45
Souls that have toiled, and wrought, and
    thought with me—
That ever with a frolic welcome took
The thunder and the sunshine, and opposed
Free hearts, free foreheads—you and I are
    old;
Old age hath yet his honor and his toil.   50
Death closes all; but something ere the end,
Some work of noble note, may yet be done,
Not unbecoming men that strove with gods.
The lights begin to twinkle from the rocks;
The long day wanes; the slow moon climbs;
    the deep   55
Moans round with many voices. Come, my
    friends.
'Tis not too late to seek a newer world.
Push off, and sitting well in order smite
The sounding furrows; for my purpose holds
To sail beyond the sunset, and the baths   60
Of all the western stars, until I die.
It may be that the gulfs will wash us down;
It may be we shall touch the Happy Isles,[2]
And see the great Achilles,[3] whom we knew.

1. *rainy Hyades* (hī'ə dēz), a group of seven stars once associated with the rainy season. 2. *Happy Isles*, the mythical Islands of the Blessed where the souls of the good were supposed to dwell after death. 3. *Achilles* (ə kil'ēz), a great Greek warrior slain in battle.

Though much is taken, much abides; and
　　though　　　65
We are not now that strength which in old
　　days
Moved earth and heaven, that which we are,
　　we are—
One equal temper of heroic hearts,
Made weak by time and fate, but strong in
　　will
To strive, to seek, to find, and not to yield. 70

from LOCKSLEY HALL

*The speaker in "Locksley Hall" is a young
man who, having been rebuffed by the woman
he loves, is determined to find solace by recap-
turing his youthful vision of a happier world.
These lines reveal both Tennyson's interest in
science and his basic faith in mankind.*

For I dipped into the future, far as human
　　eye could see,
Saw the vision of the world, and all the
　　wonder that would be;

Saw the heavens fill with commerce, argosies
　　of magic sails,
Pilots of the purple twilight, dropping down
　　with costly bales;

Heard the heavens fill with shouting, and
　　there rained a ghastly dew　　5
From the nations' airy navies grappling in the
　　central blue;

Far along the world-wide whisper of the south
　　wind rushing warm
With the standards of the people plunging
　　through the thunderstorm;

Till the war drum throbbed no longer, and
　　the battle flags were furled
In the Parliament of man, the Federation of
　　the world.　　10

There the common sense of most shall hold a
　　fretful realm in awe,
And the kindly earth shall slumber, lapped
　　in universal law.

The Poet Laureate

To the ancient Greeks, the laurel was a symbol of distinction and was used to form a
crown of honor for poets and heroes. The
English used the word *laureate* to signify
glory. In England's Middle Ages the title
"poet laureate" was applied to any eminent
poet. Thus poetic tributes referred to both
Chaucer and Spenser as "laureates."

The first poet laureates attached to the
court seem to have been Ben Jonson (for
whom the office was created by James I in
1617) and his successor, Sir William Davenant. The office did not become official, however, until John Dryden's appointment in
1670. Dryden received letters patent to the
position, a pension of three-hundred pounds,
and one-hundred-twenty-six gallons of Canary
wine.

Early duties of the poet laureate were to
produce verses on birthdays and court occasions. Many of England's better poets, feeling that the position was a trivial one, refused
it. Thus, during the seventeenth and eighteenth centuries the position was held by mere
versifiers and second-rate poets. Thomas Gray
and Sir Walter Scott have the distinction of
having declined the appointment. Robert
Southey, who accepted the office, was ridiculed by Byron in *Don Juan* for doing so.
Wordsworth took the laureateship with the
stipulation that he would not necessarily have
to write verse for court occasions, and the
office became an honorary one. Tennyson,
who followed Wordsworth into the office, was
by temperament ideally suited to the position,
and he did much to elevate the office in the
eyes of poets. Robert Bridges, Tennyson's successor, and John Masefield, who took the
office in 1930, were the latest of England's
poets to be appointed to what is now an honored and dignified position.

MORTE D'ARTHUR

So all day long the noise of battle roll'd
Among the mountains by the winter
    sea;
Until King Arthur's table, man by man,
Had fallen in Lyonnesse[1] about their lord,
King Arthur: then, because his wound was
    deep,   5
The bold Sir Bedivere uplifted him,
Sir Bedivere, the last of all his knights,
And bore him to a chapel nigh the field,
A broken chancel with a broken cross,
That stood on a dark strait of barren land.   10
On one side lay the ocean, and on one
Lay a great water, and the moon was full.

Then spake King Arthur to Sir Bedivere:
"The sequel of today unsolders all
The goodliest fellowship of famous knights   15
Whereof this world holds record. Such a sleep
They sleep—the men I loved. I think that we
Shall never more, at any future time,
Delight our souls with talk of knightly deeds,
Walking about the gardens and the halls   20
Of Camelot, as in the days that were.
I perish by this people which I made—
Tho' Merlin sware that I should come again
To rule once more—but let what will be, be,
I am so deeply smitten thro' the helm   25
That without help I cannot last till morn.
Thou therefore take my brand Excalibur,
Which was my pride: for thou rememberest
    how
In those old days, one summer noon, an arm
Rose up from out the bosom of the lake,   30
Clothed in white samite, mystic, wonderful,
Holding the sword—and how I row'd across
And took it, and have worn it, like a king:
And, wheresoever I am sung or told
In aftertime, this also shall be known: 35
But now delay not: take Excalibur,
And fling him far into the middle mere:
Watch what thou seest, and lightly bring me
    word."

To him replied the bold Sir Bedivere:
"It is not meet, Sir King, to leave thee thus, 40
Aidless, alone, and smitten thro' the helm.
A little thing may harm a wounded man.
Yet I thy hest will all perform at full,
Watch what I see, and lightly bring thee
    word."

So saying, from the ruin'd shrine he stept   45
And in the moon athwart the place of tombs,
Where lay the mighty bones of ancient men,[2]
Old knights, and over them the sea wind sang
Shrill, chill, with flakes of foam. He,
    stepping down
By zigzag paths, and juts of pointed rock,   50
Came on the shining levels of the lake.

There drew he forth the brand Excalibur,
And o'er him, drawing it, the winter moon,
Brightening the skirts of a long cloud, ran
    forth
And sparkled keen with frost against the
    hilt: 55
For all the haft twinkled with diamond
    sparks,
Myriads of topaz lights, and jacinth work
Of subtlest jewelry. He gazed so long
That both his eyes were dazzled, as he stood,
This way and that dividing the swift mind,   60
In act to throw: but at the last it seem'd
Better to leave Excalibur conceal'd
There in the many-knotted waterflags,
That whistled stiff and dry about the marge.
So strode he back slow to the wounded
    King.   65

Then spake King Arthur to Sir Bedivere:
"Hast thou perform'd my mission which I
    gave?

---

1. *Lyonnesse*, a fabled country supposedly situated in part
of what is now Cornwall. 2. *place of tombs . . . men*, probably the tombs of the early Danish invaders of Britain,
reputed to have been men of great stature.

What is it thou hast seen? or what hast
  heard?"

And answer made the bold Sir Bedivere:
"I heard the ripple washing in the reeds,   70
And the wild water lapping on the crag."

To whom replied King Arthur, faint and
  pale:
"Thou hast betray'd thy nature and thy
  name,
Not rendering true answer, as beseem'd
Thy fealty, nor like a noble knight: 75
For surer sign had follow'd, either hand,
Or voice, or else a motion of the mere.
This is a shameful thing for men to lie.
Yet now, I charge thee, quickly go again
As thou art lief and dear, and do the thing   80
I bade thee, watch, and lightly bring me
  word."

Then went Sir Bedivere the second time
Across the ridge, and paced beside the mere,
Counting the dewy pebbles, fix'd in thought;
But when he saw the wonder of the hilt,   85
How curiously and strangely chased, he smote
His palms together, and he cried aloud,

"And if indeed I cast the brand away,
Surely a precious thing, one worthy note,
Should thus be lost forever from the earth,   90
Which might have pleased the eyes of many
  men.
What good should follow this, if this were
  done?
What harm, undone? deep harm to disobey,
Seeing obedience is the bond of rule.
Were it well to obey, then, if a king
  demand   95
An act unprofitable, against himself?
The King is sick, and knows not what he
  does.
What record, or what relic of my lord
Should be to aftertime, but empty breath
And rumors of a doubt? but were this kept,   100
Stored in some treasure-house of mighty
  kings,
Some one might show it at a joust of arms,
Saying, 'King Arthur's sword, Excalibur,
Wrought by the lonely Maiden of the Lake.

Nine years she wrought it, sitting in the
  deeps   105
Upon the hidden bases of the hills.'
So might some old man speak in the aftertime
To all the people, winning reverence.

But now much honor and much fame were
  lost."
  So spake he, clouded with his own conceit,
And hid Excalibur the second time,   111
And so strode back slow to the wounded King.

Then spoke King Arthur, breathing
  heavily:
"What is it thou hast seen? or what hast
  heard?"

And answer made the bold Sir Bedivere: 115
"I heard the water lapping on the crag,
And the long ripple washing in the reeds."

To whom replied King Arthur, much in
  wrath:
"Ah, miserable and unkind, untrue,
Unknightly, traitor-hearted! Woe is me!   120
Authority forgets a dying king,
Laid widow'd of the power in his eye
That bow'd the will. I see thee what thou art,
For thou, the latest-left of all my knights,
In whom should meet the offices of all,   125
Thou wouldst betray me for the precious hilt;
Either from lust of gold, or like a girl
Valuing the giddy pleasure of the eyes.
Yet, for a man may fail in duty twice,
And the third time may prosper, get thee
  hence: 130
But, if thou spare to fling Excalibur,
I will arise and slay thee with my hands."

Then quickly rose Sir Bedivere, and ran,
And, leaping down the ridges lightly, plunged
Among the bulrush beds, and clutch'd the
  sword,   135
And strongly wheel'd and threw it. The
  great brand
Made lightnings in the splendor of the moon,
And flashing round and round, and whirl'd
  in an arch,
Shot like a streamer of the northern morn,[3]

3. *streamer . . . northern morn,* northern lights.

Seen where the moving isles of winter shock
By night, with noises of the northern sea. 141
So flash'd and fell the brand Excalibur:
But ere he dipt the surface, rose an arm
Clothed in white samite, mystic, wonderful,
And caught him by the hilt, and brandish'd
    him   145
Three times, and drew him under in the
    mere.
And lightly went the other to the King.

And spoke King Arthur, drawing thicker
    breath:
"Now see I by thine eyes that this is done.
Speak out: what is it thou hast heard, or
    seen?"   150

And answer made the bold Sir Bedivere:
"Sir King, I closed mine eyelids, lest the gems
Should blind my purpose, for I never saw,
Nor shall see, here or elsewhere, till I die,
Not tho' I live three lives of mortal men, 155
So great a miracle as yonder hilt.
Then with both hands I flung him, wheeling
    him
But when I look'd again, behold an arm,
Clothed in white samite, mystic, wonderful,
That caught him by the hilt, and brandish'd
    him   160
Three times, and drew him under in the
    mere."

And answer made King Arthur, breathing
    hard:
"My end draws nigh; 'tis time that I were
    gone.
Make broad thy shoulders to receive my
    weight,
And bear me to the margin; yet I fear   165
My wound hath taken cold, and I shall die."

So saying, from the pavement he half rose,
Slowly, with pain, reclining on his arm,
And looking wistfully with wide blue eyes
As in a picture. Him Sir Bedivere   170
Remorsefully regarded thro' his tears,
And would have spoken, but he found not
    words;
Then took with care, and kneeling on one
    knee,

O'er both his shoulders drew the languid
    hands,
And rising bore him thro' the place of
    tombs.

But, as he walk'd, King Arthur panted
    hard,   176
Like one that feels a nightmare on his bed
When all the house is mute. So sigh'd the
    King,
Muttering and murmuring at his ear, "Quick,
    quick!
I fear it is too late, and I shall die."   180
But the other swiftly strode from ridge to
    ridge,
Clothed with his breath, and looking, as he
    walk'd,
Larger than human on the frozen hills.
He heard the deep behind him, and a cry
Before. His own thought drove him, like a
    goad.   185
Dry clash'd his harness in the icy caves
And barren chasms, and all to left and right
The bare black cliff clang'd round him, as he
    based
His feet on juts of slippery crag that rang
Sharp-smitten with the dint of armed heels—
And on a sudden, lo! the level lake,   191
And the long glories of the winter moon.

Then saw they how there hove a dusky
    barge,
Dark as a funeral scarf from stem to stern,
Beneath them; and descending they were
    ware   195
That all the decks were dense with stately
    forms
Black-stoled, black-hooded, like a dream—by
    these
Three Queens with crowns of gold—and
    from them rose
A cry that shiver'd to the tingling stars,
And, as it were one voice, an agony   200
Of lamentation, like a wind, that shrills
All night in a waste land, where no one
    comes,
Or hath come, since the making of the world.

Then murmur'd Arthur, "Place me in the
    barge,"

And to the barge they came. There those three Queens   205
Put forth their hands, and took the King, and wept.
But she, that rose the tallest of them all
And fairest, laid his head upon her lap,
And loosed the shatter'd casque, and chafed his hands,
And call'd him by his name, complaining loud,   210
And dropping bitter tears against his brow
Striped with dark blood: for all his face was white
And colorless, and like the wither'd moon
Smote by the fresh beam of the springing east;
And all his greaves and cuisses dash'd with drops   215
Of onset; and the light and lustrous curls—
That made his forehead like a rising sun
High from the dais throne—were parch'd with dust;
Or, clotted into points and hanging loose,
Mix'd with the knightly growth that fringed his lips.   220
So like a shatter'd column lay the King;
Not like that Arthur who, with lance in rest,
From spur to plume a star of tournament,
Shot thro' the lists at Camelot, and charged
Before the eyes of ladies and of kings.   225

Then loudly cried the bold Sir Bedivere,
"Ah! my Lord Arthur, whither shall I go?
Where shall I hide my forehead and my eyes?
For now I see the true old times are dead,
When every morning brought a noble chance,   230
And every chance brought out a noble knight.
Such times have been not since the light that led
The holy Elders with the gift of myrrh.[4]
But now the whole Round Table is dissolved
Which was an image of the mighty world;   235
And I, the last, go forth companionless,
And the days darken round me, and the years,
Among new men, strange faces, other minds."

And slowly answered Arthur from the barge:

"The old order changeth, yielding place to new,   240
And God fulfills Himself in many ways,
Lest one good custom should corrupt the world.
Comfort thyself: what comfort is in me?
I have lived my life, and that which I have done
May He within Himself make pure! but thou,   245
If thou shouldst never see my face again,
Pray for my soul. More things are wrought by prayer
Than this world dreams of. Wherefore, let thy voice
Rise like a fountain for me night and day.   249
For what are men better than sheep or goats
That nourish a blind life within the brain,
If, knowing God, they lift not hands of prayer
Both for themselves and those who call them friend?
For so the whole round earth is every way   254
Bound by gold chains about the feet of God.
But now farewell. I am going a long way
With these thou seest—if indeed I go—
(For all my mind is clouded with a doubt)
To the island-valley of Avilion[5];
Where falls not hail, or rain, or any snow,   260
Nor ever wind blows loudly; but it lies
Deep-meadow'd, happy, fair with orchard lawns
And bowery hollows crown'd with summer sea,
Where I will heal me of my grievous wound."

So said he, and the barge with oar and sail
Moved from the brink, like some full-breasted swan   266
That, fluting a wild carol ere her death,
Ruffles her pure cold plume, and takes the flood
With swarthy webs. Long stood Sir Bedivere
Revolving many memories, till the hull   270
Look'd one black dot against the verge of dawn,
And on the mere the wailing died away.

---

4. *holy Elders . . . myrrh*, the Magi. (Matthew 2:1-12)
5. *Avilion*, Avalon, Land of the Blessed, an imaginary ocean island.

CROSSING THE BAR

Tennyson tells us that this lyric came to him "in a moment" in his eighty-first year. A few days before he died, two years later, the poet gave instructions that the lyric be placed last in all editions of his work.

Sunset and evening star,
  And one clear call for me!
And may there be no moaning of the bar,[1]
  When I put out to sea,

But such a tide as moving seems asleep, 5
  Too full for sound and foam,
When that which drew from out the boundless
    deep
  Turns again home.

Twilight and evening bell,
  And after that the dark! 10
And may there be no sadness of farewell,
  When I embark;

For though from out our bourn of time and
    place
  The flood may bear me far,
I hope to see my Pilot[2] face to face 15
  When I have crossed the bar.

1. *no moaning of the bar.* A sandbar sometimes obstructs the passage of a ship from the harbor into open water. An old superstition held that, whenever a death occurred, the outgoing tide moaned as it rolled over the bar. 2. *my Pilot.* Tennyson explained the Pilot as "that Divine and Unseen Who is always guiding us."

To increase understanding

Flower in the Crannied Wall

1. Compare the thought of "Flower in a Crannied Wall" with that expressed by William Blake in "Auguries of Innocence":

> To see a world in a grain of sand,
>   And a heaven in a wild flower;
> Hold infinity in the palm of your hand
>   And eternity in an hour.

2. In what way is the thought of "Flower in the Crannied Wall" typical of Tennyson?

Break, Break, Break and selections from In Memoriam

1. (a) How is "Break, Break, Break" related to *In Memoriam*? (b) What is its tone?

2. In stanza 1 of the "Prologue" to *In Memoriam* Tennyson speaks of "faith alone" and "Believing where we cannot prove." What facets of Victorian thought are implied by these quotations?

3. In stanzas 2-4 Tennyson gives reasons for his belief in God. (a) What reasons does he advance for this belief? (b) Cite the lines in which he implies a belief in immortality. (c) How does he relate this belief to belief in God?

4. (a) What distinction between faith and knowledge does Tennyson make in stanza 6? (b) Trace and explain the thought introduced by Tennyson's mention of knowledge as "A beam in darkness" (line 24).

5. What reference to Hallam do you find in the "Prologue"?

6. Is the prevailing tone of the "Prologue" one of faith or of doubt? Explain.

7. Explain how Section 54 illustrates the line "Believing where we cannot prove."

8. (a) What lines in Section 54 best express Tennyson's belief in a merciful God? (b) Which lines reveal his doubts?

9. In Section 55 what conflict between God and Nature troubles the poet?

10. (a) What does Tennyson mean by "the larger hope" in the last line of Section 55? (b) Is the poet's hope stronger or weaker in this section than in Section 54? Explain.

11. (a) What is the purpose of repeating "So careful of the type" (Section 55, line 7) as part of the first line of Section 56? (b) How does use of the question mark change the idea?

12. (a) Who is the speaker in lines 3-8 of Section 56? (b) What thought is here expressed? (c) Cite lines in Sections 55 and 56 which refer to the theory of evolution.

13. Explain the contrasting views of Man and Nature developed in Section 56, citing lines to illustrate the ideas.

14. (a) How does Section 106 differ in tone from the other sections of *In Memoriam* you have studied? (b) How does it differ in ideas treated?

Ulysses and selection from Locksley Hall

1. (a) Why is Ulysses dissatisfied with his present state of life? (b) Read aloud lines that express his feeling.

2. Ulysses and Telemachus represent two quite different ideals of life. (a) Discuss the advantages

and disadvantages of each way. (*b*) Explain whether in your opinion Tennyson is unbiased in his presentation of each view of living.

3. (*a*) What does Ulysses mean by saying "I am a part of all that I have met" (line 18)? (*b*) Explain the three lines following line 18.

4. Probably one reason "Ulysses" is frequently quoted is that it contains many lines which, like those cited in question 3, have a universal application. Cite and explain the meaning of other lines of this type.

5. Tennyson himself said that "Ulysses," written shortly after the death of Hallam, expressed his need of "going forward and braving the struggle of life." (*a*) How is this need reflected in the overall meaning of the poem? (*b*) What lines best summarize this theme?

6. "Locksley Hall" was written in 1842. (*a*) What specific things does Tennyson mention that were then predictions and have since become realities? (*b*) Which prophecies remain unfulfilled?

7. In what way does "Locksley Hall" reveal both Tennyson's interest in science and his faith in mankind?

Morte D'Arthur and *Crossing the Bar*

1. Tennyson's "Morte D'Arthur" is based on the portion of Malory's *Morte Darthur* printed on pages 86-87. Locate the following parallel passages and point out similarities and differences: (*a*) the description of Excalibur; (*b*) Bedivere's account of his

actions and Arthur's replies; (*c*) the casting away of the sword; (*d*) Arthur's reception on the barge; (*e*) Bedivere's lament and Arthur's reply.

2. (*a*) What details of setting does Malory's version contain? (*b*) Cite some of the lines used to describe the setting in Tennyson's poem. (*c*) Does Tennyson use setting to fulfill the same function as Malory does? Explain.

3. (*a*) Explain how Tennyson adds a moral and religious tone to the following passages: (1) Bedivere's speech as he deliberates on whether to cast away Excalibur (lines 88-109); (2) Arthur's reply (lines 119-132); (3) Arthur's speech from the barge (lines 240-264). (*b*) What can you learn about Tennyson and the age in which he wrote from these passages? (*c*) Why are there no similar passages in Malory?

4. Lines from Tennyson's "Morte D'Arthur" are frequently quoted. Select lines from the poem that you have previously heard or that you particularly like. What makes these lines quotable?

5. (*a*) What makes this poem melodious? (*b*) What use does Tennyson make of imagery and of figurative language? (*c*) What is the tone of the poem?

6. Why do you think Tennyson wished "Crossing the Bar" to be printed at the end of every edition of his works?

7. (*a*) What is the tone of "Crossing the Bar"? (*b*) Compare the attitude of the poet here with his attitude in *In Memoriam*.

Matthew Arnold 1822-1888

*Portrait of
Matthew Arnold
by G. F. Watts.*

Unlike Tennyson, who early determined to be a poet and remained a poet all his long life, Matthew Arnold sought for and attained excellence in a number of areas. He was a poet, an educator, a classical scholar, and one of the most brilliant literary critics of the Victorian Age.

Arnold's interest in education came to him naturally, for his father was the renowned headmaster of Rugby, Thomas Arnold, who in the first half of the nineteenth century did much to revolutionize secondary-school education in England. Matthew attended Rugby as a matter of course, and then went to Oxford, where the Oxford Movement was reaching its climax. The reforms of Newman and his associates left Arnold untouched, since he had little interest in organized religion. His remedy for the ills of the Victorian world was culture, and he found the culture he sought in the civilization of the ancient Greeks. Toward science, the growing god, Arnold was unsympathetic.

Shortly after leaving Oxford, Arnold became a government inspector of schools, a post he held until two years before his death. In 1859 he was made foreign assistant commissioner on education. In connection with this appointment he made an extensive study of school systems on the continent of Europe and wrote several books which have become standard texts on continental education. In 1857 he was appointed to the chair of poetry at Oxford and lectured there for ten years. Later in life he became a lecturer to the general public both in England and the United States.

Arnold was one of the most dissatisfied men of the Victorian Age. Sharply critical of the materialism of nineteenth-century civilization and of its comfort-loving devotees, he constantly preached the gospel of culture. This he defined as a compound of "sweetness and light" consisting of a knowledge of "the best that has been thought and said in the world." He referred to the Victorian middle class as "Philistines," a term he used to describe people whom he regarded as crude and uncultured. He fancied himself as a "lonely Greek," friendly to ideas of beauty which were unappreciated by his contemporaries. To the end of his life he maintained that no work of art could be great that did not possess both artistic merit and moral power. His insistence on this is particularly strong in *Essays on Criticism* (1865, 1888), *On the Study of Celtic Literature* (1867), and *The Study of Poetry* (1880).

Arnold once defined religion as "morality touched with emotion." It was this unwillingness to accept religious faith without reservations, while accepting the supreme importance of morality, that made him one of the most effective of the Victorian poets of doubt.

DOVER BEACH

The sea is calm tonight,
   The tide is full, the moon lies fair
   Upon the straits; on the French
     coast the light
Gleams and is gone; the cliffs of England
    stand,   4
Glimmering and vast, out in the tranquil bay.
Come to the window, sweet is the night air!

Only, from the long line of spray
Where the sea meets the moon-blanched land,
Listen! you hear the grating roar
Of pebbles which the waves draw back, and
    fling,   10
At their return, up the high strand,
Begin, and cease, and then again begin,
With tremulous cadence slow, and bring
The eternal note of sadness in.

Sophocles[1] long ago   15
Heard it on the Aegean, and it brought
Into his mind the turbid ebb and flow
Of human misery; we

Find also in the sound a thought,
Hearing it by this distant northern sea.   20

The Sea of Faith
Was once, too, at the full, and round earth's
    shore
Lay like the folds of a bright girdle furled.
But now I only hear
Its melancholy, long, withdrawing roar,   25
Retreating, to the breath
Of the night wind, down the vast edges drear
And naked shingles[2] of the world.

Ah, love, let us be true
To one another! for the world, which seems 30
To lie before us like a land of dreams,
So various, so beautiful, so new,
Hath really neither joy, nor love, nor light,
Nor certitude, nor peace, nor help for pain;
And we are here as on a darkling plain   35
Swept with confused alarms of struggle and
    flight,
Where ignorant armies clash by night.

---

1. *Sophocles* (sof'ə klēz), 495-406? B.C., a noted author of Greek tragedy. 2. *shingles*, beaches.

SELF-DEPENDENCE

Weary of myself, and sick of asking
What I am, and what I ought to be,
At this vessel's prow I stand, which bears me
Forwards, forwards, o'er the starlit sea.

And a look of passionate desire   5
O'er the sea and to the stars I send:
"Ye who from my childhood up have calmed
          me,
Calm me, ah, compose me to the end!

"Ah, once more," I cried, "ye stars, ye waters,
On my heart your mighty charm renew;   10
Still, still let me, as I gaze upon you,
Feel my soul becoming vast like you!"

From the intense, clear star-sown vault of
          heaven,
Over the lit sea's unquiet way,
In the rustling night air came the answer: 15
"Wouldst thou *be* as they are? *Live* as they.

"Unaffrighted by the silence round them,
Undistracted by the sights they see,
These demand not that the things without
          them
Yield them love, amusement, sympathy.   20

"And with joy the stars perform their shining,
And the sea its long moon-silvered roll;
For self-poised they live, nor pine with noting
All the fever of some differing soul.

"Bounded by themselves, and unregardful   25
In what state God's other works may be,
In their own tasks all their powers pouring,
These attain the mighty life you see."

O air-borne voice! long since, severely clear,
A cry like thine in mine own heart I hear: 30
"Resolve to be thyself; and I know that he
Who finds himself loses his misery!"

❀ To increase understanding

1. (*a*) What is the setting of "Dover Beach"?
(*b*) What is the tone of the first part of the poem?
(*c*) Where does the tone change? (*d*) What is the
dominant tone of the poem as a whole?
2. (*a*) When was the "Sea of Faith" at the full?
(*b*) Explain the analogy developed in stanza 4.
3. (*a*) Is it likely that a poem like "Dover
Beach" would have been written before the nineteenth century? (*b*) Is this theme uncommon today? Explain.
4. (*a*) Chart the rhyme scheme of the first two
stanzas of "Dover Beach." (*b*) Scan several lines
of the poem. (*c*) Explain how the irregular rhythm
and the unobtrusive rhyme help establish the tone.
5. (*a*) In "Self-Dependence" what is the reason
the poet is disconsolate? (*b*) What is his plea? (*c*)
What is the answer?
6. (*a*) Do these poems possess the "moral power"
that Arnold demanded of a work of art? Explain.
(*b*) What light do they throw on Arnold as a Victorian poet of doubt?

❀ Better reading
The effects of poetic phrasing

One of the more elusive elements a poet uses to
give his poetry form and beauty is a particular arrangement or order of words. In some poetry this
arrangement may be partly conditioned by the demands of rhythm and rhyme; but the true poet
usually manipulates words and phrases as he orders
rhythm, imagery, and figurative language to add
meaning to a poem and to underscore the tone.

In the first stanza of "Dover Beach," Matthew
Arnold makes extensive use of the *broken line*; that
is, he phrases the lines so that there is either a full
stop or a pause in the middle of the line. Read
this stanza aloud. How does the mid-line pause aid
the effect of vast calmness and quiet meditation the
poet seeks to gain here?

Contrast the second stanza with the first. Note
that the only full break within a line occurs after
the first foot of line 9. How does this break accen-
tuate the description of the sounds of the tide that
follows it? Read lines 9 through 14 aloud, pausing
at the commas and letting your voice rise and fall
naturally. How does the phrasing help the reader
sense the action of the sea? What words in line 13
give the tempo as well as the idea of the slow rhythm
of the sea?

"Morte D'Arthur" shows Tennyson's artistry at
handling blank verse in such a way that the five-

beat line never becomes monotonous. Moreover, the line moves slowly or rapidly in harmony with the idea expressed. Tennyson achieves this variety by the arrangement of words, phrases, and pauses. To note the skill with which a master craftsman can handle blank verse, read aloud lines 14 through 21. Are any of the lines end-stopped? Where do the most important breaks occur? What is the longest sequence of words between breaks? What is the shortest? What is the total effect of the passage?

Study the lines which describe Sir Bedivere's casting of the sword (lines 133-147). How would you describe the movement of the first part of this passage? Where does a change occur? What is the reason for the change?

Compare Arthur's famous last speech (lines 240-264) with lines 54-70 of "Ulysses." What differences in pace do you observe? What causes these differences? To what extent does the ordering of phrases affect the tone?

Robert Browning 1812-1889 and Elizabeth Barrett Browning 1806-1861

Robert Browning and Alfred Tennyson, the two greatest poets of the middle decades of the nineteenth century, were unlike in almost every way. Tennyson was a Victorian Englishman in his interests and his attitudes, and spent most of his long life in England. Browning was possessed of an un-Victorian optimism and lived for long periods in Italy. Tennyson's poetry was easily understood, and the grace and beauty of its form together with its high seriousness captivated the Victorian public. Browning's poetry was far harder to understand and often substituted strength and ruggedness for smoothness. Although it was less popular in the poet's own day than Tennyson's poetry, its reputation has steadily grown greater in the intervening years.

Robert Browning was one of the few English writers of modern times who never attended an English university, yet he stands among the most erudite of English poets. The son of a well-to-do clerk in the Bank of England, he received most of his education from private tutors and from reading in his father's excellent library. At the age of twenty-two he made the "grand tour" of Europe, spending much time in Russia and in Italy, a country with which he immediately fell in love. In 1835 *Paracelsus*, his first work of any importance, appeared. In this dramatic poem, based on the life of a fifteenth-century magician and alchemist, he showed for the first time both the interest in the Renaissance and in men and their motives that are dominant strains in his work. Other volumes followed during the 1840's, but most of them gained little public acclaim.

Then in 1846 occurred an event that was of major importance to Browning's life and to his work. He married the popular poet Elizabeth Barrett, an invalid. In hope of improving Elizabeth's health, the Brownings went to Italy to live, and for fifteen years, until Mrs. Browning's death in 1861, they lived an idyllic life there. They became interested in Italian politics and Italian art, and Robert Browning pursued further his interest in the Renaissance. His work steadily grew in depth and range, and in 1855 he published *Men and Women*, which contained some of his finest dramatic monologues, including "Andrea del Sarto" (page 456).

Mrs. Browning's most famous work also dates from the Italian sojourn. During her engagement to Robert Browning she had written some sonnets, and she completed the sequence during the first years of their marriage. Presented to her husband as a gift, the sequence was entitled *Sonnets from the Portuguese,* the title being a playful reference to the fact that Browning had called her his "little Portuguese" because of her dark complexion. More personal and intimate than most sonnets, this sequence of forty-four sonnets is among the finest achievements of its kind in English literature.

After Mrs. Browning's death, Robert Browning returned to England. For a time he shunned society, but in time his optimism and his courage drove him back to a more normal way of life. He published *Dramatis Personae* (1864) and the four-volume *The Ring and the Book.* His reputation rose steadily. In 1878 he returned to Italy for a visit. He spent the last years of his life in Venice, and it was there he died. He is buried in Westminster Abbey, not far from the tomb of Tennyson, who died three years later.

Twentieth-century readers, accustomed to the conciseness and obscurity of much poetry today, find Browning a strangely modern poet. The poetry which was so "difficult" to Victorian readers seems far less difficult a hundred years later. The ruggedness and force of the verse appeal to the modern reader. So too do the poet's insistence on the necessity of courage, hope, and the will to try.

SUMMUM BONUM *The Latin title of this poem (pronounced sum′əm bō′nəm) literally means "the highest good."*

All the breath and bloom of the year in the bag of one bee;
  All the wonder and wealth of the mine in the heart of one gem;
In the core of one pearl all the shade and the shine of the sea:
  Breath and bloom, shade and shine—wonder, wealth, and—how far above
      them—
        Truth, that's brighter than gem,   5
        Trust, that's purer than pearl—
Brightest truth, purest trust in the universe—all were for me
        In the kiss of one girl.

Portrait of Browning by Francis Talfourd.

HOME THOUGHTS, FROM ABROAD

Oh, to be in England
  Now that April's there,
  And whoever wakes in England
  Sees, some morning, unaware,
That the lowest boughs and the brushwood
      sheaf   5
Round the elm tree bole are in tiny leaf,
While the chaffinch sings on the orchard
      bough
In England—now!

And after April, when May follows,
And the whitethroat builds, and all the
     swallows! 10
Hark, where my blossomed pear tree in the
     hedge
Leans to the field and scatters on the clover
Blossoms and dewdrops—at the bent spray's
     edge—
That's the wise thrush; he sings each song
     twice over,
Lest you should think he never could
     recapture 15
The first fine careless rapture!
And though the fields look rough with hoary
     dew,
All will be gay when noontide wakes anew
The buttercups, the little children's dower
—Far brighter than this gaudy melon flower!

MY LAST DUCHESS

*The scene is the city of Ferrara (fə rär′ə) in
northern Italy. The time is the Renaissance.
The speaker is the Duke of Ferrara, who is
negotiating with an envoy sent by a count
about marrying the count's daughter.*

That's my last Duchess painted on the wall,
Looking as if she were alive. I call
That piece a wonder, now; Frà Pandolf's[1]
     hands
Worked busily a day, and there she stands.
Will't please you sit and look at her? I said 5
"Frà Pandolf" by design, for never read
Strangers like you that pictured countenance,
The depth and passion of its earnest glance,
But to myself they turned (since none puts by
The curtain I have drawn for you, but I) 10
And seemed as they would ask me, if they
     durst,
How such a glance came there; so, not the
     first
Are you to turn and ask thus. Sir, 'twas not
Her husband's presence, only, called that spot
Of joy into the Duchess' cheek. Perhaps 15
Frà Pandolf chanced to say, "Her mantle laps
Over my lady's wrist too much," or "Paint
Must never hope to reproduce the faint
Half-flush that dies along her throat"; such
     stuff

Was courtesy, she thought, and cause enough
For calling up that spot of joy. She had 21
A heart—how shall I say?—too soon made
     glad,
Too easily impressed: she liked whate'er
She looked on, and her looks went everywhere.
Sir, 'twas all one! My favor at her breast, 25
The dropping of the daylight in the west,
The bough of cherries some officious fool
Broke in the orchard for her, the white mule
She rode with round the terrace—all and each
Would draw from her alike the approving
     speech, 30
Or blush, at least. She thanked men—good!
     but thanked
Somehow—I know not how—as if she ranked
My gift of a nine-hundred-years-old name
With anybody's gift. Who'd stoop to blame
This sort of trifling? Even had you skill 35
In speech—(which I have not)—to make your
     will
Quite clear to such an one, and say, "Just this
Or that in you disgusts me; here you miss,
Or there exceed the mark"—and if she let
Herself be lessoned so, nor plainly set 40
Her wits to yours, forsooth, and made
     excuse—
E'en that would be some stooping; and I
     choose
Never to stoop. Oh, sir, she smiled, no doubt,
Whene'er I passed her; but who passed
     without
Much the same smile? This grew; I gave
     commands; 45
Then all smiles stopped together. There she
     stands
As if alive. Will't please you rise? We'll meet
The company below, then. I repeat,
The Count your master's known munificence
Is ample warrant that no just pretense 50
Of mine for dowry will be disallowed;
Though his fair daughter's self, as I avowed
At starting, is my object. Nay, we'll go
Together down, sir. Notice Neptune,[2] though,
Taming a sea horse, thought a rarity, 55
Which Claus of Innsbruck[3] cast in bronze for
     me!

---

1. *Fra Pandolf* (frä pän′dôlf), an imaginary artist-monk.
2. *Neptune*, a statue of the Roman god of the sea. 3.
Claus of Innsbruck, an imaginary Austrian sculptor.

ANDREA DEL SARTO

called THE FAULTLESS PAINTER

Andrea del Sarto (än drä'ə del sär'tō) was a Florentine painter who lived from 1486 to 1531, when the Italian Renaissance was at its height. Because of his superb craftsmanship he was called "the Faultless Painter." In 1512 he married Lucrezia del Fede (lü krä'tzyä del fä'dä), a beautiful woman described as vixenish, jealous, and unfaithful.

In 1519 Andrea was invited by Francis I to come to the palace of Fontainebleau (fon'tən-blō). Here he was highly honored by the French court as a great painter. When Lucrezia wrote him to return to Florence, he did so, bringing with him a large sum of money to purchase Florentine paintings, which he was to take back to France with him. However, Andrea spent the money on a house for Lucrezia. Disgraced, he could not return to France. Browning's poem is based on the account of Andrea found in Vasari's Lives of the Painters.

B ut do not let us quarrel any more,
No, my Lucrezia; bear with me for
once:
Sit down and all shall happen as you wish,
You turn your face, but does it bring your
heart?
I'll work then for your friend's friend, never
fear,   5
Treat his own subject after his own way,
Fix his own time, accept too his own price,
And shut the money into this small hand

Portrait of a Sculptor, *painted by Andrea del Sarto five years after his return to Florence. This painting, which is in the National Gallery, London, is considered his finest portrait.*

When next it takes mine. Will it? tenderly?
Oh, I'll content him—but tomorrow, Love!   10
I often am much wearier than you think,
This evening more than usual, and it seems
As if—forgive now—should you let me sit
Here by the window with your hand in mine
And look a half-hour forth on Fiesole,[1]   15
Both of one mind, as married people use,
Quietly, quietly the evening through,
I might get up tomorrow to my work
Cheerful and fresh as ever. Let us try.
Tomorrow, how you shall be glad for this!   20
Your soft hand is a woman of itself,
And mine the man's bared breast she curls
        inside.
Don't count the time lost, neither; you must
        serve
For each of the five pictures we require:
It saves a model.[2] So! keep looking so—   25
My serpentining beauty, round on rounds!
—How could you ever prick those perfect
        ears,
Even to put the pearl there! oh, so sweet—
My face, my moon, my everybody's moon,
Which everybody looks on and calls his,   30
And, I suppose, is looked on by in turn,
While she looks—no one's: very dear, no less.
You smile? why, there's my picture ready
        made,
There's what we painters call our harmony!
A common grayness silvers everything—   35
All in a twilight, you and I alike—
You, at the point of your first pride in me
(That's gone you know), but I, at every
        point;
My youth, my hope, my art, being all toned
        down
To yonder sober pleasant Fiesole.   40
There's the bell clinking from the chapel top;
That length of convent wall across the way
Holds the trees safer, huddled more inside;
The last monk leaves the garden; days
        decrease,
And autumn grows, autumn in everything.   45
Eh? the whole seems to fall into a shape
As if I saw alike my work and self
And all that I was born to be and do,
A twilight-piece. Love, we are in God's hand.
How strange now looks the life He makes us
        lead;   50

So free we seem, so fettered fast we are!
I feel He laid the fetter; let it lie!
This chamber for example—turn your head—
All that's behind us! You don't understand
Nor care to understand about my art,   55
But you can hear at least when people speak:
And that cartoon,[3] the second from the door—
It is the thing, Love! so such thing should
        be—
Behold Madonna! I am bold to say.
I can do with my pencil what I know,   60
What I see, what at bottom of my heart
I wish for, if I ever wish so deep—
Do easily, too—when I say, perfectly,
I do not boast, perhaps: yourself are judge,
Who listened to the Legate's talk[4] last week,   65
And just as much they used to say in France.
At any rate 'tis easy, all of it!
No sketches first, no studies, that's long past:
I do what many dream of all their lives—
Dream? Strive to do, and agonize to do,   70
And fail in doing. I could count twenty such
On twice your fingers, and not leave this
        town,
Who strive—you don't know how the others
        strive
To paint a little thing like that you smeared
Carelessly passing with your robes afloat—   75
Yet do much less, so much less, Someone says,
(I know his name, no matter)—so much less!
Well, less is more, Lucrezia: I am judged.
There burns a truer light of God in them,
In their vexed beating stuffed and stopped-up
        brain,   80
Heart, or whate'er else, than goes on to
        prompt
This low-pulsed forthright craftsman's hand
        of mine.
Their works drop groundward, but themselves,
        I know,
Reach many a time a heaven that's shut to
        me,
Enter and take their place there sure
        enough,   85
Though they come back and cannot tell the
        world.

1. *Fiesole*, a suburb of Florence.   2. *you must serve . . .
model*. All the women in Andrea's paintings have some of
the qualities of Lucrezia.   3. *cartoon*, a full-sized drawing
of a painting, used as a model.   4. *Legate's talk*. The Legate
was the Pope's representative.

My works are nearer heaven, but I sit here.
The sudden blood of these men! at a word—
Praise them, it boils, or blame them, it boils
    too.
I, painting from myself and to myself,   90
Know what I do, am unmoved by men's
    blame
Or their praise either. Somebody remarks
Morello's[5] outline there is wrongly traced,
His hue mistaken; what of that? or else,
Rightly traced and well ordered; what of
    that?   95
Speak as they please, what does the
    mountain care?
Ah, but a man's reach should exceed his
    grasp,
Or what's a heaven for? All is silver gray
Placid and perfect with my art: the worse!
I know both what I want and what might
    gain,   100
And yet how profitless to know, to sigh
"Had I been two, another and myself,
Our head would have o'erlooked the world!"
    No doubt.
Yonder's a work now, of that famous youth
The Urbanite[6] who died five years ago.   105
('Tis copied, George Vasari[7] sent it me.)
Well, I can fancy how he did it all,
Pouring his soul, with kings and popes to
    see,
Reaching, that heaven might so replenish
    him,
Above and through his art—for it gives way:110
That arm is wrongly put—and there again—
A fault to pardon in the drawing's lines,
Its body, so to speak: its soul is right,
He means right—that, a child may
    understand.
Still, what an arm! and I could alter it: 115
But all the play, the insight and the stretch—
Out of me, out of me! And wherefore out?
Had you enjoined them on me, given me soul,
We might have risen to Rafael, I and you!
Nay, Love, you did give all I asked, I
    think—   120
More than I merit, yes, by many times.
But had you—oh, with the same perfect
    brow,
And perfect eyes, and more than perfect
    mouth,

And the low voice my soul hears, as a bird
The fowler's pipe, and follows to the
    snare—   125
Had you, with these the same, but brought a
    mind!
Some women do so. Had the mouth there
    urged
"God and the glory! never care for gain.
The present by the future, what is that?
Live for fame, side by side with Agnolo![8] 130
Rafael is waiting: up to God, all three!"
I might have done it for you. So it seems:
Perhaps not. All is as God overrules.
Beside, incentives come from the soul's self;
The rest avail not. Why do I need you?   135
What wife had Rafael, or has Agnolo?
In this world, who can do a thing, will not;
And who would do it, cannot, I perceive:
Yet the will's somewhat—somewhat, too, the
    power—   139
And thus we half-men struggle. At the end,
God, I conclude, compensates, punishes.
'Tis safer for me, if the award be strict,
That I am something underrated here,
Poor this long while, despised, to speak the
    truth.
I dared not, do you know, leave home all
    day,   145
For fear of chancing on the Paris lords.
The best is when they pass and look aside;
But they speak sometimes; I must bear it all.
Well may they speak! That Francis,[9] that
    first time,
And that long festal year at Fontainebleau! 150
I surely then could sometimes leave the
    ground,
Put on the glory, Rafael's daily wear,
In that humane great monarch's golden look—
One finger in his beard or twisted curl
Over his mouth's good mark that made the
    smile,   155
One arm about my shoulder, round my neck,
The jingle of his gold chain in my ear,
I painting proudly with his breath on me,

---

5. *Morello*, a peak in the Apennines, north of Florence.
6. *Urbanite*, Raphael Sanzio (1483-1520), an Italian painter
and native of Urbino. 7. *George Vasari* (1512-1574), a
pupil of Andrea, who wrote *The Lives of the Most Eminent
Painters, Sculptors, and Architects.* 8. *Agnolo*, Michelangelo (1475-1564). 9. *That Francis*, Francis I (1494-1547),
king of France.

All his court round him, seeing with his
    eyes,
Such frank French eyes, and such a fire of
    souls   160
Profuse, my hand kept plying by those
    hearts—
And, best of all, this, this, this face beyond,
This in the background, waiting on my work,
To crown the issue with a last reward!
A good time, was it not, my kingly days? 165
And had you not grown restless . . . but I
    know—
'Tis done and past; 'twas right, my instinct
    said;
Too live the life grew, golden and not gray,
And I'm the weak-eyed bat no sun should
    tempt
Out of the grange whose four walls make his
    world.   170
How could it end in any other way?
You called me, and I came home to your
    heart.
The triumph was—to reach and stay there;
    since
I reached it ere the triumph, what is lost?
Let my hands frame your face in your hair's
    gold,   175
You beautiful Lucrezia that are mine!
"Rafael did this, Andrea painted that;
The Roman's[10] the better when you pray,
But still the other's Virgin was his wife"—
Men will excuse me. I am glad to judge 180
Both pictures in your presence; clearer grows
My better fortune, I resolve to think.
For, do you know, Lucrezia, as God lives,
Said one day Agnolo, his very self,
To Rafael . . . I have known it all these
    years . . .   185
(When the young man was flaming out his
    thoughts
Upon a palace wall for Rome to see,[11]
Too lifted up in heart because of it)
"Friend, there's a certain sorry little scrub
Goes up and down our Florence, none cares
    how,   190
Who, were he set to plan and execute
As you are, pricked on by your popes and
    kings,
Would bring the sweat into that brow of
    yours!"

To Rafael's! And indeed the arm is wrong.
I hardly dare . . . yet, only you to see,   195
Give the chalk here—quick, thus the line
    should go!
Ay, but the soul! he's Rafael! rub it out!
Still, all I care for, if he spoke the truth,
(What he? why, who but Michel Agnolo?
Do you forget already words like those?) 200
If really there was such a chance, so lost—
Is, whether you're—not grateful—but more
    pleased.
Well, let me think so. And you smile indeed!
This hour has been an hour! Another smile?
If you would sit thus by me every night 205
I should work better, do you comprehend?
I mean that I should earn more, give you
    more.
See it is settled dusk now; there's a star;
Morello's gone, the watch-lights show the
    wall,
The cue-owls speak the name we call them
    by.   210
Come from the window, Love, come in, at
    last,
Inside the melancholy little house
We built to be so gay with. God is just.
King Francis may forgive me; oft at nights
When I look up from painting, eyes tired
    out,   215
The walls become illumined, brick from brick
Distinct, instead of mortar, fierce bright gold,
That gold of his I did cement them with!
Let us but love each other. Must you go?
That Cousin here again? he waits outside? 220
Must see you—you, and not with me? Those
    loans?
More gaming debts to pay? you smiled for
    that?
Well, let smiles buy me! have you more to
    spend?
While hand and eye and something of a heart
Are left me, work's my ware, and what's it
    worth?   225
I'll pay my fancy. Only let me sit
The gray remainder of the evening out,
Idle, you call it, and muse perfectly
How I could paint, were I but back in France,

---

10. *The Roman's*, Raphael's. Raphael spent much of his
life in Rome. 11. *When . . . to see*, when Raphael was
painting in the Vatican.

One picture, just one more—the Virgin's
    face,   230
Not yours this time! I want you at my side
To hear them—that is, Michel Agnolo—
Judge all I do and tell you of its worth.
Will you? Tomorrow, satisfy your friend.
I take the subjects for his corridor,   235
Finish the portrait out of hand—there, there,
And throw him in another thing or two
If he demurs; the whole should prove
    enough
To pay for this same Cousin's freak. Beside,
What's better and what's all I care about, 240
Get you the thirteen scudi[12] for the ruff!
Love, does that please you? Ah, but what does
    he,
The Cousin! what does he to please you more?

    I am grown peaceful as old age tonight.
I regret little, I would change still less.   245
Since there my past life lies, why alter it?
The very wrong to Francis! It is true
I took his coin, was tempted and complied,
And built this house and sinned, and all is
    said.
My father and my mother died of want.   250
Well, had I riches of my own? You see
How one gets rich! Let each one bear his lot.
They were born poor, lived poor, and poor
    they died:
And I have labored somewhat in my time
And not been paid profusely. Some good
    son   255
Paint my two hundred pictures—let him try!
No doubt, there's something strikes a balance.
    Yes,
You loved me quite enough, it seems tonight.
This must suffice me here. What would one
    have?
In heaven, perhaps, new chances, one more
    chance—   260
Four great walls in the New Jerusalem,
Meted on each side by the angel's reed,
For Leonard,[13] Rafael, Agnolo and me
To cover—the three first without a wife,
While I have mine! So—still they over-
    come   265
Because there's still Lucrezia—as I choose.

    Again the Cousin's whistle! Go, my Love.

PROSPICE

The Latin word Prospice (pros'pi chē) means
"Look Forward!" and suggests Browning's un-
flinching attitude toward death. The last three
lines of the poem, which was written shortly
after the death of Mrs. Browning in 1861,
refer to her.

Fear death?—to feel the fog in my throat,
    The mist in my face,
When the snows begin, and the blasts denote
    I am nearing the place,   4
The power of the night, the press of the storm,
    The post of the foe;
Where he stands, the Arch Fear in a visible
    form;
    Yet the strong man must go:
For the journey is done and the summit
    attained,
    And the barriers fall,   10
Though a battle's to fight ere the guerdon be
    gained,
    The reward of it all.
I was ever a fighter, so—one fight more,
    The best and the last!
I would hate that Death bandaged my eyes,
    and forbore,   15
    And bade me creep past.
No! let me taste the whole of it, fare like my
    peers,
    The heroes of old,
Bear the brunt, in a minute pay glad life's
    arrears
    Of pain, darkness and cold.   20
For sudden the worst turns the best to the
    brave.
    The black minute's at end,
And the elements' rage, the fiend voices that
    rave,
    Shall dwindle, shall blend,
Shall change, shall become first a peace out
    of pain.   25
    Then a light, then thy breast,
O thou soul of my soul! I shall clasp thee
    again,
    And with God be the rest!

ANDREA DEL SARTO **12.** *scudi* (skü'dē), Italian coins
worth about a dollar each. **13.** *Leonard,* Leonardo Da
Vinci, a great Italian painter (1452-1519).

Summum Bonum and
Home Thoughts from Abroad

1. In "Summum Bonum" what does Browning describe as "the highest good"?

2. Browning uses "the bag of one bee" to symbolize all the delights of fragrance and color that summer brings. (*a*) Why is this an apt choice to symbolize all of summer? (*b*) Explain the other natural symbols Browning uses. (*c*) What relationship does the poet develop between the natural symbols in lines 1-4 and the remainder of the poem?

3. In "Home Thoughts from Abroad" the imagery is an important element in establishing the emotional effect. Cite images of sight and sound and point out details in these images that help create this effect.

4. Another important element in establishing the emotional effect of the poem is the tone. (*a*) How would you describe the tone? (*b*) What lines are important in creating this tone?

My Last Duchess

1. Summarize the story told in "My Last Duchess."

2. (*a*) According to the Duke, what quality of expression in the Duchess' portrait seems to arouse the greatest curiosity in anyone who views the painting? (*b*) How does the Duke explain this expression?

3. (*a*) What is the Duke's criticism of his last Duchess? (*b*) Cite the lines that in your opinion best summarize this criticism. (*c*) Why did the Duke not speak to the Duchess about the faults he found in her? (*d*) How do you interpret "I gave commands;/Then all smiles stopped together"?

Andrea del Sarto

1. (*a*) What is the situation at the opening of the poem? (*b*) What does Andrea consent to do for Lucrezia? (*c*) Why is she impatient to leave?

2. (*a*) What does Andrea say in praise of his own work? (*b*) What does he say that some less skillful painters have that he lacks? (*c*) What fault does Andrea point out in the Raphael copy? (*d*) What quality does the painting possess that he cannot attain in his own work?

3. (*a*) What is Lucrezia's attitude toward her husband's art? (*b*) What effect does this attitude have on Andrea?

4. (*a*) Andrea states that he has not dared to leave home all day for fear of meeting the Paris lords (lines 145-146). What has caused this situation? (*b*) With what attitude does he now regard his stay in France? (*c*) Cite the lines that explain why he came home. (*d*) Why does Andrea speak of the house as "the melancholy little house" (line 212)?

5. In order to create the illusion of the actual progression of thought as in a conversation, Browning has his narrator abruptly say seemingly unrelated things just as they come into his mind, or respond suddenly to something he sees or hears. Thus, for example, Andrea says "You turn your face, but does it bring your heart?" (line 4). Again he interrupts himself to say "How could you ever prick those perfect ears. . .?" (line 27). Find other interruptions. Do they advance the action or help tell the story? Explain.

6. The lines: "Ah, but a man's reach should exceed his grasp,/Or what's a heaven for?" are often quoted as expressing Browning's own attitude toward life. (*a*) What do these lines mean? (*b*) In what way do they typify the poet?

Prospice

1. (*a*) To what does Browning compare death in lines 1-12? (*b*) Explain the meaning of *Arch Fear* (line 7), *journey* (line 9), and *guerdon* (line 11).

The Poets' Corner

Geoffrey Chaucer was buried in the south transept of Westminster Abbey in the year 1400. In the more than five hundred years since his death, great men of letters from every period of English literature have been buried in this section of the abbey, which has come to be called the Poets' Corner. A small area, the Poets' Corner is crowded with statues, tablets, busts, and memorials. One American—Henry Wadsworth Longfellow—has the honor of being enshrined there. Among the Englishmen commemorated are Edmund Spenser, William Shakespeare, Ben Jonson, John Milton, John Dryden, Oliver Goldsmith, Samuel Johnson, Thomas Gray, Thomas Macaulay, Alfred Tennyson, and Robert Browning.

2. Browning gives two contrasting approaches to death in lines 15-16 and 17-20. (*a*) Explain each of these. (*b*) What is meant by "glad life's arrears" (line 19)?

3. What is the final guerdon death offers?

4. (*a*) Point out examples of imagery that you feel are particularly apt and comment on their appropriateness. (*b*) What effect is created by the use of many short, abrupt phrases?

5. (*a*) Compare the tone of "Prospice" with Tennyson's "Crossing the Bar" (page 449). (*b*) In what ways is each poem characteristic of the poet's thought, life, and personality?

 Better reading

The dramatic monologue

Browning is justly famous for his development and his mastery of the *dramatic monologue*, a lyric poem in which a speaker addresses himself to one or more persons who are present but do not reply. The dramatic monologue has three characteristics: it presents a dramatic moment in the life of the speaker; it reveals his character; and it includes a listener who does not speak but who affects the development of the monologue.

Browning did not invent the dramatic monologue. Chaucer had used some of its techniques in "The Wife of Bath's Prologue" and Tennyson had used it in "Ulysses" and in several other poems. But Browning handled it with such skill and used it so frequently that it has become identified with him. He found in this form an admirable way to re-create the attitudes and the aspirations, the beauty and the cruelty that had characterized the life of the men of the Renaissance hundreds of years before.

A dramatic monologue reveals far more than may be evident on first reading of the poem. The speaker's words tell only what he wishes to make known. Much of the truth about him—his character, his relations to the listener, his attitude toward life in general—are half hidden behind his words and await the analysis of the reader.

Think again of "My Last Duchess." Browning has seized upon a dramatic moment to open the monologue—the moment at which the Duke of Ferrara has drawn back the curtain which conceals the portrait of his last wife. He needs to make certain facts known to the envoy, and he expects that the envoy is sufficiently skilled in diplomacy to read the meaning behind the words. What is the message he wishes to impart? What picture of himself is he trying to give the envoy? But the picture of the Duke that the envoy received is not the same as the

impression Browning's Victorian readers got, or that you receive. What makes the difference? Describe the character of the Duke as completely as you can from the vantage point of the twentieth century.

The situation in "Andrea del Sarto" is quite different from that in "My Last Duchess." In the latter the listener is a wily courtier weighing the import of every word; in the former we have a half-listener, a beautiful woman who waits impatiently for her husband to finish talking about himself. David Daiches, in *A Critical History of English Literature*, writes that in the dramatic monologue "Browning seeks for the confessional moment, the crisis which forces out of a man the whole truth about himself as he sees it." Why is this an apt description of the situation in "Andrea del Sarto"?

The theme of "Andrea del Sarto" might be described as the nature of art and the artist, and the conflict that arises in the artist when he does not struggle to produce the best work of which he is capable. Toward the end of the poem (lines 245-246) Andrea says:

I regret little, I would change still less.
Since there my past life lies, why alter it?

Is this really the painter's attitude, is he trying to console himself for lost opportunities, or is he telling Lucrezia what she likes to hear? In weighing this question consider the following:

Lines 67-71. What aspect of art does Andrea speak of in these lines?

Lines 78-87. What contrast between the technical competence of the artist and his vision are expressed here? Where does Andrea stand? Locate other lines that express the aspiration necessary to great art.

Lines 134-140. What attributes must the artist have? What is the spur to great achievement?

Lines 184-202. What judgment of Andrea did Michelangelo once deliver? What is significant in the fact that Andrea has dwelt on it for many years? What does he say is the only important thing?

Lines 228-234. Why does Andrea wish to return to France? How does he attempt to keep Lucrezia a part of this dream? Why does he again mention Michelangelo?

Lines 259-266. Raphael, Michelangelo, and Leonardo da Vinci are generally regarded as the three greatest artists of the Renaissance. How does Andrea try to link his name with theirs? What truth do lines 265-266 contain?

Why does Andrea speak of all that he has done as "a twilight piece"? How does the setting reinforce this idea?

from SONNETS FROM THE PORTUGUESE

Elizabeth Barrett Browning

SONNET 26

I lived with visions for my company
Instead of men and women, years ago,
And found them gentle mates, nor thought to know
A sweeter music than they played to me.
But soon their trailing purple was not free   5
Of this world's dust, their lutes did silent grow,
And I myself grew faint and blind below
Their vanishing eyes. Then THOU didst come—to be,
Belovéd, what they seemed. Their shining fronts,
Their songs, their splendors (better, yet the same,   10
As river water hallowed into fonts),
Met in thee, and from out thee overcame
My soul with satisfaction of all wants:
Because God's gifts put man's best dreams to shame.

SONNET 43

How do I love thee? Let me count the ways.
I love thee to the depth and breadth and height
My soul can reach, when feeling out of sight
For the ends of Being and ideal Grace.
I love thee to the level of everyday's   5
Most quiet need, by sun and candlelight.
I love thee freely, as men strive for Right;
I love thee purely, as they turn from Praise.
I love thee with the passion put to use
In my old griefs, and with my childhood's faith.   10
I love thee with a love I seemed to lose
With my lost saints—I love thee with the breath,
Smiles, tears, of all my life!—and, if God choose,
I shall but love thee better after death.

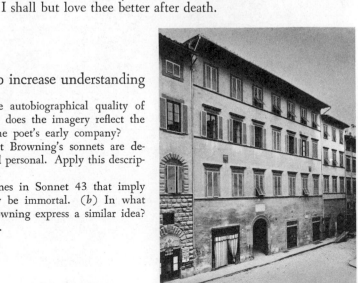

*The Brownings'
house, Florence.*

ALINARI-BROGI
PHOTO

❈ To increase understanding

1. (*a*) Explain the autobiographical quality of
Sonnet 26. (*b*) How does the imagery reflect the
visionary quality of the poet's early company?

2. Elizabeth Barrett Browning's sonnets are described as intimate and personal. Apply this description to Sonnet 43.

3. (*a*) Cite the lines in Sonnet 43 that imply
that human love may be immortal. (*b*) In what
poem does Robert Browning express a similar idea?
Cite the relevant lines.

The Pre-Raphaelite Brotherhood

Despite the rebellion of such romantic painters as Constable and Turner (see pages 374-375), most nineteenth-century artists continued to work in the conservative tradition of eighteenth-century painting. In an effort to break this tradition, a group of painters and poets who called themselves the Pre-Raphaelite Brotherhood banded together in 1848. Leader of the group was Dante Gabriel Rossetti (1828-1882), a painter and poet; among his associates were the painters Holman Hunt and John Everett Millais. The group's avowed purpose was to lead art away from the overblown fussiness and conventionality of the time and to recapture the natural simplicity and freshness found in medieval art before Raphael and the high Renaissance. In a short time the application was made to poetry as well.

One aim of the group was to pay close attention to detail. But instead of using detail to create the illusion of reality, the Pre-Raphaelites intended to employ it symbolically. Concrete details, carefully observed, would be chosen for their spiritual meanings and used to evoke an emotional-spiritual response in the viewer or reader.

Actually poetic symbolism, as the Pre-Raphaelites used it, was an inversion of its use in medieval times. In the medieval period, for example, the language of human love symbolized the worship of God, whereas Rossetti and other Pre-Raphaelite poets employed the language of mystical devotion to express human love. The Pre-Raphaelite poets differed greatly in the degree to which they adhered to the original ideas of the group, but all made extensive use of concrete detail and sensory

NATIONAL PORTRAIT GALLERY, LONDON

Self-portrait by Rossetti.

A manuscript page showing William Morris' own italic hand.

THE BODLEIAN LIBRARY, OXFORD

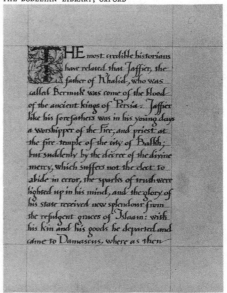

A detail from William Morris' earliest wallpaper design.

April Love, *a symbolic painting by Arthur Hughes. Besides numerous paintings, many of which were exhibited at the Royal Academy, Hughes executed illustrations for poems of Tennyson, Christina Rossetti, and others.*

imagery. In this emphasis on imagery they were influenced by John Keats. But as handled by some of the Pre-Raphaelites, the sensuous quality of the imagery often became so bold as to outrage the moral sense of the Victorian public. Rossetti was castigated for "degrading" the art of poetry.

Many critics, however, attacked the Pre-Raphaelites vigorously on another ground: their alleged practice of "art for art's sake," or sacrificing thought and moral content in poetry for the sheer beauty of form. In this tendency they were forerunners of the aesthetic poets of the last decades of the century in whose work "art for art's sake" was an absolute and freely expressed aim.

Among those who rose to defend the Pre-Raphaelites was William Morris (1834-1896), a fine craftsman and designer as well as a poet. At Oxford he had turned his attention to art and architecture, and for a time he determined to become a painter. Later, coming under the influence of Rossetti and other painters and poets of the Pre-Raphaelite Brotherhood, he decided to found a firm which would bring beauty into Victorian homes. He established a factory which became widely known for the quality and beauty of the carpets, tapestries, and furniture manufactured there. Later in life he founded the Kelmscott Press, which published books noted for beauty of print, paper, and binding. One of the finest of these was the famous Kelmscott edition of Chaucer's works.

THE CONNOISSEUR, LONDON

The "Great Parlour" of Wightwick Manor, a house preserved as a Morris period piece. Many of the furnishings, as well as the light fixtures and the wallpaper, are products of the Morris firm. The painting is Love Among the Ruins by Burne-Jones, a close friend of Rossetti and Morris.

THE BLESSED DAMOZEL   *Dante Gabriel Rossetti*

*In "The Raven" Edgar Allan Poe writes of a
lover mourning the death of a maiden "whom
the angels named Lenore." Rossetti designed
"The Blessed Damozel" as a complement to
Poe's poem. Of his poem he said: "I saw that
Poe had done the utmost possible to do with
the grief of the lover on earth, and I determined to reverse the conditions, and give utterance to the yearning of the loved one in
heaven."*

The blessed damozel leaned out
    From the gold bar of heaven;
    Her eyes were deeper than the depth
    Of waters stilled at even;
She had three lilies in her hand,   5
And the stars in her hair were seven.

Her robe, ungirt from clasp to hem,
    No wrought flowers did adorn,
But a white rose of Mary's gift,
    For service meetly worn[1];   10
Her hair that lay along her back
    Was yellow like ripe corn.

Herseemed[2] she scarce had been a day
    One of God's choristers;
The wonder was not yet quite gone   15
    From that still look of hers;
Albeit, to them she left, her day
    Had counted as ten years.

(To *one* it is ten years of years.
    . . . Yet now, and in this place,   20
Surely she leaned o'er me—her hair
    Fell all about my face. . . .
Nothing: the autumn fall of leaves.
    The whole year sets apace.)

It was the rampart of God's house   25
    That she was standing on;
By God built over the sheer depth
    The which is Space begun;
So high, that looking downward thence
    She scarce could see the sun.   30

It lies in heaven, across the flood
    Of ether, as a bridge.
Beneath, the tides of day and night
    With flame and darkness ridge
The void, as low as where this earth   35
    Spins like a fretful midge.

Around her, lovers, newly met
    'Mid deathless love's acclaims,
Spoke evermore among themselves
    Their heart-remembered names;   40
And the souls mounting up to God
    Went by her like thin flames.

And still she bowed herself and stooped
    Out of the circling charm;
Until her bosom must have made   45
    The bar she leaned on warm,
And the lilies lay as if asleep
    Along her bended arm.

From the fixed place of heaven she saw
    Time like a pulse shake fierce   50
Through all the worlds. Her gaze still strove
    Within the gulf to pierce
Its path; and now she spoke as when
    The stars sang in their spheres.[3]

The sun was gone now; the curled moon   55
    Was like a little feather
Fluttering far down the gulf; and now
    She spoke through the still weather.
Her voice was like the voice the stars
    Had when they sang together.   60

(Ah, sweet! Even now, in that bird's song,
    Strove not her accents there,
Fain to be harkened? When those bells
    Possessed the midday air,
Strove not her steps to reach my side   65
    Down all the echoing stair?)

---

1. *white rose . . . worn*, appropriately worn in the service of
the Virgin Mary.   2. *Herseemed*, it seemed to her.   3.
stars . . . spheres. At one time it was believed that stars
made music as they rotated in their spheres.

"I wish that he were come to me,
   For he will come," she said.
"Have I not prayed in heaven?—on earth,
   Lord, Lord, has he not prayed?   70
Are not two prayers a perfect strength?
   And shall I feel afraid?

"When round his head the aureole clings,
   And he is clothed in white,
I'll take his hand and go with him   75
   To the deep wells of light;
As unto a stream we will step down,
   And bathe there in God's sight.

"We two will stand beside that shrine,
   Occult, withheld, untrod,   80
Whose lamps are stirred continually
   With prayers sent up to God;
And see our old prayers, granted, melt
   Each like a little cloud.

"We two will lie i' the shadow of   85
   That living mystic tree
Within whose secret growth the Dove[4]
   Is sometimes felt to be,
While every leaf that His plumes touch
   Saith His Name audibly.   90

"And I myself will teach to him,
   I myself, lying so,
The songs I sing here; which his voice
   Shall pause in, hushed and slow,
And find some knowledge at each pause,   95
   Or some new thing to know."

(Alas! We two, we two, thou say'st!
   Yea, one wast thou with me
That once of old. But shall God lift
   To endless unity   100
The soul whose likeness with thy soul
   Was but its love for thee?)

"We two," she said, "will seek the groves
   Where the Lady Mary is,
With her five handmaidens, whose names   105
   Are five sweet symphonies,

Cecily, Gertrude, Magdalen,
   Margaret, and Rosalys.[5]

"Circlewise sit they, with bound locks
   And foreheads garlanded;   110
Into the fine cloth white like flame
   Weaving the golden thread,
To fashion the birth-robes for them
   Who are just born, being dead.

"He shall fear, haply, and be dumb;   115
   Then will I lay my cheek
To his, and tell about our love,
   Not once abashed or weak;
And the dear Mother will approve
   My pride, and let me speak.   120

"Herself shall bring us, hand in hand,
   To Him round whom all souls
Kneel, the clear-ranged unnumbered heads
   Bowed with their aureoles;
And angels meeting us shall sing   125
   To their citherns and citoles.

"There will I ask of Christ the Lord
   Thus much for him and me—
Only to live as once on earth
   With Love, only to be,   130
As then awhile, forever now,
   Together, I and he."

She gazed and listened and then said,
   Less sad of speech than mild—
"All this is when he comes." She ceased.   135
   The light thrilled toward her, filled
With angels in strong, level flight.
   Her eyes prayed, and she smiled.

(I saw her smile.) But soon their path
   Was vague in distant spheres;   140
And then she cast her arms along
   The golden barriers,
And laid her face between her hands,
   And wept. (I heard her tears.)

---

4. Dove, a symbol of the Holy Spirit, the third member of
the Trinity. 5. Cecily...Rosalys, Christian saints.

SONG *Christina Rossetti*

Dante Gabriel Rossetti's sister Christina was a favorite model for the Pre-Raphaelite painters. With her pale sensitive features and dark hair, she represented for them the ideal of feminine beauty. Her delicate lyrics show not only the love for the beauty of the world, common to the Pre-Raphaelites, but also a strong religious strain.

When I am dead, my dearest,
  Sing no sad songs for me;
Plant thou no roses at my head,
  Nor shady cypress tree.
Be the green grass above me   5
  With showers and dewdrops wet;
And if thou wilt, remember,
  And if thou wilt, forget.

I shall not see the shadows,
  I shall not feel the rain;   10
I shall not hear the nightingale
  Sing on as if in pain.
And dreaming through the twilight
  That doth not rise nor set,
Haply I may remember,   15
  And haply may forget.

To increase understanding

1. "The Blessed Damozel" is obviously a love poem. (*a*) How does the setting differ from that of most love lyrics? (*b*) Is the emphasis on mystical (religious) love, or on human love placed in an unusual setting? Explain.

2. (*a*) Cite examples of vivid imagery. (*b*) What word pictures remind you that Rossetti was also a painter?

3. In the discussion of the Pre-Raphaelite Brotherhood you read that the poets of this group "employed the language of mystical devotion to express human love" (page 464, column 2, paragraph 2). Is this statement true of "The Blessed Damozel"? Cite specific passages from the poem to justify your answer.

4. Compare Rossetti's "Blessed Damozel" with "The Raven" by Poe. (*a*) Consider rhyme, rhythm, and melody. (*b*) How do the poems differ in type of imagery? (*c*) Are they similar or different in tone? Explain.

5. (*a*) What attitude toward death does Christina Rossetti express in "Song"? (*b*) Compare and contrast the attitude toward death expressed in this poem with that voiced in other poems having the same theme.

6. Critics consider "Song" a fine lyric. What qualities does it possess that have led to this evaluation?

Edward Fitzgerald 1809-1883

Portrait of Fitzgerald by Eva Carnac.

During the nineteenth century, as the British Empire expanded throughout the Orient, there grew up in England a tremendous amount of interest in the civilizations and literatures of Eastern lands. A vogue for Chinese, Indian, and Japanese art arose, and ultimately gained such proportions that it inspired numerous satires, of which Gilbert and Sullivan's comic masterpiece, *The Mikado* (1885), remains an imperishable example. But years before the tuneful *Mikado* became the rage in London, a genuine Oriental masterpiece, *The Rubáiyát of Omar Khayyám* (1859), appeared in a translation by Edward Fitzgerald.

The original *rubáiyát* consisted of over four hundred quatrains by the Persian poet and mathematician, Omar Khayyám ("Omar the Tentmaker"), who died about 1123. Fitzgerald's translation included 101 of the quatrains. Experts agree that the translation is faithful to the original in spirit and idea, but very different in formal effect. Its success as an English poem probably depended less on Omar's original than on Fitzgerald's skill in translating, paraphrasing, and arranging selections from it. At first

The Rubáiyát of Omar Khayyám attracted little attention, but as the years passed and the Victorian public began to tire of moral earnestness, a climate for the acceptance of a skeptical and sensuous work was created. By the close of the century it was probably as widely read and quoted as any piece of literature in the British world.

Known now for *The Rubáiyát* only, inasmuch as his original poetry has long since been forgotten, Fitzgerald was a graduate of Trinity College, Cambridge, and a friend of Tennyson and Thackeray. For years he lived a quiet and scholarly life on a country estate in Suffolk. After the publication of *The Rubáiyát*, he bought a yacht and spent much of the rest of his life sailing leisurely about the North Sea.

The Rubáiyát of Omar Khayyám glories in the pleasures of the moment. Fitzgerald himself spoke of its mood as "a desperate sort of thing, unfortunately at the bottom of all thinking men's minds, but made music of." Undoubtedly it is this element—its music, along with its imagery—that has made *The Rubáiyát* popular with many who do not share its philosophy of skepticism. At any rate, it is another evidence of the complexity of the Victorian Age.

from THE RUBÁIYÁT OF OMAR KHAYYÁM

Wake! For the Sun, who scattered into
    flight
The Stars before him from the Field of Night,
  Drives Night along with them from Heav'n
    and strikes
The Sultàn's Turret with a Shaft of Light.

Come, fill the Cup, and in the fire of Spring 5
Your Winter garment of Repentance fling;
  The Bird of Time has but a little way
To flutter—and the Bird is on the Wing.

A Book of Verses underneath the Bough,
A Jug of Wine, a Loaf of Bread—and Thou 10
  Beside me singing in the Wilderness—
Oh, Wilderness were Paradise enow!

Some for the Glories of This World, and some
Sigh for the Prophet's[1] Paradise to come;
  Ah, take the Cash, and let the Credit go, 15
Nor heed the rumble of a distant Drum!

Look to the blowing[2] Rose about us—"Lo,
Laughing," she says, "into the world I blow,
  At once the silken tassel of my Purse 19
Tear, and its Treasure on the Garden throw."

And those who husbanded the Golden Grain,
And those who flung it to the winds like
    Rain,
  Alike to no such aureate Earth are turned
As, buried once, Men want dug up again.

Think, in this battered Caravanserai[3] 25
Whose Portals are alternate Night and Day,
  How Sultàn after Sultàn with his Pomp
Abode his destined Hour, and went his way.

I sometimes think that never blows so red
The Rose as where some buried Caesar[4]
    bled; 30
  That every Hyacinth[5] the Garden wears
Dropped in her Lap from some once lovely
    Head.

And this reviving Herb whose tender Green
Fledges the River-Lip on which we lean—

---

1. *Prophet's,* Mohammed's. **2.** *blowing,* blossoming. **3.** *Caravanserai* (kar′ə van′sə rä), an inn in the Orient where caravans put up for the night. **4.** *Caesar,* emperor or ruler. **5.** *Hyacinth,* the flower named after Hyacinthus (hī′ə sin′thəs), a youth killed by the Greek god Apollo, and from whose blood the flower sprang. The legend was well known in the Middle East.

Ah, lean upon it lightly! for who knows ³⁵
From what once lovely Lip it springs unseen!

Ah, make the most of what we yet may spend,
Before we too into the Dust descend;
   Dust into Dust, and under Dust, to lie,
Sans[6] Wine, sans Song, sans Singer, and—sans
   End!   40

Why, all the Saints and Sages who discussed
Of the Two Worlds so wisely—they are thrust
   Like foolish Prophets forth; their Words
      to Scorn
Are scattered, and their Mouths are stopped
   with Dust.

Myself when young did eagerly frequent   45
Doctor and Saint, and heard great argument
   About it and about; but evermore
Came out by the same door where in I went.

With them the seed of Wisdom did I sow,
And with mine own hand wrought to make it
   grow;   50
   And this was all the Harvest that I reaped—
"I came like Water, and like Wind I go."

I sent my Soul through the Invisible,
Some letter of that Afterlife to spell;
   And by and by my Soul returned to me, 55
And answered, "I Myself am Heav'n and
   Hell"—

Heav'n but the Vision of fulfilled Desire,
And Hell the Shadow from a Soul on fire
   Cast on the Darkness into which
      Ourselves,
So late emerged from, shall so soon expire. 60

We are no other than a moving row
Of Magic Shadow-shapes that come and go
   Round with the Sun-illumined Lantern
      held
In Midnight by the Master of the Show;

But helpless Pieces of the Game He plays 65
Upon this Checkerboard of Nights and Days;
   Hither and thither moves, and checks, and
      slays,
And one by one back in the Closet lays.

The Moving Finger writes, and, having writ,
Moves on; nor all your Piety nor Wit   70
   Shall lure it back to cancel half a line,
Nor all your Tears wash out a Word of it.

Oh, Thou, who Man of Baser Earth didst
   make,
And ev'n with Paradise devise the Snake,
   For all the Sin wherewith the Face of
      Man   75
Is blackened—Man's forgiveness give—
   and take!

Yet, Ah, that Spring should vanish with the
   Rose!
That Youth's sweet-scented manuscript should
   close!
   The Nightingale that in the branches
      sang,
Ah whence, and whither flown again, who
   knows!   80

Would but some wingéd Angel ere too late
Arrest the yet unfolded Roll of Fate,
   And make the stern Recorder otherwise
Enregister, or quite obliterate!   84

Ah, Love! could you and I with Him conspire
To grasp this sorry Scheme of Things entire,
   Would not we shatter it to bits—and then
Remold it nearer to the Heart's Desire!

---

6. *Sans*, without. [*French*]

✺ To increase understanding

1. The *carpe diem* theme that Robert Herrick voiced in "To the Virgins to Make Much of Time" (see pages 204, 206) pervades *The Rubáiyát*. Read aloud several quatrains in which this theme is clearly expressed.

2. Point out words and phrases which add to the sense of the fleeting or transitory quality of life.

3. *Fatalism* is a concept of life in which human beings are mere puppets, helplessly driven and controlled by overpowering Fate. Analyze lines 61-72 as an expression of fatalism, making clear the meaning of the various images.

4. Which of the stanzas do you consider the most beautiful? Consider rhythm, melody, and imagery.

THE LATE VICTORIANS

Rapidly changing social conditions in the last few decades of the nineteenth century gave rise to radical new developments in English writing. The strongly contrasting ideas and styles that had been characteristic of writers throughout the Victorian period became even more diversified.

The changes caused by the Industrial Revolution took on ever greater and more disturbing proportions. To create a market for her manufactures and to secure sources of raw material, England gradually built up the largest empire the world has ever seen. In addition to the sailors who sailed on British ships to the far corners of the world, an increasing number of merchants and civil servants lived in the outposts of the empire. This involvement of England with Asia, Africa, Australia, and the islands of the Pacific was reflected in literature. Where earlier writers had found inspiration in Europe, particularly in Italy, Rudyard Kipling, Joseph Conrad, and other writers of the late Victorian period used the far-flung British Empire as a setting for their works.

The growing interest in psychology and the relationship between behavior and social conditions had a revolutionary effect on Continental as well as English literature. Balzac, Flaubert, De Maupassant, and Zola in France, Dostoevski, Chekhov, and Tolstoi in Russia attempted to reveal man's behavior as determined by his physical and psychological environment. The realistic or naturalistic viewpoint of these writers greatly influenced Thomas Hardy and other writers of the late Victorian period and had a great effect on twentieth-century writers.

Although most writing of the late nineteenth century was realistic, the strain of romanticism, which has been strong in every major period of English literature, reappeared. Foremost among the romantic writers was Robert Louis Stevenson, poet, essayist, and storyteller. Another writer of exciting adventure was A. Conan Doyle (1859-1930), the creator of the famous detective, Sherlock Holmes.

By the last decades of the Victorian Age, popular education had made great headway. Matthew Arnold was proved to have been at least partially right in his prediction that promoting the utilitarian in education and popularizing culture would cause a lowering of intellectual standards. After 1885 almost universal elementary education coupled with the rapid growth of newspapers, periodicals, and low-cost novels had greatly increased the literacy rate; but an increasing uniformity of taste and thought —critics referred to this as "the popular mind"—had resulted. Since the percentage of highly educated people had increased little in comparison with the numbers who had attained merely a rudimentary background, pressure on writers to make their products easier, more popular, and more attuned to this new reading public increased. Thus in the closing decades of the nineteenth century, masterpieces by writers like Hardy were almost submerged in a flood of mediocre writing.

The tendencies of the late Victorian period can be traced with variations and modifications to the present day in English and American literature. It is this relationship to the twentieth century that adds a particular fascination to the study of late Victorian literature.

Robert Louis Stevenson 1850-1894

Drawing of Stevenson by P.F.S. Spence.

In his life and in his work Robert Louis Stevenson combined the moral earnestness of the Victorians with a romantic flair for adventure. Born at Edinburgh at the mid-point of the nineteenth century, he was all his life a wanderer. His father's and grandfather's profession as marine engineers and lighthouse builders early bred in him a love of the sea and of travel; and his lifelong effort to escape the ravages of tuberculosis sent him always in quest of a more congenial climate. For a time he studied law, but his heart was in writing. He first attracted attention with accounts in romantic prose of his own experiences in rambling about the Continent—*An Inland Voyage* (1878) and *Travels with a Donkey* (1879). His first volume of essays, *Virginibus Puerisque* (1881), in which "El Dorado" (page 474) appeared, showed him as a master of prose style.

On the Continent Stevenson had met an American woman, Mrs. Frances Osbourne. She became his fiancée, and he followed her to California, marrying her in 1880. The remaining fourteen years of his life were given over for the greater part to constant moving about—back to the British Isles and the Continent, to the Adirondacks (he was for a time a patient in a sanitarium at Saranac Lake, New York), and finally to the Samoan Islands in the South Pacific. Here he developed a plantation and became a friend and champion of the native Samoans, who called him Tusitala, "the teller of tales." He died suddenly—not from tuberculosis but from a cerebral hemorrhage—in Samoa late in the year 1894.

In all these years, even while seriously ill, Stevenson wrote steadily. The appearance of *Treasure Island* (1883) shot him to fame. In the 1880's he also wrote *The Strange Case of Dr. Jekyll and Mr. Hyde* and two romantic novels in the manner of Sir Walter Scott—*Kidnapped* and *The Master of Ballantrae*.

Although Stevenson wrote much poetry, including the unique and beloved *A Child's Garden of Verses* (1885), it is as a writer of prose that he deserves to be remembered. His novels, in which the late Victorian audience once again discovered that stories of pirates and seafarers and exotic places had not lost their thrill, were undeniably romantic in tone; but Stevenson had learned from the realists how to manipulate details and to handle style in such a way that even the impossible took on an aura of probability. He was undoubtedly the finest essayist of the last two decades of the nineteenth century, akin in his mastery of the familiar essay to the earlier romantic essayists. Like Charles Lamb (see page 367), he was able to put himself into his essays and to speak with warmth and humor of his own experiences. Essentially an optimist, he was aware of the currents of doubt that had been set in motion by the findings of Darwin and other scientists. In "Pulvis et Umbra" (a Latin phrase meaning "dust and shadows") he comes to grips with the problem of faith in an age of science and doubt. His style is in the tradition of elegance and eloquence. In its polish and its felicitous turns of phrase it shows the work of a master craftsman.

EL DORADO

El Dorado (el' də rä'dō) is a Spanish phrase meaning "the gilded" or "the golden." The name, originally given to a fabulous king of a wealthy city supposed to exist somewhere in South America, was later applied to the city itself. In time the term came to mean the object of any impractical quest.

It seems as if a great deal were attainable in a world where there are so many marriages and decisive battles, and where we all, at certain hours of the day, and with great gusto and dispatch, stow a portion of victuals finally and irretrievably into the bag which contains us. And it would seem also, on a hasty view, that the attainment of as much as possible was the one goal of man's contentious life. And yet, as regards the spirit, this is but a semblance. We live in an ascending scale when we live happily, one thing leading to another in an endless series. There is always a new horizon for onward-looking men, and although we dwell on a small planet, immersed in petty business and not enduring beyond a brief period of years, we are so constituted that our hopes are inaccessible, like stars, and the term of hoping is prolonged until the term of life.

To be truly happy is a question of how we begin and not of how we end, of what we want and not of what we have. An aspiration is a joy forever, a possession as solid as a landed estate, a fortune which we can never exhaust and which gives us year by year a revenue of pleasurable activity. To have many of these is to be spiritually rich. Life is only a very dull and ill-directed theater unless we have some interests in the piece; and to those who have neither art nor science, the world is a mere arrangement of colors, or a rough footway where they may very well break their shins. It is in virtue of his own desires and curiosities that any man continues to exist with even patience, that he is charmed by the look of things and people, and that he wakens every morning with a renewed appetite for work and pleasure. Desire and curiosity are the two eyes through which he sees the world in the most enchanted colors; it is they that make women beautiful or fossils interesting; and the man may squander his estate and come to beggary, but if he keeps these two amulets, he is still rich in the possibilities of pleasure. Suppose he could take one meal so compact and comprehensive that he should never hunger any more; suppose him, at a glance, to take in all the features of the world and allay the desire for knowledge; suppose him to do the like in any province of experience—would not that man be in a poor way for amusement ever after?

One who goes touring on foot with a single volume in his knapsack reads with circumspection, pausing often to reflect, and often laying the book down to contemplate the landscape or the prints in the inn parlor; for he fears to come to an end of his entertainment and be left companionless on the last stages of his journey. A young fellow recently finished the works of Thomas Carlyle, winding up, if we remember aright, with the ten notebooks upon Frederick the Great.[1] "What!" cried the young fellow, in consternation, "is there no more Carlyle? Am I left to the daily papers?" A more celebrated instance is that of Alexander, who wept bitterly because he had no more worlds to subdue. And when Gibbon had finished the *Decline and Fall*,[2] he had only a few moments of joy; and it was with a "sober melancholy" that he parted from his labors.

Happily we shoot at the moon with ineffectual arrows; our hopes are set on inaccessible El Dorado; we come to an end of nothing here below. Interests are only plucked up to sow themselves again, like mustard. You would think, when the child was born, there would be an end to trouble; and yet it is only the beginning of fresh anxieties; and when you have seen it through its teething and its education, and at last its marriage, alas! it is only

---

1. *Frederick the Great.* Carlyle's last great work was his *History of Frederick II of Prussia*, which appeared in six volumes from 1858 to 1865. Carlyle also published the notebooks that he had kept over a period of fourteen years as a preparation for writing this biography. 2. *Decline and Fall.* Edward Gibbon (1737-1794) spent twenty-four years in writing his mammoth *History of the Decline and Fall of the Roman Empire.*

to have new fears, new quivering sensibilities, with every day; and the health of your children's children grows as touching a concern as that of your own. Again, when you have married your wife, you would think you were got upon a hilltop and might begin to go downward by an easy slope. But you have only ended courting to begin marriage. Falling in love and winning love are often difficult tasks to overbearing and rebellious spirits; but to keep in love is also a business of some importance, to which both man and wife must bring kindness and good will. The true love story commences at the altar, when there lies before the married pair a most beautiful contest of wisdom and generosity, and a lifelong struggle toward an unattainable ideal. Unattainable? Aye, surely unattainable, from the very fact that they are two instead of one.

"Of making books there is no end," complained the Preacher,[3] and did not perceive how highly he was praising letters as an occupation. There is no end, indeed, to making books or experiments, or to travel, or to gathering wealth. Problem gives rise to problem. We may study forever, and we are never as learned as we would. We have never made a statue worthy of our dreams. And when we have discovered a continent, or crossed a chain of mountains, it is only to find another ocean or another plain upon the farther side. In the infinite universe there is room for our swiftest diligence and to spare. It is not like the works of Carlyle, which can be read to an end. Even in a corner of it, in a private park, or in the neighborhood of a single hamlet, the weather and the seasons keep so deftly changing that although we walk there for a lifetime there will be always something new to startle and delight us.

There is only one wish realizable on the earth; only one thing that can be perfectly attained—death. And from a variety of circumstances we have no one to tell us whether it be worth attaining.

A strange picture we make on our way to our chimeras, ceaselessly marching, grudging ourselves the time for rest; indefatigable, adventurous pioneers. It is true that we shall never reach the goal; it is even more probable that there is no such place; and if we lived for centuries and were endowed with the powers of a god, we should find ourselves not much nearer what we wanted at the end. O toiling hands of mortals! O unwearied feet, traveling ye know not whither! Soon, soon, it seems to you, you must come forth on some conspicuous hilltop, and but a little way farther, against the setting sun, descry the spires of El Dorado. Little do ye know your own blessedness; for to travel hopefully is a better thing than to arrive, and the true success is to labor.

REQUIEM

Under the wide and starry sky,
Dig the grave and let me lie.
Glad did I live and gladly die.
And I laid me down with a will.

This be the verse you grave for me: 5
Here he lies where he longed to be;
Home is the sailor, home from the sea,
And the hunter home from the hill.

EL DORADO **3.** *Preacher.* The quotation is from the twelfth chapter of Ecclesiastes, which means "The Preacher." The Preacher's theme throughout Ecclesiastes is the vanity and uselessness of the works of man.

To increase understanding

1. (*a*) What is the theme of "El Dorado"? (*b*) Cite the lines that best express this theme.

2. (*a*) What, according to Stevenson, are the "amulets" most necessary to a happy life? (*b*) What method does he use to prove the importance of these amulets?

3. In the biographical sketch Stevenson's essays are described as romantic and optimistic. Explain in what ways "El Dorado" exemplifies each of these qualities.

4. Stevenson, as you have read, is considered a master craftsman. Cite from the essay passages that might be used to show the excellence of his style and explain the reasons for your choice.

5. (*a*) Compare Stevenson's "Requiem," Tennyson's "Crossing the Bar" (page 449), and Browning's "Prospice" (page 460) as to form and tone. (*b*) In the case of each poem, what traits of the writer are suggested by the work?

The Changing English Language

Polite English of the Victorian period—especially the early years—was extremely formal. Men addressed their wives as "Mrs." and husbands were treated with equal courtesy. The utmost formality was extended to strangers, thereby implying they were solemn and important people. There were certain classes of people—the ambitious businessman, the newly rich, the aspiring student—who carried this formality to absurd lengths. They spoke an exaggerated English of their own called *genteelism*. The first and most important rule of genteelism was to avoid the common word and use instead a learned, bookish synonym. The advocates of genteelism did not help themselves to a piece of bread with jam—they assisted themselves to a portion of bread with preserves; they did not begin a meal—they commenced a collation; they did not use a toothpowder—they employed a dentrifice; they did not shut the door to a room—they closed the portal to an accommodation; and they never used *before*, *except*, or *about*—it was *ere*, *save*, and *anent*.

The rapid advance of invention and mechanization all during the Victorian Age created a need for many new words. Grammarians protested the forming of such words as *telegraph*, *typewriter*, and *gramophone* by scientists, inventors, and manufacturers, and felt that word making should be left to the etymologists. Words like *reliable* and *talented* that today are considered unquestionably acceptable were banned by those stanch protectors of the language, who judged the respectability of a word by numerous rules. Many words formed from a stem or word belonging to one language attached to a prefix or suffix belonging to another language were considered incorrect; others formed this way were acceptable. Correctness depended somewhat on whether the prefixes and suffixes were considered *living English* or *classical*. Those considered living English were many times of Latin, Greek, or French origin, but had become an integral part of the English language. Examples of this type were *-able*, *-age*, *-ic*, *-ery*, *-ation*, *-ous*, *-ness*, *a-*, and *dis-*. Those designated as classical were not used extensively and included such stems as *-ize*, *-ance*, *-ence*, *-al*, *-meter*, and *bi-*. Therefore words like *readable*, *fishery*, *plainness*, and *kindness* were considered correct because they were combinations of English elements. Words such as *amoral* and *gullible* were considered incorrect, however, because they were supposedly bad combinations of two foreign words. *Mechanize*, *biweekly*, and *speedometer* were disliked because they were combinations of English with classical elements. *Racial*, *coastal*, and *pacifist* were unacceptable because they were wrongly put together from words of the same language.

As American English grew, it often used different words from British English to denote the same thing. Compare the following words pertaining to the railroad industry—the first of each pair is American, the second is British: *railroad—railway*; *conductor—guard*; *fireman—stoker*; *car—carriage*; *track—line*; *freight—goods*; *trunk—box*; and *check—register*. Britishers were *ill*, *clever*, and *homely*; Americans were *sick*, *smart*, and *friendly*. Many words had different meanings to Americans and Britishers. A Britisher pays *rates*; an American pays *taxes*. The British use *nice* to mean "delicate," Americans use it to mean "agreeable." To *fix* in Britain means "to establish," in America it means "to repair." Some strictly American words were *sashay*, *savvy*, *scalawaggery*, *gerrymander*, *revenuer*, and *razz*.

As the language grew, when words were needed they were used with little regard for "correctness" in spite of the snobbery of genteelism and the protests of grammarians. By the end of the Victorian era the English language had grown to include almost five-hundred-thousand words.

Rudyard Kipling 1865-1936

No author has ever given more support to a monarch than did Rudyard Kipling to Queen Victoria. He believed in the Queen, the flag, and British imperialism, and felt that it was both England's right and England's duty to guide the destinies of its subject peoples all over the world. To his way of thinking it was the responsibility of the white man to lift the backward and benighted peoples of the Orient to a point where they could understand and profit from the more advanced civilization of the mother country. But he also saw the dangers of imperialism. Many times he took the side of the natives of India, and his poem "Recessional" (see page 489) is a daring rebuke of the Queen. He was a champion of the soldier and the seaman, and he recognized the benefits of the emerging world of industry.

Kipling did not form his ideals and ideas while sitting comfortably in London. Born in Bombay, India, of English parents, he lived in England and America, and traveled around the world. A good part of his early life was spent working as a newspaperman, both in England and in India, and his occupation gave him the opportunity to know these countries well. Thus he was fully aware of the grief and strife of backward India; he knew the demands these conditions made on the mind of the English soldier stationed there. This thorough knowledge of his subjects makes Kipling's writings astonishingly vital and remarkably true to life.

Kipling's career as a writer began while he was still a teen-ager, and he took the reading public by storm. Like a high gust of wind he burst through the doors of mild-mannered Victorianism. A romantic at heart, he had a streak of realism in him and did not spare his readers from the grime and grit of his subjects, nor did he lessen the blows by flowery phrases or humble apologies. His cockney soldiers use cockney English, and his natives think and act like natives. Yet he was undoubtedly the most popular British author of the 1880's and 1890's. He was a master storyteller and his glamorous plots, his exotic settings, his strong patriotic views, his realistic characters, and the brilliance and vividness of his writing possessed a vast appeal. Among his best works are *Departmental Ditties* (1886), *Plain Talk from the Hills* (1887), *Barrack-Room Ballads* (1892), from which "Ballad of East and West" (page 487) is taken, the two Jungle Books (1894, 1895), and *Kim* (1901).

The colonial society pictured so well by Kipling eventually vanished, and the glamour of imperialism has faded away, but Kipling's stories and poems remain favorites of lovers of adventure and exotic places.

This drawing executed by William Strang, etcher and portraitist, member of the Royal Academy.

NATIONAL PORTRAIT GALLERY, LONDON

THE MAN WHO WAS

The time of the story is about 1878, when England's imperial power in the Near East was steadily growing. By gaining control of the Suez Canal in 1875 England had strengthened her hold on India—and had aroused the bitter jealousy of Russia, which was striving to build up its own colonial power. British and Russian interests clashed also in the efforts of each nation to gain dominance of Afghanistan, a buffer state between India and Russia.

The story is set in the Indian city of Peshawur. The city was of strategic importance, for only a few miles away lies the entrance of the Khyber Pass, cutting through the rugged mountains and forming the chief gateway between India and Afghanistan.

L et it be clearly understood that the Russian is a delightful person till he tucks his shirt in.[1] As an Oriental he is charming. It is only when he insists upon being treated as the most easterly of Western peoples, instead of the most westerly of Easterns, that he becomes a racial anomaly extremely difficult to handle. The host never knows which side of his nature is going to turn up next.

Dirkovitch was a Russian—a Russian of the Russians, as he said—who appeared to get his bread by serving the Czar as an officer in a Cossack regiment,[2] and corresponding for a Russian newspaper with a name that was never twice the same. He was a handsome young Oriental, with a taste for wandering through unexplored portions of the earth, and he arrived in India from nowhere in particular. At least no living man could ascertain whether it was by way of Balkh, Badakhshan, Chitral, Baluchistan, Nepal,[3] or anywhere else. The Indian government, being in an unusually affable mood, gave orders that he was to be civilly treated, and shown everything that was

From *Life's Handicap* by Rudyard Kipling. Reprinted by permission of Doubleday & Company, Inc., New York; and A. P. Watt & Son, London, for Mrs. George Bambridge, The Macmillan Co. of Canada, Ltd., Toronto, and Macmillan and Co. Ltd., London.

1. *till he tucks his shirt in,* till he gives up customs or traits of his own country for those of another. When this story was written, the shirt of the Russian peasant was worn loosely over his other garments. 2. *by serving the Czar . . . Cossack regiment.* At the time of the story Russia was an empire ruled by a czar. Cossack regiments were made up of excellent horsemen from southern Russia. 3. *Balkh . . . Nepal,* cities, provinces, or kingdoms of central Asia, through any one of which persons going from Russia to India might pass.

The Khyber Pass, a narrow, highly fortified defile, famous since the time of Alexander the Great. The camel caravan is headed from the Peshawur plain toward Afghanistan.

to be seen; so he drifted, talking bad English and worse French, from one city to another till he foregathered with Her Majesty's White Hussars[4] in the city of Peshawur, which stands at the mouth of that narrow sword-cut in the hills that men call the Khyber Pass.

Dirkovitch was undoubtedly an officer, and he was decorated, after the manner of the Russians, with little enameled crosses, and he could talk, and (though this has nothing to do with his merits) he had been given up as a hopeless task or case by the Black Tyrones,[5] who, individually and collectively, with hot whiskey and honey, mulled brandy and mixed spirits of all kinds, had striven in all hospitality to make him drunk. And when the Black Tyrones, who are exclusively Irish, fail to disturb the peace of head of a foreigner, that foreigner is certain to be a superior man. This was the argument of the Black Tyrones, but they were ever an unruly and self-opinionated regiment, and they allowed junior subalterns of four years' service to choose their wines.[6] The spirits were always purchased by the colonel and a committee of majors. And a regiment that would so behave may be respected but cannot be loved.

The White Hussars were as conscientious in choosing their wine as in charging the enemy. There was a brandy that had been purchased by a cultured colonel a few years after the Battle of Waterloo.[7] It had been maturing ever since, and it was a marvelous brandy at the purchasing. The memory of that liquor would cause men to weep as they lay dying in the teak forests of upper Burma or the slime of the Irrawaddy.[8] And there was a port which was notable; and there was a champagne of an obscure brand, which always came to mess without any labels, because the White Hussars wished none to know where the source of supply might be found. The officer on whose head the champagne choosing lay was forbidden the use of tobacco for six weeks previous to sampling.

This particularity of detail is necessary to emphasize the fact that that champagne, that port, and above all, that brandy—the green and yellow and white liqueurs did not count— was placed at the absolute disposition of Dir-

kovitch, and he enjoyed himself hugely—even more than among the Black Tyrones.

But he remained distressingly European through it all. The White Hussars were—"My dear true friends," "Fellow soldiers glorious," and "Brothers inseparable." He would unburden himself by the hour on the glorious future that awaited the combined arms of England and Russia when their hearts and their territories should run side by side, and the great mission of civilizing Asia should begin. That was unsatisfactory, because Asia is not going to be civilized after the methods of the West. There is too much Asia, and she is too old. You cannot reform a lady of many lovers, and Asia has been insatiable in her flirtations aforetime. She will never attend Sunday School, or learn to vote save with swords for tickets.

Dirkovitch knew this as well as anyone else, but it suited him to talk special-correspondently[9] and to make himself as genial as he could. Now and then he volunteered a little, a very little, information about his own sotnia[10] of Cossacks, left apparently to look after themselves somewhere at the back of beyond. He had done rough work in Central Asia, and had seen rather more help-yourself fighting than most men of his years. But he was careful never to betray his superiority, and more than careful to praise on all occasions the appearance, drill, uniform, and organization of Her Majesty's White Hussars. And, indeed, they were a regiment to be admired. When Mrs. Durgan, widow of the late Sir John Durgan, arrived in their station, and after a short time had been proposed to by every single man at mess, she put the public sentiment very neatly when she explained

---

4. *Her Majesty's White Hussars* (hù zärz'), a famous cavalry regiment of Great Britain. "Her Majesty" is Queen Victoria. 5. *Black Tyrones,* an Irish regiment in the British army. It took its name from County Tyrone in Ireland. 6. *they allowed junior subalterns . . . to choose their wines.* Officers below the rank of captain (subaltern) in this regiment exercised a privilege usually reserved to higher ranking officers. 7. *Battle of Waterloo,* one of the decisive battles of the world, in which Napoleon was defeated by the Allies under the Duke of Wellington (June 18, 1815). This battle, which was fought at a village near Brussels, Belgium, brought to a close the twenty years of hostilities in Europe known as the Napoleonic Wars. 8. *Irrawaddy* (ir'ə wod'i), a river that flows through Burma. 9. *special-correspondently,* in the manner of a special newspaper correspondent. 10. *sotnia* (sot'ni ə), a cavalry squadron.

that they were all so nice that unless she could marry them all, including the colonel and some majors who were already married, she was not going to content herself with one of them. Wherefore she wedded a little man in a rifle regiment—being by nature contradictious—and the White Hussars were going to wear crape on their arms, but compromised by attending the wedding in full force, and lining the aisle with unutterable reproach. She had jilted them all—from Basset-Holmer, the senior captain, to Little Mildred, the last subaltern, and he could have given her four thousand a year and a title. He was a viscount, and on his arrival the mess had said he had better go into the Guards,[11] because they were all sons of large grocers and small clothiers in the Hussars, but Mildred begged very hard to be allowed to stay, and behaved so prettily that he was forgiven, and became a man, which is much more important than being any sort of viscount.

The only persons who did not share the general regard for the White Hussars were a few thousand gentlemen who lived across the border, and answered to the name of Pathan.[12] They had not only met the regiment officially, and for something less than twenty minutes, but the interview, which was complicated with many casualties, had filled them with prejudice. They even called the White Hussars "children of the devil," and sons of persons whom it would be perfectly impossible to meet in decent society. Yet they were not above making their aversion fill their money belts. The regiment possessed carbines, beautiful Martini-Henry carbines,[13] that would lob a bullet into an enemy's camp at one thousand yards, and were even handier than the long rifle. Therefore they were coveted all along the border, and since demand inevitably breeds supply, they were supplied at the risk of life and limb for exactly their weight in coined silver—seven and one-half pounds of rupees,[14] or sixteen pounds and a few shillings each, reckoning the rupee at par. They were stolen at night by snaky-haired thieves that crawled on their stomachs under the nose of the sentries; they disappeared mysteriously from armracks; and in the hot weather when

all the doors and windows were open, they vanished like puffs of their own smoke. The border people desired them first for their own family vendettas, and then for contingencies. But in the long, cold nights of the northern India winter they were stolen most extensively. The traffic of murder was liveliest among the hills at that season, and prices ruled high. The regimental guards were first doubled and then trebled. A trooper does not much care if he loses a weapon—government must make it good—but he deeply resents the loss of his sleep. The regiment grew very angry, and one night thief who managed to limp away bears the visible marks of their anger upon him to this hour. That incident stopped the burglaries for a time, and the guards were reduced accordingly, and the regiment devoted itself to polo with unexpected results, for it beat by two goals to one that very terrible polo corps, the Lushkar Light Horse, though the latter had four ponies apiece for a short hour's fight, as well as a native officer who played like a lambent flame across the ground.

Then they gave a dinner to celebrate the event. The Lushkar team came, and Dirkovitch came, in the fullest full uniform of a Cossack officer, which is as full as a dressing gown, and was introduced to the Lushkars, and opened his eyes as he regarded them. They were lighter men than the Hussars, and they carried themselves with the swing that is the peculiar right of the Punjab[15] frontier force and all irregular horse. Like everything else in the service, it has to be learned; but, unlike many things, it is never forgotten, and remains on the body till death.

The great beam-roofed mess room of the White Hussars was a sight to be remembered. All the mess plate was on the long table—the same table that had served up the bodies of five dead officers in a forgotten fight long and

11. *Guards,* a special group of soldiers originally assigned as bodyguards to the King.   12. *Pathan* (pǝ tän′ or pet-hän′), a member of the principal race of Afghanistan, noted for its warriors.   13. *Martini-Henry carbines,* short rifles named after Frederic Martini, a Swiss inventor, and a Scottish gunmaker named Henry.   14. *rupees* (rü pēz′), the silver coins of India, normally worth about thirty-six cents apiece.   15. *Punjab* (pun jäb′ or pun′jäb), a former province in northern India, now divided between India and Pakistan.

long ago—the dingy, battered standards faced the door of entrance, clumps of winter roses lay between the silver candlesticks, the portraits of eminent officers deceased looked down on their successors from between the heads of sambar, nilgai, markhor,[16] and pride of all the mess, two grinning snow leopards that had cost Basset-Holmer four months' leave that he might have spent in England instead of on the road to Tibet, and the daily risk of his life on ledge, snowslide, and glassy grass slope.

The servants, in spotless white muslin and the crest of their regiments on the brow of their turbans, waited behind their masters, who were clad in the scarlet and gold of the White Hussars and the cream and silver of the Lushkar Light Horse. Dirkovitch's dull green uniform was the only dark spot at the board, but his big onyx eyes made up for it. He was fraternizing effusively with the captain of the Lushkar team, who was wondering how many of Dirkovitch's Cossacks his own long, lathy down-countrymen could account for in a fair charge. But one does not speak of these things.

The talk rose higher and higher, and the regimental band played between the courses, as is the immemorial custom, till all tongues ceased for a moment with the removal of the dinner slips and the First Toast of Obligation, when the colonel, rising, said, "Mr. Vice,[17] the Queen," and Little Mildred from the bottom of the table answered, "The Queen, God bless her!" and the big spurs clanked as the big men heaved themselves up and drank the Queen, upon whose pay they were falsely supposed to pay their mess bills. That sacrament of the mess never grows old, and never ceases to bring a lump into the throat of the listener wherever he be, by land or sea. Dirkovitch rose with his "brothers glorious," but he could not understand. No one but an officer can understand what the toast means; and the bulk have more sentiment than comprehension. It all comes to the same in the end, as the enemy said when he was wriggling on a lance point. Immediately after the little silence that follows on the ceremony there entered the native officer who played for the Lushkar team. He could not of course eat with the alien,[18] but

he came in at dessert, all six feet of him, with the blue-and-silver turban atop, and the big black top boots below. The mess rose joyously as he thrust forward the hilt of his saber, in token of fealty, for the colonel of the White Hussars to touch, and dropped into a vacant chair amid shouts of "Rung Ho! Hira Singh!" (which being translated means "Go in and win!"). "Did I whack you over the knee, old man?" "Ressaldar Sahib,[19] what the devil made you play that kicking pig of a pony in the last ten minutes?" "Shabash,[20] Ressaldar Sahib!" Then the voice of the colonel, "The health of Ressaldar Hira Singh!"

After the shouting had died away, Hira Singh rose to reply, for he was the cadet of a royal house, the son of a king's son, and knew what was due on these occasions. Thus he spoke in the vernacular:

"Colonel Sahib and officers of this regiment, much honor have you done me. This will I remember. We came down from afar to play you; but we were beaten." ("No fault of yours, Ressaldar Sahib. Played on our own ground y'know. Your ponies were cramped from the railway. Don't apologize.") "Therefore perhaps we will come again if it be so ordained." ("Hear! Hear, hear, indeed! Bravo! Hsh!") "Then we will play you afresh" ("Happy to meet you") "till there are left no feet upon our ponies. Thus far for sport." He dropped one hand on his sword hilt and his eye wandered to Dirkovitch lolling back in his chair. "But if by the will of God there arises any other game which is not the polo game, then be assured, Colonel Sahib and officers, that we shall play it out side by side, though *they*" —again his eyes sought Dirkovitch—"though *they*, I say, have fifty ponies to our one horse." And with a deep-mouthed *Rung ho!* that rang like a musket butt on flagstones, he sat down amid shoutings.

16. *sambar* (sam'bər), *nilgai* (nil'gī), *markhor* (mär'kôr), respectively deer, antelope, and wild goats of Asia. 17. *Mr. Vice*, the title bestowed upon Little Mildred because he was presiding as vice-chairman of the banquet. 18. *He could not . . . with the alien.* As a devout Moslem, the native officer could not be expected to break bread with the heathen (i.e., Christians). 19. *Ressaldar Sahib* (res'əl där' sä'ib) Honorable Captain. A ressaldar is a native captain in a cavalry regiment. *Sahib* is a title of respect. 20. *Shabash* (shä'bash), bravo.

Dirkovitch, who had devoted himself steadily to the brandy—the terrible brandy aforementioned—did not understand, nor did the expurgated translations offered to him at all convey the point. Decidedly the native officer's speech was the speech of the evening, and the clamor might have continued to the dawn had it not been broken by the noise of a shot without that sent every man feeling at his defenseless left side. It is notable that Dirkovitch "reached back," after the American fashion—a gesture that set the captain of the Lushkar team wondering how Cossack officers were armed at mess. Then there was a scuffle, and a yell of pain.

"Carbine stealing again!" said the adjutant, calmly sinking back in his chair. "This comes of reducing the guards. I hope the sentries have killed him."

The feet of armed men pounded on the veranda flags,[21] and it sounded as though something was being dragged.

"Why don't they put him in the cells till morning?" said the colonel, testily. "See if they've damaged him, sergeant."

The mess sergeant fled out into the darkness, and returned with two troopers and a corporal, all very much perplexed.

"Caught a man stealin' carbines, sir," said the corporal. "Leastways 'e was crawlin' toward the barricks, sir, past the main-road sentries; and the sentry 'e says, sir——"

The limp heap of rags upheld by the three men groaned. Never was seen so destitute and demoralized an Afghan. He was turbanless, shoeless, caked with dirt, and all but dead with rough handling. Hira Singh started slightly at the sound of the man's pain. Dirkovitch took another liqueur glass of brandy.

"*What* does the sentry say?" said the colonel.

"Sez he speaks English, sir," said the corporal.

"So you brought him into mess instead of handing him over to the sergeant. If he spoke all the tongues of the Pentecost[22] you've no business——"

Again the bundle groaned and muttered. Little Mildred had risen from his place to inspect. He jumped back as though he had been shot.

"Perhaps it would be better, sir, to send the men away," said he to the colonel, for he was a much-privileged subaltern. He put his arms round the rag-bound horror as he spoke, and dropped him into a chair. It may not have been explained that the littleness of Mildred lay in his being six feet four, and big in proportion. The corporal, seeing that an officer was disposed to look after the capture, and that the colonel's eye was beginning to blaze, promptly removed himself and his men. The mess was left alone with the carbine thief, who laid his head on the table and wept bitterly, hopelessly, and inconsolably, as little children weep.

Hira Singh leaped to his feet, with a long-drawn vernacular oath. "Colonel Sahib," said he, "that man is no Afghan, for they weep '*Ai! Ai!*' Nor is he of Hindustan, for they weep '*Ow! Ho!*' He weeps after the fashion of the white men, who say '*Ow! Ow!*'"

"Now where the dickens did you get that knowledge, Hira Singh?" said the captain of the Lushkar team.

"Hear him!" said Hira Singh, simply, pointing at the crumpled figure, that wept as though it would never cease.

"He said, 'My God!'" said Little Mildred. "I heard him say it."

The colonel and the mess room looked at the man in silence. It is a horrible thing to hear a man cry. A woman can sob from the top of her palate, or her lips, or anywhere else, but a man cries from his diaphragm, and it rends him to pieces. Also, the exhibition causes the throat of the onlooker to close at the top. "Poor devil!" said the colonel, coughing tremendously.

"We ought to send him to hospital. He's been manhandled."

Now the adjutant loved his rifles. They were to him as his grandchildren—the men standing in the first place. He grunted rebelliously: "I can understand an Afghan stealing, because he's made that way. But I can't understand his crying. That makes it worse."

---

21. *flags*, flagstones, large flat stones used for paving. 22. *all the tongues . . . Pentecost.* On the seventh Sunday after Easter (the first Christian Pentecost) the Holy Ghost descended upon the Apostles in the form of tongues of fire, enabling the Apostles to speak in diverse languages.

The brandy must have affected Dirkovitch, for he lay back in his chair and stared at the ceiling. There was nothing special in the ceiling beyond the shadow as of a huge black coffin. Owing to some peculiarity in the construction of the mess room, this shadow was always thrown when the candles were lighted. It never disturbed the digestion of the White Hussars. They were, in fact, rather proud of it.

"Is he going to cry all night," said the colonel, "or are we supposed to sit with Little Mildred's guest until he feels better?"

The man in the chair threw up his head and stared at the mess. Outside, the wheels of the first of those bidden to the festivities crunched the roadway.

"Oh, my God!" said the man in the chair, and every soul in the mess rose to his feet.

Then the Lushkar captain did a deed for which he ought to have been given the Victoria Cross[23]—distinguished gallantry in a fight against overwhelming curiosity. He picked up his team with his eyes, as the hostess picks up the ladies at the opportune moment, and pausing only by the colonel's chair to say, "This isn't *our* affair, you know, sir," led the team into the veranda and the gardens. Hira Singh was the last, and he looked at Dirkovitch as he moved. But Dirkovitch had departed into a brandy paradise of his own. His lips moved without sound, and he was studying the coffin on the ceiling.

"White—white all over," said Basset-Holmer, the adjutant. "What a pernicious renegade he must be! I wonder where he came from."

The colonel shook the man gently by the arm, and "Who are you?" said he.

There was no answer. The man stared round the mess room and smiled in the colonel's face. Little Mildred, who was always more of a woman than a man till "Boot and Saddle" was sounded, repeated the question in a voice that would have drawn confidences from a geyser. The man only smiled. Dirkovitch, at the far end of the table, slid gently from his chair to the floor. No son of Adam, in this present imperfect world, can mix the Hussars' champagne with the Hussars' brandy by five and eight glasses of each without remembering the pit whence he has been digged and descending thither. The band began to play the tune with which the White Hussars, from the date of their formation, preface all their functions. They would sooner be disbanded than abandon that tune. It is a part of their system. The man straightened himself in his chair and drummed on the table with his fingers.

"I don't see why we should entertain lunatics," said the colonel; "call a guard and send him off to the cells. We'll look into the business in the morning. Give him a glass of wine first, though."

Little Mildred filled a sherry glass with the brandy and thrust it over to the man. He drank, and the tune rose louder, and he straightened himself yet more. Then he put his long-taloned hands to a piece of plate opposite and fingered it lovingly. There was a mystery connected with that piece of plate in the shape of a spring, which converted what was a seven-branched candlestick, three springs each side and one in the middle, into a sort of wheelspoke candelabrum. He found the spring, pressed it, and laughed weakly. He rose from his chair and inspected a picture on the wall, then moved on to another picture, the mess watching him without a word. When he came to the mantelpiece, he shook his head and seemed distressed. A piece of plate representing a mounted hussar in full uniform caught his eye. He pointed to it, and then to the mantelpiece, with inquiry in his eyes.

"What is it—oh, what is it?" said Little Mildred. Then, as a mother might speak to a child, "That is a horse—yes, a horse."

Very slowly came the answer, in a thick, passionless guttural, "Yes, I—have seen. But—where is *the* horse?"

You could have heard the hearts of the mess beating, as the men drew back to give the stranger full room in his wanderings. There was no question of calling the guard.

Again he spoke, very slowly, "Where is *our* horse?"

---

23. *Victoria Cross*, a bronze cross awarded to British soldiers and sailors for deeds of exceptional bravery.

There is no saying what happened after that. There is but one horse in the White Hussars, and his portrait hangs outside the door of the mess room. He is the piebald drum horse, the king of the regimental band, that served the regiment for seven-and-thirty years, and in the end was shot for old age. Half the mess tore the thing down from its place and thrust it into the man's hands. He placed it above the mantelpiece; it clattered on the ledge, as his poor hands dropped it, and he staggered toward the bottom of the table, falling into Mildred's chair. The band began to play the "River of Years" waltz, and the laughter from the gardens came into the tobacco-scented mess room. But nobody, even the youngest, was thinking of waltzes. They all spoke to one another something after this fashion: "The drum horse hasn't hung over the mantelpiece since '67." "How does he know?" "Mildred, go and speak to him again." "Colonel, what are you going to do?" "Oh, dry up, and give the poor devil a chance to pull himself together!" "It isn't possible, anyhow. The man's a lunatic."

Little Mildred stood at the colonel's side talking into his ear. "Will you be good enough to take your seats, please gentlemen?" he said, and the mess dropped into their chairs.

Only Dirkovitch's seat, next to Little Mildred's, was blank, and Little Mildred himself had found Hira Singh's place. The wide-eyed mess sergeant filled the glasses in dead silence. Once more the colonel rose, but his hand shook, and the port spilled on the table as he looked straight at the man in Little Mildred's chair and said, hoarsely, "Mr. Vice, the Queen." There was a little pause, but the man sprang to his feet and answered, without hesitation, "The Queen, God bless her!" and as he emptied the thin glass he snapped the shank between his fingers.

Long and long ago, when the Empress of India[24] was a young woman, and there were no unclean ideals in the land, it was the custom in a few messes to drink the Queen's toast in broken glass, to the huge delight of the mess contractors. The custom is now dead, because there is nothing to break anything for, except now and again the word of a govern-

ment, and that has been broken already.

"That settles it," said the colonel, with a gasp. "He's not a sergeant. What in the world is he?"

The entire mess echoed the word, and the volley of questions would have scared any man. Small wonder that the ragged, filthy invader could only smile and shake his head.

From under the table, calm and smiling urbanely, rose Dirkovitch, who had been aroused from healthful slumber by feet upon his body. By the side of the man he rose, and the man shrieked and groveled at his feet. It was a horrible sight, coming so swiftly upon the pride and glory of the toast that had brought the strayed wits together.

Dirkovitch made no offer to raise him, but Little Mildred heaved him up in an instant. It is not good that a gentleman who can answer to the Queen's toast should lie at the feet of a subaltern of Cossacks.

The hasty action tore the wretch's upper clothing nearly to the waist, and his body was seamed with dry black scars. There is only one weapon in the world that cuts in parallel lines, and it is neither the cane nor the cat.[25] Dirkovitch saw the marks, and the pupils of his eyes dilated—also, his face changed. He said something that sounded like "Shto ve takete"[26]; and the man, fawning, answered, "Chetyre."[27]

"What's that?" said everybody together.

"His number. That is number four, you know." Dirkovitch spoke very thickly.

"What has a Queen's officer to do with a qualified number?"[28] said the colonel, and there rose an unpleasant growl around the table.

"How can I tell?" said the affable Oriental, with a sweet smile. "He is a—how you have it?—escape—runaway, from over there."

He nodded toward the darkness of the night.

"Speak to him, if he'll answer you, and speak to him gently," said Little Mildred, settling the man in a chair. It seemed most im-

---

24. *Empress of India*, one of the titles of Queen Victoria. 25. *neither the cane . . . cat*, neither a stick nor the cat-o'-nine-tails, a whip with nine pieces of knotted cords, used for flogging. 26. *Shto ve takete?* Who are you? [Russian] 27. *Chetyre*, four. [Russian] 28. *a qualified number*, the number by which a prisoner was identified.

proper to all present that Dirkovitch should sip brandy as he talked in purring, spitting Russian to the creature who answered so feebly and with such evident dread. But since Dirkovitch appeared to understand, no man said a word. They breathed heavily, leaning forward, in the long gaps of the conversation. The next time that they have no engagements on hand the White Hussars intend to go to St. Petersburg[29] and learn Russian.

"He does not know how many years ago," said Dirkovitch, facing the mess, "but he says it was very long ago, in a war. I think that there was an accident. He says he was of this great and distinguished regiment in the war."

"The rolls! The rolls! Holmer, get the rolls!" said Little Mildred, and the adjutant dashed off bareheaded to the orderly room, where the rolls of the regiment were kept. He returned just in time to hear Dirkovitch conclude, "Therefore I am most sorry to say there was an accident, which would have been reparable if he had apologized to that our colonel, which he had insulted."

Another growl, which the colonel tried to beat down. The mess was in no mood to weigh insults to Russian colonels just then.

"He does not remember, but I think that there was an accident, and so he was not exchanged among the prisoners, but he was sent to another place—how do you say?—the country. *So*, he says, he came here. He does not know how he came. Eh? He was at Chepany" —the man caught the word, nodded, and shivered—"at Zhigansk and Irkutsk.[30] I cannot understand how he escaped. He says, too, that he was in the forests for many years, but how many years he has forgotten—that with many things. It was an accident, done because he did not apologize to that our colonel. Ah!"

Instead of echoing Dirkovitch's sigh of regret, it is sad to record that the White Hussars livelily exhibited unchristian delight and other emotions, hardly restrained by their sense of hospitality. Holmer flung the frayed and yellow regimental rolls on the table, and the men flung themselves atop of these.

"Steady! Fifty-six — fifty-five — fifty-four," said Holmer. "Here we are. 'Lieutenant Austin Limmason—*missing*.' That was before Sebastopol.[31] What an infernal shame! Insulted one of their colonels, and was quietly shipped off. Thirty years of his life wiped out."

"But he never apologized. Said he'd see him— first," chorused the mess.

"Poor devil! I suppose he never had the chance afterward. How did he come here?" said the colonel.

The dingy heap in the chair could give no answer.

"Do you know who you are?"

It laughed weakly.

"Do you know that you are Limmason— Lieutenant Limmason, of the White Hussars?"

Swift as a shot came the answer, in a slightly surprised tone, "Yes, I'm Limmason, of course." The light died out of his eyes, and he collapsed afresh, watching every motion of Dirkovitch with terror. A flight from Siberia may fix a few elementary facts in the mind, but it does not lead to continuity of thought. The man could not explain how, like a homing pigeon, he had found his way to his own old mess again. Of what he had suffered or seen he knew nothing. He cringed before

29. *St. Petersburg*, the capital of Russia under the czars, now called Leningrad. 30. *Chepany* (che pä'ni) . . . *Zhigansk* (zhi gänsk') . . . *Irkutsk* (ir kütsk'), towns in Siberia, the place of exile for prisoners in the days of the Russian czars. 31. *Sebastopol* (si bas'tə pōl), also *Sevastopol*. This city, an important Russian port on the Black Sea in the Crimea (kri mē'ə), was besieged and captured by Britain and France during the Crimean War (1854-1856).

Regimental badges of the Royal Berkshires, the Connaught Rangers, the Argyll and Sutherland Highlanders.

Dirkovitch as instinctively as he had pressed the spring of the candlestick, sought the picture of the drum horse, and answered to the Queen's toast.

The rest was a blank that the dreaded Russian tongue could only in part remove. His head bowed on his breast, and he giggled and cowered alternately.

The devil that lived in the brandy prompted Dirkovitch at this extremely inopportune moment to make a speech. He rose, swaying slightly, gripped the table edge, while his eyes glowed like opals, and began:

"Fellow soldiers, glorious—true friends and hospitables. It was an accident, and deplorable —most deplorable." Here he smiled sweetly all around the mess. "But you will think of this little, little thing. So little, is it not? The Czar! Posh! I snap my fingers—I snap my fingers at him. Do I believe in him? No! But the Slav who has done nothing, *him* I believe.[32] Seventy—how much?—millions that have done nothing—not one thing. Napoleon was an episode."[33] He banged a hand on the table. "Hear you, old peoples, we have done nothing in the world—out here. All our work is to do; and it shall be done, old peoples. Get away!" He waved his hand imperiously, and pointed to the man. "You see him. He is not good to see. He was just one little—oh, so little —accident, that no one remembered. Now he is *That*. So will you be, brother soldiers so brave—so will you be. But you will never come back. You will all go where he has gone, or"—he pointed to the great coffin shadow on the ceiling, and muttering "seventy millions— get away, you old people," fell asleep.

"Sweet, and to the point," said Little Mildred. "What's the use of getting wroth? Let's make the poor devil comfortable."

But that was a matter suddenly and swiftly taken from the loving hands of the White Hussars. The lieutenant had returned only to go away again three days later when the wail of the "Dead March" and the tramp of the squadrons told the wondering station, that saw no gap in the table, an officer of the regiment had resigned his new-found commission.

And Dirkovitch—bland, supple, and always genial—went away, too, by a night train. Little Mildred and another saw him off, for he was the guest of the mess, and even had he smitten the colonel with open hand, the law of the mess allowed no relaxation of hospitality.

"Good-by, Dirkovitch, and a pleasant journey," said Little Mildred.

"*Au revoir*, my true friends," said the Russian.

"Indeed! But we thought you were going home?"

"Yes; but I will come again. My friends, is that road shut?" He pointed to where the north star burned over the Khyber Pass.

"By jove! I forgot. Of course. Happy to meet you, old man, any time you like. Got everything you want—cheroots, ice, bedding? That's all right. Well, *au revoir*, Dirkovitch."

"Um," said the other man, as the tail lights of the train grew small. "Of—all—the—unmitigated——"

Little Mildred answered nothing, but watched the north star, and hummed a selection from a recent burlesque that had much delighted the White Hussars. It ran:

> I'm sorry for Mister Bluebeard,
>   I'm sorry to cause him pain;
> But a terrible spree there's sure to be
>   When he comes back again.

---

32. *But the Slav . . . I believe.* Dirkovitch is implying that Russia's true power lies in its millions of peasants, who belong to the group of people called the Slavs. 33. *Napoleon was an episode.* Napoleon's invasion of Russia in 1812, which ended in disaster for the French, was only an example of what the united Slavs can do.

THE BALLAD OF EAST AND WEST

Oh, East is East, and West is West, and never the twain shall meet,
Till Earth and Sky stand presently at God's great Judgment Seat;
But there is neither East nor West, Border, nor Breed, nor Birth,
When two strong men stand face to face, though they come from the
ends of the earth!

Kamal is out with twenty men to raise the Border side,   5
And he has lifted the Colonel's mare that is the Colonel's pride.
He has lifted her out of the stable door between the dawn and the day,
And turned the calkins upon her feet, and ridden her far away.
Then up and spoke the Colonel's son that led a troop of the Guides[1]:
"Is there never a man of all my men can say where Kamal hides?"   10
Then up and spoke Mohammed Khan, the son of the Ressaldar[2]:
"If ye know the track of the morning mist, ye know where his pickets are.
"At dusk he harries the Abazai[3]—at dawn he is into Bonair,
"But he must go by Fort Bukloh to his own place to fare.
"So if ye gallop to Fort Bukloh as fast as a bird can fly,   15
"By the favour of God ye may cut him off ere he win to the Tongue of Jagai.
"But he be past the Tongue of Jagai, right swiftly turn ye then,
"For the length and the breadth of that grisly plain is sown with Kamal's men.
"There is rock to the left, and rock to the right, and low lean thorn between,
"And ye may hear a breechbolt snick where never a man is seen."   20
The Colonel's son has taken horse, and a raw rough dun was he,
With the mouth of a bell and the heart of Hell and the head of a gallows tree.
The Colonel's son to the Fort has won, they bid him stay to eat—
Who rides at the tail of a Border thief, he sits not long at his meat.
He's up and away from Fort Bukloh as fast as he can fly,   25
Till he was aware of his father's mare in the gut of the Tongue of Jagai,
Till he was aware of his father's mare with Kamal upon her back,
And when he could spy the white of her eye, he made the pistol crack.
He has fired once, he has fired twice, but the whistling ball went wide.
"Ye shoot like a soldier," Kamal said. "Show now if ye can ride!"   30
It's up and over the Tongue of Jagai, as blown dust devils go,
The dun he fled like a stag of ten,[4] but the mare like a barren doe.
The dun he leaned against the bit and slugged his head above,
But the red mare played with the snaffle bars, as a maiden plays with a glove.
There was rock to the left and rock to the right, and low lean thorn between,   35
And thrice he heard a breechbolt snick tho' never a man was seen.
They have ridden the low moon out of the sky, their hoofs drum up the dawn,
The dun he went like a wounded bull, but the mare like a new-roused fawn.
The dun he fell at a watercourse—in a woeful heap fell he,
And Kamal has turned the red mare back, and pulled the rider free.   40
He has knocked the pistol out of his hand—small room was there to strive,

---

From *Departmental Ditties and Barrack-Room Ballads* by Rudyard Kipling. Reprinted by permission of Doubleday & Company, Inc., New York; and A. P. Watt & Son, London, for Mrs. George Bambridge, The Macmillan Co. of Canada, Ltd., Toronto, and Methuen & Co., Ltd., London.
1. *Guides*, a regiment of cavalry and infantry attached to the frontier force and acting as scouts. 2. *Ressaldar*, (res'əl där'), a Hindu leader of a group of Indian cavalry. 3. *Abazai*, an enemy tribe. 4. *stag of ten*, a stag with ten points on his antlers.

" 'Twas only by favor of mine," quoth he, "ye rode so long alive:
"There was not a rock for twenty mile, there was not a clump of tree,
"But covered a man of my own men with his rifle cocked on his knee.
"If I had raised my bridle hand, as I have held it low,   45
"The little jackals that flee so fast were feasting all in a row.
"If I had bowed my head on my breast, as I have held it high,
"The kite that whistles above us now were gorged till she could not fly."
Lightly answered the Colonel's son:"Do good to bird and beast,
"But count who come for the broken meats before thou makest a feast.   50
"If there should follow a thousand swords to carry my bones away,
"Belike the price of a jackal's meal were more than a thief could pay.
"They will feed their horse on the standing crop, their men on the garnered grain
"The thatch of the byres will serve their fires when all the cattle are slain.
"But if thou thinkest the price be fair—thy brethren wait to sup,   55
"The hound is kin to the jackal spawn—howl, dog, and call them up!
"And if thou thinkest the price be high, in steer and gear and stack,
"Give me my father's mare again, and I'll fight my own way back!"
Kamal has gripped him by the hand and set him upon his feet.
"No talk shall be of dogs," said he, "when wolf and grey wolf meet.   60
"May I eat dirt if thou hast hurt of me in deed or breath;
"What dam of lances[5] brought thee forth to jest at the dawn with Death?"
Lightly answered the Colonel's son: "I hold by the blood of my clan:
"Take up the mare for my father's gift—by God, she has carried a man!"
The red mare ran to the Colonel's son, and nuzzled against his breast;   65
"We be two strong men," said Kamal then, "but she loveth the younger best.
"So she shall go with a lifter's dower, my turquoise-studded rein,
"My 'broidered saddle and saddlecloth, and silver stirrups twain."
The Colonel's son a pistol drew, and held it muzzle-end,
"Ye have taken the one from a foe," said he. "Will ye take the mate from a friend?" 70
"A gift for a gift," said Kamal straight; "a limb for the risk of a limb.
"Thy father has sent his son to me, I'll send my son to him!"
With that he whistled his only son, that dropped from a mountain crest—
He trod the ling[6] like a buck in spring, and he looked like a lance in rest.
"Now here is thy master," Kamal said, "who leads a troop of the Guides, 75
"And thou must ride at his left side as shield on shoulder rides.
"Till Death or I cut loose the tie, at camp and board and bed,
"Thy life is his—thy fate it is to guard him with thy head.
"So, thou must eat the White Queen's meat, and all her foes are thine,
"And thou must harry thy father's hold for the peace of the Border line.   80
"And thou must make a trooper tough and hack thy way to power—
"Belike they will raise thee to Ressaldar when I am hanged in Peshawur!"[7]

They have looked each other between the eyes, and there they found no fault.
They have taken the Oath of the Brother-in-Blood on leavened bread and salt:
They have taken the Oath of the Brother-in-Blood on fire and fresh-cut sod, 85
On the hilt and the haft of the Khyber[8] knife, and the Wondrous Names of God.
The Colonel's son he rides the mare and Kamal's boy the dun,
And two have come back to Fort Bukloh where there went forth but one.

---

5. *dam of lances*, mother of fighters.   6. *ling*, heather.   7. *Peshawur*, see headnote, page 478.   8. *Khyber*, see headnote, page 478.

And when they drew to the Quarter Guard, full twenty swords flew clear—
There was not a man but carried his feud with the blood of the mountaineer.   90
"Ha' done! ha' done!" said the Colonel's son. "Put up the steel at your sides!
"Last night ye had struck at a Border thief—tonight 'tis a man of the Guides!"

Oh, East is East, and West is West, and never the twain shall meet,
Till Earth and Sky stand presently at God's great Judgment Seat;
But there is neither East nor West, Border, nor Breed, nor Birth,   95
When two strong men stand face to face, though they come from the ends of the
    earth!

RECESSIONAL

A recessional is a hymn sung as the choir leaves the church service. This poem was published in the London Times *in July, 1897, near the close of the celebration, in London, of the sixtieth anniversary of Queen Victoria —the Diamond Jubilee. High government officials and troops, as well as kings and representatives of all the important nations of the world, were assembled for the ceremonies. So, too, were soldiers from all the colonies and dominions of the British Empire; and nearly two hundred vessels of the Royal Navy were gathered in English waters. Thus it was a most appropriate time for Kipling to sound a warning, in almost Old Testament manner, to the nation dazzled by the pomp and splendor of the occasion.*

God of our fathers, known of old,
Lord of our far-flung battle line,
Beneath whose awful hand we hold
Dominion over palm and pine[1]—
Lord God of Hosts,[2] be with us yet,   5
Lest we forget[3]—lest we forget!

The tumult and the shouting dies[4];
The captains and the kings depart:
Still stands Thine ancient sacrifice,
An humble and a contrite heart.[5]   10
Lord God of Hosts, be with us yet,
Lest we forget—lest we forget!

Far-called, our navies melt away;
On dune and headland sinks the fire:
Lo, all our pomp of yesterday   15

Is one with Nineveh and Tyre![6]
Judge of the Nations, spare us yet,
Lest we forget—lest we forget!

If, drunk with sight of power, we loose
Wild tongues that have not Thee in awe,   20
Such boastings as the Gentiles use,
Or lesser breeds without the Law[7]—
Lord God of Hosts, be with us yet,
Lest we forget—lest we forget!

For heathen heart that puts her trust   25
In reeking tube and iron shard,[8]
All valiant dust that builds on dust,
And guarding, calls not Thee to guard,
For frantic boast and foolish word—
Thy mercy on Thy People, Lord!   30

"Recessional" from *The Five Nations* by Rudyard Kipling. Reprinted by permission of Doubleday & Company, Inc., New York; and A. P. Watt & Son, London, for Mrs. George Bambridge, The Macmillan Co. of Canada, Ltd., Toronto, and Methuen & Co., Ltd., London.
1. *palm and pine,* symbols of the geographical spread of the British Empire from the tropics to the northland. **2.** *Lord God of Hosts,* a common Biblical expression. **3.** *Lest we forget,* based upon the Biblical passage, "Then beware lest thou forget the Lord." (Deuteronomy 6:12.) **4.** *The tumult . . . dies,* based upon the Biblical passage, "He smelleth the battle afar off, the thunder of the captains, and the shouting." (Job 39:25.) **5.** *Thine ancient sacrifice . . . heart,* based upon the Biblical passage, "The sacrifices of God are a broken spirit; a broken and a contrite heart, O God, thou wilt not despise." (Psalms 51:17.) **6.** *Nineveh* (nin'ə və) *and Tyre* (tir). Nineveh, now buried under the sands, was the capital of ancient Assyria. Tyre, now a seaport on the coast of Palestine, was once a great city of the ancient Phoenicians. **7.** *the Gentiles . . . Law,* based upon the Biblical passage, "For when the Gentiles, which have not the law, do by nature the things contained in the law, these, having not the law, are a law unto themselves." (Romans 2:14.) In this poem Kipling thinks of the Gentiles as being those who are not English. **8.** *reeking tube and iron shard,* gun barrel and fragment of shell.

To increase understanding
The Man Who Was

1. The key to understanding the story lies in the final speech of Dirkovitch. (a) Is he sincere in addressing the British as "Fellow soldiers, glorious —true friends"? (b) What is the "deplorable accident" to which he refers? (c) What new source of Russian power does he stress? (d) Explain the significance of his statement, "All our work is to do; and it shall be done, old peoples. Get away!" (e) How does he use the pathetic figure of Limmason as a warning to the British? (f) Sum up that warning in one sentence.

2. The introduction to the story extends to page 480, column 2, paragraph 1. (a) What has the first paragraph to do with the story? (b) What attitude does Dirkovitch express toward coöperation between England and Russia in regard to Asia? (c) What is the purpose of the anecdote about Mrs. Durgan? (d) What is Kipling's purpose in relating the story about the carbine thieves?

3. (a) How does Kipling show the admiration of the British for Hira Singh as he speaks? (b) What does the last part of his speech really mean?

4. (a) How does Kipling make you see the object brought in by the sentries? (b) What discovery does Hira Singh make? (c) What is Dirkovitch's reaction? (d) What is the reaction of the Hussars?

5. What is the significance of each of the following in establishing the identity of the man: (a) a candlestick, (b) a horse, (c) a wine glass?

6. Sum up the story of what has happened to "the man who was."

7. (a) Find examples of Kipling's personal opinions in the story. (b) What feeling does this style of writing create? (c) Do you like or dislike Kipling's editorializing? Explain.

8. (a) What is the tone of the story? (b) How does the tone keep the story from becoming overly sentimental? (c) What effect does the style have on the tone?

9. Kipling was a believer in British imperialism. (a) What evidence of his attitude do you see in "The Man Who Was"? (b) In your opinion, does the story have a special significance today? Explain.

Ballad of East and West and Recessional

1. (a) What is the theme of "The Ballad of East and West"? (b) Where is it stated?

2. (a) What does the Colonel's son call Kamal in line 56? (b) What is Kamal's reaction to the insult? (c) Is this the reaction you expected? (d) How does this scene exemplify the poem's theme?

3. (a) Which is the first to be generous, Kamal or the Colonel's son? (b) Which succeeds in outdoing the other in generosity? How?

4. (a) How is this ballad like old ballads? (b) How is it unlike them?

5. Can you explain why this poem has always been one of Kipling's most popular poems?

6. What was the extent of the British Empire as suggested in the first stanza of "Recessional"?

7. (a) What fear and what prayer are expressed in the poem? (b) What is the moral?

8. What aspects of "Recessional" give it unity?

9. Why is Kipling's warning appropriate for the occasion on which the poem was written?

Better reading
Setting

If the plot element of "The Man Who Was" is considered apart from its particular setting, it becomes contrived and mechanical. In fact, the setting is an important part of the whole. A setting, such as this one, on which all actions, emotions, and moods are dependent, is called *functional*. When the setting is a particular geographic area, the concrete details of natural scenery, local traditions, customs, points of view, dialect, and peculiar types of character that give the impression of authenticity to a story are known as *local color*.

Kipling, realizing the importance of the setting to the story told in "The Man Who Was," has given it careful attention. The scene is laid in Peshawur, the capital of the northwest frontier province of British India. Peshawur's position, at the entrance of the Khyber Pass, gives it great strategic importance, and the action of the story grows naturally out of the setting. Explain why this setting may be considered functional. The presentation of the customs and manners of the isolated soldiers may appeal to the interest of the reader, but they have a more important purpose—they make the story believable. Cite examples of Kipling's use of local color and explain how they add to the plausibility of the story.

The setting of "The Ballad of East and West" is the same as that of "The Man Who Was." Do you consider the poem's setting functional? Why? What details of local color appear in the poem?

The use of local color not only lends plausibility to a story but also helps create an atmosphere of tension. Explain how this is done in both "The Man Who Was" and "The Ballad of East and West." In which is the tension the greater? Why? How does Kipling use local color to release as well as increase tensions in "The Man Who Was"?

The Victorian Woman

The stereotype of the Victorian woman is a myth. According to this stereotype she was prim and proper, serene and sheltered. She was always found seated with needlepoint work in her hands, read expurgated copies of Shakespeare, had no interests other than her home and her weekly social calls, and considered herself inferior, both mentally and physically, to her husband. Although in the early years of Victoria's reign some women did fit into this picture quite well, they were far outnumbered by a more daring and adventurous type who felt the time had come for women to declare themselves the equals of their male counterparts.

One of the first reforms came in clothing. For centuries only women of the aristocracy had paid much attention to fashion. But the style-conscious courts of Victoria in England and Napoleon III in France attracted the attention of the wealthy middle class. Fashion magazines became the vogue and spread the news of changes as fast as they occurred. Unimaginative dressmakers suddenly found themselves without clients, for women preferred those who invented new and becoming styles. Clothing manufacturers, who had previously devoted themselves exclusively to men's clothing, began to recognize the business potential in clothing women. The feeble cry of certain men that this business was contemptuous, corrupt, and entirely against the laws of nature—the male animal was meant to wear the more colorful plumage, they said—was totally unheeded by women who went from a capital X shape to a triangular shape to a bell shape during the Victorian Age.

A Victorian fashion plate.

As women entered more actively into business and sports, they found their usual clothes uncomfortable; they demanded more practical garments. But men, who had never tried to maneuver their way down a muddy street while garbed in a dress that swept the ground or attempted to play a fast game of tennis in voluminous skirts, ignored these demands. Realizing they would not be able to obtain comfortable clothing without first taking drastic steps, women abandoned all propriety and took to wearing such items as bloomers for bicycle riding. Needless to say, this was a short-lived garb, but it led to the manufacture and acceptance of sports clothes. Comfort, proper fit, and attractiveness in women's dress were here to stay.

Prior to the Victorian era, a stanch and militant feminist named Mary Wollstonecraft had fought a battle for women's rights. In

1792 she had asked that women be considered "in the grand light of human creatures, who in common with men are placed on this earth to unfold their faculties," but it was not until the latter half of the nineteenth century that this cause was actively supported by other women. Between the years 1870 and 1880 diligent campaigners for equal rights formed women's societies in every large English town and flooded Parliament with petitions containing 2,953,563 signatures requesting that the right to vote be extended to women. Because of Queen Victoria's unexplained hostility toward the idea and a widely held opinion that women were biologically incapable of casting an intelligent vote, they were defeated. Nevertheless, some gains were made, the largest of which was probably the Married Women's Property Act (1882), which gave married women the right to hold property and the right to keep money they earned.

The new position women were fighting for and gradually gaining gave rise to a new type of literature in which "the Women Question," as it was called, was examined, discussed, and argued about. While men like John Ruskin maintained that woman's function was to guide and uplift her intellectually superior husband, and while the Brownings insisted that marriages were made in heaven, Charlotte and Emily Brontë presented love honestly from a woman's point of view. Dickens, Thackeray, and George Eliot all described the heartaches of loveless marriages, but also suggested that true love would find a way. At a time when marriages were still being made over bargaining tables by ambitious parents, these romantic concepts were most reassuring and helped convince many young women that a choice of husband was an inalienable right.

Feminine fashion (below), contrasted with feminist fashion (right).

Thomas Hardy 1840-1928

R.G. Eves, who executed this portrait of Hardy, was noted for his ability to seize a characteristic expression.

Although most of the years of his long life were lived during the reign of Queen Victoria, there is little about Thomas Hardy that is typically Victorian. In the eyes of many critics he was the "first of the moderns." Hardy was born in Dorsetshire, a county in the southwest of England which coincides in part with the ancient Anglo-Saxon kingdom of Wessex, better known in our generation as "the Hardy country." Although he had aspirations toward a college education, he spent only eight years in school. At sixteen he was apprenticed to an architect; at twenty-two he was employed by a prominent London architectural firm. During his spare time he wrote poetry, but he was unable to get it published. Since he could stimulate no interest in his poetic endeavors, he turned to writing prose. Again he was unsuccessful, until the publication of *Desperate Remedies* in 1871 won him recognition as a novelist. Shortly after publication of this novel he gave up his architectural career and spent the next twenty-five years of his life writing a series of books that placed him high among English novelists. By far the best of these novels are those classified as "novels of environment and character": *Under the Greenwood Tree* (1872), *Far from the Madding Crowd* (1874), *The Return of the Native* (1878), *The Mayor of Casterbridge* (1886), *The Woodlanders* (1887), *Tess of the D'Urbervilles* (1891), and *Jude the Obscure* (1896).

Hardy also wrote short stories, many of which were first published in periodicals and later collected in book form. One of the most popular of these collections is *Wessex Tales* (1888), from which "The Three Strangers" (page 494) is taken.

Much of Hardy's prose writing is based on the belief that man is a victim of circumstance. He presents the losing struggle of individuals against the pressures of nature and social forces which gradually destroy them. Working behind the pressures is Fate—or Chance, or Hap, as Hardy calls it—malignant, relentless, and unavoidable. Hardy has often been reproached for overemphasizing the part chance plays in human life. Yet he is sympathetic, even tender-hearted, toward the victims of circumstance in his works. It is not his fault, Hardy would say, that they suffer; nor is it their fault either. They are pushed about and finally pinned down between the overwhelming forces of fate on one side and man-made society on the other. Hardy sees nature as completely indifferent to man. Many times he places it in a dominant position over man by giving it a strong and ruling personality. In *The Return of the Native*, for example, the great heath on which most of the action of the story takes place is actually one of the chief characters of the novel, perhaps the hero.[1]

This pessimistic and realistic attitude on Hardy's part offended many Victorians, and his novels and short stories were condemned and ridiculed by the majority of the critics and moralists of the period. When the publication of *Jude the Obscure* raised an outcry, Hardy turned from the writing of prose back to his greatest love, poetry, and never wrote another novel. Thus, from 1896 until his death thirty-two years later, Hardy gave full utterance to his beliefs through poetry. Unlike his prose, which is intri-

---

1. See the discussion guide for *The Return of the Native* on page 534.

cately constructed, Hardy's verse is terse, rugged, and almost naked in its lack of detail. He makes his poems conform to an exact and rigid stanza, and he imposes a rhyme scheme at all costs. The result is poetry with blood and muscle. His diction defies poetic tradition, for he writes in the same talk-flavored, sometimes salty, idiom that characterizes his prose.

Hardy's most ambitious single achievement in poetry was *The Dynasts*, a vast epic-drama about the Napoleonic wars and their impact on England. A summation of life as Hardy viewed it, the first part appeared in 1903, and the second and third sections occupied his attention for the next five years. As Hardy grew older, he continued to write poetry. At the age of eighty-three he saw his first play produced. Until his death at eighty-eight years, he reigned as the outstanding writer of his generation. His heart was buried in his native Dorset in accordance with his wishes, but his ashes were placed in the Poets' Corner of Westminster Abbey.

THE THREE STRANGERS

Among the few features of agricultural England which retain an appearance but little modified by the lapse of centuries, may be reckoned the long, grassy and furzy downs, coombs, or ewe leases,[1] as they are called according to their kind, that fill a large area of certain counties in the south and southwest. If any mark of human occupation is met with hereon, it usually takes the form of the solitary cottage of some shepherd.

Fifty years ago such a lonely cottage stood on such a down, and may possibly be standing there now. In spite of its loneliness, however, the spot, by actual measurement, was not more than five miles from a county-town. Yet that affected it little. Five miles of irregular upland, during the long inimical seasons, with their sleets, snows, rains, and mists, afford withdrawing space enough to isolate a Timon or a Nebuchadnezzar[2]; much less, in fair weather, to please that less repellent tribe, the poets, philosophers, artists and others who "conceive and meditate of pleasant things."

Some old earthen camp or barrow, some clump of trees, at least some starved fragment of ancient hedge is usually taken advantage of in the erection of these forlorn dwellings. But, in the present case, such a kind of shelter had been disregarded. Higher Crowstairs, as the house was called, stood quite detached and undefended. The only reason for its precise situation seemed to be the crossing of two footpaths at right angles hard by, which may have crossed there and thus for a good five hundred years. Hence the house was exposed to the elements on all sides. But, though the wind up here blew unmistakably when it did blow, and the rain hit hard whenever it fell, the various weathers of the winter season were not quite so formidable on the down as they were imagined to be by dwellers on low ground. The raw rimes were not so pernicious as in the hollows, and the frosts were scarcely so severe. When the shepherd and his family who tenanted the house were pitied for their sufferings from the exposure, they said that upon the whole they were less inconvenienced by "wuzzes and flames" (hoarses and phlegms) than when they had lived by the stream of a snug neighboring valley.

From *Wessex Tales* by Thomas Hardy. Reprinted by permission of The Macmillan Co. of Canada, Ltd., Toronto; Macmillan & Co., Ltd., London; St. Martin's Press, Inc. and the Trustees of the Estate of the author.
1. *furzy downs ... ewe leases.* Furzy downs are rolling lands overgrown with furze, a low, prickly, evergreen shrub with yellow flowers; coombs are small valleys or hollows; and ewe leases are sheep pastures. 2. *Timon or a Nebuchadnezzar.* Timon (ti'mon) was a Shakespearian hero who mistrusted his fellowmen and lived as a hermit. Nebuchadnezzar (neb'ū kəd nez'ər) was the king of Babylon from 605 to 562 B.C.; he spent four years alone in the wilderness living on grass.

The night of March 28, 182–, was precisely one of the nights that were wont to call forth these expressions of commiseration. The level rainstorm smote walls, slopes and hedges like the clothyard shafts of Senlac and Crecy.[3] Such sheep and outdoor animals as had no shelter stood with their buttocks to the winds; while the tails of little birds trying to roost on some scraggy thorn were blown inside out like umbrellas. The gable end of the cottage was stained with wet, and the eavesdroppings flapped against the wall. Yet never was commiseration for the shepherd more misplaced. For that cheerful rustic was entertaining a large party in glorification of the christening of his second girl.

The guests had arrived before the rain began to fall, and they were all now assembled in the chief or living room of the dwelling. A glance into the apartment at eight o'clock on this eventful evening would have resulted in the opinion that it was as cosy and comfortable a nook as could be wished for in boisterous weather. The calling of its inhabitant was proclaimed by a number of highly polished sheepcrooks without stems that were hung ornamentally over the fireplace, the curl of each shining crook varying from the antiquated type engraved in the patriarchal pictures of old family Bibles to the most approved fashion of the last local sheep fair. The room was lighted by half-a-dozen candles, having wicks only a trifle smaller than the grease which enveloped them, in candlesticks that were never used but at high days, holy days, and family feasts. The lights were scattered about the room, two of them standing on the chimney piece. This position of candles was in itself significant. Candles on the chimney piece always meant a party.

On the hearth, in front of a back brand to give substance, blazed a fire of thorns, that crackled "like the laughter of the fool."[4]

Nineteen persons were gathered here. Of these, five women, wearing gowns of various bright hues, sat in chairs along the wall; girls shy and not shy filled the window bench; four men, including Charley Jake the hedge carpenter, Elijah New the parish clerk, and John Pitcher, a neighboring dairyman, the shepherd's father-in-law, lolled in the settle; a young man and maid, who were blushing over tentative *pourparlers*[5] on a life companionship, sat beneath the corner cupboard; and an elderly engaged man of fifty or upward moved restlessly about from spots where his betrothed was not to the spot where she was. Enjoyment was pretty general, and so much the more prevailed in being unhampered by conventional restrictions. Absolute confidence in each other's good opinion begat perfect ease, while the finishing stroke of manner, amounting to a truly princely serenity, was lent to the majority by the absence of any expression or trait denoting that they wished to get on in the world, enlarge their minds, or do any eclipsing thing whatever—which nowadays so generally nips the bloom and *bonhomie* of all except the two extremes of the social scale.

Shepherd Fennel had married well, his wife being a dairyman's daughter from a vale at a distance, who brought fifty guineas in her pocket—and kept them there, till they should be required for ministering to the needs of a coming family. This frugal woman had been somewhat exercised as to the character that should be given to the gathering. A sit-still party had its advantages; but an undisturbed position of ease in chairs and settles was apt to lead on the men to such an unconscionable deal of toping that they would sometimes fairly drink the house dry. A dancing party was the alternative; but this, while avoiding the foregoing objection on the score of good drink, had a counterbalancing disadvantage in the matter of good victuals, the ravenous appetites engendered by the exercise causing immense havoc in the buttery. Shepherdess Fennel fell back upon the intermediate plan of mingling short dances with short periods of talk and singing, so as to hinder any ungovernable rage in either. But this scheme

---

3. *clothyard shafts of Senlac and Crecy.* Senlac is a hill in Sussex, England. It was the scene of the Battle of Hastings, fought in 1066. Crecy (kres′i) is a small town in the north of France, where the army of Edward III of England defeated the army of Philip VI of France in 1346. "Clothyard shafts" refers to the yard-long arrows used in both these battles. 4. *"like the laughter of the fool."* The quote is from the Old Testament, Ecclesiastes 7:6. 5. *pourparlers* (pür′pär′lā′), arrangements. [*French*]

was entirely confined to her own gentle mind: the shepherd himself was in the mood to exhibit the most reckless phases of hospitality.

The fiddler was a boy of those parts, about twelve years of age, who had a wonderful dexterity in jigs and reels, though his fingers were so small and short as to necessitate a constant shifting for the high notes, from which he scrambled back to the first position with sounds not of unmixed purity of tone. At seven the shrill tweedle-dee of this youngster had begun, accompanied by a booming ground bass from Elijah New, the parish clerk, who had thoughtfully brought with him his favorite musical instrument, the serpent.[6] Dancing was instantaneous, Mrs. Fennel privately enjoining the players on no account to let the dance exceed the length of a quarter of an hour.

But Elijah and the boy in the excitement of their position quite forgot the injunction. Moreover, Oliver Giles, a man of seventeen, one of the dancers, who was enamored of his partner, a fair girl of thirty-three rolling years, had recklessly handed a new crown piece to the musicians, as a bribe to keep going as long as they had muscle and wind. Mrs. Fennel, seeing the steam begin to generate on the countenances of her guests, crossed over and touched the fiddler's elbow and put her hand on the serpent's mouth. But they took no notice, and fearing she might lose her character of genial hostess if she were to interfere too markedly, she retired and sat down helpless. And so the dance whizzed on with cumulative fury, the performers moving in their planet-like courses, direct and retrograde, from apogee to perigee, till the hand of the well-kicked clock at the bottom of the room had traveled over the circumference of an hour.

While these cheerful events were in the course of enactment within Fennel's pastoral dwelling an incident having considerable bearing on the party had occurred in the gloomy night without. Mrs. Fennel's concern about the growing fierceness of the dance corresponded in point of time with the ascent of a human figure to the solitary hill of Higher Crowstairs from the direction of the distant town. This personage strode on through the rain without a pause, following the little-worn path which, further on in its course, skirted the shepherd's cottage.

It was nearly the time of full moon, and on this account, though the sky was lined with a uniform sheet of dripping cloud, ordinary objects out of doors were readily visible. The sad wan light revealed the lonely pedestrian to be a man of supple frame; his gait suggested that he had somewhat passed the period of perfect and instinctive agility, though not so far as to be otherwise than rapid of motion when occasion required. At a rough guess, he might have been about forty years of age. He appeared tall, but a recruiting sergeant, or other person accustomed to the judging of men's heights by the eye, would have discerned that this was chiefly owing to his gauntness, and that he was not more than five-feet-eight or nine.

Notwithstanding the regularity of his tread there was caution in it, as in that of one who mentally feels his way; and despite the fact that it was not a black coat nor a dark garment of any sort that he wore, there was something about him which suggested that he naturally belonged to the black-coated tribes of men. His clothes were of fustian, and his boots hobnailed, yet in his progress he showed not the mud-accustomed bearing of hobnailed and fustianed peasantry.

By the time that he had arrived abreast of the shepherd's premises the rain came down, or rather came along, with yet more determined violence. The outskirts of the little settlement partially broke the force of wind and rain, and this induced him to stand still. The most salient of the shepherd's domestic erections was an empty sty at the forward corner of his hedgeless garden, for in these latitudes the principle of masking the homelier features of your establishment by a conventional frontage was unknown. The traveler's

---

6. *serpent*, a bass wind instrument, now obsolete, that resembles a trumpet. It has a cupped mouthpiece and a long serpentine-twisted conical tube which is pierced with three finger holes; the tone is strong but coarse.

eye was attracted to this small building by the pallid shine of the wet slates that covered it. He turned aside, and, finding it empty, stood under the pent roof for shelter.

While he stood the boom of the serpent within the adjacent house, and the lesser strains of the fiddler, reached the spot as an accompaniment to the surging hiss of the flying rain on the sod, its louder beating on the cabbage leaves of the garden, on the straw hackles of eight or ten beehives just discernible by the path, and its dripping from the eaves into a row of buckets and pans that had been placed under the walls of the cottage. For at Higher Crowstairs, as at all such elevated domiciles, the grand difficulty of housekeeping was an insufficiency of water; and a casual rainfall was utilized by turning out, as catchers, every utensil that the house contained. Some queer stories might be told of the contrivances for economy of suds and dishwaters that are absolutely necessitated in upland habitations during the droughts of summer. But at this season there were no such exigencies; a mere acceptance of what the skies bestowed was sufficient for an abundant store.

At last the notes of the serpent ceased and the house was silent. This cessation of activity aroused the solitary pedestrian from the reverie into which he had lapsed, and, emerging from the shed, with an apparently new intention, he walked up the path to the house door. Arrived here, his first act was to kneel down on a large stone beside the row of vessels, and to drink a copious draught from one of them. Having quenched his thirst he rose and lifted his hand to knock, but paused with his eye upon the panel. Since the dark surface of the wood revealed absolutely nothing, it was evident that he must be mentally looking through the door, as if he wished to measure thereby all the possibilities that a house of this sort might include, and how they might bear upon the question of his entry.

In his indecision he turned and surveyed the scene around. Not a soul was anywhere visible. The garden path stretched downward from his feet, gleaming like the track of a snail; the roof of the little well (mostly dry), the well cover, the top rail of the garden gate, were varnished with the same dull liquid glaze; while, far away in the vale, a faint whiteness of more than usual extent showed that the rivers were high in the meads. Beyond all this winked a few bleared lamplights through the beating drops—lights that denoted the situation of the county town from which he had appeared to come. The absence of all notes of life in that direction seemed to clinch his intentions, and he knocked at the door.

Within, a desultory chat had taken the place of movement and musical sound. The hedge carpenter was suggesting a song to the company, which nobody just then was inclined to undertake, so that the knock afforded a not unwelcome diversion.

"Walk in!" said the shepherd promptly.

The latch clicked upward, and out of the night our pedestrian appeared upon the doormat. The shepherd arose, snuffed two of the nearest candles, and turned to look at him.

Their light disclosed that the stranger was dark in complexion and not unprepossessing as to feature. His hat, which for a moment he did not remove, hung low over his eyes, without concealing that they were large, open, and determined, moving with a flash rather than a glance round the room. He seemed pleased with his survey, and, baring his shaggy head, said, in a rich deep voice, "The rain is so heavy, friends, that I ask leave to come in and rest awhile."

"To be sure, stranger," said the shepherd. "And faith, you've been lucky in choosing your time, for we are having a bit of a fling for a glad cause—though, to be sure, a man could hardly wish that glad cause to happen more than once a year."

"Nor less," spoke up a woman. "For 'tis best to get your family over and done with, as soon as you can, so as to be all the earlier out of the fag o't."

"And what may be this glad cause?" asked the stranger.

"A birth and christening," said the shepherd.

The stranger hoped his host might not be made unhappy either by too many or too few of such episodes, and being invited by a gesture to pull at the mug, he readily acquiesced. His manner, which, before entering, had been so dubious, was now altogether that of a careless and candid man.

"Late to be traipsing athwart this coomb—hey?" said the engaged man of fifty.

"Late it is, master, as you say. I'll take a seat in the chimney corner, if you have nothing to urge against it, ma'am; for I am a little moist on the side that was next the rain."

Mrs. Shepherd Fennel assented, and made room for the self-invited comer, who, having got completely inside the chimney corner, stretched out his legs and his arms with the expansiveness of a person quite at home.

"Yes, I am rather cracked in the vamp," he said freely, seeing that the eyes of the shepherd's wife fell upon his boots, "and I am not well fitted either. I have had some rough times lately, and have been forced to pick up what I can get in the way of wearing, but I must find a suit better fit for working days when I reach home."

"One of hereabouts?" she inquired.

"Not quite that—further up the country."

"I thought so. And so be I; and by your tongue you come from my neighborhood."

"But you would hardly have heard of me," he said quickly. "My time would be long before yours, ma'am, you see."

This testimony to the youthfulness of his hostess had the effect of stopping her cross-examination.

"There is only one thing more wanted to make me happy," continued the newcomer. "And that is a little baccy, which I am sorry to say I am out of."

"I'll fill your pipe," said the shepherd.

"I must ask you to lend me a pipe likewise."

"A smoker, and no pipe about 'ee?"

"I have dropped it somewhere on the road."

The shepherd filled and handed him a new clay pipe, saying, as he did so, "Hand me your baccy box—I'll fill that too, now I am about it."

The man went through the movement of searching his pockets.

"Lost that too?" said his entertainer, with some surprise.

"I am afraid so," said the man with some confusion. "Give it to me in a screw of paper." Lighting his pipe at the candle with a suction that drew the whole flame into the bowl, he resettled himself in the corner and bent his looks upon the faint steam from his damp legs, as if he wished to say no more.

Meanwhile the general body of guests had been taking little notice of this visitor by reason of an absorbing discussion in which they were engaged with the band about a tune for the next dance. The matter being settled, they were about to stand up when an interruption came in the shape of another knock at the door.

At sound of the same the man in the chimney corner took up the poker and began stirring the brands as if doing it thoroughly were the one aim of his existence; and a second time the shepherd said, "Walk in!" In a moment another man stood upon the straw-woven doormat. He too was a stranger.

This individual was one of a type radically different from the first. There was more of the commonplace in his manner, and a certain jovial cosmopolitanism sat upon his features. He was several years older than the first arrival, his hair being slightly frosted, his eyebrows bristly, and his whiskers cut back from his cheeks. His face was rather full and flabby, and yet it was not altogether a face without power. A few grog blossoms marked the neighborhood of his nose. He flung back his long drab greatcoat, revealing that beneath it he wore a suit of cinder-gray shade throughout, large heavy seals, of some metal or other that would take a polish, dangling from his fob as his only personal ornament. Shaking the waterdrops from his low-crowned glazed hat, he said, "I must ask for a few minutes' shelter, comrades, or I shall be wetted to my skin before I get to Casterbridge."

"Make yourself at home, master," said the shepherd, perhaps a trifle less heartily than on the first occasion. Not that Fennel had the least tinge of niggardliness in his composition; but the room was far from large, spare chairs were not numerous, and damp companions were not altogether desirable at close quarters for the women and girls in their bright-colored gowns.

However, the second comer, after taking off his greatcoat, and hanging his hat on a nail in one of the ceiling beams as if he had been specially invited to put it there, advanced and sat down at the table. This had been pushed so closely into the chimney corner, to give all available room to the dancers, that its inner edge grazed the elbow of the man who had ensconced himself by the fire; and thus the two strangers were brought into close companionship. They nodded to each other by way of breaking the ice of unacquaintance, and the first stranger handed his neighbor the family mug—a huge vessel of brown ware, having its upper edge worn away like a threshold by the rub of whole generations of thirsty lips that had gone the way of all flesh, and bearing the following inscription burnt upon its rotund side in yellow letters:

THERE IS NO FUN
UNTiLL i CUM.

The other man, nothing loth, raised the mug to his lips, and drank on, and on, and on—till a curious blueness overspread the countenance of the shepherd's wife, who had regarded with no little surprise the first stranger's free offer to the second of what did not belong to him to dispense.

"I knew it!" said the toper to the shepherd with much satisfaction. "When I walked up your garden before coming in, and saw the hives all of a row, I said to myself, 'Where there's bees there's honey, and where there's honey there's mead.' But mead of such a truly comfortable sort as this I really didn't expect to meet in my older days." He took yet another pull at the mug, till it assumed an ominous elevation.

"Glad you enjoy it!" said the shepherd warmly.

"It is goodish mead," assented Mrs. Fennel, with an absence of enthusiasm which seemed to say that it was possible to buy praise for one's cellar at too heavy a price. "It is trouble enough to make—and really I hardly think

we shall make any more. For honey sells well, and we ourselves make shift with a drop o' small mead and metheglin for common use from the comb washings.'"[7]

"O, but you'll never have the heart!" reproachfully cried the stranger in cinder gray, after taking up the mug a third time, and setting it down empty. "I love mead, when 'tis old like this, as I love to go to church o' Sundays, or to relieve the needy any day of the week."

"Ha, ha, ha!" said the man in the chimney corner, who, in spite of the taciturnity induced by the pipe of tobacco, could not or would not refrain from this slight testimony to his comrade's humor.

Now the old mead of those days, brewed of the purest first year or maiden honey, four pounds to the gallon—with its due complement of white of eggs, cinnamon, ginger, cloves, mace, rosemary, yeast, and processes of working, bottling, and cellaring—tasted remarkably strong; but it did not taste so strong as it actually was. Hence, presently, the stranger in cinder gray at the table, moved by its creeping influence, unbuttoned his waistcoat, threw himself back in his chair, spread his legs, and made his presence felt in various ways.

"Well, well, as I say," he resumed, "I am going to Casterbridge, and to Casterbridge I must go. I should have been almost there by this time; but the rain drove me into your dwelling, and I'm not sorry for it."

"You don't live in Casterbridge?" said the shepherd.

"Not as yet; though I shortly mean to move there."

"Going to set up in trade, perhaps?"

"No, no," said the shepherd's wife. "It is easy to see that the gentleman is rich, and don't want to work at anything."

The cinder-gray stranger paused, as if to consider whether he would accept that definition of himself. He presently rejected it by answering, "Rich is not quite the word for me, dame. I do work, and I must work. And

---

7. *small mead and metheglin . . . comb washings,* drinks less potent than mead, made by pouring water over honeycomb after the salable honey has been removed.

even if I only get to Casterbridge by midnight I must begin work there at eight tomorrow morning. Yes, het or wet, blow or snow, famine or sword, my day's work tomorrow must be done."

"Poor man! Then, in spite o' seeming, you be worse off than we?" replied the shepherd's wife.

" 'Tis the nature of my trade, men and maidens. 'Tis the nature of my trade more than my poverty. . . . But really and truly I must up and off, or I shan't get a lodging in the town." However, the speaker did not move, and directly added, "There's time for one more draught of friendship before I go; and I'd perform it at once if the mug were not dry."

"Here's a mug o' small," said Mrs. Fennel. "Small, we call it, though to be sure 'tis only the first wash o' the combs."

"No," said the stranger disdainfully. "I won't spoil your first kindness by partaking o' your second."

"Certainly not," broke in Fennel. "We don't increase and multiply every day, and I'll fill the mug again." He went away to the dark place under the stairs where the barrel stood. The shepherdess followed him.

"Why should you do this?" she said reproachfully, as soon as they were alone. "He's emptied it once though it held enough for ten people; and now he's not contented wi' the small, but must needs call for more o' the strong! And a stranger unbeknown to any of us. For my part, I don't like the look o' the man at all."

"But he's in the house, my honey; and 'tis a wet night, and a christening. Daze it, what's a cup of mead more or less? There'll be plenty more next bee-burning."[8]

"Very well—this time, then," she answered, looking wistfully at the barrel. "But what is the man's calling, and where is he one of, that he should come in and join us like this?"

"I don't know. I'll ask him again."

The catastrophe of having the mug drained dry at one pull by the stranger in cinder gray was effectually guarded against this time by Mrs. Fennel. She poured out his allowance in a small cup, keeping the large one at a discreet distance from him. When he had tossed off his portion the shepherd renewed his inquiry about the stranger's occupation.

The latter did not immediately reply, and the man in the chimney corner, with sudden demonstrativeness, said, "Anybody may know my trade—I'm a wheelwright."

"A very good trade for these parts," said the shepherd.

"And anybody may know mine—if they've the sense to find it out," said the stranger in cinder gray.

"You may generally tell what a man is by his claws," observed the hedge carpenter, looking at his own hands. "My fingers be as full of thorns as an old pincushion is of pins."

The hands of the man in the chimney corner instinctively sought the shade, and he gazed into the fire as he resumed his pipe. The man at the table took up the hedge carpenter's remark, and added smartly, "True; but the oddity of my trade is that, instead of setting a mark upon me, it sets a mark upon my customers."

No observation being offered by anybody in elucidation of this enigma the shepherd's wife once more called for a song. The same obstacles presented themselves as at the former time—one had no voice, another had forgotten the first verse. The stranger at the table, whose soul had now risen to a good working temperature, relieved the difficulty by exclaiming that, to start the company, he would sing himself. Thrusting one thumb into the armhole of his waistcoat, he waved the other hand in the air, and, with an extemporizing gaze at the shining sheepcrooks above the mantelpiece, began:

> O my trade it is the rarest one,
> > Simple shepherds all—
> My trade is a sight to see;
> For my customers I tie, and take them up on high,
> > And waft 'em to a far countree!

The room was silent when he had finished the verse—with one exception, that of the man in the chimney corner, who, at the

---

8. *bee-burning.* Bee keepers use smoke as protection while taking honey from the bee hive.

singer's word, "Chorus!" joined him in a deep bass voice of musical relish—

And waft 'em to a far countree!

Oliver Giles, John Pitcher the dairyman, the parish clerk, the engaged man of fifty, the row of young women against the wall, seemed lost in thought not of the gayest kind. The shepherd looked meditatively on the ground, the shepherdess gazed keenly at the singer, and with some suspicion; she was doubting whether this stranger were merely singing an old song from recollection, or was composing one there and then for the occasion. All were as perplexed at the obscure revelation as the guests at Belshazzar's Feast,[9] except the man in the chimney corner, who quietly said, "Second verse, stranger," and smoked on.

The singer thoroughly moistened himself from his lips inwards, and went on with his next stanza as requested:

My tools are but common ones,
　　　　　　Simple shepherds all—
　My tools are no sight to see:
A little hempen string, and a post whereon to swing,
　Are implements enough for me!

Shepherd Fennel glanced round. There was no longer any doubt that the stranger was answering his question rhythmically. The guests one and all started back with suppressed exclamations. The young woman engaged to the man of fifty fainted halfway, and would have proceeded, but finding him wanting in alacrity for catching her she sat down trembling.

"O, he's the——!" whispered the people in the background, mentioning the name of an ominous public officer. "He's come to do it! 'Tis to be at Casterbridge jail tomorrow—the man for sheep stealing—the poor clockmaker we heard of, who used to live away at Shottsford and had no work to do—Timothy Summers, whose family were astarving, and so he went out of Shottsford by the highroad, and took a sheep in open daylight, defying the farmer and the farmer's wife and the farmer's lad, and every man jack among 'em. He" (and they nodded towards the stranger of the deadly trade) "is come from up the country to do it because there's not enough to do in his own county town, and he's got the place here now our own county man's dead; he's going to live in the same cottage under the prison wall."

The stranger in cinder gray took no notice of this whispered string of observations, but again wetted his lips. Seeing that his friend in the chimney corner was the only one who reciprocated his joviality in any way, he held out his cup towards that appreciative comrade, who also held out his own. They clinked together, the eyes of the rest of the room hanging upon the singer's actions. He parted his lips for the third verse; but at that moment another knock was audible upon the door. This time the knock was faint and hesitating.

The company seemed scared; the shepherd looked with consternation towards the entrance, and it was with some effort that he resisted his alarmed wife's deprecatory glance, and uttered for the third time the welcoming words, "Walk in!"

The door was gently opened, and another man stood upon the mat. He, like those who had preceded him, was a stranger. This time it was a short, small personage, of fair complexion, and dressed in a decent suit of dark clothes.

"Can you tell me the way to——?" he began: when, gazing round the room to observe the nature of the company amongst whom he had fallen, his eyes lighted on the stranger in cinder gray. It was just at the instant when the latter, who had thrown his mind into his song with such a will that he scarcely heeded the interruption, silenced all whispers and inquiries by bursting into his third verse:

Tomorrow is my working day,
　　　　　　Simple shepherds all—
　Tomorrow is a working day for me:
For the farmer's sheep is slain, and the lad who did it ta'en,
　And on his soul may God ha' merc-y!

9. *Feast,* handwriting appeared on the wall at Belshazzar's (bel shaz′ərz) feast, forecasting doom. (Daniel 5:1-24)

The stranger in the chimney corner, waving cups with the singer so heartily that his mead splashed over on the hearth, repeated in his bass voice as before:

And on his soul may God ha' merc-y!

All this time the third stranger had been standing in the doorway. Finding now that he did not come forward or go on speaking, the guests particularly regarded him. They noticed to their surprise that he stood before them the picture of abject terror—his knees trembling, his hand shaking so violently that the door latch by which he supported himself rattled audibly: his white lips were parted, and his eyes fixed on the merry officer of justice in the middle of the room. A moment more and he had turned, closed the door, and fled.

"What a man can it be?" said the shepherd.

The rest, between the awfulness of their late discovery and the odd conduct of this third visitor, looked as if they knew not what to think, and said nothing. Instinctively they withdrew further and further from the grim gentleman in their midst, whom some of them seemed to take for the Prince of Darkness himself, till they formed a remote circle, an empty space of floor being left between them and him—". . . circulus, cujus centrum diabolus."[10] The room was so silent—though there were more than twenty people in it— that nothing could be heard but the patter of the rain against the window shutters, accompanied by the occasional hiss of a stray drop that fell down the chimney into the fire, and the steady puffing of the man in the corner, who had now resumed his pipe of long clay.

The stillness was unexpectedly broken. The distant sound of a gun reverberated through the air—apparently from the direction of the county town.

"Be jiggered!" cried the stranger who had sung the song, jumping up.

"What does that mean?" asked several.

"A prisoner escaped from the jail—that's what it means."

All listened. The sound was repeated, and none of them spoke but the man in the chim-ney corner, who said quietly, "I've often been told that in this county they fire a gun at such times; but I never heard it till now."

"I wonder if it is my man?" murmured the personage in cinder gray.

"Surely it is!" said the shepherd involuntarily. "And surely we've zeed him! That little man who looked in at the door by now, and quivered like a leaf when he zeed ye and heard your song!"

"His teeth chattered, and the breath went out of his body," said the dairyman.

"And his heart seemed to sink within him like a stone," said Oliver Giles.

"And he bolted as if he'd been shot at," said the hedge carpenter.

"True—his teeth chattered, and his heart seemed to sink; and he bolted as if he'd been shot at," slowly summed up the man in the chimney corner.

"I didn't notice it," remarked the hangman.

"We were all a-wondering what made him run off in such a fright," faltered one of the women against the wall, "and now 'tis explained!"

The firing of the alarm gun went on at intervals, low and sullenly, and their suspicions became a certainty. The sinister gentleman in cinder gray roused himself. "Is there a constable here?" he asked, in thick tones. "If so, let him step forward."

The engaged man of fifty stepped quavering out from the wall, his betrothed beginning to sob on the back of the chair.

"You are a sworn constable?"

"I be, sir."

"Then pursue the criminal at once, with assistance, and bring him back here. He can't have gone far."

"I will, sir, I will—when I've got my staff. I'll go home and get it, and come sharp here, and start in a body."

"Staff! Never mind your staff; the man'll be gone!"

"But I can't do nothing without my staff— can I, William, and John, and Charles Jake? No; for there's the king's royal crown a

10. *circulus . . . diabolus*, a circle in the center of which was the devil.

painted on en in yaller and gold, and the lion and the unicorn, so as when I raise en up and hit my prisoner, 'tis made a lawful blow thereby. I wouldn't 'tempt to take up a man without my staff—no, not I. If I hadn't the law to gie me courage, why, instead o' my taking up him he might take up me!"

"Now, I'm a king's man myself, and can give you authority enough for this," said the formidable officer in gray. "Now then, all of ye, be ready. Have ye any lanterns?"

"Yes—have ye any lanterns? I demand it!" said the constable.

"And the rest of you able-bodied——"

"Able-bodied men—yes—the rest of ye!" said the constable.

"Have you some good stout staves and pitchforks——"

"Staves and pitchforks—in the name o' the law! And take 'em in yer hands and go in quest, and do as we in authority tell ye!"

Thus aroused, the men prepared to give chase. The evidence was, indeed, though circumstantial, so convincing, that but little argument was needed to show the shepherd's guests that after what they had seen it would look very much like connivance if they did not instantly pursue the unhappy third stranger, who could not as yet have gone more than a few hundred yards over such uneven country.

A shepherd is always well provided with lanterns; and, lighting these hastily, and with hurdle-staves in their hands, they poured out of the door, taking a direction along the crest of the hill, away from town, the rain having fortunately a little abated.

Disturbed by the noise, or possibly by unpleasant dreams of her baptism, the child who had been christened began to cry heart-brokenly in the room overhead. These notes of grief came down through the chinks of the floor to the ears of the women below, who jumped up one by one, and seemed glad of the excuse to ascend and comfort the baby, for the incidents of the last half-hour greatly oppressed them. Thus in the space of two or three minutes the room on the ground floor was deserted quite.

But it was not for long. Hardly had the sound of footsteps died away when a man returned round the corner of the house from the direction the pursuers had taken. Peeping in at the door, and seeing nobody there, he entered leisurely. It was the stranger of the chimney corner, who had gone out with the rest. The motive of his return was shown by his helping himself to a cut piece of skimmer cake that lay on a ledge beside where he had sat, and which he had apparently forgotten to take with him. He also poured out half a cup more mead from the quantity that remained, ravenously eating and drinking these as he stood. He had not finished when another figure came in just as quietly —his friend in cinder gray.

"O—you here?" said the latter, smiling. "I thought you had gone to help in the capture." And this speaker also revealed the object of his return by looking solicitously round for the fascinating mug of old mead.

"And I thought you had gone," said the other, continuing his skimmer cake with some effort.

"Well, on second thoughts, I felt there were enough without me," said the first confidentially, "and such a night as it is, too. Besides, 'tis the business o' the Government to take care of its criminals—not mine."

"True; so it is. And I felt as you did, that there were enough without me."

"I don't want to break my limbs running over the humps and hollows of this wild country."

"Nor I neither, between you and me."

"These shepherd people are used to it— simple-minded souls, you know, stirred up to anything in a moment. They'll have him ready for me before the morning, and no trouble to me at all."

"They'll have him, and we shall have saved ourselves all labor in the matter."

"True, true. Well, my way is to Caster-bridge; and 'tis as much as my legs will do to take me that far. Going the same way?"

"No, I am sorry to say! I have to get home over there" (he nodded indefinitely to the right), "and I feel as you do, that it is quite enough for my legs to do before bedtime."

The other had by this time finished the

mead in the mug, after which, shaking hands heartily at the door, and wishing each other well, they went their several ways.

In the meantime the company of pursuers had reached the end of the hog's-back elevation which dominated this part of the down. They had decided on no particular plan of action; and, finding that the man of the baleful trade was no longer in their company, they seemed quite unable to form any such plan now. They descended in all directions down the hill, and straightway several of the party fell into the snare set by nature for all misguided midnight ramblers over this part of the cretaceous formation. The "lanchets," or flint slopes, which belted the escarpment at intervals of a dozen yards, took the less cautious ones unawares, and losing their footing on the rubbly steep they slid sharply downwards, the lanterns rolling from their hands to the bottom, and there lying on their sides till the horn was scorched through.

When they had again gathered themselves together the shepherd, as the man who knew the country best, took the lead, and guided them round these treacherous inclines. The lanterns, which seemed rather to dazzle their eyes and warn the fugitive than to assist them in the exploration, were extinguished, due silence was observed; and in this more rational order they plunged into the vale. It was a grassy, briery, moist defile, affording some shelter to any person who had sought it; but the party perambulated it in vain, and ascended on the other side. Here they wandered apart, and after an interval closed together again to report progress. At the second time of closing in they found themselves near a lonely ash, the single tree on this part of the coomb, probably sown there by a passing bird some fifty years before. And here, standing a little to one side of the trunk, as motionless as the trunk itself, appeared the man they were in quest of, his outline being well defined against the sky beyond. The band noiselessly drew up and faced him.

"Your money or your life!" said the constable sternly to the still figure.

"No, no," whispered John Pitcher. " 'Tisn't our side ought to say that. That's the doctrine of vagabonds like him, and we be on the side of the law."

"Well, well," replied the constable impatiently; "I must say something, mustn't I? And if you had all the weight o' this undertaking upon your mind, perhaps you'd say the wrong thing too! Prisoner at the bar, surrender, in the name of the Father—the Crown, I mane!"

The man under the tree seemed now to notice them for the first time, and, giving them no opportunity whatever for exhibiting their courage, he strolled slowly towards them. He was, indeed, the little man, the third stranger; but his trepidation had in a great measure gone.

"Well, travelers," he said, "did I hear ye speak to me?"

"You did: you've got to come and be our prisoner at once!" said the constable. "We arrest 'ee on the charge of not biding in Casterbridge jail in a decent proper manner to be hung tomorrow morning. Neighbors, do your duty, and seize the culpet!"

On hearing the charge the man seemed enlightened, and, saying not another word, resigned himself with preternatural civility to the search party, who, with their staves in their hands, surrounded him on all sides, and marched him back towards the shepherd's cottage.

It was eleven o'clock by the time they arrived. The light shining from the open door, a sound of men's voices within, proclaimed to them as they approached the house that some new events had arisen in their absence. On entering they discovered the shepherd's living room to be invaded by two officers from Casterbridge jail, and a well-known magistrate who lived at the nearest country seat, intelligence of the escape having become generally circulated.

"Gentlemen," said the constable, "I have brought back your man—not without risk and danger; but every one must do his duty! He is inside this circle of able-bodied persons, who have lent me useful aid, considering their ignorance of Crown work. Men, bring forward your prisoner!" And the third stranger was led to the light.

"Who is this?" said one of the officials.

"The man," said the constable.

"Certainly not," said the turnkey; and the first corroborated his statement.

"But how can it be otherwise?" asked the constable. "Or why was he so terrified at sight o' the singing instrument of the law who sat there?" Here he related the strange behavior of the third stranger on entering the house during the hangman's song.

"Can't understand it," said the officer coolly. "All I know is that it is not the condemned man. He's quite a different character from this one; a gauntish fellow with dark hair and eyes, rather good-looking, and with a musical bass voice that if you heard once you'd never mistake as long as you lived."

"Why, souls—'twas the man in the chimney corner!"

"Hey—what?" said the magistrate, coming forward after inquiring particulars from the shepherd in the background. "Haven't you got the man after all?"

"Well, sir," said the constable, "he's the man we were in search of, that's true; and yet he's not the man we were in search of. For the man we were in search of was not the man we wanted, sir, if you understand my everyday way; for 'twas the man in the chimney corner!"

"A pretty kettle of fish altogether!" said the magistrate. "You had better start for the other man at once."

The prisoner now spoke for the first time. The mention of the man in the chimney corner seemed to have moved him as nothing else could do. "Sir," he said, stepping forward to the magistrate, "take no more trouble about me. The time is come when I may as well speak. I have done nothing; my crime is that the condemned man is my brother. Early this afternoon I left home at Shottsford to tramp it all the way to Casterbridge jail to bid him farewell. I was benighted, and called here to rest and ask the way. When I opened the door I saw before me the very man, my brother, that I thought to see in the condemned cell at Casterbridge. He was in this chimney corner; and jammed close to him, so that he could not have got out if he had

tried, was the executioner who'd come to take his life, singing a song about it and not knowing that it was his victim who was close by, joining in to save appearances. My brother threw a glance of agony at me, and I knew he meant, 'Don't reveal what you see; my life depends on it.' I was so terror-struck that I could hardly stand, and, not knowing what I did, I turned and hurried away."

The narrator's manner and tone had the stamp of truth, and his story made a great impression on all around. "And do you know where your brother is at the present time?" asked the magistrate.

"I do not. I have never seen him since I closed this door."

"I can testify to that, for we've been between ye ever since," said the constable.

"Where does he think to fly to? What is his occupation?"

"He's a watch-and-clock-maker, sir."

"'A said 'a was a wheelwright—a wicked rogue," said the constable.

"The wheels of clocks and watches he meant, no doubt," said Shepherd Fennel. "I thought his hands were palish for 's trade."

"Well, it appears to me that nothing can be gained by retaining this poor man in custody," said the magistrate; "your business lies with the other, unquestionably."

And so the little man was released offhand; but he looked nothing the less sad on that account, it being beyond the power of magistrate or constable to raze out the written troubles in his brain, for they concerned another whom he regarded with more solicitude than himself. When this was done, and the man had gone his way, the night was found to be so far advanced that it was deemed useless to renew the search before the next morning.

Next day, accordingly, the quest for the clever sheep stealer became general and keen, to all appearance at least. But the intended punishment was cruelly disproportioned to the transgression, and the sympathy of a great many country folk in that district was strongly on the side of the fugitive. Moreover, his marvelous coolness and daring in hob-and-nobbing with the hangman, under the unprecedented circumstances of the shepherd's party, won their admiration. So that it may be questioned if all those who ostensibly made themselves so busy in exploring woods and fields and lanes were quite so thorough when it came to the private examination of their own lofts and outhouses. Stories were afloat of a mysterious figure being occasionally seen in some old overgrown trackway or other, remote from turnpike roads; but when a search was instituted in any of these suspected quarters nobody was found. Thus the days and weeks passed without tidings.

In brief, the bass-voiced man of the chimney corner was never recaptured. Some said that he went across the sea, others that he did not, but buried himself in the depths of a populous city. At any rate, the gentleman in cinder gray never did his morning's work at Casterbridge, nor met anywhere at all, for business purposes, the genial comrade with whom he had passed an hour of relaxation in the lonely house on the slope of the coomb.

The grass has long been green on the graves of Shepherd Fennel and his frugal wife, the guests who made up the christening party have mainly followed their entertainers to the tomb; the baby in whose honor they all had met is a matron in the sere and yellow leaf.[11] But the arrival of the three strangers at the shepherd's that night, and the details connected therewith, is a story as well known as ever in the country about Higher Crowstairs.

---

11. *sere and yellow leaf*, old age. This is taken from Shakespeare's *Macbeth*, Act V, Scene III: "I have lived long enough: my way of life / Is fallen into the sere, the yellow leaf.

Hardy's birthplace, a cottage in Higher Bockhampton, a Dorset hamlet.

DRUMMER HODGE

The background of "Drummer Hodge" is the Boer War in South Africa in 1899-1902 between the British and the Dutch settlers, or Boers.

They throw in Drummer Hodge, to
    rest
    Uncoffined—just as found:
His landmark is a kopje crest[1]
    That breaks the veldt[2] around;
And foreign constellations west   5
    Each night above his mound.

Young Hodge the Drummer never knew—
    Fresh from his Wessex home—
The meaning of the broad Karoo,[3]
    The Bush,[4] the dusty loam,   10
And why uprose to nightly view
    Strange stars amid the gloom.

Yet portion of that unknown plain
    Will Hodge forever be;
His homely Northern breast and brain   15
    Grow to some Southern tree,
And strange-eyed constellations reign
    His stars eternally.

THE DARKLING THRUSH

This poem was written during the closing weeks of the year 1900—in other words, just before the end of the nineteenth century.

I leant upon a coppice gate
    When frost was specter-gray,
And winter's dregs made desolate
    The weakening eye of day.
The tangled bine-stems[1] scored the sky   5
    Like strings of broken lyres,
And all mankind that haunted night
    Had sought their household fires.

The land's sharp features seemed to be
    The Century's corpse outleant,   10
His crypt the cloudy canopy,
    The wind his death lament.

The ancient pulse of germ and birth
    Was shrunken hard and dry,
And every spirit upon earth   15
    Seemed fervorless as I.

At once a voice arose among
    The bleak twigs overhead
In a full-hearted evensong
    Of joy unlimited;   20
An aged thrush, frail, gaunt, and small,
    In blast-beruffled plume,
Had chosen thus to fling his soul
    Upon the growing gloom.

So little cause for carolings   25
    Of such ecstatic sound
Was written on terrestrial things
    Afar or nigh around,
That I could think there trembled through
    His happy good-night air   30
Some blessed Hope, whereof he knew
    And I was unaware.

IN TIME OF "THE BREAKING OF NATIONS"

The title is adapted from the Biblical verse: "Thou art my battle ax and weapons of war; for with thee will I break in pieces the nations; and with thee will I destroy kingdoms." (Jeremiah 51:20)

Only a man harrowing clods
    In a slow silent walk,
With an old horse that stumbles and nods
    Half asleep as they stalk.

Only thin smoke without flame   5
    From the heaps of couch grass:

DRUMMER HODGE   **1.** *kopje* (kop′i) *crest*, the top of a small hill. *Kopje* is a South African word. **2.** *veldt* (velt or felt), a tract of grassland in South Africa. **3.** *Karoo* (kar ü′), a dry elevated region in Cape Colony. **4.** *Bush,* a vast area of scrub-covered country.

THE DARKLING THRUSH   **1.** *bine-stems,* the stems of a kind of climbing plant.

Yet this will go onward the same
Though Dynasties pass.

Yonder a maid and her wight
Come whispering by;   10
War's annals will fade into night
Ere their story die.

THE MAN HE KILLED

"Had he and I but met
By some old ancient inn,
We should have set us down to wet
Right many a nipperkin![1]

"But ranged as infantry,   5
And staring face to face,
I shot at him as he at me,
And killed him in his place.

"I shot him dead because—
Because he was my foe,   10
Just so: my foe of course he was;
That's clear enough; although

"He thought he'd 'list, perhaps,
Off-hand like—just as I;
Was out of work, had sold his traps—   15
No other reason why.

"Yes; quaint and curious war is!
You shoot a fellow down
You'd treat if met where any bar is,
Or help to half-a-crown."[2]   20

"The Man He Killed" from *The Collected Poems of Thomas Hardy*. Reprinted by permission of The Macmillan Company, New York; The Macmillan Company of Canada, Ltd.; Macmillan & Co., Ltd., London; and the Trustees of the Estate of the author. Copyright 1925 by The Macmillan Company.
1. *nipperkin*, a half-pint of ale. 2. *half-a-crown*, an English coin (two shillings and a half), worth in Hardy's day about sixty-three cents.

To increase understanding
The Three Strangers

1. (*a*) Describe the character and appearance of the thief. (*b*) Of what crime is he guilty? (*c*) Is the punishment for the crime just? (*d*) Why do you think Hardy makes the punishment so severe? (*e*) How does Hardy show his sympathy for the

thief through his own statements and the remarks of the various characters?

2. Reread the paragraph in the biographical sketch (page 493) dealing with Hardy's belief that man is a victim of circumstance. (*a*) In what way is the condemned man such a victim? (*b*) What choices were open to him? (*c*) Was either of these choices acceptable in the eyes of society? Explain.

3. (*a*) To what extent are the details of setting in "The Three Strangers" functional? (*b*) Find details other than those pertaining to setting that are important. (*c*) How do these details help make the plot something more than mere coincidence?

4. Some of the detail Hardy employs in the story appears at first glance to be irrelevant. An example of this type of detail is the fact that the shepherdess is proud of her mead, yet is not anxious to serve it. Hardy does not insert this detail just to emphasize the peculiarities of the shepherdess, nor is he trying to point out the miserliness of the class of people to which the shepherdess belongs. (*a*) What connection between the condemned man's circumstances and the people at the party is Hardy pointing out? (*b*) How does this relationship help explain why the thief escapes? (*c*) Find other examples of seemingly irrelevant details and explain the function of each.

5. Cite details that would make this story one as "well known as ever in the country about Higher Crowstairs."

6. Hardy's description of the girl who decides not to faint because her betrothed is not prepared to catch her shows his use of humor in an essentially serious story. (*a*) At what moment in the tale does this description occur? (*b*) What is the reason for a humorous touch at this point? (*c*) Where else in the story does Hardy use humor? (*d*) What function does each of these humorous touches serve?

7. (*a*) What two devices does Hardy use to clear the room? (*b*) What is his purpose in clearing the room? (*c*) What reasons do the condemned man and the hangman give for their return? (*d*) What is Hardy trying to point out about the whole situation by having these two men return? (*e*) What do you learn about the character of each man upon his return?

8. (*a*) Does the heath in the story have a personality? (*b*) Does it influence the characters in any way? Explain. (*c*) What part does the storm play in the story? (*d*) What is the attitude of the characters toward nature?

9. (*a*) Why is "The Three Strangers" considered a realistic story? (*b*) Is the ending in keeping with the rest of the story? (Before answering this ques-

tion, reëxamine the characteristics and attitudes of the people involved.)

Four Poems

1. What aspect of the death of a young soldier is the theme of "Drummer Hodge"?

2. (a) How does Hardy build up an atmosphere appropriate to the subject of "The Darkling Thrush"? (b) What is the central idea of the poem? (c) Is it a poem of hope or despair?

3. "The Darkling Thrush" was written during the closing weeks of the year 1900. Why is this fact important in understanding the poem?

4. (a) What is Hardy's belief as implied in "In Time of 'The Breaking of Nations' "? (b) How do the old man, the horse, the burning grass, and the loving couple emphasize the theme?

5. (a) In "The Man He Killed," what does Hardy imply is the fundamental proof of the folly of war? (b) According to the ideas expressed in the poem, does Hardy consider war a personal or impersonal matter?

6. (a) How do these four poems differ in style, content, and tone from earlier Victorian poems? (b) What does Hardy gain by eliminating all unnecessary ornamentation? (c) Is his style suited to the subjects and tone of his poetry? (d) Do you prefer this type of poetry or that of the earlier Victorians? Explain.

7. Can you explain why Hardy might be considered the "first of the moderns"?

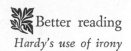

Better reading

Hardy's use of irony

Hardy leans heavily on irony to tell the story of "The Three Strangers." He not only uses *verbal irony*, or expressions which say the opposite of what is meant, but he also makes extensive use of *irony of situation*. For example, the story opens at Shepherd Fennel's house, where friends have gathered to celebrate a christening; soon a condemned man and a hangman enter. This juxtaposition of life and death forms an ironical situation that is basic in understanding the story. A second ironical factor is the close association between joy and sorrow. What happens to the party that begins so happily? Hardy also introduces irony by contrasting people as individuals with people acting as a group. What is the attitude of Shepherd Fennel and the guests to the stranger in the chimney corner? How does the group react when the supposed sheep-stealer is escaping? What does the difference in attitudes imply about the author's feeling about society?

Verbal irony is also used throughout "The Three Strangers." Where is the irony in Hardy's description of Oliver Giles and his dancing partner (page 496, column 1, paragraph 2)? Find other examples of this type of irony.

Hardy's poems also make use of irony. What is ironic about the theme of "The Man He Killed"? In what way is this theme related to one of the ideas developed in "The Three Strangers"? Point out examples of irony in other poems by Hardy.

Joseph Conrad 1857-1924

...trait of Conrad
...Sir William
...henstein,
...cipal of the
...al College
...Art.

Joseph Conrad, born Teodor Joseph Konrad Korzeniowski in the Ukraine, then part of Russian Poland, was the only writer born a foreigner to become a recognized master of the art of English prose. His parents, wealthy and cultured Poles, were exiled as a result of his father's leadership in the Polish revolution against Russia. A good education and a comfortable career were planned for him by an uncle, but Conrad had other dreams—he was determined to become an Englishman and a sailor. At sixteen he joined the French Mercantile Marine, and after three years spent in Marseilles and the West Indies, he transferred to a British ship. In 1878 he set foot on British soil for the first time; he was twenty-one years old, and he spoke no English. By the time he was twenty-seven he was a Master in the British Marine, a naturalized British citizen, and had changed his name to Joseph Conrad.

The sea fascinated Conrad. To him it was an incalculable force that scorns civilization. At sea a man stands alone, pitted against a hostile world, unprotected by organized society, freed from everything but his own conscience. Here a man must display his integrity and heroism to conquer these hostile forces, or be crushed by the terrible realities of life. Conrad remained at sea for twenty years and during that time stored up memories of incidents, experiences, impressions, and people which he used later in his writing.

Almost forty when *Almayer's Folly*, his first book, was published, Conrad was so encouraged by public and critical reception of the novel that he gave up the sea and concentrated on writing. Within the next twenty years he perfected his prose style and secured his position as one of the great masters of English fiction. Among his best works are *The Nigger of the Narcissus* (1897), *Lord Jim* (1900), *Nostromo* (1904), *Chance* (1914), *The Rescue* (1920), and *The Rover* (1923).

One of Conrad's strongest characteristics is his almost complete detachment from his stories. By playing the part of an aloof and objective observer, he creates the impression that the story actually happened and is being retold rather than invented. In order to maintain his objectivity, Conrad often tells a story within the frame of another story through the impersonal, disinterested eyes of one of his characters. For example, Marlow, a character in the novel *Lord Jim*, is used merely to help tell the story and keep the author from expressing too much of his own point of view.[1]

Conrad viewed life pessimistically, and about it he said, "If you take it to heart it becomes an unendurable tragedy," and "I would fondly believe its purpose is purely spectacular." He felt that man had it in his power to succeed in his harsh struggle with life, at least to the point of coming to terms with it, but that moral reality was stern and unavoidable, and no man could survive who failed to meet the demands of love, honor, and duty. He claimed that he was neither a romanticist nor a realist, but that he merely tried to capture the truth of life as he saw it.

---

1. For a guide to the discussion of *Lord Jim*, see page 536.

THE LAGOON

The white man, leaning with both arms over the roof of the little house in the stern of the boat, said to the steersman: "We will pass the night in Arsat's clearing. It is late."

The Malay only grunted, and went on looking fixedly at the river. The white man rested his chin on his crossed arms and gazed at the wake of the boat. At the end of the straight avenue of forests cut by the intense glitter of the river, the sun appeared unclouded and dazzling, poised low over the water that shone smoothly like a band of metal. The forests, somber and dull, stood motionless and silent on each side of the broad stream. At the foot of big, towering trees, trunkless nipa palms rose from the mud of the bank, in bunches of leaves enormous and heavy, that hung unstirring over the brown swirl of eddies. In the stillness of the air every tree, every leaf, every bough, every tendril of creeper and every petal of minute blossoms seemed to have been bewitched into an immobility perfect and final. Nothing moved on the river but the eight paddles that rose flashing regularly, dipped together with a single splash; while the steersman swept right and left with a

From *Tales of Unrest* by Joseph Conrad. Reprinted by permission of Doubleday & Company, New York; J. M. Dent & Sons Ltd., London; and the Trustees of the Estate of the author.

periodic and sudden flourish of his blade describing a glinting semicircle above his head. The churned-up water frothed alongside with a confused murmur. And the white man's canoe, advancing upstream in the short-lived disturbance of its own making, seemed to enter the portals of a land from which the very memory of motion had forever departed.

The white man, turning his back upon the setting sun, looked along the empty and broad expanse of the sea reach. For the last three miles of its course the wandering, hesitating river, as if enticed irresistibly by the freedom of an open horizon, flows straight into the sea, flows straight to the east—to the east that harbors both light and darkness. Astern of the boat the repeated call of some bird, a cry discordant and feeble, skipped along over the smooth water and lost itself, before it could reach the other shore, in the breathless silence.

The steersman dug his paddle into the stream, and held hard with stiffened arms, his body thrown forward. The water gurgled aloud; and suddenly the long straight reach seemed to pivot on its center, the forests swung in a semicircle, and the slanting beams of sunset touched the broadside of the canoe with a fiery glow, throwing the slender and distorted shadows of its crew upon the streaked glitter of the river. The white man turned to look ahead. The course of the boat had been altered at right angles to the stream, and the carved dragonhead of its prow was pointing now at a gap in the fringing bushes of the bank. It glided through, brushing the overhanging twigs, and disappeared from the river like some slim and amphibious creature leaving the water for its lair in the forests.

The narrow creek was like a ditch: tortuous, fabulously deep, filled with gloom under the thin strip of pure and shining blue of the heaven. Immense trees soared up, invisible behind the festooned draperies of creepers. Here and there, near the glistening blackness of the water, a twisted root of some tall tree showed amongst the tracery of small ferns, black and dull, writhing and motionless, like an arrested snake. The short words of the paddlers reverberated loudly between the thick and somber walls of vegetation. Darkness oozed out from between the trees, through the tangled maze of the creepers, from behind the great fantastic and unstirring leaves; the darkness, mysterious and invincible; the darkness scented and poisonous of impenetrable forests.

The men poled in the shoaling water. The creek broadened, opening out into a wide sweep of a stagnant lagoon. The forests receded from the marshy bank, leaving a level strip of bright green, reedy grass to frame the reflected blueness of the sky. A fleecy pink cloud drifted high above, trailing the delicate coloring of its image under the floating leaves and the silvery blossoms of the lotus. A little house, perched on high piles, appeared black in the distance. Near it, two tall nibong palms, that seemed to have come out of the forests in the background, leaned slightly over the ragged roof, with a suggestion of sad tenderness and care in the droop of their leafy and soaring heads.

The steersman, pointing with his paddle said, "Arsat is there. I see his canoe fast between the piles."

The polers ran along the sides of the boat glancing over their shoulders at the end of the day's journey. They would have preferred to spend the night somewhere else than on this lagoon of weird aspect and ghostly reputation. Moreover, they disliked Arsat, first as a stranger, and also because he who repairs a ruined house, and dwells in it, proclaims that he is not afraid to live amongst the spirits that haunt the places abandoned by mankind. Such a man can disturb the course of fate by glances or words; while his familiar ghosts are not easy to propitiate by casual wayfarers upon whom they long to wreak the malice of their human master. White men care not for such things, being unbelievers and in league with the Father of Evil, who leads them unharmed through the invisible dangers of this world. To the warnings of the righteous they oppose an offensive pretense of disbelief. What is there to be done?

So they thought, throwing their weight on the end of their long poles. The big canoe glided on swiftly, noiselessly, and smoothly, toward Arsat's clearing, till, in a great rattling of poles thrown down, and the loud murmurs of "Allah[1] be praised!" it came with a gentle knock against the crooked piles below the house.

The boatmen with uplifted faces shouted discordantly, "Arsat! O Arsat!" Nobody came. The white man began to climb the rude ladder giving access to the bamboo platform before the house. The juragan[2] of the boat said sulkily, "We will cook in the sampan and sleep on the water."

"Pass my blankets and the basket," said the white man, curtly.

He knelt on the edge of the platform to receive the bundle. Then the boat shoved off, and the white man, standing up, confronted Arsat, who had come out through the low door of his hut. He was a man young, powerful, with broad chest and muscular arms. He had nothing on but his sarong. His head was bare. His big, soft eyes stared eagerly at the white man, but his voice and demeanor were composed as he asked, without any words of greeting, "Have you medicine, Tuan?"[3]

"No," said the visitor in a startled tone. "No. Why? Is there sickness in the house?"

"Enter and see," replied Arsat, in the same calm manner, and turning short around, passed again through the small doorway. The white man, dropping his bundles, followed.

In the dim light of the dwelling he made out on a couch of bamboos a woman stretched on her back under a broad sheet of red cotton cloth. She lay still, as if dead; but her big eyes, wide open, glittered in the gloom, staring upward at the slender rafters, motionless and unseeing. She was in a high fever, and evidently unconscious. Her cheeks were sunk slightly, her lips were partly open, and on the young face there was the ominous and fixed expression—the absorbed, contemplating expression of the unconscious who are going to die. The two men stood looking down at her in silence.

"Has she been long ill?" asked the traveler.

"I have not slept for five nights," answered the Malay, in a deliberate tone. "At first she heard voices calling her from the water and struggled against me who held her. But since the sun of today rose she hears nothing—she

hears not me. She sees nothing. She sees not me—me!"

He remained silent for a minute, then asked softly, "Tuan, will she die?"

"I fear so," said the white man, sorrowfully. He had known Arsat years ago, in a far country in times of trouble and danger, when no friendship is to be despised. And since his Malay friend had come unexpectedly to dwell in the hut on the lagoon with a strange woman, he had slept many times there, in his journeys up and down the river. He liked the man who knew how to keep faith in council and how to fight without fear by the side of his white friend. He liked him—not so much perhaps as a man likes his favorite dog—but still he liked him well enough to help and ask no questions, to think sometimes vaguely and hazily in the midst of his own pursuits, about the lonely man and the long-haired woman with audacious face and triumphant eyes, who lived together hidden by the forests—alone and feared.

The white man came out of the hut in time to see the enormous conflagration of sunset put out by the swift and stealthy shadows that, rising like a black and impalpable vapor above the treetops, spread over the heaven, extinguishing the crimson glow of floating clouds and the red brilliance of departing daylight. In a few moments all the stars came out above the intense blackness of the earth and the great lagoon, gleaming suddenly with reflected lights, resembled an oval patch of night sky flung down into the hopeless and abysmal night of the wilderness. The white man had some supper out of the basket, then collecting a few sticks that lay about the platform, made up a small fire, not for warmth, but for the sake of the smoke, which would keep off the mosquitos. He wrapped himself in the blankets and sat with his back against the reed wall of the house, smoking thoughtfully.

Arsat came through the doorway with noiseless steps and squatted down by the fire. The white man moved his outstretched legs a little.

---

1. *Allah*, the Mohammedan term for God. 2. *juragan* (jū′rä gän), the rower chiefly responsible for steering the boat. 3. *Tuan* (tü än′), a term of respect given by Malayans to European men.

"She breathes," said Arsat in a low voice, anticipating the expected question. "She breathes and burns as if with a great fire. She speaks not; she hears not—and burns!"

He paused for a moment, then asked in a quiet, incurious tone, "Tuan . . . will she die?"

The white man moved his shoulders uneasily and muttered in a hesitating manner, "If such is her fate."

"No, Tuan," said Arsat, calmly. "If such is my fate. I hear, I see, I wait. I remember . . . Tuan, do you remember the old days? Do you remember my brother?"

"Yes," said the white man. The Malay rose suddenly and went in. The other, sitting still outside, could hear the voice in the hut. Arsat said: "Hear me! Speak!" His words were succeeded by a complete silence. "O Diamelen!" he cried, suddenly. After that cry there was a deep sigh. Arsat came out and sank down in his old place.

They sat in silence before the fire. There was no sound within the house, there was no sound near them; but far away on the lagoon they could hear the voices of the boatmen ringing fitful and distinct on the calm water. The fire in the bows of the sampan shone faintly in the distance with a hazy red glow. Then it died out. The voices ceased. The land and the water slept invisible, unstirring and mute. It was as though there had been nothing left in the world but the glitter of stars streaming, ceaseless and vain, through the black stillness of the night.

The white man gazed straight before him into the darkness with wide-open eyes. The fear and fascination, the inspiration and the wonder of death—of death near, unavoidable, and unseen, soothed the unrest of his race and stirred the most indistinct, the most intimate of his thoughts. The ever-ready suspicion of evil, the gnawing suspicion that lurks in our hearts, flowed out into the stillness round him —into the stillness profound and dumb, and made it appear untrustworthy and infamous, like the placid and impenetrable mask of an unjustifiable violence. In that fleeting and powerful disturbance of his being, the earth enfolded in the starlight peace became a shadowy country of inhuman strife, a battlefield of phantoms terrible and charming, august or ignoble, struggling ardently for the possession of our helpless hearts. An unquiet and mysterious country of inextinguishable desires and fears.

A plaintive murmur rose in the night; a murmur saddening and startling, as if the great solitudes of surrounding woods had tried to whisper into his ear the wisdom of their immense and lofty indifference. Sounds hesitating and vague floated in the air round him, shaped themselves slowly into words; and at last flowed on gently in a murmuring stream of soft and monotonous sentences. He stirred like a man waking up and changed his position slightly. Arsat, motionless and shadowy, sitting with bowed head under the stars, was speaking in a low and dreamy tone:

". . . for where can we lay down the heaviness of our trouble but in a friend's heart? A man must speak of war and of love. You, Tuan, know what war is, and you have seen me in time of danger seek death as other men seek life! A writing may be lost; a lie may be written; but what the eye has seen is truth and remains in the mind!"

"I remember," said the white man, quietly.

Arsat went on with mournful composure: "Therefore I shall speak to you of love. Speak in the night. Speak before both night and love are gone—and the eye of day looks upon my sorrow and my shame; upon my blackened face; upon my burnt-up heart."

A sigh, short and faint, marked an almost imperceptible pause, and then his words flowed on, without a stir, without a gesture.

"After the time of trouble and war was over and you went away from my country in the pursuit of your desires, which we, men of the islands, cannot understand, I and my brother became again, as we had been before, the sword-bearers of the Ruler. You know we were men of family, belonging to a ruling race, and more fit than any to carry on our right shoulder the emblem of power. And in the time of prosperity Si Dendring showed us favor, as we, in time of sorrow, had showed to him the faithfulness of our courage. It was a time of peace. A time of deer hunts and cockfights; of idle talks and foolish squabbles between men whose bellies are full and weapons are rusty. But the sower watched the young rice shoots grow up without fear, and the traders came and went, departed lean and returned fat into the river of peace. They brought news, too. Brought lies and truth mixed together, so that no man knew when to rejoice and when to be sorry. We heard from them about you also. They had seen you here and had seen you there. And I was glad to hear, for I remembered the stirring times, and I always remembered you, Tuan, till the time came when my eyes could see nothing in the past, because they had looked upon the one who is dying there—in the house."

He stopped to exclaim in an intense whisper, "O Mara bahia!⁴ O Calamity!" then went on speaking a little louder:

"There's no worse enemy and no better friend than a brother, Tuan, for one brother knows another, and in perfect knowledge is strength for good or evil. I loved my brother. I went to him and told him that I could see nothing but one face, hear nothing but one voice. He told me: 'Open your heart so that she can see what is in it—and wait. Patience is wisdom. Inchi Midah may die or our Ruler may throw off his fear of a woman!' . . . I waited! . . . You remember the lady with the veiled face, Tuan, and the fear of our Ruler before her cunning and temper. And if she wanted her servant, what could I do? But I fed the hunger of my heart on short glances and stealthy words. I loitered on the path to the bathhouses in the daytime, and when the sun had fallen behind the forest I crept along the jasmine hedges of the women's courtyard. Unseeing, we spoke to one another through the scent of flowers, through the veil of leaves, through the blades of long grass that stood still before our lips; so great was our prudence, so faint was the murmur of our great longing. The time passed swiftly . . . and there were whispers amongst women—and our enemies watched—my brother was gloomy, and I began to think of killing and of a fierce death. . . . We are of a people who take what they want—like you whites. There is a time when a man should forget loyalty and respect. Might and authority are given to rulers, but to all

men is given love and strength and courage. My brother said, 'You shall take her from their midst. We are two who are like one.' And I answered, 'Let it be soon, for I find no warmth in sunlight that does not shine upon her.'

"Our time came when the Ruler and all the great people went to the mouth of the river to fish by torchlight. There were hundreds of boats, and on the white sand, between the water and the forests, dwellings of leaves were built for the households of the rajahs. The smoke of cooking fires was like a blue mist of the evening, and many voices rang in it joyfully. While they were making the boats ready to beat up the fish, my brother came to me and said, 'Tonight!' I looked to my weapons, and when the time came our canoe took its place in the circle of boats carrying the torches. The lights blazed on the water, but behind the boats there was darkness. When the shouting began and the excitement made them like mad we dropped out. The water swallowed our fire, and we floated back to the shore that was dark, with only here and there the glimmer of embers. We could hear the talk of slave girls amongst the sheds.

"Then we found a place deserted and silent. We waited there. She came. She came running along the shore, rapid and leaving no trace, like a leaf driven by the wind into the sea. My brother said gloomily, 'Go and take her; carry her into our boat.' I lifted her in my arms. She panted. Her heart was beating against my breast. I said, 'I take you from those people. You came to the cry of my heart, but my arms take you into my boat against the will of the great!' 'It is right,' said my brother. 'We are men who take what we want and can hold it against many. We should have taken her in daylight.' I said, 'Let us be off'; for since she was in my boat I began to think of our Ruler's many men. 'Yes. Let us be off,' said my brother. 'We are cast out and this boat is our country now—and the sea is our refuge.' He lingered with his foot on the shore, and I entreated him to hasten, for I remembered the strokes of her heart against my

4. O Mara bahia (mä′rä bä he̅′ä), translated in the following phrase, "O Calamity."

breast and thought that two men cannot withstand a hundred.

"We left, paddling downstream close to the bank; and as we passed by the creek where they were fishing, the great shouting had ceased, but the murmur of voices was loud like the humming of insects flying at noonday. The boats floated, clustered together, in the red light of torches, under a black roof of smoke; and men talked of their sport. Men that boasted, and praised, and jeered—men that would have been our friends in the morning, but on that night were already our enemies. We paddled swiftly past. We had no more friends in the country of our birth. She sat in the middle of the canoe with covered face; silent as she is now; unseeing as she is now—and I had no regret at what I was leaving because I could hear her breathing close to me—as I can hear her now."

He paused, listened with his ear turned to the doorway, then shook his head and went on:

"My brother wanted to shout the cry of challenge—one cry only—to let the people know we were freeborn robbers who trusted our arms and the great sea. And again I begged him in the name of our love to be silent. Could I not hear her breathing close to me? I knew the pursuit would come quick enough. My brother loved me. He dipped his paddle without a splash. He only said, 'There is half a man in you now—the other half is in the woman. I can wait. When you are a whole man again, you will come back with me here to shout defiance. We are sons of the same mother.'

"I made no answer. All my strength and all my spirit were in my hands that held the paddle—for I longed to be with her in a safe place beyond the reach of men's anger and of women's spite. My love was so great that I thought it could guide me to a country where death was unknown, if I could only escape from Inchi Midah's fury and from our Ruler's sword. We paddled with haste, breathing through our teeth. The blades bit deep into the smooth water. We passed out of the river; we flew in clear channels amongst the shallows. We skirted the black coast; we skirted the sand beaches where the sea speaks in whispers to the land; and the gleam of white sand flashed back past our boat, so swiftly she ran upon the water. We spoke not. Only once I said, 'Sleep, Diamelen, for soon you may want all your strength.' I heard the sweetness of her voice, but I never turned my head.

"The sun rose and still we went on. Water fell from my face like rain from a cloud. We flew in the light and heat. I never looked back, but I knew that my brother's eyes, behind me, were looking steadily ahead, for the boat went as straight as a bushman's dart, when it leaves the end of the sumpitan. There was no better paddler, no better steersman than my brother. Many times, together, we had won races in that canoe. But we never had put out our strength as we did then— then, when for the last time we paddled together! There was no braver or stronger man in our country than my brother. I could not spare the strength to turn my head and look at him, but every moment I heard the hiss of his breath getting louder behind me. Still he did not speak. The sun was high. The heat clung to my back like a flame of fire. My ribs were ready to burst, but I could no longer get enough air into my chest. And then I felt I must cry out with my last breath, 'Let us rest!' . . . 'Good!' he answered; and his voice was firm. He was strong. He was brave. He knew not fear and no fatigue . . . My brother!"

A murmur powerful and gentle, a murmur vast and faint; the murmur of trembling leaves, of stirring boughs, ran through the tangled depths of the forests, ran over the starry smoothness of the lagoon, and the water between the piles lapped the slimy timber once with a sudden splash. A breath of warm air touched the two men's faces and passed on with a mournful sound—a breath loud and short like an uneasy sigh of the dreaming earth.

Arsat went on in an even, low voice.

"We ran our canoe on the white beach of a little bay close to a long tongue of land that seemed to bar our road; a long wooded cape going far into the sea. My brother knew that place. Beyond the cape a river has its entrance, and through the jungle of that land there is a narrow path. We made a fire and cooked rice. Then we lay down to sleep on the soft sand in the shade of our canoe, while she watched. No sooner had I closed my eyes than I heard her cry of alarm. We leaped up. The sun was halfway down the sky already, and coming in sight in the opening of the bay we saw a prau manned by many paddlers. We knew it at once; it was one of our rajah's praus. They were watching the shore, and saw us. They beat the gong, and turned the head of the prau into the bay.

"I felt my heart become weak within my breast. Diamelen sat on the sand and covered her face. There was no escape by sea. My brother laughed. He had the gun you had given him, Tuan, before you went away, but there was only a handful of powder. He spoke to me quickly: 'Run with her along the path. I shall keep them back, for they have no fire-arms, and landing in the face of a man with a gun is certain death for some. Run with her. On the other side of that wood there is a fisherman's house—and a canoe. When I have fired all the shots, I will follow. I am a great runner, and before they can come up we shall be gone. I will hold out as long as I can, for she is but a woman—that can neither run nor fight, but she has your heart in her weak hands.' He dropped behind the canoe. The prau was coming.

"She and I ran, and as we rushed along the path I heard shots. My brother fired—once—twice—and the booming of the gong ceased. There was silence behind us. That neck of land is narrow. Before I heard my brother fire the third shot, I saw the shelving shore, and I saw the water again; the mouth of a broad river. We crossed a grassy glade. We ran down to the water. I saw a low hut above the black mud, and a small canoe hauled up. I heard another shot behind me. I thought, 'That is his last charge.' We rushed down to the canoe; a man came running from the hut, but I leaped on him, and we rolled together in the mud. Then I got up, and he lay still at my feet. I didn't know whether I had killed him or not. I and Diamelen pushed the canoe afloat. I heard yells behind me, and I saw my brother run across the glade. Many men were bounding after him. I took her in my arms and threw her into the boat, then leaped in myself. When I looked back I saw that my brother had fallen. He fell and was up again, but the men were closing around him. He shouted, 'I am coming!' The men were close to him. I looked. Many men. Then I looked at her. Tuan, I pushed the canoe! I pushed it into deep water. She was kneeling forward looking at me, and I said, 'Take your paddle,' while I struck the water with mine. Tuan, I heard him cry. I heard him cry my name twice; and I heard voices shouting, 'Kill! Strike!' I never turned back. I heard him calling my name again with a great shriek, as when life is going out together with the voice —and I never turned my head. My own name! . . . My brother! Three times he called—but I was not afraid of life. Was she not there in that canoe? And could I not with her find a country where death is forgotten—where death is unknown!"

The white man sat up. Arsat rose and stood, an indistinct and silent figure above the dying embers of the fire. Over the lagoon a mist drifting and low had crept, erasing slowly the glittering images of the stars. And now a great expanse of white vapor covered the land; it flowed cold and gray in the darkness, eddied in noiseless whirls around the tree trunks and about the platform of the house, which seemed to float upon a restless and impalpable illusion of a sea. Only far away the tops of the trees stood outlined on the twinkle of heaven, like a somber and forbidding shore—a coast decep-tive, pitiless and black.

Arsat's voice vibrated loudly in the pro-found peace. "I had her there! I had her! To get her I would have faced all mankind. But I had her—and——"

His words went out ringing into the empty distances. He paused, and seemed to listen to them dying away very far—beyond help and beyond recall. Then he said quietly, "Tuan, I loved my brother."

A breath of wind made him shiver. High above his head, high above the silent sea of mist the drooping leaves of the palms rattled together with a mournful and expiring sound. The white man stretched his legs. His chin rested on his chest, and he murmured sadly without lifting his head, "We all love our brothers."

Arsat burst out with an intense whispering violence, "What did I care who died? I wanted peace in my own heart."

He seemed to hear a stir in the house—listened—then stepped in noiselessly. The white man stood up. A breeze was coming in fitful puffs. The stars shone paler as if they had retreated into the frozen depths of immense space. After a chill gust of wind there were a few seconds of perfect calm and absolute silence. Then from behind the black and wavy line of the forests a column of golden light shot up into the heavens and spread over the semicircle of the eastern horizon. The sun had risen. The mist lifted, broke into drifting patches, vanished into thin flying wreaths; and the unveiled lagoon lay, polished and black, in the heavy shadows at the foot of the wall of trees. A white eagle rose over it with a slanting and ponderous flight, reached the clear sunshine and appeared dazzlingly brilliant for a moment, then soaring higher, became a dark and motionless speck before it vanished into the blue as if it had left earth forever. The white man, standing gazing upward before the doorway, heard in the hut a confused and broken murmur of distracted words ending with a loud groan. Suddenly Arsat stumbled out with outstretched hands, shivered, and stood still for some time with fixed eyes. Then he said, "She burns no more."

Before his face the sun showed its edge above the treetops rising steadily. The breeze freshened; a great brilliance burst upon the lagoon, sparkled on the rippling water. The forests came out of the clear shadows of the morning, became distinct, as if they had rushed nearer—to stop short in a great stir of leaves, of nodding boughs, of swaying branches. In the merciless sunshine the whisper of unconscious life grew louder, speaking in an incomprehensible voice round the dumb darkness of that human sorrow. Arsat's eyes wandered slowly, then stared at the rising sun.

"I can see nothing," he said half aloud to himself.

"There is nothing," said the white man, moving to the edge of the platform and waving his hand to his boat. A shout came faintly over the lagoon and the sampan began to glide toward the abode of the friend of ghosts.

"If you want to come with me, I will wait all the morning," said the white man, looking away upon the water.

"No, Tuan," said Arsat, softly. "I shall not eat or sleep in this house, but I must first see my road. Now I can see nothing—see nothing! There is no light and no peace in the world; but there is death—death for many. We are sons of the same mother—and I left him in the midst of enemies; but I am going back now."

He drew a long breath and went on in a dreamy tone:

"In a little while I shall see clear enough to strike—to strike. But she has died, and . . . now . . . darkness."

He flung his arms wide open, let them fall along his body, then stood still with unmoved face and stony eyes, staring at the sun. The white man got down into his canoe. The polers ran smartly along the sides of the boat, looking over their shoulders at the beginning of a weary journey. High in the stern, his head muffled up in white rags, the juragan sat moody, letting his paddle trail in the water. The white man, leaning with both arms over the grass roof of the little cabin, looked back at the shining ripple of the boat's wake. Before the sampan passed out of the lagoon into the creek he lifted his eyes. Arsat had not moved. He stood lonely in the searching sunshine; and he looked beyond the great light of a cloudless day into the darkness of a world of illusions.

✹ To increase understanding

1. What device does Conrad use to introduce an air of foreboding before Arsat enters the story?

2. (a) Summarize the events recounted in the flashback. (b) Why is the material contained in the flashback functionally necessary to the story?

3. As Arsat concluded the account of his escape he "burst out with an intense whispering violence, 'What did I care who died? I wanted peace in my own heart.'" (a) Why has he failed to find that

peace? (*b*) What is the meaning of the last sentence of the story?

4. How does the theme developed in "The Lagoon" agree with Conrad's ideas of life as expressed in the biographical sketch?

🌿 Better reading
Singleness of effect

No one knew better than Joseph Conrad the importance of atmosphere in setting the tone of a story, or understood better the necessity of choosing just the right details to create the desired effect. A master craftsman, he realized that mere accumulation of unrelated details produces a cluttered and confused effect; singleness of effect depends upon arrangement and elimination. An excellent illustration of Conrad's method is found in the second paragraph of "The Lagoon." Here the author is concerned with capturing the one essential quality of the scene: its utter *stillness*. Example follows example: the forest "stood motionless and silent on each side of the broad brown swirl of eddies"; "in

the stillness of the air every tree, every leaf, every bough, every tendril of creeper and every petal of minute blossoms seemed to have been bewitched into immobility perfect and final"; and the canoe "seemed to enter the portals of a land from which the very memory of motion had forever departed."

Each scene is similarly drawn to create a single, unified effect. Reread the following paragraphs, deciding in each case what the effect is and enumerating the details which build up this impression:

(*a*) The paragraph beginning "The narrow creek . . ." (page 511, column 1, paragraph 3).

(*b*) The paragraph beginning "The white man . . ." (page 512, column 2, paragraph 3).

(*c*) The paragraph beginning "They sat in silence . . ." (page 513, column 1, paragraph 6).

(*d*) The paragraph beginning "Before his face . . ." (page 517, column 1, paragraph 3).

How does the last paragraph cited differ from the other three? Read the one sentence in this paragraph that relates it to the other paragraphs listed. How are these paragraphs related to the tone of the story as a whole?

Alfred Edward Housman 1859-1936

REPRODUCED BY PERMISSION OF
SIR JOHN ROTHENSTEIN, DIRECTOR
OF THE TATE GALLERY, LONDON

Drawing of Housman by Sir William Rothenstein (see page 509).

Vergil, great poet of ancient Rome, once expressed the belief that "there are tears in the very nature of things." A. E. Housman, "professor of Latin by trade" and poet for his own pleasure, found himself in full accord with that statement. Born in Worcestershire, from boyhood he loved the hills of Shropshire, which rimmed the horizon to the west. He was a shy and sensitive boy who grew into a reserved and individualistic man. Like most individualists, he wrote out of himself and for himself—there is no scene, no object, no emotion in Housman's poetry that he has not known. A lonely man, almost a recluse, he never married. Woman-hater, escapist from reality, fatalist, disillusioned sophisticate, mourner of lost youth, perfectionist—all these titles have been applied to this small, thin-lipped man, and all are in some way correct.

Housman began writing poetry while a student in classical studies at Oxford. The fact that his love for poetry overshadowed his interest in his studies probably explains why he failed to pass his final examinations. Eventually he became a professor of Latin, first at University College, London, and later at Cambridge University. Most of the poems of his first great success, *A Shropshire Lad*, were written in 1895, during a great burst of creative activity. Another collection, *Last Poems*, appeared in 1922; after his death a third group, *More Poems*, was brought out.

Housman was able to a remarkable degree to distinguish between the best and the inferior in his work. He published only the best, and these comprise some of the most hauntingly beautiful lyrics in English literature.

His poems are simple in form and expression, but they are exquisitely finished and polished. They are pervaded by a sense of the beauty of the world and the brevity of life. The swift passage of all loveliness to death and decay is a constant theme. But although Housman's poetry may be melancholy and even at times pessimistic, it is never sentimental or unrestrained. The emotion is controlled, and there is a classic elegance in the spareness and directness with which the theme unfolds. The selections presented here are typical of Housman's genius and are among the best-loved lyrics in English literature.

TO AN ATHLETE DYING YOUNG

The time you won your town the race
We chaired you through the market place;
Man and boy stood cheering by,
And home we brought you shoulder-high.

Today, the road all runners come,   5
Shoulder-high we bring you home,
And set you at your threshold down,
Townsman of a stiller town.

Smart lad, to slip betimes away
From fields where glory does not stay,   10
And early though the laurel grows
It withers quicker than the rose.

Eyes the shady night has shut
Cannot see the record cut,
And silence sounds no worse than cheers   15
After earth has stopped the ears.

Now you will not swell the rout
Of lads that wore their honors out,
Runners whom renown outran
And the name died before the man.   20

So set, before its echoes fade,
The fleet foot on the sill of shade,
And hold to the low lintel up
The still-defended challenge cup.

And round that early-laureled head   25
Will flock to gaze the strengthless dead,
And find unwithered on its curls
The garland briefer than a girl's.

WITH RUE MY HEART IS LADEN

With rue my heart is laden
  For golden friends I had,
For many a rose-lipt maiden
  And many a lightfoot lad.

By brooks too broad for leaping   5
  The lightfoot boys are laid;
The rose-lipt girls are sleeping
  In fields where roses fade.

LOVELIEST OF TREES

Loveliest of trees, the cherry now
Is hung with bloom along the bough,
And stands about the woodland ride,
Wearing white for Eastertide.

Now, of my threescore years and ten,   5
Twenty will not come again,
And take from seventy springs a score,
It only leaves me fifty more.

And since to look at things in bloom
Fifty springs are little room,   10
About the woodlands I will go
To see the cherry hung with snow.

REVEILLE

Wake! The silver dusk returning
    Up the beach of darkness brims,
And the ship of sunrise burning
    Strands upon the eastern rims.

Wake! The vaulted shadow shatters,   **5**
    Trampled to the floor it spanned,
And the tent of night in tatters
    Straws[1] the sky-pavilioned land.

Up, lad, up! 'Tis late for lying;
    Hear the drums of morning play;   **10**
Hark, the empty highways crying,
    "Who'll beyond the hills away?"

Towns and countries woo together,
    Forelands beacon, belfries call;
Never lad that trod on leather   **15**
    Lived to feast his heart with all.

Up, lad; thews that lie and cumber
    Sunlit pallets never thrive;
Morns abed and daylight slumber
    Were not meant for man alive.   **20**

Clay lies still, but blood's a rover;
    Breath's a ware that will not keep.
Up, lad; when the journey's over,
    There'll be time enough to sleep.

SOLDIER FROM THE WARS RETURNING

Soldier from the wars returning,
    Spoiler of the taken town,
Here is ease that asks not earning;
    Turn you in and sit you down.

Peace is come and wars are over,   **5**
    Welcome you and welcome all,
While the charger crops the clover
    And his bridle hangs in stall.

Now no more of winters biting,
    Filth in trench from fall to spring,   **10**
Summers full of sweat and fighting
    For the Kesar or the King.

Rest you, charger, rust you, bridle;
    Kings and kesars, keep your pay;
Soldier, sit you down and idle   **15**
    At the inn of night for aye.

REVEILLE   **1.** *Straws,* strews.

Shropshire countryside.

A. F. KERSTING

THE HALF-MOON WESTERS LOW, MY LOVE

The half-moon westers low, my love,
   And the wind brings up the rain;
And wide apart lie we, my love,
   And seas between the twain.

I know not if it rains, my love,   5
   In the land where you do lie;
And, oh, so sound you sleep, my love,
   You know no more than I.

To increase understanding

1. (a) What is the poet's point of view toward the death of the young athlete in "To an Athlete Dying Young"? (b) Explain why you agree or disagree with that point of view.

2. (a) Describe the scene pictured in the first stanza of "To an Athlete Dying Young." (b) What is the meaning of the second stanza? (c) Point out words or phrases which link the two pictures presented.

3. Explain Housman's use of the laurel as a symbol in the poem.

4. Compare "With Rue My Heart Is Laden" with Gray's "Elegy in a Country Churchyard" (page 326) as to form, tone, and theme.

5. (a) How old is the speaker in "Loveliest of Trees"? (b) Why is it important to know the speaker's age?

6. (a) What message does Housman have for youth in "Reveille"? (b) What resemblance in theme do you find between this poem and "Loveliest of Trees"? (c) Compare the theme of "Reveille" with the *carpe diem* theme of Herrick's "To the Virgins to Make Much of Time" (page 204). (d) Discuss any other poems you have read in which the *carpe diem* theme is developed.

7. (a) Find passages in "Reveille" you consider outstanding for their imagery. (b) How and when does Housman make use of personification in the poem?

8. What clues do you have that the soldier to whom "Soldier from the Wars Returning" is addressed has been killed?

9. Why do you think the poet has blended details of modern and ancient warfare in the poem?

10. (a) What phrase in "The Half-Moon Westers Low, My Love" explains the meaning of the poem? (b) What is the tone of the poem? (c) Find words that help suggest that tone.

Better reading
Housman's theory of poetry

A. E. Housman had definite ideas on the writing of poetry. In an essay entitled "The Name and Nature of Poetry," he stated (1) that the best poetry "is made out of the most ordinary words," and (2) that "the peculiar function of poetry" is "to transfuse emotion, . . . to set up in the reader's sense a vibration corresponding to what was felt by the writer."

Examination of even a single stanza of Housman's poetry will make evident how well he put these two principles to work:

> Clay lies still, but blood's a rover;
>   Breath's a ware that will not keep.
> Up, lad; when the journey's over,
>   There'll be time enough to sleep.

Certainly, in this final stanza of "Reveille," Housman is using "the most ordinary words": *clay, blood, breath, journey, sleep.* But he is using them in a special way—a way that makes them suggest far more than their ordinary meaning. *Clay* becomes not merely "a stiff, sticky kind of earth," but the symbol of inactivity; it stands in contrast to *blood,* or the dash and spirit of the lively man, the rover. And similarly Housman uses the other ordinary words of the stanza in such a way that we cannot escape the impact of his own emotion: his sense of the passionate excitement of life and the urgency of using every moment of it before it is halted by the long quiet of death.

Select other passages of Housman's poetry for similar analysis. In each passage, what special significance does he give to quite ordinary words? What is his own emotion? And how well does he succeed in "setting up in the reader's sense a vibration corresponding to what was felt by the writer"?

Extending interests

You may discover other poems by Housman that speak even more forcefully to you than those found in this book. Begin with "When I Was One-and-Twenty," "The Lads in Their Hundreds," and "On Wenlock Edge"; then follow your own inclinations. Arrange with your teacher for a time to share your discoveries with your classmates.

Housman's *Collected Poems* contains all of his poetry. Representative selections by Housman are found in *Modern British Poetry,* edited by Louis Untermeyer, and in *A Little Treasury of British Poetry,* edited by Oscar Williams.

Gerard Manley Hopkins 1844-1889

Portrait of Hopkins at the age of fifteen, by his aunt, Anne Eleanor Hopkins.

One of the most original poets of the latter Victorian period, Gerard Manley Hopkins has had a great and lasting influence on modern poetry. He was not a professional poet but a Jesuit priest who wrote his poetry in longhand—probably with no intentions of having it published. Hopkins, whose first plans were to enter the ministry of the English church, studied at Oxford University. While at the school he wrote tense and erratic verse, much of which was highly commended by his instructors. But at the age of twenty-one he came under the influence of Cardinal Newman (page 432), became a Roman Catholic, and burned all of his early poetry. Eleven years later he was ordained into the priesthood. He served as a missionary in the slums of Liverpool, as a pastor in an Oxford church, and finally as a Jesuit teacher at the Catholic University of Dublin, where he spent the last five years of his life.

Upon Hopkins' death, he left his handwritten manuscripts to Robert Bridges, friend and fellow poet, who, convinced that Hopkins' poetry would be either ignored or abused if introduced too early to the reading public, held up its publication for twenty-nine years. The eventual appearance of that slim volume of *Poems* on the literary scene caused a sensation. Hopkins was hailed as a brilliant innovator in poetic forms and style, whose spirit was closer to the twentieth century than to the Victorian Age in which he had lived. His writings became a springboard for many younger poets who admired and imitated his style. Men like W. H. Auden, Stephen Spender, and Dylan Thomas adopted many of his highly original poetic techniques into their own writings, and his works still exert a strong influence upon aspiring young poets.

Hopkins has never gained real popularity with the general reading public. In the first place his poems, mostly religious in nature, do not deal with the problems of everyday man, nor do they show any concern for these problems. Secondly, his poetry is difficult to understand. His poems are crowded with images; so quickly indeed does he rush from image to image that obscurity often results. But many of his nature lyrics are clear and unlabored, and in all of them one shares the keen exaltation that Hopkins feels in nature's varied and lovely manifestations of God.

HEAVEN—HAVEN

(A NUN TAKES THE VEIL)

I have desired to go
   Where springs not fail,
To fields where flies no sharp and sided hail,
   And a few lilies blow.

And I have asked to be   5
   Where no storms come,
Where the green swell is in the haven dumb,
   And out of the swing of the sea.

"Heaven-Haven," "Pied Beauty" and "God's Grandeur" from *Poems of Gerard Manley Hopkins.* Used by permission of the publishers, Oxford University Press, London.

PIED BEAUTY

Glory be to God for dappled things—
  For skies of couple-color as a brinded cow;
    For rose-moles all in stipple upon trout
      that swim;
Fresh-firecoal chestnut-falls[1]; finches' wings;
  Landscape plotted and pieced[2]—fold, fallow,
    and plow;   5
    And all trades, their gear and tackle and
      trim.[3]

All things counter,[4] original, spare,[5] strange;
  Whatever is fickle, freckled (who knows
    how?)
    With swift, slow; sweet, sour; adazzle,
      dim;
He fathers-forth whose beauty is past change[6]:
  Praise him.   10

PIED BEAUTY. **1.** *chestnut-falls,* chestnuts newly stripped
of their husks. **2.** *plotted and pieced,* divided into fields.
3. *trim,* equipment. **4.** *counter,* contrary to what is expected. **5.** *spare,* rare. **6.** *He . . . change.* Thought is
adapted from James 1:17: "Every good gift and every perfect gift is from above, and cometh down from the Father of
lights, with whom is no variableness, neither shadow of
turning."
GOD'S GRANDEUR. **1.** *ooze . . . Crushed,* oil from crushed
olives. **2.** *for,* despite.

GOD'S GRANDEUR

The world is charged with the grandeur of
  God.
  It will flame out, like shining from shook
    foil;
  It gathers to a greatness, like the ooze of oil
Crushed.[1] Why do men then now not reck
  his rod?
Generations have trod, have trod, have trod; 5
  And all is seared with trade; bleared,
    smeared with toil;
  And wears man's smudge and shares man's
    smell: the soil
Is bare now, nor can foot feel, being shod.

And for[2] all this, nature is never spent;
  There lives the dearest freshness deep down
    things;   10
And though the last lights off the black West
  went
  Oh, morning, at the brown brink eastward,
    springs—
Because the Holy Ghost over the bent
  World broods with warm breast and with
    ah! bright wings.

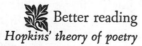
To increase understanding

1. (*a*) What sort of world is suggested to your
mind by the two words in the title "Heaven—
Haven"? (*b*) What contrasting pictures does the
poet paint of that world and of the earthly world?
2. (*a*) What does the word *pied* suggest to your
mind? (*b*) How many different examples of pied
beauty does the poet picture in the poem of that
name? (*c*) Point out words or phrases that show
his skill in describing various pied objects without
repeating the word *pied.* (*d*) Summarize the thought
of "Pied Beauty."

Better reading
Hopkins' theory of poetry

    Although Hopkins and Housman were contemporaries, their theories of poetry differ greatly. Housman's poetry is easily comprehensible, and understanding can be achieved in many cases by one reading of the poem. Hopkins, one of the few Victorian poets to make a radical change in the nature of poetic expression, did not believe poetry should be immediately intelligible, and his poetry must be studied to be understood.

    Hopkins wrote not for the eye but for the ear, and he did not consider the established forms of poetic technique suitable for reading aloud. He employed a technique based on actual speech, which he called *sprung rhythm.* Last used by the early Elizabethans, it consists of scanning by accents or stresses alone, without any regard to the number of syllables in a foot. It is measured by feet of one to four syllables with the accent always on the first syllable of the foot. In "God's Grandeur," which Hopkins claims is written in iambic pentameter, there are the usual five stresses in each line. If Hopkins were following the exact rules of iambic pentameter, line 9 would be read like this:

    And for| all this,| na ture| is nev|er spent.

But this type of scanning demolishes sound and meaning. Using the principles of sprung rhythm Hopkins specifically specified that the line should be scanned like this:

And for all |this,| na ture is |nev er| spent.

Scan other lines in the poem and determine which syllables should be stressed. You will find that reading aloud helps this kind of scanning. This innovation in which the iambic requirement is dropped but the five stresses remain is used by many modern poets.

Hopkins uses imagery for an effect opposite that for which poets such as Tennyson and Browning used it. They used it for expansion—to create a mood, to add color. Hopkins uses it for compression, not expansion. The imagery in his poetry is all connected by interrelations of meaning. The imagery in the second line of a poem draws you back to the imagery in the first line, helping to create a new understanding of the first line. This goes on throughout the poem until a total structure of meaning is developed—a meaning which suddenly *explodes* once it becomes known. The explosion is the result of the total impact of the poem, not of any one of the parts alone. Hopkins prevents the reader from forming any premature opinions as to the poem's meaning until total expression has been achieved by rearranging sentences, cramming together words and phrases, dropping verbs, prepositions, and conjunctions, using adjectives as nouns, and giving words new and/or double meanings.

This explosion theory can perhaps be better understood when studied in a poem. In "God's Grandeur" the subject is evident, but what is the poet saying about it? An analysis of the poem will lead to the meaning. What is *shook foil* (line 2)? What does it look like? What does the simile "like shining from shook foil" refer to? What new meaning does this simile give to the word *charged* in line 1? Describe the mental picture you have of God's grandeur up to this point. Hopkins uses the symbol of oozing oil to describe God's grandeur because in its use in the Old Testament it represents abundance. What is the total picture as created by these two images?

Having impressed upon the reader's mind the greatness of God's grandeur, in line 4 Hopkins asks a question. Paraphrase that question. The repetition of *have trod* in line 5 has a specific purpose: it symbolizes the plodding day-to-day existence of generations becoming more and more diverted from God by work and trade. The words *seared, bleared, smeared,* and *smudge* used in the following lines not only paint a picture of the dirtiness of human existence, but are used as a direct contrast to the imagery of flame and oil used to symbolize God's grandeur in the opening lines. As an example of man's isolation from God, Hopkins points out that even man's feet are separated from nature by the shoes he wears.

Despite all this, says Hopkins, "nature is never spent." *Spent* as used here has two meanings: "exhausted," and "spent," in a financial sense. How do both these meanings relate back to the rest of the poem? Explain lines 10-12. Explain the meaning of *bent* in line 13. Where does Hopkins return to the image of brightness with which he begins the poem? How does this help unify the poem?

What idea is expressed in this poem? What is the tone of the poem? Compare "God's Grandeur" to "The World Is Too Much with Us" (page 356) as to tone and theme.

THE DEVELOPMENT OF THE NOVEL

The Victorian Age was the period of the novel in English literature. A family gathered around the fireplace reading the latest installment of a Dickens' novel in a monthly magazine became a typical Victorian scene. But although the novel as a literary form did not develop until relatively late in the long procession of English literature, the narrative form can be traced back to the epic tale *Beowulf*. From the Middle Ages came the romances, culminating in Sir Thomas Malory's *Morte Darthur*. In the seventeenth century John Bunyan's allegory, *Pilgrim's Progress*, became a popular success largely because of its interest as a story. In the eighteenth century Jonathan Swift's bitter satire, *Gulliver's Travels*, appeared with its elements of marvelous adventure; and Daniel Defoe captured the imagination of the public with *Robinson Crusoe*. Defoe's use of accurate detail and of situations which the reader accepted as plausible anticipated the modern novel.

The modern novel is said to have begun with *Pamela: or Virtue Rewarded* (1740) by Samuel Richardson (1689-1761). This story of a poor servant girl who eventually marries her mistress' son enters into the trials and temptations of Pamela, the heroine, in such detail that four volumes were required to complete the tale. Since Pamela writes her story in the form of letters to her parents in the country, the book is autobiographical in style. Richardson said that his chief concern in writing was "to promote the cause of religion and virtue"; thus he regarded the moral of *Pamela*— virtue will be rewarded—as of prime importance. All of Richardson's novels, including his masterpiece *Clarissa Harlowe* (1748), follow the same pattern.

Henry Fielding (1707-1754), a playwright, journalist, and man of the world, was disgusted with the sentimentalities and moralizings of Richardson's *Pamela*. He began his first novel, *The History and Adventures of Joseph Andrews* (1742), as a burlesque of Richardson's novel, his hero being, presumably, Pamela's brother. But the book, which began as a joke, turned into a first-rate novel; and others followed, notably *Tom Jones* (1749). One of Fielding's important innovations was his use of the third person rather than the first person, which Richardson had used. Fielding brought a feeling of reality to the novel; his characters are distinct individuals; the background is a panorama of eighteenth-century life. His exuberant humor adds life and zest.

In *The Vicar of Wakefield* (1766) the versatile Oliver Goldsmith wrote one of the best novels of the eighteenth century. While Goldsmith returned to the first-person method of telling a story and indulged in some of the sentimentalizing of Richardson, still his novel contributed a new quality—a wholesomeness and pleasantness, a kindliness and gentleness, which readers found refreshing after the coarseness of many earlier novels. Its charm of character portrayal and its easy graceful manner of expression appealed to a host of readers in England, on the Continent, and in America.

During the last decades of the eighteenth century, novels increased in quantity and in variety. Many of these novels followed types developed by Richardson, Fielding, and other early novelists, but distinct new types also emerged. Prominent among these were the *Gothic romance, the novel of manners,* and *the historical novel.*

First of the new types of novel to emerge was the Gothic romance. The term *Gothic* suggested to the neoclassicists of the eighteenth century the wild and the primitive. Thus the Gothic novels, which were grotesque, bloodcurdling tales of horror and the supernatural, indicate the return to the romantic mode which was also apparent in the poetry of the late eighteenth century. One of the earliest and most famous of the Gothic romances is *The Castle of Otranto* (1764), written by Horace Walpole (1717-1794). Probably the best writer of this type of novel was Mrs. Anne Radcliffe (1764-1823), whose most popular work was *The Mysteries of Udolpho* (1794). *Frankenstein* (1816), by Mary Godwin Shelley (see page 383), has been revived in recent times largely because its theme —the consequences of a scientist's success in artificially creating human life—reflects the modern interest in the ultimate possibilities of science.

THE NOVEL OF MANNERS Radically different from the Gothic romance was the novel of manners. Drawing its setting, its characters, and its plot from contemporary England, the novel of manners concerned itself with delineating in detail the manners and the customs of a particular social class. The forerunners of the novel of manners had been the narratives of Defoe, with their emphasis on realistic detail, and the lusty novels of Fielding; but where these earlier novelists had used exaggeration and burlesque in describing English life, the writers of the novel of manners—the best of whom were women—employed a deft and subtle satire. First among these novelists of manners was Fanny Burney (1752-1840), a friend of Dr. Samuel Johnson. Her first novel, *Evelina; or The History of a Young Lady's Entrance into the World* (1778), pictures daily life in a middle-class city family and dwells on the frustrations Evelina suffers as she enters the world of fashion.

A far greater novelist of manners, and one of the greatest of all English novelists, was Jane Austen (1775-1817). Her novels are concerned with the upper-middle class and set in the villages and the adjoining country at a time when landowning was the most genteel of occupations. Consequently the pursuit of gentlemen with broad lands and spacious manor houses by ambitious "mamas" with marriageable daughters often provides their plot interest.

Character portrayal and analysis were Jane Austen's chief concern, as the titles of some of her best books indicate: *Sense and Sensibility* (1811), *Pride and Prejudice* (1813), and *Emma* (1816). A delicate satire is characteristic of her style; and her word-painting she herself compares to miniature-painting on ivory "on which I work with so fine a brush as produces little effect after much labor." In spite of Jane Austen's own comment on her "little effect," subsequent generations have judged her total achievement brilliant; and the influence of the novel of manners as she developed it can be seen in the work of the great Victorian novelists, William Thackeray and George Eliot.

THE HISTORICAL NOVEL The historical novel, like the Gothic novel, is romantic in concept, since it affords the writer an opportunity to deal with events whose outlines have been blurred by the passage of time. With the growth of romanticism in the later years of the eighteenth century, numerous historical novels appeared, but none of them were especially noteworthy. Sir Walter Scott (see page 371) was the first great master of the historical novel and, without doubt, the greatest romantic novelist of his age. Among those influenced by him was the first American master of the historical novel, James Fenimore Cooper.

THE VICTORIAN NOVEL Although some excellent historical novels were written in the Victorian Age, interest lay chiefly in portraying the people and events of the bustling current scene. The novel of manners attracted many novelists, among them Anthony Trollope (1815-1882), who in *The Warden, Barchester Towers,* and other novels, presented with delicate humor and satire the life and ecclesiastical intrigue in a cathedral town.

Other writers, while centering their interest in the contemporary scene, used the novel to protest against the abuses in social and economic life that had resulted from a century of too rapid growth. Preëminent among the writers of the *novel of purpose* was Charles Dickens. Still other Victorians turned to the *psychological* or *problem novel*, which attempts to analyze the motives of characters and in so doing to solve problems in human relationships. Most of George Eliot's great novels fall into this category, as do those of Thomas Hardy and Joseph Conrad.

The novels of the Brontë sisters, Charlotte and Emily, grew out of personal emotion and stand apart from any classification. Growing up on the bleak Yorkshire moors, tyrannized over by their pastor-father, the Brontës turned to writing for escape. Charlotte produced in *Jane Eyre* an exciting novel which is in parts autobiographical. *Wuthering Heights*, by Emily Brontë, is a magnificent work of imagination unlike any other major novel in English literature.

During the Victorian Age many novels appeared first in serial form, either in monthly paperbound editions or as installments in periodicals. Each installment was more or less a complete episode in itself and ended at a point of high interest. Since the first installments of a novel usually appeared before an author had completely worked out all details of his plan for the work, many Victorian novels are episodic rather than tightly constructed. This method of publishing also tended to produce long, leisurely novels in which the interest centers on characters rather than on plot.

CHARLES DICKENS First among the major Victorian novelists in time and in popularity was Charles Dickens (1812-1870). He won the hearts of people of all classes and of all tastes and intellects almost as soon as he appeared in print. With the publication of *The Pickwick Papers* (1837)[1] Dickens gained immediate fame. Originally planned as a series of sketches to illustrate a set of sporting prints, *The Pickwick Papers* began as a burlesque. The fact that like most novels of the Victorian Age it was published in installments added to its episodic character.

As Dickens gained more experience, his plot structure became more complicated, with several plots closely interrelated in each novel. He discovered also that his public enjoyed weeping with him as much as laughing, and that sentiment and melodrama were as acceptable as humor. The death of Little Nell in *The Old Curiosity Shop* (1841) was mourned by high and low. It is said that the packet carrying the last installment of the book to the United States was met at the pier by anxious readers inquiring, "Is Little Nell dead?"

Dickens drew upon his own experiences for much of the material he put into his novels. Himself a member of the lower-middle class and, as a boy, a victim of the evils of child labor, Dickens knew at first hand the suffering and hardship of the poor. He knew also the humiliation of the debtor's prison, for his father had been confined to the Marshalsea for almost a year. The bitter experiences of his boyhood are most fully described in *David Copperfield* (1850), the most autobiographical of his works and one of his finest novels.

As was natural in the impecunious Dickens family, Charles' schooling was often interrupted. Much of his education was gained through reading

1. See the discussion guide for *The Pickwick Papers* on page 531.

the eighteenth-century novels on his father's bookshelves. He taught himself shorthand, and at sixteen was skillful enough to become a reporter in the House of Commons. At twenty-two he was a reporter for the *Morning Chronicle,* and in covering his beat for this paper he doubtless met blackguards and criminals of the type he portrayed in *Oliver Twist.*

Most of Dickens' novels have a specific purpose, for he wrote not only to picture the age but also to correct it. *Oliver Twist* (1838), the first of his novels to concentrate on a particular social evil, exposes the pitiful plight of the unprotected children of the poor. Before writing *Nicholas Nickleby* (1839), he investigated the notorious schools of Yorkshire; and in both this novel and *David Copperfield* he crusaded for school reform. In *Hard Times* (1854), one of his less effective novels, he pilloried the heartless and utilitarian approach to life of some Victorian industrialists.

A Tale of Two Cities (1859), one of Dickens' most celebrated novels, is in several respects different from the body of his work. Instead of being episodic in structure, it is a tightly plotted, exciting novel. Unlike most of Dickens' novels, which deal with the contemporary scene, it is historical fiction. Its tale of the French Revolution is modeled on Carlyle's great history (see page 422).

While plot is important in *A Tale of Two Cities,* it is for characters that most of Dickens' novels are remembered. Like Chaucer and Shakespeare, Dickens rejoiced in the infinite variety of human life, and he crowded his novels with people—no two alike, all interesting. Although many of them are overdrawn and unreal, caricatures rather than individuals, it was a peculiarity of Dickens' genius that they seem real and convincing. So great is the vitality possessed by characters such as Barkis and Peggotty, Ebenezer Scrooge and Uriah Heep, Mrs. Gamp and Mr. Pecksmith, that, like Chaucer's Wife of Bath and Shakespeare's Falstaff, they are known the world over.

WILLIAM MAKEPEACE THACKERAY In contrast to Dickens who knew poverty in his early years, William Makepeace Thackeray (1811-1863) was born into a prosperous upper-middle-class family. His great-grandfather had been headmaster of Harrow, a famous school for boys, and both of his grandfathers as well as his father were in the East India service. When he was six years old, young Thackeray traveled from Calcutta, India, where he had been born, to England to be educated. From the Charterhouse School he proceeded to Trinity College at Cambridge, but he cared so little for his studies there that he left after a year. After Cambridge, Thackeray traveled on the Continent and spent some time in Paris studying art. He first attempted to earn a living as an illustrator, but after indifferent success he turned to writing. His pleasant chatty essays, miscellaneous reviews, and stories for newspapers and magazines found a ready market. Thackeray illustrated many of these pieces with amusing drawings; and the fictitious names he often used—Titmarsh, Mr. Yellowplush, Mr. Snob, and others—added to the humorous effect.

The first important work to which Thackeray signed his own name was his most famous novel, *Vanity Fair.*[2] It came out first in twenty-four

2. A guide for discussing *Vanity Fair* will be found on page 532.

monthly installments, which Thackeray himself illustrated, and then, in 1848, as a complete book. It was followed in 1850 by *Pendennis*, which, like Dickens' *David Copperfield*, is in part autobiographical. Since Thackeray was a slow and painstaking worker, he did not produce nearly the quantity of novels written by Scott and Dickens. However, every one of his novels is top quality. *Henry Esmond* (1852), a story of the early eighteenth century, is often considered the greatest of English historical novels, and many critics place it first among Thackeray's works.

While Dickens wrote almost exclusively of contemporary England, Thackeray often wrote of earlier periods. Like Dickens, however, he wrote about members of his own class, but in a far different manner. Dickens fiercely championed the lower classes; in his novels of purpose he often inveighs against the abuses suffered by them. Thackeray, on the other hand, despised the sham and hypocrisy that he felt in the upper and middle classes. From his college days, when he had contributed to a university paper called *The Snob*, he had shown himself keenly aware of the extreme class-consciousness existing in a country which called itself democratic. A kindly and genial man himself, he loathed snobbery, and in his work he used satire to prick the pretensions of the snobs and social climbers who inhabit his novels.

Thackeray was essentially a moralist. This fact is apparent not only in the little sermons he occasionally delivers to the reader, but also in the moral justice of his climaxes. Unlike Dickens, who was not above using melodramatic means to punish an evil character, Thackeray contrived scenes of retribution which seem to flow naturally and quietly from the action. He was a critic of life, and a great one. He studied human nature and had the novelist's genius for creating characters who were real individuals, puzzling combinations of good and bad, who have been remembered and talked about from his day to our own.

GEORGE ELIOT One of the truly great writers of the Victorian Age, George Eliot (1819-1880) stands with Dickens and Thackeray as a master of the novel. Born Mary Ann Evans, she grew up amid the farms and villages of Warwickshire. Her father was a highly respected surveyor and land agent for several large estates, on one of which the Evans family lived in a comfortable red brick farmhouse. There, from the age of seventeen to almost thirty, Mary Ann kept house for her widowed father. Along with her work in house and dairy she found time to study languages with private tutors, to read, and to attend school in Coventry. Later, in Coventry, where she and her father lived after his retirement, she met various intellectuals and advanced thinkers. The new and exciting ideas which stimulated the brilliant young woman led George Eliot to produce, in time, novels which surpassed all previous novels in intellectual depth and in insight into human nature.

Although like Dickens and Thackeray, George Eliot was a product of her age, she responded differently to the forces which were affecting all Victorians. She felt keenly the impact of the newly propounded scientific truths, particularly those of the biologists. She delved into moral, philosophical, and religious problems with the analytical attitude of a scientist. Her chief concern in her novels was character. She studied the motives for the actions of individuals and the problems of human relationships. The problem she dealt with in each of her works centered in the inward conflict of an individual against his own weaknesses rather than in the outward conflict of the individual or the group against a social evil. In her probing of character she may be said to have started the trend toward the psychological novel of today.

The people George Eliot wrote of were for the most part the common people of country and village whom she had known from her earliest years. In *Adam Bede* (1859), her first successful novel, there is much of her father in the title character. In *The Mill on the Floss* (1860) she and her brother appear as Tom and Maggie Tulliver. There is no exaggeration, no caricature, no satire in her handling of character. "I aspire," she says in *Adam Bede*, "to give no more than a faithful account of men and things as they have mirrored themselves in my mind. The mirror is doubtless defective; the reflection faint and confused; the outlines will be sometimes distorted; but I feel as much bound to tell you as precisely as I can what that reflection is as if I were in the witness box narrating my experience on oath." George Eliot had a keen eye for describing the physical setting of her novels and a quick ear for capturing the flavor of speech; but her greatest talent was an ability to depict characters of many types, from the villagers and gentry of *Silas Marner* (1861) to the highly educated people of *Middlemarch* (1872). The wisdom and the understanding of human nature found in all George Eliot's novels place her high among English novelists.

LATER VICTORIAN NOVELS As the Victorian Age advanced, the form of the novel gradually changed. Gone was the long, leisurely chronicle in which a group of characters were involved in a series of loosely related episodes. In its place there developed a shorter, more tightly plotted novel in which each incident was integrally related to one central idea.

The variety of the age is evident in the various kinds of novels that achieved wide popularity. The psychological novel increased in scope and claimed the attention of an increasing number of writers. George Meredith (1828-1909) in such novels as *The Ordeal of Richard Feverel* and *The Egoist* centered his attention on probing the motives of individuals and investigating the problems behind their tangled relationships. Thomas Hardy (see page 493) viewed ironically the hidden struggles of men trapped in an indifferent world.[3] Hardy's characters lived and died in England; those of Joseph Conrad (see page 509) wandered in far parts of the British Empire; but Conrad, like Hardy, was most interested in the psychological springs of action.[4] Robert Louis Stevenson (see page 473) returned to the past for his romantic novels in which interest centers on fast-paced, exciting action. Rudyard Kipling (see page 477) captured the exotic sights and sounds of distant lands and extolled the glory of British law and British order. Romantic and realistic novels, historical novels and novels of manners, psychological novels and novels of purpose were available to readers in the rich variety of the Victorian novel.

---

3. A guide for discussing Hardy's *Return of the Native* will be found on page 534.   4. See the discussion guide for Conrad's *Lord Jim* on page 536.

DISCUSSION GUIDES

The Pickwick Papers, by Charles Dickens

A clue to the points to be emphasized in discussing the novel lies in its full title: The Posthumous Papers of the Pickwick Club containing a Faithful Record of the Perambulations, Perils, Travels, Adventures and Sporting Transactions of the corresponding Members. *Here we have an indication of the form of the novel, of the fact that the novel is built around the characters, and of the tone.*

STRUCTURE. *Like many Victorian novels,* The Pickwick Papers *was published in installments.* What clue does the title give you as to the episodic nature of the work? Pick out places in the book that you believe might be the beginning and the end of an installment. What elements would an installment necessarily contain? How are the various extraneous short stories worked into the novel? Do you find these stories an irritating interruption of the action or do you feel they are justified by the overall form of the work? Explain. What strand of action is most important in giving a certain unity to the novel? What subplots build continuity?

DICKENS AND THE PICKWICKIANS. The Pickwick Papers *was originally planned as a series of sketches to illustrate a set of sporting prints.* Explain how the characters of Mr. Pickwick and the "corresponding Members" as described in the first chapters of the novel would have been suitable for this purpose. What happens to the author's attitude toward Mr. Pickwick as the story progresses? (Note particularly Mr. Pickwick's motive for travel and adventure as stated in Chapter I and his statement in the final chapter as he looks back on his experiences.) What qualities make Mr. Pickwick a beloved figure in English fiction? If Dickens' story had remained the burlesque he had originally planned, would Mr. Pickwick have become a real person to countless readers? Explain your answer.

How does the character of Mr. Winkle change after he has seriously begun his pursuit of Arabella? Discuss the change in the author's attitude toward Mr. Tupman and Mr. Snodgrass as the story progresses.

What is Sam Weller's function in the novel? Why do many readers enjoy most the pages on which he appears? Is he a mere caricature or is he something more? Explain.

Discuss the influence of the following characters in changing the basic idea of the book: (*a*) Dodsen and Fogg; (*b*) Mr. Jingle and Job Trotter; (*c*) "the Reverend" Mr. Stiggins.

Is the first part of the book or are later sections more like other novels by Dickens that you have read? In what way do Dickens' own sympathy and his natural impulse toward the novel of purpose (see page 527) gradually undermine the farcical character of the early chapters? In this connection consider the effect on Mr. Pickwick of the law proceedings in the case of *Bardell* vs. *Pickwick,* the sojourn in the Fleet Prison, and similar episodes.

DICKENS' USE OF HUMOR. *Dickens wrote* The Pickwick Papers *primarily to entertain; and though his concept of this novel changed as he worked on, and even though his demand for the reform of abuses motivated the way certain episodes are treated,* Pickwick *emerged as one of the great humorous works in the English language.* Point out examples in which each of the following devices is used for a humorous purpose: (*a*) natural dialect of a character; (*b*) misuse of words by a character; (*c*) names the author gives characters; (*d*) an exaggerated notion of prowess of a certain type in a character least likely to possess it; for example, Mr. Tupman's idea of himself as a lover; (*e*) the gullibility of a character; (*f*) the pretensions of a character to be something which he is not; (*g*) cynical hypocrisy of a character as he fleeces the gullible; (*h*) humor based on ignorance; (*i*) tongue-in-cheek remarks by the author; (*j*) ludicrous circumstances arising from mistaken identity; (*k*) self-consciousness in the relationship of the sexes; (*l*) the assertion of social status.

How does the quality of the humor change as the novel progresses? For example, how does the author's attitude toward the gullible change? Cite other examples in which the author's changed attitude is evident in the tone of the humor.

Consider Dickens' use of satire. Cite instances in which it is kindly and warm—a kind of laughing with the characters. Where does the author use satire to denounce conditions of the time?

What, in general, is the tone of the novel? What view of humanity does Dickens convey in *The Pickwick Papers?*

Vanity Fair, by William Makepeace Thackeray

In all respects Vanity Fair *is an exceedingly rich novel. The action is carried forward by a series of plots and subplots; a multitude of characters move through the pages; the setting is detailed and varied. Towering over all is Thackeray's ability to use the novel to make a pertinent comment upon life.*

STRUCTURE. *In spite of the fact that, like most Victorian novels,* Vanity Fair *was first published in installments, Thackeray has done a masterly job in fusing plots and subplots into a unified whole.* Explain the way in which in the opening chapters Thackeray combines action with exposition. (See the article on plot, page 179.) Are the events that mark the actual beginning of the rising action well motivated? Throughout the novel background information is occasionally inserted. Cite instances in which such exposition covers (*a*) past events, (*b*) new characters, (*c*) settings, (*d*) social conditions. Discuss specifically how in each case such exposition is necessary to the plot.

What constitutes the plot in *Vanity Fair?* Does it seem that there is more than one main plot in this novel? To answer this question, determine and separate the chief aims of the two principal characters, Rebecca and Amelia. What complications arise in the story of each girl? What major conflict arises in each case? Does an inter-conflict ever develop between the two girls? Are the two story lines sufficiently strong and independent to be considered separate main plots? If not, which is the main plot?

In analyzing the stories of the two principal characters, you will have to look for two climaxes, one involving Rebecca, the other, Amelia. In Rebecca's story, what is the technical climax (see page 179)? What minor climaxes add to the suspense of the rising action? Does the technical climax coincide with the dramatic climax? In Amelia's story do the technical and dramatic climaxes occur together or separately? Explain fully. What are the steps in the rising action in Amelia's story? Discuss the inevitability of the technical climax in each major strand of the plot: that is, does the climax rise naturally from the character of the individual concerned and the actions in which the character is involved, or does the author force events to satisfy a particular pattern?

Consider the subplots and their relation to the principal strands of action. Trace the story of the younger Pitt Crawley. What other characters are involved in this plot? In what sense does it form a "little story" on its own? Explain the relationship between this subplot and the Rebecca story. What does this subplot add to the novel as a whole?

To isolate other subplots, consider situations in which an independent story is woven about an important but secondary character. In addition to the Pitt Crawley story, what subplots are related to the Rebecca plot? What subplots are subordinate to Amelia's story? Explain in each case the relationship between the subplot and a main plot.

After the dramatic climax of Rebecca's story, how long is it before the *denouement* (see page 179) of this plot is taken up? What comes between? Why? In your opinion is the resolution to Rebecca's story appropriate? Judging from Becky's character and her actions throughout the novel, is the ending to her story appropriate? *In the brief biography of Thackeray on page 528, you read that Thackeray was a moralist.* Does his treatment of Becky bear this out? Explain.

Why was it necessary that the falling action of Amelia's story be so extended? What social and psychological problems had to be worked out after the technical climax?

Instead of a straight time arrangement, Thackeray occasionally uses both flashbacks and foreshadowing in developing the plot. Find examples of both and explain what effect use of these techniques has in stimulating the reader's interest.

CHARACTERIZATION. *One critical test often applied in measuring the effectiveness of characterization is the balance within the character of good and bad, strength and weakness.* Apply this criterion of balance to Becky and Amelia. What is the ratio of good to bad in Becky? If the good is somewhat lacking, what special qualities does Thackeray give Becky to hold the reader's interest and belief? What flaws in Amelia's character take the place of the selfishness, etc., that we find in Becky? Apply the criterion of balance to Rawdon Crawley, George Osborne, Lord Steyne, Jos Sedley, and Dobbin. What characters in the novel seem most balanced and lifelike? Do you find any characters that are either all good or all bad?

Whether we accept characters as lifelike de-

pends not only on their balance but also on their consistency; that is, on whether their deportment is consistent with the personal characteristics the author has given them, and whether the reasons for action follow a consistent pattern. What characteristics does Thackeray attribute to Becky in the opening chapters? What characterizes her actions in her first visit to Amelia's home? What evidence do you find of the same type of behavior as the novel progresses? Explain the consistency of Amelia's background and behavior.

If a character is consistently drawn, circumstances of setting and plot will have a logical influence on the character's behavior. Since changes in character should be caused partly by the influence of evolving circumstances, and since character in turn forces the direction of the plot, plot is necessarily conditioned by and related to character. How convincing are each of the following situations? Discuss and criticize each in detail by analyzing the motivation of the characters involved, their prior development, and the consistency of their actions: (a) Amelia's blind devotion to George, before and after his death; (b) Rebecca's conduct on Curzon Street, and her subsequent actions to the end of the novel; (c) Dobbin's patience and his attitude toward Amelia; (d) Mr. Osborne's attitude toward his son following George's marriage to Amelia, and his later change of heart; (e) Rawdon Crawley's action from his arrest to the end of the novel; (f) Jos Sedley's faithfulness to Becky after Amelia's second marriage.

In addition to the characters who play a major rôle in the story, a host of less important characters are introduced. Briefly describe each of the following: Miss Pinkerton, old Sir Pitt Crawley, Miss Crawley, Mrs. Bute Crawley, Briggs, Mr. Sedley, Mrs. Sedley, Mrs. O'Dowd, Glorvina O'Dowd, Lady Bareacres, Countess Southdown, Lady Jane Sheepshanks (later Lady Pitt Crawley), Charles Raggles. Is each of these a consistent character? Are any of them caricatures? What, collectively, do they add to the story?

THEME, PURPOSE, AND TONE. At the heart of the interaction of plot and character is the theme—the central idea about which the novel is built. Often the theme throws light on the author's purpose in writing a particular piece of literature. The tone the author employs is also indicative of his purpose. What is the theme of Vanity Fair? What clue does the title give you? You will recall that John Bunyan writes of Vanity Fair in Pilgrim's Progress (see page

225 of this anthology). What is a "vanity fair"? What characters in the novel may be regarded as shoppers at such a fair? Are there any who would be out of place at such a fair? If so, explain their function in the novel. On page 529 you read that Thackeray "despised the sham and hypocrisy that he felt in the upper and middle classes." What light does this statement shed on his purpose in writing the novel?

Thackeray pictures the world of which he is writing in Vanity Fair as a "very vain, wicked, foolish place, full of all sorts of humbugs, and falsenesses, and pretensions," where "a title and a coach-and-four are toys more precious than happiness." Cite particular characters or episodes which illustrate this attitude, in each case noting the tone. Is satire involved in the attitude of Miss Crawley's friends and relatives toward her? Explain. What evidences of satire are there in Thackeray's treatment of young Pitt before and after his father's death? What is Thackeray's tone in dealing with Jos Sedley, Lord Steyne, Mr. Osborne? What is the tone of the Brussels episode?

Find and read aloud several passages in which Thackeray speaks directly to the reader. What is the purpose of such passages? How would you describe their tone?

In Chapter III, when Becky is laying her plans to snare Jos Sedley, Thackeray writes: "I don't think . . . we have any right to blame her" because "Miss Sharp had no kind parent to arrange these delicate matters for her, and . . . if she did not get a husband for herself, there was no one else in the wide world who would take the trouble off her hands." How does Thackeray here imply that Becky is a victim of social custom? How might this attitude affect his treatment of Becky in the novel? Are there other characters whose shortcomings may be regarded to some extent as the fault of the system under which they live? Are any of the characters essentially evil—individuals who would behave in a similar manner in any society? What relationship can you discover between the essential goodness or badness of a character and Thackeray's tone in writing of him? What, in general, is the tone of Thackeray's satire in this novel? (See the article on satire on page 268.) What is he attacking? Does his satire have a universal application or is it relevant only to a particular time and place? Thackeray gave Vanity Fair the subtitle, A Novel Without a Hero. What insight does this subtitle give you into Thackeray's attitude throughout the novel?

The Return of the Native, by Thomas Hardy

When critics speak of the strong "architectural quality" of The Return of the Native, *they are alluding to the closely woven nature of the novel, the powerful integration and unity of all elements. In discussing* The Return of the Native, *it is difficult to separate such facets as plot, character, underlying meaning, and tone and to consider them as semi-independent elements.*

PLOT-CHARACTER RELATIONSHIP. *The core of the novel centers on the actions of Eustacia Vye as they affect the other characters and the events of the plot.* In Book I, through accident, a marriage between Thomasin Yeobright and Damon Wildeve fails to occur. Wildeve's apparent intention is to marry Thomasin after the weekend. Then we see Wildeve stalking into the darkness toward the signal fire. Discuss in detail the reasons that the wedding keeps being postponed. What part does Eustacia play in this?

In Book II Eustacia develops a new interest—Clym Yeobright. Discuss the circumstances leading to her interest in Clym and her strategy in meeting him. What effect does her interest in Clym have on Thomasin's future?

In Book III Clym's interest in Eustacia affects his relationship with his mother. Discuss this problem and its results.

In Book IV Mrs. Yeobright meets her death. In what way is Eustacia involved in this event? To what extent is she guilty of the death?

In Book V, following Mrs. Yeobright's death, Eustacia becomes involved in a series of events that end in catastrophe. How do these events affect Clym, Thomasin, Wildeve, and Diggory Venn? What part does Eustacia play in these events? What happens to her?

The basic condition of a dramatic situation is conflict of interest. Two characters alone can come into conflict; but the complexity of the conflict is increased by the addition of a third character. This results in a relationship called a triangle, in which two characters vie in some way for a third. In The Return of the Native, *this basic triangle situation is greatly expanded and complicated.* Eustacia, the pivotal character in the novel, is a member of the triangle with which the story opens. Who are the other members? As Eustacia withdraws, what new triangle is formed? How does the second triangle work itself out in Book II?

Simultaneously, in Book II, an entirely new triangle is made possible by Clym Yeobright's arrival. How does this triangle develop? What resolves the conflict?

What new triangle is formed in Book III? How does its development affect each of the three characters involved?

As a result of this succession of triangles, two couples have been formed and two principal characters—Mrs. Yeobright and Diggory Venn—emerge losers. Explain how a relationship threatens to develop between Eustacia and Wildeve, dooming their respective marriages, and how Mrs. Yeobright and Venn bring the plot of the novel to its climax. What is the technical climax? (See the article on plot, page 179.) What is the dramatic climax?

Book VI, which is titled "Aftercourses," consists mainly of the falling action. What happens to various important characters? How have their lives been changed by Eustacia Vye?

THE ROLE OF FATE IN THE NOVEL. *Hardy's use of Fate or Chance as a dominant element in the affairs of men is discussed on page 493. In reading* The Return of the Native *you have undoubtedly been struck by the predominant part played by chance. To begin with, the mistake involving the marriage license is simply an oversight. Diggory Venn's very presence at the time Thomasin needed transportation home is pure coincidence. The timing of Clym's arrival home is also coincidental.* Analyze and discuss the rôle chance plays in the following: (*a*) Clym's first meeting with Eustacia; (*b*) the timing of the fifth of November fires and the marriage fiasco; (*c*) the reddleman's sighting Wildeve with Eustacia following the dance; (*d*) the miscarriage of the money sent to Clym and Thomasin; (*e*) Mrs. Yeobright's attempt to visit her son and be reconciled with him; (*f*) the writing and delivery of Clym's letter to Eustacia. Cite other events that lean heavily on chance.

Many other events occur because of the personality or premeditated aim of a character. Discuss Mrs. Yeobright's quarrels with Clym, explaining how the personalities and beliefs of the mother and son naturally lead to disagreement. Eustacia's desire to find a more exciting life is also natural and well motivated. Discuss her actions in terms of her personality. On the other hand, what part did chance play in her being at this place? Cite other events that grow naturally out of the needs and emotions of the characters. Do events dependent on chance outweigh events growing out of character, or do they balance out evenly? Explain.

IRONY OF SITUATION. *In* The Return of the Native *Hardy makes use of irony of situation (see the article on page 534).* Point out situations in which an action produces a result opposite from that desired. Note particularly the actions of the reddleman and of Mrs. Yeobright. What connection do you find between Hardy's use of irony and his belief in Fate? Why is it important to understand the irony if one is to grasp the intent of the novel?

MEANING AND TONE. *In the description of Egdon Heath, with which the story opens, Hardy not only establishes the emotional tone of the book but also foreshadows the meaning of the novel.* Reread Book I, Chapter 1. Notice that there is still ample daylight but that the heath creates dark. What is the author implying by referring to the heath as "a near relation of night" (paragraph 3)? What other details in Chapter 1 support this deeper meaning? In describing the figure on the barrow toward the end of Chapter 2, Hardy writes that the figure "seemed a sort of last man among them [the Celts], musing for a moment before dropping into eternal night with the rest of his race." Comment on the treatment of the solitary figure in this and the three succeeding paragraphs. What atmosphere is the author building up? What deeper meaning is being established?

The November 5 fires being lighted in Chapter 3 supposedly commemorate Guy Fawkes Day (see page 641, footnote 2). But Hardy writes: ". . . it is pretty well known that such blazes as this the heathmen were now enjoying are rather the lineal descendants from jumbled Druidical rites and Saxon ceremonies than the invention of popular feeling about Gunpowder Plot." What does this mean? How does the idea stated here strengthen the meaning suggested in the earlier description of the heath? Why does Hardy write that "to light a fire is the instinctive and resistant act of man . . . at the winter ingress?" What symbolic meaning is suggested?

Why is the story set on Egdon Heath rather than on the cultivated lands nearby? In what way does the heath dramatize the passing generations of man? Why throughout the novel does Hardy refer to the races who have lived here?

In what way does Hardy relate these vanished peoples to the present inhabitants of the heath?

Rainbarrow dominates the landscape; it is the meeting place of the lovers. What meaning attaches to this emphasis on an ancient burial mound? In this connection consider the many tragic events which occur to the dwellers nearby —events whose control is seemingly beyond the power of the individuals involved. Could Mrs. Yeobright have prevented the crushing disappointments she suffered in Thomasin and Clym? Was it necessary that she die an embittered and broken woman? Was the heath the right place for one of Eustacia's temperament? How does Clym change between the beginning and the end of the novel? What effect does walking on the heath where "the past seized upon him with its shadowy hand" eventually have upon him?

In the discussion of Hardy as a novelist (page 534) these sentences occur: "Many times Hardy places nature in a dominant position over man by giving it a strong and ruling personality. In The Return of the Native *the great heath is actually one of the chief characters of the novel, perhaps the hero.*" Comment on this idea, using examples from the novel to substantiate your opinion. What effect does the recurring emphasis on the heath have on the tone of the novel? How would you describe the tone?

In your discussion of the novel you have noted Hardy's stress on chance happenings and the ironic outcome of many events. What light do these emphases shed on the meaning of the novel? State the idea of man and his place in the universe as developed in the novel.

PERSONAL REACTIONS. *The following questions place you in the rôle of critic. Weigh your answers carefully, substantiating them with references to the text.*

Does Hardy successfully develop his thesis in The Return of the Native? Do you accept it entirely, in part, or not at all? In view of Hardy's indictment of life, is the element of chance overstressed?

Is Clym a believable character? Consider his previous life, his reasons for returning home, his relationship with his mother, and his decision to marry Eustacia. Would an individual like Clym cling both to a girl like Eustacia and to his dedication to service? Or does the author shape the character's actions to illustrate his thesis?

Which characters are the most convincing in their development, attitudes, and actions? Which are least convincing?

Lord Jim, by Joseph Conrad

Lord Jim *is primarily the story of a man; plot is subordinate to the development of character. In order to throw as much light as possible on the reasons why this man acted as he did, Conrad uses an involved and somewhat difficult narrative technique.*

NARRATIVE POINT OF VIEW. *The first four chapters are told in the third person from a partially omniscient point of view; that is, the author explains what goes on in Jim's mind as well as what he does and says.* What information is given in these chapters about Jim's early life? Trace the steps leading to Jim's berth as chief mate on the *Patna*.

In Chapter 3 the *Patna* accident occurs. Why does the author not utilize the dramatic opportunity to develop the action of the *Patna* accident when it occurs? Where, when, and by whom are the details of this event finally related?

Why do you think the scenes at the official inquiry are included? Why, during the hearings, is the reader not given the testimony covering the actual details of action on board the *Patna*? To what important new character are Jim and the reader introduced during the hearings?

What impression of Jim does the reader gain during the hearing (Chapter 4) and in the preceding chapters? Why is use of the omniscient point of view necessary to build up an understanding of Jim?

In Chapter 5, Marlow becomes the narrator of the story. How does the information about Jim given by a narrator necessarily differ from that imparted by an author using the omniscient point of view? What reasons might Conrad have had for shifting to an objective point of view at this juncture? How does this shift affect the nature of the reader's knowledge about Jim?

Where is Marlow as he talks? At what period in time, in relation to the inquiry, is his narration taking place? What is Marlow's relationship to Jim? Discuss his private and his expressed attitudes concerning Jim as the latter discloses the details of the accident to the *Patna* and its aftermath (Chapters 7-12), citing details to justify your opinion. Can you take Jim's account of these happenings at face value, or must the personal element be considered? Compare Marlow's reaction to Jim's story with the attitude of the board of inquiry.

Often, in the course of his narrative, Marlow introduces characters who have no apparent bearing on the plot. Such a one is Captain Brierly, an assessor at Jim's hearing, who commits suicide shortly after. What sort of man is Brierly? Compare Marlow's description of him with Marlow's description of Jim. *The story of Brierly's suicide is told not directly by Marlow but by First Officer Jones, whom Marlow quotes at length.* What light does Jones throw on the reason for the suicide? Why does the author employ this third narrator, thus complicating the reader's already difficult task in following the story?

In Chapter 12 Marlow introduces the elderly French naval lieutenant whom he meets in a café in Australia. What opinion of Jim does the lieutenant express? Why does Marlow respect his opinion? In the same chapter Marlow mentions Little Bob Stanton, who is drowned trying to rescue a fear-crazed woman. Is there an implied moral relationship between Brierly, the French lieutenant, Bob Stanton, and Jim? Explain. From the technical point of view, what does the introduction of these characters of different types and nationalities add to Marlow's narrative?

Marlow's narrative ends with Chapter 35. What is Jim's situation the last time he sees him? Relate the last part of Jim's story. What devices does the author use to tell this part of the tale?

CHARACTER AND STRUCTURE. *Since character is the dominant interest in* Lord Jim, *Conrad manipulates the plot structure to throw light on his central character. Consequently he makes extensive use of flashbacks and foreshadowing.* In Chapter 1, paragraph 1, we read: "He was spotlessly neat, apparelled in immaculate white from shoes to hat, and in the various Eastern ports where he got his living as ship-chandler's water-clerk he was very popular." To what point in Jim's career does this sentence refer? What words give you a clue that one climactic event of Jim's life is behind him? What outstanding trait does the author stress in the flashback to Jim's youth? What often occupies Jim's thoughts while he is in training for the mercantile marine? On his first ship? On board the *Patna*? What impressions of Jim's character do you begin to form from his dreams of the future? Do you believe Jim is the kind of individual he thinks he is? Explain.

The most significant factor of Jim's reaction to the crisis on the *Patna* is that he becomes immobilized. What event in his earlier life foreshadows this reaction to sudden danger? What later event is foreshadowed by his action in the *Patna* crisis?

According to Jim's own story of the *Patna* incident, was he a coward? Explain. Why is the fact that the *Patna* does not sink ironic? How does this fact intensify Jim's moral dilemma? What effect does this fact have on the reader's attitude toward Jim's action?

It is obvious that Jim's regret for his action is overwhelming. What is the real cause of his regret—a conscience tortured because of abandoning the pilgrims or an ego crushed by a dishonorable act? What is his main concern for the future? What, precisely, does he hope to prove to Marlow and the world? Why does Jim leave a succession of jobs when the truth about him becomes known? What are Marlow's thoughts about Jim's motives?

The second half of the novel is concerned with the Patusan experience. What character traits does Jim show in the early episodes of this section; for example, in his escape from the Rajah and in his persuading the natives to follow his plan to drive out Sherif Ali? Contrast these acts with his earlier ones at sea. Explain how his success gradually transforms him to a seemingly different person. Does he find in Patusan that which he is really seeking? Is he satisfied that he has proved his worth and conquered his personal problems? Discuss these questions, using evidence from the novel to support your ideas. What is Marlow's opinion of Jim's success? Compare it to his attitude toward Jim after the trial.

Review Jim's talk with Brown (Chapters 41-42). What chance thrust does Brown make that startles Jim? How does Brown exploit this opening? Describe Jim's reaction to Brown's argument. What action does Jim decide to take? Explain why you think he acts in this manner.

Consider Jim's final action in rejecting love and the opportunity of escape. Is this devotion to principle or selfish pride? Is it glory or weakness? How do Tamb'Itam and the girl regard it? What is your opinion?

Does Jim admit fear anywhere in the novel? What do other characters, for example, Stein and the French lieutenant, say about fear?

In Chapter 20, just before Jim's Patusan experience begins, Stein says of him: "He is romantic—romantic . . . And that is very bad—very bad . . . Very good, too." To which Marlow replies, "But is he?" Why does Stein call Jim a romantic? Why does Marlow question this opinion? Judging from subsequent events, which man is more nearly correct in understanding Jim?

The Larger View

A. In the introduction to the Victorian Age you read that ". . . the term *Victorian* has come to stand not only for a period of time but also for a particular outlook on life" (page 412). The writers listed below represent in one way or another this particular outlook. Discuss the qualities in the work of each man that are typical of Victorian literature. Whenever possible, base your argument on particular selections you have read in class or independently.

Thomas Babington Macaulay
Thomas Henry Huxley
John Cardinal Newman
Alfred, Lord Tennyson
Matthew Arnold
Rudyard Kipling
Charles Dickens
William Makepeace Thackeray
George Eliot

B. Not all writers of the Victorian Age reflected the typical Victorian attitudes; in fact, the Victorian Age "was one of the most varied and diverse periods in the history of English life and letters" (page 411). The writers listed below differed in interests, in attitudes, or in some other regard from what is usually termed *Victorian*. Discuss the dominant characteristics of each writer and the qualities which set his work apart from the main stream of Victorian thought.

Thomas Carlyle
Robert Browning
Dante Gabriel Rossetti
Edward Fitzgerald
Robert Louis Stevenson
Thomas Hardy
Joseph Conrad
A. E. Housman
Gerard Manley Hopkins

Bibliography

AUDEN, W. H. and NORMAN HOLMES PEARSON, editors, *Poets of the English Language* (Viking) Volume V includes selections by the most prominent poets from Tennyson through Yeats.

AUSTEN, JANE, *Pride and Prejudice*. (Dodd •Collier) Miss Austen's subtle but revealing satire of eighteenth-century landed gentry is a delightful commentary on human foibles. *Sense and Sensibility* also mirrors the manners of upper- and middle-class English of that day.

BENTLEY, PHYLLIS, *The Young Brontës*. (Roy) The six Brontë children lived a lonely life under the dominance of their minister-father on the bleak Yorkshire moors. Miss Bentley's biography shows the effect on the later writing of the Brontës of their oppressive childhood.

BRONTË, CHARLOTTE, *Jane Eyre*. (Dodd •Dell) The publication of this book brought to English fiction a new type of heroine, a woman of intelligence and passion.

BRONTË, EMILY, *Wuthering Heights*. (Dodd •Dell) This violent tale of love and revenge will be popular as long as readers enjoy imaginative, romantic novels.

CARLYLE, THOMAS, *A History of the French Revolution*. (Modern Library) Regarded as a partial view of a momentous political struggle, Carlyle's work has been called a poetic unrolling of the historic drama.

COLLINS, WILKIE, *The Moonstone*. (Dodd •Doubleday) The theft of a sacred Hindu diamond and its recovery has been called the first and best detective story written.

CONRAD, JOSEPH, *Lord Jim*. (Dodd •Collier) In this powerful novel of human strengths and weaknesses, the solution to Jim's dilemma is left to the reader. *Nigger of the Narcissus* (•Collier) deals with the tensions of unavoidable death and their effect on a ship's crew.

DICKENS, CHARLES, *Pickwick Papers*. (Dodd •Washington Square) Here is Dickens at his most amusing. *Nicholas Nickleby* (Dodd) describes the terrible conditions in many private schools in Dickens' time. *A Tale of Two Cities* (Dodd •Washington Square) tells a gripping story of the French Revolution.

ELIOT, GEORGE, *Adam Bede*. (Dodd •Collier) The cause-and-effect relationship in human nature is skillfully handled in this novel of pastoral England. *The Mill on the Floss* demonstrates George Eliot's ability to portray the workings of the human heart.

HARDY, THOMAS, *Return of the Native*. (Dodd •Washington Square) Egdon Heath plays a major role in this tragedy.

HOFF, RHODA, *Why They Wrote: Dickens, Thoreau, Flaubert, Clemens, Stevenson*. (Walck) Biographical summaries emphasize the literary careers and noted works of these authors.

HOUSMAN, LAURENCE, *Victoria Regina* in *Sixteen Famous British Plays*, edited by Bennett Cerf and Van H. Cartmell. (Garden City) This dramatic biography is written by one of Queen Victoria's contemporaries.

KIPLING, RUDYARD, *The Light That Failed*. (Doubleday) A young artist and a pretty but shallow girl are the chief characters in this dramatic novel of heroism.

MEREDITH, GEORGE, *The Ordeal of Richard Feverel*. (••Modern Library) In this psychological novel, Meredith probes the relationships between individuals and the conflicts between system and instinct.

PRIESTLEY, J. B., *Charles Dickens, A Pictorial Biography*. (Viking) Numerous beautiful illustrations make this lively, sympathetic treatment of Dickens' life exceptional.

STEVENSON, ROBERT LOUIS, *Black Arrow*. (Dodd •Collier) Set in fifteenth-century England during the War of the Roses, *Black Arrow* is a swift-paced adventure. *Dr. Jekyll and Mr. Hyde* (•Dutton), eerie story of a dual personality, is an excellent example of Stevenson's masterful prose and keen insight.

THACKERAY, WILLIAM, *Vanity Fair*. (Dodd• Dell) In this novel, the author reveals the hypocrisy he found in Victorian society.

TREVELYAN, GEORGE MACAULAY, *Illustrated English Social History*, Volume 4. (McKay) This book is notable for 150 illustrations, chosen from contemporary sources, which re-create the life of the nineteenth century.

TROLLOPE, ANTHONY, *Barchester Towers*. (Dutton •Doubleday) An ironic tone, complex situations, and frequent remarks by the author pertaining to his characters' behavior add much to the enjoyment of this satire on society.

WINGFIELD-STRATFORD, ESME CECIL, *Those Earnest Victorians*. (Apollo) Impartial appraisals of Victorian values, virtues, and shortcomings can be found in this well-written work.

WINWAR, FRANCES, *The Immortal Lovers*. (Harper) Almost anything you will want to know about the Brownings can be found in this colorful and accurate biography.

•paperback   ••paperback and hardcover

part two

TWENTIETH CENTURY ENGLISH LITERATURE

In the twentieth century England has been displaced from the pinnacle of power which she achieved in Victorian times. A commonly held view of the effects of England's new position was well expressed by a staff member of the *Manchester Guardian* living in the United States. Speaking of the rigid class system that had long been established in England, he says: "Most Englishmen suffered under this system and they have profited from its defeat, but it had one advantage for both the privileged and the underprivileged—they never had any doubts about who they were. As a boy, I was rock-certain of my identity—I was a member of the working class in England and an Englishman abroad. And by Englishman abroad, I meant a proud carrier of the white man's burden, a son of the Empire. . . . But all that is over now. By overturning the system, the working class won a chance to share the opportunities; and the colonies, as symbols, were shattered. But with their loss, we have lost the identities they gave us. We are face to face with ourselves now and we don't know who we are."[1]

The social revolution in England may not have been altogether so thoroughgoing as this writer suggests; but the modern temper is one of loss of identity, and social change is one of its causes.

SOCIAL CHANGE When Queen Victoria died in 1901, England was the most powerful nation in the world. Her Empire stretched to all corners of the globe, her navy ruled the seas, and the advance of the Industrial Revolution created jobs and kept her prosperous. But during the reign of Victoria's son Edward VII, a change so gradual as to be at first imperceptible set in. The contrasts between the Captain of Industry and the aristocrat on the one hand and the common man on the other became less marked as the power and wealth of the ruling class declined, as the demands of the new technology created positions for intelligent men without regard to birth or rank, and as the vast number of British laborers obtained real political power for the first time. These changes led to a feeling of dislocation and frustration on the part of the laborer as well as of the industrialist.

Wren's St. Paul's Cathedral (far right) rises above modern London.

From government work to dock work, jobs became more specialized, narrower in scope, demanded more uniformity, and gave less satisfaction outside of the salary or wage.

The increasing rise and strength of the laboring force resulted in time in the formation of the Labour Party. It challenged the positions of both Liberals and Conservatives, who for over a hundred years had alternated in governing England, and in the second quarter of the century forced widespread changes in the very fabric of English life. The steel industry was nationalized. A vast new program of social legislation was put into effect. More liberal old-age benefits were set up, along with increased health insurance and free (or very inexpensive) hospital and medical care. To pay the huge costs of the new program, higher taxes were levied against all classes.

---

1. W. J. Weatherby, "The Lost Englishman," *The Nation*, November 10, 1962.

DISSOLUTION OF THE EMPIRE The long reign of George V (1910-1936) was a time of cataclysmic change in England and throughout the world. One of the first signs of the emerging new order was the growth of a world-wide nationalist movement, which would within a half century convert England from an empire to a commonwealth.

At the opening of the twentieth century the colonial system seemed to most Englishmen the ideal way to maintain and advance an industrial civilization. The departure of laborers from the farms to the cities throughout the nineteenth century had made it necessary for England to import much of her food. To obtain the money to buy food, exports had to be increased. Therefore, so long as England retained her colonies and her superiority in manufacture, she had not only food but wealth. The Empire supplied most of her food and raw materials and was an important market for goods made from some of those same materials.

Long before the nationalist movement swelled in India and in other distant parts of the Empire, it rose to a head in Ireland.

Throughout the nineteenth century the Irish had agitated for home rule, and by the end of the century this feeling of nationalism was becoming evident in literature as well as in politics. A remarkable group of writers, led by William Butler Yeats (see page 622), strove to awaken in the Irish people a sense of the romance of their past and the future they might achieve as a united people. To this end Gaelic, the original language of Celtic Ireland, was revived; the Irish Theatre Movement, which resulted in the founding of the renowned Abbey Theatre in Dublin, was launched; and in drama, prose, and poetry writers interpreted the life of the Irish people. This resurgence in Irish literature is called the Irish Literary Renaissance.

Writers also took an active part in the struggle which led to the establishment of the Irish Free State in 1921 and culminated in 1949 with the establishment of the Republic of Eire.

The Abbey Theatre, Dublin, symbol of the Irish Renaissance. The "No Waiting" sign on the lamppost shows the influence of the Gaelic revival; the theater billboard advertises a play by Yeats, a leader of the Irish Renaissance, a statesman, and one of the foremost modern poets.

Early in the twentieth century the urge for self-government also grew stronger in India. Mahatma Gandhi's campaign of nonviolence and civil disobedience made him a national hero. Finally in 1950 India became an independent republic. Unlike Eire, India retained many ties with England as a member of the British Commonwealth of Nations.

THE EFFECTS OF
WORLD WAR I

The world-wide surge toward independence inevitably led to war. Germany, a newly united nation, threatened England's colonial expansion, industrial monopoly, and naval supremacy. Since these factors undermined England's economic position, she initiated a system of restraints against Germany. The war which began in 1914 opened with limited objectives, but it later involved the United States and Japan and became World War I. Over the years it became invested with a sense of mission on the part of England, France, the United States, and the other Allies: it was to be a war to end wars; in its wake was to follow a recognition of the rights of peoples to govern themselves; there was to be a great Western federation under the League of Nations; the world was to be made safe for democracy. In terms of these ideals, the unprecedented violence of the war could be tolerated. When, after the Versailles Treaty, it appeared that all the ideals had been trampled underfoot in the race for vengeance and territorial expansion, a wave of profound disillusion spread over Europe, adding its impact to the spirit of the modern age. When, one by one, the democratic republics set up after the war fell into the hands

Below left: Women selling the Suffragette *newspaper in London in 1913. Below right: The barbaric intensity of World War I, that devastated thousands of square miles of farmland and forest, is revealed in this painting of trench warfare by John Northcote Nash, an artist commissioned to paint war pictures for the Imperial War Museum.*

of dictators and Europe began to divide into two armed camps, it seemed to many that at best Western civilization was coming apart at the seams. Many felt that the assumption of continuous progress and social evolution, which had been inherited from the eighteenth century, given its final form by the Darwinians, and upon which men had built for generations, had been discredited. More pessimistic individuals came to believe that all social institutions from the family to religion to international law were based on selfishness and violence; in the ideals that had long served as a spur to a more civilized life, they saw nothing but hypocrisy and sham.

THE GREAT DEPRESSION
The period of disillusion that set in after World War I was followed by the world-wide economic collapse of 1929. The northern industrial cities of England suffered most—in some nearly half of the people were out of work —and the national exchequer, heavily in debt from the war, had to support these people at the same time that money flowed out of the country to pay for food.

By 1936, the year George V died, England was beginning to emerge from the blackest years of the depression. George V's son Edward VIII ruled for less than a year before abdicating. When George VI, the father of Queen Elizabeth II, ascended the throne, England was still troubled by widespread unemployment, torn by struggles with her colonies, and confused about the future.

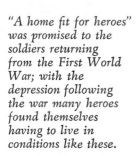

"A home fit for heroes" was promised to the soldiers returning from the First World War; with the depression following the war many heroes found themselves having to live in conditions like these.

When World War II began in September 1939, England faced its greatest crisis. In May 1940 Winston Churchill (see page 718) became Prime Minister. Speaking in the House of Commons that same month Churchill declared:

I have nothing to offer but blood, toil, tears, and sweat. . . . You ask, What is our aim? I can answer in one word: Victory —victory . . . however long and hard the road may be; for without victory there is no survival. Let that be realized; no survival for the British Empire; no survival for all that the British Empire has stood for; no survival for the urge and the impulse of the ages, that mankind will move forward to its goal. But I take up my task with buoyancy and hope.

In the early years of war Churchill stood almost alone in believing that England could endure. Norway and Denmark, Belgium and Holland, and France fell before the Nazis. Again and again London was battered by bombs. Industrial towns across England were destroyed. Only the channel across which William the Conqueror had brought his invading Normans almost nine hundred years earlier stood between England and another invading army. During these years Churchill became the symbol of Britain's bulldog determination and courage.

During the war and for some time afterwards, members of all classes, rich and poor, felt the pinch of strictly rationed food and other necessities. By the time Elizabeth II came to the throne in 1952, *austerity* had become the hated word symbolizing the continuing necessity of all Englishmen to live frugally.

Fire resulting from a bombing raid on the night of December 29, 1940, lights St. Paul's Cathedral. The great leadership of Winston Churchill helped Englishmen endure the nightly terror of these raids.

If events seemed to be conspiring to disillusion modern man, he could find even less comfort in the realm of the intellect. He found that even here the old certainties of Newtonian physics and Euclidean geometry had been found to be only approximate descriptions of the world. New concepts—relativity, particles of energy—made time, space, matter itself seem like nothing more stable than the stuff that dreams are made of. Writing in 1925 the English philosopher Alfred North Whitehead said, "The progress of science has now reached a turning point. The stable foundations of physics have broken up. . . . The old foundations of scientific thought are becoming unintelligible. Time, space, matter, material, ether, electricity, mechanism, organism, configuration, structure, pattern, function, all require reinterpretation."[2] At the same time the new study of depth psychology seemed, like the political events of the age, to say that there was irreducible evil at the core of man and the best he could do was to learn to live with it.

The modern outlook was bleak indeed. Britain had emerged from World War II only to be confronted with the continuing fact of the atomic bomb and the baffling and ever-widening revolution that is reshaping her social, economic, political, and intellectual existence. In 1947 the British-born poet W. H. Auden gave to his long philosophical poem the title *The Age of Anxiety*. In this title he has summed up the dominant tone of literature during the past half century.

THE TIMES, LONDON

2. Alfred North Whitehead, *Science and the Modern World* (Macmillan Co., 1926).

In spite of Britain's continuing economic problems, her face is set squarely toward the future. Above: A gas discharge tube at Harwell, center of research in industrial atomic energy. Below: A radio telescope at Jodrell Bank, the world's largest at the time it was built.

THE TIMES, LO

CECIL BEATON, LONDON

The official coronation photograph of Queen Elizabeth II.

chapter eight Short Story

In the age of Queen Victoria, general readers and critics alike raised an outcry over the pessimism and fatalism of Hardy's *Jude the Obscure*. But a view of man's condition that seemed an affront in the nineteenth century appeared quite natural in the light of events that occupied the first half of the twentieth century. Consequently the general tendency of most modern fiction is toward realism. Realism, however, does not necessarily imply pessimism. Far from concluding that the universe is really ruled by blind chance, many writers have worked within the framework of realism to find and express attitudes of a more positive nature based on some kind of certainty.

One common view of the trouble with modern life has been that it has become too civilized. Writers who followed in the footsteps of Joseph Conrad (see page 509) contrasted the "natural" responses and ideals of primitive peoples with those of Western men, to the disadvantage of the latter. Other writers exposed the artificiality of civilization by looking at the world from the viewpoint of an adolescent, who might be endowed with the virtues that primitive peoples were supposed to have. This viewpoint, which assumes that an adolescent has not yet been corrupted by long exposure to the conventions of modern life, is at once frank and romantic or idealistic.

The general suspicion of all social conventions that was a result of the disillusionment following World War I was welcomed by writers as an opportunity to experiment with new ways of writing. Experimentation became the hallmark of the modern short story. New forms of the short story, far less tightly plotted than, for example, the stories of Rudyard Kipling (see page 477), evolved; and new approaches to treatment of theme and character were worked out. Although experimentation produces by its very nature a wide variety of types which are difficult to summarize, it is possible to distinguish two approaches to writing that are typical of many modern stories. One is the use of myths, folk tales, and ballads in stories that in other respects are modern, often realistic; the other is the scrutiny of a character's mental state.

The study of primitive cultures, which was beginning at the time Sir Walter Scott was collecting ballads on the Scottish border (see page 371), furnished inspiration for the modern use of myth and folk tale. When it was discovered that widely separated peoples had told similar stories and had often used the same religious symbols, the theory developed that through studying folk tales and myths modern man might arrive at fundamental truths which had been obscured by civilization. Many writers sought to tap these sources by retelling folk tales and ballads in modern terms or by relating modern stories to ancient myths. James Joyce based one of his two major novels on the Greek legend of Ulysses and the other on an Irish ballad.

From the very beginnings of the novel and of the short story, one of the prime considerations of the author has been to reveal to the reader the character of the fictional individual he has created. Traditionally character is shown by actions and speech, but the studies of modern psychologists have pointed out that such conventional guides are incomplete or unreliable. The studies of Sigmund Freud (1856-1939), an Austrian psychologist, were particularly influential in changing the methods by which authors handled character. For Freud was concerned with uncovering the underlying reasons (often unconscious or semiconscious) for the emotions, reactions, and behavior of the individual. Since it seemed to many writers that only by probing such feelings could they create a real individual, they developed new techniques to expose and communicate this realm of the inner man.

Frank O'Connor   CHRISTMAS MORNING

I never really liked my brother, Sonny. From the time he was a baby he was always the mother's pet and always chasing her to tell her what mischief I was up to. Mind you, I was usually up to something. Until I was nine or ten I was never much good at school, and I really believe it was to spite me that he was so smart at his books. He seemed to know by instinct that this was what Mother had set her heart on, and you might almost say he spelt himself into her favor.

"Mummy," he'd say, "will I call Larry in to his t-e-a?" or: "Mummy, the k-e-t-e-l is boiling," and, of course, when he was wrong she'd correct him, and next time he'd have it right and there would be no standing him. "Mummy," he'd say, "aren't I a good speller?" Cripes, we could all be good spellers if we went on like that!

Mind you, it wasn't that I was stupid. Far from it. I was just restless and not able to fix my mind for long on any one thing. I'd do the lessons for the year before, or the lessons for the year after: what I couldn't stand were the lessons we were supposed to be doing at the time. In the evenings I used to go out and play with the Doherty gang. Not, again, that I was rough, but I liked the excitement, and for the life of me I couldn't see what attracted Mother about education.

"Can't you do your lessons first and play after?" she'd say, getting white with indignation. "You ought to be ashamed of yourself that your baby brother can read better than you."

She didn't seem to understand that I wasn't, because there didn't seem to me to be anything particularly praiseworthy about reading, and it struck me as an occupation better suited to a sissy kid like Sonny.

"The dear[1] knows what will become of you," she'd say. "If only you'd stick to your books, you might be something good like a clerk or an engineer."

"I'll be a clerk, Mummy," Sonny would say smugly.

"Who wants to be an old clerk?" I'd say, just to annoy him. "I'm going to be a soldier."

"The dear knows, I'm afraid that's all you'll ever be fit for," she would add with a sigh.

I couldn't help feeling at times that she wasn't all there. As if there was anything better a fellow could be!

Coming on to Christmas, with the days getting shorter and the shopping crowds bigger, I began to think of all the things I might get from Santa Claus. The Dohertys said there was no Santa Claus, only what your father and mother gave you, but the Dohertys were a rough class of children you wouldn't expect Santa to come to anyway. I was rooting round for whatever information I could pick up about him, but there didn't seem to be much. I was no hand with a pen, but if a letter would do any good I was ready to chance writing to him. I had plenty of initiative and was always writing off for free samples and prospectuses.

"Ah, I don't know will he come at all this year," Mother said with a worried air. "He has enough to do looking after steady boys who mind their lessons without bothering about the rest."

"He only comes to good spellers, Mummy," said Sonny. "Isn't that right?"

"He comes to any little boy who does his best, whether he's a good speller or not," Mother said firmly.

Well, I did my best. God knows I did! It

wasn't my fault if, four days before the holidays, Flogger Dawley gave us sums we couldn't do, and Peter Doherty and myself had to go on the lang.[2] It wasn't for love of it, for, take it from me, December is no month for mitching,[3] and we spent most of our time sheltering from the rain in a store on the quays. The only mistake we made was imagining we could keep it up till the holidays without being spotted. That showed real lack of foresight.

Of course, Flogger Dawley noticed and sent home word to know what was keeping me. When I came in on the third day the mother gave me a look I'll never forget, and said: "Your dinner is there." She was too full to talk. When I tried to explain to her about Flogger Dawley and the sums she brushed it aside and said: "You have no word." I saw then it wasn't the langing she minded but the lies, though I still didn't see how you could lang without lying. She didn't speak to me for days. And even then I couldn't make out what she saw in education, or why she wouldn't let me grow up naturally like anyone else.

To make things worse, it stuffed Sonny up more than ever. He had the air of one saying: "I don't know what they'd do without me in this blooming house." He stood at the front door, leaning against the jamb with his hands in his trouser pockets, trying to make himself look like Father, and shouted to the other kids so that he could be heard all over the road.

"Larry isn't left go out. He went on the lang with Peter Doherty and me mother isn't talking to him."

And at night, when we were in bed, he kept it up.

"Santa Claus won't bring you anything this year, aha!"

"Of course he will," I said.

"How do you know?"

"Why wouldn't he?"

"Because you went on the lang with Doherty. I wouldn't play with them Doherty fellows."

2. *on the lang*, a slang expression meaning "playing hooky."
3. *mitching*, slang for "playing hooky."

BROWN BROTHERS

Frank O'Connor   1903–1966

In *An Only Child* (1961) Frank O'Connor, who was christened Michael O'Donovan, traces his life from his birth in a slum in Cork to his release in 1923 from imprisonment as a revolutionary during the Irish fight for independence. As the autobiography makes clear, O'Connor's early life was hard, unhappy, and poverty-stricken; yet bitterness is not the outstanding note in his account of it. Rather the tone is humorous and warm with compassion. These are the qualities that are dominant in practically all O'Connor's stories.

From childhood O'Connor was keenly interested in the people and the language of his native land. His knowledge of Gaelic, which he had learned by ear from his grandmother, enabled him to collaborate with William Butler Yeats (page 622) on translations of Gaelic poems. His bicycle tours through Ireland provided him with subjects for stories and kept his ear tuned to the subtle beauties of the spoken word. In collections of stories such as *Bones of Contention* (1936) and *Crabapple Jelly* (1944) his fidelity to the patterns of Irish speech and his knowledge of the Irish people, their cities, and their green countryside are evident. His simple, loosely plotted stories are notable for their lucid, rhythmic style.

"You wouldn't be left."

"I wouldn't play with them. They're no class.[4] They had the bobbies up to the house."

"And how would Santa know I was on the lang with Peter Doherty?" I growled, losing patience with the little prig.

"Of course he'd know. Mummy would tell him."

"And how could Mummy tell him and he up at the North Pole? Poor Ireland, she's rearing them yet! 'Tis easy seen you're only an old baby."

"I'm not a baby, and I can spell better than you, and Santa won't bring you anything."

"We'll see whether he will or not," I said sarcastically, doing the old man on him.

But, to tell the God's truth, the old man was only bluff. You could never tell what powers these superhuman chaps would have of knowing what you were up to. And I had a bad conscience about the langing because I'd never before seen the mother like that.

That was the night I decided that the only sensible thing to do was to see Santa myself and explain to him. Being a man, he'd probably understand. In those days I was a good-looking kid and had a way with me when I liked. I had only to smile nicely at one old gent on the North Mall to get a penny from him, and I felt if only I could get Santa by himself I could do the same with him and maybe get something worth while from him. I wanted a model railway: I was sick of Ludo and Snakes-and-Ladders.[5]

I started to practice lying awake, counting five hundred and then a thousand, and trying to hear first eleven, then midnight, from Shandon. I felt sure Santa would be round by midnight, seeing that he'd be coming from the north, and would have the whole of the South Side to do afterwards. In some ways I was very farsighted. The only trouble was the things I was farsighted about.

I was so wrapped up in my own calculations that I had little attention to spare for Mother's difficulties. Sonny and I used to go to town with her, and while she was shopping we stood outside a toy shop in the North Main Street, arguing about what we'd like for Christmas.

On Christmas Eve when Father came home from work and gave her the housekeeping money, she stood looking at it doubtfully while her face grew white.

"Well?" he snapped, getting angry. "What's wrong with that?"

"What's wrong with it?" she muttered. "On Christmas Eve!"

"Well," he asked truculently, sticking his hands in his trouser pockets as though to guard what was left, "do you think I get more because it's Christmas?"

"Lord God," she muttered distractedly. "And not a bit of cake in the house, nor a candle, nor anything!"

"All right," he shouted, beginning to stamp. "How much will the candle be?"

"Ah, for pity's sake," she cried, "will you give me the money and not argue like that before the children? Do you think I'll leave them with nothing on the one day of the year?"

"Bad luck to you and your children!" he snarled. "Am I to be slaving from one year's end to another for you to be throwing it away on toys? Here," he added, tossing two half-crowns on the table, "that's all you're going to get, so make the most of it."

"I suppose the publicans will get the rest," she said bitterly.

Later she went into town, but did not bring us with her, and returned with a lot of parcels, including the Christmas candle. We waited for Father to come home to his tea, but he didn't, so we had our own tea and a slice of Christmas cake each, and then Mother put Sonny on a chair with the holy-water stoup to sprinkle the candle, and when he lit it she said: "The light of heaven to our souls." I could see she was upset because Father wasn't in—it should be the oldest and youngest. When we hung up our stockings at bedtime he was still out.

Then began the hardest couple of hours I ever put in. I was mad with sleep but afraid of losing the model railway, so I lay for a

---

4. *They're no class*, a slang expression for people of an inferior class. 5. *Ludo and Snakes-and-Ladders*, board games popular with children, commonly presented as Christmas gifts.

while, making up things to say to Santa when he came. They varied in tone from frivolous to grave, for some old gents like kids to be modest and well-spoken, while others prefer them with spirit. When I had rehearsed them all I tried to wake Sonny to keep me company, but that kid slept like the dead.

Eleven struck from Shandon, and soon after I heard the latch, but it was only Father coming home.

"Hello, little girl," he said, letting on to be surprised at finding Mother waiting up for him, and then broke into a self-conscious giggle. "What have you up so late?"

"Do you want your supper?" she asked shortly.

"Ah, no, no," he replied. "I had a bit of pig's cheek at Daneen's on my way up (Daneen was my uncle). I'm very fond of a bit of pig's cheek. . . . My goodness, is it that late?" he exclaimed, letting on to be astonished. "If I knew that I'd have gone to the North Chapel for midnight Mass. I'd like to hear the *Adeste* again. That's a hymn I'm very fond of—a most touching hymn."

Then he began to hum it falsetto.

Adeste fideles
Solus domus dagus.

Father was very fond of Latin hymns, particularly when he had a drop in, but as he had no notion of the words he made them up as he went along, and this always drove Mother mad.

"Ah, you disgust me!" she said in a scalded voice, and closed the room door behind her. Father laughed as if he thought it a great joke; and he struck a match to light his pipe and for a while puffed at it noisily. The light under the door dimmed and went out but he continued to sing emotionally.

Dixie medearo
Tutum tonum tantum
Venite adoremus.

He had it all wrong but the effect was the same on me. To save my life I couldn't keep awake.

Coming on to dawn, I woke with the feeling that something dreadful had happened.

The whole house was quiet, and the little bedroom that looked out on the foot and a half of back yard was pitch-dark. It was only when I glanced at the window that I saw how all the silver had drained out of the sky. I jumped out of bed to feel my stocking, well knowing that the worst had happened. Santa had come while I was asleep, and gone away with an entirely false impression of me, because all he had left me was some sort of book, folded up, a pen and pencil, and a tuppenny bag of sweets. Not even Snakes-and-Ladders! For a while I was too stunned even to think. A fellow who was able to drive over rooftops and climb down chimneys without getting stuck—God, wouldn't you think he'd know better?

Then I began to wonder what that foxy boy, Sonny, had. I went to his side of the bed and felt his stocking. For all his spelling and sucking-up he hadn't done so much better, because, apart from a bag of sweets like mine, all Santa had left him was a popgun, one that fired a cork on a piece of string and which you could get in any hunter's shop for sixpence.

All the same, the fact remained that it was a gun, and a gun was better than a book any day of the week. The Dohertys had a gang, and the gang fought the Strawberry Lane kids who tried to play football on our road. That gun would be very useful to me in many ways, while it would be lost on Sonny who wouldn't be let play with the gang, even if he wanted to.

Then I got the inspiration, as it seemed to me, direct from heaven. Suppose I took the gun and gave Sonny the book! Sonny would never be any good in the gang: he was fond of spelling, and a studious child like him could learn a lot of spellings from a book like mine. As he hadn't seen Santa any more than I had, what he hadn't seen wouldn't grieve him. I was doing no harm to anyone; in fact, if Sonny only knew, I was doing him a good turn which he might have cause to thank me for later. That was one thing I was always keen on; doing good turns. Perhaps this was Santa's intention the whole time and he had merely become confused between us. It was a mistake that might happen to anyone. So

I put the book, the pencil, and the pen into Sonny's stocking and the popgun into my own, and returned to bed and slept again. As I say, in those days I had plenty of initiative.

It was Sonny who woke me, shaking me to tell me that Santa had come and left me a gun. I let on to be surprised and rather disappointed in the gun, and to divert his mind from it made him show me his picture book, and cracked it up to the skies.

As I knew, that kid was prepared to believe anything, and nothing would do him then but to take the presents in to show Father and Mother. This was a bad moment for me. After the way she had behaved about the langing, I distrusted Mother, though I had the consolation of believing that the only person who could contradict me was now somewhere up by the North Pole. That gave me a certain confidence, so Sonny and I burst in with our presents, shouting: "Look what Santa Claus brought!"

Father and Mother woke, and Mother smiled, but only for an instant. As she looked at me her face changed. I knew that look; I knew it only too well. It was the same she had worn the day I came home from langing, when she said I had no word.

"Larry," she said in a low voice, "where did you get that gun?"

"Santa left it in my stocking, Mummy," I said, trying to put on an injured air, though it baffled me how she guessed that he hadn't. "He did, honest."

"You stole it from that poor child's stocking while he was asleep," she said, her voice quivering with indignation. "Larry, Larry, how could you be so mean?"

"Now, now, now," Father said deprecatingly, "'tis Christmas morning."

"Ah," she said with real passion, "it's easy it comes to you. Do you think I want my son to grow up a liar and a thief?"

"Ah, what thief, woman?" he said testily. "Have sense, can't you?" He was as cross if you interrupted him in his benevolent moods as if they were of the other sort, and this one was probably exacerbated by a feeling of guilt for his behavior of the night before. "Here, Larry," he said, reaching out for the money

on the bedside table, "here's sixpence for you and one for Sonny. Mind you don't lose it now!"

But I looked at Mother and saw what was in her eyes. I burst out crying, threw the popgun on the floor, and ran bawling out of the house before anyone on the road was awake. I rushed up the lane behind the house and threw myself on the wet grass.

I understood it all, and it was almost more than I could bear; that there was no Santa Claus, as the Dohertys said, only Mother trying to scrape together a few coppers from the housekeeping; that Father was mean and common and a drunkard, and that she had been relying on me to raise her out of the misery of the life she was leading. And I knew that the look in her eyes was the fear that, like my father, I should turn out to be mean and common and a drunkard.

To increase understanding

1. (a) Why does Larry think Sonny a prig? (b) What does Larry think of himself?

2. (a) Explain the source of conflict between the father and mother. (b) What is the attitude of the boys toward each parent? (c) From which parent does Sonny seem to get his sense of values? From which does Larry acquire his?

3. Frank O'Connor has said that he does not wish to shape his stories into what he considers an artificial literary pattern; he wishes simply to present the life of the common people as it is lived. Specifically, he does not approve of a sudden change of character or sudden "twist" at the end. If such a change occurs, it must be like "the twisting of an iron bar"— a change growing directly out of the circumstances, which affects the personality of the character for life. In the last paragraph of this story, Larry explains exactly what the climactic event in the story revealed to him. (a) Show how each point of this revelation does or does not grow directly out of his experiences in the story. (b) Is Larry's experience like the "twisting of an iron bar"? Explain.

4. Although the story ends in disillusionment for Larry, there is much comedy in the story. (a) Point out passages that are especially amusing. (b) Is this humor out of place in view of the ending? Why or why not?

Graham Greene I SPY

Charlie Stowe waited until he heard his mother snore before he got out of bed. Even then he moved with caution and tiptoed to the window. The front of the house was irregular, so that it was possible to see a light burning in his mother's room. But now all the windows were dark. A searchlight passed across the sky, lighting the banks of cloud and probing the dark deep spaces between, seeking enemy airships. The wind blew from the sea, and Charlie Stowe could hear behind his mother's snores the beating of the waves. A draft through the cracks in the window frame stirred his nightshirt. Charlie Stowe was frightened.

But the thought of the tobacconist's shop which his father kept down a dozen wooden stairs drew him on. He was twelve years old, and already boys at the County School mocked him because he had never smoked a cigarette. The packets were piled twelve deep below, Gold Flake and Players, De Reszke, Abdulla, Woodbines, and the little shop lay under a thin haze of stale smoke which would completely disguise his crime. That it was a crime to steal some of his father's stock Charlie Stowe had no doubt, but he did not love his father; his father was unreal to him, a wraith,

pale, thin, and indefinite, who noticed him only spasmodically and left even punishment to his mother. For his mother he felt a passionate demonstrative love; her large boisterous presence and her noisy charity filled the world for him; from her speech he judged her the friend of everyone, from the rector's wife to the "dear Queen," except the "Huns," the monsters who lurked in Zeppelins in the clouds.[1] But his father's affection and dislike were as indefinite as his movements. Tonight he had said he would be in Norwich, and yet you never knew. Charlie Stowe had no sense of safety as he crept down the wooden stairs. When they creaked he clenched his fingers on the collar of his nightshirt.

At the bottom of the stairs he came out quite suddenly into the little shop. It was too dark to see his way, and he did not dare touch the switch. For half a minute he sat

1. *the "Huns" . . . clouds.* The Huns were a people of Western Asia that overran Europe in the fifth century. During World War I the Germans were referred to as *Huns* by people of the allied nations, who viewed them as barbaric destroyers of European society. The Zeppelin, or dirigible, invented by the German Count Zeppelin, became famous during the war.

Graham Greene 1904— Graham Greene was born in Hertfordshire, the son of the headmaster at Berkhamstead School. After graduating from Oxford, he began his writing career as a subeditor on the London *Times*. His early novels were mystery thrillers, frankly designed to be popular, called "entertainments." Although Greene displayed great technical skill in these books, it was for his novels like *Brighton Rock* (1938) and *The Power and the Glory* (1940) that he attracted critical attention as a major novelist. Here his interest in terror and fear is used to express deep concern with the moral position of man in the modern world. Modern man is shown terrified when he discovers that he must find his own salvation or damnation with little help from what used to be steady moral forces in a stable society. Critic Morton Zabel has spoken of Greene's concern in this way: "Where once . . . it was society, state, kingdom, world, or the universe itself that supplied the presiding order of law or justice, it is now the isolated, betrayed, and finally indestructible integrity of the individual life that must furnish the measure."[1]

1. *Morton Zabel,* "Graham Greene," *Critiques and Essays on Modern Fiction,* ed. John W. Aldridge (New York: The Ronald Press, 1952); reprinted and revised from *The Nation,* July 3, 1943.

in despair on the bottom step with his chin cupped in his hands. Then the regular movement of the searchlight was reflected through an upper window and the boy had time to fix in memory the pile of cigarettes, the counter, and the small hole under it. The footsteps of a policeman on the pavement made him grab the first packet to his hand and dive for the hole. A light shone along the floor and a hand tried the door, then the footsteps passed on, and Charlie cowered in the darkness.

At last he got his courage back by telling himself in his curiously adult way that if he were caught now there was nothing to be done about it, and he might as well have his smoke. He put a cigarette in his mouth and then remembered that he had no matches. For a while he dared not move. Three times the searchlight lit the shop, while he muttered taunts and encouragements. "May as well be hung for a sheep,"[2] "Cowardy, cowardy custard," grown-up and childish exhortation oddly mixed.

But as he moved he heard footfalls in the street, the sound of several men walking rapidly. Charlie Stowe was old enough to feel surprise that anybody was about. The footsteps came nearer, stopped; a key was turned in the shop door, a voice said, "Let him in," and then he heard his father: "If you wouldn't mind being quiet, gentlemen. I don't want to wake up the family." There was a note unfamiliar to Charlie in the undecided voice. A torch flashed and the electric globe burst into blue light. The boy held his breath; he wondered whether his father would hear his heart beating, and he clutched his nightshirt tightly and prayed, "O God, don't let me be caught." Through a crack in the counter he could see his father where he stood, one hand held to his high stiff collar, between two men in bowler hats and belted mackintoshes. They were strangers.

"Have a cigarette," his father said in a voice dry as a biscuit. One of the men shook his head. "It wouldn't do, not when we are on duty. Thank you all the same." He spoke gently, but without kindness; Charlie Stowe thought his father must be ill.

"Mind if I put a few in my pocket?" Mr. Stowe asked, and when the man nodded he lifted a pile of Gold Flake and Players from a shelf and caressed the packets with the tips of his fingers.

"Well," he said, "there's nothing to be done about it, and I may as well have my smokes." For a moment Charlie Stowe feared discovery, his father stared round the shop so thoroughly; he might have been seeing it for the first time. "It's a good little business," he said, "for those that like it. The wife will sell out, I suppose. Else the neighbors'll be wrecking it. Well, you want to be off. A stitch in time. I'll get my coat."

"One of us'll come with you, if you don't mind," said the stranger gently.

"You needn't trouble. It's on the peg here. There, I'm all ready."

The other man said in an embarrassed way: "Don't you want to speak to your wife?" The thin voice was decided. "Not me. Never do today what you can put off till tomorrow. She'll have her chance later, won't she?"

"Yes, yes," one of the strangers said and he became very cheerful and encouraging. "Don't you worry too much. While there's life. . . ." And suddenly his father tried to laugh.

When the door had closed Charlie Stowe tiptoed upstairs and got into bed. He wondered why his father had left the house again so late at night and who the strangers were. Surprise and awe kept him for a little while awake. It was as if a familiar photograph had stepped from the frame to reproach him with neglect. He remembered how his father had held tight to his collar and fortified himself with proverbs, and he thought for the first time that, while his mother was boisterous and kindly, his father was very like himself, doing things in the dark which frightened him. It would have pleased him to go down to his father and tell him that he loved him, but he could hear through the window the quick steps going away. He was alone in the house with his mother, and he fell asleep.

---

2. *"May as well be hung for a sheep."* ". . . as a lamb" completes the proverb, which means that when one is already in trouble, he may as well get in farther.

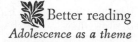

To increase understanding

1. During what period does the story take place? Cite details to support your answer.

2. (a) What are Charlie's impressions of his father in the early parts of the story? (b) Contrast Charlie's attitude toward his father with his feelings about his mother.

3. (a) Why does Charlie raid his father's shop? (b) Explain the following statement: "That it was a crime to steal some of his father's stock Charlie Stowe had no doubt, but he did not love his father" (page 555, column 1, paragraph 2). (c) Why does Charlie continue his actions in spite of his feeling of guilt?

4. (a) What happens to Charlie's father? (b) What statement does Mr. Stowe make about his shop that reveals the nature of his activities?

5. (a) What does Charlie learn about his father during the climactic scene? (b) Point out all the details that lead to this revelation.

6. What use does the author make of setting and atmosphere in showing how Charlie feels?

7. How does Charlie's feeling in the dark shop illustrate the predicament of modern man as Graham Greene sees it?

Better reading
Adolescence as a theme

Traditionally the word *theme* has meant the basic idea that underlies a piece of imaginative literature and gives it a meaning larger than the work itself. But in modern discussions of literature the term *theme* is also used to suggest a subject which frequently occurs in the works of different writers and which is useful in exploring the attitudes of characters. One modern theme is adolescence, the crucial period during which a young person evaluates his relations with his parents, the values he has inherited, and his entire social background. So important is this theme in the modern world that nearly every first major novel by the important writers in the early decades of the twentieth century deals with adolescence.

Although both "Christmas Morning" and "I Spy" use adolescence as a theme, this does not imply that the stories mean the same thing. The crisis that lies at the center of the theme of adolescence may have any of a number of outcomes. The young person may, for example, simply become disillusioned when a false picture he has of his parents is destroyed by emerging reality. Or he may fear the unknown and shrink into the security of the familiar. In other circumstances he may revolt against and leave his parents, and in so doing he may either find or destroy himself. While in neither "Christmas Morning" nor "I Spy" does the crisis result in drastic changes, nevertheless each boy emerges from his experience a somewhat different person. How is Larry's attitude likely to change in regard to (a) his father, (b) his mother, (c) the Doherty boys, (d) education, (e) his family's social and economic position? How does Charlie's discovery about his father affect him? What clues does Charlie himself have as to the kind of person he may turn out to be?

Authors may also differ in their attitudes toward the same theme. Compare the tone of "Christmas Morning" with that of "I Spy." Which writer expresses the more optimistic (or less pessimistic) view of life? Explain.

James Joyce EVELINE

She sat at the window watching the evening invade the avenue. Her head was leaned against the window curtains and in her nostrils was the odor of dusty cretonne. She was tired.

Few people passed. The man out of the last house passed on his way home; she heard his footsteps clacking along the concrete pavement and afterwards crunching on the cinder path before the new red houses. One time

Reprinted from *Dubliners* by James Joyce, by permission of The Viking Press, Inc., New York; Jonathan Cape Ltd., London; and the Executors of the Estate of the author. Originally published by B. W. Huebsch in 1916.

Portrait by
J.E. Blanche.

James Joyce   1882-1941

One of the most important novelists of the twentieth century and probably the most influential, James Joyce was born and educated in Dublin. He attended Jesuit schools, was an outstanding scholar, and for a time considered entering the priesthood. At a crucial point in his life, however, he felt he had to renounce both his religion and his native land in order to develop in his own way. From the time of this self-imposed exile, Joyce became a wanderer on the Continent, supporting his family by working as a commercial translator and as a teacher in a Berlitz language school. Most of his energies he devoted to the writing of fiction.

Joyce's first major work was a collection of short stories called *Dubliners* (1914). As the title suggests, Joyce, in spite of his exile, made Ireland the focus of his writing in this collection. This he continued to do throughout his career. In his first novel, *A Portrait of the Artist as a Young Man* (1916), he reviewed the steps that had led to his adolescent revolt. Then followed the revolutionary novel *Ulysses* (1922), a series of episodes in the lives of Irish characters who have parallels in Homer's *Odyssey*. Joyce's last novel, *Finnegans Wake* (1939), embodied many modern theories, was highly experimental, and is regarded as his masterpiece.

In form and in content much of Joyce's work was controversial. During his lifetime it was banned, burned, pirated, confiscated, and attacked. Only in more recent years has his reputation reached its present eminence.

"Eveline," a story from *Dubliners*, like much of Joyce's writing, explores the forces that drive men into exile from one another and voices his sympathy for misunderstanding and loneliness.

there used to be a field there in which they used to play every evening with other people's children. Then a man from Belfast bought the field and built houses in it—not like their little brown houses but bright brick houses with shining roofs. The children of the avenue used to play together in that field—the Devines, the Waters, the Dunns, little Keogh the cripple, she and her brothers and sisters. Ernest, however, never played: he was too grown up. Her father used often to hunt them in out of the field with his blackthorn stick; but usually little Keogh used to keep *nix*[1] and call out when he saw her father coming. Still they seemed to have been rather happy then. Her father was not so bad then; and besides, her mother was alive. That was a long time ago; she and her brothers and sisters were all grown up; her mother was dead. Tizzie Dunn was dead, too, and the Waters had gone back to England. Everything changes. Now she was going to go away like the others, to leave her home.

Home! She looked round the room, reviewing all its familiar objects which she had dusted once a week for so many years, wondering where on earth all the dust came from. Perhaps she would never see again those familiar objects from which she had never dreamed of being divided. And yet during all those years she had never found out the name of the priest whose yellowing photograph hung on the wall above the broken harmonium beside the colored print of the promises made to Blessed Margaret Mary Alacoque.[2] He had been a school friend of her father. Whenever he showed the photograph to a visitor her father used to pass it with a casual word: "He is in Melbourne now."

She had consented to go away, to leave her home. Was that wise? She tried to weigh each side of the question. In her home anyway she had shelter and food; she had those whom she had known all her life about her.

---

1. *nix*, an old slang word, originally used by thieves, to refer to the member of a gang who kept watch. 2. *promises . . . Alacoque*. Saint Margaret Mary is a saint of the Roman Catholic Church who lived in France in the seventeenth century. "The promises" are the graces Christ is said to have promised in an apparition to Margaret Mary to those who observe the devotion to the Sacred Heart.

Of course she had to work hard, both in the house and at business. What would they say of her in the Stores when they found out that she had run away with a fellow? Say she was a fool, perhaps; and her place would be filled up by advertisement. Miss Gavan would be glad. She had always had an edge on her, especially whenever there were people listening.

"Miss Hill, don't you see these ladies are waiting?"

"Look lively, Miss Hill, please."

She would not cry many tears at leaving the Stores.

But in her new home, in a distant unknown country, it would not be like that. Then she would be married—she, Eveline. People would treat her with respect then. She would not be treated as her mother had been. Even now, though she was over nineteen, she sometimes felt herself in danger of her father's violence. She knew it was that that had given her the palpitations. When they were growing up he had never gone for her, like he used to go for Harry and Ernest, because she was a girl; but latterly he had begun to threaten her and say what he would do to her only for her dead mother's sake. And now she had nobody to protect her. Ernest was dead and Harry, who was in the church decorating business, was nearly always down somewhere in the country. Besides, the invariable squabble for money on Saturday nights had begun to weary her unspeakably. She always gave her entire wages—seven shillings—and Harry always sent up what he could but the trouble was to get any money from her father. He said she used to squander the money, that she had no head, that he wasn't going to give her his hard-earned money to throw about the streets, and much more, for he was usually fairly bad on Saturday night. In the end he would give her the money and ask her had she any intention of buying Sunday's dinner. Then she had to rush out as quickly as she could and do her marketing, holding her black leather purse tightly in her hand as she elbowed her way through the crowds and returning home late under her load of provisions. She had hard work to keep the house

together and to see that the two young children who had been left to her charge went to school regularly and got their meals regularly. It was hard work—a hard life—but now that she was about to leave it she did not find it a wholly undesirable life.

She was about to explore another life with Frank. Frank was very kind, manly, openhearted. She was to go away with him by the night boat to be his wife and to live with him in Buenos Aires where he had a home waiting for her. How well she remembered the first time she had seen him; he was lodging in a house on the main road where she used to visit. It seemed a few weeks ago. He was standing at the gate, his peaked cap pushed back on his head and his hair tumbled forward over a face of bronze. Then they had come to know each other. He used to meet her outside the Stores every evening and see her home. He took her to see *The Bohemian Girl*[3] and she felt elated as she sat in an unaccustomed part of the theater with him. He was awfully fond of music and sang a little. People knew that they were courting and, when he sang about the lass that loves a sailor, she always felt pleasantly confused. He used to call her Poppens out of fun. First of all it had been an excitement for her to have a fellow and then she had begun to like him. He had tales of distant countries. He had started as a deck boy at a pound a month on a ship of the Allan Line going out to Canada. He told her the names of the ships he had been on and the names of the different services. He had sailed through the Straits of Magellan and he told her stories of the terrible Patagonians. He had fallen on his feet in Buenos Aires, he said, and had come over to the old country just for a holiday. Of course, her father had found out the affair and had forbidden her to have anything to say to him.

"I know these sailor chaps," he said.

One day he had quarreled with Frank and after that she had to meet her lover secretly.

The evening deepened in the avenue. The

---

3. "*The Bohemian Girl*," a light opera by Balfe, produced in 1843. The plot concerns a girl who is kidnaped by a band of gypsies, but is later returned to her father.

white of two letters in her lap grew indistinct. One was to Harry; the other was to her father. Ernest had been her favorite but she liked Harry too. Her father was becoming old lately, she noticed; he would miss her. Sometimes he could be very nice. Not long before, when she had been laid up for a day, he had read her out a ghost story and made toast for her at the fire. Another day, when their mother was alive, they had all gone for a picnic to the Hill of Howth. She remembered her father putting on her mother's bonnet to make the children laugh.

Her time was running out but she continued to sit by the window, leaning her head against the window curtain, inhaling the odor of dusty cretonne. Down far in the avenue she could hear a street organ playing. She knew the air. Strange that it should come that very night to remind her of the promise to her mother, her promise to keep the home together as long as she could. She remembered the last night of her mother's illness; she was again in the close dark room at the other side of the hall and outside she heard a melancholy air of Italy. The organ player had been ordered to go away and given sixpence. She remembered her father strutting back into the sickroom saying "Those Italians! coming over here!"

As she mused the pitiful vision of her mother's life laid its spell on the very quick of her being—that life of commonplace sacrifices closing in final craziness. She trembled as she heard again her mother's voice saying constantly with foolish insistence: "Derevaun Seraun! Derevaun Seraun!"[4]

She stood up in a sudden impulse of terror. Escape! She must escape! Frank would save her. He would give her life, perhaps love, too. But she wanted to live. Why should she be unhappy? She had a right to happiness. Frank would take her in his arms, fold her in his arms. He would save her.

She stood among the swaying crowd in the station at the North Wall. He held her hand and she knew that he was speaking to her, saying something about the passage over and over again. The station was full of soldiers with brown baggages. Through the wide doors of the sheds she caught a glimpse of the black mass of the boat, lying in beside the quay wall, with illumined portholes. She answered nothing. She felt her cheek pale and cold and, out of a maze of distress, she prayed to God to direct her, to show her what was her duty. The boat blew a long mournful whistle into the mist. If she went, tomorrow she would be on the sea with Frank, steaming toward Buenos Aires. Their passage had been booked. Could she still draw back after all he had done for her? Her distress awoke a nausea in her body and she kept moving her lips in silent fervent prayer.

A bell clanged upon her heart. She felt him seize her hand:

"Come!"

All the seas of the world tumbled about her heart. He was drawing her into them: he would drown her. She gripped with both hands at the iron railing.

"Come!"

No! No! No! It was impossible. Her hands clutched the iron in frenzy. Amid the seas she sent a cry of anguish.

"Eveline! Evvy!"

He rushed beyond the barrier and called to her to follow. He was shouted at to go on but he still called to her. She set her white face to him, passive, like a helpless animal. Her eyes gave him no sign of love or farewell or recognition.

4. *Derevaun ... Seraun!* a Celtic term of endearment, meaning "innocent darling."

To increase understanding

1. This story is divided into two episodes. (*a*) Where does the division take place? (*b*) In broad terms, what do the characters do in each of these two scenes?

2. (*a*) What aspects of her life make Eveline want to go away with Frank? (*b*) Which of these seems most important? Explain.

3. (*a*) What various things incline Eveline to stay? (*b*) Explain why these finally win out. (*c*) Why, in the last sentence, is Eveline compared to a helpless animal?

4. Like "Christmas Morning" and "I Spy" this story deals with the theme of adolescence. In what

ways does Joyce's treatment of this theme differ from the treatments of O'Connor and Greene? Use the article "Adolescence as a Theme" on page 557 as a guide in answering this question.

Better reading
The stream-of-consciousness technique

One aim of serious fiction is to show what it is like to be a certain kind of person confronting certain problems. Usually a character is developed by devising a situation in the plot which will best reveal the character's significant traits, and then showing how the character reacts—what he does, says, thinks, and feels about this situation.

Most fiction before the twentieth century showed the character's reaction from the outside, either as another person might have seen him or as he saw himself, looking back from a later date. A more direct and intimate method, suggested by the psychological studies of William James and Sigmund Freud, was brought to perfection by James Joyce. It involves a direct presentation of the character's consciousness, putting down everything just as the character experiences it at the moment, without the author's intruding for so much as a "he thought. . . ." Raw images, perceptions, memories come and go in seemingly random, but actually carefully controlled, fashion, just as they do in people's minds. Taking its name from a phrase by William James, this has become known as the "stream-of-consciousness" technique.

Although "Eveline" represents not the full-blown use of stream of consciousness but an early step in that direction, it does serve to show how a subjective approach can reveal the true plight of a girl understood by no one—least of all herself. Examine the first part of the story. Notice that the organization is based on one thought or image suggesting another. Cite examples. What are the majority of these images and thoughts about? Does it seem reasonable that Eveline's situation would call forth such thoughts? In what way does the working of her mind, as exhibited in the first part, suggest what her decision will be in the second? What feelings, images, or thoughts determine her "decision" at the critical moment? What do you learn about Eveline from this?

The Changing English Language

The language continues to grow. The Oxford English Dictionary is published in thirteen volumes. The word *head* now has forty meanings; the word *green* has fifty. Two world wars have added such words as *jeep* and *blitzkrieg*. The jargon used by armies has been adopted into informal speech. Science has made terms like *satellite, intercontinental, jet-propelled, nuclear,* and *missiles* familiar to most English-speaking people. Words like *stereophonic, television, radio,* and *short-wave* are household words. *Id, ego, psychoanalysis, vivisection,* and *vaccines* are no longer words used only by doctors and scientists. These are terms that anyone exposed to communication recognizes.

The language continues to change. Words have taken on new meanings. *Scan* once meant to study with great care; it now means to glance at hastily. Fifty years ago *sophistication* was a term of condemnation; today it signifies approval. A *stool pigeon* once meant a decoy used in duck hunting; now it means a police informer. Once *hassle* meant to breathe heavily; now it signifies argument. A *vulgar* man was once a member of the middle class; now he is unrefined. A *diaper* was once a geometric pattern, *hectic* once meant habitual, and a *boor* was once a farmer.

Speed and informality are the keynotes of English in the twentieth century. People once rode in *omnibuses, taximeter motor cabriolets,* and *automobiles.* Now they ride in *buses, cabs,* and *cars.* Students go to *prep schools* and study for *prelims* and *exams.* Babies ride in *buggies* and *prams.* Words like NATO, UNESCO, SEATO, and AWOL are extremely common. AAA, FDR, JFK, GB, WPA, and USSR are abbreviations understood by anyone who reads newspapers. Presidents, prime ministers, and dictators are known by their first names. A common business practice is to address clients by given names. Strangers may be greeted like old friends. Rigidity in speech is gone. The language continues to be a living, growing part of the times.

Sean O'Faolain UP THE BARE STAIRS

*A pity beyond all telling is
hid in the heart of love.*[1]

All the way from Dublin my traveling companion had not spoken a dozen words. After a casual interest in the countryside as we left Kingsbridge he had wrapped a rug about his legs, settled into his corner, and dozed.

He was a bull-shouldered man, about sixty, with coarse, sallow skin stippled with pores, furrowed by deep lines on either side of the mouth: I could imagine him dragging these little dikes open when shaving. He was dressed so conventionally that he might be a judge, a diplomat, a shopwalker,[2] a shipowner, or an old-time Shakespearean actor: black coat, striped trousers, gray spats, white slip inside his waistcoat, butterfly collar folded deeply, and a black cravat held by a gold clasp with a tiny diamond.

The backs of his fingers were hairy: he wore an amethyst ring almost as big as a bishop's. His temples were graying and brushed up in two sweeping wings—wherefore the suggestion of the actor. On the rack over his head was a leather hat case with the initials *F.J.N.* in Gothic lettering. He was obviously an Englishman who had crossed the night before. Even when the steam of the train lifted to show the black January clouds sweeping across the Galtees,[3] and a splash of sleet hit the window by his ear, he did not waken. Just then the ticket checker came in from the corridor and tipped his shoulder. As he received back his ticket he asked, "What time do we arrive in Cork?" He said the word *Cork* as only a Corkman can say it, giving the *r* its distinctively delicate palatal trill, not saying "Corrrk," or "Cohk." He was unmistakably a Corkonian.

At Mallow I came back from tea to find him stretching his legs on the platform and taking notice. He had bought the evening paper and was tapping his thigh with it as he watched, with a quizzical smile, two tipsy old countrymen in amiable dispute, nose to nose, outside the bar. A fine man on his feet; at least six foot two. I bought a paper, also, at the bookstall and as we went on our way we both read.

My eye floated from a heading about a licensing case—the usual long verbatim report, two men found hiding under the stairs, six men with bottles in the stable, much laughter in court, and so on—to a headline beside it: CORKMAN IN BIRTHDAY HONORS LIST. The paragraph referred to "Francis James Nugent, Baronet: for War Services."[4] I looked across at him.

"Did you say something?" he asked.

"No, no! Or, rather, I don't think so."

"Pretty cold," he said, in a friendly way. "Though I will say one thing for the G.S.R.,[5] they do heat their trains."

"Yes, it's nice and warm today. They're not, of course, the G.S.R. now, you know. They're called Corus Iompair Eireann."

"What's that? Irish for G.S.R.?"

"More or less."

We talked a bit about the revival of the language.[6] Not that he was interested; but he

---

"Up the Bare Stairs" by Sean O'Faolain from *The Man Who Invented Sin And Other Stories* by Sean O'Faolain, copyright 1948 by The Devin-Adair Company. Reprinted by permission of The Devin-Adair Company and Rupert Hart-Davis Limited.
1. *A pity . . . heart of love,* from the poem "The Pity of Love" by William Butler Yeats. 2. *shopwalker,* floorwalker. 3. *Galtees* (gôl´tēz), a range of mountains about three quarters of the way from Dublin to Cork. 4. *Birthday Honors List . . . . War Services.* The headlines refer to the fact that, for his services during the war, Francis Nugent was one of the commoners raised to the rank of baronet in honor of the king's birthday. 5. *G. S. R.,* Great Southern Railway. 6. *revival of the language.* One phase of the Irish national movement was the attempt to reëstablish Celtic as the native language of Ireland.

was tolerant, or perhaps the right word is indifferent. After a bit I said:

"I see there's a Corkman in the new honors list."

"Oh?" I glanced up at the rack and said, with a grin: "I see the initials on your hatbox."

He chuckled, pleased.

"I suppose I'd better plead guilty."

"Congratulations."

"Thank you."

"What does it feel like?"

He glanced out at the wheeling fields, with their lochs[7] of water and cowering cattle, and then looked back at me with a cynical smile.

"It doesn't feel any different. By the time you get it you've pretty well enjoyed everything it stands for. Still, it helps."

"I see from the paper that you went to the same school as myself."

"Are you the old Red and Green, too?"

"Up the Abbey!"

He laughed, pleased again.

"Does all that go on just the same as before?"

"It goes on. Perhaps not just the same as before."

We talked of West Abbey. I knew none of the men he knew, but he thawed out remembering them.

"Are all the old photographs still in the main hall? Chaps in the Indian Civil,[8] the Canadian Mounted, the Navy, the Indian Police? God, I used to stare at them when I was a kid."

"They're gone. They've been replaced by Confirmation groups all wearing holy medals."

He made a bored face.

"I suppose in those days you little thought you'd be coming back to Cork one day as Sir Francis Nugent."

He peered at me through his cigarette smoke and nodded sagely.

"I knew."

"You did!"

"I shouldn't have said that. I couldn't know. But I had a pretty good idea."

Then he leaned forward and let down all his reserves. As he began my heart sank. He was at the favorite theme of every successful man: "How I Began." But as he went on I felt mean and rebuked. I doubt if he had ever told anyone, and before he finished I could only guess why he chose to tell me now.

7. *loch*, lake.   8. *Indian Civil*, the Indian Civil Service. This was the department of the British government in India.

BROWN BROTHERS

Sean O'Faolain   1900— In many ways the life of Sean O'Faolain (shôn ō fal'ən) parallels that of Frank O'Connor. Both were born in Cork, were interested in Gaelic, and took an active part in the Irish revolution. But while O'Connor struggled for an education on his way up from the slums and never attended a university, O'Faolain received master's degrees from both the National University of Ireland and from Harvard University. He then taught in the United States, England, and Ireland before his success as a writer afforded him sufficient income to devote all his time to writing.

In both his first collection of short stories, *Midsummer Night Madness and Other Stories* (1932), and his first novel, *A Nest of Simple Folk* (1933), O'Faolain deals with the revolutionary period in Ireland. His best short stories are collected in *The Finest Stories of Sean O'Faolain* (1957). In recent years O'Faolain has concentrated on writing essays, biographies, and travel articles.

O'Faolain has interpreted Irish life with sympathy and understanding. However, since he has never glossed over the shortcomings of the people he writes about nor the circumstances under which they live, he has been a center of controversy in his native Ireland.

You know, it's extraordinary the things that set a fellow going. I always knew I'd get somewhere. Not merely that, but I can tell you the very day, the very hour, I made up my mind I was going to get there. I don't think I was more than fourteen or fifteen at the time. Certainly not more than fifteen. It was as simple as that"—clicking his fingers. "It was all on account of a little man named Angelo—one of the monks who was teaching us. He's gone to God by now. There was a time when I thought he was the nicest little man in the whole school. Very handsome. Cheeks as red as a girl's, black bristly hair, blue eyes, and the most perfect teeth I've ever seen between a man's lips. He was absolutely full of life, bursting with it. He was really just a big boy and that's probably why we got on so well with him. I've seen him get as much fun out of solving a quadratic equation or a problem in Euclid as a kid with a new toy. He had a marvelous trick of flinging his *cappa*[9] over one shoulder, shoving his two wrists out of his sleeves like a conjurer, snapping up a bit of chalk and saying, 'Watch what I'm going to do now,' that used to make us sit bolt upright in our desks as if . . . well, as if he was going to do a conjuring trick. And if you could only have seen the way he'd kick ball with us in the yard—you know, the old yard at the back of West Abbey—all we had was a lump of paper tied with twine—shouting and racing like any of us. He really was a good chap. We were very fond of him.

"Too fond of him, I've often thought. He knew it, you see, and it made him put too much of himself into everything we did. And the result was that we were next door to helpless without him. He made us depend on him too much. Perhaps he wasn't the best kind of teacher; perhaps he was too good a teacher—I don't know—have it whichever way you like. If he was tired, or had a headache, or sagged, we sagged. If he was away sick and somebody else had to take charge of us we were a set of duffers. They could be just as cross as he was—he was very severe, he'd take no excuses from anybody—or they could

be as merry as he was: it just wasn't the same thing. They had a job to do, and they did the best they could, but with him it wasn't a job, it was his life, it was his joy and his pleasure. You could tell how much the fellows liked him by the way they'd crowd around him at play hour, or at the end of the holidays to say good-by.

"One particularly nice thing about him was that he had no favorites, no pets, as we used to call them. Did you call them that in your time? But he was—what shall I say?—more than a little partial to me. And for a very, if you like to call it, silly reason. In those days, you see, politics were very hot in Cork city; very hot, very passionate. Of course, they were the old Irish Party days, long before your time, when politics were taken much more seriously than I've ever seen them taken anywhere else. John Redmond had one party called the Molly Maguires, and William O'Brien had another party called the All for Irelanders. Mind you, if you asked me now what it was all about I'd find it very hard to tell you, because they were all the one party at Westminster,[10] and they were all agreed about home rule,[11] but once it came to election time they tore one another to pieces. Fights in the street every night, baton charges, clashes between rival bands, instruments smashed on the pavements. One night, with my own eyes, I saw a big six-foot countryman take a running jump down the grand parade and land right on top of a big drum.

"Well, Angelo was a Molly, and I needn't tell you he was just as excited about politics as he was about everything else, and I was also a Molly and a very hot one. Not that I understood anything at all about it, but just that my father was one of the hottest Redmondites in the city of Cork. And, of course, nothing would do Angelo but to bring politics into class. He'd divide the class into Mollies and All Fors and when we'd be doing Euclid or reciting poetry he'd set one team against the other, and he'd work up the excitement until

9. *cappa*, academic cape. 10. *all the one party at West-minster.* Although the Irish differed among themselves, they had to present a united front in the British Parliament, where the Irish were in a small minority. 11. *home rule*, government of Ireland by a separate Irish Parliament.

the fellows would be clambering across the desks, and if any fellow let down his side we'd glare at him until he'd want to creep away out of sight, and if he scored a point we'd cheer him as if he'd kicked a goal in an All Ireland Final. [12]

"It was on one of these days that it happened. We were at the Eighth Problem. The Mollies wanted one point to pull even. I was the last man in—and I muffed it. And no wonder, with Angelo shouting at me like a bull, 'Come on, now, Frankie. If A.B. be placed on C.D. . . . Up the Mollies! Go on, Frankie. Go on. If A.B. . . .'

"The All Fors won. Angelo laughed it off with, 'Very good, very good, back to yeer places now. Work is work. This isn't the Old Market Place. Now for tomorrow,' and so on.

"But he kept me in after school. There I sat, alone in the empty classroom upstairs—you know the one, near the ball alley—with the crows outside in the yard picking up the crusts, and the dusk falling over the city, and Angelo, never speaking a word, walking up and down the end of the room reading his office. [13] As a rule we were let out at three. He kept me there until five o'clock rang. Then he told me to go home and went off himself up to the monastery.

"I walked out of the yard behind him, and at that moment if I had had a revolver in my hand I'd have shot him. I wouldn't have cared if he'd beaten me black and blue. I wouldn't have cared if he'd given me extra work to do at home. He deliberately got me into trouble with my father and mother, and what that meant he understood exactly. Perhaps you don't. You don't know my background as he knew it. When I tell you that my father was a tailor and my mother was a seamstress I needn't tell you any more. When a kid's mother has to work as hard as his father to push him through school you can guess the whole picture. I don't seem to remember an hour, except for Sundays, when one or other, or both, of these machines wasn't whirring in that little room where we lived, down by the distillery, sometimes until twelve or one o'clock at night. I remember that day as I walked home I kept saying to myself over

and over again, 'If only my mummy wasn't sick.' All the way. Past the distillery. Around by the tannery. You possibly know the little terrace of houses. They've been there since the eighteenth century. Dark. We had only two rooms. In the hall. I can still get that stuffy smell that had been locked up there for a hundred and fifty years—up the bare stairs. On the landing there was a tap dripping into an old leaden trough that had been there since the year dot. I could hear the machine whirring. I remember I stopped at the window and picked a dead leaf from the geraniums. I went up the last few steps and I lifted the latch. My father was bent over the machine; specs on his forehead, black skeins of thread around his neck, bare arms. My mother was wrapped in shawls in the old basket chair before the fire. I could draw that room; the two machines, my bed in one corner, my dinner waiting on the table, the tailor's goose[14] heating on the grate. The machine stopped.

"'In the name of God what happened to you, boy?' says my father. 'Is there anything wrong? What kept you? Your poor mother there is out of her head worrying about you.'

"'Ah, I was just kept in, sir,' says I, passing it off as airily as I could. 'How are you, Mummy?'

"The old man caught me by the arm.

"'Kept in?' says he, and the way he said it you'd think I was after coming out of the lockup. 'Why were you kept in?'

"'Ah, 'twas just a bit of Euclid I didn't know, that's all.'

"It was only then I noticed that the mother was asleep. I put my hand to my lips begging him not to waken her. He let a roar out of him.

"'A nice disgrace! Kept in because you didn't know your Euclid!'

"'What is it, what is it, Frankie?' she says, waking up in a fright. 'What did they do to you, boy?'

"''Twas nothing at all, Mummy, just that

---

12. *All Ireland Final*, the official championship soccer match. 13. *office*, a body of prayers, divided into various parts, that a priest or monk must read daily. 14. *goose*, a tailor's smoothing iron.

I didn't know a bit of Euclid. I had to stay back to learn it.'

" 'A nice how d'ye do! And why didn't you know Euclid?'—and he had me up against the wall and his fist raised.

" 'It wasn't really Euclid at all, Father. It was all Angelo's fault. It was all politics. He divided the class into All Fors and Mollies and because the All Fors won he kept me in out of spite. Honestly, that's all it was, Mummy, there was nothing else to it.'

" 'Holy God,' whispers the old man. 'So it wasn't only the Euclid, but lettin' down John Redmond in front of the whole class. That's what you did, is it?'

" 'Oh, for God's sake, Billy,' says the mother, 'don't mind John Redmond. 'Tis little John Redmond or any other John Redmond cares about us, 'tis the work, the work. What are we slaving for, boy, day and night, and all the rest of it? There's your poor father working himself to the bone to send you through school. And so on. Nothing matters, boy, but the work! The work!'

" ' 'Tisn't only the work,' says the old man. ' 'Tisn't only the work,' and he was sobbing over it. 'But to think of poor John Redmond fighting night after night for Ireland, standing up there in the House of Commons, and you—you brat—couldn't even do a sum in Euclid to stand by him! In your own school! Before everybody! Look at him,' he wails, with his arm up to the picture of John Redmond on the wall, with his hooked nose and his jowls like an old countrywoman. 'Look at the dacent gentleman. A man that never let down his side. A gentleman to the tips of his toes if there ever was one. And you couldn't do a simple sum in Euclid to help him! Th'other fellows could do it. The All Fors could do it. But my son couldn't do it!'

"And with that he gave me a crack that nearly sent me into the fire.

"The end of it was that I was on my knees with my head on the mother's lap, blubbering, and the old man with his two hands up to John Redmond, and the tears flowing down his face like rain, and the mother wailing, 'Won't you promise, Frankie, won't you prom-ise to work, boy?' and I promising and promising anything if she'd only stop crying.

"That was the moment that I swore to myself to get on. But wait! You won't understand why until I've finished.

"The next day Angelo took the same problem, at the same hour, and he asked me to do it again. Now, kids are no fools. I knew by the look on his face why he asked me to do it. He wanted to make friends with me, to have everything the same as if yesterday had never happened. But he didn't know what had happened inside in me the night before. I went through the problem, step by step—I knew it perfectly—down to the Q.E.D.[15]

" 'Now, isn't it a pity, Frankie,' he says, smiling at me, 'that you wouldn't do that yesterday?'

" 'Oh,' I said, in a very lordly, tired voice, 'I just didn't feel like it.'

"I knew what was coming to me, and I wanted it, and to make sure that I got it I gave him that sort of insolent smile that drives grown-ups mad with children. I've seen that smile on my own children's faces now and again, and when I see it I have to go outside the door for fear I'd knock them the length of the room. That is what Angelo did to me. I got up off the floor and I sat back in my place and I had the same insolent smile on my face.

" 'Now, if you please,' says Angelo, reaching for his cane, and he was as white as his teeth, 'will you kindly do the next problem?'

"I did it, step by step, calm as a breeze, down to the Q.E.D. I'd prepared it the night before.

" 'Right,' says Angelo, and his voice was trembling with rage. 'Do the next problem.'

"I had him where I wanted him. He was acting unfairly, and he knew it, and the class knew it. I had that problem prepared too. Just to tease him I made a couple of slips, but just as he'd be reaching for the cane I'd correct them. I was a beast, but he'd made me a beast. I did it, down to the Q.E.D., and I smiled at him, and he looked at me. We both

15. *Q. E. D.*, which was to be proved (for the Latin *quod erat demonstrandum*). In Euclidean geometry textbooks this sign is traditionally used after the conclusion.

knew that from that moment it was war to the knife.

"I worked that night until twelve o'clock; and I worked every night until I left school until twelve o'clock. I never gave him a chance. I had to, because until the day I left that place he followed me. He followed me into Middle Grade. And into Senior Grade. He made several efforts to make it up with me, but I wouldn't let him. He was too useful to me the other way. I sat for the Civil Service[16] and I got first place in the British Isles in three subjects out of five, geometry, chemistry, and history, third in mathematics, fifth in German. I did worst in German because I didn't have Angelo for German. I think I can say without arrogance that I was the most brilliant student that ever passed out of West Abbey School."

Sir Francis leaned back.

"You must have worked like a slave."

"I did."

"Well, it was worth it!"

He looked out over the fields which were now becoming colorless in the falling dusk and his voice sank to a murmur, as if he were thinking aloud.

"I don't know. For me? Yes, perhaps. I had no youth. For them? I don't know. I didn't work to get on, I worked to get out. I didn't work to please my mother or my father. I hated my mother and I hated my father from the day they made me cry. They did the one thing to me that I couldn't stand up against. They did what that little cur Angelo planned they'd do. They broke my spirit with pity. They made me cry with pity. Oh, I needn't say I didn't go on hating them. A boy doesn't nourish hatred. He has his life before him. I was too sorry for them. But that's where they lost everything. A boy can be sorry for people who are weak and pitiable, but he can't respect them. And you can't love people if you don't respect them. I pitied them and I despised them. That's the truth."

He leaned back again.

"You don't look like a man whose spirit was ever broken," I laughed, a little embarrassed.

"The spirit is always broken by pity. Oh, I patched it up pretty well. I made a man of myself. Or, rather," he said with passion, "with what was left of myself after they'd robbed me of my youth that I spent slaving to get away from them."

"You'd have slaved anyway. You were full of ambition."

"If I did I'd have done it for ambition alone. I tell you I did it for pity and hate and pride and contempt and God knows what other reason. No. They broke my spirit all right. I know it. The thing I've put in its place is a very different thing. I know it. I've met plenty of men who've got along on ambition and they're whole men. I know it. I'm full of what they put into me—pity and hate and rage and pride and contempt for the weak and anger against all bullying, but, above all, pity, chock-a-block with it. I know it. Pity is the most disintegrating of all human emotions. It's the most disgusting of all human emotions. I know it."

"What happened to Angelo?"

"I don't know. Nor care. Died, I suppose."

"And . . . your father?"

"Fifteen years after I left Cork he died. I never saw him. I brought my mother to live with me in London."

"That was good. You were fond of her."

"I was sorry for her. That's what she asked me for when I was a boy. I've been sorry for her all my life. Ah!"

His eyes lit up. I looked sideways to see what had arrested him. It was the first lights of Cork, and, mingling with the smoke over the roofs, the January night. Behind the violet hills the last cinder of the sun made a saffron horizon. As the train roared into the tunnel we could see children playing in the streets below the steep embankment, and he was staring at them thirstily, and I must have imagined that I heard their happy shouts. Then the tunnel opened and swallowed us.

There were no lights in the carriage. All I could see was the occasional glow of his cigarette. Presently the glow moved and my knee was touched. His voice said: "She's

---

16. *sat for the Civil Service*, took the Civil Service examinations.

with me on this train. My mother. I'm bringing her back to Cork."

"Will she like that?"

"She's dead."

The train roared on through the tunnel. As we passed under the first tunnel vent a drip of water fell on the roof. The tiny glow swelled and ebbed softly.

"I'm very sorry."

His voice said, in the darkness: "I meant to bury her in London. But I couldn't do it. Silly, wasn't it?"

After a while another drip of water splashed on the roof. The windows were gray.

"You did the kind thing."

His voice was so low that I barely heard it. "Kind!"

In a few more minutes we were drawing up in steam alongside the lighted platform. He was standing up, leaning over his hatbox. From it he lifted a silk topper and a dark scarf. He put on his black frock coat. "Goodby," he said politely, and beckoned for a porter.

From the platform I watched him walk down towards the luggage van where a tiny group already stood waiting. They were all poor people. There was a bent old woman there in a black shawl, and three or four humble-looking men in bowler hats and caps. As I watched him bow to them and doff his hat to the old woman and introduce himself, the yellow pine-and-brass of the coffin was already emerging from the van and the undertaker's men in their brass-buttoned coats were taking it from the porters. Among his poor relations he walked reverently, bareheaded, out into the dark station yard.

They slid the coffin into the motor hearse; he showed his relatives into the carriages, and, stooping, he went in after them. Then the little procession moved slowly out into the streets on its way to whatever chapel would take her for the night into its mortuary.

To increase understanding

1. At the point at which Sir Francis begins to tell his story the narrator comments: "As he began my heart sank. . . . But as he went on I felt mean and rebuked" (page 563, column 2, paragraph 9). Explain the narrator's sentiments.

2. (a) What does Sir Francis mean by "getting somewhere"? (b) What episode had made this aim supremely important to him? (c) What price has Sir Francis paid for achieving his ambition?

3. (a) Explain Sir Francis' own analysis of his character. (b) What does the fact that he is bringing his dead mother back to Cork indicate about his character? (c) Does his action in this situation tend to support or contradict his own view of his character? Explain.

4. (a) What is the key word in the quotation that prefaces the story? (b) In what way does the quotation illuminate the ideas of the story itself?

5. (a) What is the setting at the moment that Sir Francis makes his dramatic announcement that he is bringing his mother home—dead? (b) How does O'Faolain use the setting to heighten the drama of the announcement?

6. (a) What is the narrative point of view of "Up the Bare Stairs"? (b) What is the function of the narrator?

7. What indications are there in "Up the Bare Stairs" of O'Faolain's interest in (a) Gaelic and (b) Irish politics?

Mary Lavin

STORY OF THE WIDOW'S SON

Mary Lavin   1912—

Dairmuid Russell, the son of George Russell (page 626), has called Mary Lavin "the most promising of the younger Irish writers." With the gifts of the born storyteller she combines a penetrating insight into the human heart and an ability to see beauty in the everyday world. Although Miss Lavin was born in Walpole, Massachusetts, she must be counted as an Irish author, for she was born of Irish parents and moved to Ireland at the age of ten, where she has since lived. At first she looked toward a career in research—she received her master's degree from the National University of Ireland for a thesis on Jane Austen—but the publication of one of her short stories changed the direction of her work to the writing of fiction. The story was noticed by Lord Dunsany, who encouraged her to produce a collection. *Tales from Bective Bridge,* which appeared in 1942 with a commendatory preface by Lord Dunsany, was an immediate critical success. Although Miss Lavin has written good novels, among them *The House in Clewe Street* (1945) and *Mary O'Grady* (1950), she continues to be most successful in the short-story form.

This is the story of a widow's son, but it is a story that has two endings.

There was once a widow, living in a small neglected village at the foot of a steep hill. She had only one son, but he was the meaning of her life. She lived for his sake. She wore herself out working for him. Every day she made a hundred sacrifices in order to keep him at a good school in the town, four miles away, because there was a better teacher there than the village dullard that had taught herself.

She made great plans for Packy, but she did not tell him about her plans. Instead she threatened him, day and night, that if he didn't turn out well, she would put him to work on the roads, or in the quarry under the hill.

But as the years went by, everyone in the village, and even Packy himself, could tell by the way she watched him out of sight in the morning, and watched to see him come into sight in the evening, that he was the beat of her heart, and that her gruff words were only a cover for her pride and her joy in him.

It was for Packy's sake that she walked for hours along the road, letting her cow graze the long acre of the wayside grass, in order to spare the few poor blades that pushed up through the stones in her own field. It was for his sake she walked back and forth to the town to sell a few cabbages as soon as ever they were fit. It was for his sake that she got up in the cold dawning hours to gather mushrooms that would take the place of foods that had to be bought with money. She bent her back daily to make every penny she could, and as often happens, she made more by industry, out of her few bald acres, than many of the farmers around her made out of their great bearded meadows. Out of the money she made by selling eggs alone, she paid for Packy's clothes and for the greater number of his books.

When Packy was fourteen, he was in the

Reprinted by permission of Mary Lavin; from *Irish Harvest.*

last class in the school, and the master had great hopes of his winning a scholarship to a big college in the city. He was getting to be a tall lad, and his features were beginning to take a strong cast. His character was strengthening too, under his mother's sharp tongue. The people of the village were beginning to give him the same respect they gave to the sons of the farmers who came from their fine colleges in the summer, with blue suits and bright ties. And whenever they spoke to the widow they praised him up to the skies.

One day in June, when the air was so heavy the scent that rose up from the grass was imprisoned under the low clouds and hung in the air, the widow was waiting at the gate for Packy. There had been no rain for some days and the hens and chickens were pecking irritably at the dry ground and wandering up and down the road in bewilderment.

A neighbor passed.

"Waiting for Packy?" said the neighbor, pleasantly, and he stood for a minute to take off his hat and wipe the sweat of the day from his face. He was an old man.

"It's a hot day!" he said. "It will be a hard push for Packy on that battered old bike of his. I wouldn't like to have to face into four miles on a day like this!"

"Packy would travel three times that distance if there was a book at the other end of the road!" said the widow, with the pride of those who cannot read more than a line or two without wearying.

The minutes went by slowly. The widow kept looking up at the sun.

"I suppose the heat is better than the rain!" she said, at last.

"The heat can do a lot of harm, too, though," said the neighbor, absent-mindedly, as he pulled a long blade of grass from between the stones of the wall and began to chew the end of it. "You could get sunstroke on a day like this!" He looked up at the sun. "The sun is a terror," he said. "It could cause you to drop down dead like a stone!"

The widow strained out further over the gate. She looked up the hill in the direction of the town.

"He will have a good cool breeze on his face coming down the hill, at any rate," she said.

The man looked up the hill. "That's true. On the hottest day of the year you would get a cool breeze coming down that hill on a bicycle. You would feel the air streaming past your cheeks like silk. And in the winter it's like two knives flashing to either side of you, and peeling off your skin like you'd peel the bark off a sally-rod!"[1] He chewed the grass meditatively. "That must be one of the steepest hills in Ireland," he said. "That hill is a hill worthy of the name of a hill." He took the grass out of his mouth. "It's my belief," he said, earnestly looking at the widow —"it's my belief that that hill is to be found marked with a name in the Ordnance Survey map!"

"If that's the case," said the widow, "Packy will be able to tell you all about it. When it isn't a book he has in his hand it's a map."

"Is that so?" said the man. "That's interesting. A map is a great thing. A map is not an ordinary thing. It isn't everyone can make out a map."

The widow wasn't listening.

"I think I see Packy!" she said, and she opened the wooden gate and stepped out into the roadway.

At the top of the hill there was glitter of spokes as a bicycle came into sight. Then there was a flash of blue jersey as Packy came flying downward, gripping the handlebars of the bike, with his bright hair blown back from his forehead. The hill was so steep, and he came down so fast, that it seemed to the man and woman at the bottom of the hill that he was not moving at all, but that it was the bright trees and bushes, the bright ditches and wayside grasses that were streaming away to either side of him.

The hens and chickens clucked and squawked and ran along the road looking for a safe place in the ditches. They ran to either side with feminine fuss and chatter. Packy waved to his mother. He came nearer and nearer. They could see the freckles on his face.

---

1. *sally-rod*, a willow twig.

"Shoo!" cried Packy, at the squawking hens that had not yet left the roadway. They ran with their long necks straining forward.

"Shoo!" said Packy's mother, lifting her apron and flapping it in the air to frighten them out of his way.

It was only afterwards, when the harm was done, that the widow began to think that it might, perhaps, have been the flapping of her own apron that frightened the old clucking hen, and sent her flying out over the garden wall into the middle of the road.

The old hen appeared suddenly on top of the grassy ditch and looked with a distraught eye at the hens and chickens as they ran to right and left. Her own feathers began to stand out from her. She craned her neck forward and gave a distracted squawk, and fluttered down into the middle of the hot dusty road.

Packy jammed on the brakes. The widow screamed. There was a flurry of white feathers and a spurt of blood. The bicycle swerved and fell. Packy was thrown over the handlebars.

It was such a simple accident that, although the widow screamed, and although the old man looked around to see if there was help near, neither of them thought that Packy was very badly hurt, but when they ran over and lifted his head, and saw that he could not speak, they wiped the blood from his face and looked around, desperately, to measure the distance they would have to carry him.

It was only a few yards to the door of the cottage, but Packy was dead before they got him across the threshold.

"He's only in a weakness!" screamed the widow, and she urged the crowd that had gathered outside the door to do something for him. "Get a doctor!" she cried, pushing a young laborer towards the door. "Hurry! Hurry! The doctor will bring him around."

But the neighbors that kept coming in the door, quickly, from all sides, were crossing themselves, one after another, and falling on their knees, as soon as they laid eyes on the boy, stretched out flat on the bed, with the dust and dirt and the sweat marks of life on his dead face.

When at last the widow was convinced that her son was dead, the other women had to hold her down. She waved her arms and cried out aloud, and wrestled to get free. She wanted to wring the neck of every hen in the yard.

"I'll kill every one of them. What good are they to me, now? All the hens in the world aren't worth one drop of human blood. That old clucking hen wasn't worth more than six shillings, at the very most. What is six shillings? Is it worth poor Packy's life?"

But after a time she stopped raving, and looked from one face to another.

"Why didn't he ride over the old hen?" she asked. "Why did he try to save an old hen that wasn't worth more than six shillings? Didn't he know he was worth more to his mother than an old hen that would be going into the pot one of these days? Why did he do it? Why did he put on the brakes going down one of the worst hills in the country? Why? Why?"

The neighbors patted her arm.

"There now!" they said. "There now!" and that was all they could think of saying, and they said it over and over again. "There now! There now!"

And years afterwards, whenever the widow spoke of her son Packy to the neighbors who dropped in to keep her company for an hour or two, she always had the same question to ask—the same tireless question.

"Why did he put the price of an old clucking hen above the price of his own life?"

And the people always gave the same answer.

"There now!" they said, "There now!" And they sat as silently as the widow herself, looking into the fire.

But surely some of those neighbors must have been stirred to wonder what would have happened had Packy not yielded to his impulse of fear, and had, instead, ridden boldly over the old clucking hen? And surely some of them must have stared into the flames and pictured the scene of the accident again, altering a detail here and there as they did so, and giving the story a different end. For these people knew the widow, and they knew

Packy, and when you know people well it is as easy to guess what they would say and do in certain circumstances as it is to remember what they actually did say and do in other circumstances. In fact it is sometimes easier to invent than to remember accurately, and were this not so two great branches of creative art would wither in an hour: the art of the storyteller and the art of the gossip. So, perhaps, if I try to tell you what I myself think might have happened had Packy killed that cackling old hen, you will not accuse me of abusing my privileges as a writer. After all, what I am about to tell you is no more of a fiction than what I have already told, and I lean no heavier now upon your credulity than, with your full consent, I did in the first instance.

And moreover, in many respects the new story is the same as the old.

It begins in the same way too. There is the widow grazing her cow by the wayside, and walking the long roads to the town, weighted down with sacks of cabbages that will pay for Packy's schooling. There she is, fussing over Packy in the mornings in case he would be late for school. There she is in the evening watching the battered clock on the dresser for the hour when he will appear on the top of the hill at his return. And there too, on a hot day in June, is the old laboring man coming up the road, and pausing to talk to her, as she stood at the door. There he is dragging a blade of grass from between the stones of the wall, and putting it between his teeth to chew, before he opens his mouth.

And when he opens his mouth at last it is to utter the same remark.

"Waiting for Packy?" said the old man, and then he took off his hat and wiped the sweat from his forehead. It will be remembered that he was an old man. "It's a hot day," he said.

"It's very hot," said the widow, looking anxiously up the hill. "It's a hot day to push a bicycle four miles along a bad road with the dust rising to choke you, and sun striking spikes off the handlebars!"

"The heat is better than the rain, all the same," said the old man.

"I suppose it is," said the widow. "All the

same, there were days when Packy came home with the rain dried into his clothes so bad they stood up stiff like boards when he took them off. They stood up stiff like boards against the wall, for all the world as if he was still standing in them!"

"Is that so?" said the old man. "You may be sure he got a good petting on those days. There is no son like a widow's son. A ewe lamb!"

"Is it Packy?" said the widow, in disgust. "Packy never got a day's petting since the day he was born. I made up my mind from the first that I'd never make a soft one out of him."

The widow looked up the hill again, and set herself to raking the gravel outside the gate as if she were in the road for no other purpose. Then she gave another look up the hill.

"Here he is now!" she said, and she raised such a cloud of dust with the rake that they could hardly see the glitter of the bicycle spokes, and the flash of blue jersey as Packy came down the hill at a breakneck speed.

Nearer and nearer he came, faster and faster, waving his hand to the widow, shouting at the hens to leave the way!

The hens ran for the ditches, stretching their necks in gawky terror. And then, as the last hen squawked into the ditch, the way was clear for a moment before the whirling silver spokes.

Then, unexpectedly, up from nowhere it seemed, came an old clucking hen and, clucking despairingly, it stood for a moment on the top of the wall and then rose into the air with the clumsy flight of a ground fowl.

Packy stopped whistling. The widow screamed. Packy yelled and the widow flapped her apron. Then Packy swerved the bicycle, and a cloud of dust rose from the braked wheel.

For a minute it could not be seen what exactly had happened, but Packy put his foot down and dragged it along the ground in the dust till he brought the bicycle to a sharp stop. He threw the bicycle down with a clatter on the hard road and ran back. The widow could not bear to look. She threw her apron over her head.

"He's killed the clucking hen!" she said. "He's killed her! He's killed her!" and then she let the apron fall back into place, and began to run up the hill herself. The old man spat out the blade of grass that he had been chewing and ran after the woman.

"Did you kill it?" screamed the widow, and as she got near enough to see the blood and feathers she raised her arm over her head, and her fist was clenched till the knuckles shone white. Packy cowered down over the carcass of the fowl and hunched up his shoulders as if to shield himself from a blow. His legs were spattered with blood, and the brown and white feathers of the dead hen were stuck to his hands, and stuck to his clothes, and they were strewn all over the road. Some of the short white inner feathers were still swirling with the dust in the air.

"I couldn't help it, Mother. I couldn't help it. I didn't see her till it was too late!"

The widow caught up the hen and examined it all over, holding it by the bone of the breast, and letting the long neck dangle. Then, catching it by the leg, she raised it suddenly above her head, and brought down the bleeding body on the boy's back, in blow after blow, spattering the blood all over his face and his hands, over his clothes and over the white dust of the road around him.

"How dare you lie to me!" she screamed, gaspingly, between the blows. "You saw the hen. I know you saw it. You stopped whistling! You called out! We were watching you. We saw." She turned upon the old man. "Isn't that right?" she demanded. "He saw the hen, didn't he? He saw it?"

"It looked that way," said the old man, uncertainly, his eye on the dangling fowl in the widow's hand.

"There you are!" said the widow. She threw the hen down on the road. "You saw the hen in front of you on the road, as plain as you see it now," she accused, "but you wouldn't stop to save it because you were in too big a hurry home to fill your belly! Isn't that so?"

"No, Mother. No! I saw her all right but it was too late to do anything."

"He admits now that he saw it," said the widow, turning and nodding triumphantly at the onlookers who had gathered at the sound of the shouting.

"I never denied seeing it!" said the boy, appealing to the onlookers as to his judges.

"He doesn't deny it!" screamed the widow. "He stands there as brazen as you like, and admits for all the world to hear that he saw the hen as plain as the nose on his face, and he rode over it without a thought!"

"But what else could I do?" said the boy, throwing out his hand; appealing to the crowd now, and now appealing to the widow. "If I'd put on the brakes going down the hill at such a speed I would have been put over the handlebars!"

"And what harm would that have done you?" screamed the widow. "I often saw you taking a toss when you were wrestling with Jimmy Mack and I heard no complaints afterwards, although your elbows and knees would be running blood, and your face scraped like a gridiron!" She turned to the crowd. "That's as true as God. I often saw him come in with his nose spouting blood like a pump, and one eye closed as tight as the eye of a corpse. My hand was often stiff for a week from sopping out wet cloths to put poultices on him and try to bring his face back to rights again." She swung back to Packy again. "You're not afraid of a fall when you go climbing trees, are you? You're not afraid to go up on the roof after a cat, are you? Oh, there's more in this than you want me to know. I can see that. You killed that hen on purpose—that's what I believe! You're tired of going to school. You want to get out of going away to college. That's it! You think if you kill the few poor hens we have there will be no money in the box when the time comes to pay for books and classes. That's it!" Packy began to redden.

"It's late in the day for me to be thinking of things like that," he said. "It's long ago I should have started those tricks if that was the way I felt. But it's not true. I want to go to college. The reason I was coming down the hill so fast was to tell you that I got the scholarship. The teacher told me as I was leaving the schoolhouse. That's why I was pedaling so hard. That's why I was whistling. That's why I was waving my hand. Didn't you see me waving my hand from once I came in sight of the top of the hill?"

The widow's hands fell to her side. The wind of words died down within her and left her flat and limp. She didn't know what to say. She could feel the neighbors staring at her. She wished that they were gone away about their business. She wanted to throw out her arms to the boy, to drag him against her heart and hug him like a small child. But she thought of how the crowd would look at each other and nod and snigger. A ewe lamb! She didn't want to satisfy them. If she gave in to her feelings now they would know how much she had been counting on his getting the scholarship. She wouldn't please them! She wouldn't satisfy them!

She looked at Packy, and when she saw him standing there before her, spattered with the furious feathers and crude blood of the dead hen, she felt a fierce disappointment for the boy's own disappointment, and a fierce resentment against him for killing the hen on this day of all days, and spoiling the great news of his success.

Her mind was in confusion. She started at the blood on his face, and all at once it seemed as if the blood was a bad omen of the future that was for him. Disappointment, fear, resentment, and above all defiance, raised themselves within her like screeching animals. She looked from Packy to the onlookers.

"Scholarship! Scholarship!" she sneered, putting as much derision as she could into her voice and expression.

"I suppose you think you are a great fellow now? I suppose you think you are independent now? I suppose you think you can go off with yourself now, and look down on your poor slave of a mother who scraped and sweated for you with her cabbages and her hens? I suppose you think to yourself that it doesn't matter now whether the hens are alive or dead? Is that the way? Well, let me tell you this! You're not as independent as you think. The scholarship may pay for your books and your teacher's fees but who will pay for your clothes? Ah ha, you forgot that,

didn't you?" She put her hands on her hips. Packy hung his head. He no longer appealed to the gawking neighbors. They might have been able to save him from blows but he knew enough about life to know that no one could save him from shame.

The widow's heart burned at sight of his shamed face, as her heart burned with grief, but her temper too burned fiercer and fiercer, and she came to a point at which nothing could quell the blaze till it had burned itself out. "Who'll buy your suits?" she yelled. "Who'll buy your boots?" She paused to think of more humiliating accusations. "Who'll buy your breeches?" She paused again and her teeth bit against each other. What would wound deepest? What shame could she drag upon him? "Who'll buy your nightshirts or will you sleep in your skin?"

The neighbors laughed at that, and the tension was broken. The widow herself laughed. She held her sides and laughed, and as she laughed everything seemed to take on a newer and simpler significance. Things were not as bad as they seemed a moment before. She wanted Packy to laugh too. She looked at him. But as she looked at Packy her heart turned cold with a strange new fear.

"Get into the house!" she said, giving him a push ahead of her. She wanted him safe under her own roof. She wanted to get him away from the gaping neighbors. She hated them, man, woman and child. She felt that if they had not been there things would have been different. And she wanted to get away from the sight of the blood on the road. She wanted to mash a few potatoes and make a bit of potato cake for Packy. That would comfort him. He loved that.

Packy hardly touched the food. And even after he had washed and scrubbed himself there were stains of blood turning up in the most unexpected places: behind his ears, under his fingernails, inside the cuff of his sleeve.

"Put on your good clothes," said the widow, making a great effort to be gentle, but her manners had become as twisted and as hard as the branches of the trees across the road from her, and even the kindly offers she made sounded harsh. The boy sat on the chair in a slumped position that kept her nerves on edge and set up a further conflict of irritation and love in her heart. She hated to see him slumping there in the chair, not asking to go outside the door, but still she was uneasy whenever he as much as looked in the direction of the door. She felt safe while he was under the roof; inside the lintel under her eyes.

Next day she went in to wake him for school, but his room was empty; his bed had not been slept in, and when she ran out into the yard and called him everywhere there was no answer. She ran up and down. She called at the houses of the neighbors but he was not in any house. And she thought she could hear sniggering behind her in each house that she left, as she ran to another one. He wasn't in the village. He wasn't in the town. The master of the school said that she should let the police have a description of him. He said he never met a boy as sensitive as Packy. A boy like that took strange notions into his head from time to time.

The police did their best but there was no news of Packy that night. A few days later there was a letter saying that he was well. He asked his mother to notify the master that he would not be coming back, so that some other boy could claim the scholarship. He said that he would send the price of the hen as soon as he made some money.

Another letter in a few weeks said that he had got a job on a trawler, and that he would not be able to write very often but that he would put aside some of his pay every week and send it to his mother whenever he got into port. He said that he wanted to pay her back for all she had done for him. He gave no address. He kept his promise about the money but he never gave any address when he wrote. . . . And so the people may have let their thoughts run on, as they sat by the fire with the widow, many a night, listening to her complaining voice saying the same thing over and over. "Why did he put the price of an old hen above the price of his own life?" And it is possible that their version of the story has a certain element of truth about it

too. Perhaps all our actions have this double quality about them; this possibility of alternative, and that it is only by careful watching and absolute sincerity, that we follow the path that is destined for us, and, no matter how tragic that may be, it is better than the tragedy we bring upon ourselves.

To increase understanding

1. In the first sentence of the story Mary Lavin writes, "This is the story of a widow's son, but it is a story that has two endings." (a) What is the first ending? (b) What is the second ending? (c) What detail is altered to produce this second ending? (d) What subtle distinction is there between "story of a widow's son" and "story that has two endings"?

2. In "The Story of the Widow's Son" Mary Lavin uses the technique of the storyteller narrating an old tale to a group of neighbors. (a) Cite passages in the story up to the first ending (page 571 column 2, paragraph 10) that are reminiscent of the folk tale. (b) What idea does this part of the story give you about the relations between the widow and her son? (c) If, as in a conventional tale, the first ending had concluded the story, how would you interpret the widow's remark: "That old clucking hen wasn't worth more than six shillings, at the very most. What is six shillings? Is it worth poor Packy's life?" (page 571, column 2, paragraph 2).

3. Reread the paragraph beginning "but surely some of these neighbors. . ." (page 571, column 2, paragraph 11). (a) Why does the author here speak directly to the reader? (b) What is the function of this paragraph?

4. In the paragraph noted in the preceding question, the author says some of the neighbors must have "pictured the scene of the accident again, altering a detail here and there as they did so." (a) What significant changes in the conversation between the widow and the old laborer prepare for the second ending? (b) What important change is there in the description of the coming of the old clucking hen? (c) In the context of the second telling of the story, how do you interpret the widow's earlier remarks about the value of an "old clucking hen"?

5. (a) Trace the widow's emotions from the time she discovers that the old hen is dead until she finds that Packy has disappeared. (b) What is the importance of the presence of the neighbors?

6. Explain the meaning of the last two sentences in the story.

Twentieth-Century Art

The same forces that brought about radical changes in the writing of fiction in this century acted upon other forms of art as well. Nowhere is the break with the past more obvious than in modern painting and sculpture. A first glance at the illustrations on these pages reveals the marked contrast between modern English art—which is part of an international movement—and previous art, as illustrated earlier in this book. The one aspect of modern art that, more than any other, produces this contrast is the marked tendency of modern painters to minimize or eliminate recognizable subjects.

In its beginnings modern art was in part a revolt against the somewhat artificial rules developed by both the British and French academies of art. Many modern painters felt that the public in general, since they had learned to admire paintings only insofar as they followed these rules, had largely lost the capacity to enjoy the paintings themselves. Through the efforts of the academies people had come to look primarily for flawless realism and high moral tone in art. Modern artists argued, however, that the beauty of a work of art is really similar to the beauty of a natural object. A sunset, they said, is not admired because one can find in it a resemblance to a camel or a weasel or a whale, or because it is uplifting; it is admired for its own beau-

ties of form and color. A painting, they argued, should be admired for similar reasons—not because it looks like a man or a dog or a landscape, or because it has a high moral tone, but because it is simply beautiful, moving, or otherwise valuable in itself. To prevent the viewer from looking for the wrong things in their paintings many of these painters eliminated the subject altogether, while others transformed the subject to emphasize its abstract qualities of form, color, pattern of motion, and so forth.

The sudden liberation from outmoded, restrictive rules unleashed a bewildering variety of styles. Artists felt free to experiment widely with all kinds of materials and techniques in an effort to find the most direct way of ex-

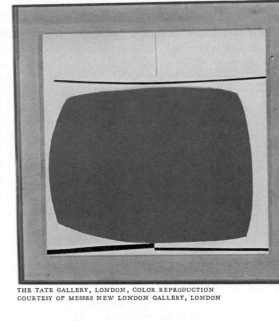

THE TATE GALLERY, LONDON, COLOR REPRODUCTION
COURTESY OF MESSRS NEW LONDON GALLERY, LONDON

Right below: Sculptor Henry Moore uses the human figure as a starting point for most of his expressive forms.
Right above: Yellow Abstract, *by Victor Pasmore, explores basic qualities of color, mass, and line.*

MARLBOROUGH FINE ART, LONDON

pressing modern values. Experimentation has ranged from the creation of visual forms for their own sakes to a fanatically detailed realism; from attempts to depict nightmares, to attempts to express pure thought processes directly; from the intellectual analysis of an object into lines and planes to a direct, emotional record of the motion of the painter's body. There have also been many attempts to apply the techniques of the early experimenters to more conventional subjects. That these experimental efforts have often failed is not surprising; what is surprising is that they have succeeded so often, and that they have succeeded so well as to make the first half of the twentieth century a rich period in the history of English, and of Western, art.

Above: The subject predominates in the Industrial Landscape *by William Ware, though it is distorted to emphasize the artist's experience of it. Below: Interlocking planes of subtle texture and color make up this painting by Ben Nicholson, though a suggestion of subject—glassware on a table—remains.*

Katherine Mansfield
MISS BRILL

Katherine Mansfield   1888-1923

Kathleen Mansfield Beauchamp, who wrote under the name of Katherine Mansfield, was the daughter of a banker in Wellington, New Zealand. By 1908, having completed her formal education at Queen's College, London, she had determined on writing as a career. Depressed by the failure of a brief, unhappy marriage, by difficulty in getting her first stories published, and by serious financial worries, she joined a traveling operatic troupe. The rigors of this occupation undermined her delicate health, and she was forced to spend much of the rest of her short life traveling in search of relief from the tuberculosis that eventually developed. It has been suggested that her consciousness of the imminence of death heightened her awareness and helps account for the highly sensitive style for which her writing is noted.

The first resort Miss Mansfield sought out was in Germany. Here she wrote her first important stories, which were collected in book form under the title *In a German Pension*. Here also she met the critic John Middleton Murry, with whom she collaborated on a short-lived literary review, and whom she later married.

After the collapse of the magazine, Miss Mansfield wrote no more for several years. During the war year 1915 her brother Leslie, on furlough from his army duties in France, visited her in London. Hours of quiet and happy talk about their childhood in New Zealand rekindled Katherine's desire to write. When Leslie was killed in action shortly thereafter, she dedicated her life to writing in tribute to the "lovely time when we were both alive." In 1920 she achieved her first marked success with *Bliss and Other Stories*. This was followed in 1922 by her best-known collection, *The Garden Party and Other Stories*, which included "Miss Brill." *The Dove's Nest* followed in 1923.

Most of Miss Mansfield's stories are set in New Zealand or on the French Riviera or in London, but the locale means little; the mood and the psychological understanding are everything. The true objective of literature, she once wrote, is that of "subjecting its readers to a real and at the same time illuminating experience."

Although it was so brilliantly fine —the blue sky powdered with gold and great spots of light like white wine splashed over the Jardins Publiques[1]—Miss Brill was glad that she had decided on her fur. The air was motionless, but when you opened your mouth there was just a faint chill, like the chill from a glass of iced water before you sip, and now and again a leaf came drifting—from nowhere, from the sky.

Miss Brill put up her hand and touched her fur. Dear little thing! It was nice to feel it again. She had taken it out of its box that afternoon, shaken out the moth powder, given it a good brush, and rubbed the life back into the dim little eyes. "What has been happening to me?" said the sad little eyes. Oh, how sweet it was to see them snap at her again from the red eider down! . . . But the nose, which was of some black composition, wasn't at all firm. It must have had a knock, somehow. Never mind—a little dab of black sealing wax when the time came— when it was absolutely necessary. . . . Little rogue! Yes, she really felt like that about it. Little rogue biting its tail just by her left ear. She could have taken it off and laid it on her lap and stroked it. She felt a tingling in her hands and arms, but that came from walking, she supposed. And when she breathed, something light and sad—no, not sad, exactly— something gentle seemed to move in her bosom.

There were a number of people out this afternoon, far more than last Sunday. And the band sounded louder and gayer. That was because the Season had begun. For although the band played all the year round on Sundays, out of season it was never the same. It was like someone playing with only the family to listen; it didn't care how it played if there weren't any strangers present. Wasn't the conductor wearing a new coat, too? She was sure it was new. He scraped with his foot and flapped his arms like a rooster about to crow, and the bandsmen sitting in the green rotunda blew out their cheeks and glared at the music.

Now there came a little "flutey" bit—very pretty!—a little chain of bright drops. She was sure it would be repeated. It was; she lifted her head and smiled.

Only two people shared her "special" seat; a fine old man in a velvet coat, his hands clasped over a huge carved walking stick, and a big old woman, sitting upright, with a roll of knitting on her embroidered apron. They did not speak. This was disappointing, for Miss Brill always looked forward to the conversation. She had become really quite expert, she thought, at listening as though she didn't listen, at sitting in other people's lives just for a minute while they talked round her.

She glanced, sideways, at the old couple. Perhaps they would go soon. Last Sunday, too, hadn't been as interesting as usual. An Englishman and his wife, he wearing a dreadful Panama hat and she button boots. And she'd gone on the whole time about how she ought to wear spectacles; she knew she needed them; but that it was no good getting any; they'd be sure to break and they'd never keep on. And he'd been so patient. He'd suggested everything—gold rims, the kind that curved around your ears, little pads inside the bridge. No, nothing would please her. "They'll always be sliding down my nose!" Miss Brill had wanted to shake her.

The old people sat on the bench, still as statues. Never mind, there was always the crowd to watch. To and fro, in front of the flower beds and the band rotunda, the couples and groups paraded, stopped to talk, to greet, to buy a handful of flowers from the old beggar who had his tray fixed to the railings. Little children ran among them, swooping and laughing; little boys with big white silk bows under their chins, little girls, little French dolls, dressed up in velvet and lace.

Reprinted from *The Short Stories of Katherine Mansfield*, by permission of Alfred A. Knopf, Inc. and The Society of Authors as the literary representative of the Estate of the late Katherine Mansfield. Copyright 1922, 1937 by Alfred A. Knopf, Inc.

1. *Jardins Publiques* (zhär daN′ pʏ blēk′), public gardens. [French]

And sometimes a tiny staggerer came suddenly rocking into the open from under the trees, stopped, stared, as suddenly sat down "flop," until its small high-stepping mother, like a young hen, rushed scolding to its rescue. Other people sat on the benches and green chairs, but they were nearly always the same, Sunday after Sunday, and—Miss Brill had often noticed—there was something funny about nearly all of them. They were odd, silent, nearly all old, and from the way they stared they looked as though they'd just come from dark little rooms or even—even cupboards.

Behind the rotunda the slender trees with yellow leaves down drooping, and through them just a line of sea, and beyond the blue sky with gold-veined clouds.

Tum-tum-tum tiddle-um! tiddle-um! tum tiddley-um tum ta! blew the band.

Two young girls in red came by and two young soldiers in blue met them, and they laughed and paired and went off arm in arm. Two peasant women with funny straw hats passed, gravely, leading beautiful smoke-colored donkeys. A cold, pale nun hurried by. A beautiful woman came along and dropped her bunch of violets, and a little boy ran after to hand them to her, and she took them and threw them away as if they'd been poisoned. Dear me! Miss Brill didn't know whether to admire that or not!

And now an ermine toque and a gentleman in gray met just in front of her. He was tall, stiff, dignified, and she was wearing the ermine toque she'd bought when her hair was yellow. Now everything, her hair, her face, even her eyes, was the same color as the shabby ermine, and her hand in its cleaned glove, lifted to dab her lips, was a tiny yellowish paw. Oh, she was so pleased to see him—delighted! She rather thought they were going to meet that afternoon. She described where she'd been—everywhere, here, there, along by the sea. The day was so charming—didn't he agree? And wouldn't he, perhaps? . . . But he shook his head—lighted a cigarette, slowly breathed a great deep puff into her face, and, even while she was still talking and laughing, flicked the match away and walked

on. The ermine toque was alone; she smiled more brightly than ever. But even the band seemed to know what she was feeling and played more softly, played tenderly, and the drum beat, "The Brute! The Brute!" over and over. What would she do? What was going to happen now? But as Miss Brill wondered, the ermine toque turned, raised her hand as though she'd seen someone else, much nicer, just over there, and pattered away. And the band changed again and played more quickly, more gaily than ever, and the old couple on Miss Brill's seat got up and marched away, and such a funny old man with long whiskers hobbled along in time to the music and was nearly knocked over by four girls walking abreast.

Oh, how fascinating it was! How she enjoyed it! How she loved sitting here, watching it all! It was like a play. It was exactly like a play. Who could believe the sky at the back wasn't painted? But it wasn't till a little brown dog trotted on solemnly and then slowly trotted off, like a little "theater" dog, a little dog that had been drugged, that Miss Brill discovered what it was that made it so exciting. They were all on the stage. They weren't only the audience, not only looking on; they were acting. Even she had a part and came every Sunday. No doubt somebody would have noticed if she hadn't been there; she was part of the performance after all.

How strange she'd never thought of it like that before! And yet it explained why she made such a point of starting from home at just the same time each week—so as not to be late for the performance—and it also explained why she had quite a queer, shy feeling at telling her English pupils how she spent her Sunday afternoons. No wonder! Miss Brill nearly laughed out loud. She was on the stage. She thought of the old invalid gentleman to whom she read the newspaper four afternoons a week while he slept in the garden. She had got quite used to the frail head on the cotton pillow, the hollowed eyes, the open mouth and the high pinched nose. If he'd been dead she mightn't have noticed for weeks; she wouldn't have minded. But suddenly he knew he was having the paper read to him by an actress! "An actress!" The old head lifted; two points of light quivered in the old eyes. "An actress—are ye?" And Miss Brill smoothed the newspaper as though it were the manuscript of her part and said gently: "Yes, I have been an actress for a long time."

The band had been having a rest. Now they started again. And what they played was warm, sunny, yet there was just a faint chill—a something, what was it?—not sadness—no, not sadness—a something that made you want to sing. The tune lifted, lifted, the light shone; and it seemed to Miss Brill that in another moment all of them, all the whole company, would begin singing. The young ones, the laughing ones who were moving together, they would begin, and the men's voices, very resolute and brave, would join them. And then she too, she too, and the others on the benches—they would come in with a kind of accompaniment—something low, that scarcely rose or fell, something so beautiful—moving. . . . And Miss Brill's eyes filled with tears and she looked smiling at all the other members of the company. Yes, we understand, we understand, she thought—though what they understood she didn't know.

Just at that moment a boy and girl came and sat down where the old couple had been. They were beautifully dressed; they were in love. The hero and heroine, of course, just arrived from his father's yacht. And still soundlessly singing, still with that trembling smile, Miss Brill prepared to listen.

"No, not now," said the girl. "Not here, I can't."

"But why? Because of that stupid old thing at the end there?" asked the boy. "Why does she come here at all—who wants her? Why doesn't she keep her silly old mug at home?"

"It's her fu-fur which is so funny," giggled the girl. "It's exactly like a fried whiting."

"Ah, be off with you!" said the boy in an angry whisper. Then: "Tell me, *ma petite chérie*[2]——"

"No, not here," said the girl. "Not *yet*."

On her way home she usually bought a slice of honeycake at the baker's. It was her Sunday treat. Sometimes there was an almond in her slice, sometimes not. It made a great difference. If there was an almond, it was like carrying home a tiny present—a surprise—something that might very well not have been there. She hurried on the almond Sundays and struck the match for the kettle in quite a dashing way.

But today she passed the baker's by, climbed the stairs, went into the little dark room—her room like a cupboard—and sat down on the red eider down. She sat there for a long time. The box that the fur came out of was on the bed. She unclasped the necklet quickly; quickly, without looking, laid it inside. But when she put the lid on she thought she heard something crying.

2. *ma petite chérie* (mä pə tēt′ chā′rē′), my little darling. [*French*]

❋ To increase understanding

1. (a) What is Miss Brill's mood in the first three paragraphs of the story? (b) What things are responsible for this mood?

2. (a) Why does Miss Brill feel disappointment in the two people who share her special seat? (b) Describe the woman whom Miss Brill thinks of as the "ermine toque." (c) Why is Miss Brill sympathetically inclined to the ermine toque? (d) Why does the name *ermine toque* imply a comparison between this woman's situation and that of Miss Brill?

3. (a) What "discovery" does Miss Brill make when "a little brown dog trotted on solemnly and then slowly trotted off" (page 580, column 2, paragraph 1)? (b) How does this discovery affect her? (c) How does she relate this discovery to her everyday life?

4. Miss Brill's first discovery is followed immediately by a second revelation. What is this second revelation?

5. (a) What is symbolized by Miss Brill's failure to buy a slice of almond honeycake on her way home? (b) How has Miss Mansfield used the fur neckpiece as a symbol of the change in Miss Brill's feelings from the moment she removes it from its box to the moment she replaces it?

6. Do you find any evidence of the stream-of-consciousness technique in Katherine Mansfield's development of Miss Brill? Explain.

Evelyn Waugh   BELLA FLEACE GAVE A PARTY

Ballingar is four-and-a-half hours from Dublin if you catch the early train from Broadstone Station and five-and-a-quarter if you wait until the afternoon. It is the market town of a large and comparatively well-populated district. There is a pretty Protestant Church in 1820 Gothic on one side of the square and a vast, unfinished Catholic cathedral opposite it, conceived in that irresponsible medley of architectural orders that is so dear to the hearts of transmontane pietists.[1] Celtic lettering of a sort is beginning to take the place of the Latin alphabet on the shop fronts that complete the square. These all deal in identical goods in varying degrees of dilapidation; Mulligan's Store, Flannigan's Store, Riley's Store, each sells thick black boots, hanging in bundles, soapy colonial cheese, hardware and haberdashery, oil and saddlery, and each is licensed to sell ale and porter for consumption on or off the premises. The shell of the barracks stands with empty window frames and blackened interior as a monument to emancipation.[2] A typical Irish town.

Fleacetown is fifteen miles from Ballingar, on a direct uneven road through typical Irish country; vague purple hills in the far distance and towards them, on one side of the road, fitfully visible among drifting patches of white mist, unbroken miles of bog, dotted with occasional stacks of cut peat. On the other side the ground slopes up to the north, divided irregularly into spare fields by banks and stone walls over which the Ballingar hounds have some of their most eventful hunting. Moss lies on everything; in a rough green rug on the walls and banks, soft green velvet on the timber—blurring the transitions so that there is no knowing where the ground ends and trunk and masonry begin. All the way from Ballingar there is a succession of whitewashed cabins and a dozen or so fair-size farmhouses; but there is no gentleman's house, for all this

was Fleace property in the days before the Land Commission.[3] The demesne land[4] is all that belongs to Fleacetown now, and this is let for pasture to neighboring farmers. Only a few beds are cultivated in the walled kitchen garden; the rest has run to rot, thorned bushes barren of edible fruit spreading everywhere among weedy flowers reverting rankly to type. The hothouses have been drafty skeletons for ten years. The great gates set in their Georgian arch are permanently padlocked, the lodges are derelict, and the line of the main drive is only just discernible through the meadows. Access to the house is half a mile further up through a farm gate, along a track befouled by cattle.

But the house itself, at the date with which we are dealing, was in a condition of comparatively good repair; compared, that is to say, with Ballingar House or Castle Boycott or Knode Hall. It did not, of course, set up to rival Gordontown, where the American Lady Gordon had installed electric light, central heating and a lift, or Mock House or Newhill, which were leased to sporting Englishmen, or Castle Mockstock, since Lord Mockstock married beneath him. These four houses with their neatly raked gravel, bathrooms and dynamos, were the wonder and

Reprinted from *Mr. Lovejoy's Little Outing* by Evelyn Waugh, by permission of Little, Brown & Company, New York; Chapman & Hall Ltd., London; and the author.
1. *irresponsible medley ... transmontane pietists.* The architectural styles or orders used in the temples of ancient Greece and Rome were distinctive and consistent throughout. As church architecture developed north of the Alps (*transmontani* was the Latin word for those living "across the mountains"), many different styles were often incorporated into the same cathedral. 2. *shell of the barracks ... emancipation.* To quell the Irish rebellion of 1918 to 1920, the English sent a special army, popularly known as the "Black and Tans." There was much violence on both sides—to which these burned barracks testify—before the Irish Free State was established in 1922. 3. *Land Commission,* part of the reform established by England just after the turn of the century. The land commission was able to offer inducements to the land owners to sell and then offer land to the tenants on easy terms. 4. *demesne* (di mān') *land,* that land which was reserved to the landlord for his own use, the remainder being occupied by tenants.

ridicule of the country. But Fleacetown, in fair competition with the essentially Irish houses of the Free State, was unusually habitable.

Its roof was intact; and it is the roof which makes the difference between the second and third grades of Irish country houses. Once that goes you have moss in the bedrooms, ferns on the stairs and cows in the library, and in a very few years you have to move into the dairy or one of the lodges. But so long as he has, literally, a roof over his head, an Irishman's house is still his castle. There were weak bits in Fleacetown, but general opinion held that the leads were good for another twenty years and would certainly survive the present owner.

Miss Annabel Rochfort-Doyle-Fleace, to give her the full name under which she appeared in books of reference, though she was known to the entire countryside as Bella Fleace, was the last of her family. There had been Fleaces and Fleysers living about Ballingar since the days of Strongbow,[5] and farm buildings marked the spot where they had inhabited a stockaded fort two centuries before the immigration of the Boycotts or Gordons or Mockstocks. A family tree emblazed by a nineteenth-century genealogist, showing how the original stock had merged with the equally ancient Rochforts and the respectable though more recent Doyles, hung in the billiard room. The present home had been built on extravagant lines in the middle of the eighteenth century, when the family, though enervated, was still wealthy and influential. It would be tedious to trace its gradual decline from fortune; enough to say that it was due to no heroic debauchery. The Fleaces just got unobtrusively poorer in the way that families do who make no effort to help themselves. In the last generations, too, there had been marked traces of eccentricity. Bella Fleace's mother—an O'Hara of Newhill—had from the day of her marriage until her death suffered from the delusion that she was a Negress. Her brother, from whom she had inherited, devoted himself to oil painting; his mind ran on the simple subject of assassina-

MESSRS CHAPMAN & HALL LTD., LONDON

Evelyn Waugh 1903–1966

Evelyn Waugh, the son of a London publisher, attended Oxford, where he became known for his brilliance and for his pose as a fashionable playboy. He first became famous for the barbed satire of his novels describing London high society of the 1920's and 1930's. Later, disillusioned by the hollowness of the society he portrayed with such polish in his work, Waugh felt the need for a positive moral base. This led to his conversion to Catholicism in 1930. The fervor with which he embraced his new faith alienated some of his former readers; but, partially as a result of his changed outlook, in novels like *A Handful of Dust* (1934) his satire became deeper and more thought-provoking. *Brideshead Revisited* (1945), a novel about the decline of an aristocratic English Catholic family, broadened his popularity because of its absorbing story; however, it displeased readers who see Waugh's greatest gifts as those of the satirist. Also apparent in *Brideshead Revisited* is Waugh's conservatism, a romantic love of the past that has become increasingly notable in his later writings.

At the beginning of World War II, Waugh enlisted in the Royal Marines. Later he transferred to the Commandos and was parachuted into Yugoslavia. Out of his war experiences has come the trilogy *Men at Arms* (1952), *Officers and Gentlemen* (1955), and *End of the Battle* (1961).

5. *Strongbow*, the Anglo-Norman earl who in 1169 began the conquest of Ireland.

tion, and before his death he had executed pictures of practically every such incident in history from Julius Caesar to General Wilson.[6] He was at work on a painting, his own murder, at the time of the troubles,[7] when he was, in fact, ambushed and done to death with a shotgun on his own drive.

It was under one of her brother's paintings —Abraham Lincoln in his box at the theater— that Miss Fleace was sitting one colorless morning in November when the idea came to her to give a Christmas party. It would be unnecessary to describe her appearance closely, and somewhat confusing, because it seemed in contradiction to much of her character. She was over eighty, very untidy and very red; streaky gray hair was twisted behind her head into a horsy bun, wisps hung round her cheeks; her nose was prominent and blue-veined; her eyes pale blue, blank and mad; she had a lively smile and spoke with a marked Irish intonation. She walked with the aid of a stick, having been lamed many years back when her horse rolled her among loose stones late in a long day with the Ballingar Hounds; a tipsy sporting doctor had completed the mischief, and she had not been able to ride again. She would appear on foot when hounds drew the Fleacetown coverts and loudly criticize the conduct of the huntsman, but every year fewer of her old friends turned out; strange faces appeared.

They knew Bella, though she did not know them. She had become a byword in the neighborhood, a much valued joke.

"A rotten day," they would report. "We found our fox, but lost again almost at once. But we saw Bella. Wonder how long the old girl will last. She must be nearly ninety. My father remembers when she used to hunt— went like smoke, too."

Indeed, Bella herself was becoming increasingly occupied with the prospect of death. In the winter before the one we are talking of, she had been extremely ill. She emerged in April, rosy-cheeked as ever, but slower in her movements and mind. She gave instructions that better attention must be paid to her father's and brother's graves, and in June took the unprecedented step of inviting her heir

to visit her. She had always refused to see this young man up till now. He was an Englishman, a very distant cousin, named Banks. He lived in South Kensington and occupied himself in the Museum. He arrived in August and wrote long and very amusing letters to all his friends describing his visit, and later translated his experiences into a short story for the *Spectator*. Bella disliked him from the moment he arrived. He had horn-rimmed spectacles and a BBC[8] voice. He spent most of his time photographing the Fleacetown chimney pieces and the molding of the doors. One day he came to Bella bearing a pile of calf-bound volumes from the library.

"I say, did you know you had these?" he asked.

"I did," Bella lied.

"All first editions. They must be extremely valuable."

"You put them back where you found them."

Later, when he wrote to thank her for his visit—enclosing prints of some of his photographs—he mentioned the books again. This set Bella thinking. Why should that young puppy go poking round the house putting a price on everything? She wasn't dead yet, Bella thought. And the more she thought of it, the more repugnant it became to think of Archie Banks carrying off her books to South Kensington and removing the chimney pieces and, as he threatened, writing an essay about the house for the *Architectural Review*. She had often heard that the books were valuable. Well, there were plenty of books in the library and she did not see why Archie Banks should profit by them. So she wrote a letter to a Dublin bookseller. He came to look through the library, and after a while he offered her twelve hundred pounds for the lot, or a thousand for the six books which had attracted

6. *General Wilson*, noted English general during World War I, hostile to the Irish nationalist movement, who was assassinated by an Irish extremist in London, in 1922. 7. *the troubles*, probably refers to the period immediately after the establishment of the Irish Free State when the extremists continued a civil war against the new national government, agitating for complete independence. 8. BBC, British Broadcasting Corporation. This entire description of Banks marks him as a sophisticated Londoner, quite unsympathetic to Bella's world of aristocratic Ireland.

Archie Banks' attention. Bella was not sure that she had the right to sell things out of the house; a wholesale clearance would be noticed. So she kept the sermons and military history which made up most of the collection, the Dublin bookseller went off with the first editions, which eventually fetched rather less than he had given, and Bella was left with winter coming on and a thousand pounds in hand.

It was then that it occurred to her to give a party. There were always several parties given round Ballingar at Christmas-time, but of late years Bella had not been invited to any, partly because many of her neighbors had never spoken to her, partly because they did not think she would want to come, and partly because they would not have known what to do with her if she had. As a matter of fact she loved parties. She liked sitting down to supper in a noisy room, she liked dance music and gossip about which of the girls was pretty and who was in love with them, and she liked drink and having things brought to her by men in pink evening coats. And though she tried to console herself with contemptuous reflections about the ancestry of the hostesses, it annoyed her very much whenever she heard of a party being given in the neighborhood to which she was not asked.

And so it came about that, sitting with the *Irish Times* under the picture of Abraham Lincoln and gazing across the bare trees of the park to the hills beyond, Bella took it into her head to give a party. She rose immediately and hobbled across the room to the bell rope. Presently her butler came into the morning room; he wore the green baize apron in which he cleaned the silver and in his hand he carried the plate brush to emphasize the irregularity of the summons.

"Was it yourself ringing?" he asked.

"It was, who else?"

"And I at the silver!"

"Riley," said Bella with some solemnity, "I propose to give a ball at Christmas."

"Indeed!" said her butler. "And for what would you want to be dancing at your age?" But as Bella adumbrated her idea, a sympathetic light began to glitter in Riley's eye.

"There's not been such a ball in the country for twenty-five years. It will cost a fortune."

"It will cost a thousand pounds," said Bella proudly.

The preparations were necessarily stupendous. Seven new servants were recruited in the village and set to work dusting and cleaning and polishing, clearing out furniture and pulling up carpets. Their industry served only to reveal fresh requirements; plaster moldings, long rotten, crumbled under the feather brooms, worm-eaten mahogany floor-boards came up with the tin tacks; bare brick was disclosed behind the cabinets in the great drawing room. A second wave of the invasion brought painters, paperhangers and plumbers, and in a moment of enthusiasm Bella had the cornice and the capitals of the pillars in the hall regilded; windows were reglazed, banisters fitted into gaping sockets, and the stair carpets shifted so that the worn strips were less noticeable.

In all these works Bella was indefatigable. She trotted from drawing room to hall, down the long gallery, up the staircase, admonishing the hireling servants, lending a hand with the lighter objects of furniture, sliding, when the time came, up and down the mahogany floor of the drawing room to work in the French chalk. She unloaded chests of silver in the attics, found long-forgotten services of china, went down with Riley into the cellars to count the few remaining and now flat and acid bottles of champagne. And in the evenings when the manual laborers had retired exhausted to their gross recreations, Bella sat up far into the night turning the pages of cookery books, comparing the estimates of rival caterers, inditing long and detailed letters to the agents for dance bands and, most important of all, drawing up her list of guests and addressing the high double piles of engraved cards that stood in her escritoire.

Distance counts for little in Ireland. People will readily drive three hours to pay an afternoon call, and for a dance of such importance no journey was too great. Bella had her list painfully compiled from works of reference, Riley's more up-to-date social knowledge and her own suddenly animated memory. Cheerfully, in a steady childish handwriting, she transferred the names to the cards and addressed the envelopes. It was the work of several late sittings. Many of those whose names were transcribed were dead or bedridden; some whom she just remembered seeing as small children were reaching retiring age in remote corners of the globe; many of the houses she wrote down were blackened shells, burned during the troubles and never rebuilt; some had "no one living in them, only farmers." But at last, none too early, the last envelope was addressed. A final lap with the stamps and then later than usual she rose from the desk. Her limbs were stiff, her eyes dazzled, her tongue cloyed with the gum of the Free State post office; she felt a little dizzy, but she locked her desk that evening with the knowledge that the most serious part of the work of the party was over. There had been several notable and deliberate omissions from that list.

"What's all this I hear about Bella giving a party?" said Lady Gordon to Lady Mockstock. "I haven't had a card."

"Neither have I yet. I hope the old thing hasn't forgotten me. I certainly intend to go. I've never been inside the house. I believe she's got some lovely things."

With true English reserve the lady whose husband had leased Mock Hall never betrayed the knowledge that any party was in the air at all at Fleacetown.

As the last days approached Bella concentrated more upon her own appearance. She had bought few clothes of recent years, and the Dublin dressmaker with whom she used to deal had shut up shop. For a delirious instant she played with the idea of a journey to London and even Paris, and considerations of time alone obliged her to abandon it. In the end she discovered a shop to suit her, and purchased a very magnificent gown of crimson satin; to this she added long white gloves and satin shoes. There was no tiara, alas! among her jewels, but she unearthed large numbers of bright, nondescript Victorian rings, some chains and lockets, pearl brooches, turquoise earrings, and a collar of garnets. She ordered a coiffeur down from Dublin to dress her hair.

On the day of the ball she woke early, slightly feverish with nervous excitement, and wriggled in bed till she was called, restlessly rehearsing in her mind every detail of the arrangements. Before noon she had been to supervise the setting of hundreds of candles in the sconces round the ballroom and supper room, and in the three great chandeliers of cut Waterford glass; she had seen the supper tables laid out with silver and glass and stood the massive wine coolers by the buffet; she had helped bank the staircase and hall with chrysanthemums. She had no luncheon that day, though Riley urged her with samples of the delicacies already arrived from the caterer's. She felt a little faint; lay down for a short time, but soon rallied to sew with her own hands the crested buttons on to the liveries of the hired servants.

The invitations were timed for eight o'clock. She wondered whether that would be too early—she had heard tales of parties that began very late—but as the afternoon dragged on unendurably, and rich twilight enveloped the house, Bella became glad that she had set a short term on this exhausting wait.

At six she went up to dress. The hairdresser was there with a bag full of tongs and combs. He brushed and coiled her hair and whiffed it up and generally manipulated it until it became orderly and formal and apparently far more copious. She put on all her jewelry and, standing before the cheval glass in her room, could not forbear a gasp of surprise. Then she limped downstairs.

The house looked magnificent in the candlelight. The band was there, the twelve hired footmen, Riley in knee breeches and black silk stockings.

It struck eight. Bella waited. Nobody came.

She sat down on a gilt chair at the head of

the stairs, looked steadily before her with her blank, blue eyes. In the hall, in the cloakroom, in the supper room, the hired footmen looked at one another with knowing winks. "What does the old girl expect? No one'll have finished dinner before ten."

The linkmen on the steps stamped and chafed their hands.

At half-past twelve Bella rose from her chair. Her face gave no indication of what she was thinking.

"Riley, I think I will have some supper. I am not feeling altogether well."

She hobbled slowly to the dining room.

"Give me a stuffed quail and a glass of wine. Tell the band to start playing."

The *Blue Danube* waltz flooded the house. Bella smiled approval and swayed her head a little to the rhythm.

"Riley, I am really quite hungry. I've had nothing all day. Give me another quail and some more champagne."

Alone among the candles and the hired footmen, Riley served his mistress with an immense supper. She enjoyed every mouthful.

Presently she rose. "I am afraid there must be some mistake. No one seems to be coming to the ball. It is very disappointing after all our trouble. You may tell the band to go home."

But just as the band was leaving the dining room there was a stir in the hall. Guests were arriving. With wild resolution Bella swung herself up the stairs. She must get to the top before the guests were announced. One hand on the banister, one on her stick, pounding heart, two steps at a time. At last she reached the landing and turned to face the company. There was a mist before her eyes and a singing in her ears. She breathed with effort, but dimly she saw four figures advancing and saw Riley meet them and heard him announce

"Lord and Lady Mockstock, Sir Samuel and Lady Gordon."

Suddenly the daze in which she had been moving cleared. Here on the stairs were the two women she had not invited—Lady Mockstock the draper's daughter, Lady Gordon the American.

She drew herself up and fixed them with her blank, blue eyes.

"I had not expected this honor," she said. "Please forgive me if I am unable to entertain you."

The Mockstocks and the Gordons stood aghast; saw the mad blue eyes of their hostess, her crimson dress; the ballroom beyond, looking immense in its emptiness; heard the dance music echoing through the empty house. The air was charged with the scent of chrysanthemums. And then the drama and unreality of the scene were dispelled. Miss Fleace suddenly sat down, and holding out her hands to her butler, said, "I don't quite know what's happening."

He and two of the hired footmen carried the old lady to a sofa. She spoke only once more. Her mind was still on the same subject. "They came uninvited, those two . . . and nobody else."

A day later she died.

Mr. Banks arrived for the funeral and spent a week sorting out her effects. Among them he found in her escritoire, stamped, addressed, but unposted, the invitations to the ball.

To increase understanding

1. (a) At the end of the first paragraph of "Bella Fleace Gave a Party" Waugh sums up Ballingar as "A typical Irish town." Describe this town. (b) At the beginning of the second paragraph the author mentions that the road to Fleacetown runs "through typical Irish country." What details in this description are most significant? (c) Paragraph 3 deals with Irish country houses. What evidences of satire do you find? (d) What purposes does this lengthy introduction to the story serve?

2. (a) Before Waugh mentions Bella Fleace's idea of giving a Christmas party, he describes her background and family history. Why is this discussion important in light of the direction the story takes? (b) How is the description of Bella's family

closely linked in the narrative to her first idea of giving a ball? (*c*) What detail of Bella's appearance is most signficant?

3. What is the function of the flashback that introduces Mr. Banks?

4. (*a*) How does Riley react to Bella's idea of having a Christmas ball? (*b*) Using his reaction as a guide, explain Bella's intense excitement over the ball.

5. (*a*) After rereading the account of those to whom Bella sent invitations (page 585, column 2, paragraph 5), describe what the ball would probably have been like had the invitations been mailed. (*b*) How did you learn that certain neighbors had been omitted?

6. (*a*) What is the effect of the scene in which Bella waits for her guests in the empty hall? (*b*) From the time she decides to have dinner until the time the uninvited guests arrive, does Bella enjoy her party? Explain your answer.

7. Critic Edmund Wilson has pointed out that one of Evelyn Waugh's characteristics is the ability "to combine the outrageous with the plausible without offending our sense of truth." (*a*) What is, in a sense, outrageous about the fact revealed in the last paragraph of the story? (*b*) Why is its discovery by Mr. Banks plausible? (*c*) How has the author prepared throughout the story for a fact of this type? (*d*) Does the fact itself offend the reader's sense of truth?

8. (*a*) What is the author's attitude toward (1) Bella Fleace, (2) Mr. Banks, (3) the Gordons and the Mockstocks? (*b*) How would you describe the tone of the story?

🌸 Words!

In the medieval morality plays common nouns denoting a class or an abstract quality were often used as the names of characters—*Everyman, Death, Mankind, Mercy.* A good part of the power of these early dramas comes from this obvious device: giving highly individualized characters names of general significance. The technique has been taken up by later writers, and, indeed, has become a cherished tradition in English fiction. While some writers like John Bunyan (see pages 223-229) have continued to use these names in obvious, allegorical ways, some have been more subtle, making up names that are combinations or parts of ordinary words, or new words that sound very much like familiar ones. Dickens is famous for names that suggest the personality of a character: *Bumble, Murdstone, Chuzzlewit, Steerforth.*

Modern writers sometimes are able to suggest still more complex ideas about their characters by naming them in this way. Reread the first sentence of "Miss Brill" (page 579). What does the name *Miss Brill* immediately suggest about Katherine Mansfield's heroine? In view of her fate, what irony does this name take on? What does Evelyn Waugh convey about his characters through the names *Mockstock* and *Banks*? *Bella Fleace* is more complex. *Fleace,* of course, is a homonym for *fleece.* What meaning of *fleece* might suggest the way the family fortune and social position had been maintained? Why might *woolgathering* be suggested by Bella Fleace's name? In what ways does the name *Bella* underline the irony and pathos of her last, grand act?

H. H. Munro (Saki) LAURA

You are not really dying, are you?" asked Amanda.

"I have the doctor's permission to live till Tuesday," said Laura.

"But today is Saturday; this is serious!" gasped Amanda.

"I don't know about it being serious; it is certainly Saturday," said Laura.

"Death is always serious," said Amanda.

"I never said I was going to die. I am presumably going to leave off being Laura, but I shall go on being something. An animal of some kind, I suppose. You see, when one hasn't been very good in the life one has just lived, one reincarnates in some lower organism. And I haven't been very good, when one comes to think of it. I've been petty and mean and vindictive and all that sort of thing when circumstances have seemed to warrant it."

"Circumstances never warrant that sort of thing," said Amanda hastily.

"If you don't mind my saying so," observed Laura, "Egbert is a circumstance that would warrant any amount of that sort of thing. You're married to him—that's different; you've sworn to love, honor, and endure him: I haven't."

"I don't see what's wrong with Egbert," protested Amanda.

"Oh, I daresay the wrongness has been on my part," admitted Laura dispassionately; "he has merely been the extenuating circumstance. He made a thin, peevish kind of fuss, for instance, when I took the collie puppies from the farm out for a run the other day."

"They chased his young broods of speckled Sussex[1] and drove two sitting hens off their nests, besides running all over the flower beds. You know how devoted he is to his poultry and garden."

"Anyhow, he needn't have gone on about it for the entire evening and then have said, 'Let's say no more about it' just when I was beginning to enjoy the discussion. That's where one of my petty vindictive revenges came in," added Laura with an unrepentant chuckle; "I turned the entire family of speckled Sussex into his seedling shed the day after the puppy episode."

"How could you?" exclaimed Amanda.

"It came quite easy," said Laura; "two of the hens pretended to be laying at the time, but I was firm."

"And we thought it was an accident!"

"You see," resumed Laura, "I really *have* some grounds for supposing that my next incarnation will be in a lower organism. I shall be an animal of some kind. On the other hand, I haven't been a bad sort in my way, so I think I may count on being a nice animal, something elegant and lively, with a love of fun. An otter, perhaps."

"I can't imagine you as an otter," said Amanda.

"Well, I don't suppose you can imagine me as an angel, if it comes to that," said Laura.

Amanda was silent. She couldn't.

"Personally I think an otter life would be rather enjoyable," continued Laura; "salmon to eat all the year round, and the satisfaction of being able to fetch the trout in their own homes without having to wait for hours till they condescend to rise to the fly you've been dangling before them; and an elegant svelte figure——"

"Think of the otter hounds," interposed Amanda; "how dreadful to be hunted and harried and finally worried to death!"

"Rather fun with half the neighborhood looking on, and anyhow not worse than this Saturday-to-Tuesday business of dying by inches; and then I should go into something else. If I had been a moderately good otter, I suppose I should get back into human shape of some sort; probably something rather primitive—a little brown, unclothed Nubian boy,[2] I should think."

"I wish you would be serious," sighed Amanda; "you really ought to be if you're only going to live till Tuesday."

As a matter of fact, Laura died on Monday.

"So dreadfully upsetting," Amanda complained to her uncle-in-law, Sir Lulworth Quayne. "I've asked quite a lot of people down for golf and fishing, and the rhododendrons are just looking their best."

"Laura always was inconsiderate," said Sir Lulworth; "she was born during Goodwood week,[3] with an Ambassador staying in the house who hated babies."

"She had the maddest kind of ideas," said Amanda; "do you know if there was any insanity in her family?"

"Insanity? No, I never heard of any. Her father lives in West Kensington, but I believe he's sane on all other subjects."[4]

"She had an idea that she was going to be reincarnated as an otter," said Amanda.

"One meets with those ideas of reincarna-

---

1. *speckled Sussex*, an English breed of poultry, noted for the excellence of its flesh. 2. *Nubian boy*, a native of Nubia (nü′bi ə or nü′bi ə), a region in northeast Africa. 3. *Goodwood week*, the last week in July, when races are held in Goodwood Park near Chichester, England. 4. *Her father . . . subjects.* Sir Lulworth enjoys playing the rôle of the country gentleman who scorns anyone who lives in the city—even in the fashionable district of West Kensington.

tion so frequently, even in the West," said Sir Lulworth, "that one can hardly set them down as being mad. And Laura was such an unaccountable person in this life that I should not like to lay down definite rules as to what she might be doing in an afterstate."

PHOTOGRAPH BY E. O. HOPPE, LONDON

H. H. Munro (Saki)   1870-1916

Hector Hugh Munro was born in Burma, the son of an inspector-general of police. His mother died when he was two, and he was sent home to Scotland. His formal education ended with grammar school, but he traveled widely with his father for a tutor. In 1893 his father secured him a post in the Burma police. His delicate health, however, forced him to return to Britain, where he took up a career in writing. It was while doing political sketches for the *Westminster Gazette* that he adopted the pen name *Saki*—the name of the cup-bearer in *The Rubáiyát*.

After serving for a time as a foreign correspondent for the *Morning Post*, he returned to London in 1908 to devote himself to the writing of stories and novels. In 1910 *Reginald in Russia*, a collection of stories, appeared, followed in 1912 by a novel, *The Unbearable Bassington* and, in 1914, by another group of stories, *Beasts and Super-Beasts*.

When World War I began, Munro declined several offers of commissions and enlisted as a private. He was killed in action in 1916.

A master of the short-story form, Saki is best known today for stories in which with macabre humor and flashes of satire he moves unerringly to an abrupt but subtly prepared climax.

"You think she really might have passed into some animal form?" asked Amanda. She was one of those who shape their opinions rather readily from the standpoint of those around them.

Just then Egbert entered the breakfast room, wearing an air of bereavement that Laura's demise would have been insufficient, in itself, to account for.

"Four of my speckled Sussex have been killed," he exclaimed; "the very four that were to go to the show on Friday. One of them was dragged away and eaten right in the middle of that new carnation bed that I've been to such trouble and expense over. My best flower bed and my best fowls singled out for destruction; it almost seems as if the brute that did the deed had special knowledge how to be as devastating as possible in a short space of time."

"Was it a fox, do you think?" asked Amanda.

"Sounds more like a polecat," said Sir Lulworth.

"No," said Egbert, "there were marks of webbed feet all over the place, and we followed the tracks down to the stream at the bottom of the garden; evidently an otter."

Amanda looked quickly and furtively across at Sir Lulworth.

Egbert was too agitated to eat any breakfast, and went out to superintend the strengthening of the poultry-yard defenses.

"I think she might at least have waited till the funeral was over," said Amanda in a scandalized voice.

"It's her own funeral, you know," said Sir Lulworth; "it's a nice point in etiquette how far one ought to show respect to one's own mortal remains."

Disregard for mortuary convention was carried to further lengths next day; during the absence of the family at the funeral ceremony the remaining survivors of the speckled Sussex were massacred. The marauder's line of retreat seemed to have embraced most of the flower beds on the lawn, but the strawberry beds in the lower garden had also suffered.

"I shall get the otter hounds to come here at the earliest possible moment," said Egbert savagely.

"On no account! You can't dream of such a

thing!" exclaimed Amanda. "I mean, it wouldn't do, so soon after a funeral in the house."

"It's a case of necessity," said Egbert; "once an otter takes to that sort of thing, it won't stop."

"Perhaps it will go elsewhere now that there are no more fowls left," suggested Amanda.

"One would think you wanted to shield the beast," said Egbert.

"There's been so little water in the stream lately," objected Amanda; "it seems hardly sporting to hunt an animal when it has so little chance of taking refuge anywhere."

"Good gracious!" fumed Egbert, "I'm not thinking about sport. I want to have the animal killed as soon as possible."

Even Amanda's opposition weakened when, during church time on the following Sunday, the otter made its way into the house, raided half a salmon from the larder and worried it into scaly fragments on the Persian rug in Egbert's studio.

"We shall have it hiding under our beds and biting pieces out of our feet before long," said Egbert, and from what Amanda knew of this particular otter she felt that the possibility was not a remote one.

On the evening preceding the day fixed for the hunt Amanda spent a solitary hour walking by the banks of the stream making what she imagined to be hound noises. It was charitably supposed by those who overheard her performance that she was practicing for farmyard imitations at the forthcoming village entertainment.

It was her friend and neighbor, Aurora Burret, who brought her news of the day's sport.

"Pity you weren't out; we had quite a good day. We found it at once, in the pool just below your garden."

"Did you—kill?" asked Amanda.

"Rather. A fine she-otter. Your husband got rather badly bitten in trying to 'tail it.' Poor beast, I felt quite sorry for it, it had such a human look in its eyes when it was killed. You'll call me silly, but do you know who the look reminded me of? My dear woman, what is the matter?"

When Amanda had recovered to a certain extent from her attack of nervous prostration, Egbert took her to the Nile Valley to recuperate. Change of scene speedily brought about the desired recovery of health and mental balance. The escapades of an adventurous otter in search of a variation of diet were viewed in their proper light. Amanda's normally placid temperament reasserted itself. Even a hurricane of shouted curses, coming from her husband's dressing room, in her husband's voice, but hardly in his usual vocabulary, failed to disturb her serenity as she made a leisurely toilet one evening in a Cairo hotel.

"What is the matter? What has happened?" she asked in amused curiosity.

"The little beast has thrown all my clean shirts into the bath! Wait till I catch you, you little——"

"What little beast?" asked Amanda, suppressing a desire to laugh; Egbert's language was so hopelessly inadequate to express his outraged feelings.

"A little beast of a naked brown Nubian boy," spluttered Egbert.

And now Amanda is seriously ill.

To increase understanding

1. (a) What serious subject is introduced at the very beginning of the story? (b) What is surprising about each character's attitude toward this subject?

2. (a) What evidence does Laura cite to show that she has indeed been "petty and mean and vindictive"? (b) Is she repentant? Explain.

3. (a) What events caused Amanda to become seriously ill? (b) Why did they have this effect? (c) How had these events been foreshadowed?

4. (a) Point out some remarks made by the author or by the characters that are particularly funny. (b) What is being satirized in this story?

5. The critic William York Tindall writes of Saki: "The callousness of his short stories . . . is that of a sadistic child. His effect depends in part upon regarding the affairs of the adult world with the cold-blooded eyes of such a child." (a) Explain this remark. (b) As regards "Laura," do you agree or disagree with Tindall's opinion?

W. Somerset Maugham   LOUISE

I could never understand why Louise bothered with me. She disliked me and I knew that behind my back, in that gentle way of hers, she seldom lost the opportunity of saying a disagreeable thing about me. She had too much delicacy ever to make a direct statement, but with a hint and a sigh and a little flutter of her beautiful hands she was able to make her meaning plain. She was a mistress of cold praise. It was true that we had known one another almost intimately, for five-and-twenty years, but it was impossible for me to believe that she could be affected by the claims of old association. She thought me a coarse, brutal, cynical and vulgar fellow. I was puzzled at her not taking the obvious course and dropping me. She did nothing of the kind; indeed, she would not leave me alone; she was constantly asking me to lunch and dine with her and once or twice a year invited me to spend a weekend at her house in the country. At last I thought that I had discovered her motive. She had an uneasy suspicion that I did not believe in her; and if that was why she did not like me, it was also why she sought my acquaintance: it galled her that I alone should look upon her as a comic figure and she could not rest till I acknowledged myself mistaken and defeated. Perhaps she had an inkling that I saw the face behind the mask and because I alone held out was determined that sooner or later I too should take the mask for the face. I was never quite certain that she was a complete humbug. I wondered whether she fooled herself as thoroughly as she fooled the world or whether there was some spark of humor at the bottom of her heart. If there was it might be that she was attracted to me, as a pair of crooks might be attracted to one another, by the knowledge that we shared a secret that was hidden from everybody else.

I knew Louise before she married. She was then a frail, delicate girl with large and melancholy eyes. Her father and mother worshipped her with an anxious adoration, for some illness, scarlet fever I think, had left her with a weak heart and she had to take

THE TATE GALLERY, LONDON

Portrait of Maugham by Graham Sutherland.

W. Somerset Maugham   1874–1965

William Somerset Maugham was born in Paris, where his father held a post at the British Embassy. When he was ten years old, he returned to England to attend school. Later, because his parents had destined him for the medical profession, he spent several years at St. Thomas Hospital in London. His experiences treating the sick in the slums of London gave him material for *Lisa of Lambeth* (1897), a realistic novel which shocked the conventional readers of the day but showed great promise in its power of photographic portraiture. By the time Maugham took his degree in medicine, he had decided to devote his life to writing.

Success first came to him in the theater with the production of his play *Lady Frederick* (1907).

the greatest care of herself. When Tom Maitland proposed to her they were dismayed, for they were convinced that she was much too delicate for the strenuous state of marriage. But they were not too well off and Tom Maitland was rich. He promised to do everything in the world for Louise and finally they entrusted her to him as a sacred charge. Tom Maitland was a big, husky fellow, very good looking, and a fine athlete. He doted on Louise. With her weak heart he could not hope to keep her with him long and he made up his mind to do everything he could to make her few years on earth happy. He gave up the games he excelled in, not because she wished him to, she was glad that he should play golf and hunt, but because by a coincidence she had a heart attack whenever he proposed to leave her for a day. If they had a difference of opinion she gave in to him at once, for she was the most submissive wife a man could have, but her heart failed her and she would be laid up, sweet and uncomplaining, for a week. He could not be such a brute as to cross her. Then they would have quite a little tussle about which should yield and it was only with difficulty that at last he persuaded her to have her own way. On one occasion seeing her walk eight miles on an expedition that she particularly wanted to make, I suggested to Tom Maitland that she

was stronger than one would have thought. He shook his head and sighed.

"No, no, she's dreadfully delicate. She's been to all the best heart specialists in the world and they all say that her life hangs on a thread. But she has an unconquerable spirit."

He told her that I had remarked on her endurance.

"I shall pay for it tomorrow," she said to me in her plaintive way. "I shall be at death's door."

"I sometimes think that you're quite strong enough to do the things you want to," I murmured.

I had noticed that if a party was amusing, she could dance till five in the morning, but if it was dull she felt very poorly and Tom had to take her home early. I am afraid she did not like my reply, for though she gave me a pathetic little smile I saw no amusement in her large blue eyes.

"You can't very well expect me to fall down dead just to please you," she answered.

Louise outlived her husband. He caught his death of cold one day when they were sailing and Louise needed all the rugs there were to keep her warm. He left her a comfortable fortune and a daughter. Louise was inconsolable. It was wonderful that she managed to survive the shock. Her friends ex-

---

Cynically writing plays for the express purpose of making money, he became a highly successful and popular playwright.

It was with his autobiographical novel, *Of Human Bondage* (1915), that Maugham received recognition as a literary artist. This novel, which is in the naturalist tradition, is still considered his masterpiece. Like a number of other important first novels, *Of Human Bondage* deals with adolescence—a theme to which Maugham returned in *The Razor's Edge* (1944).

During World War I, Maugham was a British agent. After the war he traveled widely. He visited the South Seas to determine the reason for their great fascination. The result of his sojourn there was *The Moon and Sixpence* (1919), a novel based primarily on the life of the French artist Paul

Gauguin, who had gone in 1891 to the South Sea Islands and adopted the primitive life of the natives. Two new volumes of excellent short stories, together with the grim play *East of Suez* (1922), followed in quick succession and established Maugham as the most important contemporary interpreter of the white man gone native in tropical way stations east of Suez. In sharp contrast to Rudyard Kipling (page 477), Maugham never entertained any illusions about the white man—in the tropics or anywhere else. Often his white characters are distinctly inferior to the natives of the Oriental and Polynesian locales that are frequently the settings of his stories. However, it was Maugham's ability to catch the essence of a character, whether London matron or Singapore innkeeper, that has made his novels and short stories outstanding.

pected her speedily to follow poor Tom Maitland to the grave. Indeed they already felt dreadfully sorry for Iris, her daughter, who would be left an orphan. They redoubled their attentions towards Louise. They would not let her stir a finger; they insisted on doing everything in the world to save her trouble. They had to, because if she was called upon to do anything tiresome or inconvenient her heart went back on her and there she was at death's door. She was entirely lost without a man to take care of her, she said, and she did not know how, with her delicate health, she was going to bring up her dear Iris. Her friends asked why she did not marry again. Oh, with her heart it was out of the question, though of course she knew that dear Tom would have wished her to, and perhaps it would be the best thing for Iris if she did; but who would want to be bothered with a wretched invalid like herself? Oddly enough more than one young man showed himself quite ready to undertake the charge and a year after Tom's death she allowed George Hobhouse to lead her to the altar. He was a fine, upstanding fellow and he was not at all badly off. I never saw anyone so grateful as he for the privilege of being allowed to take care of this frail little thing.

"I shan't live to trouble you long," she said.

He was a soldier and an ambitious one, but he resigned his commission. Louise's health forced her to spend the winter at Monte Carlo and the summer at Deauville.[1] He hesitated a little at throwing up his career, and Louise at first would not hear of it; but at last she yielded as she always yielded, and he prepared to make his wife's last few years as happy as might be.

"It can't be very long now," she said. "I'll try not to be troublesome."

For the next two or three years Louise managed, notwithstanding her weak heart, to go beautifully dressed to all the most lively parties, to gamble very heavily, to dance, and even to flirt with tall slim young men. But George Hobhouse had not the stamina of Louise's first husband and he had to brace himself now and then with a stiff drink for his day's work as Louise's second husband.

It is possible that the habit would have grown on him, which Louise would not have liked at all, but very fortunately (for her) the war broke out. He rejoined his regiment and three months later was killed. It was a great shock to Louise. She felt, however, that in such a crisis she must not give way to a private grief; and if she had a heart attack nobody heard of it. In order to distract her mind she turned her villa at Monte Carlo into a hospital for convalescent officers. Her friends told her that she would never survive the strain.

"Of course it will kill me," she said, "I know that. But what does it matter? I must do my bit."

It didn't kill her. She had the time of her life. There was no convalescent home in France that was more popular. I met her by chance in Paris. She was lunching at the Ritz with a tall and very handsome young Frenchman. She explained that she was there on business connected with the hospital. She told me that the officers were too charming to her. They knew how delicate she was and they wouldn't let her do a single thing. They took care of her, well—as though they were all her husbands. She sighed.

"Poor George, who would ever have thought that I with my heart should survive him?"

"And poor Tom!" I said.

I don't know why she didn't like my saying that. She gave me her plaintive smile and her beautiful eyes filled with tears.

"You always speak as though you grudged me the few years that I can expect to live."

"By the way, your heart's much better, isn't it?"

"It'll never be better. I saw a specialist this morning and he said I must be prepared for the worst."

"Oh, well, you've been prepared for that for nearly twenty years now, haven't you?"

When the war came to an end Louise settled in London. She was now a woman of

---

1. *Monte Carlo . . . Deauville* (dō'vil). Because of its location on the Mediterranean Sea, Monte Carlo is a famous winter resort. Deauville is a French summer resort on the English Channel.

over forty, thin and frail still, with large eyes and pale cheeks, but she did not look a day more than twenty-five. Iris, who had been at school and was now grown up, came to live with her.

"She'll take care of me," said Louise. "Of course it'll be hard on her to live with such a great invalid as I am, but it can only be for such a little while, I'm sure she won't mind."

Iris was a nice girl. She had been brought up with the knowledge that her mother's health was precarious. As a child she had never been allowed to make a noise. She had always realized that her mother must on no account be upset. And though Louise told her now that she would not hear of her sacrificing herself for a tiresome old woman the girl simply would not listen. It wasn't a question of sacrificing herself, it was a happiness to do what she could for her poor dear mother. With a sigh her mother let her do a great deal.

"It pleases the child to think she's making herself useful," she said.

"Don't you think she ought to go out and about more?" I asked.

"That's what I'm always telling her. I can't get her to enjoy herself. Heaven knows, I never want anyone to put themselves out on my account."

And Iris, when I remonstrated with her, said: "Poor dear mother, she wants me to go and stay with friends and go to parties, but the moment I start off anywhere she has one of her heart attacks, so I much prefer to stay at home."

But presently she fell in love. A young friend of mine, a very good lad, asked her to marry him and she consented. I liked the child and was glad that she was to be given at last the chance to lead a life of her own. She had never seemed to suspect that such a thing was possible. But one day the young man came to me in great distress and told me that his marriage was indefinitely postponed. Iris felt that she could not desert her mother. Of course it was really no business of mine, but I made the opportunity to go and see Louise. She was always glad to receive her

friends at tea time and now that she was older she cultivated the society of painters and writers.

"Well, I hear that Iris isn't going to be married," I said after a little.

"I don't know about that. She's not going to be married quite as soon as I could have wished. I've begged her on my bended knees not to consider me, but she absolutely refuses to leave me."

"Don't you think it's rather hard on her?"

"Dreadfully. Of course it can only be for a few months, but I hate the thought of anyone sacrificing themselves for me."

"My dear Louise, you've buried two husbands, I can't see the least reason why you shouldn't bury at least two more."

"Do you think that's funny?" she asked me in a tone that she made as offensive as she could.

"I suppose it's never struck you as strange that you're always strong enough to do anything you want to and that your weak heart only prevents you from doing things that bore you?"

"Oh, I know, I know what you've always thought of me. You've never believed that I had anything the matter with me, have you?"

I looked at her full and square.

"Never. I think you've carried out for twenty-five years a stupendous bluff. I think you're the most selfish and monstrous woman I have ever known. You ruined the lives of those two wretched men you married and now you're going to ruin the life of your daughter."

I should not have been surprised if Louise had had a heart attack then. I fully expected her to fly into a passion. She merely gave me a gentle smile.

"My poor friend, one of these days you'll be so dreadfully sorry you said this to me."

"Have you quite determined that Iris shall not marry this boy?"

"I've begged her to marry him. I know it'll kill me, but I don't mind. Nobody cares for me. I'm just a burden to everybody."

"Did you tell her it would kill you?"

"She made me."

"As if anyone ever made you do anything

that you were not yourself quite determined to do."

"She can marry her young man tomorrow if she likes. If it kills me, it kills me."

"Well, let's risk it, shall we?"

"Haven't you got any compassion for me?"

"One can't pity anyone who amuses one as much as you amuse me," I answered.

A faint spot of color appeared on Louise's pale cheeks and though she smiled still her eyes were hard and angry.

"Iris shall marry in a month's time," she said, "and if anything happens to me I hope you and she will be able to forgive yourselves."

Louise was as good as her word. A date was fixed, a trousseau of great magnificence was ordered, and invitations were issued. Iris and the very good lad were radiant. On the wedding-day, at ten o'clock in the morning, Louise, that devilish woman, had one of her heart attacks—and died. She died gently forgiving Iris for having killed her.

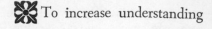 To increase understanding

1. (a) Cite phrases or sentences in the opening paragraph that raise the reader's interest in Louise. (b) In the last sentence of this paragraph the narrator suggests that he and Louise share a secret. When does the reader first begin to understand the nature of this secret?

2. How is Louise able to beg her husbands and her daughter not to consider her, and yet force them to give her her own way?

3. (a) What is Louise's opinion of the narrator? (b) Why does she continue to see him?

4. What causes Louise finally to be crossed?

5. (a) In the first paragraph the narrator wonders whether Louise "was a complete humbug." Was she? Explain. (b) To what extent does she succeed in forcing the narrator to acknowledge himself "mistaken and defeated"? How?

6. Maugham's famous, sophisticated style abounds in ironic statements that say one thing while meaning another. (a) Point out statements of this type. (b) Why is irony an especially appropriate device for developing the character of Louise?

John Galsworthy THE JAPANESE QUINCE

As Mr. Nilson, well known in the City,[1] opened the window of his dressing room on Campden Hill, he experienced a peculiar sweetish sensation in the back of his throat, and a feeling of emptiness just under his fifth rib. Hooking the window back, he noticed that a little tree in the Square Gardens had come out in blossom, and that the thermometer stood at sixty. "Perfect morning," he thought; "spring at last!"

Resuming some meditations on the price of Tintos, he took up an ivory-backed handglass and scrutinized his face. His firm, well-colored cheeks, with their neat brown mustaches, and his round, well-opened, clear grey eyes wore a reassuring appearance of good health.

Putting on his black frock coat, he went downstairs.

In the dining room his morning paper was laid out on the sideboard. Mr. Nilson had scarcely taken it in his hand when he again became aware of that queer feeling. Somewhat concerned, he went to the French window and descended the scrolled iron steps into the fresh air. A cuckoo clock struck eight.

"Half an hour to breakfast," he thought; "I'll take a turn in the Gardens."

He had them to himself, and proceeded to pace the circular path with his morning paper clasped behind him. He had scarcely made two revolutions, however, when it was borne

"The Japanese Quince" is reprinted with the permission of Charles Scribner's Sons and William Heinemann Ltd. from *A Motley* by John Galsworthy. Copyright 1910 Charles Scribner's Sons; renewal copyright 1938 Ada Galsworthy.
1. *the City*, the financial district of London.

in on him that, instead of going away in the fresh air, the feeling had increased. He drew several deep breaths, having heard deep breathing recommended by his wife's doctor; but they augmented rather than diminished the sensation—as of some sweetish liquor in course within him, together with a faint aching just above his heart. Running over what he had eaten the night before, he could recollect no unusual dish, and it occurred to him that it might possibly be some smell affecting him. But he could detect nothing except a faint sweet lemony scent, rather agreeable than otherwise, which evidently emanated from the bushes budding in the sunshine. He was on the point of resuming his promenade, when a blackbird close by burst into song, and, looking up, Mr. Nilson saw at a distance of perhaps five yards a little tree, in the heart of whose branches the bird was perched. He stood staring curiously at this tree, recognizing it for that which he had noticed from his window. It was covered with young blossoms, pink and white, and little bright green leaves both round and spiky; and on all this blossom and these leaves the sunlight glistened. Mr. Nilson smiled; the little tree was so alive and pretty! And instead of passing on, he stayed there smiling at the tree.

"Morning like this!" he thought; "and here I am the only person in the Square who has the—— to come out and—— !" But he had no sooner conceived this thought than he saw quite near him a man with his hands behind him, who was also staring up and smiling at the little tree. Rather taken aback, Mr. Nilson ceased to smile, and looked furtively at the stranger. It was his next-door neighbor, Mr. Tandram, well known in the City, who had occupied the adjoining house for some five years. Mr. Nilson perceived at once the awkwardness of his position, for, being married, they had not yet had occasion to speak to one another. Doubtful as to his proper conduct, he decided at last to murmur: "Fine morning!" and was passing on, when Mr. Tandram answered, "Beautiful, for the time of year!" Detecting a slight nervousness in his neighbor's voice, Mr. Nilson was emboldened to

John Galsworthy   1867-1933

Galsworthy was born in Coombe, Surrey, of an old Devonshire county family. He was educated at Harrow, where he made a name for himself as an athlete, and at Oxford, where he graduated with honors in law. Since he had enough money to live comfortably, he never practiced law. Instead he took to traveling extensively. On one voyage he read a fragment of a novel written by the captain of the ship and encouraged him to continue writing. The captain was Joseph Conrad; the friendship between Galsworthy and Conrad lasted until Conrad's death.

Galsworthy then settled down in Devonshire and began to write. His early novels were written between 1897 and 1901, but it was not until he published *Island Pharisees* that he found the subject which was to bring him renown—the effects of commercialism on personality in the upper-middle class. His next novel, *The Man of Property* (1906), was the first of a group of novels which, together with a series of connective links or "interludes," was published in 1922 as a single work, *The Forsyte Saga*. In this, his acknowledged masterpiece, Galsworthy traces the fortunes of the Forsyte family from the Victorian Age well into the twentieth century and makes clear the shifting tastes, moral standards, and economic values of several successive generations.

The year *The Man of Property* was published also saw the first of Galsworthy's numerous popular plays. In these, as in his novels, social criticism is the dominant theme, but in the plays his intention is more obvious. No one mistook the criticisms embodied in *Justice* (1910), *The Skin Game* (1920), or *Loyalties* (1922), all dealing with injustice and prejudice, but there were people who mistook *The Forsyte Saga* for a eulogy of property and the propertied classes!

Honor followed fame. In 1929, having earlier refused a knighthood, Galsworthy accepted the Order of Merit, and in 1932, the year before his death, he was awarded the Nobel Prize for literature.

regard him openly. He was of about Mr. Nilson's own height, with firm, well-colored cheeks, neat brown mustaches, and round, well-opened, clear grey eyes; and he was wearing a black frock coat. Mr. Nilson noticed that he had his morning paper clasped behind him as he looked up at the little tree. And, visited somehow by the feeling that he had been caught out, he said abruptly: "Er—can you give me the name of that tree?"

Mr. Tandram answered: "'I was about to ask you that," and stepped towards it. Mr. Nilson also approached the tree.

"Sure to have its name on, I should think," he said.

Mr. Tandram was the first to see the little label, close to where the blackbird had been sitting. He read it out. "Japanese quince!"

"Ah!" said Mr. Nilson, "thought so. Early flowerers."

"Very," assented Mr. Tandram, and added: "Quite a feelin' in the air today."

Mr. Nilson nodded. "It was a blackbird singin'," he said.

"Blackbirds," answered Mr. Tandram. "I prefer them to thrushes myself; more body in the note." And he looked at Mr. Nilson in an almost friendly way.

"Quite," murmured Mr. Nilson. "These exotics, they don't bear fruit. Pretty blossom!" and he again glanced up at the blossom, thinking: "Nice fellow, this, I rather like him."

Mr. Tandram also gazed at the blossom. And the little tree, as if appreciating their attention, quivered and glowed. From a distance the blackbird gave a loud, clear call. Mr. Nilson dropped his eyes. It struck him suddenly that Mr. Tandram looked a little foolish; and, as if he had seen himself, he said: "I must be going in. Good morning!"

A shade passed over Mr. Tandram's face, as if he, too, had suddenly noticed something about Mr. Nilson.

"Good morning," he replied, and clasping their journals to their backs they separated.

Mr. Nilson retraced his steps towards his garden window, walking slowly so as to avoid arriving at the same time as his neighbor. Having seen Mr. Tandram mount his scrolled iron steps, he ascended his own in turn. On the top step he paused.

With the slanting spring sunlight darting and quivering into it, the Japanese quince seemed more living than a tree. The blackbird had returned to it, and was chanting out his heart.

Mr. Nilson sighed; again he felt that queer sensation, that choky feeling in his throat.

The sound of a cough or sigh attracted his attention. There, in the shadow of his French window, stood Mr. Tandram, also looking forth across the Gardens at the little quince tree.

Unaccountably upset, Mr. Nilson turned abruptly into the house, and opened his morning paper.

✼ To increase understanding

1. (a) Why is Mr. Nilson prompted to go outside? (b) To what causes does he attribute his distress? (c) What does this reveal about his character?

2. As Mr. Nilson stands beside the quince tree he thinks: "Morning like this! . . . and here I am the only person in the Square who has the——to come out and——!" (page 597, column 1, paragraph 1). (a) How would he have completed this thought, had he been able? (b) What does his inability to complete it suggest about his character?

3. (a) What is humorous about the meeting between Mr. Nilson and Mr. Tandram? (b) Why are both men nervous?

4. As the two men stand beside the tree, Mr. Nilson is suddenly struck by the fact "that Mr. Tandram looked a little foolish; and, *as if he had seen himself*, he said: " 'I must be going in' " (page 598, column 1, paragraph 9). (a) What is the force of the italicized words? (b) Cite details or passages from the story that describe the two men, their occupations, and the circumstances of their lives, and explain why, in your opinion, Galsworthy has handled these details in this particular manner.

5. (a) What does the Japanese quince symbolize? (b) Why does it attract Mr. Nilson? (c) Why does it make him uncomfortable?

6. (a) What is the theme of the story? (b) Which of the following elements do you regard as most important in this story: plot, character, setting, theme? Give reasons for your answer.

Elizabeth Bowen   THE DEMON LOVER

Toward the end of her day in London Mrs. Drover went round to her shut-up house to look for several things she wanted to take away. Some belonged to herself, some to her family, who were by now used to their country life. It was late August; it had been a steamy, showery day; at the moment the trees down the pavement glittered in an escape of humid yellow afternoon sun. Against the next batch of clouds, already piling up ink-dark, broken chimneys and parapets stood out. In her once familiar street, as in any unused channel, an unfamiliar queerness had silted up; a cat wove itself in and out of railings but no human eye watched Mrs. Drover's return. Shifting some parcels under her arm, she slowly forced round her latchkey in an unwilling lock, then gave the door, which had warped, a push with her knee. Dead air came out to meet her as she went in.

The staircase window having been boarded up, no light came down into the hall. But one door, she could just see, stood ajar, so she went quickly through into the room and unshuttered the big window in there. Now the prosaic woman, looking about her, was more perplexed than she knew by everything that she saw, by traces of her long former habit of life—the yellow smoke stain up the white marble mantelpiece, the ring left by a vase on the top of the escritoire; the bruise in the wallpaper where, on the door being thrown open widely, the china handle had always hit the wall. The piano, having gone away to be stored, had left what looked like claw marks on its part of the parquet. Though not much dust had seeped in, each object wore a film of another kind; and, the only ventilation being the chimney, the whole drawing room smelled of the cold hearth. Mrs. Drover put down her parcels on the escritoire and left the room to proceed upstairs; the things she wanted were in a bedroom chest.

She had been anxious to see how the house was—the part-time caretaker she shared with some neighbors was away this week on his holiday, known to be not yet back. At the best of times he did not look in often, and she was never sure that she trusted him. There were some cracks in the structure, left by the last bombing, on which she was anxious to keep an eye. Not that one could do anything——

A shaft of refracted daylight now lay across the hall. She stopped dead and stared at the hall table—on this lay a letter addressed to her.

She thought first—then the caretaker *must* be back. All the same, who, seeing the house shuttered, would have dropped a letter in the box? It was not a circular, it was not a bill. And the post office redirected, to the address

Elizabeth Bowen   1899–1973

Although she was born in Dublin, Elizabeth Bowen lived most of her life in or near London, making winter trips to Italy in her early years, and, since she inherited her ancestral home in County Cork, summer trips to Ireland. Miss Bowen first moved to London at the age of nineteen, when she left home to devote herself to a life of writing. So successful was she that most critics consider her one of Britain's very best writers.

During World War II Miss Bowen worked days for the Ministry of Information; her nights were spent on duty as an air-raid warden; and in every cranny of time she wrote. Her writings of this period are a remarkable record of the reactions of individuals to the stress of living under bombardment. Never concentrating on the actual events of war, she penetrates instead to the depths of a character's consciousness. Both the collection of short stories assembled in *The Demon Lover* in 1941 (published in the United States under the title *Ivy Gripped the Steps*) and the novel *The Heat of the Day* (1949) are set in the framework of war.

in the country, everything for her that came through the post. The caretaker (even if he *were* back) did not know she was due in London today—her call here had been planned to be a surprise—so his negligence in the manner of this letter, leaving it to wait in the dusk and the dust, annoyed her. Annoyed, she picked up the letter which bore no stamp. But it cannot be important, or they would know. . . . She took the letter rapidly upstairs with her, without a stop to look at the writing till she reached what had been her bedroom, where she let in light. The room looked over the garden and other gardens; the sun had gone in; as the clouds sharpened and lowered, the trees and rank lawns seemed already to smoke with dark. Her reluctance to look again at the letter came from the fact that she felt intruded upon—and by someone contemptuous of her ways. However, in the tenseness preceding the fall of rain she read it; it was a few lines.

Dear Kathleen,
  You will not have forgotten that today is our anniversary, and the day we said. The years have gone by at once slowly and fast. In view of the fact that nothing has changed, I shall rely upon you to keep your promise. I was sorry to see you leave London, but was satisfied that you would be back in time. You may expect me, therefore, at the hour arranged.
                    Until then . . .
                              K.

Mrs. Drover looked for the date; it was today's. She dropped the letter onto the bedsprings, then picked it up to see the writing again—her lips, beneath the remains of lipstick, beginning to go white. She felt so much the change in her own face that she went to the mirror, polished a clear patch in it and looked at once urgently and stealthily in. She was confronted by a woman of forty-four, with eyes staring out under a hat brim that had been rather carelessly pulled down. She had not put on any more powder since she left the shop where she ate her solitary tea. The pearls her husband had given her on their marriage hung loose round her now rather thinner throat, slipping into the V of the pink wool jumper her sister knitted last autumn as

they sat round the fire. Mrs. Drover's most normal expression was one of controlled worry, but of assent. Since the birth of the third of her little boys, attended by a quite serious illness, she had had an intermittent muscular flicker to the left of her mouth, but in spite of this she could always sustain a manner that was at once energetic and calm.

Turning from her own face as precipitately as she had gone to meet it, she went to the chest where the things were, unlocked it, threw up the lid, and knelt to search. But as rain began to come crashing down she could not keep from looking over her shoulder at the stripped bed on which the letter lay. Behind the blanket of rain the clock of the

THE DEMON LOVER

The ballad known as "The Demon Lover" has been found throughout the English-speaking world in many versions. This text, traditional in Scotland and Ireland, was collected by Sir Walter Scott (see page 371), and published in his Minstrelsy of the Scottish Border.

"O where have you been, my long, long love,
  This long seven years and mair?"
"O I'm come to seek my former vows
  Ye granted me before."

"O hold your tongue of your former vows, 5
  For they will breed sad strife;
O hold your tongue of your former vows
  For I am become a wife."

He turnd him right and round about,
  And the tear blinded his ee: 10
"I wad never hae trodden on Irish ground,
  If it had not been for thee.

"I might hae had a king's daughter,
  Far, far beyond the sea;
I might have had a king's daughter, 15
  Had it not been for love o thee."

church that still stood struck six—with rapidly heightening apprehension she counted each of the slow strokes, "The hour arranged . . . My God," she said, "*what* hour? How should I . . . ? After twenty-five years, . . ."

The young girl talking to the soldier in the garden had not ever completely seen his face. It was dark; they were saying good-by under a tree. Now and then—for it felt, from not seeing him at this intense moment, as though she had never seen him at all—she verified his presence for these few moments longer by putting out a hand, which he each time pressed, without very much kindness, and painfully, onto one of the breast buttons of his uniform. That cut of the button on the palm of her hand was, principally, what she was to carry away. This was so near the end of a leave from France that she could only wish him already gone. It was August, 1916. Being not kissed, being drawn away from and looked at intimidated Kathleen till she imagined spectral glitters in the place of his eyes. Turning away, and looking back up the lawn she saw, through branches of trees, the drawing-room window alight; she caught a breath for the moment when she could go running back there into the safe arms of her mother and sister, and cry: "What shall I do, what shall I do? He has gone."

"If ye might have had a king's daughter,
    Yer sel ye had to blame;
Ye might have taken the king's daughter,
    For ye kend that I was nane.   20

"If I was to leave my husband dear,
    And my two babes also,
O what have you to take me to,
    If with you I should go?"

"I hae seven ships upon the sea—   25
    And the eighth brought me to land—
With four-and-twenty bold mariners,
    And music on every hand."

She has taken up her two little babes,
    Kissed them baith cheek and chin: 30
"O fair ye weel, my ain two babes,
    For I'll never see you again."

She set her foot upon the ship,
    No mariners could she behold;
But the sails were o the taffetie,   35
    And the masts o beaten gold.

She had not sailed a league, a league,
    A league but barely three,

When dismal grew his countenance,
    And drumlie grew his ee.   40

They had not sailed a league, a league,
    A league but barely three,
Until she espied his cloven foot,
    And she wept right bitterlie.

"O hold your tongue of your weeping," says he,
    "Of your weeping now let me be;   46
I will show you how the lilies grow
    On the banks of Italy."

"O what hills are yon, yon pleasant hills,
    That the sun shines sweetly on?"   50
"O yon are the hills of heaven," he said,
    "Where you will never win."

"O whaten a mountain is yon," she said,
    "All so dreary wi frost and snow?"
"O yon is the mountain of hell," he cried, 55
    "Where you and I will go."

He strack the tap-mast wi his hand,
    The fore-masts wi his knee,
And he brake that gallant ship in twain,
    And sank her in the sea.   60

Hearing her catch her breath, her fiancé said, without feeling, "Cold?"

"You're going away such a long way."

"Not so far as you think."

"I don't understand?"

"You don't have to," he said. "You will. You know what we said."

"But that was—suppose you—I mean, suppose."

"I shall be with you," he said, "sooner or later. You won't forget that. You need do nothing but wait."

Only a little more than a minute later she was free to run up the silent lawn. Looking in through the window at her mother and sister, who did not for the moment perceive her, she already felt that unnatural promise drive down between her and the rest of all humankind. No other way of having given herself could have made her feel so apart, lost and foresworn. She could not have plighted a more sinister troth.

Kathleen behaved well when, some months later, her fiancé was reported missing, presumed killed. Her family not only supported her but were able to praise her courage without stint because they could not regret, as a husband for her, the man they knew almost nothing about. They hoped she would, in a year or two, console herself—and had it been only a question of consolation things might have gone much straighter ahead. But her trouble, behind just a little grief, was a complete dislocation from everything. She did not reject other lovers, for these failed to appear; for years she failed to attract men—and with the approach of her thirties she became natural enough to share her family's anxiousness on this score. She began to put herself out, to wonder; and at thirty-two she was very greatly relieved to find herself being courted by William Drover. She married him, and the two of them settled down in this quiet, arboreal part of Kensington; in this house the years piled up, her children were born and they all lived till they were driven out by the bombs of the next war. Her movements as Mrs. Drover were circumscribed, and she dismissed any idea that they were still watched.

As things were—dead or living, the letter writer sent her only a threat. Unable, for some minutes to go on kneeling with her back exposed to the empty room, Mrs. Drover rose from the chest to sit on an upright chair whose back was firmly against the wall. The desuetude of her former bedroom, her married London home's whole air of being a cracked cup from which memory, with its reassuring power, had either evaporated or leaked away, made a crisis—and at just this crisis the letter writer had, knowledgeably, struck. The hollowness of the house this evening canceled years on years of voices, habits, and steps. Through the shut windows she only heard rain fall on the roofs around. To rally herself, she said she was in a mood—and, for two or three seconds shutting her eyes, told herself that she had imagined the letter. But she opened them—there it lay on the bed.

On the supernatural side of the letter's entrance she was not permitting her mind to dwell. Who, in London, knew she meant to call at the house today? Evidently, however, this had been known. The caretaker, *had* he come back, had had no cause to expect her: he would have taken the letter in his pocket, to forward it, at his own time, through the post. There was no other sign that the caretaker had been in—but, if not? Letters dropped in at doors of deserted houses do not fly or walk to tables in halls. They do not sit on the dust of empty tables with the air of certainty that they will be found. There is needed some human hand—but nobody but the caretaker had a key. Under circumstances she did not care to consider, a house can be entered without a key. It was possible that she was not alone now. She might be waited for, downstairs. Waited for—until when? Until "the hour arranged." At least that was not six o'clock; six had struck.

She rose from the chair and went over and locked the door.

The thing was, to get out. To fly? No, not that: she had to catch her train. As a woman whose utter dependability was the keystone of her family life, she was not willing to return to the country, to her husband, her little boys and her sister, without the objects she had come to fetch.

Resuming work at the chest she set about making up a number of parcels in a rapid, fumbling-decisive way. These, with her shopping parcels, would be too much to carry; these meant a taxi—at the thought of the taxi her heart went up and her normal breathing resumed. I will ring up the taxi now; the taxi cannot come too soon: I shall hear the taxi out there running its engine, till I walk calmly down to it through the hall. I'll ring up—But no: the telephone is cut off. . . . She tugged at a knot she had tied wrong.

The idea of flight . . . He was never kind to me, not really. I don't remember him kind at all. Mother said he never considered me. He was set on me, that was what it was—not love. Not love, not meaning a person well. What did he do, to make me promise like that? I can't remember—— But she found that she could.

She remembered with such dreadful acuteness that the twenty-five years since then dissolved like smoke and she instinctively looked for the weal left by the button on the palm of her hand. She remembered not only all that he said and did, but the complete suspension of *her* existence during that August week. I was not myself—they all told me so at the time. She remembered—but with one white burning blank as where acid has been dropped on a photograph; *under no conditions* could she remember his face.

So, wherever he may be waiting I shall not know him. You have no time to run from a face you do not expect.

The thing was to get to the taxi before any clock struck what could be the hour. She would slip down the street and round the side of the square to where the square gave on the main road. She would return in the taxi, safe, to her own door, and bring the solid driver into the house with her to pick up the parcels from room to room. The idea of the taxi driver made her decisive, bold; she unlocked the door, went to the top of the staircase, and listened down.

She heard nothing—but while she was hearing nothing the *passé* air of the staircase was disturbed by a draft that traveled up to her face. It emanated from the basement; down there a door or window was being opened by someone who chose this moment to leave the house.

The rain had stopped; the pavements steamily shone as Mrs. Drover let herself out by inches from her own front door into the empty street. The unoccupied houses opposite continued to meet her look with their damaged stare. Making toward the thoroughfare and the taxi, she tried not to keep looking behind. Indeed, the silence was so intense—one of those creeks of London silence exaggerated this summer by the damage of war—that no tread could have gained on hers unheard. Where her street debouched on the square where people went on living she grew conscious of and checked her unnatural pace. Across the open end of the square two buses impassively passed each other; women, a perambulator, cyclists, a man wheeling a barrow signalized, once again, the ordinary flow of life.

At the square's most populous corner should be—and was—the short taxi rank. This evening, only one taxi—but this, although it presented its blank rump, appeared already to be alertly waiting for her. Indeed, without looking round the driver started his engine as she panted up from behind and put her hand on the door. As she did so, the clock struck seven. The taxi faced the main road; to make the trip back to her house it would have to turn—and she settled back on the seat and the taxi *had* turned before she, surprised by its knowing movement, recollected that she had not "said where." She leaned forward to scratch at the glass panel that divided the driver's seat from her own.

The driver braked to what was almost a stop, turned round, and slid the glass panel back; the jolt of this flung Mrs. Drover forward till her face was almost into the glass. Through the aperture driver and passenger, not six inches between them, remained for an eternity eye to eye. Mrs. Drover's mouth hung open for some seconds before she could issue her first scream. After that she continued to scream freely and to beat with her gloved hands on the glass all round as the taxi, accelerating without mercy, made off with her into the hinterland of deserted streets.

To increase understanding

1. Like any good ghost story, "The Demon Lover" builds up tension and excitement steadily toward a climax. (a) How does the setting contribute to this effect? (b) Point out other means by which excitement is built up.

2. Why did Kathleen marry Mr. Drover?

3. (a) What kind of life has Mrs. Drover led since her marriage? (b) Compare it, in its satisfactions and limitations, with that of Mr. Nilson in "The Japanese Quince."

4. (a) What events are recounted in the flashback beginning on page 601, column 1, paragraph 1? (b) What is the purpose of this flashback?

5. (a) What were Kathleen's feelings when her fiancé left? (b) Why does he now appear to her

as a threat? (c) To what extent is Mrs. Drover in control of her thoughts and feelings? Support your answer with examples from the story.

6. Miss Bowen makes use of the old ballad "The Demon Lover" to suggest the ghostly character of her story and to probe beyond the conscious thoughts and feelings of an individual haunted by the continuing stress of war. (a) In what way is Mrs. Drover's situation like that of the heroine of the ballad? (b) What lines in the ballad suggest Mrs. Drover's memories of her fiancé? (c) The author reports that after Kathleen's fiancé was reported missing, she suffered "a complete dislocation from everything." What does this mean? (d) How might World War II affect the state of mind of an individual who was once in this condition?

7. Compare the tone of the story with the tone of the old ballad.

E. M. Forster THE CELESTIAL OMNIBUS

The boy who resided at Agathox Lodge, 28, Buckingham Park Road, Surbiton, had often been puzzled by the old signpost that stood almost opposite. He asked his mother about it, and she replied that it was a joke, and not a very nice one, which had been made many years back by some naughty young men, and that the police ought to remove it. For there were two strange things about this signpost: firstly, it pointed up a blank alley, and, secondly, it had painted on it, in faded characters, the words, "To Heaven."

"What kind of young men were they?" he asked.

"I think your father told me that one of them wrote verses, and was expelled from the University and came to grief in other ways. Still, it was a long time ago. You must ask your father about it. He will say the same as I do, that it was put up as a joke."

"So it doesn't mean anything at all?"

She sent him upstairs to put on his best things, for the Bonses were coming to tea, and he was to hand the cakestand.

It struck him, as he wrenched on his tight-

ening trousers, that he might do worse than ask Mr. Bons about the signpost. His father, though very kind, always laughed at him—shrieked with laughter whenever he or any other child asked a question or spoke. But Mr. Bons was serious as well as kind. He had a beautiful house and lent one books; he was a churchwarden, and a candidate for the County Council; he had donated to the Free Library enormously, he presided over the Literary Society, and had Members of Parliament to stop with him—in short, he was probably the wisest person alive.

Yet even Mr. Bons could only say that the signpost was a joke—the joke of a person named Shelley.

"Of course!" cried the mother; "I told you so, dear. That was the name."

"Had you never heard of Shelley?" asked Mr. Bons.

"No," said the boy, and hung his head.

"But is there no Shelley in the house?"

"Why, yes!" exclaimed the lady, in much agitation. "Dear Mr. Bons, we aren't such

Reprinted from The Collected Tales of E. M. Forster, by permission of Alfred A. Knopf, Inc., New York; and Sidgwick & Jackson Ltd., London. Copyright 1947 by Alfred A. Knopf, Inc.

Philistines[1] as that. Two at the least. One a wedding present, and the other, smaller print, in one of the spare rooms."

"I believe we have seven Shelleys," said Mr. Bons, with a slow smile. Then he brushed the cake crumbs off his stomach, and, together with his daughter, rose to go.

The boy, obeying a wink from his mother, saw them all the way to the garden gate, and when they had gone he did not at once return to the house, but gazed for a little up and down Buckingham Park Road.

His parents lived at the right end of it. After No. 39 the quality of the houses dropped very suddenly, and 64 had not even a separate servants' entrance. But at the present moment the whole road looked rather pretty, for the sun had just set in splendor, and the inequalities of rent were drowned in a saffron afterglow. Small birds twittered, and the breadwinners' train shrieked musically down through the cutting—that wonderful cutting which has drawn to itself the whole beauty out of Surbiton, and clad itself, like any Alpine valley, with the glory of the fir and the silver birch and the primrose. It was this cutting that had first stirred desires within the boy—desires for something just a little different, he knew not what, desires that would return whenever things were sunlit, as they were this evening, running up and down inside him, up and down, up and down, till he would feel quite unusual all over, and as likely as not would want to cry. This evening he was even sillier, and he slipped across the road towards the signpost and began to run up the blank alley.

The alley runs between high walls—the walls of the gardens of "Ivanhoe" and "Belle Vista"[2] respectively. It smells a little all the way, and is scarcely twenty yards long, including the turn at the end. So not unnaturally the boy soon came to a standstill. "I'd like to kick that Shelley," he exclaimed, and

---

1. *Philistines.* In Biblical times the Philistines were an enemy of the Israelites. Matthew Arnold adapted the term from the word *Philister,* used by students in the German universities to express their contempt for the townspeople. Hence a Philistine is a person lacking culture. **2.** *"Ivanhoe" and "Belle Vista."* It is a widespread custom in England to give names to houses.

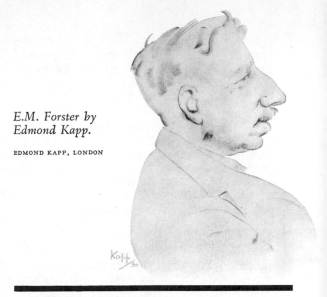

E.M. Forster by Edmond Kapp.

E. M. Forster 1879-1970

Although he wrote only a few novels, E. M. Forster is regarded as one of the major novelists of the first half of the twentieth century. Born in London, he was educated at Tonbridge School and at Cambridge, where he spent his last years. After his graduation from the university, he lived for a time in Italy. While there he worked on two novels—*Where Angels Fear to Tread* (1905) and *A Room with a View* (1908)—both of which have an Italian background. After returning to England in 1907, he wrote *Howard's End* (1910), the most mature work he had thus far produced.

In 1911 he traveled to India with a former Cambridge tutor and friend. He spent World War I in Alexandria, Egypt, returning to England after the fighting to write reviews for the *New Statesman* and *Spectator.* As the years passed he devoted more and more of his time to criticism, winning an enviable reputation in this field.

Forster returned to India in 1921, and from impressions of his two visits there he wrought his most famous novel, *A Passage to India* (1924). In this, his last novel and his greatest work, he lays bare the difficulties of establishing ordinary social contact between a cultivated Englishman and an Indian of a similar class. In *A Passage to India,* as in most of his work, his aim is similar to Galsworthy's—through satire and irony to expose flaws in the values cherished by the upper-middle class to which he himself belonged. In "The Celestial Omnibus," as in a number of his novels and most of his short stories, the shortcomings of the conventionally educated and conforming adult are shown up by the natural life-loving enthusiasm of children or primitive foreigners.

glanced idly at a piece of paper which was pasted on the wall. Rather an odd piece of paper, and he read it carefully before he turned back. This is what he read:

S. and C. R. C. C.
Alteration in Service

Owing to lack of patronage the Company are regretfully compelled to suspend the hourly service, and to retain only the

Sunrise and Sunset Omnibuses,

which will run as usual. It is to be hoped that the public will patronize an arrangement which is intended for their convenience. As an extra inducement, the Company will, for the first time, now issue

Return tickets!

(available one day only), which may be obtained of the driver. Passengers are again reminded that no *tickets are issued at the other end, and that no complaints in this connection will receive consideration from the Company. Nor will the Company be responsible for any negligence or stupidity on the part of Passengers, nor for Hailstorms, Lightning, Loss of Tickets, nor for any Act of God.*

§ *For the Direction.*

Now he had never seen this notice before, nor could he imagine where the omnibus went to. S. of course was for "Surbiton," and R. C. C. meant "Road Car Company." But what was the meaning of the other C.? "Coombe and Malden," perhaps, or possibly "City." Yet it could not hope to compete with the South-Western. The whole thing, the boy reflected, was run on hopelessly unbusinesslike lines. Why not tickets from the other end? And what an hour to start! Then he realized that unless the notice was a hoax, an omnibus must have been starting just as he was wishing the Bonses goodby. He peered at the ground through the gathering dusk, and there he saw what might or might not be the marks of wheels. Yet nothing had come out of the alley. And he had never seen an omnibus at any time in the Buckingham Park Road. No: it must be a hoax, like the signposts, like the fairy tales, like the dreams upon which he would wake suddenly in the night. And with a sigh he stepped from the alley—right into the arms of his father.

Oh, how his father laughed! "Poor, poor Popsey!" he cried. "Diddums! Diddums! Diddums think he'd walky-palky up to Evvink!" And his mother, also convulsed wth laughter, appeared on the steps of Agathox Lodge. "Don't, Bob!" she gasped. "Don't be so naughty! Oh, you'll kill me! Oh, leave the boy alone!"

But all that evening the joke was kept up. The father implored to be taken too. Was it a very tiring walk? Need one wipe one's shoes on the doormat? And the boy went to bed feeling faint and sore, and thankful for only one thing—that he had not said a word about the omnibus. It was a hoax, yet through his dreams it grew more and more real, and the streets of Surbiton, through which he saw it driving, seemed instead to become hoaxes and shadows. And very early in the morning he woke with a cry, for he had had a glimpse of its destination.

He struck a match, and its light fell not only on his watch but also on his calendar, so that he knew it to be half-an-hour to sunrise. It was pitch dark, for the fog had come down from London in the night, and all Surbiton was wrapped in its embrace. Yet he sprang out and dressed himself, for he was determined to settle once for all which was real, the omnibus or the streets. "I shall be a fool one way or the other," he thought, "until I know." Soon he was shivering in the road under the gas lamp that guarded the entrance to the alley.

To enter the alley itself required some courage. Not only was it horribly dark, but he now realized that it was an impossible terminus for an omnibus. If it had not been for a policeman, whom he heard approaching through the fog, he would never have made the attempt. The next moment he had made the attempt and failed. Nothing. Nothing but a blank alley and a very silly boy gaping at its dirty floor. It *was* a hoax. "I'll tell papa and mamma," he decided. "I deserve it. I deserve that they should know. I am too silly to be alive." And he went back to the gate of Agathox Lodge.

There he remembered that his watch was fast. The sun was not risen; it would not rise for two minutes. "Give the bus every chance," he thought cynically, and returned into the alley.

But the omnibus was there.

I t had two horses, whose sides were still smoking from their journey, and its two great lamps shone through the fog against the alley's walls, changing their cobwebs and moss into tissues of fairyland. The driver was huddled up in a cape. He faced the blank wall, and how he had managed to drive in so neatly and so silently was one of the many things that the boy never discovered. Nor could he imagine how ever he would drive out.

"Please," his voice quavered through the foul brown air, "Please, is that an omnibus?"

"Omnibus est,"[3] said the driver, without turning around. There was a moment's silence. The policeman passed, coughing, by the entrance of the alley. The boy crouched in the shadow, for he did not want to be found out. He was pretty sure, too, that it was a Pirate; nothing else, he reasoned, would go from such odd places and at such odd hours.

"About when do you start?" He tried to sound nonchalant.

"At sunrise."

"How far do you go?"

"The whole way."

"And can I have a return ticket which will bring me all the way back?"

---

3. "*Omnibus est.*" The driver answers the boy's question with a play on the English and Latin meanings of the word *omnibus*. Using the English meaning, *omnibus est* would mean "It is an omnibus"; the original Latin meaning is "It is for everybody."

Wagner's *Ring*

Richard Wagner (1813-1883) was a great German opera composer, deeply interested in German nationalism, Germanic myths, and art. His major work is a vast cycle of four operas called *Der Ring des Nibelungen*, which is based on a group of old Scandinavian legends. This opera cycle centers around a magic ring of gold stolen from the Rhine maidens by the Nibelungs—dwarfs who dwell in the land of darkness and mists. The ring, which symbolizes all wealth and power, brings a curse to all who gain it.

The first of the operas, *Das Rheingold* (*The Rhine Gold*), serves as an introduction to the rest, telling the origin of the ring and introducing the gods. Chief among the gods is Wotan, who steals the ring, thereby bringing its curse down upon himself and all the other gods. In the spectacular finale of this first opera the gods cross the rainbow bridge into their fabulous palace, Valhalla.

It was in *Das Rheingold* that Wagner first brought to perfection his philosophy of music and art generally. Since his aim was to provide a grand fusion of drama, music, and spectacle, the long flowing lines of harmony are designed to be the musical counterpart of the characters, actions, ideas, and scenes presented on the stage. In a sense the listener can see what is happening through hearing the music. The most famous device used by Wagner to achieve this effect is the *leitmotif*. This is simply a passage of music which is used throughout the selection to represent a single character or idea.

The remaining three operas in the cycle— *Die Walküre* (*The Valkyr*), *Siegfried*, and *Götterdämmerung* (*The Twilight of the Gods*)—show the working out of the curse, symbolic of the destruction that accompanies sacrificing other interests to that of gaining wealth and power. In the end even Valhalla with all the gods is destroyed by fire, and the ring of gold returns to the bottom of the Rhine River, where it is guarded once again by its original possessors, the Rhine maidens.

"You can."

"Do you know, I half think I'll come." The driver made no answer. The sun must have risen, for he unhitched the brake. And scarcely had the boy jumped in before the omnibus was off.

How? Did it turn? There was no room. Did it go forward? There was a blank wall. Yet it was moving—moving at a stately pace through the fog, which had turned from brown to yellow. The thought of warm bed and warmer breakfast made the boy feel faint. He wished he had not come. His parents would not have approved. He would have gone back to them if the weather had not made it impossible. The solitude was terrible; he was the only passenger. And the omnibus, though well built, was cold and somewhat musty. He drew his coat round him, and in so doing chanced to feel his pocket. It was empty. He had forgotten his purse.

"Stop!" he shouted. "Stop!" And then, being of a polite disposition, he glanced up at the painted notice-board so that he might call the driver by name. "Mr. Browne! stop; O, do please stop!"

Mr. Browne did not stop, but he opened a little window and looked in at the boy. His face was a surprise, so kind it was and modest.

"Mr. Browne, I've left my purse behind. I've not got a penny. I can't pay for the ticket. Will you take my watch, please? I am in the most awful hole."

"Tickets on this line," said the driver, "whether single or return, can be purchased by coinage from no terrene mint. And a chronometer, though it had solaced the vigils of Charlemagne, or measured the slumbers of Laura,[4] can acquire by no mutation the double-cake that charms the fangless Cerberus of Heaven!"[5] So saying, he handed in the necessary ticket, and, while the boy said "Thank you," continued: "Titular pretensions, I know it well, are vanity. Yet they merit no censure when uttered on a laughing lip, and in an homonymous world are in some sort useful, since they do serve to distinguish one Jack from his fellow. Remember me, therefore, as Sir Thomas Browne."[6]

"Are you a *Sir*? Oh, sorry!" He had heard of these gentlemen drivers. "It *is* good of you about the ticket. But if you go on at this rate, however does your bus pay?"

"It does not pay. It was not intended to pay. Many are the faults of my equipage; it is compounded too curiously of foreign woods; its cushions tickle erudition rather than promote repose; and my horses are nourished not on the evergreen pastures of the moment, but on the dried bents and clovers of Latinity. But that it pays! —that error at all events was never intended and never attained."

"Sorry again," said the boy rather hopelessly. Sir Thomas looked sad, fearing that, even for a moment, he had been the cause of sadness. He invited the boy to come up and sit beside him on the box, and together they journeyed on through the fog, which was now changing from yellow to white. There were no houses by the road; so it must be either Putney Heath or Wimbledon Common.[7]

"Have you been a driver always?"

"I was a physician once."

"But why did you stop? Weren't you good?"

"As a healer of bodies I had scant success, and several score of my patients preceded me. But as a healer of the spirit I have succeeded beyond my hopes and my deserts. For though my draughts were not better nor subtler than those of other men, yet, by reason of the cunning goblets wherein I offered them, the queasy soul was ofttimes tempted to sip and be refreshed."

"The queasy soul," he murmured; "if the sun sets with trees in front of it, and you suddenly come strange all over, is that a queasy soul?"

"Have you felt that?"

4. *Laura*, a French lady celebrated in the sonnets of the great fourteenth-century Italian poet, Petrarch. 5. *double-cake . . . Heaven*. In Roman mythology Cerberus was the three-headed dog that guarded the gates to the abode of the dead. When Aeneas made his trip to this land, according to Vergil's *Aeneid*, Cerberus was lulled to sleep with a cake seasoned with poppies and honey. 6. *Sir Thomas Browne*, seventeenth-century physician, famous as one of the great English prose stylists. As this passage indicates, his prose is based on Latin vocabulary and structure, and is shot through with classical allusions. 7. *Putney Heath or Wimbledon Common*, large open areas between Surbiton and London.

"Why yes."

After a pause he told the boy a little, a very little, about the journey's end. But they did not chatter much, for the boy, when he liked a person, would as soon sit silent in his company as speak, and this, he discovered, was also the mind of Sir Thomas Browne and of many others with whom he was to be acquainted. He heard, however, about the young man Shelley, who was now quite a famous person, with a carriage of his own, and about some of the other drivers who are in the service of the Company. Meanwhile the light grew stronger, though the fog did not disperse. It was now more like mist than fog, and at times would travel quickly across them, as if it was part of a cloud. They had been ascending, too, in a most puzzling way; for over two hours the horses had been pulling against the collar, and even if it were Richmond Hill[8] they ought to have been at the top long ago. Perhaps it was Epsom, or even the North Downs[9]; yet the air seemed keener than that which blows on either. And as to the name of their destination, Sir Thomas Browne was silent.

Crash!

"Thunder, by Jove!" said the boy, "and not so far off either. Listen to the echoes! It's more like mountains."

He thought, not very vividly, of his father and mother. He saw them sitting down to sausages and listening to the storm. He saw his own empty place. Then there would be questions, alarms, theories, jokes, consolations. They would expect him back at lunch. To lunch he would not come, nor to tea, but he would be in for dinner, and so his day's truancy would be over. If he had had his purse he would have bought them presents—not that he should have known what to get them.

Crash!

The peal and the lightning came together. The cloud quivered as if it were alive, and torn streamers of mist rushed past. "Are you afraid?" asked Sir Thomas Browne.

"What is there to be afraid of? Is it much farther?"

The horses of the omnibus stopped just as a ball of fire burst up and exploded with a ringing noise that was deafening but clear, like the noise of a blacksmith's forge. All the cloud was shattered.

"Oh, listen, Sir Thomas Browne! No, I mean look; we shall get a view at last. No, I mean listen; that sounds like a rainbow!"

The noise had died into the faintest murmur, beneath which another murmur grew, spreading stealthily, steadily, in a curve that widened but did not vary. And in widening curves a rainbow was spreading from the horses' feet into the dissolving mists.

"But how beautiful! What colors! Where will it stop? It is more like the rainbows you can tread on. More like dreams."

The color and the sound grew together. The rainbow spanned an enormous gulf. Clouds rushed under it and were pierced by it, and still it grew, reaching forward, conquering the darkness, until it touched something that seemed more solid than a cloud.

The boy stood up. "What is that out there?" he called. "What does it rest on, out at that other end?"

In the morning sunshine a precipice shone forth beyond the gulf. A precipice—or was it a castle? The horses moved. They set their feet upon the rainbow.

"Oh, look!" the boy shouted. "Oh, listen! Those caves—or are they gateways? Oh, look between those cliffs at those ledges. I see people! I see trees!"

"Look also below," whispered Sir Thomas. "Neglect not the diviner Acheron."[10]

The boy looked below, past the flames of the rainbow that licked against their wheels. The gulf also had cleared, and in its depths there flowed an everlasting river. One sunbeam entered and struck a green pool, and as they passed over he saw three maidens rise to the surface of the pool, singing, and playing with something that glistened like a ring.

"You down in the water——" he called.

They answered, "You up on the bridge——" There was a burst of music. "You up on the

8. *Richmond Hill,* a hill in a large park near London. 9. *Epsom, or even the North Downs,* tracts of open land several miles south of London. 10. *Acheron.* This word had two meanings for the Greeks and Romans. *Acheron* was used to refer to all of the lower world; it also was the name of one of the rivers that flowed through the lower world.

bridge, good luck to you. Truth in the depth, truth on the height."

"You down in the water, what are you doing?"

Sir Thomas Browne replied: "They sport in the mancipiary possession of their gold"; and the omnibus arrived.

The boy was in disgrace. He sat locked up in the nursery of Agathox Lodge, learning poetry for a punishment. His father had said, "My boy! I can pardon anything but untruthfulness," and had caned him, saying at each stroke, "There is *no* omnibus, *no* driver, *no* bridge, *no* mountain; you are a *truant*, a *guttersnipe*, a *liar*." His father could be very stern at times. His mother had begged him to say he was sorry. But he could not say that. It was the greatest day of his life, in spite of the caning and the poetry at the end of it.

He had returned punctually at sunset—driven not by Sir Thomas Browne, but by a maiden lady who was full of quiet fun. They had talked of omnibuses and also of barouche landaus. How far away her gentle voice seemed now! Yet it was scarcely three hours since he had left her up the alley.

His mother called through the door. "Dear, you are to come down and to bring your poetry with you."

He came down, and found that Mr. Bons was in the smoking room with his father. It had been a dinner party.

"Here is the great traveler!" said his father grimly. "Here is the young gentleman who drives in an omnibus over rainbows, while young ladies sing to him." Pleased with his wit, he laughed.

"After all," said Mr. Bons, smiling, "there is something a little like it in Wagner.[11] It is odd how, in quite illiterate minds, you will find glimmers of Artistic Truth. The case interests me. Let me plead for the culprit. We have all romanced in our time, haven't we?"

"Hear how kind Mr. Bons is," said his mother, while his father said, "Very well. Let

him say his poem, and that will do. He is going away to my sister on Tuesday, and *she* will cure him of this alley-slopering."[12] (Laughter.) "Say your poem."

The boy began. " 'Standing aloof in giant ignorance.' "

His father laughed again—roared. "One for you, my son! 'Standing aloof in giant ignorance!' I never knew these poets talked sense. Just describes you. Here, Bons, you go in for poetry. Put him through it, will you, while I fetch up the whisky?"

"Yes, give me the Keats," said Mr. Bons. "Let him say his Keats to me."

So for a few moments the wise man and the ignorant boy were left alone in the smoking room.

" 'Standing aloof in giant ignorance, of thee I dream and of the Cyclades, as one who sits ashore and longs perchance to visit——' "[13]

"Quite right. To visit what?"

" 'To visit dolphin coral in deep seas,' " said the boy, and burst into tears.

"Come, come! why do you cry?"

"Because—because all these words that only rhymed before, now that I've come back they're me."

Mr. Bons laid the Keats down. The case was more interesting than he had expected. "*You?*" he exclaimed. "This sonnet, *you?*"

"Yes—and look further on: 'Aye, on the shores of darkness there is light, and precipices show untrodden green.' It *is* so, sir. All these things are true."

"I never doubted it," said Mr. Bons, with closed eyes.

"You—then you believe me? You believe in the omnibus and the driver and the storm and that return ticket I got for nothing and——"

"Tut, tut! No more of your yarns, my boy. I meant that I never doubted the essential truth of poetry. Some day, when you have read more, you will understand what I mean."

"But Mr. Bons, it *is* so. There *is* light upon the shores of darkness. I have seen it coming. Light and a wind."

---

11. *Wagner*. See "Wagner's Ring," page 607. 12. *alley-slopering*. Used in the colloquial sense, the verb *slope*, means "amble." 13. *"Standing aloof . . . to visit____,"* lines from Keats' sonnet "To Homer."

"Nonsense," said Mr. Bons.

"If I had stopped! They tempted me. They told me to give up my ticket—for you cannot come back if you lose your ticket. They called from the river for it, and indeed I was tempted, for I have never been so happy as among those precipices. But I thought of my mother and father, and that I must fetch them. Yet they will not come, though the road starts opposite our house. It has all happened as the people up there warned me, and Mr. Bons has disbelieved me like every one else. I have been caned. I shall never see that mountain again."

"What's that about me?" said Mr. Bons, sitting up in his chair very suddenly.

"I told them about you, and how clever you were, and how many books you had, and they said, 'Mr. Bons will certainly disbelieve you.'"

"Stuff and nonsense, my young friend. You grow impertinent. I—well—I will settle the matter. Not a word to your father. I will cure you. Tomorrow evening I will myself call here to take you for a walk, and at sunset we will go up this alley opposite and hunt for your omnibus, you silly little boy."

His face grew serious, for the boy was not disconcerted, but leapt about the room singing, "Joy! joy! I told them you would believe me. We will drive together over the rainbow. I told them that you would come." After all, could there be anything in the story! Wagner? Keats? Shelley? Sir Thomas Browne? Certainly the case was interesting.

And on the morrow evening, though it was pouring with rain, Mr. Bons did not omit to call at Agathox Lodge.

The boy was ready, bubbling with excitement, and skipping about in a way that vexed the President of the Literary Society. They took a turn down Buckingham Park Road, and then—having seen that no one was watching them—slipped up the alley. Naturally enough (for the sun was setting) they ran straight against the omnibus.

"Good heavens!" exclaimed Mr. Bons. "Good gracious heavens!"

It was not the omnibus in which the boy had driven first, not yet that in which he had returned. There were three horses—black, gray, and white, the gray being the finest. The driver, who turned round at the mention of goodness and of heaven, was a sallow man with terrifying jaws and sunken eyes. Mr. Bons, on seeing him, gave a cry as if of recognition, and began to tremble violently.

The boy jumped in.

"Is it possible?" cried Mr. Bons. "Is the impossible possible?"

"Sir; come in, sir. It is such a fine omnibus. Oh, here is his name—Dan some one."

Mr. Bons sprang in too. A blast of wind immediately slammed the omnibus door, and the shock jerked down all the omnibus blinds, which were very weak on their springs.

"Dan . . . show me. Good gracious heavens! we're moving."

"Hooray!" said the boy.

Mr. Bons became flustered. He had not intended to be kidnapped. He could not find the door handle, nor push up the blinds. The omnibus was quite dark, and by the time he had struck a match, night had come on outside also. They were moving rapidly.

"A strange, a memorable adventure," he said, surveying the interior of the omnibus, which was large, roomy, and constructed with extreme regularity, every part exactly answering to every other part. Over the door (the handle of which was outside) was written, *Lasciate ogni baldanza voi che entrate*—at least, that was what was written, but Mr. Bons said that it was Lashy arty something, and that *baldanza* was a mistake for *speranza*.[14] His voice sounded as if he was in church. Meanwhile, the boy called to the cadaverous driver for two return tickets. They were handed in without a word. Mr. Bons covered his face with his hand and again trembled. "Do you know who that is!" he whispered, when the little window had shut upon them. "It is the impossible."

---

14. *Lasciate ogni . . . speranza.* This famous quotation identifies the driver ("Dan some one") as Dante, author of the great Italian epic, the *Divine Comedy.* In that poem the inscription, using the word *speranza* ("hope"), appears over the gates of Hell and means, "Abandon all hope, you who enter here." Mr. Bons quite naturally misses the point of the substituted word *baldanza*, which means "arrogance."

"Well, I don't like him as much as Sir Thomas Browne, though I shouldn't be surprised if he had even more in him."

"More in him?" He stamped irritably. "By accident you have made the greatest discovery of the century, and all you can say is that there is more in this man. Do you remember those vellum books in my library, stamped with red lilies? This—sit still, I bring you stupendous news! —*this is the man who wrote them*."

The boy sat quite still. "I wonder if we shall see Mrs. Gamp?" he asked, after a civil pause.

"Mrs.——?"

"Mrs. Gamp and Mrs. Harris.[15] I like Mrs. Harris. I came upon them quite suddenly. Mrs. Gamp's bandboxes have moved over the rainbow so badly. All the bottoms have fallen out, and two of the pippins off her bedstead tumbled into the stream."

"Out there sits the man who wrote my vellum books!" thundered Mr. Bons, "and you talk to me of Dickens and of Mrs. Gamp?"

"I know Mrs. Gamp so well," he apologized. "I could not help being glad to see her. I recognized her voice. She was telling Mrs. Harris about Mrs. Prig."

"Did you spend the whole day in her elevating company?"

"Oh, no. I raced. I met a man who took me out beyond to a race course. You run, and there are dolphins out at sea."

"Indeed. Do you remember the man's name?"

"Achilles. No; he was later. Tom Jones."[16]

Mr. Bons sighed heavily. "Well, my lad, you have made a miserable mess of it. Think of a cultured person with your opportunities! A cultured person would have known all these characters and known what to have said to each. He would not have wasted his time with a Mrs. Gamp or a Tom Jones. The creations of Homer, of Shakespeare, and of Him who drives us now, would alone have contented him. He would not have raced. He would have asked intelligent questions."

"But, Mr. Bons," said the boy humbly, "you will be a cultured person. I told them so."

"True, true, and I beg you not to disgrace me when we arrive. No gossiping. No running. Keep close to my side, and never speak to these Immortals unless they speak to you. Yes, and give me the return tickets. You will be losing them."

The boy surrendered the tickets, but felt a little sore. After all, he had found the way to this place. It was hard first to be disbelieved and then to be lectured. Meanwhile, the rain had stopped, and moonlight crept into the omnibus through the cracks in the blinds.

"But how is there to be a rainbow?" cried the boy.

"You distract me," snapped Mr. Bons. "I wish to meditate on beauty. I wish to goodness I was with a reverent and sympathetic person."

The lad bit his lip. He made a hundred good resolutions. He would imitate Mr. Bons all the visit. He would not laugh, or run, or sing, or do any of the vulgar things that must have disgusted his new friends last time. He would be very careful to pronounce their names properly, and to remember who knew whom. Achilles did not know Tom Jones— at least, so Mr. Bons said. The Duchess of Malfi[17] was older than Mrs. Gamp—at least, so Mr. Bons said. He would be self-conscious, reticent, and prim. He would never say he liked any one. Yet, when the blind flew up at a chance touch of his head, all these good resolutions went to the winds, for the omnibus had reached the summit of a moonlit hill, and there was the chasm, and there, across it, stood the old precipices, dreaming, with their feet in the everlasting river. He exclaimed, "The mountain! Listen to the new tune in the water! Look at the camp fires in the ravines," and Mr. Bons, after a hasty glance, retorted, "Water? Camp fires? Ridiculous rubbish. Hold your tongue. There is nothing at all."

Yet, under his eyes, a rainbow formed, compounded not of sunlight and storm, but

---

15. *Mrs. Gamp and Mrs. Harris*, coarse but delightful low-life characters in Dickens' *Martin Chuzzlewit*. 16. *Tom Jones*, the adventurous and likable hero of Henry Fielding's novel of that name. 17. *Duchess of Malfi*, heroine of John Webster's seventeenth-century tragedy of the same name.

of moonlight and the spray of the river. The three horses put their feet upon it. He thought it the finest rainbow he had seen, but did not dare to say so, since Mr. Bons said that nothing was there. He leant out—the window had opened—and sang the tune that rose from the sleeping waters.

"The prelude to *Rheingold?*" said Mr. Bons suddenly. "Who taught you these *leitmotifs?*"[18] He, too, looked out of the window. Then he behaved very oddly. He gave a choking cry, and fell back on the omnibus floor. He writhed and kicked. His face was green.

"Does the bridge make you dizzy?" the boy asked.

"Dizzy!" gasped Mr. Bons. "I want to go back. Tell the driver." But the driver shook his head.

"We are nearly there," said the boy. "They are asleep. Shall I call? They will be so pleased to see you, for I have prepared them."

Mr. Bons moaned. They moved over the lunar rainbow, which ever and ever broke away behind their wheels. How still the night was! Who would be sentry at the Gate?

"I am coming," he shouted, again forgetting the hundred resolutions. "I am returning—I, the boy."

"The boy is returning," cried a voice to other voices, who repeated, "The boy is returning."

"I am bringing Mr. Bons with me."

Silence.

"I should have said Mr. Bons is bringing me with him."

Profound silence.

"Who stands sentry?"

"Achilles."

And on the rocky causeway, close to the springing of the rainbow bridge, he saw a young man who carried a wonderful shield.

"Mr. Bons, it is Achilles, armed."

"I want to go back," said Mr. Bons.

The last fragment of the rainbow melted, the wheels sang upon the living rock, the door of the omnibus burst open. Out leapt the boy—he could not resist—and sprang to meet the warrior, who, stooping suddenly, caught him on his shield.

"Achilles!" he cried, "let me get down, for I am ignorant and vulgar, and I must wait for that Mr. Bons of whom I told you yesterday."

But Achilles raised him aloft. He crouched on the wonderful shield,[19] on heroes and burning cities, on vineyards graven in gold, on every dear passion, every joy, on the entire image of the Mountain that he had discovered, encircled, like it, with an everlasting stream. "No, no," he protested, "I am not worthy. It is Mr. Bons who must be up here."

But Mr. Bons was whimpering, and Achilles trumpeted and cried, "Stand upright upon my shield!"

"Sir, I did not mean to stand! something made me stand. Sir, why do you delay? Here is only the great Achilles, whom you know."

Mr. Bons screamed, "I see no one. I see nothing. I want to go back." Then he cried to the driver, "Save me! Let me stop in your chariot. I have honored you. I have quoted you. I have bound you in vellum. Take me back to my world."

The driver replied, "I am the means and not the end. I am the food and not the life. Stand by yourself, as that boy has stood. I cannot save you. For poetry is a spirit; and they that would worship it must worship in spirit and in truth."

Mr. Bons—he could not resist—crawled out of the beautiful omnibus. His face appeared, gaping horribly. His hands followed, one gripping the step, the other beating the air. Now his shoulders emerged, his chest, his stomach. With a shriek of "I see London," he fell—fell against the hard, moonlit rock, fell into it as if it were water, fell through it, vanished, and was seen by the boy no more.

"Where have you fallen to, Mr. Bons? Here is a procession arriving to honor you with music and torches. Here come the men and women whose names you know. The mountain is awake, the river is awake, over the race course the sea is awaking those dolphins, and it is all for you. They want you——"

---

18. *leitmotifs.* See the explanation of this term in the article on page 607. 19. *the wonderful shield.* A long passage in the *Iliad* describes the elaborate sculpturing on Achilles' shield.

There was the touch of fresh leaves on his forehead. Some one had crowned him.

ΤΕΛΟΣ²⁰

From the *Kingston Gazette, Surbiton Times*, and *Raynes Park Observer.*

The body of Mr. Septimus Bons has been found in a shockingly mutilated condition in the vicinity of the Bermondsey gasworks. The deceased's pockets contained a sovereign purse, a silver cigar case, a bijou pronouncing dictionary, and a couple of omnibus tickets. The unfortunate gentleman had apparently been hurled from a considerable height. Foul play is suspected, and a thorough investigation is pending by the authorities.

---

20. *telos* (tel'os) the end. [*Greek*]

To increase understanding

1. (*a*) What is the starting point of the omnibus? (*b*) Where does it go?

2. Reread the information about the omnibus that the boy found posted on the wall of the alley (page 606, column 1, paragraph 1). (*a*) What is satiric about the announcement that service has been curtailed "owing to lack of patronage"? (*b*) How do the boy's experiences with his family and their friends show why patronage would be lacking?

3. (*a*) Who are the drivers of the omnibuses? (*b*) Following the clues given in the descriptions of the carriages on pages 608 and 611, explain what the carriages represent. A further clue to the meaning of the carriages is the fact that the drivers "transport" people to such a heaven.

4. Reread the conversation that takes place between the boy and the driver when the boy first journeys on the omnibus (page 608, column 1, paragraph 4 to page 610, column 1, paragraph 3). (*a*) What is the driver's name? (*b*) What was his original profession? (*c*) Why did he become a writer? (*d*) How does Forster indicate the style of his writing? (*e*) What does the driver mean by saying "For though my draughts were not better nor subtler than those of other men, yet by reason of the cunning goblets wherein I offered them, the queasy soul was ofttimes tempted to sip and be refreshed"? (*f*) How does the boy define a "queasy soul"? (*g*) How do you interpret the boy's saying, "No, I mean listen; that sounds like a rainbow"? (*h*) What do you learn about the boy from this conversation with the driver?

5. Describe the boy's father and mother, paying attention to their social class, the way they treat their son, their attitude toward poetry and the world of imagination. Consider the following specific points from the story in answering the question:

(*a*) The boy's mother says the signpost is "a joke and not a very nice one, which had been made many years back by some naughty young men, and that the police ought to remove it" (page 604, column 1, paragraph 1).

(*b*) His mother is agitated when Mr. Bons queries whether "there is no Shelley in the house" and answers, "Dear Mr. Bons, we aren't such Philistines as that. Two at the least. One a wedding present, and the other, smaller print, in one of the spare rooms" (page 604, column 2, paragraph 6).

(*c*) The boy, gazing down Buckingham Road, reflects that he "lived at the right end of it" (page 605, column 1, paragraph 3).

(*d*) The boy, after studying the poster advertising the omnibus, reflects that it "was run on hopelessly unbusinesslike lines" (page 606, column 1, last paragraph).

(*e*) The boy's father teases him about the alley (page 606, column 2, paragraph 1).

(*f*) On his return from the first journey, the boy is set to learning poetry as a punishment for lying (page 610, column 1, paragraph 3).

(*g*) The boy's father twits him as "the great traveler . . . who drives in an omnibus over rainbows," and is pleased with his wit (page 610, column 1, paragraph 7).

(*h*) The boy's father laughs when he tells Mr. Bons the boy is being sent away for "alley-sloping" and roars with laughter as the boy recites the poem he has learned for punishment (page 610, column 1, paragraph 9).

6. (*a*) Why does Mr. Bons finally agree to look for the omnibus? (*b*) Why does he keep this fact secret from the boy's father and mother?

7. (*a*) Why, when Mr. Bons discovers who the driver of the omnibus is, does his voice sound "as if he was in church"? (*b*) Why, when the boy mentions Mrs. Gamp, does Mr. Bons become irritated with him? (*c*) What is significant about the fact that there is no reply when the boy shouts to the dwellers in heaven that he is bringing Mr. Bons with him? (*d*) What happens to Mr. Bons? Why does this happen?

8. Contrast Mr. Bons' enjoyment of literature with that of the boy. Relate your answer to the second driver's statement in the paragraph beginning: "The driver replied, 'I am the means and not the end . .' !" (page 613, column 2, paragraph 6).

9. What does the story mean?

The Larger View

A. Listed below are some statements from the introduction to this chapter. Each statement is followed by questions. Answering the questions may help you relate particular literary works to the general ideas about modern short stories developed in the introduction.

1. . . . *the general tendency of most modern fiction is toward realism.* Which stories in this chapter do you consider realistic? Are there any you consider pessimistic or fatalistic? Would you classify any of the stories as romantic?

2. Other writers exposed the artificiality of civilization by looking at the world from the viewpoint of an adolescent. Which stories have adolescence as a theme? Is this necessarily the same as writing from "the viewpoint of an adolescent"? Do any of the stories expose "the artificiality of civilization"?

3. New forms of the short story, far less tightly plotted than, for example, the stories of Rudyard Kipling, evolved. Which of the stories have a closely knitted plot rising to a conventional climax? Which of the stories seem plotless by older standards?

4. Many writers sought [to retell] folk tales and ballads in modern terms or [to relate] modern stories to ancient myths. Do any of the stories show the influence of myth or of folklore? How is such material used?

5. [Writers] developed new techniques to expose and communicate this realm of the inner man. What stories are primarily concerned with laying bare the attitudes and emotions of an individual? What techniques does the author use to accomplish this?

B. A critic says: "It is probably true that in no previous era in English literature has the Irish contribution been so considerable or the number of Irish writers proportionately so numerous as in the modern period."

1. What forces have contributed to this growth of Irish literature?

2. What stories in this chapter are by Irish writers?

3. Are there any qualities of style, theme, tone, or form that seem to be characteristic of these writers as a group? Explain.

C. Compare the short stories in this chapter with American short stories you have studied. Do you find modern English short stories in general similar to or different from American short stories in form? Are the same themes predominant? Are the same approaches to literature evident in American short stories as the approaches you have noted in these English stories?

Bibliography

BENNETT, ARNOLD, *Buried Alive*. (•Dolphin) The adventure of a shy English painter who uses an assumed name after his supposed death forms the plot of this amusing story.

BOWEN, ELIZABETH, *Stories*. (•Vintage) This compact volume will furnish much additional pleasure for readers who enjoyed *The Demon Lover*.

CARY, JOYCE, *Spring Song, and other Stories*. (Harper) This collection contains tales which show the author's skill in handling a wide variety of settings and characters.

CHESTERTON, G. K., *The Amazing Adventures of Father Brown*. (•Dell) In the fifty-two years since the first Father Brown story appeared, the detective-priest has never lost his popularity. The stories in this collection will show you why.

DOYLE, ARTHUR CONAN, *The Adventures of Sherlock Holmes*. (•Collier) Fans of this famous amateur sleuth and his crony, Dr. Watson, tend to forget that the pair are as fictitious as the thrilling mysteries they solve.

FORSTER, E. M., *A Passage to India*. (Harcourt) This novel mirrors the conflicts which arise when two divergent cultures, in this case, British and East Indian, attempt to coexist. Romantic and unromantic elements of the Indian setting form the background.

GALSWORTHY, JOHN, *The Forsyte Saga*. (Scribner) Originally published as three separate novels, this great story traces a wealthy English family through several generations. As time passes, the conservative Victorian character of the Forsytes is undermined by the moral upheaval of World War I.

GREENE, GRAHAM, *Nineteen Stories* (•Bantam) Most of the works in this collection deal with the conflict between good and evil in the human heart.

HAVIGHURST, WALTER, editor, *Masters of the Modern Short Story*. (•Harcourt) Stories by Conrad, Forster, O'Connor, James Joyce, Virginia Woolf, Graham Greene, Aldous Huxley, Maugham, O'Faolain and Mansfield are included in this collection.

GARRITY, DEVIN A., editor, *Forty-four Irish Short Stories: An Anthology of Irish Short Fiction from Yeats to Frank O'Connor*. (Devin) The top stories of such authors as Joyce, Shaw, and Wilde are in this lively, humorous collection.

LAVIN, MARY, *The Great Wave and Other Stories*. (Macmillan) Plot is less important than character in these sympathetic stories. Although the setting is Irish, the situations are universal.

LLEWELLYN, RICHARD, *How Green Was My Valley*. (•Macmillan) Hew Morgan's story is also the chronicle of a fertile Welsh valley which grew barren as Hew passed through boyhood, manhood, and into old age there.

MANSFIELD, KATHERINE, *Stories of Katherine Mansfield*, edited by Elizabeth Bowen. (•Vintage) Miss Mansfield's followers will enjoy this collection edited by a fellow teller of tales.

MAUGHAM, W. SOMERSET, *Of Human Bondage*. (•Vintage) In bondage with himself because of a birth defect, Philip Carey's ability to face life is clouded by his sensitivity to his physical handicap. His effort to find himself has given this novel tremendous appeal to readers of all ages.

MUNRO, HECTOR (Saki), *The Best of Saki*, compiled and edited by Graham Greene. (•Viking) The stories in this collection are characteristic of Saki's sometimes weird and supernatural twists of plot.

O'CONNOR, FRANK, *An Only Child*. (Knopf) An autobiography of the author's youth in Cork slums and his role in the Irish revolution, this is one of O'Connor's finest works. For those who want more O'Connor reading, *Stories* (•Vintage) is a compact edition.

O'CONNOR, FRANK, editor, *Mirror in the Roadway*. (Knopf) This study of the modern novel and leading novelists is said to reveal almost as much about the author as about the writers he discusses. He includes selections by the novelists represented.

O'FAOLAIN, SEAN, *The Finest Stories of Sean O'Faolain*. (•Bantam) Twenty-seven of this author's tales, some chillingly depressing, are contained in this volume.

PRIESTLEY, J. B., *The Thirty-first of June*. (Doubleday) The humorous adventures of a modern man in King Arthur's era and of Arthurian people in contemporary life make this short novel appealing.

SCHWEIKERT, HARRY C., editor, *Short Stories*. (Harcourt) Bennett, Galsworthy, Mansfield, J. M. Barrie, Doyle, and Conrad are a few of the authors in this anthology.

WAGENKNECHT, EDWARD, *Cavalcade of the English Novel*. (Holt) This excellent reference provides a critical appraisal of English fiction. Nearly one hundred lesser novelists are included.

WAUGH, EVELYN, *The World of Evelyn Waugh*, edited by Charles J. Rolo. (Little) In this collection, two short stories, the complete novel *The Loved One*, and excerpts from other Waugh writings show the variety of his creative talent.

WELLS, H. G., *Seven Science Fiction Novels*. (Dover) This noted historian was an early writer of space fiction, as this group of short novels indicates.

WISE, HERBERT A., and PHYLLIS FRASER, editors, *Great Tales of Terror and the Supernatural*. (Modern Library) In this anthology of thrillers by noted authors are stories by Munro (Saki), Kipling, Wells, De la Mare, Forster, Bulwer-Lytton, and many others.

•paperback

chapter nine Poetry

When Queen Victoria died in 1901, the Victorian Age came officially to an end. Actually, however, the ideas that would characterize the twentieth century and set it distinctly apart from the Victorian era were being formulated about twenty years before the turn of the century. In these years the psychiatrist Sigmund Freud was in Vienna working out his theories (see page 549), and Gerard Manley Hopkins (page 522) was writing poetry that would have a strong influence on the poets of the 1920's. But in 1901 most Englishmen had heard of neither Freud nor Hopkins, since neither had achieved fame until the publication of later works; and literature remained predominantly Victorian. Even if most Englishmen were not so secure as is indicated by Henley's often quoted lines:

> I am the master of my fate:
> I am the captain of my soul

the late Victorians felt comfortable with the familiar sentiments and rhythm of the poem. Within twenty years, however, poets and novelists began to concentrate on what modern man was thinking and how he felt about life. The result was a literature as distinct from that of preceding ages as life in this century is different from that of preceding centuries.

For the most part the subjects that twentieth-century poets wrote about were the same ones that had engaged the poet's imagination since *Beowulf* —love, war, friendship, nature, jealousy, the struggle for existence, and curiosity about the unknown. But in past ages certain subjects were not considered fit for poetry. The twentieth century abolished these pre-scriptions. In addition, the method of treating a subject was changed by the impact of psychology; poets were challenged to explore new dimensions in the people and situations they were writing about. The form of poetry also changed radically. Instead of being governed by certain limited if not rigid rules of rhyme and rhythm, the poet gained freedom to couch his thoughts in the form that best suited the idea.

The first great flowering of twentieth-century poetry took place in the 1920's. It was preceded by a series of experimental movements, the first of which began to form in the 1890's. These movements usually origi-nated among a group of young poets who published their experimental poetry in magazines that were sympathetic to their ideas. These groups formed and dissolved rather quickly as they reached the limits of what they had to offer or as new groups with different ideas pushed to the front. Some of these experimental groups made important contributions to the growth of modern poetry; taken together they help explain why and how poetry became "modern."

The first and one of the most important of these groups consisted of young Irish poets. Some of them lived in Ireland and took an active part in the Irish movement for independence (see page 542); others lived in London. Dissatisfied with conditions in Ireland and with life generally, they turned to a world of dreams and visions for material for their poetry, and wrote mystically of their search for a better world.

Another group of poets rebelled against the "smugness, false piety, and sentimentality" of the Victorian Age. In their poetry they tried to copy the zest and enthusiasm for life that Elizabethan poetry had cap-tured. But it was a poor imitation. The twentieth-century man was too introspective and self-conscious to be as carefree as his Elizabethan counter-part.

The Georgians, a group so-called because they came into existence about 1910 at the beginning of the reign of George V, disagreed with the Victorian outlook on life and scorned the atmosphere of the new machine age. They wrote about what they considered the ideal existence, a life of rural simplicity. Their favorite subject was the beauties of nature. They were soon succeeded by the Anti-Georgians who protested that "primroses and budding trees" were no longer acceptable "as a solution of, or consolation for, human misery." With their sarcasm they buried the most fragile and flowery poetry of the Georgians.

The Imagists, a group which appeared in 1912, had an important effect on the emergence of modern poetry. In a manifesto which stated their objectives, the Imagists said they wanted above all to avoid "indefinite" or "decorative" poetry. They believed that by the use of exact language an entire statement could be embodied in one concrete image. This idea of concentrated speech—the essence of all poetry—was not new, but the Imagists felt it had been lost sight of in the rambling thought and moralizing of much Victorian poetry. Another of the Imagist tenets was to "allow absolute freedom in the choice of subject" and "to create new rhythms—as the expression of new moods." Sometimes the Imagists failed to live up to their own creed, but nevertheless they pushed verse a great step toward what was to become modern poetry. In the United States also, where Amy Lowell preached the gospel of the Imagists from coast to coast, they forced the acceptance of concrete images and free-verse forms, and opened the door for other experimentalists.

Experimentalism in poetry flourished in the 1920's. Poets became so engrossed in the technical aspects of writing that in their involvement with *how* something was said, *what* was said sometimes became lost. Poetry abounded in isolated images and allusions. The commentary for literary references sometimes occupied as much space as the poems themselves. If these new techniques were skillfully used, the result was poetry. If they were unskillfully used, the result was verbiage. From among the poets and versifiers of the 1920's, two towering figures emerged: William Butler Yeats and T. S. Eliot. Yeats through his use of symbols created poetry that beautifully combined the mainsprings of twentieth-century poetry—romantic imagination and intellect. Eliot set the tone for much of modern poetry; his "hollow man" has become a conventional symbol for the futility that many people believe underlies modern life.

During the 1920's the concern of many poets with form rather than substance created a chasm between the poet and his audience. The public accused the poets of being obscure, uninterested in the ordinary man, and of placing a value on intellectualism for its own sake. The poets reacted to this censure by ignoring the public and writing for themselves. Whether the poets alienated the public or the public ignored the poets may be argued; but by the 1930's there was often little communication between poet and public.

During the 1930's the Great Depression (see page 544) and the threats of coming war again changed the character of poetry. Issues more immediate than verse technique began to occupy the minds of poets. There was a new emphasis on emotion, lyric intensity, and rich colorful language, producing a warmth, boldness, and romanticism which much of the poetry of the previous decades had lacked. The leader of this newest group of romantic poets was the Welsh poet Dylan (dil′ən) Thomas. His exuberant personality and the warmth and vigor of his poetry made him a powerful force. He was in his writing prime when he died in 1953 at the age of thirty-nine, but he has had a strong influence on today's poets.

Today we are far enough removed from the early part of the century to review the major influences on modern poetry and to trace its development. Free verse, precise images, irony, language ranging from learned to slang, suggestion rather than statement, and extensive use of symbols are some of its characteristics. More important than particular techniques, however, is the fact that the freedom to choose from among numerous modes and styles has allowed such poets as Yeats, Eliot, Thomas, and many others to describe with vigor and honesty contemporary man and his relation to his world.

IRISH TOURIST BOARD, DUBLIN

William Butler Yeats

THE LAKE ISLE OF INNISFREE

I will arise and go now, and go to Innisfree,
  And a small cabin build there, of clay and wattles made;
Nine bean rows[1] will I have there, a hive for the honeybee,
  And live alone in the bee-loud glade.

And I shall have some peace there, for peace comes dropping slow,   5
  Dropping from the veils of the morning to where the cricket sings;
There midnight's all a-glimmer, and noon a purple glow,
  And evening full of the linnet's wings.

I will arise and go now, for always night and day
  I hear lake water lapping with low sounds by the shore;   10
While I stand on the roadway, or on the pavements gray,
  I hear it in the deep heart's core.

WHEN YOU ARE OLD

When you are old and gray and full of sleep,
  And nodding by the fire, take down this book,
  And slowly read, and dream of the soft look
Your eyes had once, and of their shadows deep;

How many loved your moments of glad grace,   5
  And loved your beauty with love false or true;
  But one man loved the pilgrim soul in you,
And loved the sorrows of your changing face;

And bending down beside the glowing bars,
  Murmur, a little sadly, how love fled   10
  And paced upon the mountains overhead
And hid his face amid a crowd of stars.

THE LAKE ISLE OF INNISFREE **1.** *Nine ... rows.* The Celtic poets liked to use definite numbers. Favorites were the mystic three, five, and seven, and their multiples. The bean rows are an allusion to the chapter entitled "The Bean-Field" in Thoreau's *Walden*, which Yeats had read just before he wrote this poem.

INTO THE TWILIGHT

Outworn heart, in a time outworn,
  Come clear of the nets of wrong and right;
  Laugh, heart, again in the gray twilight,
Sigh, heart, again in the dew of the morn.

Your mother Eire is always young,   5
  Dew ever shining and twilight gray;
  Though hope fall from you and love decay,
Burning in fires of a slanderous tongue.

Come, heart, where hill is heaped upon hill:
  For there the mystical brotherhood   10
  Of sun and moon and hollow and wood
And river and stream work out their will;

And God stands winding His lonely horn,
  And time and the world are ever in flight;
  And love is less kind than the gray twilight,   15
And hope is less dear than the dew of the morn.

RED HANRAHAN'S SONG ABOUT IRELAND[1]

The old brown thorn-trees break in two[2] high over Cummen Strand,[3]
Under a bitter black wind that blows from the left hand;
Our courage breaks like an old tree in a black wind and dies,
But we have hidden in our hearts the flame out of the eyes
Of Cathleen, the daughter of Houlihan.[4]   5

The wind has bundled up the clouds high over Knocknarea,
And thrown the thunder on the stones for all that Maeve[5] can say.
Angers that are like noisy clouds have set our hearts abeat;
But we have all bent low and low and kissed the quiet feet
Of Cathleen, the daughter of Houlihan.   10

The yellow pool has overflowed high up on Clooth-na-Bare,[6]
For the wet winds are blowing out of the clinging air;
Like heavy flooded waters our bodies and our blood;
But purer than a tall candle before the Holy Rood[7]
Is Cathleen, the daughter of Houlihan.   15

RED HANRAHAN'S SONG ABOUT IRELAND. 1. *Red ... Ireland.* In Yeats' short stories Red Hanrahan is a gambler, poet, and schoolmaster. He symbolizes the poet, who is constantly aware of the separation of the ideal and reality. 2. *thorn-trees ... two.* The tree was one of Yeats' favorite symbols. A broken tree often symbolized disorder or undesirable change. 3. *Cummen Strand,* shoreline in Sligo. 4. *Cathleen ... Houlihan.* Cathleen ni Houlihan was a character in one of Yeats' plays who symbolized Ireland. 5. *Maeve* (māv). On the summit of Knocknarea is a monument to Maeve, an early Celtic fairy queen. 6. *Clooth-na-Bare* (klüth nä bã′rə), a mountain named after a folklore creature who went all over the world looking for a lake deep enough to drown her fairy life. She found the deepest water in a little lake on the top of this mountain in Sligo. 7. *Holy Rood,* the Holy Cross.

SAILING TO BYZANTIUM

I

That is no country for old men. The young
In one another's arms, birds in the trees,
—Those dying generations—at their song,
The salmon-falls, the mackerel-crowded seas,
Fish, flesh, or fowl, commend all summer
     long   5
Whatever is begotten, born, and dies.
Caught in that sensual music all neglect
Monuments of unaging intellect.

II

An aged man is but a paltry thing,
A tattered coat upon a stick, unless   10
Soul clap its hands and sing, and louder sing
For every tatter in its mortal dress,
Nor is there singing school but studying
Monuments of its own magnificence;
And therefore I have sailed the seas and
     come   15
To the holy city of Byzantium.

III

O sages standing in God's holy fire
As in the gold mosaic of a wall,
Come from the holy fire, perne in a gyre,
And be the singing-masters of my soul.   20
Consume my heart away; sick with desire
And fastened to a dying animal
It knows not what it is; and gather me
Into the artifice of eternity.

IV

Once out of nature I shall never take   25
My bodily form from any natural thing,
But such a form as Grecian goldsmiths make
Of hammered gold and gold enameling
To keep a drowsy Emperor awake;
Or set upon a golden bough to sing   30
To lords and ladies of Byzantium
Of what is past, or passing, or to come.

"Sailing to Byzantium" from *Collected Poems* by William Butler Yeats. Reprinted by permission of The Macmillan Company, New York; and A. P. Watt & Son, London, for Mr. M. B. Yeats, The Macmillan Co. of Canada Ltd., Toronto, and Macmillan & Co. Ltd., London. Copyright 1928 by The Macmillan Company; Copyright 1956 by Georgie Yeats.

William Butler Yeats 1865-1939

William Butler Yeats was the acknowledged leader of the Irish Literary Renaissance (see page 542). Yeats was born in Sandymount, a suburb of Dublin; but the family's principal residence during the first ten years of Yeats' life was County Sligo in the west of Ireland—an area which Yeats loved and which forms the setting for many of his poems. Although he studied art in Dublin, his interest in painting was soon overshadowed by his success in writing poetry and plays. After having achieved some notice in Ireland, he went to London with his family in 1887. There he became associated with a group of writers whom he later organized into the Rhymer's Club. He felt shy in London and probably would not have stayed had he not met Maude Gonne, a majestic woman (she was more than six feet tall) who was an ardent Irish nationalist. Yeats met her in 1889 and fell in love with her. Through her influence he became immersed in Irish politics and the theater. One of his most famous plays, *Cathleen ni Houlihan* (1902), was written for Maude Gonne, who played Cathleen, the character symbolizing Ireland.

For thirteen years Yeats pursued Maude Gonne, but she refused his continued offers of marriage. Even after she married Major John MacBride in 1903, Yeats continued to revere her. After MacBride's death in 1917, Yeats proposed a final time, and was again refused. He married Georgie Hyde-Lees soon afterward. In losing Maude, Yeats did not, however, lose his interest in the politics and literature of Ireland: in 1922 he was elected a member of the senate of the new Irish Free State; he became a successful playwright and helped to found the Abbey Theater; and in 1923 he was awarded the highest honor in the literary world, the Nobel Prize for Literature.

After 1903 Yeats turned his attention to writing a different kind of poetry, one which he felt was more significant than his earlier efforts. His early poetry had been romantic, imbued with a love of faraway places, a feeling for the supernatural, and a mourning over the separation of art from life. Because of his two-fold career as poet and government official, he felt this separation keenly. As Yeats grew older, he learned to reconcile the disparity between life as one might desire it to be and life as it actually is. He wrote less of the need to escape to havens like Innisfree. He revised his thinking about art and its relation to life, coming ultimately to see art not as separated from life but as transcending life. Thus through art, reality and the ideal could be united.

The compression of language through symbol in Yeats' later poems gives them an emotional intensity lacking in his earlier work. All his poetry shows that mastery of language which identifies a good poet. It was his unique ability to combine mastery of language and the various techniques of poetry with ideas and feeling that marks him as one of the outstanding writers of the twentieth century.

To increase understanding

1. (a) What mood do you think the following details in "The Lake Isle of Innisfree" suggest: the honeybee in the bee-loud glade, cricket singing, lake water lapping with low sounds, evening full of the linnet's wings? (b) Why is the reference to Thoreau's *Walden* appropriate to this mood? (c) What makes an island particularly suitable to the mood of the poem?

2. When Yeats moved to London, he often thought with affection and nostalgia of Sligo County and Lough (lōн) Gill with its island of Innisfree. One day, after passing a shop that had a little fountain displayed in the window, he wrote: "I . . . began to remember lake water. From the sudden remembrance came my poem Innisfree." (a) What images indicate that Yeats is longing for something more than an actual place? (b) What is it that Yeats longs for? (c) What line indicates that the desire is sincere and not just romantic wool-gathering?

3. "When You Are Old" is the best of several poems Yeats wrote to Maude Gonne. (a) How would you describe the poet's feeling for Maude? (b) What is the tone of the poem?

4. (a) Explain the reference to "pilgrim soul" in line 7 of "When You Are Old." (b) What glimpses of Maude Gonne does the poem give you?

5. (a) What does the first line of "Into the Twilight" tell you about the poet's reaction to the contemporary world? (b) What times of day are mentioned in the first stanza? (c) What is significant about the poet's choice of these particular periods?

6. The twentieth-century world is a world of science and of fact. (a) In "Into the Twilight" how does "Mother Eire" symbolize the escape from a practical world? (b) How do "twilight gray" and "shining dew" strengthen the idea? (c) Judging from the last two lines, does the poet prefer the natural world of love and hope and their consequences or the ideal world of Mother Eire?

7. Which lines in "Into the Twilight" seem to you most successful in catching the essential spirit of romanticism?

8. Conflict between what actually is and what should be is suggested in the three poems already discussed. In "Red Hanrahan's Song About Ireland" it becomes the central theme. Each stanza treats of two subjects—disorder and change (actuality) and order and steadfastness (what should be). (a) What images does Yeats use to suggest disorder and change? (b) What symbol suggests order and steadfastness?

9. What can you learn from "Red Hanrahan's Song" about Yeats' own attitude toward Ireland?

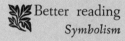 Better reading
Symbolism

"To hear all the talk about it," quipped the American poet Robert Frost, "you'd think the symbol had just been invented!" As Frost implied, the symbol has been in existence as long as man has been around to associate characteristics with objects. But because modern writers use symbolism extensively and because they often develop a symbol system of their own invention rather than use conventional symbols, some special study is necessary.

A symbol is a close relative of the simile and the metaphor. The simile and metaphor take the place of statements. For example, the simile "How like a winter hath my absence been from thee" could be paraphrased in three or four statements explaining how cold and bleak life is away from someone beloved. Some of the implications would be lost in the paraphrase, but the meaning would be clear. A paraphrase can also be made of the metaphor "My mind to me a kingdom is."

But the power of the symbol is that it implies more than a statement can put into words. This is one reason poetry cannot be "translated" into prose without damaging the meaning and the feeling. Symbolism in modern writing becomes especially complex because a work is often symbolic in every respect: setting, characters, action, and language.

Yeats' poem "Sailing to Byzantium" affords an excellent opportunity to study the use of symbolism in a modern poem. The word *Byzantium*, which was the ancient name of the city that became Constantinople and finally Istanbul, suggests distance in time as well as place. Of Byzantium Yeats writes: "I think that in early Byzantium, maybe never before or since in recorded history, religious, aesthetic and practical life were one, that architect and artifices . . . spoke to the multitude and the few alike." Byzantium then, to Yeats, becomes not a place but an ideal, a symbol of the unity of all aspects of life. It is a "holy city," literally because it was the capital of Eastern Christendom, symbolically because it fostered that development of intellect and imagination which produces artistic perfection.

In "Sailing to Byzantium" the first fourteen lines deal with the country upon which the poet is turning his back; the remainder of the poem treats of the "holy city of Byzantium." The imagery used in each section helps the reader grasp the symbolism.

Notice that all the images and details in the first stanza suggest the natural world of birth, change, and death. Cite details that bring concretely alive this sensual world. Of what do the birds sing? What is neglected in this world? How does an aged man in this country regard himself (stanza 2)? Why is the poet "sailing to Byzantium"?

How do the images in stanzas 3 and 4 differ from those in the earlier stanzas? What images suggest an atmosphere of timelessness? What plea does the poet make in stanza 3? Why is "the artifice of eternity" an apt phrase in its context?

Describe the bird introduced in the fourth stanza. To whom does this bird sing? What line in the first stanza does this song echo? How has the time the song includes been expanded in this second song? Why should this bird's song reflect the timelessness of art?

Reread the first line of the poem. What is symbolized by the word *country* in this line? What do the seas in line 15 symbolize? Trace the changing symbolism of the bird.

The poem cannot be "translated." The symbols, however, lend insight to what the poem is saying. The "meaning" of the poem is what you experience as you read it. The more insights you have, the greater will be the poem's meaning for you.

George William Russell (Æ)

PROMISE

Be not so desolate
Because thy dreams have flown
And the hall of the heart is empty
And silent as stone
As age left by children   5
Sad and alone.

Those delicate children,
Thy dreams, still endure:
All pure and lovely things
Wend to the Pure.   10
Sigh not: unto the fold
Their way was sure.

Thy gentlest dreams, thy frailest,
Even those that were
Born and lost in a heartbeat,   15
Shall meet thee there.
They are become immortal
In shining air.

The unattainable beauty
The thought of which was pain,   20
That flickered in eyes and on lips
And vanished again;
That fugitive beauty
Thou shalt attain.

The lights innumerable   25
That led thee on and on,
The Masque of Time[1] ended,
Shall glow into one.
It shall be with thee forever,
Thy travel done.   30

"Promise" from *Collected Poems* by George William Russell. Reprinted by permission of A. M. Heath & Company, Ltd., London.
1. *Masque of Time*, earthly life, which is only a brief masquerade in the endless pageant of eternity.

Padraic Colum

AN OLD WOMAN OF THE ROADS

Oh, to have a little house!
To own the hearth and stool and all!
The heaped-up sods upon the fire,
The pile of turf against the wall!

To have a clock with weights and chains   5
And pendulum swinging up and down!
A dresser filled with shining delph,
Speckled and white and blue and brown!

I could be busy all the day
Clearing and sweeping hearth and floor,   10
And fixing on their shelf again
My white and blue and speckled store!

I could be quiet there at night
Beside the fire and by myself,
Sure of a bed and loath to leave   15
The ticking clock and the shining delph!

Och! but I'm weary of mist and dark,
And roads where there's never a house nor
    bush,
And tired I am of bog and road,
And the crying wind and the lonesome
    hush!   20

And I am praying to God on high,
And I am praying Him night and day,
For a little house—a house of my own—
Out of the wind's and the rain's way.

James Stephens

THE SHELL

And then I pressed the shell
Close to my ear
And listened well,
And straightway like a bell
Came low and clear   5
The slow, sad murmur of the distant seas,
Whipped by an icy breeze
Upon a shore
Wind-swept and desolate.
It was a sunless strand that never bore   10
The footprint of a man,
Nor felt the weight
Since time began
Of any human quality or stir
Save what the dreary winds and waves incur.
And in the hush of waters was the sound   16
Of pebbles rolling round,
Forever rolling with a hollow sound.
And bubbling seaweeds as the waters go
Swish to and fro   20
Their long, cold tentacles of slimy gray.
There was no day,
Nor ever came a night
Setting the stars alight
To wonder at the moon;   25
Was twilight only and the frightened croon,
Smitten to whimpers, of the dreary wind
And waves that journeyed blind—
And then I loosed my ear . . . Oh, it was sweet
To hear a cart go jolting down the street.   30

IN WASTE PLACES

As a naked man I go
Through the desert, sore afraid;
Holding high my head, although
I'm as frightened as a maid.

The lion crouches there! I saw   5
In barren rocks his amber eye!
He parts the cactus with his paw!
He stares at me as I go by!

He would pad upon my trace
If he thought I was afraid!   10
If he knew my hardy face
Veils the terrors of a maid.

He rises in the nighttime, and
He stretches forth! He snuffs the air!
He roars! He leaps along the sand!   15
He creeps! He watches everywhere!

His burning eyes, his eyes of bale
Through the darkness I can see!
He lashes fiercely with his tail!
He makes again to spring at me!   20

I am the lion, and his lair!
I am the fear that frightens me!
I am the desert of despair!
And the night of agony!

Night or day, whate'er befall,   25
I must walk that desert land,
Until I dare my fear and call
The lion out to lick my hand.

Reprinted with the permission of The Macmillan Company,
Macmillan & Co. Ltd., The Macmillan Company of
Canada, Ltd., and Mrs. Iris Wise from *Collected Poems* by
James Stephens. Copyright 1915 by The Macmillan
Company. Copyright 1943 by James Stephens.

George William Russell "AE" 1867-1935

Second only to Yeats as a lyric poet of the Irish Renaissance, at various periods in his life George Russell was artist, poet, philosopher, journalist, and economist. He was active in Irish political affairs and wrote many books on politics and economics.

His romantic poetry and his public life remained apart from each other, as his poetry never became concerned with daily realities, but was set in a world of visions and dreams. He was given to trances and visions, and his pen name "AE" was from *Aeon*, a word which came to him in a vision as the name of a spiritual being. "Promise" is typical of the romantic tone of most of his poetry.

Padraic Colum 1881-1972

Like the other leaders of the Irish Renaissance, Padraic (pôᴛн'rig) Colum drew on Celtic folklore for themes for his plays and poems. Within Ireland he is well known for the peasant plays which he wrote for the Irish National Theatre; outside of his native Eire he is best known for his masterly retelling of folk tales and for his poetry. Simple, lyrical, and compelling, Colum's poetry shows great understanding of the common people of Ireland and of the emotional needs of people everywhere.

James Stephens 1882-1950

By virtue of sheer will and optimism, James Stephens survived a bitter childhood of extreme poverty and a dreary financial struggle in his youth. Another Dubliner, AE, encouraged him to write. Although he brought out a volume of poetry, *Insurrections*, in 1909, he was virtually unknown until the publication of his most famous novel, *The Crock of Gold*, in 1912.

In both his poetry and his novels Stephens combines fantasy and realism; leprechauns mingle comfortably with more usual inhabitants of the world. His tone is sympathetic, and although he is known for his Irish wit, he can also write perceptively about the inner life, the "waste places" of the soul.

❁ To increase understanding

1. (*a*) For what loss is the poet trying to console the person to whom "Promise" is addressed? (*b*) What is the "promise" of the title?
2. (*a*) Cite details in the first four stanzas of "An Old Woman of the Roads" that show Colum's intimate knowledge of Irish life. (*b*) How do the

last two stanzas contrast with the first four? (c) Why, in spite of its use of realistic details, is "An Old Woman of the Roads" considered a romantic poem?

3. (a) Explain the setting James Stephens supposes in "The Shell." (b) Why does he keep details of this setting hidden until the last two lines?

4. (a) What sounds does the poet hear in the shell? (b) Trace the way the poet's imagination carries him from sound to sight. (c) What mood do sound and sight combined suggest?

5. How does the idea implied in "The Shell" differ from the theme of "The Lake Isle of Innisfree"?

6. (a) What does the lion in "In Waste Places" symbolize? (b) What does the poem mean? (c) Which lines most clearly express the theme?

7. What resemblances do you find between "In Waste Places" and "The Tiger" by William Blake (page 339)?

8. (a) In the introduction to this chapter you read that the poets of the Irish Literary Renaissance "turned to a world of dreams and visions for material for their poetry, and wrote mystically of their search for a better world" (page 618). What poems of Yeats, AE, Colum, or Stephens show this tendency? (b) What other evidences of romanticism do you find in the poems by these Irish writers?

Walter de la Mare 1873-1956

Walter de la Mare holds an almost unique position among twentieth-century poets. His poems for children are written with such sensitive imagery and delicate rhythm that they appeal to adults as well; and in a world in which realism is dominant he was an unabashed romantic, writing of the world of fantasy and of the supernatural.

De la Mare was born in Kent and educated at St. Paul's School in London. For eighteen years he was a clerk with the British division of Standard Oil Company before he retired to devote all his time to writing poems, stories, and novels. His most famous collection of stories and verses for children is *Peacock Pie* (1913). The collection entitled *The Listeners* (1912) illustrates his gift for writing about the supernatural world in such a way that the strange and the fantastic seem familiar. His best-known novel is *Memoirs of a Midget* (1921).

Walter de la Mare

NOD

Softly along the road of evening,
  In a twilight dim with rose,
Wrinkled with age and drenched with dew,
  Old Nod, the shepherd, goes.

His drowsy flock streams on before him,   5
  Their fleeces charged with gold,
To where the sun's last beam leans low
  On Nod the shepherd's fold.

The hedge is quick and green with briar,
  From their sand the conies creep;   10
And all the birds that fly in heaven
  Flock singing home to sleep.

His lambs outnumber a noon's roses,
  Yet, when night's shadows fall,
His blind old sheep dog, Slumber-soon,   15
  Misses not one of all.

His are the quiet steeps of dreamland,
  The waters of no-more-pain;
His ram's bell rings 'neath an arch of stars,
  "Rest, rest, and rest again."   20

SILVER

Slowly, silently, now the moon
Walks the night in her silver shoon;
This way, and that, she peers, and sees
Silver fruit upon silver trees;
One by one the casements catch   5
Her beams beneath the silvery thatch;
Couched in his kennel, like a log,
With paws of silver sleeps the dog;

"Nod" and "Silver" reprinted by permission of The Literary Trustees of Walter de la Mare and The Society of Authors as their representative.

From their shadowy cote the white breasts
    peep
Of doves in silver-feathered sleep;   10
A harvest mouse goes scampering by,
With silver claws and a silver eye;
And moveless fish in the water gleam,
By silver reeds in a silver stream.

THE LISTENERS

"Is there anybody there?" said the Traveler,
    Knocking on the moonlit door;
And his horse in the silence champed the
    grasses
Of the forest's ferny floor;
And a bird flew up out of the turret,   5
    Above the Traveler's head;
And he smote upon the door again a second
    time;
    "Is there anybody there?" he said.
But no one descended to the Traveler;
    No head from the leaf-fringed sill   10
Leaned over and looked into his gray eyes,
    Where he stood perplexed and still.
But only a host of phantom listeners
    That dwelt in the lone house then   14
Stood listening in the quiet of the moonlight

To that voice from the world of men;
Stood thronging the faint moonbeams on the
    dark stair,
    That goes down to the empty hall,
Hearkening in an air stirred and shaken
    By the lonely Traveler's call.   20
And he felt in his heart their strangeness,
    Their stillness answering his cry,
While his horse moved, cropping the dark
    turf,
    'Neath the starred and leafy sky;
For he suddenly smote on the door, even   25
    Louder, and lifted his head—
"Tell them I came, and no one
    answered,
    That I kept my word," he said.
Never the least stir made the listeners,
    Though every word he spake   30
Fell echoing through the shadowiness of the
    still house
    From the one man left awake.
Aye, they heard his foot upon the stirrup,
    And the sound of iron on stone,
And how the silence surged softly
    backward,   35
    When the plunging hoofs were gone.

To increase understanding

1. (a) What idea is developed in "Nod"? (b)
Why is Nod personified as a shepherd? (c) Who
are the sheep? (d) Why is the sheep dog blind?

2. (a) What is the basic meter of "Nod"? (b)
How has the poet created its slowly moving effect?

3. (a) How does the poet suggest an atmosphere
of silence in "Silver"? (b) What movement is
mentioned? (c) Why does the mention of specific
movement intensify the general feeling of quiet?

4. What devices are important in making "Silver" musical?

5. (a) What is the tone of "Silver"? (b) Compare the tone with that of "Nod."

6. (a) What story does "The Listeners" tell?
(b) What mysteries does it suggest?

7. Critic Louis Untermeyer has said of "The
Listeners": "Never . . . has the symbolism of man's
courage facing the cryptic riddle of life been more
memorably expressed." (a) Explain Untermeyer's
statement with reference to the poem. (b) Explain
why you agree or disagree with this interpretation
of "The Listeners." (c) Why, in your opinion, is
the poem widely regarded as a masterpiece in its
expression of the mysterious?

John Masefield

SPANISH
WATERS

Spanish waters, Spanish waters, you are ringing in my ears,
Like a slow sweet piece of music from the gray forgotten years;
Telling tales, and beating tunes, and bringing weary thoughts to me
Of the sandy beach at Muertos,[1] where I would that I could be.

There's a surf breaks on Los Muertos, and it never stops to roar,   5
And it's there we came to anchor, and it's there we went ashore,
Where the blue lagoon is silent amid snags of rotting trees,
Dropping like the clothes of corpses cast up by the seas.

We anchored at Los Muertos when the dipping sun was red,
We left her half-a-mile to sea, to west of Nigger Head[2];   10
And before the mist was on the cay, before the day was done,
We were all ashore on Muertos with the gold that we had won.

We bore it through the marshes in a half-score battered chests,
Sinking, in the sucking quagmires, to the sunburn on our breasts,
Heaving over tree trunks, gasping, damning at the flies and heat,   15
Longing for a long drink, out of silver, in the ship's cool lazareet.[3]

The moon came white and ghostly as we laid the treasure down,
There was gear there'd make a beggarman as rich as Lima Town,[4]
Copper charms and silver trinkets from the chests of Spanish crews,
Gold doubloons and double moidores;[5] louis d'ors[6] and portagues,[7]   20

Clumsy yellow-metal earrings from the Indians of Brazil,
Uncut emeralds out of Rio,[8] bezoar stones from Guayaquil[9];
Silver, in the crude and fashioned, pots of old Arica bronze,[10]
Jewels from the bones of Incas desecrated by the Dons.[11]

We smoothed the place with mattocks, and we took and blazed the tree, 25
Which marks yon where the gear is hid that none will ever see,

1. *Muertos*, Los Muertos (lōs mwer′tōs), a small island off the eastern coast of Panama. *Los Muertos* means "dead men."   2. *Nigger Head*, a prominent cape off Los Muertos.   3. *lazareet* (laz′ə rēt′), usually *lazaretto* (laz′ə ret′ō), a place near the stern of a ship where supplies are kept.   4. *Lima* (lē′mə) *Town*; Lima, Peru, once the wealthiest city of the Spanish Empire.   5. *doubloons* (dub lünz′) . . . *moidores* (moi′dôrz). Doubloons were Spanish gold coins varying in value from five to sixteen dollars. Moidores were Portuguese gold coins worth about $6.50.   6. *louis d'ors* (lü′i dôrz′), old French gold coins worth a little over four dollars.   7. *portagues* (pôr′tə güz) obsolete Portuguese gold coins worth from seventeen to twenty-two dollars.   8. *Rio*, Rio de Janeiro, Brazil.   9. *bezoar* (bē′zōr) *stones from Guayaquil*. Bezoar stones were believed to be an antidote to poison. They were hard masses of organic matter taken, in this instance, from the llama. They were gathered in Guayaquil, the principal seaport of Ecuador, for shipment.   10. *Arica* (ä rē′kä) *bronze*. Arica, a seaport in northern Chile, was once ruled by the Inca Indians. Rich deposits of tin and copper in the vicinity gave rise to the making of fine bronze.   11. *the bones of Incas . . . Dons*. The graves of the Incas, the highly civilized Indians of Peru, were robbed by the Spanish conquerors (dons).

And we laid aboard the ship again, and south away we steers,
Through the loud surf of Los Muertos which is beating in my ears.

I'm the last alive that knows it. All the rest have gone their ways—
Killed, or died, or come to anchor in the old Mulatas Cays,[12]   30
And I go singing, fiddling, old and starved and in despair,
And I know where all that gold is hid, if I were only there.

It's not the way to end it all. I'm old, and nearly blind,
And an old man's past's a strange thing, for it never leaves his mind.
And I see in dreams, awhiles, the beach, the sun's disk dipping red,   35
And the tall ship, under topsails, swaying in past Nigger Head.

I'd be glad to step ashore there. Glad to take a pick and go
To the lone blazed coco palm tree in the place no others know,
And lift the gold and silver that has moldered there for years
By the loud surf of Los Muertos which is beating in my ears.   40

SEA-FEVER
I must go down to the seas again, to the lonely sea and the sky,
And all I ask is a tall ship and a star to steer her by,
And the wheel's kick and the wind's song and the white sail's shaking,
And a gray mist on the sea's face and a gray dawn breaking.

I must go down to the seas again, for the call of the running tide   5
Is a wild call and a clear call that may not be denied;
And all I ask is a windy day with the white clouds flying,
And the flung spray and the blown spume and the sea gulls crying.

Reprinted with the permission of the publisher, The Society of Authors and Dr. John Masefield O.M. from *Poems* by John Masefield. Copyright 1912 by The Macmillan Company. Copyright 1940 by John Masefield.

SPANISH WATERS. **12.** *Mulatas* (mü lä'täs) *Cays*, the chain of little islands off the coast of Panama which includes the island of Los Muertos.

John Masefield 1878-1967

The man who was to become Poet Laureate of England in 1930 was a restless boy who ran away from home and put to sea at the age of thirteen. At sixteen he was aboard a windjammer looking for adventure on the seven seas. Long after illness forced him to leave the sea, his love of ships and the sea remained and is reflected in some of his best poetry.

After leaving his life aboard ship, Masefield spent some years in New York working at odd jobs. In 1897 he returned to England. The previous year, after reading Chaucer, he had determined to become a poet. His first collection of poetry, *Salt-Water Ballads* (1902), contained many poems, including "Sea-Fever," that have remained among his

Portrait by William Strang (see page 477).

I must go down to the seas again to the vagrant gypsy life,
To the gull's way and the whale's way where the wind's like a whetted
        knife;   10
And all I ask is a merry yarn from a laughing fellow-rover,
And quiet sleep and a sweet dream when the long trick's over.

CARGOES   Quinquireme of Nineveh from distant Ophir,[1]
            Rowing home to haven in sunny Palestine,
            With a cargo of ivory,
            And apes and peacocks,
            Sandalwood, cedarwood, and sweet white wine.   5

            Stately Spanish galleon coming from the Isthmus,[2]
            Dipping through the Tropics by the palm-green shores,
            With a cargo of diamonds,
            Emeralds, amethysts,
            Topazes, and cinnamon, and gold moidores.[3]   10

            Dirty British coaster with a salt-caked smokestack,
            Butting through the Channel in the mad March days,
            With a cargo of Tyne coal,[4]
            Road rails, pig lead,
            Firewood, ironware, and cheap tin trays.   15

CARGOES. **1.** *Quinquireme* (kwing'kwi rēm) *of Nineveh* (nin'ə və) . . . *Ophir* (ō'fər). A quinquireme was a large ancient galley with five banks of oars. Nineveh was a wealthy and luxurious Assyrian city on the Tigris River in what is now Iraq. Ophir was the place from which Solomon obtained his gold. (I Kings 9:28) **2.** *Isthmus*, Panama. **3.** *moidores*. See footnote 5 on page 629. **4.** *Tyne* (tin) *coal*, coal from the Tyne River country in northeastern England.

most popular. Later, influenced by his reading of Chaucer, he wrote several long narrative poems including *Dauber* (1912) and *Reynard the Fox* (1919). He also wrote short stories, biographies, plays, novels, and historical studies.

✿ To increase understanding

1. "Spanish Waters" is an implied narrative poem; the poet relates part of a story and merely suggests the remainder. Who is the speaker and what is the story he implies?

2. What makes "Spanish Waters" a romantic poem?

3. Many people remember lines from "Sea-Fever" or can quote the entire poem. What reasons can you advance for this wide popular appeal?

4. What period of history is suggested by each stanza of "Cargoes"?

5. (*a*) Compare and contrast the three stanzas of "Cargoes" as to (1) type of imagery, (2) rhythm, and (3) melody. (*b*) In what way do the differences between stanzas add to the effectiveness of the poem as a whole?

6. (*a*) What glimpses of Masefield's experiences as a youth do you gain from these poems? (*b*) Do you think the personal element has anything to do with the quality of the poetry? Explain.

Kew Gardens in spring.

Alfred Noyes

THE BARREL ORGAN

There's a barrel organ caroling across a
    golden street
    In the City[1] as the sun sinks low;
And the music's not immortal; but the world ·
    has made it sweet
    And fulfilled it with the sunset glow;
And it pulses through the pleasures of the
    City and the pain   5
    That surround the singing organ like a
    large eternal light;
And they've given it a glory and a part to
    play again
    In the Symphony that rules the day and
    night.

And now it's marching onward through the
    realms of old romance,
    And trolling out a fond familiar tune,   10
And now it's roaring cannon down to fight
    the King of France,
    And now it's prattling softly to the moon.
And all around the organ there's a sea
    without a shore
    Of human joys and wonders and regrets;
To remember and to recompense the music
    evermore   15
    For what the cold machinery forgets . . .

    Yes; as the music changes,
      Like a prismatic glass,
    It takes the light and ranges
      Through all the moods that pass;   20
    Dissects the common carnival
      Of passions and regrets,
    And gives the world a glimpse of all
      The colors it forgets.

Alfred Noyes 1880-1958

Born in Staffordshire and educated at Oxford,
Alfred Noyes served with the British trawlers in
World War I, using his own exciting experiences
as the basis for his poems "Open Boat" and "Songs
of the Trawlers." A forceful and entertaining
speaker, he was Professor of Poetry at Princeton
from 1914 to 1923, and was a popular figure on the
American lecture platform for many years.

His first book, published when he was twenty-
two, was favorably received by critics and established poets, and he was popular enough with the
public to be one of the few poets who could earn
his living by writing poetry. His later poetry was
not so well accepted as some of his earlier work and
has been criticized for its sentimentality.

"The Barrel Organ," however, as well as his well-
known "Highwayman," is a happy example of his
finer work. The nostalgic effect of the sounds of
a hurdy-gurdy he achieves in "The Barrel Organ"
shows his skill with handling rhythms and visual
color through language.

"The Barrel Organ" from *Collected Poems in One Volume*
by Alfred Noyes. Reprinted by permission of J. B. Lippincott Company, New York; and Mr. Hugh Noyes. Copyright 1906, 1922, 1947 by Alfred Noyes.
1. *the City*, the old part of London, most of which was once
enclosed within the Roman wall. It is now a business
section.

And there *La Traviata*[2] sighs   25
  Another sadder song;
And there *Il Trovatore*[3] cries
  A tale of deeper wrong;
And bolder knights to battle go
  With sword and shield and lance   30
Than ever here on earth below
  Have whirled into—*a dance!*—

Go down to Kew[4] in lilac time, in lilac time,
  in lilac time;
  Go down to Kew in lilac time (it isn't far
  from London!)
And you shall wander hand in hand with
  love in summer's wonderland;   35
  Go down to Kew in lilac time (it isn't far
  from London!)

The cherry trees are seas of bloom and soft
  perfume and sweet perfume,
  The cherry trees are seas of bloom (and
  oh, so near to London!)
And there they say, when dawn is high and
  all the world's a blaze of sky
  The cuckoo, though he's very shy, will
  sing a song for London.   40

The Dorian nightingale[5] is rare, and yet they
  say you'll hear him there
  At Kew, at Kew in lilac time (and oh, so
  near to London!)
The linnet and the throstle, too, and after
  dark the long halloo
  And golden-eyed *tu-whit, tu-whoo,* of owls
  that ogle London.

For Noah hardly knew a bird of any kind
  that isn't heard   45
  At Kew, at Kew in lilac time (and oh, so
  near to London!)
And when the rose begins to pout, and all
  the chestnut spires are out,
  You'll hear the rest without a doubt, all
  chorusing for London:

Come down to Kew in lilac time, in lilac
  time, in lilac time;
  Come down to Kew in lilac time (it isn't
  far from London!)   50

And you shall wander hand in hand with
  love in summer's wonderland;
  Come down to Kew in lilac time (it isn't
  far from London!)

And then the troubadour begins to thrill the
  golden street,
  In the City as the sun sinks low;
And in all the gaudy busses there are scores
  of weary feet   55
Marking time, sweet time, with a dull
  mechanic beat,
And a thousand hearts are plunging to a
  love they'll never meet,
Through the meadows of the sunset, through
  the poppies and the wheat,
  In the land where the dead dreams go.

Verdi, Verdi, when you wrote *Il Trovatore*
  did you dream   60
  Of the City when the sun sinks low,
Of the organ and the monkey and the
  many-colored stream
On the Piccadilly[6] pavement, of the myriad
  eyes that seem
To be litten[7] for a moment with a wild
  Italian gleam
As *A che la morte*[8] parodies the world's
  eternal theme   65
  And pulses with the sunset glow?

There's a thief, perhaps, that listens with a
  face of frozen stone
  In the City as the sun sinks low,
There's a portly man of business with a
  balance of his own,

---

2. *La Traviata* (lä trä'vē ä'tä), an extremely popular opera by Giuseppe Verdi (jü zep'pe vär'di), an Italian composer (1813-1901). Its story concerns a woman with a past who gives up the man she loves to avoid ruining his life. 3. *Il Trovatore* (ēl trō'vä tō're), another opera by Verdi. The tragic story concerns concealed identities and violent death in medieval Spain. 4. *Kew* (kū), a village near London, where there is a famous botanical garden. 5. *Dorian nightingale*, an allusion to the classical legend of Philomela (fĭl'ə mē'lə), a princess who was transformed into a nightingale. Dorian refers to Doris, a district in ancient Greece. 6. *Piccadilly*, one of the principal business streets in London. 7. *litten*, lighted up. 8. A *che la morte* (ä kä lä môr'te), the opening words (meaning "To whom death") of the "Miserere" (mĭz'ə rār'ĭ), the most famous aria in Verdi's opera *Il Trovatore*.

There's a clerk and there's a butcher of a soft
    reposeful tone,   70
And they're all of them returning to the
    heavens they have known;
They are crammed and jammed in busses
    and—they're each of them alone
In the land where the dead dreams go.

There's a very modish woman, and her smile
    is very bland
In the City as the sun sinks low;   75
And her hansom jingles onward, but her
    little jeweled hand
Is clenched a little tighter, and she cannot
    understand
What she wants or why she wanders to that
    undiscovered land,
For the parties there are not at all the sort of
    thing she planned,
In the land where the dead dreams go.   80

There's an Oxford man that listens, and his
    heart is crying out
In the City as the sun sinks low,
For the barge, the eight, the Isis,[9] and the
    coach's whoop and shout,
For the minute gun, the counting, and the
    long disheveled rout,
For the howl along the towpath and a fate
    that's still in doubt,   85
For a roughened oar to handle and a race to
    think about
In the land where the dead dreams go.

There's a laborer that listens to the voices of
    the dead
In the City as the sun sinks low;
And his hand begins to tremble and his face
    is rather red   90
As he sees a loafer watching him and—there
    he turns his head
And stares into the sunset where his April
    love is fled,
For he hears her softly singing, and his
    lonely soul is led
Through the land where the dead dreams go.

There's an old and haggard demirep; it's
    ringing in her ears,   95

In the City as the sun sinks low;
With the wild and empty sorrow of the love
    that blights and sears,
Oh, and if she hurries onward, then be sure,
    be sure she hears,
Hears and bears the bitter burden of the
    unforgotten years,
And her laugh's a little harsher, and her eyes
    are brimmed with tears   100
For the land where the dead dreams go.

There's a barrel organ caroling across a
    golden street
In the City as the sun sinks low;
Though the music's only Verdi, there's a
    world to make it sweet,
Just as yonder yellow sunset where the earth
    and heaven meet   105
Mellows all the sooty City! Hark, a hundred
    thousand feet
Are marching on to glory through the
    poppies and the wheat
In the land where the dead dreams go.

    So it's Jeremiah, Jeremiah,
        What have you to say   110
    When you meet the garland girls
        Tripping on their way?

    All around my gala hat
        I wear a wreath of roses;
    (A long and lonely year it is   115
        I've waited for the May!)

    If anyone should ask you,
        The reason why I wear it is—
    My own love, my true love
        Is coming home today.   120

And it's buy a bunch of violets for the lady
    (It's lilac time in London; it's lilac time in
    London!)
Buy a bunch of violets for the lady,
    While the sky burns blue above;

---

9. *For the barge, the eight, the Isis* (ī′sis). The upper stretches
of the Thames River at Oxford and above are called the
Isis. "The barge," "the eight," and the reference to racing
crews in the remainder of the stanza are a reminder of the
fact that Noyes rowed with the Oxford crew on the Isis.

On the other side the street you'll find it
    shady   125
    (It's lilac time in London; it's lilac time in
    London!)
But buy a bunch of violets for the lady,
    And tell her she's your own true love.

There's a barrel organ caroling across a
    golden street
    In the City as the sun sinks glittering and
    slow;   130
And the music's not immortal; but the world
    has made it sweet
And enriched it with the harmonies that
    make a song complete
In the deeper heavens of music where the
    night and morning meet
As it dies into the sunset glow;
And it pulses through the pleasures of the
    City and the pain   135
    That surround the singing organ like a
    large eternal light,
And they've given it a glory and a part to
    play again
    In the Symphony that rules the day and
    night.

And there, as the music changes,
    The song runs round again;   140
Once more it turns and ranges
    Through all its joy and pain,
Dissects the common carnival
    Of passions and regrets;   144
And the wheeling world remembers all
    The wheeling song forgets.

Once more La Traviata sighs
    Another sadder song;
Once more Il Trovatore cries
    A tale of deeper wrong;   150
Once more the knights to battle go
    With sword and shield and lance
Till once, once more, the shattered foe
    Has whirled into—a dance!

Come down to Kew in lilac time, in lilac
    time, in lilac time;   155
Come down to Kew in lilac time (it isn't far
    from London!)
And you shall wander hand in hand with
    love in summer's wonderland;
Come down to Kew in lilac time (it isn't far
    from London!)

🌼To increase understanding

1. (a) Where is the barrel organ playing? (b) What is the time of day? (c) What types of music are being played? (d) Who are some of the people hearing the barrel organ? (e) How do they react to the music? (f) What connection is there between the listeners and "the land where the dead dreams go"? (g) What relation is there between the time of day, the type of music, and "the land where the dead dreams go"?

2. There is a close relationship between the rhythm and rhyme of this poem and the ideas expressed. (a) What is the basic meter of the first part of the poem? (b) Where does the rhythm change? Why? (c) Where is the third rhythmic pattern introduced? (d) What effect is produced by the use of internal rhyme in this section? (e) Where does the rhythm of the first part reappear? (f) Explain the return to this rhythm. (g) What effect is produced by the twelve lines beginning "So it's Jeremiah, Jeremiah" (line 109)? (h) Why, in your opinion, does the poem end with the Kew refrain?

3. (a) In addition to rhyme and rhythm what other devices does Noyes use to add melody? Give examples. (b) Which section of the poem do you think is richest in melody? Give reasons for your answer.

Rupert Brooke

THE SOLDIER

If I should die, think only this of me:
That there's some corner of a foreign field
That is forever England. There shall be
In that rich earth a richer dust concealed;

A dust whom England bore, shaped, made
    aware,   **5**
Gave, once, her flowers to love, her ways to
    roam,
A body of England's breathing English air,
Washed by the rivers, blest by suns of home.

And think, this heart, all evil shed away,
A pulse in the eternal mind, no less,   **10**
Gives somewhere back the thoughts by
    England given:
Her sights and sound; dreams happy as her
    day;
And laughter, learnt of friends; and
    gentleness,
In hearts at peace, under an English heaven.

THE DEAD

These hearts were woven of human joys and
    cares,
Washed marvelously with sorrow, swift to
    mirth.
The years had given them kindness. Dawn
    was theirs,
And sunset, and the colors of the earth.
These had seen movement, and heard music;
    known   **5**
Slumber and waking; loved; gone proudly
    friended;
Felt the quick stir of wonder; sat alone;
Touched flowers and furs and cheeks. All
    this is ended.
There are waters blown by changing winds
    to laughter   **9**
And lit by the rich skies, all day. And after,
Frost, with a gesture, stays the waves that
    dance
And wandering loveliness. He leaves a white
Unbroken glory, a gathered radiance,
A width, a shining peace, under the night.

CULVER PICTURES

Rupert Brooke 1887-1915

Rupert Brooke, handsome and athletic, published his first poems in 1911, shortly before the storm clouds of World War I rolled over the horizon. When the war came, he enlisted with enthusiasm. In the Dardanelles campaign of 1915 he died—not on the field of battle, ironically enough, but of an infection from an insect bite.

Brooke's poems were collected in the year that he died. His body was buried on the Aegean island of Skyros, thus giving reality to the thought expressed in the first three lines of "The Soldier."

Wilfred Owen

FUTILITY

Move him into the sun—
Gently its touch awoke him once,
At home, whispering of fields unsown.
Always it woke him, even in France,
Until this morning and this snow.　　　　**5**
If anything might rouse him now
The kind old sun will know.

Think how it wakes the seeds—
Woke, once, the clays of a cold star.
Are limbs, so dear-achieved, are sides,　　　**10**
Full-nerved—still warm—too hard to stir?
Was it for this the clay grew tall?
—O what made fatuous sunbeams toil
To break earth's sleep at all?

IMPERIAL WAR MUSEUM, LONDON

Wilfred Owen 1893-1918

Wilfred Owen was born in Shropshire—the English county celebrated by A. E. Housman. He was killed just a week before the armistice of November 1918, as he was leading a group of British soldiers across the Sambre Canal in Flanders.

Owen received little formal education. But with an inborn love of poetry and undoubted talents, he had made a name for himself a year or more before his death. Today he is considered by most critics the finest poet of World War I and one of the first poets to use the techniques of modern poetry with artistry and assurance.

To increase understanding

1. (*a*) What is the theme of "The Soldier"? (*b*) What verse form does Rupert Brooke use? (*c*) What is the tone of the poem?

2. In the sestet of "The Dead" water and frost are used as symbols. Explain the symbolism.

3. The war poems of both Brooke and Owen included here turn back to memories of England. (*a*) For what effect does Owen use references to England? (*b*) How does his purpose in using memories of the past differ from Brooke's? (*c*) What one word in "Futility" best expresses the reason for the title of the poem?

4. (*a*) Contrast the attitudes toward war and its dead expressed by Owen and Brooke. (*b*) Would the word *patriotic* be more apt to be applied to Owen's poem or to Brooke's? Explain.

Better reading
Imperfect rhyme

Although poets of earlier times occasionally used *imperfect* or *slant rhyme* (see page 392, column 2, paragraph 2), this technique has assumed greater significance than ever before in twentieth-century poetry. Unlike conventional rhyme, which makes use of words which match exactly in vowel and consonant sounds (*field/concealed*), imperfect rhyme is a deliberate use of words in which the vowel and consonant sounds differ but are similar (*blade/blood*, *flash/flesh*, *teeth/death*).

Wilfred Owen makes frequent use of slant rhyme. Find examples of this rhyme in "Futility." What examples of conventional rhyme can you find? What purposes does this change in rhyme pattern serve? What connection can you see between the slant rhymes in "Futility" and the theme of the poem?

Robert Bridges

NIGHTINGALES   Beautiful must be the mountains whence ye come,
        And bright in the fruitful valleys the streams wherefrom
            Ye learn your song:
        Where are those starry woods? O might I wander there,
            Among the flowers, which in that heavenly air   5
            Bloom the year long!

        Nay, barren are those mountains and spent the streams:
        Our song is the voice of desire, that haunts our dreams,
            A throe of the heart,
        Whose pining visions dim, forbidden hopes profound,   10
            No dying cadence nor long sigh can sound,
            For all our art.

        Alone, aloud in the raptured ear of men
        We pour our dark nocturnal secret; and then,
            As night is withdrawn   15
        From these sweet-springing meads and bursting boughs of May,
            Dream, while the innumerable choir of day
            Welcome the dawn.

From *The Poetical Works of Robert Bridges*. Reprinted by permission of The Clarendon Press, Oxford, England.

Robert Bridges   1844-1930

While he was a doctor at St. Bartholomew's Hospital in London, Robert Bridges began to write the poetry which eventually led him to the position of Poet Laureate of England. When he was thirty-eight years old, he gave up the practice of medicine in order to spend all of his time writing; but at the time he was appointed Poet Laureate in 1913, he was still comparatively unknown to the British public. Called the "silent laureate" because he refused to write the occasional verse demanded by his position, he concentrated upon his own numerous projects—the writing of critical essays, the promotion of spelling reform, and the writing of his philosophy *The Testament of Beauty* (1929). Bridges also edited the poetry of his friend Gerard Manley Hopkins (see page 522), and succeeded in having it published in 1918. Before he died at the age of eighty-six, Bridges requested that no biographies of him be written. Whatever the public needed to know about his life, he said, could be found in his book *Three Friends*.

Like his friend Hopkins, Bridges was an innovator in metrics, experimenting with the use of free verse based on the natural accents of speech. The craftsmanship of his verse is outstanding; a master of diction, he often speaks with the dignity and formality of the eighteenth century.

Robert Graves

ROCKY ACRES

This is a wild land, country of my choice,
With harsh craggy mountain, moor ample
    and bare.
Seldom in these acres is heard any voice
But voice of cold water that runs here and
    there
Through rocks and lank heather growing
    without care.   5
No mice in the heath run, no songbirds fly
For fear of the buzzard that floats in the sky.

He soars and he hovers, rocking on his wings,
He scans his wide parish with a sharp eye,
He catches the trembling of small hidden
    things,   10
He tears them in pieces, dropping them from
    the sky;
Tenderness and pity the heart will deny,
Where life is but nourished by water and
    rock—
A hardy adventure, full of fear and shock.

Time has never journeyed to this lost land,   15
Crakeberry and heather bloom out of date,
The rocks jut, the streams flow singing on
    either hand,
Careless if the season be early or late,
The skies wander overhead, now blue, now
    slate;   19
Winter would be known by his cutting snow
If June did not borrow his armor also.

Yet this is my country, beloved by me best,
The first land that rose from Chaos and the
    Flood,
Nursing no valleys for comfort and rest,
Trampled by no shod hooves, bought with
    no blood.   25
Sempiternal country whose barrows have
    stood
Stronghold for demigods when on earth they
    go,
Terror for fat burghers on far plains below.

G. K. Chesterton

THE DONKEY

When fishes flew and forests
    walked
    And figs grew upon thorn,
Some moment when the moon was
    blood,
    Then surely I was born;

With monstrous head and sickening cry   5
    And ears like errant wings,
The devil's walking parody
    On all four-footed things.

The tattered outlaw of the earth,
    Of ancient crooked will;   10
Starve, scourge, deride me: I am dumb,
    I keep my secret still.

Fools! For I also had my hour,
    One far fierce hour and sweet:
There was a shout about my ears,   15
    And palms before my feet!

"Rocky Acres" by Robert Graves. From *Collected Poems
1955* published by Doubleday & Company, Inc. Reprinted
by permission of Willis Kingsley Wing, New York. Copyright © 1955 International Authors N.V.
From the book *The Wild Knight And Other Poems* by G. K.
Chesterton. Published by E. P. Dutton & Co., Inc. and
reprinted with their permission and that of Miss D. E.
Collins and J. M. Dent & Sons Ltd.

Robert Graves

Robert Graves   1895-

In 1929 Robert Graves wrote an autobiography called *Good-by To All That* and set off for the island of Majorca (mə jôr′kə), Spain, where he has lived ever since. "All That" of the title included quite a lot. He had been a member of the British Expeditionary Forces during World War I and wrote bitter poetry about his experiences. Upon returning from the war he married, finished his education at Oxford, and, since profits from his writing were not sufficient for his expenses, became a shopkeeper. He liked sports and before the war had been a prize winner in the Olympic games.

Except for an interlude during the Spanish Civil War, Graves has lived in the Majorcan fishing village of Deyá since 1929, writing books which now fill an eight-foot-long bookshelf. In 1934 he won the Hawthornden and James Tait Black prizes for his exciting fictional account of a Roman emperor, *I, Claudius*. Many of his other books have been created from his interest in myth and history, including *Hercules, My Shipmate* (1945) and *King Jesus* (1946).

There have been frequent publications of Graves' collected poems to make available the many new poems he writes each year. One of the latest volumes is a 1959 edition of *Collected Poems*. Some of his early poetry has been called "flippant," a term which cannot be applied to his later poetry, which is much more speculative and frequently paradoxical.

G. K. Chesterton   1874-1936

G. K. Chesterton was one of the most colorful personalities of the literary London of his day. A versatile writer, he dealt with almost every form of literary composition. He began writing as an art-book reviewer, turned to literary criticism, and then wrote novels and short stories about the fanciful and fantastic. He created one of the best-known detectives of modern mystery fiction—Father Brown—and wrote a series of stories about him, the first of which was *The Innocence of Father Brown* (1911).

His verse varies from ballads to near epigrams. He delights in paradox. His light verse sparkles with wit. In his more serious poetry he speaks with conviction and emotion.

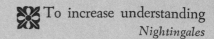 To increase understanding

Nightingales

1. (*a*) In the poem "Nightingales," what assumption does the speaker make in the first stanza? (*b*) What causes him to make this assumption?

2. (*a*) Who speaks in the second stanza? (*b*) What causes the nightingales' beautiful song?

3. "Dark nocturnal secret" (line 14) suggests both night and the sad reality behind the song. (*a*) What is the song, or "secret," of the nightingales contrasted with? (*b*) The poet implies that the song of the nightingales is more beautiful than the songs of "the innumerable choir of day." From what does the beauty of the nightingales' song result?

4. What is the poem's theme?

5. "Nightingales" is a very musical poem. Explain as well as you can how Bridges achieves this effect.

6. Compare this poem with Keats' "Ode to a Nightingale" (page 395). (*a*) How does Keats regard the nightingale? (*b*) Which poem is more romantic? Explain your answer.

Rocky Acres

1. Describe the country Graves writes of in "Rocky Acres," citing details that you feel best catch its dominant characteristics.

2. (*a*) Why is the "wild land" the buzzard's "parish" (line 7)? (*b*) In what way does the buzzard symbolize this land?

3. (*a*) Why is this land a "Stronghold for demi-gods" (line 27)? (*b*) What is the poet's attitude toward the "burghers on far plains below" (line 28)? (*c*) Who are the "burghers"?

4. Compare the theme of "Rocky Acres" with that of Bridges' "Nightingales."

The Donkey

1. Who is the speaker in "The Donkey"?

2. (*a*) Why must the donkey have been born when "fishes flew" and "forests walked"? (*b*) Explain why the donkey is the "devil's walking parody" (line 7). (*c*) Explain the relevance to the poem of the donkey as a "tattered outlaw" of "ancient crooked will" (lines 9-10).

3. (*a*) What is alluded to in the last stanza? (*b*) What other title for this poem can you suggest?

T. S. Eliot

THE HOLLOW MEN

Mistah Kurtz—he dead.[1]

A penny for the Old Guy.[2]

I

We are the hollow men
We are the stuffed men
Leaning together
Headpiece filled with straw. Alas!
Our dried voices, when   5
We whisper together
Are quiet and meaningless
As wind in dry grass
Or rats' feet over broken glass
In our dry cellar   10

Shape without form, shade without color,
Paralysed force, gesture without motion;

Those who have crossed
With direct eyes,[3] to death's other Kingdom
Remember us—if at all—not as lost   15
Violent souls, but only
As the hollow men
The stuffed men.

II

Eyes[4] I dare not meet in dreams
In death's dream kingdom   20
These do not appear:
There, the eyes are
Sunlight on a broken column
There, is a tree swinging
And voices are   25
In the wind's singing
More distant and more solemn
Than a fading star.

Let me be no nearer
In death's dream kingdom   30
Let me also wear
Such deliberate disguises
Rat's coat, crowskin, crossed staves
In a field
Behaving as the wind behaves   35
No nearer—

Not that final meeting
In the twilight kingdom.[5]

III

This is the dead land
This is cactus land   40
Here the stone images
Are raised, here they receive
The supplication of a dead man's hand
Under the twinkle of a fading star.

Is it like this   45
In death's other kingdom

1. *Mistah Kurtz—he dead*, a quotation from Joseph Conrad's novel, *Heart of Darkness*. Mr. Kurtz was a European trader who had gone into "the heart of darkness" —the central African wilderness—with European standards of life and conduct. Because he was "hollow at the core" and had no moral or spiritual strength to sustain him, he was soon turned into a barbarian.   2. *A penny . . . Guy*, the cry of English children taking part in the annual celebration of Guy Fawkes Day, November 5. On this date in 1605 the traitor Guy Fawkes was thwarted in his "gunpowder plot" to blow up both Houses of Parliament. In modern celebrations of the deliverance of Parliament, effigies of Guy Fawkes are burned, and children beg for pennies, in the name of the "Old Guy," to buy firecrackers.   3. *Those . . . direct eyes*, those who have somehow represented something positive (direct), either for good or bad.   4. *Eyes*, an allusion to the eyes of the dead Beatrice in Dante's *Divine Comedy*, which are symbolic of spiritual reality. But among "the hollow men," who would, in Dante's scheme of things, belong in Limbo (the first circle of Hell), there is no reality and therefore no spiritual challenge. On the contrary, the hollow men dread to see anything that suggests reality.   5. *Not . . . kingdom*. The hollow men do not want to face the final meeting in Hell, where the eyes of spiritual reality will be on them and make them flinch.

Waking alone
At the hour when we are
Trembling with tenderness
Lips that would kiss   50
Form prayers to broken stone.

IV

The eyes are not here
There are no eyes here
In this valley of dying stars
In this hollow valley   55
This broken jaw of our lost kingdoms

In this last of meeting places
We grope together
And avoid speech
Gathered on this beach of the tumid river   60

Sightless, unless
The eyes reappear
As the perpetual star
Multifoliate rose
Of death's twilight kingdom   65
The hope only
Of empty men.

V

Here we go round the prickly pear
Prickly pear prickly pear
Here we go round the prickly pear   70
At five o'clock in the morning.

Between the idea
And the reality
Between the motion
And the act   75
Falls the Shadow
                    For Thine is the Kingdom

Between the conception
And the creation
Between the emotion   80
And the response
Falls the Shadow
                              Life is very long

Between the desire
And the spasm   85
Between the potency
And the existence
Between the essence
And the descent
Falls the Shadow   90
                    For Thine is the Kingdom

For Thine is
Life is
For Thine is the

This is the way the world ends   95
This is the way the world ends
This is the way the world ends
Not with a bang but a whimper.

T. S. Eliot   1888-1965

In his dual rôles as poet and critic T. S. Eliot had a greater influence on twentieth-century poetry both in England and the United States than any other individual. Born in St. Louis, Missouri, Eliot studied at Harvard University. In 1914 he went to England where he took up residence. He became a British subject in 1927.

While he was still a student at Harvard, Eliot wrote one of the most famous poems of the twentieth century, "The Love Song of J. Alfred Prufrock." In "Prufrock" he offered his conception of the modern intellectual—timid, blasé, mediocre, and defeatist. This poem appeared in *Prufrock and Other Observations* in 1917, a volume which made evident Eliot's complete break with romanticism.

He discussed his distaste for romanticism and the emotion which is one of its essentials in his criticism. He believed that the intellect must be dominant in the writing of poetry. He valued finish in form, balance and symmetry in expression. He saw satire as a valuable antidote to sentimentalism. To him poetry was not an outburst but a deliberately constructed object which creates or reproduces emotion through a series of images and the use of appropriate rhythm. In such poems as *The Waste Land* (1922) and "The Hollow Men" he used these techniques in presenting his idea of modern man as an ineffective defeatist living in a sterile, uncreative world. Eliot's images are often based on allusions. In the 403 lines of *The Waste Land* there are allusions to or quotations from more than thirty-five different writers as well as words and phrases

CHORUS 3
from
THE ROCK

The word of the LORD came unto me, saying:
O miserable cities of designing men,
O wretched generation of enlightened men,
Betrayed in the mazes of your ingenuities,
Sold by the proceeds of your proper inventions:
I have given you hands which you turn from worship,
I have given you speech, for endless palaver,
I have given you my Law, and you set up commissions,
I have given you lips, to express friendly sentiments,
I have given you hearts, for reciprocal distrust.   10
I have given you power of choice, and you only alternate
Between futile speculation and unconsidered action.
Many are engaged in writing books and printing them,
Many desire to see their names in print,
Many read nothing but the race reports.   15
Much is your reading, but not the Word of GOD.
Much is your building, but not the House of GOD.
Will you build me a house of plaster, with corrugated roofing,
To be filled with a litter of Sunday newspapers?

1ST MALE VOICE:

A Cry from the East: 20
What shall be done to the shore of smoky ships?
Will you leave my people forgetful and forgotten
To idleness, labor, and delirious stupor?
There shall be left the broken chimney,
The peeled hull, a pile of rusty iron,   25
In a street of scattered brick where the goat climbs,
Where My Word is unspoken.

---

from six different languages. In spite of its difficulty, *The Waste Land* is a very effective poem. So aptly did it catch the spirit of disillusionment and pessimism prevailing after the First World War that it gave its name to a major trend in the poetry of the 1920's and early 1930's.

Eliot set the tone for the poetry of the period. Young poets with less skill than he mimicked his style. The result was often confusion and obscurity. Eliot's tastes in poetry were imitated. Because he favored the Elizabethan writers and praised John Donne highly, Donne's sonnets (see page 184) became extremely popular. When Eliot criticized Milton, Milton lost favor with the young intellectuals.

Shortly after Eliot became a British subject in 1927, he announced himself as "an Anglo-Catholic in religion," "a classicist in literature and a royalist in politics." Such sweeping changes in his personal outlook made a great change in his writing. He turned to religion as the one possible solution for modern man. In the poem *Ash Wednesday* (1930) and the verse pageant *The Rock* (1934) he insisted powerfully upon a mood of repentance and of faith in the Church ("the Rock"). His poetic drama *Murder in the Cathedral* (1935), which tells the story of Thomas à Becket, repeated the theme that only in religion can man find salvation. In *The Family Reunion* (1939) he suggested that the evils facing the family and society in modern times can be corrected only through religious faith.

<table>
<tr><td>2ND MALE VOICE:</td><td>A Cry from the North, from the West and from the South</td><td></td></tr>
</table>

2ND MALE VOICE: A Cry from the North, from the West and from the South
Whence thousands travel daily to the timekept City;
Where My Word is unspoken,   30
In the land of lobelias and tennis flannels
The rabbit shall burrow and the thorn revisit,
The nettle shall flourish on the gravel court,
And the wind shall say: "Here were decent godless people:
Their only monument the asphalt road   35
And a thousand lost golf balls."

CHORUS: We build in vain unless the LORD build with us.
Can you keep the City that the LORD keeps not with you?
A thousand policemen directing the traffic
Cannot tell you why you come or where you go.
A colony of cavies or a horde of active marmots   41
Build better than they that build without the LORD.
Shall we lift up our feet among perpetual ruins?
I have loved the beauty of Thy House, the peace of Thy Sanctuary,
I have swept the floors and garnished the altars.   45
Where there is no temple there shall be no homes,
Though you have shelters and institutions,
Precarious lodgings while the rent is paid,
Subsiding basements where the rat breeds
Or sanitary dwellings with numbered doors   50
Or a house a little better than your neighbor's;
When the Stranger says: "What is the meaning of this city?
Do you huddle close together because you love each other?"
What will you answer? "We all dwell together
To make money from each other"? or "This is a community"?   55
And the Stranger will depart and return to the desert.
O my soul, be prepared for the coming of the Stranger,
Be prepared for him who knows how to ask questions.
O weariness of men who turn from GOD
To the grandeur of your mind and the glory of your action,   60
To arts and inventions and daring enterprises,
To schemes of human greatness thoroughly discredited,
Binding the earth and the water to your service,
Exploiting the seas and developing the mountains,
Dividing the stars into common and preferred,[1]   65
Engaged in devising the perfect refrigerator,
Engaged in working out a rational morality,
Engaged in printing as many books as possible,
Plotting of happiness and flinging empty bottles,
Turning from your vacancy to fevered enthusiasm   70
For nation or race or what you call humanity;
Though you forget the way to the Temple,
There is one who remembers the way to your door:
Life you may evade, but Death you shall not.
You shall not deny the Stranger.   75

---

1. *preferred*, classifying stars as if they were "common" and "preferred" stocks in business.

To increase understanding

The Hollow Men

1. (*a*) Explain the origin of Eliot's term "the hollow men." (*b*) In modern England who is "the Old Guy"? (*c*) In what way are the ideas suggested by "the hollow men" and "the Old Guy" united in lines 1-12?

2. (*a*) What are some of the images Eliot uses to describe the hollow men? (*b*) Cite images that show the hollow men as having no purpose or will. (*c*) What is it that the hollow men fear in "death's other Kingdom"?

3. Sections III and IV treat of "the dead land." (*a*) What lines best express the hopelessness of this land? (*b*) Who are the inhabitants of this land?

4. (*a*) What nursery rhyme is the basis of the opening lines of Section V? (*b*) How does Eliot's substitution of "prickly pear" link this section with the two preceding ones?

5. In Section V Eliot quotes from the Lord's Prayer ("For Thine is the Kingdom"). At the end of each stanza he uses the refrain "Falls the Shadow." (*a*) What is the Shadow? (*b*) In the context of the poem does the quotation from the Lord's Prayer express belief or disbelief? Explain. (*c*) What is the effect of the cut-off references to earlier quotations in lines 92-94?

6. The last two lines of "The Hollow Men" are among the most quoted lines in twentieth-century poetry. (*a*) What do they mean? (*b*) How do they epitomize the spirit of the hollow men?

Chorus from The Rock

1. (*a*) In this portion of *The Rock* Eliot uses satire to condemn modern society. Cite lines that you feel are most apt in pointing out flaws. (*b*) How does the tone of Eliot's criticism here differ from the tone of "The Hollow Men"?

2. (*a*) What is meant by "the Stranger"? (*b*) What questions does the Stranger ask? (*c*) What answers does modern man give to his questions? (*d*) Are these answers adequate?

3. (*a*) How does the poet's attitude in *The Rock* differ from his attitude in "The Hollow Men"? (*b*) Relate these poems to the work of different periods in Eliot's life.

PHOTOGRAPH BY ANGUS MCBEAN

T.S. Eliot.

CHORUS

from THE FAMILY REUNION

From: Part II, Scene III
Scene: The Library in a Country House in the North of England, After Dinner

CHORUS: We do not like to look out of the same window, and see quite a different landscape.
We do not like to climb a stair, and find that it takes us down.
We do not like to walk out of a door, and find ourselves back in the same room.
We do not like the maze in the garden, because it too closely resembles the maze in the brain.
We do not like what happens when we are awake, because it too closely resembles what happens when we are asleep. ⁵
We understand the ordinary business of living,
We know how to work the machine,
We can usually avoid accidents,

We are insured against fire,
Against larceny and illness,   10
Against defective plumbing,
But not against the act of God.
We know various spells and enchantments,
And minor forms of sorcery,
Divination and chiromancy,   15
Specifics against insomnia,
Lumbago, and the loss of money.
But the circle of our understanding
Is a very restricted area.
Except for a limited number   20
Of strictly practical purposes
We do not know what we are doing;
And even, when you think of it,
We do not know much about thinking.
What is happening outside of the circle?   25
And what is the meaning of happening?
What ambush lies beyond the heather
And behind the Standing Stones?
Beyond the Heaviside Layer
And behind the smiling moon?   30
And what is being done to us?
And what are we, and what are we doing?
To each and all of these questions
There is no conceivable answer.
We have suffered far more than a personal
    loss—   35
We have lost our way in the dark.

GROWLTIGER'S LAST STAND

GROWLTIGER was a Bravo Cat, who lived
    upon a barge:
In fact he was the roughest cat that ever
    roamed at large.
From Gravesend up to Oxford he pursued
    his evil aims,
Rejoicing in his title of "The Terror of the
    Thames."

His manners and appearance did not
    calculate to please;   5
His coat was torn and seedy, he was baggy
    at the knees;
One ear was somewhat missing, no need to
    tell you why,
And he scowled upon a hostile world from
    one forbidding eye.

The cottagers of Rotherhithe knew
    something of his fame,
At Hammersmith and Putney people
    shuddered at his name.   10
They would fortify the hen-house, lock up
    the silly goose,
When the rumor ran along the shore:
    GROWLTIGER'S ON THE LOOSE!

Woe to the weak canary, that fluttered
    from its cage;
Woe to the pampered Pekinese, that faced
    Growltiger's rage.
Woe to the bristly Bandicoot, that lurks on
    foreign ships,   15
And woe to any Cat with whom Growltiger
    came to grips!

But most to Cats of foreign race his hatred
    had been vowed;
To Cats of foreign name and race no quarter
    was allowed.
The Persian and the Siamese regarded him
    with fear—
Because it was a Siamese had mauled his
    missing ear.   20

Now on a peaceful summer night, all
    nature seemed at play,
The tender moon was shining bright, the
    barge at Molesey lay.
All in the balmy moonlight it lay rocking on
    the tide—
And Growltiger was disposed to show his
    sentimental side.

His bucko mate, GRUMBUSKIN, long since
    had disappeared,   25
For to the Bell at Hampton he had gone to
    wet his beard;
And his bosun, TUMBLEBRUTUS, he too had
    stol'n away—
In the yard behind the Lion he was prowling
    for his prey.

In the forepeak of the vessel Growltiger
sate alone,
Concentrating his attention on the Lady
GRIDDLEBONE.   30
And his raffish crew were sleeping in their
barrels and their bunks—
As the Siamese came creeping in their
sampans and their junks.

Growltiger had no eye or ear for aught
but Griddlebone,
And the Lady seemed enraptured by his
manly baritone,
Disposed to relaxation, and awaiting no
surprise—   35
But the moonlight shone reflected from a
thousand bright blue eyes.

And closer still and closer the sampans
circled round,
And yet from all the enemy there was not
heard a sound.
The lovers sang their last duet, in danger of
their lives—
For the foe was armed with toasting forks
and cruel carving knives.   40

Then GILBERT gave the signal to his fierce
Mongolian horde;
With a frightful burst of fireworks the
Chinks they swarmed aboard.

Abandoning their sampans, and their
pullaways and junks,
They battened down the hatches on the
crew within their bunks.

Then Griddlebone she gave a screech, for
she was badly skeered;   45
I am sorry to admit it, but she quickly
disappeared.
She probably escaped with ease, I'm sure she
was not drowned—
But a serried ring of flashing steel Growltiger
did surround.

The ruthless foe pressed forward, in
stubborn rank on rank;
Growltiger to his vast surprise was forced to
walk the plank.   50
He who a hundred victims had driven to
that drop,
At the end of all his crimes was forced to go
ker-flip, ker-flop.

Oh there was joy in Wapping when the
news flew through the land;
At Maidenhead and Henley there was
dancing on the strand.
Rats were roasted whole at Brentford, and at
Victoria Dock,   55
And a day of celebration was commanded in
Bangkok.

Chorus from The Family Reunion

1. The first five lines of the chorus from *The Family Reunion* are a series of paradoxes. (*a*) Explain these paradoxes. (*b*) What do they tell you about the speakers in the chorus?

2. (*a*) The speakers say they understand "the ordinary business of living" (line 6). What is here included? (*b*) What do they not know? (*c*) What impact is modern science having upon them?

3. What similarities do you find between this chorus and other poems by Eliot you have studied?

Growltiger's Last Stand

1. (*a*) Whose "last stand" is famous in American history? (*b*) Judging from the title "Growltiger's Last Stand," what do you anticipate the tone of the poem will be?

2. "Growltiger's Last Stand" is the tale of a hero, his lady love, and the battle he must fight to preserve his fame. In these narrative elements and in the form of the verse, "Growltiger's Last Stand" is a ballad. (*a*) How does the hero differ from the typical ballad hero? (*b*) How does the lady differ from the usual ballad heroine? (*c*) Does the hero's end follow ballad convention? (*d*) How does the tone of the poem differ from the conventional ballad?

3. "Growltiger's Last Stand" is taken from Eliot's *Old Possum's Book of Practical Cats.* (*a*) What additional insight on the poet do you get from "Growltiger"? (*b*) Do you find here any qualities you noted in other poems by Eliot? Explain.

Coventry Cathedral

After dark on November 14, 1940, five hundred German bombers flew over Coventry, England, dropping incendiaries and bombs until above the city there was "a mile-high fiery cloud shining red in the sky in the brightness of the moon-drenched night." The extent of the damage is indicated by the word coined the next day—*to coventrize*, which meant "to destroy utterly." During the twelve-hour raid one of Coventry's most famous landmarks fell victim to the fire and bombs, and by morning all that remained of the fourteenth-century St. Michael's Cathedral was the 303-foot spire overlooking a shell of smoldering timbers. Shortly after dawn one of the townspeople formed two of the timbers into a cross, placed them where the altar had been, and into the ruins scratched the words "Father forgive." From that day the idea of rebuilding Coventry's cathedral became a symbol of resurrection—not only of the building itself but of man's faith and hope.

Ten years after the destruction of St. Michael's a competition was opened for designs for a new cathedral. Basil Spence, a Scottish architect, went to Coventry and walked around the cathedral ruins trying to envision how the new church should be built. He decided that the architect's task would be "to design a new building linked to the old which would stand for the triumph of the Resurrection. The ruins were the Old Testament, the new cathedral would be the New." Basil Spence's designs, based on these ideas, won over 218 other entries. Construction was begun in 1954.

In America as well as England the public was anxious to see the new cathedral, and to answer the question in their minds, "How can the traditional Christian symbolism and the awesomeness of a medieval cathedral be expressed in modern terms?" When the cathedral was finally completed and dedicated in May 1962, the result was generally acclaimed a success.

The new St. Michael's Cathedral is joined at right angles to the old by a wide, pillared porch. From the porch one enters the cathedral through a seventy-foot-high wall of glass etched with frosted figures of saints and angels. The worshiper may look to the altar of the new cathedral, then turn, and look through the glass wall to the ruins of the old. Standing in the nave, he notices that the walls and black marble floor are covered with multicolored light which directs his eye to the altar; yet no windows are visible. The source of light can only be seen from the altar. Standing here and facing the nave, he sees the windows—magnificent windows of stained glass which give the illusion that the roof is supported only by multicolored light. The windows' abstract designs symbolize man's journey through life to the City of God. The greens represent youth, red stands for young manhood, multicolored light represents the many sides of maturity, purple signifies old age, and gold represents the afterlife.

Behind the altar is the tapestry "Christ in Majesty," designed by the painter Graham Sutherland. This tapestry, supposedly the

Ruins of the old Coventry Cathedral.

largest in the world, was made by fourteen weavers who worked on it for three years.

One of the three small chapels in the new cathedral is the Chapel of Christ the Servant, also called the Chapel of Industry. From the long windows of this chapel, which is dedicated to Coventry's ancient guilds, trade unions, and management associations, can be seen the industrial area of modern Coventry.

In June 1962, a grand music festival was held to honor the new St. Michael's. The most moving moments of the festival were during the presentation of "War Requiem," a composition written for Coventry by the twentieth-century composer Benjamin Britten, who used as part of his text the war poetry of Wilfred Owen (see page 637). The composition moves from passages of war's destruction to the pity of war, and ends with an assertion of faith expressed in the "In Paradisum." This work emphasized one of the most interesting facets of the new Coventry cathedral, the fact that from the beginning it has been a symbol not only of rebirth, but also of unity. Artisan, architect, painter, sculptor, musician, and poet have combined their specialized talents into a unified expression of twentieth-century faith.

Right: The only exterior design is this sculpture by Sir Jacob Epstein of St. Michael standing in triumph over the chained devil. Below: The baptistry window, designed by John Piper. The blue symbolizes the sky, the reds and greens represent the fire that destroyed the church and the weeds which grew in the ruins, and the gold in the center stands for the rebirth of the cathedral.

Edith Sitwell

PRAISE WE GREAT MEN

for Benjamin Britten[1]

Praise we the Gods of Sound—
From all the hearths and homes of men,
    from hives
Of honey-making lives;
Praise with our music those
Who bring the morning light   5
To the hearts of men, those households of
    high heaven! Praise

We the great Gods of Sound
Who stole the honey red, the frozen fire—
Oh, beyond all delight and all desire—
From gilded hives upon Mount Parnassus[2]   10
(Hives gilded by the light), who brought to
    us
That fire compressed into such holy forms
As those of the gold wanderers in heaven!
    Praise

Those who can raise
Gold spirits of mankind from the rough
    ape-dust, and can show   15
The planetary system in the atom, and great
    suns
Hid in a speck of dust. Praise we the just
Who have not come to judge, but come to
    bless
Immortal things in our poor earthly dress
And ripen lives and rule our hearts and
    rhythms,   20
Immortal hungers in the veins and heart.

Praise be to those who sing
Green hymns of the great waters to the dry
And tearless deserts in the souls of men, until
Under the fertilization of their singing
    breath   25
Even the grayness and the dust of Death
Seem the gray pollen of the long September
    heat. Oh, praise

With lion music such as that heard in the air
When the roaring golden lion that roams
    the heavens
Devours the dark, and multitudes and
    magnitudes respond   30
To that lion music . . . and on wings
Of music let us rise
Like velvet honey-flies
To praise the Gods of Sound with those bee
    murmurings
The sound of violins   35
And the clear sound of flutes
As round as honeyed fruits
And like the water Phoenix[3] ever rising
For wanderers in the lonely desert sand.

Praise we these earthly Gods—   40
Praise with the trumpet's purple sound,
Praise with the trumpet flower
And with that flower the long five-petaled
    hand
That sweeps the strings. Praise with that
    angel of High God, the voice!
Oh, let us still rejoice   45
And praise we these great men from the
    first hour
Of the spirit's birth until our earthly setting
Into the night of Death.
Praise with our last breath
These earthly Gods who bring   50
All sounds, all faiths, delights and splendors
    lost
Beneath the winter's frost
Back to the hearts, the hearths, and homes
    of men.

Fires on the hearth, fires in the skies, fires
    in the human heart—
Praise we Great Men!   55

1. *Benjamin Britten* (1913-), English composer, pianist and conductor. In 1954 he wrote *Canticle III* for Edith Sitwell's poem "Still Falls the Rain." 2. *Mount Parnassus* (pär nas'əs), in southern Greece. In classical Greece, it was hallowed by the worship of Apollo (sun god) and the Muses. 3. *Phoenix*, Greek name for an Egyptian mythological bird which lived for 500-600 year periods, then was consumed in fire. From the ashes came forth a new Phoenix. In Christian symbolism it represents resurrection and immortality.

Edith Sitwell   1887-1964

Dame Edith Sitwell (sister of writers Osbert and Sacheverell Sitwell) was the oldest child of Sir George and Lady Ida Sitwell. She was educated privately, or "in secrecy," as she called it, at Renishaw, the more than six-hundred-year-old family estate in Yorkshire.

Miss Sitwell enveloped herself in the tradition of eccentricity fostered by the Sitwells. In her turban hats, long brocaded or silk gowns, and with her fingers covered by large, jeweled rings, she fit the fancied conception of what a poet should look like. Her behavior was sometimes as unusual as her appearance. On one occasion she sent a stuffed owl to a critic she considered "too stuffy."

Miss Sitwell's reputation as an eccentric sometimes obscured the fact that she was a serious poet. In her poetry she experimented constantly. The lines of her verse are as heavily adorned with rich sounds and intricate rhythms as her medieval brocaded gowns were ornamented with color and intricately woven patterns. Because of this romantic richness, some critics have thought her verse too contrived and superficial. Others agree that in her control of sound and rhythm she was a master. Some of her later poetry—her war poetry, for example— is less ornate. As technically skillful as her earlier work, it is more thoughtful and compassionate.

In her prose Miss Sitwell often returned for subject matter to the period her attire suggested. *Fanfare for Elizabeth* (1946) treats of the first Queen Elizabeth and *The Queens and the Hive* (1962) is a colorful account of rival queens of the Elizabethan Age.

❊ To increase understanding

1. (*a*) Who are the *Gods of Sound*? (*b*) What does the poet mean by *morning light*? (*c*) Explain what the poet is implying by describing hearts as *households of high heaven*.

2. In the second stanza there is an allusion to the gift of fire from Prometheus, which is compared to the gift of music from the Gods of Sound. (*a*) Was the gift of fire valuable to man? (*b*) What, then, is implied about the gift of music? (*c*) Why is it called *frozen* fire? (*d*) What other image in this stanza extends the idea of the form of the gift? (*e*) Why is Mt. Parnassus an appropriate image to use with the Gods of Sound?

3. The poem is particularly rich in color imagery, which Miss Sitwell uses to give unity to the poem. (*a*) Find lines that illustrate use of color imagery. (*b*) What is the dominant color in the poem? (*c*) How is Apollo associated with Mt. Parnassus? (*d*) What color is associated with him? Why? (*e*) What is the *golden lion that roams the heavens* (line 29)? (*f*) What associations can be made with Apollo and the *golden lion*?

4. (*a*) What are traditional associations with the Phoenix? (*b*) In line 38 the poet uses the Phoenix to represent a continual issuing forth of water to quench thirst. What lines in stanza three prepare for this image? (*c*) Explain the significance of water and desert used as symbols. (*d*) How does the Phoenix continue the image of *frozen fire* in line 8?

5. Edith Sitwell uses other conventional symbols in this poem. (*a*) Explain the meaning of *night of Death* (line 48). (*b*) Explain the significance of *winter's frost* (line 52). (*c*) *Light* and *fire* are important images in the poem. What is the symbolical meaning of light? fire?

6. State the idea of the poem.

7. Compare this poem with Dryden's "A Song for St. Cecilia's Day" (page 236). What similarities do you find in tone, theme, and versification?

Stephen Spender

I THINK CONTINUALLY OF THOSE

I think continually of those who were truly
    great.
Who, from the womb, remembered the soul's
    history
Through corridors of light where the hours
    are suns
Endless and singing. Whose lovely ambition
Was that their lips, still touched with fire,   5
Should tell of the Spirit clothed from head
    to foot in song.
And who hoarded from the Spring branches
The desires falling across their bodies like
    blossoms.

What is precious is never to forget
The essential delight of the blood drawn
    from ageless springs   10
Breaking through rocks in worlds before our
    earth;
Never to deny its pleasure in the morning
    simple light,
Nor its grave evening demand for love;
Never to allow gradually the traffic to smother
With noise and fog the flowering of the
    spirit.   15

Near the snow, near the sun, in the highest
    fields
See how these names are feted by the waving
    grass
And by the streamers of white cloud
And whispers of wind in the listening sky;
The names of those who in their lives fought
    for life   20
Who wore at their hearts the fire's center.
Born of the sun they traveled a short while
    toward the sun,
And left the vivid air signed with their honor.

"I Think Continually of Those" and "The Express"
from *Collected Poems 1928-1953* by Stephen Spender. Reprinted by permission of Random House, Inc., New York;
and Faber and Faber Ltd., London. Copyright 1934 and
renewed 1961 by Stephen Spender.

THE EXPRESS

After the first powerful plain manifesto
The black statement of pistons, without more
    fuss
But gliding like a queen, she leaves the
    station.
Without bowing and with restrained
    unconcern
She passes the houses which humbly crowd
    outside,   5
The gasworks and at last the heavy page
Of death, printed by gravestones in the
    cemetery.
Beyond the town there lies the open country
Where, gathering speed, she acquires mystery,
The luminous self-possession of ships on
    ocean.   10
It is now she begins to sing—at first quite
    low
Then loud, and at last with a jazzy madness—
The song of her whistle screaming at curves,
Of deafening tunnels, brakes, innumerable
    bolts.
And always light, aerial, underneath   15
Goes the elate meter of her wheels.
Steaming through metal landscape on her
    lines
She plunges new eras of wild happiness
Where speed throws up strange shapes, broad
    curves
And parallels clean like the steel of guns.   20
At last, further than Edinburgh or Rome,
Beyond the crest of the world, she reaches
    night
Where only a low streamline brightness
Of phosphorus on the tossing hills is white.
Ah, like a comet through flames she moves
    entranced   25
Wrapt in her music no bird song, no, nor
    bough
Breaking with honey buds, shall ever equal.

Stephen Spender by Edmond Kapp.

EDMOND KAPP, LONDON

3. "I Think Continually of Those" and Edith Sitwell's "Praise We Great Men" have not only similar themes but similar imagery. Cite images which are similar and explain their function in each poem.

4. (*a*) What is the usual meaning of *manifesto*? (*b*) What metaphorical meaning has Spender given it in line 1 of "The Express"? (*c*) What statement do the pistons make?

5. (*a*) Point out other effective uses of metaphorical language in "The Express." (*b*) How does each one help you get the "feel" of the express at some point of its journey?

6. (*a*) Explain the meaning of the last three lines of "The Express." (*b*) What is Spender's attitude toward the machine age, as represented by a fast train?

Stephen Spender 1909-

The son of a novelist-journalist, Stephen Spender was born near London and educated at Oxford University. For a while he considered painting as a career and there is probably some correlation between this interest in painting and the fact that one of the most arresting aspects of his poetry is his skill in the use of imagery. While attending classes at Oxford he helped edit one of the Oxford anthologies of poetry, and he also published his first verse.

By the 1930's Spender was one of the most important figures in English poetry. His poetry, like that of other poets of the time, generally reflected a concern for social and political reforms and an interest in the problems of the common man. As time passed, Spender became less a critic of the social order and more a poet. He came to believe that a poem should not be an instrument with which to champion a cause, but should speak about what lies closest to the poet's heart.

In addition to poetry, Spender has written travel journals, short stories, verse drama, and criticism; he has also edited magazines. His autobiography, *World Within World*, was published in 1951.

To increase understanding

1. In the poem "I Think Continually of Those," whom does Spender regard as the "truly great"?

2. Spender does not list qualities that accompany greatness. Rather through the use of symbolism and imagery he suggests certain characteristics. Select lines Spender uses to describe greatness and tell what qualities are implied.

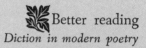

Better reading
Diction in modern poetry

If, when looking at random through a volume of poetry, you were to come upon the line

Of deafening tunnels, brakes, innumerable bolts

you would probably conclude that the poem had been written in the modern era. What would lead you to this conclusion? The words themselves are not new. *Tunnel* and *brake* appear in eighteenth-century prose, and *bolt* is at least a century older. It is not the words but their use in poetry that is new. Once poets differentiated between poetic and unpoetic words, but modern poets believe that if poetry is to speak to men with vitality and truth it must speak in accents that they understand. Today any word that helps the poet say things accurately and well has a place in poetry. Thus Eliot in *The Rock* writes of

. . . the broken chimney,
The peeled hull, a pile of rusty iron,
In a street of scattered brick . . .

Because machinery is an important element of the age in which he lives, Spender often brings machinery into his poetry. In "The Express," in addition to brakes and bolts, the poet writes of pistons, whistles, wheels, and the gasworks.

Select a passage from a poem by one of the modern poets you have studied which contains words that would have been considered unpoetic a hundred years ago. Point out these words and explain why you think the modern poet has used them. What is your personal opinion of the fitness of such words in poetry?

Dylan Thomas

POEM IN OCTOBER *This poem resulted from Dylan Thomas' visit on his thirtieth birthday to his boyhood home in Wales. Dylan, which in Welsh means "tide" or "water," is the name of the Welsh god of the waves. Throughout the poem Dylan Thomas plays with the word* water, *an evidence of his fascination with the limitless meanings in words.*

It was my thirtieth year to heaven
Woke to my hearing from harbor and neighbor wood
   And the mussel pooled and the heron
        Priested shore
        The morning beckon   5
With water praying and call of seagull and rook
And the knock of sailing boats on the net webbed wall
     Myself to set foot
        That second
In the still sleeping town and set forth.   10

   My birthday began with the water—
Birds and the birds of the winged trees flying my name
   Above the farms and the white horses
        And I rose
     In the rainy autumn   15
And walked abroad in a shower of all my days.
High tide and the heron dived when I took the road
     Over the border
        And the gates
Of the town closed as the town awoke.   20

   A springful of larks in a rolling
Cloud and the roadside bushes brimming with whistling
   Blackbirds and the sun of October
        Summery

On the hill's shoulder,   25
Here were fond climates and sweet singers suddenly
Come in the morning where I wandered and listened
    To the rain wringing
      Wind blow cold
In the wood faraway under me.   30

    Pale rain over the dwindling harbor
And over the sea wet church the size of a snail
    With its horns through mist and the castle
        Brown as owls
    But all the gardens   35
Of spring and summer were blooming in the tall tales
Beyond the border and under the lark full cloud.
    There could I marvel
      My birthday
Away but the weather turned around.   40

    It turned away from the blithe country
And down the other air and the blue altered sky
    Streamed again a wonder of summer
        With apples
    Pears and red currants   45
And I saw in the turning so clearly a child's
Forgotten mornings when he walked with his mother
    Through the parables
      Of sun light
And the legends of the green chapels   50

    And the twice told fields of infancy
That his tears burned my cheeks and his heart moved in mine.
    These were the woods the river and sea
        Where a boy
    In the listening   55
Summertime of the dead whispered the truth of his joy
To the trees and the stones and the fish in the tide.
    And the mystery
      Sang alive
Still in the water and singingbirds.   60

    And there could I marvel my birthday
Away but the weather turned around. And the true
    Joy of the long dead child sang burning
        In the sun.
    It was my thirtieth   65
Year to heaven stood there then in the summer noon
Though the town below lay leaved with October blood.
    O may my heart's truth
      Still be sung
On this high hill in a year's turning.   70

DO NOT GO GENTLE INTO
THAT GOOD NIGHT

When Dylan Thomas wrote this poem, he had a feeling that his father had only a short time to live.

Do not go gentle into that good night,
Old age should burn and rave at close of
　　　day;
Rage, rage against the dying of the light.

Though wise men at their end know dark is
　　　right,
Because their words had forked no lightning
　　　they　　　　　　　　　　　　　　　　5
Do not go gentle into that good night.

Good men, the last wave by, crying how
　　　bright
Their frail deeds might have danced in a
　　　green bay,
Rage, rage against the dying of the light.

Wild men who caught and sang the sun in
　　　flight,　　　　　　　　　　　　　　10
And learn, too late, they grieved it on its way,
Do not go gentle into that good night.

Grave men, near death, who see with
　　　blinding sight
Blind eyes could blaze like meteors and be
　　　gay,
Rage, rage against the dying of the light.　15

And you, my father, there on the sad height,
Curse, bless, me now with your fierce tears,
　　　I pray.
Do not go gentle into that good night.
Rage, rage against the dying of the light.

Dylan Thomas　1914-1953

The major influence on English poetry written during and after the 1950's was that of Dylan (dil'ən) Thomas. Born and educated in Swansea, a seacoast town in southern Wales, Thomas began writing poetry when still a boy, and his first small volume was published when he was only nineteen. The qualities of his poetry which so attracted certain London editors seeking to encourage new poets were the same qualities which later brought Thomas international fame: freshness, originality, warmth, exuberance, an almost embarrassing richness of feeling. The sights and sounds and smells of his native Wales flicker through his highly personal poetry. His use of imagery and word play is so masterful that Stephen Spender has called him a "linguistic genius."

After leaving school at sixteen, Thomas tried reporting for a local newspaper for one year, but his heart was in writing poetry. He published some volumes of poetry in the 1930's. During World War II he was a documentary film editor for the British Broadcasting Company. He had a wonderful reading voice and for some time earned his living reading poetry, stories, and essays over the B.B.C. His biggest earnings, however, came through lecture tours in the United States in 1950 and 1952. He liked America and the Americans, and the youth of the United States looked to him as the leading poet of their generation. In 1953 on his third trip to the United States, Dylan Thomas died suddenly in New York City at the age of thirty-nine.

Like the earlier romantic poets Shelley, Keats, and Byron, Dylan Thomas produced a remarkable body of work in a relatively short time. In addition to his poetry he wrote short stories and essays that in their rhythm and imagery are as rich and evocative as his poetry. *Quite Early One Morning*, published posthumously in 1954, contains lyrical reminiscences about his childhood and holidays at Swansea and sketches of Welsh poets. *Under Milk Wood* (1954), a verse play, is rich in imagery and symbolism. Much of his best poetry has been assembled in *Collected Poems 1934-1952* (1953).

To increase understanding
Poem in October

1. Because of inverted word order, Thomas' poems often require several rereadings if they are to be understood. The fact that in "Poem in October" no commas are used adds to the difficulty. (a) The first two stanzas are concerned mainly with the present. What does the poet say "Woke

to my hearing" (line 2)? (*b*) The verb *beckon* (line 5) is third person plural. What is its subject? (*c*) What is the setting as the poet sets forth?

2. In the way he uses imagery, Dylan Thomas shows the influence of Gerard Manley Hopkins. (See the discussion of imagery in "Hopkins' Theory of Poetry," page 523.) (*a*) How do you understand "heron/Priested shore" (lines 3-4)? (*b*) In what words is the idea suggested by *priested* repeated? (*c*) What causes the poet to speak of "winged trees" (line 12)? (*d*) What word in line 12 continues the image? (*e*) How does "the rainy autumn" (line 15) prepare for "a shower of all my days" (line 16)?

3. In stanzas 3-6 the poet recalls happy childhood hours spent at Fern Hill, a highland farm. With this in mind explain the meaning of "I . . . walked abroad in a shower of all my days."

4. (*a*) Cite images in stanzas 3-6 that refer to the past. (*b*) What do these images have in common? (*c*) What lines describe the present? (*d*) How do these lines differ in tone from the lines dealing with the past?

5. In describing the child's long-ago walks with his mother, Thomas speaks of "parables/Of sun light" (lines 48-49). (*a*) What words in the following lines echo the figure begun in the word *parables*? (*b*) Paraphrase lines 46-52.

6. (*a*) What is the theme of the poem? (*b*) What is the tone?

Do Not Go Gentle into That Good Night

1. Stanzas 2-5 speak of different classes of men. What class is the subject of each of these stanzas?

2. (*a*) Why do wise men know that "dark is right"? (*b*) What image communicates the thought that the wise men have not been able to transmit their ideas to the world?

3. The idea of water is in both *wave* (line 7) and "green bay" (line 8) but the suggested image is different. With this difference in mind explain why the good men believe their "frail deeds might have danced in a green bay."

4. (*a*) How have the wild men spent their time? (*b*) What do the grave men now see "with blinding sight" (line 13)?

5. Contrasting images of dark and light unify the poem. Cite examples of such imagery.

6. Unlike much modern poetry, "Do Not Go Gentle into That Good Night" is written in conventional meter and makes use of rhyme and a refrain. (*a*) What is the meter? (*b*) What is the rhyme scheme? (*c*) Where do the lines used as alternating refrains first appear? (*d*) Where are they last used? (*e*) What is the purpose of these refrains?

John Betjeman

DEATH IN LEAMINGTON

She died in the upstairs bedroom
  By the light of the ev'ning star
That shone through the plate glass window
  From over Leamington Spa.[1]

Beside her the lonely crochet   5
  Lay patiently and unstirred,
But the fingers that would have work'd it
  Were dead as the spoken word.

And Nurse came in with the tea-things
  Breast high 'mid the stands and chairs— 10
But Nurse was alone with her own little soul,
  And the things were alone with theirs.

She bolted the big round window,
  She let the blinds unroll,
She set a match to the mantle,   15
  She covered the fire with coal.

And "Tea!" she said in a tiny voice
  "Wake up! It's nearly *five*."
Oh! Chintzy, chintzy cheeriness,
  Half dead and half alive!   20

Do you know that the stucco is peeling?
  Do you know that the heart will stop?
From those yellow Italianate arches
  Do you hear the plaster drop?

Nurse looked at the silent bedstead,   25
  At the gray, decaying face,
As the calm of a Leamington ev'ning
  Drifted into the place.

She moved the table of bottles
  Away from the bed to the wall;   30
And tiptoeing gently over the stairs
  Turned down the gas in the hall.

"Death in Leamington" from *Collected Poems* by John Betjeman. Reprinted by permission of Houghton Mifflin Company, Boston; and John Murray Ltd., London.
1. *Leamington Spa*, a health resort on the river Leam in central England noted for its healing springs. The English pronounce *spa* to rhyme with *star*.

George Barker

SONNET TO
MY MOTHER

Most near, most dear, most loved and most far,
Under the window where I often found her
Sitting as huge as Asia, seismic with laughter,
Gin and chicken helpless in her Irish hand,
Irresistible as Rabelais[1] but most tender for 5
The lame dogs and hurt birds that surround her,—
She is a procession no one can follow after
But be like a little dog following a brass band.
She will not glance up at the bomber or condescend
To drop her gin and scuttle to a cellar, 10
But lean on the mahogany table like a mountain
Whom only faith can move, and so I send
O all my faith and all my love to tell her
That she will move from mourning into morning.

Ted Hughes

VIEW OF A PIG

The pig lay on a barrow dead.
It weighed, they said, as much as three men.
Its eyes closed, pink white eyelashes.
Its trotters stuck straight out.

Such weight and thick pink bulk 5
Set in death seemed not just dead.
It was less than lifeless, further off.
It was like a sack of wheat.

I thumped it without feeling remorse.
One feels guilty insulting the dead, 10
Walking on graves. But this pig
Did not seem able to accuse.

It was too dead. Just so much
A poundage of lard and pork.
Its last dignity had entirely gone. 15
It was not a figure of fun.

Too dead now to pity.
To remember its life, din, stronghold
Of earthly pleasure as it had been,
Seemed a false effort, and off the point. 20

Too deadly factual. Its weight
Oppressed me—how could it be moved?

And the trouble of cutting it up!
The gash in its throat was shocking, but not
pathetic.

Once I ran at a fair in the noise 25
To catch a greased piglet
That was faster and nimbler than a cat,
Its squeal was the rending of metal.

Pigs must have hot blood, they feel like ovens.
Their bite is worse than a horse's— 30
They chop a half-moon clean out.
They eat cinders, dead cats.

Distinctions and admirations such
As this one was long finished with.
I stared at it a long time. They were going 35
to scald it,
Scald it and scour it like a doorstep.

SONNET TO MY MOTHER. 1. *Rabelais* (rab'ə lā), François (1495?-1553). French author of *Gargantua and Pantagruel*, famous for robust humor and satire.

John Betjeman 1906-

Poet John Betjeman (bet′jə mən) represents to the British public what Robert Frost represented to Americans, in that his poetry has captured the traditions and mannerisms that Britishers feel are peculiarly their own. His nostalgic descriptions of the past are usually accompanied with enough irony to have gained for him a reputation as a light verse writer.

Betjeman has become an authority on church architecture, and he has written guides for travel in the English countryside, as well as essays and poetry. Probably his best-known volume in America is *Summoned by Bells*, an autobiography written in verse which was published in 1960. His *Collected Poems* were published in 1958.

George Barker 1913-

Among English poets who have been writing for the past fifteen years, George Barker has been ranked second only to Dylan Thomas. Barker, too, is a lover of words, and his poems are a tumble of imagery and emotion.

George Barker was educated in London. He has traveled extensively since he left school, and has lived in Japan, where he taught school, and in America. In 1941 he published *Selected Poems;* this was followed by *Sacred and Secular Elegies* in 1944. His later verse in *Love Poems* (1947) and *Collected Poems 1930-1955* is more subdued in tone than his earlier poetry, and the language less tempestuous; yet even in his later poetry he is not analytical or apart from his subject. Like Thomas, he makes no effort to hide his personal involvement in his poetry.

Ted Hughes 1930-

Still comparatively unknown to a wide audience, Ted Hughes has published only three small volumes of poetry. When his first book, *Hawk in the Rain* (1957), appeared in America, it was unanimously chosen for an award honoring an outstanding first publication.

Reviewers of his second book, *Lupercal* (1960), from which "View of a Pig" (page 658) is taken, noted that the bumpy Anglo-Saxon rhythms and words gave his poetry a certain roughness of tone. Most of the poems in this book are about nature, and more especially about animals. By analogy they acknowledge and find exciting the unthinking, animal nature of man. Hughes' third volume, *Meet My Folks*, was published in 1961.

❧ To increase understanding
Death in Leamington

1. Tell in one or two sentences what happens in the poem.

2. (*a*) Cite the lines that describe the various things the nurse does from the moment she enters the room. (*b*) What details specifically describe the nurse? (*c*) What idea of the nurse does the poet give you through combining a chronicle of actions with direct comments?

3. The fact of the woman's death is mentioned in the first two words of the poem and never directly spoken of again. (*a*) What references throughout the poem remind the reader of death? (*b*) What is ironic about the fact that a poem entitled "Death in Leamington" is filled with homely housekeeping details? (*c*) What is the poet implying about the effect of death on the living?

4. (*a*) Explain why the meter of the poem is appropriate to the surface activities described. (*b*) How does it differ from the type of rhythm usual in a poem about death? (*c*) How does the form of the poem contribute to its ironic tone?

Sonnet to My Mother

1. "Sonnet to My Mother" was written during World War II when England was being bombed. What references to this fact do you find in the poem?

2. A *hyperbole* is an extravagant exaggeration of fact used to produce an effect. (*a*) Cite examples of hyperbole in the poet's description of his mother. (*b*) What effect is he attempting to produce? (*c*) What is his attitude toward his mother?

3. Even though "Sonnet to My Mother" is cast in one of the oldest verse forms, it is essentially a modern poem. What evidence do you have that this is so? In your answer consider (*a*) diction, (*b*) type of rhymes used, (*c*) selection of details, and (*d*) tone.

View of a Pig

1. (*a*) In describing the dead pig does the poet rely mainly on literal or figurative expressions? (*b*) What words does he use that would have been considered unpoetic in past centuries? (*c*) What effect does this method of description produce?

2. (*a*) What is the poet's attitude toward the dead pig? Cite phrases to explain your answer. (*b*) State in your own words the idea developed in the poem.

Words!

The word *pig*, as you learned in studying the growth of the English language, is an Old English or Anglo-Saxon word—a word which has been a part of the English language since the Angles and Saxons invaded England fifteen hundred years ago. Among the other Anglo-Saxon words Ted Hughes uses in "View of a Pig" are the following: *barrow, eye, dead, wheat, guilty, grave, pound, din, life, earth, weight, throat, hot, oven, horse, cat,* and *cinder.* The words *stronghold* and *doorstep* are made by combining two Old English words to form a new word.

How would you describe these words as a class? Explain ways in which they differ in general from words derived from Latin. Why are these Anglo-Saxon words appropriate in "View of a Pig"? How do they affect the rhythm and tone of the poem?

The Larger View

A. A critic has said that the difference between the poetry of past centuries and twentieth-century poetry is not in the choice of subject matter, but in the way this subject is treated. In the past many poets tended to emphasize the romantic aspects of a subject; the modern poet is often concerned with its tragic and ironic phases. Discuss to what extent you think this is true, based on poetry you have studied.

B. The literature of a period lends insight into people's ideas and general way of life. Find two or three poems in this chapter that seem to express ideas or feelings about life in the twentieth century. What ideas do they express? What poems express an affirmation of life? What poems are more pessimistic?

C. Many modern poems develop a theme different from what the title would lead one to expect. Select one of the poems listed below. State its theme as clearly as possible. Does the poet use symbolism in developing this theme? If so, explain the symbols and how they are used. What is the tone of the poem? How is imagery used in establishing this tone? Does the theme or tone differ from what the title would lead one to expect? Explain.

Rocky Acres
Nightingales
        Death in Leamington
        Sailing to Byzantium
    Sonnet to My Mother

Bibliography

BETJEMAN, JOHN, *Collected Poems.* (Houghton) Selections in this book show Betjeman as a skilled craftsman of various verse forms.

ELIOT, T. S., *Complete Poems and Plays, 1909-1950.* (Harcourt) This assemblage of works by a major writer speaks for itself.

ENGLE, PAUL, and WARREN CARRIER, editors, *Reading Modern Poetry.* (Scott, Foresman) Among the English poets represented in this collection are Joyce, Housman, Hardy, Yeats, Spender, Bridges, Eliot, Hopkins, Barker, and Thomas.

MACDONAGH, DONAGH, and LENNOX ROBINSON, editors, *Oxford Book of Irish Verse, XVIIth Century-XXth Century.* (Oxford) This anthology is noted for the number of younger modern poets represented.

MASEFIELD, JOHN, *Salt-Water Poems and Ballads.* (••Macmillan) This collection of early works mirrors the author's life at sea.

SPENDER, STEPHEN, *Collected Poems, 1928-1935.* (Random) The author has arranged his most valued works in this volume.

THOMAS, DYLAN, *Collected Poems of Dylan Thomas.* (New Directions) This is a keepsake for readers who find Thomas a spokesman for our times.

UNTERMEYER, LOUIS, *Modern British Poetry.* (Harcourt) An anthology that treats of poetry from Hardy to the present, this volume has a short biography and critique of each poet represented.

WILLIAMS, OSCAR, editor, *A Treasury of Modern Poetry.* (Scribner) Numerous portraits illustrate this anthology of English and American verse. *A Little Treasury of British Poetry* (Scribner) contains 350 pages of modern works. Mr. Williams has also edited the *Pocket Book of Modern Verse* (•Washington Square).

YEATS, WILLIAM BUTLER, *Collected Poems.* (Macmillan) This definitive edition contains the poet's final revisions.

YEATS, WILLIAM BUTLER, editor, *Oxford Book of Modern Verse, 1892-1935.* (Oxford) Yeats includes selections from the works of ninety-eight poets in this fine and varied collection. Seventy-seven of these poets are not represented in the *Oxford Book of English Verse.*

•paperback   ••paperback and hard cover

chapter ten Drama

Only a few ages in history—the Athens of Pericles, the Elizabethan Age, the reign of Louis XIV—have seen the creation of great drama. Although the twentieth century has not been such a period, in drama there has been a fresh spirit of change and experimentation since shortly before 1900.

Today's plays are the results of reaction against the "well-made play" of the 1800's. The well-made play consisted of a logical sequence of events into which a complication was introduced; and then, sometimes by sleight of hand, all troublesome issues were resolved in the last act. Alan S. Downer has noted that the busiest and hardest working member of the cast of a well-made play was the postman, because it was he that delivered all the letters that conveniently contained solutions for the hero's problems. This type of play raised no social issues nor did it explore character.

Toward the end of the century a Norwegian playwright, Henrik Ibsen, wrote a new kind of drama focusing attention on social issues, especially as they concerned the middle class. His characters were complex, and often revealed aspects of human nature that the Victorian audiences thought would be more comfortably forgotten. Ibsen's plays were banned on the Continent because they had "destructive tendencies"—destructive because they destroyed the illusion of the virtues of social conventions.

The public found his plays uncomfortable, the press took up its cudgels; but in spite of both, his drama moved into England.

Since 1737 no play has been allowed public presentation in England without a license from the Lord Chamberlain. The Lord Chamberlain, reacting to public sentiment, promptly refused to license Ibsen's plays. British playwrights revolted. They were not only interested in Ibsen's drama but they also wanted to free themselves from the Lord Chamberlain's censorship in order to experiment with new types of drama. To gain their ends, they formed the Independent Theatre in 1891 as a private club with a subscription audience. Here they were free to present Ibsen's plays as well as to experiment with original drama.

The main changes in British drama in the twentieth century have been in tone and subject matter. Of the new playwrights, James Barrie (*Peter Pan, What Every Woman Knows*) was closest to the Victorians in his emphasis on sentiment. His fantasies had enough gentle satire, however, to claim a relationship with the more realistic plays of Galsworthy and Shaw. The dominant theme of the new plays was the moral vacuum of the times. In serious drama John Galsworthy (page 597) confronted his audiences with plots based on social issues and left them to think out their own solutions. Awakening the social conscience was a risky way to earn a living, however, and some playwrights found there was a profit in making depressing realities palatable through comedy. The British audiences who squirmed uncomfortably in their seats through presentations of serious drama loved comedy, and playwrights like Oscar Wilde, Somerset Maugham (page 592), and Noel Coward created what the public wanted. The humor of their plays, however, was affected by the new feeling for realism, and differed from nineteenth-century humor in being less sentimental and more ironic and lively in tone. Masterbuilder of the play fusing comedy and social issues was the man whom Yeats called "the smiling sewing machine," George Bernard Shaw.

Other modern English playwrights have shown an interest in the form of play popular in the Elizabethan Age, the verse play. T. S. Eliot's *The Cocktail Party* and Christopher Fry's poetic comedy *The Lady's Not for Burning* have both been very successful on the stage. Some critics feel that the great drama of the future will probably be the verse play.

While the free theater movement was being established in England, the Renaissance of the arts in Ireland was producing a strong Irish drama based on Irish folklore. (See pages 542 and 618 for a fuller discussion of the Irish Renaissance.) Under the leadership of Lady Augusta Gregory, herself a playwright, a group which included William Butler Yeats and Padraic Colum founded the famous Abbey Theatre in Dublin in 1904. The Abbey developed one of the most distinguished theatrical companies in the world. It has produced two of the best playwrights of the century: John M. Synge (*Riders to the Sea*) and Sean O'Casey (*Juno and the Paycock, The Plough and the Stars*).

Drama more than any of the other arts is a group art. The playwright, the director, the actors, and finally the audience have a part in its creation. What concerns twentieth-century dramatists is that point of perfection which must be reached in each of these elements before great plays can be created.

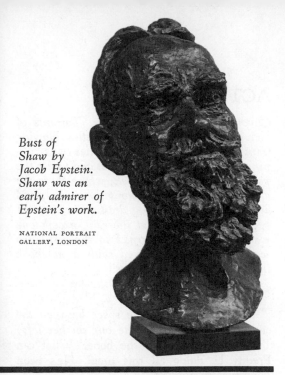

Bust of Shaw by Jacob Epstein. Shaw was an early admirer of Epstein's work.

NATIONAL PORTRAIT
GALLERY, LONDON

George Bernard Shaw   1856-1950

"Things have not happened to me," said George Bernard Shaw; "on the contrary it is I who have happened to things."[1] For more than fifty years Shaw directed his wit and satire at things traditionally considered too sacred to be ridiculed, such as marriage, heroism, and parenthood. With witty aplomb this "self-appointed headmaster to the universe" lectured his contemporaries on the errors of their social viewpoints and instructed them in the proper methods of setting themselves and the world right. If he often baffled and irritated his critics, he succeeded in stinging them to a realization that they were living, not in the dead world of the past, but in the twentieth century. His chief weapon in doing so was what he called "my most cherished possession, my gift of ridicule." To a friend he once said, "Being naturally of a serious disposition, I soon saw the world for what it was and was not in the least deceived by the peace and prosperity of Victorian days. The peace was the peace of a lunatic living in the world of fantasy, and the prosperity was the prosperity of the vulture. I laughed Victorianism out of existence."[2]

Shaw was born in Dublin of a middle-class English family. He arrived in London in 1876 and for the next few years was barely able to earn his living as an art critic, a music critic, and a literary editor and reviewer. From the 1880's until 1911 he was a leader in the Fabian Society of London, which advocated gradual social reform through constructive legislation. It was his conviction that the human race can solve its problems by controlling the productive forces in the interests of the common good.

His first play appeared in 1893, but Shaw discovered that audiences did not like to see themselves ridiculed. He soon had no stage for his plays, so he published them with elaborate stage directions and prefaces hoping that he might at least reach a reading public. His skill in argumentation and sense of the comic eventually won the public's enthusiasm and provoked an interest in seeing the works performed.

Shaw became the high priest of those who preach that things are not always what they seem, that what is conventionally regarded as bad or wicked may actually contain nobility, and that preconceived notions about human character may in reality be very far from the truth. Thus in *Widowers' Houses* (1893) he presents the paradox of a genuinely honest man who owns tenements which are nothing less than social ulcers. In *Arms and the Man* (1898) a soldier demonstrates that military heroism is largely the creation of the civilian mind. According to *You Never Can Tell* (1898), the authority of parents— a sacred object of belief among Victorians—is an outworn fiction. It is customary to consider a man as the leader in courtship; actually, Shaw says in *Man and Superman* (1903), it is the woman who takes the initiative. In a society based on money, it is simply hypocritical to think that poverty is anything but a dreadful vice—this is the message of *Major Barbara* (1907). *Pygmalion* (1912) considers some of the illusions of class distinction.

Shaw had two main interests in his lifetime: the theater and his desire for a reformed alphabet. He wryly commented that the existing English lettering system was an "ancient Phoenician alphabet" that cost his country millions a year in time wasted in printing and writing superfluous letters. He proposed a phonetic alphabet of forty-four letters, each representing a sound. When he died, his will stipulated that his money was to be used to promote such a reform.

Behind Shaw's mask of wit and humor we can discern his serious concern to make the imperfect world a better place. All his life he tried to stir up the passive inhabitants of that world. "O God, who madest this beautiful world," cries the heroine of Shaw's *Saint Joan* (1924), "when will it be ready to receive Thy Saints? How long, O Lord, how long?"

---

1. George Bernard Shaw, *Sixteen Self-Sketches*, Dodd, Mead & Company, 1949. 2. Stephen Winsten, *Days with Bernard Shaw*, Vanguard Press, Inc., 1949.

Pygmalion

Greek mythology has always been a rich source of legend for writers to draw upon. One of the favorite myths is the story of Pygmalion (pig mā′li ən), a sculptor who created a statue so beautiful that he fell in love with it. The goddess of love transformed the statue into a real woman, Galatea (gal′ə tē′ə), whom Pygmalion married.

Shaw uses the Pygmalion myth as the basis of his play about a man to whom phonetics is the dominant interest in life. In the preface to the play he writes: ". . . The English have no respect for their language, and will not teach their children to speak it. They spell it so abominably that no man can teach himself what it sounds like. It is impossible for an Englishman to open his mouth without making some other Englishman hate or despise him. German and Spanish are accessible to foreigners: English is not accessible even to Englishmen. The reformer England needs today is an energetic phonetic enthusiast: that is why I have made such a one the hero of a popular play . . . . if the play makes the public aware that there are such people as phoneticians, and that they are among the most important people in England at present, it will serve its turn. . . ."

CAST OF CHARACTERS

THE DAUGHTER—Miss Eynsford Hill (Clara)
THE MOTHER—Mrs. Eynsford Hill
FREDDY—Mr. Eynsford Hill, *her son*
THE FLOWER GIRL—Eliza (Liza) Doolittle
THE GENTLEMAN—Colonel Pickering
THE NOTE TAKER—Henry Higgins, *a professor of phonetics*
A BYSTANDER
A SARCASTIC BYSTANDER
GENERAL BYSTANDERS
MRS. PEARCE, *Henry Higgins' housekeeper*
ALFRED DOOLITTLE, *Eliza's father*
MRS. HIGGINS, *Henry Higgins' mother*
THE PARLOR-MAID

ACT ONE

Covent Garden[1] *at 11.15 p.m. Torrents of heavy summer rain. Cab whistles blowing frantically in all directions. Pedestrians running for shelter into the market and under the portico of St Paul's Church, where there are already several people, among them a lady and her daughter in evening dress. They are all peering out gloomily at the rain, except one man with his back turned to the rest, who seems wholly preoccupied with a notebook in which he is writing busily.*

The church clock strikes the first quarter.

The Daughter (*in the space between the central pillars, close to the one on her left*) I'm getting chilled to the bone. What can Freddy be doing all this time? He's been gone twenty minutes.

The Mother (*on her daughter's right*) Not so long. But he ought to have got us a cab by this.

A Bystander (*on the lady's right*) He wont[2] get no cab not until half-past eleven, missus, when they come back after dropping their theatre fares.

The Mother. But we must have a cab. We cant stand here until half-past eleven. It's too bad.

The Bystander. Well, it aint my fault, missus.

The Daughter. If Freddy had a bit of gumption, he would have got one at the theatre door.

The Mother. What could he have done, poor boy?

1. *Covent Garden,* chief fruit, vegetable, and flower-market district of London. It originally was a "convent garden" of Westminster Abbey. The area also includes St. Paul's Church (not to be confused with St. Paul's Cathedral), and the famous theater, Covent Garden Opera House. 2. *wont.* One of the spelling reforms advocated by Shaw was the omission of apostrophes in contractions. He retained the punctuation when omission would be confusing (*I'll* rather than *Ill*), or if omission would change pronunciation (*he's* rather than *hes*).

The Daughter. Other people got cabs. Why couldnt he?

Freddy rushes in out of the rain from the Southampton Street side, and comes between them closing a dripping umbrella. He is a young man of twenty, in evening dress, very wet round the ankles.

The Daughter. Well, havnt you got a cab?

Freddy. Theres not one to be had for love or money.

The Mother. Oh, Freddy, there must be one. You cant have tried.

The Daughter. It's too tiresome. Do you expect us to go and get one ourselves?

Freddy. I tell you theyre all engaged. The rain was so sudden: nobody was prepared; and everybody had to take a cab. Ive been to Charing Cross one way and nearly to Ludgate Circus the other; and they were all engaged.

The Mother. Did you try Trafalgar Square?

Freddy. There wasnt one at Trafalgar Square.

The Daughter. Did you try?

Freddy. I tried as far as Charing Cross Station. Did you expect me to walk to Hammersmith?

The Daughter. You havnt tried at all.

The Mother. You really are very helpless, Freddy. Go again; and dont come back until you have found a cab.

Freddy. I shall simply get soaked for nothing.

The Daughter. And what about us? Are we to stay here all night in this draught, with next to nothing on? You selfish pig—

Freddy. Oh, very well: I'll go, I'll go. (*He opens his umbrella and dashes off Strand-wards,[3] but comes into collision with a flower girl, who is hurrying in for shelter, knocking her basket out of her hands. A blinding flash of lightning, followed instantly by a rattling peal of thunder, orchestrates the incident*).

The Flower Girl. Nah then, Freddy: look wh' y' gowin, deah.

Freddy. Sorry (*he rushes off*).

The Flower Girl (*picking up her scattered flowers and replacing them in the basket*) Theres menners f' yer! Te-oo banches o voylets trod into the mad. (*She sits down on the plinth of the column, sorting her flowers, on the lady's right. She is not at all an attractive person. She is perhaps eighteen, perhaps twenty, hardly older. She wears a little sailor hat of black straw that has long been exposed to the dust and soot of London and has seldom if ever been brushed. Her hair needs washing rather badly: its mousy color can hardly be natural. She wears a shoddy black coat that reaches nearly to her knees and is shaped to her waist. She has a brown skirt with a coarse apron. Her boots are much the worse for wear. She is no doubt as clean as she can afford to be; but compared to the ladies she is very dirty. Her features are no worse than theirs; but their condition leaves something to be desired; and she needs the services of a dentist*).

The Mother. How do you know that my son's name is Freddy, pray?

The Flower Girl. Ow, eez ye-ooa san, is e? Wal, fewd dan y' de-ooty bawmz a mather should, eed now bettern to spawl a pore gel's flahrzn than ran awy athaht pyin. Will ye-oo py me f' them? (*Here, with apologies, this desperate attempt to represent her dialect without a phonetic alphabet must be abandoned as unintelligible outside London*).

The Daughter. Do nothing of the sort, mother. The idea!

The Mother. Please allow me, Clara. Have you any pennies?

The Daughter. No. Ive nothing smaller than sixpence.

The Flower Girl (*hopefully*) I can give you change for a tanner,[4] kind lady.

The Mother (*to Clara*) Give it to me. (*Clara parts reluctantly*). Now (*to the girl*) this is for your flowers.

The Flower Girl. Thank you kindly, lady.

The Daughter. Make her give you the change. These things are only a penny a bunch.

The Mother. Do hold your tongue, Clara. (*To the girl*) You can keep the change.

The Flower Girl. Oh, thank you, lady.

---

3. *Strandwards.* The Strand is the main thoroughfare between the West End, the fashionable residential area, and the business and commercial center of London. St. Paul's Church is two blocks from the Strand. 4. *tanner*, sixpence. [*British Slang*]

The Mother. Now tell me how you know that young gentleman's name.

The Flower Girl. I didnt.

The Mother. I heard you call him by it. Dont try to deceive me.

The Flower Girl (protesting) Who's trying to deceive you? I called him Freddy or Charlie same as you might yourself if you was talking to a stranger and wished to be pleasant. (She sits down beside her basket).

The Daughter. Sixpence thrown away! Really, mamma, you might have spared Freddy that. (She retreats in disgust behind the pillar).

An elderly gentleman of the amiable military type rushes into the shelter, and closes a dripping umbrella. He is in the same plight as Freddy, very wet about the ankles. He is in evening dress, with a light overcoat. He takes the place left vacant by the daughter's retirement.

The Gentleman. Phew!

The Mother (to the gentleman) Oh, sir, is there any sign of its stopping?

The Gentleman. I'm afraid not. It started worse than ever about two minutes ago. (He goes to the plinth beside the flower girl; puts up his foot on it; and stoops to turn down his trouser ends).

The Mother. Oh dear! (She retires sadly and joins her daughter).

The Flower Girl (taking advantage of the military gentleman's proximity to establish friendly relations with him) If it's worse, it's a sign it's nearly over. So cheer up, Captain; and buy a flower off a poor girl.

The Gentleman. I'm sorry. I havnt any change.

The Flower Girl. I can give you change, Captain.

The Gentleman. For a sovereign? Ive nothing less.

The Flower Girl. Garn! Oh do buy a flower off me, Captain. I can change half-a-crown. Take this for tuppence.

The Gentleman. Now dont be troublesome: theres a good girl. (Trying his pockets) I really havnt any change—Stop: heres three hapence, if thats any use to you (he retreats to the other pillar).

The Flower Girl (disappointed, but thinking three half-pence better than nothing) Thank you, sir.

The Bystander (to the girl) You be careful: give him a flower for it. Theres a bloke here behind taking down every blessed word youre saying. (All turn to the man who is taking notes).

The Flower Girl (springing up terrified) I aint done nothing wrong by speaking to the gentleman. Ive a right to sell flowers if I keep off the kerb. (Hysterically) I'm a respectable girl: so help me, I never spoke to him except to ask him to buy a flower off me. (General hubbub, mostly sympathetic to the flower girl, but deprecating her excessive sensibility. Cries of Dont start hollerin. Who's hurting you? Nobody's going to touch you. Whats the good of fussing? Steady on. Easy easy, etc., come from the elderly staid spectators, who pat her comfortingly. Less patient ones bid her shut her head, or ask her roughly what is wrong with her. A remoter group, not knowing what the matter is, crowd in and increase the noise with question and answer: Whats the row? Whatshe do? Where is he? A tec[5] taking her down. What! him? Yes: him over there: Took money off the gentleman, etc. The flower girl, distraught and mobbed, breaks through them to the gentleman, crying wildly) Oh, sir, dont let him charge me.[6] You dunno what it means to me. Theyll take away my character and drive me on the streets for speaking to gentlemen. They—

The Note Taker (coming forward on her right, the rest crowding after him) There, there, there, there! who's hurting you, you silly girl? What do you take me for?

The Bystander. It's all right: he's a gentleman: look at his boots. (Explaining to the note taker) She thought you was a copper's nark, sir.

The Note Taker (with quick interest) Whats a copper's nark?

The Bystander (inapt at definition) It's a—well, it's a copper's nark, as you might say.

---

5. tec, detective. [British Slang] 6. charge me, bring an accusation against me.

What else would you call it? A sort of informer.

The Flower Girl (still hysterical) I take my Bible oath I never said a word—

The Note Taker (overbearing but good-humored) Oh, shut up, shut up. Do I look like a policeman?

The Flower Girl (far from reassured) Then what did you take down my words for? How do I know whether you took me down right? You just shew me what youve wrote about me. (*The note taker opens his book and holds it steadily under her nose, though the pressure of the mob trying to read it over his shoulders would upset a weaker man*). Whats that? That aint proper writing. I cant read that.

The Note Taker. I can. (*Reads, reproducing her pronunciation exactly*) "Cheer ap, Keptin; n' baw ya flahr orf a pore gel."

The Flower Girl (much distressed) It's because I called him Captain. I meant no harm. (*To the gentleman*) Oh, sir, dont let him lay a charge agen me for a word like that. You—

The Gentleman. Charge! I make no charge. (*To the note taker*) Really, sir, if you are a detective, you need not begin protecting me against molestation by young women until I ask you. Anybody could see that the girl meant no harm.

The Bystanders Generally (demonstrating against police espionage) Course they could. What business is it of yours? You mind your own affairs. He wants promotion, he does. Taking down people's words! Girl never said a word to him. What harm if she did? Nice thing a girl cant shelter from the rain without being insulted, etc., etc., etc. (*She is conducted by the more sympathetic demonstrators back to her plinth, where she resumes her seat and struggles with her emotion*).

The Bystander. He aint a tec. He's a blooming busybody: thats what he is. I tell you, look at his boots.

The Note Taker (turning on him genially) And how are all your people down at Selsey?

The Bystander (suspiciously) Who told you my people come from Selsey?

The Note Taker. Never you mind. They did. (*To the girl*) How do you come to be up so far east? You were born in Lisson Grove.

The Flower Girl (appalled) Oh, what harm is there in my leaving Lisson Grove? It wasnt fit for a pig to live in; and I had to pay four-and-six a week. (*In tears*) Oh, boo—hoo—oo—

The Note Taker. Live where you like; but stop that noise.

The Gentleman (to the girl) Come, come! he cant touch you: you have a right to live where you please.

A Sarcastic Bystander (thrusting himself between the note taker and the gentleman) Park Lane, for instance. I'd like to go into the Housing Question with you, I would.

The Flower Girl (subsiding into a brooding melancholy over her basket, and talking very low-spiritedly to herself) I'm a good girl, I am.

The Sarcastic Bystander (not attending to her) Do you know where I come from?

The Note Taker (promptly) Hoxton.

Titterings. Popular interest in the note taker's performance increases.

The Sarcastic One (amazed) Well, who said I didnt? Bly me! You know everything, you do.

The Flower Girl (still nursing her sense of injury) Aint no call to meddle with me, he aint.

The Bystander (to her) Of course he aint. Dont you stand it from him. (*To the note taker*) See here: what call have you to know about people what never offered to meddle with you? Wheres your warrant?

Several Bystanders (encouraged by this seeming point of law) Yes: wheres your warrant?

The Flower Girl. Let him say what he likes. I dont want to have no truck with him.

The Bystander. You take us for dirt under your feet, dont you? Catch you taking liberties with a gentleman!

The Sarcastic Bystander. Yes: tell him where he come from if you want to go fortune-telling.

The Note Taker. Cheltenham, Harrow, Cambridge, and India.

The Gentleman. Quite right. (*Great laughter. Reaction in the note taker's favor. Exclamations of* He knows all about it. Told him proper. Hear him tell the toff where he come from? etc.). May I ask, sir, do you do this for your living at a music hall?

The Note Taker. Ive thought of that. Perhaps I shall some day.

The rain has stopped; and the persons on the outside of the crowd begin to drop off.

The Flower Girl (resenting the reaction) He's no gentleman, he aint, to interfere with a poor girl.

The Daughter (out of patience, pushing her way rudely to the front and displacing the gentleman, who politely retires to the other side of the pillar) What on earth is Freddy doing? I shall get pneumonia if I stay in this draught any longer.

The Note Taker (to himself, hastily making a note of her pronunciation of "monia") Earlscourt.

The Daughter (violently) Will you please keep your impertinent remarks to yourself.

The Note Taker. Did I say that out loud? I didnt mean to. I beg your pardon. Your mother's Epsom, unmistakably.

The Mother (advancing between her daughter and the note taker) How very curious! I was brought up in Largelady Park, near Epsom.

The Note Taker (uproariously amused) Ha! Ha! What a devil of a name! Excuse me. (*To the daughter*) You want a cab, do you?

The Daughter. Dont dare speak to me.

The Mother. Oh please, please, Clara. (*Her daughter repudiates her with an angry shrug and retires haughtily*). We should be so grateful to you, sir, if you found us a cab. (*The note taker produces a whistle*). Oh, thank you. (*She joins her daughter*).

The note taker blows a piercing blast.

The Sarcastic Bystander. There! I knowed he was a plain-clothes copper.

The Bystander. That aint a police whistle: thats a sporting whistle.

The Flower Girl (still preoccupied with her wounded feelings) He's no right to take away my character. My character is the same to me as any lady's.

The Note Taker. I dont know whether youve noticed it; but the rain stopped about two minutes ago.

The Bystander. So it has. Why didnt you say so before? and us losing our time listening to your silliness! (*He walks off towards the Strand*).

The Sarcastic Bystander. I can tell where you come from. You come from Anwell. Go back there.

The Note Taker (helpfully) Hanwell.

The Sarcastic Bystander (affecting great distinction of speech) Thenk you, teacher. Haw haw! So long (*he touches his hat with mock respect and strolls off*).

The Flower Girl. Frightening people like that! How would he like it himself?

The Mother. It's quite fine now, Clara. We can walk to a motor bus. Come. (*She gathers her skirts above her ankles and hurries off towards the Strand*).

The Daughter. But the cab—(*her mother is out of hearing*). Oh, how tiresome! (*She follows angrily*).

All the rest have gone except the note taker, the gentleman, and the flower girl, who sits arranging her basket and still pitying herself in murmurs.

The Flower Girl. Poor girl! Hard enough for her to live without being worried and chivied.

The Gentleman (returning to his former place on the note taker's left) How do you do it, if I may ask?

The Note Taker. Simply phonetics. The science of speech. Thats my profession: also my hobby. Happy is the man who can make a living by his hobby! You can spot an Irishman or a Yorkshireman by his brogue. *I* can place any man within six miles. I can place him within two miles in London. Sometimes within two streets.

The Flower Girl. Ought to be ashamed of himself, unmanly coward!

The Gentleman. But is there a living in that?

The Note Taker. Oh yes. Quite a fat one. This is an age of upstarts. Men begin in Kentish Town with £80 a year, and end in Park Lane with a hundred thousand. They want to drop Kentish Town; but they give themselves away every time they open their mouths. Now I can teach them—

The Flower Girl. Let him mind his own business and leave a poor girl—

The Note Taker (explosively) Woman: cease this detestable boohooing instantly; or else seek the shelter of some other place of worship.

The Flower Girl (with feeble defiance) Ive a right to be here if I like, same as you.

The Note Taker. A woman who utters such depressing and disgusting sounds has no right to be anywhere—no right to live. Remember that you are a human being with a soul and the divine gift of articulate speech: that your native language is the language of Shakespeare and Milton and The Bible: and dont sit there crooning like a bilious pigeon.

The Flower Girl (quite overwhelmed, looking up at him in mingled wonder and deprecation without daring to raise her head) Ah-ah-ah-ow-ow-ow-oo!

The Note Taker (whipping out his book) Heavens! what a sound! (*He writes; then holds out the book and reads, reproducing her vowels exactly*) Ah-ah-ah-ow-ow-ow-oo!

The Flower Girl (tickled by the performance, and laughing in spite of herself) Garn!

The Note Taker. You see this creature with her kerbstone English: the English that will keep her in the gutter to the end of her days. Well, sir, in three months I could pass that girl off as a duchess at an ambassador's garden party. I could even get her a place as lady's maid or shop assistant, which requires better English. Thats the sort of thing I do for commercial millionaires. And on the profits of it I do genuine scientific work in phonetics, and a little as a poet on Miltonic lines.

The Gentleman. I am myself a student of Indian dialects; and—

The Note Taker (eagerly) Are you? Do you know Colonel Pickering, the author of Spoken Sanscrit?

The Gentleman. I am Colonel Pickering. Who are you?

The Note Taker. Henry Higgins, author of Higgins' Universal Alphabet.

Pickering (with enthusiasm) I came from India to meet you.

Higgins. I was going to India to meet you.

Pickering. Where do you live?

Higgins. 27A Wimpole Street. Come and see me to-morrow.

Pickering. I'm at the Carlton. Come with me now and lets have a jaw over some supper.

Higgins. Right you are.

The Flower Girl (to Pickering, as he passes her) Buy a flower, kind gentleman. I'm short for my lodging.

Pickering. I really havnt any change. I'm sorry (*he goes away*).

Higgins (shocked at the girl's mendacity) Liar. You said you could change half-a-crown.

The Flower Girl (rising in desperation) You ought to be stuffed with nails, you ought. (*Flinging the basket at his feet*) Take the whole blooming basket for sixpence.

The church clock strikes the second quarter.

Higgins (hearing in it the voice of God, rebuking him for his Pharisaic want of charity to the poor girl) A reminder. (*He raises his hat solemnly; then throws a handful of money into the basket and follows Pickering*).

The Flower Girl (picking up a half-crown) Ah-ow-ooh! (*Picking up a couple of florins*) Aaah-ow-ooh! (*Picking up several coins*) Aaaaaah-ow-ooh! (*Picking up a half-sovereign*) Aaaaaaaaaaaah-ow-ooh!!!

Freddy (springing out of a taxicab) Got one at last. Hallo! (*To the girl*) Where are the two ladies that were here?

The Flower Girl. They walked to the bus when the rain stopped.

Freddy. And left me with a cab on my hands! Damnation!

The Flower Girl (with grandeur) Never mind, young man. I'm going home in a taxi. (*She sails off to the cab. The driver puts his hand behind him and holds the door firmly shut against her. Quite understanding his mistrust, she shews him her handful of money*). Eightpence aint no object to me, Charlie. (*He grins and opens the door*). Angel Court, Drury Lane, round the corner of Micklejohn's oil shop. Lets see how fast you can make her hop it. (*She gets in and pulls the door to with a slam as the taxicab starts*).

Freddy. Well, I'm dashed!

1. Why do you think Shaw elected to open the play with the shelter scene?
2. (*a*) What social class is represented by the daughter, mother, and son Freddy? (*b*) Does Shaw present a sympathetic or unsympathetic picture of the daughter? (*c*) Through what actions does he reveal her character?
3. (*a*) What class is represented by the by-standers? (*b*) Why are they generally sympathetic to the flower girl? (*c*) What causes them to switch their sympathies to the note taker?
4. (*a*) How does the note taker make a living from his hobby of phonetics? (*b*) What is his attitude toward the flower girl? (*c*) According to his theory, what will keep the flower girl in the lower class?

Lilli Marberd as Liza in the first production of Pygmalion. *Because of the criticism Shaw had received in England, this production took place in Vienna, where it was an immediate success. The play was then "imported" to London the next year (1914).*

THE RAYMOND MANDER AND JOE MITCHENSON THEATER COLLECTION, LONDON

ACT TWO

Next day at 11 a.m. Higgins's laboratory in Wimpole Street. It is a room on the first floor, looking on the street, and was meant for the drawing room. The double doors are in the middle of the back wall; and persons entering find in the corner to their right two tall file cabinets at right angles to one another against the walls. In this corner stands a flat writing table, on which are a phonograph, a laryngoscope, a row of tiny organ pipes with bellows, a set of lamp chimneys for singing flames with burners attached to a gas plug in the wall by an indiarubber tube, several tuning-forks of different sizes, a lifesize image of half a human head, shewing in section the vocal organs, and a box containing a supply of wax cylinders for the phonograph.

Further down the room, on the same side, is a fireplace, with a comfortable leather-covered easy-chair at the side of the hearth nearest the door, and a coal-scuttle. There is a clock on the mantelpiece. Between the fire-place and the phonograph table is a stand for newspapers.

On the other side of the central door, to the left of the visitor, is a cabinet of shallow drawers. On it is a telephone and the telephone directory. The corner beyond, and most of the side wall, is occupied by a grand piano, with the keyboard at the end furthest from the door, and a bench for the player extending the full length of the keyboard. On the piano is a dessert dish heaped with fruit and sweets, mostly chocolates.

The middle of the room is clear. Besides the easy-chair, the piano bench, and two chairs at the phonograph table, there is one stray chair. It stands near the fireplace. On the walls, engravings: mostly Piranesis and mezzo-tint portraits.[1] No paintings.

Pickering is seated at the table, putting down some cards and a tuning-fork which he

---

1. *Piranesis and mezzotint portraits.* Giovanni Battista Piranesi (1720-78), an Italian draftsman and etcher, is noted for his large prints of buildings of classical and post-classical Rome, and views of Greek temples. A mezzotint is a picture engraved on a roughened copper or steel plate. Light areas are obtained by scraping away and burnishing parts of the plate.

has been using. Higgins is standing up near him, closing two or three file drawers which are hanging out. He appears in the morning light as a robust, vital, appetizing sort of man of forty or thereabouts, dressed in a professional-looking black frock-coat with a white linen collar and black silk tie. He is of the energetic, scientific type, heartily, even violently interested in everything that can be studied as a scientific subject, and careless about himself and other people, including their feelings. He is, in fact, but for his years and size, rather like a very impetuous baby "taking notice" eagerly and loudly, and requiring almost as much watching to keep him out of unintended mischief. His manner varies from genial bullying when he is in a good humor to stormy petulance when anything goes wrong; but he is so entirely frank and void of malice that he remains likeable even in his least reasonable moments.

Higgins (as he shuts the last drawer) Well, I think thats the whole show.

Pickering. It's really amazing. I havnt taken half of it in, you know.

Higgins. Would you like to go over any of it again?

Pickering (rising and coming to the fireplace, where he plants himself with his back to the fire) No, thank you; not now. I'm quite done up for this morning.

Higgins (following him, and standing beside him on his left) Tired of listening to sounds?

Pickering. Yes. It's a fearful strain. I rather fancied myself because I can pronounce twenty-four distinct vowel sounds; but your hundred and thirty beat me. I cant hear a bit of difference between most of them.

Higgins (chuckling, and going over to the piano to eat sweets) Oh, that comes with practice. You hear no difference at first; but you keep on listening, and presently you find theyre all as different as A from B. (*Mrs Pearce looks in: she is Higgins's housekeeper*). Whats the matter?

Mrs Pearce (hesitating, evidently perplexed) A young woman wants to see you, sir.

Higgins. A young woman! What does she want?

Mrs Pearce. Well, sir, she says youll be glad to see her when you know what she's come about. She's quite a common girl, sir. Very common indeed. I should have sent her away, only I thought perhaps you wanted her to talk into your machines. I hope Ive not done wrong; but really you see such queer people sometimes—youll excuse me, I'm sure, sir—

Higgins. Oh, thats all right, Mrs Pearce. Has she an interesting accent?

Mrs Pearce. Oh, something dreadful, sir, really. I dont know how you can take an interest in it.

Higgins (to Pickering) Lets have her up. Shew her up, Mrs Pearce (*he rushes across to his working table and picks out a cylinder to use on the phonograph*).

Mrs Pearce (only half resigned to it) Very well, sir. It's for you to say. (*She goes downstairs*).

Higgins. This is rather a bit of luck. I'll shew you how I make records. We'll set her talking; and I'll take it down first in Bell's Visible Speech; then in broad Romic; and then we'll get her on the phonograph so that you can turn her on as often as you like with the written transcript before you.

Mrs Pearce (returning) This is the young woman, sir.

The flower girl enters in state. She has a hat with three ostrich feathers, orange, sky-blue, and red. She has a nearly clean apron, and the shoddy coat has been tidied a little. The pathos of this deplorable figure, with its innocent vanity and consequential air, touches Pickering, who has already straightened himself in the presence of Mrs Pearce. But as to Higgins, the only distinction he makes between men and women is that when he is neither bullying nor exclaiming to the heavens against some feather-weight cross, he coaxes women as a child coaxes its nurse when it wants to get anything out of her.

Higgins (brusquely, recognizing her with unconcealed disappointment, and at once, babylike, making an intolerable grievance of it) Why, this is the girl I jotted down last night. She's no use: Ive got all the records I want of the Lisson Grove lingo; and I'm not going to waste another cylinder on it. (*To the girl*) Be off with you: I dont want you.

The Flower Girl. Dont you be so saucy. You aint heard what I come for yet. (*To Mrs Pearce, who is waiting at the door for further instructions*) Did you tell him I come in a taxi?

Mrs Pearce. Nonsense, girl! what do you think a gentleman like Mr Higgins cares what you came in?

The Flower Girl. Oh, we are proud! He aint above giving lessons, not him: I heard him say so. Well, I aint come here to ask for any compliment; and if my money's not good enough I can go elsewhere.

Higgins. Good enough for what?

The Flower Girl. Good enough for ye-oo. Now you know, dont you? I'm come to have lessons, I am. And to pay for em too: make no mistake.

Higgins (*stupent*) Well!!! (*Recovering his breath with a gasp*) What do you expect me to say to you?

The Flower Girl. Well, if you was a gentleman, you might ask me to sit down, I think. Dont I tell you I'm bringing you business?

Higgins. Pickering: shall we ask this baggage to sit down, or shall we throw her out of the window?

The Flower Girl (*running away in terror to the piano, where she turns at bay*) Ah-ah-oh-ow-ow-ow-oo! (*Wounded and whimpering*) I wont be called a baggage when Ive offered to pay like any lady.

Motionless, the two men stare at her from the other side of the room, amazed.

Pickering (*gently*) What is it you want, my girl?

The Flower Girl. I want to be a lady in a flower shop stead of selling at the corner of Tottenham Court Road. But they wont take me unless I can talk more genteel. He said he could teach me. Well, here I am ready to pay him—not asking any favor—and he treats me as if I was dirt.

Mrs Pearce. How can you be such a foolish ignorant girl as to think you could afford to pay Mr Higgins?

The Flower Girl. Why shouldnt I? I know what lessons cost as well as you do; and I'm ready to pay.

Higgins. How much?

The Flower Girl (*coming back to him, triumphant*) Now youre talking! I thought youd come off it when you saw a chance of getting back a bit of what you chucked at me last night. (*Confidentially*) Youd had a drop in, hadnt you?

Higgins (*peremptorily*) Sit down.

The Flower Girl. Oh, if youre going to make a compliment of it—

Higgins (*thundering at her*) Sit down.

Mrs Pearce (*severely*) Sit down, girl. Do as youre told. (*She places the stray chair near the hearthrug between Higgins and Pickering, and stands behind it waiting for the girl to sit down*).

The Flower Girl. Ah-ah-ah-ow-ow-oo! (*She stands, half rebellious, half bewildered*).

Pickering (*very courteous*) Wont you sit down?

The Flower Girl (*coyly*) Dont mind if I do. (*She sits down. Pickering returns to the hearthrug*).

Higgins. Whats your name?

The Flower Girl. Liza Doolittle.

Higgins (*declaiming gravely*)
　　Eliza, Elizabeth, Betsy and Bess,
　　They went to the woods to get a bird's nes':

Pickering. They found a nest with four eggs in it:

Higgins. They took one apiece, and left three in it.

They laugh heartily at their own wit.

Liza. Oh, dont be silly.

Mrs Pearce. You mustnt speak to the gentleman like that.

Liza. Well, why wont he speak sensible to me?

Higgins. Come back to business. How much do you propose to pay me for the lessons?

Liza. Oh, I know whats right. A lady friend of mine gets French lessons for eighteenpence an hour from a real French gentleman. Well, you wouldnt have the face to ask me the same for teaching me my own language as you would for French; so I wont give more than a shilling. Take it or leave it.

Higgins (walking up and down the room, rattling his keys and his cash in his pockets) You know, Pickering, if you consider a shilling, not as a simple shilling, but as a percentage of this girl's income, it works out as fully equivalent to sixty or seventy guineas from a millionaire.

Pickering. How so?

Higgins. Figure it out. A millionaire has about £150 a day. She earns about half-a-crown.

Liza (haughtily) Who told you I only—

Higgins (continuing) She offers me two-fifths of her day's income for a lesson. Two-fifths of a millionaire's income for a day would be somewhere about £60. It's handsome. By George, it's enormous! it's the biggest offer I ever had.

Liza (rising, terrified) Sixty pounds! What are you talking about? I never offered you sixty pounds. Where would I get—

Higgins. Hold your tongue.

Liza (weeping) But I aint got sixty pounds. Oh—

Mrs Pearce. Dont cry, you silly girl. Sit down. Nobody is going to touch your money.

Higgins. Somebody is going to touch you, with a broomstick, if you dont stop snivelling. Sit down.

Liza (obeying slowly) Ah-ah-ah-ow-oo-o! One would think you was my father.

Higgins. If I decide to teach you, I'll be worse than two fathers to you. Here (*he offers her his silk handkerchief*)!

Liza. Whats this for?

Higgins. To wipe your eyes. To wipe any part of your face that feels moist. Remember: thats your handkerchief; and thats your sleeve. Dont mistake the one for the other if you wish to become a lady in a shop.

Liza, utterly bewildered, stares helplessly at him.

Mrs Pearce. It's no use talking to her like that, Mr Higgins: she doesnt understand you. Besides, youre quite wrong: she doesnt do it that way at all (*she takes the handkerchief*).

Liza (snatching it) Here! You give me that handkerchief. He give it to me, not to you.

Pickering (laughing) He did. I think it must be regarded as her property, Mrs Pearce.

Mrs Pearce (resigning herself) Serve you right, Mr Higgins.

Pickering. Higgins: I'm interested. What about the ambassador's garden party? I'll say youre the greatest teacher alive if you make that good. I'll bet you all the expenses of the experiment you cant do it. And I'll pay for the lessons.

Liza. Oh, you are real good. Thank you, Captain.

Higgins (tempted, looking at her) It's almost irresistible. She's so deliciously low—so horribly dirty—

Liza (protesting extremely) Ah-ah-ah-ah-ow-ow-oo-oo!!! I aint dirty: I washed my face and hands afore I come, I did.

Pickering. Youre certainly not going to turn her head with flattery, Higgins.

Mrs Pearce (uneasy) Oh, dont say that, sir: theres more ways than one of turning a girl's head; and nobody can do it better than Mr Higgins, though he may not always mean it. I do hope, sir, you wont encourage him to do anything foolish.

Higgins (becoming excited as the idea grows on him) What is life but a series of inspired follies? The difficulty is to find them to do. Never lose a chance: it doesnt come every day. I shall make a duchess of this draggletailed guttersnipe.

Liza (strongly deprecating this view of her) Ah-ah-ah-ow-ow-oo!

Higgins (carried away) Yes: in six months —in three if she has a good ear and a quick tongue—I'll take her anywhere and pass her off as anything. We'll start today: now! this moment! Take her away and clean her, Mrs Pearce. Monkey Brand, if it wont come off any other way. Is there a good fire in the kitchen?

Mrs Pearce (protesting) Yes; but—

Higgins (storming on) Take all her clothes off and burn them. Ring up Whiteley or somebody for new ones. Wrap her up in brown paper til they come.

Liza. Youre no gentleman, youre not, to talk of such things. I'm a good girl, I am; and I know what the like of you are, I do.

Higgins. We want none of your Lisson Grove prudery here, young woman. Youve got to learn to behave like a duchess. Take her away, Mrs Pearce. If she gives you any trouble, wallop her.

Liza (springing up and running between Pickering and Mrs Pearce for protection) No! I'll call the police, I will.

Mrs Pearce. But Ive no place to put her.

Higgins. Put her in the dustbin.

Liza. Ah-ah-ah-ow-ow-oo!

Pickering. Oh come, Higgins! be reasonable.

Mrs Pearce (resolutely) You must be reasonable, Mr Higgins: really you must. You cant walk over everybody like this.

Higgins, thus scolded, subsides. The hurricane is succeeded by a zephyr of amiable surprise.

Higgins (with professional exquisiteness of modulation) I walk over everybody! My dear Mrs Pearce, my dear Pickering, I never had the slightest intention of walking over anyone. All I propose is that we should be kind to this poor girl. We must help her to prepare and fit herself for her new station in life. If I did not express myself clearly it was because I did not wish to hurt her delicacy, or yours.

Liza, reassured, steals back to her chair.

Mrs Pearce (to Pickering) Well, did you ever hear anything like that, sir?

Pickering (laughing heartily) Never, Mrs Pearce: never.

Higgins (patiently) Whats the matter?

Mrs Pearce. Well, the matter is, sir, that you cant take a girl up like that as if you were picking up a pebble on the beach.

Higgins. Why not?

Mrs Pearce. Why not! But you dont know anything about her. What about her parents? She may be married.

Liza. Garn!

Higgins. There! As the girl very properly says, Garn! Married indeed! Dont you know that a woman of that class looks a worn out drudge of fifty a year after she's married?

Liza. Whood marry me?

Higgins (suddenly resorting to the most thrillingly beautiful low tones in his best elocutionary style) By George, Eliza, the streets will be strewn with the bodies of men shooting themselves for your sake before Ive done with you.

Mrs Pearce. Nonsense, sir. You mustnt talk like that to her.

Liza (rising and squaring herself determinedly) I'm going away. He's off his chump, he is. I dont want no balmies teaching me.

Higgins (wounded in his tenderest point by her insensibility to his elocution) Oh, indeed! I'm mad, am I? Very well, Mrs Pearce: you neednt order the new clothes for her. Throw her out.

Liza (whimpering) Nah-ow. You got no right to touch me.

Mrs Pearce. You see now what comes of being saucy. (Indicating the door) This way, please.

Liza (almost in tears) I didnt want no clothes. I wouldnt have taken them (she throws away the handkerchief). I can buy my own clothes.

Higgins (deftly retrieving the handkerchief and intercepting her on her reluctant way to the door) Youre an ungrateful wicked girl. This is my return for offering to take you out of the gutter and dress you beautifully and make a lady of you.

Mrs Pearce. Stop, Mr Higgins. I wont allow it. It's you that are wicked. Go home to your parents, girl; and tell them to take better care of you.

Liza. I aint got no parents. They told me I was big enough to earn my own living and turned me out.

Mrs Pearce. Wheres your mother?

Liza. I aint got no mother. Her that turned me out was my sixth stepmother. But I done without them. And I'm a good girl, I am.

Higgins. Very well, then, what on earth is all this fuss about? The girl doesnt belong to anybody—is no use to anybody but me. (He goes to Mrs Pearce and begins coaxing). You can adopt her, Mrs Pearce: I'm sure a daughter would be a great amusement to you. Now dont make any more fuss. Take her downstairs; and—

Mrs Pearce. But whats to become of her? Is she to be paid anything? Do be sensible, sir.

Higgins. Oh, pay her whatever is necessary: put it down in the housekeeping book. (*Impatiently*) What on earth will she want with money? She'll have her food and her clothes. She'll only drink if you give her money.

Liza (*turning on him*) Oh you are a brute. It's a lie: nobody ever saw the sign of liquor on me. (*She goes back to her chair and plants herself there defiantly*).

Pickering (*in good-humored remonstrance*) Does it occur to you, Higgins, that the girl has some feelings?

Higgins (*looking critically at her*) Oh no, I dont think so. Not any feelings that we need bother about. (*Cheerily*) Have you, Eliza?

Liza. I got my feelings same as anyone else.

Higgins (*to Pickering, reflectively*) You see the difficulty?

Pickering. Eh? What difficulty?

Higgins. To get her to talk grammar. The mere pronunciation is easy enough.

Liza. I dont want to talk grammar. I want to talk like a lady.

Mrs Pearce. Will you please keep to the point, Mr Higgins? I want to know on what terms the girl is to be here. Is she to have any wages? And what is to become of her when youve finished your teaching? You must look ahead a little.

Higgins (*impatiently*) Whats to become of her if I leave her in the gutter? Tell me that, Mrs Pearce.

Mrs Pearce. Thats her own business, not yours, Mr Higgins.

Higgins. Well, when Ive done with her, we can throw her back into the gutter; and then it will be her own business again; so thats all right.

Liza. Oh, youve no feeling heart in you: you dont care for nothing but yourself (*she rises and takes the floor resolutely*). Here! Ive had enough of this. I'm going (*making for the door*). You ought to be ashamed of yourself, you ought.

Higgins (*snatching a chocolate cream from the piano, his eyes suddenly beginning to twinkle with mischief*) Have some chocolates, Eliza.

Liza (*halting, tempted*) How do I know what might be in them? Ive heard of girls being drugged by the like of you.

Higgins whips out his penknife; cuts a chocolate in two; puts one half into his mouth and bolts it; and offers her the other half.

Higgins. Pledge of good faith, Eliza. I eat one half: you eat the other. (*Liza opens her mouth to retort: he pops the half chocolate into it*). You shall have boxes of them, barrels of them, every day. You shall live on them. Eh?

Liza (*who has disposed of the chocolate after being nearly choked by it*) I wouldnt have ate it, only I'm too ladylike to take it out of my mouth.

Higgins. Listen, Eliza. I think you said you came in a taxi.

Liza. Well, what if I did? Ive as good a right to take a taxi as anyone else.

Higgins. You have, Eliza; and in future you shall have as many taxis as you want. You shall go up and down and round the town in a taxi every day. Think of that, Eliza.

Mrs Pearce. Mr Higgins: youre tempting the girl. It's not right. She should think of the future.

Higgins. At her age! Nonsense! Time enough to think of the future when you havnt any future to think of. No, Eliza: do as this lady does: think of other people's futures; but never think of your own. Think of chocolates, and taxis, and gold, and diamonds.

Liza. No: I dont want no gold and no diamonds. I'm a good girl, I am. (*She sits down again, with an attempt at dignity*).

Higgins. You shall remain so, Eliza, under the care of Mrs Pearce. And you shall marry an officer in the Guards, with a beautiful moustache: the son of a marquis, who will disinherit him for marrying you, but will relent when he sees your beauty and goodness—

Pickering. Excuse me, Higgins; but I really must interfere. Mrs Pearce is quite right. If this girl is to put herself in your hands for six months for an experiment in teaching, she must understand thoroughly what she's doing.

Higgins. How can she? She's incapable of understanding anything. Besides, do any of us understand what we are doing? If we did, would we ever do it?

Pickering. Very clever, Higgins; but not sound sense. (*To Eliza*) Miss Doolittle—

Liza (*overwhelmed*) Ah-ah-ow-oo!

Higgins. There! Thats all youll get out of Eliza. Ah-ah-ow-oo! No use explaining. As a military man you ought to know that. Give her her orders: thats what she wants. Eliza: you are to live here for the next six months, learning how to speak beautifully, like a lady in a florist's shop. If youre good and do whatever youre told, you shall sleep in a proper bedroom, and have lots to eat, and money to buy chocolates and take rides in taxis. If youre naughty and idle you will sleep in the back kitchen among the black beetles, and be walloped by Mrs Pearce with a broomstick. At the end of six months you shall go to Buckingham Palace in a carriage, beautifully dressed. If the King finds out youre not a lady, you will be taken by the police to the Tower of London, where your head will be cut off as a warning to other presumptuous flower girls. If you are not found out, you shall have a present of seven-and-sixpence to start life with as a lady in a shop. If you refuse this offer you will be a most ungrateful and wicked girl; and the angels will weep for you. (*To Pickering*) Now are you satisfied, Pickering? (*To Mrs Pearce*) Can I put it more plainly and fairly, Mrs Pearce?

Mrs Pearce (*patiently*) I think youd better let me speak to the girl properly in private. I dont know that I can take charge of her or consent to the arrangement at all. Of course I know you dont mean her any harm; but when you get what you call interested in people's accents, you never think or care what may happen to them or you. Come with me, Eliza.

Higgins. Thats all right. Thank you, Mrs Pearce. Bundle her off to the bathroom.

Liza (*rising reluctantly and suspiciously*) Youre a great bully, you are. I wont stay here if I dont like. I wont let nobody wallop me. I never asked to go to Bucknam Palace, I didnt. I was never in trouble with the police, not me. I'm a good girl—

Mrs Pearce. Dont answer back, girl. You dont understand the gentleman. Come with me. (*She leads the way to the door, and holds it open for Eliza*).

Liza (*as she goes out*) Well, what I say is right. I wont go near the King, not if I'm going to have my head cut off. If I'd known what I was letting myself in for, I wouldnt have come here. I always been a good girl; and I never offered to say a word to him; and I dont owe him nothing; and I dont care; and I wont be put upon; and I have my feelings the same as anyone else—

Mrs Pearce shuts the door; and Eliza's plaints are no longer audible. Pickering comes from the hearth to the chair and sits astride it with his arms on the back.

Pickering. Excuse the straight question, Higgins. Are you a man of good character where women are concerned?

Higgins (*moodily*) Have you ever met a man of good character where women are concerned?

Pickering. Yes: very frequently.

Higgins (*dogmatically, lifting himself on his hands to the level of the piano, and sitting on it with a bounce*) Well, I havnt. I find that the moment I let a woman make friends with me, she becomes jealous, exacting, suspicious, and a damned nuisance. I find that the moment I let myself make friends with a woman, I become selfish and tyrannical. Women upset everything. When you let them into your life, you find that the woman is driving at one thing and youre driving at another.

Pickering. At what, for example?

Higgins (*coming off the piano restlessly*) Oh, Lord knows! I suppose the woman wants to live her own life; and the man wants to live his; and each tries to drag the other on to the wrong track. One wants to go north and the other south; and the result is that both have to go east, though they both hate the east wind. (*He sits down on the bench at the keyboard*). So here I am, a confirmed old bachelor, and likely to remain so.

Pickering (*rising and standing over him gravely*) Come, Higgins! You know what I mean. If I'm to be in this business I shall feel responsible for that girl. I hope it's understood that no advantage is to be taken of her position.

Higgins. What! That thing! Sacred, I assure you. (*Rising to explain*) You see, she'll be a pupil; and teaching would be impossible unless pupils were sacred. Ive taught scores of American millionairesses how to speak English: the best looking women in the world. I'm seasoned. They might as well be blocks of wood. *I* might as well be a block of wood. It's—

Mrs Pearce opens the door. She has Eliza's hat in her hand. Pickering retires to the easy-chair at the hearth and sits down.

Higgins (*eagerly*) Well, Mrs Pearce: is it all right?

Mrs Pearce (*at the door*) I just wish to trouble you with a word, if I may, Mr Higgins.

Higgins. Yes, certainly. Come in. (*She comes forward*). Dont burn that, Mrs Pearce. I'll keep it as a curiosity. (*He takes the hat*).

Mrs Pearce. Handle it carefully, sir, please. I had to promise her not to burn it; but I had better put it in the oven for a while.

Higgins (*putting it down hastily on the piano*) Oh! thank you. Well, what have you to say to me?

Pickering. Am I in the way?

Mrs Pearce. Not at all, sir. Mr Higgins: will you please be very particular what you say before the girl?

Higgins (*sternly*) Of course. I'm always particular about what I say. Why do you say this to me?

Mrs Pearce (*unmoved*) No, sir: youre not at all particular when youve mislaid anything or when you get a little impatient. Now it doesnt matter before me: I'm used to it. But you really must not swear before the girl.

Higgins (*indignantly*) I swear! (*Most emphatically*) I never swear. I detest the habit. What the devil do you mean?

Mrs Pearce (*stolidly*) Thats what I mean, sir. You swear a great deal too much. I dont mind your damning and blasting, and what the devil and where the devil and who the devil—

Higgins. Mrs Pearce: this language from your lips! Really!

Mrs Pearce (*not to be put off*)—but there is a certain word I must ask you not to use. The girl has just used it herself because the bath was too hot. It begins with the same letter as bath. She knows no better: she learnt it at her mother's knee. But she must not hear it from your lips.

Higgins (*loftily*) I cannot charge myself with having ever uttered it, Mrs Pearce. (*She looks at him steadfastly. He adds, hiding an uneasy conscience with a judicial air*) Except perhaps in a moment of extreme and justifiable excitement.

Mrs Pearce. Only this morning, sir, you applied it to your boots, to the butter, and to the brown bread.

Higgins. Oh, that! Mere alliteration, Mrs Pearce, natural to a poet.

Mrs Pearce. Well, sir, whatever you choose to call it, I beg you not to let the girl hear you repeat it.

Higgins. Oh, very well, very well. Is that all?

Mrs Pearce. No, sir. We shall have to be very particular with this girl as to personal cleanliness.

Higgins. Certainly. Quite right. Most important.

Mrs Pearce. I mean not to be slovenly about her dress or untidy in leaving things about.

Higgins (*going to her solemnly*) Just so. I intended to call your attention to that. (*He passes on to Pickering, who is enjoying the conversation immensely*). It is these little things that matter, Pickering. Take care of the pence and the pounds will take care of themselves is as true of personal habits as of money. (*He comes to anchor on the hearthrug, with the air of a man in an unassailable position*).

Mrs Pearce. Yes, sir. Then might I ask you not to come down to breakfast in your dressing-gown, or at any rate not to use it as a napkin to the extent you do, sir. And if you would be so good as not to eat everything off the same plate, and to remember not to put the porridge saucepan out of your hand on the clean tablecloth, it would be a better example to the girl. You know you nearly choked yourself with a fishbone in the jam only last week.

Higgins (*routed from the hearthrug and drifting back to the piano*) I may do these things sometimes in absence of mind; but surely I dont do them habitually. (*Angrily*) By the way: my dressing-gown smells most damnably of benzine.

Mrs Pearce. No doubt it does, Mr Higgins. But if you will wipe your fingers—

Higgins (*yelling*) Oh very well, very well: I'll wipe them in my hair in future.

Mrs Pearce. I hope youre not offended, Mr Higgins.

Higgins (*shocked at finding himself thought capable of an unamiable sentiment*) Not at all, not at all. Youre quite right, Mrs Pearce: I shall be particularly careful before the girl. Is that all?

Mrs Pearce. No, sir. Might she use some of those Japanese dresses you brought from abroad? I really cant put her back into her old things.

Higgins. Certainly. Anything you like. Is that all?

Mrs Pearce. Thank you, sir. Thats all. (*She goes out*).

Higgins. You know, Pickering, that woman has the most extraordinary ideas about me. Here I am, a shy, diffident sort of man. Ive never been able to feel really grown-up and tremendous, like other chaps. And yet she's firmly persuaded that I'm an arbitrary overbearing bossing kind of person. I cant account for it.

Mrs Pearce returns.

Mrs Pearce. If you please, sir, the trouble's beginning already. Theres a dustman[2] downstairs, Alfred Doolittle, wants to see you. He says you have his daughter here.

Pickering (*rising*) Phew! I say! (*He retreats to the hearthrug*).

Higgins (*promptly*) Send the blackguard up.

Mrs Pearce. Oh, very well, sir. (*She goes out*).

Pickering. He may not be a blackguard, Higgins.

Higgins. Nonsense. Of course he's a blackguard.

Pickering. Whether he is or not, I'm afraid we shall have some trouble with him.

Higgins (*confidently*) Oh no: I think not. If theres any trouble he shall have it with me, not I with him. And we are sure to get something interesting out of him.

Pickering. About the girl?

Higgins. No. I mean his dialect.

Pickering. Oh!

Mrs Pearce (*at the door*) Doolittle, sir. (*She admits Doolittle and retires*).

Alfred Doolittle is an elderly but vigorous dustman, clad in the costume of his profession, including a hat with a black brim covering his neck and shoulders. He has well marked and rather interesting features, and seems equally free from fear and conscience. He has a remarkably expressive voice, the result of a habit of giving vent to his feelings without reserve. His present pose is that of wounded honor and stern resolution.

Doolittle (*at the door, uncertain which of the two gentlemen is his man*) Professor Higgins?

Higgins. Here. Good morning. Sit down.

Doolittle. Morning, Governor. (*He sits down magisterially*) I come about a very serious matter, Governor.

Higgins (*to Pickering*) Brought up in Hounslow. Mother Welsh, I should think. (*Doolittle opens his mouth, amazed. Higgins continues*) What do you want, Doolittle?

Doolittle (*menacingly*) I want my daughter: thats what I want. See?

Higgins. Of course you do. Youre her father, arnt you? You dont suppose anyone else wants her, do you? I'm glad to see you have some spark of family feeling left. She's upstairs. Take her away at once.

Doolittle (*rising, fearfully taken aback*) What!

Higgins. Take her away. Do you suppose I'm going to keep your daughter for you?

Doolittle (*remonstrating*) Now, now, look here, Governor. Is this reasonable? Is it fairity to take advantage of a man like this? The girl belongs to me. You got her. Where do I come in? (*He sits down again*).

Higgins. Your daughter had the audacity to come to my house and ask me to teach her

---

2. *dustman*, trash or garbage collector. [British]

how to speak properly so that she could get a place in a flower-shop. This gentleman and my housekeeper have been here all the time. (*Bullying him*) How dare you come here and attempt to blackmail me? You sent her here on purpose.

Doolittle (*protesting*) No, Governor.

Higgins. You must have. How else could you possibly know that she is here?

Doolittle. Dont take a man up like that, Governor.

Higgins. The police shall take you up. This is a plant—a plot to extort money by threats. I shall telephone for the police. (*He goes resolutely to the telephone and opens the directory*).

Doolittle. Have I asked you for a brass farthing? I leave it to the gentleman here: have I said a word about money?

Higgins (*throwing the book aside and marching down on Doolittle with a poser*) What else did you come for?

Doolittle (*sweetly*) Well, what would a man come for? Be human, Governor.

Higgins (*disarmed*) Alfred: did you put her up to it?

Doolittle. So help me, Governor, I never did. I take my Bible oath I aint seen the girl these two months past.

Higgins. Then how did you know she was here?

Doolittle (*"most musical, most melancholy"*[3]) I'll tell you, Governor, if youll only let me get a word in. I'm willing to tell you. I'm wanting to tell you. I'm waiting to tell you.

Higgins. Pickering: this chap has a certain natural gift of rhetoric. Observe the rhythm of his native woodnotes wild. "I'm willing to tell you: I'm wanting to tell you: I'm waiting to tell you." Sentimental rhetoric! thats the Welsh strain in him. It also accounts for his mendacity and dishonesty.

Pickering. Oh, please, Higgins: I'm west country myself. (*To Doolittle*) How did you know the girl was here if you didnt send her?

Doolittle. It was like this, Governor. The girl took a boy in the taxi to give him a jaunt. Son of her landlady, he is. He hung about on the chance of her giving him another ride home. Well, she sent him back for her luggage when she heard you was willing for her to stop here. I met the boy at the corner of Long Acre and Endell Street.

Higgins. Public house. Yes?

Doolittle. The poor man's club, Governor: why shouldnt I?

Pickering. Do let him tell his story, Higgins.

Doolittle. He told me what was up. And I ask you, what was my feelings and my duty as a father? I says to the boy, "You bring me the luggage," I says—

Pickering. Why didnt you go for it yourself?

Doolittle. Landlady wouldnt have trusted me with it, Governor. She's that kind of woman: you know. I had to give the boy a penny afore he trusted me with it, the little swine. I brought it to her just to oblige you like, and make myself agreeable. Thats all.

Higgins. How much luggage?

Doolittle. Musical instrument, Governor. A few pictures, a trifle of jewelry, and a bird-cage. She said she didnt want no clothes. What was I to think from that, Governor? I ask you as a parent what was I to think?

Higgins. So you came to rescue her from worse than death, eh?

Doolittle (*appreciatively: relieved at being so well understood*) Just so, Governor. Thats right.

Pickering. But why did you bring her luggage if you intended to take her away?

Doolittle. Have I said a word about taking her away? Have I now?

Higgins (*determinedly*) Youre going to take her away, double quick. (*He crosses to the hearth and rings the bell*).

Doolittle (*rising*) No, Governor. Dont say that. I'm not the man to stand in my girl's light. Heres a career opening for her, as you might say; and—

Mrs Pearce opens the door and awaits orders.

Higgins. Mrs Pearce: this is Eliza's father. He has come to take her away. Give her to

---

3. *most . . . melancholy,* line 62 from Milton's "Il Penseroso" (see page 213).

him. (*He goes back to the piano, with an air of washing his hands of the whole affair*).

Doolittle. No. This is a misunderstanding. Listen here—

Mrs Pearce. He cant take her away, Mr Higgins: how can he? You told me to burn her clothes.

Doolittle. Thats right. I cant carry the girl through the streets like a blooming monkey, can I? I put it to you.

Higgins. You have put it to me that you want your daughter. Take your daughter. If she has no clothes go out and buy her some.

Doolittle (*desperate*) Wheres the clothes she come in? Did I burn them or did your missus here?

Mrs Pearce. I am the housekeeper, if you please. I have sent for some clothes for your girl. When they come you can take her away. You can wait in the kitchen. This way, please.

Doolittle, much troubled, accompanies her to the door; then hesitates; finally turns confidently to Higgins.

Doolittle. Listen here, Governor. You and me is men of the world, aint we?

Higgins. Oh! Men of the world, are we? Youd better go, Mrs Pearce.

Mrs Pearce. I think so, indeed, sir. (*She goes, with dignity*).

Pickering. The floor is yours, Mr Doolittle.

Doolittle (*to Pickering*) I thank you, Governor. (*To Higgins, who takes refuge on the piano bench, a little overwhelmed by the proximity of his visitor; for Doolittle has a professional flavor of dust about him*). Well, the truth is, Ive taken a sort of fancy to you, Governor; and if you want the girl, I'm not so set on having her back home again but what I might be open to an arrangement. Regarded in the light of a young woman, she's a fine handsome girl. As a daughter she's not worth her keep; and so I tell you straight. All I ask is my rights as a father; and youre the last man alive to expect me to let her go for nothing; for I can see youre one of the straight sort, Governor. Well, whats a five-pound note to you? And whats Eliza to me? (*He returns to his chair and sits down judicially*).

Pickering. I think you ought to know,

Doolittle, that Mr Higgins's intentions are entirely honorable.

Doolittle. Course they are, Governor. If I thought they wasnt, I'd ask fifty.

Higgins (*revolted*) Do you mean to say, you callous rascal, that you would sell your daughter for £50?

Doolittle. Not in a general way I wouldnt; but to oblige a gentleman like you I'd do a good deal, I do assure you.

Pickering. Have you no morals, man?

Doolittle (*unabashed*) Cant afford them, Governor. Neither could you if you was as poor as me. Not that I mean any harm, you know. But if Liza is going to have a bit out of this, why not me too?

Higgins (*troubled*) I dont know what to do, Pickering. There can be no question that as a matter of morals it's a positive crime to give this chap a farthing. And yet I feel a sort of rough justice in his claim.

Doolittle. Thats it, Governor. Thats all I say. A father's heart, as it were.

Pickering. Well, I know the feeling; but really it seems hardly right—

Doolittle. Dont say that, Governor. Dont look at it that way. What am I, Governors both? I ask you, what am I? I'm one of the undeserving poor: thats what I am. Think of what that means to a man. It means that he's up agen middle class morality all the time. If theres anything going, and I put in for a bit of it, it's always the same story: "Youre undeserving; so you cant have it." But my needs is as great as the most deserving widow's that ever got money out of six different charities in one week for the death of the same husband. I dont need less than a deserving man: I need more. I dont eat less hearty than him; and I drink a lot more. I want a bit of amusement, cause I'm a thinking man. I want cheerfulness and a song and a band when I feel low. Well, they charge me just the same for everything as they charge the deserving. What is middle class morality? Just an excuse for never giving me anything. Therefore, I ask you, as two gentlemen, not to play that game on me. I'm playing straight with you. I aint pretending to be deserving. I'm undeserving; and I mean to go on being undeserving. I like it; and thats the truth. Will you take advantage of a man's nature to do him out of the price of his own daughter what he's brought up and fed and clothed by the sweat of his brow until she's growed big enough to be interesting to you two gentlemen? Is five pounds unreasonable? I put it to you; and I leave it to you.

Higgins (*rising, and going over to Pickering*) Pickering: if we were to take this man in hand for three months, he could choose between a seat in the Cabinet and a popular pulpit in Wales.

Pickering. What do you say to that, Doolittle?

Doolittle. Not me, Governor, thank you kindly. Ive heard all the preachers and all the prime ministers—for I'm a thinking man and game for politics or religion or social reform same as all the other amusements—and I tell you it's a dog's life any way you look at it. Undeserving poverty is my line. Taking one station in society with another, it's—it's—well, it's the only one that has any ginger in it, to my taste.

Higgins. I suppose we must give him a fiver.

Pickering. He'll make a bad use of it, I'm afraid.

Doolittle. Not me, Governor, so help me I wont. Dont you be afraid that I'll save it and spare it and live idle on it. There wont be a penny of it left by Monday: I'll have to go to work same as if I'd never had it. It wont pauperize me, you bet. Just one good spree for myself and the missus, giving pleasure to ourselves and employment to others, and satisfaction to you to think it's not been throwed away. You couldnt spend it better.

Higgins (*taking out his pocket book and coming between Doolittle and the piano*) This is irresistible. Lets give him ten. (*He offers two notes to the dustman*).

Doolittle. No, Governor. She wouldnt have the heart to spend ten; and perhaps I shouldnt neither. Ten pounds is a lot of money: it makes a man feel prudent like; and then goodbye to happiness. You give me what I ask you, Governor: not a penny more, and not a penny less.

Pickering. Why dont you marry that missus of yours? I rather draw the line at encouraging that sort of immorality.

Doolittle. Tell her so, Governor; tell her so. I'm willing. It's me that suffers by it. Ive no hold on her. I got to be agreeable to her. I got to give her presents. I got to buy her clothes something sinful. I'm a slave to that woman, Governor, just because I'm not her lawful husband. And she knows it too. Catch her marrying me! Take my advice, Governor: marry Eliza while she's young and dont know no better. If you dont youll be sorry for it after. If you do, she'll be sorry for it after; but better her than you, because youre a man, and she's only a woman and dont know how to be happy anyhow.

Higgins. Pickering: if we listen to this man another minute, we shall have no convictions left. (*To Doolittle*) Five pounds I think you said.

Doolittle. Thank you kindly, Governor.

Higgins. Youre sure you wont take ten?

Doolittle. Not now. Another time, Governor.

Higgins (*handing him a five-pound note*) Here you are.

Doolittle. Thank you, Governor. Good morning. (*He hurries to the door, anxious to get away with his booty. When he opens it he is confronted with a dainty and exquisitely clean young Japanese lady in a simple blue cotton kimono printed cunningly with small white jasmine blossoms. Mrs Pearce is with her. He gets out of her way deferentially and apologizes*). Beg pardon, miss.

The Japanese Lady. Garn! Dont you know your own daughter?

Doolittle		exclaiming		Bly me! it's Eliza!
Higgins	}	simul-	{	Whats that! This!
Pickering		taneously		By Jove!

Liza. Dont I look silly?

Higgins. Silly?

Mrs Pearce (*at the door*) Now, Mr Higgins, please dont say anything to make the girl conceited about herself.

Higgins (*conscientiously*) Oh! Quite right, Mrs Pearce. (*To Eliza*) Yes: damned silly.

Mrs Pearce. Please, sir.

Higgins (*correcting himself*) I mean extremely silly.

Liza. I should look all right with my hat on. (*She takes up her hat; puts it on; and walks across the room to the fireplace with a fashionable air*).

Higgins. A new fashion, by George! And it ought to look horrible!

Doolittle (*with fatherly pride*) Well, I never thought she'd clean up as good looking as that, Governor. She's a credit to me, aint she?

Liza. I tell you, it's easy to clean up here. Hot and cold water on tap, just as much as you like, there is. Woolly towels, there is; and a towel horse so hot, it burns your fingers. Soft brushes to scrub yourself, and a wooden bowl of soap smelling like primroses. Now I know why ladies is so clean. Washing's a treat for them. Wish they saw what it is for the like of me!

Higgins. I'm glad the bathroom met with your approval.

Liza. It didnt: not all of it; and I dont care who hears me say it. Mrs Pearce knows.

Higgins. What was wrong, Mrs Pearce?

Mrs Pearce (*blandly*) Oh, nothing, sir. It doesnt matter.

Liza. I had a good mind to break it. I didnt know which way to look. But I hung a towel over it, I did.

Higgins. Over what?

Mrs Pearce. Over the looking glass, sir.

Higgins. Doolittle: you have brought your daughter up too strictly.

Doolittle. Me! I never brought her up at all, except to give her a lick of a strap now and again. Dont put it on me, Governor. She aint accustomed to it, you see: thats all. But she'll soon pick up your free-and-easy ways.

Liza. I'm a good girl, I am; and I wont pick up no free-and-easy ways.

Higgins. Eliza: if you say again that youre a good girl, your father shall take you home.

Liza. Not him. You dont know my father. All he come here for was to touch you for some money to get drunk on.

Doolittle. Well, what else would I want money for? To put into the plate in church,

I suppose. (*She puts out her tongue at him. He is so incensed by this that Pickering presently finds it necessary to step between them*). Dont you give me none of your lip; and dont let me hear you giving this gentleman any of it neither, or youll hear from me about it. See?

Higgins. Have you any further advice to give her before you go, Doolittle? Your blessing, for instance.

Doolittle. No, Governor, I aint such a mug as to put up my children to all I know myself. Hard enough to hold them in without that. If you want Eliza's mind improved, Governor, you do it yourself with a strap. So long, gentlemen. (*He turns to go*).

Higgins (*impressively*) Stop. Youll come regularly to see your daughter. It's your duty, you know. My brother is a clergyman; and he could help you in your talks with her.

Doolittle (*evasively*) Certainly. I'll come, Governor. Not just this week, because I have a job at a distance. But later on you may depend on me. Afternoon, gentlemen. Afternoon, maam. (*He takes off his hat to Mrs Pearce, who disdains the salutation and goes out. He winks at Higgins, thinking him probably a fellow-sufferer from Mrs Pearce's difficult disposition, and follows her*).

Liza. Dont you believe the old liar. He'd as soon you set a bull-dog on him as a clergyman. You wont see him again in a hurry.

Higgins. I dont want to, Eliza. Do you?

Liza. Not me. I dont want never to see him again, I dont. He's a disgrace to me, he is, collecting dust, instead of working at his trade.

Pickering. What is his trade, Eliza?

Liza. Taking money out of other people's pockets into his own. His proper trade's a navvy[4]; and he works at it sometimes too—for exercise—and earns good money at it. Aint you going to call me Miss Doolittle any more?

Pickering. I beg your pardon, Miss Doolittle. It was a slip of the tongue.

Liza. Oh, I dont mind; only it sounded so genteel. I should just like to take a taxi to

---

4. *navvy,* unskilled laborer, especially one doing excavation or construction work. [*British*]

the corner of Tottenham Court Road and get out there and tell it to wait for me, just to put the girls in their place a bit. I wouldnt speak to them, you know.

Pickering. Better wait til we get you something really fashionable.

Higgins. Besides, you shouldnt cut your old friends now that you have risen in the world. Thats what we call snobbery.

Liza. You dont call the like of them my friends now, I should hope. Theyve took it out of me often enough with their ridicule when they had the chance; and now I mean to get a bit of my own back. But if I'm to have fashionable clothes, I'll wait. I should like to have some. Mrs Pearce says youre going to give me some to wear in bed at night different to what I wear in the daytime; but it do seem a waste of money when you could get something to shew. Besides, I never could fancy changing into cold things on a winter night.

Mrs Pearce (coming back) Now, Eliza. The new things have come for you to try on.

Liza. Ah-ow-oo-ooh! (*She rushes out*).

Mrs Pearce (following her) Oh, dont rush about like that, girl. (*She shuts the door behind her*).

Higgins. Pickering: we have taken on a stiff job.

Pickering (with conviction) Higgins: we have.

To increase understanding

1. Why has Eliza come to see Professor Higgins?
2. Professor Higgins says that he will make "a duchess of this draggletailed guttersnipe." (*a*) What does he mean, and what does the statement reveal about him? (*b*) What arguments are put forth against using Eliza as a guinea pig? (*c*) How does Professor Higgins answer each objection? (*d*) What do his arguments reveal about his personality?
3. How does Colonel Pickering's personality differ from Higgins'?
4. (*a*) Why has Alfred Doolittle come to see Professor Higgins? (*b*) Why does Higgins offer him ten pounds? (*c*) Why won't Doolittle accept it?

Better reading
Comedy of ideas

The gay Elizabethan era gave rise to *romantic comedy,* a type of play in which love's smooth course is constantly set awry by obstacles until the last scene, when all ends well. The social conventions of the seventeenth and eighteenth centuries provided character types and plots for the *comedy of manners* (page 324). Good comedy did not appear again until the twentieth century, and the form in which it has been best developed in England is the *comedy of ideas.* Shaw is undeniably its master.

The main difference between the *comedy of ideas* and other forms of comedy is that it does not depend on situation or intrigue for its humor. Instead of laughing at an unexpected situation, we laugh at unexpected ideas which are cleverly expressed and developed. The humor, which appeals to the intellect, is created for a serious purpose. This form of comedy is especially appropriate for modern audiences since more people are able to read plays than to see them performed, and the humor depends more on a mental process than on a visual one.

The plot of *Pygmalion* advances but little in Act II, and it is Shaw's sallies into the world of ideas that make the act exciting. He comments upon several ideas which are only incidentally related to the plot, although they are related to the theme. For instance, the plot in Act II consists of Eliza's decision to study phonetics with Professor Higgins and the arrangements under which this is to be accomplished. From such a small wedge Shaw leads his characters into critical conversations on Victorian ideals of manners, marriage, parenthood, and morals. Since the middle and upper classes, at whom these criticisms are aimed, comprise his audiences, he softens his criticisms through comedy.

Eliza makes comments about "being a lady." We know she is objective because she speaks as an outsider. What, according to her comments, makes the difference between someone who is a lady and someone who is not? If you find her ideas amusing, you are amused by the absurdity of social manners which you ordinarily accept with seriousness. Is Shaw making fun of Eliza or of you, the audience?

It is through Alfred Doolittle that Shaw expresses most of his ideas. What are Doolittle's views on marriage? What does Professor Higgins have to say about this subject? What does Doolittle have to say about the Victorian ideals of the authority of parenthood? Doolittle's most famous views are about middle-class morality. How does he define it? What does he mean when he says he can't afford to have morals? What class or classes seem to be the main objects of Shaw's satire here?

ACT THREE

It is Mrs Higgins's at-home day. Nobody has yet arrived. Her drawing room, in a flat on Chelsea Embankment,[1] has three windows looking on the river; and the ceiling is not so lofty as it would be in an older house of the same pretension. The windows are open, giving access to a balcony with flowers in pots. If you stand with your face to the windows, you have the fireplace on your left and the door in the right-hand wall close to the corner nearest the windows.

Mrs Higgins was brought up on Morris and Burne Jones;[2] and her room, which is very unlike her son's room in Wimpole Street, is not crowded with furniture and little tables and nicknacks. In the middle of the room there is a big ottoman; and this, with the carpet, the Morris wall-papers, and the Morris chintz window curtains and brocade covers of the ottoman and its cushions, supply all the ornament, and are much too handsome to be hidden by odds and ends of useless things. A few good oil-paintings from the exhibitions in the Grosvenor Gallery thirty years ago (the Burne Jones, not the Whistler side of them) are on the walls. The only landscape is a Cecil Lawson on the scale of a Rubens. There is a portrait of Mrs Higgins as she was when she defied fashion in her youth in one of the beautiful Rosettian costumes which, when caricatured by people who did not understand, led to the absurdities of popular estheticism in the eighteen-seventies.

In the corner diagonally opposite the door Mrs Higgins, now over sixty and long past taking the trouble to dress out of the fashion, sits writing at an elegantly simple writing-table with a bell button within reach of her hand. There is a Chippendale chair further back in the room between her and the window nearest her side. At the other side of the room, further forward, is an Elizabethan chair roughly carved in the taste of Inigo Jones. On the same side a piano in a decorated case. The corner between the fireplace and the window is occupied by a divan cushioned in Morris chintz.

It is between four and five in the afternoon.

The door is opened violently; and Higgins enters with his hat on.

Mrs Higgins (dismayed) Henry (scolding him)! What are you doing here to-day? It is my at-home day: you promised not to come. (As he bends to kiss her, she takes his hat off, and presents it to him).

Higgins. Oh bother! (He throws the hat down on the table).

Mrs Higgins. Go home at once.

Higgins (kissing her) I know, mother. I came on purpose.

Mrs Higgins. But you mustnt. I'm serious, Henry. You offend all my friends: they stop coming whenever they meet you.

Higgins. Nonsense! I know I have no small talk; but people dont mind. (He sits on the settee).

Mrs Higgins. Oh! dont they? Small talk indeed! What about your large talk? Really, dear, you mustnt stay.

Higgins. I must. Ive a job for you. A phonetic job.

Mrs Higgins. No use, dear. I'm sorry; but I cant get round your vowels; and though I like to get pretty postcards in your patent shorthand, I always have to read the copies in ordinary writing you so thoughtfully send me.

Higgins. Well, this isnt a phonetic job.

Mrs Higgins. You said it was.

Higgins. Not your part of it. Ive picked up a girl.

Mrs Higgins. Does that mean that some girl has picked you up?

Higgins. Not at all. I dont mean a love affair.

Mrs Higgins. What a pity!

Higgins. Why?

Mrs Higgins. Well, you never fall in love with anyone under forty-five. When will you

---

1. *Chelsea Embankment.* Chelsea is a pleasant residential district along the bank of the Thames. 2. *Morris and Burne Jones.* William Morris and Burne Jones (1833-1898) were members of a decorating firm noted for fine carvings, stained glass, metalwork, paper hangings, chintzes and carpets. (See the article "The Pre-Raphaelite Brotherhood," page 464.)

discover that there are some rather nice-looking young women about?

Higgins. Oh, I cant be bothered with young women. My idea of a lovable woman is something as like you as possible. I shall never get into the way of seriously liking young women: some habits lie too deep to be changed. (*Rising abruptly and walking about, jingling his money and his keys in his trouser pockets*) Besides, theyre all idiots.

Mrs Higgins. Do you know what you would do if you really loved me, Henry?

Higgins. Oh bother! What? Marry, I suppose?

Mrs Higgins. No. Stop fidgeting and take your hands out of your pockets. (*With a gesture of despair, he obeys and sits down again*). Thats a good boy. Now tell me about the girl.

Higgins. She's coming to see you.

Mrs Higgins. I dont remember asking her.

Higgins. You didnt. *I* asked her. If youd known her you wouldnt have asked her.

Mrs Higgins. Indeed! Why?

Higgins. Well, it's like this. She's a common flower girl. I picked her off the kerbstone.

Mrs Higgins. And invited her to my at-home!

Higgins (*rising and coming to her to coax her*) Oh, thatll be all right. Ive taught her to speak properly; and she has strict orders as to her behavior. She's to keep to two subjects: the weather and everybody's health— Fine day and How do you do, you know— and not to let herself go on things in general. That will be safe.

Mrs Higgins. Safe! To talk about our health! about our insides! perhaps about our outsides! How could you be so silly, Henry?

Higgins (*impatiently*) Well, she must talk about something. (*He controls himself and sits down again*). Oh, she'll be all right: dont you fuss. Pickering is in it with me. Ive a sort of bet on that I'll pass her off as a duchess in six months. I started on her some months ago; and she's getting on like a house on fire. I shall win my bet. She has a quick ear; and she's been easier to teach than my middle class pupils because she's had to learn a com-

plete new language. She talks English almost as you talk French.

Mrs Higgins. Thats satisfactory, at all events.

Higgins. Well, it is and it isnt.

Mrs Higgins. What does that mean?

Higgins. You see, Ive got her pronunciation all right; but you have to consider not only how a girl pronounces, but what she pronounces; and thats where—

They are interrupted by the parlor-maid, announcing guests.

The Parlor-Maid. Mrs and Miss Eynsford Hill. (*She withdraws*).

Higgins. Oh Lord! (*He rises; snatches his hat from the table; and makes for the door; but before he reaches it his mother introduces him*).

Mrs and Miss Eynsford Hill are the mother and daughter who sheltered from the rain in Covent Garden. The mother is well bred, quiet, and has the habitual anxiety of straitened means. The daughter has acquired a gay air of being very much at home in society: the bravado of genteel poverty.

Mrs Eynsford Hill (*to Mrs Higgins*) How do you do? (*They shake hands*).

Miss Eynsford Hill. How d'you do? (*She shakes*).

Mrs Higgins (*introducing*) My son Henry.

Mrs Eynsford Hill. Your celebrated son! I have so longed to meet you, Professor Higgins.

Higgins (*glumly, making no movement in her direction*) Delighted. (*He backs against the piano and bows brusquely*).

Miss Eynsford Hill (*going to him with confident familiarity*) How do you do?

Higgins (*staring at her*) Ive seen you before somewhere. I havnt the ghost of a notion where; but Ive heard your voice. (*Drearily*) It doesnt matter. Youd better sit down.

Mrs Higgins. I'm sorry to say that my celebrated son has no manners. You mustnt mind him.

Miss Eynsford Hill (*gaily*) I dont. (*She sits in the Elizabethan chair*).

Mrs Eynsford Hill (*a little bewildered*) Not at all. (*She sits on the ottoman between her daughter and Mrs Higgins, who has *turned her chair away from the writing-table*).

Higgins. Oh, have I been rude? I didnt mean to be.

He goes to the central window, through which, with his back to the company, he contemplates the river and the flowers in Battersea Park on the opposite bank as if they were a frozen desert.

The parlor-maid returns, ushering in Pickering.

The Parlor-Maid. Colonel Pickering. (*She withdraws*).

Pickering. How do you do, Mrs Higgins?

Mrs Higgins. So glad youve come. Do you know Mrs Eynsford Hill—Miss Eynsford Hill? (*Exchange of bows. The Colonel brings the Chippendale chair a little forward between Mrs Hill and Mrs Higgins, and sits down*).

Pickering. Has Henry told you what weve come for?

Higgins (*over his shoulder*) We were interrupted: damn it!

Mrs Higgins. Oh Henry, Henry, really!

Mrs Eynsford Hill (*half rising*) Are we in the way?

Mrs Higgins (*rising and making her sit down again*) No, no. You couldnt have come more fortunately: we want you to meet a friend of ours.

Higgins (*turning hopefully*) Yes, by George! We want two or three people. Youll do as well as anybody else.

The parlor-maid returns, ushering Freddy.

The Parlor-Maid. Mr Eynsford Hill.

Higgins (*almost audibly, past endurance*) God of Heaven! another of them.

Freddy (*shaking hands with Mrs Higgins*) Ahdedo?

Mrs Higgins. Very good of you to come. (*Introducing*) Colonel Pickering.

Freddy (*bowing*) Ahdedo?

Mrs Higgins. I dont think you know my son, Professor Higgins.

Freddy (*going to Higgins*) Ahdedo?

Higgins (*looking at him much as if he were a pickpocket*) I'll take my oath Ive met you before somewhere. Where was it?

Freddy. I dont think so.

Higgins (*resignedly*) It dont matter, anyhow. Sit down.

He shakes Freddy's hand, and almost slings him on to the ottoman with his face to the windows; then comes round to the other side of it.

Higgins. Well, here we are, anyhow! (*He sits down on the ottoman next Mrs Eynsford Hill, on her left*). And now, what the devil are we going to talk about until Eliza comes?

Mrs Higgins. Henry: you are the life and soul of the Royal Society's soirées; but really youre rather trying on more commonplace occasions.

Higgins. Am I? Very sorry. (*Beaming suddenly*) I suppose I am, you know. (*Uproariously*) Ha, ha!

Miss Eynsford Hill (*who considers Higgins quite eligible matrimonially*) I sympathize. I havnt any small talk. If people would only be frank and say what they really think!

Higgins (*relapsing into gloom*) Lord forbid!

Mrs Eynsford Hill (*taking up her daughter's cue*) But why?

Higgins. What they think they ought to think is bad enough, Lord knows; but what they really think would break up the whole show. Do you suppose it would be really agreeable if I were to come out now with what I really think?

Miss Eynsford Hill (*gaily*) Is it so very cynical?

Higgins. Cynical! Who the dickens said it was cynical? I mean it wouldnt be decent.

Mrs Eynsford Hill (*seriously*) Oh! I'm sure you dont mean that, Mr Higgins.

Higgins. You see, we're all savages, more or less. We're supposed to be civilized and cultured—to know all about poetry and philosophy and art and science, and so on; but how many of us know even the meanings of these names? (*To Miss Hill*) What do you know of poetry? (*To Mrs Hill*) What do you know of science? (*Indicating Freddy*) What does he know of art or science or anything else? What the devil do you imagine I know of philosophy?

Mrs Higgins (*warningly*) Or of manners, Henry?

The Parlor-Maid (*opening the door*) Miss Doolittle. (*She withdraws*).

Higgins (*rising hastily and running to Mrs Higgins*) Here she is, mother. (*He stands on tiptoe and makes signs over his mother's head to Eliza to indicate to her which lady is her hostess*).

Eliza, *who is exquisitely dressed, produces an impression of such remarkable distinction and beauty as she enters that they all rise, quite fluttered. Guided by Higgins's signals, she comes to Mrs Higgins with studied grace.*

Liza (*speaking with pedantic correctness of pronunciation and great beauty of tone*) How do you do, Mrs Higgins? (*She gasps slightly in making sure of the H in Higgins, but is quite successful*). Mr Higgins told me I might come.

Mrs Higgins (*cordially*) Quite right: I'm very glad indeed to see you.

Pickering. How do you do, Miss Doolittle?

Liza (*shaking hands with him*) Colonel Pickering, is it not?

Mrs Eynsford Hill. I feel sure we have met before, Miss Doolittle. I remember your eyes.

Liza. How do you do? (*She sits down on the ottoman gracefully in the place just left vacant by Higgins*).

Mrs Eynsford Hill (*introducing*) My daughter Clara.

Liza. How do you do?

Clara (*impulsively*) How do you do? (*She sits down on the ottoman beside Eliza, devouring her with her eyes*).

Freddy (*coming to their side of the ottoman*) Ive certainly had the pleasure.

Mrs Eynsford Hill (*introducing*) My son Freddy.

Liza. How do you do?

Freddy bows and sits down in the Elizabethan chair, infatuated.

Higgins (*suddenly*) By George, yes: it all comes back to me! (*They stare at him*). Covent Garden! (*Lamentably*) What a damned thing!

Mrs Higgins. Henry, please! (*He is about to sit on the edge of the table*) Dont sit on my writing-table: youll break it.

Higgins (*sulkily*) Sorry.

He goes to the divan, stumbling into the fender and over the fire-irons on his way; extricating himself with muttered imprecations; and finishing his disastrous journey by throwing himself so impatiently on the divan that he almost breaks it. Mrs Higgins looks at him, but controls herself and says nothing.

A long and painful pause ensues.

Mrs Higgins (*at last, conversationally*) Will it rain, do you think?

Liza. The shallow depression in the west of these islands is likely to move slowly in an easterly direction. There are no indications of any great change in the barometrical situation.

Freddy. Ha! ha! how awfully funny!

Liza. What is wrong with that, young man? I bet I got it right.

Freddy. Killing!

Mrs Eynsford Hill. I'm sure I hope it wont turn cold. Theres so much influenza about. It runs right through our whole family regularly every spring.

Liza (*darkly*) My aunt died of influenza: so they said.

Mrs Eynsford Hill (*clicks her tongue sympathetically*)!!!

Liza (*in the same tragic tone*) But it's my belief they done the old woman in.

Mrs Higgins (*puzzled*) Done her in?

Liza. Y-e-e-e-es, Lord love you! Why should she die of influenza? She come through diphtheria right enough the year before. I saw her with my own eyes. Fairly blue with it, she was. They all thought she was dead; but my father he kept ladling gin down her throat til she came to so sudden that she bit the bowl off the spoon.

Mrs Eynsford Hill (*startled*) Dear me!

Liza (*piling up the indictment*) What call would a woman with that strength in her have to die of influenza? What become of her new straw hat that should have come to me? Somebody pinched it; and what I say is, them as pinched it done her in.

Mrs Eynsford Hill. What does doing her in mean?

Higgins (*hastily*) Oh, thats the new small talk. To do a person in means to kill them.

Mrs Eynsford Hill (*to Eliza, horrified*) You surely dont believe that your aunt was killed?

Liza. Do I not! Them she lived with would have killed her for a hat-pin, let alone a hat.

Mrs Eynsford Hill. But it cant have been right for your father to pour spirits down her throat like that. It might have killed her.

Liza. Not her. Gin was mother's milk to her. Besides, he'd poured so much down his own throat that he knew the good of it.

Mrs Eynsford Hill. Do you mean that he drank?

Liza. Drank! My word! Something chronic.

Mrs Eynsford Hill. How dreadful for you!

Liza. Not a bit. It never did him no harm what I could see. But then he did not keep it up regular. (*Cheerfully*) On the burst, as you might say, from time to time. And always more agreeable when he had a drop in. When he was out of work, my mother used to give him fourpence and tell him to go out and not come back until he'd drunk himself cheerful and loving-like. Theres lots of women has to make their husbands drunk to make them fit to live with. (*Now quite at her ease*) You see, it's like this. If a man has a bit of a conscience, it always takes him when he's sober; and then it makes him low-spirited. A drop of booze just takes that off and makes him happy. (*To Freddy, who is in convulsions of suppressed laughter*) Here! what are you sniggering at?

Freddy. The new small talk. You do it so awfully well.

Liza. If I was doing it proper, what was you laughing at? (*To Higgins*) Have I said anything I oughtnt?

Mrs Higgins (*interposing*) Not at all, Miss Doolittle.

Liza. Well, thats a mercy, anyhow. (*Expansively*) What I always say is—

Higgins (*rising and looking at his watch*) Ahem!

Liza (*looking round at him; taking the hint; and rising*) Well: I must go. (*They all*

rise, *Freddy goes to the door*). So pleased to have met you. Goodbye. (*She shakes hands with Mrs Higgins*).

Mrs Higgins. Goodbye.

Liza. Goodbye, Colonel Pickering.

Pickering. Goodbye, Miss Doolittle. (*They shake hands*).

Liza (*nodding to the others*) Goodbye, all.

Freddy (*opening the door for her*) Are you walking across the Park, Miss Doolittle? If so—

Liza. Walk! Not bloody likely. (*Sensation*). I am going in a taxi. (*She goes out*).

Pickering gasps and sits down. Freddy goes out on the balcony to catch another glimpse of Eliza.

Mrs Eynsford Hill (*suffering from shock*) Well, I really cant get used to the new ways.

Clara (*throwing herself discontentedly into the Elizabethan chair*) Oh, it's all right, mamma, quite right. People will think we never go anywhere or see anybody if you are so old-fashioned.

Mrs Eynsford Hill. I daresay I am very old-fashioned; but I do hope you wont begin using that expression, Clara. I have got accustomed to hear you talking about men as rotters, and calling everything filthy and beastly; though I do think it horrible and unladylike. But this last is really too much. Dont you think so, Colonel Pickering?

Pickering. Dont ask me. Ive been away in India for several years; and manners have changed so much that I sometimes dont know whether I'm at a respectable dinner-table or in a ship's forecastle.

Clara. It's all a matter of habit. Theres no right or wrong in it. Nobody means anything by it. And it's so quaint, and gives such a smart emphasis to things that are not in themselves very witty. I find the new small talk delightful and quite innocent.

Mrs Eynsford Hill (*rising*) Well, after that, I think it's time for us to go.

Pickering and Higgins rise.

Clara (*rising*) Oh yes: we have three at-homes to go to still. Goodbye, Mrs Higgins. Goodbye, Colonel Pickering. Goodbye, Professor Higgins.

Higgins (*coming grimly at her from the*

divan, and accompanying her to the door) Goodbye. Be sure you try on that small talk at the three at-homes. Dont be nervous about it. Pitch it in strong.

Clara (all smiles) I will. Goodbye. Such nonsense, all this early Victorian prudery!

Higgins (tempting her) Such damned nonsense!

Clara. Such bloody nonsense!

Mrs Eynsford Hill (convulsively) Clara!

Clara. Ha! ha! *(She goes out radiant, conscious of being thoroughly up to date, and is heard descending the stairs in a stream of silvery laughter).*

Freddy (to the heavens at large) Well, I ask you— *(He gives it up, and comes to Mrs Higgins).* Goodbye.

Mrs Higgins (shaking hands) Goodbye. Would you like to meet Miss Doolittle again?

Freddy (eagerly) Yes, I should, most awfully.

Mrs Higgins. Well, you know my days.

Freddy. Yes. Thanks awfully. Goodbye. *(He goes out).*

Mrs Eynsford Hill. Goodbye, Mr Higgins.

Higgins. Goodbye. Goodbye.

Mrs Eynsford Hill (to Pickering) It's no use. I shall never be able to bring myself to use that word.

Pickering. Dont. It's not compulsory, you know. Youll get on quite well without it.

Mrs Eynsford Hill. Only, Clara is so down on me if I am not positively reeking with the latest slang. Goodbye.

Pickering. Goodbye. *(They shake hands).*

Mrs Eynsford Hill (to Mrs Higgins) You mustnt mind Clara. *(Pickering, catching from her lowered tone that this is not meant for him to hear, discreetly joins Higgins at the window).* We're so poor! and she gets so few parties, poor child! She doesnt quite know. *(Mrs Higgins, seeing that her eyes are moist, takes her hand sympathetically and goes with her to the door).* But the boy is nice. Dont you think so?

Mrs Higgins. Oh, quite nice. I shall always be delighted to see him.

Mrs Eynsford Hill. Thank you, dear. Goodbye. *(She goes out).*

Higgins (eagerly) Well? Is Eliza presentable? *(He swoops on his mother and drags her to the ottoman, where she sits down in Eliza's place with her son on her left).*

Pickering returns to his chair on her right.

Mrs Higgins. You silly boy, of course she's not presentable. She's a triumph of your art and of her dressmaker's; but if you suppose for a moment that she doesnt give herself away in every sentence she utters, you must be perfectly cracked about her.

Pickering. But dont you think something might be done? I mean something to eliminate the sanguinary element from her conversation.

Mrs Higgins. Not as long as she is in Henry's hands.

Higgins (aggrieved) Do you mean that my language is improper?

Mrs Higgins. No, dearest: it would be quite proper—say on a canal barge; but it would not be proper for her at a garden party.

Higgins (deeply injured) Well I must say—

Pickering (interrupting him) Come, Higgins: you must learn to know yourself. I havnt heard such language as yours since we used to review the volunteers in Hyde Park twenty years ago.

Higgins (sulkily) Oh, well, if you say so, I suppose I dont always talk like a bishop.

Mrs Higgins (quieting Henry with a touch) Colonel Pickering: will you tell me what is the exact state of things in Wimpole Street?

Pickering (cheerfully: as if this completely changed the subject) Well, I have come to live there with Henry. We work together at my Indian Dialects; and we think it more convenient—

Mrs Higgins. Quite so. I know all about that: it's an excellent arrangement. But where does this girl live?

Higgins. With us, of course. Where should she live?

Mrs Higgins. But on what terms? Is she a servant? If not, what is she?

Pickering (slowly) I think I know what you mean, Mrs Higgins.

Higgins. Well, dash me if *I* do! Ive had

to work at the girl every day for months to get her to her present pitch. Besides, she's useful. She knows where my things are, and remembers my appointments and so forth.

Mrs Higgins. How does your housekeeper get on with her?

Higgins. Mrs Pearce? Oh, she's jolly glad to get so much taken off her hands; for before Eliza came, she used to have to find things and remind me of my appointments. But she's got some silly bee in her bonnet about Eliza. She keeps saying "You dont think, sir": doesnt she, Pick?

Pickering. Yes: thats the formula. "You dont think, sir." Thats the end of every conversation about Eliza.

Higgins. As if I ever stop thinking about the girl and her confounded vowels and consonants. I'm worn out, thinking about her, and watching her lips and her teeth and her tongue, not to mention her soul, which is the quaintest of the lot.

Mrs Higgins. You certainly are a pretty pair of babies, playing with your live doll.

Higgins. Playing! The hardest job I ever tackled: make no mistake about that, mother. But you have no idea how frightfully interesting it is to take a human being and change her into a quite different human being by creating a new speech for her. It's filling up the deepest gulf that separates class from class and soul from soul.

Pickering (drawing his chair closer to Mrs Higgins and bending over to her eagerly) Yes: it's enormously interesting. I assure you, Mrs Higgins, we take Eliza very seriously. Every week—every day almost—there is some new change. (*Closer again*) We keep records of every stage—dozens of gramophone disks and photographs—

Higgins (assailing her at the other ear) Yes, by George: it's the most absorbing experiment I ever tackled. She regularly fills our lives up: doesn't she, Pick?

Pickering. We're always talking Eliza.

Higgins. Teaching Eliza.

Pickering. Dressing Eliza.

Mrs Higgins. What!

Higgins. Inventing new Elizas.

	Higgins.	*Pickering.*
(*speaking together*)	You know, she has the most extraordinary quickness of ear:	I assure you, my dear Mrs Higgins, that girl
	just like a parrot. Ive tried her with every	is a genius. She can play the piano quite beautifully.
	possible sort of sound that a human being can make—	We have taken her to classical concerts and to music
	Continental dialects, African dialects, Hottentot	halls; and it's all the same to her: she plays everything
	clicks, things it took me years to get hold of; and	she hears right off when she comes home, whether it's
	she picks them up like a shot, right away, as if she had	Beethoven and Brahms or Lehar and Lionel Monckton;
	been at it all her life.	though six months ago, she'd never as much as touched a piano—

Mrs Higgins (putting her fingers in her ears, as they are by this time shouting one another down with an intolerable noise) Sh-sh-sh-sh! *(They stop)*.

Pickering. I beg your pardon. *(He draws his chair back apologetically)*.

Higgins. Sorry. When Pickering starts shouting nobody can get a word in edgeways.

Mrs Higgins. Be quiet, Henry. Colonel Pickering: dont you realize that when Eliza walked into Wimpole Street, something walked in with her?

Pickering. Her father did. But Henry soon got rid of him.

Mrs Higgins. It would have been more to the point if her mother had. But as her mother didnt something else did.

Pickering. But what?

Mrs Higgins (unconsciously dating herself by the word) A problem.

Pickering. Oh, I see. The problem of how to pass her off as a lady.

Higgins. I'll solve that problem. Ive half solved it already.

Mrs Higgins. No, you two infinitely stupid male creatures; the problem of what is to be done with her afterwards.

Higgins. I dont see anything in that. She can go her own way, with all the advantages I have given her.

Mrs Higgins. The advantages of that poor woman who was here just now! The manners and habits that disqualify a fine lady from earning her own living without giving her a fine lady's income! Is that what you mean?

Pickering (indulgently, being rather bored) Oh, that will be all right, Mrs Higgins. *(He rises to go)*.

Higgins (rising also) We'll find her some light employment.

Pickering. She's happy enough. Dont you worry about her. Goodbye. *(He shakes hands as if he were consoling a frightened child, and makes for the door)*.

Higgins. Anyhow, theres no good bothering now. The thing's done. Goodbye, mother. *(He kisses her, and follows Pickering)*.

Pickering (turning for a final consolation) There are plenty of openings. We'll do whats right. Goodbye.

A London production.

Higgins (to Pickering as they go out together) Let's take her to the Shakespear exhibition at Earls Court.

Pickering. Yes: lets. Her remarks will be delicious.

Higgins. She'll mimic all the people for us when we get home.

Pickering. Ripping. *(Both are heard laughing as they go downstairs)*.

Mrs Higgins (rises with an impatient bounce, and returns to her work at the writing table. She sweeps a litter of disarranged papers out of her way; snatches a sheet of paper from her stationery case; and tries resolutely to write. At the third line she gives it up; flings down her pen; grips the table angrily and exclaims) Oh, men! men!! men!!!

❈ To increase understanding

1. (*a*) Describe Mrs. Higgins, drawing inferences from what she says and does in this act. (*b*) What is the attitude of Professor Higgins toward his mother? (*c*) How does she regard him? (*d*) Why has Higgins brought Eliza to his mother?

2. (*a*) Cite passages to show that Eliza has not entirely mastered social amenities. (*b*) To whom does Eliza seem a complete success? (*c*) What effect does Eliza produce on Clara?

3. (*a*) What class of society is Shaw criticizing in this act? (*b*) Cite lines that show what characteristics of that class he is satirizing.

4. Explain the reason for Mrs. Higgins' anger at the end of the act.

ACT FOUR

The Wimpole Street laboratory. Midnight. Nobody in the room. The clock on the mantelpiece strikes twelve. The fire is not alight: it is a summer night.

Presently Higgins and Pickering are heard on the stairs.

Higgins (calling down to Pickering) I say, Pick: lock up, will you? I shant be going out again.

Pickering. Right. Can Mrs Pearce go to bed? We dont want anything more, do we?

Higgins. Lord, no!

Eliza opens the door and is seen on the lighted landing in opera cloak, brilliant evening dress, and diamonds, with fan, flowers, and all accessories. She comes to the hearth, and switches on the electric lights there. She is tired: her pallor contrasts strongly with her dark eyes and hair; and her expression is almost tragic. She takes off her cloak; puts her fan and flowers on the piano; and sits down on the bench, brooding and silent. Higgins, in evening dress, with overcoat and hat, comes in, carrying a smoking jacket which he has picked up downstairs. He takes off the hat and overcoat; throws them carelessly on the newspaper stand; disposes of his coat in the same way; puts on the smoking jacket; and throws himself wearily into the easy-chair at the hearth. Pickering, similarly attired, comes in. He also takes off his hat and overcoat, and is about to throw them on Higgins's when he hesitates.

Pickering. I say: Mrs Pearce will row if we leave these things lying about in the drawing room.

Higgins. Oh, chuck them over the bannisters into the hall. She'll find them there in the morning and put them away all right. She'll think we were drunk.

Pickering. We are, slightly. Are there any letters?

Higgins. I didnt look. (Pickering takes the overcoats and hats and goes downstairs. Higgins begins half singing half yawning an air from La Fanciulla del Golden West.[1] Suddenly he stops and exclaims) I wonder where the devil my slippers are!

Eliza looks at him darkly; then rises suddenly and leaves the room.

Higgins yawns again, and resumes his song.

Pickering returns, with the contents of the letter-box in his hand.

Pickering. Only circulars, and this coroneted billet-doux for you. (He throws the circulars into the fender, and posts himself on the hearthrug, with his back to the grate).

Higgins (glancing at the billet-doux) Money-lender. (He throws the letter after the circulars).

Eliza returns with a pair of large down-at-heel slippers. She places them on the carpet before Higgins, and sits as before without a word.

Higgins (yawning again) Oh Lord! What an evening! What a crew! What a silly tomfoolery! (He raises his shoe to unlace it, and catches sight of the slippers. He stops unlacing and looks at them as if they had appeared there of their own accord). Oh! theyre there, are they?

Pickering (stretching himself) Well, I feel a bit tired. It's been a long day. The garden party, a dinner party, and the opera! Rather too much of a good thing. But youve won your bet, Higgins. Eliza did the trick, and something to spare, eh?

Higgins (fervently) Thank God it's over!

Eliza flinches violently; but they take no notice of her; and she recovers herself and sits stonily as before.

Pickering. Were you nervous at the garden party! I was. Eliza didnt seem a bit nervous.

Higgins. Oh, she wasnt nervous. I knew she'd be all right. No: it's the strain of putting the job through all these months that has told on me. It was interesting enough at first, while we were at the phonetics; but after that I got deadly sick of it. If I hadnt backed myself to do it I should have chucked the whole thing up two months ago. It was a silly notion: the whole thing has been a bore.

Pickering. Oh come! the garden party was

1. La Fanciulla del Golden West, The Girl of the Golden West, an opera by Puccini that opened in New York in 1910.

frightfully exciting. My heart began beating like anything.

Higgins. Yes, for the first three minutes. But when I saw we were going to win hands down, I felt like a bear in a cage, hanging about doing nothing. The dinner was worse: sitting gorging there for over an hour, with nobody but a damned fool of a fashionable woman to talk to! I tell you, Pickering, never again for me. No more artificial duchesses. The whole thing has been simple purgatory.

Pickering. Youve never been broken in properly to the social routine. (*Strolling over to the piano*) I rather enjoy dipping into it occasionally myself: it makes me feel young again. Anyhow, it was a great success: an immense success. I was quite frightened once or twice because Eliza was doing it so well. You see, lots of the real people cant do it at all: theyre such fools that they think style comes by nature to people in their position; and so they never learn. Theres always something professional about doing a thing superlatively well.

Higgins. Yes: thats what drives me mad: the silly people dont know their own silly business. (*Rising*) However, it's over and done with; and now I can go to bed at last without dreading tomorrow.

Eliza's beauty becomes murderous.

Pickering. I think I shall turn in too. Still, it's been a great occasion: a triumph for you. Goodnight. (*He goes*).

Higgins (following him) Goodnight. (*Over his shoulder, at the door*) Put out the lights, Eliza; and tell Mrs Pearce not to make coffee for me in the morning: I'll take tea. (*He goes out*).

Eliza tries to control herself and feel indifferent as she rises and walks across to the hearth to switch off the lights. By the time she gets there she is on the point of screaming. She sits down in Higgins's chair and holds on hard to the arms. Finally she gives way and flings herself furiously on the floor, raging.

Higgins (in despairing wrath outside) What the devil have I done with my slippers? (*He appears at the door*).

Liza (snatching up the slippers, and hurling them at him one after the other with all her force) There are your slippers. And there. Take your slippers; and may you never have a day's luck with them!

Higgins (astounded) What on earth—! (*He comes to her*). What's the matter? Get up. (*He pulls her up*). Anything wrong?

Liza (breathless) Nothing wrong—with you. Ive won your bet for you, havnt I? Thats enough for you. *I* dont matter, I suppose.

Higgins. You won my bet! You! Presumptuous insect! *I* won it. What did you throw those slippers at me for?

Liza. Because I wanted to smash your face. I'd like to kill you, you selfish brute. Why didnt you leave me where you picked me out of—in the gutter? You thank God it's all over, and that now you can throw me back again there, do you? (*She crisps her fingers frantically*).

Higgins (looking at her in cool wonder) The creature is nervous, after all.

Liza (gives a suffocated scream of fury, and instinctively darts her nails at his face)!!

Higgins (catching her wrists) Ah! would you? Claws in, you cat. How dare you shew your temper to me? Sit down and be quiet. (*He throws her roughly into the easy-chair*).

Liza (crushed by superior strength and weight) Whats to become of me? Whats to become of me?

Higgins. How the devil do I know whats to become of you? What does it matter what becomes of you?

Liza. You dont care. I know you dont care. you wouldnt care if I was dead. I'm nothing to you—not so much as them slippers.

Higgins (thundering) Those slippers.

Liza (with bitter submission) Those slippers. I didnt think it made any difference now.

A pause. Eliza hopeless and crushed. Higgins a little uneasy.

Higgins (in his loftiest manner) Why have you begun going on like this? May I ask whether you complain of your treatment here?

Liza. No.

Higgins. Has anybody behaved badly to you? Colonel Pickering? Mrs Pearce? Any of the servants?

Liza. No.

Higgins. I presume you dont pretend that I have treated you badly?

Liza. No.

Higgins. I am glad to hear it. (*He moderates his tone*). Perhaps youre tired after the strain of the day. Will you have a glass of champagne? (*He moves towards the door*).

Liza. No. (*Recollecting her manners*) Thank you.

Higgins (*good-humored again*) This has been coming on you for some days. I suppose it was natural for you to be anxious about the garden party. But thats all over now. (*He pats her kindly on the shoulder. She writhes*). Theres nothing more to worry about.

Liza. No. Nothing more for you to worry about. (*She suddenly rises and gets away from him by going to the piano bench, where she sits and hides her face*). Oh God! I wish I was dead.

Higgins (*staring after her in sincere surprise*) Why? In heaven's name, why? (*Reasonably, going to her*) Listen to me, Eliza. All this irritation is purely subjective.

Liza. I dont understand. I'm too ignorant.

Higgins. It's only imagination. Low spirits and nothing else. Nobody's hurting you. Nothing's wrong. You go to bed like a good girl and sleep it off. Have a little cry and say your prayers: that will make you comfortable.

Liza. I heard your prayers. "Thank God it's all over!"

Higgins (*impatiently*) Well, dont you thank God it's all over? Now you are free and can do what you like.

Liza (*pulling herself together in desperation*) What am I fit for? What have you left me fit for? Where am I to go? What am I to do? Whats to become of me?

Higgins (*enlightened, but not at all impressed*) Oh thats whats worrying you, is it? (*He thrusts his hands into his pockets, and walks about in his usual manner, rattling the contents of his pockets, as if condescending to a trivial subject out of pure kindness*). I shouldnt bother about it if I were you. I should imagine you wont have much difficulty in settling yourself somewhere or other,

though I hadnt quite realized that you were going away. (*She looks quickly at him: he does not look at her, but examines the dessert stand on the piano and decides that he will eat an apple*). You might marry, you know. (*He bites a large piece out of the apple and munches it noisily*). You see, Eliza, all men are not confirmed old bachelors like me and the Colonel. Most men are the marrying sort (poor devils!); and youre not bad-looking: it's quite a pleasure to look at you sometimes—not now, of course, because youre crying and looking as ugly as the very devil; but when youre all right and quite yourself, youre what I should call attractive. That is, to the people in the marrying line, you understand. You go to bed and have a good nice rest; and then get up and look at yourself in the glass; and you wont feel so cheap.

Eliza again looks at him, speechless, and does not stir.

The look is quite lost on him: he eats his apple with a dreamy expression of happiness, as it is quite a good one.

Higgins (*a genial afterthought occurring to him*) I daresay my mother could find some chap or other who would do very well.

Liza. We were above that at the corner of Tottenham Court Road.

Higgins (*waking up*) What do you mean?

Liza. I sold flowers. I didnt sell myself. Now youve made a lady of me I'm not fit to sell anything else. I wish youd left me where you found me.

Higgins (*slinging the core of the apple decisively into the grate*) Tosh, Eliza. Dont you insult human relations by dragging all this cant about buying and selling into it. You neednt marry the fellow if you dont like him.

Liza. What else am I to do?

Higgins. Oh, lots of things. What about your old idea of a florist's shop? Pickering could set you up in one: he's lots of money. (*Chuckling*) He'll have to pay for all those togs you have been wearing to-day; and that, with the hire of the jewellery, will make a big hole in two hundred pounds. Why, six months ago you would have thought it the millennium to have a flower shop of your own. Come! youll be all right. I must clear off to bed: I'm devilish sleepy. By the way, I came down for something: I forget what it was.

Liza. Your slippers.

Higgins. Oh yes, of course. You shied them at me. (*He picks them up, and is going out when she rises and speaks to him*).

Liza. Before you go, sir—

Higgins (*dropping the slippers in his surprise at her calling him Sir*) Eh?

Liza. Do my clothes belong to me or to Colonel Pickering?

Higgins (*coming back into the room as if her question were the very climax of unreason*) What the devil use would they be to Pickering?

Liza. He might want them for the next girl you pick up to experiment on.

Higgins (*shocked and hurt*) Is that the way you feel towards us?

Liza. I dont want to hear anything more about that. All I want to know is whether anything belongs to me. My own clothes were burnt.

Higgins. But what does it matter? Why need you start bothering about that in the middle of the night?

Liza. I want to know what I may take away with me. I dont want to be accused of stealing.

Higgins (*now deeply wounded*) Stealing! You shouldnt have said that, Eliza. That shews a want of feeling.

Liza. I'm sorry. I'm only a common ignorant girl; and in my station I have to be careful. There cant be any feelings between the like of you and the like of me. Please will you tell me what belongs to me and what doesnt?

Higgins (*very sulky*) You may take the whole damned houseful if you like. Except the jewels. Theyre hired. Will that satisfy you? (*He turns on his heel and is about to go in extreme dudgeon*).

Liza (*drinking in his emotion like nectar, and nagging him to provoke a further supply*) Stop, please. (*She takes off her jewels*). Will you take these to your room and keep them safe? I dont want to run the risk of their being missing.

Higgins (*furious*) Hand them over. (*She puts them into his hands*). If these belonged to me instead of to the jeweller, I'd ram them down your ungrateful throat. (*He perfunctorily thrusts them into his pockets, unconsciously decorating himself with the protruding ends of the chains*).

Liza (*taking a ring off*) This ring isnt the jeweller's: it's the one you bought me in Brighton. I dont want it now. (*Higgins dashes the ring violently into the fireplace, and turns on her so threateningly that she crouches over the piano with her hands over her face, and exclaims*) Dont you hit me.

Higgins. Hit you! You infamous creature, how dare you accuse me of such a thing? It is you who have hit me. You have wounded me to the heart.

Liza (*thrilling with hidden joy*) I'm glad. Ive got a little of my own back, anyhow.

Higgins (*with dignity, in his finest professional style*) You have caused me to lose my temper: a thing that has hardly ever happened to me before. I prefer to say nothing more to-night. I am going to bed.

Liza (*pertly*) Youd better leave a note for Mrs Pearce about the coffee; for she wont be told by me.

Higgins (*formally*) Damn Mrs Pearce; and damn the coffee; and damn you; and damn my own folly in having lavished hard-earned knowledge and the treasure of my regard and intimacy on a heartless guttersnipe. (*He goes out with impressive decorum, and spoils it by slamming the door savagely*).

Eliza smiles for the first time; expresses her feelings by a wild pantomime in which an imitation of Higgins's exit is confused with her own triumph; and finally goes down on her knees on the hearthrug to look for the ring.

To increase understanding

1. How does Higgins react to Eliza's success at the garden party?

2. Consider the relationship of Act IV to the development of the play. (*a*) Is it more important to the development of the plot, exposition of ideas, or development of comedy effects? (*b*) What two conflicts reach a climax in Act IV? (*c*) How are they resolved? (*d*) What must the next act resolve?

ACT FIVE

Mrs Higgins's drawing room. She is at her writing-table as before. The parlor-maid comes in.

The Parlor-Maid (at the door) Mr Henry, maam, is downstairs with Colonel Pickering.

Mrs Higgins. Well, shew them up.

The Parlor-Maid. Theyre using the telephone, maam. Telephoning to the police, I think.

Mrs Higgins. What!

The Parlor-Maid (coming further in and lowering her voice) Mr Henry is in a state, maam. I thought I'd better tell you.

Mrs Higgins. If you had told me that Mr Henry was not in a state it would have been more surprising. Tell them to come up when theyve finished with the police. I suppose he's lost something.

The Parlor-Maid. Yes, maam *(going).*

Mrs Higgins. Go upstairs and tell Miss Doolittle that Mr Henry and the Colonel are here. Ask her not to come down til I send for her.

The Parlor-Maid. Yes, maam.

Higgins bursts in. He is, as the parlor-maid has said, in a state.

Higgins. Look here, mother: heres a confounded thing!

Mrs Higgins. Yes, dear. Good morning. *(He checks his impatience and kisses her, whilst the parlor-maid goes out).* What is it?

Higgins. Eliza's bolted.

Mrs Higgins (calmly continuing her writing) You must have frightened her.

Higgins. Frightened her! nonsense! She was left last night, as usual, to turn out the lights and all that; and instead of going to bed she changed her clothes and went right off: her bed wasnt slept in. She came in a cab for her things before seven this morning; and that fool Mrs Pearce let her have them without telling me a word about it. What am I to do?

Mrs Higgins. Do without, I'm afraid, Henry. The girl has a perfect right to leave if she chooses.

Higgins (wandering distractedly across the room) But I cant find anything. I dont know what appointments Ive got. I'm—*(Pickering comes in. Mrs Higgins puts down her pen and turns away from the writing-table).*

Pickering (shaking hands) Good morning, Mrs Higgins. Has Henry told you? *(He sits down on the ottoman).*

Higgins. What does that ass of an inspector say? Have you offered a reward?

Mrs Higgins (rising in indignant amazement) You dont mean to say you have set the police after Eliza.

Higgins. Of course. What are the police for? What else could we do? *(He sits in the Elizabethan chair).*

Pickering. The inspector made a lot of difficulties. I really think he suspected us of some improper purpose.

Mrs Higgins. Well, of course he did. What right have you to go to the police and give the girl's name as if she were a thief, or a lost umbrella, or something? Really! *(She sits down again, deeply vexed).*

Higgins. But we want to find her.

Pickering. We cant let her go like this, you know, Mrs Higgins. What were we to do?

Mrs Higgins. You have no more sense, either of you, than two children. Why—

The parlor-maid comes in and breaks off the conversation.

The Parlor-Maid. Mr Henry: a gentleman wants to see you very particular. He's been sent on from Wimpole Street.

Higgins. Oh, bother! I cant see anyone now. Who is it?

The Parlor-Maid. A Mr Doolittle, sir.

Pickering. Doolittle! Do you mean the dustman?

The Parlor-Maid. Dustman! Oh no, sir: a gentleman.

Higgins (springing up excitedly) By George, Pick, it's some relative of hers that she's gone to. Somebody we know nothing about. *(To the parlor-maid)* Send him up, quick.

The Parlor-Maid. Yes, sir. *(She goes).*

Higgins (eagerly, going to his mother) Genteel relatives! now we shall hear something. *(He sits down in the Chippendale chair).*

Mrs Higgins. Do you know any of her people?

Pickering. Only her father: the fellow we told you about.

The Parlor-Maid (announcing) Mr Doolittle. *(She withdraws).*

Doolittle enters. He is brilliantly dressed in a new fashionable frock-coat, with white waistcoat and grey trousers. A flower in his buttonhole, a dazzling silk hat, and patent leather shoes complete the effect. He is too concerned with the business he has come on to notice Mrs Higgins. He walks straight to Higgins, and accosts him with vehement reproach.

Doolittle (indicating his own person) See here! Do you see this? You done this.

Higgins. Done what, man?

Doolittle. This, I tell you. Look at it. Look at this hat. Look at this coat.

Pickering. Has Eliza been buying you clothes?

Doolittle. Eliza! not she. Not half. Why would she buy me clothes?

Mrs Higgins. Good morning, Mr Doolittle. Wont you sit down?

Doolittle (taken aback as he becomes conscious that he has forgotten his hostess) Asking your pardon, maam. *(He approaches her and shakes her proffered hand).* Thank you. *(He sits down on the ottoman, on Pickering's right).* I am that full of what has happened to me that I cant think of anything else.

Higgins. What the dickens has happened to you?

Doolittle. I shouldnt mind if it had only happened to me: anything might happen to anybody and nobody to blame but Providence, as you might say. But this is something that you done to me: yes, you, Henry Higgins.

Higgins. Have you found Eliza? Thats the point.

Doolittle. Have you lost her?

Higgins. Yes.

Doolittle. You have all the luck, you have. I aint found her; but she'll find me quick enough now after what you done to me.

Mrs Higgins. But what has my son done to you, Mr Doolittle?

Doolittle. Done to me! Ruined me. Destroyed my happiness. Tied me up and delivered me into the hands of middle class morality.

Higgins (rising intolerantly and standing over Doolittle) Youre raving. Youre drunk. Youre mad. I gave you five pounds. After that I had two conversations with you, at half-a-crown an hour. Ive never seen you since.

Doolittle. Oh! Drunk! am I? Mad? am I? Tell me this. Did you or did you not write a letter to an old blighter in America that was giving five millions to found Moral Reform Societies all over the world, and that wanted you to invent a universal language for him?

Higgins. What! Ezra D. Wannafeller! He's dead. *(He sits down again carelessly).*

Doolittle. Yes: he's dead; and I'm done for. Now did you or did you not write a letter to him to say that the most original moralist at present in England, to the best of your knowledge, was Alfred Doolittle, a common dustman.

Higgins. Oh, after your last visit I remember making some silly joke of the kind.

Doolittle. Ah! you may well call it a silly joke. It put the lid on me right enough. Just give him the chance he wanted to shew that Americans is not like us: that they recognize and respect merit in every class of life, however humble. Them words is in his blooming will, in which, Henry Higgins, thanks to your silly joking, he leaves me a share in his Pre-digested Cheese Trust worth three thousand a year on condition that I lecture for his Wannafeller Moral Reform World League as often as they ask me up to six times a year.

Higgins. The devil he does! Whew! *(Brightening suddenly)* What a lark!

Pickering. A safe thing for you, Doolittle. They wont ask you twice.

Doolittle. It aint the lecturing I mind. I'll lecture them blue in the face, I will, and not turn a hair. It's making a gentleman of me that I object to. Who asked him to make a gentleman of me? I was happy. I was free. I touched pretty nigh everybody for money when I wanted it, same as I touched you, Henry Higgins. Now I am worrited; tied neck and heels; and everybody touches me for money. It's a fine thing for you, says my solicitor. Is it? says I. You mean it's a good thing for you, I says. When I was a poor man and had a solicitor once when they found a pram in the dust cart, he got me off, and got shut of me and got me shut of him as quick as he could. Same with the doctors: used to shove me out of the hospital before I could hardly stand on my legs, and nothing to pay. Now they finds out that I'm not a healthy man and cant live unless they looks after me twice a day. In the house I'm not let do a hand's turn for myself: somebody else must do it and touch me for it. A year ago I hadnt a relative in the world except two or three that wouldnt speak to me. Now Ive fifty, and not a decent week's wages among the lot of them. I have to live for others and not for myself: thats middle class morality. You talk of losing Eliza. Dont you be anxious: I bet she's on my doorstep by this: she that could support herself easy by selling flowers if I wasnt respectable. And the next one to touch me will be you, Henry Higgins. I'll have to learn to speak middle class language from you, instead of speaking proper English. Thats where youll come in; and I daresay thats what you done it for.

Mrs Higgins. But, my dear Mr Doolittle, you need not suffer all this if you are really in earnest. Nobody can force you to accept this bequest. You can repudiate it. Isnt that so, Colonel Pickering?

Pickering. I believe so.

Doolittle (softening his manner in deference to her sex) Thats the tragedy of it, maam. It's easy to say chuck it; but I havnt the nerve. Which of us has? We're all intimidated. Intimidated, maam: thats what we are. What is there for me if I chuck it but the workhouse in my old age? I have to dye my hair already to keep my job as a dustman. If I was one of the deserving poor, and had put by a bit, I could chuck it; but then why should I, acause the deserving poor might as well be millionaires for all the happiness they ever has. They dont know what

happiness is. But I, as one of the undeserving poor, have nothing between me and the pauper's uniform but this here blasted three thousand a year that shoves me into the middle class. (Excuse the expression, maam: youd use it yourself if you had my provocation.) Theyve got you every way you turn: it's a choice between the Skilly of the workhouse and the Char Bydis of the middle class[1]; and I havnt the nerve for the workhouse. Intimidated: thats what I am. Broke. Brought up. Happier men than me will call for my dust, and touch me for their tip; and I'll look on helpless, and envy them. And thats what your son has brought me to. (*He is overcome by emotion*).

Mrs Higgins. Well, I'm very glad youre not going to do anything foolish, Mr Doolittle. For this solves the problem of Eliza's future. You can provide for her now.

Doolittle (with melancholy resignation) Yes, maam: I'm expected to provide for everyone now, out of three thousand a year.

Higgins (jumping up) Nonsense! he cant provide for her. He shant provide for her. She doesnt belong to him. I paid him five pounds for her. Doolittle: either youre an honest man or a rogue.

Doolittle (tolerantly) A little of both, Henry, like the rest of us: a little of both.

Higgins. Well, you took that money for the girl; and you have no right to take her as well.

Mrs Higgins. Henry: dont be absurd. If you want to know where Eliza is, she is upstairs.

Higgins (amazed) Upstairs!!! Then I shall jolly soon fetch her downstairs. (*He makes resolutely for the door*).

Mrs Higgins (rising and following him) Be quiet, Henry. Sit down.

Higgins. I—

---

1. *Skilly . . . Char Bydis of the middle class.* Doolittle is referring to Scylla (sil'ə) and Charybdis (kə rib'dis). In the narrow strait that separates Italy and Sicily there is a dangerous rock and a whirlpool, which the ancient Greeks named Scylla and Charybdis. The expression "to be between Scylla and Charybdis" means to be between two evils, either one of which can be safely avoided only by risking the other.

Mrs Higgins. Sit down, dear; and listen to me.

Higgins. Oh very well, very well, very well. (*He throws himself ungraciously on the ottoman, with his face towards the windows*). But I think you might have told us this half an hour ago.

Mrs Higgins. Eliza came to me this morning. She passed the night partly walking about in a rage, partly trying to throw herself into the river and being afraid to, and partly in the Carlton Hotel. She told me of the brutal way you two treated her.

Higgins (bounding up again) What!

Pickering (rising also) My dear Mrs Higgins, she's been telling you stories. We didnt treat her brutally. We hardly said a word to her; and we parted on particularly good terms. (*Turning on Higgins*) Higgins: did you bully her after I went to bed?

Higgins. Just the other way about. She threw my slippers in my face. She behaved in the most outrageous way. I never gave her the slightest provocation. The slippers came bang into my face the moment I entered the room—before I had uttered a word. And used perfectly awful language.

Pickering (astonished) But why? What did we do to her?

Mrs Higgins. I think I know pretty well what you did. The girl is naturally rather affectionate, I think. Isnt she, Mr Doolittle?

Doolittle. Very tender-hearted, maam. Takes after me.

Mrs Higgins. Just so. She had become attached to you both. She worked very hard for you, Henry! I dont think you quite realize what anything in the nature of brain work means to a girl like that. Well, it seems that when the great day of trial came, and she did this wonderful thing for you without making a single mistake, you two sat there and never said a word to her, but talked together of how glad you were that it was all over and how you had been bored with the whole thing. And then you were surprised because she threw your slippers at you! *I* should have thrown the fire-irons at you.

Higgins. We said nothing except that we were tired and wanted to go to bed. Did we, Pick?

Pickering (shrugging his shoulders) That was all.

Mrs Higgins (ironically) Quite sure?

Pickering. Absolutely. Really, that was all.

Mrs Higgins. You didnt thank her, or pet her, or admire her, or tell her how splendid she'd been.

Higgins (impatiently) But she knew all about that. We didnt make speeches to her, if thats what you mean.

Pickering (conscience stricken) Perhaps we were a little inconsiderate. Is she very angry?

Mrs Higgins (returning to her place at the writing-table) Well, I'm afraid she wont go back to Wimpole Street, especially now that Mr Doolittle is able to keep up the position you have thrust on her; but she says she is quite willing to meet you on friendly terms and to let bygones be bygones.

Higgins (furious) Is she, by George? Ho!

Mrs Higgins. If you promise to behave yourself, Henry, I'll ask her to come down. If not, go home; for you have taken up quite enough of my time.

Higgins. Oh, all right. Very well. Pick: you behave yourself. Let us put on our best Sunday manners for this creature that we picked out of the mud. (*He flings himself sulkily into the Elizabethan chair*).

Doolittle (remonstrating) Now, now, Henry Higgins! have some consideration for my feelings as a middle class man.

Mrs Higgins. Remember your promise, Henry. (*She presses the bell-button on the writing-table*). Mr Doolittle: will you be so good as to step out on the balcony for a moment. I dont want Eliza to have the shock of your news until she has made it up with these two gentlemen. Would you mind?

Doolittle. As you wish, lady. Anything to help Henry to keep her off my hands. (*He disappears through the window*).

The parlor-maid answers the bell. Pickering sits down in Doolittle's place.

Mrs Higgins. Ask Miss Doolittle to come down, please.

The Parlor-Maid. Yes, maam. (*She goes out*).

Mrs Higgins. Now, Henry: be good.

Higgins. I am behaving myself perfectly.

Pickering. He is doing his best, Mrs Higgins.

A pause. Higgins throws back his head; stretches out his legs; and begins to whistle.

Mrs Higgins. Henry, dearest, you dont look at all nice in that attitude.

Higgins (pulling himself together) I was not trying to look nice, mother.

Mrs Higgins. It doesnt matter, dear. I only wanted to make you speak.

Higgins. Why?

Mrs Higgins. Because you cant speak and whistle at the same time.

Higgins groans. Another very trying pause.

Higgins (springing up, out of patience) Where the devil is that girl? Are we to wait here all day?

Eliza enters, sunny, self-possessed, and giving a staggeringly convincing exhibition of ease of manner. She carries a little work-basket, and is very much at home. Pickering is too much taken aback to rise.

Liza. How do you do, Professor Higgins? Are you quite well?

Higgins (choking) Am I—(*He can say no more*).

Liza. But of course you are: you are never ill. So glad to see you again, Colonel Pickering. (*He rises hastily; and they shake hands*). Quite chilly this morning, isnt it? (*She sits down on his left. He sits beside her*).

Higgins. Dont you dare try this game on me. I taught it to you; and it doesnt take me in. Get up and come home; and dont be a fool.

Eliza takes a piece of needlework from her basket, and begins to stitch at it, without taking the least notice of this outburst.

Mrs Higgins. Very nicely put, indeed, Henry. No woman could resist such an invitation.

Higgins. You let her alone, mother. Let her speak for herself. You will jolly soon see whether she has an idea that I havnt put into her head or a word that I havnt put into her mouth. I tell you I have created this thing out of the squashed cabbage leaves of Covent Gardens; and now she pretends to play the fine lady with me.

Mrs Higgins (placidly) Yes, dear; but youll sit down, wont you?

Higgins sits down again, savagely.

Liza (to Pickering, taking no apparent notice of Higgins, and working away deftly) Will you drop me altogether now that the experiment is over, Colonel Pickering?

Pickering. Oh dont. You mustnt think of it as an experiment. It shocks me, somehow.

Liza. Oh, I'm only a squashed cabbage leaf—

Pickering (impulsively) No.

Liza (continuing quietly)—but I owe so much to you that I should be very unhappy if you forgot me.

Pickering. It's very kind of you to say so, Miss Doolittle.

Liza. It's not because you paid for my dresses. I know you are generous to everybody with money. But it was from you that I learnt really nice manners; and that is what makes one a lady, isn't it? You see it was so very difficult for me with the example of Professor Higgins always before me. I was brought up to be just like him, unable to control myself, and using bad language on the slightest provocation. And I should never have known that ladies and gentlemen didnt behave like that if you hadnt been there.

Higgins. Well!!

Pickering. Oh, thats only his way, you know. He doesnt mean it.

Liza. Oh, I didnt mean it either, when I was a flower girl. It was only my way. But you see I did it; and thats what makes the difference after all.

Pickering. No doubt. Still, he taught you to speak; and I couldnt have done that, you know.

Liza (trivially) Of course: that is his profession.

Higgins. Damnation!

Liza (continuing) It was just like learning to dance in the fashionable way: there was nothing more than that in it. But do you know what began my real education?

Pickering. What?

Liza (stopping her work for a moment) Your calling me Miss Doolittle that day when I first came to Wimpole Street. That was the beginning of self-respect for me. (*She resumes her stitching*). And there were a hundred little things you never noticed, because they came naturally to you. Things about standing up and taking off your hat and opening doors—

Pickering. Oh, that was nothing.

Liza. Yes: things that shewed you thought and felt about me as if I were something better than a scullery-maid; though of course I know you would have been just the same to a scullery-maid if she had been let into the drawing room. You never took off your boots in the dining room when I was there.

Pickering. You mustnt mind that. Higgins takes off his boots all over the place.

Liza. I know. I am not blaming him. It is his way, isnt it? But it made such a difference to me that you didnt do it. You see, really and truly, apart from the things anyone can pick up (the dressing and the proper way of speaking, and so on), the difference between a lady and a flower girl is not how she behaves, but how she's treated. I shall always be a flower girl to Professor Higgins, because he always treats me as a flower girl, and always will; but I know I can be a lady to you, because you always treat me as a lady, and always will.

Mrs Higgins. Please dont grind your teeth, Henry.

Pickering. Well, this is really very nice of you, Miss Doolittle.

Liza. I should like you to call me Eliza, now, if you would.

Pickering. Thank you, Eliza, of course.

Liza. And I should like Professor Higgins to call me Miss Doolittle.

Higgins. I'll see you damned first.

Mrs Higgins. Henry! Henry!

Pickering (laughing) Why dont you slang back at him? Dont stand it. It would do him a lot of good.

Liza. I cant. I could have done it once; but now I cant go back to it. Last night, when I was wandering about, a girl spoke to me; and I tried to get back into the old way with her; but it was no use. You told me, you know, that when a child is brought to a foreign country, it picks up the language in a few weeks, and forgets its own. Well, I am a child in your country. I have forgotten my own language, and can speak nothing but yours. Thats the real break-off with the corner of Tottenham Court Road. Leaving Wimpole Street finishes it.

Pickering (much alarmed) Oh! but youre coming back to Wimpole Street, arnt you? Youll forgive Higgins?

Higgins (rising) Forgive! Will she, by George! Let her go. Let her find out how she can get on without us. She will relapse into the gutter in three weeks without me at her elbow.

Doolittle appears at the centre window. With a look of dignified reproach at Higgins, he comes slowly and silently to his daughter, who, with her back to the window, is unconscious of his approach.

Pickering. He's incorrigible, Eliza. You wont relapse, will you?

Liza. No: not now. Never again. I have learnt my lesson. I dont believe I could utter one of the old sounds if I tried. (*Doolittle touches her on her left shoulder. She drops her work, losing her self-possession utterly at the spectacle of her father's splendor*) A-a-a-a-a-ah-ow-ooh!

Higgins (with a crow of triumph) Aha! Just so. A-a-a-a-ahowooh! A-a-a-a-ahowooh! A-a-a-a-ahowooh! Victory! Victory! (*He throws himself on the divan, folding his arms, and spraddling arrogantly*).

Doolittle. Can you blame the girl? Dont look at me like that, Eliza. It aint my fault. Ive come into some money.

Liza. You must have touched a millionaire this time, dad.

Doolittle. I have. But I'm dressed something special today. I'm going to St George's, Hanover Square. Your stepmother is going to marry me.

Liza (angrily) Youre going to let yourself down to marry that low common woman!

Pickering (quietly) He ought to, Eliza. (*To Doolittle*) Why has she changed her mind?

Doolittle (*sadly*) Intimidated, Governor. Intimidated. Middle class morality claims its victim. Wont you put on your hat, Liza, and come and see me turned off?

Liza. If the Colonel says I must, I—I'll (*almost sobbing*) I'll demean myself. And get insulted for my pains, like enough.

Doolittle. Dont be afraid: she never comes to words with anyone now, poor woman! respectability has broke all the spirit out of her.

Pickering (*squeezing Eliza's elbow gently*) Be kind to them, Eliza. Make the best of it.

Liza (*forcing a little smile for him through her vexation*) Oh well, just to shew theres no ill feeling. I'll be back in a moment. (*She goes out*).

Doolittle (*sitting down beside Pickering*) I feel uncommon nervous about the ceremony, Colonel. I wish youd come and see me through it.

Pickering. But youve been through it before, man. You were married to Eliza's mother.

Doolittle. Who told you that, Colonel?

Pickering. Well, nobody told me. But I concluded—naturally—

Doolittle. No: that aint the natural way, Colonel: it's only the middle class way. My way was always the undeserving way. But dont say nothing to Eliza. She dont know: I aways had a delicacy about telling her.

Pickering. Quite right. We'll leave it so, if you dont mind.

Doolittle. And youll come to the church, Colonel, and put me through straight?

Pickering. With pleasure. As far as a bachelor can.

Mrs Higgins. May I come, Mr Doolittle? I should be very sorry to miss your wedding.

Doolittle. I should indeed be honored by your condescension, maam; and my poor old woman would take it as a tremenjous compliment. She's been very low, thinking of the happy days that are no more.

Mrs Higgins (*rising*) I'll order the carriage and get ready. (*The men rise, except Higgins*). I shant be more than fifteen minutes. (*As she goes to the door Eliza comes in, hatted and buttoning her gloves*). I'm going to the church to see your father married, Eliza. You had better come in the brougham with me. Colonel Pickering can go on with the bridegroom.

Mrs Higgins goes out. Eliza comes to the middle of the room between the centre window and the ottoman. Pickering joins her.

Doolittle. Bridegroom! What a word! It makes a man realize his position, somehow. (*He takes up his hat and goes towards the door*).

Pickering. Before I go, Eliza, do forgive him and come back to us.

Liza. I dont think papa would allow me. Would you, dad?

Doolittle (*sad but magnanimous*) They played you off very cunning, Eliza, them two sportsmen. If it had been only one of them, you could have nailed him. But you see, there was two; and one of them chaperoned the other, as you might say. (*To Pickering*) It was artful of you, Colonel; but I bear no malice: I should have done the same myself. I been the victim of one woman after another all my life; and I dont grudge you two getting the better of Eliza. I shant interfere. It's time for us to go, Colonel. So long, Henry. See you in St George's, Eliza. (*He goes out*).

Pickering (*coaxing*) Do stay with us, Eliza. (*He follows Doolittle*).

Eliza goes out on the balcony to avoid being alone with Higgins. He rises and joins her there. She immediately comes back into the room and makes for the door; but he goes along the balcony quickly and gets his back to the door before she reaches it.

Higgins. Well, Eliza, youve had a bit of your own back, as you call it. Have you had enough? and are you going to be reasonable? Or do you want any more?

Liza. You want me back only to pick up your slippers and put up with your tempers and fetch and carry for you.

Higgins. I havnt said I wanted you back at all.

Liza. Oh, indeed. Then what are we talking about?

Higgins. About you, not about me. If you come back I shall treat you just as I have always treated you. I cant change my nature; and I dont intend to change my manners. My manners are exactly the same as Colonel Pickering's.

Liza. Thats not true. He treats a flower girl as if she was a duchess.

Higgins. And I treat a duchess as if she was a flower girl.

Liza. I see. (*She turns away composedly, and sits on the ottoman, facing the window*). The same to everybody.

Higgins. Just so.

Liza. Like father.

Higgins (*grinning, a little taken down*) Without accepting the comparison at all points, Eliza, it's quite true that your father is not a snob, and that he will be quite at home in any station of life to which his eccentric destiny may call him. (*Seriously*) The great secret, Eliza, is not having bad manners or good manners or any other particular sort of manners, but having the same manner for all human souls: in short, behaving as if you were in Heaven, where there are no third-class carriages, and one soul is as good as another.

Liza. Amen. You are a born preacher.

Higgins (*irritated*) The question is not whether I treat you rudely, but whether you ever heard me treat anyone else better.

Liza (*with sudden sincerity*) I dont care how you treat me. I dont mind your swearing at me. I dont mind a black eye: Ive had one before this. But (*standing up and facing him*) I wont be passed over.

Higgins. Then get out of my way; for I wont stop for you. You talk about me as if I were a motor bus.

Liza. So you are a motor bus: all bounce and go, and no consideration for anyone. But I can do without you: dont think I cant.

Higgins. I know you can. I told you you could.

Liza (*wounded, getting away from him to the other side of the ottoman with her face to the hearth*) I know you did, you brute. You wanted to get rid of me.

Higgins. Liar.

Liza. Thank you. (*She sits down with dignity*).

Higgins. You never asked yourself, I suppose, whether *I* could do without you.

Liza (*earnestly*) Dont you try to get round me. Youll have to do without me.

Higgins (*arrogant*) I can do without anybody. I have my own soul: my own spark of divine fire. But (*with sudden humility*) I shall miss you, Eliza. (*He sits down near her on the ottoman*). I have learnt something from your idiotic notions: I confess that humbly and gratefully. And I have grown accustomed to your voice and appearance. I like them, rather.

Liza. Well, you have both of them on your gramophone and in your book of photographs. When you feel lonely without me, you can turn the machine on. It's got no feelings to hurt.

Higgins. I cant turn your soul on. Leave me those feelings; and you can take away the voice and the face. They are not you.

Liza. Oh, you are a devil. You can twist the heart in a girl as easy as some could twist her arms to hurt her. Mrs Pearce warned me. Time and again she has wanted to leave you; and you always got round her at the last minute. And you dont care a bit for her. And you dont care a bit for me.

Higgins. I care for life, for humanity; and you are a part of it that has come my way and been built into my house. What more can you or anyone ask?

Liza. I wont care for anybody that doesnt care for me.

Higgins. Commercial principles, Eliza. Like (*reproducing her Covent Garden pronunciation with professional exactness*) s'yol-lin voylets (*selling violets*), isn't it?

Liza. Dont sneer at me. It's mean to sneer at me.

Higgins. I have never sneered in my life. Sneering doesnt become either the human face or the human soul. I am expressing my righteous contempt for Commercialism. I dont and wont trade in affection. You call me a brute because you couldnt buy a claim on me by fetching my slippers and finding my spectacles. You were a fool: I think a woman fetching a man's slippers is a disgusting sight: did I ever fetch your slippers?

I think a good deal more of you for throwing them in my face. No use slaving for me and then saying you want to be cared for: who cares for a slave? If you come back, come back for the sake of good fellowship; for youll get nothing else. Youve had a thousand times as much out of me as I have out of you; and if you dare to set up your little dog's tricks of fetching and carrying slippers against my creation of a Duchess Eliza, I'll slam the door in your silly face.

Liza. What did you do it for if you didnt care for me?

Higgins (heartily) Why, because it was my job.

Liza. You never thought of the trouble it would make for me.

Higgins. Would the world ever have been made if its maker had been afraid of making trouble? Making life means making trouble. Theres only one way of escaping trouble; and thats killing things. Cowards, you notice, are always shrieking to have troublesome people killed.

Liza. I'm no preacher: I dont notice things like that. I notice that you dont notice me.

Higgins (jumping up and walking about intolerantly) Eliza: youre an idiot. I waste the treasures of my Miltonic mind by spreading them before you. Once for all, understand that I go my way and do my work without caring twopence what happens to either of us. I am not intimidated, like your father and your stepmother. So you can come back or go to the devil: which you please.

Liza. What am I to come back for?

Higgins (bouncing up on his knees on the ottoman and leaning over it to her) For the fun of it. Thats why I took you on.

Liza (with averted face) And you may throw me out to-morrow if I dont do everything you want me to?

Higgins. Yes; and you may walk out to-morrow if I don't do everything you want me to.

Liza. And live with my stepmother?

Higgins. Yes, or sell flowers.

Liza. Oh! if I only could go back to my flower basket! I should be independent of both you and father and all the world!

Why did you take my independence from me? Why did I give it up? I'm a slave now, for all my fine clothes.

Higgins. Not a bit. I'll adopt you as my daughter and settle money on you if you like. Or would you rather marry Pickering?

Liza (looking fiercely round at him) I wouldnt marry you if you asked me; and youre nearer my age than what he is.

Higgins (gently) Than he is: not "than what he is."

Liza (losing her temper and rising) I'll talk as I like. Youre not my teacher now.

Higgins (reflectively) I dont suppose Pickering would, though. He's as confirmed an old bachelor as I am.

Liza. Thats not what I want; and dont you think it. Ive always had chaps enough wanting me that way. Freddy Hill writes to me twice and three times a day, sheets and sheets.

Higgins (disagreeably surprised) Damn his impudence! (*He recoils and finds himself sitting on his heels*).

Liza. He has a right to if he likes, poor lad. And he does love me.

Higgins (getting off the ottoman) You have no right to encourage him.

Liza. Every girl has a right to be loved.

Higgins. What! By fools like that?

Liza. Freddy's not a fool. And if he's weak and poor and wants me, may be he'd make me happier than my betters that bully me and dont want me.

Higgins. Can he make anything of you? Thats the point.

Liza. Perhaps I could make something of him. But I never thought of us making anything of one another; and you never think of anything else. I only want to be natural.

Higgins. In short, you want me to be as infatuated about you as Freddy? Is that it?

Liza. No I dont. Thats not the sort of feeling I want from you. And dont you be too sure of yourself or of me. I could have been a bad girl if I'd liked. Ive seen more of some things than you, for all your learning. Girls like me can drag gentlemen down to make love to them easy enough. And they wish each other dead the next minute.

Higgins. Of course they do. Then what in thunder are we quarrelling about?

Liza (much troubled) I want a little kindness. I know I'm a common ignorant girl, and you a book-learned gentleman; but I'm not dirt under your feet. What I done *(correcting herself)* what I did was not for the dresses and the taxis: I did it because we were pleasant together and I come—came—to care for you; not to want you to make love to me, and not forgetting the difference between us, but more friendly like.

Higgins. Well, of course. Thats just how I feel. And how Pickering feels. Eliza: youre a fool.

Liza. Thats not a proper answer to give me *(she sinks on the chair at the writing-table in tears)*.

Higgins. It's all youll get until you stop being a common idiot. If youre going to be a lady, youll have to give up feeling neglected if the men you know dont spend half their time snivelling over you and the other half giving you black eyes. If you cant stand the coldness of my sort of life, and the strain of it, go back to the gutter. Work til you are more a brute than a human being; and then cuddle and squabble and drink til you fall asleep. Oh, it's a fine life, the life of the gutter. It's real: it's warm: it's violent: you can feel it through the thickest skin: you can taste it and smell it without any training or any work. Not like Science and Literature and Classical Music and Philosophy and Art. You find me cold, unfeeling, selfish, dont you? Very well: be off with you to the sort of people you like. Marry some sentimental hog or other with lots of money, and a thick pair of lips to kiss you with and a thick pair of boots to kick you with. If you cant appreciate what youve got, youd better get what you can appreciate.

Liza (desperate) Oh, you are a cruel tyrant. I cant talk to you: you turn everything against me: I'm always in the wrong. But you know very well all the time that youre nothing but a bully. You know I cant go back to the gutter, as you call it, and that I have no real friends in the world but you and the Colonel. You know well I couldnt bear to live with a low common man after you two; and it's wicked and cruel of you to insult me by pretending I could. You think I must go back to Wimpole Street because I have nowhere else to go but father's. But dont you be too sure that you have me under your feet to be trampled on and talked down. I'll marry Freddy, I will, as soon as he's able to support me.

Higgins (sitting down beside her) Rubbish! you shall marry an ambassador. You shall marry the Governor-General of India or the Lord-Lieutenant of Ireland, or somebody who wants a deputy-queen. I'm not going to have my masterpiece thrown away on Freddy.

Liza. You think I like you to say that. But I havnt forgot what you said a minute ago; and I wont be coaxed round as if I was a baby or a puppy. If I cant have kindness, I'll have independence.

Higgins. Independence? That's middle class blasphemy. We are all dependent on one another, every soul of us on earth.

Liza (rising determinedly) I'll let you see whether I'm dependent on you. If you can preach, I can teach. I'll go and be a teacher.

Higgins. Whatll you teach, in heaven's name?

Liza. What you taught me. I'll teach phonetics.

Higgins. Ha! ha! ha!

Liza. I'll offer myself as an assistant to Professor Nepean.

Higgins (rising in a fury) What! That impostor! that humbug! that toadying ignoramus! Teach him my methods! my discoveries! You take one step in his direction and I'll wring your neck. *(He lays hands on her).* Do you hear?

Liza (defiantly non-resistant) Wring away. What do I care? I knew youd strike me some day. *(He lets her go, stamping with rage at having forgotten himself, and recoils so hastily that he stumbles back into his seat on the ottoman).* Aha! Now I know how to deal with you. What a fool I was not to think of it before! You cant take away the knowledge you gave me. You said I had a finer ear than you. And I can be civil and kind to people, which is more than you can. Aha!

Thats done you, Henry Higgins, it has. Now I dont care that (*snapping her fingers*) for your bullying and your big talk. I'll advertize it in the papers that your duchess is only a flower girl that you taught, and that she'll teach anybody to be a duchess just the same in six months for a thousand guineas. Oh, when I think of myself crawling under your feet and being trampled on and called names, when all the time I had only to lift up my finger to be as good as you, I could just kick myself.

Higgins (*wondering at her*) You damned impudent slut, you! But it's better than snivelling; better than fetching slippers and finding spectacles, isnt it? (*Rising*) By George, Eliza, I said I'd make a woman of you; and I have. I like you like this.

Liza. Yes: you turn round and make up to me now that I'm not afraid of you, and can do without you.

Higgins. Of course I do, you little fool. Five minutes ago you were like a millstone round my neck. Now youre a tower of strength: a consort battleship. You and I and Pickering will be three old bachelors together instead of only two men and a silly girl.

Mrs Higgins returns, dressed for the wedding. Eliza instantly becomes cool and elegant.

Mrs Higgins. The carriage is waiting, Eliza. Are you ready?

Liza. Quite. Is the Professor coming?

Mrs Higgins. Certainly not. He cant behave himself in church. He makes remarks out loud all the time on the clergyman's pronunciation.

Liza. Then I shall not see you again, Professor. Goodbye. (*She goes to the door*).

Mrs Higgins (*coming to Higgins*) Goodbye, dear.

Higgins. Goodbye, mother. (*He is about to kiss her, when he recollects something*). Oh, by the way, Eliza, order a ham and a Stilton cheese, will you? And buy me a pair of reindeer gloves, number eights, and a tie to match that new suit of mine, at Eale & Binman's. You can choose the color. (*His cheerful, careless, vigorous voice shows that he is incorrigible*).

Liza (*disdainfully*) Buy them yourself. (*She sweeps out*).

Mrs Higgins. I'm afraid youve spoiled that girl, Henry. But never mind, dear: I'll buy you the tie and gloves.

Higgins (*sunnily*) Oh, dont bother. She'll buy em all right enough. Goodbye.

They kiss. Mrs Higgins runs out. Higgins, left alone, rattles his cash in his pocket; chuckles; and disports himself in a highly self-satisfied manner.

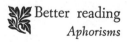
To increase understanding

1. (*a*) What circumstances have brought about Doolittle's change of fortune? (*b*) Cite some of the lines in which Doolittle explains why he doesn't want to become a gentleman. (*c*) Cite lines in which Doolittle explains why he can't refuse the money. (*d*) According to Doolittle, what is the difference between the middle class and the undeserving poor?

2. (*a*) Eliza says that it is manners that make one a lady; but what does she think is the biggest difference between a flower girl and a lady? (*b*) Cite the lines in which Higgins explains manners.

3. In Acts IV and V Eliza becomes more of a person than a character. Cite speeches or actions in which we can see the human qualities she possesses.

4. (*a*) Have all the problems presented in the play been resolved? Explain. (*b*) How do you think the story ends?

5. Shaw called his play a "Romance in Five Acts." Do you consider it a romance? Explain.

6. (*a*) Explain why Shaw called this play *Pygmalion*. (*b*) In what way is the title related to the theme?

Better reading
Aphorisms

The *aphorism* is a bit of shrewd insight into an important truth expressed in a concise statement; it is a wry observation about life. It is similar to the proverb, maxim, or adage, but differs in its higher degree of intellectual ingenuity and sophistication. The author of an aphorism is generally known, whereas a proverb is usually an anonymous product of folklore. The purpose of a maxim is to teach a moral, but this is not necessarily the purpose of an aphorism. The expression, "Take care of the pence and the pounds will take care of themselves," for example, is so deliberately instructive that it is classified as a maxim. If an aphorism is instructive at all, it is likely to be in a negative or ironic sense, as is Ambrose Bierce's famous saying, *"Men never do evil so completely and cheerfully as when they do it from religious conviction."* Another example of aphoristic needling is the following quotation from the educator, R. M. Hutchins: *"We do not know what education could do for us, because we have never tried it."*

It is paradoxical that we like aphorisms for the same reasons that we distrust them. We enjoy the quick flash of insight that seemingly gives us a complete answer about something. At the same time, we suspect that a complex idea cannot be stated so simply, and that closer scrutiny will undoubtedly show up the aphorism's weak points.

Much of Bernard Shaw's writing, like Francis Bacon's (see page 186), is aphoristic in style. Study the following passages from *Pygmalion* and answer the following questions about each: What idea does the aphorism express? Will the idea stand up under close scrutiny? Can you present valid arguments to show its weak points?

What is middle class morality? Just an excuse for never giving me anything.

(Alfred Doolittle, Act II)

There's only one way of escaping trouble; and that's killing things. Cowards, you notice, are always shrieking to have troublesome people killed.

(Higgins, Act V)

The poor can't afford to have morals.

(Doolittle, Act II)

. . . the difference between a lady and a flower girl is not how she behaves, but how she's treated.

(Eliza, Act V)

EPILOGUE

The rest of the story need not be shewn in action, and indeed, would hardly need telling if our imaginations were not so enfeebled by their lazy dependence on the ready-mades and reach-me-downs of the ragshop in which Romance keeps its stock of "happy endings" to misfit all stories. Now, the history of Eliza Doolittle, though called a romance because the transfiguration it records seems exceedingly improbable, is common enough. Such transfigurations have been achieved by hundreds of resolutely ambitious young women since Nell Gwynne set them the example by playing queens and fascinating kings in the theatre in which she began by selling oranges. Nevertheless, people in all directions have assumed, for no other reason than that she became the heroine of a romance, that she must have married the hero of it. This is unbearable, not only because her little drama, if acted on such a thoughtless assumption, must be spoiled, but because the true sequel is patent to anyone with a sense of human nature in general, and of feminine instinct in particular.

Eliza, in telling Higgins she would not marry him if he asked her, was not coquetting: she was announcing a well-considered decision. When a bachelor interests, and dominates, and teaches, and becomes important to a spinster, as Higgins with Eliza, she always, if she has character enough to be capable of it, considers very seriously indeed whether she will play for becoming that bachelor's wife, especially if he is so little interested in marriage that a determined and devoted woman might capture him if she set herself resolutely to do it. Her decision will depend a good deal on whether she is really free to choose; and that, again, will depend on her age and income. If she is at the end of her youth, and has no security for her livelihood, she will marry him because she must marry anybody who will provide for her. But at Eliza's age a good-looking girl does not feel that pressure: she feels free to pick and choose. She is therefore guided by her instinct in the matter. Eliza's instinct tells her not to marry Higgins. It does not tell her to give him up. It is not in the slightest doubt as to his remaining one of the strongest personal interests in her life. It would be very sorely strained if there was another woman likely to supplant her with him. But as she feels sure of him on that last point, she has no doubt at all as to her course, and would not have any, even if the difference of twenty years in age, which seems so great to youth, did not exist between them.

As our own instincts are not appealed to by her conclusion, let us see whether we cannot discover some reason in it. When Higgins excused his indifference to young women on the ground that they had an irresistible rival in his mother, he gave the clue to his inveterate old-bachelordom. The case is uncommon only to the extent that remarkable mothers are uncommon. If an imaginative boy has a sufficiently rich mother who has intelligence, personal grace, dignity of character without harshness, and a cultivated sense of the best art of her time to enable her to make her house beautiful, she sets a standard for him against which very few women can struggle, besides effecting for him a disengagement of his affections, his sense of beauty, and his idealism from his specifically sexual impulses. This makes him a standing puzzle to the huge number of uncultivated people who have been brought up in tasteless homes by commonplace or disagreeable parents, and to whom, consequently, literature, painting, sculpture, music, and affectionate personal relations come as modes of sex if they come at all. The word passion means nothing else to them; and that Higgins could have a passion for phonetics and idealize his mother instead of Eliza, would seem to them absurd and unnatural. Nevertheless, when we look round and see that hardly anyone is too ugly or disagreeable to find a wife or a husband if he or she wants one, whilst many old maids and bachelors are above the average in quality and culture, we cannot help suspecting that the disentanglement of sex from the associations with which it is so commonly confused, a disentanglement which persons of genius achieve by sheer intellectual analysis, is sometimes produced or aided by parental fascination.

Now, though Eliza was incapable of thus explaining to herself Higgins's formidable powers of resistance to the charm that prostrated Freddy at the first glance, she was instinctively aware that she could never obtain a complete grip of him, or come between him and his mother (the first necessity of the married woman). To put it shortly, she knew that for some mysterious reason he had not the makings of a married man in him, according to her conception of a husband as one to whom she would be his nearest and fondest and warmest interest. Even had there been no mother-rival, she would still have refused to accept an interest in herself that was secondary to philosophic interests. Had Mrs Higgins died, there would still have been Milton and the Universal Alphabet. Landor's remark that to those who have the greatest power of loving, love is a secondary affair, would not have recommended Landor to Eliza. Put that along with her resentment of Higgins's domineering superiority, and her mistrust of his coaxing cleverness in getting round her and evading her wrath when he had gone too far with his impetuous bullying, and you will see that Eliza's instinct had good grounds for warning her not to marry her Pygmalion.

And now, whom did Eliza marry? For if Higgins was a predestinate old bachelor, she was most certainly not a predestinate old maid. Well, that can be told very shortly to those who have not guessed it from the indications she has herself given them.

Almost immediately after Eliza is stung into proclaiming her considered determination not to marry Higgins, she mentions the fact that young Mr Frederick Eynsford Hill is pouring out his love for her daily through the post. Now Freddy is young, practically twenty years younger than Higgins: he is a gentleman (or, as Eliza would qualify him, a toff), and speaks like one; he is nicely dressed, is treated by the Colonel as an equal, loves her unaffectedly, and is not her master, nor ever likely to dominate her in spite of his advantage of social standing. Eliza has no use for the foolish romantic tradition that all women love to be mastered, if not actually bullied and beaten. "When you go to women," says Nietzsche, "take your whip with you." Sensible despots have never confined that precaution to women: they have taken their whips with them when they have dealt with men, and been slavishly idealized by the men over whom they have flourished the whip much more than by women. No doubt there are slavish women as well as slavish men: and women, like men, admire those that are stronger than themselves. But to admire a strong person and to live under that strong person's thumb are two different things. The weak may not be admired and hero-worshipped; but they are by no means disliked or shunned; and they never seem to have the least difficulty in marrying people who are too good for them. They may fail in emergencies; but life is not one long emergency: it is mostly a string of situations for which no exceptional strength is needed, and with which even rather weak people can cope if they have a stronger partner to help them out. Accordingly, it is a truth everywhere in evidence that strong people, masculine or feminine, not only do not marry stronger people, but do not shew any preference for them in selecting their friends. When a lion meets another with a louder roar "the first lion thinks the last a bore." The man or woman who feels strong enough for two, seeks for every other quality in a partner than strength.

The converse is also true. Weak people want to marry strong people who do not frighten them too much; and this often leads them to make the mistake we describe metaphorically as "biting off more than they can chew." They want too much for too little; and when the bargain is unreasonable beyond all bearing, the union becomes impossible: it ends in the weaker party being either discarded or borne as a cross, which is worse. People who are not only weak, but silly or obtuse as well, are often in these difficulties.

This being the state of human affairs, what is Eliza fairly sure to do when she is placed between Freddy and Higgins? Will she look forward to a lifetime of fetching Higgins's slippers or to a lifetime of Freddy fetching hers? There can be no doubt about the answer. Unless Freddy is biologically repulsive to her, and Higgins biologically attractive to a degree that overwhelms all her other instincts, she will, if she marries either of them, marry Freddy.

And that is just what Eliza did.

Complications ensued; but they were economic, not romantic. Freddy had no money and no occupation. His mother's jointure, a last relic of the opulence of Largelady Park, had enabled her to struggle along in Earlscourt with an air of gentility, but not to procure any serious secondary education for her children, much less give the boy a profession. A clerkship at thirty shillings a week was beneath Freddy's dignity, and extremely distasteful to him besides. His prospects consisted of a hope that if he kept up appearances somebody would do something for him. The something appeared vaguely to his imagination as a private secretaryship or a sinecure of some sort. To his mother it perhaps appeared as a marriage to some lady of means who could not resist her boy's niceness. Fancy her feelings when he married a flower girl who had become déclassée under extraordinary circumstances which were now notorious!

It is true that Eliza's situation did not seem wholly ineligible. Her father, though formerly a dustman, and now fantastically disclassed, had become extremely popular in the smartest society by a social talent which triumphed over every prejudice and every disadvantage. Rejected by the middle class, which he loathed, he had shot up at once into the highest circles by his wit, his dustmanship (which he carried like a banner), and his Nietzschean transcendence of good and evil. At intimate ducal dinners he sat on the right hand of the Duchess; and in country houses he smoked in the pantry and was made much of by the butler when he was not feeding in the dining room and being consulted by cabinet ministers. But he found it almost as hard to do all this on four thousand a year as Mrs Eynsford Hill to live in Earlscourt on an income so pitiably smaller that I have not the heart to disclose its exact figure. He absolutely refused to add the last straw to his burden by contributing to Eliza's support.

Thus Freddy and Eliza, now Mr and Mrs Eynsford Hill, would have spent a penniless honeymoon but for a wedding present of £500 from the Colonel to Eliza. It lasted a long time because Freddy did not know how to spend money, never having had any to spend, and Eliza, socially trained by a pair of old bachelors, wore her clothes as long as they held together and looked pretty, without the least regard to their being many months out of fashion. Still, £500 will not last two young people for ever; and they both knew, and Eliza felt as well, that they must shift for themselves in the end. She could quarter herself on Wimpole Street because it had come to be her home; but she was quite aware that she ought not to quarter Freddy there, and that it would not be good for his character if she did.

Not that the Wimpole Street bachelors objected. When she consulted them, Higgins declined to be bothered about her housing problem when that solution was so simple. Eliza's desire to have Freddy in the house with her seemed of no more importance than if she had wanted an extra piece of bedroom furniture. Pleas as to Freddy's character, and the moral obligation on him to earn his own living, were lost on Higgins. He denied that Freddy had any character, and declared that if he tried to do any useful work some competent person would have the trouble of undoing it: a procedure involving a net loss to the community, and great unhappiness to Freddy himself, who was obviously intended by Nature for such light work as amusing Eliza, which, Higgins declared, was a much more useful and honorable occupation than working in the city. When Eliza referred again to her project of teaching phonetics, Higgins abated not a jot of his violent opposition to it. He said she was not within ten years of being qualified to meddle with his pet subject; and as it was evident that the Colonel agreed with him, she felt she could not go against them in this grave matter, and that she had no right, without Higgins's consent, to exploit the knowledge he had given her; for his knowledge seemed to her as much his private property as his watch: Eliza was no communist. Besides, she was superstitiously devoted to them both, more entirely and frankly after her marriage than before it.

It was the Colonel who finally solved the problem, which had cost him much perplexed cogitation. He one day asked Eliza, rather shyly, whether she had quite given up her notion of keeping a flower shop. She replied that she had thought of it, but had put it out of her head, because the Colonel had said, that day at Mrs Higgins's, that it would never do. The Colonel confessed that when he said that, he had not quite recovered from the dazzling impression of the day before. They broke the matter to Higgins that evening. The sole comment vouchsafed by him very nearly led to a serious quarrel with Eliza. It was to the effect that she would have in Freddy an ideal errand boy.

Freddy himself was next sounded on the subject. He said he had been thinking of a shop himself; though it had presented itself to his pennilessness as a small place in which Eliza should sell tobacco at one counter whilst he sold newspapers at the opposite one. But he agreed that it would be extraordinarily jolly to go early every morning with Eliza to Covent Garden and buy flowers on the scene of their first meeting: a sentiment which earned him many kisses from his wife. . . .

Now here is a last opportunity for romance. Would you not like to be assured that the shop was an immense success, thanks to Eliza's charms and her early business experience in Covent Garden? Alas! the truth is the truth: the shop did not pay for a long time, simply because Eliza and her Freddy did not know how to keep it. True, Eliza had not to begin at the very beginning: she knew the names and prices of the cheaper flowers; and her elation was unbounded when she found that Freddy, like all youths educated at cheap, pretentious, and thoroughly inefficient schools, knew a little Latin. It was very little, but enough to make him appear to her a Porson or Bentley,[1] and to put him at his ease with botanical nomenclature. Unfortunately he knew nothing else; and Eliza, though she could count money up to eighteen shillings or so, and had acquired a certain familiarity with the language of Milton from her struggles to qualify herself for winning Higgins's

1. *Porson or Bentley.* Richard Porson (1759-1808), professor of Greek at Cambridge University, was a famous English scholar. Richard Bentley (1662-1742) was a well-known classical scholar.

bet, could not write out a bill without utterly disgracing the establishment. Freddy's power of stating in Latin that Balbus built a wall and that Gaul was divided into three parts did not carry with it the slightest knowledge of accounts or business: Colonel Pickering had to explain to him what a cheque book and a bank account meant. And the pair were by no means easily teachable. Freddy backed up Eliza in her obstinate refusal to believe that they could save money by engaging a book-keeper with some knowledge of the business. How, they argued, could you possibly save money by going to extra expense when you already could not make both ends meet? But the Colonel, after making the ends meet over and over again, at last gently insisted; and Eliza, humbled to the dust by having to beg from him so often, and stung by the uproarious derision of Higgins, to whom the notion of Freddy succeeding at anything was a joke that never palled, grasped the fact that business, like phonetics, has to be learned.

On the piteous spectacle of the pair spending their evenings in shorthand schools and polytechnic classes, learning bookkeeping and typewriting with incipient junior clerks, male and female, from the elementary schools, let me not dwell. There were even classes at the London School of Economics, and a humble personal appeal to the director of that institution to recommend a course bearing on the flower business. He, being a humorist, explained to them the method of the celebrated Dickensian essay on Chinese Metaphysics by the gentleman who read an article on China and an article on Metaphysics and combined the information. He suggested that they should combine the London School with Kew Gardens. Eliza, to whom the procedure of the Dickensian gentleman seemed perfectly correct (as in fact it was) and not in the least funny (which was only her ignorance), took his advice with entire gravity. But the effort that cost her the deepest humiliation was a request to Higgins, whose pet artistic fancy, next to Milton's verse, was calligraphy, and who himself wrote a most beautiful Italian hand, that he would teach her to write. He declared that she was congenitally incapable of forming a single letter worthy of the least of Milton's words; but she persisted; and again he suddenly threw himself into the task of teaching her with a combination of stormy intensity, concentrated patience, and occasional bursts of interesting disquisition on the beauty and nobility, the august mission and destiny, of human handwriting. Eliza ended by acquiring an extremely uncommercial script which was a positive extension of her personal beauty, and spending three times as much on stationery as anyone else because certain qualities and shapes of paper became indispensable to her. She could not even address an envelope in the usual way because it made the margins all wrong.

Their commercial schooldays were a period of disgrace and despair for the young couple. They seemed to be learning nothing about flower shops. At last they gave it up as hopeless, and shook the dust of the shorthand schools, and the polytechnics, and the London School of Economics from their feet for ever. Besides, the business was in some mysterious way beginning to take care of itself. They had somehow forgotten their objections to employing other people. They came to the conclusion that their own way was the best, and that they had really a remarkable talent for business. The Colonel, who had been compelled for some years to keep a sufficient sum on current account at his bankers to make up their deficits, found that the provision was unnecessary: the young people were prospering. It is true that there was not quite fair play between them and their competitors in trade. Their week-ends in the country cost them nothing, and saved them the price of their Sunday dinners; for the motor car was the Colonel's; and he and Higgins paid the hotel bills. Mr F. Hill, florist and greengrocer (they soon discovered that there was money in asparagus; and asparagus led to other vegetables), had an air which stamped the business as classy; and in private life he was still Frederick Eynsford Hill, Esquire. Not that there was any swank about him: nobody but Eliza knew that he had been christened Frederick Challoner. Eliza herself swanked like anything.

That is all. That is how it turned out. It is astonishing how much Eliza still manages to meddle in housekeeping at Wimpole Street in spite of the shop and her own family. And it is notable that though she never nags her husband, and frankly loves the Colonel as if she were his favorite daughter, she has never got out of the habit of nagging Higgins that was established on the fatal night when she won his bet for him. She snaps his head off on the faintest provocation, or on none. He no longer dares to tease her by assuming an abysmal inferiority of Freddy's mind to his own. He storms and bullies and derides: but she stands up to him so ruthlessly that the Colonel has to ask her from time to time to be kinder to Higgins; and it is the only request of his that brings a mulish expression into her face. Nothing but some emergency or calamity great enough to break down all likes and dislikes, and throw them both back on their common humanity—and may they be spared any such trial!—will ever alter this. She knows that Higgins does not need her, just as her father did not need her. The very scrupulousness with which he told her that day that he had become used to having her there, and dependent on her for all sorts of little services, and that he should miss her if she went away (it would never have occurred to Freddy or the Colonel to say anything of the sort) deepens her inner certainty that she is "no more to him than them slippers"; yet she has a sense, too, that his indifference is deeper than the infatuation of commoner souls. She is immensely interested in him. She has even secret mischievous moments in which she wishes she could get him alone, on a desert island, away from all ties and with nobody else in the world to consider, and just drag him off his pedestal and see him making love like any common man. We all have private imaginations of that sort. But when it comes to business, to the life that she really leads as distinguished from the life of dreams and fancies, she likes Freddy and she likes the Colonel; and she does not like Higgins and Mr Doolittle. Galatea never does quite like Pygmalion: his relation to her is too godlike to be altogether agreeable.

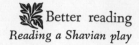 Better reading
Reading a Shavian play

Shaw said once that he would rather write the whole dialogue of *Hamlet* than manage the entrance and exit of the Ghost. The stage business of skillfully arranging the entrance or exit of characters which bothered Shaw was of little concern to Shakespeare, who surmised that the actors would themselves work out their "business." He designed his plays to be acted and probably never realized that succeeding generations would find in them the best of reading matter. In contrast, Shaw knew from the beginning that far more people would read his plays than would see them acted, and so he consciously designed his dramas for the enlightenment of the reader as well as for the delight of the spectator. He wrote descriptions of rôles which are in themselves brilliant miniature character sketches; he wrote stage directions as witty or as provocative as the lines of the actors; and he wrote long prefaces and epilogues, some of which have become as famous as the plays they accompany.

The Elizabethans who crowded the Globe to see *Hamlet*, and the eighteenth-century sophisticates who laughed at *She Stoops to Conquer* had no analysis by Shakespeare or Goldsmith to help them interpret a character's thoughts or motives. They understood a character by what was said and done on the stage. The actors had very nearly complete control over the interpretation of a character's personality. But in a Shavian play the playwright himself has much to say about interpretation.

Reread the entrance and description of Alfred Doolittle on page 678. Before Doolittle says a word, Shaw sketches his personality. What effect does the word *pose* have on the reader's picture of Doolittle? What has Shaw indicated are Doolittle's outstanding characteristics? Does Doolittle's character change in the rest of the play? Why is extensive character development not so essential in *Pygmalion* as in *Hamlet*?

What other characters does Shaw sketch in stage directions? Find other examples of shorter stage directions which reveal character.

Find examples of stage directions which seem to exist only to delight the wit of the reader and which would be lost to the audience in an actual production.

Shaw wrote the prefaces and epilogues to his plays independently of the plays themselves. When he felt that a subject was too large to be fully dealt with on the stage, he wrote essays which he appended to his plays. Why did he think *Pygmalion* needed a sequel?

Explain Shaw's reasons for considering *Pygmalion* a romance.

What reasons does he give for the fact that Eliza does not marry Higgins? He says that Eliza was "instinctively aware that she could never obtain a complete grip of him [Higgins]." What prevented her from getting a complete grip of him? In Acts II and V Professor Higgins and Doolittle comment on marriage and the romantic notions of love. Are their attitudes about marriage sentimental ones? How does the sequel bear out these attitudes? How does the ending of the musical version of *Pygmalion*, "My Fair Lady," differ from Shaw's play? Would Shaw have approved? Why or why not?

Bibliography

BARNET, SYLVAN, and others, editors, *The Genius of the Later English Theater*. (•Mentor) This collection includes plays by Shaw and Wilde. An unusual feature is *The Brass Butterfly*, a play by novelist William Golding, author of *Lord of the Flies*.

BARRIE, JAMES M., *The Plays of J. M. Barrie*. (Scribner) *Dear Brutus, The Admirable Crichton*, and *Peter Pan* are among the familiar plays in this collection of well-loved dramas.

CERF, BENNETT, and VAN H. CARTMELL, editors, *Twenty-Four Favorite One-Act Plays*. (Doubleday) Synge, Yeats, Wilde, A. A. Milne, Lord Dunsany, and Lady Gregory are among the British dramatists represented in this fine collection.

FRY, CHRISTOPHER, *The Lady's Not for Burning; A Comedy*. (Oxford) The medieval English setting has not diminished the universal quality or popularity of this comedy about witchcraft.

GREGORY, LADY AUGUSTA, *Lady Gregory: Selected Plays*, chosen and edited by Elizabeth Coxhead. (Hill and Wang) Here Miss Coxhead has collected dramas created by the woman who helped establish Dublin's Abbey Theatre.

LERNER, ALAN JAY, *My Fair Lady*. (•Signet) The tremendously popular musical version of *Pygmalion* retains much of Shaw's original satirical humor.

NATHAN, GEORGE JEAN, editor, *Five Great Irish Plays*. (Modern Library) P. V. Carroll, Sean O'Casey, Lady Gregory, and Synge are the playwrights represented in this book.

PEARSON, HESKETH, *G. B. S., A Full Length Portrait*. (Harper) This is a combined reprint of Pearson's two books on Shaw. It contains excerpts from Shaw's published and unpublished correspondence and other vivid quotations.

SHAW, GEORGE BERNARD, *Four Plays by Shaw*. (•Dell) This collection contains *The Devil's Disciple, Caesar and Cleopatra, Candida*, and *Captain Brassbound's Conversion*. Another collection of three Shaw dramas is bound under the title *St. Joan; Major Barbara; Androcles and the Lion* (Modern Library). All are splendid Shavian reading.

SHENFIELD, MARGARET, *Bernard Shaw*. (Viking) This well-written text is enhanced by one hundred photographs of Shaw's colorful life.

THOMAS, DYLAN, *Under Milk Wood*. (•New Direction) The rhythm and beauty of this verse play, the only one Thomas wrote, show clearly that his untimely death deprived the world of a fine dramatist.

WILDE, OSCAR, *Five Plays by Oscar Wilde*. (•Bantam) The wit of plays like *The Importance of Being Earnest* has won this Irish satirist a wide following in England and America.

WILLIAMS, EMLYN, *The Collected Plays of Emlyn Williams*. (Random) Readers who are familiar with *Night Must Fall* and *The Corn Is Green* may want to read other dramas by this author.

YEATS, WILLIAM BUTLER, *Collected Plays*. (Macmillan) Among the works in this volume are *Deidre, Full Moon in March, King of the Great Clock Tower, Herne's Egg*, and *Land of Heart's Desire*.

•paperback

chapter eleven
Non-Fiction

The term *nonfiction* covers many different kinds of writing, including biography, essay, history, and travel. Most inclusive of these categories is the essay, which has enjoyed a long and continuous life in England since the time of Bacon (see page 187). The only restrictions on this form are that it should be relatively short and that it should be, as the name implies, an "attempt," not a fully worked out, formal treatise. The essay has proved to be a form of writing which is adaptable to any subject, any point of view. It is for this reason that, unlike most other literary forms, the English essay has not undergone a period of revolutionary experimentation in the twentieth century.

A second category of nonfiction, which also had its beginnings in sixteenth-century England, is biography, a form of writing which has been strongly affected by the revolutionary viewpoints of the present. From its earliest beginnings, biography has been associated with history, moral teaching, and the commemoration of the dead. All three kinds of biography were prominent in Victorian times. Carlyle gave the historical view of biography new emphasis in this era (see page 422, paragraph 4). There has never been any lack of people who, regarding biography primarily as moral teaching, told about the lives of great men in such a way that they might be an inspiration to the young. And the commemorative biography, that praised the dead in such a way as to shed honor upon the surviving members of the family, became a fixture of Victorian libraries. So popular had these forms of biography become by late Victorian times, that the real lives of many famous persons seemed in danger of becoming obscured by writers who wanted to prove a point or create a myth.

In the twentieth century it was Lytton Strachey who revived the great art of Boswell—the biography that reveals the man as he actually was with all his faults as well as virtues—from the evil days it had fallen upon in the later Victorian period. "Those two fat volumes," he wrote, "with which it is our custom to commemorate the dead—who does not know them, with their ill-digested masses of material, their slipshod style, their tone of tedious panegyric, their lamentable lack of selection, of detachment, of design?" Strachey's revolution was not complete; the family biography and the "great-man" biography still find a place in English letters. But Strachey's influence has carried forward the great tradition of the literary biography in England.

Aldous Huxley TIME AND THE MACHINE

Time, as we know it, is a very recent invention. The modern time-sense is hardly older than the United States. It is a by-product of industrialism—a sort of psychological analogue of synthetic perfumes and aniline dyes.

Time is our tyrant. We are chronically aware of the moving minute hand, even of the moving second hand. We have to be. There are trains to be caught, clocks to be punched, tasks to be done in specified periods, records to be broken by fractions of a second, machines that set the pace and have to be kept up with. Our consciousness of the smallest units of time is now acute. To us, for example, the moment 8:17 A.M. means something—something very important, if it happens to be the starting time of our daily train. To our ancestors, such an odd eccentric instant was without significance—did not even exist. In inventing the locomotive, Watt and Stephenson[1] were part inventors of time.

Another time-emphasizing entity is the factory and its dependent, the office. Factories exist for the purpose of getting certain quantities of goods made in a certain time. The old artisan worked as it suited him, with the result that consumers generally had to wait for the goods they had ordered from him. The factory is a device for making workmen hurry. The machine revolves so often each minute; so many movements have to be made, so many pieces produced each hour. Result: the factory worker (and the same is true of the office worker) is compelled to know time in its smallest fractions. In the handwork age there was no such compulsion to be aware of minutes and seconds.

Our awareness of time has reached such a pitch of intensity that we suffer acutely whenever our travels take us into some corner of the world where people are not interested in minutes and seconds. The unpunctuality of the Orient, for example, is appalling to those who come freshly from a land of fixed meal-times and regular train services. For a modern American or Englishman, waiting is a psychological torture. An Indian accepts the blank hours with resignation, even with satisfaction. He has not lost the fine art of doing nothing. Our notion of time as a collection of minutes, each of which must be filled with some business or amusement, is wholly alien to the Oriental just as it was wholly alien to the Greek. For the man who lives in a preindustrial world, time moves at a slow and easy pace; he does not care about each minute, for the good reason that he has not been made conscious of the existence of minutes.

This brings us to a seeming paradox. Acutely aware of the smallest constituent particles of time—of time, as measured by clockwork and train arrivals and the revolutions of machines—industrialized man has to a great extent lost the old awareness of time in its larger divisions. The time of which we have knowledge is artificial, machine-made time. Of natural, cosmic time, as it is measured out by sun and moon, we are for the most part almost wholly unconscious. Preindustrial people know time in its daily, monthly, and seasonal rhythms. They are aware of sunrise, noon, and sunset; of the full moon and the new; of equinox and solstice; of spring and summer, autumn and winter. All the old religions have insisted on this daily and seasonal rhythm. Preindustrial man was never allowed to forget the majestic movement of cosmic time.

Industrialism and urbanism have changed all this. One can live and work in a town without being aware of the daily march of the sun across the sky; without ever seeing the

1. Watt and Stephenson, James Watt (1736-1819), who invented the condensing steam engine in 1765, and George Stephenson (1781-1848), who invented the steam locomotive in 1814.

moon and stars. Broadway and Piccadilly[2] are our Milky Way; our constellations are outlined in neon tubes. Even changes of season affect the townsman very little. He is the inhabitant of an artificial universe that is, to a great extent, walled off from the world of nature. Outside the walls, time is cosmic and moves with the motion of sun and stars. Within, it is an affair of revolving wheels and is measured in seconds and minutes—at its longest, in eight-hour days and six-day weeks. We have a new consciousness; but it has been purchased at the expense of the old consciousness.

---

2. *Piccadilly*, one of the main business streets of London.

Aldous Huxley   1894–1963

On his father's side, Aldous Huxley was the grandson of Thomas Henry Huxley (see page 427), the biologist; on his mother's side, he was the great-nephew of Matthew Arnold (see page 450), the poet and essayist. This distinguished ancestry makes clear Huxley's interest in both science and literature.

It was to the scientific side of this inheritance that Huxley first turned, majoring in biology at Eton, until he developed eye trouble that left him almost blind. While trying to recover part of his lost vision, young Huxley wrote a novel in Braille. This was the turning point of his career. He decided to become a writer rather than a scientist.

Huxley shared the general disillusionment that followed in the wake of World War I. His early novels, *Chrome Yellow* (1921), *Antic Hay* (1923), and *Point Counter Point* (1928), reflecting this attitude, are bitter, mocking, and cynical. Civilization, he felt, had proved self-destructive, and science bore an important part of the responsibility for its breakdown.

Most of Huxley's later works—*Brave New World* (1932), *Eyeless in Gaza* (1936), *Brave New World Revisited* (1958)—show his search for meaning beyond the pale of rational science. In *Point Counter Point* a character who is very like Huxley himself remarks that he is "not a congenital novelist" but rather an essayist clothing his ideas in the form of novels. This suggestion is borne out by Huxley's works; and it is therefore not surprising that Huxley *was* a congenital essayist, with many successful volumes of essays to his credit.

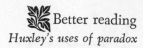 Better reading
Huxley's uses of paradox

A paradox is usually thought of as simply a rhetorical device—a statement that seems contradictory, but upon reflection reveals a subtle truth. The word *paradox*, however, is often used to refer to other things than epigrammatic statements of this kind. We speak of a paradoxical situation—one which is the contrary of what we should expect, but which is nonetheless true. Some modern writers go so far as to view paradox as a basic ingredient in life. In "Time and the Machine" Huxley has organized an entire essay around a central paradox. He states this central paradox in the paragraph beginning, "This brings us to a seeming paradox . . ." (page 715, column 2). In what way is the situation he describes contrary to the way one normally thinks of time? What examples does Huxley cite to show that it is nonetheless true? How widely does the influence of this paradox extend? What aspect of modern life does Huxley believe to be responsible for this paradoxical situation? What seems to be Huxley's general point of view about twentieth-century life?

The essay begins with a statement that is a paradox in the narrower sense described above: "Time, as we know it, is a very recent invention." The rest of the essay may be seen as revealing the truth and the implications that lie behind this superficially absurd treatment. In the course of the essay Huxley uses a number of other paradoxical statements, some of which help to explain the central paradox of the essay, others of which are used as rhetorical devices to attract attention or emphasize a point. For each of the following paradoxical statements explain (*a*) what seems contradictory about it, and (*b*) what truth lies behind the apparent contradiction. Then determine whether the purpose of the statement is to help explain the central paradox or to make the idea more effective.

(*a*) . . . machines that set the pace and have to be kept up with (page 715, column 1, paragraph 2).

(*b*) In inventing the locomotive, Watt and Stephenson were part inventors of time (page 715, column 1, paragraph 2).

(*c*) . . . the factory and its dependent, the office (page 715, column 1, paragraph 3).

(*d*) He has not lost the fine art of doing nothing (page 715, column 2, line 5).

(*e*) Broadway and Piccadilly are our Milky Way; our constellations are outlined in neon tubes (page 716, column 1, lines 1-3).

Winston Churchill DUNKIRK

In May 1940 the Germans forced the surrender of the Dutch and Belgian armies, thus leaving the British and French forces in France and Belgium in a perilous situation. After temporarily defending the French port of Dunkirk, close to the Belgian border, the Allied troops began, on May 29, the most famous retreat in history. British naval vessels, supplemented by thousands of privately owned vessels of all descriptions, stood off the beaches of Dunkirk, where the Allied troops were pinned down by a crossfire of German artillery and airplanes. Yet, with the protection provided by the Royal Air Force, the fleet of British vessels succeeded in embarking many thousands of troops and bringing them safely to England. Churchill reported these facts to the House of Commons in the following speech on June 4.

From the moment that the French defenses at Sedan and on the Meuse[1] were broken at the end of the second week of May, only a rapid retreat to Amiens[2] and the south could have saved the British and French armies who had entered Belgium at the appeal of the Belgian king; but this strategic fact was not immediately realized. The French High Command hoped they would be able to close the gap, and the Armies of the North[3] were under their orders. Moreover, a retirement of this kind would have involved almost certainly the destruction of the fine Belgian army of over twenty divisions and the abandonment of the whole of Belgium. Therefore, when the force and scope of the German penetration were realized, ... an effort was made by the French and British armies in Belgium to keep on holding the right hand of the Belgians and to give their own right hand to a newly created French army which was to have advanced across the Somme in great strength to grasp it.

However, the German eruption swept like a sharp scythe around the right and rear of the Armies of the North. Eight or nine armored divisions, each of about four hundred armored vehicles of different kinds, ... cut off all communications between us and the main French armies. It severed our own communications for food and ammunition, which ran first to Amiens and afterward through Abbeville,[4] and it shore[5] its way up the coast to Boulogne and Calais,[6] and almost to Dunkirk. Behind this armored and mechanized onslaught came a number of German divisions in lorries, and behind them again there plodded comparatively slowly the dull brute mass of the ordinary German army and German people, always so ready to be led to the trampling down in other lands of liberties and comforts which they have never known in their own.

I have said this armored scythe-stroke almost reached Dunkirk—almost but not quite. Boulogne and Calais were the scenes of desperate fighting. The Guards[7] defended Boulogne for a while and were then withdrawn by orders from this country. The Rifle Brigade, the 60th Rifles, and the Queen Victoria's Rifles,[8] with a battalion of British tanks and one thousand Frenchmen, in all about four thousand strong, defended Calais to the last. The British brigadier was given an hour to surrender. He spurned the offer, and four days of intense street fighting passed before

---

From *Blood, Sweat and Tears* by Winston S. Churchill. Reprinted by permission of G. P. Putnam's Sons, New York; and Cassell and Company Ltd., London. Copyright 1941 by Winston S. Churchill.
1. *Sedan and on the Meuse.* Sedan is a city on the Meuse River in northern France near the Belgian border. The Meuse River, which flows into Belgium, was one of the principal Belgian lines of defense against invasion from Germany. 2. *Amiens* (am'i ənz; *French* ä myaɴ'), an important city on the Somme River in northern France, west of Sedan. 3. *Armies of the North,* the entire British Expeditionary Force and two French armies. 4. *Abbeville* (ab'vēl'), an industrial city on the Somme between Amiens and the English Channel. 5. *shore,* an archaic past tense of *shear.* 6. *Boulogne* (bü lōn') *and Calais* (ka lā'), two French seaports on the English Channel. 7. *Guards,* certain famous regiments in the regular British army. 8. *Rifle Brigade ... Queen Victoria's Rifles,* bodies of soldiers armed with rifles, referred to later as "light divisions."

silence reigned over Calais, which marked the end of a memorable resistance. Only thirty unwounded survivors were brought off by the navy, and we do not know the fate of their comrades. Their sacrifice, however, was not in vain. At least two armored divisions, which otherwise would have been turned against the

---

Winston Churchill 1874-1965

Winston Churchill was sixty-five when he became Prime Minister of England. This was in 1940. In him, family tradition and experience combined with the tenacity of John Bull himself to produce a great leader in Britain's darkest hour.

Churchill, whose mother was an American, was born in an eighteenth-century manor house built by his ancestor, the Duke of Marlborough—a brilliant general who became a key minister in Queen Anne's reign. Young Churchill was educated for public service at Harrow and for military service at Sandhurst; then, following somewhat in the pattern of his great ancestor, he participated in a number of military campaigns before being sent to the House of Commons, there to move into several ministerial posts before becoming Prime Minister at last. A stanch conservative with a strong sense of history, Churchill held tenaciously to his belief in the Empire. It was largely for this reason that, in spite of his great personal popularity, he and his party were voted out of office immediately after World War II. Six years later, however, at the age of seventy-seven, he was returned to office and kept there until his resignation in 1955. In 1953 Churchill was raised to the peerage and made a Knight of the Garter.

Churchill's writings, like his political philosophy, are marked by an interest in history and a pervading sense of the long tradition of great English prose. He wrote a noted biography of the first Duke of Marlborough. He wrote of the history he helped to shape in *The World Crisis* (1923-1929) and in the six-volume *Second World War* (1948-1953), for which he received the Nobel Prize for Literature. In 1958 he completed *A History of the English Speaking Peoples*.

His orations delivered during the course of World War II also contributed to his literary fame. His voice became the voice of England. His fellow countrymen, their backs to the wall, heard that voice, and it brought to them the courage to stand and fight, to look with hope and confidence to the future.

British Expeditionary Force, had to be sent to overcome them. They have added another page to the glories of the light divisions, and the time gained enabled the Gravelines water lines[9] to be flooded and to be held by the French troops.

Thus it was that the port of Dunkirk was kept open. When it was found impossible for the Armies of the North to reopen their communications to Amiens with the main French armies, only one choice remained. It seemed indeed forlorn. The Belgian, British, and French armies were almost surrounded. Their sole line of retreat was to a single port and to its neighboring beaches. They were pressed on every side by heavy attacks and far outnumbered in the air.

When, a week ago today, I asked the House to fix this afternoon as the occasion for a statement, I feared it would be my hard lot to announce the greatest military disaster in our long history. I thought—and some good judges agreed with me—that perhaps 20,000 or 30,000 men might be reëmbarked. But it certainly seemed that the whole of the French First Army and the whole of the British Expeditionary Force north of the Amiens-Abbeville gap would be broken up in the open field or else would have to capitulate for lack of food and ammunition. These were the hard and heavy tidings for which I called upon the House and the nation to prepare themselves a week ago. The whole root and core and brain of the British army, on which and around which we were to build, and are to build, the great British armies in the later years of the war, seemed about to perish upon the field or to be led into an ignominious and starving captivity.

That was the prospect a week ago. But another blow which might well have proved final was yet to fall upon us. The King of the Belgians had called upon us to come to his aid. Had not this ruler and his government severed themselves from the Allies, who rescued their country from extinction in the late

---

9. *Gravelines* (gräv′lēn′) *water lines*. Gravelines is a strongly fortified seaport town twelve miles northeast of Calais. By means of sluices the whole adjacent country may be flooded.

war,[10] and had they not sought refuge in what has proved to be a fatal neutrality, the French and British armies might well at the outset have saved not only Belgium but perhaps even Poland.[11] Yet at the last moment, when Belgium was already invaded, King Leopold called upon us to come to his aid, and even at the last moment we came. He and his brave, efficient army, nearly half a million strong, guarded our left flank and thus kept open our only line of retreat to the sea. Suddenly, without prior consultation, with the least possible notice, without the advice of his ministers and upon his own personal act, he sent a plenipotentiary to the German Command, surrendered his army, and exposed our whole flank and means of retreat.

I asked the House a week ago to suspend its judgment because the facts were not clear, but I do not feel that any reason now exists why we should not form our own opinions upon this pitiful episode. The surrender of the Belgian army compelled the British at the shortest notice to cover a flank to the sea more than thirty miles in length. Otherwise all would have been cut off, and all would have shared the fate to which King Leopold had condemned the finest army his country had ever formed. So in doing this and in exposing this flank, as anyone who followed the operations on the map will see, contact was lost between the British and two out of the three corps forming the First French Army, who were still farther from the coast than we were, and it seemed impossible that any large number of Allied troops could reach the coast.

The enemy attacked on all sides with great strength and fierceness, and their main power, the power of their far more numerous air force, was thrown into the battle or else concentrated upon Dunkirk and the beaches. Pressing in upon the narrow exit, both from the east and from the west, the enemy began to fire with cannon upon the beaches by which alone the shipping could approach or depart. They sowed magnetic mines in the channels and seas; they sent repeated waves of hostile aircraft, sometimes more than a hundred strong in one formation, to cast their bombs upon the single pier that remained, and upon the sand dunes upon which the troops had their eyes for shelter. Their U-boats, one of which was sunk, and their motor launches took their toll of the vast traffic which now began. For four or five days an intense struggle reigned. All their armored divisions—or what was left of them—together with great masses of infantry and artillery, hurled themselves in vain upon the ever-narrowing, ever-contracting appendix within which the British and French armies fought.

Meanwhile, the Royal Navy, with the willing help of countless merchant seamen, strained every nerve to embark the British and Allied troops; 220 light warships and 650 other vessels were engaged. They had to operate upon the difficult coast, often in adverse weather, under an almost ceaseless hail of bombs and an increasing concentration of artillery fire. Nor were the seas, as I have said, themselves free from mines and torpedoes. It was in conditions such as these that our men carried on, with little or no rest, for days and nights on end, making trip after trip across the dangerous waters, bringing with them always men whom they had rescued. The numbers they have brought back are the measure of their devotion and their courage. The hospital ships, which brought off many thousands of British and French wounded, being so plainly marked were a special target for Nazi bombs; but the men and women on board them never faltered in their duty.

Meanwhile, the Royal Air Force, which had already been intervening in the battle, so far as its range would allow, from home bases, now used part of its main metropolitan fighter strength, and struck at the German bombers and at the fighters which in large numbers protected them. This struggle was protracted and fierce. Suddenly the scene has cleared, the crash and thunder has for the moment—but only for the moment—died away. A miracle of deliverance, achieved by valor, by perseverance, by perfect discipline, by faultless service, by resource, by skill, by unconquerable fidel-

---

10. *late war*, World War I. 11. *might well . . . even Poland*. World War II had started on September 1, 1939, when Germany suddenly attacked Poland. Before the allies of Poland had agreed on coming to her aid, Poland had been crushed by the Germans.

ity, is manifest to us all. The enemy was hurled back by the retreating British and French troops. He was so roughly handled that he did not hurry their departure seriously. The Royal Air Force engaged the main strength of the German air force, and inflicted upon them losses of at least four to one; and the navy, using nearly 1000 ships of all kinds, carried over 335,000 men, French and British, out of the jaws of death and shame, to their native land and to the tasks which lie immediately ahead.

We must be very careful not to assign to this deliverance the attributes of a victory. Wars are not won by evacuations. But there was a victory inside this deliverance, which should be noted. It was gained by the air force. Many of our soldiers coming back have not seen the air force at work; they saw only the bombers which escaped its protective attack. They underrate its achievements. I have heard much talk of this; that is why I go out of my way to say this. I will tell you about it.

This was a great trial of strength between the British and German air forces. Can you conceive a greater objective for the Germans in the air than to make evacuation from these beaches impossible, and to sink all these ships which were displayed, almost to the extent of thousands? Could there have been an objective of greater military importance and significance for the whole purpose of the war than this? They tried hard, and they were beaten back; they were frustrated in their task. We got the army away; and they have paid fourfold for any losses which they have inflicted. Very large formations of German airplanes—and we know that they are a very brave race—have turned on several occasions from the attack of one-quarter of their number of the Royal Air Force, and have dispersed in different directions. Twelve airplanes have been hunted by two. One airplane was driven into the water and cast away by the mere charge of a British airplane, which had no more ammunition. All of our types—the Hurricane, the Spitfire, and the new Defiant—and all our pilots have been vindicated as superior to what they have at present to face.

When we consider how much greater would be our advantage in defending the air above this island against an overseas attack, I must say that I find in these facts a sure basis upon which practical and reassuring thoughts may rest. I will pay my tribute to these young airmen. The great French army was very largely, for the time being, cast back and disturbed by the onrush of a few thousands of armored vehicles. May it not also be that the cause of civilization itself will be defended by the skill and devotion of a few thousand airmen? There never has been, I suppose, in all the world, in all the history of war, such an opportunity for youth. The Knights of the Round Table, the Crusaders, all fall back into the past—not only distant but prosaic; these young men, going forth every morn to guard their native land and all that we stand for, holding in their hands these instruments of colossal and shattering power, of whom it may be said that

Every morn brought forth a noble chance
And every chance brought forth a noble knight,[12]

deserve our gratitude, as do all of the brave men who, in so many ways and on so many occasions, are ready, and continue ready, to give life and all for their native land.

I return to the army. In the long series of very fierce battles, now on this front, now on that, fighting on three fronts at once, battles fought by two or three divisions against an equal or somewhat larger number of the enemy, and fought fiercely on some of the old grounds that so many of us knew so well—in these battles our losses in men have exceeded 30,000 killed, wounded, and missing. I take occasion to express the sympathy of the House to all who have suffered bereavement or who are still anxious. The President of the Board of Trade[13] is not here today. His son has been killed, and many in the House have felt the pangs of affliction in the sharpest form. But I will say this about the missing: we have had a large number of wounded come home safely to this country, but I would say about the

12. *Every . . . knight.* These lines, slightly misquoted, are from "The Passing of Arthur" in Tennyson's *Idylls of the King.* 13. *President . . . Board of Trade,* Sir Andrew Duncan. In England the Board of Trade is a department of the government in charge of commerce and industry.

missing that there may be very many reported missing who will come back home, some day, in one way or another. In the confusion of this fight it is inevitable that many have been left in positions where honor required no further resistance from them.

Against this loss of over 30,000 men, we can set a far heavier loss certainly inflicted upon the enemy. But our losses in material are enormous. We have perhaps lost one-third of the men we lost in the opening days of the battle of 21 March 1918, but we have lost nearly as many guns—nearly one thousand— and all our transport, all the armored vehicles that were with the army in the north. This loss will impose a further delay on the expansion of our military strength. That expansion had not been proceeding as fast as we had hoped. The best of all we had to give had gone to the British Expeditionary Force, and although they had not the numbers of tanks and some articles of equipment which were desirable, they were a very well and finely equipped army. They had the first fruits of all that our industry had to give, and that is gone. And now here is this further delay. How long it will be, how long it will last, depends upon the exertions which we make in this island. An effort the like of which has never been seen in our records is now being made. Work is proceeding everywhere, night and day, Sundays and weekdays. Capital and Labor have cast aside their interests, rights, and customs and put them into the common stock. Already the flow of munitions has leaped forward. There is no reason why we should not in a few months overtake the sudden and serious loss that has come upon us, without retarding the development of our general program.

Nevertheless, our thankfulness at the escape of our army and so many men, whose loved ones have passed through an agonizing week, must not blind us to the fact that what has happened in France and Belgium is a colossal military disaster. The French army has been weakened, the Belgian army has been lost, a large part of those fortified lines upon which so much faith had been reposed is gone, many valuable mining districts and factories have passed into the enemy's possession, the whole of the Channel ports are in his hands, with all the tragic consequences that follow from that, and we must expect another blow to be struck almost immediately at us or at France. We are told that Herr Hitler has a plan for invading the British Isles. This has often been thought of before. When Napoleon lay at Boulogne for a year[14] with his flat-bottomed boats and his Grand Army, he was told by someone, "There are bitter weeds in England." There are certainly a great many more of them since the British Expeditionary Force returned.

The whole question of home defense against invasion is, of course, powerfully affected by the fact that we have for the time being in this island incomparably more powerful military forces than we have ever had at any moment in this war or the last. . . . I would observe that there has never been a period in all these long centuries of which we boast when an absolute guarantee against invasion, still less against serious raids, could have been given to our people. In the days of Napoleon the same wind which would have carried his transports across the Channel might have driven away the blockading fleet. There was always the chance, and it is that chance which has excited and befooled the imaginations of many Continental tyrants. Many are the tales that are told. We are assured that novel methods will be adopted, and when we see the originality of malice, the ingenuity of aggression, which our enemy displays, we may certainly prepare ourselves for every kind of novel stratagem and every kind of brutal and treacherous maneuver. I think that no idea is so outlandish that it should not be considered and viewed with a searching—but at the same time, I hope, with a steady—eye. We must never forget the solid assurances of sea power and those which belong to air power if it can be locally exercised.

I have, myself, full confidence that if all do their duty, if nothing is neglected, and if the best arrangements are made, as they are being made, we shall prove ourselves once again able to defend our island home, to ride out the

14. *Napoleon . . . year.* In 1805 Napoleon's army lay ready to cross the Channel and invade England.

storm of war, and to outlive the menace of tyranny, if necessary for years, if necessary alone. At any rate, that is what we are going to try to do. That is the resolve of His Majesty's Government—every man of them. That is the will of Parliament and the nation. The British Empire and the French Republic, linked together in their cause and in their need, will defend to the death their native soil, aiding each other like good comrades to the utmost of their strength. Even though large tracts of Europe and many old and famous states have fallen or may fall into the grip of the Gestapo[15] and all the odious apparatus of Nazi rule, we shall not flag or fail. We shall go on to the end, we shall fight in France, we shall fight on the seas and oceans, we shall fight with growing confidence and growing strength in the air, we shall defend our island, whatever the cost may be, we shall fight on the beaches, we shall fight on the landing grounds, we shall fight in the fields and in the streets, we shall fight in the hills; we shall never surrender, and even if, which I do not for a moment believe, this island or a large part of it were subjugated and starving, then our Empire beyond the seas, armed and guarded by the British fleet, would carry on the struggle, until, in God's good time, the New World, with all its power and might, steps forth to the rescue and the liberation of the old.

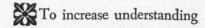 To increase understanding

1. Summarize the losses that had been suffered by the British. Why, despite these losses, was Mr. Churchill optimistic about the future?

2. As an orator Churchill has displayed an extraordinary power to move and sway his audiences. Examine each of the following quotations, determining (1) what the main purpose of the statement is in terms of the speech as a whole, and (2) what the special effect of the italicized words is.

(*a*) . . . an effort was made by the French and British armies in Belgium to keep on *holding the right hand* of the Belgians and *to give their own right hand* to a newly created French army (page 717, column 1, paragraph 1).

(*b*) The *Knights of the Round Table*, the *Crusaders*, all fall back into the past (page 720, column 2, lines 14-16).

(*c*) . . . *we shall fight* on the beaches, *we shall fight* on the landing grounds, *we shall fight* in the fields and in the streets, *we shall fight* in the hills; *we shall* never surrender (page 722, column 1, lines 20-24).

(*d*) . . . until, *in God's good time*, the New World, with all its power and might, *steps forth* to the rescue and the liberation of the old (page 722, column 1, lines 29-31).

3. In reviewing *Blood, Sweat and Tears*, the collection of Churchill's speeches in which "Dunkirk" appeared, a critic said: "Mr. Churchill's speeches are battle cries, dirges for the fallen, and hymns of victory." Do you agree that these terms aptly fit "Dunkirk"? If so, how?

Arnold Toynbee CAN WE LIVE IN PEACE?

Can our Western world and the communist world live at peace with each other side by side? Is their peaceful coexistence something desirable from our Western point of view? And, if we come to the conclusion that it is desirable, as well as possible, for these two worlds to put up with one another's presence on the face of the same planet, on what terms can we look forward to seeing them live and let live?

I suppose, among all current questions, these three are about the most highly controversial ones that anybody could pick out for discussion. What is *possible* is controversial; what is *desirable* is controversial. The most that any of us can do is to say what he personally expects and personally hopes.

I suppose one of the few points on which all of us in the West are in agreement with each other today is just this point that we must

"Can We Live in Peace?" by Arnold Toynbee from *New Republic* (December 1951). Reprinted by permission of the author.

DUNKIRK **15.** *Gestapo*, the Nazi secret police of Germany, assigned to discover and arrest persons opposed to the policies of the government.

be firm, that we must rearm, that we must be vigilantly on our guard. But it does not follow from any of this that we must resign ourselves to the prospect of a third world war as being something inevitable. As I see it, it is just as important for us now to keep on reminding ourselves that a third world war is really not inevitable, as it is important for us now to be firm and energetic and on the watch.

In saying this, I have another historical precedent in mind. I am thinking of the history of Anglo-Russian relations during the years 1856-1885. In the Crimean War the Western powers had foiled an attempt of Russia's to put Turkey in her pocket. They had inflicted on Russia a humiliating defeat which the Russians naturally wanted to reverse, as the Germans, after 1918, wanted to reverse *their* defeat after the First World War. So, like Germany in the 1930's, Russia in the 1860's began to expand eastward overland, in a quarter where the British navy could not operate; and this expansion of Russia's in Asia in the nineteenth century, like her present expansion, was taken very hard in the liberal Western world. At least twice within the thirty years ending in 1885, Great Britain found herself on the verge of going to war with Russia again. The first occasion was in 1878, when Russia had fought another war with Turkey and had beaten Turkey to its knees. The second occasion was in 1885, when the Russian advance in Central Asia reached the northwestern frontiers of Afghanistan. At those two dates, at least, another Anglo-Russian war seemed inevitable. And then, after all, it did not happen this time.

After reaching a final peak of intensity in 1885, the long drawn-out nineteenth-century tension between Britain and Russia began to relax. Within twenty-two years the two powers had entered into an entente with each other in face of a new menace to both of them from Germany. And between 1907 and now they have twice been allies in a world war, first in 1914-1917 and then for a second time in 1941-1945.

My point in bringing up these episodes of past history is this. It is possible that our present tension with Russia may end in another war, as our tension with Germany after the First World War ended in a Second World War. It is also possible that our present tension with Russia may end in a relaxation of the tension, as our tension with Russia after the Crimean War eventually relaxed without ending in another war between the two powers.

At the present moment, no doubt, it is impossible for us to foresee in which of these two possible alternative ways the present tension between the Western world and Russia is going to end. We must be prepared for the less happy as well as for the more happy possibility; but we must surely be prepared for both possibilities. In facing the possibility of an-

---

Arnold Toynbee   1889—

Arnold Toynbee was educated at Winchester and later at Balliol College, Oxford. He served for a time as tutor at Balliol; and during World War I he joined the British Intelligence Department. He sat in on the Paris Peace Conference following the war, and from 1919 until his retirement in 1955 was a professor of history at the University of London.

Toynbee has won recognition as the leading "broadview" historian of his generation. In his most important historical writings he has centered his attention, not on single nations or periods, but on the rise and fall (or survival) of the major civilizations in all periods of human history. Toynbee's belief is that entire societies move in broad patterns which can be recognized and predicted on the basis of similar patterns which have occurred in the past.

The most important of Toynbee's works is *A Study of History*, published in twelve volumes between 1934 and 1961. Abridgments of this detailed analysis have proved popular in both England and the United States. Even more popular was the collection of essays entitled *Civilization on Trial* (1948). Facing a future marked by uncertainty and doubt, people of the Western world turned to Toynbee's pages to see what message they offered. That message, they discovered, is a contradictory one. On the one hand, Toynbee is inclined to foresee the eventual decline of present-day civilizations. On the other hand, he admits the possibility, however slim, that mankind may somehow arise from its present confusion and evolve a superior civilization. If so, he believes that religion will be a powerful factor in this progress.

other 1939, we must not lose sight of the possibility of another 1885.

But is it possible for a democratic free Western world and a communist totalitarian Russia to live and let live on the face of a planet that has now become physically "one world" as a result of "the annihilation of distance" by new-fangled methods of mechanical transport? Well, yes, this *is* possible, as I see it. I see this possibility in the light of another historical precedent. I am thinking of the one world, stretching from Britain to India, which was called into existence by the expansion of the ancient Greek civilization in and after the time of Alexander the Great.

For about seven centuries, running from the last century B.C. to the seventh century of the Christian Era, that ancient world was partitioned between a Western and an Eastern power: the Roman Empire in the West and a rival Oriental Empire in Persia. It is true that Rome and her Iranian[1] rivals did go to war with one another from time to time; but to the point is that each of them soon discovered that it was beyond its strength to conquer, subjugate, and annex the other. Each of them did make the attempt, only to find that it must give it up because the effort was straining its own resources to breaking point. So those two ancient powers resigned themselves to the necessity of their coexisting, and they did go on living in one world side by side for nearly seven hundred years. When they fell into a life-and-death struggle with one another at last, they had to pay for this mistake, cash down, by both immediately succumbing to a common new enemy: the Saracens.[2] Why should it not be possible, in our modern world, for the West and the Union of Soviet Russia to repeat that episode of ancient history?

Granting for the moment that this may be *possible*, do we *want* to see it happen? As I see it, the peaceful coexistence of our Western civilization and a Russian communist society is not merely possible: it is also highly desirable for two good reasons, one negative and one positive.

My negative reason is my belief that a third world war fought with atomic weapons would plunge our planet into a chaos which would be beyond even America's power to bring into order again. I am assuming that America would win a third world war hands down; and I will also make the further assumption that the United States would come out of such a war without grave damage to herself (though I find few Americans so optimistic as that about their country's prospects of coming through unscathed). But I take it for granted that, at the end of a third world war in which Russia had been knocked out by America, the whole of the Old World would have been laid flat—not only Russia, but Europe, Asia, and Africa as well. And would even an undamaged United States have the strength, by herself, to set the whole of the rest of the world on its feet again?

My positive reason for thinking a third world war undesirable is that, even if that fearful world-wide destruction could eventually be repaired by a victorious United States, it would not, as I see it, be healthy for the world, or healthy for America herself, for there only to be one sole surviving power in the world. In order to keep morally fit, human nature needs to be exercised and kept in training by some devil or other; and our Western world today is having this indispensable, though very disagreeable, service performed for her by Russia. The other way around, too, if we can submit with a good grace to the practical joke of seeing ourselves for a moment as Russian eyes see us, I fancy that the capitalist world, dressed up in horns, hooves, forked tail and the devil's other stage properties, is a bogy that communist Russia needs just as much as a democratic West needs the bogy of Russian totalitarianism to keep her up to the mark. In fact, neither of these two incongruous neighbors would find it easy to keep in good health if the other were entirely eliminated.

What kind of *modus vivendi*[3] can we imagine? I cannot imagine any formal agreement between us to behave to each other as good

1. *Iranian*, Persian. 2. *the Saracens* (sar'ə sənz), the Arabs. Soon after Mohammed had founded Islam, or the Mohammedan religion, early in the seventh century, the Arabs began a holy war against the non-Mohammedan world. 3. *modus vivendi* (mō'dəs vi ven'dī), way of getting along. [Latin]

neighbors; but I can imagine an unspoken determination on either side not to fall into a shooting war with the other party. The kind of peaceful coexistence that consists merely in the avoidance of a shooting war between the principal parties may well prove to be a state of extremely painful stress, anxiety, and discomfort.

There might be other *local* shooting wars like the war in Korea. And I personally feel sure that, even if we manage to avoid dropping atom bombs on each other, we shall continue to wage our present missionary war—I mean, the competitive propaganda of our rival ideas and ideals. This, I fancy, will go on until Asia becomes formidable enough to the rest of us to make the English-speaking people begin to look upon Russia as "the white man's hope"; and, even if that eventually happens, we shall then merely be exchanging a Russian peril for an Asian one, as we have exchanged a Russian peril for a German one, and then a German peril for a Russian one, within living memory.

You will see that I am not doing you the disservice of prophesying to you smooth things. I am prophesying a continuance of toil and trouble for as long as we can peer ahead into our future; and, as I see it, this prophecy is a safe one to make; for I personally agree with Eliphaz the Temanite's[4] view that "man is born unto trouble, as the sparks fly upward." Indeed I will go farther than Eliphaz goes in

the Book of Job. I will put it to you that, if ever man does manage to elude trouble, he merely brings trouble on himself, because trouble, after all, is the necessary salt of life without which life loses its savor. So perhaps the unwritten condition on which we and the Russians are going to coexist is that each party shall go on serving as the other party's devil.

To increase understanding

1. This essay was originally delivered as a radio address. Explain why, in your opinion, the general tenor of Toynbee's remarks would bring hope or discouragement to his listeners in England and America.

2. What are the three questions considered in this essay?

3. (*a*) What historical illustrations does Toynbee introduce in his arguments? (*b*) What does he try to show through these examples from the past? (*c*) Do you find that this particular use of historical examples is convincing? Why, or why not?

4. (*a*) What two "good reasons" does Toynbee give for believing that the peaceful coexistence of the Western world and the communist world is both possible and desirable? (*b*) Does Toynbee use historical arguments to support his assertions here, or other kinds of arguments? Explain.

5. (*a*) What are the two most prominent features of the future relationship Toynbee foresees between Russia and the Western world? (*b*) In what way are these features related to the reasons he believes coexistence to be possible and desirable? (*c*) To what extent does his reasoning appear to be convincing?

Virginia Woolf THREE PICTURES

The First Picture

It is impossible that one should not see pictures; because if my father was a blacksmith and yours was a peer of the realm, we must needs be pictures to each other. We cannot possibly break out of the frame of the picture by speaking natural words. You see me leaning against the door of the smithy with a horseshoe in my hand and you think as you go by: "How

picturesque!" I, seeing you sitting so much at your ease in the car, almost as if you were going to bow to the populace, think what a picture of old luxurious aristocratical England! We are both quite wrong in our judgments no doubt, but that is inevitable.

CAN WE LIVE IN PEACE? 4. *Eliphaz* (el'i faz) *the Temanite* (tē'mən it), a friend who came to console Job in his troubles.

So now at the turn of the road I saw one of these pictures. It might have been called "The Sailor's Homecoming" or some such title. A fine young sailor carrying a bundle; a girl with her hand on his arm; neighbours gathering round; a cottage garden ablaze with flowers; as one passed one read at the bottom of that picture that the sailor was back from China, and there was a fine spread waiting

---

Virginia Woolf 1882-1941

Upon Virginia Woolf's birth, her godfather wrote some verses for the infant girl and prayed she would grow up to be "a sample of Heredity." His was no small wish. For Virginia, the daughter of critic Sir Leslie Stephens, was related to such writers and thinkers as Thackeray, Darwin, and Macaulay. But she did fulfill her godfather's hopes: today Virginia Woolf is considered one of the world's greatest woman writers.

In 1912, Virginia married Leonard Woolf; simply for amusement, the Woolfs founded the Hogarth Press. The press' first publication was a pamphlet entitled *Two Stories* by V. and L. Woolf. Much to the Woolfs' surprise, the little book sold out almost immediately. Soon the Woolf home became the meeting place for the Bloomsbury Group—young intellectuals interested in the esoteric aspects of literature and art.

But despite what must have been a rewarding life, Mrs. Woolf was a troubled woman. While in her thirties, she suffered a mental breakdown; from that point on she worried the illness would strike again. When, in her late fifties, she began to feel the symptoms of another collapse, she feared it would this time be permanent. On March 28, 1941, she wrote a suicide note and disappeared from her home; her drowned body was later recovered.

Virginia Woolf believed that much imaginative literature is false to life because it relates episodes in a straight line: "This happened first, and next that, and finally that." Our experiences, she claimed, do not move forward in such well-measured steps, but flow together like a stream. Any one single instant in our lives calls forth an awareness of the past that engulfs it, and this awareness links together events that occur apart. Plot, setting, character development —the "necessities" of narrative to most writers—she discarded almost completely. Time, the web that binds a life together, was her primary concern in both her novels and her essays. She tried to capture its flow, and in her best works (*Mrs. Dalloway, To the Lighthouse*) she succeeded admirably.

for him in the parlour; and he had a present for his young wife in his bundle; and she was soon going to bear him their first child. Everything was right and good and as it should be, one felt about that picture. There was something wholesome and satisfactory in the sight of such happiness; life seemed sweeter and more enviable than before.

So thinking I passed them, filling in the picture as fully, as completely as I could, noticing the colour of her dress, of his eyes, seeing the sandy cat slinking round the cottage door.

For some time the picture floated in my eyes, making most things appear much brighter, warmer, and simpler than usual; and making some things appear foolish; and some things wrong and some things right, and more full of meaning than before. At odd moments during that day and the next the picture returned to one's mind, and one thought with envy, but with kindness, of the happy sailor and his wife; one wondered what they were doing, what they were saying now. The imagination supplied other pictures springing from that first one, a picture of the sailor cutting firewood, drawing water; and they talked about China; and the girl set his present on the chimney piece where everyone who came could see it; and she sewed at her baby clothes, and all the doors and windows were open into the garden so that the birds were flittering and the bees humming, and Rogers —that was his name—could not say how much to his liking all this was after the China seas. As he smoked his pipe, with his foot in the garden.

The Second Picture

In the middle of the night a loud cry rang through the village. Then there was a sound of something scuffling; and then dead silence. All that could be seen out of the window was the branch of lilac tree hanging motionless and ponderous across the road. It was a hot still night. There was no moon. The cry made everything seem ominous. Who had cried? Why had she cried? It was a woman's voice, made by some extremity of feeling almost sexless, almost expressionless. It was as if human nature had cried out against some iniquity, some inexpressible horror. There was dead silence. The stars shone perfectly steadily. The fields lay still. The trees were motionless. Yet all seemed guilty, convicted, ominous. One felt that something ought to be done. Some light ought to appear tossing, moving agitatedly. Someone ought to come running down the road. There should be lights in the cottage windows. And then perhaps another cry, but less sexless, less wordless, comforted, appeased. But no light came. No feet were heard. There was no second cry. The first had been swallowed up, and there was dead silence.

One lay in the dark listening intently. It had been merely a voice. There was nothing to connect it with. No picture of any sort came to interpret it, to make it intelligible to the mind. But as the dark arose at last all one saw was an obscure human form, almost without shape, raising a gigantic arm in vain against some overwhelming iniquity.

The Third Picture

The fine weather remained unbroken. Had it not been for that single cry in the night one would have felt that the earth had put into harbour; that life had ceased to drive before the wind; that it had reached some quiet cove and there lay anchored, hardly moving, on the quiet waters. But the sound persisted. Wherever one went, it might be for a long walk up into the hills, something seemed to turn uneasily beneath the surface, making the peace, the stability all round one seem a little unreal. There were the sheep clustered on the side of the hill; the valley broke in long tapering waves like the fall of smooth waters. One came on solitary farmhouses. The puppy rolled in the yard. The butterflies gambolled over the gorse. All was as quiet, as safe could be. Yet, one kept thinking, a cry had rent it; all this beauty had been an accomplice that night; had consented to remain calm, to be still beautiful; at any moment it might be sundered again. This goodness, this safety were only on the surface.

And then to cheer oneself out of this apprehensive mood one turned to the picture of the sailor's homecoming. One saw it all over again producing various little details—the blue colour of her dress, the shadow that fell from the yellow flowering tree—that one had not used before. So they had stood at the cottage door, he with his bundle on his back, she just lightly touching his sleeve with her hand. And a sandy cat had slunk round the door. Thus gradually going over the picture in every detail, one persuaded oneself by degrees that it was far more likely that this calm and content and good will lay beneath the surface than anything treacherous, sinister. The sheep grazing, the waves of the valley, the farmhouse, the puppy, the dancing butterflies were in fact like that all through. And so one turned back home, with one's mind fixed on the sailor and his wife, making up picture after picture of them so that one picture after another of happiness and satisfaction might be laid over that unrest, that hideous cry, until it was crushed and silenced by their pressure out of existence.

Here at last was the village, and the churchyard through which one must pass; and the usual thought came, as one entered it, of the peacefulness of the place, with its shady yews, its rubbed tombstones, its nameless graves. Death is cheerful here, one felt. Indeed, look at that picture! A man was digging a grave, and children were picnicking at the side of it while he worked. As the shovels of yellow earth were thrown up, the children were sprawling about eating bread and jam and drinking milk out of large mugs. The gravedigger's wife, a fat fair woman, had propped herself against a tombstone and spread her apron on the grass by the open grave to serve as a tea-table. Some lumps of clay had fallen among the tea things. Who was going to be buried, I asked. Had old Mr. Dodson died at last? "Oh! no. It's for young Rogers, the sailor," the woman answered, staring at me. "He died two nights ago, of some foreign fever. Didn't you hear his wife? She rushed into the road and cried out. . . . Here, Tommy, you're all covered with earth!"

What a picture it made!

1. (*a*) Summarize the scene described in the first picture. (*b*) What is the speaker's reaction to it?

2. A cry in the night is, perhaps, most terrifying when it breaks through complete silence. (*a*) In the paragraph describing the effect of the cry, which words and phrases help create an atmosphere of silence? (*b*) Which sentence best expresses the speaker's reaction to the second picture?

3. (*a*) What picture is referred to in the last sentence of the essay? (*b*) Why might the speaker have chosen not to describe his reaction to it?

4. (*a*) Describe the tone of "Three Pictures." (*b*) In one sentence, state the feeling Woolf wishes this essay to create in the reader. (*c*) Explain the relationship between the opening paragraph and the rest of the essay.

5. (*a*) Characterize the sentence patterns in the description of the first picture. (*b*) Are these patterns suited to the content of the picture? Why or why not?

6. (*a*) What sentence pattern predominates in the description of the second picture? (*b*) Show the relationship between the effect of the picture on the speaker and the dominant sentence pattern.

7. How does the variety of sentence patterns used in the first paragraph of the third section reflect the speaker's feelings?

8. Discuss the importance of imagery in creating the three pictures.

9. Comment on the (*a*) clarity, (*b*) conciseness, (*c*) pace, and (*d*) rhythm of Virginia Woolf's style as displayed in this essay.

10. This essay seems to contrast surfaces and depths—or pictures and reality. (*a*) What does it suggest about our awareness of other people? (*b*) What does it suggest about the complexity of reality?

Kingsley Amis   *from* SCIENCE FICTION: A PRACTICAL NIGHTMARE

It might have been the cover pictures that did it—starscapes, space-suited heroes advancing through unlikely jungles with blasters at the ready, tentacled Things with eyes on stalks and an evident penchant for blondes. Or was it sampling the stories themselves?—the psychotic robots, the Martian plagues, the carnivorous weed that got up and chased people, the giant indestructible amoeba that ate battleships. The art work was vulgar and sensational, the prose style revolting, but at the age of twelve, I didn't notice. However it happened, my first five minutes' experience of science-fiction magazines was enough: I was hooked.

Readiness to enjoy horror and terror and strangeness is a basic requirement for enjoying science fiction. The same group of feelings, obviously, can be appealed to by straight horror stories, fairy tales in the Grimm vein, black-magic stories, voodoo stories. These leave me, and many others, cold, and I think that much of their territory has been annexed by science fiction. At any rate, I'm not interested in the doings of magicians who make up their own rules. My marvels and terrors must be presented as possible, as maintaining some connection with experience and reason. It seems clear that *Nineteen Eighty-Four*, for instance, depends for its effect upon our recognizing our own world in the nightmarish future that Orwell portrays. Big Brother; Newspeak, the barbarous official jargon aimed at suppressing thought; O'Brien, brainwasher-in-chief and aesthete of power—none of them would mean much to us if we weren't able to see in them some of the nastier tendencies of modern politics, and also of human nature at large.

"Science Fiction: A Practical Nightmare" by Kingsley Amis from *Holiday* (February 1965). Reprinted by permission of the author.

Two functions seem to me fundamental to science fiction: it stimulates the fancy without bypassing the intellect—it methodizes the fairy tale, so to speak; and while speculating about the future it can tell us something about mid-twentieth-century man and society. We are in fact pretty close here to a definition of the medium. For completeness, I should add that the writer's typical concern is with a situation that couldn't arise in the world we know, but is shown as arising out of some development in science or technology—anything from interplanetary travel to four-wall television. Very often, though, the new situation simply happens—a comet appears on a collision course for Earth, a virus attacks all grain crops—without science having anything to do with it. For this and other reasons, notably recent accelerations in real science which tend to make its fictional projections look rather prosaic, the "science" part of the science-fiction label is on the wane. To cope with this, some pundits suggest a switch of nomenclature to "possibility" fiction, or "context-manipulation" fiction. It sounds fine; but the effort required to get the switch accepted would compare with that needed to stop everyone saying *Hamlet* and make them call the thing *The Prince of Denmark* instead.

By trying to make its marvels plausible science fiction enhances their power. The most lyrical fantasy about what it's like on the moon would be less compelling than Arthur C. Clarke's accounts, which half persuade us the author has been there himself. A robot that we can believe in as remotely practicable —Isaac Asimov's stories are the example here— surpasses Frankenstein's monster by adding an extra component to the feelings of distrust and dread aroused by any form of pseudo-life. A science-fiction situation gives a new force to Freud's definition of the uncanny as the quality objects have when we're not sure whether they're alive or not. Other such comparisons can be made. Wyman Guin has a story, *Beyond Bedlam*, in which schizophrenia has become the social norm, with every brain occupied for alternating periods by two totally distinct personalities. Because it uses the terms we know and plays on fears we recognize, this is more disquieting than any account of, say, demoniacal possession I have come across.

Science fiction applies its realism not only to what is wonderful but also to what is disturbing, dismaying, frightening. This is no longer an escapist medium; nobody takes any further notice of little green men from Venus; Buck Rogers is dead. What we have now is a form of writing in which contemporary man can identify and spotlight the various forces that make his life difficult and dangerous. These forces may range from the internal pressures of neurosis to the external threats of power politics, but they are all very much of our own day. A French authority, Jean-Louis Curtis, recently noted:

Science fiction is the only literary form through which writers can express their rejection of certain aspects of the modern world (alienation of man by public power-groups, by mechanization, technology, propaganda, conditioning by advertising), the revolt of their conscience against everything that would like to enslave it, their reaffirmation of liberty. In these different ways, it is absolutely modern.

Kingsley Amis 1922-

Kingsley Amis, poet, novelist, and essayist, was born and raised in a working-class section of London. In 1954, he published *Lucky Jim,* a comic novel about college life. The book brought Amis international recognition and earned him a top position among the group of young British writers called the "Angry Young Men." These writers, most of whom gained literary prominence in the 1950's, are for the most part, like Amis, of working-class backgrounds. In their writings they reflect the frustrations and problems of modern English society. While Amis' fiction frequently deals with contemporary social problems, he does not consider himself a social critic. "I don't really like being thought of as a 'social novelist,'" he once said. "I have ideas about society naturally, but human behavior is what I see myself writing about."

As he states in "Science Fiction: A Practical Nightmare," Amis developed his interest in science fiction at an early age. He has edited several volumes of science-fiction short stories and has written a science fiction radio play entitled "Something Strange."

I agree with that as far as it goes, but there's a danger in taking the highbrow line here, however justified it may be and however understandable in view of the rough treatment science fiction still gets at the hands of the snootier critics. The danger is that the potential convert, given the impression that if he picks up *Amazing Stories* he's in for a dose of political and moral lecturing, may forgivably grope for a Western instead to see him through a rainy Sunday.

Fortunately it isn't that bad: the average science-fiction story is still an action story, and although the present-day monster is a more sophisticated creature than the kind that shook his tentacles at me in my youth, he remains satisfactorily monstrous. It's worth stressing the fact that, alongside these peeps into the unconscious and conjurings-up of the demons of the affluent society, science fiction offers qualities, such as speed, suspense, surprise, that have become rather rare in fiction of the main stream.

The idea that science fiction rates being talked about in any kind of elevated terms is admittedly hard to hang on to when you see what sort of covers the magazines still have. They are almost without exception crude and garish, badly executed and badly produced, their subjects ranging from feebly menacing ape-men to would-be poetic evocations of the grandeur of space. And if, after this hefty deterrent, you can bring yourself to glance at the contents, your expectations will fall further. More vile artwork, ads for the Rosicrucians,[1] garrulous and pun-riddled editorial introductions to the stories—the whole thing looks like carefully designed moron-fodder.

Small wonder if the intelligent inquirer, having reached this point, shudders and passes on. He may find it hard to believe that all the good writers in the field, including some whose hard-cover editions meet respectful attention from reviewers of general fiction, publish in these pulpy pages virtually everything they write. This is rather as if *True Life Romances* were the regular outlet for Saul Bellow or Salinger.[2]

Attempts to put over science fiction via movies and TV have almost always failed. This is not surprising, in that no other type of subject, except perhaps the battle epic and the musical, requires such a lavish expenditure of production money if any but a few themes are to be attempted. The small screen has tended to concentrate on these few easily and cheaply stageable themes—stories about electronic brains or missile tracking stations—and has soon exhausted them. Movie makers, understandably anxious that their costs should be recovered, have played it safe and low with stuff about giant birds and giant bees. Blatant menace can be fun, but it leaves out nearly all the good things that science fiction offers. A few splendid efforts (*The War of the Worlds, Forbidden Planet, Them!*) did manage to struggle onto film, though none of these is recent. All of them showed the characteristic, common to every kind of popular art, of switching with blinding suddenness from predictable banality to exciting novelty and back again. No doubt the situation will pick up, if we wait around long enough.

With his public image made to look cheap in these and other ways, the science-fiction writer is apt to feel embattled. Those who forget to call him a vulgarian are sure to call him a crank. Sometimes, of course, he *is* a crank. He will found or join a "mental science" cult, experiment with a telepathy machine, dabble in reincarnation. And he tends to see science fiction in some improbable roles, as the destined and early successor of the whole of serious fiction, as recruitment propaganda for the space services. But far more often he—only very rarely is it she—regards his chosen medium with appropriate seriousness, delighting in its novel powers yet critically concerned with its aims and standards, making few concessions to sex or horror sensationalism. This is the more admirable in view of the meager financial reward he enjoys. He must write sixteen hours a day or live in a tent or have another job: teaching or researching in some branch of science or technology, producing popular science articles or detec-

1. *Rosicrucians*, a secret society whose members claim to have occult powers. 2. *Bellow and Salinger*, highly respected American novelists.

tive stories. He goes for the third choice. There are no full-time science-fiction writers.

The fact is that science fiction is a popular art only in a restricted sense. Its practitioners are as ill-paid, and as unknown to the wider public, as its circulation is restricted—to very much less than one percent of the American population. Its content is not bland or reassuring or wish-fulfilling. It does not, unlike its second cousin, thriller or police or private-eye fiction, serve largely as the casual, occasional amusement of a wide non-specialist audience. Science fiction is popular only in so far as it is recent and gauche, with no tradition or accepted conventions of discussion, appealing above all to a readership scattered through every social and educational level. Like jazz—with which, more than with any kind of fiction, it can most helpfully be compared—it finds its addicts among truck drivers and professors, executives and elevator men....

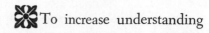 To increase understanding

1. Amplify the following statements, using your own reading experiences as well as Amis' comments to do so:

(*a*) Readiness to enjoy horror and terror and strangeness is a basic requirement for enjoying science fiction (page 728, column 1, paragraph 2).

(*b*) . . . it [science fiction] stimulates the fancy without bypassing the intellect . . . and while speculating about the future it can tell us something about mid-twentieth-century man and society (page 729, column 1, paragraph 1).

(*c*) This is no longer an escapist medium . . . (page 729, column 2, paragraph 2).

(*d*) Like jazz—with which, more than any kind of fiction, it can most helpfully be compared . . . (page 731, column 1, paragraph 1).

2. The Jean-Louis Curtis quotation (page 729) makes serious claims for science fiction. (*a*) What are these claims? (*b*) Amis calls Curtis' comment the "highbrow line," but he endorses the claims. Are they really justified? Explain. (*c*) Why does Amis call them highbrow?

Dylan Thomas MEMORIES OF AN AUGUST BANK HOLIDAY

August Bank Holiday, which falls on the first Monday in August each year, is a legal holiday in England. On this day there is a mass exodus from the cities to the seacoast.

(For a biography of Dylan Thomas, see page 656.)

Aug020ust Bank Holiday.—A tune on an ice cream cornet.[1] A slap of sea and a tickle of sand. A fanfare of sunshades opening. A wince and whinny of bathers dancing into deceptive water. A tuck of dresses. A rolling of trousers. A compromise of paddlers.

A sunburn of girls and a lark of boys. A silent hullabaloo of balloons.

I remember the sea telling lies in a shell held to my ear for a whole harmonious, hollow minute by a small, wet girl in an enormous bathing suit marked Corporation Property.

I remember sharing the last of my moist buns with a boy and a lion. Tawny and savage, with cruel nails and capacious mouth, the little boy tore and devoured. Wild as seedcake, ferocious as a hearthrug, the depressed and verminous lion nibbled like a

1. *ice cream cornet*, ice cream cone.

mouse at his half a bun and hiccupped in the sad dusk of his cage.

I remember a man like an alderman or a bailiff, bowlered and collarless, with a bag of monkeynuts in his hand, crying "Ride 'em, cowboy!" time and again as he whirled in his chairaplane giddily above the upturned laughing faces of the town girls bold as brass and the boys with padded shoulders and shoes sharp as knives; and the monkeynuts flew through the air like salty hail.

Children all day capered or squealed by the glazed or bashing sea, and the steam organ wheezed its waltzes in the threadbare playground and the waste lot, where the dodgems[2] dodged, behind the pickle factory.

And mothers loudly warned their proud pink daughters or sons to put that jellyfish down; and fathers spread newspapers over their faces; and sandfleas hopped on the picnic lettuce; and someone had forgotten the salt.

In those always radiant, rainless, lazily rowdy and skyblue summers departed, I remember August Monday from the rising of the sun over the stained and royal town to the husky hushing of the roundabout music and the drowsing of the naphtha jets[3] in the seaside fair. From bubble-and-squeak[4] to the last of the sandy sandwiches.

There was no need, that holiday morning, for the sluggardly boys to be shouted down to breakfast; out of their jumbled beds they tumbled and scrambled into their rumpled clothes; quickly at the bathroom basin they catlicked their hands and faces, but never forgot to run the water loud and long as though they washed like colliers[5]; in front of the cracked looking glass, bordered with cigarette cards, in their treasure-trove bedrooms, they whisked a gap-tooth comb through their surly hair; and with shining cheeks and noses and tide-marked necks, they took the stairs three at a time.

But for all their scramble and scamper, clamor on the landing, catlick and toothbrush flick, hair-whisk and stair-jump, their sisters were always there before them. Up with the lady lark, they had prinked and frizzed and hot-ironed; and smug in their blossoming dresses, ribboned for the sun, in gymshoes white as the blancoed[6] snow, neat and silly with doilies and tomatoes they helped in the higgledy kitchen. They were calm; they were virtuous; they had washed their necks; they did not romp, or fidget; and only the smallest sister put out her tongue at the noisy boys.

And the woman who lived next door came into the kitchen and said that her mother, an ancient uncertain body who wore a hat with cherries, was having one of her days and had insisted, that very holiday morning, in carrying, all the way to the tram stop, a photograph album and the cutglass fruit bowl from the front room.

This was the morning when father, mending one hole in the thermos flask, made three; when the sun declared war on the butter, and the butter ran; when dogs, with all the sweet-binned backyards to wag and sniff and bicker in, chased their tails in the jostling kitchen, worried sandshoes, snapped at flies, writhed between legs, scratched among towels, sat smiling on hampers.

And if you could have listened at some of the open doors of some of the houses in the street you might have heard:—

"Uncle Owen says he can't find the bottle opener—"

"Has he looked under the hallstand?"

"Willy's cut his finger—"

"Got your spade?"

"If somebody doesn't kill that dog—"

"Uncle Owen says why should the bottle opener be under the hallstand?"

"Never again, never again—"

"I know I put the pepper somewhere—"

"Willy's bleeding—"

"Look, there's a bootlace in my bucket—"

"Oh come *on*, come *on*—"

"Let's have a look at the bootlace in your bucket—"

"If I lay my hands on that dog—"

---

2. *dodgems*, small electric cars at amusement parks that are driven around a rink and bumped into one another. 3. *roundabout music . . . naphtha jets*. A roundabout is a merry-go-round. Naphtha jets are lamps that burn naphtha, a volatile oil containing gasoline. 4. *bubble-and-squeak*, potatoes, cabbage, and meat fried together. 5. *colliers*, coal miners. 6. *blancoed*, whitened, as with the whitener used by the British army for cleaning belts and so forth, called *Blanco*.

"Uncle Owen's found the bottle opener—"
"Willy's bleeding over the cheese—"
And the trams that hissed like ganders took us all to the beautiful beach.

There was cricket on the sand, and sand in the sponge cake, sandflies in the water cress, and foolish, mulish, religious donkeys on the unwilling trot. Girls undressed in slipping tents of propriety; under invisible umbrellas, stout ladies dressed for the male and immoral sea. Little naked navvies dug canals; children with spades and no ambition built fleeting castles; wispy young men, outside the bathing huts, whistled at substantial young women and dogs who desired thrown stones more than the bones of elephants. Recalcitrant uncles huddled, over luke ale, in the tiger-striped marquees. Mothers in black, like wobbling mountains, gasped under the discarded dresses of daughters who shrilly braved the gobbling waves. And fathers, in the once-a-year sun, took fifty winks. Oh, think of all the fifty winks along the paper-bagged sand.

Licorice allsorts, and Welsh hearts, were melting. And the sticks of rock, that we all sucked, were like barbers' poles made of rhubarb.

In the distance, surrounded by disappointed theoreticians and an ironmonger with a drum, a cross man on an orange box shouted that holidays were wrong. And the waves rolled in, with rubber ducks and clerks upon them.

I remember the patient, laborious, and enamoring hobby, or profession, of burying relatives in sand.

I remember the princely pastime of pouring sand, from cupped hands or bucket, down collars of tops of dresses; the shriek, the shake, the slap.

I can remember the boy by himself, the beachcombing lone wolf, hungrily waiting at the edge of family cricket; the friendless fielder, the boy uninvited to bat or to tea.

I remember the smell of sea and seaweed, wet flesh, wet hair, wet bathing dresses, the warm smell as of a rabbity field after rain, the smell of pop and splashed sunshades and toffee, the stable-and-straw smell of hot, tossed, tumbled, dug and trodden sand, the swill-and-gaslamp smell of Saturday night, though the sun shone strong, from the bellying beer-tents, and smell of the vinegar on shelled cockles, winklesmell, shrimp-smell, the dripping-oily backstreet winter-smell of chips in newspapers, the smell of ships from the sundazed docks round the corner of the sand hills, the smell of the known and paddled-in sea moving, full of the drowned and herrings, out and away and beyond and further still towards the antipodes that hung their koala bears and maoris, kangaroos and boomerangs, upside down over the backs of the stars.

And the noise of pummeling Punch and Judy falling, and a clock tolling or telling no time in the tenantless town, now and again a bell from a lost tower or a train on the lines behind us clearing its throat, and always the hopeless, ravenous swearing and pleading of the gulls, donkey-bray and hawker-cry, harmonicas and toy trumpets, shouting and laughing and singing, hooting of tugs and tramps, the clip of the chair attendant's puncher, the motorboat coughing in the bay, and the same hymn and washing of the sea that was heard in the Bible.

"If it could only just, if it could only just?" your lips said again and again as you scooped, in the hob-hot sand, dungeons, garages, torture chambers, train tunnels, arsenals, hangars for zeppelins, witches' kitchens, vampires' parlors, smugglers' cellars, trolls' grog shops, sewers, under the ponderous and cracking castle, "If it could only just be like this for ever and ever amen." August Monday all over the earth, from Mumbles[7] where the aunties grew like ladies on a seaside tree to brown, bear-hugging Henty-land and the turtled Ballantyne Islands.[8]

"Could donkeys go on the ice?"
"Only if they got snowshoes."
We snowshoed a meek, complaining donkey and galloped him off in the wake of the ten-foot-tall and Atlas-muscled Mounties, rifled and pemmicanned, who always, in the White Gold Rush wastes, got their black-oathed-and-bearded Man.

---

7. *Mumbles*, seaside resort near Swansea on the south coast of Wales. 8. *Henty-land . . . Ballantyne Islands*, references to both the fictional worlds created by two writers of boys' stories, George Alfred Henty and Robert Michael Ballantyne, and to actual geographical locations.

"Are there donkeys on desert islands?"

"Only sort-of donkeys."

"What d'you mean, sort-of donkeys?"

"Native donkeys. They hunt things on them!"

"Sort-of walruses and seals and things?"

"Donkeys can't swim!"

"These donkeys can. They swim like whales, they swim like anything, they swim like—"

"Liar."

"Liar yourself."

And two small boys fought fiercely and silently in the sand, rolling together in a ball of legs and bottoms.

Then they went and saw the Pierrots,[9] or bought vanilla ices.

Lolling or larriking[10] that unsoiled, boiling beauty of a common day, great gods with their braces over their vests sang, spat pipes, puffed smoke at wasps, gulped and ogled, forgot the rent, embraced, posed for the dickybird, were coarse, had rainbow-colored armpits, winked, belched, blamed the radishes, played hymns on paper and comb, peeled bananas, found seaweed in their panamas, blew up paper bags and banged them, wished for nothing.

But over all the beautiful beach I remember most the children playing, boys and girls tumbling, moving jewels, who might never be happy again. And "happy as a sandboy"[11] is true as the heat of the sun.

Dusk came down; or grew up out of the sands and the sea; or curled around us from the calling docks and the bloodily smoking sun. The day was done, the sand brushed and ruffled suddenly with a seabroom of cold wind.

And we gathered together all the spades and buckets and towels, empty hampers and bottles, umbrellas and fish frails,[12] bats and balls and knitting, and went—oh, listen, Dad!—to the Fair in the dusk on the bald seaside field.

Fairs were no good in the day; then they were shoddy and tired; the voices of hoopla girls were crimped as elocutionists; no cannonball could shake the roosting coconuts; the gondolas mechanically repeated their sober lurch; the Wall of Death was safe as a gov-

erness cart; the wooden animals were waiting for the night.

But in the night, the hoopla girls, like operatic crows croaked at the coming moon; whizz, whirl, and ten for a tanner,[13] the coconuts rained from their sawdust like grouse from the Highland sky; tipsy the griffon-prowed gondolas weaved on dizzy rails and the Wall of Death was a spinning rim of ruin, and the neighing wooden horses took, to a haunting hunting tune, a thousand Beecher's Brooks[14] as easily and breezily as hooved swallows.

Approaching, at dusk, the Fair field from the beach, we scorched and gritty boys heard above the belaboring of the batherless sea the siren voices of the raucous, horsy barkers. Roll up, roll up! In her tent and her rolls of flesh the Fattest Woman in the World sat sewing her winter frock, another tent, and fixed her little eyes, blackcurrants in blancmange, on the skeletons who filed and sniggered by. Roll up, roll up, roll to see the Largest Rat on the Earth. Here scampered the smallest pony, like a Shetland shrew. And here the Most Intelligent Fleas, trained, reined, bridled, and bitted, minutely cavorted in their glass corral.

Round galleries and shies[15] and stalls, pennies were burning holes in a hundred pockets.

Pale young men with larded hair and Valentino-black side whiskers, fags stuck to their lower lips, squinted along their swivel-sighted rifles and aimed at Ping-pong balls dancing on fountains.

In knife-creased, silver-gray, skirt-like Oxford bags, and a sleeveless, scarlet, zip-fastened shirt with yellow horizontal stripes, a collier at the strength machine spat on his hands, raised the hammer, and brought it, Thor-ing down.[16] The bell rang for Blaina.

Outside his booth stood a bitten-eared and barn-door-chested pug with a nose like a

9. *Pierrots*, a type of clown with whitened face and white, oversize costume. 10. *larriking*, a word commonly used in Australia meaning "in a rowdy manner." 11. *happy as a sandboy*, a slang expression meaning "happy as a simpleton." 12. *frails*, baskets made of woven rushes. 13. *tanner*, sixpence. 14. *Beecher's Brooks*, Beecher's Brook is the name of the most difficult jump in the Grand National Steeplechase in England. 15. *shies*, a carnival game in which balls are thrown at other objects. 16. *Thor-ing down*, to come down with the force of Thor's hammer. Thor was the second principal god in Norse mythology, the god of thunder.

twisted swede[17] and hair that startled from his eyebrows and three teeth yellow as a camel's, inviting any sportsman to a sudden and sickening basting in the sandy ring or a quid[18] if he lasted a round: and, wiry, cocky, bow-legged, coal-scarred, boozed, sportsmen by the dozen strutted in and reeled out; and still those three teeth remained, chipped and camel-yellow in the bored, teak face.

Draggled and stout-wanting mothers, with hap-hazard hats, hostile hatpins, buns awry, bursting bags, and children at their skirts like pop-filled and jam-smeared limpets, screamed, before distorting mirrors, at their suddenly tapering or tubular bodies and huge ballooning heads, and the children gayly bellowed at their own reflected bogies withering and bulging in the glass.

Old men, smelling of Milford Haven[19] in the rain, shuffled, badgering and cadging, round the edges of the swaggering crowd, their only wares a handful of damp confetti.

A daring dash of schoolboys, safely, shoulder to shoulder, with their fathers' trilbies cocked at a desperate angle over one eye, winked at and whistled after the procession past the swings of two girls arm in arm: always one pert and pretty, and always one with glasses.

Girls in skulled and cross-boned tunnels shrieked, and were comforted.

Young men, heroic after pints, stood up on the flying chairaplanes, tousled, crimson, and against the rules.

Jaunty girls gave sailors sauce.

All the Fun of the Fair in the hot, bubbling night. The Man in the sandyellow Moon over the hurdy of gurdies. The swingboats swimming to and fro like slices of the moon. Dragons and hippogriffs and the prows of the gondolas breathing fire and Sousa.[20] Midnight roundabout riders tantivying[21] under the fairylights, huntsmen on billygoats and zebras halooing under a circle of glowworms.

And as we climbed home, up the gas-lit hill, to the still house over the mumbling bay, we heard the music die and the voices drift like sand. And we saw the lights of the Fair fade. And, at the far end of the seaside field, they lit their lamps, one by one, in the caravans.

17. *swede*, a swede turnip, or rutabaga. 18. *quid*, a pound sterling. 19. *Milford Haven*, a fishing port, on the southwest coast of Wales. 20. *Sousa*, John Philip Sousa, famous composer of band marches. 21. *tantivying*, going at a wild gallop.

❈ To increase understanding

1. Dylan Thomas uses a multitude of vivid appeals to all the senses to re-create the mood of the August Bank Holidays of his childhood in Wales. Mention some images that seem particularly vivid in their appeal to the senses of sight, hearing, smell, and touch.

2. This essay also presents several ages and types of people. Mention and describe as many as you can.

3. In the biographical sketch of Thomas (page 656) you read that his short stories and essays "in their rhythm and imagery are as rich and evocative as his poetry." With this statement in mind, examine closely the paragraph beginning "Lolling or larriking . . ." (page 734) and the two paragraphs following it. Comment on your findings.

4. Dylan Thomas is noted for his highly individual use of words. Nearly every one of the sentences in the first paragraph of the essay contains a word which is surprising at first sight, but which seems singularly appropriate upon reflection. Point out as many of these as you can, telling why each is surprising, and why appropriate.

5. Both "Three Pictures" and "August Bank Holiday" are concerned with time, but each author has his own distinctive attitude toward time. Contrast the tone of these two essays.

6. In contrast to "Science Fiction: A Practical Nightmare," "August Bank Holiday" is a familiar essay. Kingsley Amis' intent in the article on science fiction was to relate facts, expound ideas, and argue for a particular point of view. What difference in intent do you see in the Thomas essay that might characterize it as "familiar"?

Lytton Strachey *from* FLORENCE NIGHTINGALE

Of the four subjects that Strachey chose for his Eminent Victorians, Florence Nightingale, *perhaps, comes off best. Here, while avoiding caricature, he managed to cut through the mists of sentimentality which had surrounded Miss Nightingale, turning her into the saintly "lady with the lamp" celebrated in Longfellow's poem "Santa Filomena."*

Although Florence Nightingale had a long and productive life, it was her early work in the Crimean War that made her famous. In 1854 the British and French entered the war between Turkey and Russia on the side of Turkey, and these allies determined to carry the war into Russian territory. They invaded the Crimean Peninsula, across the Black Sea from Turkey, but, unable to gain more than a foothold, were forced to settle down to a seige, transporting the wounded all the way back to Turkey. It was into this sudden crisis that Florence Nightingale was called.

1

Everyone knows the popular conception of Florence Nightingale. The saintly, self-sacrificing woman, the delicate maiden of high degree who threw aside the pleasures of a life of ease to succor the afflicted, the Lady with the Lamp, gliding through the horrors of the hospital at Scutari,[1] and consecrating with the radiance of her goodness the dying soldier's couch—the vision is familiar to all. But the truth was different. The Miss Nightingale of fact was not as facile fancy painted her. She worked in another fashion, and toward another end; she moved under the stress of an impetus which finds no place in the popular imagination. A Demon[2] possessed her. Now demons, whatever else they may be, are full of interest. And so it happens that in the real Miss Nightingale there was more that was interesting than in the legendary one; there was also less that was agreeable.

Her family was extremely well-to-do, and connected by marriage with a spreading circle of other well-to-do families. There was a large country house in Derbyshire; there was another in the New Forest;[3] there were Mayfair rooms for the London season[4] and all its finest parties; there were tours on the Continent with even more than the usual number of Italian operas and of glimpses at the celebrities of Paris. Brought up among such advantages, it was only natural to suppose that Florence would show a proper appreciation of them by doing her duty in that state of life unto which it had pleased God to call her—in other words, by marrying, after a fitting number of dances and dinner parties, an eligible gentleman, and living happily ever afterward. Her sister, her cousins, all the young ladies of her acquaintance, were either getting ready to do this or had already done it. It was inconceivable that Florence should dream of anything else; yet dream she did.

Ah! To do her duty in that state of life unto which it had pleased God to call her! Assuredly she would not be behindhand in doing her duty; but unto what state of life *had* it pleased God to call her? That was the question. God's calls are many, and they are strange. Unto what state of life had it pleased Him to call Charlotte Corday,[5] or Elizabeth

From *Eminent Victorians* by Lytton Strachey. Reprinted by permission of Harcourt, Brace & World, Inc., New York; and Chatto and Windus Ltd., London.
1. *Scutari* (skü´tä ri), now generally called Uskudar (üs kü dar´), is a suburb across the Bosporus from Istanbul, about 350 miles across the Black Sea from the scene of operations in the Crimean War. 2. *Demon*. The word is used here in the sense of a spirit that takes possession of a human being, and acts as a guiding spirit or driving force. 3. *Derbyshire* (där´bi shir) . . . *New Forest*. Derbyshire is a county in northwestern England; New Forest is extensive wooded land in Hampshire County. 4. *Mayfair rooms . . . London season*. From May to July, the season when social life in London was at its height, the Nightingale family lived in Mayfair, a fashionable district of London. 5. *Charlotte Corday*, a heroine of the French Revolution who assassinated the bloody factional leader Marat (mä rä´), in 1793.

of Hungary?[6] What was that secret voice in her ear, if it was not a call? Why had she felt, from her earliest years, those mysterious promptings toward . . . she hardly knew what but certainly toward something very different from anything around her? Why, as a child in the nursery, when her sister had shown a healthy pleasure in tearing her dolls to pieces, had *she* shown an almost morbid one in sewing them up again? Why was she driven now to minister to the poor in their cottages, to watch by sickbeds, to put her dog's wounded paw into elaborate splints as if it was a human being? Why was her head filled with queer imaginations of the country house at Embley[7] turned, by some enchantment, into a hospital, with herself as matron moving about among the beds? Why was even her vision of heaven itself filled with suffering patients to whom she was being useful? So she dreamed and wondered, and, taking out her diary, she

poured into it the agitations of her soul. And then the bell rang, and it was time to go and dress for dinner.

As the years passed, a restlessness began to grow upon her. She was unhappy, and at last she knew it. Mrs. Nightingale, too, began to notice that there was something wrong. It was very odd; what could be the matter with dear Flo? Mr. Nightingale suggested that a husband might be advisable; but the curious thing was that she seemed to take no interest in husbands. And with her attractions, and her accomplishments, too! There was nothing in the world to prevent her making a really brilliant match. But no! She would think of nothing but how to satisfy that singular craving of hers to be *doing* something. As if there was not plenty to do in any case, in the ordinary way, at home. There was the china to look after, and there was her father to be read to after dinner.

Mrs. Nightingale could not understand it; and then one day her perplexity was changed to consternation and alarm. Florence announced an extreme desire to go to Salisbury Hospital for several months as a nurse; and she confessed to some visionary plan of eventually setting up in a house of her own in a neighboring village, and there founding "something like a Protestant Sisterhood, without vows, for women of educated feelings." The whole scheme was summarily brushed aside as preposterous; and Mrs. Nightingale, after the first shock of terror, was able to settle down again more or less comfortably to her embroidery. But Florence, who was now twenty-five and felt that the dream of her life had been shattered, came near to desperation.

And, indeed, the difficulties in her path were great. For not only was it an almost unimaginable thing in those days for a woman of means to make her own way in the world and to live in independence, but the particular profession for which Florence was clearly marked out both by her instincts and her capacities was at that time a peculiarly disrepu-

---

Lytton Strachey   1880–1932

It is interesting that the man who first achieved fame by "debunking" certain eminent Victorians should have had for a father a man who had helped build the Empire and whose life coincided almost exactly with that of Queen Victoria. Lytton Strachey, son of Sir Richard Strachey, was brought up in accordance with his father's position and educated at Trinity College, Cambridge. While at Cambridge, he tried his hand at writing verse and drama, but feeling unsure of his ability to create, he turned first to the history and criticism of French literature, and then to biography. In biography he centered his attention on the attitudes of the Victorians. The result was a hotly controversial volume called *Eminent Victorians* (1918), in which Strachey used the rapier techniques that he admired in French literature to deflate the pomposity and sentimentality that surrounded many heroes of the Victorian Age.

The instant success of *Eminent Victorians* was due largely to its sensationalism. It was only with the publication of his biography *Queen Victoria* (1921), conceded to be his masterpiece, that the solid contribution of both books to the art of biography became clear. While some of the portraits in *Victorians* tended to caricature, his *Queen Victoria*, although still merciless in its treatment of hypocrisy, dullness, and mediocrity, is a balanced portrait.

---

6. *Elizabeth of Hungary,* a noble lady of the thirteenth century noted for her gifts to the poor, later canonized St. Elizabeth of Hungary.   7. *Embley.* Embley Park was the New Forest home of the Nightingales.

table one. A "nurse" meant then a coarse old woman, always ignorant, usually dirty, often brutal, a Mrs. Gamp,[8] in bunched-up sordid garments, tippling at the brandy bottle or indulging in worse irregularities. The nurses in the hospitals were especially notorious for immoral conduct; sobriety was almost unknown among them; and they could hardly be trusted to carry out the simplest medical duties. Certainly, things have changed since those days; and that they *have* changed is due, far more than to any other human being, to Miss Nightingale herself. It is not to be wondered at that her parents should have shuddered at the notion of their daughter devoting her life to such an occupation. "It was as if," she herself said afterward, "I had wanted to be a kitchen maid." Yet the want, absurd, impracticable as it was, not only remained fixed immovably in her heart, but grew in intensity day by day. . . .

Three more years passed, and then at last the pressure of time told; her family seemed to realize that she was old enough and strong enough to have her way; and she became the superintendent of a charitable nursing home in Harley Street.[9] She had gained her independence, though it was in a meager sphere enough; and her mother was still not quite resigned: surely Florence might at least spend the summer in the country. At times, indeed, among her intimates, Mrs. Nightingale almost wept. "We are ducks," she said with tears in her eyes, "who have hatched a wild swan." But the poor lady was wrong; it was not a swan that they had hatched; it was an eagle.

2

Miss Nightingale had been a year in her nursing home in Harley Street, when Fate knocked at the door. The Crimean War broke out; the battle of the Alma[10] was fought; and the terrible condition of our military hospitals at Scutari began to be known in England. It sometimes happens that the plans of Providence are a little difficult to follow, but on this occasion all was plain; there was a perfect coördination of events. For years Miss Nightingale had been getting ready; at last she was prepared—experienced, free, mature, yet still

young—she was thirty-four—desirous to serve, accustomed to command: at that precise moment the desperate need of a great nation came, and she was there to satisfy it. . . .

When the war had begun, the gallant British officers in control of affairs had other things to think about than the petty details of medical organization. Who had bothered with such trifles in the Peninsula?[11] And surely, on that occasion we had done pretty well. Thus the most obvious precautions were neglected, the most necessary preparations put off from day to day. The principal medical officer of the army, Dr. Hall, was summoned from India at a moment's notice, and was unable to visit England before taking up his duties at the front. And it was not until after the battle of the Alma, when we had been at war for many months, that we acquired hospital accommodations at Scutari for more than a thousand men. Errors, follies, and vices on the part of individuals there doubtless were; but, in general reckoning, they were of small account—insignificant symptoms of the deep disease of the body politic—the enormous calamity of administrative collapse.

Miss Nightingale arrived at Scutari—a suburb of Constantinople, on the Asiatic side of the Bosporus—on November 4th, 1854; it was ten days after the battle of Balaclava, and the day before the battle of Inkerman.[12] The organization of the hospitals, which had already given way under the stress of the battle of Alma, was now to be subjected to the further pressure which these two desperate and bloody engagements implied. Great detachments of wounded were already beginning to pour in. The men, after receiving such summary treatment as could be given them at the smaller hospitals in the Crimea itself, were forthwith

---

8. *Mrs. Gamp*, a coarse, amusing character in the novel *Martin Chuzzlewit*, by Charles Dickens. 9. *Harley Street*, a street in London where many specialists in surgery and medicine have their offices. 10. *battle of the Alma*, a famous victory won by the allied British and French armies over the Russians at the Alma River in 1854, early in the Crimean War. 11. *in the Peninsula*, in the Peninsular Campaign of the Duke of Wellington in Spain against the armies of Napoleon (1809-1813). 12. *battle of Balaclava . . . Inkerman*, two great battles of the Crimean War, fought in the autumn of 1854. The battle of Balaclava is celebrated in Tennyson's "Charge of the Light Brigade."

shipped in batches of two hundred across the Black Sea to Scutari. This voyage was in normal times one of four days and a half; but the times were no longer normal, and now the transit often lasted for a fortnight or three weeks. It received, not without reason, the name of "the middle passage."[13]

Between, and sometimes on the decks, the wounded, the sick, and the dying were crowded—men who had just undergone the amputation of limbs, men in the clutches of fever or of frostbite, men in the last stages of dysentery and cholera—without beds, sometimes without blankets, often hardly clothed. The one or two surgeons on board did what they could; but medical stores were lacking, and the only form of nursing available was that provided by a handful of invalid soldiers, who were usually themselves prostrate by the end of the voyage. There was no other food besides the ordinary salt rations of ship diet; and even the water was sometimes so stored that it was out of reach of the weak. For many months, the average of deaths during these voyages was seventy-four in the thousand; the corpses were shot out into the waters; and who shall say that they were the most unfortunate?

At Scutari, the landing stage, constructed with all the perverseness of Oriental ingenuity, could only be approached with great difficulty, and, in rough weather, not at all. When it was reached, what remained of the men in the ships had first to be disembarked, and then conveyed up a steep slope of a quarter of a mile to the nearest of the hospitals. The most serious cases might be put upon stretchers —for there were far too few for all; the rest were carried or dragged up the hill by such convalescent soldiers as could be got together, who were not too obviously infirm for the work. At last the journey was accomplished; slowly, one by one, living or dying, the wounded were carried up into the hospital. And in the hospital what did they find?

Lasciate ogni speranza, voi ch'entrate:[14] the delusive doors bore no such inscription; and yet behind them Hell yawned. Want, neglect, confusion, misery—in every shape and in every degree of intensity—filled the endless corridors

and the vast apartments of the gigantic barrack house, which, without forethought or preparation, had been hurriedly set aside as the chief shelter for the victims of the war. The very building itself was radically defective. Huge sewers underlay it, and cesspools loaded with filth wafted their poison into the upper rooms. The floors were in so rotten a condition that many of them could not be scrubbed; the walls were thick with dirt; incredible multitudes of vermin swarmed everywhere. And, enormous as the building was, it was yet too small. It contained four miles of beds, crushed together so close that there was but just room to pass between them.

Under such conditions, the most elaborate system of ventilation might well have been at fault; but here there was no ventilation. The stench was indescribable. "I have been well acquainted," said Miss Nightingale, "with the dwellings of the worst parts of most of the great cities in Europe, but have never been in any atmosphere which I could compare with that of the Barrack Hospital at night."

The structural defects were equaled by the deficiencies in the commonest objects of hospital use. There were not enough bedsteads; the sheets were of canvas, and so coarse that the wounded men recoiled from them, begging to be left in their blankets; there was no bedroom furniture of any kind, and empty beer bottles were used for candlesticks. There were no basins, no towels, no soap, no brooms, no mops, no trays, no plates; there were neither slippers nor scissors, neither shoe-brushes nor blacking; there were no knives or forks or spoons. The supply of fuel was constantly deficient. The cooking arrangements were preposterously inadequate, and the laundry was a farce. As for purely medical materials, the tale was no better. Stretchers, splints, bandages—all were lacking; and so were the most ordinary drugs.

To replace such wants, to struggle against such difficulties, there was a handful of men

<hr>

13. *the middle passage.* The term originated in reference to the transatlantic passage of slave ships. 14. *Lasciate . . . ch'entrate,* "abandon all hope, you that enter here," the inscription over the portal to Hell in Dante's *Inferno.*

overburdened by the strain of ceaseless work, bound down by the traditions of official routine, and enfeebled either by old age or inexperience or sheer incompetence. They had proved utterly unequal to their task. The principal doctor was lost in the imbecilities of a senile optimism. The wretched official whose business it was to provide for the wants of the hospital was tied fast hand and foot by red tape. A few of the younger doctors struggled valiantly, but what could they do? Unprepared, disorganized, with such help only as they could find among the miserable band of convalescent soldiers drafted off to tend their sick comrades, they were faced with disease, mutilation, and death in all their most appalling forms, crowded multitudinously about them in an ever increasing mass. They were like men in a shipwreck, fighting, not for safety, but for the next moment's bare existence—to gain, by yet another frenzied effort, some brief respite from the waters of destruction.

In these surroundings, those who had been long inured to scenes of human suffering—surgeons with a world-wide knowledge of agonies, soldiers familiar with fields of carnage, missionaries with remembrances of famine and of plague—yet found a depth of horror which they had never known before. There were moments, there were places, in the Barrack Hospital at Scutari, where the strongest hand was struck with trembling, and the boldest eye would turn away its gaze.

Miss Nightingale came, and she, at any rate, in that inferno, did not abandon hope. For one thing, she brought material succor. Before she left London she had consulted Dr. Andrew Smith, the head of the Army Medical Board, as to whether it would be useful to take out stores of any kind to Scutari; and Dr. Andrew Smith had told her that "nothing was needed." Even Sidney Herbert[15] had given her similar assurances; possibly, owing to an oversight, there might have been some delay in the delivery of the medical stores, which, he said, had been sent out from England "in profusion," but "four days would have remedied this." She preferred to trust her own instincts, and at Marseilles purchased a large quantity of miscellaneous provisions, which were of the utmost use at Scutari.

She came, too, amply provided with money —in all, during her stay in the East, about £7000 reached her from private sources; and, in addition, she was able to avail herself of another valuable means of help. At the same time as herself, Mr. Macdonald, of the *Times*, had arrived at Scutari, charged with the duty of administering the large sums of money collected through the agency of that newspaper in aid of the sick and wounded; and Mr. Macdonald had the sense to see that the best use he could make of the *Times* Fund was to put it at the disposal of Miss Nightingale.

I cannot conceive (wrote an eyewitness), as I now calmly look back on the first three weeks after the arrival of the wounded from Inkerman, how it could have been possible to have avoided a state of things too disastrous to contemplate, had not Miss Nightingale been there, with the means placed at her disposal by Mr. Macdonald.

But the official view was different. What! Was the public service to admit, by accepting outside charity, that it was unable to discharge its own duties without the assistance of private and irregular benevolence? Never! And accordingly when Lord Stratford de Redcliffe, our Ambassador at Constantinople, was asked by Mr. Macdonald to indicate how the *Times* Fund could best be employed, he answered that there was indeed one object to which it might very well be devoted—the building of an English Protestant Church at Pera.

Mr. Macdonald did not waste further time with Lord Stratford, and immediately joined forces with Miss Nightingale. But, with such a frame of mind in highest quarters, it is easy to imagine the kind of disgust and alarm with which the sudden intrusion of a band of amateurs and females must have filled the minds of the ordinary officer and the ordinary military surgeon. They could not understand it; what had women to do with war? Honest colonels relieved their spleen by the cracking of heavy jokes about "the Bird"; while poor

15. *Sidney Herbert*, Secretary of War at the time of the Crimean War and a close personal friend of Florence Nightingale.

Dr. Hall, a rough terrier of a man, who had worried his way to the top of his profession, was struck speechless with astonishment, and at last observed that Miss Nightingale's appointment was extremely droll.

Her position was, indeed, an official one, but it was hardly the easier for that. In the hospitals it was her duty to provide the services of herself and her nurses when they were asked for by the doctors, and not until then. At first some of the surgeons would have nothing to say to her, and, though she was welcomed by others, the majority were hostile and suspicious. But gradually she gained ground. Her good will could not be denied, and her capacity could not be disregarded. With consummate tact, with all the gentleness of supreme strength, she managed at last to impose her personality upon the susceptible, overwrought, discouraged, and helpless group of men in authority who surrounded her. She stood firm; she was a rock in the angry ocean; with her alone was safety, comfort, life.

And so it was that hope dawned at Scutari. The reign of chaos and old night[16] began to dwindle; order came upon the scene, and common sense, and forethought, and decision, radiating out from the little room off the great gallery in the Barrack Hospital where, day and night, the Lady Superintendent was at her task. Progress might be slow, but it was sure. The first sign of a great change came with the appearance of some of those necessary objects with which the hospitals had been unprovided for months. The sick men began to enjoy the use of towels and soap, knives and forks, combs and toothbrushes. Dr. Hall might snort when he heard of it, asking, with a growl, what a soldier wanted with a toothbrush; but the good work went on.

Eventually the whole business of purveying to the hospitals was, in effect, carried out by Miss Nightingale. She alone, it seemed, whatever the contingency, knew where to lay her hands on what was wanted; she alone could dispense her stores with readiness; above all she alone possessed the art of circumventing the pernicious influences of official etiquette. This was her greatest enemy, and sometimes even she was baffled by it. On one occasion

27,000 shirts sent out at her instance by the Home Government, arrived, were landed, and were only waiting to be unpacked. But the official "purveyor" intervened; "he could not unpack them," he said, "without a Board."[17]

Miss Nightingale pleaded in vain; the sick and wounded lay half-naked shivering for want of clothing; and three weeks elapsed before the Board released the shirts. A little later, however, on a similar occasion, Miss Nightingale felt that she could assert her own authority. She ordered a government consignment to be forcibly opened, while the miserable "purveyor" stood by, wringing his hands in departmental agony.

Vast quantities of valuable stores sent from England lay, she found, engulfed in the bottomless abyss of the Turkish Customs House. Other shiploads, buried beneath munitions of war destined for Balaclava, passed Scutari without a sign, and thus hospital materials were sometimes carried to and fro three times over the Black Sea, before they reached their destination. The whole system was clearly at fault, and Miss Nightingale suggested to the home authorities that a Government Store House should be instituted at Scutari for the reception and distribution of the consignments. Six months after her arrival this was done.

In the meantime she had reorganized the kitchens and the laundries in the hospitals. The ill-cooked hunks of meat, vilely served at irregular intervals, which had hitherto been the only diet for the sick men, were replaced by punctual meals, well-prepared and appetizing, while strengthening extra foods—soups and wines and jellies ("preposterous luxuries," snarled Dr. Hall)—were distributed to those who needed them. One thing, however, she could not effect. The separation of the bones from the meat was no part of official cookery: the rule was that the food must be divided into equal portions, and if some of the portions were all bone—well, every man must take his chance. The rule, perhaps, was not a very good one; but there it was. "It would require

16. *chaos and old night*, a state of utter confusion. In Milton's *Paradise Lost* Chaos and Old Night are two allegorical figures that reign over the vast space of unformed matter between Earth and Hell.   17. *without a Board*, without an order from an official committee.

a new regulation of the service," she was told, "to bone the meat."

As for the washing arrangements, they were revolutionized. Up to the time of Miss Nightingale's arrival the number of shirts which the authorities had succeeded in washing was seven. The hospital bedding, she found, was "washed" in cold water. She took a Turkish house, had boilers installed, and employed soldiers' wives to do the laundry work. The expenses were defrayed from her own funds and that of the *Times;* and henceforward the sick and wounded had the comfort of clean linen.

Then she turned her attention to their clothing. Owing to military exigencies the greater number of the men had abandoned their kit; their knapsacks were lost forever; they possessed nothing but what was on their persons, and that was usually only fit for speedy destruction. The "purveyor," of course, pointed out that, according to the regulations, all soldiers should bring with them into the hospital an adequate supply of clothing, and he declared that it was no business of his to make good their deficiencies. Apparently, it was the business of Miss Nightingale. She procured socks, boots, and shirts in enormous quantities; she had trousers made, she rigged up dressing gowns. "The fact is," she told Sidney Herbert, "I am now clothing the British army."

All at once, word came from the Crimea that a great new contingent of sick and wounded might shortly be expected. Where were they to go? Every available inch in the wards was occupied; the affair was serious and pressing, and the authorities stood aghast. There were some dilapidated rooms in the Barrack Hospital, unfit for human habitation, but Miss Nightingale believed that if measures were promptly taken they might be made capable of accommodating several hundred beds. One of the doctors agreed with her; the rest of the officials were irresolute: it would be a very expensive job, they said; it would involve building; and who could take the responsibility? The proper course was that a representation should be made to the Director-General of the Army Medical Department in London; then the Director-General would apply to the Horse Guards, the Horse Guards would move the Ordnance, the Ordnance would lay the matter before the Treasury, and, if the Treasury gave its consent, the work might be correctly carried through, several months after the necessity for it had disappeared.

Miss Nightingale, however, had made up her mind, and she persuaded Lord Stratford— or thought she had persuaded him—to give his sanction to the required expenditure. A hundred and twenty-five workmen were immediately engaged, and the work was begun. The workmen struck; whereupon Lord Stratford washed his hands of the whole business. Miss Nightingale engaged two hundred other workmen on her own authority, and paid the bill out of her own resources. The wards were ready by the required date; five hundred sick men were received in them; and all the utensils, including knives, forks, spoons, cans, and towels, were supplied by Miss Nightingale.

This remarkable woman was in truth performing the function of an administrative chief. How had this come about? Was she not in reality merely a nurse? Was it not her duty simply to tend to the sick? And indeed, was it not as a ministering angel, a gentle "lady with a lamp" that she actually impressed the minds of her contemporaries? No doubt that was so; and yet it is no less certain that, as she herself said, the specific business of nursing was "the least important of the functions into which she had been forced." It was clear that in the state of disorganization into which the hospitals at Scutari had fallen the most pressing, the really vital, need was for something more than nursing; it was for the necessary elements of civilized life—the commonest material objects, the most ordinary cleanliness, the rudimentary habits of order and authority.

"Oh, dear Miss Nightingale," said one of her party as they were approaching Constantinople, "when we land, let there be no delays, let us get straight to nursing the poor fellows!"

"The strongest will be wanted at the washtub," was Miss Nightingale's answer. And it was upon the washtub, and all that the washtub stood for, that she expended her greatest energies. Yet to say that is perhaps to say too much. For to those who watched her at work among the sick, moving day and night from bed to bed, with that unflinching courage, with that indefatigable vigilance, it seemed as if the concentrated force of an undivided and unparalleled devotion could hardly suffice for that portion of her task alone. Wherever, in those vast wards, suffering was at its worst and the need for help was greatest, there, as if by magic, was Miss Nightingale. Her superhuman equanimity would, at the moment of some ghastly operation, nerve the victim to endure and almost to hope. Her sympathy would assuage the pangs of dying and bring back to those still living something of the forgotten charm of life. Over and over again her untiring efforts rescued those whom the surgeons had abandoned as beyond the possibility of cure. Her mere presence brought with it a strange influence.

A passionate idolatry spread among the men; they kissed her shadow as it passed. They did more. "Before she came," said a soldier, "there was cussin' and swearin', but after that it was as 'oly as a church." The most cherished privilege of the fighting man was abandoned for the sake of Miss Nightingale. In those "lowest sinks of human misery," as she herself put it, she never heard the use of one expression "which could distress a gentlewoman."

She was heroic, and these were the humble tributes paid by those of grosser mold to that high quality. Certainly, she was heroic. Yet her heroism was not of that simple sort so dear to the readers of novels and the compilers of hagiologies—the romantic sentimental heroism with which mankind loves to invest its chosen darlings. It was made of sterner stuff. To the wounded soldier on his couch of agony she might well appear in the guise of a gracious angel of mercy; but the military surgeons, and the orderlies, and her own nurses, and the "purveyor," and Dr. Hall, and even Lord Stratford himself could tell a different story. It was not by gentle sweetness and womanly self-abnegation that she had brought order out of chaos in the Scutari hospitals, that, from her own resources, she had clothed the British army, that she had spread her dominion over the serried and reluctant powers of the official

world; it was by strict method, by stern discipline, by rigid attention to detail, by ceaseless labor, by the fixed determination of an indomitable will. . . .

As for her voice, it was true of it, even more than of her countenance, that it "had that in it one must fain call master." Those clear tones were in no need of emphasis: "I never heard her raise her voice," said one of her companions. Only, when she had spoken, it seemed as if nothing could follow but obedience. Once, when she had given some direction, a doctor ventured to remark that the thing could not be done. "But it must be done," said Miss Nightingale. A chance bystander, who heard the words, never forgot through all his life the irresistible authority of them. And they were spoken quietly—very quietly indeed. . . .

And so the months passed, and that fell winter which had begun with Inkerman and had dragged itself out through the long agony of the investment of Sebastopol, at last was over. In May, 1855, after six months of labor, Miss Nightingale could look with something like satisfaction at the condition of the Scutari hospitals. Had they done nothing more than survive the terrible strain which had been put upon them, it would have been a matter for congratulation; but they had done much more than that; they had marvelously improved. The confusion and the pressure in the wards had come to an end; order reigned in them, and cleanliness; the supplies were bountiful and prompt; important sanitary works had been carried out.

One simple comparison of figures was enough to reveal the extraordinary change: the rate of mortality among the cases treated had fallen from 42 per cent to 22 per thousand. But still the indefatigable lady was not satisfied. The main problem had been solved —the physical needs of the men had been provided for; their mental and spiritual needs remained. She set up and furnished reading rooms and recreation rooms. She started classes and lectures. Officers were amazed to see her treating their men as if they were human beings, and assured her that she would only end by "spoiling the brutes." But that was not Miss Nightingale's opinion, and she was justified. The private soldier began to drink less, and even—though that seemed impossible—to save his pay. Miss Nightingale became a banker for the army, receiving and sending home large sums of money every month. At last, reluctantly, the government followed suit, and established machinery of its own for the remission of money. Lord Panmuir, however, remained skeptical; "It will do no good," he pronounced; "the British soldier is not a remitting animal." But, in fact, during the next six months, £71,000 was sent home.

Amid all these activities, Miss Nightingale took up the further task of inspecting the hospitals in the Crimea itself. The labor was extreme, and the conditions of life were almost intolerable. She spent whole days in the saddle, or was driven over those bleak and rocky heights in a baggage cart. Sometimes she stood for hours in the heavily falling snow, and would only reach her hut at dead of night after walking for miles through perilous ravines. Her powers of resistance seemed incredible, but at last they were exhausted. She was attacked by fever, and for a moment came very near to death. Yet she worked on; if she could not move, she could at least write; and write she did until her mind had left her; and after it had left her, in what seemed the delirious trance of death itself, she still wrote. When, after many weeks, she was strong enough to travel, she was to return to England, but she utterly refused. She would not go back, she said, before the last of the soldiers had left Scutari.

This happy moment had almost arrived, when suddenly the smoldering hostilities of the medical authorities burst out into a flame. Dr. Hall's labors had been rewarded by a K.C.B.[18]—letters which, as Miss Nightingale told Sidney Herbert, she could only suppose to mean "Knight of the Crimean Burial-grounds" —and the honor had turned his head. He was Sir John, and he would be thwarted no longer. Disputes had lately arisen between Miss Nightingale and some of the nurses in the Crimean hospitals. The situation had been embittered by rumors of religious dissensions, for, while the Crimean nurses were Roman Catholics, many of those at Scutari were suspected of a regrettable propensity toward the tenets of Dr. Pusey.[19]

Miss Nightingale was by no means disturbed by these sectarian differences, but any suggestion that her supreme authority over all the nurses with the army was in doubt was enough to rouse her to fury. . . . Dr. Hall, she declared, was doing his best to "root her out of the Crimea." She would bear it no longer; the War Office was playing her false; there was only one thing to be done—Sidney Herbert must move for the production of papers in the House of Commons,[20] so that the public might be able to judge between her and her enemies. Sidney Herbert with great difficulty calmed her down. Orders were immediately dispatched putting her supremacy beyond doubt.

Sir John, however, was more tenacious. A few weeks later, Miss Nightingale and her nurses visited the Crimea for the last time, and the brilliant idea occurred to him that he could crush her by a very simple expedient—he would starve her into submission; and he actually ordered that no rations of any kind should be supplied to her. He had already tried this plan with great effect upon an unfortunate medical man whose presence in the Crimea he had considered an intrusion; but he was now to learn that such tricks were thrown away upon Miss Nightingale. With extraordinary foresight, she had brought with her a great supply of food; she succeeded in obtaining more at her own expense and by her own exertions; and thus for ten days, in that inhospitable country, she was able to feed herself and twenty-four nurses. Eventually the military authorities intervened in her favor, and Sir John had to confess that he was beaten.

It was not until July, 1856—four months after the Declaration of Peace—that Miss

18. *K.C.B.*, Knight Commander of the order of the Bath, a royal honorary order. 19. *Dr. Pusey* (pū'zi). Edward B. Pusey, an English clergyman, was a leader in the Oxford Movement and an associate of Newman. He was suspended from the office of university preacher for heresy. 20. *move . . . House of Commons.* Florence Nightingale wished to have the entire controversy and the official records placed before the House of Commons.

Nightingale left Scutari for England. Her reputation was now enormous, and the enthusiasm of the public was unbounded. The Royal approbation was expressed by the gift of a brooch, accompanied by a private letter:

You are, I know, well aware (wrote Her Majesty) of the high sense I entertain of the Christian devotion which you have displayed during this great and bloody war, and I need hardly repeat to you how warm my admiration is for your services, which are fully equal to those of my dear and brave soldiers, whose sufferings you have had the *privilege* of alleviating in so merciful a manner. I am, however, anxious of marking my feelings in a manner which I trust will be agreeable to you, and therefore send you with this letter a brooch, the form and emblems of which commemorate your great and blessed work, and which I hope you will wear as a mark of the high approbation of your Sovereign!

"It will be a very great satisfaction to me," Her Majesty added, "to make the acquaintance of one who has set so bright an example to our sex."

The brooch, which was designed by the Prince Consort, bore a St. George's cross[21] in red enamel, and the Royal cipher surmounted by diamonds. The whole was encircled by the inscription, "Blessed are the Merciful."

---

21. *St. George's cross,* a red cross with all arms of equal length on a white field.

To increase understanding

1. How did Florence Nightingale's girlhood ambitions conflict with the Victorian standards of conduct for a young lady of good family?

2. (*a*) What specific things did Miss Nightingale do as a young woman to perfect herself professionally? (*b*) What impelled her to continue this difficult course?

3. (*a*) Describe the conditions in the Scutari hospitals before Miss Nightingale took charge. (*b*) What specific improvements in the care of the sick and the wounded had Miss Nightingale effected at the end of six months?

4. How do you account (*a*) for the placid indifference of the authorities at home; (*b*) for the hostility of army doctors and surgeons in Scutari;

(*c*) for the irritating obstructions on the part of the officials all along the way?

5. What is the force of Miss Nightingale's reply to the nurse who said, ". . . let us get straight to nursing the poor fellows" (page 742, column 2, paragraph 3)?

6. (*a*) What does Strachey emphasize as being Florence Nightingale's most remarkable talent? (*b*) What does he see as her leading character trait? (*c*) Do you agree with the author that the real Florence Nightingale was more interesting than the legend? Explain.

Better reading
Strachey as biographer

Nothing delighted the "moderns" of the twentieth century so much as deflating the heroes of the preceding era. When Lytton Strachey showed them one way it could be done, he was followed by a host of lesser imitators, who were too often unscrupulous in their methods. This group was called the "debunking" school of biography. Strachey himself is not always fair, though he is accurate in his facts. His devastating ridicule comes in the way he presents his facts. Notice the rapier thrust in his brief description of Dr. Hall (page 744, column 1, lines 1-2). The *Dictionary of National Biography* speaks of Sir John Hall as an army surgeon, who received his M.D. from St. Andrews in 1845; who became principal medical officer in Kaffraria and in the Crimea; who was made Knight Commander of the Order of the Bath and inspector-general of hospitals; and who defended·the medical service in the Crimea in 1858. What a different aspect Strachey gives to this life, when he speaks of Dr. Hall as "a rough terrier of a man, who had worried his way to the top of his profession"! The first part of this statement might be mistaken for a compliment, if it were not for the last part that indirectly casts suspicion on Dr. Hall's motives and, what is worse, by conjuring up the image of a dog worrying a bone, makes him ridiculous. In this selection Strachey's barbs are directed less against individuals than against the gross inefficiencies of the War Office—the bulwark of the Empire—which he elsewhere describes as "that tropical jungle of festooned obstructiveness, of intertwisted irresponsibilities, of crouching prejudices, of abuses grown stiff and rigid with antiquity." Point out a number of places where Strachey ridicules the entire organization. What advantage does he gain by using his wit to ridicule these ills, rather than chastizing them in a tone of moral indignation?

Hesketh Pearson
from GILBERT: HIS LIFE AND STRIFE

In 1871 occurred the now famous meeting between the promising composer Arthur Sullivan and the popular writer of light verse and farcical plays, William S. Gilbert. That same year saw the production of a musical burlesque, Thespis, *with story and lyrics by Gilbert and music by Sullivan. Four years later the theater manager Richard D'Oyly Carte promoted the first of the famous Gilbert and Sullivan operettas,* Trial by Jury. *This popular satire was followed by* The Sorcerer, H.M.S. Pinafore, The Pirates of Penzance, *and, in 1881, by* Patience, *a satire on Oscar Wilde, the Pre-Raphaelites, and the "art-for-art's-sake" movement.*

Perhaps no works were ever produced at the cost of so much mental travail and in the course of so much physical pain as those of Gilbert and Sullivan. The libretti were written out as stories, revised, rewritten, reconsidered, redrafted, a score of times; and the dialogue and lyrics were subjected to an equally laborious process, from conception to completion, over a prolonged period. The music was often composed with astonishing swiftness, welling out as spontaneously as the words had been churned out arduously, though not seldom accompanied by bodily torments. The composer however took longer than usual over his contribution to the next Savoy opera.[1]

The financial rewards of *Patience*[2] were so considerable that Sullivan moved into an expensive flat in Queen's Mansions, Victoria Street, and Gilbert started to build a house in Harrington Gardens, South Kensington. Naturally the opera had been pirated in the United States, and the partners made up their minds to have their next produced simultaneously in both countries. The first act did not please Sullivan and he wanted to discuss it with Gilbert, who at the time was yachting off the south coast. They spent an afternoon together in the coffee room of the Half Moon Hotel, Exeter, and revised the act to their mutual satisfaction. To prevent piracy and newspaper gossip, the music was locked up between rehearsals and the opera misnamed. Even the cast were kept in the dark about the title until the final dress rehearsal, when they were told that the word they had been speaking, *Periola*, must be changed to *Iolanthe* the following evening. Those concerned protested that they would almost certainly confuse the names on the first night. "Never mind, so long as you sing the music," said Sullivan. "Use any name that happens to come first to you. Nobody in the audience will be any the wiser except Mr. Gilbert, and he won't be there." Gilbert cannot have been there when Sullivan delivered this advice.

The really popular writer drifts with the trend of public feeling, giving the impression that he is leading it by making articulate the sentiment of the majority. In *Patience* Gilbert had shown the public exactly what they wished to ridicule in poetry. In *Iolanthe* he showed them precisely what they wished to deride in politics. The Liberal Party under Gladstone[3] had come to power and the idea was gaining ground that the House of Lords obstructed progress. Gilbert wittily expressed the popular view in *Iolanthe*, while providing some fun at the expense of the House of Commons to placate those rich or titled playgoers who might have complained of a class

---

From *Gilbert: His Life and Strife* by Hesketh Pearson. Reprinted by permission of Harper & Row, Publishers, and The Society of Authors. Copyright 1957 by Hesketh Pearson.
1. *Savoy opera.* The Savoy is an area of London that gave its name to the Savoy Theatre, where Richard D'Oyly Carte produced the Gilbert and Sullivan operas. Hence these operas came to be called Savoy operas, and any member of the company, a Savoyard. 2. *Patience,* an opera in which Gilbert had satirized the art-for-art's-sake movement (see page 466). 3. *Liberal Party . . . Gladstone.* Gladstone led the Liberal Party to victory for the second time in 1880 (see page 414).

distinction in gray matter. Everybody was pleased, and the opera, first seen on November 25, 1882, was repeated for more than a year. Gilbert very sensibly refused to regard his satire as an index to his opinions. Twenty-seven years after he had written *Iolanthe* the Liberal Party were campaigning against the House of Lords and a section of it wished to use his verses as propaganda. He wrote sharply: "I cannot permit the verses from *Iolanthe* to be used for electioneering purposes. They do not at all express my own views. They are supposed to be the views of the wrongheaded donkey who sings them."

The collaborators had now performed a feat unparalleled in the annals of the theater: they had produced four extremely remunerative comic operas in succession. It seemed that whatever they did together would fill a theater for at least a year; and in those days very few plays, let alone operas, ran for half that time, one hundred performances constituting a success. They felt in 1883 that they could aestivate at ease, careless of the future. Gilbert lazily

---

Hesketh Pearson   1887–

Hesketh Pearson, today one of England's most popular biographers, was once a successful actor, specializing in the rôles of Shakespeare's villains. After World War I, in which he rose from the rank of private to that of captain, he began writing biographical portraits in his spare time. In 1931 he left the stage, taking other jobs that left him more time for writing. Pearson's first biographies were unsuccessful, partly because of the continuing popularity of Lytton Strachey and his imitators. Pearson's work was of a more traditional cut, in direct reaction against Strachey's influence. Success came at last, however, with his life of Bernard Shaw in 1942. Able now to devote himself entirely to writing, Pearson proved to be a prolific biographer, and his delightful, often witty style has won him a wide audience. Particularly notable among his works are *Oscar Wilde* (1946), *Dickens* (1949), and *Dizzy: The Life and Personality of Benjamin Disraeli* (1951). In 1957 he published *Gilbert: His Life and Strife*, from which this selection is taken, and the following year a double biography of Boswell and Johnson.

adapted his play *The Princess* to the needs of the Savoy and produced an opera in blank verse. Sullivan jibbed at first but assented at last. In May 1883, at the age of forty-one, he was knighted, and his birthday party on Whitsunday included the Prince of Wales, the Duke of Edinburgh, a brace of peers, Ferdinand Rothschild, J. C. Millais,[4] F. C. Burnand (editor of *Punch*) and Gilbert. Having concluded a musical entertainment, to which Madame Albani and Paolo Tosti[5] contributed, Sullivan treated his guests to a selection of songs from *Iolanthe*. The company had gone to the theater for the purpose, and the guests in Victoria Street listened in with the aid of an electrophone.[6]

That year Gilbert moved into his new house, which had been fitted up luxuriously with paneled walls, thickly molded ceilings, richly embellished wallpapers, ornate tapestries, and some windows of stained glass. More useful additions were electric light, central heating, a telephone, and a bathroom on each floor. Delays and disappointments in connection with such an elaborate establishment were inevitable. Several tart letters were addressed to one company that supplied a dado and a chimney piece, and on July 2, 1883, Gilbert wrote to the firm chiefly responsible for the interior arrangements:

Gentlemen

I write to inform you that I intend to move into my house in Harrington Gardens on 1st October next, as I am selling this house from that date. To enable me to make this move it is necessary that the hall, dining-room, morning-room on half landing, library, our bedroom and dressing-rooms, 3 servants' bedrooms, and the basement should be completed. I would suggest that you put all your strength to the completion of this work, as I shall commence occupation on the 1st October, in whatever condition the premises may be. I shall also reckon demurrage as from

---

4. *Ferdinand Rothschild, J. C. Millais.* Ferdinand Rothschild, a member of the famous banking family, was a noted art collector. J. C. Millais, a painter, president of the Royal Academy, was one of the founders of the Pre-Raphaelite Movement. 5. *Madame Albani and Paolo Tosti.* Albani was a singer with the Royal Italian Opera at Covent Garden; Tosti, an Italian composer, was teacher of singing to the royal family. 6. *electrophone,* a public address system.

that date, as regards the rooms I have specified, and such other rooms as may be essential to my comfort.

Yours truly
W. S. Gilbert

In the same year he took a furnished country-house called Breakspears, at Harefield near Uxbridge, for which he paid £800 per annum. Here he spent many summer weeks and spring weekends for the next seven years, playing tennis on an outsize court and entertaining those friends who did not provoke friction, of which there was always sufficient in the theater and the world of business.

The preparation of the next opera, *Princess Ida,* provided more friction than usual, possibly because the blank verse irritated the actors. "Look here, sir, I will *not* be bullied! I know my lines," rasped one of them. "That may be, but you don't know mine," Gilbert snapped back. George Grossmith[7] was roused to exclaim indignantly, "I beg your pardon!" after one of the author's acid remarks. "I accept the apology," Gilbert blandly replied; "let's get on with the rehearsal." Having repeated one scene almost twenty times, Grossmith struck: "I've rehearsed this confounded business until I feel a perfect fool!" Gilbert soothed him: "Ah, now we can talk on equal terms." As usual, Sullivan was late with the music and made himself ill with overwork when time pressed. On the date of production, January 5, 1884, he was clearly unfit to conduct. After two injections of morphia he struggled to the theater in a semiconscious condition. Braced by his reception he managed to get through the evening, but collapsed after the curtain call. The opera only lasted nine months, which the authors considered a failure. The theme was not acceptable, being a variation on that of *Love's Labour's Lost.* Shakespeare's male characters and Gilbert's female characters seclude themselves from the other sex to study philosophy; but playgoers had not yet been sufficiently indoctrinated by Ibsen to regard the independent woman as pleasant or natural.[8] Gilbert's satire was blunted by verse, though it happened that his lyrical gift was displayed at its finest in *Prin-* *cess Ida,* wherein one song is as charming as anything by Robert Herrick, as perfect as anything by John Suckling, its absence from anthologies being due to editorial ignorance:

> Whom thou has chained must wear his chain,
>   Thou canst not set him free,
> He wrestles with his bonds in vain
>   Who lives by loving thee!
> If heart of stone for heart of fire,
>   Be all thou hast to give,
> If dead to me my heart's desire,
>   Why should I wish to live?

> No word of thine—no stern command
>   Can teach my heart to rove,
> Then rather perish by thy hand,
>   Than live without thy love!
> A loveless life apart from thee
>   Were hopeless slavery,
> If kindly death will set me free,
>   Why should I fear to die?

The relative failure of this opera caused disruption in the partnership, though the ostensible reasons were of another kind. The one thing that bound the pair together was their dual success. Without that Sullivan would much rather write what was known as "serious music": namely, oratorios, grand operas, symphonies, and so on. From the throne to the professors of music, from friends to critics, he was incited to solemnity; and now that he had been knighted he felt that he must do better than set comic words to music, that he should justify his sovereign's confidence in him as another Mendelssohn. Yet his nature craved for all the things that money brought him, and it was impossible to grow rich on oratorios. The ambition to write music that would be approved by those who believed that music should be improving, and the desire to earn enough money for the life of gambling and hospitality enjoyed by his aristocratic friends: these were the two main

7. *George Grossmith,* famous entertainer who took many of the principal rôles in the operas. 8. *playgoers had not . . . natural.* The plays of the great Norwegian playwright Henrik Ibsen, which showed women acting according to their own interests rather than those of their fathers or husbands, shocked Victorian theatergoers. It was Shaw, primarily, that finally made this image of the "modern woman" popular.

strands in his nature, and they were irreconcilable. Sometimes one was the stronger, sometimes the other, but the struggle between the two was never resolved. Gilbert's situation was different. Though he too felt convinced that he was made for better things than the writing of humorous libretti, he was an older man who believed that he had put his best work into his plays[9] and was now solely concerned with comfort and financial security. Their different aims, coupled with Sullivan's sense of frustration and Gilbert's natural irritation, explains the first rift in their association.

Shortly after the appearance of *Princess Ida* Sullivan informed D'Oyly Carte that he had written his last work for the Savoy Theatre. Carte was upset but felt that Sullivan, temporarily under the weather, would reconsider his decision after a holiday; and when in March the opera showed signs of failure, he wrote to remind the composer of their contract whereby he had to give the collaborators six months' notice when a new opera would be required. He now gave this notice to both of them. Sullivan answered from Brussels that he could not undertake another piece "of the character of those already written by Gilbert and myself." Carte wondered what Gilbert would have to say. Gilbert said it to Sullivan: "I learnt from Carte yesterday, to my unbounded surprise, that you do not intend to write any more operas of the class with which you and I have so long been identified." He warned Sullivan that if they failed in their agreement with Carte they would be responsible for any losses resulting from their default, and he declared that he had already started work on a new libretto:

In all the pieces we have written together I have invariably subordinated my views to your own; you have often expatiated to me, and to others, on the thorough good feeling with which we have worked together for so many years. Nothing, as far as I am aware, has occurred to induce you to change your views on this point, and I am therefore absolutely at a loss to account for the decision.

Sullivan replied from Paris that his music was becoming repetitive, that his share of the work dissatisfied him, and that what he now wanted was a story of human interest and probability, where the comedy, drama and sentiment would be separated each from the other. "Your reflections on the character of the libretti with which I have supplied you have caused me considerable pain," returned Gilbert:

However, I cannot suppose that you have intended to gall and wound me, when you wrote as you did. I must assume that your letter was written hurriedly. When you tell me that your desire is that I shall write a libretto in which the humorous words will come in a humorous situation, and in which a tender or dramatic situation will be treated tenderly and dramatically, you teach me the ABC of my profession. It is inconceivable that any sane author should ever write otherwise than as you propose I should write in future.

They met in April at Sullivan's flat and had a long talk. The theme of Gilbert's new libretto was not new: one variation of it had appeared in his first play *Dulcamara*, another in *The Sorcerer*, and it would continue to haunt his fancy during the remainder of his life, for it was based on a feeling, engrafted in childhood, that the world would be a better place if its inhabitants could change their natures. The version he now proposed to Sullivan was that every character in the new piece would become what he or she pretended to be by the simple process of absorbing a lozenge. Two years before Sullivan had rejected the same idea, though on that occasion the means of metamorphosis had been a coin. The substitution of a lozenge for a medal did not make the circumstance any more lifelike, and Sullivan again rejected it. A day or two later Gilbert proposed that Sullivan should write his next opera to someone else's words, since "your objections to my libretto really seem arbitrary and capricious." Sullivan declined to consider such a proposal. Again they met but Gilbert remained faithful to his lozenge, and though Sullivan did his utmost to swallow it he found that it would not go

---

9. *plays.* Before turning to comic opera, Gilbert had written several plays.

down. He reported as much to Gilbert, who replied:

Anxious as I am, and have always been, to give due weight to your suggestions, the time has arrived when I must state—and I do so with great reluctance—that I cannot consent to construct another plot for the next Opera.

Sullivan regretted this decision and a frantic Carte went from one to the other for several days in an agitated attempt to reach a compromise.

With their weekly returns from the Savoy steadily diminishing, each would have seized any excuse to do another work together; and a Japanese exhibition in Knightsbridge turned Gilbert's thoughts from his lozenge libretto. Japanese prints, designs, and what not, were rapidly becoming the fashion, and the public would surely jump at a Japanese opera. He wrote the good news to his partner, who was inexpressibly relieved, replying that if the plot were to be devoid of supernatural and improbable elements he would "gladly undertake to set it without further discussing the matter, or asking what the subject is to be." It cannot be said that the plot and people of *The Mikado*, which Gilbert at once started to write, are noticeably natural or probable, but at least they are not made less so by a lozenge.

An example of the vogue for Chinese objects in England is this fine, eighteenth-century vase. THE MOUNT TRUST COLLECTION OF CHINESE ART

Though Gilbert declared that the idea for this opera entered his head when a Japanese sword fell from the wall of his study, it seems more likely that the idea was germinating within him before that accident, the crash of the falling weapon merely fixing it in his mind. Extremely susceptible to the atmosphere of his age, he must often have envisaged a Japanese setting, because the taste for oriental prints and pots, started in England by Whistler in the sixties and advertised by himself and Rossetti in the seventies, had become fairly general by the eighties, and Gilbert knew to a fad how the popular taste could be exploited. The sureness of his instinct, coupled with the creative harmony between librettist and composer, was again demonstrated when the country went *Mikado*-mad.

Like all the operas, it was produced by Gilbert with the utmost care, if possible with greater care than usual because of the necessity to recover the ground lost by *Princess Ida*. Weedon Grossmith, brother of George, once remarked that the difference between the methods of production at the Lyceum[10] and those at the Savoy was that at every rehearsal Henry Irving groped for perfection, while Gilbert arrived at each rehearsal with perfection in his pocket: the first saw what he wanted in fitful gleams, the second in a hard steady light. In other words Gilbert knew exactly what he wanted before he started to produce. He worked it all out on a model stage with wooden blocks for the actors; and though he occasionally improvised during rehearsals, all the positions, stage business, exits, entrances, even the word inflections, were clear in his mind's eye before the practical work began.

He was an exacting but patient producer. Knowing what he wanted, he took endless pains to get it, occasionally repeating a word twenty or thirty times before the actor could speak it rightly, often doing a scene over and over again until the performers were breaking under the strain. His energy never flagged. He could show the chorus how to dance with the efficiency of a ballet master and instruct

---

10. *Lyceum*, a rival theater for musical comedy.

them how to pronounce the words and maintain the rhythm with the skill of a music master, though he always asserted that he knew nothing about music and could scarcely distinguish between one tune and another. Whenever he thought that a performer was not trying to obtain the effect he desired, his patience gave way to temper and his sarcasms were relentless; but knowing that most people can only do their best under persuasion, he seldom attempted to bully them into subjection. Nevertheless the drilling to which they were exposed was of a military kind. Nothing was left to chance, and the company had to go through its evolutions at the word of command, repeating them, as on a parade ground, until the process became automatic. Once, at any rate, his method nearly caused disaster. George Grossmith had a highly sensitive nature, and the rehearsals of *The Mikado* shattered his nerves. To such a condition had he been reduced that, according to Sullivan, he "nearly upset the piece" on the first night. He forestalled the repetition of such an alarming event by deadening his nerves with drugs.

Though no one would have guessed it, another martyr to first-night agitation was Gilbert, whose forebodings took the form of going the round of the dressing rooms and imparting his last words of advice to the players, thus adding to their own misgivings. A score

of things he had told and repeated to the stage-manager were recapitulated, and even the property man came in for a series of warnings. He heard the roar of applause that greeted Sullivan's appearance in the orchestra, made a final survey of the scenery and chorus, and on the rise of the curtain quitted the theater. "What I suffered during those hours, no man can tell," he said. "I have spent them at the club; I once went to a theater alone to see a play; I have walked up and down the street; but no matter where I was, agony and apprehension possessed me."

The yells for librettist and composer when the final curtain descended on *The Mikado* were louder than usual. They entered from different sides, Gilbert with reluctance, Sullivan with readiness. The first frowned at the audience and nodded his head curtly; the second smiled with pleasure and bowed with grace. This time their success was unquestionable. *The Mikado*, produced on March 14, 1885, ran for nearly two years and made more money for the partners than any other of their operas. Oddly enough one of its most popular songs—

> My object all sublime
> I shall achieve in time—
> To let the punishment fit the crime—
> The punishment fit the crime—

was nearly omitted. Gilbert did not like it at the final dress rehearsal and said that it must be cut out. But Richard Temple, who sang it as the Mikado, backed by the members of the chorus, begged for its retention, and the author gave way.

After the production of all his operas the relief and reaction were so considerable that, with one exception, Gilbert never again witnessed a performance from the front. Having devoted months to the writing and weeks to the rehearsals, he felt sick of a work by the time it was ready for the public. But the public, unconscious of his birth pangs, have never shared his feeling. . . .

On one point he was never in doubt: his belief in the lozenge was almost religious, and while *The Mikado* was still packing the Savoy he again brought it up. Sullivan very

Playbill for the opening night of The Mikado, *on March 14, 1885.*

courteously begged him to forget it. In January 1886 Gilbert arrived at Sullivan's flat in a snow blizzard with a non-lozenge plot. Sullivan was delighted and agreed to coöperate, but first he had to produce an oratorio for the Leeds Festival. He did so, and *The Golden Legend* created a sensation, Sullivan undergoing the unique experience of a conductor being pelted with flowers by his orchestra. This time he was called the Mozart of England and mildly reprimanded for wasting his genius on Savoy opera. Gilbert wrote: "I congratulate you heartily on the success of the Cantata which appears from all accounts to be the biggest thing you've done." But Gilbert was solely concerned with the little thing that he himself had done, and sent the libretto of *Ruddigore* to his partner. At rehearsals each of them thought that the other had too large a share of the work, Sullivan describing it as a play with a few songs, Gilbert convinced that the words were overshadowed by the music. At the fall of the curtain on the first performance, January 22, 1887, several occupants of the gallery expressed disapprobation; and the critics said it was not half so good as *The Mikado*; whereupon Gilbert suggested that they should re-entitle it *Kensington Gore: or Not Half So Good as The Mikado*. Though a number of alterations were made to please the public, the opera only ran for ten months. Ancestral ghosts were in the air

just then, possibly because the daughters of certain impoverished peers had recently been married to wealthy Americans, and less than a month after the appearance of *Ruddigore* a magazine published *The Canterville Ghost* by Oscar Wilde; but somehow the theme failed to catch the popular fancy, and Gilbert's share of the profits on the original run was a measly £7000, which any other author would have thought a windfall. . . .

❀ To increase understanding

1. How does Pearson characterize Gilbert's style of living and his ambitions?

2. (*a*) How does Pearson portray the differences in personality between Gilbert and Sullivan and their personal relations? (*b*) How does Pearson set forth the differences in the creative methods of the two men and the way in which they worked together? (*c*) What facts does the author cite to illustrate the differences and the relations between Gilbert and Sullivan?

3. Explain in what light, according to Pearson, Gilbert viewed his work and how he approached it. Be sure to examine both phases of Gilbert's work: the working out of the story and lyrics, and the production of the opera.

4. One of the reasons for Pearson's popularity is his wit. (*a*) Point out some examples cited by the author that you found particularly amusing. (*b*) In each case tell what the example seems designed to illustrate.

J. B. Priestley *from* MARGIN RELEASED

More than half a century ago, living then in Toller Lane, Bradford, but all in another world, I was sixteen and I had to make a choice. I had to leave school that summer or I had to stay there to work for a university scholarship. No compromise was possible. There was not a chance of hanging on at school for a year or two, not doing very much. Neither the school nor my father, who had once taught there,

would have tolerated it. You stayed on to begin some systematic hard slogging for a scholarship. Contrary to some reports, I have never been at any age a systematic hard slogger. I have seemed to myself at all times to be lacking in determination and self-discipline. If I have never been called indolent and irresolute, that is because hardly anybody knows anything. I have a reputation for en-

Reprinted by permission of A. D. Peters & Co.

ergy and fertility, but chiefly among fellow writers who are neither energetic nor fertile, do not want to be, and probably dislike me anyhow. If I have written a great deal, this is largely because I have always had ideas for work to lure me on and on. Not all these ideas were good; many were indifferent, some terrible. But I have never been without them. They were just beginning to beckon then,

---

J. B. Priestley 1894-

John Boynton Priestley describes himself as amiable and shy, but many who know him are more apt to call him blunt, brusque, and downright difficult. He says he is a lazy man, but, again, few people would agree with that judgment. One of England's most prolific living writers, his books number several dozen and include novels, essay collections, plays, personal history, and social criticism. In addition to this extraordinary literary output, Priestley travels extensively, lectures, works as a radio commentator and as a television writer, handles his own voluminous correspondence, takes an active part in political affairs, and plays a hard game of lawn tennis.

Priestley began writing at sixteen and used the money he earned to pay his way through Cambridge. During the years of World War I he served in the infantry; he was wounded three times. His war experiences had little effect on the content of his writing, but, as revealed in *Margin Released*, they were a deciding influence in his personal life. For after the war he no longer felt at home in Bradford; and in 1922 he went to London, where he quickly became known and respected as a reviewer, critic, and essayist.

As a novelist, Priestley's first great success was *The Good Companions,* a book which has become one of the best-sellers of the century. He followed up *The Good Companions* with *Angel Pavement,* which has been almost equally successful. In all, Priestley has published some twenty novels; their total sales run into the millions.

In 1932, Priestley wrote his first play, *Dangerous Corner.* Unlike his novels, which adhere strongly to traditional standards, his plays are often highly experimental in form. Although these unconventional dramatic works have stimulated much praise—some consider Priestley a master of dramatic construction— they have aroused an equal amount of controversy and adverse criticism.

about 1910; they are still beckoning now. One of them lured me into this chronicle beginning at the end of my schooldays, to which I must now return.

There was of course no certainty of my winning a scholarship to Oxford or Cambridge, but that did not worry me. Though lazy and quite incapable of applying myself to subjects that bored me, I had always done very well at school; I brought to the subjects I did like, such as English and History, a great deal that I discovered for myself outside school. In coming to a decision I was not influenced by any dread of failure; one thing I possessed, perhaps to the point of brashness, was self-confidence. No, the trouble was that even the prospect of success was not enticing. Nothing beckoned there. I didn't see myself in courts or quads, under dreaming spires[1]; and nine years and a long war later, when finally I did arrive in Cambridge, I still didn't see myself there, never felt at home. Statutes about not playing marbles on the Senate House steps, that kind of thing, never made me giggle cosily; they merely irritated me. Unlike some of my school friends toiling not for a degree and a better job but already under the spell of tradition, that great English hocus-pocus, I felt even then alienated rather than attracted by everything that had been long established. I do not claim this lack of response to tradition as a virtue; in some respects it is a weakness, closing the mind to a whole range of feeling; though it does help one to examine the English social scene with detachment or a certain useful scepticism, especially when the traditional has become the bogus, power and money playing charades. Unbeckoned then, I decided to leave school.

One school friend, George, stayed on and won a scholarship to Cambridge. His father worked as a joiner in one of the big mills. His mother, a wiry little woman with excited black eyes and a curious hoarse voice, came from somewhere in the Midlands and brought with her an odd trick of speech, 'singing' be-

---

1. *in courts or quads, under dreaming spires.* The architecture of both Oxford and Cambridge universities is characterized by buildings with pointed towers, or spires, formally arranged around open courtyards, or quadrangles.

coming 'sin-Ging'. We did a lot of sin-Ging in their small front room on Saturday and Sunday nights. George and I both played the piano in the same slap-dash style, but he had no voice and I had a loud one, not unsuitable for baritone ballads but happiest in noisy comic songs. He became my accompanist, both at home and elsewhere. Once I earned a guinea, with his assistance, at a Saturday night variety concert at the Mechanics Institute, where I forgot too many words and was not a success. This must have been particularly disappointing to the impresario—a seedy old pro, who billed me as *Jack Croly, of the leading London and Provincial Halls*—because he was a believer in phrenology and before engaging me insisted upon feeling my bumps; so that I must have been a phrenological disappointment too. George and I only hit the top of our form, I suspect, in that packed front room. Fortunately both his parents delighted in company and noise and family jokes, people coming and going, casual hospitality, the party spirit. I borrowed a few touches of his father for Jess Oakroyd in *The Good Companions,* but his mother, never downcast, always blazing-eyed, about six-and-a-half stone[2] of indomitable femininity, was the greater character. And several months after George had left for Cambridge, after I had dutifully admired all the things he had to take with him, the flannels, the dinner jacket and the rest, I caught sight of her one very cold morning on my way to work. She was coming out of an office building, for once looking shrunken and fagged, after the cleaning she must have taken on to help pay for all those things so necessary in Cambridge. When George came home in the vacs we still made a lot of noise in the front room; now there were Cambridge jokes as well, about no-marbles-playing and eccentric dons[3] and cap-and-gown exploits; good evenings still, but never to me quite the same. And later I arrived in Cambridge without flannels and dinner jacket, and rather grimly paid my way.

My life at school had been neither a joy nor a torment, mostly rather boring. It was not until years afterwards, when I listened with astonishment to men talking in clubs, that I realised how important schooldays were to the English. In the later Twenties, when I lived in Hampstead, I used to play a lot of lawn tennis, and between sets all the talk was of schools—'Both our boys are at So-and-so—where is your boy going?' It seemed, and still seems, idiotic to me, all this school talk. But then of course I did not live at school; perhaps nobody should. Games I enjoyed, and even collected three medals, which vanished years ago. (But where do such indestructible things go?) Gymnastics I detested then and have never admired since; those Czech mass antics seem to me a horror, halfway to the anthill. Most of the hours spent in classrooms were tedious. I had a quick impatient mind and it fretted when some point had to be made over and over again. Later, in the Army, and much later still at conferences, I discovered the same reaction in myself, the same mixture of irritation and boredom. There was nothing wrong with the masters, but only one of them seemed to me to bring his subject, English, to life.

His name was Richard Pendlebury—a good name in my ears—and he died, long before he ought to have done, over forty years ago. He was tall, intensely dark, as handsome and commanding as an ideal Spanish grandee. His qualifications were modest, below our present standards; he had no Ph.D. for a thesis on the use of the semi-colon in the later works of George Eliot, but he loved good writing, and he knew how to communicate and share that love. Perhaps my feeling for literature could hardly be separated from my liking and admiration for Pendlebury himself. Probably I felt obscurely that the poems and plays and essays he read and discussed with us had helped to make him what he was, had given his glance a flash of fire, had brought a grave courtesy into his manner, had put glints of humour and a cutting edge into his talk. I can see and hear him again, quite clearly,

2. *six-and-a-half stone.* A *stone* is a British measure of weight equal to fourteen pounds avoirdupois. George's mother weighed about ninety-one pounds. 3. *dons*, heads, tutors, or administrators of any college of Oxford or Cambridge.

across years that changed all human history; and if his influence on me was far greater, as indeed it was, than that of all the professors and lecturers I heard later in Cambridge and the critics I met in London, that was because I sat in a classroom, at the right time, with a teacher who loved good writing. But at school there would have been no more Pendlebury; I was already outside his orbit.

So I left school, tired of it. I wanted to write—though ready to conduct symphony orchestras and do a little great acting from time to time—and I believed that the world outside classrooms and labs would help me to become a writer. Certificates and degrees, I felt, had nothing to do with authorship. Moreover, not one of the living writers whose work excited me most had been to Oxford or Cambridge. No class feeling came into all this; I was neither a snob nor an anti-snob. This must seem strange now, when we are always reading—or at least are being asked to read—books and articles about the English class system. The truth is that in these early years I was barely conscious of its existence. When, about thirty years ago, Bernard Shaw came back from a visit to Russia, he told me it was a wonderful relief to be in a country that had no ladies and gentlemen. I said that I had spent the first twenty years of my life without meeting any of those ladies and gentlemen. This was true. I had been brought up in a West Riding industrial community, where to a youngster the social hierarchy was invisible. I am not pretending we had a miniature classless society there, but we probably came nearer to having one than anybody born in southern England can even imagine. Wool men who gambled and won generally left Bradford before they acquired a title and began entertaining the County.[4] If they had come back, a lot of men wearing cloth caps and mufflers would still have called them Sam and Joe. It was not until I took a commission, later in the War, that I discovered that the class structure, with all its tangle of superiorities and inferiorities, was not simply something useful to novelists and playwrights, almost like wills and wards and missing heirs, but something one might have to live with. I felt somewhat

bewildered then, half-amused, half-indignant; and I think I have stayed like that ever since.

No, I simply wanted to have done with formal education. I was tired of people telling me things and then asking me how much I remembered. What I wanted was to look around and find things out myself, then try to write. Here, no doubt, I was pulling away from my father, as a lad of sixteen should do. My father was a schoolmaster, and I could never imagine him as anything else: teaching was his vocation. After teaching children all day he was ready to spend half his nights and nearly all his week-ends teaching adults. People he met in trains, country pubs, seaside boarding houses, found themselves being taught by him. He was no dictatorial and boring pedant; he was lively-minded and companionable, always eager to learn himself; but what he knew—and he knew a lot—he had to teach. He believed in Education as few people nowadays believe in anything. He and his father, a mill worker who probably earned about thirty shillings a week, together performed some little miracle of thrift so that he was able to go to a teachers' training college in London, some time in the Eighties; and there he found Education, a prize, a jewel, not a modern convenience laid on like hot and cold water. He belonged to a generation that believed we could educate ourselves out of muddle and wretchedness and black despair into the sunlight for ever. Its spokesman was H. G. Wells, one of my father's favourite authors, at least before *Ann Veronica* brought sex in, and sound Baptist chapel men,[5] like my father, began shaking their heads. And of course it is true that Education can take us all from darkness into light, that is, so long as we are not thinking about actual schools, colleges, courses, examinations, degrees, but have in mind some rather vague dark-into-light process that may be called educational. Most of the demands for more and more education I have read these last few years do not suggest anybody is worrying about our civilisa-

---

4. *County*, members of the English nobility who hold a rank of earl or better.   5. *chapel men*, a term used by the English to designate all members of any religious faith other than that of the Church of England.

tion, and the sort of minds at work on it, but only about competing for bigger or cheaper bombs and rockets, faster jets, cars that have telephones, and electric shoe-cleaners. Sometimes I think that every time the school makes one move up, the street outside, representing the environment that must win in the end, makes three moves down. Even before 1924, when he died, my father had lost some confidence. If he were alive now, he would be half out of his mind.

I was very fond of my father, indeed I loved him. He was unselfish, brave, honourable, public-spirited. He was the man socialists have in mind when they write about socialism. Bradford, after often hearing what he thought of it, came at last to cherish him; among the older citizens up there I have never really lived up to him, merely represent a showy falling-off. But he was not all of a piece; there were odd mixed elements in him. Though largely tolerant and humorous, there was a curious puritanical streak in him. One of our differences was that from childhood I was fascinated by any form of professional entertainment, whereas he was suspicious of it, considering it at best a waste of time and possibly a danger to sound character-building. Again, though not a pious type, he was one of the most conscientious and hard-working members of our Baptist chapel and its Sunday school, both of which I detested at all ages. He was also a fanatical sabbatarian,[6] so that by the time I reached my teens and spotted the illogicalities he soon lost his temper in any argument we had about the Lord's Day.

He had in fact an explosive temper, and with it a terrifying trick of suddenly breaking into violence, sweeping everything off a breakfast table, for example, or hurling an open suitcase down a flight of stairs. Any preparations for travel brought the flashpoint nearer, and the Priestley family often began its holidays in tears. But any storm soon passed; he was never sulky, silent, cold, sarcastic. He wanted to teach, to counsel, to guide, but not to gather and use power. Indeed, except during his occasional berserk moments, my father was a most lovable man.

Like so many good men—and unlike all the men I have known who have been corrupted in some way—my father was not afraid, at the right time and in the right place, to let go of his dignity and be a clown. He was never artfully funny; just downright frankly silly, like a boy among boys. He baulked at nothing in charades, which I helped to organise as soon as I was old enough to command any attention. In those days, before the wholesale and retail trades took over Christmas, there used to be parties every night or so, and many a time I laughed myself into a red haze and a danger of choking. (This may be happening now to small boys; perhaps I don't go to the right parties.) Until my middle teens, when I naturally wanted to go my own way and so had some sharp differences of opinion with my father, I was happy at home. My mother died not long after I was born, but I had a step-mother who defied tradition by always being kind, gentle, loving. Indeed, it was she who excused my teenage eccentricities, declaring, with that sardonic over-emphasis peculiar to women in the North, great flatterers of male pretensions, that I was a genius and therefore might be excused. (But you have to hear that 'geeenius'.) Yes, I was happy there, so, wherever my desire to write came from, it certainly did not come out of any frustrated, wretched childhood. I was outside the fashionable literary movement before I even began. But at home I did hear too much about Education.

This was inevitable. Many of my father's friends were teachers too, belonging to the same generation of educational enthusiasts. Our house, where there was a great deal of that casual hospitality which largely vanished in the First War, was noisy with the claims and protests of the teaching profession, all the noisier because these teachers, once they were warm in argument, could not help using their classroom voices. I lingered among their pipes and, in winter, toddy, for which we had those silver sugar-crushers (and, remember, whisky was three-and-sixpence a bottle then), hearing too much about Education but enjoying the visitors as comic characters. I think

---

6. *sabbatarian,* here used to mean a Christian who favors a very strict observance of Sunday.

people who cannot appreciate such characters in literature, finding them overdrawn, out of scale, larger and simpler than life, must have lost all memory of their childhood or had one that was unusually narrow and cheerless. When we are very young, it is the friends of our parents, so enormously themselves and so seemingly unchanging, like immortals, who create for us our first comic characters. Later, when fiction and drama present us with such characters, they take us back to a time when all available rooms have been tidied and cleared and the fires are burning bright, and we are anything between six and twelve years old, giggling and scuffling in the background while the great drolls arrive. It is useless to insist, as austere and unimaginative criticism often does, that people are not really like that, for there is a time when they are, and it is a time that continues to exist out of reach of critical opinion, a time we remember when we no longer recall which critic said what. But though my father's friends did not fail me as comic characters, nevertheless they talked too much about Education. I was tired of it. I needed a change of atmosphere.

Now that I look back I am surprised that my father was not violently angry nor even sadly reproachful when I told him I wanted to leave school. (Or were there some scenes that memory has blotted out?) I should like to think he had never made a plan in which I went to a university. There may have been in him a conflict between his bookishness, which later accepted with pride anything of mine that got into print, and his West Riding insistence upon livings being earned, corn being carried, and no monkey business and hanky-panky. I can understand now why my teenage antics should make him feel uneasy. His own family were mill workers, both men and women, but a solid steady sort; but he had plucked my mother, my real mother, about whom I know nothing except that she was high-spirited and witty, from the clogs and shawls 'back o't mill', a free and easy, rather raffish kind of working-class life, where in the grim little back-to-back houses they shouted and screamed, laughed and cried, and sent out a jug for more beer. He must have

felt that it needed only a bit too much hanky-panky, just a few years trying this and that, with no corn to be carried, and down I would go, putting on a cloth cap and muffler to fetch another jugful of beer. Certainly something of the sort must have been at the back of his mind, for when I told him I wanted to leave school, without any immediate plan of earning a living, he announced that I must go into the Bradford trade, the wool business.

It was as if a fanatical teetotaller had told his son to get a job as a barman. My father himself would no more have gone into the wool trade than he would have joined the Foreign Legion. To him and his friends there was a composite and symbolic 'wool man'—and I can still hear them pronouncing the words with scorn—who was the enemy of teachers and the good life. There were of course some 'wool men' among my father's large acquaintance, but not one among his friends. He had, I suspect, a mental image of a 'wool man' that could have been used to represent capitalism in a socialist cartoon. A few of the richer dealers in raw wool, who had brought off some lucky gambles, were indeed fat and red-faced and loose-lipped and went off to the races behind enormous cigars. It was such men who infuriated my father and his friends by declaring that teachers were overpaid for what they did and had too many holidays. However, the wool trade, which began with bids in distant auction-rooms for the raw material and ended with the delivery of the dyed and finished cloth (and a sound Bradford man never accepted any cloth a tailor offered him, but picked his own suit length elsewhere) and so contained many different skills and levels of buying and selling, was Bradford's own trade, where there was solid brass among the muck. Any youth with a suspected weakness for hanky-panky might at least stand on his own two feet there. If he had 'anything about him'—a phrase I seem to remember—he could learn and then earn somewhere among the wool merchants, the combers, the spinners, the weavers, the dyers and finishers, the exporters; he could acquire a nice girl, a house of his own, a bedroom suite, a piano and a pram, with whist drives and chapel high-teas-and-concerts in the winter, and the summer rising to a peak in ten days at Scarborough or Morecambe.[7] So into the wool trade I must go.

I agreed, partly to stop my father worrying, partly because I had no plan of my own. I knew that, in the Bradfordian sense, I hadn't anything about me: I was crammed with hanky-panky. I wanted to write but I had just enough sense to know that I must spend at least the next few years trying my hand at it. I also knew—and this was clever of me at sixteen—that work on a newspaper was no use to me, otherwise I would have rejected the wool trade and bluffed or wheedled myself into one of our three local dailies. I was already acquainted with several young reporters, whose sophistication seemed to me almost satanic; they could take the city to pieces over a coffee and roll-and-butter at Lyons's; they had even interviewed delectable beings appearing at the Theatre Royal or the Empire; they were already men of the world to my stammering oaf; but somehow I knew that what I wanted to do, whatever that might be, had to be kept clear of what they were doing. So for the time being it had to be the wool trade; any branch of it, for tops, noils, yarns, pieces, were all the same to me, I cared for none of these things. Letters were exchanged; I was seen and questioned and—probably because I didn't really care what happened—was given the job. I left school to become a very junior clerk with Helm and Company, Swan Arcade, Bradford.

---

7. *Scarborough or Morecambe*, popular English watering places, or resorts.

✺ To increase understanding

1. (*a*) In this self-portrait, do you feel that Priestley gives a generally honest appraisal of himself as a youth? Why or why not? (*b*) What characteristics does he reveal? (*c*) Can you find any evidence of the type of glorification of the individual which Strachey criticizes in biographies?

2. (*a*) What various rôles did George, Pendlebury, and the elder Priestley play in shaping the writer's attitude toward higher education? (*b*) Discuss your impressions of these three men. (*c*) Are Priestley's sketches of all three sufficiently well-rounded to give you an adequate picture of them? Explain.

3. Priestley, who is known to have strong opinions, expresses his viewpoints on a variety of subjects in *Margin Released*. Defend or criticize the following of these viewpoints, all contained in the chapter of the book you have just read:

(*a*) . . . the traditional has become the bogus, power and money playing charades (page 753, column 2, paragraph 1).

(*b*) Certificates and degrees, I felt, had nothing to do with authorship (page 755, column 1, paragraph 1).

(*c*) Most of the demands for more and more education I have read these last few years do not suggest anybody is worrying about our civilisation, and the sort of minds at work on it, but only about competing for bigger or cheaper bombs and rockets, faster jets, cars that have telephones, and electric shoe-cleaners. Sometimes I think that every time the school makes one move up, the street outside, representing the environment that must win in the end, makes three moves down (page 755, column 2, paragraph 1 and page 756, column 1, lines 1-8).

(*d*) I think people who cannot appreciate such [comic] characters in literature, finding them overdrawn, out of scale, larger and simpler than life, must have lost all memory of their childhood or had one that was unusually narrow and cheerless (page 756, column 2, paragraph 1, and page 757, column 1, lines 1-5).

4. In discussing his reasons for leaving school, Priestley implies that education is little more than having someone tell you things and then asking you how much you have remembered (page 755, column 2, paragraph 1). Do you accept this view? Why or why not?

5. Priestley's desire to write appears to be the motivating force behind his life. (*a*) How does this desire shape and arrange the events of his life? (*b*) How does this element in his life affect the organization of this selection?

6. Priestley claims that *Margin Released* is not an autobiography, but a *memoir,* an author's account of the times he lived in and the personalities who influenced him. In the cutting which appears in the text, find evidence to support this claim.

7. The biographical sketch on page 753 comments on the immense popularity of Priestley's many works. Discuss what you consider the reasons for this popularity; in your discussion, comment on the author's style, tone, and ability as a craftsman.

V. S. *Pritchett*   THAMES—RIVER OF HISTORY

River life is male: Father Tiber; Old Man River; Father Thames. On the banks of rivers, civilizations are begotten. English civilization is the Thames. It is the preëminent British river.

It is small, but the British specialty is, notoriously, smallness. The Thames could be swallowed whole by the Rhine, the Danube or the Volga; from its estuary far down on the east coast of England, to its source in the west among the hills of Gloucestershire, it is only 209 miles long; it is only 50 yards wide at Oxford, 250 yards at London Bridge, and 700 at Gravesend and Tilbury. Twenty-odd miles farther down is the estuary and the Nore Light Tower where the river ends its journey to the sea.

A ship bound for London will pass the Nore Light and pick up the river pilot off Gravesend Pier, where the river narrows. There are another twenty-four miles to travel before she can dock in the Pool below London Bridge in the center of the city. The pilot will take her past Greenwich on the south bank, and the Isle of Dogs—an island of docks, in fact—on the north, where Limehouse Reach begins. Beyond is Tower Bridge, cutting the Pool in half, and beyond London Bridge she cannot go. The journey farther up

must be done by river steamer or launch. These craft pass under the bridges of Blackfriars, Waterloo, Westminster, Lambeth, Vauxhall and the rest, until we breathe less polluted air in the suburban greenery of Kew, Hampton Court and Richmond.

At Teddington the tidal water and the rule of the Port of London Authority end; then we are free for the pastoral river—for Windsor, Hampton Court and Richmond, for the pleasure waters of Maidenhead, the straight racing mile of Henley and its regatta, for Goring and Oxford, and so into the west of England, through Lechlade, Cricklade to the source.

The secret of the power and prestige of the Thames lies in its location: the estuary is immediately opposite the mouths of three great rivers of continental Europe—the Elbe, the Scheldt and the Rhine. Handily placed at the crossing of the sea routes, the Thames turned the port of London into a huge warehouse and center of transshipment. Half the being of the river is mercantile; it is heavy with wealth and the advantages of trade and politics. To follow the Thames from estuary to source is to cut through the dense accumu-

Tower Bridge.

lation of English political history into the vegetative rumination and poetry of English life.

So we can say that the Thames is really two rivers: London river, which is the river of merchants and government, and, above that, the "sweete Themmes" of poetry and pleasure. Let us look at London river first. It stretches from the Nore Light Tower in the estuary to London Bridge, just over forty-seven miles of muddy and polluted water poor in oxygen—a River Policeman told me there is none at all—where no fish live. They get five hundred tons of driftwood, broken boxes mainly, out of this part of the river every year. The water is sometimes sadly silvered, but most often it is brown to look at, like dark ale, and very murky, fit only for rats. Indeed, a pair of kestrels made a nest and brought up

---

V. S. Pritchett 1900—

Victor Sawdon Pritchett, known in England primarily as a fiction writer and in the United States primarily as an essayist, may best be described simply as a man of letters. Pritchett was born at Ipswich, educated in London, and after two or three odd jobs, found himself working as a newspaper reporter in France during the early 1920's. From France he went to Spain, where he was commissioned to write articles giving his impressions of that country. At the same time he was working on his first novel, *Claire Drummer* (1929). This and succeeding novels, in the tradition of Dickens, quickly established Pritchett's reputation. In recent years he has turned more to the writing of short stories.

Rounding out Pritchett's literary career are his critical essays, written, for the most part, for the *New Statesman* and *Nation* and collected from time to time. Critical essays in *My Good Books* (1942), *Living Novel* (1947), and *Books in General* (1953) delight through that sense of learning lightly carried which has been a characteristic of most masters of the informal English essay since the seventeenth century.

Over the past several years Pritchett has combined his skill as an essayist with his early experiences as a reporter on the Continent to produce travel articles for magazines. "Thames—River of History," which appeared in *Holiday* magazine in 1961, is such an article.

a family in the roof of the Savoy Hotel in the Strand a year or two back, and lived off the rats of the Thames mud. . . .

As with many important English things, there is nothing appropriately grand about the entry to the river from the sea. The estuary is wide and open, but narrows to five-and-a-half miles at the Nore Light Tower. Joseph Conrad has described what it's like to bring a ship into London. The pilot comes down to meet you, he says, and takes the ship through Queens Channel, Princess Channel or the Four Fathoms; sometimes he comes up to the Swin from the north. Conrad said that, of all the rivers he knew, this one lacked romance and grandeur in its outer approaches. Its quality, he said, was mysteriousness. There was no sign of a great city, no clatter of work, but the silence of low sea wall and marsh, broken here and there by chalk bluff. His ship, he said, went deeper and deeper inland as if it were being lured. He saw more sky than land.

The entry is most mysterious in a light sea fog, when an extra brush stroke of unearthliness may be given by the sight of the high brown sails of one of the few remaining sailing barges of the river—some "bricky," low in the water, still surviving against the competition of the roads, making for the Essex or the Kentish brickfields, or carrying a cargo of rubbish and clinker. Tall, melancholy, these stained and rusted sails rise over craft that seem to be standing still until, as you pass one, you can just hear the whisper of the water at the stern. I believe there are not more than half a dozen of them left. Presently, as you move upstream, the oil stores, the power and gas plants appear in the marshes, standing up like cathedrals. If you should ever walk across these flats you will come upon gunnery ranges, forgotten lime workings, factories abandoned generations ago and broken up; this desolate country is a natural scene for the writer of thrillers.

It is not until Gravesend, with its old fort on the midstream island and the thickening of industrial chimneys, that the Thames really begins. This was the nearest point to the sea at which the river could be defended by shore batteries. The Norse raiders and invaders got this far without hindrance; after that they met trouble—although, as we know, some of them settled down: the *hythe* of the nearby river towns of Greenhithe and Rotherhithe is their language.

At Gravesend the sea pilot drops off and goes ashore to the Pilot Station at Royal Terrace Pier. Here he reports, no doubt, to the officer known as Ruler of Pilots—with no definite article, as if he were Ruler of Heaven and Earth. He has a den in that green-painted row of offices on the pier down which the north wind blows. You will notice a strong smell of tea here. There are hundreds of parked bicycles: you are confronting the touchy bureaucracy of the river, with its ancient pomps, privileges and jealousies. The Port of London Authority, founded in 1908, now rules, administers, preserves and improves the Port of London as far as Teddington, the tidal limit; but the old hard-won rights and privileges, dating from the time of the trade guilds of the Tudors when every trade defended itself by charter, still have their place. . . .

Just above the Royal Terrace Pier is the Gravesend Ferry, and on the opposite shore is Tilbury, the first dock one reaches coming up the river, where the Oriental liners lie at rest, flashing white like new hotels. Here begin the cement works, the paper mills, the power stations; the drab processions of wharves, dock gates, warehouses and factories will continue for twenty-four miles to London Bridge, in the middle of the City. It is a long way—a packed, populous, smoking, clattering stretch, with only one or two patches of green and no fine building to relieve the eye until Wren's superb, cold, grand Naval College at Greenwich, and beside it, the first Queen Elizabeth's charming house at the end of its classical vista.

Gravesend is a pretty little town, with a good deal of Regency about it and the air of having been drawn by Cruikshank[1] and populated by Dickens. Indeed, all this part of the Thames is full of Dickens—from Rotherhithe, where Bill Sikes hanged himself, to Gadshill, where the novelist lived; from Rochester to the Medway, from which Mr. Micawber[2] hoped for something to turn up. At Gravesend the shops sell shrimps, cockles and winkles from the estuary flats. There is talk of "up-anchoring" in the pubs. River life has even affected the parking lots, for on the wall of a boat house are the words "Please park pretty." Customers in the bar of the Clarendon Royal raise their tankards and, as they do so, cannot resist a sideways glance at the river to note the ships going by, two a minute at high tide, and to listen to the peremptory blasphemies of the tugs.

From now on up to the Pool there will be no silence on the river, but a day-long, night-long cacophony carrying briskly across the water; an orchestra of phutting cranes, rattling conveyors, shovelings, chuggings, whinings, the clanking and croak of anchors, the spining of winches and the fizz of steam— broken every now and then by the whistles of ships' officers to their crews or occasionally by a plain human voice uttering an unprintable word. . . .

The lighters are the distinguishing craft of the Thames, marking its difference from all other rivers. They are moored by the score, all over the stream, forming vague low islands and archipelagos. It is the commonest sight of the river to see a tug rushing along with a double row of these poor, black, blind hulks behind her; they never sheer or get out of the line of tow; they pass under bridges and dodge the traffic with the ease of skaters. The big ships must unload in the docks, but whatever can be dropped overside onto lighters saves port dues.

It is surprising to stare at one of those ugly, seemingly rotting islands of craft which look as though they have been lying there for years, and then suddenly see a couple of tugs appear

1. *Regency . . . Cruikshank.* The English Regency extended from 1811, when George III became permanently insane, to 1820, when he died. His son was regent during this period, which was one of rugged individualism combined with the evils of the early Industrial Revolution. Dickens grew up during the Regency; George Cruikshank, a satirist, was famous for his illustrations of Dickens' *Oliver Twist.* 2. *Bill Sikes . . . Mr. Micawber*, characters in *Oliver Twist* and *David Copperfield*, respectively.

and a dozen men spring off. In a few minutes of shouting and rushing work the island splits into pieces, and in a quarter of an hour it has gone. They are mostly "dumb," these barges—that is to say they have no engines. One of the grotesque sights of the Thames is to see a barge adrift and askew on the tide with one or two men in the stern, steering with their long oars. Their job looks hopeless. The lump looks as though it will foul all traffic and blunder into the piers of any bridge in its way. But the Thames waterman has not just tumbled into his job. He has been apprenticed; he has had to earn his license.

The waterman at his long oar reminds us that at one time the Thames was London's only convenient or safe road from one end of the city to the other. The whole population used it. Kings and queens went up by river to the palaces at the Tower of London or at Greenwich, for royal and naval London lay east not west until the eighteenth century. The royal barges, graceful gondolas in green and red with golden canopies, lie in the National Maritime Museum at Greenwich. The present queen has twice made a royal river progress—at the end of the last war and again at her coronation. Shakespeare's Globe Theater was on the South Bank between London Bridge and Blackfriars; the actors and the theater crowds, who mostly lived on the north side, had to go "over the water"—a phrase still used in London life. The wherries were the taxicabs of those years: indeed when the roads became safe and coaches and carriages came in, the London watermen were powerful enough to prevent these interlopers from getting licenses for more than a generation. The Thames was marked by "stairs" and "gates," where the wherries picked up their passengers. Many still exist: Wapping Old Stairs, for example and the stairs at London Bridge where Nancy took the boat in *Oliver Twist*. The old trick was not to tell the passenger his fare until he was in the middle of the river and at the wherryman's mercy. These rows and quarrels and blusterings were, and are, perpetual in British life; British liberty seems to be based on bloody-minded acrimony; this mild race has a talent for digging its toes in.

The old Watermen's & Lightermen's Company, founded in 1555 to stop these arguments about fares, still licenses the apprentice lightermen under the Port of London Authority. The pretty Georgian building of the Watermen's and Lightermen's Company, crammed between fish warehouses down in Billingsgate —London's treasures are often stuck away in terrible places—has a portrait of one of its Masters whose lonely distinction it was to be called "The Honest Waterman." Honesty was a matter for astonishment, till the River Police were started at the end of the eighteenth century: they claimed to be the oldest police force in the world.

Shakespeare's actors were a particular thorn in the flesh of the watermen, but in fact the uneasy alliance between stage and wherry was eventually celebrated in a happy fashion in 1715, when an actor called Thomas Doggett founded a prize called Doggett's Coat and Badge for an annual rowing race of Thames Watermen. The race has been held every year since then, although wherries are no longer used: it is now rowed in gigs, from the site of the Old Swan public house near London Bridge to Cadogan Pier at Chelsea, and it is claimed to be the oldest and longest rowing race in the world, the course being four miles seven furlongs. . . .

The docks break up east London into grimy little Venices. How do you imagine the Isle of Dogs? It is about three miles down the river from Tower Bridge—a collection of high black prison walls and streets without feature. Over one of these walls will appear, perhaps, in huge white letters the startling single word *Philosopher,* or some other just as strange: you are looking at the name of a ship whose black bow overhangs the wall of the graving dock, dwarfing trains, buses, houses, everything. The funnels and the masts stand up between the new blocks of flats that have gone up since dockland was burned out during the Blitz.[3] It is exciting to see ships, lightly domesticated, careless look-

3. Blitz, the bombing of Britain by the Germans in World War II.

ing, gay and trim, rising with the clean paint of the sea among London's dirty brick. . . .

The destruction on the Isle of Dogs during the war was terrible, but no one could get the inhabitants to move. This was true of all the other dockland neighborhoods—Stepney, Limehouse, Poplar, Wapping, Deptford, Woolwich and Rotherhithe: the river people are as tenacious and as closed to the outside world as villagers. They have grown out of a rich and a picaresque past, in which honest work went on beside the piracy and pilfering enjoyed by gangs who were subtly divided into river pirates, night plunderers, light horsemen, heavy horsemen, scuffle-hunters and mudlarks.

The amount of thieving on the Thames in the days before the docks were built in the nineteenth century was due to the enormous congestion in the Pool below London Bridge; the docks and the River Police brought it slowly to an end, or nearly so. You hear tales today of ambitious rogues making off with a lighter of copper, or modest ones collaring a few cans of rabbit.[4] But the bloodcurdling tales of the Ratcliff Highway and Limehouse Causeway; the general atmosphere of robbery, murder and brothels; the story of Execution Dock, where pirates were left for three tides to pass over them—all this is history now. The *Town of Ramsgate* pub, where criminals were given a good feed the night before their execution, still stands snugly at Wapping Old Stairs, and still does a good lunch. . . . And *The Angel* in Cherry Garden Street, where Pepys used to gather cherries when all this dock area was countryside, has been modernized. The *New Jolly Caulkers* by the Surrey Commercial Docks commemorates the site if not the actual house of Dickens' *Three Jolly Fellowship Porters*.[5] The past of the whole region lives on in street names, with their whiff of sea life: Dockhead, Muscovy Street, Cathay Street, Pickle Herring Street and Shad Thames. There is Free Trade Wharf, dating back to the battles fought by the river folk against an old monopoly; there is New Fresh Wharf, where the banana boats unload in the middle of the city, just as the bacon and butter and hide trades are unloading on the southern side opposite. Down near Lon-

don Bridge is the site of the Old Clink prison. The approach road to old London Bridge—Pepys described the houses burning on it in the Fire—goes through the churchyard of Wren's beautiful St. Magnus the Martyr, and anyone on a tug or a police launch will show you how the water breaks a little, a few yards east of London Bridge, over the site of the old piers.

This "absurd old bridge," as it was called, with its four-story houses, stood unsteadily for 650 years. If things are unsteady enough, they last. It was deadly to navigators and some of its arches used to be jammed with the bodies of dead starlings. Starlings have nowadays moved westward with civilization to Trafalgar Square. The old houses came down in 1750;

---

4. *rabbit*, any property stolen from the Royal Dockyards. [British slang] 5. *Three Jolly Fellowship Porters*. The Fellowship of Porters, members of an organization of dock porters, frequented a tavern called *The Six Jolly Porters*, with which Dickens was familiar. This tavern forms part of the setting for Dickens' late novel, *Our Mutual Friend*.

Docks in the Pool, the center of the industrial river.

the present London Bridge, packed tight with City clerks ten abreast at eight-thirty in the morning when the suburban trains get in, was finished in 1831. T. S. Eliot recorded these clerks in *The Waste Land*:

Sighs, short and infrequent, were exhaled,
And each man fixed his eyes before his feet.

Kipling was sardonic also:

Twenty bridges from Tower to Kew
Wanted to know what the River knew.

Tower Bridge, that strange Victorian Gothic contraption in stone and steel—fake fortress, part cathedral, part machine, which suits well with the Tower of London nearby, is the first bridge you meet as you come upriver. Below this point, the Thames is crossed by tunnel or by ferry. . . .

This corner by the Tower is the most intense point of the river, the Pool; intense because the river work is thickest here, but also because the Tower exists as a lasting image in the minds of all who have been children in London. Those school visits with the history teacher. Your armor period; your Crown Jewels period; your spy and prisoner period; your almost traumatic preoccupation with smothered children, executioners' axes and heroes unjustly passing to doom under Traitors' Gate. Somehow the Thames looks sinister and greenish under the low arch of Traitors' Gate and one winces at the half-sly smile which the wobbling reflection of the water makes on the stone archway. A good part of the bloody history of England is contained in this fortress, and I confess to getting a nasty thrill out of the thought that spies have been sent here in the last two wars.

But it is not until the Londoner has grown out of childhood and got over the boredom of guidebook history, that he wakes up to the fact that the Tower is one of the marvels of Europe. Every time you see it, it seems to have got larger, and its walls, curtains, screens, towers and ramparts, built of a stone as gray and cruel as frost, give you the fright of something impregnable and of enormous weight. It is said to be the largest and most complete surviving medieval fortress in Europe. A king's palace and court, in flushed royal red brick, are at the center where the ravens walk like dilapidated Tudors on the lawns; a belt of medieval town is set about the court; and then the outer belt of fortress with its screens and moats. In its hollow, the Tower is dwarfed by office buildings; but how many such modern steel things were blown up or burned out eighteen years ago, while the Tower stood? . . .

My temperament is the trader's. I keep a glance for the Tower, but thousands of hours I must have passed staring at the Pool. I always have to take one more look down the river at the cranes: twenty-four miles of cranes —forty-eight if you can reckon both banks— from Gravesend to London Bridge, and they are thickest in the Pool, like a nation of grasshoppers sticking up against the sky. I wait, in a stupor, for one of these insects to move a leg or alter the angle of its antennae; and then for it to drop a bale into a ship's hold, as dead straight and sudden as a die. . . .

They take ships up to ten thousand tons into the Pool below London Bridge but as we move on above the bridge commerce thins out, the State and the Law impose their Portland stone. Modern architecture is leveling the Victorian skyline of low-built cities, but the Thames has St. Paul's on its hill and all Wren's pigeon-gray spires. We pass Wren's little house squeezed behind wharves near Blackfriars. It has a bright red door now. We pass under the bridges at Waterloo, get one more salute from a passing police launch, and look at the noble façade of Somerset House in the Strand, once a duke's mansion, now a mixture of University, Record Office and the home of those sad, dedicated mathematicians, the Commissioners of Inland Revenue,[6] the stateliest building on the Thames, indeed I would say the finest in London. This curving reach of the Thames to Westminster impresses, though the South Bank is mostly an industrial mess. On the north bank the Victorian outline, the Victorian statues and monuments predominate; there is something heavily Londonish and official about the Embankment.

---

6. *Commissioners of Inland Revenue*, British government agency similar to the American Internal Revenue Service.

In this stretch the Thames lacks the grace and lightness of the Seine, but the flowers in the Embankment Gardens and the lawns, like all southern English flowers and lawns, are beautiful. Coal lighters go up past Westminster to Chelsea, and even far beyond, and there the river sweeps beautifully, often silver, to encourage painters, and there is green on the banks. We go on to the rowing and sailing Thames of sport and pleasure has begun at last.

We are in the waters of the Oxford and Cambridge boat-race course, where in March the crowds climb on the walls, run shouting along the towpaths, and spit down from the bridges, as people do—by some peculiar human impulse—from all the bridges in the world. We round the big bend to Kew and Richmond, and it is well to go ashore here and climb Richmond Hill, for there we have the finest of all the views of a silver river curving

with elegance through the parkland and sumptuous woods of its valley. And so to Hampton Court, Magna Carta Island, the mass of Windsor Castle, and Eton College. The associations are overpowering. We are looking at the "sweete Themmes" of Spenser's poem,[7] at last.

Nor is Spenser so remote, for whether we English have embellished the river with palaces, courts, great houses and pretty towns, or ruined it with industrial suburbs, some regard for nature is still left in us. One ice-clear winter afternoon I was looking at Hampton Court. It is a ruddy-faced, comfortable, quietly splendid palace like some agreeable wine-fed king, with its small Tudor panes like tears of cold in old eyes. The red sun was dropping

---

7. *Spenser's poem*, the *Prothalamion*, which celebrates the beauties of the Thames.

Swans on the Thames by Richmond Bridge at the foot of Richmond Hill.

into the mists that rise early here in the river valley, breaking into lilacs, violets and grays so soft one cannot speak of them. The green of the riverbanks grew more vivid as the evening closed; the miles of wiry willows were gray and brown; the air still and the straight river like a low stairway rising to some imperceptible entrance to the sky. And then—I saw them: Spenser's swans coming down the stream, their eyes and necks seigneurial and their bodies like boats beneath them on the water.

So purely white they were
That even the gentle streame, the which them
    bear, seem'd foul to them,
And bade his billowes spare
To wet their silken feathers, lest they might
Soyle their fayre plumes with water not so fayre,
And marre their beauties bright,
That shone as heaven's light
Against their Brydale day, which was not long:
Sweete Themmes! rune softly, till I end my Song.

Day after day of your journey up the Thames you see them. They belong to the Queen. On the last Monday in July every year the quaint ceremony or lark—whatever you like—called *swan-upping* begins at Romney Lock, where the river turns north to Windsor. It simply means that the young swans are caught and marked, and nicked on the side of the beak by emissaries of the Dyers' and Vintners' Companies who have some historic right under royal license to the birds they can catch and nick. To catch a swan takes some doing, and, since all unmarked birds belong to the Queen, her property increases every year under the genial incompetence of the lark.

From Putney to Henley the Thames is a pleasant resort, as packed in some places as the lakes of Berlin. Sometime in the last quarter of the nineteenth century the office workers, shop workers and factory hands became aquatic, taking to the river on weekends. Today, painted houseboats with jaunty names, cabin cruisers, tied-up barges, and converted troop carriers, landing craft and torpedo boats are littered along the towpaths. There are the shack cafés and bungalows of the weekend parties, with radios and record players

going hard, and the riverside pubs that have had to enlarge their bars to cater for the busloads of tourists. The grand mansion façade of Ham House, a fine example of seventeenth-century architecture and now a museum, looks down between the trees and through its great iron gates, upon a river that at times resembles a merry-go-round.

On hot Sundays, the punts line up by the hundred to go through the locks, their occupants cursing the wash of the flashing cruisers or the packed steamers that ply regularly from Kingston to Oxford. The Londoner is a water animal—Henry James[8] noted it and, taking time off from his addiction to country-house visiting, he was surprisingly delighted by the vulgar gaieties of the river.

To hire a punt, after haggling with a rosy, sentimental and rapacious waterside dealer who looks as innocent as honeysuckle—and then to pole or paddle the craft along under branches of overhanging willow, with a girl, a sunshade and a radio, is a kind of heaven—if the sun doesn't go in, if the midges don't bite, and if insensitive bargees don't wreck the affair with their wake and with brutal comments on love, which seems to have no appeal for them. Punting on the Thames enhances the beauty of the male. Tall, sunburned, in flashing flannels, he is Hamlet's waterfly[9] in person as he stands poised on the small platform at the stern of the punt, silhouetted against the sky and the luxurious summer trees. He lets the long pole slide vertically between his hands, until it just taps—he hopes—a gravel bottom; and then, adeptly moving his weight, he pushes effortlessly yet forcefully on the bottom and, as the punt glides forward, draws in his shishing pole at the prettiest low angle to renew the stroke—without, he hopes, getting a quart of water down his sleeve, or soaking the lady, or without any of those accidents that come to the self-admiring, such as being hung up on the low branches of a passing tree, or getting the pole stuck in the river bed so that he remains,

8. *Henry James*, American-born novelist, later a British subject, who was fascinated by the relations between the American upper classes and the English aristocracy. 9. *Hamlet's waterfly.* See Hamlet, Act V, Scene ii, line 84, and the accompanying footnote.

slowly sinking, at the top of it, while the punt and its heavenly load shoots on like a passing smile of farewell, beyond him.

Two hundred and nine miles from the Nore Light Tower, in the softer and wetter climate of the West of England where the hills rise higher, there is a soggy meadow and a tree on which some one has cut the letters т. н. Not far off is a dried up Roman well, and near that the embankment of the Fosse Way, the Roman Road from Cirencester to Bath; under the embankment is a small tunnel. They have called the culvert Thames Head Bridge. Somewhere here is the source of the river, the childish stream that is to grow into the Father. In its progress from here to the sea it has its pastoral, its academic, its poetic, its sporting, its royal and its mercantile phases. Pastorally it is a curl of silver clasping the parklands and the great houses, running through fields of buttercups and cooling the cows. It has its odd villages and odder churches: at Dorchester Abbey there is an epitaph to a lady who died "a martyr to excessive sensibility," uncalmed by the rural stream. Oxford rules its academic and poetic life: there it belongs to poets and undergraduates—and there, by some freak of English pedantry, tradition, or local tenacity, it changes its name to Isis. Why? Was it a splitting up of the old name Themesis or Tamesis? Or a corruption of the common English names for a river—Ouse or Isca, so that people said Thames Ouse or Thames Isca for Thames River? Here, too, when it does not belong to the undergraduates who go to Salter's boat landing to talk of dinghies, gigs, skiffs, scullers, randans, whiffs, Roys, funnies and other such vessels, it belongs to the poets.

Shelley heard a skylark at Bablock Hythe, Keats planned Endymion's journey hereabouts, Southey "sailed unskillfully" at Nuneham, Pope translated the *Iliad*, and Wordsworth listened to that oldest and most delicate of Thames sounds, "the dripping of the oar suspended."

But if we start drifting down the literature of the Thames or indeed its historical anecdotage, we shall never end until we pass Falstaff dining at his inn at Windsor, Wolsey filling Hampton Court with four hundred guests, Henry VIII calmly stealing the property from him, and Magna Carta being signed at Runnymede all over again.

The sky is the least of the things that is reflected in Thames water; the light on its water is the long light of time itself. It bears away British history and habit of life. No great falls break its course; no high mountains dominate; it runs into no lakes; has no great islands; its weirs are mild, its locks domestic, its bridges without drama. It has no splendor, no wildness and no mythology. It is simply a sly, idle stream that has enticed a civilization and a lot of swans.

To increase understanding

1. (*a*) What is unusual about the Thames in contrast to other great rivers of the world? (*b*) Why has English civilization centered around the Thames?

2. What distinction does the author make between the character and uses of the upper river and the lower?

3. How does a trip up the Thames serve the author as an excellent means of showing a cross section of English life, both (*a*) in its various aspects today and (*b*) as it has been at various periods in history?

4. Tell briefly the character of each of the following sections of the river, and cite some of the observed details and historical recollections by which the author evokes that character:

    (*a*) The estuary, to Gravesend
    (*b*) From Gravesend to the Pool
    (*c*) The Pool around Tower Bridge
    (*d*) London River above London Bridge
    (*e*) The area around Richmond Hill
    (*f*) From Putney to Henley
    (*g*) Through Oxford
    (*h*) The headwater region

5. In the biographical sketch on page 760 you read that one of the distinctions of the best writers of the informal essay is a "sense of learning lightly carried." Find at least three places in this essay dealing with historical or literary facts that you found particularly interesting. Examine each passage in detail to see how Pritchett succeeds in introducing these facts gracefully and how his manner of presenting them sustains the reader's interest.

The Larger View

In "Thames—River of History," V. S. Pritchett views the Thames as a link that binds modern England to the cultural traditions of the past. Similarly, the reader can perceive in the modern selections in this chapter relationships with the ideas and the types of older English literature.

1. Compare the character sketches of Florence Nightingale and W. S. Gilbert with Boswell's descriptions of Dr. Johnson and Oliver Goldsmith (pages 277, 280). What similarities and differences do you find in the personal qualities that are admired or ridiculed?

2. Compare the tone of Thomas' "August Bank Holiday" with the tone of Charles Lamb's "Dream Children" (page 368).

3. Toynbee in "Can We Live in Peace?" presents certain ideas from the standpoint of a historian that John Donne, in "Meditation 17" (page 184), presented from the standpoint of a churchman in Elizabethan times. Compare the ideas in these essays. Contrast their styles and their points of view. In what ways are these styles and viewpoints typical of the times in which the men wrote?

4. Churchill's "Dunkirk" and the selections from Pepys' Diary (page 230) give us brief glimpses of the workings of government separated by nearly three centuries. What contrasts strike you most forcibly?

5. In "Time and the Machine," Aldous Huxley examines certain aspects of the industrial and scientific revolution from the vantage point of the twentieth century. Compare the findings in this essay with those made by Macaulay in "England in 1685" (page 419) and Carlyle in "Midas" (page 423).

Bibliography

BEERBOHM, MAX, And Even Now. (••Dutton) In these essays, Beerbohm writes in his inimitable way about books and writers.

BELLOC, HILAIRE, Selected Essays. (•Penguin) The writings of this versatile author cover history, travel, criticisms, and other subjects.

CHURCHILL, WINSTON, and the editors of LIFE, The Second World War. (Golden Press) This two-volume abridgement of Churchill's six-volume work retains the force and flavor of the original. Another side of Churchill is seen in Painting as a Pastime (•Cornerstone).

HUXLEY, ALDOUS, Collected Essays of Aldous Huxley. (Harper •Bantam) These essays show the author's wide scope of interests and unpretentious scholarship.

JORGENSON, PAUL A., and FREDERICK B. SHROYER, The Informal Essay. (•Norton) Huxley, Beerbohm, Thomas, Orwell, Forster, Woolf, Leacock, and Russell are represented in this collection which illustrates the relaxed style of the essay form.

MACDONALD, DWIGHT, editor, Parodies; An Anthology from Chaucer to Beerbohm and After. (Random House) Amusing parodies on writers and institutions by many well-known authors are in this collection.

MOOREHEAD, ALAN, Winston Churchill: A Pictorial Biography. (Viking) The text is warmly written without undue adulation.

PARKER, ELINOR, editor, I Was Just Thinking. (Crowell) This is a fine collection of all types of essays by established writers.

PEARSON, HESKETH, Gilbert: His Life and Strife. (Harper) A warm, sincere account of W. S. Gilbert, this book is well illustrated. Another refreshing Pearson biography is Sir Walter Scott: His Life and Personality.

PRITCHETT, V. S., London Perceived. (Harcourt) More than one hundred photographs illustrate this panoramic view of London's history, art, literature, and daily life through three centuries.

SNOW, C. P., The Two Cultures and the Scientific Revolution. (Cambridge) The gulf between scientists and other thinking people and the gulf between wealth and poverty are Snow's concern in this volume.

STRACHEY, LYTTON, Eminent Victorians. (Modern Library) If you enjoyed the excerpt from Florence Nightingale, you will want to read other biographies in this collection. Queen Victoria (Harcourt) is a fascinating portrait of a great queen and her court.

THOMAS, DYLAN, Quite Early One Morning. (•New Directions) This book is as nearly autobiographical as any that Thomas wrote.

TOYNBEE, ARNOLD, War and Civilization, edited by Albert V. Fowler. (Oxford) These nine papers from Toynbee's six-volume Study of History emphasize his view of the suicidal outcome of militarism.

WOOLF, VIRGINIA, Granite and Rainbow. (Harcourt) This posthumous collection of essays concentrates on fiction and biography.

•paperback   ••paperback and hard cover

Composition Guide

Don Otto

Literature presupposes both idea and form. To find a place among the masters of English literature, a writer must have important things to say and the ability to voice his ideas clearly, precisely, and well. Studying the works of those who have proved themselves masters of the writer's craft is an excellent way to improve your own writing.

This composition guide contains sixteen lessons, each of which is made up of two assignments. Some of the lessons also provide a third optional assignment for ambitious students or students who are particularly interested in writing. In most of the lessons Assignment 1 is relatively short, usually from one to three paragraphs, while Assignment 2 often calls for a paper of from 300 to 500 words. Lesson Thirteen lists ideas for a research paper. In the greater number of lessons both the first and second assignments cover the same type of writing. Therefore, in situations in which time does not permit the working out of all the thirty-two compositions suggested, it is possible to use only one part of a lesson without completely omitting practice in a certain type of writing.

Wherever possible the lessons offer a type of writing practice that allows the material in this anthology to serve as a model. Thus that kind of exposition that deals with explanation of a process is taught in conjunction with Huxley's "Method of Scientific Investigation" and work on the formal essay accompanies the study of Bacon's "Of Studies." The subject matter of most of the lessons is drawn from ideas suggested by the selections being studied. You will find writing a paragraph comparing the ancient and the modern idea of a hero a natural sequel to the study of *Beowulf*. And with *Pygmalion* freshly in memory, a paper evaluating the qualities that have made this play an enduring success becomes an interesting assignment.

Printed below are the titles of the lessons in the composition guide, and the chapters in the anthology which they are designed to accompany.

One: Comparison and Contrast	Chapter 1: Anglo-Saxon England
Two: Description	Chapter 2: Medieval England
Three: Interpretation—Poetry	Chapter 3: The Elizabethan Age
Four: Analysis—Drama	
Five: The Formal Essay	
Six: Personal Reactions	Chapter 4: The Seventeenth Century
Seven: Argument	Chapter 5: The Eighteenth Century
Eight: Literary Criticism	
Nine: Paraphrase and Analysis	Chapter 6: The Romantic Revolt
Ten: Exposition and Précis	Chapter 7: The Victorian Age
Eleven: Exposition	
Twelve: Book Review	
Thirteen: The Research Paper	Chapter 8: Short Story
Fourteen: Analyzing Ideas—Poetry	Chapter 9: Poetry
Fifteen: Evaluation	Chapter 10: Drama
Sixteen: Analysis and Evaluation	Chapter 11: Nonfiction

LESSON ONE: Comparison and Contrast

ASSIGNMENT 1. *Based on* Beowulf, *pages 26-30.*

If the popularity of certain programs on television is an accurate index to taste, the general public has not changed its appetites greatly since the days when *Beowulf* was chanted by *scops* in eighth-century banquet halls. The hero has changed his helmet and his Viking ship for a Western hat and a horse; the opponent may be a crooked gunslinger or a twentieth-century mobster instead of a dragon. But the central physical conflict is still important, and the odds against the hero have changed but little.

Imagine a character from *Beowulf* and a modern television character side by side. (If you don't watch television, use a character from a Western novel.) Think of the traits they have in common and the aspects in which they differ. Then in a paragraph or two write an analysis of these similarities and differences. If you are doubtful about how to develop a paragraph of this type, consult your language text. Use one of the topics below or a topic of your own choice.

1. Beowulf and a Western Marshal.
2. Grendel and a Gunslinger.
3. The Fire-Dragon and an Angry Mob.
4. The Hero-King and the Private Eye.

After you have written a careful first draft, examine each sentence for completeness and clarity. Cross out trite expressions and substitute original phrases. When you are doubtful of the spelling of a word, look it up in the dictionary. This part of writing—revision—will give you more insight into the improvement of your writing than will any other single phase of the composition process.

ASSIGNMENT 2. *Based on "Anglo-Saxon England," pages 16-43.*

Literature throws an interesting light not only on the heroes and villains of the past but also on the people who listened to the tales—what they believed in, the ideals they held before them, and how they lived. In a longer composition (not more than 500 words) develop one of the following assignments.

1. Outline the plot of an episode from *Beowulf* and the plot of an episode of a television adventure program (or an episode from an adventure story). After studying the two outlines carefully, write an analysis of their similarities and differences. Pay particular attention to the following factors: introduction, suspense techniques, dramatic action, climactic scene, and outcome.

2. Analyze the implied character, attitudes, and personal standards of a television hero, determining from this analysis the qualities the average television viewer demands in a hero. Compare the qualities and characteristics of the television hero with the standards of conduct and the characteristics of the Anglo-Saxon hero. State your conclusions as to the progress man has made.

3. Using "A Colloquy on the Occupations" as a guide, write a sketch on modern occupations and conditions. Present the interviewer as either the master of ceremonies on a television or radio audience-participation show or as an opinion pollster getting information about the average man. Have the interviewer ask four or five different "men on the street" to explain what they actually do in their occupations, each answer to be given in the form of a short paragraph. You may wish to select persons interviewed from classifications similar to those in "A Colloquy on the Occupations": farmer, cowboy, fisherman, merchant, mechanic, carpenter, and pupil.

OPTIONAL ASSIGNMENT

Later this year you may be assigned a research paper on literature. The following suggestions, expanded or reduced, may be helpful in guiding you toward a topic for such a paper. If you think you would like to do research on one of these subjects, begin reading in this area now. Be sure to jot down the names of the books or magazines you use and pertinent information as to pages, issues of magazines, etc. It is well also to keep a record of topics treated in each reference.

1. Changing Heroes in English Literature.
2. Changing Ideas of Entertainment in England.
3. Changing Social Positions in England.
4. The Art of Book Production, Monastery Manuscript to Modern Times.
5. English Schools, Ancient and Modern.

LESSON TWO: Description

ASSIGNMENT 1. *Based on selections by Chaucer, pages 68-82.*

Chaucer was a master of the art of describing human beings. So perceptive and so lively were his word portraits that individuals like the Wife of Bath, the Prioress, the Friar, and many others seem living individuals even today. Figures of speech, images, and subtly significant details abound in Chaucer's descriptions. Examine the sketch of the Franklin (page 73). Immediately after introducing him, Chaucer mentions a dominant physical feature: "Whiter could never daisy petal be/Than was his beard." Then he points out a revealing detail: "His ruddy face gave sign/He liked his morning sop of toast in wine." Then follow a few words about his fondness for comfort, ". . . he was a true son of Epicurus . . .," and details about his hospitality—"He was St. Julian to his countryside." Such descriptive devices create a more memorable picture of the subject than would a simple statement that the Franklin was a man with a white beard, who liked wine, good food, and other luxuries, and offered hospitality to other men of similar tastes.

In a single paragraph describe from memory in your own words one of the characters listed below. Remember the rôle that careful choice of details, imagery, and figurative language play in making a description interesting.

1. The Knight
2. The Squire
3. The Prioress
4. The Parson
5. The Student
6. The Wife of Bath
7. The Friar
8. The Miller

After you have written your paragraph, revise it carefully. Ask another student to see how many inaccuracies he can find in comparing your description with Chaucer's. Revise the paragraph before turning it in to your teacher.

ASSIGNMENT 2. *Based on "Medieval England," pages 44-89.*

When you were writing descriptions of Chaucer's pilgrims, your difficulty consisted in trying to describe in a new and fresh way an individual who had already been described by a master. Few writers of the past give the reader the wealth of descriptive details Chaucer makes use of. Sir Thomas Malory describes his knights and ladies in general terms; and the anonymous singers of the ballads were far more interested in action than in dwelling on the physical appearance and the personality of either hero or villain.

Write a paragraph or two on one of the characters listed below. Reread the selection in which this character appears for clues to his personality, but let your imagination supply the details.

1. Edward
2. Sir Patrick Spens
3. The Wife of Usher's Well
4. Lord Douglas
5. Lord Percy
6. Lady Percy
7. Bonnie George Campbell
8. Sir Bedivere

You can improve the total effect of your paragraph by substituting better descriptive words and phrases for those you have used in your first draft. Consult your language text for ways to use adjectives effectively; check the information your text offers on concrete words, loaded words, figures of speech, trite words, and connotation.

OPTIONAL ASSIGNMENT

The ballad is one of the most popular English verse forms and one of the easiest to write. Study the information on the ballad form (page 52) and the ballads in this text to learn the technique. Then try writing a ballad about a school event such as a football game, an election campaign, or some other contest involving individuals in conflict.

LESSON THREE: Interpretation—Poetry

ASSIGNMENT 1. *Based on "The Passionate Shepherd to His Love" and "The Nymph's Reply to the Shepherd," page 101.*

In one episode of Izaak Walton's *The Compleat Angler*, the fisherman tells a friend of an unexpected happening at the close of a successful day's fishing: "As I left this place and entered into the next field, a second pleasure entertained me; 'twas a handsome milk-maid, that had not yet attained so much age and wisdom as to load her mind with any fears of many things that will never be, as too many men too often do; but she cast away all care, and sung like a nightingale. Her voice was good, and the ditty fitted for it; it was that smooth song which was made by Kit Marlow, now at least fifty years ago; and the milk-maid's mother sung an answer to it, which was made by Sir Walter Raleigh, in his younger days." (The two songs, of course, are "The Passionate Shepherd" and "The Nymph's Reply.") As the fisherman finishes his account, he sees the milk-maid and her mother and compliments them on their singing. The mother replies: "I learned the first part in my golden age, when I was about the age of my poor daughter; and the latter part, which indeed fits me best now, but two or three years ago, when the cares of the world began to take hold of me."

The mother in this little episode is interpreting poetry at a high level. She is not only getting a general meaning from the lines but she is applying the meaning specifically to her own life.

Reread the songs the two women sang. Then write two paragraphs, setting in a modern frame the basic situation developed in the poems. Let your first paragraph be a marriage proposal and your second the young lady's reasons for postponing such plans. Keep as close to the spirit of Marlowe and Raleigh as possible, but use modern language and contemporary examples of both promises and problems.

ASSIGNMENT 2. *Based on Elizabethan sonnets, pages 104-110.*

Not all poetry is so easy to interpret as "The Passionate Shepherd" and "The Nymph's Reply." The very brevity demanded by the sonnet form forces a conciseness of speech that often makes interpretation difficult. Elaborate figures of speech sometimes obscure the meaning. Choose one of the sonnets you have discussed in class or a sonnet that is new to you. Read it slowly and silently several times; then read it aloud. After you have determined what the theme is, note how it is developed. Decide what words best describe the tone. Then write a paragraph in which you explain as clearly as possible your understanding of the meaning of the poem.

OPTIONAL ASSIGNMENT

Writing a sonnet is one of the most challenging tasks the field of poetry offers. It requires dealing simultaneously with rhyme, meter, diction, and thought. It demands conciseness in expression and a relationship between thought and poetic structure. Nevertheless, if you like poetry, you will enjoy learning more about it through attempting to write it. Review the technical requirements for the sonnet (page 106). Choose a theme and try writing a sonnet in either the Petrarchan or the Shakespearean form.

LESSON FOUR: Analysis—Drama

ASSIGNMENT 1. *Based on* Hamlet, Act I, *pages 114-129.*

In the opening scenes of a play, the reader or audience is given a number of hints about the previous history of the principal characters. Some information about past events is stated quite clearly; other things must be inferred.

Write a paragraph on one of the following subjects, explaining what you know about this topic from fairly clear references and what you may reasonably assume from scattered allusions.

1. Old King Hamlet As a Ruler.
2. Young Hamlet's Plans for His Future.
3. Ophelia's Previous Life.
4. The Activities of Claudius.
5. Past Relations Between Denmark and Norway.

After you have finished your first draft, examine carefully every possible reference in the act that tends to verify or contradict your conclusions. Eliminate any statements that have no foundation outside your own imagination. To check your analysis, compare notes with classmates who have written on the same subject.

ASSIGNMENT 2. *Based on* Hamlet, *pages 114-182.*

Using the same study of direct statements and incidental allusions, review the entire play preparatory to writing a more comprehensive essay (300-500 words) on one of the following subjects or on a similar topic of your own choice. Do not use the opinions of critics as evidence. In this paper rely solely on evidence in the play itself.

1. The Role of Poison in *Hamlet*.
2. The Reasons for Hamlet's Apparent Delay in Seeking Revenge.
3. The Evidence Against Claudius.
4. The Nature of the Queen's Guilt.
5. The Case for Hamlet As a Man of Courage.

Since this paper is in the nature of a critical study and demands a somewhat formal approach, plan it carefully, using a detailed outline. The outline below may offer suggestions.

  I. Introduction. State your subject precisely and how you expect to find the answers.

 II. Investigation or Analysis.
    A. Summarize initial impressions gained from a first reading of the play. Cite the most obvious lines, incidents, or actions that illustrate the subject.
    B. Cite and explain additional references obtained through more careful reading. Present the supplementary information you feel may be admitted on the basis of this evidence.
    C. Cite references that furnish evidence of a doubtful validity. Explain the conditions that make these references capable of more than one interpretation. State any further conclusions that may be developed from this evidence and point out hazards attendant upon such conclusions.

III. Summary. State in brief the total inferences you feel justified in making about the subject as a result of examining all the evidence. Note evidence that may tend to contradict some of these inferences.

IV. Conclusion. State your conclusions as to what one may legitimately infer about the topic from the evidence within the play. Point out also what must be left to conjecture because of lack of certain evidence.

OPTIONAL ASSIGNMENT

If this type of detective work intrigues you, you may wish later to develop a full-scale research paper on a similar study of a topic in one of Shakespeare's other plays. For such a paper you should examine critical interpretations of the play as well as the play itself. The following topics may suggest others for you to investigate.

1. The Rôle of Fate in the Story of Romeo and Juliet. (*To what extent did chance determine the destinies of Shakespeare's "star-crossed lovers"?*)
2. The Character of Brutus. (*Was he "the noblest Roman of them all"?*)
3. The Motives of Cassius in Joining the Conspiracy. (*Was he as honorable as Brutus?*)
4. The Relative Guilt of Macbeth and Lady Macbeth.
5. Macbeth's Courage. (*Weigh evidence for and against.*)
6. Banquo's Knowledge of Macbeth's Guilt. (*How much did he know and how soon?*)

LESSON FIVE: The Formal Essay

ASSIGNMENT 1. *Based on "The Elizabethan Age," pages 90-192.*

Francis Bacon, the first great master of the formal essay, still stands in the front rank of English essayists. His essays are regarded as models of the logical organization of thought and the careful transition from one idea to the next that characterize this literary form.

Review the "Better Reading" article on the essay on page 187. Then write a single paragraph developing the idea suggested in one of the following quotations. Remember the formal essay is not necessarily long. Bacon's "Of Studies" consists of only one paragraph.

1. . . . to thine own self be true
   And it must follow as the night the day,
   Thou can'st not then be false to any man.
   (Hamlet, page 123)
2. . . . the apparel oft proclaims the man.
   (Hamlet, page 123)
3. Give every man thy ear, but few thy voice.
   (Hamlet, page 123)
4. No man is an island, entire of itself.
   (John Donne, "Meditation 17," page 185)
5. And now abideth faith, hope and charity, these three; but the greatest of these is charity.

   (King James Bible, page 189)

ASSIGNMENT 2. *Based on "Of Studies," page 186.*

Although essay styles have changed somewhat since the time of Bacon, the subjects about which essays are written have altered little. Man still asks the same general questions as those Bacon examined. Truth, death, adversity, love, envy, and other topics on which Bacon wrote are still timely subjects for essays today.

The following topics are adapted from the titles of some of Bacon's essays. Plan to write an essay of no more than 500 words on one of them.

1. Of Honesty in School.
2. Of Parents and Children.
3. Of Ambition Frustrated.
4. Of Friendship As Wealth.
5. Of the Value of Literary Study.
6. Of Flattery As Temptation.
7. Of Pride and Its Hazards.
8. Of Success As Power.

You may have noticed that instead of merely generalizing on a subject Bacon uses analogies or cites specific examples to make his idea clear. Thus in "Of Studies," after stating that each subject promotes a different skill, he continues: "Nay, there is no stand or impediment in the wit but may be wrought out by fit studies; like as diseases of the body may have appropriate exercises." There follows a catalogue of exercises that the Elizabethan man believed guarded against specific ills. This sort of departure from purely abstract writing gives liveliness to Bacon's essays even though his purpose is serious.

Since the essay you are to write will be a formal one with the logical development of ideas this form demands, it will be necessary to construct an outline before writing. Such an outline not only helps in organizing ideas but also aids in apportioning the space to be devoted to the various parts of the essay. Ordinarily the subject of an essay determines its length; but since in college writing assignments and in composition examinations a particular length is often stipulated, it is well occasionally to practice writing to a predetermined length. Consult your language text for help on making an outline suitable to a formal essay.

After you have written your essay, use the following outline to help you review its thought pattern. Revise accordingly.

I. Introduction. *Does your opening paragraph present a summary statement indicating both your topic and the point of view or attitude you are taking toward it?*

II. Body (or Development). *Have you presented various aspects of the topic in an orderly sequence? Have you used specific examples or anecdotes and commented on their pertinence to the topic?*

III. Summary. *Have you recapitulated in new phrasing the most important observations you have previously made?*

IV. Conclusion. *Have you left the reader with a unified impression of your ideas on the topic?*

LESSON SIX: Personal Reactions

ASSIGNMENT 1. *Based on poems by the Cavalier Poets, pages 204-206.*

A part of critical reading is testing the worth of the ideas presented by the writer. As you have read the lyrics of the sometimes cynical, sometimes intensely dedicated Cavalier Poets, you have doubtless thought at times not of seventeenth-century circumstances but of your own experiences. For although ways of life and social custom change from generation to generation, basic ideas may be understood in somewhat the same way in any time.

Not infrequently the Cavaliers were either not sincere or only half so in poems that have lasted rather for beauty of their expression than for the wisdom of their advice. Measure the truth of the following lines by the standard of your own observation of human nature. Choose the idea to which you react most strongly and state in a paragraph or so your own reactions to the idea presented.

1. That age is best which is the first.
   (Herrick, "To the Virgins to Make Much of Time," page 204)
2. I could not love thee, dear, so much
   Loved I not honor more.
   (Lovelace, "To Lucasta," page 204)
3. Stone walls do not a prison make
   Nor iron bars a cage.
   (Lovelace, "To Althea," page 205)
4. Will, when looking well can't move her,
   Looking ill prevail?
   (Suckling, "Why So Pale and Wan?" page 205)

You may prefer to concentrate on the wisdom and sincerity of an entire poem rather than on your personal reaction to a single idea presented in the poem. If so, choose a poem by one of the Cavalier Poets, analyze its tone, and write a paragraph explaining what you think the poet's attitude is. Use an example or two from your own experiences or those of your friends to strengthen your argument.

ASSIGNMENT 2. *Based on "L'Allegro" and "Il Penseroso," pages 211-215.*

In "L'Allegro" and "Il Penseroso" Milton sketched companion portraits of the cheerful man and the thoughtful man. Study what Milton has to say about these two different attitudes toward life and the type of life shaped by each attitude. Then, after considering the rewards for those who choose these ways of life in modern times, write a theme of three or four paragraphs on one or the other mode. If you prefer, you may write on one of the other subjects listed below or on a subject of a similar nature.

1. The Cheerful Man. (*Where would he be found today? What are his activities? What are the rewards for his chosen way of existence?*)
2. The Meditative Man. (*Does he still exist? Where would you find him?*)
3. The Man of Action. (*Is this a special type?*)
4. The Pessimist. (*Are there any rewards for him?*)
5. The Timid Man.
6. The Insecure Man.

The outline below may suggest one way of approaching your topic.

I. Introduction. *Briefly explain what you mean by the title chosen.*
II. Body. *Cite specific illustrations of the joys or satisfactions to be derived from the kind of life you are writing about. Suggest also the frustrations and disappointments the person of this type may encounter today.*
III. Conclusion. *Offer in brief your personal conclusions about what rewards a man of this type would find in life.*

As you would in checking any paper, before revising examine this one carefully for mechanical errors, errors in logic or in organization, and factors not contributing to a unified total effect.

LESSON SEVEN: Argument

ASSIGNMENT 1. *Based on prose by Addison and Steele, pages 252-259.*

Reporting the passing parade has always been a principal function of the writers of nonfiction. In such literary spectators as Addison, Steele, Defoe, and Swift, the eighteenth century in England saw some remarkably astute observers of contemporary conditions.

Joseph Addison's observations about the constant shifting of party patches could perhaps be applied in the twentieth century to current changes in fashion. Probably no environment reflects such changes more immediately than does the campus. It is possible that you agree with the soundness of every fashion you have seen come and go in your high-school career. On the other hand, you may at some time have been critical of a current fad or fashion, particularly of a fashion adopted by the opposite sex. To suggest names of such fashions would date any book hopelessly, for few students either can or care to name all the fads or popular songs even of last semester. However, you do remember the names of fashions which you have felt strongly for or against, and you can talk readily about them.

Write a paragraph, or two or three if you care to, on one of the following topics, filling in the blank, where necessary, with the name of the fad or fashion you wish to discuss.

1. The Insanity of Wearing_____(*hair, jewelry, sweaters, etc.*) in the Current Style.
2. A Fashion the World Could Do Without.
3. Why I Like_____.
4. Youth Faces the Future in_____.
5. Campus Politics and Styles of Dress.

You should probably write such a theme rapidly in the moment of inspiration. Its revision should perhaps wait until you are calm and reasonable again. Any essay will be more convincing if it obeys the sensible standards of good style and good taste.

ASSIGNMENT 2. *Based on biographies of and selections by Defoe, Swift, Chesterfield, Pope, and Johnson, pages 260-276.*

Daniel Defoe's essay advocating the education of women may have seemed shocking in his day. A few years ago a popular magazine writer (a man) attempted to shock the readers of a national periodical with the proposal that the college-class-room shortage be solved by denying higher education to most women. Defoe would have enjoyed this article, for he could write readily on any side of a question; unfortunately, he sometimes did just that—for money.

Although Defoe's commercial expediency in his literary loyalties is not recommended, supporting an opinion with which one does not agree gives the writer an insight into the arguments available to the other side. Just for fun, support the "wrong" side (to you) of one of the arguments below in a paper of several paragraphs. If you are to be convincing in presenting your case, it is best to outline your argument before beginning to write.

1. Women should (should not) have college educations.
2. The holding of public office should (should not) be based on party politics.
3. A man (woman) should (should not) be judged primarily by manners and social accomplishments.
4. The system under which a literary man depended on a patron should (should not) be revived.
5. Men should (should not) pay the cost of dates.
6. Seniors should (should not) be given special privileges.

OPTIONAL ASSIGNMENT

You have read about the versatility of eighteenth-century coffee houses, which served as places of business, entertainment, politics, and conversation on all subjects. Probably you and your friends get together in your leisure time at informally designated meeting places such as hamburger stands, soda fountains, youth centers, and the like. Imagine your favorite gathering place as a twentieth-century coffee house—Will's, which Addison and Pope frequented, or the Turk's Head Tavern, where Dr. Johnson's famous circle met. Write an essay describing for a reader outside your community the kinds of individuals who frequent your meeting place, their interests, their conversational topics, and their common problems and attitudes.

LESSON EIGHT: Literary Criticism

ASSIGNMENT 1. *Based on* She Stoops to Conquer, Acts I-III, *pages 287-309.*

In *She Stoops to Conquer* Oliver Goldsmith wrote a comic commentary on the eccentricities of the society in which he lived. Through characters like the socially ambitious Mrs. Hardcastle, her adored son Tony, and Charles Marlow, who changes his manners according to the company he keeps, he satirized the standards dictated for society by the cult of sentiment.

How much truth is there in Goldsmith's satire? For example, do you believe acquaintances of your own adjust their standards of conduct to suit the circumstances, or do they maintain the same set of standards for all occasions? Does a man show the same degree of courtesy toward others when he is driving a car that he demonstrates in ordinary business and social contacts? Think about this question and others suggested below. Then write a paragraph or so in which you express your opinion on the subject. Defend your ideas by pointing out illustrations from your own experience.

1. Do your contemporaries use more than one standard of conduct?
2. Do parents today try to act as matchmakers for their children?
3. Would a modern girl go to the lengths Kate Hardcastle did to win a particular man?
4. Do parents today spoil children to the extent that Mrs. Hardcastle spoiled Tony?
5. Do you believe a young man might be as brave in certain situations and as timid in others as Charles Marlow was?
6. Can you find in the modern world the same types of characters that are presented by Goldsmith in *She Stoops to Conquer?*

ASSIGNMENT 2. *Based on* She Stoops to Conquer, *pages 287-324.*

When people talk over a play they have seen, interest often centers on the author's intent in writing the drama and his success or failure in achieving this purpose. Various elements of the play are mentioned with respect as to how well they function in developing the overall concept.

Write a report on *She Stoops to Conquer*, expressing and defending your opinion about various aspects of the drama. Be sure to offer evidence from the play to substantiate your opinions. The questions below may help you write your report. Arrange them in any order that will help you develop your ideas.

1. What is Goldsmith's purpose in the play?
2. What is the tone of the play?
3. Are the characters believable? (*Cite examples to justify your opinion.*)
4. Do you have reason to believe that the dialogue is characteristic of the times?
5. Do the situations in the play grow logically from the characters presented?
6. Is suspense sustained throughout the rising action?
7. Does the author omit necessary scenes or include unnecessary passages?
8. Does the presentation of social classes seem accurate?
9. Do you think the play would be entertaining to a modern audience?

If you wish to concentrate your criticism on only a few elements of the drama, develop these at greater length and indicate your ideas on other aspects of the play only incidentally. Consult your language text for help in making an outline that will aid you in writing a unified and logical criticism.

OPTIONAL ASSIGNMENT

If you are interested in the drama of the eighteenth century as a reflection of the life of the period, you may wish to investigate topics for research papers in this area. Prepare for a paper of this type by studying several plays of the period by such dramatists as John Gay, Richard Brinsley Sheridan, and William Congreve, and by reading a number of references on the thought and manners of the time.

LESSON NINE: Paraphrase and Analysis

ASSIGNMENT 1. *Based on poetry by Wordsworth, pages 352-361.*

The poetry of Wordsworth varies greatly in difficulty. Some poems—for example, "Lines Written in Early Spring"—can be understood after a single careful reading. Other poems like "Tintern Abbey" and "Ode on Intimations of Immortality" require detailed study if the reader is to grasp the philosophical ideas that underlie the beauty of imagery and melody. The poetry of Wordsworth is not unique in this necessity for analysis; the poems of Shelley and Keats, as well as much of the great poetry of any age, require detailed reading, if one is to probe their deeper meanings. The best way to discover such meanings is through writing a paraphrase. You will find that such an exercise will also make you more aware of the poem's beauties of form and diction.

Write a paraphrase of one of the following:

1. One Summer Evening (page 352).
2. To a Skylark (page 352).
3. Tintern Abbey, lines 22-48 (page 353).
4. Tintern Abbey, lines 134-159 (page 355).
5. Ode on Intimations of Immortality, Stanza 5 (page 358).
6. Ode on Intimations of Immortality, Stanza 9 (page 360).

Before beginning to write, review the information in your language text on writing a paraphrase. Remember that a good paraphrase involves interpretation. You must ferret out and state ideas that the poet merely implies. However, be certain that for every expanded thought in your paraphrase you are able to cite a specific reference in the poem itself.

ASSIGNMENT 2. *Based on poetry by Gray, Burns, and Blake, pages 326-340, and "The Triumph of Romantic Revolt," pages 342-409.*

In the introduction to the chapter on the romantic poets you read that certain broad characteristics typified the poetry of this period. Now that you have studied the poetry, you realize that the possession of certain characteristics in common did not lead the poets of the period to produce poetry that was alike in tone, form, or theme. Scott is different from Coleridge; Shelley differs from Keats. They are all romantics, but they differ in the themes they emphasize and the aspects of these themes they develop.

Write a composition on one of the topics listed below or on a similar topic of your own choice. Let your subject determine the length of your paper, but do not write more than 500 words. Be sure to use an outline to get your ideas in order before you begin writing.

1. Nature in Poetry of the Romantic Period. (*What does nature mean to Wordsworth? How does Byron regard nature? What aspects of nature is Shelley interested in? Is love of nature apparent in Keats' poetry? What about Thomas Gray, Robert Burns, and William Blake—did they share the feeling for nature of the later romantics? Cite poems to support your opinion.*)
2. The Interest of the Romantics in Humble Life. (*Were all of the romantics interested in this theme? In the work of which poets is it most important? What differences are there in the aspects of the theme treated by various poets?*)
3. The Glamour of the Past. (*What period of the past is the favorite of the romantics? What makes this period interesting to them? How do they treat the period in their writing? What other past eras do the romantics turn toward? Which poets are most strongly affected by the glamour of past times?*)
4. The Spirit of Freedom. (*Which poets reacted most positively to the revolutionary spirit of the late eighteenth and early nineteenth centuries? Cite poems in which this spirit is evident. How do the poems differ in the aspect of freedom they glorify?*)
5. Verse Forms in Poetry of the Romantic Period. (*Does any one verse form assume the importance in the Romantic Age that the heroic couplet held in the eighteenth century? What verse forms are frequently used?*)

OPTIONAL ASSIGNMENT

In working out the preceding assignment, you have probably discovered that your topic contained ample material for a research paper. You might like to explore this topic, or one of the others in Assignment 2, as the subject of a research paper. Begin by reading widely in the works of the poets with whom you are dealing; then read critical opinions on their works.

LESSON TEN: Exposition and Précis

ASSIGNMENT 1. *Based on "The Method of Scientific Investigation," pages 428-431.*

Thomas Henry Huxley explains in "The Method of Scientific Investigation" just how scientists go about their work. In so doing, he demonstrates one of the most common types of exposition—the explanation of a process. Explaining clearly and directly in writing how to perform a simple process is excellent practice for much of the writing you will do in college. You undoubtedly know how to perform one of the tasks listed below. Choose one with which you are thoroughly familiar. Make notes that will remind you of the steps in the process and arrange the steps in order. Then write out the explanation in no more than three paragraphs. Use one paragraph if you can explain the process efficiently in such small space. Be sure that your directions are so clear that no reader can make a mistake as he follows your instructions.

1. How to Start a Car. (*Specify the kind of car to simplify the problem.*)
2. How to Prepare Coffee.
3. How to Start a Fire in the Fireplace.
4. How to Sew On a Button.
5. How to Shine Shoes.
6. How to Tie a Bow. (*This is very difficult to explain in writing.*)

ASSIGNMENT 2. *Based on selections by Macaulay, Carlyle, Huxley, and Newman, pages 418-438.*

Just what does Newman believe the function of a university to be? If you were to attempt to write a brief summary of his thoughts on this subject, keeping his organization and his point of view but omitting all the examples he uses to make his ideas clear, you would be writing a *précis*. Reread rapidly the selections in your text by Macaulay, Carlyle, Huxley, and Newman. Choose one of them as the subject for a précis. Then consult your language text for more detailed information on how to write a précis. Pay particular attention to the proper steps to take in preparation for writing a précis, the form the précis should take, and its approximate length in relation to the article summarized.

LESSON ELEVEN: Exposition

ASSIGNMENT 1. *Based on "The Victorian Age," pages 410-471.*

As you have learned from study of your language text, expository writing may serve various purposes. It explains how to do things, defines terms, and gives information. It is used for such diverse purposes as sketching in the historical background of the Victorian Age and explaining the origin of "the Pre-Raphaelite Brotherhood." Write an expository theme of several paragraphs (300 to 500 words) on one of the following subjects or on a similar subject of your own choice. You will find material to supplement that in your text in encyclopedias and histories.

1. Society for Promoting Christian Knowledge.
2. The Code of Conduct in Victorian England.
3. The Great Exposition of 1851.
4. Living Conditions in Factory Towns.
5. Treatment of the Poor in Victorian England.
6. Child Labor.
7. The Oxford Movement.

ASSIGNMENT 2. *Based on "The Victorian Age," pages 410-471.*

What does the term *Victorian* mean? Using the material in your text as a basis, write a paper analyzing some aspect of this complex age. The topics listed below will suggest areas you might explore. Before beginning to write, make an outline to get your ideas in order. In the paper itself use several short quotations from literature to emphasize the points you are making.

1. Victorian Attitudes Toward Death.
2. Victorian Attitudes Toward Religion.
3. Victorian Attitudes Toward Progress.
4. Victorian Ideas of Social Reform.

If these topics are too broad, you may narrow the subject of your essay by discussing one of the subjects listed as it appears in a single piece of literature, for example, "Tennyson's Attitude Toward Faith As Expressed in *In Memoriam*," or "Victorian Doubt in Arnold's 'Dover Beach.' "

LESSON TWELVE: Book Review

ASSIGNMENT 1. *Based on "The Victorian Age," pages 472-538.*

Imagine that you are living in the day when the novels of the Victorian giants of prose fiction are first meeting the eyes of readers and critics. You are a reviewer for the *Westminster Review, Fraser's Magazine,* or *The Cornhill Magazine.* It is your job to report to your readers on the worth of a new novel by Dickens, Thackeray, George Eliot, Stevenson, Hardy, Conrad, or one of the Brontës. From among the great novels produced by this group choose one that you have actually read. In no more than 300 words write an informal or impressionistic review of the novel.

In this sort of review you should indicate to your readers what the book is about, naming important characters and giving an idea of plot and setting. Emphasize those elements of the novel that you think will most interest the reader. You should also tell the reader how well the novelist achieves what he has set out to do. Choose the best elements of the book for special praise, and point out also the weaknesses, as you see them. Since it is never sufficient to offer an opinion without supporting evidence, your praise and criticism should include examples, either summarized or quoted directly, from the novel. Another way of indicating the strengths and weaknesses of the novel is comparing it with other books of the same type. Your review must accomplish one other result: because it is to appear in a magazine, it must entertain, or at least interest, the reader. Writing a good book review is not an easy assignment.

ASSIGNMENT 2. *Based on "The Development of the Novel" and Novel Discussion Guides, pages 524-537.*

The account in your text of the development of the English novel stresses the fact that different types of novels became popular in different periods and that most novelists are affected by the social, economic, and political conditions of their age. Even the manner in which books appear has an effect on their structure; note, for example, that because they were published in installments, most of the early Victorian novels are long and episodic rather than short and closely knit, as are many modern novels. In consider-

ing an individual novelist the material in your text focuses attention on the purpose of this author in writing, on his particular attitudes, and on the aspects of the novel in which he excels. Thus Dickens is extolled for his ability to create many and diverse characters, who, although they may be overdrawn, still seem real and convincing.

In writing a formal book review, it is necessary to temper your judgments by placing the novel in its frame of time and place and by considering the author's purpose. Judged against an absolute standard, *Vanity Fair* may be considered overly long, but the criticism against the individual book is lessened when judged in the context of its time. You may say, and with reason, that *The Pickwick Papers* is extremely weak in plot; yet Dickens' original purpose in writing the novel should also be noted since it helps explain this circumstance. (Note that the Discussion Guide for *The Pickwick Papers* centers attention on character, the area in which Dickens excels.)

Write a formal book report on a book by a novelist discussed in "The Development of the Novel," or, with your teacher's permission, on a modern English or American novel. (Do not treat the same novel you wrote of in Assignment 1.) You may use your own outline in preparing your notes, but study the following suggestions first.

1. Introduction. (*Name the author of the book, give any information about him that bears on the novel, mention date of publication.*)
2. Theme. (*Is it convincingly worked out?*)
3. Setting. (*Is it functional? What does it add to the novel?*)
4. Characters. (*Are they real individuals with a balance of good and bad traits? Are they consistently drawn? Are they interesting?*)
5. Plot. (*Is it believable? Does the climax grow naturally from the actions of the characters? What part does coincidence play? What use is made of subplots?*)
6. Narrative point of view. (*Does it add to the effectiveness of the novel? Does it unify the novel? Does the author ever speak directly to the reader?*)
7. Tone. (*Describe the tone. What is its relation to the narrative point of view?*)
8. Conclusion. (*What do you regard as strong and weak points of the novel?*)

LESSON THIRTEEN: The Research Paper

ASSIGNMENT 1. *To accompany "Short Story," pages 548-616.*

Like many realistic writers, Somerset Maugham observed carefully and kept precise notes on his observations. Some of these notes became direct sources for the characters, settings, and plots in his novels and short stories. In *Liza of Lambeth*, for example, he drew largely on his experiences in treating the poor of the London slums.

Whether gathering material for a novel or assembling information for a biography or a travel article, the researcher finds that his first task is to select and define his problem. As you prepare to work on a research paper, your first step is to write a concise, clear paragraph stating your problem exactly and explaining the methods you will apply in completing it. Submit this paragraph to your teacher, who will then decide: (*a*) whether the subject is satisfactory as it stands or whether it needs to be enlarged or narrowed; (*b*) whether material necessary for working out such a paper is available or can be secured; and (*c*) whether the method of work you have outlined will function efficiently.

SUGGESTED SUBJECTS FOR A RESEARCH PAPER

The lists of topics below will guide you in choosing a subject for a research paper. You will find other suggestions in the "Optional Assignment" sections of Lessons 1, 4, 8, and 9. Your teacher will specify the approximate length. Your language text will offer detailed suggestions for planning the paper and conducting the research, as well as for the form to be followed in the actual writing.

The kinds of topics listed below are general; you will have to limit them to fit your particular interest, the length of the paper assigned, and the available materials.

1. Analyses of Techniques. (*The nature of the sonnet, the elegy, the ode, the heroic couplet, blank verse; the verse essay as developed by Pope, Dryden, etc.; symbolism in modern poetry, in the modern short story; the rhythms of free verse; dialogue in modern fiction; plot in modern English short stories; the stream-of-consciousness technique; the uses of irony; euphuism.*

2. Schools and Types of Writing. (*The medieval romances; the development of pre-Elizabethan drama; the novel of manners; the Gothic romance; the cult of sentiment; famous British satires; British detective stories; the drama of the Irish Renaissance.*)

3. Analyses of Language. (*This anthology, your language text, and similar references will suggest techniques for the study of language, diction, sentence structure, and the like. You may study the language of a single author, of several authors in a particular period, of prose of various periods, of poetic diction through the centuries. You may also study the dialogue in dramas written at various times as an indication of differing language patterns. In analyzing language you will find it best to limit yourself to a few representative samples; an intensive study of a few pages from each of four or five authors could represent a great deal of work.*)

4. The Relationship Between Literature and _____. (*You may wish to study the effect of contemporary trends on the literature of a given time. An examination of the political, aesthetic, social, economic, religious, or philosophical movements and their effect on literature will offer many possibilities.*)

5. Studies of Individual Authors. (*You may learn a good deal from research on the work of one of the authors mentioned in your textbook. Such a paper should focus on the author's work rather than on his life. If you have developed critical standards, you may wish to apply them to an intensive study of a single work. If there is enough material available, you may analyze a single aspect of a major work, such as the historical accuracy of one of Shakespeare's dramas, or the part irony plays in one of Hardy's novels.*)

6. Defending Propositions. (*In discussions in class and in your reading of critical materials, you may have encountered statements that you believe are open to challenge. Topics of this sort often involve cause-effect relationships, questions of literary merit, and questions of correct interpretation of literature. If you choose to write on such a question, remember a scientific attitude is necessary. You must be prepared to change your mind if the evidence you uncover points away from your original position.*)

LESSON FOURTEEN: Analyzing Ideas—Poetry

ASSIGNMENT 1. *Based on "Poetry," pages 620-636.*

Although realism is the dominant note in twentieth-century writing, a strain of romanticism persists. And while romantic poetry of the present may differ in various ways from romantic poetry of the past, in one particular it varies not at all—it still involves the reader in an intense emotional experience.

Glance again over the poems included on the pages listed above. Choose the poem to which you react most strongly—the one in which the idea and mood of the poet communicate themselves to you with clarity and force—and write a paragraph or more concerning it. Explain first the idea of the poem. Then identify as accurately as possible the emotion you feel upon reading it and explain the elements that have caused this feeling on your part. Try to locate the specific details that do most to create this emotional reaction. Your own personal experiences may have helped build up your reaction to the poem; if this is the case, refer to these experiences in your analysis.

ASSIGNMENT 2. *Based on "Poetry," pages 617-660.*

Whatever form it may take, good literature is alive with ideas. These ideas challenge you as you read, and whether the writer is Chaucer, Shakespeare, Shelley, or a twentieth-century poet, you question the ideas proposed by the writer.

Write a paper of from 300 to 500 words analyzing and evaluating the ideas postulated in one of the poems in this chapter. Reread the poem several times, examining the ideas carefully. Then state what seems to be the poet's opinion about the idea or problem considered in the poem. After you have stated the poet's opinion, relate his idea to specific examples in life. Finally, assess the validity of his hypothesis on the basis of its apparent truth when applied to concrete situations. The following suggestions, which are based on poems whose basic premises often arouse strong feelings of agreement or dissent, will help you choose an idea for analysis. You may adapt any pertinent suggestions to a poem of your own choice.

1. William Butler Yeats, "The Lake Isle of Innisfree." (*Is escape from the modern world possible? Is it desirable?*)
2. William Butler Yeats, "Sailing to Byzantium." (*What does Yeats see as the ideal life? What is your reaction to the ideas suggested here?*)
3. James Stephens, "In Waste Places." (*What, essentially, is the view of life advanced here? How may life be lived successfully? Comment on the poet's idea.*)
4. Wilfred Owen, "Futility." (*Weigh the poet's implications about the value of dying on the battlefield.*)
5. Robert Bridges, "Nightingales." (*What does the voice of the nightingale symbolize? Comment on the philosophy of life that gives rise to this idea.*)
6. Robert Graves, "Rocky Acres." (*Discuss the implications about the best way of life.*)
7. T. S. Eliot, "The Hollow Men." (*Examine the poet's criticism of contemporary civilization. Do you think this criticism is valid?*)
8. T. S. Eliot, "Chorus 3 from The Rock." (*Comment on Eliot's criticism of society. Do you agree or disagree with the solution offered to mend the ills of contemporary life?*)
9. T. S. Eliot, "Chorus from The Family Reunion." (*Why does the poet believe men have "lost their way in the dark"? Comment on his reasons for so believing.*)
10. Stephen Spender, "I Think Continually of Those." (*Do you agree or disagree with Spender as to what men are "truly great"?*)
11. Dylan Thomas, "Do Not Go Gentle into That Good Night." (*Comment on the idea here presented as to the way death should be approached. How do you react to this idea?*)

LESSON FIFTEEN: Evaluation

ASSIGNMENT 1. *Based on* Pygmalion, Acts I-III, *pages 664-691.*

One of the reasons for the popularity of *Pygmalion* doubtless lies in its humor. Yet Shaw had a serious purpose in writing the play. Through the characters of Henry Higgins, Eliza Doolittle, Alfred Doolittle, and other men and women of various social classes he comments upon contemporary life as he views it. But the way Shaw views life is not necessarily the only way to see it. You, as reader or as audience, have every right to examine the playwright's ideas and come to your own conclusions. Select one of the topics listed below. Glance through the first three acts of *Pygmalion* to refresh your memory as to Shaw's ideas on this particular subject. (Remember you must read what Shaw says carefully and be aware of his satire if you are to interpret his ideas correctly.) Then in a paper of several paragraphs summarize Shaw's ideas on the subject and evaluate them in the light of your own experience.

1. The English have no respect for their language. (*Review the quotation from the preface to* Pygmalion, *Eliza's first speeches and Shaw's comments upon them, as well as the speeches of various bystanders.*)
2. An individual's social position is determined primarily by the way he speaks his language.
3. The lower classes fear and mistrust the police and all those representing authority.
4. Conventional ideas of marriage and parenthood are based on middle-class views rather than on standards of right and wrong.
5. Cleanliness is a luxury.
6. The needs of the undeserving poor are as urgent as those of the deserving poor.
7. Trying to seem sophisticated may make one appear ridiculous.
8. Training a person to the manners and habits of the upper classes may disqualify him from earning a living.

ASSIGNMENT 2. *Based on* Pygmalion, *pages 661-712.*

Shaw's *Pygmalion* first appeared on the London stage in 1914. More than forty years later, audiences stood in line to obtain tickets for a musical version of the same play. In *My Fair Lady* they watched the same characters moving through the same plot and even saying many of the same lines that had previously entertained the audiences for *Pygmalion.* Some members of the audience would have predicted happily that the charm of *Pygmalion* would be equally strong after another forty years.

Having read *Pygmalion,* you are in a position to evaluate the importance of various elements in making this drama an enduring success. What qualities of this play kept the interest of both professional and amateur groups alive for a half century and formed the basis of one of the most successful musicals ever produced? Was it the plot, the theme, the characters, the wit of Shaw's lines, some other element, or a combination of several elements?

Write an essay of three or four paragraphs on the following subject: Why *Pygmalion* Interests Contemporary Audiences. Draw on your knowledge of literature as well as on your understanding of the demands of both readers and audiences today in your explanation of the lasting success of this play. Stick to the point, be clear, and cite specific examples from the play itself to prove your points.

LESSON SIXTEEN: Analysis and Evaluation

ASSIGNMENT 1. *Based on "Time and the Machine," "Dunkirk," "Can We Live in Peace?" and "Three Pictures," pages 715-727.*

Nonfiction has many faces and embraces subject matter of all types and various degrees of importance. Yet certain qualities may be demanded of most good writing in this category: logical organization of ideas, clarity of expression, dramatic placement of important points, and a style suited to the subject.

Write a critical analysis of several paragraphs on one of the selections listed above. In this paper consider both the content of the selection and the manner in which this content is treated. The following outline may be helpful.

I. Introduction. State the name of the author, his subject, his qualifications to write on this particular subject, and his purpose in writing.

II. Evaluate the content. (*Is the subject worth writing about? What is the author's viewpoint? Are the arguments supporting this viewpoint convincing?*)

III. Evaluate the method. (*Is the material well organized? Do the ideas follow logically one from another? Is the language clear and vivid?*)

IV. Summarize the good and bad qualities of this piece of nonfiction.

After revising your paper, read it again carefully. Have you presented the kind of criticism you would expect a reasonable person to make on one of your essays?

ASSIGNMENT 2. *Based on "Nonfiction," pages 714-768.*

Few readers really like all of the literature in an anthology of this type, which seeks to sample the best of English writing through the centuries.

Most intelligent readers understand, however, that to continue to merit inclusion in an anthology after the lapse of many years, any specimen of writing must have certain qualities that assure its status as literature. Often a reader may broaden his understanding of literature by seeking reasons for the continued praise of writing that he personally does not like.

Choose the piece of literature that you like best from each of the four periods listed below. Decide why you think it deserves a place in modern anthologies.

1. Before 1625.
2. 1625-1797.
3. 1798-1901.
4. 1902—Present.

After you have prepared to defend your choice for each period, outline and write a theme of from 300 to 500 words in which you explain why in your opinion these four pieces of literature deserve continued respect. Be prepared to counter attacks from other students. You may wish to work from an outline like that below.

I. Introduction. Name your four choices and explain what general standards have guided you in making your selections. State to what degree you really like each selection and name alternate choices you have considered and omitted.

II. Defense of choices. For each choice present reasons that would convince other readers that your choice, even if not the best writing in its period, deserves to be read.

III. Summary. State the qualities common to these selections that make them worth preserving and reading today.

IV. Conclusion. Briefly state your personal conclusions as to what you seek in literature and the qualities that constitute "good literature" for you.

Glossary and Index of Literary Terms

Words in italics indicate other entries in the glossary. Numbers after an entry refer to the pages in the text on which additional information can be found.

ACCENT, stress on a syllable, a basic element of *rhythm.*

ACTION, the happenings in a *narrative.*

ALEXANDRINE, twelve-syllable *iambic* line. 406.

ALLEGORY, a narrative in which characters, action, and sometimes setting represent abstract concepts or moral qualities. 229.

ALLITERATION, repetition of consonant sounds at the beginnings of words or accented syllables.

ALLUSION, a brief, often indirect reference to a person, place, event, or work of art.

ANALOGY, a comparison of points of likeness between two otherwise dissimilar things. An analogy uses the more familiar to explain or enforce the less familiar.

ANAPEST, three-syllable metrical *foot,* consisting of two unaccented syllables followed by an accented syllable.

ANTAGONIST, a character opposing the *protagonist,* or hero.

APHORISM, a short, pithy saying. 187, 706-707.

APOSTROPHE, a *figure of speech* in which an absent person, an abstract concept, or an inanimate object is addressed directly.

ART FOR ART'S SAKE, the view that a work of literature or art need serve no practical purpose, such as moral teaching: it is its own justification. 466.

ASSONANCE, repetition of vowel sounds. 364.

ATMOSPHERE, a pervading emotional quality developed by the handling of the *setting.* The atmosphere of a work is *functional* in establishing *tone.*

AUTOBIOGRAPHY, a biographical account of at least a part of the writer's own life. 282-283.

BALLAD, a narrative song handed down in oral tradition (see also *literary ballad*). The traditional ballad stanza is a *quatrain,* alternating lines of *iambic tetrameter* and *trimeter.* 52-53.

BIOGRAPHY, the full account of a man's life and character. 282-283, 714.

BLANK VERSE, unrhymed *iambic pentameter,* often written in sections of varying length, without regular *stanzaic* form.

BURLESQUE, a means of ridiculing people, actions, or literary works by mimicking.

CADENCE, a natural rhythm above and beyond any formal one.

CAESURA, pause felt by the reader in a line of verse.

CARICATURE, a character development which exaggerates prominent features of appearance or character.

CATASTROPHE, the final stage of a *tragedy* in which the hero meets his unhappy fate. 181.

CATHARSIS, purgation of emotion, especially that experienced in watching or reading a *tragedy.* 181-182.

CHARACTER, a fictional personality created by an author. 180-181.

CHARACTERIZATION, techniques used by the writer in creating a character. 180-181.

CLASSICAL, specifically, any part of the culture of the ancient Greeks and Romans; generally, anything resembling that culture.

CLIMAX. The technical climax is the decisive point in a series of happenings. (See *dramatic climax.*) 179.

COMEDY, a play in which the *complications* are designed to amuse or interest the audience without evoking the deep sympathy of *tragedy.*

COMEDY OF IDEAS, a comedy in which the humor lies in ideas more than in situations. 683.

COMEDY OF MANNERS, a comedy in which the humor arises largely from violations of the conventions of a sophisticated society. 324.

COMPLICATION, the introduction of the *conflict* into the plot.

CONCEIT, an elaborate and surprising *figure of speech* comparing two very dissimilar things. 101.

CONFLICT, the interplay between opposing forces, a central element in most *plots.* 179.

CONNOTATION, the feeling or attitude associated with a word above and beyond its literal meaning, or *denotation.* 82-83.

CONVENTION, any artful technique widely accepted as appropriate to a given type of literature.

CORONACH, a ballad lament. 52-53.

COUPLET, a *verse form* of two rhyming lines.

CRITICISM, a type of formal essay writing in which literature is analyzed and evaluated.

CYCLE, any group of writings, each complete in itself, which together form one long narrative. 111-112, 607.

DACTYL, three-syllable metrical *foot*, consisting of one accented syllable followed by two unaccented syllables.

DENOTATION, the literal meaning of a word.

DENOUEMENT, the final untying of the *plot*. 179.

DIALECT, the imitation of regional speech in writing, using altered, phonetic spelling.

DIALOGUE, the direct presentation of conversation between two or more characters.

DIARY, a record of daily happenings written by a person for his own use. (Compare *journal* and *memoir*.) 282-283.

DICTION, the particular choice of words in a work. 140-141, 653.

DISTICH, an *aphoristic* couplet.

DRAMA, the literary form designed for presentation in a theater by actors representing the characters. 111-113, 179-182, 661-662.

DRAMATIC, a term used to describe any action presented directly, rather than told about, and often implying conflict and excitement.

DRAMATIC CLIMAX, the point of most intense excitement in a narrative. (See *climax*.) 179.

DRAMATIC IRONY, a situation in which facts known to the reader and some of the characters are unknown to other characters. 309.

DRAMATIC MONOLOGUE, poem in which the speaker addresses one or more persons who are present but whose replies are not recorded. 462.

ELEGAIC, a term used to refer to any writing which has the *tone* of an *elegy*. 329.

ELEGY, a traditional poetic form that treats of death in a formal, philosophic way. 31, 329.

END RHYME, the rhyming of words at the ends of lines of verse. (Compare *internal rhyme*.)

END-STOPPED, a term applied to a line or a couplet which exactly contains a complete thought, thus necessitating the use of a semicolon or period at the end. 273.

EPIC, a long narrative poem—originally handed down in oral tradition, later a traditional literary form—dealing with national heroes, having a world-wide or cosmic setting, and written in a deliberately ceremonial style. By extension *epic* may refer to any writing with similar qualities. 217.

EPIGRAM, originally, an inscription; later, any very short, highly polished verse or saying, usually ending with a witty turn.

EPILOGUE, concluding section added to a work, serving to round out or interpret it.

EPISODE, an event in a narrative.

EPISODIC, a narrative largely composed of loosely related events.

ESSAY, a brief piece of nonfiction which presents a personal point of view either through informal discourse or formal analysis and argument. 187, 367, 370-371, 714.

EXPOSITION, that part of a narrative, usually at the beginning, that sketches in the background of the characters and the action. 179.

FALLING ACTION, the action in a narrative which represents the working out of the decisive action of the *climax*. 179.

FARCE, comedy which aims above all at laughter, usually at the expense of realism and conventions. 324.

FIGURATIVE LANGUAGE, language used in such a way as to force words out of their literal meanings and, by emphasizing their *connotations*, to bring new insight to the subject described.

FIGURES OF SPEECH, specific devices, such as *metaphors* and *similes*, for achieving the effects of *figurative language*.

FLASHBACK, interruption of the narrative to show an episode that happened prior to the story.

FOLK SONG, a song handed down in oral tradition.

FOLKLORE, the customs, legends, songs, tales of a people or nation.

FOOT, a metrical division consisting of one accented syllable and all unaccented syllables associated with it. (Exception: the *spondee*.)

FORESHADOWING, implication by the author of events to come later in a narrative.

FRAME, a narrative device presenting a story or group of stories within the frame of a larger narrative. 510.

FREE VERSE, poetry written with *rhythm* and other poetic devices, but without *meter* or regular *rhyme scheme*.

FUNCTIONAL, a term applied to elements in a work which are effectively related to other elements or to the unity of the work as a whole.

GOTHIC NOVEL, type of novel which aims at evoking terror through a gloomy setting and sensational, supernatural action. 525.

HACK, writer whose primary aim is making money, and who is not concerned with the literary value of his writing.

786

HEROIC COUPLET, a pair of rhymed verse lines in *iambic pentameter.*

HEROIC SIMILE, a *simile* sustained for several lines and giving a *connotation* of heroic stature.

HEXAMETER, a verse line of six *feet.*

HISTORICAL NOVEL, novel using fictional characters in an accurately reproduced historical setting. 526.

HOMILY, a sermon, or serious moral talk.

HYPERBOLE, a *figure of speech* involving great exaggeration for expressive or comic effect. 659.

IAMB, two-syllable metrical *foot* consisting of one unaccented syllable followed by one accented syllable.

IDYL or IDYLL, a *pastoral poem.*

IMAGERY, the use of vivid, concrete, sensory details. 155, 223.

IMAGISM, the view that poetic expression is best achieved by the use of sharply detailed *imagery.* 618-619.

IMPERFECT RHYME, *rhyme* in which the vowel sounds are not quite identical. 392, 637.

INTERNAL RHYME, rhyming of words within, rather than at the end of, lines.

IRONY. An ironic tone is one in which the author seems, superficially, to mask his real intention. In a more restricted sense *irony* refers to a statement that says the opposite of what is really implied. This is sometimes called *verbal irony* in order to distinguish it from *irony of situation, dramatic irony,* etc. 82, 509.

IRONY OF SITUATION, a happening contrary to that which is appropriate. 509.

JOURNAL, a formal record of a person's daily experiences. 282-283.

KENNING, metaphorical compound word used as a poetic *convention.* 25, 30.

LAY, a short narrative song; also, a *ballad.* 19.

LEGEND, a traditional story about a particular person, place, or deity, often popularly accepted as history. 25.

LETTERS, literary culture as a whole.

LITERARY BALLAD, a poem composed in imitation of the folk *ballad.* 405.

LOCAL COLOR, use in fiction of the speech, customs, and setting of a particular region for their own interest. 490.

LYRIC, any short poem, or passage in a poem, intended mainly to express a state of mind.

MANUSCRIPT, hand written (or typewritten) copy of a book or other work.

MASQUE, an elaborate entertainment combining fine costumes, scenery, music, and dancing. 206.

MAXIM, a brief saying embodying a moral. (Compare *aphorism* and *proverb.*) 706-707.

MELODRAMA, a kind of pretentious tragedy in which realism and convention may be sacrificed for the primary aim of emotional effect.

MEMOIR, a partial *autobiography*, dealing with events of public importance by a person who has figured notably in them. 282-283.

METAPHOR, a *figure of speech* involving an implied comparison. (Compare *simile.*)

METER, any regular pattern of *rhythm.*

MIRACLE PLAY, medieval verse drama dealing with a subject from the Bible or the life of a saint. 111.

MOCK EPIC, a *satire* using the form of an *epic* poem to develop a trivial incident. 270.

MONOLOGUE, an extended speech by one character.

MORALITY PLAY, medieval drama in which the characters are *personifications* of virtues and vices. 112.

MOTIF, a character, incident, or idea that recurs frequently in various works or in various parts of the same work.

MYSTERY PLAY, another term for *miracle play.*

MYTH, a traditional story connected with the religion of a people, usually attempting to account for something in nature.

NARRATIVE, any writing which concerns a series of happenings.

NARRATIVE POINT OF VIEW, the relation assumed between the author and the characters. This includes specifically the extent to which the narrator shows himself to be aware of what each character thinks and feels.

NARRATOR, the teller of a story, usually either a character or an anonymous voice used by the author.

NATURALISM, a form of *realism* embodying a fatalistic view of man. 472.

NEOCLASSICISM, writing that shows the influence of Greek and Roman *classics.* 273.

NONFICTION, prose writing that seeks to inform, expound a point of view, or argue a point. 714.

NOVEL, an extended piece of narrative prose fiction which usually explores the values of a large segment of society. 524-530.

NOVEL OF MANNERS, a novel making use of the

fashions and conventions of a particular class. 526.

NOVEL OF PURPOSE, novel designed to effect social change. 526-527.

OCTAVE, first eight lines of a *sonnet*, particularly the Italian sonnet. 106.

ODE, a long *lyric* poem, formal in style and complex in form, often written for a special occasion.

OMNISCIENT POINT OF VIEW, *narrative point of view* in which the author may tell anything he wishes about the characters' thoughts and feelings.

ONOMATOPOEIA, words used in such a way that the sound of the words imitates the sound of the thing spoken about.

PARADOX, a statement that is self-contradictory on the surface, but which reveals a subtler meaning on reflection. 206, 716.

PARODY, a kind of *burlesque* aimed particularly at making the style of an author ridiculous.

PASTORAL POETRY, a conventional form of *lyric* poetry using an idealized picture of rural life. 102.

PENTAMETER, metrical line of five *feet*. 106.

PERSONIFICATION, *figure of speech* in which a thing or an abstraction is treated as a person. 112.

PHILISTINISM, lack of culture. 451, *footnote* 605.

PLOT, the pattern of happenings in a narrative. 179.

POETRY, the communication of feeling and thought through the carefully organized arrangement of words for their sounds, rhythm, and connotation, as well as their meaning. 617-619.

POINT OF VIEW. (See *narrative point of view*.)

PROLOGUE, section of a work preceding the main part, serving as an introduction.

PROPERTIES, any kind of movable pieces used in staging a play.

PROTAGONIST, the hero, or most appealing character of a story.

PROVERB, a brief, traditional saying. (Compare *aphorism* and *maxim*.) 706.

PSYCHOLOGICAL NOVEL, a novel largely concerned with analyzing the motives of the characters. 527.

PUN, simultaneous use of two or more different senses of the same word for expressive or humorous effect. 167.

QUATRAIN, verse *stanza* of four lines. 106.

REALISM, the tendency to emphasize the limitations that real life imposes on humanity, and to show how those limitations affect life. 472.

REFRAIN, the repetition of one or more lines in each stanza of a poem.

REPETITION, the deliberate repeating of any element in a literary work for a particular effect.

RHETORIC, conventional techniques used in prose to heighten an effect. The term is sometimes used to disparage overblown language.

RHYME, exact repetition of sounds in at least the final accented syllables of two or more words.

RHYME SCHEME, any pattern of rhymes in a stanza which is a conventional pattern or which is repeated in another stanza.

RHYTHM, a series of stresses or emphases in a group of words, arranged so that the reader expects a similar series to follow. These emphases may be of grammatical structure, meaning, imagery, or feeling, as well as of sound.

RISING ACTION, the section of most narratives during which the tension between opposing characters or forces builds toward a *climax*.

ROMANCE, a long narrative in verse or prose that originated in the Middle Ages. Its main elements are adventure, love, and magic. 85.

ROMANTIC COMEDY, play with idealized characters, and complications arising from a love affair. 683.

ROMANTICISM, a broad, often vague term that may be applied to any work that tends to be unconventional, subjective, exotic, or idealistic. 325, 337, 345-347.

SARCASM, the use of exaggerated praise to imply dispraise. Similar to *irony*, but more specific in intent, and heavier, less subtle in tone.

SATIRE, use of witty techniques to ridicule a subject. *Irony* and *sarcasm* are common weapons of satire. 268.

SCANSION, marking off a line of verse into *feet*, indicating the stressed and unstressed syllables.

SCENE, the setting for a given event in a narrative, or the shortest major division of a play.

SCOP, professional reciter of poems at tribal feasts in Anglo-Saxon times. 19.

SENTIMENT, term used in the eighteenth century to mean exaggerated feelings of pity and tenderness. 303.

SENTIMENTAL COMEDY, comedy that attempts moral reform by setting a good example in the hero and heroine and by lavish use of *sentiment*. 303.

SESTET, the concluding six lines of a *sonnet*, particularly the Italian sonnet. 106.

SETTING, the represented place and time of an event in a literary work. 490.

SHORT STORY, a brief, concentrated piece of narrative prose fiction. 548-549.

SIMILE, a *figure of speech* involving a comparison made explicit by the use of the word *like* or *as*. (Compare *metaphor*.)

SLANT RHYME, *imperfect rhyme*.

SOLILOQUY, a dramatic *convention* which allows a character to speak his thoughts aloud, apparently unheard by others who may be on stage. 180.

SONNET, a *lyric* poem with a traditional form of fourteen *iambic pentameter* lines. 106.

SONNET SEQUENCE, a series of sonnets written as a group with a common theme or subject.

SPENSERIAN STANZA, a stanza of nine *iambic* lines, eight of which have five *feet*, the ninth line, six, rhyming *ababbcbcc*. 406.

SPONDEE, metrical *foot* of two accented syllables.

SPRUNG RHYTHM, metrical form which prescribes only the number of the accented syllables in a line. 523-524.

STAGE DIRECTIONS, a dramatist's written directions as to how scenes are to be set and how the play is to be produced. 712.

STANZA, the smallest division of a poem having a *rhyme scheme*. The word *stanza* is sometimes extended to refer to similar divisions in *blank verse* or *free verse*, even though in these there is no rhyme scheme.

STOCK CHARACTER, a definite type of character conventionally used in a particular literary form. 303.

STREAM OF CONSCIOUSNESS, narrative technique that presents only the subjective impressions that a character has. 561.

STYLE, the distinctive handling of the language by a given author. 437-438.

SUBPLOT, a *plot* of secondary importance carried on in partial or complete independence of the main plot.

SUBSTITUTE FOOT, a metrical foot different from the one prevailing in a line or stanza.

SYMBOL, something relatively concrete, such as an object, action, character, or scene, which signifies something relatively abstract, such as a concept or an idea. 623-624.

TALE, a short narrative with at least the appearance of naïve simplicity.

TECHNICAL CLIMAX, the main turning point in a narrative. (See *climax*.)

TERZA RIMA, verse form with a three line *stanza* rhyming *aba, bcb, cdc*, etc. 392.

TETRAMETER, metrical line of four *feet*.

THEME, the idea of a literary work; also, a broad subject, especially one that recurs in the same work or different works. 557.

TONE, author's attitude toward his material as expressed in a work. 82.

TRACT, a short book or pamphlet treating a religious or political issue, usually in a partisan way.

TRAGEDY, in its most general sense, a term referring to any narrative writing in which the *protagonist* suffers disaster after a serious and significant struggle, but faces his downfall in such a way as to attain heroic stature. In its more restricted sense, *tragedy* refers to a play of this nature. 181-182.

TRAGIC FLAW, flaw of character in a tragic hero which precipitates his downfall. 182.

TREATISE, an extended formal essay treating a subject in a systematic way from the standpoint of an expert.

TRIMETER, metrical line of three *feet*.

TROCHEE, metrical *foot* made up of one accented syllable followed by an unaccented syllable.

TYPE CHARACTER, an uncomplicated, "flat" character, having only a single, predictable motivation.

UNITIES. Classical dramatic criticism insisted that a good play must have (*a*) a unified action, taking place during (*b*) a single continuous time, in (*c*) one place. These criteria are known as the three *unities*. 235.

UNITY, the quality achieved by an artistic work when all its elements are so interrelated as to form a complete whole.

VERSE. In its most general sense *verse* is a synonym for *poetry*. *Verse* also may be used to refer to poetry carefully composed as to rhythm and rhyme scheme, but of inferior literary value. Finally, *verse* may mean a single line of poetry.

VERSE FORM, a specific pattern of rhythm and rhyme.

WELL-MADE PLAY, tightly plotted play in which the interest is centered on the resolution of the *complication* of plot, often to the exclusion of character development or depth of thought and feeling. 661.

Glossary

The pronunciation of each word is shown just after the word, in this way:
ab bre vi ate (ə brē′vi āt). The letters and signs used are pronounced as in the words
below. The mark ′ is placed after a syllable with primary or strong accent, as in the
example above. The mark ′ after a syllable shows a secondary or lighter accent, as
in **ab bre vi a tion** (ə brē′vi ā′shən).

Some words, taken from foreign languages, are spoken with sounds that otherwise
do not occur in English. Symbols for these sounds are given at the end of the table
as "Foreign Sounds."

a	hat, cap	o	hot, rock	ə represents:	
ā	age, face	ō	open, go	a in about	
ã	care, air	ô	order, all	e in taken	
ä	father, far	oi	oil, voice	i in pencil	
		ou	house, out	o in lemon	
b	bad, rob			u in circus	
ch	child, much				
d	did, red	p	paper, cup		
		r	run, try		
e	let, best	s	say, yes	FOREIGN SOUNDS	
ē	equal, see	sh	she, rush		
ėr	term, learn	t	tell, it	Y	as in French du. Pronounce ē with the lips rounded as for English ü in **rule.**
		th	thin, both		
f	fat, if	ŦH	then, smooth		
g	go, bag			œ	as in French peu. Pronounce ā with the lips rounded as for ō.
h	he, how	u	cup, butter		
		u̇	full, put		
i	it, pin	ü	rule, move		
ī	ice, five	ū	use, music	N	as in French bon. The N is not pronounced, but shows that the vowel before it is nasal.
j	jam, enjoy				
k	kind, seek	v	very, save		
l	land, coal	w	will, woman		
m	me, am	y	young, yet	H	as in German ach. Pronounce k without closing the breath passage.
n	no, in	z	zero, breeze		
ng	long, bring	zh	measure, seizure		

ETYMOLOGY KEY

<	from, derived from, taken from	*dial.*	dialect	*neut.*	neuter
		dim.	diminutive	*pp.*	past participle
?	possibly	*fem.*	feminine	*ppr.*	present participle
abl.	ablative	*gen.*	genitive	*pt.*	past tense
accus.	accusative	*lang.*	language	*ult.*	ultimately
cf.	compare	*masc.*	masculine	*var.*	variant

790

LANGUAGE ABBREVIATIONS

AF	Anglo-French (= Anglo-Norman, the dialect of French spoken by the Normans in England, esp. 1066-c. 1164)
Am.E	American English (word originating in the United States)
Am.Ind.	American Indian
Am.Sp.	American Spanish
E	English
F	French
G	German
Gk.	Greek (from Homer to 300 A.D.)
Gmc.	Germanic (parent language of Gothic, Scandinavian, English, Dutch, German)
HG	High German (speech of Central and Southern Germany)
Hindu.	Hindustani (the commonest language of India)
Ital.	Italian
L	Latin (Classical Latin 200 B.C.-300 A.D.)
LG	Low German (speech of Northern Germany)
LGk.	Late Greek (300-700)
LL	Late Latin (300-700)
M	Middle
ME	Middle English (1100-1500)
Med.	Medieval
Med.Gk.	Medieval Greek (700-1500)
Med.L	Medieval Latin (700-1500)
MF	Middle French (1400-1600)
MHG	Middle High German (1100-1450)
MLG	Middle Low German (1100-1450)
NL	New Latin (after 1500)
O	Old
OE	Old English (before 1100)
OF	Old French (before 1400)
OHG	Old High German (before 1100)
Pg.	Portuguese
Scand.	Scandinavian (one of the languages of Northern Europe before Middle English times; Old Norse unless otherwise specified)
Skt.	Sanskrit (the ancient literary language of India, from the same parent language as Persian, Greek, Latin, Germanic, Slavonic, and Celtic)
Sp.	Spanish
VL	Vulgar Latin (a popular form of Latin, the main source of French, Spanish, Italian, Portuguese, and Rumanian)

OTHER ABBREVIATIONS

adj.	adjective	*E*	Eastern	*pron.*	pronoun
adv.	adverb	*esp.*	especially	*sing.*	singular
Anat.	anatomy	*interj.*	interjection	*SW*	Southwestern
Ant.	antonym	*n.*	noun	*Syn.*	synonym
Brit.	British	*pl.*	plural	*U.S.*	United States
conj.	conjunction	*prep.*	preposition	*v.*	verb

The pronunciation key and language abbreviations are from the *Thorndike-Barnhart High School Dictionary*, copyright ©1962 by Scott, Foresman and Company.

a base ment (ə bās′mənt), *n.* humiliation; degradation.

a bate (ə bāt′), *v.* **1.** make less in amount, intensity, etc.: *The medicine abated his pain.* **2.** become less violent, intense, etc. **3.** put an end to (a nuisance, an action, or a writ). [< OF *abatre* beat down < *a-* to (< L *ad-*) + *batre* beat < L *batuere*] —**Syn. 1, 2.** decrease, diminish. **3.** stop.

a bate ment (ə bāt′mənt), *n.* **1.** decrease; lessening. **2.** putting an end to. **3.** amount abated; reduction.

ab ject (ab′jekt or ab jekt′), *adj.* **1.** wretched; miserable. **2.** deserving contempt; degraded. **3.** slavish. [< L *abjectus*, pp. of *abjicere* < *ab-* down + *jacere* throw]

ab jure (ab jür′), *v.* renounce on oath; repudiate; swear to give up: *abjure one's religion.*

ab so lu tion (ab′sə lü′shən), *n.* **1.** a freeing or freedom from guilt and punishment for sin; forgiveness. A person who confesses and is sorry for his sins and promises to do penance is granted absolution by a priest. **2.** a freeing or freedom from guilt or blame. **3.** release from a duty or promise.

a bys mal (ə biz′məl), *adj.* too deep to be measured; bottomless.

ac quit tance (ə kwit′əns), *n.* **1.** release from a debt or obligation. **2.** payment of a debt; settlement of a claim. **3.** written statement showing that a debt has been paid.

ac ri mo ni ous (ak′rə mō′ni əs), *adj.* sharp or bitter in temper, language, or manner.

ad a man tine (ad′ə man′tin, ad′ə man′tēn, or ad′-ə man′tīn), *adj.* **1.** too hard to be cut or broken. **2.** unyielding; firm; immovable.

ad dress (ə dres′), *n.* **1.** speech, especially a formal one. **2. addresses,** *pl.* attentions paid in courtship.

ad ju tant (aj′ù tənt), *n.* **1.** army officer who assists a commanding officer by sending out orders, writing letters, giving messages, etc. **2.** helper; assistant. —*adj.* helping.

ad um brate (ad um′brāt or ad′əm brāt), *v.* **1.** indicate faintly; outline. **2.** foreshadow. **3.** overshadow; obscure. [< L *adumbrare* overshadow < *ad-* + *umbra* shade]

a ë re al (*adj.* ãr′i əl or ā ēr′i əl; *n.* ãr′i əl), *adj.* **1.** in the air. **2.** of or having to do with the air. **3.** like air; thin and light as air. **4.** ideal; imaginary. **5.** relating to aircraft in any way. Also, **aerial.**

aer ie or **aer y** (ãr′i or ēr′i), *n.* **1.** the lofty nest of an eagle or other bird of prey. **2.** young eagles or the young of other birds of prey. **3.** house, castle, etc., built in a high place.

aes thete (es′thēt), *n.* **1.** person who pretends to care a great deal about beauty; person who gives too much attention to beauty. **2.** person who is sensitive to beauty; lover of beauty. Also **esthete.**

af fec tion (ə fek′shən), *n.* **1.** friendly feeling; fondness; tenderness; love. **2.** feeling; inclination. **3.** *Archaic.* disposition; tendency.

af flu ence (af′lü əns), *n.* **1.** wealth; riches. **2.** abundant supply; great abundance.

af front (ə frunt′), *n.* a word or act that openly expresses intentional disrespect. —*v.* **1.** insult openly; offend purposely. **2.** meet face to face; confront. [< OF *afronter* < *a front* against the forehead < L *ad frontem*]

a gen cy (ā′jən si), *n.* **1.** means; action: *Snow is drifted by the agency of the wind.* **2.** business of a person or company that has the authority to act for another.

a gue (ā′gū), *n.* **1.** a malarial fever with chills and sweating that occur at regular intervals. **2.** a fit of shivering; chill.

al be it (ôl bē′it), *conj.* although; even though. [ME *al be it* although it be]

al lay (ə lā′), *v.* **1.** put at rest; quiet. **2.** relieve; check: *Her fever was allayed by the medicine.* **3.** make less; weaken.

am i ty (am′ə ti), *n.* peace and friendship; friendly relations. [< MF *amitie*, ult. < L *amicus* friend]

am u let (am′ū lit), *n.* some object worn as a magic charm against evil.

a nal o gous (ə nal′ə gəs), *adj.* **1.** alike in some way; similar; comparable. **2.** in biology, corresponding in function, but not in structure and origin.

an a logue (an′ə lôg or an′ə log), *n.* something analogous.

an i line (an′ə lin or an′ə līn), *n.* a poisonous, oily liquid used in making dyes, plastics, etc. —*adj.* made from aniline.

an i mad ver sion (an′ə mad vėr′zhən), *n.* criticism; blame; unfavorable comment.

an nals (an′əlz), *n.pl.* **1.** a written account of events year by year. **2.** historical records; history.

an o dyne (an′ə dīn), *n.* anything that lessens pain. [< L < Gk. *anodynos* < *an-* without + *odyne* pain]

a nom a ly (ə nom′ə li), *n.* **1.** departure from a general rule; irregularity. **2.** something abnormal.

a non (ə non′), *adv.* **1.** in a little while; soon. **2.** at another time; again.

an ti quar i an (an′tə kwãr′i ən), *adj.* having to do with antiques or antiquaries: *The antiquarian section of the museum was full of old furniture and dishes.* —*n.* antiquary.

an ti pode (an′tə pōd), *n.* anything exactly opposite; direct opposite.

a pace (ə pās′), *adv.* swiftly; quickly; fast.

ape (āp), *n.* **1.** any large, tailless monkey that can stand almost erect and walk on two feet. **2.** any monkey. **3.** person who imitates or mimics. —*v.* imitate; mimic.

ap o gee (ap′ə jē), *n.* **1.** point farthest from the earth in the orbit of a planet, comet, etc. **2.** furthermost point; highest point. [< F *apogée* < Gk. *apogaion* < *apo-* away from + *ge* or *gaia* earth]

a poth e car y (ə poth′ə ker′i), *n.* **1.** druggist. **2.** *Brit.* formerly, a person who prescribed medicines and sold them.

ap pel la tion (ap′ə lā′shən), *n.* name; title. In "John the Baptist," the appellation of *John* is *the Baptist.*

ap pur te nance (ə pėr′tə nəns), *n.* **1.** addition to something more important; added thing; accessory. **2.** a minor right or privilege belonging to another that is more important.

apt (apt), *adj.* **1.** fitted by nature; likely: *A careless person is apt to make mistakes.* **2.** suitable; fitting. **3.** quick to learn: *an apt pupil.* —**Syn. 3.** prompt, ready, clever.

ar bi trar y (är′bə trer′i), *adj.* **1.** based on one's own wishes, notions, or will; not going by rule or law. **2.** capricious. **3.** tyrannical: *an arbitrary king.*

ar bo re al (är bô′ri əl or är bō′ri əl), *adj.* **1.** of trees; like trees. **2.** living in or among trees.

ar go sy (är′gə si), *n.* **1.** a large merchant ship. **2.** fleet of such ships.

ar gu ment (är′gū mənt), *n.* **1.** discussion by persons who disagree. **2.** giving reasons for or against something. **3.** reason or reasons given for or against something. **4.** short statement of what is in a book, etc.

< = from, taken from; cf., compare; dial., dialect; dim., diminutive; pp., past participle; ppr., present participle; pt., past tense; ult., ultimately; var., variant; ?=possibly.

ar raign (ə rān′), v. 1. bring before a law court for trial. 2. call in question; find fault with. —**Syn.** 2. accuse.

ar rant (ar′ənt), adj. thoroughgoing; downright: He was such an arrant liar that nobody believed him.

ar ras (ar′əs), n. 1. kind of tapestry. 2. curtain or hangings of tapestry.

ar tic u late (adj. är tik′ū lit; v. är tik′ū lāt), adj. 1. uttered in distinct syllables of words. 2. able to put one's thoughts into words. 3. made up of distinct parts; distinct. —v. speak distinctly.

ar ti fice (är′tə fis), n. 1. a clever device; trick. 2. trickery; craft. [< F < L artificium < ars, artis art + facere make]

art less (ärt′lis), adj. 1. without awareness of conventions; simple: Small children ask many artless questions. 2. natural; not artificial. 3. without art; unskilled. 4. without guile or deceit.

as a fet i da or **as a foet i da** (as′ə fet′ə də), n. gum resin with a garliclike odor, used in medicine to prevent spasms.

as per i ty (as per′ə ti), n. roughness; harshness; severity: She spoke with her usual asperity. [< OF asprete < L asperitas < asper rough]

as say (ə sā′ or as′ā), v. 1. analyze (an ore, alloy, etc.) to find out the quantity of gold, silver, or other metal in it. 2. try; test; examine. 3. Archaic. attempt. —n. 1. analysis of an ore, alloy, etc., to find out the amount of metal in it. 2. trial; test; examination. 3. the substance analyzed or tested. 4. a list of the results of assaying. [< OF a(s)sayer, ult. < LL < VL exagere weigh]

as si du i ty (as′ə dü′ə ti or as′ə dū′ə ti), n. careful and steady attention; diligence.

as sid u ous (ə sij′ü əs), adj. careful and attentive; diligent. —**as sid′u ous ly,** adv.

as size (ə sīz′), n. session of a law court. [< OF as(s)ise < aseeir < VL assedere sit at < L assidere]

as siz es (ə sīz′iz), n.pl. periodical sessions of court held in each county of England.

a thwart (ə thwôrt′), adv. crosswise; across from side to side. —prep. 1. across. 2. across the line or course of. 3. in opposition to; against.

at tent (ə tent′), adj. attentive; heedful.

au gu ry (ô′gū ri), n. 1. art or practice of foretelling the future by the flight of birds, thunder and lightning, etc. 2. prediction; indication; sign; omen. 3. rite or ceremony performed by an augur.

au gust (ô gust′), adj. inspiring reverence and admiration; majestic; venerable.

au re ole (ô′ri ōl), n. 1. encircling radiance; halo. 2. a ring of light surrounding the sun. [< L aureola (corona) golden (crown) < aurum gold]

a ve (ā′vi or ä′vā), interj. Latin. hail! farewell! —n. Ave, the prayer Ave Maria.

av o ca tion (av′ə kā′shən), n. 1. something that a person does besides his regular business; minor occupation; hobby: Mr. Brown is a lawyer, but writing stories is his avocation. 2. Informal. regular business; occupation.

a vouch (ə vouch′), v. 1. declare to be true. 2. guarantee. 3. acknowledge; affirm. [< OF avochier < a- to (< L ad-) + vochier call < L vocare]

a wry (ə rī′), adv., adj. 1. with a twist or turn to one side: Her hat was blown awry by the wind. 2. wrong: Our plans have gone awry.

aye (ā), adv. always; ever.

back brand (bak′ brand), n. a large log at the back of a wood fire.

bag a telle (bag′ə tel′), n. 1. a mere trifle; thing of no importance. 2. game somewhat like billiards. [< F < Ital. bagatella, dim. of baga berry]

bairn (bārn), n. Scottish. child. [OE bearn]

baize (bāz), n. a thick woolen cloth used for curtains, table covers, etc.

bale¹ (bāl), n. Poetic or Archaic. 1. evil; harm. 2. sorrow; pain. [OE bealu]

bale² (bāl), n. Archaic. a blazing pile, esp. a funeral pyre.

bale ful (bāl′fəl), adj. evil; harmful.

ba nal i ty (bə nal′ə ti), n. commonplaceness; triteness; triviality.

ban di coot (ban′də küt), n. 1. a very large rat of India that is about two feet long. 2. a small ratlike animal in Australia that carries its young in a pouch. [< Indian dial. pandikokku pig-rat]

bard (bärd), n. 1. a poet and singer of long ago. Bards sang their own poems to the music of their harps. 2. poet.

bark (bärk), n. 1. ship with three masts, square-rigged on the first two masts and fore-and-aft-rigged on the other. 2. Poetic. boat; ship.

ba rouche lan dau (bə rüsh′ lan dô), n. a four-wheeled carriage with two seats facing each other and a folding top.

bar row (bar′ō), n. mound of earth or stones over an ancient grave.

bat ten (bat′ən), n. 1. board used for flooring. 2. strip of wood. Battens are nailed across parallel boards to strengthen them. They are also used to nail down the canvas over a ship's hatchway and to cover cracks between boards. —v. fasten down or strengthen with strips of wood.

beard (bērd), v. face boldly; defy.

bee tle (bē′təl), v. project; overhang: Great cliffs beetled above the narrow path.

be guile (bi gīl′), v. 1. deceive; cheat: His pleasant ways beguiled me into thinking that he was my friend. 2. take away from deceitfully or cunningly. 3. entertain; amuse. 4. while away (time) pleasantly.

be hold ing (bi hōl′ding), adj. Archaic. indebted; dependent.

be la bor (bi lā′bər), v. 1. beat vigorously; hit or whip: The man belabored his poor donkey. 2. beat with words; abuse; ridicule.

bel dam (bel′dəm), n. 1. an old woman. 2. an ugly old woman; hag.

be lie (bi lī′), v. 1. give a false idea of; misrepresent. 2. show to be false; prove to be mistaken. 3. fail to come up to; disappoint.

be like (bi līk′), adv. Archaic. very likely; probably; perhaps.

be night ed (bi nīt′id), adj. 1. not knowing right and wrong; ignorant. 2. overtaken by night; being in darkness.

bent¹ (bent), v. pt. and pp. of bend. —adj. 1. not straight. 2. strongly inclined; determined. —n. inclination; tendency: a bent for drawing.

bent² (bent), n. 1. a stiff, wiry grass that grows on sandy or waste land. 2. Archaic. heath; moor.

be seem (bi sēm′), v. be proper for; be fitting to: It does not beseem you to leave your friend without help.

bil ious (bil′yəs), adj. 1. having to do with bile. 2. suffering from or caused by some trouble with bile or the liver. 3. peevish; cross; bad-tempered.

---

hat, āge, cāre, fär; let, ēqual, tėrm; it, īce; hot, ōpen, ôrder; oil, out; cup, pùt, rüle, ūse; th, thin; ₮H, then; zh, measure; ə represents a in about, e in taken, i in pencil, o in lemon, u in circus.

bil let-doux (bil′i dü or bil′ä dü), *n.*, *pl.* **bil lets-doux** (bil′i düz′ or bil′ä düz′). a love letter. [< F]

bird lime (bėrd′līm′), *n.* a sticky substance smeared on twigs to catch small birds that light on it.

bit tern (bit′ərn), *n.* a small kind of heron that lives in marshes and has a peculiar boom-ing cry.

blanch (blanch or blänch), *v.* 1. make white; bleach. 2. turn white or pale. [< OF *blanchir* < *blanc* white < Gmc.]

blanc mange (blə mänzh′), *n.* a sweet dessert made of milk thickened with gelatin, cornstarch, etc. [< OF *blanc-manger* white food]

bla tant (blā′tənt), *adj.* 1. noisy; loud-mouthed. 2. showy in dress, manner, etc.

blear (blēr), *adj.* dim; blurred. —*v.* make dim or blurred.

blench[1] (blench), *v.* draw back; shrink away. [apparently OE *blencan* deceive]

blench[2] (blench), *v.* 1. turn pale. 2. make white. [var. of *blanch*]

bock (bok), *n.* a strong, dark beer, usually brewed in the spring.

bode (bōd), *v.* be a sign of; indicate be-forehand: *Dark clouds boded rain.* [OE *bodian* < *boda* messenger]

bod ice (bod′is), *n.* 1. the close-fitting waist of a dress. 2. a wide girdle worn over a dress and laced up the front. Some Euro-pean peasant women wear bodices. [var. of pl. of *body*, part of a dress]

bo gy (bō′gi), *n.* 1. goblin; evil spirit. 2. person or thing that is feared; bugbear. Also, **bogey, bogie.**

bole (bōl), *n.* trunk of a tree.

bon ho mie (bon′ə mē′), *n.* good nature; courteous and pleasant ways. [< F *bonhomie* < *bonhomme* good fellow]

boot less (büt′lis), *adj.* useless.

boss (bôs or bos), *n.* a raised ornament of silver, ivory, or other material on a flat surface. —*v.* decorate with bosses.

bourn or **bourne** (bôrn, bōrn, or būrn) *n.* 1. Ar-chaic. boundary; limit. 2. goal.

bowl er (bōl′ər), *n.* 1. person who bowls. 2. *Brit.* a derby hat.

brace (brās), *n.* 1. thing that holds parts together or in place. 2. pair; couple: *a brace of ducks.* 3. **braces,** *pl. Brit.* suspenders. 4. Often, **braces,** *pl.* a metal wire used to straighten crooked teeth. —*v.* support.

brand (brand), *n. Archaic* and *Poetic.* sword.

breech bolt (brēch′ bōlt′), *n.* a bolt behind the barrel of a gun, to which the mainspring, safety lock, etc., are attached.

brin ded (brin′dəd), *adj. Archaic.* gray, tan, or tawny with darker streaks and spots.

brook (brük), *v.* put up with; endure; tolerate: *Her pride would not brook such insults.* [OE *brūcan* use]

buck ler (buk′lər), *n.* 1. a small, round shield. 2. protection; defense.

buf fet (buf′it), *n.* 1. blow of the hand or fist. 2. any blow; affliction. —*v.* 1. strike with the hand or fist. 2. knock about; hurt.

bung hole (bung′hōl′), *n.* hole in the side or end of a

Bittern (30 in. long)

Bodice (def. 2)

barrel, keg, or cask through which it is filled and emptied.

bur lesque (bėr lesk′), *n.* 1. a literary or dramatic composition in which a serious subject is treated ridicu-lously, or with mock seriousness. 2. *U.S.* a cheap, vul-gar kind of vaudeville. 3. a kind of theatrical entertain-ment characterized by broad humor, slapstick comedy, imitations, light songs. —*v.* imitate so as to ridicule. [< F < Ital. *burlesco* < *burla* jest]

bur then (bėr′ᴛʜən), *n.*, *v. Archaic.* burden.

but ter y (but′ər i or but′ri), *n.* pantry.

bux om (buk′səm), *adj.* 1. plump and good to look at. 2. lively, merry.

byre (bīr), *n.* cow house.

cadge (kaj), *v.* 1. *Dialect.* peddle. 2. *Informal.* beg. [origin uncertain]

ca jole (kə jōl′), *v.* persuade by pleasant words; flat-tery, or false promises; coax.

calk in (kôk′ən or kal′kən), *n.* a pointed metal piece projecting downward on the shoe of a horse, etc., to prevent slipping.

cal lig ra phy (kə lig′rə fi), *n.* 1. handwriting. 2. beautiful handwriting. [< Gk. *kalligraphia* < *kallos* beauty + *graphein* write]

cal um ny (kal′əm ni), *n.* a false statement made to injure someone's reputation; slander.

can ker (kang′kər), *n.* 1. a spreading sore, especially one in the mouth. 2. disease of plants that causes slow decay. 3. anything that causes decay, rotting, or grad-ual eating away.

can on ize (kan′ən īz), *v.* 1. declare (a dead person) to be a saint; place in the official list of saints. 2. bury according to church rules.

cant (kant), *n.* 1. insincere talk; moral and religious statements that many people make, but few really believe or follow. 2. the peculiar language of a special group, using many strange words: *thieves' cant.* [< L *cantus* song]

ca per (kā′pər), *n.* 1. a prickly shrub of the Mediter-ranean region. 2. **capers,** *pl.* the green flower buds of this shrub, pickled and used for seasoning.

cap i tal[1] (kap′ə təl), *n.* 1. city where the govern-ment of a country or State is located. 2. A, B, C, D, or any similar large letter. 3. amount of money or property that a company or a person uses in carrying on a busi-ness. —*adj.* 1. having to do with capital. 2. im-portant; leading. 3. main. 4. excellent. 5. involving death; punishable by death: *Murder is a capital crime in most countries.*

cap i tal[2] (kap′ə təl), *n.* the top part of a column or pillar.

care ful (kãr′fəl), *adj.* 1. taking pains; watchful; cautious. 2. exact; thorough. 3. *Archaic.* anxious; worried.

car nage (kär′nij), *n.* slaughter of a great number of people. [< F < Ital. *carnaggio* < L *caro* flesh]

car nal (kär′nəl), *adj.* 1. worldly; not spiritual. 2. bodily; sensual: *Gluttony and drunkenness have been called carnal vices.*

case ment (kās′mənt), *n.* 1. window opening on hinges like a door. 2. *Poetic.* any window.

ca si no (kə sē′nō), *n.* 1. a building or room for pub-lic shows, dancing, gambling, etc. 2. cassino, a card game. [< Ital. *casino*, dim. of *casa* house < L *casa*]

casque (kask), *n.* helmet.

cat a ract (kat′ə rakt), *n.* 1. a large, steep waterfall.

< = from, taken from;   cf., compare;   dial., dialect;   dim., diminutive;   pp., past participle; ppr., present participle;   pt., past tense;   ult., ultimately;   var., variant;   ?=possibly.

2. a violent rush or downpour of water; flood. 3. an opaque condition in the lens of the eye, or its capsule, that causes partial or total blindness. [< L *cataracta* < Gk. *kataraktes* < *kata-* down + *arassein* dash]

cate (kāt), *n.* *Archaic.* a delicacy; dainty.

cause way (kôz′wā′), *n.* 1. a raised road or path, usually built across wet ground, shallow water, etc. 2. a paved road; highway.

cav i ar or **cav i are** (kav′i är or kä′vi är), *n.* 1. a salty relish made from the eggs of sturgeon or other large fish. 2. **caviar to the general,** too good a thing to be appreciated by ordinary people.

ca vort (kə vôrt′), *v.* *U.S. Informal.* prance about; jump around: *The horses cavorted with excitement.*

ca vy (kā′vi), *n.* any of a group of South American rodents, the best known being the guinea pig.

cel lar age (sel′ər ij), *n.* 1. space in a cellar. 2. cellars. 3. charge for storage in a cellar.

Celt ic (sel′tik; *esp. Brit.* kel′tik), *adj.* of the Celts or their language. —*n.* the group of languages spoken by the Celts, including Irish, Gaelic, Welsh, and Breton.

cen ser (sen′sər), *n.* container in which incense is burned.

cen so ri ous (sen sô′ri əs or sen sō′ri əs), *adj.* too ready to find fault; severely critical.

cen sure (sen′shər), *n.* act of blaming; expression of disapproval; criticism. —*v.* express disapproval of; find fault with; blame; criticize. [< L *censura* < *censere* appraise]

cere ment (sēr′mənt), *n.* Usually, **cerements,** *pl.* cloth or garment in which a dead person is wrapped for burial.

chaff¹ (chaf or chäf), *n.* 1. husks of wheat, oats, rye, etc., separated from grain by threshing. 2. hay or straw cut fine for feeding cattle. 3. worthless stuff. [OE *ceaf*]

chaff² (chaf or chäf), *v.* make fun of in a good-natured way before one's face. —*n.* good-natured joking about a person to his face. [origin uncertain]

chan son (shäN sôN′), *n. French.* song.

cha os (kā′os), *n.* 1. great confusion; complete disorder: *The whirlwind left chaos behind it.* 2. the infinite space or formless matter before the universe existed.

chap fall en (chop′fôl′ən or chap′fôl′ən), *adj.* dejected; discouraged; humiliated. Also, **chopfallen.**

char y (chār′i), *adj.* 1. careful. 2. shy. 3. sparing; stingy. [OE *cearig* < *caru* care] —**Syn.** 3. frugal.

chase (chās), *v.,* **chased, chas ing.** engrave. [var. of *enchase*]

chasm (kaz′əm), *n.* a deep opening or crack in the earth; gap.

chas tise (chas tīz′), *v.* 1. punish; beat. 2. *Archaic.* correct the faults of. 3. *Archaic.* purify; refine.

chaunt (chônt or chänt), *n., v., Archaic.* chant.

che root (shə rüt′), *n.* cigar cut off square at both ends.

che val glass (shə val′ glas′), a tall mirror mounted in a frame so that it swings between its supports. [*cheval* < F *cheval* horse, support < L *caballus* horse]

chi me ra (kə mēr′ə or kī mēr′ə), *n.* 1. Often, **Chimera.** in Greek legend, a monster with a lion's head, a goat's body, and a serpent's tail, supposed to breathe out fire. 2. a horrible creature of the imagination. 3. an absurd or impossible idea; wild fancy: *The hope of changing dirt to gold was a chimera.*

chine (chīn), *n.* 1. backbone; spine. 2. piece of an animal's backbone with the meat on it, for cooking. 3. ridge.

chip (chip), *n.* 1. a small, thin piece cut or broken off. 2. place where a small, thin piece has been cut or broken off. 3. a small, thin piece of food or candy. Potato chips are fried slices of potatoes. 4. a round, flat piece used for counting in games. —*v.* 1. cut or break off in small, thin pieces. 2. shape by cutting at the surface or edge with an ax or chisel.

chi ro man cy (kī′rə man′si), *n.* palmistry; fortunetelling by examination of the hand.

chol er (kol′ər), *n.* an irritable disposition; anger.

chron i cal ly (kron′ik li), *adv.* in a chronic manner; always; constantly.

chro nom e ter (krə nom′ə tər), *n.* clock or watch that keeps very accurate time. A ship's chronometer is used in determining longitude. [< Gk. *chronos* time + E *-meter*]

churl ish (chėr′lish), *adj.* rude; surly: *a churlish reply.* —**churl′ish ly,** *adv.* —**churl′ish ness,** *n.*

cic a trice (sik′ə tris), *n.* cicatrix.

cic a trix (sik′ə triks or sə kā′triks), *n., pl.* **cic a-trix ces** (sik′e trī′sēz). 1. scar left by a healed wound. 2. scar left on a tree or plant by a fallen leaf, branch, etc. 3. scar on a seed where it was attached to the pod or seed container.

cir cum scribe (sėr′kəm skrīb′ or sėr′kəm skrīb), *v.* 1. draw a line around; mark the boundaries of. 2. surround. 3. limit; restrict: *A prisoner's activities are circumscribed.* [< L *circumscribere* < *circum* around + *scribere* write]

cir cum spect (sėr′kəm spekt), *adj.* careful; cautious; prudent. [< L *circumspectus,* pp. of *circumspicere* < *circum* around + *specere* look] —**cir′cum spect′ly,** *adv.* —**cir′cum spect′ness,** *n.*

cir cum spec tion (sėr′kəm spek′shən), *n.* care; caution; prudence.

cir cum vent (sėr′kəm vent′), *v.* 1. get the better of; defeat by trickery. 2. go around. 3. catch in a trap. [< L *circumventus,* pp. of *circumvenire* < *circum* around + *venire* come]

cit a del (sit′ə dəl or sit′ə del), *n.* 1. fortress commanding a city. 2. a strongly fortified place. 3. a strong, safe place; refuge.

cith ern (sith′ərn), *n.* a musical instrument somewhat like a guitar, popular in the 16th and 17th centuries.

cit ole (sit′ōl or si tōl′), *n.* a small musical instrument having wires stretched over a sounding board. It is played with two light hammers.

clar i on (klar′i ən), *adj.* clear and shrill. —*n.* 1. a trumpet with clear, shrill tones. 2. *Poetic.* sound made by this trumpet. 3. *Poetic.* a clear, shrill sound like it. [< Med.L *clario, -onis* < L *clarus* clear]

cleave (klēv), *v.,* **cleft** or **cleaved** or **clove, cleft** or **cleaved** or **clo ven, cleav ing.** 1. split; divide. 2. pass through; pierce; penetrate. 3. make by cutting.

clem en cy (klem′ən si), *n.* 1. mercy. 2. mildness.

cli ma ture (klī′mə chər), *n.* *Archaic.* a region or its inhabitants.

clime (klīm), *n.* *Poetic.* country; region; climate.

clos et (kloz′it), *n.* 1. a small room used for storing clothes or household supplies, such as canned food, china, or linen. 2. cupboard for holding china, linen, etc. 3. a small, private room for prayer, study, or interviews.

clout (klout), *n.* *Informal.* a hit with the hand; rap; knock; cuff. —*v.* *Informal.* hit with the hand; rap; knock; cuff.

cloy (kloi), *v.* 1. weary by too much, too sweet, or too

hat, āge, cãre, fär; let, ēqual, tėrm; it, īce; hot, ōpen, ôrder; oil, out; cup, pút, rüle, ūse; th, thin; ᵺ, then; zh, measure; ə represents *a* in about, *e* in taken, *i* in pencil, *o* in lemon, *u* in circus.

795

rich food. **2.** weary by too much of anything pleasant.

cock le (kok′əl), *n.*   an edible salt-water animal with two ridged shells that are somewhat heart-shaped.

cof fer (kôf′ər or kof′ər), *n.* **1.** box, chest, or trunk, especially one used to hold money or other valuable things. **2.** an ornamental panel in a ceiling, etc. **3. coffers,** *pl.* treasury; funds.

cog i ta tion (koj′ə tā′shən), *n.*   deep thought; pondering; meditation.

coign (koin), *n.*   a projecting corner.

col lat er al (kə lat′ər əl), *adj.* **1.** parallel; side by side. **2.** related but less important; secondary; indirect. **3.** secured by stocks, bonds, etc. —*n.*   stocks, bonds, etc., pledged as security for a loan.

come ly (kum′li), *adj.* **1.** having a pleasant appearance; attractive. **2.** fitting; suitable; proper.

com mis er a tion (kə miz′ər ā′shən), *n.*   pity; sympathy.

com mune (*v.* kə mūn′), *v.* **1.** talk intimately. **2.** receive Holy Communion. **3.** *Archaic.* share.

com mu tu al (kə mū′chü əl), *adj.*   reciprocal; mutual; united.

com pass (kum′pəs), *n.* **1.** boundary; circumference. **2.** space within limits; extent; range. **3.** range of a voice or musical instrument. —*v.* **1.** do; accomplish; get. **2.** plot; scheme.

com post (kom′pōst), *n.* **1.** mixture. **2.** mixture of leaves, manure, etc., for fertilizing land.

com pul sa to ry (kəm pəl′sə tô′ri), *adj.*   compulsory.

con cil i ate (kən sil′i āt), *v.* **1.** win over; soothe. **2.** gain (good will, regard, favor, etc.) by friendly acts. **3.** reconcile; bring into harmony.

con fed er ate (*adj., n.* kən fed′ər it or kən fed′rit; *v.* kən fed′ər āt), *adj.* joined together for a special purpose; allied. —*n.* **1.** ally; companion. **2.** accomplice; partner in crime. —*v.* join together for a special purpose; ally. [< L *confoederatus,* pp. of *confoederare* unite in a league < *com-* together + *foedus* league]

con found ed (kon′foun′did or kən foun′did), *adj.* **1.** damned. **2.** hateful; detestable.

con fute (kən fūt′), *v.* **1.** prove (an argument, testimony, etc.) to be false or incorrect. **2.** prove (a person) to be wrong; overcome by argument.

con gen i tal ly (kən jen′ə təl i), *adv.* from the time of birth.

co ny (kō′ni), *n.* **1.** rabbit fur. **2.** rabbit. **3.** a small rabbitlike animal.

con ju ra tion (kon′jù rā′shən), *n.* **1.** act of invoking by a sacred name. **2.** a magic form of words used in conjuring; magic spell. **3.** *Archaic.* a solemn appeal.

con jure (kun′jər or kon′jər *for 1-5;* kən jür′ *for 6*), *v.* **1. conjure up, a.** cause to appear in a magic way. **b.** cause to appear in the mind. **2.** compel (a spirit, devil, etc.) to appear or disappear by magic words. **3.** summon a devil, spirit, etc. **4.** cause to be or happen by magic or as if by magic. **5.** perform tricks by skill and quickness in moving the hands. **6.** make a solemn appeal to; request earnestly; entreat: *I conjure you not to betray your country.*

con science (kon′shəns), *n. Archaic.* examination of one's own thoughts and feelings. [< OF < L *conscientia* < *conscire* < *com-* + *scire* know]

con se crate (kon′sə krāt), *v.* **1.** set apart as sacred; make holy: *A church is consecrated to worship.* **2.** devote to a purpose. [< L *consecrare* < *com-* + *sacer* sacred] —**Syn.** *v.* **1.** sanctify.

con se quen tial (kon′sə kwen′shəl), *adj.* **1.** fol-

lowing as an effect; resulting. **2.** self-important; pompous.

con ster na tion (kon′stər nā′shən), *n.* great dismay; paralyzing terror or amazement.

con straint (kən strānt′), *n.* **1.** confinement. **2.** restraint. **3.** forced or unnatural manner; embarrassment. **4.** force; compulsion.

con sum mate (*v.* kon′sə māt; *adj.* kən sum′it), *v.* complete; fulfill. —*adj.* complete; perfect; in the highest degree. [< L *consummare* bring to a peak < *com-* + *summa* highest degree]

con sum ma tion (kon′sə mā′shən), *n.* completion; fulfillment.

conte (kônt; *French* kôɴt), *n.* **1.** short story; tale. **2.** formerly, short fictional tale of adventure.

con temn (kən tem′), *v.* treat with contempt; despise; scorn. [< L *contemnere* < *com-* + *temnere* disdain, originally, cut]

con ten tion (kən ten′shən), *n.* **1.** argument; dispute; quarrel. **2.** statement or point that one has argued for; statement maintained as true. **3.** disputing; quarreling. **4.** struggle; contest.

con ten tious (kən ten′shəs), *adj.* **1.** quarrelsome; fond of arguing; given to disputing. **2.** characterized by contention: *a contentious campaign.*

con tin gen cy (kən tin′jən si), *n.* **1.** uncertainty of occurrence. **2.** an accidental happening; unexpected event. **3.** a happening or event depending on something that is uncertain; possibility: *The explorer carried supplies for every contingency.*

con tin gent (kən tin′jənt), *adj.* **1.** conditional; depending on something not certain. **2.** liable to happen or not to happen; uncertain. **3.** accidental; unexpected. —*n.* **1.** share of soldiers, laborers, etc., furnished to a force from other sources. **2.** group that is part of a larger group. **3.** an accidental or unexpected event. [< L *contingens, -entis* touching, ppr. of *contingere*]

con tro vert (kon′trə vèrt or kon′trə vèrt′), *v.* **1.** dispute; deny; oppose: *The statement of the last witness controverts the evidence of the first two.* **2.** discuss; debate. [< L *contro-* against + *vertere* turn]

con tu me ly (kon′tü mə li, kon′tü mə li, kən tü′mə li, or kən tü′mə li), *n.* **1.** insolent contempt; insulting words or actions; humiliating treatment. **2.** a humiliating insult.

con ver sant (kən vèr′sənt or kon′vər sənt), *adj.* familiar by use or study; acquainted.

con verse (*v.* kən vèrs′; *n.* kon′vèrs), *v.* talk informally together. —*n.* conversation.

con vey ance (kən vā′əns), *n.* **1.** act of carrying; transportation; transmission. **2.** thing that carries people and goods; vehicle. **3.** communication. **4.** transfer of the ownership of property from one person to another. **5.** a written statement that shows such a transfer; deed. **6.** *Archaic.* convoy.

con vo ca tion (kon′və kā′shən), *n.* **1.** a calling together; an assembling by a summons. **2.** assembly; number of persons met in answer to a summons.

cope (kōp), *n.* **1.** a long cape worn by priests during certain religious rites. **2.** anything like a cope; cloaklike covering, such as a canopy, a high, arched roof, or the sky.

co pi ous (kō′pi əs), *adj.* **1.** plentiful; abundant. **2.** containing much matter.

cop pice (kop′is), *n.* a thicket of small bushes, trees, shrubs, etc.

cor nice (kôr′nis), *n.* **1.** an ornamental molding that projects along the top of a wall, pillar, building, etc.

< = from, taken from;   cf., compare;   dial., dialect;   dim., diminutive;   pp., past participle; ppr., present participle;   pt., past tense;   ult., ultimately;   var., variant;   ?=possibly.

2. molding around the walls of a room just below the ceiling.

cor o nal (*n.* kôr′ə nəl or kor′ə nəl; *adj.* kə rō′nəl, kôr′ə nəl, or kor′ə nəl), *n.* **1.** crown or coronet. **2.** garland.

cor o net (kôr′ə net or kor′ə net), *n.* **1.** a small crown worn as a mark of high rank. **2.** circle of gold, jewels, or flowers worn around the head as an ornament.

cor po re al (kôr pô′ri əl or kôr pō′ri əl), *adj.* **1.** of or for the body; bodily. **2.** material; tangible. [< L *corporeus* < *corpus* body]

corse (kôrs), *n.* *Archaic* and *Poetic.* corpse.

corse let (kôrs′lit *for 1;* kôr′sə let′ *for 2*), *n.* **1.** armor for the body. **2.** a woman's undergarment somewhat like a corset.

cos mic (koz′mik), *adj.* **1.** of or belonging to the cosmos; having to do with the whole universe. **2.** vast. [< Gk. *kosmikos* < *kosmos* order, world]

co til lion (kə til′yən), *n.* *Esp. U.S.* a dance with complicated steps and much changing of partners, led by one couple.

coul ter (kōl′tər), *n.* a sharp blade or disc on a plow.

coun te nance (koun′tə nəns), *n.* **1.** expression of the face. **2.** face; features. **3.** approval; encouragement. **4.** calmness; composure. —*v.* approve or encourage.

cov ert (kuv′ərt), *adj.* secret; hidden; disguised. —*n.* **1.** shelter; hiding place. **2.** thicket in which animals hide.

coz en (kuz′ən), *v.* cheat; deceive; beguile.

crank (krangk), *n.* **1.** part or handle of a machine connected at right angles to a shaft to transmit motion. **2.** humorous turn of speech or thought. **3.** *Informal.* a cross or ill-tempered person.

cra ven (krā′vən), *adj.* cowardly. —*n.* coward.

cre dent (krē′dənt), *adj.* believing; inclined to believe.

cre ta ceous (kri tā′shəs), *adj.* **1.** like chalk; containing chalk. **2. Cretaceous,** of or having to do with the geological period when most of the chalk deposits were made or with rocks formed in this period. [< L *cretaceus* < *creta* chalk]

cre tonne (kri ton′ or krē′ton), *n.* a strong cotton cloth with designs printed in colors on one or both sides, used for curtains, furniture covers, etc.

crone (krōn), *n.* a withered old woman.

cudg el (kuj′əl), *n.* a short, thick stick used as a weapon; club. —*v.* **1.** beat with a cudgel. **2. cudgel one's brains,** try very hard to think.

cuisse (kwis), *n.* piece of armor to protect the thigh.

cull (kul), *v.* **1.** pick out; select: *The lawyer culled important facts from the mass of evidence.* **2.** pick over; make selections from.

cum ber (kum′bər), *v.* **1.** burden; trouble: *Household cares cumber a busy mother.* **2.** hinder; hamper. —*n.* hindrance. [probably < OF *combrer* impede < *combre* barrier < Celtic]

curd (kėrd), *n.* Often, **curds,** *pl.* the thick part of milk which separates from the watery part when milk sours.

cur lew (kėr′lü), *n.*, *pl.* **-lews** or (*esp. collectively*) **-lew.** a wading bird with a long, thin bill.

cut ting (kut′ing), *n.* **1.** thing cut off or cut out. **2.** place cut through high ground for a road, track, etc.

cy no sure (sī′nə shür or sin′ə shür), *n.* **1.** center of attraction, interest, or attention. **2.** something used for guidance or direction.

cy press lawn (sī′prəs lôn′), *n.* a transparent material. When black it is used for mourning garments.

da is (dā′is; *esp. Brit.* dās), *n.* a raised platform at one end of a hall or large room. A throne, seats of honor, a lecture desk, etc., are set on a dais.

dal li ance (dal′i əns), *n.* **1.** flirtation. **2.** a playing; trifling. **3.** amorous play.

dark ling (därk′ling), *adv.* in the dark. —*adj.* dark.

dearth (dėrth), *n.* **1.** scarcity; lack; too small a supply. **2.** scarcity of food; famine. **3.** *Archaic.* costliness; highness of price.

de bauch er y (di bôch′ər i or di bôch′ri), *n.* **1.** excessive indulgence in sensual pleasures. **2.** seduction from duty, virtue, or morality.

deb o nair or **deb o naire** (deb′ə nãr′), *adj.* **1.** gay; cheerful. **2.** pleasant; courteous. [< OF *debonaire* < *de bon aire* of good disposition]

de bouch (di büsh′), *v.* **1.** come out from a narrow or confined place into open country: *The soldiers debouched from the valley into the plain.* **2.** come forth; emerge. [< F *deboucher* < *dé-* parting from (< L *dis-*) + *bouche* mouth < L *bucca*]

dé clas sé (dā′klə sā′), *adj.* lowered in social status; having lost class.

de duc tion (di duk′shən), *n.* **1.** act of taking away; subtraction. **2.** amount deducted. **3.** inference from a general rule or principle. A person using deduction reasons from general laws to particular cases.
→ **Deduction, induction** are names of opposite processes of reasoning, the two ways in which we think. **Deduction** applies to the process by which one starts with a general principle that is accepted as true, applies it to a particular case, and arrives at a conclusion that is true if the starting principle was true: *All animals die; this is an animal; therefore, this will die.* **Induction** applies to the process by which one collects many particular cases, finds out by experiment what is common to all of them, and forms a general rule or principle which is probably true: *Every animal I have tested died; probably all animals die.*

def er en tial (def′ər en′shəl), *adj.* showing a yielding in opinion, judgment, wishes, etc.; respectful. —**def′er en′tial ly,** *adv.*

de file[1] (di fīl′), *v.* **1.** make filthy or dirty; make disgusting in any way. **2.** corrupt. [alteration of *defoul* (< OF *defouler* trample down, violate) after obsolete *file* befoul < OE *fȳlan* < *fūl* foul] —**de fil′er,** *n.*

de file[2] (di fīl′ or dē′fīl), *n.* steep and narrow valley. [< F *défilé,* special use of pp. of *défiler* march by files < *dé-* off + *file* file[1]]

de lu sive (di lü′siv), *adj.* misleading; deceptive; false.

de mean (di mēn′), *v.* behave or conduct (oneself).

de mesne (di mān′ or di mēn′), *n.* **1.** in law, the possession of land as one's own. **2.** land or land and buildings possessed as one's own. **3.** house and land belonging to a lord and used by him. **4.** domain; realm. [< AF *demesne,* a respelling of OF *demeine* domain. Doublet of DOMAIN.]

dem i rep (dem′i rep′), *n.* woman of doubtful reputation.

de mise (di mīz′), *n.* **1.** death. **2.** transfer of an estate by a will or lease. **3.** transfer of royal power by death or abdication.

dep re cate (dep′rə kāt), *v.* express strong disapproval of; protest against: *Lovers of peace deprecate war.* [< L *deprecari* plead in excuse, avert by prayer < *de-* + *precari* pray] —**dep′re cat′ing ly,** *adv.* —**dep′re ca′tor,** *n.*

dep re ca tion (dep′rə kā′shən), *n.* a strong expression of disapproval; protesting against something.

dep re ca to ry (dep′rə kə tô′ri or dep′rə kə tō′ri), *adj.* deprecating.

---

hat, āge, cãre, fär; let, ēqual, tėrm; it, īce; hot, ōpen, ôrder; oil, out; cup, pùt, rüle, ūse; th, thin; ŦH, then; zh, measure; ə represents *a* in about, *e* in taken, *i* in pencil, *o* in lemon, *u* in circus.

dep u ty (dep′ū ti), *n.*   person appointed to do the work of or to act in the place of another.

der e lict (der′ə likt), *adj.*   1. abandoned; deserted; forsaken: *a derelict ship.* 2. failing in one's duty; negligent. —*n.* 1. ship abandoned at sea. 2. any deserted person or thing.

de scry (di skrī′), *v.*   catch sight of; be able to see; make out: *The shipwrecked sailor at last descried an island far away on the horizon.*

de spoil (di spoil′), *v.*   rob; plunder.

des ue tude (des′wə tüd or des′wə tūd), *n.*   disuse. [< F < L *desuetudo* < *de-* dis- + *suescere* accustom]

des ul to ry (des′əl tô′ri or des′əl tō′ri), *adj.* jumping from one thing to another; unconnected. [< L *desultorius* of a leaper, ult. < *de-* down + *salire* leap]

di a dem (dī′ə dem), *n.* 1. crown. 2. an ornamental band of cloth formerly worn as a crown. 3. royal power, authority, or dignity [< L < Gk. *diadema* < *diadeein* < *dia-* across + *deein* bind]

di a pa son (dī′ə pā′zən or dī′ə pā′sən), *n.* 1. harmony. 2. melody; strain. 3. a swelling musical sound. 4. the whole range of a voice or instrument. 5. a fixed standard of musical pitch. [< L < Gk. *diapason* < *dia pason* (*chordon*) across all (the notes of the scale)]

dight (dīt), *v.*, **dight** or **dight ed, dight ing.** *Archaic.* 1. dress; adorn. 2. equip.

dint (dint), *n.* 1. force: *By dint of hard work the man became successful.* 2. dent.

dire (dīr), *adj.*   causing great fear or suffering; dreadful. [< L *dirus*]

dirge (dėrj), *n.*   a funeral song or tune.

dis com fit (dis kum′fit), *v.* 1. overthrow completely; defeat; rout. 2. defeat the plans or hopes of; frustrate. 3. embarrass greatly; confuse; disconcert. —**Syn.** 1. vanquish. 3. baffle, abash.

dis con cert ed (dis′kən sėr′tid), *adj.*   disturbed; confused. —**dis′con cert′ed ly,** *adv.*

dis cre tion (dis kresh′ən), *n.* 1. freedom to judge or choose: *Making final plans was left to the president's discretion.* 2. quality of being discreet; good judgment; carefulness in speech or action; wise caution.

dis in ter est ed (dis in′tər is tid, dis in′tris tid, or dis in′tər es′tid), *adj.*   free from selfish motives; impartial; fair.

> **Disinterested** and **uninterested** should not be confused. *Disinterested* means having no selfish interest or personal feelings in a matter and therefore having no reason or desire to be anything but strictly impartial and fair: *A judge should be disinterested.* *Uninterested* means not interested in any way, having no concern or feelings about the matter and paying no attention: *An uninterested boy can spoil a class.*

dis par age ment (dis par′ij mənt), *n.* 1. act of belittling or discrediting. 2. something that lowers a thing or person in worth or importance.

dis qui si tion (dis′kwə zish′ən), *n.*   a long or formal speech or writing about a subject.

dis sem ble (di sem′bəl), *v.* 1. disguise or hide (one's real feelings, thoughts, plans, etc.). 2. conceal one's motives, etc. 3. pretend; feign. 4. disregard; ignore. —**dis sem′bler,** *n.*

dis sim u la tion (di sim′ū lā′shən), *n.*   act of dissembling; hypocrisy; pretense; deceit.

dis tem per (dis tem′pər), *n.* 1. an infectious disease of dogs and other animals. 2. sickness of the mind or body. 3. disturbance.

dis tich (dis′tik), *n.*   two lines of verse forming a stanza, and usually making complete sense; couplet.

dis tract (dis trakt′), *adj. Archaic.* distracted; mad; insane.

dis traught (dis trôt′), *adj.* 1. in a state of mental conflict and confusion. 2. crazed.

di vers (dī′vərz), *adj.* several different; various.

div i na tion (div′ə nā′shən), *n.* 1. act of foreseeing the future or foretelling the unknown. 2. a skillful guess or prediction.

dole (dōl), *n.* 1. portion of money, food, etc., given in charity. 2. a small portion. 3. relief money given by a government to unemployed workers. —*v.* 1. deal out in portions to the poor. 2. give in small portions.

dole ful (dōl′fəl), *adj.* sad; mournful; dreary; dismal.

dot age (dōt′ij), *n.* 1. weak-minded and childish condition caused by old age. 2. *Archaic.* foolish utterance; folly.

dow er (dou′ər), *n.* 1. a widow's share for life of her dead husband's property. 2. dowry. 3. a natural gift, talent, or quality; endowment. —*v.* provide with a dower.

drab (drab), *n.* 1. a dirty, untidy woman. 2. prostitute.

drap er (drāp′ər), *n. Esp. Brit.* dealer in cloth or dry goods.

draught (draft or dräft), *n.* 1. act of drinking. 2. amount taken in one drink. [ME *draht* < OE *dragan* draw]

drone (drōn), *n.* 1. a male honeybee. Drones do not work. 2. person not willing to work; idler; loafer. —*v.* spend time idly; loaf.

dross (drôs or dros), *n.* 1. waste or scum that comes to the surface of melting metals. 2. waste material; rubbish.

duc at (duk′ət), *n.*   a gold or silver coin formerly used in some European countries.

dudg eon (duj′ən), *n.* 1. anger; resentment. 2. in high dudgeon, very angry; resentful.

duff er (duf′ər), *n. Slang.* a useless, clumsy, or stupid person.

dust dev il (dust′ dev′əl), *n.*   a moving column of sand.

eb on (eb′ən), *n.* ebony. —*adj. Poetic* 1. made of ebony. 2. dark; black.

ef fu sive (i fū′siv), *adj.* showing too much feeling; too emotional in expression. —**ef fu′sive ly,** *adv.* —**ef fu′sive ness,** *n.*

eft (eft), *adv.* again; afterwards.

eg lan tine (eg′lən tin or eg′lən tēn), *n.* a wild rose with a tall, prickly stem and single, pink flowers; sweetbrier.

eke (ēk), *adv., conj. Archaic.* also; moreover.

el o cu tion ist (el′ə kū′shən ist), *n.* 1. person skilled in elocution, the art of public speaking. 2. teacher of elocution.

em bla zon (em blā′zən), *v.* 1. display conspicuously; picture in bright colors. 2. decorate; adorn. 3. praise highly; honor publicly.

em bowed (em bōd′), *adj.* bent like a bow; arched.

en clave (en′klāv), *n.* country or district surrounded by territory of another country. [< F *enclave* < *enclaver* enclose]

en er vate (en′ər vāt), *v.* lessen the vigor or strength of; weaken: *A hot, damp climate enervates people who are not used to it.* [< L *enervare* < *ex-* away + *nervus* sinew, nerve]

en graff (en graf′), *v.* 1. insert or graft (a shoot from one tree or plant) into or on another. 2. add permanently; implant.

en join (en join′), *v.* order; direct; urge.

< = from, taken from;   cf., compare;   dial., dialect;   dim., diminutive;   pp., past participle;   ppr., present participle;   pt., past tense;   ult., ultimately;   var., variant;   ?=possibly.

en sconce (en skons'), *v.* **1.** shelter safely; hide. **2.** settle comfortably and firmly: *The cat ensconced itself in the armchair.*

en tente (än tänt'), *n. French.* an understanding; agreement between two or more governments.

en toil (en toil'), *v.* to ensnare; trap.

e qui nox (ē'kwə noks), *n.* either of the two times in the year when the center of the sun crosses the celestial equator, and day and night are of equal length all over the earth, occurring about March 21 and September 22. [< Med.L *equinoxium* < L *aequinoctium* < *aequus* equal + *nox* night]

eq ui page (ek'wə pij), *n.* **1.** carriage. **2.** carriage with its horses, driver, and servants. **3.** equipment; outfit.

e quiv o cal (i kwiv'ə kəl), *adj.* **1.** having two or more meanings; intentionally vague or ambiguous. **2.** undecided; uncertain. **3.** questionable; rousing suspicion [< LL *aequivocus* ambiguous < L *aequus* equal + *vocare* call] **—Syn. 1.** doubtful. **—Ant. 1.** clear, evident, definite.

e quiv o ca tion (i kwiv'ə kā'shən), *n.* **1.** use of ambiguous expressions in order to mislead. **2.** an intentionally vague expression.

er rant (er'ənt), *adj.* **1.** traveling in search of adventure; wandering. **2.** mistaken; incorrect.

Erse (èrs), *n.* **1.** the Celtic language of the Scottish Highlanders; Scotch Gaelic. **2.** less accurately, the Celtic language of Ireland; Irish Gaelic. **—adj.** of either of these languages. [Scottish var. of *Irish*]

erst (èrst), *adv. Archaic.* formerly; long ago.

es carp ment (es kärp'mənt), *n.* **1.** a steep slope; cliff. **2.** ground made into a steep slope as part of a fortification.

es cri toire (es'krə twär' or es'krə twär), *n.* a writing desk. [< F < LL *scriptorium* < L *scribere* write]

es cutch eon (es kuch'ən), *n.* shield or shield-shaped surface on which a coat of arms is put. [< OF *escuchon* < L *scutum* shield]

Escutcheon

es py (es pī'), *v.* see; spy.

es thet i cism (es thet'ə siz əm), *n.* doctrine or cult of beauty and good taste rather than usefulness.

e ther (ē'thər), *n.* **1.** a colorless, strong-smelling liquid that burns and evaporates readily. Its fumes cause unconsciousness when deeply inhaled. **2.** the upper regions of space beyond the earth's atmosphere; clear sky. **3.** the invisible, elastic substance supposed to be distributed evenly through all space and to conduct light waves, electric waves, etc. [< L *aether* < Gk. *aither* upper air]

ewe (ū), *n.* a female sheep.

ex ac er bate (eg zas'ər bāt or eks as'ər bāt), *v.* **1.** make worse; aggravate (pain, disease, anger). **2.** irritate (a person's feelings).

ex cise man (ek sīz'mən), *n.* official of the British government who collects excise taxes and enforces the laws having to do with them.

ex e cra tion (ek'sə krā'shən), *n.* **1.** abhorrence; loathing; detestation. **2.** a cursing. **3.** a curse: *The mob shouted angry execrations.* **4.** person or thing execrated.

ex hort (eg zôrt'), *v.* urge strongly; advise or warn earnestly. [< L *exhortari* < *ex-* + *hortari* urge strongly]

ex hor ta tion (eg'zôr tā'shən or ek'sôr tā'shən), *n.* strong urging; earnest advice or warning.

ex i gence (ek'sə jəns), *n.* exigency.

ex i gen cy (ek'sə jən si), *n.* **1.** Usually, **exigencies,** *pl.* an urgent need; demand for immediate action or at-

tention: *The exigencies of business kept him from leaving town.* **2.** situation demanding immediate attention.

ex pos tu late (eks pos'chü lāt), *v.* reason earnestly with a person, protesting against something he means to do or has done. **2.** discuss; examine.

ex pur gate (eks'pər gāt), *v.* remove objectionable passages or words from (a book, letter, etc.); purify. [< L *expurgare* < *ex-* out + *purgare* purge]

ex ten u ate (eks ten'ū āt), *v.* **1.** make (a fault, offense, etc.) seem less; excuse in part: *His foreign bringing-up extenuates his faulty pronunciation.* **2.** make thin or weak; diminish. [< L *extenuare* < *ex-* out + *tenuis* thin]

ey as (ī'əs), *n.* **1.** a young hawk taken from the nest for training as a falcon. **2.** nestling.

fag[1] (fag), *v.,* **fagged, fag ging,** *n.* **—v. 1.** work hard or until wearied: *Tom fagged away at his arithmetic.* **2.** tire by work: *The horse was fagged.* **3.** act as a fag. **—n. 1.** *Brit.* hard, uninteresting work. **2.** person who does hard work. **3.** boy who waits on an older boy in English schools.

fag[2] (fag), *n. Esp. Brit. Slang.* cigarette.

fain (fān), *Archaic* and *Poetic.* **—adv.** by choice; gladly. **—adj. 1.** glad; willing. **2.** eager; desirous.

fal low (fal'ō), *adj.* uncultivated; inactive. **—n. 1.** land plowed and left unseeded for a season or more. **2.** the plowing of land without seeding it for a season in order to destroy weeds, improve the soil, etc.

fane (fān), *n. Archaic* and *Poetic.* temple; church.

fat u ous (fach'ü əs), *adj.* stupid but self-satisfied; foolish; silly. [< L *fatuus* foolish]

fawn (fôn), *v.* **1.** cringe and bow; act slavishly: *Many flattering relatives fawned on the rich old man.* **2.** of dogs, etc., show fondness by crouching, wagging the tail, licking the hand, etc.

fay[1] (fā), *n.* fairy. [< OF *fae, fee,* ult. < L *fatum* (thing) spoken (i.e., by the gods), pp. neut. of *fari* speak]

fay[2] (fā), *n. Archaic.* faith. [< OF *fei* < L *fides.* Doublet of FAITH.]

fe al ty (fē'əl ti), *n.* **1.** loyalty and duty owed by a vassal to his feudal lord. **2.** loyalty; faithfulness; allegiance.

fe lic i ty (fə lis'ə ti), *n.* **1.** happiness; bliss. **2.** good fortune; blessing. **3.** a pleasing aptness in expression; appropriateness; grace. [< L *felicitas* < *felix* happy]

fell (fel), *adj.* **1.** cruel; fierce; terrible: *a fell blow.* **2.** deadly; destructive: *a fell disease.*

fen (fen), *n. Brit.* marsh; swamp; bog [OE *fenn*]

fet ter (fet'ər), *n.* **1.** chain or shackle for the feet to prevent escape. **2.** Usually, **fetters,** *pl.* anything that shackles or binds; restraint. **—v. 1.** bind with fetters. **2.** bind; restrain. **—Syn. v. 2.** confine, hamper, impede.

fi at (fī'ət or fī'at), *n.* **1.** an authoritative order or command; decree. **2.** sanction. [< L *fiat* let it be done]

fine (fīn), *n.* **1.** sum of money paid as a punishment. **2. in fine,** *a.* finally. *b.* in a few words; briefly. **—v.** cause to pay a fine.

fin ger (fing'gər), *v.* steal.

fi nite (fī'nīt), *adj.* having limits or bounds; not infinite: *Death ends man's finite existence.* **—n.** something finite. [< L *finitus,* pp. of *finire* finish]

fir ma ment (fèr'mə mənt), *n.* arch of the heavens; sky.

fish mon ger (fish'mung'gər or fish'mong'gər), *n. Esp. Brit.* dealer in fish.

flag (flag), *v.* get tired; grow weak.

flag on (flag'ən), *n.* **1.** container for liquids, usually

---

hat, āge, cãre, fär; let, ēqual, tèrm; it, īce; hot, ōpen, ôrder; oil, out; cup, pùt, rüle, ūse; th, thin; ŦH, then; zh, measure; ə represents *a* in about, *e* in taken, *i* in pencil, *o* in lemon, *u* in circus.

having a handle and a spout, and often a cover. **2.** a large bottle, holding about two quarts. **3.** contents of a flagon. [< OF *flascon*. Akin to *flask*.]

flor in (flôr/ən or flor/ən), *n.* **1.** an English silver coin worth 2 shillings. **2.** a gold coin issued at Florence in 1252. **3.** any of various gold or silver coins used in different countries of Europe since then.

fob (fob), *n.* **1.** a small pocket in trousers or breeches to hold a watch, etc. **2.** a short watch chain, ribbon, etc., that hangs out of a watch pocket. **3.** ornament worn at the end of such a chain, ribbon, etc.

fo li ate (*adj.* fō/li it or fō/li āt; *v.* fō/li āt), *adj.* having leaves; covered with leaves. —*v.* **1.** put forth leaves. **2.** decorate with leaflike ornaments. [< L *foliatus* < *folia* leaves]

fond (fond), *adj.* **1.** liking. **2.** loving. **3.** loving foolishly or too much. **4.** cherished. **5.** *Archaic.* foolish; foolishly ready to believe or hope. [ME *fonned*, pp. of *fonne(n)* be foolish; origin uncertain] —**fond/ly,** *adv.* —**fond/ness,** *n.*

fop per y (fop/ər i), *n.* foppish behavior; fine clothes, affected manners, etc., suitable for a fop, a vain, empty-headed man.

fore land (fôr/land/ or fōr/land/), *n.* cape; headland; promontory.

for sooth (fôr sūth/), *adv.* *Archaic.* in truth; indeed. [OE *forsōth* < *for* for + *sōth* sooth, truth]

fraught (frôt), *adj.* loaded; filled: *A battlefield is fraught with horror.* [pp. of obsolete *fraught* load, v. use of n., < MDutch or MLG *vracht* freight]

fret[1] (fret), *v.* **1.** be peevish, unhappy, discontented, or worried. **2.** make peevish, unhappy, discontented, or worried. **3.** eat away; wear; rub. **4.** to be agitated; to be in commotion: *The stream fretted over the rocks.* [OE *fretan* eat]

fret[2] (fret), *n.* an ornamental pattern made of straight lines bent or combined at angles. —*v.* decorate with fretwork. [? < OF *frete*]

front (frunt), *n.* **1.** foremost part. **2.** part that faces forward. **3.** thing fastened or worn on the front. **4.** forehead.

frounce (frouns), *v.* *Archaic.* to frizzle or curl (the hair).

fur bish (fér/bish), *v.* **1.** polish. **2.** restore to good condition.

gall[1] (gôl), *n.* **1.** a bitter yellow, brown, or greenish liquid secreted by the liver and stored in the gall bladder. **2.** gall bladder. **3.** anything very bitter or harsh. **4.** bitterness; hate. [OE *galla*]

gall[2] (gôl), *v.* **1.** make or become sore by rubbing. **2.** annoy; irritate. —*n.* **1.** a sore spot on the skin caused by rubbing. **2.** cause of annoyance or irritation. [extended use of *gall*[1]]

gam bol (gam/bəl), *n.* a running and jumping about in play; caper; frolic. —*v.* frisk about; run and jump about, as in play. [< F *gambade* < Ital. *gambata* < *gamba* leg]

gan net (gan/it), *n.* a large, fish-eating sea bird with long, pointed wings.

gar ner (gär/nər), *v.* gather and store away: *Wheat is cut and garnered at harvest time.* —*n.* **1.** storehouse for grain. **2.** a store of anything.

gar ni ture (gär/nə chər), *n.* decoration; garnish.

gauche (gōsh), *adj.* awkward; clumsy; tactless.

ge nie (jē/ni), *n.* spirit; jinni: *When Aladdin rubbed his lamp, the genie came and did what Aladdin asked.*

ge ni i (jē/ni i), *n.* a pl. of *genius.*

gen ius (jēn/yəs or jē/ni əs), *n., pl.* **gen ius es** *for 1-4,* **ge ni i** *for 5-7.* **1.** very great natural power of mind. **2.** person having such power. **3.** great natural ability of some special kind. **4.** the special character or spirit of a person, nation, age, language, etc. **5.** a guardian spirit of a person, place, institution, etc. **6.** either of two spirits, one good and one evil, supposed to influence a person's fate. **7.** spirit; jinn. [< L *genius* tutelary spirit, male generative power, ult. < *gignere* beget]

gen try (jen/tri), *n.* **1.** people of good family and social position. The English gentry are next below the nobility. **2.** people of any particular class. **3.** qualities appropriate to people of good family, such as courtesy.

gibe (jīb), *v., n.* jeer; scoff; sneer. Also, **jibe.** [? < OF *giber* handle roughly < *gibe* staff] —**Syn.** *v.* mock, taunt.

gie (gē or gi), *v.* British Dialect or Scottish. give.

gir dle (gér/dəl), *n.* **1.** belt, sash, cord, etc., worn around the waist, often used as a means of carrying things, such as keys or a sword. **2.** anything that surrounds or encloses. **3.** support like a corset worn about the hips or waist.

glebe (glēb), *n.* *Poetic.* soil; earth; field.

gloam (glōm), *n.* *Poetic.* twilight; gloaming.

goad (gōd), *n.* **1.** a sharp-pointed stick for driving cattle, etc.; **2.** anything that drives or urges one on. —*v.* drive or urge on; act as a goad to.

gran dam (gran/dam), *n.* **1.** grandmother. **2.** an old woman.

gran dame (gran/dām), *n.* grandam.

grange (grānj), *n.* **1.** farm with its buildings. **2.** farmhouse with its barn and other buildings. [< OF < VL *granica* < L *granum* grain]

greave (grēv), *n.* armor for the leg below the knee.

grif fin (grif/ən), *n.* a mythical creature with the head, wings, and forelegs of an eagle, and the body, hind legs, and tail of a lion.

grif fon (grif/ən), *n.* griffin.

gris ly (griz/li), *adj.* frightful; horrible; ghastly.

griz zled (griz/əld), *adj.* **1.** grayish; gray. **2.** gray-haired.

grog blos som (grog/ blos/əm), *n.* *Informal.* a redness or an eruption on the nose or face of someone who drinks liquor to excess.

gross (grōs), *adj.* **1.** with nothing taken out; whole; entire. **2.** very bad; easy to see: *She makes gross errors in pronouncing words.* **3.** coarse; vulgar: *Her manners are too gross for a lady.* **4.** thick; heavy.

grouse (grous), *n., pl.* **grouse.** a game bird with feathered legs. The prairie chicken, sage hen, and ruffed grouse of the United States are different kinds.

gut (gut), *n.* a narrow channel or gully.

gyre (jīr), *n.* a circular or spiral form.

hab er dash er (hab/ər dash/ər) *n.* **1.** *U.S.* dealer in men's furnishings, such as hats, ties, shirts, socks, etc. **2.** dealer in small articles, such as buttons, needles, trimmings, etc.

hab er dash er y (hab/ər dash/ər i or hab/ər dash/-ri), *n.* **1.** articles sold by a haberdasher. **2.** shop of a haberdasher.

hab it (hab/it), *n.* **1.** usual way of acting. **2.** the distinctive dress or costume worn by members of a religious order. **3.** dress; attire; garb. **4.** *Archaic.* piece of apparel; garment.

haft (haft or häft), *n.* handle (of a knife, sword, etc.). —*v.* furnish with a handle or hilt; set in a haft.

hag i ol o gy (hag/i ol/ə ji or hā/ji ol/ə ji), *n.* **1.** lit-

---

< = from, taken from;   cf., compare;   dial., dialect;   dim., diminutive;   pp., past participle; ppr., present participle;   pt., past tense;   ult., ultimately;   var., variant;   ?=possibly.

hamlet   incipient

erature that deals with the lives and legends of saints. **2.** book on this subject. **3.** list of saints. [< Gk. *hagios* holy + E -*logy*]

ham let (ham′lit), *n.*   a small village; little group of houses in the country.

hap ly (hap′li), *adv.* *Archaic.* perhaps; by chance.

har bin ger (här′bin jər), *n.*   one that goes ahead to announce another's coming; forerunner: *The robin is a harbinger of spring.* —*v.* announce beforehand.

hard (härd), *adj.* **1.** solid and firm. **2.** difficult. **3.** causing much trouble, care, etc.; severe. —*adv.* **1.** so as to be solid and firm. **2.** with effort. **3.** close; near.

har lot (här′lət), *n.* prostitute. [< OF *harlot* vagabond]

har lot ry (här′lət ri), *n.* prostitution.

har mo ni um (här mō′ni əm), *n.* a small organ with metal reeds.

har ness (här′nis), *n.*   *Archaic.* armor for a knight, soldier, or horse.

har row (har′ō), *n.*   a heavy frame with iron teeth or upright disks. —*v.* **1.** draw a harrow over (land, etc.). **2.** hurt; wound. **3.** distress; torment.

hart (härt), *n.*, *pl.* **harts** or (*esp. collectively*) **hart.** a male deer; stag. A hart is usually a male red deer after its fifth year.

hatch ment (hach′mənt), *n.*   a square tablet set diagonally, bearing the coat of arms of a dead person. [earlier *atcheament*, *achement*, var. of *achievement*]

hay cock (hā′kok′), *n.* *Esp. Brit.*   a small, cone-shaped pile of hay in a field.

Heb ri des (heb′rə dēz), *n.pl.*   group of Scotch islands off NW Scotland.

hec tic (hek′tik), *adj.* **1.** flushed. **2.** feverish.

hest (hest), *n.* *Archaic.* behest; command.

het (het), *n.* *Dialect.* heat.

hi er ar chy (hī′ər är′ki), *n.* organization of persons or things that has higher and lower ranks.

high day (hī′ dā′), *n.* holy or feast day.

hin ter land (hin′tər land′), *n.* **1.** land or district behind a coast; back country. **2.** remote parts; background.

hire ling (hīr′ling), *n.* **1.** person who works only for money, without interest or pride in the task. **2.** person hired to do whatever another orders him to do. —*adj.* to be had for hire; mercenary.

hist (hist), *v.*   to say "Hist" to or to urge by, or as if by, that sound.

hoar (hôr or hōr), *adj.* **1.** white or light gray. **2.** white or gray with age. **3.** old; ancient.

hob (hob), *n.* shelf at the back or side of a fireplace.

hock-cart (hok′ kärt′), *n.*   the last cart loaded at harvest.

ho mon y mous (hō mon′ə mus), *adj.* alike; referring to people, words, etc., that are alike.

hulk (hulk), *n.* **1.** body of an old or worn-out ship. **2.** ship used as a prison. **3.** a big, clumsy person or thing.

hus band (huz′bənd), *n.* **1.** married man. **2.** *Archaic.* manager. —*v.* **1.** manage carefully; be saving of. **2.** marry. **3.** *Archaic.* till (soil); cultivate (plants).

hus band ry (huz′bənd ri), *n.* **1.** farming. **2.** management of one's affairs or resources. **3.** careful management; thrift.

hy me ne al (hī′mə nē′əl), *adj.*   having to do with marriage. —*n.* a wedding song.

id i om (id′i əm), *n.* **1.** phrase or expression whose meaning cannot be understood from the ordinary mean-

ings of the words in it: *"How do you do?"* and *"I have caught cold"* are English idioms. **2.** dialect. **3.** a people's way of expressing themselves: *The French idiom "of a rapidity" means "rapid."* [< LL < Gk. *idioma*, ult. < *idios* one's own]

ig no ble (ig nō′bəl), *adj.* **1.** mean; base; without honor. **2.** of low birth. [< L *ignobilis* < *in-* not + OL *gnobilis* noble]

ig no min i ous (ig′nə min′i əs), *adj.* **1.** shameful; disgraceful; dishonorable; humiliating. **2.** contemptible.

ig no min y (ig′nə min′i), *n.* **1.** dishonor. **2.** shameful action or conduct.

im pal pa ble (im pal′pə bəl), *adj.* **1.** that cannot be perceived by the sense of touch: *Sunbeams are impalpable.* **2.** very hard for the mind to grasp.

im pec ca ble (im pek′ə bəl), *adj.* **1.** faultless. **2.** sinless. [< LL *impeccabilis* < *in-* not + *peccare* sin]

im pe ri ous (im pēr′i əs), *adj.* **1.** haughty; arrogant; domineering; overbearing. **2.** necessary; urgent. [< L *imperiosus* commanding] —**Syn. 1.** dictatorial.

im pe tus (im′pə təs), *n.* **1.** force with which a moving body tends to maintain its velocity and overcome resistance. **2.** a driving force; incentive. [< L *impetus* attack < *impetere* to attack < *in-* + *petere* aim for]

im pla ca ble (im plā′kə bəl or im plak′ə bəl), *adj.* that cannot be placated, pacified, or appeased.

im por tu nate (im pôr′chə nit), *adj.* **1.** asking repeatedly; annoyingly persistent; urgent. **2.** *Archaic.* burdensome; troublesome.

im por tune (im′pôr tün′, im′pôr tūn′, or im pôr′chən), *v.*   ask urgently or repeatedly; trouble with demands. [< MF < L *importunus* inconvenient]

im por tu ni ty (im′pôr tü′nə ti or im′pôr tū′nə ti), *n.* persistence in asking; act of demanding again and again.

im pre ca tion (im′prə kā′shən), *n.* **1.** act of calling down curses, evil, etc. **2.** a curse.

im pre sa ri o (im′prə sä′ri ō), *n.* organizer or manager of an opera or concert company. [< Ital. *impresario* < *impresa* undertaking, ult. < L *in-* on + *prehendere* take]

im pu ta tion (im′pū tā′shən), *n.* **1.** an imputing. **2.** charge or hint of wrongdoing. **3.** anything imputed; reputation.

im pute (im pūt′), *v.*   consider as belonging; attribute; charge (a fault, etc.) to a person; blame: *I impute his failure to laziness.*

in a ni tion (in′ə nish′ən), *n.* **1.** emptiness. **2.** weakness from lack of food. [< LL *inanitio*, -*onis* < L *inanire* to empty < *inanis* empty]

in an i ty (in an′ə ti), *n.* **1.** lack of sense. **2.** a silly or senseless act, practice, remark, etc. **3.** emptiness.

in ar tic u late (in′är tik′ū lit), *adj.* **1.** not distinct; not like regular speech: *an inarticulate mutter.* **2.** unable to speak in words; unable to say what one thinks.

in can ta tion (in′kan tā′shən), *n.* **1.** set of words spoken as a magic charm or to cast a magic spell. **2.** use of such words.

in cense (in sens′), *v.*   make very angry; fill with rage. [< L *incensus*, pp. of *incendere* kindle]

in cest (in′sest), *n.*   crime of sexual intercourse between persons so closely related that their marriage is prohibited by law.

in ces tu ous (in ses′chü əs), *adj.* **1.** involving incest. **2.** guilty of incest.

in cip i ent (in sip′i ənt), *adj.*   just beginning; in an early stage. [< L *incipiens*, -*entis*, ppr. of *incipere* begin < *in-* on + *capere* take]

---

hat, āge, cāre, fär;   let, ēqual, tėrm;   it, īce;   hot, ōpen, ôrder;   oil, out;   cup, pùt, rüle, ūse; th, thin;   ŦH, then;   zh, measure;   ə represents *a* in about, *e* in taken, *i* in pencil, *o* in lemon, *u* in circus.

801

incontinency

in con ti nen cy (in kon/tə nən si), *n.* 1. lack of self-restraint. 2. lack of chastity.

in cor po re al (in/kôr pô/ri əl or in/kôr pō/ri əl), *adj.* not made of any material substance; spiritual.

in cum bent (in kum/bənt), *adj.* 1. lying, leaning, or pressing (on). 2. resting (on a person) as a duty. 3. *Poetic.* overhanging. [< L *incumbens, -entis,* ppr. of *incumbere* lie down on]

in den ture (in den/chər), *n.* 1. a written agreement. 2. contract by which a person is bound to serve someone else. 3. indentation. 4. legal contract. —*v.* bind by a contract to serve someone else.

in dict ment (in dīt/mənt), *n.* 1. a formal accusation; especially, a legal accusation. 2. accusation.

in dif fer ent (in dif/ər ənt or in dif/rənt), *adj.* 1. having no feeling for or against. 2. impartial. 3. unimportant. 4. neither good nor bad; just fair. 5. *Archaic.* ordinary.

in di gent (in/də jənt), *adj.* poor; needy. [< L *indigens, -entis,* ppr. of *indigere* need]

in di rec tion (in/də rek/shən or in/dī rek/shən), *n.* 1. a roundabout act or method. 2. deceit.

in dite (in dīt/), *v.* put in words or writing; compose: *indite a letter.*

in duc tion (in duk/shən), *n.* 1. process by which an object having electrical or magnetic properties produces similar properties in a nearby object, without direct contact. 2. reasoning from particular facts to a general rule or principle. 3. conclusion reached in this way. ➔See **deduction** for usage note.

in due (in dü/ or in dū/), *v.* 1. provide with a quality or power. 2. put on. 3. clothe. 4. *Archaic.* put or be in harmony with.

in fal li ble (in fal/ə bəl), *adj.* 1. free from error. 2. absolutely reliable; sure. —**in fal/li bly,** *adv.*

in gen u ous (in jen/ū əs), *adj.* 1. frank; open; sincere. 2. simple; natural; innocent.

in im i cal (in im/ə kəl), *adj.* 1. unfriendly; hostile. 2. adverse; unfavorable; harmful. [< LL *inimicalis* < L *inimicus* < *in-* not + *amicus* friendly]

in junc tion (in jungk/shən), *n.* 1. command; order. 2. a formal order issued by a law court ordering a person or group to do, or refrain from doing, something.

in oc u late (in ok/ū lāt), *v.* 1. use disease germs to prevent or cure diseases. 2. *Archaic.* insert a bud into; graft (a tree, etc.) by budding.

in or di nate ly (in ôr/də nit li), *adv.* excessively.

in sen si ble (in sen/sə bəl), *adj.* 1. not sensitive; not able to feel or observe: *A blind man is insensible to colors.* 2. not aware.

in sip id (in sip/id), *adj.* 1. without much taste. 2. dull; uninteresting. [< LL *insipidus* < L *in-* not + *sapidus* tasty]

in ter (in tėr/), *v.* bury. [< OF *enterrer* < L *interrare* < *in-* in + *terra* earth]

in ter im (in/tər im), *n.* meantime; time between.

in ter mit (in/tər mit/), *v.* stop for a time. [< L *intermittere* < *inter-* between + *mittere* leave]

in tre pid i ty (in/trə pid/ə ti), *n.* fearlessness.

in ure (in ùr/), *v.* toughen or harden; accustom; habituate.

in vest ment (in vest/mənt), *n.* 1. an investing; a laying out of money. 2. amount of money invested. 3. a surrounding with soldiers or ships; siege.

in vet er a cy (in vet/ər ə si), *n.* settled, fixed condition; habitualness.

in vet er ate (in vet/ər it), *adj.* 1. habitual. 2. long and firmly established. [< L *inveteratus,* pp. of *inveter-*

laurel

ascere make old < *in-* in + *veterascere* grow old < *vetus* old]

i ron mon ger (ī/ərn mung/gər or ī/ərn mong/gər), *n. Esp. Brit.* dealer in ironware or hardware.

ir re mis sive (ir/i mis/iv), *adj. Archaic.* that cannot be decreased or lessened.

ja cinth (jā/sinth or jas/inth), *n.* a reddish-orange gem.

joc und (jok/ənd or jō/kənd), *adj.* cheerful; merry; gay.

join ture (join/chər), *n.* property given to a woman at the time of her marriage.

jo rum (jô/rəm or jō/rəm), *n.* 1. a large drinking bowl. 2. its contents.

Jove (jōv), *n.* the god Jupiter, chief divinity of the ancient Romans.

ken (ken), *n.* 1. range of sight. 2. range of knowledge: *What happens on Mars is beyond our ken.* —*v. Scottish.* know.

kirk (kėrk), *n. Scottish.* church.

kir tle (kėr/təl), *n. Archaic.* 1. skirt or dress. 2. a man's short coat.

kite (kīt), *n.* 1. a light wooden frame covered with paper or cloth. 2. hawk with long pointed wings. 3. any of the very high, light sails of a ship.

knave (nāv), *n.* 1. a tricky, dishonest person; rascal. 2. *Archaic.* a male servant; man of humble birth or position. [OE *cnafa* boy]

knell (nel), *n.* 1. sound of a bell rung slowly after a death or at a funeral. 2. a warning sign of death, failure, etc. 3. a mournful sound. —*v.* 1. ring slowly. 2. give a warning sign of death, failure, etc. 3. make a mournful sound.

ko a la (kō ä/lə), *n.* a gray, furry mammal of Australia that carries its young in a pouch. Koalas live in trees. [< Australian lang.]

lam bent (lam/bənt), *adj.* 1. moving lightly over a surface: *a lambent flame.* 2. playing lightly and brilliantly over a subject: *a lambent wit.* 3. softly bright: *Moonlight is lambent.*

lan guid (lang/gwid), *adj.* 1. drooping; weary. 2. without interest or enthusiasm; indifferent. 3. sluggish; dull; not brisk or lively. [< L *languidus* < *languere* be faint]

lan guor (lang/gər), *n.* 1. weariness. 2. lack of interest or enthusiasm. 3. softness or tenderness of mood. 4. quietness; stillness: *the languor of a summer afternoon.* 5. sluggishness.

lard (lärd), *n.* fat of pigs, melted down and made clear. —*v.* 1. insert strips of bacon or salt pork in (meat) before cooking. 2. give variety to; enrich: *lard a long speech with stories.*

la ryn go scope (lə ring/gə skōp/), *n.* an instrument for examining the larynx.

lath y (lath/i), *adj.* long and slender; thin.

lat ten (la/tən), *n.* a kind of brass or brasslike metal hammered into thin sheets.

lat tice (lat/is), *n.* 1. structure of crossed wooden or metal strips with open spaces between them. 2. window, gate, etc., having a lattice. —*v.* 1. make like a lattice. 2. furnish with a lattice.

laud a ble (lôd/ə bəl), *adj.* worthy of praise; commendable: *Unselfishness is laudable.*

lau rel (lô/rəl or lor/əl), *n.* 1. a small evergreen tree with smooth, shiny leaves; bay tree. 2. the leaves. The

---

< = from, taken from; cf., compare; dial., dialect; dim., diminutive; pp., past participle; ppr., present participle; pt., past tense; ult., ultimately; var., variant; ?=possibly.

ancient Greeks and Romans crowned victors with wreaths of laurel. **3.** Usually, **laurels,** *pl.* **a.** honor; fame. **b.** victory.

lay (lā), *n.* **1.** short poem to be sung; poem. **2.** song; tune.

lea (lē), *n.* a grassy field; meadow; pasture.

lead (led), *n.* **1.** a heavy, easily melted, bluish-gray metal. **2.** something made of this metal or one of its alloys. **3. leads,** *pl.* **a.** strips of lead used to cover roofs. **b.** frames of lead in which panes of glass are set. —*adj.* made of lead.

leav en (lev′ən), *v.* **1.** raise with yeast, etc. **2.** spread through and transform. [< OF *levain* < L *levamen* a lifting < *levare* raise]

lech er y (lech′ər i or lech′ri), *n.* lewdness; gross indulgence of lust.

lee (lē), *n.* **1.** shelter. **2.** side sheltered from the wind. **3.** side away from the wind. —*adj.* **1.** sheltered from the wind. **2.** on the side away from the wind. **3.** in the direction toward which the wind is blowing.

leek (lēk), *n.* vegetable somewhat like an onion.

lees (lēz), *n.pl.* dregs; sediment. [< F *lie* < Celtic]

Lent en or **lent en** (len′tən), *adj.* **1.** of Lent; suitable for Lent. **2.** *Archaic.* dull.

let (let), *v. Archaic.* prevent; hinder; obstruct. —*n.* prevention; hindrance.

let ter (let′ər), *n.* **1.** mark or sign that stands for any one of the sounds that make up words. **2.** a written message. **3.** exact wording; actual terms: *He kept the letter of the law but not the spirit.* **4. letters,** *pl.* **a.** literature. **b.** knowledge of literature; literary culture. **c.** profession of an author.

le vi a than (lə vī′ə thən), *n.* **1.** in the Bible, a huge sea animal. **2.** a huge ship. **3.** any great and powerful person or thing.

lev i ty (lev′ə ti), *n.* lightness of mind, character, or behavior; lack of proper seriousness or earnestness. [< L *levitas* < *levis* light] —**Syn.** flippancy, frivolity.

lev y (lev′i), *v.* **1.** order to be paid. **2.** collect (men) for an army. —*n.* **1.** money collected by authority or force. **2.** men collected for an army.

lib er tine (lib′ər tēn), *n.* person without moral restraints; man who does not respect women. —*adj.* without moral restraint. [< L *libertinus* freedman < *libertus* made free < *liber* free]

lief (lēf), *adv.* willing. —*adj.* **1.** willing. **2.** *Archaic.* beloved; precious. [OE *lēof* dear]

liege (lēj), *n.* **1.** lord having a right to the homage and loyal service of his vassals. **2.** vassal obliged to give homage and loyal service to his lord.

liege lord (lēj′ lôrd′), *n.* a feudal lord.

lift (lift), *n. Esp. Brit.* elevator.

light er (līt′ər), *n.* a flat-bottomed barge mainly used for loading and unloading ships.

light ly (līt′li), *adv.* **1.** with little weight, force, etc. **2.** to a small degree or extent. **3.** quickly.

lim pet (lim′pit), *n.* a small shellfish that sticks to rocks, used for bait and sometimes for food.

link man (link′mən), *n., pl.* **-men.** *Archaic.* attendant who summons vehicles and escorts people to and from them, as at theaters and hotels.

lin net (lin′it), *n.* a small songbird of Europe, Asia, and Africa.

lin tel (lin′təl), *n.* a horizontal beam or stone over a door, window, etc., to support the structure above it.

lists (lists), *n.pl.* **1.** place where knights fought in tournaments. **2.** barriers enclosing such a field. **3.** any place or scene of combat.

lit a ny (lit′ə ni), *n.* series of prayers by the minister with responses by the congregation.

liv er y (liv′ər i or liv′ri), *n.* **1.** any special uniform provided for the servants of a household, or adopted by any group or profession. **2.** any characteristic dress, garb, or outward appearance.

liv id (liv′id), *adj.* **1.** having a dull-bluish or leaden color. **2.** discolored by a bruise.

loath (lōth), *adj.* **1.** unwilling; reluctant. **2. nothing loath,** willing; willingly. Also, **loth.** [OE *lāth* hostile]

lode star (lōd′stär′), *n.* **1.** star that shows the way. **2.** polestar; North Star. **3.** guiding principle; center of attraction.

lor ry (lôr′i or lor′i), *n. Brit.* automobile truck.

loth (lōth), *adj.* loath.

lu cent (lü′sənt), *adj.* **1.** shining; luminous. **2.** letting the light through; clear. [< L *lucens, -entis,* ppr. of *lucere* shine]

lu rid (lür′id), *adj.* **1.** lighted up with a red or fiery glare. **2.** terrible; sensational; startling: *lurid crimes.*

lyre (līr), *n.* an ancient stringed musical instrument somewhat like a small harp.

mace¹ (mās), *n.* **1.** a war club used in the Middle Ages. **2.** staff used as a symbol of authority. [< OF < VL *mattea* < L *matteola* kind of hammer]

mace² (mās), *n.* spice made from the dried outer covering of nutmegs. [< OF *macis* < L *macir* reddish rind of an Indian root < Gk. *makir*]

mad ding (mad′ing), *adj.* **1.** mad; acting as if mad: *"the madding crowd's ignoble strife."* **2.** making mad.

Ma gel lan (mə jel′ən), *n.* **1.** Ferdinand, 1480?-1521, Portuguese navigator. **2. Strait of,** strait at the S tip of South America.

mag is te ri al (maj′is tēr′i əl), *adj.* **1.** showing authority: *The captain spoke with a magisterial voice.* **2.** domineering; overbearing. [< Med.L *magisterialis,* ult. < L *magister* master] —**mag′is te′ri al ly,** *adv.* —**Syn.** 2. haughty, arrogant.

mail (māl), *n.* **1.** armor made of metal rings, or small loops of chain, linked together. **2.** armor; protective covering. [< OF *maille* < L *macula* a mesh in network]

mal e fac tion (mal′ə fak′shən), *n.* crime; evil deed.

ma lig ni ty (mə lig′nə ti), *n.* **1.** extreme hate. **2.** great harmfulness; dangerous quality; deadliness.

man ci pi ar y (man si′pi ar′i), *adj.* referring to a taking by the hand.

man date (*n.* man′dāt or man′dit; *v.* man′dāt), *n., v.,* command; order.

man i fes to (man′ə fes′tō), *n., pl.* **-toes.** a public declaration of intentions by an important person or group; proclamation. [< Ital.]

Ma o ri (mä′ō ri or mou′ri), *n.* **1.** member of the native brown race of New Zealand. **2.** their language. **3.** the rainbow fish.

ma raud (mə rôd′), *v.* go about in search of plunder; make raids on for booty. —**ma raud′er,** *n.*

marge (märj), *n. Poetic.* edge; border.

marl (märl), *n.* **1.** soil containing clay and calcium carbonate, used in making fertilizer. **2.** *Poetic.* earth.

mar mot (mär′mət), *n.* rodent with a thick body and a bushy tail. Woodchucks and prairie dogs are marmots. [Am.E; < F *marmotte* < *marmottaine* < Med. L. *mus* (*muris*) *montanus* mouse of the mountains]

mar ry (mar′i), *interj. Archaic.* exclamation showing surprise, indignation, etc. [< (the Virgin) *Mary*]

mass y (mas′i), *adj.* massive.

hat, āge, cãre, fär;   let, ēqual, tèrm;   it, īce;   hot, ōpen, ôrder;   oil, out;   cup, pùt, rüle, ūse; th, thin;   ŦH, then;   zh, measure;   ə represents *a* in about, *e* in taken, *i* in pencil, *o* in lemon, *u* in circus.

803

ma tins (mat′ənz), *n.pl.* Also, **matin**, *Poetic.* morning song. [< OF < LL *matutinus* of or in the morning <*Matuta* dawn goddess < *matu-* early, originally, good]

mead¹ (mēd), *n. Poetic.* meadow. [OE *mǣd*]

mead² (mēd), *n.* an alcoholic drink made from fermented honey and water. [OE *medu*]

mean (mēn), *adj.* **1.** low in quality or grade. **2.** low in social position or rank. **3.** of little importance or value: *the meanest flower.* **4.** of poor appearance. **5.** small-minded; ignoble: *mean thoughts.* **6.** stingy. **7.** *Informal.* humiliated; ashamed. **8.** *Informal.* troublesome; bad-tempered. **9.** *Informal.* in poor physical condition; unwell. [OE (*ge*)*mǣne* common]

mean ness (mēn′nis), *n.* **1.** being mean in grade or quality; poorness. **2.** stinginess. **3.** a mean act.

men dac i ty (men das′ə ti), *n.* **1.** habit of telling lies; untruthfulness. **2.** a lie.

mer ce nar y (mèr′sə ner′i), *adj.* done for money or gain. —*n.* **1.** soldier serving for pay in a foreign army. **2.** *Archaic.* one who works solely for pay. [< L *mercenarius* < *merces* wages]

mere¹ (mēr), *adj.* nothing else than; only; simple. [< L *merus* pure]

mere² (mēr), *n. Poetic* or *Dialect.* lake; pond. [OE]

met a phys i cal (met′ə fiz′ə kəl), *adj.* **1.** of metaphysics; about the real nature of things. **2.** highly abstract; hard to understand.

mete¹ (mēt), *v.,* **met ed, met ing. 1.** give to each a share; distribute; allot. **2.** *Poetic.* measure. [OE *metan*]

mete² (mēt), *n.* **1.** boundary. **2.** a boundary stone. [< OF < L *meta*]

mick le (mik′əl), *adj., adv., n. Archaic* or *Dialect.* much.

midge (mij), *n.* **1.** a kind of very small insect; gnat. **2.** a very small person.

mis chie vous (mis′chə vəs), *adj.* **1.** harmful: *a mischievous belief.* **2.** full of pranks and teasing fun.

mis sal (mis′əl), *n.* book containing the prayers, etc., for celebrating Mass throughout the year.

mold er (mōl′dər), *v.* crumble; waste away.

mol li fy (mol′ə fī), *v.* soften; appease; mitigate: *mollify a person or his wrath.* [< F < LL *mollificare* < *mollis* soft + *facere* make]

mon key nut (mung′ki nut′), *n.* peanut.

mor dant (môr′dənt), *adj.* biting; cutting; sarcastic. [< OF *mordant,* ppr. of *mordre* bite < L *mordere*]

mor tise (môr′tis), *n.* hole in one piece of wood cut to receive a projection on another piece. —*v.* fasten by mortise: *Good furniture is mortised together, not nailed.*

mor tu a ry (môr′chü er′i), *n.* **1.** building or room where dead bodies are kept until burial. **2.** morgue. [< Med.L *mortuarium,* ult. < L *mors* death]

mote (mōt), *n.* small particle, as a speck of dust.

mou jik (mü zhik′ or mü′zhik), *n.* a Russian peasant.

moun te bank (moun′tə bangk), *n.* **1.** person who sells quack medicines in public, appealing to his audience by tricks, stories, jokes, etc. **2.** anybody who tries to deceive people by tricks, stories, and jokes. [< Ital. *montambanco* for *monta in banco* mount-on-bench]

mull (mul), *v.* make (wine, beer, etc.) into a warm drink, with sugar, spices, etc.

mul ti far i ous (mul′tə fãr′i əs), *adj.* **1.** having many different parts, forms, etc. **2.** many and various.

mu nif i cence (mü nif′ə səns), *n.* very great generosity. [< L *munificentia* < *munificus* generous, ult. < *munus* gift + *facere* make]

muse (mūz), *v.* **1.** think in a dreamy way; think; meditate. **2.** look thoughtfully. **3.** say thoughtfully. [< OF *muser* loiter]

mus sel (mus′əl), *n.* an edible salt-water animal that looks like a small clam, with black shells.

mu ta tion (mū tā′shən), *n.* **1.** change; alteration. **2.** a new feature that appears suddenly in animals or plants and can be inherited. **3.** a new variety of animal or plant formed in this way. [< L *mutatio, -onis* < *mutare* change]

nave (nāv), *n.* hub; central part of a wheel.

nav vy (nav′i), *n. Brit.* an unskilled laborer who works on canals, railways, roads, etc.

neg li gi ble (neg′lə jə bəl), *adj.* that can be disregarded.

Ne an der thal man (ni an′dər täl), an extinct race, widespread in Europe in the early Stone Age. [from *Neanderthal,* a valley in West Germany, where evidence of this race was found]

ne o lith ic (nē′ə lith′ik), *adj.* of the later Stone Age, when polished stone weapons and tools were made and used: *neolithic man.* [< *neo-* + Gk. *lithos* stone]

ni bong palm (nē′bong päm′), *n.* Malayan tree whose leaves have a featherlike arrangement.

nig gard ly (nig′ərd li), *adj.* **1.** stingy. **2.** meanly small or scanty: *a niggardly gift.* —*adv.* stingily. —**nig′gard li ness,** *n.*

ni pa palm (nē′pə or nī′pə päm′), *n.* low East Indian tree which is common along tidal rivers.

no men cla ture (nō′mən klā′chər or nō men′klə-chər), *n.* set or system of names or terms: *the nomenclature of music.* [< L *nomenclatura* < *nomen* name + *calare* to call]

nurs ling (nèrs′ling), *n.* **1.** baby that is being nursed. **2.** any person or thing that is having tender care.

ob du rate (ob′dù rit or ob′dū rit), *adj.* **1.** stubborn; unyielding. **2.** hardened in feelings or heart; not repentant. [< L *obduratus,* pp. of *obdurare* < *ob-* against + *durare* harden]

ob liv i on (əb liv′i ən), *n.* **1.** condition of being entirely forgotten. **2.** forgetfulness.

ob liv i ous (əb liv′i əs), *adj.* **1.** forgetful; not mindful: *The book was so interesting that I was oblivious of my surroundings.* **2.** bringing or causing forgetfulness. —Syn. **1.** unmindful, heedless.

ob se quies (ob′sə kwiz), *n.pl.* funeral rites or ceremonies.

ob se qui ous (əb sē′kwi əs), *adj.* polite or obedient from hope of gain or from fear; servile; fawning.

ob tuse (əb tüs′ or əb tūs′), *adj.* **1.** not sharp or acute; blunt. **2.** slow in understanding; stupid. **3.** not sensitive; dull.

oc cult (o kult′ or ok′ult), *adj.* **1.** beyond the bounds of ordinary knowledge; mysterious. **2.** outside the laws of the natural world; magical. —Syn. **1.** secret, hidden.

of fal (ôf′əl or of′əl), *n.* **1.** the waste parts of an animal killed for food. **2.** garbage; refuse. [< *off* + *fall*]

of fi cious (ə fish′əs), *adj.* too ready to offer services or advice; minding other people's business.

o gle (ō′gəl), *v.* **1.** look at with desire; make eyes at. **2.** look with desire; make eyes. —*n.* an ogling look. [< Dutch *oogelen* < *oog* eye]

O lym pi an (ō lim′pi ən), *adj.* **1.** having to do with Olympia, where the ancient Greek games were held, or with Mount Olympus, where the greater Greek gods were

---

< = from, taken from;   cf., compare;   dial., dialect;   dim., diminutive;   pp., past participle; ppr., present participle;   pt., past tense;   ult., ultimately;   var., variant;   ?=possibly.

supposed to live. **2.** like a god; heavenly. **3.** magnificent; superior: *Olympian calm.* —*n.* **1.** one of the major Greek gods. **2.** contender in the Olympic games.

on set (on′set′ or ôn′set′), *n.* **1.** attack: *The onset of the enemy took us by surprise.* **2.** beginning: *the onset of a disease.* —*Syn.* **1.** assault. **2.** commencement.

on yx (on′iks), *n.* a semiprecious variety of quartz with layers of different colors and shades.

Onyx

o pi ate (ō′pi it or ō′pi āt), *n.* **1.** drug that contains opium and so dulls pain or brings sleep. **2.** anything that quiets. —*adj.* **1.** containing opium. **2.** bringing sleep or ease. [< Med. L *opiatus* < L *opium* opium]

op u lence (op′ū ləns), *n.* **1.** wealth. **2.** abundance.

or a to ry (ôr′ə tô′ri), *n.* a small chapel; room set apart for prayer. [< LL *oratorium* < *orare* pray. Doublet of ORATORIO.]

orb (ôrb), *n.* **1.** sphere; globe. **2.** sun, moon, planet, or star. **3.** *Esp. Poetic.* eyeball or eye.

ord nance (ôrd′nəns), *n.* **1.** cannon; artillery. **2.** military weapons of all kinds.

or i son (ôr′ə zən or or′ə zən), *n.* *Archaic* or *Poetic.* prayer.

os ten si bly (os ten′sə bli), *adv.* apparently.

pack thread (pak′thred′), *n.* a strong thread or twine for sewing or tying up packages.

pal a tal (pal′ə təl), *adj.* **1.** of or having to do with the palate. **2.** of speech sounds, made with the tongue near or touching the hard palate. The *y* in *yet* is a palatal sound. —*n.* a palatal sound.

pa lav er (pə lav′ər or pə lä′vər), *n.* **1.** parley or conference. **2.** talk. **3.** smooth, persuading talk; fluent talk; flattery. —*v.* **1.** talk. **2.** talk fluently or flatteringly. [< Pg. *palavra* < L *parabola* story, parable. Doublet of PARABLE, PAROLE.]

pale (pāl), *n.* **1.** boundary: *outside the pale of civilized society.* **2.** *Archaic.* space having bounds; enclosure.

pal frey (pôl′fri), *n.* a gentle riding horse, especially one used by ladies.

pall[1] (pôl), *n.* **1.** a heavy cloth of black, purple, or white velvet spread over a coffin, a hearse, or a tomb. **2.** a dark, gloomy covering. **3.** *Archaic.* splendid robe. [OE *pæll* < L *pallium* cloak]

pall[2] (pôl), *v.* **1.** become distasteful or very tiresome because there has been too much of it. **2.** cloy. [var. of *appall*]

pal let[1] (pal′it), *n.* bed of straw; poor bed. [< OF *paillet* < *paille* straw < L *palea*]

pal let[2] (pal′it), *n.* **1.** a flat blade used by potters and others. **2.** a painter's palette. **3.** projection on a pawl. [var. of *palette*]

pal li a tive (pal′i ā′tiv), *adj.* useful to lessen or soften; excusing. —*n.* something that lessens, softens, or excuses.

palm y (päm′i or päl′mi), *adj.* **1.** abounding in palms. **2.** flourishing; prosperous.

pal pi ta tion (pal′pə tā′shən), *n.* **1.** very rapid beating of the heart. **2.** a quivering; trembling.

pal sy (pôl′zi), *n.* paralysis. —*v.* paralyze.

pal try (pôl′tri), *adj.* almost worthless; trifling; petty; mean.

par a dox (par′ə doks), *n.* statement that may be true but seems to say two opposite things: "*More haste, less speed*" and "*The child is father of the man*" are para-

doxes. **2.** person or thing that seems to be full of contradictions. [< L < Gk. *paradoxos* < *para-* contrary to + *doxa* opinion]

par a gon (par′ə gon), *n.* model of excellence or perfection.

par a pet (par′ə pet or par′ə pit), *n.* **1.** a low wall or mound of stone, earth, etc., to protect soldiers. **2.** a low wall at the edge of a balcony, roof, bridge, etc.

par o dy (par′ə di), *n.* **1.** a humorous imitation of a serious writing. A parody follows the form of the original, but changes its sense to nonsense. **2.** a poor imitation. —*v.* **1.** make a parody on. **2.** imitate poorly.

par quet (pär kā′ or pär ket′), *n.* **1.** an inlaid wooden flooring. **2.** the main floor of a theater. —*v.* make or put down (an inlaid wooden floor).

par terre (pär târ′), *n.* **1.** *U.S.* the part of the main floor of a theater under the balcony. **2.** an ornamental arrangement of flower beds.

pas sé (pa sā′ or pas′ā), *adj.* **1.** past. **2.** past its usefulness; out of date; worn. [< F *passé* passed]

Pat a go ni an (pat′ə gō′ni ən or pat′ə gōn′yən), *adj.* of or having to do with Patagonia, a region in the extreme south of South America. —*n.* **1.** native or inhabitant of Patagonia. **2.** member of a very tall Indian race living in Patagonia.

pate (pāt), *n.* **1.** top of the head; head. **2.** brains.

pa ter nal ism (pə tèr′nəl iz əm), *n.* principle or practice of managing the affairs of a country or group of people as a father manages the affairs of children.

pa tri ar chal (pā′tri är′kəl), *adj.* having to do with a patriarch, a father, ruler of a tribe, or venerable old man.

pa thos (pā′thos), *n.* quality in speech, writing, music, events, or a scene that arouses a feeling of pity or sadness. [< Gk. *pathos* suffering, feeling]

peat (pēt), *n.* kind of turf, used as fuel after being dried. Peat is made of partly rotted moss and plants.

ped a gogue (ped′ə gog or ped′ə gôg), *n.* **1.** teacher. **2.** a narrow-minded teacher.

ped ant (ped′ənt), *n.* **1.** person who displays his knowledge in an unnecessary or tiresome way. **2.** a dull, narrow-minded teacher or scholar.

pe dan tic (pi dan′tik), *adj.* **1.** displaying one's knowledge more than is necessary. **2.** tediously learned; scholarly in a dull and narrow way.

pelf (pelf), *n.* money or riches, thought of as bad or degrading. [< OF *pelfre* spoils]

pem mi can (pem′ə kən), *n.* dried meat pounded into a paste with melted fat. [Am.E; < Cree (N Am. Ind.) *pimikan* < *pimikew* he makes grease]

pen chant (pen′chənt), *n.* a strong taste or liking.

pend ent (pen′dənt), *adj.* **1.** hanging: *the pendent branches of a willow.* **2.** overhanging. **3.** pending.

pen sion er (pen′shən ər), *n.* **1.** person who receives a pension. **2.** a hireling; dependent.

pent roof (pent′ rüf′), *n.* **1.** a sloping roof projecting from a building. **2.** shed with a sloping roof attached to a building.

pen u ry (pen′ū ri), *n.* great poverty. [< L *penuria*]

per chance (pər chans′ or pər chäns′), *adv.* *Archaic* or *Poetic.* perhaps.

per di tion (pər dish′ən), *n.* **1.** loss of one's soul and the joys of heaven. **2.** hell. **3.** utter loss. [< L *perditio, -onis* < *perdere* destroy < *per-* destruction + *dare* give]

per emp to ry (pər emp′tə ri or per′əmp tō′ri), *adj.* **1.** positive: *a peremptory teacher.* **2.** allowing no denial or refusal: *a peremptory command.* **3.** decisive; final. —**per emp′to ri ly,** *adv.* —**per emp′to ri ness,** *n.*

hat, āge, cãre, fär; let, ēqual, tèrm; it, ĭce; hot, ōpen, ôrder; oil, out; cup, pùt, rüle, ūse; th, thin; ŦH, then; zh, measure; ə represents *a* in about, *e* in taken, *i* in pencil, *o* in lemon, *u* in circus.

perfidious | prerogative

per fid i ous (pər fid/i əs), *adj.* deliberately faithless; treacherous.

per func to ry (pər fungk/tə ri), *adj.* **1.** done merely for the sake of getting rid of the duty; mechanical; indifferent: *The little boy gave his face a perfunctory washing.* **2.** acting in a perfunctory way. —**per func/to ri ly,** *adv.* —**per func/to ri ness,** *n.* —**Syn. 1.** careless, superficial.

per i gee (per/ə jē), *n.* point in the orbit of a heavenly body where it comes closest to the earth. [< F < NL < Gk. *perigeion* < *peri-* near + *ge* earth]

per i win kle[1] (per/i wing/kəl), *n.* a trailing plant with blue flowers.

per i win kle[2] (per/i wing/kəl), *n.* a sea snail with a thick, cone-shaped, spiral shell, used for food in Europe. [OE *pinewincle; pine-* ? < L *pina* mussel < Gk. *pine*]

perne (pèrn), *v.* turn; wind around.

per ni cious (pər nish/əs), *adj.* **1.** that will destroy or ruin; causing great harm or damage. **2.** fatal. [< L *perniciosus,* ult. < *per-* + *nex* death]

per spi cu i ty (per/spə kū/ə ti), *n.* clearness in expression; ease in being understood. —**Syn.** lucidity.

pe ruse (pə rüz/), *v.* **1.** read through carefully. **2.** read. **3.** *Archaic.* examine carefully. [originally, use up, < L *per-* to the end + E *use*]

pes ti lent (pes/tə lənt), *adj.* **1.** often causing death. **2.** harmful to morals; destroying peace. **3.** troublesome; annoying. [< L *pestilens, -entis* < *pestis* pest]

pet u lance (pech/ù ləns), *n.* peevishness; bad humor; being irritated by trifles.

Phar i sa ic (far/ə sā/ik), *adj.* **1.** of or having to do with the Pharisees. **2. pharisaic, a.** making an outward show of religion or morals without the real spirit. **b.** thinking oneself more moral than others.

phre nol o gy (fri nol/ə ji), *n.* theory that the shape of the skull shows what sort of mind and character a person has; practice of reading character from the shape of the skull. [Am.E; < Gk. *phren* mind + E *-logy*]

pick et (pik/it), *n.* a small body of troops, or a single man, posted at some place to watch for the enemy and guard against surprise.

pie bald (pī/bôld/), *adj.* spotted in two colors, especially black and white. —*n.* a spotted horse.

pied (pīd), *adj.* **1.** having patches of two or more colors; many-colored. **2.** spotted.

pip pin (pip/ən), *n.* any of several kinds of apple, such as Grimes' golden pippin, the Newtown pippin, the white pippin.

pitch (pich), *n.* height; in falconry, the height to which the falcon rises before swooping on its prey.

plaice (plās), *n.* a flounder or various flatfishes.

plain tive (plān/tiv), *adj.* mournful; sad.

plait (plāt or plat *for 1;* plāt or plēt *for 2*), *n., v.* **1.** braid. **2.** pleat. [< OF *pleit,* ult. < L *plicare* to fold]

plau si ble (plô/zə bəl), *adj.* **1.** appearing true, reasonable, or fair. **2.** apparently worthy of confidence but often not really so: *a plausible liar.* **3.** *Archaic.* worthy of applause or approval. [< L *plausibilis* deserving applause, pleasing < *plaudere* applaud]

plen i po ten ti ar y (plen/ə pə ten/shi er/i or plen/-ə pə ten/shə ri), *n.* a diplomatic agent having full power or authority —*adj.* having or giving full power and authority. [< Med.L *plenipotentiarius,* ult. < L *plenus* full + *potens* powerful]

ple thor ic (ple thôr/ik or pleth/ə rik), *adj.* **1.** too full; inflated. **2.** having too much blood or too many red corpuscles in the blood.

plight (plīt), *v.* **1.** pledge; promise. **2. plight one's**

---

troth, a. promise to be faithful. **b.** promise to marry. —*n.* a solemn promise; pledge.

plinth (plinth), *n.* **1.** the lower, square part of the base of a column. **2.** a square base of a pedestal.

pol i tic (pol/ə tik), *adj.* **1.** wise in looking out for one's own interests; prudent: *A politic person tries not to offend people.* **2.** scheming; crafty. **3.** political. [< L *politicus* < Gk. *politikos,* ult. < *polis* city-state]

poll (pōl), *n.* the head, especially the part of it on which the hair grows.

pom mel (pum/əl or pom/əl), *n.* **1.** part of a saddle that sticks up at the front. **2.** a rounded knob on the hilt of a sword, dagger, etc.

por ten tous (pôr ten/təs or pōr ten/təs), *adj.* **1.** indicating evil to come; ominous; threatening. **2.** amazing; extraordinary. —**Syn. 1.** foreboding. **2.** wonderful, marvelous.

por ti co (pôr/tə kō or pōr/tə kō), *n., pl.* **-coes** or **-cos.** roof supported by columns, forming a porch or a covered walk.

port man teau (pôrt man/tō or pōrt man/tō), *n., pl.* **-teaus** or **-teaux** (-tōz). *Esp. Brit.* a stiff, oblong traveling bag with two compartments opening like a book.

pos set (pos/it), *n.* a hot drink made of milk, alcoholic liquor, and spices.

post chaise (pōst/ chāz/), *n.* a hired carriage that was used for traveling before there were railroads.

po ten tate (pō/tən tāt), *n.* **1.** person having great power. **2.** ruler. Kings, queens, and emperors were potentates.

poth er (po#/ər), *n.* **1.** confusion; disturbance; fuss. **2.** a choking cloud of dust or smoke. —*v.* bother; fuss.

preb end (preb/ənd), *n.* clergyman connected with a cathedral or a collegiate church.

prec e dent (*n.* pres/ə dənt; *adj.* pri sēd/ənt or pres/ə dənt), *n.* case that may serve as an example or reason for a later case. —*adj.* preceding.

pre cinct (prē/singkt), *n.* **1.** district within certain boundaries, for governmental, administrative, or other purposes. **2.** space within a boundary. **3.** Often, **precincts,** *pl.* boundary; limit.

pre cip i tate (*v.* pri sip/ə tāt; *adj., n.* pri sip/ə tāt or pri sip/ə tit), *v.* **1.** bring about suddenly. **2.** throw headlong; hurl. —*adj.* **1.** very hurried; sudden. **2.** with great haste and force; hasty; rash. —**pre cip/-i tate ly,** *adv.* —**pre cip/i ta/tor,** *n.*

pre curse (prē kûrs/), *n. Archaic.* a foreshadowing; forerunning.

pre des ti nate (prē des/tə nāt), *v.* **1.** decree or ordain beforehand. **2.** foreordain by divine purpose.

pre fer ment (pri fèr/mənt), *n.* **1.** advancement; promotion. **2.** position or office giving social or financial advancement, especially one in the church.

preg nant (preg/nənt), *adj.* **1.** having an embryo or embryos developing in the uterus. **2.** filled; loaded. **3.** fertile; rich; abounding. **4.** filled with meaning; very significant. [< L *praegnans, -antis* < *prae-* before + *gen-* to bear]

prel ate (prel/it), *n.* clergyman of high rank, such as a bishop.

prem ise (prem/is), *n.* in logic, a statement assumed to be true and used to draw a conclusion. *Example:* Major premise: Children should go to school. Minor premise: He is a child. Conclusion: He should go to school.

pre rog a tive (pri rog/ə tiv), *n.* right or privilege

< = from, taken from; cf., compare; dial., dialect; dim., diminutive; pp., past participle; ppr., present participle; pt., past tense; ult., ultimately; var., variant; ?=possibly.

that nobody else has: *The government has the prerogative of coining money.* —*adj.* having or exercising a prerogative.

pre sume (pri züm′), *v.* 1. suppose. 2. take upon oneself; venture; dare. 3. take an unfair advantage (used with *on* or *upon*). 4. go beyond what is proper or to be expected. [< L *praesumere* take for granted < *prae-* before + *sumere* take]

pre ter nat u ral (prē′tər nach′ə rəl or prē′tərnach′rəl), *adj.* 1. out of the ordinary course of nature; abnormal. 2. due to something above or beyond nature; supernatural. [< L Med.L *praeternaturalis,* ult. < L *praeter-* beyond + *natura* nature]

pri mal (prī′məl), *adj.* 1. of early times; first, primeval. 2. chief; fundamental. [< Med.L *primalis* < L *primus* first]

prime (prīm), *adj.* 1. first in rank; chief. 2. first in time or order; fundamental. 3. first in quality. —*n.* 1. the best time; best condition. 2. the best part. 3. the first part; beginning. 4. the second of the seven canonical hours, or the service for it, originally fixed for the first hour of the day (beginning at 6 A.M.).

pri or ess (prī′ər is), *n.* head of a convent.

priv y (priv′i), *adj.* 1. private. 2. *Archaic.* secret; hidden. 3. **privy to,** having secret or private knowledge of.

pro bi ty (prō′bə ti or prob′ə ti), *n.* uprightness; honesty; high principle.

prod i gal (prod′ə gəl), *adj.* 1. wasting money or other resources. 2. abundant; lavish. —*n.* person who is wasteful or extravagant; spendthrift. —Syn. *adj.* 1. extravagant. —Ant. *adj.* 1. frugal.

pro di gious (prə dij′əs), *adj.* 1. very great; huge. 2. wonderful; marvelous.

pro pi ti ate (prə pish′i āt), *v.* prevent or reduce the anger of; win the favor of; appease or conciliate.

pro sa ic (prō zā′ik), *adj.* like prose; matter-of-fact; ordinary; not exciting. —Syn. commonplace, humdrum.

pros pect (pros′pekt), *n.* 1. thing expected or looked forward to. 2. act of looking forward. 3. outlook for the future. 4. view; scene: *The prospect from the mountain was grand.* [< L *prospectus,* ult. < *pro-* forward + *specere* to look]

pro spec tus (prə spek′təs), *n.* a printed statement describing and advertising something.

prov i dence (prov′ə dəns), *n.* 1. God's care and help. 2. instance of God's care and help. 3. care for the future. 4. *Archaic.* foresight. 5. **Providence,** God.

prox im i ty (proks im′ə ti), *n.* nearness; closeness.

pru dence (prü′dəns), *n.* 1. wise thought before acting; good judgment. 2. good management; economy.

pru dent (prü′dənt), *adj.* planning carefully ahead of time; sensible; discreet: *A prudent man saves part of his wages.* —pru′dent ly, *adv.* —Syn. judicious, wise. —Ant. foolish, thoughtless.

prune (prün), *v.* 1. cut out useless or undesirable parts from. 2. cut superfluous or undesirable twigs or branches from (a bush, tree, etc.). 3. cut off or out.

pub li can (pub′lə kən), *n.* 1. *Brit.* keeper of a pub. 2. a tax collector of ancient Rome.

pum ice (pum′is), *n.* a light, spongy stone thrown up from volcanoes, used for cleaning, smoothing, and polishing. —*v.* clean, smooth, or polish with pumice.

pur ga tion (pėr gā′shən), *n.* a purging; cleansing.

pur port (pėr′pôrt or pėr′pōrt), *n.* meaning; main idea. [< AF *purporter* < *pur-* forth (< *pro-*) + *porter* carry < L *portare*] —Syn. sense, gist, signification.

quaint (kwānt), *adj.* 1. strange or odd, especially in an interesting, pleasing, or amusing way. 2. *Archaic.* crafty; wily. —**quaint′ly,** *adv.* —**quaint′ness,** *n.*

qua ver ous (kwā′vər us), *adj.* characterized by shaking and trembling.

quea sy (kwē′zi), *adj.* 1. inclined to nausea; easily upset. 2. tending to unsettle the stomach. 3. uneasy; uncomfortable. 4. squeamish; fastidious.

quick (kwik), *n.* 1. the tender, sensitive flesh under a fingernail or toenail. 2. the tender, sensitive part of one's feelings. 3. living persons. [OE *cwic* alive]

quick set (kwik′set′), *n. Esp. Brit.* plant or cutting, especially of hawthorn, set to grow in a hedge.

quince (kwins), *n.* 1. a hard, yellowish acid fruit, used for preserves. 2. tree it grows on. 3. a similar shrub or tree grown for its blossoms.

quin tes sence (kwin tes′əns), *n.* 1. pure essence; purest form. 2. the most perfect example of something. [< Med.L *quinta essentia* fifth essence, translation of Gk. *pempte ousia*]

quire (kwīr), *n. Archaic.* choir.

quiz zi cal (kwiz′ə kəl), *adj.* 1. odd; comical. 2. teasing.

rack (rak), *n.* flying, broken clouds driven by the wind.

raff ish (raf′ish), *adj.* 1. vulgar; common. 2. disreputable; low; worthless.

ral ly (ral′i), *v.* make fun of; tease.

ram part (ram′pärt), *n.* 1. a wide bank of earth, often with a wall on top, built around a fort to help defend it. 2. anything that defends; defense; protection.

rank (rangk), *adj.* 1. large and coarse: *rank grass.* 2. growing richly. 3. having a strong, bad smell or taste. 4. extreme: *rank nonsense.* 5. coarse; not decent. —Syn. 3. rancid. 5. obscene, indecent.

ra pi er (rā′pi ər), *n.* a light sword used for thrusting.

rav age (rav′ij), *v.* lay waste; destroy. —*n.* violence; destruction.

ra vine (rə vēn′), *n.* 1. a long, deep, narrow gorge worn by running water. 2. *Archaic.* impetus; rush. [< F *ravine* < OF *ravine* violent rush, robbery]

rav ish (rav′ish), *v.* 1. fill with delight. 2. carry off by force. 3. rape. —Syn. 1. enrapture, enchant.

raze (rāz), *v.* tear down; destroy completely.

re bec or **re beck** (rē′bek), *n.* a musical instrument, somewhat like a violin, used in the Middle Ages.

re cal ci trant (ri kal′sə trənt), *adj.* resisting authority or control; disobedient. [< L *recalcitrans, -antis,* ppr. of *recalcitrare* kick back, ult. < *re-* back + *calx* heel]

re ceipt (ri sēt′), *n.* 1. a written statement that money, a package, a letter, etc., has been received. 2. recipe. 3. remedy; cure.

reck (rek), *v. Archaic.* 1. care; heed. 2. be important or interesting; matter. [OE *reccan*]

re cog ni zance (ri kog′nə zəns or ri kon′ə zəns), in law: **a.** bond binding a person to do some particular act. **b.** sum of money to be forfeited if the act is not performed.

re dress (*v.* ri dres′; *n.* rē′dres or ri dress′), *v.* set right; repair; remedy. —*n.* a setting right; reparation. [< F *redresser* < *re-* again + *dresser* straighten, arrange]

re mand (ri mand′ or ri mänd′), *v.* 1. send back. 2. send back (a prisoner or an accused person) to prison. —*n.* a remanding. [< LL *remandare* < L *re-* back + *mandare* consign]

re miss (ri mis′), *adj.* careless; neglectful.

---

hat, āge, cãre, fär; let, ēqual, tėrm; it, īce; hot, ōpen, ôrder; oil, out; cup, pút, rüle, ūse; th, thin; ŦH, then; zh, measure; ə represents *a* in about, *e* in taken, *i* in pencil, *o* in lemon, *u* in circus.

re plete (ri plēt′), *adj.* abundantly supplied; filled.

re trench (ri trench′), *v.* **1.** cut down; reduce (expenses, words, etc.). **2.** reduce expenses. [< MF *retrencher < re-* back + *trencher* cut]

ret ro grade (ret′rə grād), *adj.* **1.** moving backward; retreating. **2.** becoming worse. —*v.* **1.** move or go backward. **2.** fall back toward a worse condition. [< L *retrogradus < retrogradi*, ult. < *retro-* backward + *gradi* go]

rime (rīm), *n.* white frost; hoarfrost. —*v.* cover with rime.

rive (rīv), *v.* tear apart; split; cleave.

ro bus tious (rō bus′chəs), *adj. Archaic* or *Humorous.* **1.** rough; rude; boisterous. **2.** robust; strong; stout.

roe[1] (rō), *n.* fish eggs. [ME *rowe*]

roe[2] (rō), *n., pl.* **roes** or (*esp. collectively*) **roe.** a small deer of Europe and Asia, with forked antlers. [OE *rā*]

rose mar y (rōz′mâr′i), *n.* an evergreen shrub whose leaves yield a fragrant oil used in making perfume. Rosemary is a symbol of remembrance. [< L *ros maris,* literally, dew of the sea; associated with *rose* and *Mary*]

rude (rüd), *adj.* **1.** impolite. **2.** roughly made or done. **3.** rough in manner or behavior; violent; harsh. **4.** of the poor or uncultured people; simple.

run a gate (run′ə gāt), *n. Archaic.* **1.** runaway. **2.** vagabond; wanderer. [< *run* + *agate* away; influenced by *renegat* renegade]

rust y (rus′ti), *adj.* **1.** rusted. **2.** made by rust. **3.** colored like rust. **4.** faded.

sa ble (sā′bəl), *adj. Poetic.* black; dark.

sack (sak), *n.* sherry or other strong, light-colored wine. [< F (*vin*) *sec* dry (wine) < L *siccus*]

sa li ent (sā′li ənt or sāl′yənt), *adj.* **1.** standing out; prominent; striking: *the salient features in a landscape, the salient points in a speech.* **2.** projecting: *a salient angle.* —*n.* a salient angle or part. —**Syn.** *adj.* **1.** noticeable, conspicuous.

sal ly (sal′i), *n.* **1.** a sudden attack on an enemy made from a defensive position. **2.** a sudden rushing forth. **3.** a going forth; trip. **4.** a sudden start into activity. **5.** outburst. —*v.* **1.** go suddenly from a defensive position to attack an enemy. **2.** rush forth suddenly; go out. **3.** go on a trip. [< F *saillie,* ult. < L *salire* to leap]

sa lu bri ty (sə lü′brə ti), *n.* healthfulness; wholesomeness.

sa lute (sə lüt′), *v.* **1.** meet with kind words, a bow, a kiss, etc.; greet. **2.** make a bow, gesture, or the like to. [< L *salutare* greet < *salus* good health]

sal ver (sal′vər), *n.* tray.

sam ite (sam′īt or sā′mīt), *n.* a heavy, rich silk fabric, sometimes interwoven with gold, worn in the Middle Ages.

san guine (sang′gwin), *adj.* **1.** naturally cheerful and hopeful. **2.** confident; hopeful. **3.** having a healthy red color; ruddy: *a sanguine complexion.* [< L *sanguineus < sanguis* blood]

sar don ic (sär don′ik), *adj.* bitter; sarcastic; scornful; mocking: *a fiend's sardonic laugh.* [< F < L < Gk. *Sardonios,* a supposed Sardinian plant that produced hysterical convulsions] —**sar don′i cal ly,** *adv.*

sark (särk), *n.* body garment, such as a shirt, robe, etc.

sate (sāt or sat), *v. Archaic.* a pt. and a pp. of **sit.**

sa ti e ty (sə tī′ə ti), *n.* the feeling of having had too much; disgust or weariness caused by excess. [< L *satietas < satis* enough]

sat ur nine (sat′ər nīn), *adj.* gloomy; grave; reserved. [< *Saturn;* those born under the planet's sign are supposed to be morose]

saw (sô), *n.* a wise saying; proverb. [OE *sagu.* Related to *say.*]

scarp (skärp), *n.* **1.** a steep slope. **2.** the inner slope or side of a ditch surrounding a fortification. —*v.* make into a steep slope; slope steeply.

sconce (skons), *n.* bracket projecting from a wall, used to hold a candle or other light.

Sconce

scul lion (skul′yən), *n. Archaic.* **1.** servant who does the dirty, rough work in a kitchen. **2.** a low, contemptible person. [< OF *escouillon* swab, cloth < *escouve* broom < L *scopa*]

scutch eon (skuch′ən), *n.* escutcheon.

sea mew (sē′mū′), *n.* sea gull.

sec tar i an (sek târ′i ən), *adj.* **1.** of or having to do with a sect. **2.** characteristic of one sect only; strongly prejudiced in favor of a certain sect.

se cure (si kūr′), *adj. Archaic.* careless; care-free.

sedge (sej), *n.* a grasslike plant that grows in wet places.

se duce (si düs′ or si dūs′), *v.* **1.** tempt to wrongdoing; persuade to do wrong: *General Arnold, seduced by the offer of great wealth, betrayed his country to the enemy.* **2.** lead astray. **3.** entice to a surrender of chastity. [< L *seducere < se-* aside + *ducere* lead]

seis mic (sīz′mik or sīs′mik), *adj.* **1.** of earthquakes; having to do with an earthquake. **2.** caused by an earthquake. [< Gk. *seismos* earthquake < *seiein* shake]

sem pi ter nal (sem′pi tẽr′nəl), *adj.* everlasting; eternal. [< LL *sempiternalis,* ult. < L *semper* forever]

sen si bil i ty (sen′sə bil′ə ti), *n.* **1.** ability to feel or perceive. **2.** sensitiveness. **3.** fineness of feeling: *She has an unusual sensibility for colors.* **4.** Usually, **sensibilities,** *pl.* sensitive feelings. **5.** tendency to feel hurt or offended too easily. **6.** awareness; consciousness. —**Syn.** **2.** impressibility.

sen si ble (sen′sə bəl), *adj.* **1.** having or showing good judgment; wise. **2.** aware; conscious: *I am sensible of your kindness.* **3.** can be perceived by the senses. **4.** sensitive. [< LL *sensibilis,* ult. < L *sentire* feel]

sen si bly (sen′sə bli), *adv.* **1.** in a sensible manner; with good sense. **2.** so as to be felt.

sen su al (sen′shü əl), *adj.* **1.** having to do with the bodily senses rather than with the mind or soul: *sensual pleasures.* **2.** caring too much for the pleasures of the senses. **3.** lustful. **4.** of or having to do with the senses or sensation.

Syn. **1, 2. Sensual, sensuous** mean of or concerned with the senses. **Sensual** describes things that give pleasurable satisfaction to the bodily senses and appetites and people who indulge their desires and feelings for pure physical pleasure: *A glutton derives sensual pleasure from eating.* **Sensuous** describes people highly sensitive to beauty and the pleasure of the senses and feelings, but never of appetite, and things that give pleasure through the senses: *She derives sensuous delight from old church music.*

se quent (sē′kwənt), *adj.* **1.** following; subsequent. **2.** following in order. **3.** following as a result. [< L *sequens, -entis,* ppr. of *sequi* follow]

se ques ter (si kwes′tər), *v.* **1.** remove or withdraw from public use or from public view: *The shy old lady sequestered herself from all strangers.* **2.** seize by authority. [< L *sequestrare < sequester* trustee, mediator < *sequi* follow]

< = from, taken from;   cf., compare;   dial., dialect;   dim., diminutive;   pp., past participle; ppr., present participle;   pt., past tense;   ult., ultimately;   var., variant;   ?=possibly.

ser aph (ser′əf), *n.*, *pl.* **-aphs** or **-a phim.** one of the highest order of angels.

ser ried (ser′id), *adj.* crowded closely together; pressed together. [< F *serré*, pp. of *serrer* press close]

set tle (set′əl), *n.* a long bench.

sex ton (seks′tən), *n.* man who takes care of a church. A sexton's duties sometimes include ringing the bell, digging graves, etc.

shard (shärd), *n.* **1.** a broken piece; fragment. **2.** piece of broken earthenware or pottery.

shin gle (shing′gəl), *n.* *Esp. Brit.* **1.** loose stones or pebbles such as lie on the seashore; coarse gravel. **2.** beach or other place covered with this.

shire (shīr), *n.* one of the counties into which Great Britain is divided. [OE *scīr*]

shoal (shōl), *n.* **1.** place where the water is shallow. **2.** sandbank or sand bar that makes the water shallow. —*adj.* shallow. —*v.* become shallow. [OE *sceald* shallow]

shoon (shün), *n.* *Archaic.* a pl. of shoe.

shrewd (shrüd), *adj.* **1.** having a sharp mind; clever. **2.** keen; sharp.

shrive (shrīv), *v.*, **shrove** or **shrived**, **shriv en** or **shrived, shriv ing.** *Archaic.* **1.** hear the confession of, impose penance on, and grant absolution to. **2.** make confession. **3.** hear confessions.

sift (sift), *v.* **1.** separate large pieces of from small by shaking in a sieve. **2.** put through a sieve. **3.** fall through, or as if through, a sieve. **4.** examine very carefully: *The jury sifted the evidence to decide if the man was guilty.* [OE *siftan* < *sife* sieve]

sig nal ly (sig′nəl i), *adv.* remarkably; strikingly.

sig net (sig′nit), *n.* a small seal: *The order was sealed with the king's signet.* [< OF *signet*, ult. < L *signum* seal]

si ne cure (sī′nə kūr or sin′ə kūr), *n.* an extremely easy job; position requiring little or no work and usually paying well.

sith (sith), *Archaic. adv.*, *prep.*, *conj.* since.

skirt (skėrt), *n.* **1.** border; edge. **2.** the outer part of a place, group of people, etc.

sleight (slīt), *n.* **1.** skill; dexterity. **2.** a clever trick. [< Scand. *slægth* < *slægr* sly]

sloe (slō), *n.* a dark-purple, plumlike fruit.

sloth (slōth or slôth), *n.* **1.** laziness; idleness. **2.** *Archaic.* slowness. **3.** a very slow-moving mammal of South and Central America that lives in trees.

slough (slou), *n.* a soft, deep muddy place.

snaf fle (snaf′əl), *n.* a slender, jointed bit used on a bridle. —*v.* control or manage by a snaffle. [cf. Dutch *snavel* beak]

soi ree or **soi rée** (swä rā′), *n.* an evening party or social gathering. [< F *soirée* < *soir* evening]

so lic it ous (sə lis′ə təs), *adj.* **1.** showing care or concern: *Parents are solicitous for their children's progress.* **2.** desirous; eager. —**so lic′it ous ly,** *adv.* —**so lic′it ous ness,** *n.*

so lic i tude (sə lis′ə tüd or sə lis′ə tūd), *n.* anxious care; anxiety; concern.

sol stice (sol′stis), *n.* either of the two times in the year when the sun is at its greatest distance from the celestial equator. In the Northern Hemisphere, June 21 or 22 is the longest day of the year and December 21 or 22 is the shortest. [< OF < L *solstitium*, ult. < *sol* sun + *sistere* stand still]

sooth (süth), *Archaic.* —*n.* truth. —*adj.* true.

sore (sôr or sōr), *adj.* **1.** painful. **2.** sad; distressed:

The suffering of the poor makes her heart sore. **3.** easily angered or offended. **4.** causing pain, misery, anger, or offense. **5.** severe; distressing. —*n.* **1.** a painful place on the body where the skin or flesh is broken or bruised. **2.** cause of pain, sorrow, sadness, anger, offense, etc. —*adv. Archaic.* in a sore manner.

spawn (spôn), *n.* **1.** eggs of fish, frogs, shellfish, etc. **2.** young newly hatched from such eggs. **3.** a swarming brood; offspring. **4.** product; result. —*v.* **1.** produce eggs. **2.** bring forth; give birth to.

spec tral (spek′trəl), *adj.* **1.** of or like a specter; ghostly. **2.** of or produced by the spectrum: *spectral colors.*

springe (sprinj), *n.*, *v.*, **springed, spring ing.** —*n.* snare for catching small game. —*v.* catch in a snare. [< OE *sprengan* cause to spring]

stack (stak), *n.* **1.** a large pile of anything. **2.** number of rifles arranged to form a cone or pyramid.

stave (stāv), *n.*, *v.*, **staved** or **stove, stav ing.** —*n.* **1.** one of the curved pieces of wood that form the sides of a barrel, tub, etc. **2.** stick or staff. **3.** rung of a ladder. —*v.* **1.** break a hole in (a barrel, boat, etc.). **2.** become smashed or broken in. **3.** furnish with staves. [< *staves*, pl. of *staff*]

staves (stāvz), *n.* **1.** a pl. of **staff. 2.** pl. of **stave.**

stew ard (stü′ərd or stū′ərd), *n.* **1.** man who manages another's property: *He is the steward of that great estate.* **2.** man who takes charge of the food and table service for a club, ship, etc. **3.** servant on a ship. **4.** person appointed to manage a ball, show, etc. [OE *stigweard* < *stig* hall + *weard* keeper, ward]

stile (stīl), *n.* **1.** step or steps for getting over a fence or wall. **2.** turnstile. **3.** a vertical piece in a door, paneled wall, etc. [OE *stigel;* related to *stīgan* climb]

still (stil), *adj.* **1.** quiet. **2.** soft; low; subdued. —*v.* **1.** make quiet. **2.** make quiet. **3.** calm; relieve. —*n.* **1.** *Poetic.* silence. **2.** photograph of a person or other subject at rest. —*adv.* **1.** at this or that time: *He came yesterday and he is still here.* **2.** up to this or that time. **3.** in the future as in the past: *It will still be here.* **4.** even; yet. **5.** *Archaic* or *Poetic.* steadily; constantly; always. —*conj.* yet; nevertheless.

stip ple (stip′əl), *v.* **1.** paint, draw, or engrave by dots. **2.** produce a stippled effect on. —*n.* **1.** the method of painting, drawing, or engraving by stippling. **2.** effect produced by this method.

Sto i cism (stō′ə siz əm), *n.* **1.** philosophy of the Stoics, members of a school of philosophy which taught that virtue is the highest good and that men should be free from passion and unmoved by life's happenings. **2. stoicism,** patient endurance; indifference to pleasure and pain.

stole (stōl), *n.* **1.** a narrow strip of silk or other material worn around the neck by a clergyman during certain church functions. **2.** a woman's collar or scarf of fur or cloth with ends hanging down in front. **3.** *Archaic.* a long robe.

stoup (stüp), *n.* **1.** a drinking vessel of varying size for liquids, such as a cup, flagon, or tankard. **2.** amount it holds. **3.** basin for holy water at the entrance of a church. [< Scand. *staup*]

stout (stout), *adj.* **1.** fat and large. **2.** strongly built; firm; strong. **3.** brave; bold. **4.** not yielding; stubborn: *stout resistance.* —*n.* a strong, dark-brown beer.

strait en (strāt′ən), *v.* **1.** limit by the lack of something; restrict. **2.** make narrow. **3. in straitened circumstances,** needing money badly.

---

hat, āge, cãre, fär; let, ēqual, tėrm; it, īce; hot, ōpen, ôrder; oil, out; cup, pùt, rüle, ūse; th, thin; ᴛʜ, then; zh, measure; ə represents *a* in about, *e* in taken, *i* in pencil, *o* in lemon, *u* in circus.

strand   throe

strand (strand), *n.* *Poetic.* shore; land bordering a sea, lake, or river.

stu pent (stü′pənt), *adj.* *Archaic.* stupefied; dumfounded.

sub jec tive (səb jek′tiv), *adj.* 1. existing in the mind; belonging to the person thinking rather than to the object thought of: *Base your subjective opinions on objective facts.* 2. about the thoughts and feelings of the speaker, writer, painter, etc.; personal: *a subjective poem.* —**sub jec′tive ly,** *adv.* —**sub jec′tive ness,** *n.*

sub join (səb join′), *v.* 1. add at the end; append. 2. place in immediate sequence to something else. [< MF *subjoindre* < L *subjungere* < *sub-* under + *jungere* join]

sub lime (səb līm′), *adj.* lofty; noble; majestic; exalted. —*n.* that which is lofty, noble, exalted, etc. —*v.* 1. heat (a solid substance) and condense the vapor given off; purify; refine. 2. pass off as a vapor and condense as a solid; become purified or refined. 3. elevate; exalt. 4. *Archaic.* raise on high.

suf fer ance (suf′ər əns or suf′rəns), *n.* 1. permission or consent given only by a failure to object or prevent. 2. power to bear or endure; patient endurance.

sul ly (sul′i), *v., n.* soil; stain; tarnish. [OE *sōlian* < *sōl* dirty]

sum ma ri ly (sum′ə rə li or sə mer′ə li), *adv.* in a summary manner; briefly; without delay.

sum pi tan (sum′pi tan), *n.* a kind of blowgun used to discharge a dart, which is often poisoned. The weapon is used in Borneo and the Malayan islands.

su per flu ous (sù pėr′flü əs), *adj.* 1. more than is needed. 2. needless. [< L *superfluus*, ult. < *super-* over + *fluere* flow] —**Syn.** 1. excessive, surplus. 2. unnecessary.

su per nal (sù pėr′nəl), *adj.* 1. heavenly; divine. 2. lofty; exalted. [< L *supernus* < *super* above]

su pine (*adj.* sü pīn′; *n.* sü′pīn), *adj.* 1. lying flat on the back. 2. lazily inactive; listless. —**Syn.** 2. languid, inert.

sup ple (sup′əl), *adj.* 1. bending easily: *a supple birch tree.* 2. readily adaptable to different ideas, circumstances, people, etc.; yielding: *a supple mind.*

sur mise (*v.* sər mīz′; *n.* sər mīz′ or sėr′mīz), *v.* guess: *We surmised that the delay was caused by some accident.* —*n.* formation of an idea with very little or no evidence; a guessing: *His guilt was a matter of surmise; there was no proof.* —**Syn.** *v.* infer, suppose.

sus pi ra tion (sus′pə rā′shən), *n.* a sigh.

swill (swil), *n.* 1. kitchen refuse, especially when partly liquid; garbage; slops. 2. a deep drink. —*v.* 1. drink greedily. 2. fill with drink. 3. wash by flooding with water.

syl lo gism (sil′ə jəm), *n.* 1. a form of argument or reasoning, consisting of two statements and a conclusion drawn from them. *Example:* All trees have roots; an oak is a tree; therefore, an oak has roots. 2. reasoning in this form; deduction. [< L < Gk. *syllogismos,* originally, inference, ult. < *syn-* together + *logos* a reckoning]

syl van (sil′vən), *adj.* of the woods; in the woods; consisting of woods; having woods. [< L *silvanus* < *silva* forest]

syn od (sin′əd), *n.* 1. assembly called together under authority to discuss and decide church affairs; church council. 2. assembly; convention; council. [< LL < Gk. *synodos* assembly, meeting < *syn-* together + *hodos* a going]

ta bor (tā′bər), *n.* a small drum, used especially to accompany a pipe or fife. [< OF *tabur;* of Oriental origin Cf. Persian *tabūrāk* drum.]

tac i tur ni ty (tas′ə tėr′nə ti), *n.* habit of keeping silent; disinclination to talk much

tam bour (tam′bür), *n.* 1. a drum. 2. frame for holding in place cloth to be embroidered. [< F < Arabic < Persian *tanbūr.* Akin to *tabor.*]

targe (tärj), *n.* *Archaic.* shield or buckler.

taut (tôt), *adj.* 1. tightly drawn; tense: *a taut rope.* 2. in neat condition; tidy. [earlier *taught,* apparently var. of *tight*]

taw dry (tô′dri), *adj.* showy and cheap; gaudy. [ult. alteration of *St. Audrey,* from cheap laces sold at St. Audrey's fair in Ely, England]

teak (tēk), *n.* 1. a large tree of the East Indies with a hard, durable, yellowish-brown wood. 2. this wood. [< Pg. < Malayalam *tēkka*]

tem per (tem′pər), *n.* 1. the hardness, toughness, etc., of a mixture given by tempering: *The temper of the clay was right for shaping.* 2. substance added to something to modify its properties or qualities.

te na cious (ti nā′shəs), *adj.* 1. holding fast. 2. stubborn; persistent. 3. holding fast together; not easily pulled apart. [< L *tenax, -acis* < *tenere* hold]

ten der (ten′dər), *n.* 1. formal offer. 2. thing offered.

ten or (ten′ər), *n.* 1. the general tendency; course: *The calm tenor of her life has never been disturbed by excitement or trouble.* 2. the general meaning or drift. [< L *tenor,* originally, a holding on < *tenere* hold]

ten ure (ten′yər), *n.* 1. a holding; possessing. 2. length of time of holding or possessing: *The tenure of office of the president of our club is one year.* 3. manner of holding land, buildings, etc., from a feudal lord or superior. 4. conditions, terms, etc., on which anything is held or occupied. [< OF *tenure,* ult. < L *tenere* hold]

ter ma gant (tėr′mə gənt), *n.* a violent, quarreling, scolding woman. —*adj.* violent; quarreling; scolding.

tern (tėrn), *n.* a sea bird like a gull but with a more slender body and bill and a long, forked tail.

ter rene (tə rēn′), *adj.* having to do with the earth; earthly.

tes ty (tes′ti), *adj.* easily irritated; impatient. —**tes′ti ly,** *adv.* —**tes′ti ness,** *n.* —**Syn.** peevish, cross.

teth er (teᴛʜ′ər), *n.* rope or chain for fastening an animal so that it can graze only within certain limits. —*v.* fasten with a tether.

tet ter (tet′ər), *n.* an itching skin disease. Eczema is a tetter. [OE *teter*]

thane (thān), *n.* 1. man who ranked between an earl and an ordinary freeman in early England. Thanes held lands of the king or lord and gave military service in return. 2. among the Anglo-Saxons and Danes, one of a class of free servants. [OE *thegn*]

thence (ᴛʜens), *adv.* 1. from that place; from there: *A few miles thence is a river.* 2. for that reason; therefore. 3. from that time; from then.

thews (thüz), *n.pl.* 1. muscles. 2. sinews.

Thor (thôr), *n.* the ancient Scandinavian god of thunder.

thorn (thôrn), *n.* 1. a sharp-pointed growth on a stem or branch of a tree or plant. 2. tree or plant that has thorns on it. [OE]

thrall (thrôl), *n.* 1. person in bondage; slave. 2. thralldom; bondage; slavery.

throe (thrō), *n.* 1. a violent pang; great pain. 2. **throes,** *pl.* **a.** anguish; agony. **b.** a desperate struggle; violent disturbance.

< = from, taken from; cf., compare; dial., dialect; dim., diminutive; pp., past participle; ppr., present participle; pt., past tense; ult., ultimately; var., variant; ?=possibly.

ti ar a (tĭ är′ə or ti ä′rə), *n.* band of gold, jewels, or flowers worn around the head as an ornament.

tim brel (tim′brəl), *n.* tambourine.

tip ple (tip′əl), *v.* drink (alcoholic liquor) often. —*n.* an alcoholic liquor.

tithe (tĭFH), *n.* **1.** one tenth. **2.** Often, **tithes,** *pl. Brit.* tax of one tenth of the yearly produce of land, animals, and personal work, paid for the support of the church and the clergy. **3.** any small tax, levy, etc. —*v.* **1.** put a tax of a tenth on. **2.** pay a tithe on. **3.** give one tenth of one's income to the church or to charity. [OE *teogotha* tenth]

tit u lar (tich′ü lər or tit′ü lər), *adj.* **1.** in title or name only. **2.** having a title. **3.** having to do with a title. [< L *titulus* title]

toff (tof), *n. British. Slang.* a dandy; fop; man who pays too much attention to his clothes and appearance.

to paz (tō′paz), *n.* a crystalline mineral that occurs in various forms and colors. Transparent yellow topaz is used as a gem.

tope (tōp), *v. Archaic.* to drink much or frequently; drink to excess.

toque (tōk), *n.* hat without a brim; small hat with very little brim.

torch (tôrch), *n.* **1.** light to be carried around or stuck in a holder on a wall. **2.** device for producing a very hot flame, used especially to burn off paint, to solder metal, and to melt metal. **3.** *Brit.* a stick-shaped electric lamp; flashlight.

tor por (tôr′pər), *n.* **1.** dull, inactive, sluggish condition. **2.** condition of numbness. [< L *torpor* < *torpere* be numb]

tort (tôrt), *n.* a civil (not criminal) wrong for which the law requires damages (except a breach of contract): *If a man's automobile breaks the glass of a shopwindow, he has committed a tort against the shopowner.* [< OF < Med.L *tortum* injustice < L *torquere* turn awry, twist]

tor tu ous (tôr′chü əs), *adj.* **1.** full of twists, turns, or bends; winding. **2.** mentally or morally crooked; not straightforward: *tortuous reasoning.* [< L *tortuosus,* ult. < *torquere* twist]

to ward (*prep.* tôrd, tōrd, or tə wôrd′; *adj.* tôrd or tōrd), *prep.* **1.** in the direction of. **2.** regarding; about; concerning. **3.** for. —*adj.* **1.** about to happen; impending. **2.** *Archaic.* promising, hopeful, or apt; docile.

tow path (tō′path′ or tō′päth′), *n.* path along the bank of a canal or river for use in towing boats.

tram (tram), *n.* **1.** *Esp. Brit.* streetcar. **2.** tramway. **3.** train in a coal mine.

trans gress (trans gres′ or tranz gres′), *v.* **1.** break a law, command, etc.; sin. **2.** go contrary to; sin against. **3.** go beyond (a limit or bound): *Her manners transgressed the bounds of good taste.*

tran sient (tran′shənt), *adj.* **1.** passing soon; not lasting. **2.** passing through and not staying long: *a transient guest in a hotel.* —*n.* visitor or boarder who stays for a short time. [< L *transiens, -entis,* ppr. of *transire* pass through < *trans-* through + *ire* go]

trap pings (trap′ingz), *n.pl.* **1.** ornamental coverings for a horse. **2.** things worn; ornaments: *trappings of a king and his court.*

trench er (tren′chər), *n.* a wooden platter on which meat was formerly served and carved. [< OF *trencheor* knife, ult. < *trenchier* cut.]

trep i da tion (trep′ə dā′shən), *n* **1.** nervous dread; fear; fright. **2.** a trembling.

trib u tar y (trib′ü ter′i), *n.* **1.** stream that flows into a larger stream or body of water. **2.** one that pays tribute. —*adj.* **1.** flowing into a larger stream or body of water. **2.** paying tribute; required to pay tribute. **3.** paid as tribute. **4.** contributing; helping.

trib ute (trib′üt), *n* **1.** money paid by one nation to another for peace or protection or because of some agreement. **2.** any forced payment. **3.** compliment. [< L *tributum* < *tribuere* allot < *tribus* tribe]

trick (trik), *n.* **1.** something done to deceive or cheat. **2.** illusion. **3.** a clever act; feat of skill. **4.** prank. —*v.* **1.** deceive; cheat. **2.** play tricks. **3.** dress. **4. trick out.** dress up; ornament.

tril by (tril′bi), *n. Brit.* a kind of soft felt hat.

trot ter (trot′ər), *n.* **1.** a horse bred and trained to trot. **2.** the foot of a sheep or a pig used for food.

truc u lent (truk′ü lənt or trü′kü lənt), *adj.* savagely threatening or bullying; fierce and cruel.

trump er y (trump′ər i or trump′ri), something showy but without value; worthless ornaments; nonsense. —*adj.* showy but without value; nonsensical. [< F *tromperie* < *tromper* deceive]

tu mid (tü′mid or tū′mid), *adj.* **1.** swollen. **2.** swollen with big words; pompous. [< L *tumidus* < *tumere* swell]

tur bid (tèr′bid), *adj.* **1.** muddy; thick; not clear. **2.** confused; disordered: *a turbid imagination.* [< L *turbidus* < *turba* turmoil]

turn key (tèrn′kē′), *n.* person in charge of the keys of a prison; keeper of a prison.

twain (twān), *n., adj. Archaic* or *Poetic.* two.

tzar ist (tsär′ist), *n* **1.** having to do with the tsars of Russia. **2.** having to do with tsars; autocratic.

ul ti ma tum (ul′tə mā′təm), *n., pl.* **-tums, -ta** (-tə). **1.** a final proposal or statement of conditions. **2.** the ultimate; final point or stage to be reached.

un co (ung′kō), *Scottish.* —*adv.* remarkably; very; extremely. —*adj.* **1.** unknown, strange, or unusual. **2.** remarkable, extraordinary, or great. [ult. var. of *uncouth*]

un con scion a ble (un kon′shən ə bəl), *adj.* **1.** not influenced or guided by conscience. **2.** unreasonable; very great: *wait an unconscionable time for someone.*

un couth (un küth′), *adj.* **1.** awkward; clumsy; crude: *uncouth manners.* **2.** unusual and unpleasant; strange.

unc tion (ungk′shən), *n.* **1.** an anointing with oil, ointment, or the like, for medical purposes or as a religious rite. **2.** the oil, ointment, or the like, used for anointing. **3.** something soothing or comforting. [< L *unctio, -onis* < *unguere* anoint]

un mit i gat ed (un mit′ə gāt′id), *adj.* **1.** not softened or lessened: *unmitigated harshness.* **2.** unqualified or absolute: *an unmitigated fraud.*

un pre pos sess ing (un′prē pə zes′ing), *adj.* not creating at first a favorable impression.

un pre tend ing (un′pri ten′ding), *adj.* unassuming; modest.

un time ly (un tĭm′li), *adj.* at a wrong time or season. —*adv.* not at the natural or usual time; too early; too soon: *His death came untimely at 32.*

up braid ing (up brād′ing), *n.* a severe reproof; scolding. —*adj.* full of reproach.

ur bane (èr bān′), *adj.* **1.** courteous; refined; elegant. **2.** smoothly polite. —**ur bane′ly,** *adv.* —**ur bane′ness,** *n.*

ur chin (èr′chən), *n.* **1.** a small boy. **2.** a mischievous boy. **3.** a poor, ragged child. **4.** *Archaic.* elf.

ush er (ush′ər), *n.* **1.** person who shows people to

their seats in a church, theater, etc. **2.** *Brit.* an assistant teacher in an English school. —*v.* conduct; escort; show.

u surp (ū zėrp´ or ū sėrp´), *v.* seize and hold (power, position, authority, etc.) by force or without right. [< L *usurpare,* ult. < *usu,* abl., through use + *rapere* seize] —**Syn.** appropriate.

vail (vāl), *v., Archaic.* **1.** lower; cause or allow to fall. **2.** take off; doff. **3.** yield; bow. [< OF *valer,* or < *avale* < OF *avaler,* both ult. < L *ad vallem* to the valley]

vale (vāl), *n. Poetic.* valley.

vamp (vamp), *n.* **1.** the upper front part of a shoe or foot. **2.** piece or patch added to an old thing to make it look new. —*v.* **1.** furnish with a vamp. **2.** patch up; make (an old thing) look new.

van tage (van´tij or vän´tij), *n.* a better position or condition; advantage.

var let (vär´lit), *n. Archaic.* a low fellow; rascal.

vas sal (vas´əl), *n.* **1.** person who held land from a lord or superior, to whom in return he gave help in war or some other service. **2.** servant.

vaunt (vônt or vänt), *v., n.* boast. [< F < LL *vanitare* < *vanus* vain]

vel lum (vel´əm), *n.* **1.** the finest kind of parchment, used for writing, binding books, etc. **2.** paper or cloth imitating such parchment. —*adj.* of vellum.

ven det ta (ven det´ə), *n.* feud in which a murdered man's relatives try to kill the slayer or his relatives. [< Ital. < L *vindicta* revenge, ult. < *vindex* protector, avenger]

vent age (ven´tij), *n.* vent; small hole, especially for the escape or passage of air. The finger holes of a flute are ventages.

ver ba tim (vėr bā´tim), *adv., adj.* word for word; in exactly the same words. [< Med.L *verbatim* < L *verbum* word]

ver dur ous (vėr´jər əs), *adj.* green and fresh.

verge (vėrj), *n.* **1.** edge; rim; brink: *His business is on the verge of ruin.* **2.** a limiting belt, strip, or border of something. **3.** rod, staff, etc. —*v.* be on the verge; border.

ver i ty (ver´ə ti), *n* **1.** truth. **2.** a true statement or fact. **3.** reality. [< L *veritas* < *verus* true]

ver meil (vėr´məl), *n., adj.* **1.** *Poetic.* vermilion; bright-red. **2.** silver or bronze coated with gilt.

ver nac u lar (vər nak´ū lər), *n.* **1.** a native language; language used by the people of a certain country or place. **2.** informal speech. **3.** language of a profession, trade, etc. —*adj.* **1.** used by the people of a certain country, place, etc. **2.** of or in the native language, rather than a literary or learned language. [< L *vernaculus* domestic, native < *verna* home-born slave]

ver nal (vėr´nəl), *adj.* **1.** of spring; having to do with spring: *vernal flowers, vernal months.* **2.** like spring; suggesting spring. **3.** youthful. [< L *vernalis* < *ver* spring]

ves pers or **Ves pers** (ves´pərz), *n.pl.* a church service held in the late afternoon or in the evening. [< Med.L < L *vespera* evening]

vi al (vī´əl), *n.* a small glass bottle for holding medicines or the like; bottle. [var. of *phial*]

vi cious (vish´əs), *adj.* **1.** evil; wicked. **2.** having bad habits or a bad disposition. **3.** not correct; having faults: *This argument contains vicious reasoning.* **4.** spiteful; malicious.

vict ual (vit´əl), *n.* Usually, **victuals,** *pl. Informal* or *Dialect.* food. [< OF *vitaille* < L *victualia,* pl., ult. < *vivere* live]

vil i fy (vil´ə fī), *v.* speak evil of; revile; slander. [< LL *vilificare* < L *vilis* vile + *facere* make]

vin di ca tion (vin´də kā´shən), *n.* a vindicating or being vindicated; defense; justification.

vin tage (vin´tij), *n.* **1.** the wine from a certain crop of grapes: *The finest vintages cost much more than others.* **2.** a year's crop of grapes. **3.** the gathering of grapes for making wine.

vir u lent (vir´ū lənt or vir´ə lənt), *adj.* **1.** very poisonous or harmful; deadly: *a virulent form of a disease.* **2.** intensely bitter or spiteful; violently hostile. [< L *virulentus* < *virus* poison]

vis age (viz´ij), *n.* **1.** face. **2.** appearance. [< OF *visage* < *vis* face < L *visus* a look < *videre* see]

vol u ble (vol´ū bəl), *adj.* **1.** tending to talk much; fond of talking. **2.** having a smooth, rapid flow of words. [< L *volubilis,* originally, rolling < *volvere* roll]

vo lup tu ous (və lup´chū əs), *adj.* **1.** caring much for the pleasures of the senses. **2.** giving pleasure to the senses: *voluptuous music or beauty.*

vouch (vouch), *v.* **1.** be responsible; give a guarantee (for): *I can vouch for the truth of the story.* **2.** answer for; confirm; guarantee.

vouch er (vouch´ər), *n.* **1.** person or thing that vouches for something. **2.** a written evidence of payment; receipt. Canceled checks returned from one's bank are vouchers.

vouch safe (vouch sāf´), *v.* be willing to grant or give; deign (to do or give): *The proud man vouchsafed no reply when we spoke to him.* [original meaning "guarantee," to *vouch* for as *safe*]

wake (wāk), *v.,* **waked** or **woke, waked** or (*Archaic and Dialect*) **wo ken, wak ing,** *n.* —*v.* **1.** stop sleeping. **2.** cause to stop sleeping. **3.** become alive or active. **4.** keep watch. **5.** keep watch over. —*n.* **1.** a watching. **2.** an all-night watch kept beside the body of a dead person. [OE *wacian*]

wal let (wol´it or wôl´it), *n.* **1.** a small, flat leather case for carrying paper money, cards, etc., in one's pocket. **2.** bag for carrying food and small articles for personal use when on a journey.

wan (won), *adj.* **1.** pale; lacking natural color: *Her face looked wan after her long illness.* **2.** looking worn or tired; faint; weak. [OE *wann* dark]

wan ton (won´tən), *adj.* **1.** reckless; heartless. **2.** without reason or excuse. **3.** not moral. **4.** *Poetic.* frolicsome; playful: *a wanton breeze, a wanton child.* **5.** *Poetic.* not restrained: *a wanton mood.* —*n.* a wanton person. —*v.* act in a wanton manner. —**wan´ton ly,** *adv.* —**wan´ton ness,** *n.*

ward (wôrd), *n.* **1.** a division of a hospital or prison. **2.** a district of a city or town. **3.** person under the care of a guardian or of a court. **4.** *Archaic.* one who guards. [OE *weard,* fem., a guarding] —*v. Archaic.* keep watch over. [OE *weardian* guard. Akin to *guard.*]

war rant (wôr´ənt or wor´ənt), *n.* **1.** that which gives a right; authority. **2.** a written order giving authority for something. **3.** a good and sufficient reason; promise; guarantee. **4.** a document certifying something, especially to a purchaser. —*v.* **1.** authorize. **2.** justify: *Nothing can warrant such rudeness.* **3.** give one's word for; guarantee; promise: *The storekeeper warranted the quality of the coffee.* —**Syn.** *n.* **1.** sanction, authorization. —*v.* **1.** sanction. **3.** assure.

war ran ty (wôr´ən ti or wor´ən ti), *n.* **1.** warrant; authority; justification. **2.** guarantee.

< = from, taken from;   cf., compare;   dial., dialect;   dim., diminutive;   pp., past participle; ppr., present participle;   pt., past tense;   ult., ultimately;   var., variant;   ?=possibly.

war ren (wôr**′**ən or wor**′**ən), *n.* piece of ground filled with burrows, where rabbits live or are raised.

was sail (wos**′**əl or was**′**əl), *n.* **1.** a drinking party; revel with drinking of healths. **2.** spiced ale or other liquor drunk at a wassail. **3.** a salutation meaning "Your health!" —*v.* **1.** take part in a wassail; revel. **2.** drink to the health of. —*interj.* "Your health!" [< Scand. *ves heill* be healthy!]

was sail er (wos**′**əl ər or was**′**əl ər), *n.* **1.** reveler. **2.** drinker of healths.

wa ter flag (wô**′**tər flag**′**), *n.* the yellow or blue iris.

wat tle (wot**′**əl), *n.* **1.** Also, **wattles,** *pl.* sticks interwoven with twigs or branches; framework of wicker. **2.** in Australia, the acacia, used to make wattles and in tanning.

wax (waks), *v.* **1.** grow bigger or greater; increase. **2.** become: *The party waxed merry.* [OE *weaxan*]

weal[1] (wēl), *n.* *Archaic.* well-being; prosperity; happiness: *Good citizens act for the public weal.* [OE *wela*]

weal[2] (wēl), *n.* streak or ridge on the skin made by a stick or whip; welt. [var. of *wale*]

ween (wēn), *v.* *Archaic.* think; suppose; believe; expect. [OE *wēnan*]

wel ter (wel**′**tər), *v.* **1.** roll or toss about; wallow. **2.** lie soaked; be drenched. —*n.* **1.** a rolling and tossing. **2.** confusion; commotion.

wheel wright (hwēl**′**rīt**′**), *n.* man whose work is making or repairing wheels, carriages, and wagons.

whelp (hwelp), *n.* **1.** puppy or cub; young dog, wolf, bear, lion, tiger, etc. **2.** a good-for-nothing boy or young man. —*v.* give birth to (whelps).

whet (hwet), *v.* **1.** sharpen by rubbing: *whet a knife.* **2.** make keen or eager; stimulate: *The smell of food whetted my appetite.*

whist (hwist), *n.* a card game somewhat like bridge for two pairs of players. Auction and contract bridge developed from it.

wight (wīt), *n.* **1.** *Archaic* or *Dialect.* a human being; person; man. **2.** *Archaic.* supernatural creature, such as a fairy, witch, etc.

wile (wīl), *n.* **1.** a trick to deceive; cunning way: *The serpent by his wiles persuaded Eve to eat the apple.* **2.** subtle trickery; slyness; craftiness. —*v.* coax; lure; entice. [OE *wigle* magic]

win kle (wing**′**kəl), *n.* a sea snail used for food.

wist (wist), *v.* *Archaic.* pt. and pp. of **wit,** to know.

with al (wiꞮH ôl**′** or with ôl**′**), *Archaic.* —*adv.* with it all; as well; besides; also: *The lady is rich and fair and wise withal.* —*prep.* with. [<*with* + *all*]

woe be gone (wō**′**bi gôn**′** or wō**′**bi gon**′**), *adj.* looking sad, sorrowful, or wretched.

wont (wunt or wōnt), *adj.* accustomed: *He was wont to read the paper at breakfast.* —*n.* custom; habit: *He rose early, as was his wont.* [originally pp., ult. < OE *wunian* be accustomed]

wont ed (wun**′**tid or wōn**′**tid), *adj.* accustomed; customary; usual.

woof (wŭf), *n.* **1.** the threads running from side to side across a woven fabric. The woof crosses the warp. **2.** fabric; cloth; texture.

wor ry (wėr**′**i), *v.* **1.** feel anxious or uneasy. **2.** cause to feel anxious or troubled. **3.** annoy; bother. **4.** seize and shake with the teeth; bite at; snap at: *A cat will worry a mouse.* —*n.* **1.** anxiety; uneasiness; trouble; care. **2.** cause of trouble or care. [OE *wyrgan* strangle]

wraith (rāth), *n.* **1.** ghost of a person seen before or soon after his death. **2.** specter; ghost.

wroth (rôth or roth), *adj.* angry. [OE *wrāth*]

y clept or **y cleped** (i klept**′**), *adj.* *Archaic.* called; named; styled. [OE *geclipod* named]

yew (ū), *n.* **1.** an evergreen tree native to Europe and Asia. **2.** the wood of this tree. Bows used to be made of yew. [OE *īw*]

yo kel (yō**′**kəl), *n.* a country fellow.

ze nith (zē**′**nith), *n.* **1.** the point in the heavens directly overhead. **2.** the highest point.

Zep pe lin or **zep pe lin** (zep**′**ə lən or zep**′**lən), *n.* a large dirigible balloon shaped like a cigar with pointed ends. It has compartments for gas, engines, passengers, etc. [named after F. von *Zeppelin*]

Zeppelin moored

zone (zōn), *n.* **1.** any of the five great divisions of the earth's surface, bounded by lines parallel to the equator. **2.** any region or area especially considered or set off. **3.** belt; girdle. —*v.* **1.** divide into zones. **2.** be formed into zones. **3.** surround like a belt or girdle. **4.** surround with a belt or girdle. [< L *zona* < Gk. *zone*, originally, girdle]

---

hat, āge, cãre, fär; let, ēqual, tèrm; it, ĭce; hot, ōpen, ôrder; oil, out; cup, pùt, rüle, ūse; th, thin; ꞮH, then; zh, measure; ə represents *a* in about, *e* in taken, *i* in pencil, *o* in lemon, *u* in circus.

Index of Types of Literature

son, 272; *Praise We Great Men*, 650; *The Prologue to the Canterbury Tales, From*, 68; *Promise*, 624; *Prospice*, 460; *Proud Maisie*, 372; *Psalm 1*, 190; *Psalm 24*, 190; *Psalm 91*, 190; *Psalm 100*, 191; *Recessional*, 489; *Red Hanrahan's Song About Ireland*, 621; *A Red, Red Rose*, 331; *Requiem*, 475; *Reveille*, 520; *The Rock, Chorus 3*, 643; *Rocky Acres*, 639; *The Rubáiyát of Omar Khayyám, From*, 470; *Sailing to Byzantium*, 622; *The Seafarer, From*, 31; *Sea-Fever*, 630; *Self-Dependence*, 452; *The Shell*, 625; *She Walks in Beauty*, 377; *Shield*, 33; *Sigh No More*, 100; *Silver*, 627; *The Soldier*, 636; *Soldier from the Wars Returning*, 520; *Soldier, Rest! Thy Warfare O'er*, 373; *The Solitary Reaper*, 355; *Song: Go and catch a falling star*, 184; *Song: When I am dead, my dearest*, 469; *A Song for St. Cecilia's Day*, 236; *Song to Celia*, 99; *Song to the Men of England*, 384; *Sonnets 26, 43 (Elizabeth Barrett Browning)*, 463; *Sonnets 18, 29, 116, 146 (Shakespeare)*, 109, 110; *Sonnets 31, 41 (Sidney)*, 104, 105; *Sonnets 34, 75 (Spenser)*, 106; *Sonnet on Chillon*, 378; *Sonnet to My Mother*, 658; *Spanish Waters*, 629; *Stanzas for Music*, 377; *Summum Bonum*, 454; *Swan*, 33; *Tam o' Shanter*, 334; *There Is a Lady Sweet and Kind*, 100; *The Tiger*, 339; *To —*, 385; *To a Louse*, 333; *To Althea, from Prison*, 205; *To a Mouse*, 332; *To an Athlete Dying Young*, 519; *To a Skylark (Shelley)*, 386; *To a Skylark (Wordsworth)*, 352; *To Lucasta, on Going to the Wars*, 204; *To the Virgins to Make Much of Time*, 204; *The Triumph of Charis*, 99; *Ulysses*, 443; *Under the Greenwood Tree*, 99; *View of a Pig*, 658; *When You Are Old*, 620; *Who Is Silvia?* 99; *Why So Pale and Wan?* 205; *With Rue My Heart Is Laden*, 519; *The World Is Too Much with Us*, 356

ROMANCE. *Morte Darthur, From*, 86

SHORT STORY. *Bella Fleace Gave a Party*, 582; *The Celestial Omnibus*, 604; *Christmas Morning*, 550; *The Demon Lover*, 599; *Eveline*, 557; *I Spy*, 555; *The Japanese Quince*, 596; *The Lagoon*, 510; *Laura*, 588; *Louise*, 592; *The Man Who Was*, 478; *Miss Brill*, 579; *Story of the Widow's Son*, 569; *The Three Strangers*, 494; *Up the Bare Stairs*, 562

General Index

Names of authors represented in the text appear in capital letters; titles of selections printed in the text are italicized. General topics, including names of authors and selections discussed but not represented in the text, are printed in regular type.

10 11 12 13 14 15 16 17 18 19 20 21 22 23 24 25   82 81 80 79 78 77 76 75 74 73

A Literary Map of England

NORTH SEA

ATLANTIC OCEAN

ORKNEY IS.

HEBRIDES

NORTHERN

Inverness

Aberdeen

SCOTLAND

LOCH KATRINE

BANNOCKBURN x

INCHCAPE ROCK
(BELL ROCK)

Glasgow

Edinburgh

Kilmarnock

Doon

Afton

CRAIGENPUTTOCK □

Ecclefechan

Tweed

ABBOTSFORD □

OTTERBOURNE
x

HADRIAN'S WALL

Durham

Londonderry